EXCAVATIONS AT TELL ES-SWEYHAT, SYRIA
VOLUME 2, PART 2: FIGURES AND PLATES

# ARCHAEOLOGY OF THE BRONZE AGE, HELLENISTIC, AND ROMAN REMAINS AT AN ANCIENT TOWN ON THE EUPHRATES RIVER

*by*

THOMAS A. HOLLAND

*with contributions by*

Martha Goodway *and* Michael Roaf

ORIENTAL INSTITUTE PUBLICATIONS • VOLUME 125
THE ORIENTAL INSTITUTE OF THE UNIVERSITY OF CHICAGO

Library of Congress Control Number: 2006938967

ISBN: 1-885923-33-3

ISSN: 0069-3367

©2006 by The University of Chicago. All rights reserved.
Published 2006. Printed in the United States of America.

*The Oriental Institute, Chicago*

*Co-managing Editors*
Thomas A. Holland *and* Thomas G. Urban

*Series Editors' Acknowledgments*

The assistance of Katherine Strange Burke, Lindsay DeCarlo, Katie L. Johnson, and Alexandra Witsell is acknowledged in the production of this volume.

*Spine Illustration:* Model horse figurine (SW. 770; see p. 229 for description; Part II, fig. 157: 6 and pl. 116a)

*Printed by Edwards Brothers, Ann Arbor, Michigan*

The paper used in this publication meets the minimum requirements of American National Standard for Infor-

# LIST OF FIGURES

1. Map of Syria Showing Position of Tell es-Sweyhat in Its Near Eastern Setting
2. Map of the Tabqa Dam Reservoir Area in Syria Showing Lake Assad and Positions of Sites Excavated
3. Map of the Sweyhat Plain Showing Regional Position of Tell es-Sweyhat and Neighboring Sites
4. Contour Plan of Tell es-Sweyhat Showing Areas and Operations of Excavations
5. Cross Sections of Central Mound of Tell es-Sweyhat: East–West Elevation and North–South Elevation
6. Holland/Whitcomb 1972 Euphrates Survey Pottery: Site A, Site K (Tell Hajji Ibrahim), Site F, Nafileh, Site C (Tell Othman), and Shams ed-Din, Lower Site
7. Holland/Whitcomb 1972 Euphrates Survey Pottery from the Shams ed-Din Cemetery
8. Holland/Whitcomb 1972 Euphrates Survey Pottery: Mazraʿat Hadidi, Site H (Mishrifah Saghir), Tell Hadidi, Site D (Khirbet al-Hamrah), Site E, Site G (Khirbet Haj Hassan), Site J (Zarob), Rasm el-ʿAbd Mustaha, Tell Sheikh Hassan, and Umm Jehash
9. Holland/Whitcomb 1972 Euphrates Survey Pottery: Shams ed-Din Central Tell, Tell Walid Asaf, and Ramalah
10. Pottery from Sounding 1 (Phase 3; Period E — Early Bronze Age IVb) and Sounding 2 (Phases 1 and 2; Periods F and E — Early Bronze Age IVa and Early Bronze Age IVb)
11. Pottery from Sounding t.1 (Phases 1 to 5; Periods F and E — Early Bronze Age IVa and Early Bronze Age IVb)
12. Pottery from Trench VIA (Phases 1, 4, and 5; Periods F, E, and E–D — Early Bronze Age IVa, Early Bronze Age IVb, and Early–Middle Bronze Age)
13. Pottery from Trenches VIIA and VIIB (Phases 1–5; Periods F, E, and E–D — Early Bronze Age IVa, Early Bronze Age IVb, and Early–Middle Bronze Age)
14. Pottery from Trenches VIIIA and VIIIB (Phases 1–3; Periods F and E — Early Bronze Age IVa and Early Bronze Age IVb)
15. Pottery from Trenches XIA and XIB (Phases 1–3; Period B — Roman)
16. Trench IC (Phases 1 and 2, Period K — Late Chalcolithic)
17. Pottery from Trench IC (Phase 3; Period J — Early Bronze Age I)
18. Pottery from Trench IC (Phase 4; Period H — Early Bronze Age II)
19. Pottery from Trench IC (Phase 4; Period H — Early Bronze Age II) (cont.)
20. Pottery from Trench IC (Phase 4; Period H — Early Bronze Age II) (cont.)
21. Pottery from Trench IC (Phase 5; Period F — Early Bronze Age IVa)
22. Pottery from Trench IC (Phase 5; Period F — Early Bronze Age IVa) (cont.)
23. Pottery from Trench IC (Phase 6; Period E — Early Bronze Age IVb)
24. Pottery from Trench IC (Phase 7; Period E — Early Bronze Age IVb)
25. Pottery from Trench IC (Phase 8; Period E — Early Bronze Age IVb)
26. Pottery from Trench IC (Phase 9; Period E–D — Early–Middle Bronze Age)
27. Pottery from Trench IC (Phase 10; Period B — Mixed Early Bronze Age, Early–Middle Bronze Age, Hellenistic, and Roman): Bronze Age, Hellenistic Period, Roman Period, Various Periods
28. Miscellaneous Small Finds from Trench IC (Phases 3–8 and 10; Periods J, H, F, E, and B — Early Bronze Age I, Early Bronze Age II, Early Bronze Age IVa, Early Bronze Age IVb, and Roman), Trench IA2 (Phase 2; Period B — Roman), and Trench IA2 (Phases 2–3; Period B — Roman)
29. Pottery from Trench IIA (Phase 1; Period J — Early Bronze Age I)
30. Pottery from Trench IIA, Room 4 (Phase 2; Period J — Early Bronze Age I)
31. Pottery from Trench IIA (Phase 3; Period J — Early Bronze Age I)

## LIST OF FIGURES

32. Pottery from Trench IIA (Phase 4; Period H — Early Bronze Age II)
33. Pottery from Trench IIA (Phase 5; Period H — Early Bronze Age II)
34. Pottery from Trench IIA, Rooms 9–12 (Phase 6; Period G — Early Bronze Age III)
35. Pottery from Trench IIA, Hellenistic Pits B1 and B2 (Period C — Hellenistic) Cut into Early Bronze Age Pottery Level, and Debris above Phase 6 (Phase 7; Period G — Derived Early Bronze Age): Hellenistic, Derived Early Bronze Age
36. Pottery from Trench IIA, Courtyard/Working Area (Phase 8; Period G — Early Bronze Age III), and Pit D Cut into Phase 8 Pottery Level (Period C — Hellenistic)
37. Pottery from Trench IIA (Phase 9; Period C — Hellenistic)
38. Pottery from Trench IIA, Pits 7.1, 7.2, and 7.3 (Phase 10; Period C — Hellenistic)
39. Pottery from Trench IIA, Loci Disturbed by Hellenistic Pits 7.2, 7.3, and Locus 7.12 (Phase 10; Period C — Derived Early Bronze Age)
40. Pottery from Trench IIA, Street and Associated Remains (Phase 11; Period C — Hellenistic)
41. Pottery from Trench IIA, Pit C (Phase 12; Period C — Hellenistic)
42. Pottery from Trench IIA, Pit C (Phase 12; Period C — Hellenistic) (*cont.*)
43. Pottery from Trench IIA, Pit C (Phase 12; Period C — Derived Early Bronze Age)
44. Pottery from Trenches IIA and IIB (Phase 13; Period C — Hellenistic)
45. Pottery from Trenches IIA and IIB (Phase 13; Period C — Hellenistic [*cont.*] and Derived Early Bronze–Middle Bronze Age)
46. Pottery from Trenches IIA and IIB (Phase 14; Period C — Hellenistic)
47. Pottery from Trenches IIA and IIB (Phase 14; Period C — Hellenistic) (*cont.*)
48. Pottery from Trench IIA (Phase 14; Period C — Derived Early Bronze Age)
49. Pottery from Trenches IIA and IIB (Phase 15; Period C — Hellenistic)
50. Pottery from Trenches IIA and IIB (Phase 15; Period C — Hellenistic) (*cont.*)
51. Miscellaneous Clay Small Finds and Greek Ostracon from Trenches IIA and IIB
52. Miscellaneous Small Finds of Various Materials from Trench IIA
53. Miscellaneous Stone Vessels and Tools from Trench IIA
54. Miscellaneous Stone Vessels and Tools from Trenches IIA and IIB
55. Pottery from Trench IVM, Sounding Below Room 7 (Phase 1A; Period J — Early Bronze Age I)
56. Pottery from Trench IVM, Sounding Below Room 7 (Phase 1B; Period H — Early Bronze Age II)
57. Area IV, Operation 6, Sounding Below Room 16 (Phase 1B; Period H — Early Bronze Age II)
58. Pottery from Trench IVB, Sounding Through Town Wall Tower and Trenches IVC, D, J, M, and Z(S) (Phase 1C; Period G — Early Bronze Age III)
59. Pottery from Trench IVP, Operation 6, Sounding Below Courtyard Room 9 (Phase 1C; Period G — Early Bronze Age III)
60. Pottery from Area IV, Operation 6, Sounding Below Room 16 (Phase 1C, Period G — Early Bronze Age III)
61. Pottery from Trench XA, Operation 11, Sounding Below Room 15 (Phase 1C; Period G — Early Bronze Age III)
62. Pottery from Trenches IVA; IVB, Room 1 and Tower Foundations; and IVC, Room 7 (Phase 2A; Period F — Early Bronze Age IVa)
63. Pottery from Trench IVE, Room 2 (Phase 2A; Period F — Early Bronze Age IVa)
64. Pottery from Trench IVF, Room 1 and Doorway Between Rooms 1 and 8 (Phase 2A; Period F — Early Bronze Age IVa)
65. Pottery from Trench IVG, Northwest Corner of Room 3 (Phase 2A; Period F — Early Bronze Age IVa)
66. Pottery from Trench IVJ, Room 4 and Room 5 Bin (Phase 2A; Period F — Early Bronze Age IVa)
67. Pottery from Trench IVL, Room 3 (Phase 2A; Period F — Early Bronze Age IVa)
68. Pottery from Trenches IVM, IVX, and IVC, Room 7 (Phase 2A; Period F — Early Bronze Age IVa)

## LIST OF FIGURES

69. Pottery from Trench IVX = Northern Half of Trench IVM, Room 7 (Phase 2A; Period F — Early Bronze Age IVa)
70. Pottery from Trench IVN, Rooms 8 and 18 (Phase 2A; Period F — Early Bronze Age IVa)
71. Pottery from Trench IVN, Operation 10, Rooms 8 and 18 (Phase 2A; Period F — Early Bronze Age IVa)
72. Pottery from Trench IVO, Room 10 (Phase 2A; Period F — Early Bronze Age IVa)
73. Pottery from Trench IVP, Courtyard Room 9 (Phase 2A; Period F — Early Bronze Age IVa)
74. Pottery from Trench IVP, Operation 6, Courtyard Room 9 (Phase 2A; Period F — Early Bronze Age IVa)
75. Pottery from Area IV, Operation 6, Room 16 (Phase 2A; Period F — Early Bronze Age IVa)
76. Pottery from Area IV, Operation 6, Room 17 (Phase 2A; Period F — Early Bronze Age IVa)
77. Pottery from Trench IVQ, Room 6 (Phase 2A; Period F — Early Bronze Age IVa)
78. Pottery from Trenches IVR, Room 11, and IVS, Room 12 (Phase 2A; Period F — Early Bronze Age IVa)
79. Pottery from Trenches IVW, Sounding, and IVM, Room 7, Pit A (Phase 2A; Period F — Early Bronze Age IVa)
80. Pottery from Area IV, Operation 7, Room 34 (Phase 2A(a); Period F — Early Bronze Age IVa)
81. Pottery from Trenches IVZ(S) and IVZ(N1) (Phase 2A; Period F — Early Bronze Age IVa)
82. Pottery from Trench IXA (Phase 2A; Period F — Early Bronze Age IVa)
83. Pottery from Trench XA, Room 15 (Phase 2A; Period F — Early Bronze Age IVa)
84. Pottery from Trench IVA (Phase 2B; Period F — Early Bronze Age IVa)
85. Pottery from Trench IVB = Southwest Corner of Trench IVF, Room 1 (Phase 2B; Period F — Early Bronze Age IVa)
86. Pottery from Trench IVC, North and West Side of Town Wall Tower, Pit 1.6 and Room 7, and Trench IVD, West Side of Town Wall (Phase 2B; Period F — Early Bronze Age IVa)
87. Pottery from Trench IVD, Room 2 (Phase 2B; Period F — Early Bronze Age IVa)
88. Pottery from Trench IVE, Rooms 3 and 4 (Phase 2B; Period F — Early Bronze Age IVa)
89. Pottery from Trench IVF, Southeast Corner of Room 1 (Phase 2B; Period F — Early Bronze Age IVa)
90. Pottery from Trench IVF/N, Doorway Between Rooms 1 and 8; Trench IVG, Northwest Corner of Trench IVL, Room 3; Trench IVH, Southeast Corner of Area IVL, Room 3; and Trench IVL = Central Portion, Room 3 (Phase 2B; Period F — Early Bronze Age IVa)
91. Pottery from Trench IVJ, Room 4 and Room 5 Bin (Phase 2B; Period F — Early Bronze Age IVa)
92. Pottery from Trench IVK, Room 2 (Phase 2B; Period F — Early Bronze Age IVa)
93. Pottery from Trenches IVM and IVC, Room 7 (Phase 2B; Period F — Early Bronze Age IVa
94. Pottery from Trench IVN, Room 8, and Operation 10, Northeast Corner of Room 8 (Phase 2B; Period F — Early Bronze Age IVa)
95. Pottery from Trench IVP, Courtyard Room 9 (Phase 2B; Period F — Early Bronze Age IVa)
96. Pottery from Area IV, Operation 6, Courtyard Room 9 (Phase 2B; Period F — Early Bronze Age IVa)
97. Pottery from Trench IVQ, Room 6 (Phase 2B; Period F — Early Bronze Age IVa)
98. Pottery from Trench IVO, Room 11; Trench IVS, Room 13; Sounding IVW; Trench IVX, Room 14; and Sounding IVY (Phase 2B; Period F — Early Bronze Age IVa)
99. Pottery from Trench IVX = North Side of Trench IVM, Room 7 (Phase 2B; Period F — Early Bronze Age IVa)
100. Pottery from Trench IVZ(S), (N1), and (N2), Room 21 (Phase 2B; Period F — Early Bronze Age IVa)
101. Pottery from Trenches IXA and IXB, Modern Water Barrel Pit (Phase 2B; Period F — Early Bronze Age IVa)
102. Pottery from Trench XA, Room 15 (Phase 2B; Period F — Early Bronze Age IVa)
103. Pottery from Trench XA, Operation 11, Rooms 19 and 20 (Phase 2B; Period F — Early Bronze Age IVa)
104. Pottery from Trenches IVA and IVB (= Southwest Corner of Trench IVF, Room 1A; Phase 3; Period E — Early Bronze Age IVb)
105. Pottery from Trench IVC (= Town Wall Tower; Phase 3; Period E — Early Bronze Age IVb)
106. Pottery from Trench IVF, Room 1A (Phase 3; Period E — Early Bronze Age IVb)

# LIST OF FIGURES

107. Pottery from Trench IVF, Room 1A (Phase 3; Period E — Early Bronze Age IVb) (*cont.*)
108. Pottery from Trench IVG, Room 3A (Phase 3; Period E — Early Bronze Age IVb)
109. Pottery from Trench IVJ, Room 4A (Phase 3; Period E — Early Bronze Age IVb)
110. Pottery from Trench IVJ Bin, Room 5A (Phase 3; Period E — Early Bronze Age IVb)
111. Pottery from Trench IVK, Room 2A (Phase 3; Period E — Early Bronze Age IVb)
112. Pottery from Trench IVL, Room 3A (Phase 3; Period E — Early Bronze Age IVb)
113. Pottery from Trench IVL/P, Pit Cutting Wall North of Door Between Rooms 3 and 9 (Phase 3; Period E — Early Bronze Age IVb)
114. Pottery from Trench IVP, Operation 6, Room 22, Above Courtyard Room 9 (Phase 3; Period E — Early Bronze Age IVb)
115. Area IV, Operation 6, Room 24 and Alley (Phase 3; Period E — Early Bronze Age IVb)
116. Pottery from Trench IVM, Room 7A (Phase 3; Period E — Early Bronze Age IVb)
117. Pottery from Area IVN, Rooms 8A/18A (Phase 3; Period E — Early Bronze Age IVb)
118. Pottery from Trench IVN, Operation 10, Northeast Corner of Room 8A (Phase 3; Period E — Early Bronze Age IVb)
119. Pottery from Trench IVO, Fill Above Rooms 10A and 11 (Phase 3; Period E — Early Bronze Age IVb)
120. Pottery from Trench IVP, Room 9A (Phase 3; Period E — Early Bronze Age IVb)
121. Pottery from Trench IVR, Rooms 11A and 12A (Phase 3; Period E — Early Bronze Age IVb)
122. Pottery from Trench IVS, Room 12A, IVX, Room 14A, and Soundings IVW and IVY (Phase 3; Period E — Early Bronze Age IVb)
123. Pottery from Trench IVZ(N1), (N2), and (S) (Phase 3; Period E — Early Bronze Age IVb)
124. Pottery from Trench IXA (Phase 3; Period E — Early Bronze Age IVb)
125. Pottery from Trench IXB, Modern Water Barrel Pit (Phase 3; Period E — Early Bronze Age IVb)
126. Pottery from Trench XA, Room 15A (Phase 3; Period E — Early Bronze Age IVb)
127. Pottery from Trench XA, Operation 11, Rooms 15A and 19A (Phase 3; Period E — Early Bronze Age IVb)
128. Pottery from Trench IVB, Southwest Corner of Trench IVF, Room 1B; Trench IVC, Town Wall Tower; Trench IVD, Above Town Wall and Pit in Wall; Trench IVE, Room 3B; and Trench IVF, Room 1B (Phase 4; Period E — Early Bronze Age IVb)
129. Pottery from Trench IVJ, Room 4B (Phase 4; Period E — Early Bronze Age IVb)
130. Pottery from Trench IVK, Room 2B; Trench IVL, Room 3B; and Trench IVM, Room 7B (Phase 4; Period E — Early Bronze Age IVb)
131. Pottery from Trench IVN, Rooms 8B and 18B (Phase 4; Period E — Early Bronze Age IVb)
132. Pottery from Trench IVN, Operation 10, Room 8B, Northeast Corner (Phase 4; Period E–D — Early–Middle Bronze Age)
133. Pottery from Trench IVO, Room 10B (Phase 4; Period E — Early Bronze Age IVb)
134. Pottery from Trench IVP, Room 9B (Phase 4; Period E — Early Bronze Age IVb)
135. Pottery from Area IV, Operation 6, Room 31, Built Over Room 22 (Phase 4; Period E–D — Early–Middle Bronze Age)
136. Pottery from Area IV, Operation 6, Room 32, Built Over Room 23 (Phase 4; Period E–D — Early–Middle Bronze Age)
137. Trench IVQ, Room 25, and Soundings IVV, W, and Y Above and South of Operation 7 Street (Phase 4; Period E — Early Bronze Age IVb)
138. Pottery from Trench IVT, Sounding (Phase 4; Period E — Early Bronze Age IVb)
139. Pottery from Trench IVZ(N1), (N2), and (S) (Phase 4; Period E — Early Bronze Age IVb)
140. Pottery from Trench IXA (Phase 4; Period E–D — Early–Middle Bronze Age)
141. Pottery from Trench XA, Above Room 15A and Operation 11, Above Rooms 19A and 20A (Phase 4; Period E–D — Early–Middle Bronze Age)

142. Pottery from Area IV, Lower and Upper Surface Layers (Phase 5; Periods E–D to D — Early–Middle Bronze Age to Middle Bronze Age I)
143. Pottery from Area IV, Operation 7 (Phase 2A(a); Period F — Early Bronze Age IVa)
144. Pottery from Area IV, Operation 7 (Phase 2A(a); Period F — Early Bronze Age IVa) (cont.)
145. Pottery from Area IV, Operation 7 (Phase 2A(a); Period F — Early Bronze Age IVa) (cont.)
146. Pottery from Area IV, Operation 7 Extramural Areas (Phase 2A(b); Period F — Early Bronze Age IVa)
147. Pottery from Area IV, Operation 7, Room 40, Pit (Phase 2B(a); Period E — Early Bronze Age IVb)
148. Pottery from Area IV, Operation 7, Rooms 37–40, Courtyard, and Extramural (Phase 2B(b); Period E — Early Bronze Age IVb)
149. Pottery from Area IV, Operation 7, Courtyard, and Extramural (Phase 3; Period E — Early Bronze Age IVb)
150. Pottery from Area IV, Operation 7 (Phase 4; Period E–D — Early–Middle Bronze Age)
151. Pottery from Area IV, Operation 8, Room 29 (Phase 3; Period E — Early Bronze Age IVb)
152. Pottery from Area IV, Operation 8, Room 29A (Phase 4; Period E–D — Early–Middle Bronze Age)
153. Miscellaneous Incised Pottery Sherds from Area IIA (Phases 11, 13, 14, and 15; Period C — Hellenistic)
154. Area IV (Phases 2A, 2B, 3, 4, and 5; Periods F to E–D) Early Bronze Age IVa to Early–Middle Bronze Age, Miscellaneous Incised Pottery Sherds, Potters' Marks, and an Applied-band Sherd
155. Human Figurines from Area IV (Phases 2–3; Periods F and E — Early Bronze Age IVa and Early Bronze Age IVb)
156. Human Figurines from Area IV (Phases 2–4; Periods F, E, and E–D — Early Bronze Age IVa, Early Bronze Age IVb, and Early–Middle Bronze Age)
157. Animal Figurines from Area IV (Phases 2–4; Periods F and E — Early Bronze Age IVa and Early Bronze Age IVb)
158. Animal Figurines from Area IV (Phases 2–5; Periods F to E–D — Early Bronze Age IVa to Early Bronze–Middle Bronze Age)
159. Model Chariots and Wheels from Area IV (Phases 1C–4; Periods G–E — Early Bronze Age III to Early Bronze Age IVb)
160. Miscellaneous Clay Objects from Area IV (Phases 2A–4; Periods F to E–D — Early Bronze Age IVa to Early Bronze–Middle Bronze Age)
161. Metal Objects from Area IV (Phases 2A–3; Periods F and E — Early Bronze Age IVa and Early Bronze Age IVb)
162. Metal Objects from Area IV (Phases 2A–4; Periods F to E–D — Early Bronze Age IVa to Early Bronze–Middle Bronze Age)
163. Stone Objects from Area IV (Phases 1C–2B; Periods G and F — Early Bronze Age III and Early Bronze Age IVa)
164. Stone Objects from Area IV (Phases 2B–5; Periods F to E–D — Early Bronze Age IVb to Early Bronze–Middle Bronze Age)
165. Clay Sling Bullets from Area IVK, Room 2A (Phase 3; Period E — Early Bronze Age IVb)
166. Clay Sling Bullets from Area IV, Room 2A (Phase 3; Period E — Early Bronze Age IVb)
167. Stone Pestle/Pounder Tool and Stone Sling Bullets from Area IV (Phases 2A–3; Periods F and E — Early Bronze Age IVa and Early Bronze Age IVb)
168. Flint Tools and Weapons from Area IV (Phases 1C–2B; Periods G and F — Early Bronze Age III and Early Bronze Age IVa)
169. Beads and Pendants from Area IV (Phases 2A–4; Periods F to E–D — Early Bronze Age IVa to Early–Middle Bronze Age)
170. Miscellaneous Vessels and Objects from Area IV (Phases 1B, 2A–5; Periods H, F, E, and E–D — Early Bronze Age II, Early Bronze Age IVa, Early Bronze Age IVb, and Early–Middle Bronze Age)
171. Stone Mortars, Type SF.3a, from Area IV (Phases 2A–4; Periods F to E–D — Early Bronze Age IVa to Early–Middle Bronze Age)

172. Grinding Stones, Type SF.3a, from Area IV (Phases 2A–4; Periods F to E–D — Early Bronze Age IVa to Early–Middle Bronze Age)

173. Stone Pounders and Grinder/Pounder Tools, Type SF.3a, from Area IV (Phases 2A–5; Periods F to E–D — Early Bronze Age IVa to Early–Middle Bronze Age)

174. Stone Weights and Miscellaneous Stone Objects from Area IV (Phases 1C–5; Periods G to E–D — Early Bronze Age III to Early–Middle Bronze Age)

175. Various Small Finds from Area IXA (Phases 2A–4; Periods F to E–D — Early Bronze Age IVa to Early–Middle Bronze Age)

176. Pottery from Area IIIA, Rooms 4A and 4B (Phase 3; Period F — Early Bronze Age IVa)

177. Pottery from Area IIIA, Rooms 8A, 8B, and 11 (Phase 4; Period E — Early Bronze Age IVb)

178. Pottery from Trench IIIA, Rooms 8A, 8B, and 11 (Phase 4; Period E — Early Bronze Age IVb Pottery)(*cont.*)

179. Pottery from Trench IIIA (Phase 5; Period E — Early Bronze Age IVb)

180. Pottery in Trench IIIA (Phase 6; Period E–D — Early–Middle Bronze Age)

181. Pottery from Trench IIIA (Phase 7; Period D — Middle Bronze Age I)

182. Pottery from Trench IIIB (Phase 1B; Period G — Early Bronze Age III)

183. Pottery from Trench IIIB (Phases 1C and 2; Periods G and F — Early Bronze Age III and Early Bronze Age IVa)

184. Pottery from Trench Area IIIB, Rooms 1A/B and 1B (Phase 3; Period F — Early Bronze Age IVa)

185. Pottery from Trench IIIB, Rooms 6 and 7 (Phase 4; Period E — Early Bronze Age IVb)

186. Pottery from Trench IIIB (Phase 5; Period E — Early Bronze Age IVb)

187. Pottery from Trench IIIB (Phase 6; Period E–D — Early–Middle Bronze Age)

188. Pottery from Trench IIIB (Phase 7; Period D — Middle Bronze Age I)

189. Pottery from Trench IIIC, Room 9 (Phase 4; Period E — Early Bronze Age IVb)

190. Pottery from Trench IIIC, Rooms 19A, 19B, and 19C (Phase 5; Period E — Early Bronze Age IVb)

191. Pottery from Trench IIIC (Phase 6; Period E–D — Early–Middle Bronze Age)

192. Pottery from Trench IIIC (Phase 7; Period D — Middle Bronze Age I)

193. Pottery from Trench IIID, Rooms 11A, 12, and 13 (Phase 4; Period E — Early Bronze Age IVb)

194. Pottery from Trench IIID, Rooms 11A, 12, and 13 (Phase 4; Period E — Early Bronze Age IVb) (*cont.*)

195. Pottery from Trench IIID, Rooms 20/21 (Phase 5; Period E — Early Bronze Age IVb)

196. Pottery from Trench IIID (Phase 6; Period E–D — Early–Middle Bronze Age)

197. Pottery from Trench IIID (Phase 7; Period D — Middle Bronze Age I)

198. Pottery from Trench IIIE, Room 5 (Phase 4; Period E — Early Bronze Age IVb)

199. Pottery from Trench IIIE, Room 15 and Courtyard Room 14 (Phase 5; Period E — Early Bronze Age IVb)

200. Pottery from Trench IIIE (Phase 6/7; Period E–D — Early–Middle Bronze Age)

201. Pottery from Trench IIIF, Room 16, Floors, and Alley (Phases 3 and 4; Periods F and E — Early Bronze Age IVa and Early Bronze Age IVb)

202. Pottery from Trench IIIF (Phase 5; Period E — Early Bronze Age IVb)

203. Pottery from Trench IIIF (Phase 6/7, Period E–D — Early–Middle Bronze Age)

204. Pottery from Trench IIIG (Phases 4 and 5; Period E — Early Bronze Age IVb)

205. Pottery from Trench IIIG Extramural (Phase 6/7; Period E–D — Early–Middle Bronze Age)

206. Pottery from Trench IIIG/H (Phases 1C and 2; Periods G and F — Early Bronze Age III and Early Bronze Age IVa)

207. Pottery from Trench IIIG/H, Rooms 3A and 3B (Phase 3; Period F — Early Bronze Age IVa)

208. Pottery from Trench IIIG/H, Rooms 17, 17A, and 18 (Phase 4; Period E — Early Bronze Age IVb)

209. Pottery from Trench IIIG/H, Rooms 22A, 22B, and 22A/B Extramural (Phase 5; Period E — Early Bronze Age IVb)

210. Pottery from Trench IIIG/H, Rooms 22A, 22B, and Rooms 22A/B Extramural (Phase 5; Period E — Early Bronze Age IVb) (*cont.*)

211. Pottery from Trench IIIG/H, Rooms 23, 24, and Extramural Courtyard (Phases 6 and 7A; Periods E–D and D — Early–Middle Bronze Age and Middle Bronze Age I)

212. Pottery from Trench IIIH, Town Wall Debris (Phase 5; Period E — Early Bronze Age IVb)

213. Pottery from Trench IIIH (Phase 6/7; Period E–D — Early–Middle Bronze Age)

214. Pottery from Trench IIIJ (Phase 3; Period F — Early Bronze Age IVa)

215. Pottery from Trench IIIJ (Phases 4 and 5, Period E — Early Bronze Age IVb)

216. Pottery from Trench IIIJ (Phase 6/7; Period E–D — Early–Middle Bronze Age)

217. Pottery from Trench IIIK (Phase 6/7; Period E–D — Early–Middle Bronze Age)

218. Pottery from Trench IIIL, Walls 1 and 2 (Phase 5; Period E — Early Bronze Age IVb)

219. Pottery from Trench IIIL (Phase 6/7; Period E–D — Early–Middle Bronze Age)

220. Pottery from Area III, Unstratified Early Bronze Age

221. Human Figurines, Types SF.1a and SF.1c, from Area III (Phases 3–7A; Periods F to D — Early Bronze Age IVa to Middle Bronze Age I)

222. Animal Figurines, Model Chariots, Model Wheels, and Miscellaneous Clay Objects from Area III (Phases 3–6/7; Periods F, E, and E–D — Early Bronze Age IVa, Early Bronze Age IVb, and Early–Middle Bronze Age)

223. Beads and Pendants from Area III (Phases 3–6; Periods F, E, and E–D — Early Bronze Age IVa, Early Bronze Age IVb, and Early–Middle Bronze Age)

224. Metal Objects from Area III (Phases 4–6; Periods E and E–D — Early Bronze Age IVb and Early–Middle Bronze Age)

225. Flint Tools from Area III (Phases 3, 4, 6, and 7B; Periods F to D — Early Bronze Age IVb to Middle Bronze Age I)

226. Stone Pestles and Pounders from Area III (Phases 1B, 2–4, 6–7A; Periods G to D — Early Bronze Age III to Middle Bronze Age I)

227. Stone Mortars and Grinder from Area III (Phase 4; Period E — Early Bronze Age IVb)

228. Stone Grinders from Area III (Phases 1C and 3–7A; Periods G to D — Early Bronze Age III to Middle Bronze Age I)

229. Miscellaneous Stone Vessels and Objects from Area III (Phases 1C and 4–7; Periods G, E, E–D, and D — Early Bronze Age III, Early Bronze Age IVb, Early–Middle Bronze Age, and Middle Bronze Age I)

230. Pottery from Operation 5 (Phase 1; Period H — Early Bronze Age II)

231. Pottery from Operation 5 (Phase 2; Period G — Early Bronze Age III)

232. Pottery from Operation 5 (Phase 3; Period G — Early Bronze Age III)

233. Pottery from Operation 5 (Phase 4; Period F — Early Bronze Age IVa)

234. Pottery from Operation 5 (Phase 4, Period F) Early Bronze Age IVa (*cont.*)

235. Pottery from Operation 5 (Phase 4; Period F — Early Bronze Age IVa) (*cont.*)

236. Pottery from Operation 5 (Phase 4; Period F — Early Bronze Age IVa) (*cont.*)

237. Pottery from Operation 5 (Phase 4; Period F — Early Bronze Age IVa) (*cont.*)

238. Pottery from Operation 5, Pit 17.3 (Phase 4; Period F — Early Bronze Age IVa)

239. Pottery from Operation 5, Pit 17.3 (Phase 4; Period F — Early Bronze Age IVa) (*cont.*)

240. Pottery from Operation 5 (Phase 5; Period B — Early Roman)

241. Pottery from Operation 5 (Phase 5; Period B — Early Roman [*cont.*] and Derived Early Bronze Age)

242. Pottery from Operation 5 (Phase 5; Period B — Derived Early Bronze Age)

243. Pottery from Operation 5 (Phase 6; Period B — Late Roman)

244. Pottery from Operation 5 (Phase 6; Period B — Late Roman) (*cont.*)

245. Pottery from Operation 5 (Phase 6; Period B — Derived Early Bronze Age)

246. Pottery from Operation 5 (Phase 7, Period B — Late Roman)

247. Pottery from Operation 5 (Phase 7; Period B — Late Roman) (*cont.*)
248. Pottery from Operation 5 (Unstratified; Roman and Early Bronze Age)
249. Figurines, Model Chariot, and Model Chariot Wheel from Operation 5 (Phases 2 and 4–7; Periods G, F, and B — Early Bronze Age III, Early Bronze Age IVa, and Roman)
250. Stone Objects from Operation 5 (Phases 2 and 4–7; Periods G, F, and B — Early Bronze Age III, Early Bronze Age IVa, and Roman)
251. Bone, Metal, and Stone Objects from Operation 5 (Phases 3–7; Periods G, F, and B — Early Bronze Age III, Early Bronze Age IVa, and Roman)
252. Miscellaneous Clay Objects from Operation 5 (Phases 2, 4, 5, and 7; Periods G, F, and B — Early Bronze Age III, Early Bronze Age IVa, and Roman)
253. Glass, Flint, and Special Clay Vessels or Objects from Operation 5 (Phases 4–7; Periods F and B — Early Bronze Age IVa and Roman)
254. Wall Painting Fragment, WP.92.38, Depicting a Bovine with Suckling Calf Standing on a Mountainside from Operation 5 (Phase 2; Period G — Early Bronze Age III)
255. Wall Painting Fragments Depicting Stylized Human Figures from Operation 5 (Phase 2; Period G — Early Bronze Age III)
256. Wall Painting Fragments Depicting Stylized Human Figures from Operation 5 (Phase 2; Period G — Early Bronze Age III)
257. Wall Painting Fragments Depicting Geometric Patterns from Operation 5 (Phase 2; Period G — Early Bronze Age III)
258. Plan and East Section of Trench IA1
259. Plan and East Section of Trench IA2
260. Pottery from Trenches IA1 and IA2 (Phase 1, Period B — Derived Early Bronze Age and Roman)
261. Pottery from Trenches IA1 and IA2 (Phase 2; Period B — Derived Early Bronze Age, Roman, and Hellenistic)
262. Pottery from Trenches IA1 and IA2 (Phase 3; Period B — Derived Early Bronze Age and Roman)
263. Pottery from Trenches IA1 and IA2 (Phase 4; Period B — Derived Early Bronze Age and Roman)
264. Plan and West Section of Trench IB
265. Pottery from Trench IB (Phases 2 to 4, Period B — Derived Early Bronze Age and Roman)
266. Plan of Area I Trenches and Phase 2 Plan of Trench ID
267. South Section and Key to Phase Hatching of Trench IE Sections; Trench IE, Phase 1 Plan; Trench IE, Phase 2 Plan; Trench IE, Phases 3 and 4 (Pit 1.9) Plan; and Trench IE, Phases 5 and 6 Plan
268. Trench IF, West Section; Trench IF, Phases 1, 3, and 4 Plan; Trench IF, Phase 3 Plan; and Trench IF, Phase 4 Plan
269. Trench IG, West Section; Trench IG, Phases 1–4 Plan; and Trench IG, East Section
270. Trench IH, Phases 1 and 2 Plan, and Trench IJ, Phase 1 Plan
271. Trench IE, Phase 1, and Trench IF, Phase 1
272. Trench IF, Phases 1–3, and Trench IF, Phases 1–6
273. Trench IG, Phases 1–6 (North View); Trench IG, Phases 1–6 (South View); and Trenches IH and IJ, Phases 1–2 (South View)
274. Pottery from Trench ID (Phase 2; Period B — Derived Early Bronze Age and Roman)
275. Pottery from Trench IE (Phase 1; Period F — Early Bronze Age IVa)
276. Pottery from Trench IE (Phase 2; Period E — Early Bronze Age IVb)
277. Pottery from Trench IE (Phase 3; Period E — Early Bronze Age IVb)
278. Pottery from Trenches IC (Phase 4 = IE, Loci 1.40, 1.41, Period H — EBII) and Trench IE (Phase 4; Period E — Early Bronze Age IVb)
279. Pottery from Trench IE (Phase 5; Period E–D — Early–Middle Bronze Age and Roman)
280. Pottery from Trench IE (Phase 6; Period B — Derived Early–Middle Bronze Age and Roman)

281. Pottery from Trench IF (Phases 1 and 2; Periods F and E — Early Bronze Age IVa and Early Bronze Age IVb)
282. Pottery from Trench IF (Phases 3 and 4; Period E — Early Bronze Age IVb)
283. Pottery from Trench IF (Phase 5; Period E–D — Early–Middle Bronze Age)
284. Pottery from Trench IF (Phase 6; Period B — Derived Early–Middle Bronze Age and Roman)
285. Pottery from Trench IF/G (Phases 2, 3, and 6; Periods E and B — Early Bronze Age IVb, Derived Early–Middle Bronze Age, and Roman)
286. Pottery from Trench IG (Phase 1; Period F — Early Bronze Age IVa)
287. Pottery from Trench IG (Phase 2; Period E — Early Bronze Age IVb)
288. Pottery from Trench IG (Phase 3; Period E — Early Bronze Age IVb)
289. Pottery from Trench IG (Phase 4; Period E — Early Bronze Age IVb and Derived Roman)
290. Pottery from Trench IG (Phase 6; Period B — Derived Early Bronze Age, Early–Middle Bronze Age, and Roman)
291. Pottery from Trench IH (Phase 2; Period B — Derived Early Bronze Age, Early–Middle Bronze Age, and Roman)
292. Pottery from Trench IJ (Phase 1; Period E–D — Early–Middle Bronze Age)
293. Pottery from Trench IJ (Phase 2; Period B — Derived Early–Middle Bronze Age and Roman)
294. Glass and Stone Small Finds from Trench IA1 (Phases 1–3; Period B — Roman)
295. Stone and Pottery Small Finds from Trench IA1 (Phase 3; Period B — Late Roman)
296. Glass, Pottery, and Stone Small Finds from Trench IA2 (Phases 1–4; Period B — Early and Late Roman)
297. Glass, Metal, Pottery, and Stone Small Finds from Trench IB (Phases 2–4; Period B — Early and Late Roman)
298. Pottery and Stone Small Finds from Trenches ID, E, F, H, and J (Phases 2–3 and 5–6; Periods E, E–D, and B — Early Bronze Age, Early–Middle Bronze Age, and Late Roman)
299. Key to East Sections of Area V Step Trenches
300. East Sections of Trenches VG, VF, and VE with Key to Hatching of Phases 1–9
301. East Sections of Trenches VD, VC, VB, and VA
302. Plans of Trenches VA (Phase 1), VB (Phase 4), VC (Phases 1 and 4), and VC (Phase 2)
303. Plans of Trenches VD (Phase 3), VE (Phases 3 and 4), VF (Phases 5 and 6), and VG (Phases 5 and 6)
304. Highest, Southern Portion of Trenches VE, VF, and VG. Stone Mortar from Trench VE in situ at Bottom Left Foreground
305. Lowest, Northern Portion of Trenches VD, VC, VB, and VA
306. Pottery from Trench VA (Phase 3; Period E — Early Bronze Age IVb)
307. Pottery from Trench VA (Phase 4; Period C — Hellenistic)
308. Pottery from Area V, Trench Baulk A/B (Phases 2–4; Periods E and C — Early Bronze Age IVb and Hellenistic)
309. Pottery from Trench VB (Phase 3; Period E — Early Bronze Age IVb and Derived Hellenistic)
310. Pottery from Trench VB (Phase 4; Period C — Hellenistic and Derived Early Bronze Age IVb)
311. Pottery from Trench VC (Phase 3; Periods F and E — Early Bronze Age IVa, Early Bronze Age IVb, and Derived Hellenistic)
312. Pottery from Trench VC (Phase 4; Period C — Hellenistic and Derived Early Bronze Age IVb)
313. Pottery from Trench VD (Phase 4; Period E — Early Bronze Age IVb)
314. Pottery from Trench VD (Phase 5; Period C — Hellenistic and Derived Early Bronze Age IVb)
315. Pottery from Trench VD from the Bottom of Hellenistic Pit 2.4 (Phase 9; Period C — Derived Early Bronze Age II–III and Early Bronze Age IVb)
316. Pottery from Trench VE (Phase 3 Pit; Periods G and F — Mixed Early Bronze Age II, Early Bronze Age III, and Early Bronze Age IVa)
317. Pottery from Trench VE (Phase 4; Period E — Early Bronze Age IVb)

318. Pottery from Trench VE (Phase 5; Period C — Hellenistic and Derived Early Bronze Age IVb)
319. Pottery from Trench VE (Phase 9; Period C — Hellenistic and Derived Early Bronze Age IVb)
320. Pottery from Trench VF (Phase 4; Period E — Early Bronze Age IVb)
321. Pottery from Trench VF (Phase 5; Period E — Early Bronze Age IVb)
322. Pottery from Trench VF (Phase 6; Period E — Early Bronze Age IVb and Derived Hellenistic)
323. Pottery from Trench VF (Phase 9; Period C — Hellenistic and Derived Early Bronze Age IVb)
324. Pottery from Area V, Trench Baulk F/G (Phases 8 and 9; Period C — Hellenistic and Derived Early Bronze Age IVb)
325. Pottery from Trench VG (Phase 5; Period F — Early Bronze Age IVa)
326. Pottery from Trench VG (Phase 6; Period E — Early Bronze Age IVb and Derived Hellenistic)
327. Pottery from Trench VG (Phase 7; Period E — Early Bronze Age IVb and Derived Hellenistic)
328. Pottery from Trench VG (Phase 8; Period E — Early Bronze Age IVb Pottery and Derived Hellenistic)
329. Pottery from Trench VG (Phase 9; Period C — Hellenistic)
330. Small Finds from Area V Step Trenches (Phases 3–7, 9; Periods E and C — Early Bronze Age IVb and Hellenistic)
331. Miscellaneous Small Finds from Area I, Trench IIB, Area V, and Trench VIA (Early Bronze Age, Early–Middle Bronze Age, and Hellenistic/Roman)
332. Miscellaneous Small Finds from Area I, Trench IIB, Areas V, VI, VII, and VIII, and Surface (Early Bronze Age IVa–Roman)
333. Potters' Marks on Miscellaneous Vessels and Sherds from Areas I, II, III, IV, and V
334. Selected Pottery from the Western Sector of the Lower Town, Operation 4 (Phase 1; Period F — Early Bronze Age IVa)

# LIST OF PLATES

1. Aerial View (ca. mid-1960s) of Tell es-Sweyhat and View of the Central Mound from the Southwest with Uppermost Bluffs Surrounding the Sweyhat Plain East of the Mound

2. View of the Central Mound from the Southwest Showing Area IV on the Extreme Left, Area I in the Center, and Lower Town in the Foreground; Aerial View of Khirbet Dhiman, an Islamic Site Southwest of Tell es-Sweyhat; and Aerial View of Khirbet al-Hamrah, an Islamic Site Northeast of Tell es-Sweyhat

3. General North View of Trench VIA, Surface Stone Foundations, Wall 1, and General East View of Trench VIA, Phase 5, Mudbrick Wall Remains

4. General View of Trench VIA, Southeast End of the Area Investigated with Inner City Mound in the Background to the Northwest, and Close-up View of Trench VIA, Phase 3, Wall 6 Stone Foundations, and Phase 1, Mudbrick Wall 5 and South Portion of the West Section

5. Trench VIA, Phase 1 Wall 5 (center right), with Excavated Pit for a Cooking Pot in Right Lower Foreground, and Close-up View of Trench VIA, Top of Wall 6 Stone Foundations and Remains of Mudbrick Superstructure in the East Section

6. General View of Trench VIIB to Left and Trench VIIA to Right Viewed Toward the Euphrates River and Jebel Aruda in Far Left Background, and Close-up West View of Trench VIIA, Stone Foundations for Phase 4, Wall 1, in Foreground, and Wall 3 Against the North Section

7. Close-up of Trench VIIA, Phase 4 Wall 1 Stone Foundations and Partial Excavation of Phase 3 Occupation Below (West View), and General East View of Trench VIIA, Phases 3, 4, and 5 Occupation Levels

8. General North View of Trench VIIIB Across Northern Portion of Outer Defensive Wall and Trench VIIIA Across Southern Portion of Defensive Wall in Foreground, and Close-up View of Trench VIIIA, Buttress Wall 3 North of Wall 1

9. South View from Trench VIIIB Toward Trench VIIIA, Phase 1, Wall 1, and Trench VIIIA, Phases 1 and 2, Occupation Levels Between Walls 1 and 2 Viewed to the North

10. Close-up South View of Trench VIIIA, Buttress Wall 3 and Phase 2, Occupation Levels to the Right, and Trench VIIIA, Phases 1, 2, and 3, Occupation Levels Viewed to the East

11. General North View of Trench VIIIB from Trench VIIIA with Stone Wall 4 in Far Background, and Close-up South View of Stone Wall 4 with Trench VIIIA in Background Below Level of the Landrover

12. General Southeastern View of Trench XIB and Surface Stone Enclosure Walls on the Central Mound with Nefilah Village in the Distant Background, and Close-up Southeastern View of Trench XIA, Locus 1.3 Stone Wall Foundations

13. Trench IC, Pit B at Base of Deep Sounding Through the Western Half of the $5.00 \times 5.00$ m Square (East View), and Trench IC, Upper Surviving Course of Mudbrick Wall D (Northwest View)

14. South End of Trench IC, West Section Showing Remains of Mudbrick Wall D (West View), and Trench IC, North End of the West Section Showing Remains of Mudbrick Wall D and Top of Pit A (West View)

15. Trench IC, Stone Foundations of the Latest Excavated Walls A and B with Trench IB in Background (East View), and Trench IC, Stone Foundations of the Latest Excavated Walls A and B (North View)

16. Trench IIA, Close-up View of the $5.00 \times 5.00$ m Square after Removal of the Topsoil (Northwest View), and General View of Trench IIA, Deep Sounding, West End with 3 m High Access Ladder Showing Lowest Undercut Phases 1 and 2 (Southwest View)

17. General View of Trench IIA, Deep Sounding, East End Showing Phases 1, 2, and 3 in the Lowest Levels (East View), and Trench IIA, Deep Sounding, West Section Showing Successive Rebuilding of Walls B and Y During Phases 1 to 4 (West View)

18. Trench IIA, Deep Sounding, Phase 3, Stone Foundations for Wall Y (Southwest View), and Trench IIA, Deep Sounding, Phase 6, Room 9 Walls and Doorway (East View)

## LIST OF PLATES

19. Trench IIA, Deep Sounding, Phase 10, Pit 7.2 (South View), and Trench IIA, Deep Sounding, Phase 11, Hellenistic Stone-paved Street and Stone Collapse (Southeast View)

20. Trench IIA, Deep Sounding, Phase 11, Hellenistic Stone-paved Street and Top Western Edge of Pit C (Northwest View), and Trench IIA, East Quadrant of Square, Phase 12, Hellenistic Pit C in East Section (East View)

21. Trench IIA, Deep Sounding, Phase 13, Hellenistic Pit B in South Section (South View), and Trench IIA, Latest Surviving Occupation Level with Architecture, Phase 14, Hellenistic Room and Enclosures (Southwest View)

22. General View of Area IV from the Outer Town (Southeast View) and Aerial Kite View of Area IV and Operations 1, 2, 6, 7, and 8, Photographed during the 1991 Excavations by Anwar Ghafour (Aleppo National Museum)

23. General View of Trenches IVC, B, and D Showing Mudbrick Fortification Tower and Inner City Town Wall (East View), and Trench IVC, Stone Foundations Under Western Side of Mudbrick Fortification Tower (East View)

24. Trench IVB, Sounding in Mudbrick Fortification Tower Showing Stone Foundations (East View), and Trench IVD, Pit Cut into Town Wall in Foreground and East Section Showing Collapsed Wall Mudbricks into Trench IVK, Room 2 (East View)

25. Trench IVB, East Section Showing East–West Wall Between Trench IVF, Room 1, and Trench IVK, Room 2 (East View), and Trench IVF, Room 1, Phases 2A and 2B, East Wall Connecting Room 1, and Trench IVN, Room 8 (East View)

26. Trench IVF, Room 1, Phase 2A, Floor and East Wall North of Central Door (East View), and Trench IVF, Room 1, Phase 2A, Floor and East Wall South of Central Door with Upturned Stone Door Socket (East View)

27. Trenches IVF and IVN, Rooms 1 and 8, Completely Excavated Doorway Showing Paving Stones in Front of Unexcavated Workbench in Room 8 (Southeast View)

28. Trenches IVF and IVM, Phase 2B, Doorway Connecting Rooms 1 and 7 (North View), and Trench IVF, Room 1, Phase 2A, Niche in Eastern Side of Town Wall and Stone Door Socket on the Floor (West View)

29. Trenches IVJ, K, L, and Q, Rooms 2–6, Phase 2A, General View Showing Partially Excavated Storage Bin (Room 5) in Foreground, Rooms 4 and 6 in Midground, and North Walls of Rooms 2 and 3 Shown Behind and to the Right of the Vertical Foot Scale in the Background (North View); and Trenches IVL and IVP, Rooms 3 and 9, General View Showing Partially Excavated Rooms (North View)

30. View of Trench IVJ, Room 4, Phase 2A, Stone-built Bench Constructed Against Inner Face of Town Wall (West View), and Trench IVJ, Room 4, Phase 2B: Pottery in situ on Clay Platform Between Town Wall and Buttress (North View)

31. Trench IVJ, Room 4, Phase 2A, Door Between Rooms 4 and 2 with Buttress to the Left of the Door (North View), and Trench IVJ, Room 4, Phase 2A, Floor and Remaining Plaster Coating on East Wall of Room (East View)

32. Trench IVJ, Room 4, Phase 2A, Northeast Corner of Room with Jar in Doorway and Small Jar in Northeast Corner (East View); and Trench IVJ, Room 4, Phase 2A, South Side of Room with Pottery Vessels in situ (East View)

33. Trench IVJ, Room 4, Phase 2A, South Side of Room with Pottery Vessels in situ (South View)

34. Trench IVJ, Storage Bin, Room 5, Phase 2A, Jar and Cup in situ on Floor (East View), and Trench IVJ, Storage Bin, Room 5, and Trench IVO, Room 10 to Right of the South Wall (East View)

35. Trench IVK, Room 2, Phase 2A, Stone-built Bench Constructed Against Inner Face of Town Wall (West View), and Trench IVK, Room 2, Phase 2B, General View of Floor in Northeastern Sector of Room with Pottery in situ and Trench IVD Sounding into Phase 2A in Foreground (Northeast View)

36. Trench IVK, Room 2, Phase 2B, Close-up View of Floor in Northeastern Sector of Room with Mudbricks Used as Working Surfaces (East View), and Trench IVL, Room 3, Buttress Supporting Western Wall North of the Doorway (West View)

37. Trench IVL, Room 3, Plaster-covered Workbench in Northeast Corner of Room, Wall Niche Above and Left of Bench, and a Phase 3 Pit Cut through a Portion of the East Wall to the Right (North View), and Trench IVL, Room 3, Unexcavated Door in Center of East Wall Showing Position of Northern Doorjamb and Posthole (East View)

38. Trenches IVM and X, Room 7, Sounding in Western Side of Room Showing North Section of Phases 1A, 1B (Cooking Pot to right of meter pole), and 1C; North Half of Trench IVX in Upper Background (North View)

## LIST OF PLATES

39. Trench IVM, Room 7, Large Niche in Western Wall (eastern face of Town Wall) of Room (West View), and Trench IVM, Room 7, Phase 1A, Pit C Cut into Bedrock (South View)

40. Trench IVM, Room 7, Southeast Quadrant of Room Showing Threshold of Doorway into Trench IVN, Room 8 (East View, scale pole in feet), and Trench IVM, Room 7, Southeast Quadrant of Room Showing Phase 2A Pit A in Right Foreground (East View)

41. Trench IVN, Room 18, View of Partially Excavated North Side of Arch and Adjoining Bench at Lower Left with Remains of South Side of Arch Extending Out from the South Section Behind the Meter Pole to the Right (East View), and Trench IVN, Rooms 8 and 18, General View of the South Section Showing Remains of the Mudbrick-built Arch at the Far Left with Collapsed Mudbricks from the Eastern Wall Over the Arch and into the Western Sector of the Rooms (South View, scale pole in feet)

42. Trench IVN, Rooms 8 and 18, General View of the North Section Showing the Collapsed Mudbricks from the Eastern Wall Over the Arch and into the Western Sector of the Rooms (modern access steps cut into the ancient debris depicted to the right of the foot scale pole), and Trench IVN, Room 18, Lower Courses of the North Side of the Arch and Bench in the Center of Room 18 (East View)

43. Trench IVN, Room 18, South Side of Arch and Doorway into Trench IVP, Room 9 (South View), and Trench IVN (Operation 10), Rooms 18 and 8, Jar Support Hole in Floor of Southeast Corner of Room 18, Stone Foundations of Southern Half of Arch, Doorway into Room 9, and Workbench Against Southern Wall of Room 8 Excavated During the 1992 Season (South View)

44. Trench IVN (Operation 10), Room 18 in Foreground and Western Portion of Room 8 in Background Showing Completely Excavated Workbench along the Base of the Southern Wall to the Left (West View), and Trench IVN, Room 8, Western End of the Workbench Excavated in 1975 with Stone Grinders and Strainer Bowl in situ (South View)

45. Trench IVN, Room 8, Close-up of Central Portion of Workbench and Numerous Plastered Floor Surfaces with Large Flat Paving Stones in Front and Vessel Support Holes in the Floor (South View), and Trench IVN (Operation 10), Room 18, General View Showing Completely Excavated Room (East View)

46. Trench IVN (Operation 10), Room 8, General View Showing Base of Northern Side of Arch and Doorway to the Right into Room 8 (North View), and Trench IVN (Operation 10), Room 18, Close-up View of Northeastern Doorway Partially Blocked with Stones and One Half of a Grinding Stone on the Right-hand Side of the Base of the Arch (North View)

47. Trench IVN (Operation 10), Sounding Northeast of Room 18, Stone Foundations and Remains of Mudbrick Superstructure of East–West Wall Likely Constructed on Top of the North, Unexcavated, Wall of Room 8 (North View)

48. Trench IVQ, Room 6, General View of South Side of Room Showing Phase 2A Bench and Working Platform, Phase 2B Destruction, and Phase 3 Stone Foundations Built on Top of the Southern Wall of Room 6 (South View), and Trench IVQ, Room 6, Close-up View of the Phase 3 Foundation Trench for the Stones Supporting the Mudbrick Wall Constructed on Top of the Southern Wall of Room 6 in Use During Phases 2A and 2B (Southeast View)

49. Trench IVQ, Room 6, Stone Door Socket in situ on Phase 2A Floor (South View), and Trench IVQ, Room 6, Phase 2A Pottery Vessels in situ on the Floor (Southeast View)

50. Trench IVO, Room 10, General View of East Wall of the Room Showing Unexcavated Doorway in the Middle (East View, scale pole in feet), and Trench IVR, Room 11A, Phase 3 Type Series Jar in situ in the Southwest Side of the Room (North View)

51. Trench IVP, Room 9, Western End of Room Showing Unexcavated Central Doorway to Right of Scale Pole and North Side of Western Wall Destroyed by Later Pit; South End of Western Wall Removed During Excavation of Trench IVH (West View, scale pole in feet), and Trench IVP, Room 9, Northwest Corner of Room Showing the Phase 2A Doorway into Room 18 Blocked and Plastered during Phase 2B and Unexcavated Square Niche to Right of Meter Pole (North View)

52. Trench IVP, Room 9, Northwest Corner of Room Showing the Blocked and Partially Excavated Phase 2A Doorway into Room 18 (North View), and Trench IVP, Room 9, Northwest Corner of Room Showing Full Extent of the Phase 2A Doorway into Room 18 Blocked on the South with a Large Jar and Mudbricks (North View)

53. Area IV (Operation 6), Courtyard Room 9, General View of the Phase 2B Oven (Southeast View)

## LIST OF PLATES

54. Area IV (Operation 6), Rooms 16 and 17, General View Upon Completion of Excavation (Southeast View), and Area IV (Operation 6), Rooms 16 and 17, Close-up View Showing Stone Foundations of Phase 3 Mudbrick Walls in the Foreground with the Excavator, Emma Murray, Sitting on the Surviving Portion of the Phases 2A and 2B Wall (Northwest View)

55. Area IV (Operation 6), Room 16, General View Showing the Phase 2A Room with Bench Against the Western Wall and the Sounding into Phases 1B and 1C (North View), and Area IV (Operation 6), General View Showing the Buttress in Courtyard Room 9 at the Center Right and the Operation 2 Trench to the Right with the Inner Town Ring Road (North View)

56. Area IV (Operation 6), General View North Showing Partial Collapse of the Fill in the Unexcavated Northeast Doorway of Room 9 (North View), and Area IV (Operation 6): Close-up View Showing the Buttress (center right) and Partial Collapse of the Fill in the Unexcavated Northeast Doorway of Room 9 (in center background, left of the Draughtsman, John Ellsworth) (Northwest View)

57. Area IV (Operation 7), General View of 10.00 × 10.00 m Square with Phase 2B Architectural Remains on the Left Side and Phase 2A Architectural Remains on the Right Side (West View, scale pole in feet)

58. Area IV (Operation 7), General View of 10.00 × 10.00 m Square with Phase 2A Architectural Remains on the Left Side and Phase 2B Remains on the Right Side (East View, scale pole in feet), and Area IV (Operation 7), General View of 10.00 × 10.00 m Square with Partially Excavated Town Wall, Upper Left, and Partially Excavated Phases 2A, B, and 3 in Upper Background (North View, scale pole in feet)

59. Trench IXA: Phase 4, Pottery in situ (South View), and Trench IXA: Phase 4, Pottery in situ (West View)

60. Trench IXA, General East View of Trench (scale pole in feet), and Trench IXA, Close-up View of East End of Trench (scale poles in meters)

61. Trench IXA, General West View of Trench (scale pole in feet), and Trench IXA, Close-up View of West End of Trench (scale poles in meters)

62. Trench IXA, General South View of Phase 2A Stone Foundations for Walls 6 and 8 and Wall 7 and Phase 4 Pit A in the South Section (scale pole in feet), and Trench IXA, Close-up View of West Side of Pit A and Wall 7 Stone Foundations Extending into the South Section (scale pole in feet)

63. Trench XA, Room 15, Inner Mudbrick Face of Phase 2A Town Wall with Stone Foundations of Later Phase 3 Wall on Top and Room 15 in the Foreground (West View), and Trench XA, Room 15, Southern Mudbrick Wall of Room 15 Shown Obliquely in the South Section with its Stone Foundations in the Foreground after the Removal of the Mudbrick Superstructure (South View)

64. Trench XA, Room 15, Close-up of the Stone Foundations for the South and West Mudbrick Walls 3 and 2 (South View), and Trench XA (Operation 11), General View of Enlarged North Side of Trench XA During 1992 Showing the Remains of Mudbrick Wall 3 at Far Right (Northeast View)

65. Trench XA (Operation 11), General View of Operation 11 Showing Partially Excavated Phase 2B Room 20 at Far Left and Room 17 to the Right of the North–South Wall Topped with Phase 3 Wall Foundation Stones (South View), and Trench XA (Operation 11), General Central Eastern View Showing Sounding into Phases 2A and 1C to the Left of Wall 3 (East View)

66. Trench XA (Operation 11), Close-up of the Sounding into Phases 2A and 1C (Northeast View), and Trench XA (Operation 11), Phase 3 Stone Basin in situ with Phase 4 Wall Foundation Stones in Foreground (East View)

67. Trench IVZ(S), Phase 3, Wall with Flat Stone Threshold and Pottery in situ on Floor (West View), and Trench IVZ(N1): Phase 2B Wall C at Left and Phase 2A Stone Wall Foundations at Right (South View)

68. Trench IVZ(N2), Phase 3, Portion of Room 21 with Stone Wall Foundations and Threshold in Foreground and Some Pottery Vessels in situ (Southeast View), and South Sector of the Central Mound Showing the Stone Foundations of the Roman Period Buildings Protruding from the Modern Surface Soil (South View)

69. Area III, General View from Top of Central Mound (Northeast View), and Area III, General View of Squares A–E at Right Foreground and Step Trench, Area V, at Left Foreground (North View)

70. Trench IIIA, Phase 3, Wall 5 (South View), and Trench IIIA, Phase 4, Walls 1 and 2 Showing Door and Socket Stone (South View)

71. Trench IIIB, Phase 3, Destruction Levels Above the Phase 2B Occupation Shown in the Western Part of the North Section (North View), and Trench IIIB, Phase 3, Destruction Levels Above the Phase 2B Occupation Shown in the Eastern Part of the North Section (North View)

LIST OF PLATES                                                                                          xix

72. Trench IIIB, Phase 2B, Stone Foundations for Wall 3 (West View), and Trench IIIB, Phase 5, Stones on Top of Storage Pit (West View)

73. Trench IIIB, Phase 4, Wall 1 (Southeast View), and Trench IIIB, Phase 5, Close-up View of Hearth Attached to Wall 1 (Southeast View)

74. Trench IIIC, Phase 4, Walls 13 and 15 (Foreground Left), 14 (Center), and Wall 8A, Below Phase 5 Wall 8B (Right Background) (South View), and Trench IIIC, General View of Phases 4 and 5 Walls (West View)

75. Trench IIID, Stone Foundations of Phase 5 Walls 1, 2, and 4 (Northwest View), and Trench IIID, Stone Foundations of Phase 4 Walls 7 (Left) and 8 (Central Background) and Phase 5 Walls 1 and 2 (Southeast View)

76. Trench IIID, Pottery and Stone Objects in situ on Phase 4, Floor 5.6, Bounded by Walls 7 and 8 (Northwest View), and Trench IIID, General View of Phase 4, Floor 5.6, After Removal of the Finds (Northwest View)

77. Trench IIIG/H, Close-up View of Plastered Face of Phase 3 Wall P in Courtyard Room 1 (Southeast View), and Trench IIIG/H, Close-up View from Above Storage Pit 1.11 of Phase 3 in Courtyard Room 1

78. Trench IIIG/H, Phase 4, Room 17A, Cooking Pot in situ with a Child Burial Inside in situ (East View), and Trench IIIG/H, Stone Working Surface on North Side of Phase 5, Room 3 (North View)

79. Trench IIIG/H, General View of Phase 6 Stone Wall Foundations (South View), and Trench IIIG/H, General View of Phase 7, Walls E and F (South View)

80. Trench IIIG/H, Phase 6, Courtyard Locus 1.4 Showing Burned Patch in Vicinity of a Flint Deposit (West View), and Trench IIIL, Stone Foundations of Phase 5, Wall 1 (Foreground) and Wall 2 (Background Right; East View)

81. Operation 5, General North View of Quadrant D, Phases 3, 4 (Pits 17.3 and 18.6), and 5 in Right Foreground and Quadrant C, Phase 3, Roman Pit and Phase 4, Wall 13.1 in Background, and Operation 5, General South View of Quadrant C, Phase 4, Floors in Foreground and Quadrant D, Phase 4, Pits 18.6 and 17.3, in Background

82. Operation 5, Close-up North View of Quadrant D, Phase 5, Wall 19.2 in Right Foreground, and Phase 4, Pits 17.3 and 18.6, in Background, and Operation 5, Close-up West View of Phase 4, Pits 18.6, in Foreground, and 17.3, in Background

83. Operation 5, General West View of Quadrant C, Phase 4, Wall 13.1, Cut by Roman Pit 14.9, and Operation 5, General Northeast View of Quadrant C, Phase 2, Surviving Top of Mudbrick Wall 21.2 with Buttress A in Center of Photograph

84. Operation 5, General East View of Quadrant C, Phase 2, Mudbrick Wall 21.2 After Clearance of Fallen Wall Painting Fragments from the Face of the Wall and Buttress C; and Operation 5, Close-up View of North Top of Wall 21.2 with Unpainted Eastern Plaster Face of the Wall in situ in the Northeast Corner of Quadrant C

85. Operation 5, Close-up East View of Quadrant C, Phase 2, Floor Between Buttresses A and B of Wall 21.2, and Operation 5: Close-up South View of Phase 1 Sounding in Southwest Corner of Quadrant C with Top of Jar in situ at Floor Level

86. Operation 5, Close-up East View of Quadrant C, Phase 2, Buttress A with Topmost Surviving Layer of Wall Painting Fragments in situ, and Operation 5: Close-up South View of Quadrant C, Phase 2, North Face of Buttress A with Wall Painting Fragments Under Consolidation for Removal from the Soil

87. Operation 5, Close-up South View of Quadrant C, Phase 2, Wall Painting Fragments in situ with Reused Jar Sherd Spindle Whorl, and Operation 5, Close-up East View of Quadrant C, Phase 2 Buttress A to Right with Wall Painting Fragment WP. 92.61 (pl. 131a) in Foreground

88. Operation 5, General West View of Quadrant C, West Section Showing Phase 5, Pit 11.8, Cutting Through the Phase 4 Occupation Levels and Floor 13.7, and Operation 5, General West View of Quadrant C, Phase 2, Floor 32.5, Showing Mudbrick Offering or Working Platforms in situ on the Floor

89. Bronze Age Pottery Types. Miniature Bowl: MBR. A.I.a (SW. 483, pl. 204:1), Top and Side Views; Small Bowls: SBR. A.I.a (SW. 569, fig. 66:1), SBR. A.I.b (SW. 382, pl. 205:2); and Bowls: BR. E.III.a (SW. 496, pl. 214:7), and BR. R.I.a (SW. 501, pl. 222:1)

90. Bronze Age Pottery Type. Crucible Bowl: CBR. A.I.a (SW. 381, pl. 223:1)

91. Bronze Age Pottery Types. Small Jars: SJR. B.II.j (SW. 519, fig. 68:3), SJR. C.II.d (SW. 102, pl. 226:12), and SJR. C.II.i (SW. 10 = TS. 848, pl. 226:17)

92. Bronze Age Pottery Types. Small Jars: SJR. C.II.k (SW. 395 = TS. 1767, pl. 226:19), SJR. C.II.m (SW. 723, pl. 226:21); Jar: JR. E.II.r (SW. 524, pl. 243:10)

93. Bronze Age Pottery Type. Jar JR. H.I.g (SW. 294, fig. 64:4): General View and Close-up View of Eagle under the Hole of the Missing Spout
94. Bronze Age Pottery Type. Jar JR. J.I.e (SW. 292, pl. 251:5)
95. Bronze Age Pottery Types. Jars: JR. J.I.h (SW. 733, pl. 251:8), JR. J.III.a (SW. 293, fig. 62:6), JR. J.III.t (SW. 567, pls. 34a, 254:1), and JR. J.III.v (SW. 309, pl. 254:3)
96. Bronze Age Pottery Types. Jars: JR. J.IV.a (SW. 649, pl. 255:1), JR. L.I.a (SW. 676, pl. 259:1), JR. L.II.a (SW. 651, pl. 259:2), and JR. O.II.a (SW. 624, pl. 263:1)
97. Bronze Age Pottery Types. Flasks: FL. A.II.a (SW. 722, pl. 274:3), FL. A.II.b (SW. 706, pl. 274:5), and FL. B.I.a (SW. 272, fig. 88:5), Pot Stand: PS. A.I.a (SW. 560, pl. 289:1), and Windowed Pot or Pedestal Stand: WPS. B (TS. 3197 = TS. 3269, fig. 74:9)
98. Bronze Age Pottery Types. Strainer Bowls: SR. B.I.b (SW. 558, pl. 290:8), SR. C.I.a (SW. 725, pl. 290:16); Cooking Pots: Reconstruction of Cooking Pot SW. 539, CP. A.II.a (SW. 539, pl. 276:1), and CP. B.IV.c (SW. 761, pl. 280:3)
99. Bronze Age Pottery, Miscellaneous. Small Jar or Covered Model Wagon: SJR. C.I.a (SW. 820, fig. 136 text, cf. pl. 119c); Incised Jar Sherds: Incised "Warrior" (SW. 627, fig. 154:6), and Incised "Horse" (SW. 630, fig. 154:13)
100. Bronze Age Pottery. Rim and Body Sherds with Miscellaneous Decoration and Potters' Marks: Mythical-type Incised Animals (TS. 1733, fig. 90:3), Applied Snake-like Rope Band (TS. 1597, fig. 129:5), Incised Floral Decoration, Bowl BR. L.I.h (TS. 1610, pl. 219:8), Potter's Mark on Jar Sherd (TS. 1586, fig. 64:13), Tree or Wheat Stalk Pattern on Jar Sherd (TS. 2573, fig. 154:11), and Potter's Mark on Jar Sherd (TS. 1734, fig. 64:14)
101. Bronze Age Pottery. Types with Incised Potters' Marks: Jar Base BE. E.I.c [PM. C.14] (TS. 1609, pl. 292:3), Jar JR. O.I.a [PM. D.6] (SW. 695, pl. 261), Jar JR. O.II.m [PM. C.5] (SW. 644, fig. 77:4), Jar JR. O.III.e [PM. D.1] (SW. 638, fig. 77:5), and Jar Sherd, JR. Sh. [PM. D.17] (TS. 1774, fig. 77:10)
102. Bronze Age Pottery. Jar Types with Incised Potters' Marks and Comb-incised Decoration: JR. P.II.a [PM. C.7] (SW. 666, fig. 64:10), JR. P.II.a [PM. D.15] (TS. 2810, fig. 91:10), Jar Sherd, Jr. Sh. [IP (G.1) B.I.a] (TS. 1655, fig. 112:14), and Jar Sherd, Jr. Sh. [IP (G.1) C.IV.a] (TS. 1651, fig. 130:7)
103. Bronze Age Vessels. Zoomorphic Clay Figures, Type SV.3: SW. 655 (IVN, fig. 170:8), Vessel Fragment with Bird-like Spout, Right Side and Frontal Views; SW. 460 (IC, fig. 28:2), Boar's Head, Front of Head and Nostril Views; and SW. 840 (Operation 4, fig. 335:15), Boar's Head, Front of Head and Nostril Views
104. Bronze Age Figurines (Area III). Clay Human Female, Type SF.1a: SW. 135 (IIID, fig. 221:5), SW. 192 (IIIB, fig. 221:4), SW. 46 (IIIA, fig. 221:1), Front and Back Views, and SW. 546 (IIIG/H, fig. 221:6), Right Side, Front, and Back Views
105. Bronze Age Figurines (Areas III, VI, and IX). Clay Human Female, Type SF.1c: SW. 223 (IIIE, fig. 221:3), SW. 401 (IIIG/H, fig. 221:9), Front and Back Views, SW. 389 (VIA, fig. 258:4), SW. 385 (VIA, fig. 258:6), and SW. 479 (IXA, fig. 175:2)
106. Bronze Age Figurines (Area III). Clay Human Female, Type SF.1c: SW. 476 (IIIG/H, fig. 221:7), Front and Back Views, and SW. 366 (IIIG/H, fig. 221:8), Front, Left Side, and Back Views
107. Bronze Age Figurine (Unknown Provenance). Two-headed Human Attached to Four-legged Basin: Front, Back, Top, Frontal Detail of Heads, Right Side, and Left Side
108. Bronze Age Figurines (Area IV). Clay Human Female, Type SF.1a: SW. 318 (IVG, Unstratified, fig. 155:2), Right Side, Front, and Back Views; TS. 3292 (Operation 6, fig. 156:12), Right Side, Front, Left Side, and Back Views; and SW. 814 (Operation 7, fig. 155:12), Right Side, Front, and Back Views
109. Bronze Age Figurines (Area IV). Clay Human Female, Type SF.1a: SW. 766 (Operation 7, fig. 156:8), Top of Head, Right Side, Front, Left Side, and Back Views, and SW. 383 (IVF, fig. 155:3), Front and Back Views
110. Bronze Age Figurines (Area IV). Clay Human Female, Type SF.1a: SW. 714 (IVX, fig. 155:4), SW. 811 (Operation 6, fig. 156:13), Front and Back Views, and SW. 836 (Operation 7, fig. 155:13), Front and Back Views
111. Bronze Age Figurines (Area IV). Clay Human Female, Types SF.1a and 1c: Type SF.1a (SW. 556, IVL/P Baulk, fig. 156:5), Type SF.1a (FN. 45, Operation 7, fig. 156 Text), Type SF.1a (SW. 765, Operation 7, fig. 156:7), and Type SF.1c (SW. 815, Operation 7, fig. 156 Text), Front and Back Views
112. Bronze Age Figurine (Operation 5). Clay Human Female, Type SF.1a: SW. 835 (fig. 249:1), Front and Back Views

# LIST OF PLATES

113. Bronze Age Figurines (Operation 5). Clay Human Figurine, Types SF.1c and 1b: Type SF.1c, Female Torso Fragment (FN. 13, fig. 249:3), and Type SF.1b, Male Head Fragment (SW. 817, fig. 249:2), Right Side, Front, and Left Side Views

114. Bronze Age Figurines and Miniature Mortars (Operation 5). Clay Figurines: Type SF.1c, Human Female Figurine (FN. 175, fig. 249:4), Front and Back Views; Type SF.1c, Human Figurine Pillar Stand (FN. 149, fig. 249 Text); and Type SF.1d, Model Horse Figurine Fragment (FN. 24, fig. 249 Text); Miniature Mortars: Type SF.6g, Two Clay Mortars (FN. 169 and FN. 170, fig. 252:3, 4), Top and Bottom Views

115. Bronze Age and Hellenistic Figurines (Areas II, III, and IV). Bronze Age Clay Female Figurine Pillar- and Plaque-type Stands: Type SF.1c (SW. 111, IIA, fig. 51:3), Type SF.1c (SW. 112, IIA, fig. 51:4), Type SF.1c (SW. 402, IIIG/H, fig. 221:14 ), Type SF.1c (SW. 200, IIIB, fig. 221:12), Type SF.1c (SW. 141, IIIC, fig. 221:15), Type SF.1c (SW. 548, IVP, fig. 155:11), Type SF.1c (SW. 42, IIIB, fig. 221:13), and Type SF.1c (SW. 481, IVJ, fig. 155:6); Hellenistic Figurines: Type SF.1c, Human Figurine Torso (SW. 153, IIB, fig. 258:12), Type SF.1d, Model Bull's Head (SW. 85, IIA, fig. 51:9), and Type SF.1d, Dove Figurine (SW. 87, IIA, fig. 51:6)

116. Bronze Age Clay Animal Figurines (Area IV and Operation 10). Type SF.1d: Horse (SW. 770, Operation 10, fig. 157:6), Top, Left Side, Underside, and Right Side Views; Horse or Onager Head (SW. 396, IVF, fig. 157:1), Right Side and Frontal Views; and Bovine Head (SW. 555, IVP, Unstratified, fig. 158:6), Top of Head and Snout Views

117. Bronze Age Clay Animal Figurines (Areas II, III, and IV): Type SF.1d (SW. 51, IIIA, fig. 222:1), Type SF.1d (SW. 204, IIIF, fig. 222:3), Type SF.1d (SW. 93, IIIC, fig. 222:4), Type SF.1d (SW. 418, IVN, fig. 158:5), Type SF.1d (SW. 232, IVE, fig. 157:9), Type SF.1d (SW. 713, IVP, fig. 157:4), Type SF.1d (SW. 518, IVL, fig. 157:3), Type SF.1e (SW. 79, IIA, fig. 51:7), and Type SF.1e (SW. 48, IIIA, fig. 222:2)

118. Bronze Age Clay Animal Figurines (Areas III, IV, IX, and Operation 5): Type SF.1d (SW. 592, IVD, fig. 157:10), Type SF.1e (SW. 387, IVC, fig. 158:1), Type SF.1d (SW. 436, IXA, fig. 175:3), Type SF.1e (SW. 712, IVM, fig. 157:5), Type SF.1d (SW. 83, IIIA, fig. 222:5), Top and Right Side Views, and Type SF.1d (SW. 826, Operation 5, fig. 249:8), Eyes, Forehead, and Ears (Top), Right Side, Front Mouth, and Left Side Views

119. Bronze Age Clay Model Chariots and Model Wheels (Areas IC, IV, X, and Operation 6). Model Chariots, Type SF.2a: SW. 522 (XA, fig. 159:1), Left Side View, SW. 393 (IVK, fig. 159:2), Front and Right Side Views, and SW. 842 (Operation 6, fig. 159:3), Right Side and Front Views; Model Wheels, Type SF.2b: SW. 392 (IVK, fig. 159:4), SW. 475 (IVN, fig. 159:5), SW. 459 (IC, fig. 28:3), and SW. 547 (XA, fig. 159:8)

120. Bronze Age Clay Model Wheel and Miscellaneous Objects (Areas IV and X): Model Wheel, Type SF.2b (SW. 549, XA, fig. 159:9), Unfired Mold Fragment, Type SF.6d (SW. 660, IVM, fig. 160:2), Offering Stand, Type SF.6g (SW. 553, IVL/P, Baulk, fig. 160:4), Compartment Vessel or Model House, Type SF.2c (SW. 521, XA, fig. 170:6), Top and Oblique Side Views, and Unbaked Sling Bullets, Types SF.6a.1–4, 8 (SW. 420a–e, IVK, fig. 165:1–5)

121. Bronze Age Metal Objects (Area IV Rooms and Operation 7). Type SF.5: Tongs, Type SF.5a (SW. 234, IVK, fig. 161:1), Collar for Pottery Jar, Type SF.5b (SW. 598, IVJ, fig. 161:2), Toilet Knife, Type SF.5h (SW. 606, IVL, fig. 162:15), Mushroom-headed Pin Type with Eyelet Hole, Type SF.5c (SW. 619, IVJ, fig. 161:3), Lynch Pin, Type SF.5d (SW. 720, IVN, fig. 161:11), Lynch Pin, Type SF.5d (SW. 721, IVN, fig. 161:12), and Pin Shaft, Type SF.5c (SW. 802, Operation 7, fig. 162:12)

122. Roman Period Metal and Stone Objects and Coins (Operation 5 and Area I). Bronze Spatula, Type SF.5g (SW. 801, Operation 5, fig. 251:3), Stone Tool or Weapon Mold, Type SF.3f (SW. 830, Operation 5, fig. 250:7), and Roman Coins, Type SF.5j (SW. 235, SW. 236, Area IA2, fig. 28 Text), Obverse and Reverse Views

123. Bronze Age Stone Objects (Area IV Rooms and Operation 11). Limestone Cylinder Seal and Plaster-rolled Impression of Its Decoration, Type SF.3f (SW. 647, IVL, fig. 163:4), One Mana Cuneiform Inscribed Stone Weight, Types SF.3e and SF.10 (SW. 585, IVL, fig. 163:2), Plaster Impression of One Mana Cuneiform Inscribed Weight, Stone Pivot or Potter's Wheel, Type SF.3f (SW. 767, Operation 11, fig. 163:1), and Limestone Bowl with Engraved Decoration, Type SF.3c (SW. 471, IVN, fig. 163:5)

124. Bronze Age Miscellaneous Objects (Area IV and Operation 6 Rooms). Flint Arrowhead, Type SF.12b (SW. 593, IVM, fig. 168:1), Shell Pendant, Type SF.4c (SW. 823, Operation 6, fig. 169 Text), Inside Decorated and Outside Views; and Stone Jewelry Mold, Type SF.3f (SW. 833, Operation 6, fig. 164:5), Top, Outside, Bottom, and Inside Views

125. Bronze Age Stone Objects (Operations 6 and 7 Rooms). Cosmetic Tray, Type SF.3c (SW. 804, Operation 6, fig. 164:6), Top and Side Views, and Fishing Net Weight or Loom Weight, Type SF.3e (SW. 822, Operation 7, fig. 164:7), Obverse and Reverse Views

126. Bronze Age Stone Objects (Operation 6 Rooms). Pounding Tool, Type SF.3a (SW. 805, Operation 6, fig. 173:10), Broad and Flat Side Views, Loom Weight, Type SF.3e (FN. 125, Operation 6, fig. 164 Text), Obverse and Reverse Views; and Footed Mortar, Type SF.3c (SW. 821, Operation 6, fig. 171:7)

127. Bronze Age Objects (Area IXA). Clay Animal Pull-toy, Type SF.1f (SW. 458, fig. 175:4): Right-hand Side, Complete, Left-hand Side, Incomplete; and Three-footed Limestone Mortar, Type SF.3c (SW. 448, fig. 175:8)

128. Bronze Age Stone and Clay Objects (Areas III, IV). Mortar, Type SF.3c, with Grinder, Type SF.3a, Found in situ (SW. 349a, b; IIID, fig. 227:1a, b), and Two Unfired Clay Objects, Type SF.6g (SW. 648, IVJ/O Baulk, fig. 170:5a, b)

129. Bronze Age Mat Impressions on Fallen Roof *Libn* (IVQ, Room 6, Phase 2B). Photograph of Two Segments, and Line Drawing Showing Mat Impressions and Pattern of Weaving on the Two Segments (by Donald Whitcomb)

130. Wall Painting Fragments (Operation 5). WP. 92.38 (fig. 254), Photograph Showing a Bovine with Suckling Calf Standing on a Mountainside, WP. 91.18, Photograph Showing Border and Tree Pattern, and Possible Reconstruction of Part of One Painting

131. Wall Painting Fragments Depicting Human and Geometric Designs (Operation 5). WP. 92.61 (fig. 255c), Photograph Showing Human Figures, WP. 91.9 (fig. 257:1), Photograph Showing Tree Branches, WP. 92.74a and WP. 92.74b (fig. 257:3, 4), Photograph Showing Border Patterns, and Possible Reconstruction of Part of a Second Painting

132. Hellenistic and Roman Finds (Area I, II, and 1972 Survey of Romala, fig. 9 Text). Greek Ostracon (SW. 196, IIB, fig. 51:15), Aramaic Inscription (SW. 105, IA2, fig. 28:8), Geometric Stamp Seal Impression (Romala Survey), Stamped Jar Handle (Romala Survey), Male Human Figurine (Romala Survey), Female Plaque-type Figurine (Romala Survey), and Hollow-molded Figure of a Female Riding a Horse or Camel (SW. 178, IIA, fig. 51:1)

133. Plan of South Slope of Central Mound Showing Surface Stone Wall Foundations Dated to the Roman Period, Positions of Area I Trenches A to J, Operation 5, XIB Sounding, and Later Surface Stone Enclosure Walls on the Lower Southeast Portion of the Tell with Position of Sounding XIA

134. Plan of Trench XIA, Phase 2, and Plan of Trench XIB, Phases 1 and 2

135. Lower Town and Outer Fortification Soundings: S.1, Phase 3 Plan; S.1, Phase 2 Plan; S.2, Phase 2 Plan; S.2, Phase 1 Plan; t.1, North Section, Phases 1–5; and t.1, Key to Hatching of Phases on North Section

136. Key to Plans and Positions of Sections of Trench VIA and Key to Hatching of Phases on Section Drawings of Trench VIA

137. Plan of Trench VIA, Phase 1, and Plan of Trench VIA, Phase 2

138. Plan of Trench VIA, Phase 3, and Plan of Trench VIA, Phase 4

139. Trench VIA, West Section, Trench VIA, East Section, and Trench VIA, South Section

140. Plan of Trenches VIIA and B and Key to Hatching of Phases on Section Drawings of Trench VIIA

141. Trench VIIA, South Section, Trench VIIA, East Section, and Trench VIIA, Southeast Section

142. Plan of Trenches VIIIA and B and Key to Hatching of Phases on Section Drawings of Trenches VIIIA and B

143. Trench VIIIA, East Section, and Trench VIIIB, West Section

144. Key to Plan and Sections of Trench IC and Trench IC, West Section

145. Trench IC, North Section, Key to Hatching of Phases on Section Drawings of Trench IC, and Trench IC, East Section

146. Keys to Plans and Sections of Trench IIA and Keys to Plans and Sections of Trench IIB

147. Area IIA, West Section, Area IIA, North Section, and Key to Hatching of Phases on Section Drawings of Trenches IIA and IIB

148. Trench IIA, East Section

149. Trench IIA, South Section, Trench IIB, East Section, and Trench IIB, South Section

150. Plan of Trench IIA, Phase 1, Plan of Trench IIA, Phase 2, Plan of Trench IIA, Phase 3, and Plan of Trench IIA, Phase 4

151. Plan of Trench IIA, Phase 5, Plan of Trench IIA, Phase 6, Plan of Trench IIA, Phase 7, and Plan of Trench IIA, Phase 8

152. Plan of Trench IIA, Phase 9, Plan of Trench IIA, Phase 10, and Plan of Trench IIA, Phase 11

## LIST OF PLATES

153. Plan of Trench IIA, Phase 12, and Plan of Trench IIA, Phase 13
154. Plan of Trench IIA, Phase 14, and Plan of Trench IIB, Phases 13, 14, and 15
155. Schematic Plan Showing Locations of Trenches, Operations, and Rooms in Area IV and Trench XA, and Key to Hatching of Phases on Section Drawings of Area IV and Trench XA
156. Trench IVA, South Section, Trench IVB, East Section of Sounding into Western Portions of Trench IVF (Room 1) and Trench IVK (Room 2), Trench IVC, South Section Abutting Southwest Corner of Town Wall Tower, and Trench IVD, North Section Showing Position of Town Wall and Western Portion of Trench IVK (Room 2)
157. Trench IVD, East Section Showing Central Portion of Trench IVK (Room 2), Trench IVD, South Section Showing Position of Town Wall and Western Portion of Trench IVK (Room 2), and Trench IVE, East Section of Sounding into Portions of Trench IVL (Room 3) and Trench IVQ (Room 6)
158. Trench IVF, East Section Along Walls and Door Between IVF (Room 1) and IVN (Room 8), Trench IVF, South Section of First Sounding in the North Portion of Room 1, Trench IVJ, North Section Showing Position of Pottery on Platform in Northwestern Portion of Room 4, Trench IVJ, South Section of Sounding on Southern Side of Room 4, Trench IVJ, West Section of Sounding on Southern Side of Room 4, and Trench IVJ, East Section Through Central Upper Portion of the Storage Bin (Room 5)
159. Trench IVL, East Section Along Wall and Door Between Trench IVL (Room 3) and Trench IVP (Courtyard Room 9), Trench IVM, North Section 1 Across Full Length of the Northern Portion of Room 7, and Trench IVM, North Section 2 Showing Remains of North Wall (Room 7) and Sounding Below the Wall of Room 7
160. Trench IVM, East Section of Southwest Portion of Room 7 and Sounding Below the Wall of Room 7, and Trench IVM, South Section Across the Central East–West Portion of Room 7
161. Plan of Rooms 8 and 18 in Trench IVN and the Operation 10 Sounding at the Northeast Corner of Trench IVN, Plan of Top View of Arch in Trench IVN, and Elevation Plan of West Side of Arch in Trench IVN
162. Trench IVN, South Section of Rooms 8 and 18, Operation 10, West Section, Operation 10, North Section, Trench IVQ, South Section 1 of Southeast Quadrant of Room 6, Trench IVQ, East Section of Southeast Quadrant of Room 6, and Trench IVQ, South Section 2 Along South Wall of Room 6
163. Trenches IVO and R, East Section along Walls and Door of Rooms 10 and 11, Trench IVR, Plan of Portions of Rooms 11 and 12 and the Town Wall, and Trench IVS, North Section through the Middle of Room 12
164. Phase 2A Plan of Courtyard Trench IVP, Room 9, and Operation 6, Rooms 16 and 17
165. Phase 2B Plan of Trench IVP, Courtyard Room 9, and Operation 6, Oven 16.1 and Room 17
166. Phase 3 Plan of Operation 6, Rooms 22–28
167. Phase 4 Plan of Operation 6, Rooms 31–33
168. Trench IVP, Courtyard Room 9, North Section Showing Phases IC, 2A, and 2B, Operation 6, Room 16, East Section, Operation 6, Room 16, South Section, and Operation 6, Room 16, West Section
169. Trench IVZ(N1), East Section, Trench IVZ(N1), South Section, Trench IVZ(N2), South Section, Trench IVZ(S), South Section, and Trench IVZ(S), West Section
170. Plan of Operation 7, Rooms 34–36, Gateway, and Street through West Side of Town Wall During Phases 2A(a) and 2A(b)
171. Phase 2B(a) Plan of Operation 7, Pits and Room 40, and Phase 2B(b), and Plan of Operation 7, Rooms 37–39
172. Plan of Operation 7, Phase 3 Walls and Phase 4 Stone Collapse, Loci 9.1 and 9.2
173. Operation 7, East Section, Operation 7, South Section, and Operation 7, West Section
174. Phases 3 and 4 Plan of Operation 8, Portions of Rooms 26, 29, and 30
175. Key to Plans and Positions of Sections in Trench IXA and Key to Hatching of Phases on Sections
176. Phases 2A and 3 Plan of Trench IXA and Phase 4 Plan of Trench IXA
177. Trench IXA, North Section, and Trench IXA, South Section
178. Trench IXA, West Section, Trench IXA, East Section 1, and Trench IXA, East Section 2
179. Key to Plans and Sections of Trench XA and Operation 11 and Plan of Trench XA, Phase 2A Town Wall and Southwestern Portion of Room 15

xxiv  *LIST OF PLATES*

180. Trench XA, West Section Against Inner Face of Town Wall, Trench XA, North Section, Trench XA, East Section, and Trench XA, South Section
181. Composite Plan of Trench XA and Operation 11 Showing Phases 1C and 2A Sounding, Phase 2B Rooms 15, 19, and 20, and Portions of Phase 3 Walls Belonging to Rooms 15A and 20A; and Operation 11, East Section
182. Key to Plans and Sections of Area III and Key to Hatching of Phases on Sections
183. Phase 3 Plan of Trench IIIA, Rooms 4A and 4B, Showing Walls 4, 5, and 5A, and Phase 4 Plan of Trench IIIA, Rooms 8A, 8B, and 11, Showing Walls 1, 2, and 3
184. Trench IIIA, North Section, Trench IIIA, South Section, and Trench IIIA, West Section
185. Phases 2 and 3 Plan of Trench IIIB, Room 1A, Showing Walls 2 and 3 with Phase 4 Wall 1 in situ, Phase 4 Plan of Trench IIIB, Rooms 6 and 7, Showing Walls 1, 1A, and 1B and Phase 5 Stone Capping on Pit 4.1 and 4.2, and Trench IIIB, North Section
186. Trench IIIB, West Section, Phase 4 Plan of Trench IIIC, Rooms 9, 10, and 11A, Showing Walls 8A, 13, 14, and 15, Trench IIIC, North Section, and Trench IIIC, East Section
187. Trench IIIC, South Section, Trench IIIC, West Section, and Phase 5 Plan of Trench IIIC, Rooms 19A–C, Showing Walls 8B, 11, 12, 12A, and 15A
188. Phase 4 Plan of Trench IIID, Rooms 11A, 12, and 13, Showing Walls 6, 7, 8, 9 and Position of Unexcavated Wall 10, Phase 5 Plan of Trench IIID, Rooms 20 and 21, Showing Walls 1–5, and Trench IIID, North Section
189. Trench IIID, East Section; Trench IIID, South Section; Phase III Plan of Trench IIIE, Room 5, Showing Wall 2 and Unexcavated Portion of Trench; Phase 4 Plan of Trench IIIE, Courtyard Room 14 and Room 15, Showing Walls 1, 1A, 1B, and 1C; and Trench IIIE, North Section
190. Trench IIIE, East Section; Trench IIIE, South Section; Phase 4 Plan of Trench IIIF, Alley and Room 16, Showing Walls 1 and 2; and Trench IIIF, North Section
191. Key to Plan of Trenches IIIG, H, and Expanded Trench III G/H Showing Positions of Sections
192. Plan of Trench IIIG/H, Phase 1C Storage Pit and Phase 2 Rooms 2A and 2B, Showing Walls N and O and Positions of Walls P and Q; and Plan of Trench IIIG/H, Phase 3 Rooms 3A and 3B, Showing Reused Walls N and O and Positions of Reused Walls P and Q
193. Phase 4 Plan of Trench IIIG/H, Rooms 17, 17A, and 18, Showing Walls D1, D2, and R and Positions of Unexcavated Walls A1 and H and Remains of Mudbrick Town Wall on the Northeastern Side of the Main Mound; and Trench IIIG/H, North Section
194. Phase 5 Plan of Trench IIIG/H, Rooms 22A and 22B, Showing Walls A2, C2, and E; and Trench IIIG/H, South Section
195. Phase 6 Plan of Trench IIIG/H Showing Fragmentary Walls K, L, and M; and Phase 7A Plan of Trench IIIG/H, Rooms 23 and 24, Showing Walls B1 and B2 and Reused Wall E
196. Phase 7B Plan of Trench IIIG/H, Reused Rooms 23 and 24, Showing Reused Walls B1, B2, E, and Additional Wall F; Trench IIIG, East Section; Trench IIIH, East Section, Trench IIIG/H, West Section; and Trench IIIG/H, Northeast Section
197. Plan of Trench IIIJ Phase 4 Showing Wall 1 and Hearth; Trench IIIJ, South Section; and Phase 5 Plan of Trench IIIL Showing Walls 1 and 2
198. Key to Plans and Sections of Operation 5
199. Plan of Operation 5, Phase 2 Mudbrick Wall 21.2 with Fallen Wall Painting Fragments and Phase 1 Sounding in Southwest Corner of Quadrant C; Key to Hatching of Phases on Sections; and Operation 5, North Section of Quadrant C
200. Operation 5, North Section of Quadrant B; Operation 5, Southwest Section of Quadrant C; and Operation 5, West Section of Quadrants D and C
201. Plan of Operation 5, Quadrant C, Showing Remnants of Phases 4 and 5; and Plan of Operation 5, Quadrant D, Showing Phase 4 Pits 17.3 and 18.6 and Phases 3, 4 (Walls 14.3, 18.1) and 5 Walls
202. Plan of Operation 5, Quadrant D, Showing Phase 5 Roman Ovens 9.2 and 9.4 and Wall 19.2; and Operation 5, Quadrant D South Section through Roman Ovens 9.2 and 9.4
203. Plan of Operation 5, Quadrants A–D, Showing Phases 6 and 7

204. Bronze Age Miniature Bowl (MBR) Types A–D
205. Bronze Age Small Bowl/Cup (SBR) Type A
206. Bronze Age Small Bowl/Cup (SBR) Type B
207. Bronze Age Small Bowl/Cup (SBR) Type C
208. Bronze Age Small Bowl (SBR) Type D
209. Bronze Age Small Bowl (SBR) Types E, F, and G
210. Bronze Age Bowl (BR) Type A
211. Bronze Age Bowl (BR) Type B
212. Bronze Age Bowl (BR) Type C
213. Bronze Age Bowl (BR) Type D
214. Bronze Age Bowl (BR) Type E
215. Bronze Age Bowl (BR) Type F
216. Bronze Age Bowl (BR) Type G
217. Bronze Age Bowl (BR) Type H
218. Bronze Age Bowl (BR) Types J and K
219. Bronze Age Bowl (BR) Type L
220. Bronze Age Bowl (BR) Types M and N
221. Bronze Age Bowl (BR) Types O, P, and Q
222. Bronze Age Bowl (BR) Types R, S, and T
223. Bronze Age Crucible Bowl (CBR) Type A and Miniature Jar (MJR) Types (Not Classified)
224. Bronze Age Small Jar (SJR) Type A
225. Bronze Age Small Jar (SJR) Type B
226. Bronze Age Small Jar (SJR) Type C
227. Bronze Age Small Jar (SJR) Types D, E, and F
228. Bronze Age Jar (JR) Type A
229. Bronze Age Jar (JR) Types B.I and B.II
230. Bronze Age Jar (JR) Type B.III
231. Bronze Age Jar (JR) Type B.IV
232. Bronze Age Jar (JR) Types B.V and B.VI
233. Bronze Age Jar (JR) Types C.I and C.II
234. Bronze Age Jar (JR) Types C.III and C.IV
235. Bronze Age Jar (JR) Types C.V and C.VI
236. Bronze Age Jar (JR) Type D.I
237. Bronze Age Jar (JR) Types D.II and D.III
238. Bronze Age Jar (JR) Types D.IV and D.V
239. Bronze Age Jar (JR) Types D.VI and D.VII
240. Bronze Age Jar (JR) Types D.VIII, D.IX, and D.X
241. Bronze Age Jar (JR) Type E.I
242. Bronze Age Jar (JR) Types E.II.a to E.II.h
243. Bronze Age Jar (JR) Types E.II.i to E.II.z
244. Bronze Age Jar (JR) Type F.I
245. Bronze Age Jar (JR) Types F.II and F.III
246. Bronze Age Jar (JR) Types G.I, G.II, and G.III
247. Bronze Age Jar (JR) Type H.I

248. Bronze Age Jar (JR) Type H.II
249. Bronze Age Jar (JR) Types H.III.a to H.III.h
250. Bronze Age Jar (JR) Types H.III.i to H.III.z
251. Bronze Age Jar (JR) Type J.I
252. Bronze Age Jar (JR) Type J.II
253. Bronze Age Jar (JR) Types J.III.a to J.III.s
254. Bronze Age Jar (JR) Types J.III.t to J.III.ae
255. Bronze Age Jar (JR) Type J.IV
256. Bronze Age Jar (JR) Types J.V and J.VI
257. Bronze Age Jar (JR) Type K.I
258. Bronze Age Jar (JR) Type K.II
259. Bronze Age Jar (JR) Type L
260. Bronze Age Jar (JR) Types M and N
261. Bronze Age Jar (JR) Type O.I.a
262. Bronze Age Jar (JR) Types O.I.b to O.I.i
263. Bronze Age Jar (JR) Types O.II.a to O.II.f
264. Bronze Age Jar (JR) Types O.II.g to O.II.l
265. Bronze Age Jar (JR) Type O.II.m
266. Bronze Age Jar (JR) Type O.III
267. Bronze Age Jar (JR) Type P.I
268. Bronze Age Jar (JR) Types P.II.a to P.II.i
269. Bronze Age Jar (JR) Types P.II.j to P.II.l
270. Bronze Age Jar (JR) Types P.II.m to P.II.s
271. Bronze Age Jar (JR) Type P.III
272. Bronze Age Jar (JR) Type Q
273. Bronze Age Jar (JR) Type R
274. Bronze Age Flask (FL) Types A and B
275. Bronze Age Cooking Pot (CP) Type A.I
276. Bronze Age Cooking Pot (CP) Types A.II and A.III
277. Bronze Age Cooking Pot (CP) Type B.I
278. Bronze Age Cooking Pot (CP) Type B.II
279. Bronze Age Cooking Pot (CP) Type B.III
280. Bronze Age Cooking Pot (CP) Types B.IV and B.V
281. Bronze Age Cooking Pot (CP) Types C.I.a to C.I.c
282. Bronze Age Cooking Pot (CP) Types C.I.d to C.I.g
283. Bronze Age Cooking Pot (CP) Type C.II
284. Bronze Age Cooking Pot Lid (CP.Ld) Type A
285. Bronze Age Bottle (Bt.) Types A and B
286. Bronze Age Jug (Jg.) Types A–C
287. Bronze Age Lid (Ld.) Types A–C
288. Bronze Age Lamp (Lp.) Types A and B
289. Bronze Age Pot Stand (PS) Types A and B
290. Bronze Age Strainer Bowl (SR) Types A — C and Strainer Bowl Base (SB) Type A
291. Bronze Age Base (BE) Types A.I to D.IV

292. Bronze Age Base (BE) Types E.I.a to E.I.m
293. Bronze Age Base (BE) Types E.II.a to E.II.l
294. Bronze Age Base (BE) Types F.I.a to F.IV.b
295. Bronze Age Base (BE) Types F.V.a to J
296. Bronze Age Applied Band Sherd (ABS) Types A–C
297. Bronze Age Handle (Hd.) Types A–G
298. Bronze Age Windowed Pedestal Stand (WPS) Types A–C
299. Hellenistic Miniature Bowl (H.MBR) and Small Bowl (H.SBR) Types A–C
300. Hellenistic Bowl (H.BR) Type A
301. Hellenistic Bowl (H.BR) Type B
302. Hellenistic Bowl (H.BR) Type C
303. Hellenistic Red Slip Bowl (H.RSB) Types A.I.a to E.III.a and Red Slip Jar (H.RSJ) Types A.I.a to C.I.a
304. Hellenistic Burnished Gray Bowl (H.BGB) Types A and B
305. Hellenistic Small Jar (H.SJR) Types A and B
306. Hellenistic Jar (H.JR) Type A
307. Hellenistic Jar (H.JR) Type B
308. Hellenistic Jar (H.JR) Type C
309. Hellenistic Jar (H.JR) Type D
310. Hellenistic Jar (H.JR) Type E
311. Hellenistic Jar (H.JR) Type F
312. Hellenistic Jar (H.JR) Type G
313. Hellenistic Jug (H.Jg.) Types A–C
314. Hellenistic Storage Jar (H.St.J) Type A
315. Hellenistic Storage Jar (H.St.J) Type B
316. Hellenistic Cooking Pot (H.CP) Types A–E
317. Hellenistic Base (BE) Types A–E
318. Hellenistic Miscellaneous Pottery Types (Unclassified): Bottles (H.Bt.), Pot Stands (H.PS), Handles (H.Hd.) Lids (H.Ld.), Lamps (H.Lp.), and Applied-band Sherd (H.ABS) Types A–E
319. Roman Miniature Bowl (R.MBR) Types 1–5 and Roman Small Bowl (R.SBR) Types A and B
320. Roman Bowl (R.BR) Type A
321. Roman Bowl (R.BR) Type B
322. Roman Bowl (R.BR) Type C
323. Roman Bowl (R.BR) Type D
324. Roman Bowl (R.BR) Type E
325. Roman Small Jar (R.SJR) Types A–C
326. Roman Jar (R.JR) Type A
327. Roman Jar (R.JR) Type B
328. Roman Jar (R.JR) Type C
329. Roman Holemouth Jar (R.HMJ) Type A
330. Roman Holemouth Jar (R.HMJ) Types B and C
331. Roman Storage Jar (R.St.J) Types A–C
332. Roman Jug (R.Jg.) Type A
333. Roman Jug (R.Jg.) Type B
334. Roman Jug (R.Jg.) Type C
335. Roman Cooking Pot (R.CP) Types A and B

336. Roman Bottle (R.Bt.) Types A–C
337. Roman Lamp (R.Lp.) Types (Unclassified) and Roman Lid (R.Ld.) Types (Unclassified)
338. Roman Pot Stands (R.PS) Types (Unclassified)
339. Roman Base (R.BE) Types A–C
340. Incised Pottery (IP) Typology Groups G.1 to G.4

## POCKET PLANS

1. Area IV: Key to Plans and Sections of Area IVA–H, J–N, P, Q, X, and Operations 1, 2, 6, and 10
2. Areas IVO, R, S, V, W, Y, and Z and Operations 7 and 8: Key to Plans and Sections
3. Areas IVF (Room 1), IVK (Room 2), IVJ (Rooms 4 and 5): (a) Phase 2B Plan and (b) East Section Through Middle of the Rooms Showing Phases 1C to 5

# LIST OF GENERAL ABBREVIATIONS

| | |
|---|---|
| A | ash |
| AB | animal burrow |
| App. | appendix |
| BN | bone |
| BR. [br.] | brick (mudbrick) |
| ch. | chapter |
| cm | centimeter |
| CP (cp.) | cooking pot |
| dec. | decorated |
| diam. | diameter |
| E | east |
| Exc. | Excavation |
| F | flint |
| fig(s). | figure(s) |
| FL | floor |
| FN. | Field Number |
| Fndt(s). | foundation(s) |
| Gen. | General |
| GL | glass |
| loc. | locus (loci) |
| m | meter |
| MB | Mudbrick |
| mm | millimeter |
| MT | metal |
| N | north |
| NE | Northeast |
| occ. | occupation |
| OP | Operation |
| P | Potsherd(s) |
| PL. | Plaster |
| pl(s). | plate(s) |
| pt. | painted |
| PT | pottery |
| RM | room |
| S | south |
| SC | Study Collection |
| SE | Southeast |
| SF | small find |
| Sh. | sherd |
| SH | shell |
| ST (st.) | stone |
| SW | Sweyhat |
| tab.(s) | table(s) |
| Tr. | trench |
| TS | Type Series |
| TW | Town Wall |
| W | west |
| WP | wall painting, fragment |

Figure 1

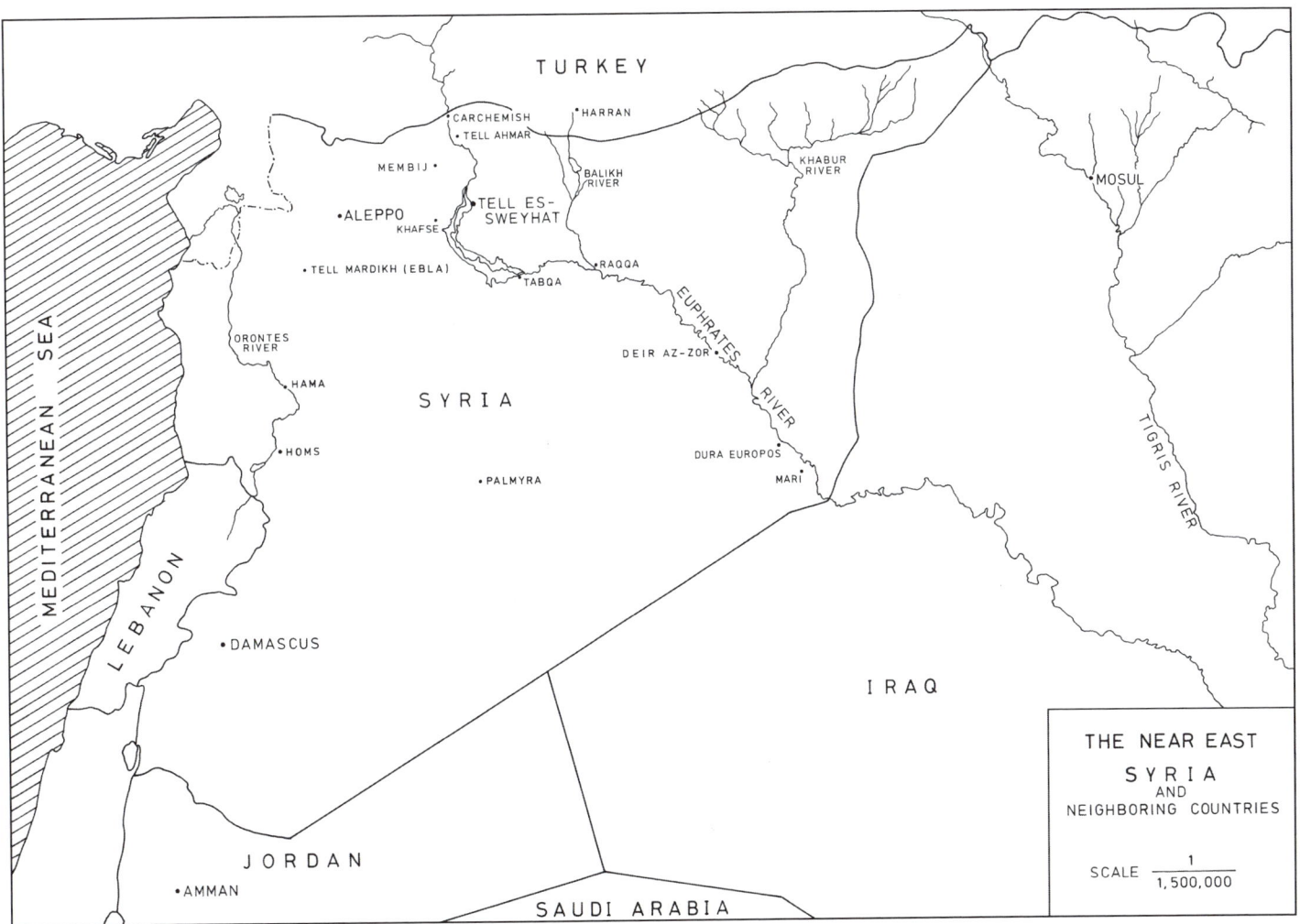

Map of Syria Showing Position of Tell es-Sweyhat in Its Near Eastern Setting

Figure 2

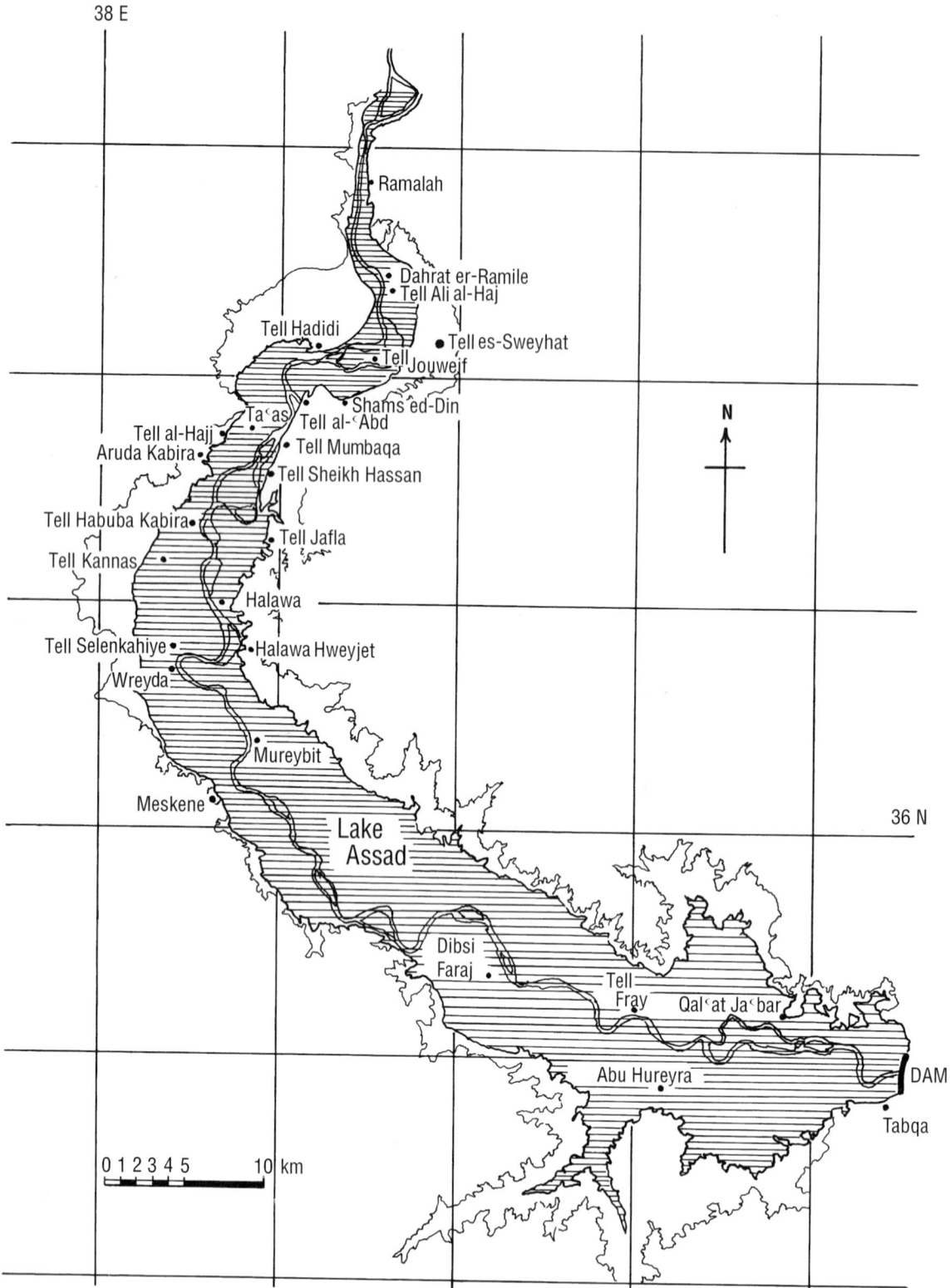

Map of the Tabqa Dam Reservoir Area in Syria Showing Lake Assad and Positions of Sites Excavated

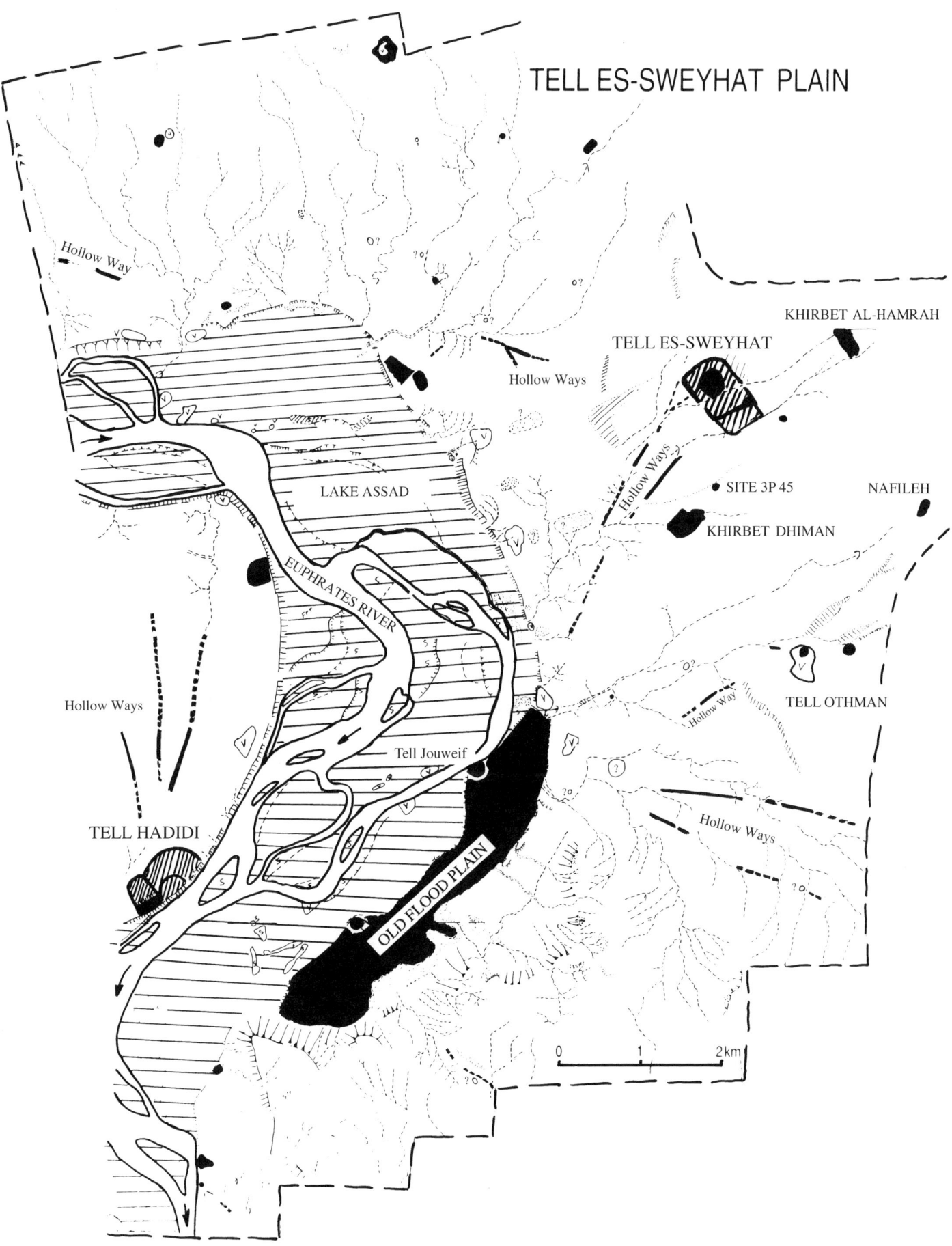

Map of the Sweyhat Plain Showing Regional Position of Tell es-Sweyhat and Neighboring Sites (after T. J. Wilkinson)

Figure 4

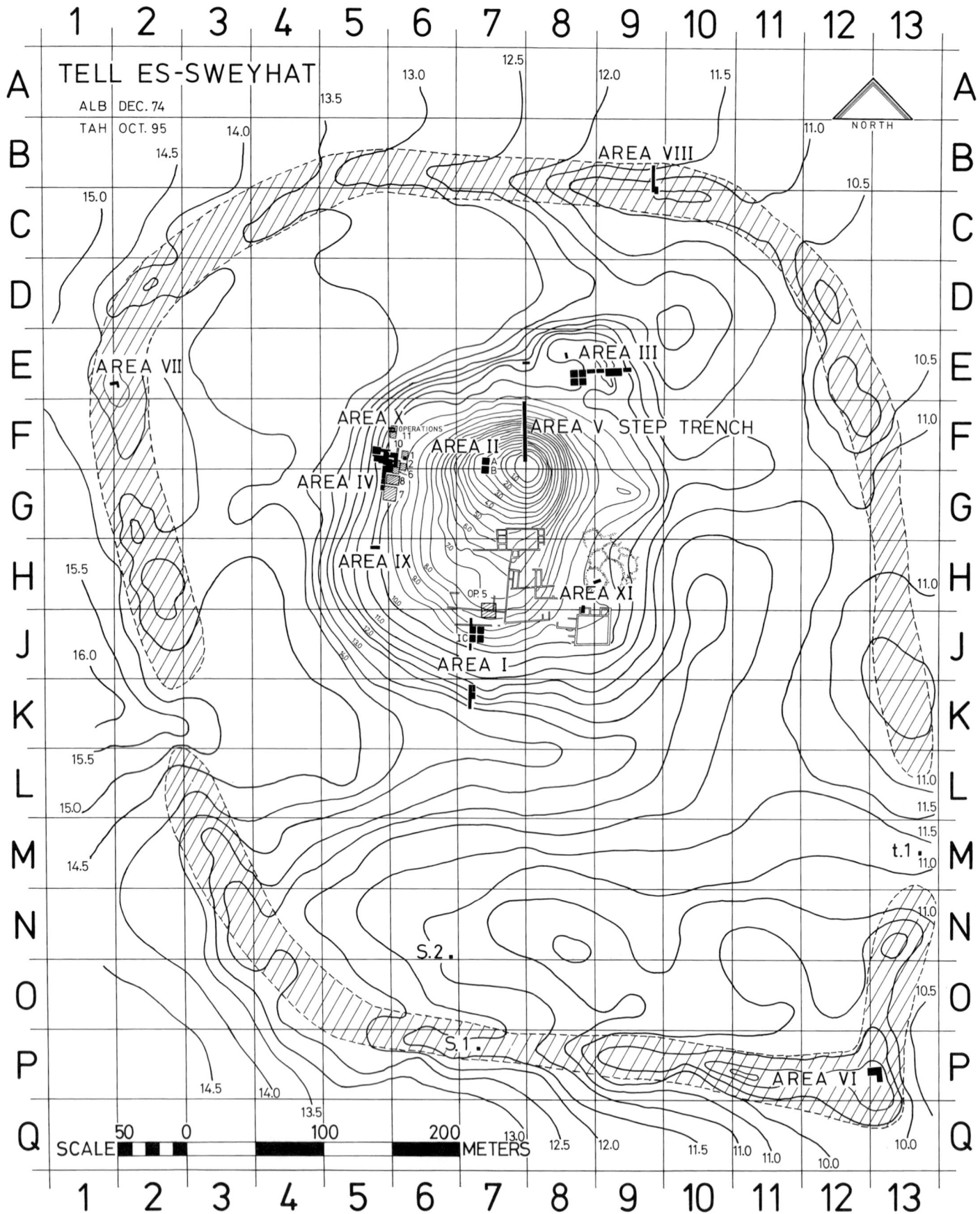

Contour Plan of Tell es-Sweyhat Showing Areas and Operations of Excavations (original plan by Alec L. Bellerby)

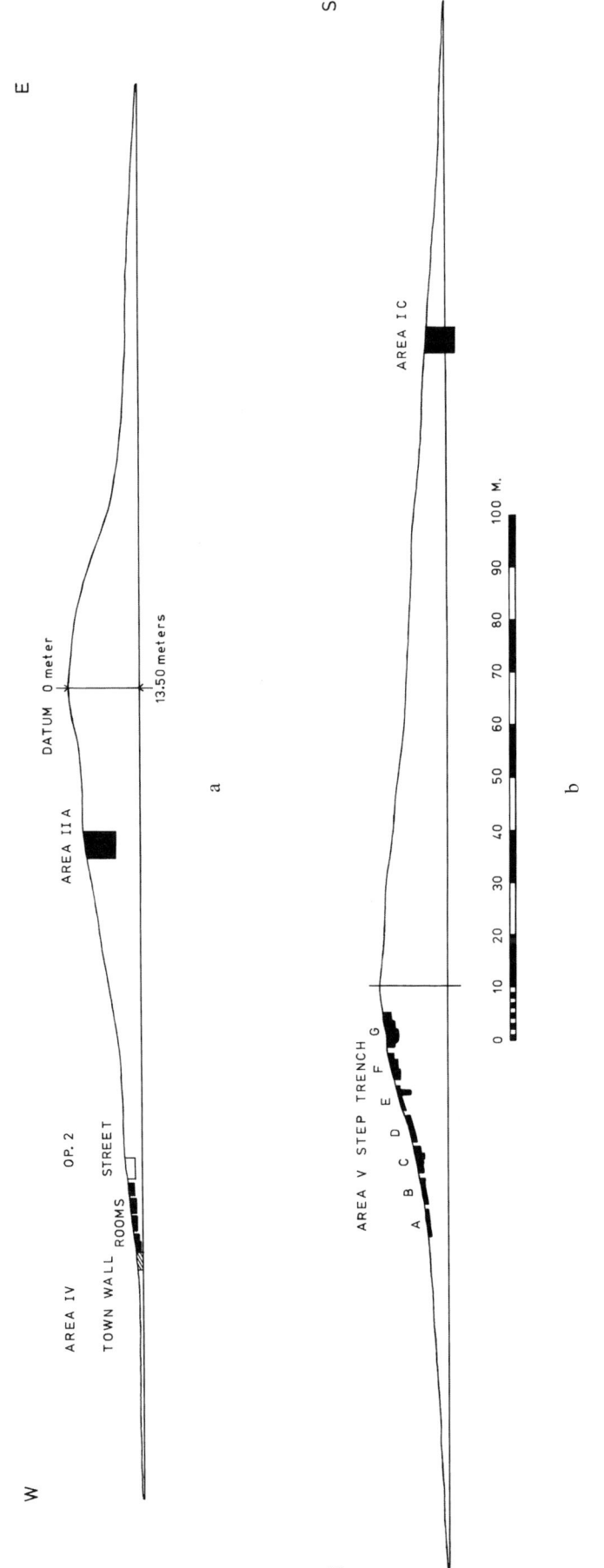

Figure 5 Cross Sections of Central Mound of Tell es-Sweyhat: (a) East–West Elevation and (b) North–South Elevation

Figure 6. Holland/Whitcomb 1972 Euphrates Survey Pottery: (1–2) Site A, (3–4) Site K (Tell Hajji Ibrahim), (5–6) Site F, (7) Nafileh, (8–13) Site C (Tell Othman), and (14–18) Shams ed-Din (SD), Lower Site

1. BR. E.III.c (Site A/1). About 1/6 rim and most of wall profile. Slightly coarse pinkish-buff ware, evenly fired. Creamy-buff slip in and out.
2. CP. A.III.a (Site A/2). Small rim, neck, and shoulder segment. Coarse gritty brown ware, unevenly fired orange on outside surface. Self slip in and out.
3. JR. J.V.b (Site K/1). About 1/6 rim and upper neck segment. Fairly fine buff ware, evenly fired. Creamy-buff slip in and out. Comb-incised decoration below rim outside.
4. JR. F.I.e (Site K/2). Small rim, neck, and upper shoulder segment. Slightly coarse and gritty pinkish-buff ware, evenly fired. Self slip out.
5. SJR. A.III.b (Site F/1). About 1/6 rim and upper shoulder segment. Slightly coarse and gritty ware, unevenly fired with gray core and pinkish-gray at surface out. Very smooth burnished self slip out.
6. JR. E.I.d (Site F/2). About 2/5 rim, neck, and shoulder segment. Slightly coarse and gritty creamy-buff ware, evenly fired. Self slip in and out.
7. BR. A.IV.a (Nafileh/1). Mended to complete profile. Ware description unavailable.
8. BR. L.I.a (Site C/3). Mended to complete profile. Potter's mark (Type PM. A.8) above outside of base incised before firing. Slightly coarse and gritty pinkish-buff ware, evenly fired. Cream slip in and out.
9. SJR. A.III.d (Site C/2). Small rim and shoulder segment. Slightly coarse pinkish-buff ware, evenly fired. Self slip in and out.
10. JR. G.II.b (Site C/5). About 1/6 rim, neck, and upper shoulder segment. Fine pinkish-buff ware, evenly fired. Cream slip in and out.
11. JR. F.II.c (Site C/4). Small rim, neck, and shoulder segment. Slightly coarse buff ware, evenly fired. Cream slip in and out.
12. JR. C.III.d (Site C/1). Small rim and upper shoulder segment. Fairly fine ware, unevenly fired with gray core and pinkish-buff on outside surface and gray on inside surface.
13. JR. H.III.r (Site C/6). About 1/4 rim, neck, and middle body segment with attached strap handle. Slightly coarse pinkish-brown ware, evenly fired. Buff slip out.
14. SBR. C.IV.a (Jouweif = SD, lower site/2). Small rim and most of body profile. Fairly fine buff ware, evenly fired. Creamy-buff slip in and out.
15. SBR. C.IV.a (Jouweif = SD, lower site/3). About 1/8 rim and 2/3 wall profile. Incomplete potter's mark (Type PM. A.5) on outside wall incised before firing. Fairly fine buff ware, evenly fired. Self slip in and out.
16. BR. F.IV.d (Jouweif = SD, lower site/1). About 1/8 rim and upper wall segment. Slightly coarse and gritty ware, unevenly fired pinkish-red in section and light gray on outside surface. Buff slip out.
17. SJR. A.III.a (Jouweif = SD, lower site/4). Small rim and shoulder segment. Fine pinkish-brown ware, evenly fired. Self slip in and out.
18. JR. E.II.a (SD, lower site/5). Small rim, neck, and upper shoulder segment. Close, slightly gritty pinkish-orange ware, evenly fired. Cream slip out.

Figure 6

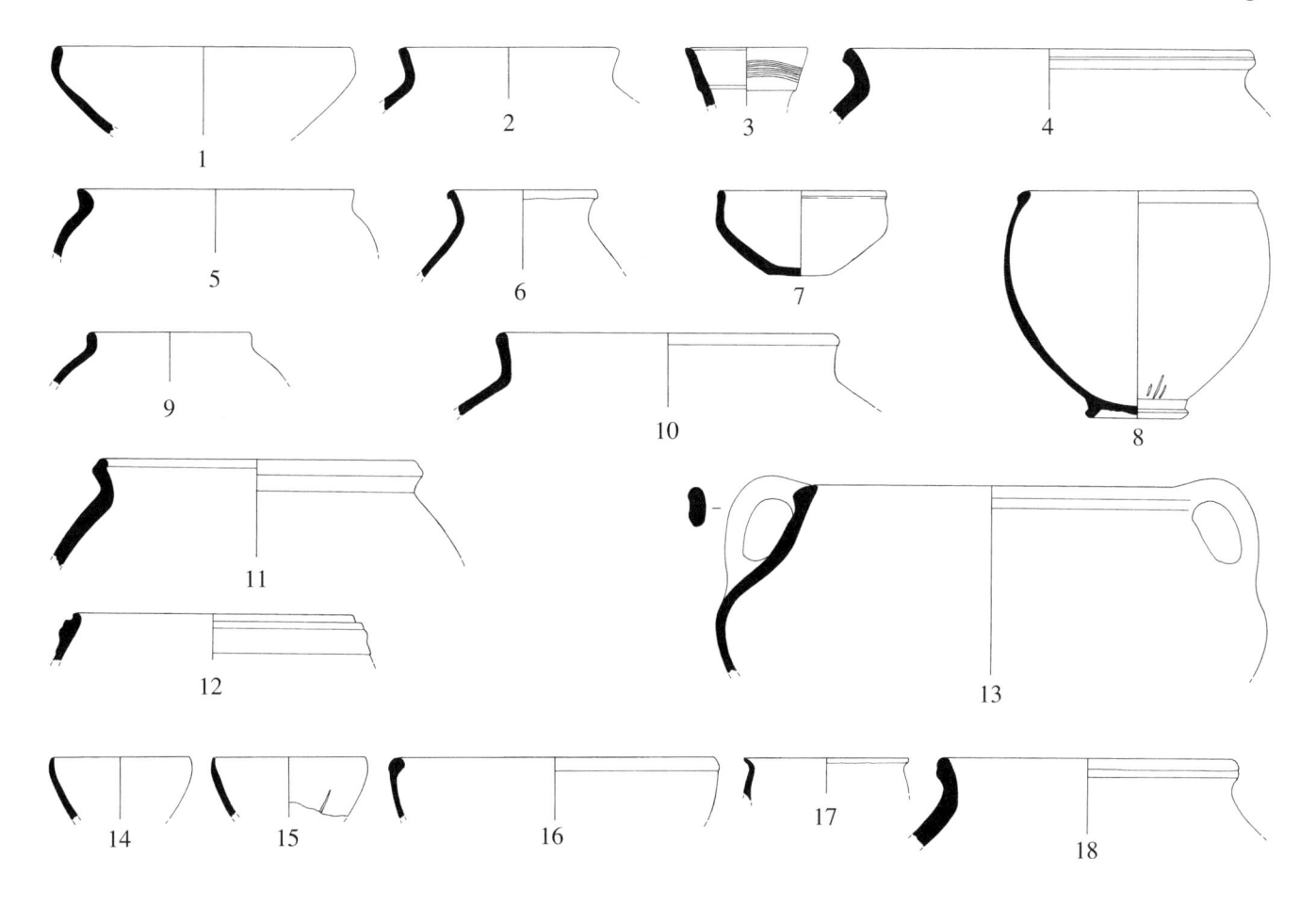

Holland/Whitcomb 1972 Euphrates Survey Pottery: (1–2) Site A, (3–4) Site K (Tell Hajji Ibrahim), (5–6) Site F, (7) Nafileh, (8–13) Site C (Tell Othman), and (14–18) Shams ed-Din, Lower Site. Scale 1:5

Figure 7. Holland/Whitcomb 1972 Euphrates Survey Pottery from the Shams ed-Din Cemetery

1. SBR. B.I.j (SDC/15). Small rim and upper wall segment. Fairly coarse and gritty buff ware, evenly fired. Self slip in and out.
2. SBR. C.II.b (SDC/9). About 1/2 rim and most of wall profile. Slightly coarse creamy-green ware, evenly fired, Self slip in and out.
3. SBR. A.I.h (SDC/13). About 1/5 rim and most of wall profile. Slightly coarse creamy-green ware, evenly fired. Self slip in and out.
4. BR. A.I.d (SDC/12). About 1/8 rim and upper half of wall segment. Slightly coarse ware, unevenly fired with buff core and creamy-green at surfaces in and out. Creamy-green slip in and out.
5. BR. A.I.b (SDC/11). About 1/6 rim and most of wall profile. Fairly fine buff ware, evenly fired. Creamy-green slip in and out.
6. SBR. E.I.b (SDC/17). Two small non-joining rim segments and most of wall profile. Slightly coarse and gritty pinkish-orange ware, evenly fired. Pink slip in and out.
7. BR. A.II.g (SDC/25). About 1/3 rim, three joining fragments, and upper wall segment. Fairly fine grayish-buff ware, evenly fired. Possibly creamy-green slip in and out, but much worn.
8. BR. D.II.c (SDC/18). About 1/6 rim and most of wall profile. Fairly fine pinkish-buff ware, evenly fired. Self slip in and out.
9. BR. C.I.a (SDC/30). About 1/3 rim and most of wall profile. Slightly coarse pinkish-buff ware, evenly fired. Self slip in and out.
10. BR. D.VI.a (SDC/19). Small rim segment attached to wall and 1/2 of base forming complete profile. Fairly fine, light green ware, evenly fired. Self slip in and out.
11. BR. F.IV.a (SDC/20). About 1/6 rim and most of wall profile. Fairly fine pinkish-brown ware, evenly fired. Wheel ring burnished on outside wall.
12. BR. F.I.d (SDC/5). About 1/4 rim segment attached to wall and nearly complete base forming complete profile. Fairly fine, slightly gritty, greenish ware, evenly fired. Self wash or slip out and over rim in.
13. SJR. B.II.d (SDC/24). About 1/2 rim and most of wall profile. Slightly coarse buff ware, evenly fired. Creamy-buff slip out and over rim in.
14. JR. C.II.b (SDC/6). Small rim, neck, and upper wall segment. Fairly fine pinkish-buff ware, evenly fired. Creamy-green slip in and out.
15. SJR. A.II.b (SDC/14). Small rim, neck, and upper wall segment. Slightly coarse and gritty buff ware, evenly fired. Creamy-buff slip in and out.
16. SJR. A.II.f (SDC/28). About 1/2 rim, neck, and upper wall segment. Fairly coarse creamy-green ware, evenly fired. Self slip in and out.
17. SJR. C.II.u (SDC/3). About 1/4 rim, neck, and upper half of wall segment. Fine pink ware, evenly fired. Pinkish-buff slip out with crisscross burnish lines on body, vertical burnish lines on the neck, and horizontal burnish on the ribbed collar.
18. JR. F.II.f (SDC/7). Two small non-joining rim segments, both attached to neck and upper wall segments. Fairly coarse green ware, evenly fired. Self slip in and out, very worn.
19. JR. F.II.f (SDC/21). About 1/6 rim, neck, and shoulder segment. Fairly coarse light green ware, evenly fired. Self slip in and out.
20. JR. F.II.c (SDC/8). About 1/4 rim, neck, and shoulder segment. Slightly coarse pinkish-buff ware, evenly fired. Creamy-buff slip in and out.
21. JR. F.I.a (SDC/4). Nearly complete rim attached to most of neck and 2/3 of shoulder. Fairly fine, slightly gritty pinkish-buff ware, evenly fired. Cream slip out.
22. JR. J.IV.g (SDC/27). About 2/5 rim, neck, and shoulder segment with a potter's mark (Type PM. A.5) at juncture of neck and shoulder, incised before firing. Slightly coarse and gritty pinkish-buff ware, fairly evenly fired. Creamy-orange slip in and out.
23. JR. J.II.c (SDC/16). About 1/3 rim, neck, and shoulder segment. Slightly coarse pinkish-buff ware, evenly fired. Creamy-buff slip out.
24. JR. J.III.z (SDC/22). Small rim, neck, and upper shoulder segment. Fairly fine pinkish-buff ware, evenly fired. Creamy-green slip out.
25. JR. H.I.e (SDC/29). About 1/3 rim and upper shoulder segment. Fairly fine pinkish-buff ware, evenly fired. Creamy-green slip out.
26. JR. H.I.h (SDC/10). Two small non-joining rim and upper shoulder segments. Potter's mark or decoration incised on shoulder before firing. Fairly fine pinkish-buff ware, evenly fired. Creamy-green slip out.
27. CP. A.I.c (SDC/23). Small rim, neck, and shoulder segment with rounded ledge handle, triangular in section, attached to lip of rim. Fairly coarse, slightly gritty ware, unevenly fired with gray core and pinkish-brown at surfaces in and out.
28. CP. B.III.c (SDC/26). Two joining rim, neck, and upper shoulder segments; about 1/3 rim. Coarse, gritty pinkish-brown ware, evenly fired. Self slip in and out.
29. BE. F.III.b (SDC/1–2). About 1/2 of a pedestal stand attached to the lower portion of probably a bowl. Slightly coarse pinkish-buff ware, evenly fired. Self slip in and out.

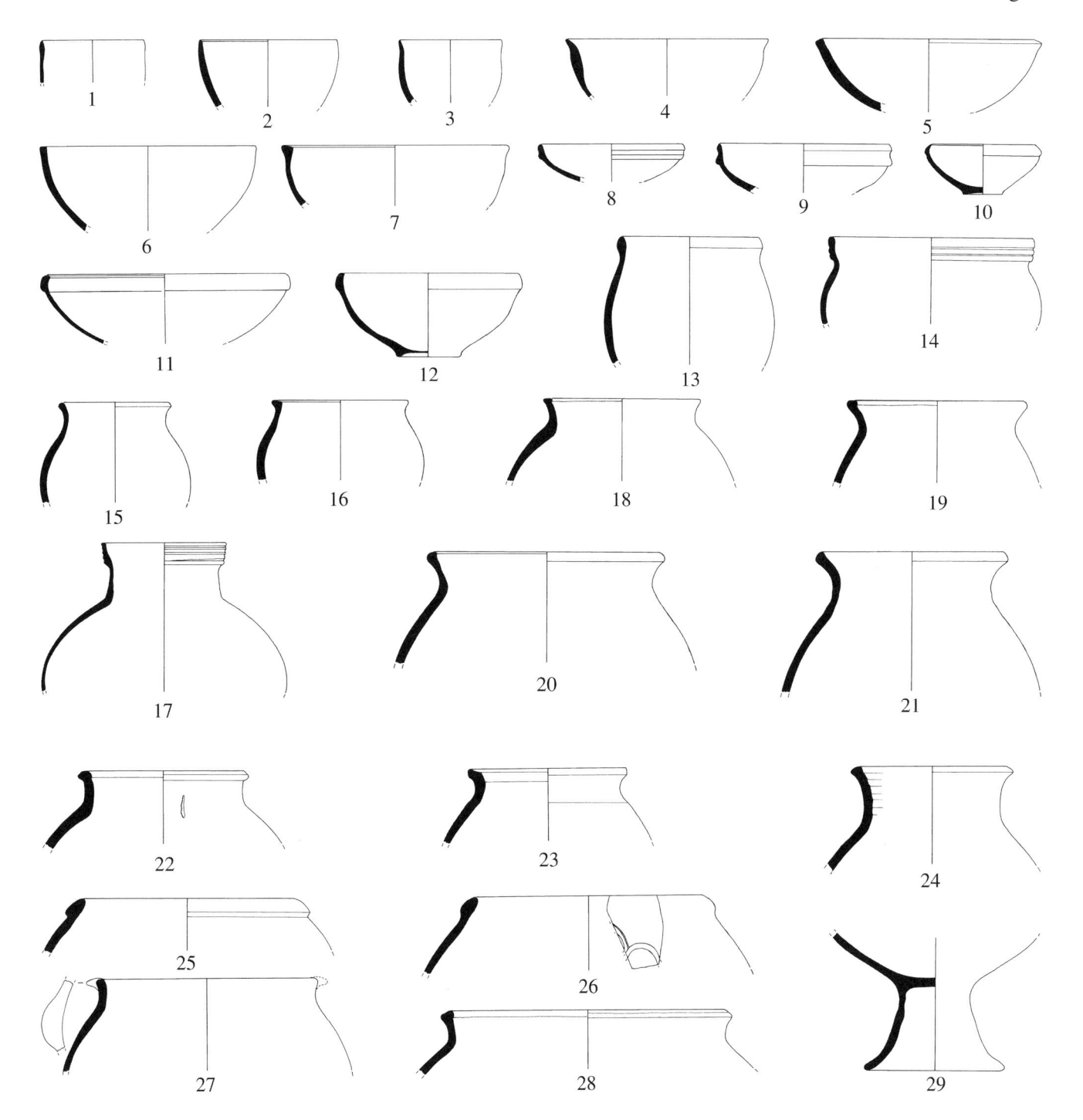

Figure 7

Holland/Whitcomb 1972 Euphrates Survey Pottery from the Shams ed-Din Cemetery. Scale 1:5

Figure 8. Holland/Whitcomb 1972 Euphrates Survey Pottery: (1–5) Mazraʿat Hadidi, (6–7) Site H (Mishrifah Saghir), (8–14) Tell Hadidi, (15–17) Site D (Khirbet al-Hamrah), (18) Site E, (19) Site G (Khirbet Haj Hassan), (20–21) Site J (Zarob), (22–23) Rasm el-ʿAbd Mustaha, (24–26) Tell Sheikh Hassan, and (27–28) Umm Jehash

1. SBR. C.II.c (MH/2). Small rim and upper wall segment. Slightly coarse, chaff-tempered, pinkish-buff ware, evenly fired. Creamy-buff slip in and out.
2. SBR. A.I.h (MH/3). Small rim and most of wall profile. Fairly fine creamy-buff ware, fairly evenly fired. Self slip in and out.
3. JR. J.II.b (MH/1). Small rim, neck, and shoulder segment. Slightly coarse pinkish-buff ware, evenly fired. Cream slip out and just over rim in.
4. JR. H.III.f (MH/4). Small rim and upper shoulder segment. Fairly coarse, chaff-tempered, creamy-green ware, evenly fired. Self slip in and out.
5. JR. J.II.j (MH/5). About 1/8 rim, neck, and upper shoulder segment. Slightly coarse, chaff-tempered ware, unevenly fired with some gray core and pinkish-buff at surfaces in and out. Possibly self slip in and out.
—. SJR.Sh. (IP [G.1] B.I.a; MH/6; SC. 3299). Small jar body sherd. Decorated outside with two sets of deep, two-grooved horizontal incisions above a thin wavy line to a depth of 2 cm below. Fairly fine pinkish-buff ware with a few silver-colored mica and black and white lime grits, evenly fired. Creamy-buff slip out.
6. SJR. B.II.i (Site H/1). Small rim, neck, and upper shoulder segment. Fairly fine, slightly gritty ware, unevenly fired with buff core and pinkish-buff at surfaces in and out. Creamy-buff slip in and out.
7. JR. J.II.n (Site H/2). About 1/4 rim, neck, and upper shoulder segment. Fairly coarse green ware, evenly fired. Self creamy-green slip in and out.
8. SBR. A.I.d (TH/5). Small rim and upper wall segment. Fine pinkish-buff ware, evenly fired. Cream slip in and out.
9. JR. H.II.b (TH/3). About 1/8 rim, neck, and upper shoulder segment. Fairly fine, slightly gritty, grayish-buff ware, evenly fired. Possibly self slip in and out, but very worn.
10. JR. J.II.i (TH/7). Nearly 1/2 rim, neck, and upper shoulder segment with horizontal comb-incised lines on shoulder. Slightly coarse pinkish-buff ware, evenly fired. Self slip in and out.
11. BR. (not typed, TH/2). About 1/10 rim and most of wall profile. Fine pink ware, evenly fired. Self wash in and out.
12. R.JR. B.II.c (TH/4). Small rim, neck, and upper wall segment with horizontal and wavy comb-incised decoration round upper part of wall. Slightly coarse and gritty pinkish-buff ware, evenly fired. Cream slip out and on top of rim.
13. R.BR. E.I.b (TH/1). About 1/8 rim and most of wall profile. Fairly fine buff ware, evenly fired. Cream slip in and out.
14. R.CP. B.II.b (TH/6). Two joining rim and neck segments, about 1/3 rim. Fairly coarse ware, unevenly fired with gray core and reddish-brown at surfaces in and out. Self slip in and out.
15. Isl.BR. (not typed, Site D/1). About 1/16 rim and upper wall segment. Fairly fine creamy-green ware, evenly fired. Self slip in and out. Impressed repeating decorative pattern on top of rim.
16. Isl.BR. (not typed, Site D/2). Small rim and upper wall segment. Slightly coarse and gritty pinkish ware, fairly evenly fired. Creamy-buff slip in and out.
—. JR.Sh. (IP [G.1] C.V.a; Site D/3; SC. 3297). Jar body sherd. Decorated outside with one comb-incised band (seven grooves extant) above a very wide horizontal band (nineteen grooves). Fairly coarse buff ware with small lime grits and burnt-out vegetable temper. Creamy-green slip out.
17. H.JR. D.II.a (Site D/4; SC. 3256). About 1/12 rim and neck segment. Fairly fine pinkish-buff ware with a few lime grit inclusions, evenly fired. Self slip in and out. Decorative pattern incised around the neck before firing may represent a fish and a fishnet.
18. R.BR. (not typed, Site E/1). Two small joining rim and upper wall segments. Fairly coarse reddish-brown ware, unevenly fired. Purplish-colored slip in and out. Remains of a wide strap handle just below rim.
—. JR.Sh. (IP [G.1] D.III.a; Site E/2; SC. 3298). Jar body sherd. Decorated outside with two (three grooves) wavy comb-incised bands (top one not continuous) above one horizontal five-grooved band. Slightly coarse buff ware with small black and white lime grits, evenly fired. Creamy-buff slip in and out.
19. R.PS.2 (Site G/1). Small rim and wall segment of a pedestal or pot stand. Fairly coarse pinkish-orange ware, evenly fired. Self slip in and out.
20. Isl.BR. (not typed, Site J/1). About 1/8 rim and upper wall segment. Fairly fine buff ware, evenly fired. Ivory-colored glaze in and out.
21. Isl.JR. (not typed, Site J/2). About 1/4 rim, neck, and upper shoulder segment. Fairly coarse ware, unevenly fired with black core and green at surfaces in and out. Self green slip in and out.
22. H.BR. B.I.c (RM/1). Small rim and upper wall segment. Slightly coarse buff ware, evenly fired. Creamy-buff slip in and out.
23. H.JR. G.II.b (RM/2). About 1/8 rim and upper shoulder segment. Fairly coarse and gritty buff-brown ware, evenly fired. Possibly self slip in and out. Burned outside and on rim.
24. H.St.J. (not typed, SH/1). Small rim and neck segment. Fairly fine creamy-green ware, evenly fired. Self slip in and out.
25. H.St.J. B.I.d (SH/3). Small rim and neck segment. Fairly fine pinkish-buff ware, evenly fired. Creamy slip in and out.
26. H.St.J. (not typed, SH/2). Small rim and neck segment. Fairly fine salmon-pink ware, evenly fired. Red slip in and out.
27. H.BR. C.II.d (UJ/1). About 1/16 rim and upper wall segment with incised wavy line decoration on top of rim. Fairly fine, non gritty, ware, unevenly fired with light buff core and pinkish-buff at surfaces in and out. Cream slip in and out.
28. H.CP. C.I.b (UJ/2). Small rim and neck segment. Coarse gritty ware, unevenly fired with gray core and pinkish-brown at surfaces in and out. Self slip in and out.

Figure 8

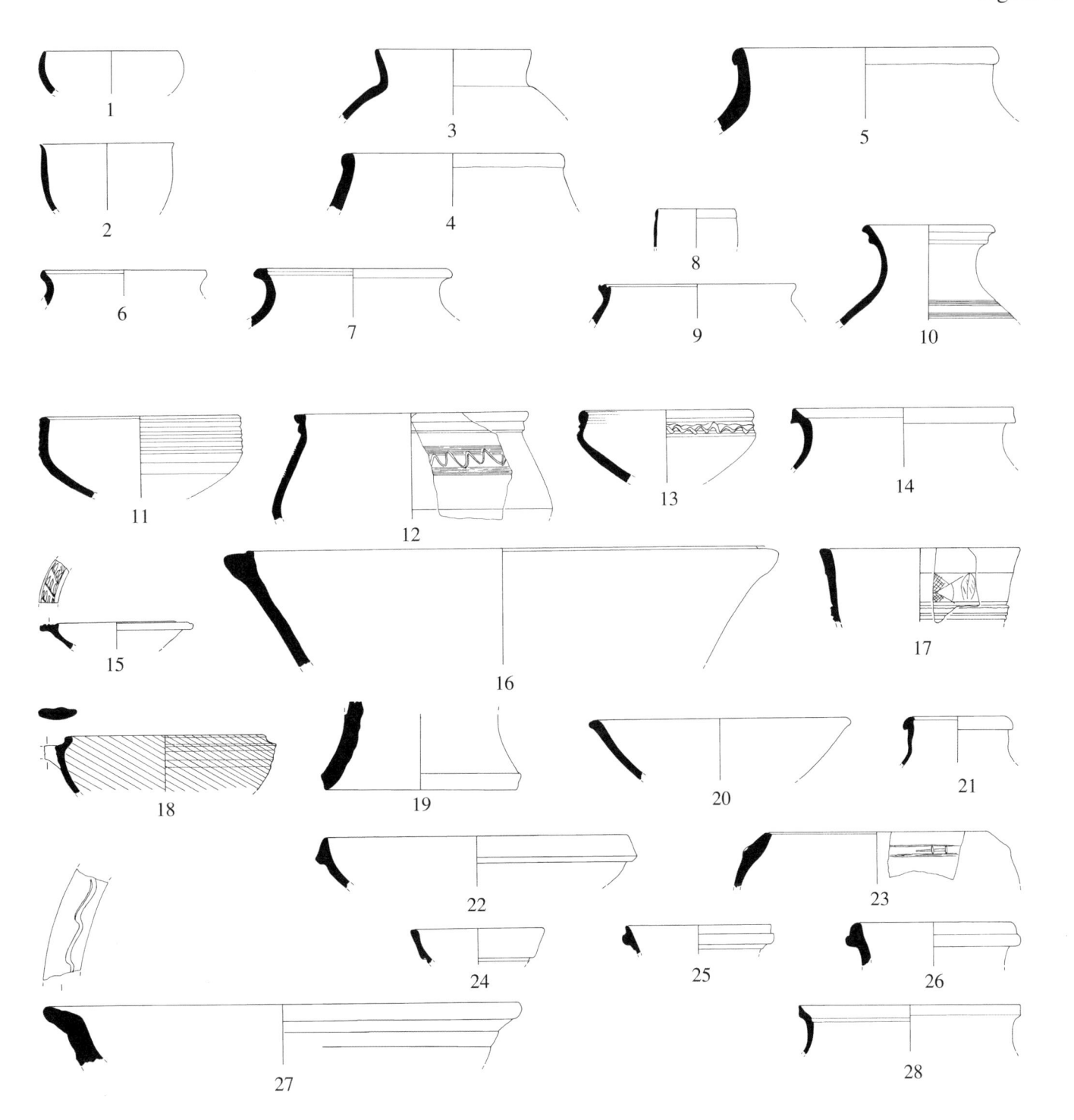

Holland/Whitcomb 1972 Euphrates Survey Pottery: (1–5) Mazraʿat Hadidi, (6–7) Site H (Mishrifah Saghir), (8–14) Tell Hadidi, (15–17) Site D (Khirbet al-Hamrah), (18) Site E, (19) Site G (Khirbet Haj Hassan), (20–21) Site J (Zarob), (22–23) Rasm el-ʿAbd Mustaha, (24–26) Tell Sheikh Hassan, and (27–28) Umm Jehash
Scale 1:5

Figure 9

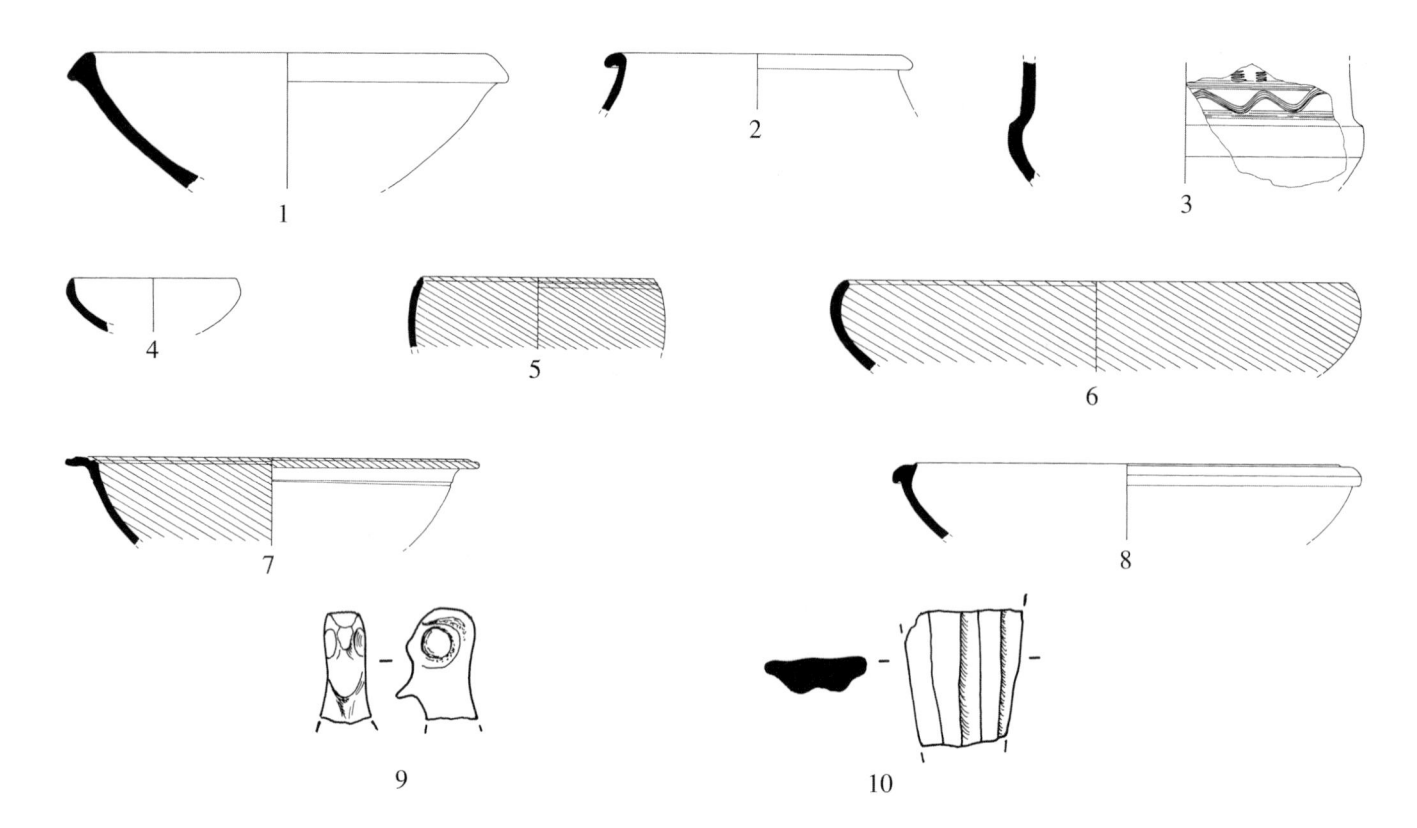

Holland/Whitcomb 1972 Euphrates Survey Pottery: (1–3) Shams ed-Din Central Tell, (4–8) Tell Walid Asaf, and (9–10) Ramalah. Scale 1:5

1. BR. G.I.c (SDCT/3). About 1/8 rim and most of wall profile. Slightly coarse and gritty pinkish-buff ware, evenly fired. Traces of a possible cream slip in and out, but much worn.
2. JR. H.III.q (SDCT/2). About 1/8 rim and upper shoulder segment. Fairly fine pinkish-buff ware, evenly fired. Creamy-buff slip in and out.
3. JR.Sh. (IP [G.1] F.I.a; SDCT/1). Large body segment with fingernail-incised vertical bands above horizontal and wavy comb-incised linear decoration. Slightly coarse and gritty pinkish-brown ware, evenly fired. Self slip in and out.
—. JR.Sh. (IP [G.1] C.IV.a; SDCT/4; SC. 3295). Jar body sherd. Decorated outside with one wavy comb-incised five-grooved band above one six-grooved horizontal band. Slightly coarse pinkish-buff ware with small gold-colored mica and lime grits, evenly fired. Creamy-buff slip out.
—. JR.Sh. (IP [G.1] C.VI.a; SDCT/5; SC. 3296). Jar body sherd. Decorated outside with a single wide-looped tool-incised band, 3–5 mm in width, covering a depth of 3 cm. Fairly coarse buff ware with fine gold- and silver-colored mica grits and burnt-out vegetable temper, evenly fired. Creamy-buff slip out.
4. H.BGB. B.I.d (WA/1). Small rim and most of wall profile. Fairly fine grayish-brown ware. Fine gray slip burnished horizontally in and out.
5. H.RSB. C.II.b (WA/2). Small rim and upper wall segment. Fine pinkish-orange ware, evenly fired. Red slip in and out.
6. H.RSB. D.II.a (WA/3). Small rim and upper wall segment. Fine ware, unevenly fired with buff core and pink at surfaces in and out. Red slip in and out.
7. H.RSB. B.II.a (WA/4). About 1/6 rim and most of wall profile. Fine salmon-pink ware, evenly fired. Red slip in and just over rim out.
8. H.BR. B.III.k (WA/5). Small rim and upper wall segment. Fairly fine buff ware, evenly fired. Creamy-buff slip in and on top of rim.
9. Type SF.1b (R/2). Head of bearded male figurine (see pl. 132e).
10. Type SF.1c (R/3). Fragment of human plaque-type figurine depicting only the central leg portion (see pl. 132f).
—. H.Hd. (R/5). Rhodian-type Stamped wine jar handle with a trident flanked with name, δαρασ, on right side of the trident (see pl. 132d).
—. Type SF.1e (R/4). Hellenistic. Fragment of a horse and rider figurine.
—. H.Sh. (Geometric Stamp Impression; R/6). Hellenistic. Probably a jar body sherd (see pl. 132c). Compare Athenian Agora stamped jar handle: Grace 1934, no. 282.
—. H.JR.Sh. (IP [G.1] L.I.a; R/1; SC. 3300). Hellenistic. Jar body sherd. Decorated outside with two single tool-incised wavy bands separated by two horizontal bands. Slightly coarse pinkish-buff ware with a few visible silver-colored mica and small lime grits, evenly fired. Buff slip out.

Figure 10

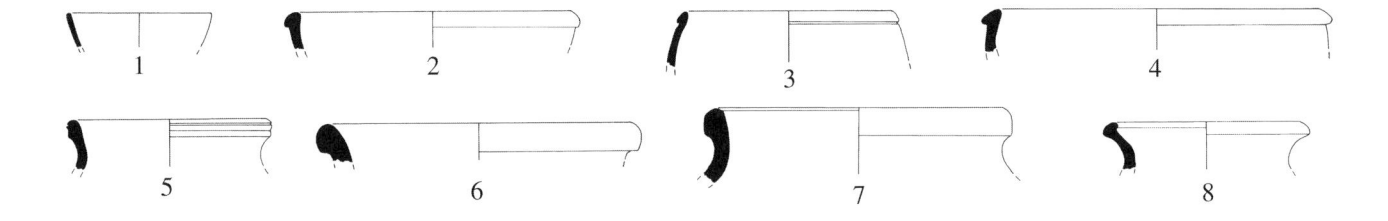

Pottery from (1–2) Sounding 1 (Phase 3; Period E — Early Bronze Age IVb) and (3–8) Sounding 2 (Phases 1 and 2; Periods F and E — Early Bronze Age IVa and Early Bronze Age IVb). Scale 1:5

1. SBR. B.I.b (TS. 4207; S1, 1.2). Sounding 1, Phase 3. About 1/12 rim and upper wall segment. Fine, hard, dark buff ware with a few small silver-colored mica and lime grits, evenly fired; horizontally burnished on outside wall. Self slip in and out.
2. BR. F.III.a (TS. 4206; S1, 1.2). Sounding 1, Phase 3. About 1/20 rim and upper wall segment. Slightly coarse pinkish-buff ware with vegetable temper burned out of surfaces during firing, evenly fired. Self slip in and out.
3. SBR. A.I.d (TS. 4214; S2, 1.3). Sounding 2, Phase 1. About 1/12 rim and upper wall segment. Fine light pink ware with mica and lime grit temper, evenly fired. Cream slip out.
4. BR. F.III.c (TS. 4220; S2, 1.3). Sounding 2, Phase 1. About 1/20 rim and upper wall segment. Fairly coarse buff ware with silver-colored mica grits and burned out vegetable temper, unevenly fired pink at surfaces. Surfaces very worn.
5. SJR. C.II.g (TS. 4210; S2, 1.2). Sounding 2, Phase 2. About 1/16 rim and neck segment. Very hard grayish-buff ware with a few small lime grits, evenly fired. Creamy-green slip out.
6. JR. J.II.d (TS. 4215; S2, 1.3). Sounding 2, Phase 1. About 1/10 rim and upper neck segment. Very hard greenish-buff ware with lime and mica temper, evenly fired. Creamy-buff slip out.
7. JR. J.II.h (TS. 1063; S2, 1.2). Sounding 2, Phase 2. About 1/20 rim and neck segment. Very hard brownish-buff ware with black and white lime grits, evenly fired. Self slip in and out.
8. JR. J.III.y (TS. 732; S2, 1.2). Sounding 2, Phase 2. About 1/12 rim, neck, and upper shoulder segment. Fine greenish-buff ware with vegetable temper burned out during firing. Creamy-green self slip in and out. Very light in weight.

Other Examples Not Illustrated from Sounding 2:
    Phase 1— (1) SBR. A.I.a (TS. 4217), (2) SBR. B.I.h (TS. 4218), (3) SJR. B.I.a (TS. 4219), (4) JR. E.I.c (TS. 4216).
    Phase 2— (1) SBR. B.I.m (TS. 4212), (2) SBR. B.I.q (TS. 4211), (3) SJR. C.I.f (TS. 4209), (4) SJR. C.II.o (TS. 4208), (5) BE. E.I.f (TS. 4213).

Figure 11. Pottery from Sounding t.1 (Phases 1 to 5; Periods F and E — Early Bronze Age IVa and Early Bronze Age IVb)

1. SBR. B.I.c (TS. 2895; t.1, 11p.89). Phase 1. Small rim and most of wall profile. Slightly coarse yellow-buff ware, evenly fired. Cream slip in and out.
2. SJR. B.II.c (TS. 2894; t.1, 10p.89). Phase 2. Small rim and neck segment. Fairly fine pinkish-orange ware, evenly fired. Possibly self slip in and out, but very worn.
3. SJR. C.II.c (TS. 2892; t.1, 9p.89). Phase 2. About 1/4 rim and complete neck profile. Fine, dark buff ware, evenly fired. Self slip in and out.
4. JR. J.III.ab (TS. 2893; t.1, 9p.89). Phase 2. Small rim and complete neck profile. Slightly coarse creamy-green ware, evenly fired. Self slip in and out.
5. SBR. B.I.h (TS. 2877; t.1, 5p.89). Phase 3. Small rim and upper wall segment. Fine buff-brown ware, evenly fired. Cream slip out and over rim in.
6. BR. F.III.d (TS. 2880; t.1, 6p.89). Phase 3. Small rim and upper wall segment. Slightly coarse buff ware, evenly fired. Cream slip in and out.
7. BR. F.III.e (TS. 2882; t.1, 7p.89). Phase 3. Small rim and upper wall segment. Fairly fine pinkish-buff ware, evenly fired. Creamy-buff slip in and out.
8. BR. F.III.e (TS. 2888; t.1, 8p.89). Phase 3. Small rim and upper wall segment. Fairly fine pink ware, evenly fired. Remains of self slip in and out.
9. BR. F.IV.d (TS. 2886; t.1, 8p.89). Phase 3. Small rim and upper wall segment. Slightly coarse pinkish-buff ware, evenly fired. Cream slip in and out.
10. SJR. C.II.d (TS. 2881; t.1, 7p.89 and 8p.89). Phase 3. About 2/5 rim and neck made up of four joining segments. Fairly fine pinkish-buff ware, evenly fired. Self slip in and out.
11. JR. E.II.j (TS. 2875; t.1, 5p.89). Phase 3. Small rim and neck segment. Fairly fine pinkish-buff ware, evenly fired. Buff slip in and out.
12. JR. E.II.m (TS. 2884; t.1, 8p.89). Phase 3. About 1/5 rim, neck, and upper shoulder segment. Fairly fine pinkish-buff ware, evenly fired. Cream slip out.
13. JR. E.II.w (TS. 2890; t.1, 8p.89). Phase 3. Small rim and neck segment. Slightly coarse buff ware, evenly fired. Creamy-green slip in and out.
14. JR. F.II.b (TS. 2891; t.1, 8p.89). Phase 3. Small rim and upper neck segment. Slightly coarse buff ware, evenly fired. Cream slip in and out.
15. JR. F.III.c (TS. 2879; t.1, 6p.89). Phase 3. Small rim and upper shoulder segment. Slightly coarse buff ware, evenly fired. Creamy-green slip in and out.
16. JR. J.III.v (TS. 2885; t.1, 6p.89 and 8p.89). Phase 3. About 1/2 rim made up of three segments, one from 6p.89. Fairly fine pinkish-buff ware, evenly fired. Creamy-buff slip in and out.
17. JR. J.IV.j (TS. 2889; t.1, 8p.89). Phase 3. Small rim and neck segment. Slightly coarse greenish-buff ware, evenly fired. Self slip in and out.
18. JR. P.II.q (TS. 2887; t.1, 8p.89). Phase 3. Small rim and neck segment. Slightly coarse light green ware, evenly fired. Self slip in and out.
19. BE. E.II.i (TS. 3084; t.1, 7p.89). Phase 3. Complete ring base with lower segment of wall preserved. Fairly fine pinkish-buff ware, evenly fired. Self slip in and out.
20. BR. E.I.a (TS. 2874; t.1, 4p.89). Phase 4. Small rim and upper wall segment. Fairly fine pink ware, evenly fired. Cream slip in and out.
21. JR. J.III.e (TS. 2876; t.1, 4p.89). Phase 4. Small rim and complete neck profile. Fairly fine pinkish-brown ware, unevenly fired pinkish-red at surfaces. Self slip in and out.
22. JR. G.I.c (TS. 2873; t.1, 3p.89). Phase 5. Small rim and complete neck profile. Slightly coarse pink ware, evenly fired. Cream slip in and out.
23. JR. J.I.f (TS. 2872; t.1, 2p.89). Phase 5. Small rim and neck segment. Slightly coarse buff ware, unevenly fired pink and gray at surfaces.

Other Bronze Age Type Series Examples (see pls. 204–98):
    Phase 1 — (1) SJR. A.III.c (TS. 2896).
    Phase 2 — (1) SJR. D.I.d (TS. 2898).
    Phase 3 — (1) SJR. C.II.u (TS. 2878), (2) JR. J.III.ac (TS. 2883).
Other Study Collection Examples Not Illustrated:
    Phase 3 — (1) SJR. B.II.d (SC. 2510), (2) SJR. C.II.d (SC. 2583).
    Phase 5 — (1) SJR. C.II.n (SC. 2602).

Figure 11

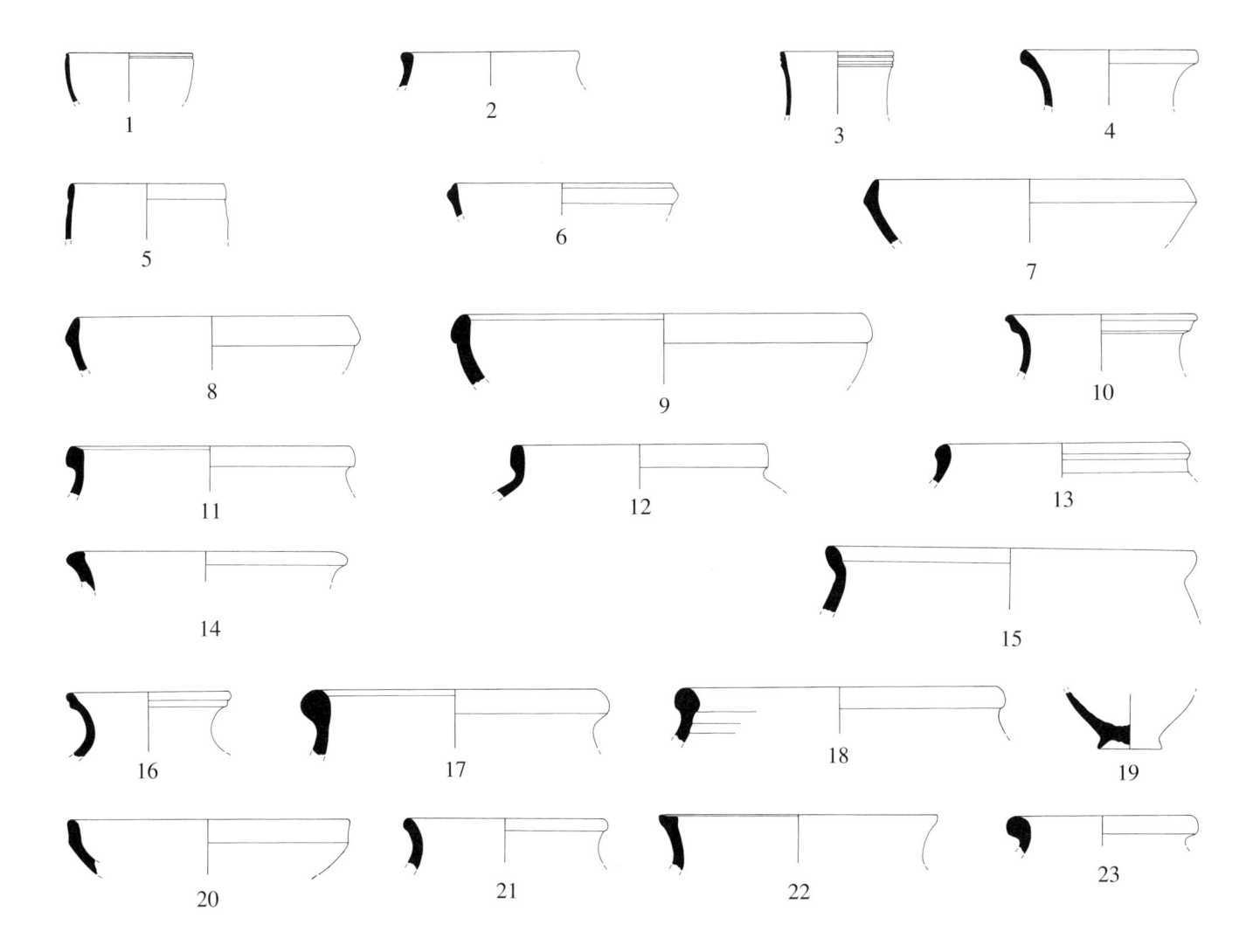

Pottery from Sounding t.1 (Phases 1 to 5; Periods F and E — Early Bronze Age IVa and Early Bronze Age IVb). Scale 1:5

Figure 12. Pottery from Trench VIA (Phases 1, 4, and 5; Periods F, E, and E–D — Early Bronze Age IVa, Early Bronze Age IVb, and Early–Middle Bronze Age)

1. CP. B.IV.b (TS. 2786; VIA, 3.7). Phase 1. About 1/5 rim, neck, and upper shoulder with most of round-shaped base not mended. Fairly coarse gritty brown ware, evenly fired. Self slip out and over rim in.
2. SJR. C.I.a (TS. 845; VIA, 1.2). Phase 4. About 1/10 rim and neck segment. Fairly fine pinkish-buff ware, evenly fired. Thin cream slip out and just over rim in.
3. SJR. C.I.f (TS. 705; VIA, 3.3). Phase 4. About 1/20 rim and neck segment. Fairly fine pink ware, evenly fired. Cream slip in and out.
4. SBR. A.I.b (TS. 701; VIA, 3.1a). Phase 5. About 1/16 rim and upper wall segment. Fairly coarse buff ware, evenly fired. Cream slip in and out.
5. BR. A.II.e (TS. 2490; VIA, 3.1a). Phase 5. About 1/10 rim and upper wall segment. Slightly coarse buff ware, evenly fired. Creamy-buff slip in and out.
6. BR. F.IV.b (TS. 709; VIA, 3.1a). Phase 5. About 1/28 rim and upper wall segment. Fairly coarse cream ware, evenly fired.
7. BR. G.I.f (IP [G.3] A.II.a; TS. 783; VIA, 3.1). Phase 5. About 1/20 rim and upper wall segment. Incised herringbone pattern on top of rim. Coarse buff ware, evenly fired. Cream slip in and traces out.
8. BR. L.III.c (TS. 690; VIA, 3.1a). Phase 5. About 1/24 rim and upper wall segment. Fairly coarse pinkish-buff ware, evenly fired. Buff slip in and out.
9. JR. D.V.c (TS. 2220; VIA, 3.1 + 3.1a). Phase 5. Two joining rim and neck segments. Slightly coarse buff ware, evenly fired. Creamy-buff slip in and out.
10. JR. H.I.j (PM. E.2; TS. 702; VIA, 3.1a). Phase 5. About 1/12 rim and shoulder segment with incomplete potter's mark incised on outside shoulder before firing. Fairly coarse pink ware, evenly fired. Creamy-buff slip out.
11. JR. H.III.o (SC. 3302; VIA, 3.1a). Phase 5. Small rim and upper shoulder segment. Very hard-fired pinkish-buff ware with small lime and gold-colored mica grits, evenly fired. Self slip, partially straw-wiped on outer surface.
12. JR. J.I.f (TS. 726; VIA, 3.1). Phase 5. About 1/6 rim and upper neck segment. Fairly coarse pink ware, evenly fired. Cream slip in and out.
13. JR. J.III.a (TS. 2317; VIA, 3.1a). Phase 5. About 1/6 rim, neck, and upper shoulder segment. Slightly coarse pink ware, evenly fired. Creamy-buff slip out and just over rim in.
14. JR. O.III.b (TS. 2413; VIA, 3.1a). Phase 5. About 1/8 rim and upper shoulder segment. Fairly coarse yellowish-green ware, unevenly fired yellow-buff on outside surface. Creamy-buff slip out.

Other Type Series Examples:

Phase 4 — (1) JR. K.I.f (TS. 901).

Phase 5 — (1) Jg. C.4 (SC. 3301), (2) BE. E.II.g (TS. 687).

Other Study Collection Examples:

Phase 4 — (1) SJR. B.II.h (SC. 2513), (2) JR. H.I.d (SC. 1259), (3) JR. J.I.c (SC. 2113), (4) JR. J.III.g (SC. 1389), (5) JR. J.III.g (SC. 1390), (6) JR. J.III.ab (SC. 2369), (7) JR. J.IV.g (SC. 1537), (8) JR. O.I.d (SC. 1615)

Phase 5 — (1) SBR. A.I.a (SC. 197), (2) SBR. A.I.b (SC. 201), (3) SBR. B.I.b (SC. 354), (4) SBR. B.I.g (SC. 364), (5) SBR. B.I.g (SC. 368), (6) BR. A.II.e (SC. 713), (7) BR. L.II.b (SC. 848), (8) SJR. (not typed, SC. 97), (9) JR. B.III.a (SC. 932), (10) JR. D.I.b (SC. 1043), (11) JR. E.II.d (SC. 2019), (12) JR. E.II.j (SC. 1153), (13) JR. H.I.c (SC. 1251), (14) JR. H.I.k (SC. 1280), (15) JR. J.III.m (SC. 1424), (16) JR. J.IV.g (SC. 1532), (17) BE. E.I.e (SC. 3170); Derived Hellenistic — (1) RSB. B.II.a (SC. 2851).

Figure 12

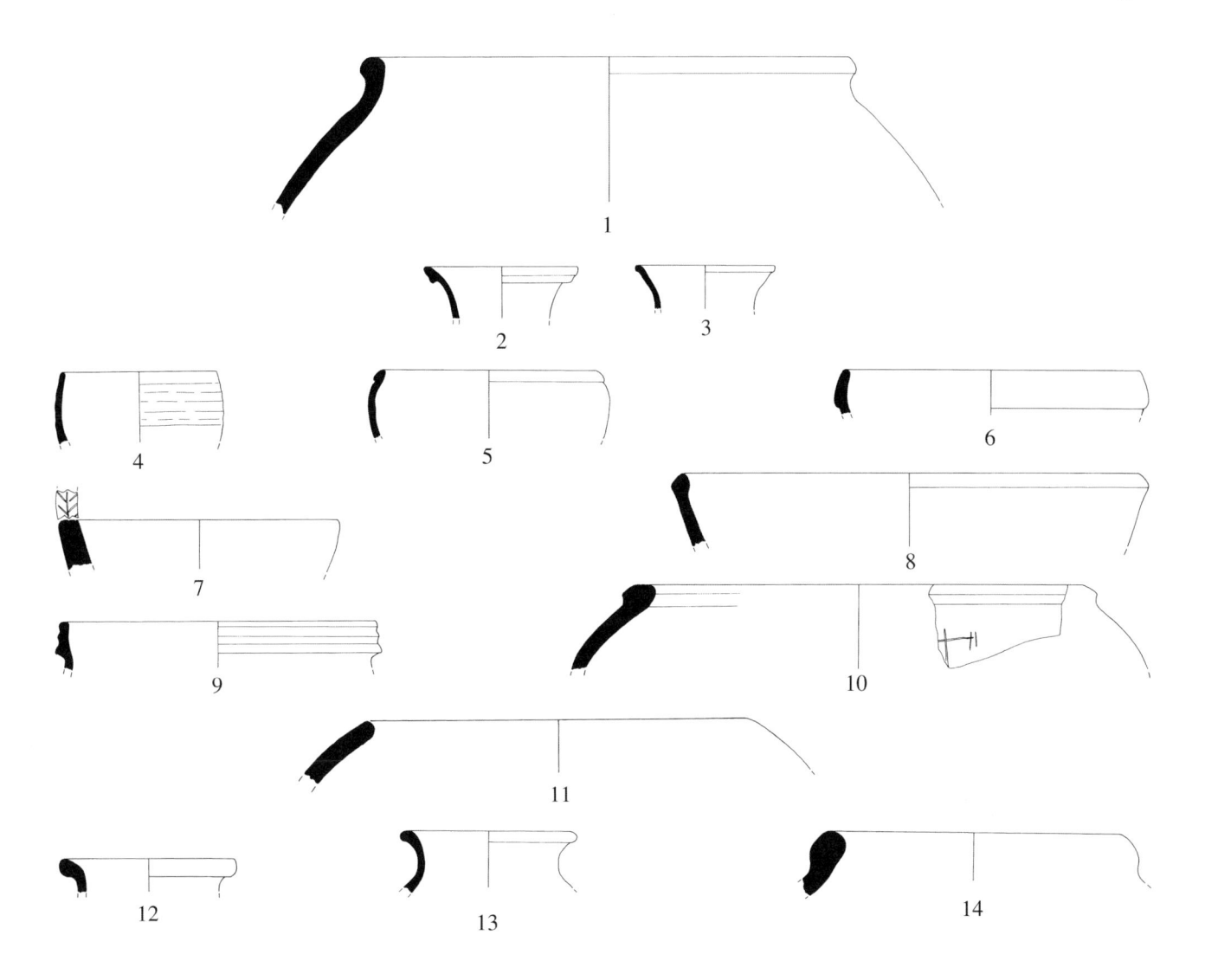

Pottery from Trench VIA (Phases 1, 4, and 5; Periods F, E, and E–D — Early Bronze Age IVa, Early Bronze Age IVb, and Early–Middle Bronze Age). Scale 1:5

Figure 13. Pottery from Trenches VIIA and VIIB (Phases 1–5; Periods F, E, and E–D — Early Bronze Age IVa, Early Bronze Age IVb, and Early–Middle Bronze Age)

1. BR. F.III.e (TS. 711; VIIA, 1.7 and 1.8). Phase 1. About 1/16 rim and upper wall segment; two joining sherds. Fairly coarse buff ware, evenly fired. Cream slip in and out.
2. BR. L.I.a (TS. 568 = TS. 788; VIIA, 1.6, 1.7, and 1.8). Phase 1. About 1/3 rim and most of wall profile; three joining segments. Fairly coarse buff ware, evenly fired. Cream slip in and out. Partly blackened by fire in and out.
3. SJR. C.I.f (SC. 3303; VIIA, 1.8). Phase 1. About 1/10 rim and neck segment. Slightly coarse pinkish-orange ware with many gold-colored mica grits, evenly fired. Traces of pinkish-buff slip in and out.
4. JR. J.III.j (TS. 692; VIIA, 2.6). Phase 1. About 1/5 rim and neck segment. Fairly coarse pink ware, evenly fired. Cream slip in and out.
5. SBR. B.I.e (TS. 686; VIIA, 4.4). Phase 2. About 1/8 rim and upper wall segment. Fairly coarse pink ware, evenly fired. Cream slip out.
6. BR. A.II.e (TS. 678; VIIA, 4.4). Phase 2. About 1/16 rim and upper wall segment. Fairly fine light brown ware, evenly fired. Light creamy-buff slip out.
7. JR. G.I.b (TS. 2050; VIIA, 1.5). Phase 2. Large rim, neck, and upper shoulder segment. Hard, fairly fine pinkish-orange ware, evenly fired. Self slip in and out.
8. FL. B.I.a (TS. 578; VIIA, 2.4). Phase 2. Complete loop handle on shoulder sherd of a two-handled flask type jar. Fairly fine pink ware, evenly fired. Cream slip out.
9. BR. A.II.e (SC. 721; VIIA, 3.2). Phase 3. About 1/10 rim and upper wall segment. Fairly fine buff ware with small gold- and silver-colored mica grits, evenly fired. Creamy-buff slip in and out.
10. JR. J.I.b (SC. 2096; VIIA, 3.2). Phase 3. About 1/12 rim and neck segment. Hard, slightly coarse creamy-green ware with small lime grits, evenly fired. Self slip on outside of neck wet-smoothed and horizontally burnished.
11. JR. J.I.i (SC. 2129; VIIA, 1.3). Phase 3. About 1/16 rim and neck segment. Fairly coarse pinkish-buff ware with lime grits, evenly fired. Thick creamy-green slip in and out.
12. BE. B.II (TS. 674; VIIA, 3.2). Phase 3. About 1/3 base and small segment of lower wall of vessel. Fairly fine cream ware, evenly fired.
13. SBR. A.I.b (TS. 2530; VIIA, 4.1/4.2). Phase 4. About 1/4 rim and most of wall profile. Fairly fine buff-brown ware, evenly fired. Self slip in and out.
14. BR. D.VI.b (TS. 698; VIIA, 3.1). Phase 4. About 1/16 rim segment. Fairly fine pink ware, evenly fired. Cream slip in and out.
15. SJR. A.II.h (TS. 718; VIIA, 2.1). Phase 4. About 1/10 rim and upper shoulder segment. Fairly coarse pink ware, unevenly fired with light brown core. Cream slip partially present on outside surface.
16. JR. K.I.b (TS. 721; VIIA, 2.1). Phase 4. About 1/6 rim and neck segment. Fairly coarse buff ware, evenly fired. Cream slip out.
17. BE. E.I.d (TS. 681; VIIA, 1.2). Phase 4. About 1/4 ring base and portion of lower wall of vessel. Fairly coarse cream ware, evenly fired.
18. JR.Sh. (IP [G.4] F.III.a; TS. 566; VIIA, 1.1 and 1.2). Phases 5 and 4. Large jar sherd from Locus 1.2 and two smaller sherds from loci 1.1 and 1.2 with incised animal decoration on outside surface. Fairly coarse buff ware, evenly fired. Cream slip out.
—. SJR. D.I.a (TS. 4224; VIIA, 1.1). Phase 5. Very small rim and upper shoulder segment. Fine buff ware with small white lime grits, evenly fired. Smooth creamy-buff slip in and out.
19. SR. A.I.b (SC. 3304; VIIB, 1.1). Phase 5. Very small rim and upper wall segment with remains of one drainage hole in body wall. Fine light creamy-buff ware with small lime grits, evenly fired.
20. BE. H (TS. 682; VIIA, 1.1). Phase 5. Complete string-cut knob-like base. Fairly fine buff ware, evenly fired. Cream slip in and out.
21. JR.Sh. (IP [G.4] F.III.a; TS. 680; VIIA, 1.1). Phase 5. Jar body sherd with incised animal decoration on outside wall. Fairly coarse pink ware, evenly fired. Cream slip in and out.

Other Type Series Examples from Area VIIA and VIIB:

Area VIIA:

Phase 1— (1) BR. E.III.g (TS. 2201), (2) BR. L.I.f (TS. 2468), (3) Bt. B.I.2 (TS. 1215).

Phase 2 — (1) Derived Hellenistic: H.RSB. A.II.b (TS. 685).

Phase 3 — (1) SBR. D.II.g (TS. 539), (2) Derived Hellenistic: H.BR. B.IV.b (TS. 727).

Phase 4 — (1) BR. L.III.f (TS. 706), (2) WPS. A.I.a (TS. 704).

Area VIIB:

Phase 5 — (1) BR. L.II.f (TS. 2467).

Other Study Collection Examples Not Illustrated from Area VIIA and Area VIIB.

Area VIIA:

Phase 1— (1) SBR. B.I.g (SC. 369).

Phase 2 — (1) SBR. C.III.a (SC. 603), (2) BR. L.II.d (SC. 860), (3) JR. D.I.b (SC. 1041), (4) JR. H.I.c (SC. 1250), (5) JR. K.I.c (SC. 1580).

Phase 3 — (1) SBR. B.I.g (SC. 362), (2) SBR. B.I.h (SC. 469), (3) SBR. C.III.b (SC. 617).

Phase 4 — (1) SBR. B.I.c (SC. 276), (2) SBR. B.I.h (SC. 517), (3) SBR. B.I.i (SC. 527), (4) SJR. C.II.k (SC. 2596), (5) JR. C.VI.b (SC. 1032), (6) JR. O.III.c (SC. 1672), (7) WPS. A.II (SC. 1952), (8) ABS. C (SC. 3245).

Phase 5 — (1) BR. F.I.c (SC. 1962), (2) JR. C.V.d (SC. 1024), (3) JR. J.II.j (SC. 1355), (4) JR. J.III.d (SC. 2228).

Area VIIB:

Phase 5 — (1) JR. J.III.q (SC. 2353).

Figure 13

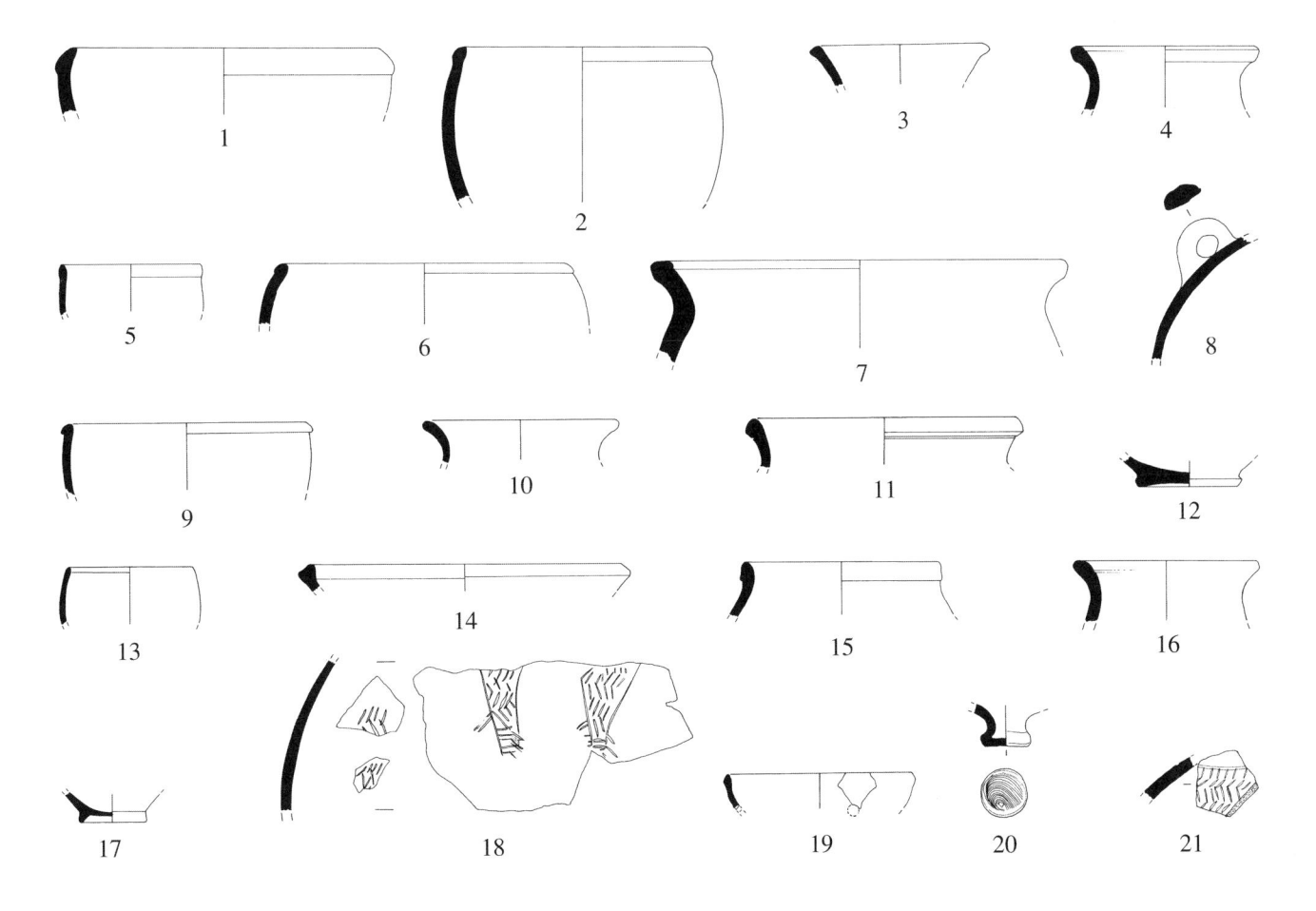

Pottery from Trenches VIIA and VIIB (Phases 1–5; Periods F, E, and E–D — Early Bronze Age IVa, Early Bronze Age IVb, and Early–Middle Bronze Age). Scale 1:5

Figure 14. Pottery from Trenches VIIIA and VIIIB (Phases 1–3; Periods F and E — Early Bronze Age IVa and Early Bronze Age IVb)

1. BR. F.IV.a (TS. 695; VIIIA, 2.3). Phase 1. About 1/36 rim and upper wall segment. Fairly coarse buff ware, evenly fired. Cream slip out.
2. BR. L.I.d (TS. 689; VIIIA, 2.3). Phase 1. About 1/28 rim and upper wall segment. Fairly coarse pink ware, evenly fired. Cream slip in and out.
3. SJR. A.II.c (SC. 3305; VIIIA, 2.3). Phase 1. Small neck and upper should segment. Fine, hard-fired dark pinkish-orange ware with small lime and gold-colored mica grits, evenly fired. Self slip out, highly burnished horizontally around neck and body.
4. JR. F.I.a (SC. 1188; VIIIA, 2.3). Phase 1. About 1/30 rim and upper neck segment. Slightly coarse pinkish-buff ware with very fine mica and lime grits, evenly fired. Creamy-buff slip in and out.
5. JR. J.I.h (TS. 2341; VIIIA, 2.2). Phase 1. About 1/8 rim and neck segment. Slightly coarse buff ware, evenly fired. Creamy-yellow slip in and out.
6. BE. D.III (TS. 840; VIIIA, 2.2). Phase 1. About 1/6 segment of a flat base and lower wall of vessel. Handmade. Coarse pink ware, evenly fired. Thick cream slip in.
7. BE. E.II.i (TS. 694; VIIIA, 2.2). Phase 1. About 1/3 of a ring base with lower portion of wall. Fine reddish-brown ware, unevenly fired with brown core.
8. BE. E.II.k (TS. 1014; VIIIA, 2.2). Phase 1. About 1/2 of a ring base with lower portion of wall. Fairly coarse cream ware, evenly fired.
9. BR. L.I.a (SW. 550; VIIIA, 2.1/2.2). Phase 2. About 1/2 rim and most of wall profile. Fairly coarse creamy-buff ware, evenly fired.
10. BR. L.II.b (TS. 1123; VIIIB, 1.2). Phase 2. About 1/12 rim and upper wall segment. Fairly coarse pinkish-buff ware, evenly fired. Cream slip in and out.
11. JR. E.II.g (TS. 683; VIIIA, 2.1). Phase 2. About 1/12 rim, neck, and shoulder segment. Fairly coarse pinkish-buff ware, evenly fired. Cream slip out.
12. JR. J.III.v (TS. 630; VIIIA, 2.1). Phase 2. About 1/8 rim, neck, and shoulder segment. Fairly fine pink ware, unevenly fired with lighter pink core. Cream slip in and out.
13. JR. O.II.a (TS. 2410; VIIIA, 2.1). Phase 2. About 1/8 rim and upper shoulder segment. Hard, fairly coarse grayish-buff ware, evenly fired. Creamy-green slip out.
14. BE. D.III (TS. 703; VIIIA, 2.1). Phase 2. About 1/2 of a flat base and lower half of wall of vessel with remains of a drainage hole in the base. Fairly fine grayware, evenly fired. Cream slip out.
15. BE. E.I.d (TS. 693; VIIIA, 2.1). Phase 2. Complete ring base and about 1/3 of lower wall of vessel. Fine pink ware, evenly fired. Creamy-buff slip out.
16. BR. B.I.a (TS. 792; VIIIA, 1.1). Phase 3. About 1/12 rim and upper wall segment. Fairly coarse buff ware, evenly fired. Cream slip in and out.
17. JR. B.VI.a (TS. 673; VIIIA, 1.1). Phase 3. About 1/8 rim, neck, and upper shoulder segment. Fairly coarse pink ware, evenly fired. Cream slip in and out.
18. JR. H.I.b (TS. 929; VIIIA, 1.1). Phase 3. About 1/20 rim and shoulder segment. Fairly coarse pinkish-buff ware, evenly fired. Cream slip out.
19. JR. O.I.g (TS. 891; VIIIA, 1.1). Phase 3. About 1/28 rim and neck segment. Fairly coarse pinkish-buff ware, evenly fired. Horizontally burnished below rim and around the neck inside. Cream slip out.
20. BE. E.II.b (TS. 691; VIIIA, 1.1). Phase 3. About 1/6 of a ring base with portion of lower wall of vessel. Fairly coarse pink ware, evenly fired. Cream slip out.

Other Type Series Examples from Area VIIIA and VIIIB:

Phase 2 — (1) BR. L.II.b (TS. 1123), (2) BR. L.II.c (TS. 699), (3) SR. B.II.c (SW. 346).
Phase 3 — (1) BR. A.IV.d (TS. 928), (2) Derived Hellenistic: H.JR. C.I.j (TS. 802), (3) Derived Roman: R.Jg. B.II.b (TS. 804).

Other Study Collection Examples Not Illustrated from Area VIIIA:

Phase 1 — (1) SBR. A.I.f (SC. 228), (2) BR. O.I.c (SC. 867), (3) SJR. A.II.b (SC. 2485), (4) JR. F.II.f (SC. 1228), (5) JR. G.I.b (SC. 2035), (6) CP. B.II.i (SC. 1853).
Phase 2 — (1) SBR. B (SC. 17), (2) SBR. B.I.g (SC. 374), (3) SBR. B.I.h (SC. 667), (4) BR. L.I.d (SC. 834), (5) SJR. (not typed, SC. 58), (6) JR. B.III.b (SC. 938), (7) JR. B.III.d (SC. 942), (8) JR. C.I.h (SC. 2802), (9) JR. D.V.c (SC. 1088), (10) JR. D.V.f (SC. 1102), (11) JR. D.VI.b (SC. 1108), (12) JR. G.I.c (SC. 1238), (13) JR. H.I.c (SC. 1249), (14) JR. K.I.d (SC. 2397), (15) JR. O.I.d (SC. 1613), (16) JR. P.II.f (SC. 1731), (17) ABS. A (SC. 3241).
Phase 3 — (1) SBR. B.I.h (SC. 493), (2) SJR. A.I.a (SC. 2475), (3) JR. C.I.f (SC. 996), (4) JR. D.I.d (SC. 2748), (5) JR. F.I.c (SC. 2650), (6) JR. G.I.b (SC. 2048), (7) JR. H.I.b (SC. 2061), (8) JR. J.I.a (SC. 1300), (9) JR. J.III.g (SC. 1394), (10) JR. J.III.h (SC. 2292), (11) JR. O.II.a (SC. 2412), (12) JR. P.II.m (SC. 1753), (13) BE. C.I (SC. 1911), (14) ABS. A (SC. 3243), (15) WPS. B (SC. 1950).

Figure 14

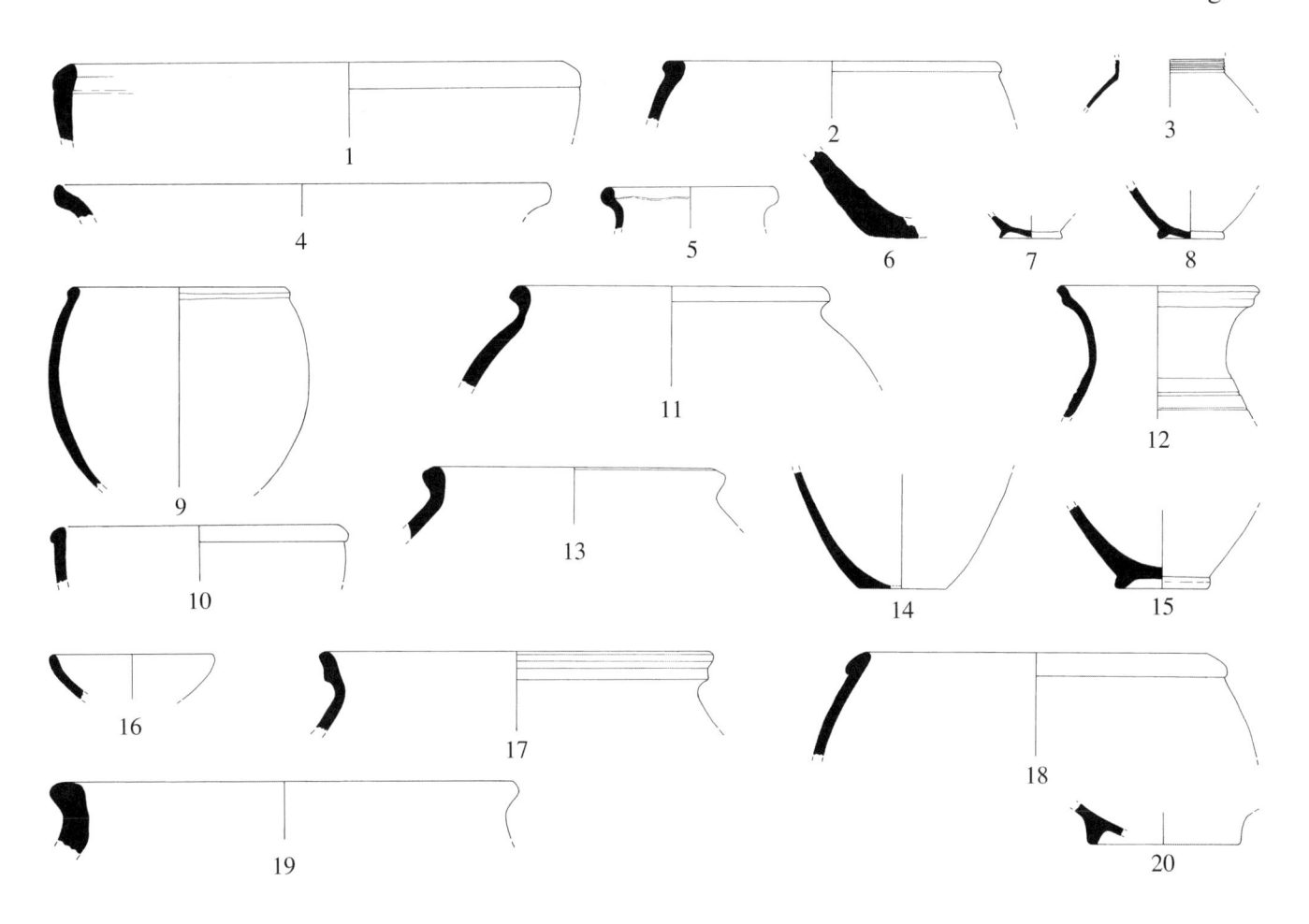

Pottery from Trenches VIIIA and VIIIB (Phases 1–3; Periods F and E — Early Bronze Age IVa and Early Bronze Age IVb). Scale 1:5

Figure 15

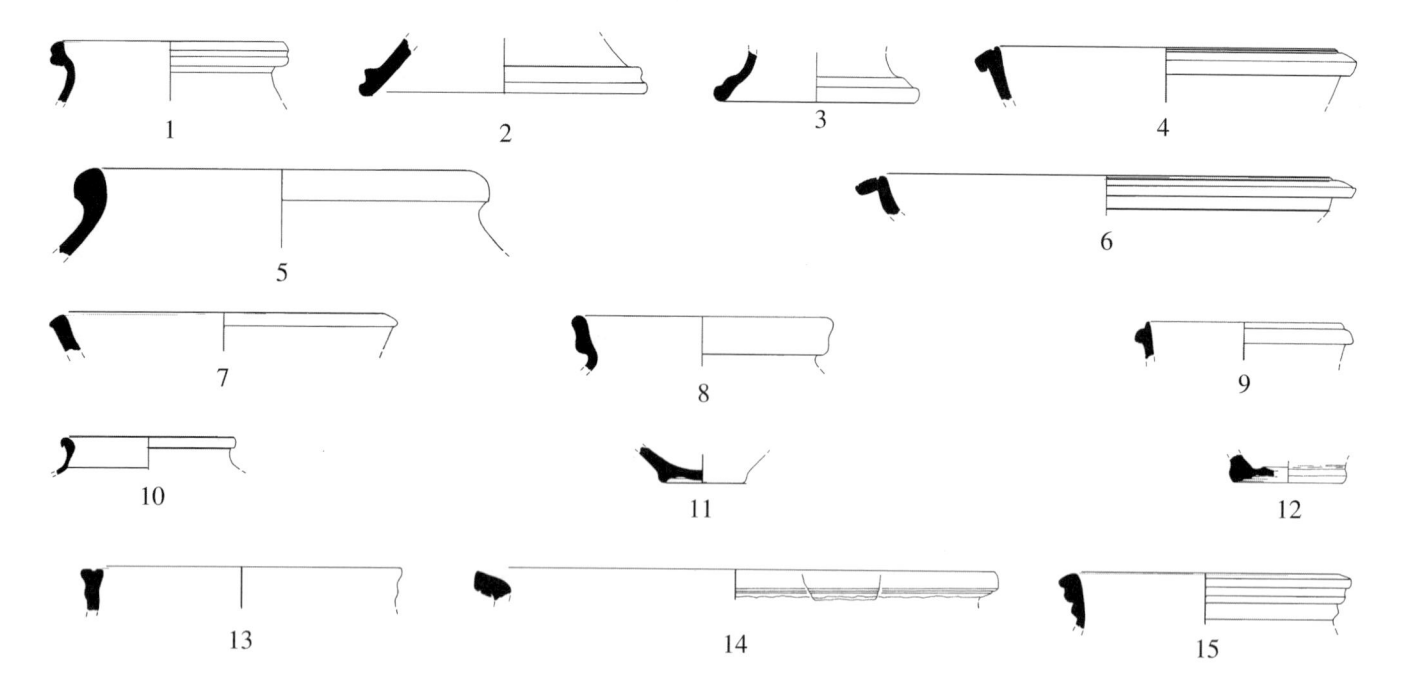

Pottery from Trenches XIA and XIB (Phases 1–3; Period B — Roman). Scale 1:5

1. R.Jg. B.I.a (TS. 999; XIA, 1.4). Phase 1. About 1/16 rim, neck, and shoulder segment. Fairly coarse buff ware, evenly fired. Cream slip in and out.
2. R.PS.4 (SC. 3308; XIA, 1.4). Phase 1. Small rim and wall segment of base or top of stand. Fairly fine hard-fired buff ware with small lime grits, evenly fired. Self slip in and out.
3. R.PS.4 (TS. 997; XIA, 1.4). Phase 1. About 1/8 rim and wall segment. Fairly coarse pink ware, evenly fired. Cream slip in and out.
4. R.BR. B.I.b (SC. 2919; XIA, 1.3). Phase 2. About 1/10 rim and upper wall segment. Slightly coarse light pinkish-buff ware with black and white lime grits, evenly fired. Self slip in and out.
5. R.St.J. B.I.a (SC. 1698; XIA, 1.3). Phase 2. About 1/6 rim, neck, and upper shoulder segment. Coarse dark buff ware with black and white lime grits, evenly fired. Creamy-green slip in and out.
6. R.BR. B.I.b (SC. 2918; XIA, 1.2). Phase 3. About 1/20 rim and upper wall segment. Slightly coarse light buff ware with black and white lime grits, evenly fired. Thick creamy-buff slip in and out.
7. R.BR. B.I.e (SC. 3309; XIA, 1.2). Phase 3. Very small rim and upper wall segment. Slightly coarse, hard-fired pinkish-orange ware with black and white lime grits, evenly fired. Pinkish-buff slip in and out.
8. R.JR. A.I.f (SC. 978; XIA, 1.2). Phase 3. About 1/12 rim and neck segment. Slightly coarse light pinkish-buff ware with a few mica and lime grits, evenly fired. Self slip in and out.
9. R.JR. C.II.b (SC. 3311; XIA, 1.2). Phase 3. About 1/8 rim and upper wall segment. Slightly coarse pinkish-buff ware with small lime grits, evenly fired. Creamy-buff slip in and out.
10. R.CP. A.V.a (SC. 3060; XIA, 1.2). Phase 3. About 1/16 rim and neck segment. Hard, slightly coarse red-brown ware with lime grits, unevenly fired black round the outside of the rim. Self slip in and out.
11. R.BE. B.I.a (TS. 3088; XIA, 1.1). Phase 3. About 1/2 of a low ring base. Very hard, fine, grayish-buff ware, evenly fired. Burnished brown slip in.
12. R.BE. B.I.a (TS. 3089; XIA, 1.1). Phase 3. About 1/3 of a shallow ring base. Hard, slightly coarse reddish-brown ware, evenly fired. Self slip in and out.
13. R.BR. C.II.a (SC. 3310; XIB, 2.1). Phase 1. Very small rim and neck segment. Fairly coarse pinkish-brown ware with lime and gold- and silver-colored mica grits, evenly fired. Creamy-buff slip out, on top of rim and traces below lip of rim inside.
14. R.BR. C.II.c (SC. 2930; XIB, 2.1). Phase 1. About 1/40 rim segment. Fairly fine pinkish-orange ware with small black and white lime grits, evenly fired. Creamy-buff slip in and out.
15. R.SJR. A.I.b (SC. 1117; XIB, 1.1). Phase 2. About 1/18 rim segment. Slightly coarse light pinkish-buff ware with small black and white lime grits, evenly fired. Self slip in and out.

Other Type Series Examples (see pls. 299–318 for the Hellenistic Type Series and pls. 319–39 for the Roman Type Series):
    Area XIA — Roman: (1) R.SJR. C.I.a (SC. 3312), (2) R.Jg. A.II.b (TS. 951), (3) R.Jg. B.II.e (TS. 1064), (4) R.Bt. C.I.b (TS. 3166); Derived Hellenistic: (1) H.JR. E.III.a (TS. 1005).
    Area XIB — Derived Hellenistic: (1) H.JR. B.I.b (TS. 952).

Other Study Collection Examples:
    Area XIA:
    Phase 2 — (1) R.Jg. B.I.a (SC. 1927), (2) R.HMJ. B.II.e (SC. 1665).
    Phase 3 — (1) R.BR. A.II.a (SC. 2915), (2) R.BR. C.II.c (SC. 2932), (3) R.Jg. A.II.a (SC. 2950), (4) R.Jg. B.II.l (SC. 3011), (5) R.Jg. B.II.q (SC. 3028), (6) R.HMJ. A.I.a (SC. 2057), (7) R.St.J. B.I.a (SC. 1655).

Miscellaneous Find: Area XIA, Phase 3 — (1) Glass fragment, 0.5 × 0.15 × 1.5 cm. Type SF.7b (SW. 503).

Figure 16

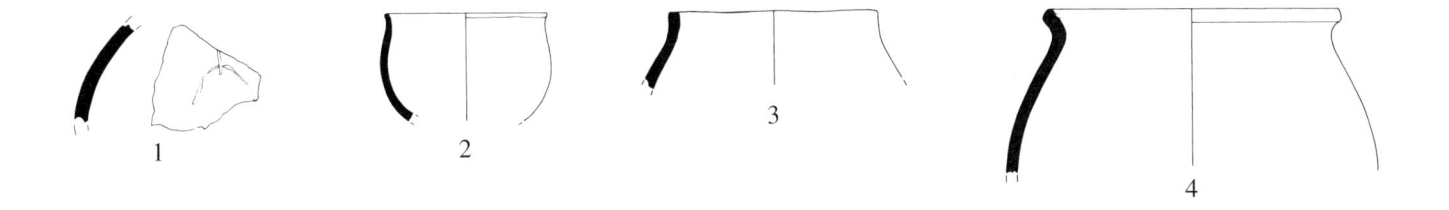

Trench IC (Phases 1 and 2, Period K — Late Chalcolithic). Scale 1:5

1. JR.Sh. (PM. C.16; TS. 1181; IC, 1.62). Phase 1. Jar body sherd with potter's mark, incomplete, incised before firing. Hard, well levigated, grayish ware with fine lime and mica grit composition, evenly fired. Buff slip outside.
2. SBR. A.I.h (TS. 2049; IC, 1.56). Phase 2. Nearly complete rim and wall profile; base missing. Slightly coarse buff ware, evenly fired. Thick self slip in and out.
3. SJR. B.II.e (TS. 1098; IC, 1.56). Phase 2. See also pl. 225: 9. About 1/6 rim and shoulder segment. Handmade, slightly gritty grayware, unevenly fired brown at surfaces. Self slip in and out, irregularly straw-wiped in and out during leather-hard stage of manufacture.
4. CP. B.I.b (TS. 820; IC, 1.56). Phase 2. See also pl. 277: 2. About 1/2 rim and upper body segment. Very coarse ware with large grits, unevenly fired with gray core and brown at surfaces.

Other Unillustrated Examples:

Phase 1— (1) CP. Body Sherds (not numbered, discarded; IC, 1.61), (2) CP. and JR. Body Sherds (not numbered, discarded; IC, 1.62).

Phase 2 — (1) CP. Rim and shoulder segment; sherd lost; untyped (TS. 830; IC, 1.56), (2) CP. Body Sherds (TS. 732; IC, 1.59), (3) JR. Body Sherds (not numbered, discarded; IC, 1.59a).

Another Study Collection Example:

Phase 2 — (1) Bt.Sh. = Bt. A.I.a (SC. 3537).

Figure 17. Pottery from Trench IC (Phase 3; Period J — Early Bronze Age I)

1. SBR. C.II.a (TS. 1043; IC, 1.48). About 1/4 rim and most of wall profile. Fairly fine pinkish-buff ware, evenly fired. Cream slip in and out.
2. SBR. C.II.a (TS. 2440; IC, 1.47). About 1/2 rim and most of wall profile. Slightly coarse pinkish-brown ware, evenly fired. Self slip in and out.
3. SBR. C.II.c (TS. 1039; IC, 1.48). See also pl. 207:4. About 1/5 rim and most of wall profile. Fairly coarse pink ware, evenly fired.
4. BR. B.I.a (SW. 474; IC, 1.48). See also pl. 211:1. About 1/2 rim with complete profile of body. Fairly coarse brownish-buff ware, evenly fired.
5. BR. B.I.a (TS. 569=TS. 873; IC, 1.47 + 1.48). Mended to about 1/2 vessel. Fairly coarse pink ware, evenly fired. Cream slip out.
6. BR. B.I.a (TS. 875; IC, 1.47). About 1/6 rim and most of wall profile. Fairly coarse pink ware, evenly fired. Cream slip out.
7. SJR. A.I.a (TS. 927; IC, 1.48). About 1/24 rim and shoulder segment. Fairly fine pink ware, evenly fired. Buff slip out. Partially blackened out.
8. SJR. A.III.a (TS. 806 = TS. 889; IC, 1.47 + 1.48). See also pl. 224:14. About 1/4 diameter of two non-joining rim and shoulder segments. Slightly coarse pinkish-buff ware, evenly fired. Cream slip in and out.
9. JR. E.I.c (TS. 2210; IC, 1.48). Large rim, neck, and shoulder segment. Slightly coarse brownish-buff ware, fairly evenly fired. Creamy-green slip out.
10. JR. E.II.a (TS. 800; IC, 1.48). About 1/3 rim, neck, and shoulder segment. Fairly fine buff ware, unevenly fired with pink core. Light creamy-buff slip in and out.
11. JR. F.I.a (PM. D.29; TS. 1567; IC, 1.54). About 1/12 rim, neck, and upper shoulder segment. Fairly compact grayish-buff ware with fine lime and mica grits, evenly fired. Creamy-buff slip in and out. Remains of potter's mark on shoulder, incised before firing.
12. JR. F.I.a (PM. A.12; TS. 2053; IC, 1.48). About 1/6 rim, neck, and upper shoulder segment. Incomplete potter's mark on shoulder incised before firing. Slightly coarse pinkish-buff ware, fairly evenly fired. Creamy-buff slip in and out.
13. JR. F.I.c (TS. 801; IC, 1.48). See also pl. 244:3. About 1/16 rim and shoulder segment. Fairly coarse buff ware, fairly evenly fired. Light cream slip out.
14. JR. F.II.d (TS. 924; IC, 1.58). About 1/24 rim, neck, and upper shoulder segment. Fairly fine pinkish-buff ware, fairly evenly fired. Light cream slip in and out.
15. JR. F.III.a (TS. 798; IC, 1.48). See also pl. 245:7. About 1/4 rim, neck, and upper shoulder segment, two joining fragments. Fairly fine buff ware, evenly fired. Light cream slip in and out.
16. JR. G.I.c (TS. 1566; IC, 1.54 + IE, 1.41). Two small rim, neck, and upper shoulder segments Fairly fine pinkish-buff ware with lime and mica grits, evenly fired. Tannish-buff slip out and over rim.
17. JR. J.II.b (TS. 925; IC,1.54). About 1/8 rim, neck, and upper shoulder segment. Fairly fine brown ware, evenly fired. Cream slip in and out. Blackened from fire in and out.
18. JR. J.III.g (PM. C.11; TS. 794; IC, 1.48). See also pl. 253:7. About 1/4 rim, neck, and shoulder segment. Incomplete potter's mark on shoulder incised before firing. Fairly fine buff ware, evenly fired. Light cream slip out.
19. JR. O.I.c (TS. 791; IC, 1.54). See also pl. 262:2. About 1/20 of rim and neck segment. Coarse buff ware, fairly evenly fired. Cream slip in and out.
20. CP. A.I.h (PM. A.15; TS. 859; IC, 1.52). See also pl. 275:8. About 1/8 rim and shoulder segment plus one body sherd, both with a potter's mark incised before firing. Coarse brown ware with lime and mica grits, well burnished in and out and also blackened from fire.
21. JR.Sh. (PM. D.7; TS. 1182; IC, 1.54). Jar base sherd with potter's mark, incised before firing. Hard, slightly coarse ware, unevenly fired with light gray core and reddish-brown in and pinkish brown out.
22. JR.Sh. (PM. C.4; TS. 918; IC, 1.48). Jar body sherd. Potter's mark incised before firing. Fairly coarse creamy-buff ware, evenly fired. Cream self slip in and out.
23. JR.Sh. (PM. D.10; TS. 922; IC, 1.48). Jar body sherd. Incomplete potter's mark incised before firing. Fairly fine creamy-buff ware, evenly fired. Blackened in and out.

Another Type Series Example: (1) SBR. C.II.a (PM. B.1; TS. 1042).

Other Study Collection Examples: (1) JR. F.I.a (SC. 1175), (2) JR. F.I.e (SC. 1214), (3) BE. D.III (SC. 3142).

Figure 17

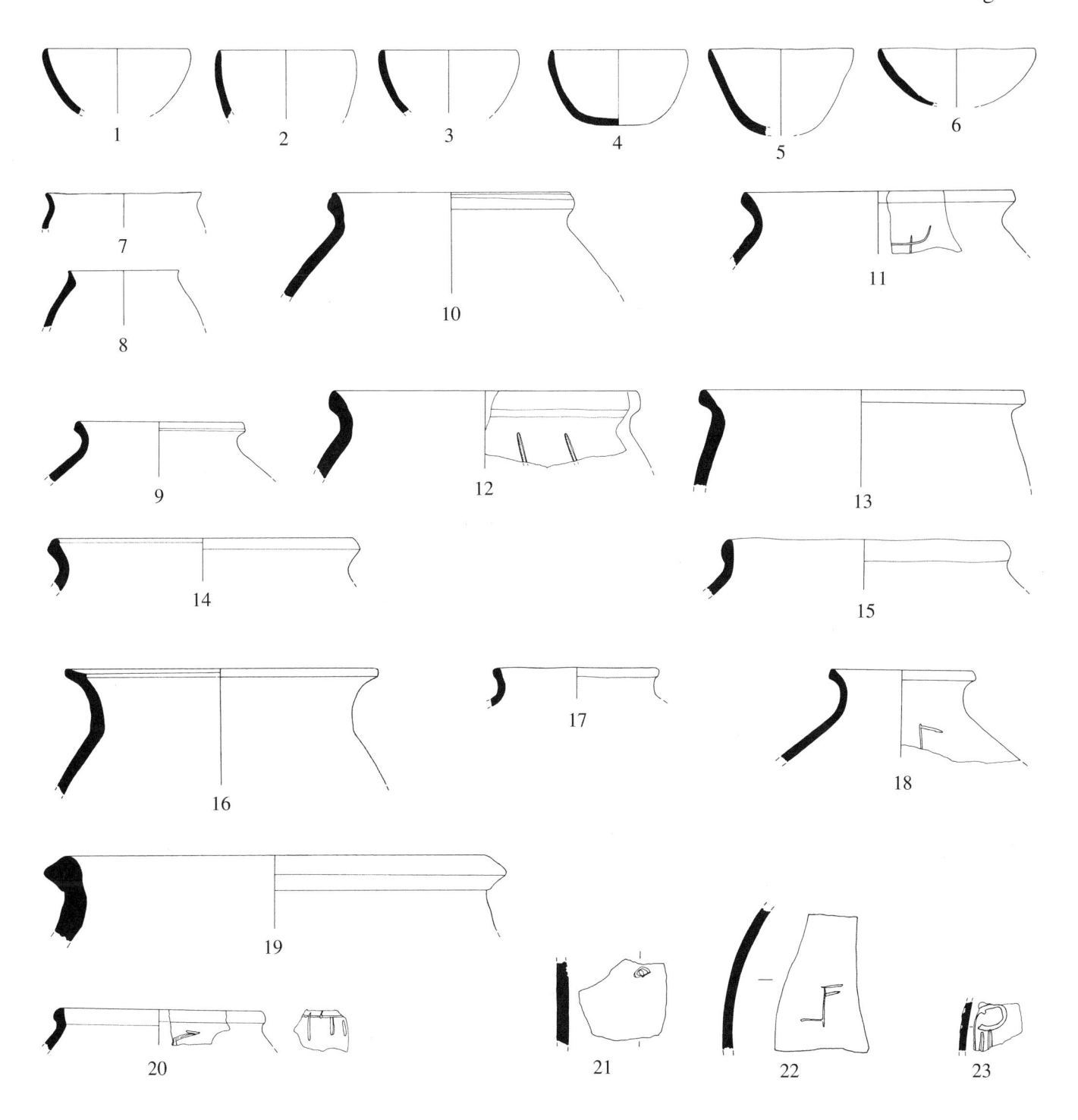

Pottery from Trench IC (Phase 3; Period J — Early Bronze Age I). Scale 1:5

Figure 18. Pottery from Trench IC (Phase 4; Period H — Early Bronze Age II) (See also fig. 278)

1. SBR. B.I.a (TS. 814; IC, 1.40). About 1/40 rim and upper wall segment. Fairly coarse pink ware, evenly fired. Cream slip out.
2. SBR. B.I.h (TS. 2227; IC, 1.43). Small rim and upper wall segment. Fairly fine buff ware, evenly fired. Creamy-buff slip out.
3. SBR. B.I.i (TS. 714; IC, 1.43). About 1/16 rim and upper wall segment. Fairly fine buff ware, evenly fired. Cream slip in and out.
4. SBR. B.I.i (TS. 742; IC, 1.43). About 1/12 and most of wall profile. Fairly fine creamy-buff ware, evenly fired. Cream slip in and out.
5. SBR. B.I.j (TS. 2482; IC, 1.41). About 1/10 rim and upper wall segment. Fairly fine pink ware, evenly fired. Pinkish-buff slip in and out.
6. SBR. B.I.m (TS. 815; IC, 1.40). See also pl. 206:13. About 1/32 rim and upper wall segment. Fairly coarse pink ware, unevenly fired with buff core. Cream slip out.
7. SBR. D.I.e (TS. 781; IC, 1.42). About 1/12 rim and upper wall segment. Fairly fine buff ware, evenly fired. Thin reddish slip out.
8. SBR. D.I.g (TS. 2522; IC, 1.41). About 1/12 rim segment. Hard, fairly compact grayish-brown ware, evenly fired. Possibly self burnished outside while on the potter's wheel.
9. BR. B.I.a (TS. 826; IC, 1.44). About 1/16 rim and upper wall segment. Fairly fine pink ware, unevenly fired with lighter core. Cream slip out.
10. BR. F.I.b (TS. 906; IC, 1.40). See also pl. 215:2. About 1/32 rim and upper wall segment. Fairly fine pink ware, evenly fired.
11. BR. F.II.c (TS. 2418; IC, 1.42). See also pl. 215:8. About 1/20 rim and upper wall segment. Fairly coarse pink ware, evenly fired. Creamy-yellow slip in and out.
12. BR. F.III.g (TS. 2420; IC, 1.43). About 1/12 rim and upper wall segment. Fairly fine pinkish-brown ware, evenly fired. Cream slip out.
13. BR. F.IV.e (TS. 741; IC, 1.43). About 1/12 rim and upper wall segment. Fairly fine buff ware, evenly fired. Cream slip in and out.
14. BR. O.I.a (TS. 715; IC, 1.43). About 1/16 rim and upper wall segment. Possible mending hole tool-drilled into wall of sherd from opposing sides. Fairly coarse pink ware, unevenly fired with pinkish-buff core. Buff slip out and thinly applied in.
15. BR. Q.I.a (TS. 771; IC, 1.32C + 1.43). See also pl. 221:6. About 1/24 rim and upper wall segment; two joining sherds. Fairly coarse pink ware, evenly fired. Cream slip in and out.
16. BR. S.I.a (TS. 775; IC, 1.42). See also pl. 222:3. About 1/12 rim and upper wall segment with rounded ledge handle attached to the top of the rim. Fairly coarse pink ware, evenly fired. Buff slip in and out.
17. SJR. B.III.a (TS. 751; IC, 1.41). See also pl. 225:16. About 1/12 rim and neck segment. Fairly fine pink ware, evenly fired.
18. SJR. C.I.a + BE. B.II (SW. 499; IC, 1.43). About 1/4 rim and neck segment and complete base and about 1/2 of body. Fairly fine cream ware, evenly fired.
19. SJR. C.II.e (TS. 2222; IC, 1.43). Small rim and neck segment. Fine, close ware, unevenly fired with pink core and buff at surfaces. Creamy-buff slip in and out.

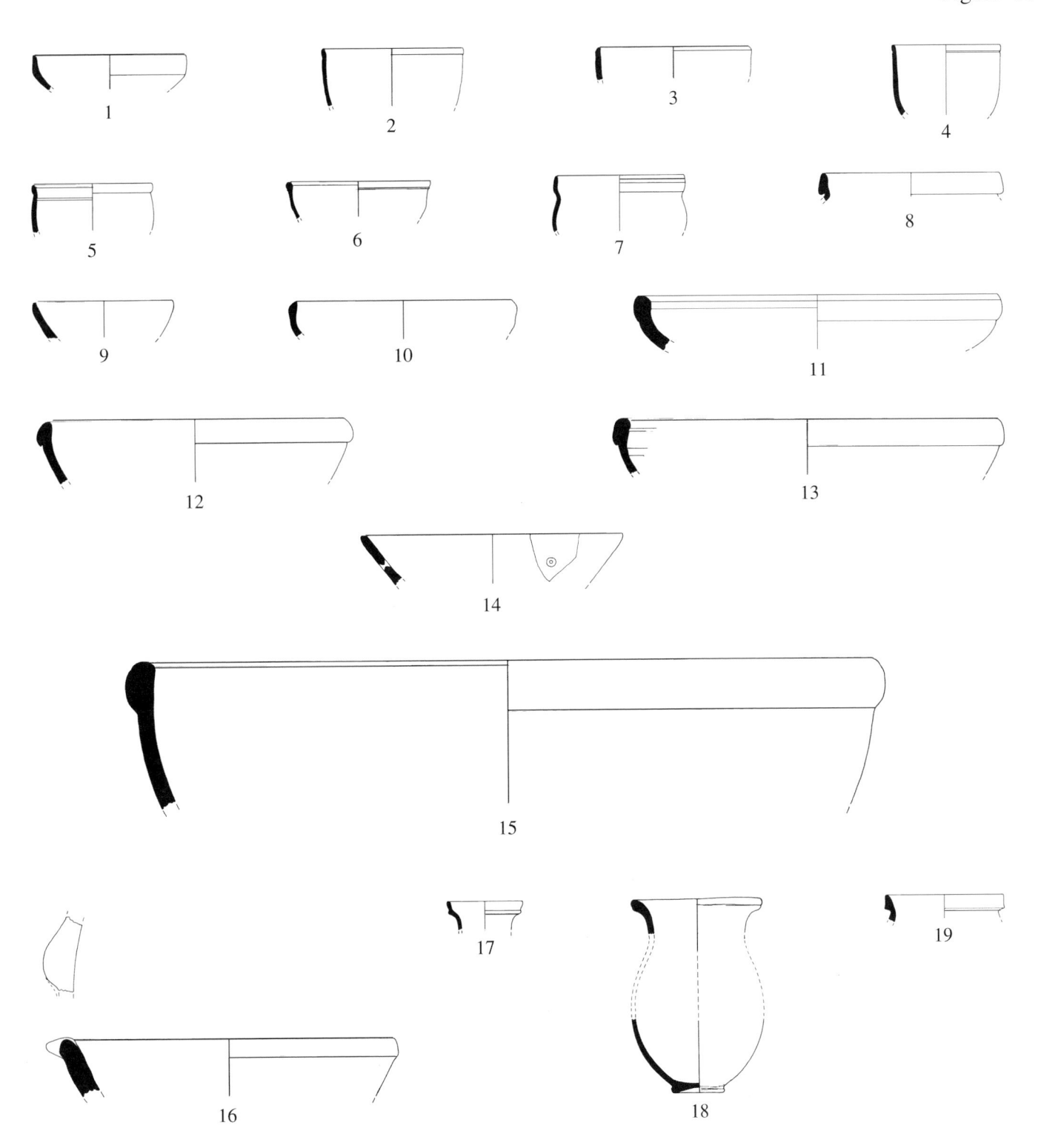

Figure 18

Pottery from Trench IC (Phase 4; Period H — Early Bronze Age II). Scale 1:5

Figure 19. Pottery from Trench IC (Phase 4; Period H — Early Bronze Age II) (*cont.*)

1. JR. D.I.g (TS. 754; IC, 1.41). See also pl. 236:7. Fairly large rim and upper shoulder segment. Fairly coarse buff ware, evenly fired. Cream slip out.
2. JR. E.I.c (TS. 780; IC, 1.42). About 1/8 rim and neck segment with two joining parts. Fairly fine pink ware, unevenly fired with buff core. Buff slip out.
3. JR. E.II.c (TS. 740; IC, 1.43). See also pl. 242:3. About 1/8 rim, neck, and upper shoulder segment. Fairly fine pinkish-buff ware, evenly fired. Buff slip in and out.
4. JR. E.II.g (TS. 2552; IC, 1.43). About 1/10 rim, neck, and upper shoulder segment. Fairly close dark pinkish-buff ware, evenly fired. Creamy-green slip in and out.
5. JR. E.II.g (TS. 2553; IC, 1.42). About 1/12 and neck segment. Hard, close brownish-buff ware, evenly fired. Creamy-green slip in and out.
6. JR. E.II.h (TS. 1078; IC, 1.42). See also pl. 242:8. About 1/20 rim and shoulder segment. Fairly coarse pink ware, evenly fired. Cream slip out.
7. JR. F.I.a (TS. 774; IC, 1.43). See also pl. 244:1. About 1/40 rim, neck, and shoulder segment. Fairly coarse pinkish-buff ware, evenly fired.
8. JR. F.I.d (TS. 2209; IC, 1.43). Small rim and shoulder segment. Fairly close buff ware, evenly fired. Creamy-buff slip in and out.
9. JR. F.II.f (TS. 2200; IC, 1.43). About 1/6 rim and neck segment. Fairly close pink ware, evenly fired. Creamy-buff slip out and on top of rim.
10. JR. F.III.f (TS. 764; IC, 1.42). About 1/6 rim, neck, and upper shoulder segment. Fairly fine brown ware, unevenly fired with darker core. Greenish-buff slip out and over rim in.
11. JR. G.I.b (TS. 770; IC, 1.42). See also pl. 246:2. About 1/8 rim, neck, and shoulder segment. Fairly fine pink ware, evenly fired. Light cream slip out.
12. JR. G.I.c (TS. 743; IC, 1.43). About 1/10 rim and neck segment. Fairly fine pinkish-buff ware, evenly fired. Light tan slip out.
13. JR. H.I.b (TS. 2242; IC, 1.40). See also pl. 247:2. Small rim and upper shoulder segment. Slightly coarse pinkish-red ware, evenly fired. Creamy-pink slip out.
14. JR. H.I.d (TS. 756; IC, 1.43). About 1/24 rim and upper shoulder segment. Fairly fine ware, unevenly fired with dark brown core and pink at surfaces.
15. JR. H.I.i (TS. 2423; IC, 1.43). About 1/20 rim and upper shoulder segment. Fairly fine pinkish-brown ware, evenly fired. Cream slip in and out.
16. JR. H.III.f (TS. 734; IC, 1.43). See also pl. 249:6. About 1/12 rim and shoulder segment. Fairly coarse pinkish-buff ware, evenly fired. Cream slip out and applied thinly in.
17. JR. H.III.i (TS. 2243; IC, 1.43). See also pl. 250:1. Small rim and upper shoulder segment. Fairly coarse gritty pink ware, evenly fired. Self slip irregularly burnished in and out.
18. JR. J.I.h (TS. 2233; IC, 1.42). Small rim and neck segment. Fairly coarse creamy-yellow-green ware, evenly fired. Self slip in and out.
19. JR. J.I.h (TS. 2273; IC, 1.42). About 1/3 rim and neck segment. Fairly fine pale pinkish-buff ware, evenly fired. Creamy buff slip out.
20. JR. J.II.k (TS. 2396; IC, 1.42). See also pl. 252:11. About 1/10 rim and neck segment. Slightly coarse buff-brown ware, evenly fired. Creamy-green slip out and over rim in.
21. JR. J.III.a (TS. 2280; IC, 1.41). About 1/4 rim, neck, and upper shoulder segment. Fairly fine buff ware, evenly fired. Creamy-green slip out and over rim in.
22. JR. J.III.g (TS. 2320; IC, 1.42). About 1/90 rim and neck segment. Fairly coarse buff ware, unevenly fired pinkish at surfaces. Creamy-buff slip out and just over rim in.
23. JR. J.III.m (TS. 2350; IC, 1.43). About 1/10 rim and neck segment. Fairly fine buff-brown ware, evenly fired. Self slip out and over rim in to base of neck.
24. JR. J.III.ab (TS. 2283; IC, 1.40). See also pl. 254:9. About 1/5 rim, neck, and upper shoulder segment. Fine pink ware, evenly fired. Cream slip out and over rim in.
25. JR. J.IV.i (TS. 2213; IC, 1.42). See also pl. 255:9. Small rim, neck, and upper shoulder segment. Hard, close reddish-brown ware, evenly fired. Creamy-buff slip out.
26. JR. K.I.b (TS. 2337; IC, 1.44). See also pl. 257:2. About 1/10 rim and neck segment. Fairly coarse yellowish-buff ware, evenly fired. Self slip in and out.
27. JR. K.II.e (TS. 844; IC, 1.42). About 1/10 rim, neck, and upper shoulder segment. Fine green ware, evenly fired.
28. JR. P.II.a (TS. 2383; IC, 1.41). About 1/8 rim, neck, and upper shoulder segment. Slightly coarse ware, unevenly fired with pink core and brown at surfaces. Creamy-green slip out.
29. JR. P.II.n (TS. 2393; IC, 1.41). See also pl. 270:2. About 1/10 rim, neck, and shoulder segment. Hard, close pinkish-brown ware, unevenly fired with some gray core. Buff slip out and over rim in.

Figure 19

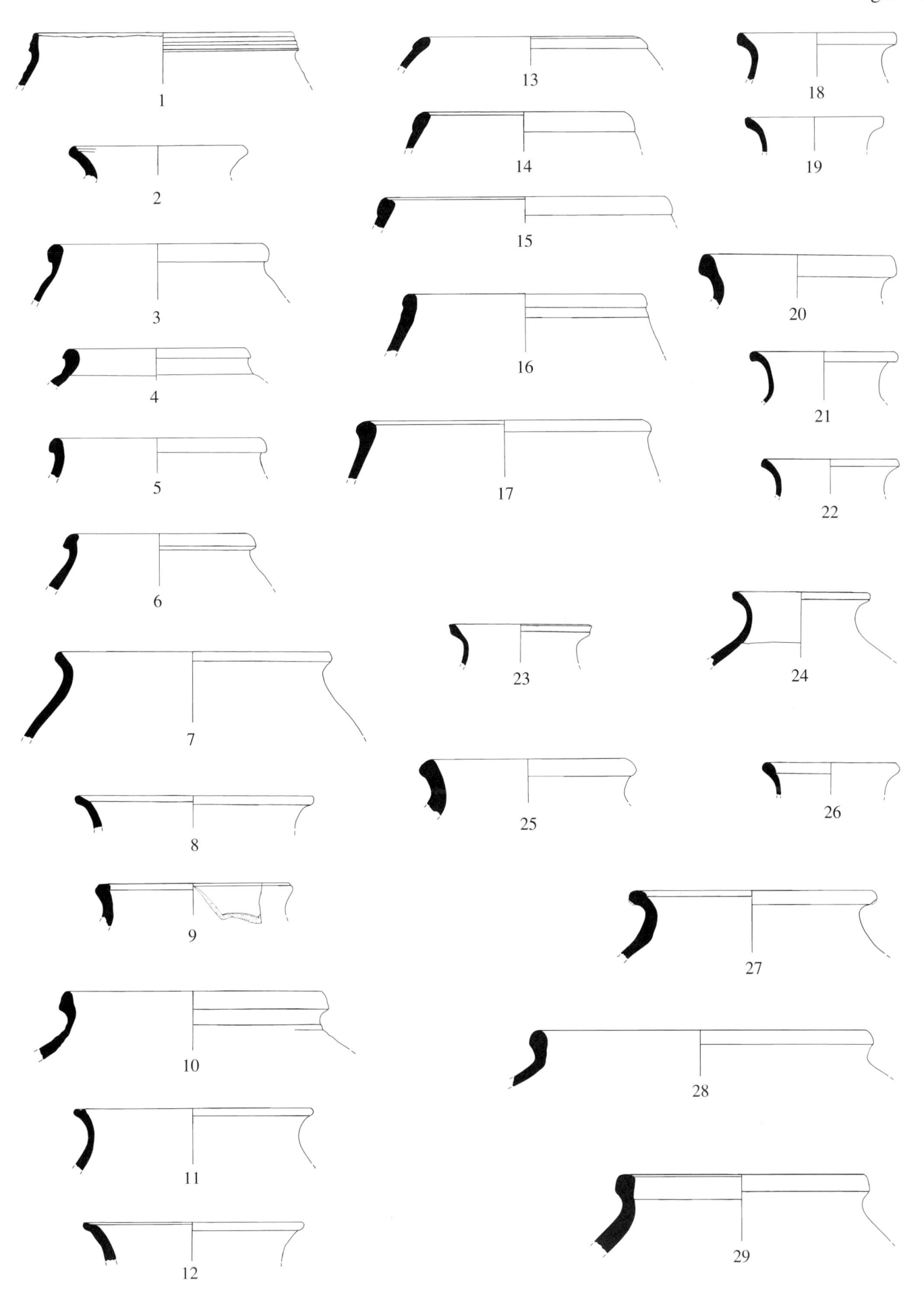

Pottery from Trench IC (Phase 4; Period H — Early Bronze Age II) (*cont.*). Scale 1:5

Figure 20. Pottery from Trench IC (Phase 4; Period H — Early Bronze Age II) (*cont.*)

1. CP. A.I.c (TS. 776; IC, 1.43). See also pl. 275:3. About 1/12 rim and neck segment with ledge handle on rim. Very coarse pink ware with lime and mica grits, fairly evenly fired. Burnished in and out.
2. CP.Ld. A.II.a (TS. 882; IC, 1.40). See also pl. 284:2. About 1/40 rim and portion of wall segment. Coarse pinkish-brown ware, unevenly fired with dark core. Light brown slip out.
3. Ld. B.II.a (TS. 987; IC, 1.41). See also pl. 287:5. Perforated lid fragment with broad loop handle. Fairly coarse buff ware, evenly fired. Cream slip in and out.
4. PS. B.I.a (TS. 753; IC, 1.43). About 1/16 rim and 1/2 wall segment with applied band round wall decorated with thumb impresssions. Fairly coarse pink ware, evenly fired. Cream slip out.
5. BE. B.II (TS. 570; IC, 1.40). Complete base and lower body of a cup or small jar. Fairly coarse cream ware, evenly fired.
6. BE. D.II (TS. 757; IC, 1.42). Complete base and portion of lower wall of vessel. Fairly coarse pinkish-buff ware, evenly fired.
7. BE. E.II.i (TS. 747; IC, 1.43). About 1/2 of base and portion of lower wall of vessel. Fairly coarse buff ware, evenly fired. Cream slip in and out.
8. BE. E.II.i (TS. 762; IC, 1.41). About 3/4 of base and portion of lower wall of vessel. Fine reddish-colored ware, evenly fired.
9. SV.2 (TS. 760; IC, 1.41). Spout. Complete. Fairly coarse pink ware, evenly fired. Cream slip in and out.
10. JR.Sh. (PM. D.4; TS. 2174; IC, 1.42). Jar shoulder sherd. Incomplete potter's mark incised before firing. Slightly coarse creamy-buff ware, evenly fired. Self slip in and out.

Other Study Collection Examples: (1) SBR. A.I.a (SC. 176), (2) SBR. B.I.d (SC. 297), (3) SBR. B.I.e (SC. 312), (4) SBR. B.I.e (SC. 313), (5) SBR. B.I.g (SC. 417), (6) SBR. B.I.h (SC. 431), (7) SBR. B.I.h (SC. 494), (8) SBR. B.I.j (SC. 539), (9) SBR. C.II.a (SC. 597), (10) SBR. C.II.a (SC. 598), (11) SBR. C.II.a (SC. 599), (12) SBR. C.II.a (SC. 600), (13) SBR. C.III.a (SC. 606), (14) SBR. C.III.a (SC. 607), (15) BR. F.II.a (SC. 785), (16) BR. F.III.d (SC. 812), (17) SJR. A.I.a (variant, SC. 3490), (18) SJR. C.I.e (SC. 2633), (19) SJR. C.I.h (SC. 2636), (20) SJR. C.II.s (SC. 2616), (21) JR. E.II.r (SC. 3393), (22) JR. F.I.a (SC. 1176), (23) JR. F.I.a (SC. 1183), (24) JR. F.I.e (SC. 1215), (25) JR. F.I.e (SC. 1216), (26) JR. F.II.a (SC. 1217), (27) JR. F. (Gen. Type, SC. 81), (28) JR. H.I.e (SC. 1286), (29) JR. H.I.e (SC. 2074), (30) JR. J.II.g (SC. 2152), (31) JR. J.II.i (SC. 2172), (32) JR. J.III.e (SC. 1381), (33) JR. J.III.u (SC. 1495), (34) JR. K.II.d (SC. 1772), (35) JR. K.II.e (SC. 1600), (36) JR. O.II.m (SC. 1663), (37) JR. (not typed, SC. 79), (38) CP. B.II.h (SC. 1852), (39) Bt.Sh. = Bt. A.I.a (SC. 3536), (40) Bt.Sh. (not typed, SC. 3782), (41) BE. A.I (SC. 3094), thick coat of bitumen lining on the inside of the wall, (42) BE. B.I (SC. 3106), (43) BE. B.II (SC. 3116), (44) BE. E.I.c (SC. 3156), (45) BE. E.I.e (SC. 3165), (46) BE. E.II.b (SC. 3196).

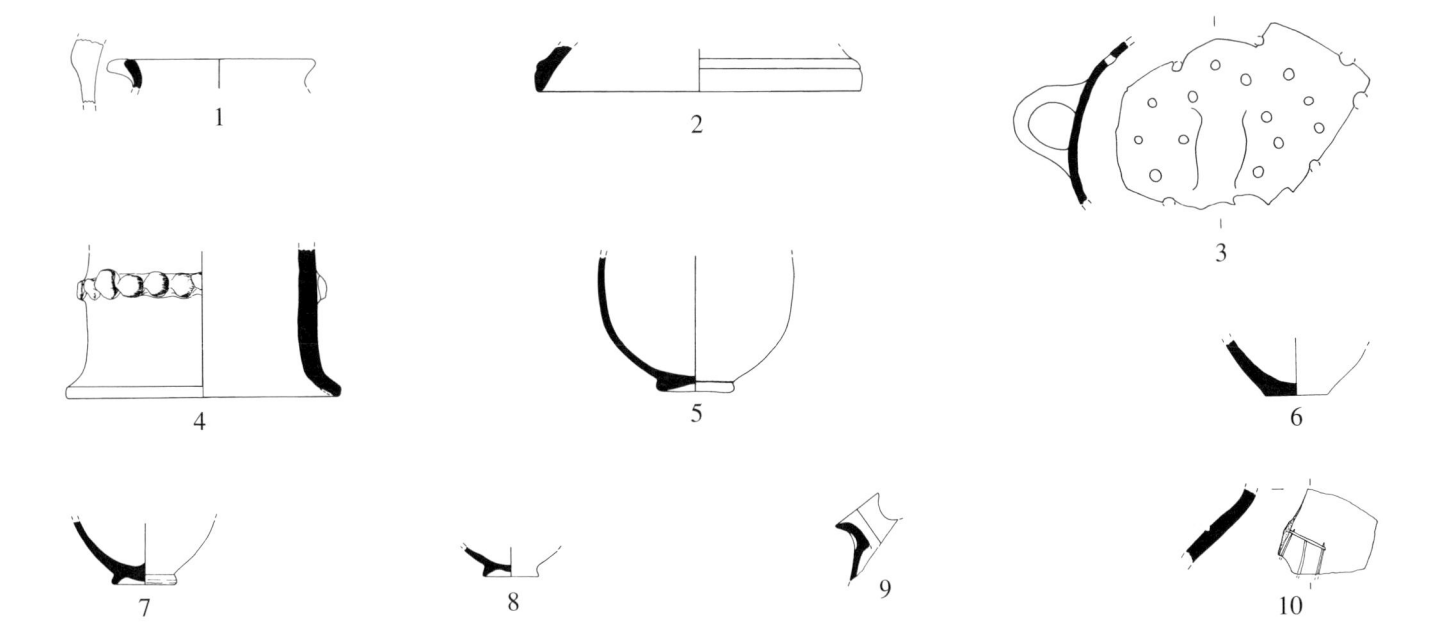

Figure 20

Pottery from Trench IC (Phase 4; Period H — Early Bronze Age II) (*cont.*). Scale 1:5

Figure 21. Pottery from Trench IC (Phase 5; Period F — Early Bronze Age IVa)

1. SBR. A.I.d (TS. 2453; IC, 1.39 + IE, 1.40). About 1/6 rim and upper wall segment. Slightly coarse buff ware, evenly fired. Cream slip out and possibly in, but very worn.
2. SBR. B.I.i (TS. 2483; IC, 1.39). About 1/6 rim and upper wall segment. Fairly fine brownish-buff ware, evenly fired. Creamy-buff slip in and out.
3. SBR. D.I.c (TS. 777; IC, 1.39). About 1/12 rim and upper wall segment. Fairly fine pink ware, evenly fired. Buff slip in and out.
4. SBR. D.I.c (TS. 772; IC, 1.33). About 1/6 rim and shoulder segment. Fairly coarse creamy-buff ware, evenly fired.
5. SBR. D.I.i (TS. 2474; IC, 1.33). Small rim and upper shoulder segment. Fine buff ware, evenly fired. Self slip in and out.
6. BR. F.II.d (TS. 2422; IC, 1.33) About 1/20 rim and upper wall segment. Fairly coarse pinkish-buff ware, evenly fired. Buff slip out.
7. BR. F.III.d (TS. 2421; IC, 1.35). About 1/15 rim and upper wall segment. Fairly fine pinkish-brown ware, evenly fired. Pinkish-buff slip out.
8. BR. G.I.c (TS. 769; IC, 1.34). See also pl. 216:3. About 1/12 rim and upper wall segment. Fairly coarse pink ware, evenly fired. Cream slip out.
9. SJR. A.II.f (TS. 782 = TS. 885; IC, 1.34, 1.35, 1.36). Two small, non-joining, rim, neck, and upper segments. Fairly fine buff ware, evenly fired. Cream slip in and out.
10. SJR. C.I.e (TS. 2312; IC, 1.35). About 1/6 rim and neck segment. Fairly fine buff ware, evenly fired. Self slip in and out.
11. JR. E.I.a (TS. 2125; IC, 1.35). See also pl. 241:1. About 1/3 rim and shoulder segment. Hard, fairly close light greenish-buff ware, evenly fired. Self slip in and out.
12. JR. E.II.b (TS. 2248; IC, 1.34). Large rim and shoulder segment. Hard, close pinkish-buff ware, evenly fired. Creamy-buff slip out.
13. JR. E.II.j (TS. 2346; IC, 1.35). About 1/10 rim, neck, and upper shoulder segment. Slightly coarse ware, unevenly fired with grayish-buff core and pink at surfaces. Creamy-yellow slip out and just over rim in.
14. JR. H.I.h (TS. 2419; IC, 1.34). About 1/10 rim and shoulder segment. Fairly fine buff ware, evenly fired. Self slip in and out.
15. JR. H.II.b (TS. 759; IC, 1.39). See also pl. 248:2. About 1/12 rim, neck, and shoulder segment. Fairly coarse creamy-buff ware, evenly fired. Self slip out.
16. JR. J.III.c (TS. 2259; IC, 1.35 + 1.39). Two small joining rim and neck segments. Fairly fine pale buff ware, evenly fired. Self slip in and out.
17. JR. J.III.g (TS. 768; IC, 1.39). About 1/4 rim and neck segment. Fairly coarse pink ware, evenly fired. Cream slip in and out.
18. JR. J.III.j (TS. 2268; IC, 1.33). Large rim, neck, and shoulder segment. Fairly coarse pinkish-buff ware, evenly fired. Creamy-green slip out and over rim to base of neck in.
19. JR. J.III.m (TS. 1079; IC, 1.35). About 1/6 rim, neck, and shoulder segment. Fairly coarse pink ware, evenly fired. Cream slip out just over rim in.
20. JR. J.III.o (TS. 1045; IC, 1.39 and 1.40). See also pl. 253:15. About 1/3 rim, neck, and 1/2 body segment plus non-joining body sherds. Fairly coarse pink ware, evenly fired. Cream slip out and just over rim; buff slip inside below rim.
21. JR. J.III.o (SW. 456; IC, 1.34 + 1.35, 1.36, 1.38, 1.39). About 1/6 rim, neck, and shoulder segment with five joining rim fragments. Hard, fairly coarse cream ware, evenly fired.
22. JR. J.III.o (TS. 1090; IC, 1.36). Complete rim, neck, and shoulder mended plus many unmended body sherds. Fairly coarse pinkish-buff ware, evenly fired. Cream slip in and out.

Figure 21

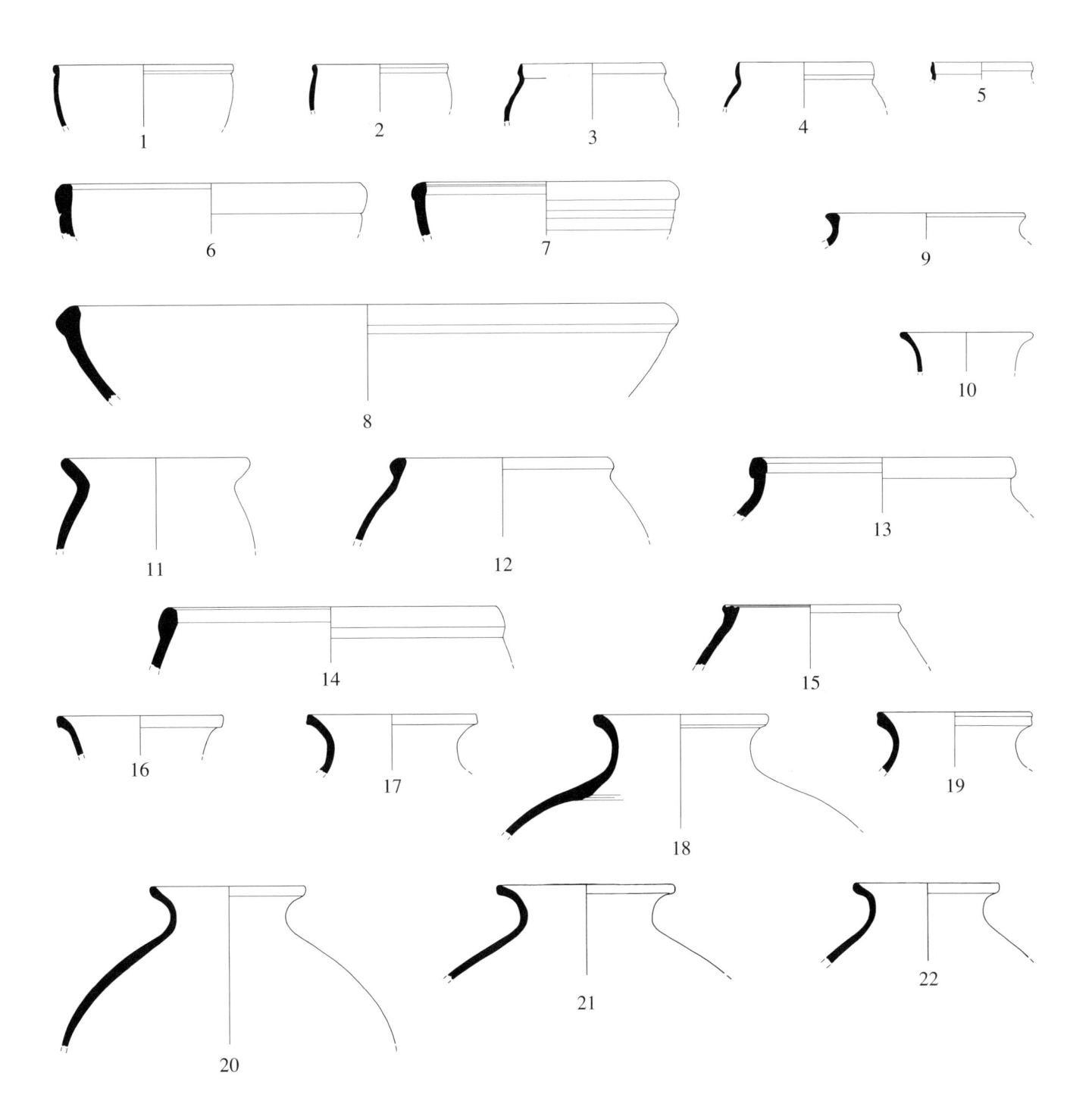

Pottery from Trench IC (Phase 5; Period F — Early Bronze Age IVa). Scale 1:5

Figure 22

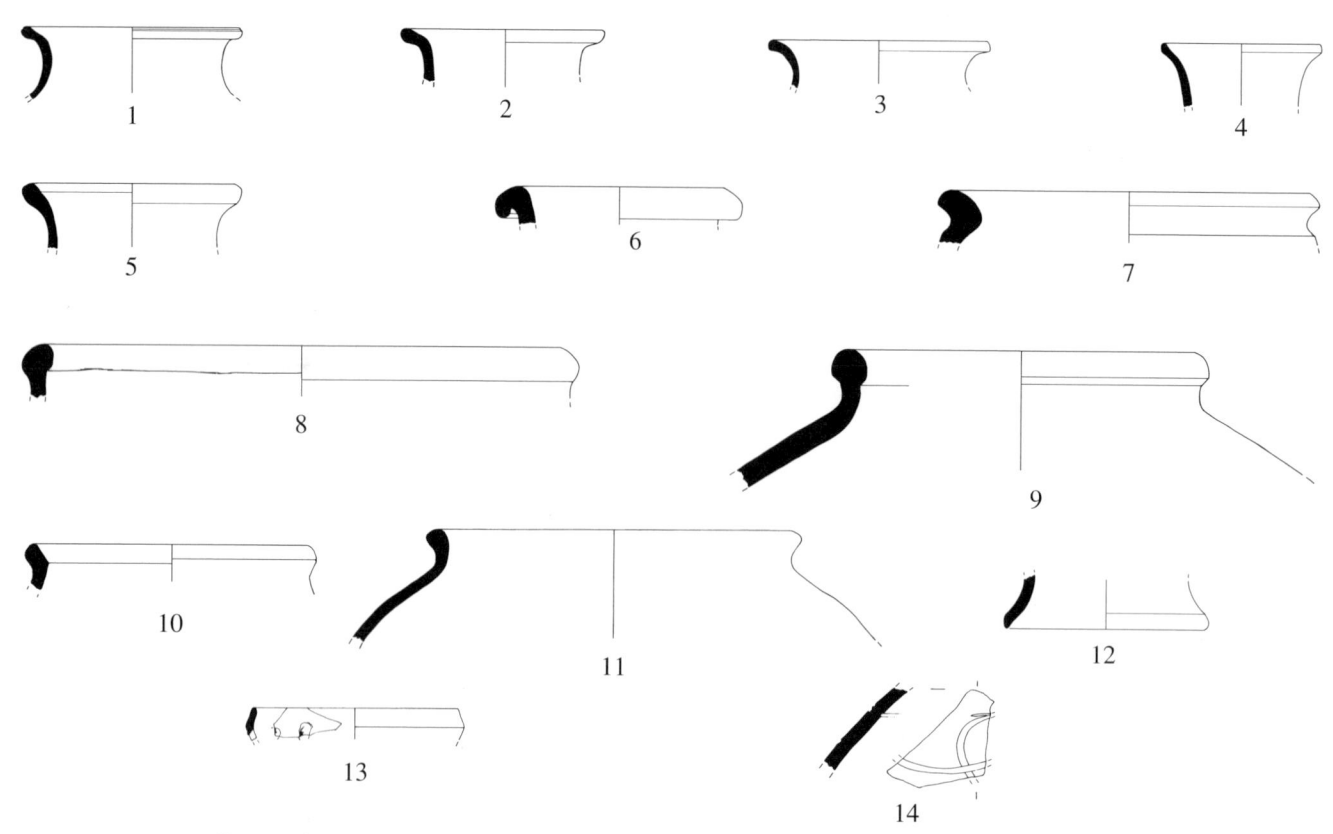

Pottery from Trench IC (Phase 5; Period F — Early Bronze Age IVa) (*cont.*). Scale 1:5

1. JR. J.III.o (TS. 860; IC, 1.36). About 1/4 rim, neck, and upper shoulder segment. Fairly fine buff ware, evenly fired. Cream slip in and out.
2. JR. J.III.o (TS. 871; IC, 1.36). About 1/5 rim and neck segment. Fairly coarse buff ware, evenly fired. Light cream slip in and out.
3. JR. J.III.p (TS. 2324; IC, 1.36 + 1.39). See also pl. 253:16. About 1/6 rim and neck segment of two joining fragments. Fine yellow-buff ware, evenly fired. Self slip in and out.
4. JR. J.III.t (TS. 2311; IC, 1.33). About 1/5 rim and neck segment. Fairly coarse buff ware, evenly fired. Self slip in and out.
5. JR. J.III.u (TS. 2274; IC, 1.34). About 1/5 rim and neck segment. Slightly coarse pinkish-buff ware, evenly fired. Pale green slip in and out.
6. JR. J.IV.f (TS. 2138; IC, 1.38). See also pl. 255:6. Small rim and upper neck segment. Coarse pinkish-buff ware, evenly fired. Pale creamy-green slip in and out.
7. JR. O.I.a (TS. 2129; IC, 1.35). Small rim and upper shoulder segment. Hard, close grayware, unevenly fired pinkish-buff at surfaces.
8. JR. P.II.g (TS. 2358; IC, 1.35). See also pl. 268:7. About 1/10 rim and neck segment. Fairly coarse and gritty dark pink ware, evenly fired. Creamy-buff slip in and out.
9. JR. Q.II.a (TS. 765; IC, 1.39). About 1/6 rim, neck, and shoulder segment. Fairly coarse pink ware, evenly fired. Cream slip out.
10. CP. B.I.i (TS. 4188; IC, 1.39). Small rim and neck segment. Fairly coarse dark brown ware with many mica and lime grits, unevenly fired gray on inside surface. Horizontally burnished in and out.
11. CP. B.II.a (TS. 822; IC, 1.39 + 1.40). See also pl. 278:1. About 1/4 rim, neck, and shoulder segment; two joining fragments. Coarse pink ware with lime and mica grits, evenly fired. Self burnished in and out.
12. PS. A.II.c (TS. 2540; IC, 1.33). About 1/8 rim and 1/2 of body segment. Slightly coarse pinkish-brown ware, evenly fired. Self slip in and out.
13. SR. B.II.a (TS. 2101; IC, 1.35). Small rim and upper wall segment.with remains of two strainer holes in the wall of the vessel. Fairly fine buff ware, evenly fired. Cream slip in and out.
14. JR.Sh. (PM. E.2; TS. 2173; IC, 1.33). Jar sherd with linear decoration incised before firing. Hard, close light pinkish-buff ware, evenly fired. Buff slip in and out.

Other Study Collection Examples: (1) SBR. A.I.a (SC. 172), (2) SBR. A.I.a (SC. 180), (3) SBR. A.I.a (SC. 182), (4) SBR. A.I.b (SC. 212), (5) SBR. A.I.d (SC. 3489), (6) SBR. A. (Gen. Type, SC. 9), (7) SBR. B.I.d (SC. 293), (8) SBR. B.I.h (SC. 502), (9) SBR. B.I.i (SC. 529), (10) SBR. B. (Gen. Type, SC. 18), (11) SBR. D.I.c (SC. 640), (12) SJR. B.I.a (SC. 2494), (13) SJR. C.I.a (SC. 2545), (14) SJR. C.II.c (SC. 2581), (15) SJR. C.II.m (SC. 3533), (16) JR. E.II.f (SC. 1149), (17) JR. F.I.c (SC. 1208), (18) JR. H.I.b (SC. 1247), (19) JR. H.I.d (SC. 2069), (20) JR. J.I.a (SC. 3498), (21) JR. J.I.b (SC. 2095), (22) JR. J.I.f (SC. 3500), (23) JR. J.II.b (SC. 3391), (24) JR. J.II.h (SC. 2157), (25) JR. J.II.m (SC. 2195), (26) FL.Sh. Pt. = FL. A.II.b (SC. 3535), (27) CP. A.II.e (SC. 1806), (28) CP. B.I.f (SC. 1832), (29) CP. B.II.e (SC. 1851), (30) BE. A.II (SC. 3099), (31) BE. B.I (SC. 3103), (32) BE. D.II (SC. 3138), (33) BE. E.I.i (SC. 3185).

Figure 23

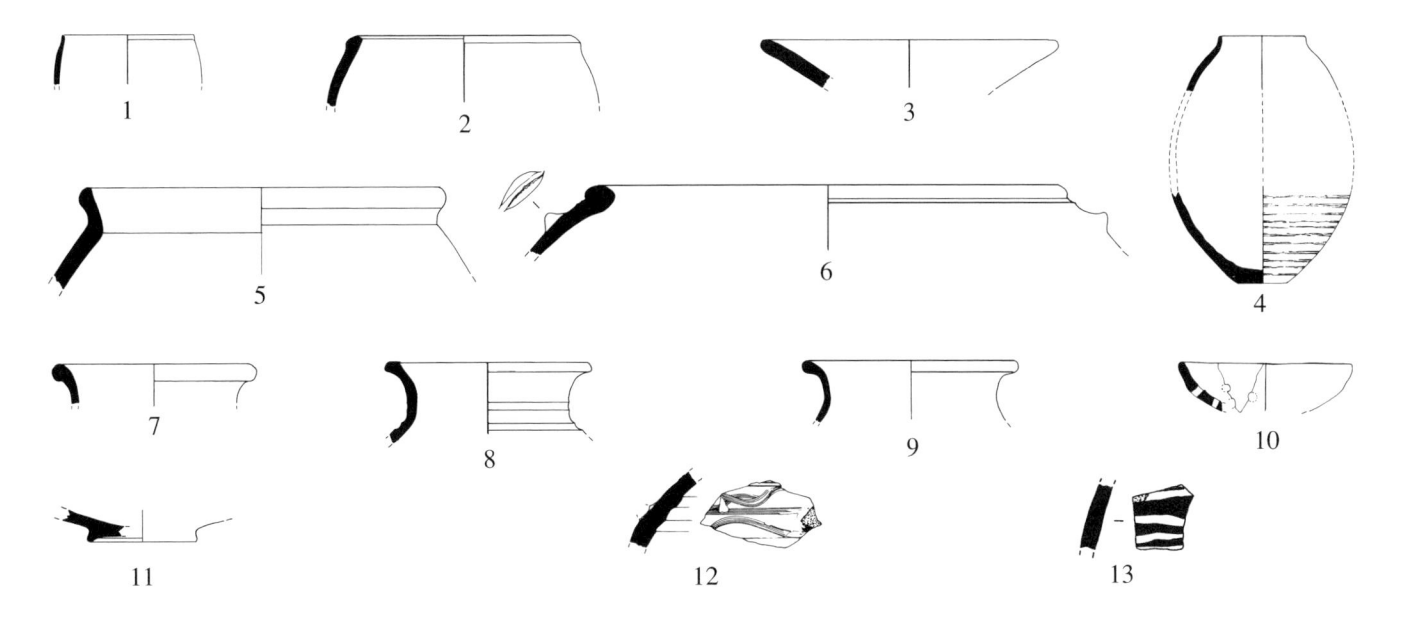

Pottery from Trench IC (Phase 6; Period E — Early Bronze Age IVb). Scale 1:5

1. SBR. A.I.a (TS. 2449; IC, 1.28). About 1/2 rim and upper wall segment. Fairly fine buff ware, evenly fired. Light creamy-green slip out.
2. BR. L.I.g (TS. 2458; IC, 1.28). See also pl. 219:7. About 1/6 rim and upper wall segment. Fairly coarse grayish-buff ware, evenly fired. Self slip in and out.
3. BR. O.I.a (TS. 653; IC, 1.25). About 1/20 rim and upper wall segment. Fairly fine buff ware, evenly fired. Light cream slip out.
4. SJR. E.I.a (SW. 303; IC, 1.28). Vessel reconstructed from rim and upper shoulder segment and complete base with portion of lower wall. Fairly close ware with black and white lime grits, unevenly fired gray in, drab out. Grayish-brown self slip out horizontally burnished with narrow black rings.
5. JR. F.I.b (TS. 622; IC, 1.26). About 1/20 rim, neck, and shoulder segment. Fairly coarse pink ware, evenly fired. Cream slip out, blackened in.
6. JR. H.I.g (TS. 590; IC, 1.27). About 1/12 rim and shoulder segment with vestigial ledge handle on shoulder. Coarse pink ware with lime and mica grits, unevenly fired. Cream slip out.
7. JR. J.III.e (TS. 2298; IC, 1.26). About 1/5 rim and neck segment. Fairly fine pinkish ware, evenly fired. Self slip in and out.
8. JR. J.III.k (TS. 556; IC, 1.26). About 1/6 rim, neck, and shoulder segment. Fairly coarse pink ware, evenly fired. Cream slip in and out.
9. JR. J.III.o (TS. 2323; IC, 1.28). About 1/6 rim, neck, and upper shoulder segment. Fairly fine yellow-buff ware, evenly fired. Self slip out and over rim in to base of neck.
10. SR. A.I.b (TS. 2104; IC, 1.25). See also pl. 290:2. Small rim and wall segment with remains of three strainer holes. Slightly coarse pinkish-buff ware, evenly fired.
11. BE. E.I.g (TS. 624; IC, 1.28). About 1/3 of the base ring and small segment of lower wall of the vessel. Fairly fine grayware, evenly fired. Self slip burinished in and out.
12. JR.Sh. (IP [G.1] E.I.a; TS. 567; IC, 1.26). Jar body sherd decorated with comb-incised wavy and horizontal line decoration. Fairly coarse buff ware, evenly fired. Cream slip in and out. Remains of a loop handle.
13. JR.Sh. Pt. (SC. 3534; IC, 1.28). Jar shoulder sherd with grayish-buff slip out painted with irregular-shaped black horizontal bands. Slightly coarse grayware with lime grits, fired pinkish-purple on inside wall.

Another Type Series Example (Derived Roman Bottle): (1) R.Bt. A.I.a (TS. 655).

Other Study Collection Examples: (1) SBR. A.I.a (SC. 179), (2) SBR. B.I.c (SC. 273), (3) SBR. B.I.d (SC. 302), (4) SBR. B.I.e (SC. 327), (5) SBR. B.I.g (SC. 358), (6) SBR. B.I.h (SC. 491), (7) SBR. B.I.l (SC. 584), (8) BR. B.II.d (SC. 733), (9) SJR. B.I.c (SC. 2505), (10) SJR. C.I.a (SC. 2541), (11) SJR. C.I.a (SC. 2548), (12) SJR. C.I.e (SC. 2551), (13) SJR. C.I.e (SC. 2553), (14) SJR. C.II.k (SC. 2601), (15) JR. A.III.c (SC. 904), (16) JR. D (Gen. Type, SC. 87), (17) JR. J.I.b (SC. 3497), (18) JR. J.I.h (SC. 2126), (19) JR. J.III.ab (SC. 3496), (20) JR. Q.II.d (SC. 1769), (21) CP. A.I.h (SC. 1793), (22) CP. A.II.c (SC. 1804), (23) CP. B.IV.d (SC. 1888), (24) Ld. C.II.a (SC. 3499), (25) BE. B.II (SC. 3119), (26) Hd. B (SC. 3272).

Figure 24. Pottery from Trench IC (Phase 7; Period E — Early Bronze Age IVb)

1. SBR. A.I.a (TS. 2462; IC, 1.32A). Small rim and upper wall segment. Fine yellow-buff ware, fairly evenly fired. Cream slip out.
2. SBR. A.I.d (TS. 2965; IC, 1.21). Small rim rim and upper shoulder segment and about half of base of a cup (reconstructed profile). Fairly fine dark pink ware, evenly fired. Buff slip in and out.
3. SBR. B.I.j (TS. 2450; IC, 1.32C). About 1/4 rim and upper wall segment. Fairly fine buff ware, evenly fired. Cream slip out.
4. BR. A.IV.c (TS. 841 = TS. 1057; IC, 1.32C). About 1/20 rim and upper wall; two joining segments. Fairly coarse greenish-buff ware, unevenly fired with gray core.
5. BR. B.II.d (TS. 2088; IC, 1.32C). Small rim and upper wall segment. Fairly close pinkish-buff ware, evenly fired. Light greenish-buff slip in and out.
6. BR. D.I.b (TS. 1083; IC, 1.32B). About 1/24 rim and wall segment. Fairly coarse creamy-buff ware, evenly fired.
7. BR. D.VI.a (TS. 828; IC, 1.32C). About 1/16 rim and upper wall segment. Fairly fine reddish ware, unevenly fired with dark brown core. Burnished buff slip out.
8. BR. E.I.a (TS. 584; IC, 1.21). About 1/6 rim and most of wall profile. Coarse pink ware, evenly fired.
9. BR. H.I.b (TS. 579; IC, 1.21). See also pl. 217:2. About 1/12 rim, upper wall and small portion of lower wall segment. Coarse pink ware, evenly fired.
10. BR. L.II.a (TS. 2056; IC, 1.21). See also pl. 219:11. About 1/4 rim and wall segment. Fairly coarse gray-buff ware, evenly fired. Self slip in and out.
11. SJR. A.III.d (TS. 2452; IC, 1.21). See also pl. 224:17. About 1/6 rim and shoulder segment. Slightly coarse pinkish-buff ware, evenly fired. Cream slip out.
12. SJR. B.I.a (TS. 1027; IC, 1.22). About 1/28 rim and upper neck segment. Fairly coarse grayware. Horizontally burnished black out and below rim in.
13. SJR. B.II.k (TS. 2326; IC, 1.32C). See also pl. 225:15. About 1/8 rim and neck segment. Fairly coarse grayish-buff ware, unevenly fired. Self slip burnished on top of rim and out.
14. SJR. C.I.h (TS. 2545; IC, 1.32B). See also pl. 226:8. About 1/6 rim and neck segment. Hard, close green ware, evenly fired. Self slip in and out.
15. SJR. C.II.q (TS. 2547; IC, 1.32C and 1.39). About 1/6 rim and neck, two joining segments. Hard, fine ware, unevenly fired with pale brown core and flesh pink at surfaces. Self slip out and just over rim in.
16. JR. C.V.b (TS. 2205; IC, 1.21). Small rim and upper shoulder segment. Fairly close dark pink ware, evenly fired. Creamy-buff slip out.
17. JR. D.I.b (TS. 2052; IC, 1.32A). See also pl. 236:2. Large rim and upper wall segment. Fairly coarse grayish-buff ware, evenly fired. Creamy-green slip out and over rim in.
18. JR. D.V.b (TS. 607; IC, 1.21). See also pl. 238:3. About 1/12 rim and upper shoulder segment. Coarse pink ware, unevenly fired with buff core. Cream slip in and out.
19. JR. D.V.c (TS. 1086; IC, 1.32C). About 1/6 rim and upper wall segment. Fairly coarse pink ware, evenly fired. Cream slip out.
20. JR. H.I.e (TS. 2415; IC, 1.21). About 1/10 rim and shoulder segment. Hard, fairly close pink ware, evenly fired. Creamy-buff slip out and over rim in.
21. JR. H.I.g (TS. 825; IC, 1.32A). About 1/16 rim and shoulder segment with remains of a spout. Fairly coarse pinkish-buff ware, fairly evenly fired. Creamy-green slip out.
22. JR. H.III.b (TS. 2239; IC, 1.32A). See also pl. 249:2. Small rim and shoulder segment. Fairly coarse gritty buff-brown ware, evenly fired. Creamy-buff slip in and out.
23. JR. J.II.g (TS. 2289; IC, 1.32C). See also pl. 252:7. About 1/4 rim, neck, and upper shoulder segment. Hard, close ware, unevenly fired with grayish core and buff-green at surfaces. Creamy-green slip in and out.
24. JR. J.III.e (TS. 2071; IC, 1.22). About 1/3 rim, neck, and shoulder segment. Fairly coarse pinkish-brown ware, evenly fired. Creamy-green slip in and out.
25. JR. O.II.e (TS. 2364; IC, 1.32C). About 1/20 rim and upper shoulder segment. Slightly coarse pink ware, evenly fired. Cream slip in and out.
26. CP. B.II.h (TS. 1058; IC, 1.32A + 1.32B). See also pl. 278:8. About 1/20 of non-joining rim and shoulder segments. Coarse pink ware, unevenly fired with brown core. Burnished inside and blackened by fire outside and inside to below concavity under rim.
27. CP. B.III.e (TS. 1068; IC, 1.32C and 1.43). About 1/12 of joining rim and neck segments. Coarse pink ware, evenly fired. Light brown slip in and out. Burnished in and out.
28. JR.Sh. (IP [G.2] A.II.a; TS. 2176; IC, 1.21). Jar shoulder sherd with linear decoration incised before firing. Fairly close buff ware, evenly fired. Self slip in and out.
29. JR.Sh. Pt. (TS. 962; IC, 1.32C). Jar sherd painted with dark brown pattern consisting of horizontal bands with filled in triangles below the two extant bands. Hard, fine gray-buff ware, fairly evenly fired.

Other Study Collection Examples: (1) SBR. A.I.a (SC. 3488), (2) SBR. B.I.b (SC. 253), (3) SBR. B.I.f (SC. 338), (4) SBR. B.I.h (SC. 669), (5) BR. F.II.a (SC. 800), (6) BR. (not typed, SC. 25), (7) SJR. C.I.f (SC. 2565), (8) JR. A.III.d (SC. 906), (9) JR. B.III.a (SC. 1983), (10) JR. B. (Gen. Type, SC. 89), (11) JR. C.I.a (SC. 987), (12) JR. H.I.d (SC. 1252), (13) JR. H.I.h (SC. 1277), (14) JR. H.I.l (SC. 1285), (15) JR. J.II.i (variant, SC. 3520), (16) JR. J.III.d (SC. 2222), (17) JR. J.III.j (SC. 1410), (18) JR. J.III.o (SC. 2654), (19) JR. J.III.v (SC. 2360), (20) JR. O.I.f (SC. 1617), (21) JR. O.II.l (SC. 1659), (22) JR. P.II.b (SC. 1719), (23) JR. (not typed, SC. 101), (24) CP. B.I.a (SC. 1815), (25) BE. D.IV (SC. 3150).

Figure 24

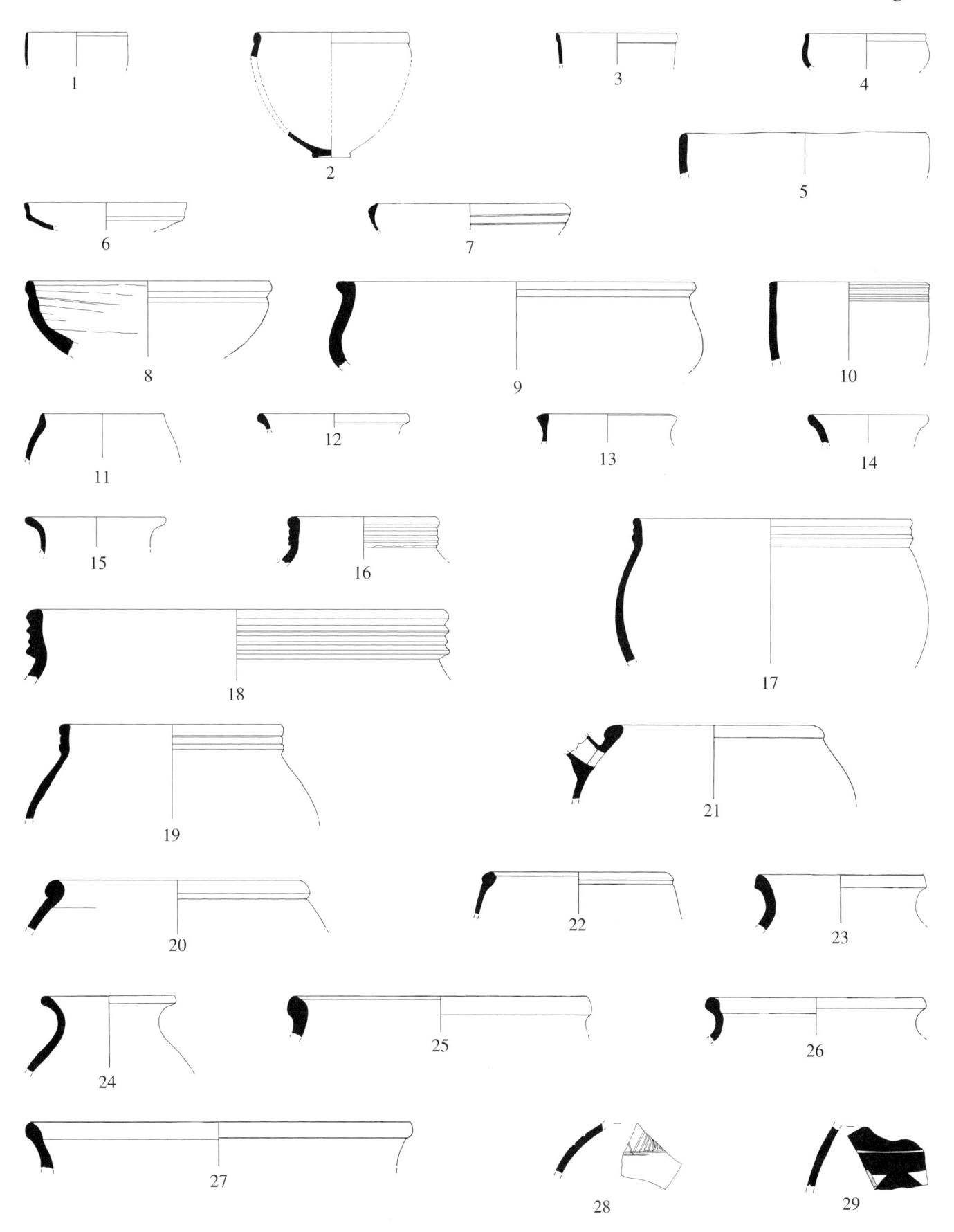

Pottery from Trench IC (Phase 7; Period E — Early Bronze Age IVb). Scale 1:5

Figure 25

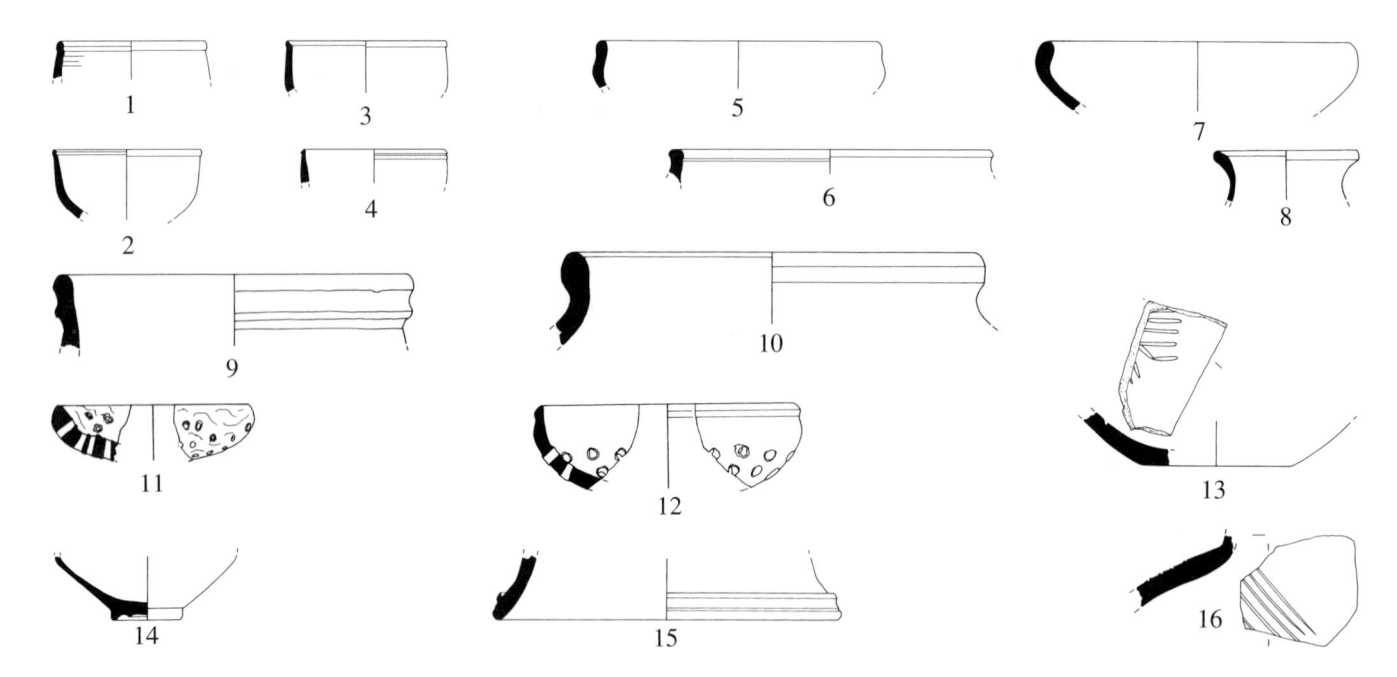

Pottery from Trench IC (Phase 8; Period E — Early Bronze Age IVb). Scale 1:5

1. SBR. B.I.g (TS. 2507; IC, 1.7). About 1/8 rim and upper wall segment. Slightly coarse buff ware, evenly fired. Creamy-buff slip in and out.
2. SBR. B.I.k (TS. 2506; IC, 1.7). About 1/10 rim and most of wall profile. Slightly coarse buff ware, evenly fired. Creamy-buff slip in and out.
3. SBR. B.I.p (TS. 2459; IC, 1.7). Small rim and upper wall segment. Fairly coarse light grayware, evenly fired. Creamy-gray self slip out.
4. SBR. B.I.r (TS. 2509; IC, 1.7). See also pl. 206:18. Small rim and upper wall segment. Fairly coarse grayware, evenly fired. Self slip in and out.
5. BR. A.IV.a (TS. 2508; IC, 1.7). About 1/10 rim and upper wall segment. Fairly fine grayish-brown ware, unevenly fired pink at surfaces.
6. BR. C.I.c (TS. 2510; IC, 1.7). About 1/10 rim and upper wall segment. Slightly coarse pink ware, evenly fired. Creamy-pink slip out and just over rim in.
7. BR. E.III.c (TS. 2497; IC, 1.7). About 1/10 rim and upper wall segment. Slightly coarse buff ware, evenly fired. Cream slip out.
8. SJR. C.I.g (TS. 2436; IC, 1.15). See also pl. 226:7. About 1/4 rim and neck segment. Coarse buff ware, evenly fired. Creamy-buff slip in and out.
9. JR. B.VI.c (TS. 619; IC, 1.15). About 1/16 rim and neck segment. Fairly coarse pink ware, evenly fired. Cream slip out.
10. JR. O.II.k (TS. 2370; IC, 1.15). About 1/6 rim and shoulder segment. Fairly coarse pinkish-buff ware, evenly fired. Cream slip out.
11. SR. A.I.a (SW. 201; IC, 1.7). About 1/8 rim and wall segment with nine extant strainer holes pierced from outside wall before firing. Pinkish-buff ware with many small mineral grits and vegetable temper, fairly evenly fired.
12. SR. B.I.a (TS. 547; IC, 1.18). About 1/4 rim and wall segment with seven extant strainer holes pierced from inside wall before firing. Coarse pink ware with lime and mica grits, fairly evenly fired. Cream slip out.
13. BE. D.III (IP [G.4] D.I; PM. D.19; TS. 2126; IC, 1.7). About 1/5 base and lower wall of vessel with tree pattern incised inside before firing. Fairly coarse light greenish-grayware, evenly fired. Self slip in.
14. BE. E.II.k (TS. 537; IC, 1.7). Complete base and most of lower wall of vessel. Coarse pink ware, fairly evenly fired. Traces of cream slip in and out.
15. WPS. C (TS. 636; IC, 1.7). Small segment with portion of smoothed side of one extant window in the wall of the vessel (not illustrated on the drawing). Fairly coarse buff-cream ware, evenly fired.
16. JR.Sh. (PM. A.19; TS. 2172; IC, 1.7). Jar sherd with potter's mark incised on the shoulder before firing. Hard, fairly close buff ware, evenly fired. Self slip out.

Other Type Series Examples: Derived Roman — (1) R.JR. B.II.a (TS. 659), (2) R.Lp. (SW. 193).

Other Study Collection Examples: (1) SBR. A.I.c (SC. 222), (2) SBR. B.I.d (SC. 301), (3) SBR. B.I.e (SC. 315), (4) SBR. B.I.e (SC. 330), (5) SBR. B.I.e (SC. 331), (6) BR. C.I.d (SC. 744), (7) BR. F.III.g (SC. 814), (8) BR. L.I.b (SC. 833), (9) SJR. A.II.e (SC. 2488), (10) SJR. C.I.h (SC. 3495), (11) JR. A.I.a (SC. 889), (12) JR. A.III.b (SC. 1978), (13) JR. A. (Gen. Type, SC. 86), (14) JR. B.I.a (SC. 925), (15) JR. B.IV.c (SC. 961), (16) JR. B.IV.c (SC. 964), (17) JR. C.I.d (SC. 994), (18) JR. H.I.a (SC. 1245), (19) JR. H.I.d (SC. 1255), (20) JR. J.III.e (SC. 1380), (21) JR. J.III.e (SC. 1382), (22) JR. J.III.e (SC. 1384), (23) JR. J.III.n (SC. 1354), (24) JR. J.III.n (SC. 1450), (25) JR. K.I.a (SC. 2385), (26) JR. K.I.c (SC. 1582), (27) CP. B.IV.c (SC. 1876), (28) BE. A.I (SC. 3089), (29) BE. D.III (SC. 3141), (30) Ld. C.III.c (SC. 1944), (31) Hd. B (SC. 3372).

Figure 26

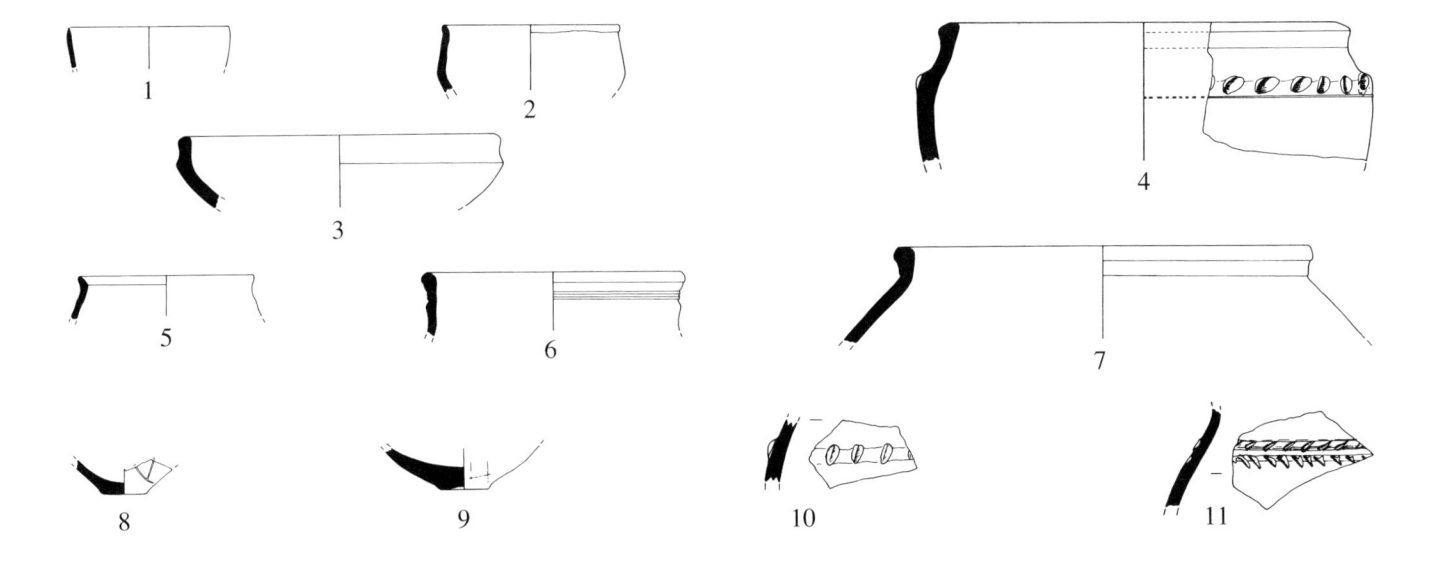

Pottery from Trench IC (Phase 9; Period E–D — Early–Middle Bronze Age). Scale 1:5

1. SBR. A.I.a (TS. 2503; IC, 1.5). About 1/8 rim and upper wall segment. Fine buff ware, evenly fired. Creamy-buff slip out.
2. SBR. F.I.b (TS. 631; IC, 1.5). About 1/8 rim and portion of upper and lower wall segment. Fairly coarse buff ware, evenly fired. Cream slip in and out.
3. BR. C.I.d (TS. 2499; IC, 1.5). Small rim and portion of upper and lower wall segment. Slightly coarse pinkish-buff ware, evenly fired. Cream slip out and just over rim in.
4. BR. N.II.b (TS. 542; IC, 1.5). See also pl. 220:7. About 1/8 rim and upper wall segment with applied, finger-impressed band of decoration around the shoulder. Coarse brownish-buff ware, evenly fired. Cream slip out.
5. SJR. A.III.b (TS. 2109; IC, 1.6). Small rim and shoulder segment. Fairly fine buff ware, evenly fired. Self slip in and out.
6. JR. C.I.g (TS. 2197; IC, 1.6). Small rim and neck segment. Fairly coarse pink ware, evenly fired. Creamy-buff slip in and out.
7. CP. B.IV.d (TS. 516; IC, 1.6). About 1/10 rim and shoulder segment. Dark brown, coarse, ware with lime grits, evenly fired. Darkish buff slip in and out.
8. BE. B.II (PM. C.15; TS. 2091; IC, 1.6). Complete disk base with remains of potter's mark on lower outside wall, incised before firing. Slightly coarse buff ware, evenly fired. Self slip out.
9. BE. B.II (PM. D.14; TS. 528; IC, 1.5). Complete disk base with potter's mark on lower outside wall, incised before firing. Fairly coarse pink ware, evenly fired. Cream slip out and with some traces in.
10. ABS. C (TS. 610; IC, 1.5). Bowl or Jar body sherd. Small segment with applied and finger-impressed decorative band round outside wall. Fairly coarse pink ware, evenly fired. Cream slip in and out.
11. JR.Sh. (IP [G.4] B.II.a; TS. 641; IC, 1.5). Jar shoulder sherd. Segment with double row of tool-impressed, wedge-shaped decorative bands. Fairly coarse pinkish-buff ware, evenly fired. Cream slip out.

Other Study Collection Examples: (1) BR. A.IV.a (SC. 728), (2) SJR. A.I.a (SC. 2469), (3) JR. A.III.d (SC. 910), (4) JR. A.III.d (SC. 911), (5) JR. B.I.a (SC. 926), (6) JR. B.IV.c (SC. 969), (7) JR. B.IV.c (SC. 970), (8) JR. C.VI.b (SC. 3392), (9) JR. D.V.c (SC. 1089), (10) JR. D.V.d (SC. 1098), (11) JR. E.I.a (variant, SC. 2722), (12) JR. J.I.d (SC. 1322), (13) JR. J.I.f (SC. 2697), (14) JR. J.III.h (SC. 1395), (15) JR. J.III.k (SC. 2303), (16) JR. J.III.o (SC. 1470), (17) JR. J.IV.a (SC. 1519), (18) JR. O.I.d (SC. 2404).

Other Type Series Examples: Derived Roman — (1) R.JR. B.II.e (TS. 2081), (2) R.HMJ. A.I.a (TS. 3160).

Other Study Collection Examples: Derived Hellenistic — (1) H.Jg. B.II.e (SC. 2776); Derived Roman — (1) R.BR. A.II.c (SC. 3389).

Figure 27. Pottery from Trench IC (Phase 10; Period B — Mixed Earloy Bronze Age, Early–Middle Bronze Age, Hellenistic, and Roman): Bronze Age: 1–9, Hellenistic Period: 10, Roman Period: 11–17, Various Periods: 18–21

1. SBR. A.I.c (TS. 2494; IC, 1.1). About 1/4 rim and upper wall segment. Slightly coarse pinkish-buff ware, evenly fired. Creamy-buff slip out.
2. BR. A.II.d (TS. 2496; IC, 1.1). About 1/8 rim and upper wall segment. Slightly coarse pinkish-buff ware, evenly fired. Cream slip out.
3. BR. L.I.e (TS. 2489; IC, 1.1). About 1/8 rim and upper wall segment. Fairly coarse pinkish-buff ware, evenly fired. Creamy-buff slip out and just over rim in.
4. BR. N.II.a (TS. 562; IC, 1.1). About 1/8 rim and upper wall segment with finger-impressed decorative band around the shoulder. Fairly coarse pink ware, evenly fired. Buff slip in and out.
5. SJR. C.II.p (PM. A.14; TS. 520; IC, 1.1). See also pl. 226:24. About 1/10 rim, neck, and shoulder segment with potter's mark incised on neck before firing. Fairly coarse pink ware, unevenly fired. Self burnished on shoulder with irregular horizontal bands.
6. JR. E.II.m (TS. 2554; IC, 1.1). About 1/8 rim and shoulder segment. Slightly coarse pinkish-buff ware, evenly fired. Self slip in and out.
7. JR. J.II.e (TS. 2060; IC, 1.1). Small rim and upper shoulder segment. Fine buff ware, evenly fired.
8. JR. P.I.e (TS. 2367; IC, 1.1). About 1/10 rim and shoulder segment. Fairly coarse pinkish-brown ware, evenly fired. Creamy-green slip out.
9. BE. F.VIII.a (IP [G.2] A.II.a; SW. 107; IC, 1.1). Nearly complete pedestal base decorated with linear decorative chevron patterns incised before firing. Coarse buff ware with black temper, fairly evenly fired. Light greenish-buff slip in and out.
—. H.St.J. B.II.e (TS. 522, IC, 1.1). Description unavailable.
10. H.St.J. B.II.l (TS. 563; IC, 1.1). About 1/12 rim and neck segment. Fairly coarse pink ware, unevenly fired with a lighter core. Creamy-buff slip out.
11. R.BR. A.II.a (TS. 644; IC, 1.1). About 1/20 rim and upper wall segment. Fairly coarse buff ware, evenly fired.
12. R.BR. A.II.a (TS. 650; IC, 1.1). About 1/28 rim and upper wall segment. Fairly coarse pink ware, evenly fired. Cream slip in and out.
13. R.BR. B.I.b (TS. 588; IC, 1.1) About 1/16 rim and upper wall segment. Fairly coarse pink ware, evenly fired. Thin cream slip in and out.
14. R.BR. B.I.b (TS. 576; IC, 1.1). About 1/20 rim and upper wall segment. Coarse pink ware, evenly fired. Buff slip in and out.
15. R.JR. A.I.a (TS. 2058; IC, 1.1). About 1/3 rim and shoulder segment. Slightly coarse pinkish-buff ware, evenly fired. Buff slip out. Inner wall and rim covered with bitumen-like sealing substance.
16. R.JR. A.I.b (TS. 549; IC, 1.1). About 1/6 rim, neck, and shoulder segment. Fairly coarse pink ware, evenly fired. Cream slip in and out.
17. R.CP. A.V.a (TS. 658; IC, 1.1). About 1/16 rim and shoulder segment. Fairly coarse reddish ware, evenly fired.
18. JR.Sh. (IP [G.1] D.III.a; TS. 581; IC, 1.1). Jar body sherd with comb-incised horizontal and wavy line decoration applied before firing. Coarse buff ware, evenly fired. Self slip in and out.
19. JR.Sh. (IP [G.1] F.I.a; TS. 558; IC, 1.1). Jar body sherd with comb-incised horizontal and columnar line decoration applied before firing. Fairly coarse pink ware, evenly fired. Cream slip out.
20. JR.Sh. (IP [G.1] I.I.a; TS. 612; IC, 1.1). Jar body sherd with incised linear decorative patterns applied before firing. Fairly coarse pink ware, evenly fired.
21. JR.Sh. (IP [G.4] D.III; PM. D.19; TS. 609; IC, 1.1). Jar body sherd with incised tree or wheat stalk pattern applied before firing. Fairly coarse pink ware, evenly fired.

Other Type Series Examples:

Mixed Early and Early–Middle Bronze — (1) ABS. D (SC. 3377).

Hellenistic Period — (1) H.BR. A.I.b (TS. 2122).

Roman Period — (1) R.SJR. A.I.a (TS. 587), (2) R.JR. B.I.e (TS. 2108), (3) R.HMJ. A.II.f (TS. 564), (4) R.Jg. B.II.f (TS. 554), (5) R.Jg. B.III.d (SC. 3519), (6) R.Jg. C.I.a (TS. 583), (7) R.Jg. C.I.g (SC. 3394), (8) R.CP. A.VI.a (TS. 3165), (9) R.CP. B.III.a (TS. 625).

Unstratified — (1) BR. B.II.a (TS. 2055), (2) BR. E.III.b (TS. 2054), (3) JR. J.I.h (TS. 2051).

Other Study Collection Examples:

Mixed Early and Early–Middle Bronze — (1) SBR. A.I.b (SC. 3485), (2) SBR. B.I.d (SC. 292), (3) SBR. B.I.e (SC. 317), (4) SBR. B.I.f (SC. 345), (5) SBR. B.I.i (SC. 3486), (6) SBR. B.I.k (SC. 562), (7) SBR. B.I.k (SC. 569), (8) SBR. D.II.c (SC. 654), (9) SBR. F.I.c (SC. 3482), (10) BR. A.II.b (SC. 2811), (11) BR. A.III.a (SC. 2812), (12) BR. A.IV.d (SC. 3430), (13) BR. C.I.e (SC. 1967), (14) BR. D.II.b (SC. 3431), (15) BR. F.II.a (SC. 787), (16) BR. F.II.a (SC. 793), (17) BR. F.II.a (SC. 797), (18) BR. F.III.d (SC. 809), (19) SJR. A.I.c (SC. 2481), (20) SJR. B.I.a (SC. 2496), (21) SJR. B.I.a (SC. 3494), (22) SJR. D.I.a (SC. 2623), (23) JR. A.III.c (SC. 903), (24) JR. A.V.b (SC. 915), (25) JR. B.I.b (SC. 927), (26) JR. B.III.b (SC. 939), (27) JR. B.IV.c (SC. 974), (28) JR. B.V.c (SC. 3390), (29) JR. C.I.d (SC. 993), (30) JR. D.I.a (SC. 1035), (31) JR. D.III.b (SC. 1063), (32) JR. D.V.b (SC. 1084), (33) JR. D.V.c (SC. 1091), (34) JR. D.V.d (SC. 1095), (35) JR. D.V.d (SC. 1096), (36) JR. D.V.d (SC. 1097), (37) JR. E.II.d (SC. 1145), (38) JR. E.II.v (SC. 1169), (39) JR. F.I.a (SC. 1193), (40) JR. F.I.c (SC. 1210), (41) JR. G.II.b (SC. 2755), (42) JR. H.I.e (SC. 2073), (43) JR. H.II.e (SC. 1292), (44) JR. H.III.i (SC. 2082), (45) JR. J.III.f (SC. 1387), (46) JR. J.III.h (SC. 1399), (47) JR. J.III.n (SC. 1460), (48) JR. J.IV.i (SC. 1540), (49) JR. J.IV.j (SC. 1546), (50) JR. J.VI.a (SC. 1555), (51) JR. K.I.b (SC. 1574), (52) JR. K.I.c (SC. 1581), (53) JR. K.I.e (SC. 1591), (54) JR. O.II.e (SC. 2419), (55) JR. O.II.f (SC. 1645), (56) JR. O.II.h (SC. 1649), (57) JR. O.II.h (SC. 1650), (58) JR. P.II.e (SC. 1729), (59) BE. A.I (SC. 3090).

Hellenistic Period — (1) H.RSB. D.II.d (SC. 2903), (2) H.St.J. A.I.g (SC. 2659).

Roman Period — (1) R.SBR. A.III.a (SC. 3484), (2) R.BR. A.I.b (SC. 2910), (3) R.BR. B.I.b (SC. 2917), (4) R.BR. B.I.d (SC. 2922), (5) R.BR. C.II.f (variant, SC. 3483), (6) R.JR. B.II.d (SC. 2943), (7) R.HMJ. A.II.d (SC. 3038), (8) R.HMJ. B.II.b (SC. 3045), (9) R.Jg. A.II.b (SC. 2957), (10) R.Jg. B.I.b (SC. 2960), (11) R.Jg. B.II.b (SC. 3063), (12) R.Jg. B.II.b (SC. 3395 = SC. 3487), (13) R.Jg. B.II.c (SC. 2978), (14) R.Jg. B.II.g (SC. 2990), (15) R.Jg. B.II.p (SC. 3388), (16) R.Jg. B.II.q (SC. 3026), (17) R.CP. A.IV.b (SC. 3532), (18) R.Bt. B.I.a (SC. 2953).

Unstratified — (1) JR. E.I.c (SC. 2644).

Figure 27

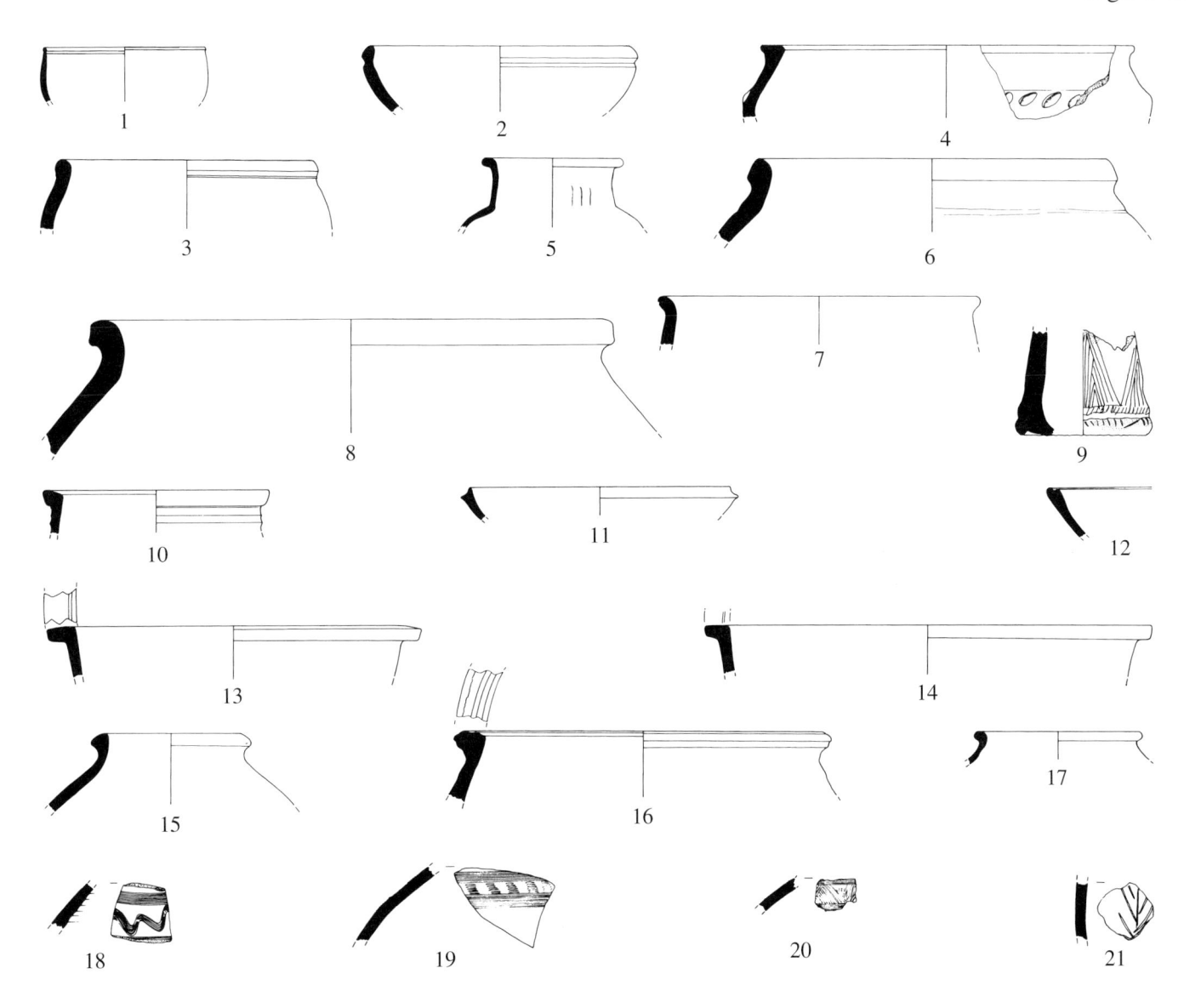

Pottery from Trench IC (Phase 10; Period B — Mixed Early Bronze Age, Early–Middle Bronze Age, Hellenistic, and Roman): Bronze Age: 1–9, Hellenistic Period: 10, Roman Period: 11–17, Various Periods: 18–21. Scale 1:5

Figure 28. Miscellaneous Small Finds from Trench IC (Phases 3–8 and 10; Periods J, H, F, E, and B — Early Bronze Age I, Early Bronze Age II, Early Bronze Age IVa, Early Bronze Age IVb, and Roman), Trench IA2 (Phase 2; Period B — Roman), and Trench IA2 (Phases 2–3; Period B — Roman)

1. Type SF.4c (SW. 447; IC, 1.48; Phase 3, Period J). Ceramic pendant. Fine, soft buff-white ware, evenly fired.
—. Type SF.3a (SW. 535; IC, 1.52; Phase 3, Period J). Limestone mortar. Parabolic cross section. Measurements: 20 × 22 × 33 cm.
—. Type SF.6e (SC. 328; IC, 1.48; Phase 3, Period J). Disk (ca. 6 × 6 mm). Nearly one half of a reworked sherd. Hole (10 mm wide on external surfaces) drilled from both sides for use as a spindle whorl. Fairly fine pinkish-buff ware with very small lime and gold-colored mica grits, evenly fired. Creamy-buff slip on outer surface.
—. Type SF.6e (SC. 3285; IC, 1.48; Phase 3, Period J). Disk (4.5 × 5 mm). Irregular-shaped reworked sherd with an incomplete drill hole (7 mm wide and 3 mm deep) started on the outside of the sherd wall. Fairly fine pinkish-buff ware with small lime and gold-colored mica grits, evenly fired. Light pink self slip in and out.
2. Type SV.3 (SW. 460; IC, 1.41; Phase 4, Period H; see pl. 103b). Zoomorphic pottery vessel fragment. Fragment of head. Coarse pink ware with lime and mica grits, unevenly fired with brown core. Cream slip on outer surface. Impressed holes for eyes and nostrils; appliqué eyebrows; and ridges over tusks with impressed linear decoration.
3. Type SF.2b (SW. 459; IC, 1.41; Phase 4, Period H; see pl. 119f). Model chariot wheel. Coarse creamy-buff ware, fairly evenly fired.
4. Type SF.3e (SW. 379; IC, 1.41; Phase 4, Period H). Ring-shaped igneous stone object (possibly a loom weight). Dark gray color, fine grained.
—. Type SF.3a (SW. 417; IC, 1.41; Phase 4, Period H). Grinding stone fragment. Cream-colored limestone. Roughly rectangular shaped with a flattened working surface. Measurements: 6 × 12 × 18 cm.
—. Type SF.1c (SC. 3330; IC, 1.33; Phase 5, Period F). Human figurine pillar stand fragment, 1.5 cm thick × 2.5 cm wide × 4 cm high. Fairly fine pinkish-buff ware with small black and white lime grits, evenly fired. Thick creamy-green slip on surfaces.
5. Type SF.4c (SW. 240; IC, 1.28; Phase 6, Period E). Pierced stone pendant. Soft chalky-white fragment with remains of two bored holes.
6. Type SF.6b (SW. 219; IC, 1.28; Phase 6, Period E). Spindle whorl fragment made from reused potsherd. Yellowish ware with black, white, silver, red, and gray mineral grits, unevenly fired with a gray core.
—. Type SF.1e (SC. 3329; IC, 1.32B; Phase 7, Period E). Animal figurine leg fragment. 1.5 cm diam. × 3 cm high. Fairly fine buff ware with fine lime grits, evenly fired. Creamy-green slip on surfaces.
—. Type SF.3a (SW. 450; IC, 1.11; Phase 8, Period E). Grinding stone fragment. Vesicular basalt. Dark gray color.
7. Type R.SF.4c (SW. 84; IC, 1.1; Phase 10, Period B). Pendant. Cream stone with gray markings on surface and hole pierced through one end.
8. Type SF.10 (SW. 105; IA2, 4.4; Phase 2, Period B). Jar shoulder sherd incised with fragment of an Aramaic inscription dated to the Roman period (see pl. 132b; Holland 1976, p. 38, pl. 8A; Chapter 5). Slightly coarse buff ware with black lime and gold-colored mica grits, evenly fired. Light yellow-buff slip on outside.
—. Type SF.5j (SW. 235, SW. 236; IA2, 3.3; Phase 3, Period B; see pl. 122c, d). Two Roman coins. For discussion and description, see Holland 1976:38; and Chapter 5.

Figure 28

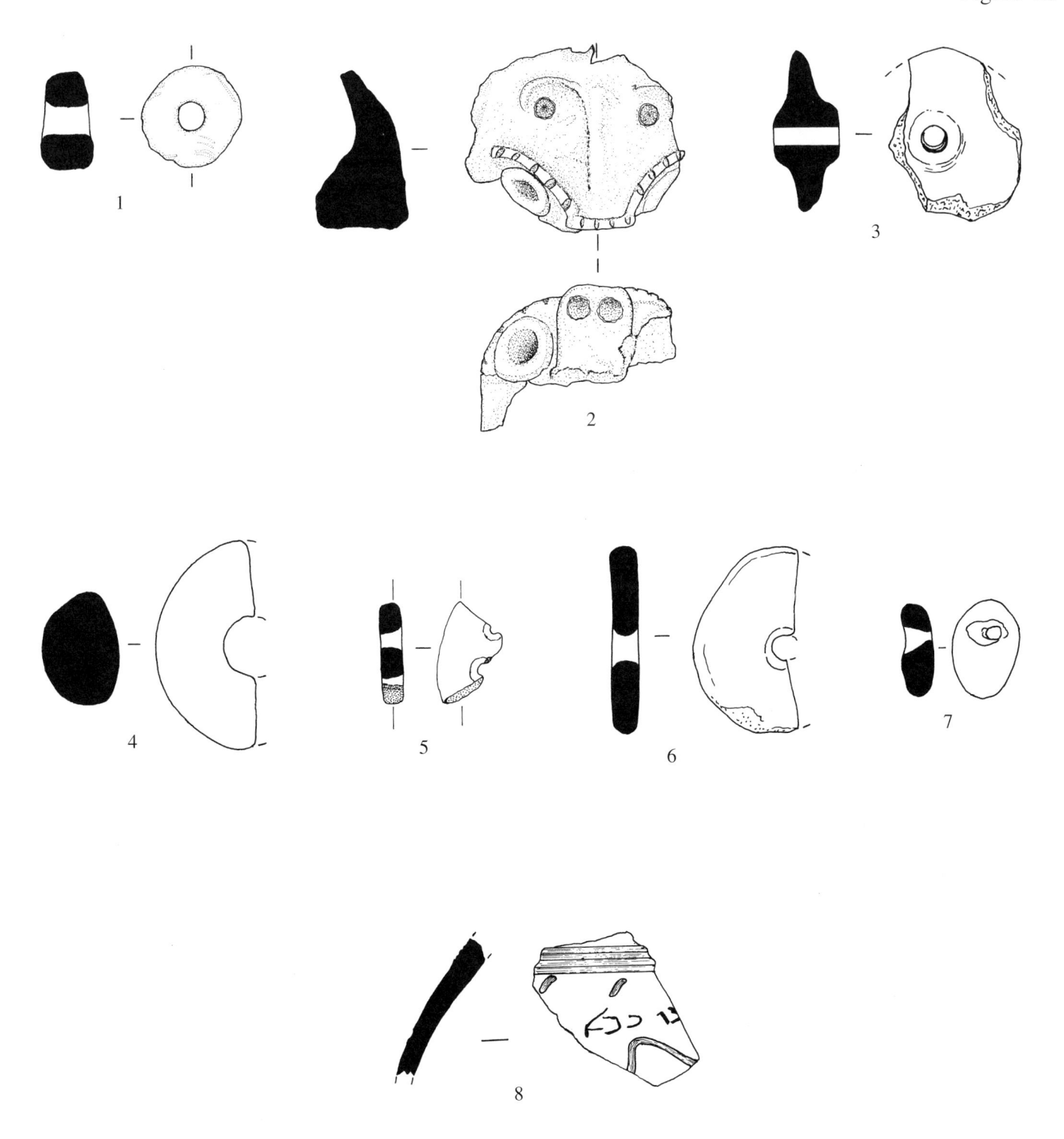

Miscellaneous Small Finds from Trench IC (Phases 3–8 and 10; Periods J, H, F, E, and B — Early Bronze Age I, Early Bronze Age II, Early Bronze Age IVa, Early Bronze Age IVb, and Roman), Trench IA2 (Phase 2; Period B — Roman), and Trench IA2 (Phases 2–3; Period B — Roman). Scale 1:2

Figure 29

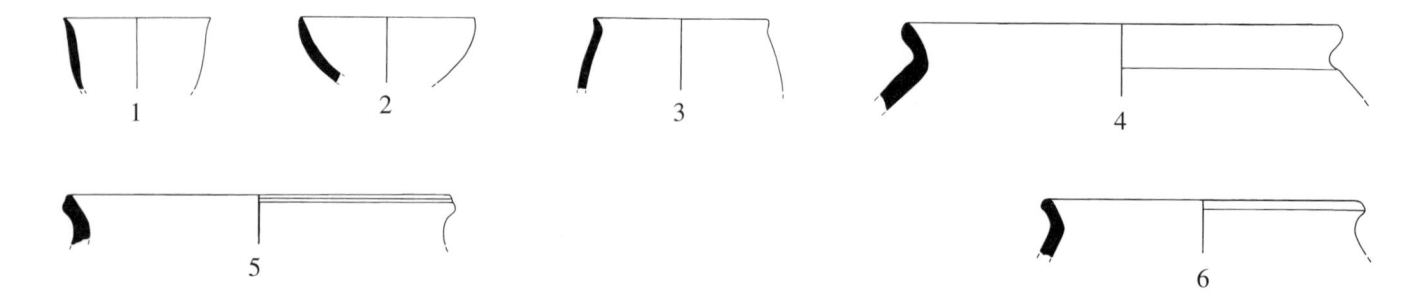

Pottery from Trench IIA (Phase 1; Period J — Early Bronze Age I). Scale 1:5

1. SBR. A.I.h (TS. 2004; IIA, 9.6, Room 2). Small segment. Fairly close pink ware evenly fired. Creamy-buff slip in and out.
2. SBR. C.III.a (TS. 1554; IIA, 9.9, Room 1). Small rim segment and most of wall profile. Fine pinkish-buff ware, evenly fired. Creamy-buff slip out. Traces of burning on rim and in.
3. SJR. A.III.a (TS. 1573; IIA, 9.6, Room 2). Small rim and upper wall segment. Slightly coarse pinkish-buff ware with lime and mica grits, evenly fired. Creamy-buff slip out.
4. JR. F.I.a (TS. 1552; IIA, 9.7, Room 3). Small rim, neck, and upper shoulder segment. Close buff ware with fine lime and mica grits, evenly fired. Creamy-buff slip in and out.
5. JR. F.I.c (TS. 1558; IIA, 8.7). Small rim and neck segment. Close buff ware with fine lime and mica grits, evenly fired. Creamy-buff slip in and out.
6. CP. B.II.g (TS. 1583; IIA, 9.6, Room 2). Small rim, neck, and upper shoulder segment. Coarse ware with lime and mica grits, unevenly fired with gray core and dark brown at surfaces. Burned below rim in and out.

Other Type Series Examples:
    Room 1— (1) SBR. C.II.b (SW. 300), (2) SBR. C.III.b (SW. 299), (3) SJR. D.I.a (TS. 1556), (4) JR. F.II.e (TS. 1555), (5) CP. B.III.d (TS. 1557).
    Room 3 — (1) JR. E.II.q (TS. 2000).

Other Study Collection Examples:
    Room 1: (1) SBR. C.III.a (SC. 696), (2) SBR. C.III.a (SC. 698).

Figure 30

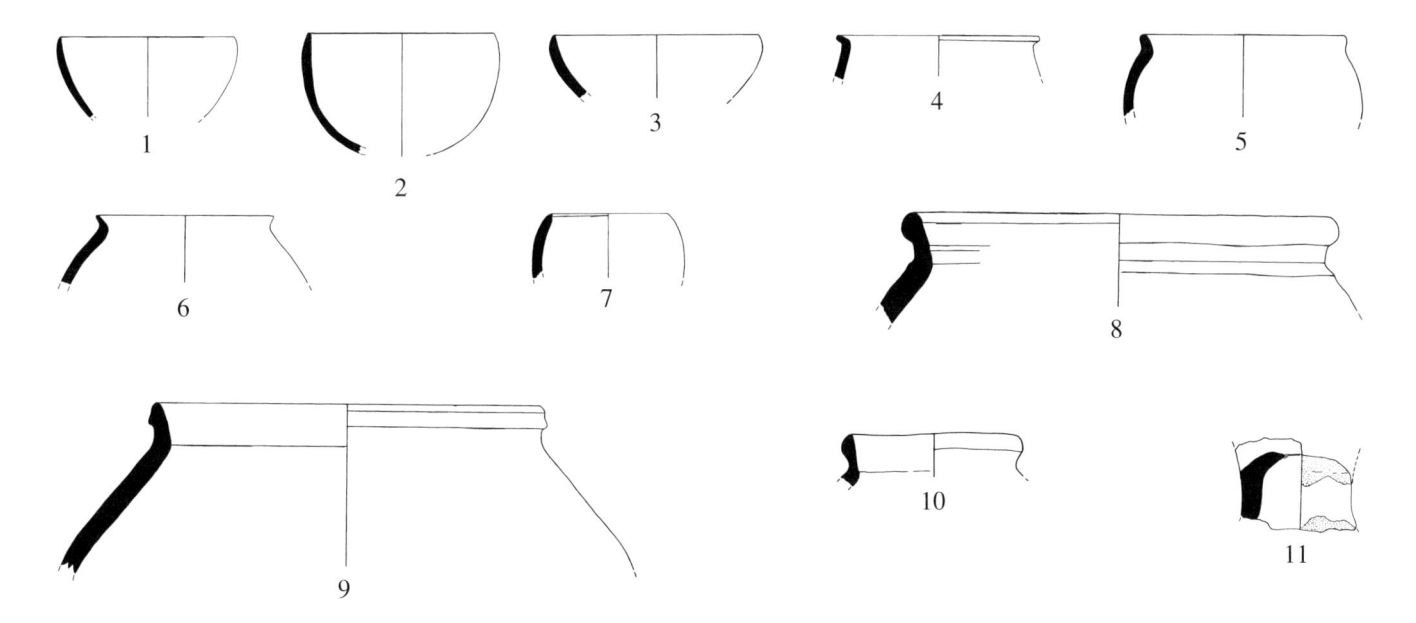

Pottery from Trench IIA, Room 4 (Phase 2; Period J — Early Bronze Age I). Scale 1:5

1. SBR. C.II.a (TS. 2202; IIA, 9.8). Small rim segment and most of wall profile. Fairly fine buff ware, unevenly fired with light pink core. Self slip in and out.
2. SBR. C.III.a (SW. 302; IIA, 9.8 and 9.9). About 1/3 rim segment and most of wall profile. Fairly fine pinkish-buff ware with lime and gold-colored mica grits, unevenly fired creamy-buff at surfaces. Self slip in and out.
3. SBR. C.III.a (TS. 1553; IIA, 9.8). Small rim and upper wall segment. Fairly fine buff ware with fine lime and mica grits, evenly fired. Creamy-buff slip in and out.
4. SJR. A.II.a (TS. 2001; IIA, 9.8). Small rim and shoulder segment. Fairly fine pinkish-buff ware, unevenly fired. Creamy-buff slip out.
5. SJR. A.III.a. (TS. 1550; IIA, 9.8). Small rim and upper wall segment. Fairly fine ware with fine lime and mica grits, unevenly fired with pinkish core and buff at surfaces. Creamy-buff slip out.
6. SJR. A.III.a (TS. 1565; IIA, 9.8). Small rim and shoulder segment. Fairly fine buff ware with fine lime and mica grits, evenly fired. Creamy-slip out.
7. SJR. D.I.a (TS. 2003; IIA, 9.8). Small rim and upper wall segment with possible remains of a lug handle just below the rim. Fairly fine buff ware, evenly fired. Self slip in and out.
8. JR. F.I.b (TS. 1551; IIA, 9.8). Small rim, neck, and upper shoulder segment. Hard, fairly fine pinkish-buff ware with fine lime and mica grits, evenly fired. Creamy-buff slip out.
9. JR. F.III.f (SW. 304; IIA, 9.8). About 1/6 rim, neck, and upper wall segment. Pinkish-orange ware with mica and lime grits, evenly fired. Cream slip out.
10. JR. J.I.h (TS. 1575; IIA, 9.8). Small rim, neck, and upper shoulder segment. Fine pinkish-buff ware with fine lime and mica grits, fairly evenly fired. Creamy-white slip in and out.
11. BE. F.VIII.c (TS. 526; IIA, 9.8). Segment of a pedestal type stand with portion of lower wall of bowl on top. Fairly fine pinkish-buff ware, unevenly fired with light brown core. Remains of bitumen in and out.

Other Type Series Examples: (1) BR. B.II.a (TS. 1568), (2) JR. F.III.b (SW. 305), (3) CP. A.III.a (TS. 1169), (4) CP. B.II.g (TS. 1997), (5) BE. F.I.a (TS. 1559).

Other Study Collection Examples: (1) SBR. C.III.a (SC. 692), (2) SBR. C.III.a (SC. 697), (3) SBR. C.III.a (SC. 700).

Figure 31

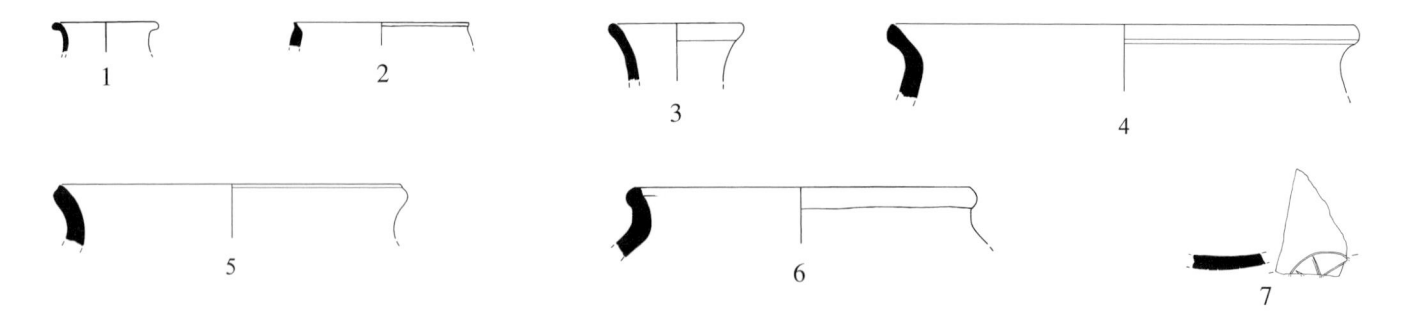

Pottery from Trench IIA (Phase 3; Period J — Early Bronze Age I). Scale 1:5

1. SJR. A.II.b (TS. 178; IIA, 8.8, Room 7). Small rim and neck segment. Fairly fine light buff ware with lime and mica grits, evenly fired. Self slip in and out.
2. SJR. A.III.a (TS. 1988; IIA, 9.4, Courtyard). Small rim and upper shoulder segment. Fine pink ware, evenly fired. Self slip in and out.
3. SJR. C.I.e (TS. 176; IIA, 8.8, Room 7). About 1/5 rim and neck segment. Salmon-pink ware with lime and mica grits, evenly fired. Creamy-pink slip in and out.
4. JR. F.I.a (SC. 1174; IIA, 9.5, Wall Q2). About 1/12 rim, neck, and shoulder segment. Hard, fairly fine ware with small silver-colored mica and lime grits, unevenly fired with light gray core and pinkish-buff at surfaces. Creamy-buff self slip in and out.
5. JR. F.I.c (SC. 1198; IIA, 8.6). Small rim, neck, and upper shoulder segment. Slightly coarse dark buff ware with gold- and silver-colored mica and lime grits, evenly fired. Creamy-buff slip in and out.
6. JR. F.II.b (TS. 1582; IIA, 9.5, Wall Q2). Small rim, neck, and upper shoulder segment. Fine grayish-buff ware with lime and mica grits, evenly fired. Creamy-buff slip out.
7. BE. A.I (PM. D.5; TS. 1250; IIA, 9.5, Wall Q2). Jar base fragment with remains of a potter's mark incised on the outside before firing. Hard, close buff ware, evenly fired.

Another Type Series Example: (1) CP. B.II.k (TS. 175).

Another Study Collection Example: (1) SBR. C.IV.a (SC. 703).

Figure 32

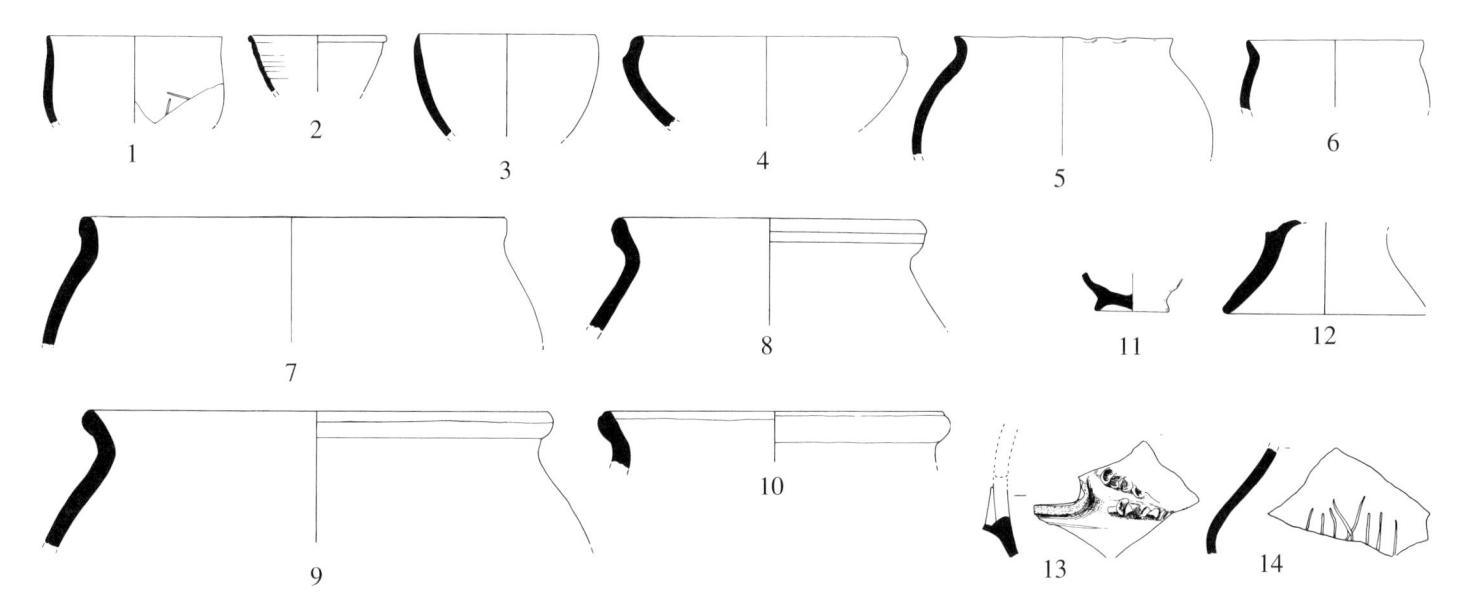

Pottery from Trench IIA (Phase 4; Period H — Early Bronze Age II). Scale 1:5

1. SBR. A.I.h (PM. D.3; TS. 1563; IIA, 9.3, Room 8). About 1/2 rim and most of wall profile with portion of a potter's mark incised on the lower outer wall before firing. Fine buff ware with lime and mica grits, unevenly fired pink at surfaces. Creamy-buff slip in and out.
2. SBR. B.I.g (TS. 174; IIA, 8.5, Room 7). About 1/6 rim and most of wall profile. Fine brick-red ware with lime and mica grits, evenly fired.
3. SBR. C.III.a (TS. 1561; IIA, 9.3, Room 8). Small rim and most of wall profile. Close buff ware with fine lime and mica grits, evenly fired. Self slip in and out.
4. BR. E.II.a (TS. 125; IIA, 8.5, Room 7). Small rim and upper wall segment. Slighly coarse pinkish-buff ware with lime and mica grits, evenly fired. Self slip in and out.
5. SJR. A.III.a (TS. 126; IIA, 8.5, Room 7). Small rim, neck, and upper wall segment with two finger-impressions on lip of rim. Slightly coarse pinkish-brown ware with lime and mica grits, evenly fired. Creamy-buff slip in and out.
6. SJR. A.III.a. (TS. 1562; IIA, 9.3, Room 8). Small rim and upper wall segment. Slightly coarse buff ware with lime and mica grits, evenly fired. Self slip in and out.
7. JR. B.II.c (TS. 127; IIA, 8.5, Room 7). Large rim, neck, and shoulder segment. Hard, fairly fine pinkish-brown ware with silver-colored mica and lime grits, evenly fired. Buff slip out.
8. JR. E.I.g (TS. 172; IIA, 8.5, Room 7). Large rim and shoulder segment. Fairly fine light brown ware with lime and mica grits, unevenly fired pinkish-brown at surfaces. Creamy-buff slip out.
9. JR. F.I.a (TS. 1560; IIA, 9.3, Room 8). Large rim, neck, and shoulder segment. Fairly close pinkish-brown ware with fine lime and mica grits, evenly fired. Self slip in and out.
10. JR. F.I.c (TS. 323; IIA, 8.20, Room 8). Small rim and neck segment. Fairly fine buff ware with lime and mica grits, evenly fired. Self slip in and out.
11. BE. E.II.i. (TS. 130; IIA, 8.5, Room 7). About 1/2 of base and lower wall segment of vessel. Fairly fine buff ware with lime and mica grits, evenly fired. Self slip out.
12. BE. F.I.a (TS. 1576; IIA, 9.1, Room 7). Large rim segment and complete wall profile of a pedestal base. Fairly close pinkish-buff ware with lime and mica grits, evenly fired. Creamy-buff slip in and out.
13. ABS. C (TS. 128; IIA, 8.5, Room 7). Spouted Jar body fragment with applied band decoration. Fairly fine pinkish-brown ware with lime and mica grits, evenly fired. Buff slip in and out.
14. JR.Sh. (IP [G.4] D.III; PM. E.2; TS. 161; IIA, 8.5, Room 7). Jar body sherd with linear decoration incised before firing. Slightly coarse pinkish-buff ware with lime and mica grits, evenly fired. Creamy-buff slip out.

Other Type Series Examples:
Room 7 — (1) JR. H.III.r (TS. 124).
Room 8 — (1) MBR. C.I.a (SW. 227), (2) Ld. C.III.d (TS. 1564).

Other Study Collection Examples:
Room 7 — (1) SBR. C.II.e (SC. 688), (2) BR. N.II.b (SC. 3321), (3) JR. F.II.a (SC. 1219), (4) JR. J.III.e (SC. 2236), (5) JR. J.III.q (SC. 1481), (6) JR. O.II.a (SC. 2411), (7) JR.Sh. (IP (G.1) A.II.c; SC. 3248).
Room 8 — (1) SBR. A.I.h (SC. 2640), (2) SBR. C.II.a (SC. 683), (3) SBR. C.III.a (SC. 695; 4) JR.Sh. (PM. E.2; SC. 3263; see fig. 333:13).

Intrusive Early Bronze Age IV Example: (1) JR. C.II.a (SW. 274; IIA, 8.5, Room 7). For illustration, see Holland 1976: fig. 5:8. Nearly complete vessel. Pinkish-buff ware with fine lime grits, fairly evenly fired. (n.b. This vessel is an intrusive late Period F or early Period E type, which may have been mixed with the earlier assemblage, Period H, pottery from Area IIA, Phase 4, vessels during the pottery cleaning stage and most likely came from one of the Area III pottery assemblage.)

Figure 33. Pottery from Trench IIA (Phase 5; Period H — Early Bronze Age II)

1. BR. B.II.d (TS. 322; IIA, 8.18, Pit E). Small rim and upper wall segment. Grayish-buff ware, evenly fired. Self slip in and out.
2. BR. B.II.d (TS. 1574; IIA, 9.2, Pit E). Small rim and upper wall segment. Fairly close pinkish-buff ware with lime and mica grits, evenly fired. Light greenish-buff slip in and out.
3. SJR. A.III.d (TS. 316; IIA, 8.19, Courtyard). About 1/12 rim and upper wall segment. Fine pinkish-buff ware with lime and mica grits, evenly fired. Cream slip out.
4. JR. F.I.a (TS. 1581; IIA, 9.2, Pit E). Small rim, neck, and upper shoulder segment. Fine ware with lime and mica grits, unevenly fired with light gray core and pink at surfaces. Creamy-buff slip out.
5. JR. F.I.b (TS. 1580; IIA, 9.2, Pit E). Small rim and upper shoulder segment. Hard, fine light grayware with lime and mica grits, evenly fired. Greenish-buff slip out.
6. JR. F.I.c (TS. 1584; IIA, 9.2, Pit E). Small rim, neck, and upper shoulder segment. Fairly fine greenish-buff ware with lime and mica grits, evenly fired. Creamy-buff slip out and over rim in.
7. JR. F.II.a (TS. 1570; IIA, 8.18, Pit E). Small rim and neck segment. Fine grayish-buff ware with lime and mica grits, fairly evenly fired. Creamy-buff slip in and out.
8. JR. J.I.j (TS. 1578; IIA, 9.2, Pit E). Small rim, neck, and upper shoulder segment. Hard, fine buff ware with fine lime and mica grits, evenly fired. Creamy-green slip in and out.
9. CP. B.II.g (TS. 320; IIA, 8.19, Courtyard). Small rim, neck, and upper shoulder segment. Brown ware with many lime and mica grits, evenly fired.
10. JR.Sh. (PM. D.19; TS. 1248; IIA, 8.18, Pit E). Jar sherd with remains of a potter's mark incised on the shoulder before firing. Hard, fairly fine pink ware, evenly fired. Creamy-buff slip in and out.
11. JR.Sh. (PM. B.10; TS. 1251; IIA, 9.2, Pit E). Jar sherd with remains of a potter's mark incised on the shoulder before firing. Hard, fine buff ware, evenly fired. Self slip out.

Other Type Series Examples:
Pit E — (1) SBR. E.I.c (TS. 1572), (2) JR. F.I.f (TS. 1585), (3) JR. J.I.g (TS. 311), (4) JR. Q.I.a (TS. 1579), (5) BE. E.II.a (TS. 3075).

Other Study Collection Examples:
Pit E — (1) JR. F.I.c (SC. 1203), (2) JR. F.I.c (SC. 2648), (3) JR.Sh. (PM. C.14; SC. 3267; see fig. 333:14).
Courtyard — (1) BE. A.II (SC. 3097).

Figure 33

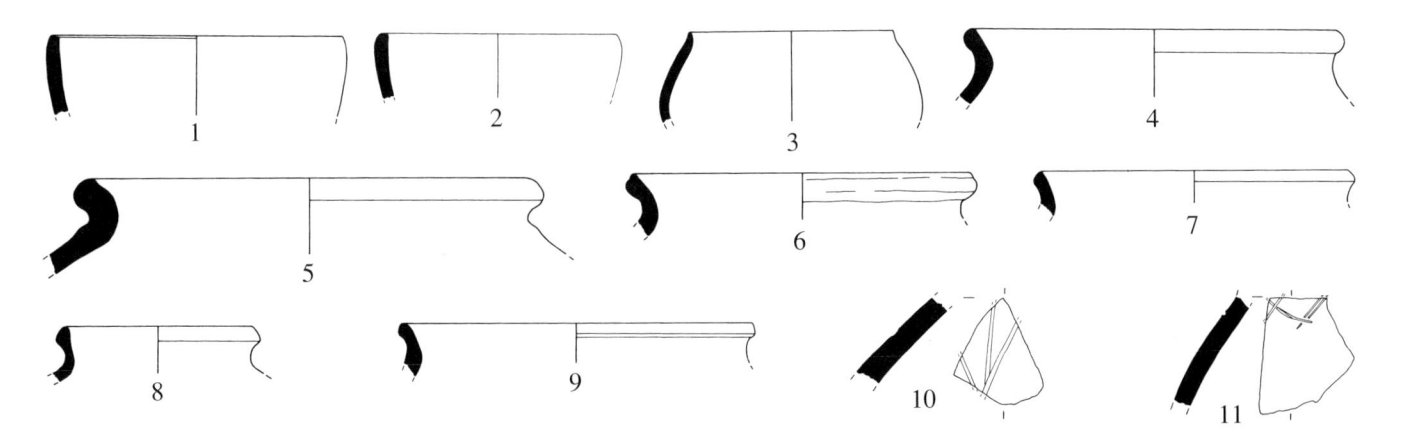

Pottery from Trench IIA (Phase 5; Period H — Early Bronze Age II). Scale 1:5

Figure 34. Pottery from Trench IIA, Rooms 9–12 (Phase 6; Period G — Early Bronze Age III)

1. SBR. C.III.a (TS. 1535; IIA, 10.2, Room 12). Small rim and upper wall segment. Fairly fine creamy-buff ware with lime and mica grits, evenly fired. Creamy-white slip out.
2. BR. B.II.b (TS. 1577; IIA, 8.4, Room 9). Small rim segment and about 2/3 of wall profile. Fairly fine pink ware with lime and mica grits, unevenly fired with lighter core. Creamy-buff slip out.
3. BR. B.II.c (TS. 81; IIA, 8.4, Room 9). Small rim and upper wall segment. Slightly coarse brown ware with lime and mica grits, evenly fired. Creamy-buff slip in and out.
4. BR. B.II.c (TS. 168 = TS. 201; IIA, 8.4, Room 9, + 8.7, Debris). Two small joining rim and upper wall segments. Slightly coarse pinkish-buff ware with lime and mica grits, evenly fired. Buff slip in and out.
5. BR. B.II.c (TS. 318; IIA, 8.15, Room 9). About 1/10 rim and upper wall segment. Fairly fine pinkish-buff ware with lime and mica grits, evenly fired. Creamy-buff slip in and out.
6. BR. E.III.a (TS. 1170; IIA, 10.2, Room 12). Large rim and upper wall segment. Fairly fine ware with lime and mica grits, unevenly fired buff out and pinkish-buff in. Creamy-buff slip in and out.
7. SJR. A.III.a (TS. 78; IIA, 8.4, Room 9). About 1/10 rim and shoulder segment. Fairly fine pinkish-buff ware with lime and mica grits, evenly fired. Creamy-buff slip in and out.
8. SJR. A.III.a (TS. 2444; IIA, 8.12, Room 10). Small rim and upper shoulder segment. Fairly fine grayware, evenly fired. Horizontally burnished out.
9. SJR. A.III.b (TS. 313; IIA, 8.17, Room 12). Small rim and upper wall segment. Slightly coarse light buff ware with lime and mica grits, evenly fired. Creamy-buff slip in and out.
10. SJR. A.III.c (TS. 77; IIA, 8.4, Room 9). About 1/8 rim and upper wall segment. Fairly fine creamy-buff ware with lime and mica grits, evenly fired. Cream slip in and out.
11. SJR. A.III.d (TS. 203; IIA, 8.12, Room 10). Small rim and shoulder segment. Slightly coarse buff ware with lime and mica grits, evenly fired. Creamy-buff slip out.
12. JR. E.II.a (TS. 173; IIA, 8.4, Room 9). Small rim, neck, and upper shoulder segment. Fairly fine pinkish-brown ware with lime and mica grits, evenly fired. Creamy-buff slip out and over rim in.
13. JR. F.I.b (TS. 321; IIA, 8.15, Room 9). Small rim, neck, and upper shoulder segment. Grayish-buff ware, evenly fired.
14. JR. F.II.b (TS. 164; IIA, 8.4, Room 9). Large rim, neck, and shoulder segment with remains of impressed decoration around the rim. Hard, slightly coarse greenish-grayware with lime and mica grits, evenly fired. Hand smoothed diagonally below neck out. Buff slip out.
15. JR. F.II.e (TS. 1536; IIA, 8.17, Room 12). Small rim, neck, and upper shoulder segment. Fairly fine pinkish-buff ware with gold-colored mica and lime grits, evenly fired. Creamy-buff slip out.
16. JR. F.III.a (PM. A.11; TS. 202; IIA, 8.12, Room 10). Large rim, neck, and upper shoulder segment. Fairly fine light brown ware with lime and mica grits, unevenly fired pinkish at surfaces. Creamy-buff slip out.
17. JR. J.II.a (TS. 76; IIA, 8.4, Room 9). Small rim, neck, and upper shoulder segment. Fairly fine grayish-buff ware with lime and mica grits, evenly fired. Self slip in and out.
18. JR. J.III.x (TS. 171; IIA, 8.10, Room 10 debris). Large rim, neck, and upper shoulder segment. Slightly coarse reddish-brown ware with lime and mica grits, unevenly fired with light brown core and pinkish-brown at surfaces.
19. CP. B.I.b (SW. 297; IIA, 10.1, Room 11). About 1/4 rim and shoulder segment. Coarse, pitted, drab ware with large gray and white lime grits, evenly fired.
20. JR.Sh. (PM. D.13; TS. 1177; IIA, 8.4, Room 9). Jar body sherd with remains of a potter's mark incised on outside wall before firing. Hard, close salmon-pink ware with fine lime and mica grits, evenly fired. Creamy-buff slip out.
21. JR.Sh. (PM. A.14; TS. 1999; IIA, 8.12, Room 10). Jar shoulder sherd with remains of a potter's mark incised on outside wall before firing. Fairly close grayish-buff ware, unevenly fired light pinkish-buff in.
22. JR.Sh. (PM. D.18; TS. 1983; IIA, 8.17, Room 12). Jar body sherds (two joining fragments) with remains of an oval-shaped potter's mark or decoration incised on outside wall before firing. Slightly coarse pinkish-buff ware, evenly fired. Self slip out.

Other Type Series Examples:
Room 9 — (1) SBR. C.I.a (TS. 169), (2) SBR. C.IV.a (TS. 1984).
Room 12 — (1) SBR. C.II.d (TS. 312 = TS. 319), (2) BR. B.II.d (TS. 1534), (3) JR. H.III.n (TS. 314).

Other Study Collection Examples:
Room 9 — (1) SBR. C.III.a (SC. 693), (2) JR. F.I.a (SC. 1181), (3) JR. J.I.b (SC. 2724).
Room 10 — (1) SBR. C.I.a (SC. 678), (2) SBR. C.IV.a (SC. 704), (3) SBR. C.IV.a (SC. 705).
Room 12 — (1) JR. F.I.a (SC. 1178), (2) BE. A.I (SC. 3095).

Figure 34

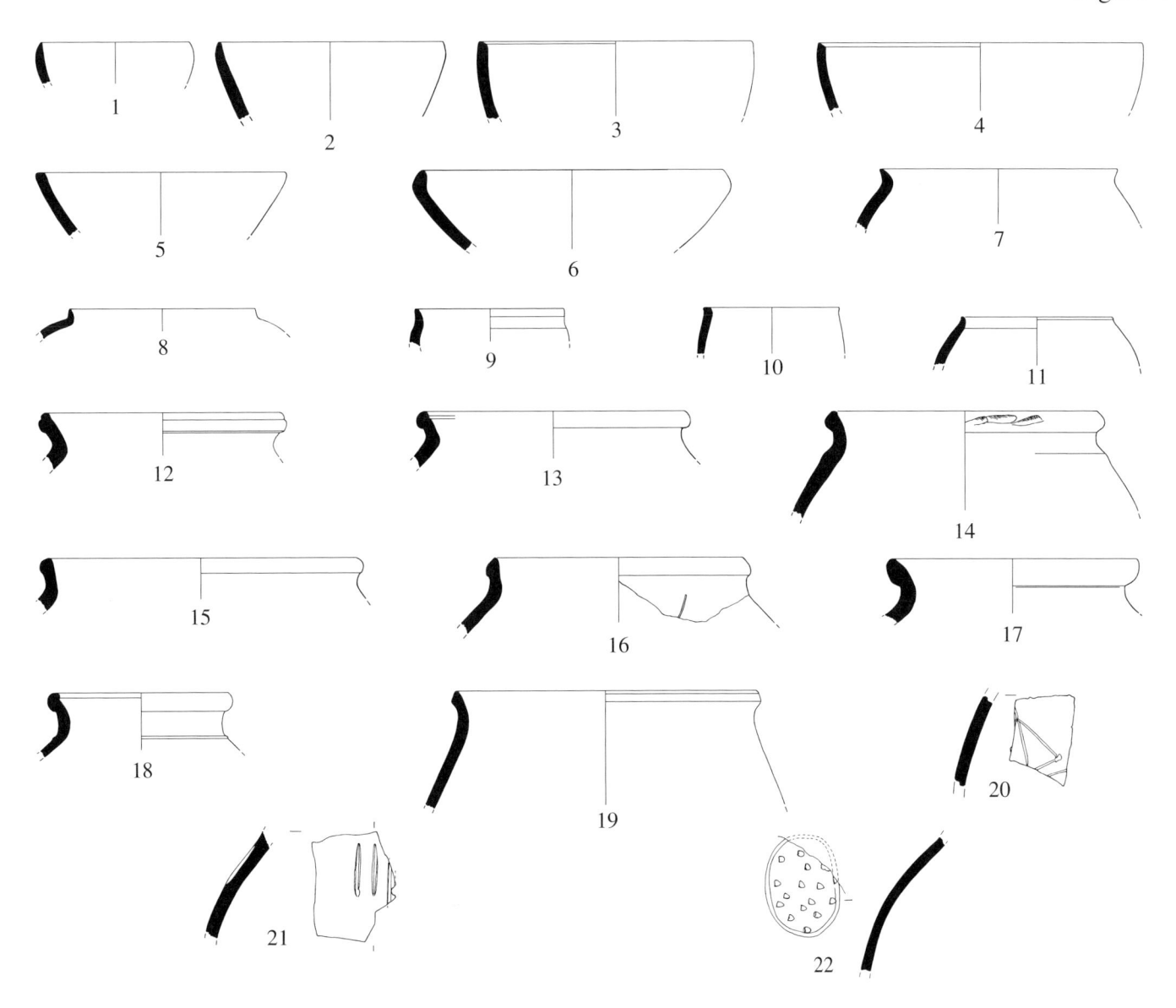

Pottery from Trench IIA, Rooms 9–12 (Phase 6; Period G — Early Bronze Age III). Scale 1:5

Figure 35

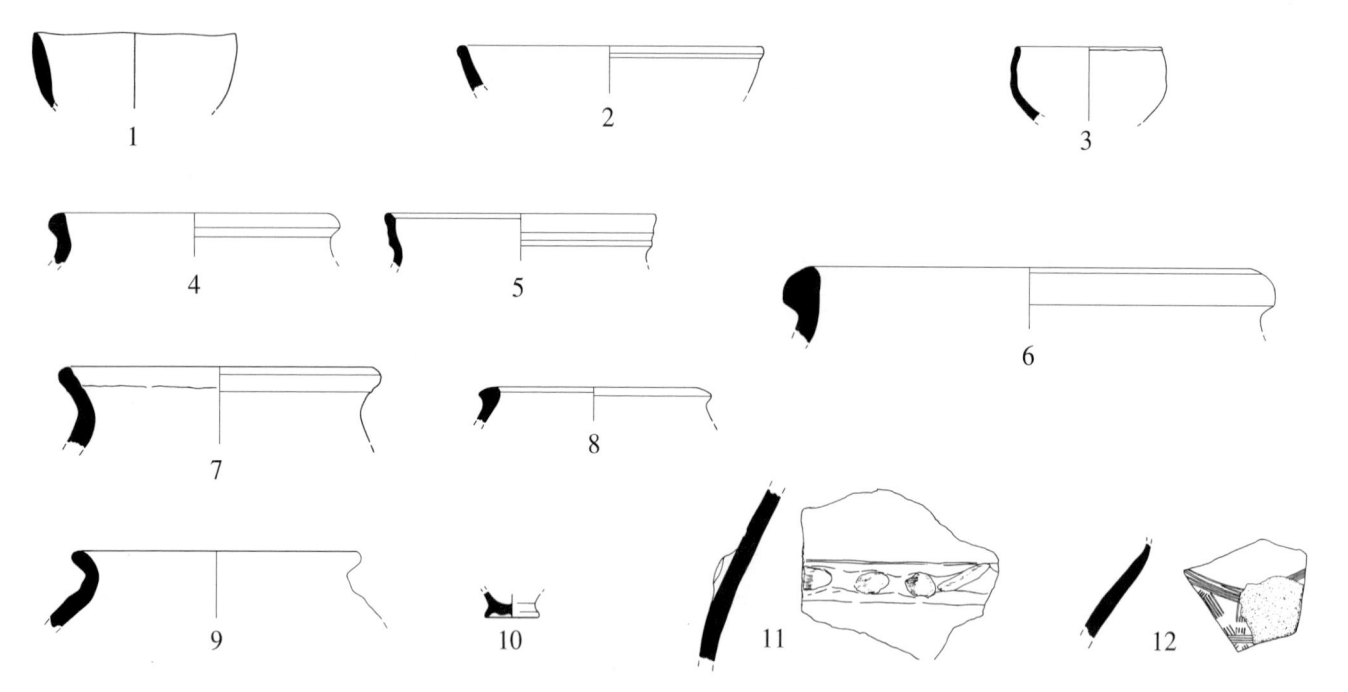

Pottery from Trench IIA, Hellenistic Pits B1 and B2 (Period C — Hellenistic) Cut into Early Bronze Age Pottery Level, and Debris above Phase 6 (Phase 7; Period G — Derived Early Bronze Age): Hellenistic: 1–8, 10; Derived Early Bronze Age: 9, 11–12. Scale 1:5

1. H.SBR. A.III.a (TS. 166; IIA, 8.3, Debris). Small rim and upper wall segment. Fairly fine creamy-buff ware with some lime grits, evenly fired. Self slip in and out.
2. H.BR. A.II.a (TS. 177; IIA, 8.7, Debris). Small rim and upper wall segment. Fairly fine buff ware with lime and mica grits, evenly fired. Self slip in and out.
3. H.BR. A.III.b (TS. 74; IIA, 5.21, Pit B1). About 1/2 rim segment and most of wall profile. Hard, metallic-like, grayware with lime and mica grits, evenly fired. Gray self slip in and out.
4. H.JR. A.II.e (TS. 317; IIA, 8.7, Debris). Small rim and upper shoulder segment. Pinkish-brown ware, evenly fired. Creamy-buff slip out.
5. H.JR. B.I.b (TS. 2219; IIA, 5.21, Pit B1). Small rim and neck segment. Slightly coarse grayish-buff ware, fairly evenly fired. Buff slip in and out.
6. H.JR. C.I.g (TS. 2377; IIA, 5.21, Pit B1). About 1/6 rim and neck segment. Fairly coarse light pink ware, evenly fired. Buff slip out.
7. H.JR. D.II.b (TS. 162; IIA, 8.3, Debris). About 1/3 rim, neck, and upper shoulder segment. Hard, close pinkish-buff ware with lime and mica grits, evenly fired. Creamy-buff slip in and out.
8. H.JR. G.I.b (TS. 205; IIA, 8.7, Debris). Small rim and upper shoulder segment. Slightly coarse buff ware, evenly fired. Burnished on rim and horizontally out. Self slip out.
9. JR. M.I.b (TS. 315; IIA, 8.7, Debris). See also pl. 260:2. Large rim, neck, and upper shoulder segment. Light brown ware, evenly fired. Slightly burnished inside the rim.
10. H.BE. B.I.a (TS. 179; IIA, 8.3, Debris). Nearly complete ring base with small segment of lower wall. Fine greenish-buff ware with fine lime grits, evenly fired. Yellowish-buff slip in and out.
11. ABS. C (TS. 207; IIA, 8.7, Debris). Derived EBA Jar sherd with applied band with thumb-impressed decoration. Coarse pinkish-brown ware, evenly fired. Pinkish-buff slip in.
12. JR.Sh. (IP [G.1] H.I.a; TS. 159; IIA, 8.3, Debris). Derived EBA jar shoulder sherd with geometric decoration incised before firing. Hard, slightly coarse buff ware with lime and mica grits, evenly fired. Self slip out.

Other Hellenistic Type Series Examples:
Pit B1 — (1) H.BR. B.IV.c (TS. 55), (2) H.St.J. A.I.1 (TS. 54).
Pit B2 — (1) H.RSB. A.I.b (TS. 44), (2) H.RSB. D.II.c (SW. 252).
Debris above Phase 6:
(1) H.JR. G.I.a (TS. 79).

Other Derived EBA Study Collection Examples:
Pit B1 — (1) JR. D.II.a (SC. 2733), (2) JR. J.III.e (SC. 2240).
Pit B2 —(1) SBR. C.III.b (SC. 701).

Figure 36. Pottery from Trench IIA, Courtyard/Working Area (Phase 8; Period G — Early Bronze Age III), and Pit D Cut into Phase 8 Pottery Level (Period C — Hellenistic)

1. SBR. C.II.a (TS. 90; IIA, 8.2, Courtyard/Working Area). Small rim and upper wall segment. Fine pinkish-buff ware with gold-colored mica and lime grits, evenly fired. Self slip in and out.
2. SBR. C.II.c (TS. 89; IIA, 8.2, Courtyard/Working Area). Small rim and upper wall segment. Fairly fine pinkish-buff ware with gold-colored mica and lime grits, evenly fired. Creamy-buff slip out and over rim in.
3. SBR. C.III.a (TS. 94; IIA, 8.2, Courtyard/Working Area). About 1/6 rim and upper wall segment. Fine buff ware with mica grit and organic temper, evenly fired. Creamy-buff slip in and out.

Figure 36

4. SBR. C.IV.a (TS. 88; IIA, 8.2, Courtyard/Working Area). Small rim and upper wall segment. Fairly fine pinkish-buff ware with gold-colored mica and lime grits, evenly fired. Creamy-buff slip in and out.
5. SBR. C.IV.a (TS. 170; IIA, 8.2, Courtyard/Working Area). About 1/4 rim segment and most of wall profile. Fine grayish-buff ware with lime and mica grits, evenly fired. Self slip in and out.
6. BR. B.II.a (TS. 95; IIA, 8.2, Courtyard/Working Area). Small rim and upper wall segment. Fairly fine grayware with lime and mica grits, unevenly fired dark gray in and light gray out. Buff slip in and out.
7. BR. B.II.c (TS. 87 = TS. 2002; IIA, 8.2, Courtyard/Working Area). Two joining small rim and upper wall segments. Fairly coarse yellow-buff ware, evenly fired. Creamy-buff slip in and out.
8. BR. B.II.e (TS. 86; IIA, 8.2, Courtyard/Working Area). Small rim and upper wall segment. Fairly fine light pink ware with lime and silver-colored mica grits, evenly fired. Creamy-buff slip in and out.
9. BR. O.I.a (TS. 96; IIA, 8.2, Courtyard/Working Area). Small rim and upper wall segment. Fine, light pink ware with mica grits, evenly fired. Creamy-buff slip in and out.
10. JR. F.I.a (TS. 1; IIA, 7.6, Pit D, Upper). About 1/10 rim, neck, and upper shoulder segment. Fine buff ware, evenly fired. Cream slip in and out.
11. JR. F.I.c (TS. 93; IIA, 8.2, Courtyard/Working Area). Small rim, neck, and upper shoulder segment. Fairly fine pinkish-buff ware with lime and mica grits, evenly fired. Creamy-buff slip out and over rim in.
12. JR. F.II.d (TS. 85; IIA, 8.2, Courtyard/Working Area). Small rim and neck segment. Fine buff ware with lime and gold-colored mica grits, evenly fired. Creamy-buff slip out and over rim in.
13. CP. A.III.b (TS. 324; IIA, 8.2, Courtyard/Working Area). Small rim and neck segment. Coarse, gritty, grayish ware, evenly fired.
14. CP. B.III.a (PM. C.4; TS. 64; IIA, 5.13, Courtyard/Working Area). Large rim, neck, and shoulder segment. Coarse light brown ware with lime and mica grits, evenly fired. Incomplete potter's mark incised on outside wall before firing.
15. JR.Sh. (PM. D.23; TS. 160; IIA, 8.2, Courtyard/Working Area). Jar sherd with remains of a potter's mark incised on upper shoulder before firing. Slightly coarse pinkish-buff ware with lime and mica grits, evenly fired.
16. JR.Sh. (PM. D.6; TS. 1180; IIA, 8.2, Courtyard/Working Area). Jar sherd with remains of a potter's mark incised on the upper shoulder before firing. Hard, close pinkish-buff ware with fine lime and mica grits, evenly fired.
17. H.SBR. A.II.a (TS. 2; IIA, 7.6, Pit D, Upper). About 1/8 rim and upper wall segment. Slightly coarse pinkish-buff ware with mica grits, evenly fired. Traces of burning outside. Self slip.

Other Type Series Examples:
  Early Bronze Age
    Courtyard — (1) SBR. C.II.e (TS. 116), (2) BR. G.I.b (TS. 56), (3) JR. G.II.c (TS. 91), (4) JR. J.II.b (TS. 92), (5) CP. B.III.a (TS. 165), (6) CP. B.III.c (TS. 325).
  Hellenistic Period
    Pit D, Lower Level — (1) H.SBR. C.I.a (TS. 3008).

Other Study Collection Examples:
  Early Bronze Age
    Courtyard — (1) JR. J.I.h (SC. 2124), (2) JR. J.III.t (SC. 2355), (3) JR.Sh. (PM. D.17; SC. 3262; see fig. 333:15).
    Pit D, Upper Level — (1) CP. A.I.c (SC. 1787).

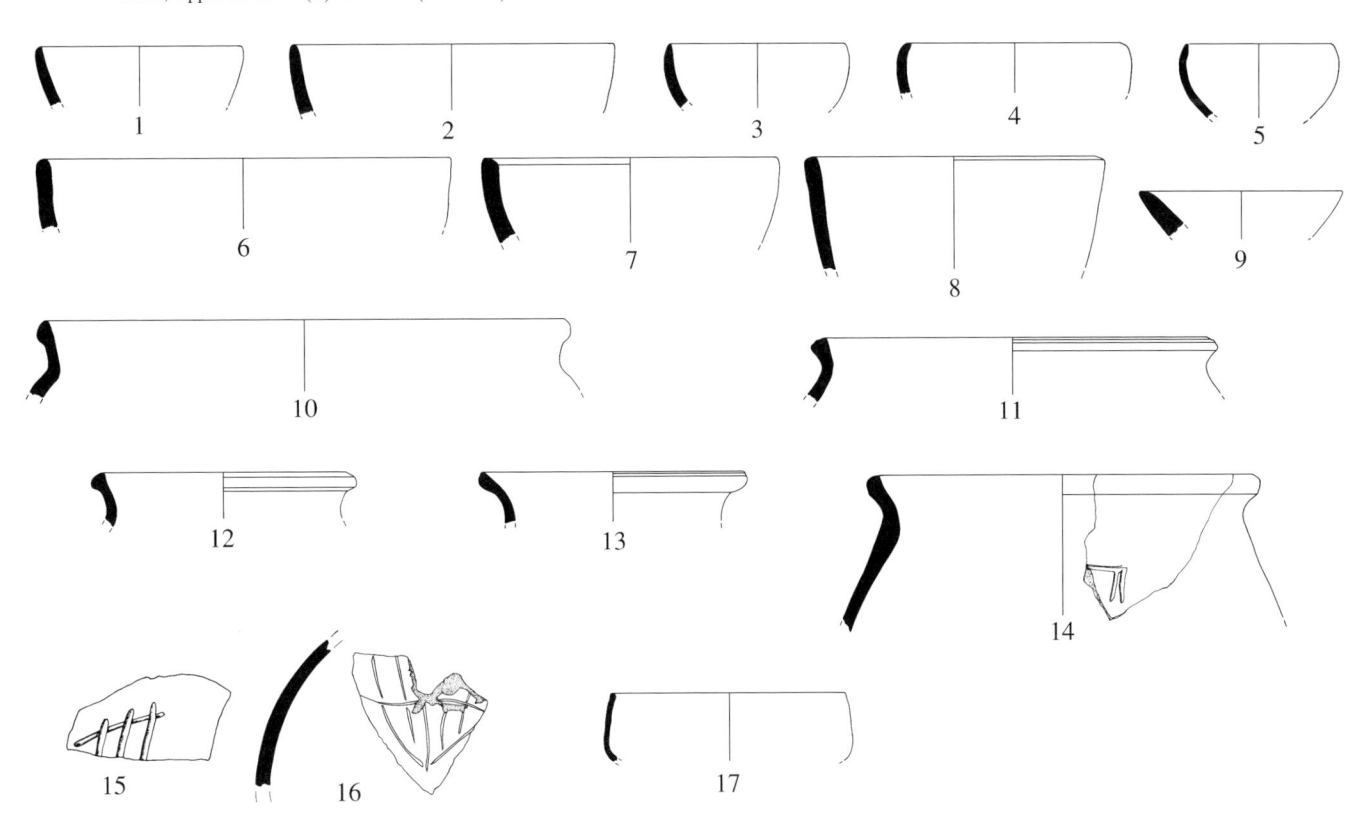

Pottery from Trench IIA, Courtyard/Working Area (Phase 8; Period G — Early Bronze Age III), and Pit D Cut into Phase 8 Pottery Level (Period C — Hellenistic). Scale 1:5

Figure 37. Pottery from Trench IIA (Phase 9; Period C — Hellenistic)

1. H.SBR. A.II.b (TS. 61; IIA, 5.9). About 1/5 rim segment and most of wall profile. Slightly coarse buff ware with lime and mica grits, evenly fired. Self slip in and out.
2. H.BR. A.III.b (TS. 72; IIA, 5.8). Small rim and upper wall segment. Fairly fine pinkish-brown ware with lime and mica grits, evenly fired. Creamy-buff slip in and out.
3. H.BR. B.I.c (TS. 27; IIA, 5.20). Small rim and upper wall segment. Fine pink ware with lime and mica grits, evenly fired. Pinkish-buff slip in and out.
4. H.BR. B.I.d (TS. 1549; IIA, 8.1, Pit C1). Small rim and upper wall segment. Slightly coarse drab ware with lime and mica grits, evenly fired. Irregularly self burnished horizontally in and out.
5. H.BR. B.I.e (TS. 26; IIA, 5.20). Small rim and upper wall segment. Fairly fine buff ware with lime and mica grits, evenly fired.
6. H.RSB. B.II.c (TS. 25; IIA, 5.20). About 1/6 rim and upper wall segment. Fine pinkish-brown ware with micaceous grit temper, evenly fired. Red slip in and out.
7. H.RSB. D.II.c (TS. 24; IIA, 5.20). About 1/8 rim segment with upper and lower wall. Fine pinkish-buff ware with lime and mica grits, evenly fired. Red slip on upper wall in and out with irregular drip lines out. Slip partially oxidized black below rim in and in patches out.
8. H.JR. D.I.a (TS. 1545; IIA, 8.1, Pit C1). Small rim, neck, and upper shoulder segment. Close buff ware with fine lime and mica grits, evenly fired. Creamy-buff slip in and out.
9. H.Jg. B.I.a (SW. 260; IIA, 5.20). Trefoil rim and neck segment broken at juncture of missing strap handle. Hard, fairly fine pinkish-buff ware with fine lime and mica grits, evenly fired. Creamy-buff slip out and over rim in.
10. H.Jgt. BE. (not typed; TS. 2536; IIA, 8.1, Pit C1). Complete pointed juglet base. Fine salmon-pink ware, evenly fired. Self slip in and out.
11. H.St.J. A.I.e (TS. 31; IIA, 5.20). About 1/5 rim and neck segment. Fairly fine pinkish-buff ware with lime and mica grits, evenly fired. Creamy-buff slip in and out.
12. H.St.J. A.I.e (TS. 36; IIA, 5.20). About 1/5 rim, neck, and upper shoulder segment. Fairly fine light brown ware with lime and mica grits, evenly fired. Creamy-buff slip out.
13. H.St.J. A.I.e (TS. 1187; IIA, 5.20). Small rim, neck, and upper shoulder segment. Close pinkish-buff ware, evenly fired.
14. H.St.J. A.I.i (TS. 37; IIA, 5.20). About 1/3 rim and shoulder segment. Fairly fine buff ware with gold-colored mica grits, evenly fired. Creamy-buff slip in and out.
15. H.St.J. B.I.d (TS. 33; IIA, 5.20). About 1/5 rim and neck segment, burned in and out. Hard, fine grayware with lime and mica grits, evenly fired. Buff slip in and out.
16. H.CP. A.III.b (TS. 1548; IIA, 8.1, Pit C1). See also pl. 276:7. Small rim and neck segment. Slightly coarse drab ware, evenly fired.
17. H.CP. B.II.a (TS. 62; IIA, 5.8). Small rim and upper shoulder segment. Coarse brown ware with many lime and mica grits, evenly fired. Self slip in and out.
18. H.PS.1 (TS. 63; IIA, 5.9). Small rim and wall segment. Fairly fine buff ware with mica and lime grits, unevenly fired pink out. Creamy-buff slip out and just over rim in.
19. H.JR.Sh. (IP [G.1] C.IV.a; TS. 2007; IIA, 5.20). Jar body sherd with comb-incised grouped horizontal and wavy line decoration. Fairly coarse pinkish-buff ware, evenly fired.
20. H.JR.Sh. (Dec.; SC. 3342; IIA, 5.19, Pit B). Jar body sherd with vertical tool-impressed decoration on outside wall. Fine dark buff ware with small mica grits, unevenly fired gray and dark red on outside surface. Dark red slip inside and discolored red and black outside.

Other Type Series Examples:
  Pit B — (1) H.JR. F.II.d (TS. 46).
  Pit C1 — (1) H.BR. C.II.f (TS. 1544).
  Locus 5.8 — (1) H.CP. D.I.c (TS. 49), (2) H.PS. 4 (TS. 51).

Other Hellenistic Study Collection Examples:
  Pit C1 — (1) H.Jg. B.II.a (SC. 2769).
  Locus 5.20 — (1) H.BR. (not typed, SC. 146), (2) H.Jg. A.II.a (SC. 2954), (3) H.Jg. B.II.a (SC. 2772), (4) H.Jg. B.III.c (SC. 2780), (5) H.St.J. B.II.f (SC. 2706).

Other Derived EBA Study Collection Examples:
  Pit B — (1) BR. L.III.e (SC. 865).
  Pit C1 — (1) SBR. C.I.a (SC. 677), (2) SBR. C.II.a (SC. 680), (3) SBR. C.II.b (SC. 684), (4) SBR. C.II.b (SC. 685), (5) SBR. C.II.e (SC. 687), (6) SBR. C.II.e (SC. 690), (7) SBR. C.II.e (SC. 691), (8) SBR. C.III.b (SC. 702), (9) BR. B.II.e (SC. 734), (10) JR. B.V.c (SC. 956), (11) JR. D.I.d (SC. 2731), (12) JR. F.II.e (SC. 1224), (13) JR. P.III.c (SC. 2442), (14) CP. A.II.b (SC. 1799).
  Locus 5.20 — (1) SBR. C.II.a (SC. 6).

Figure 37

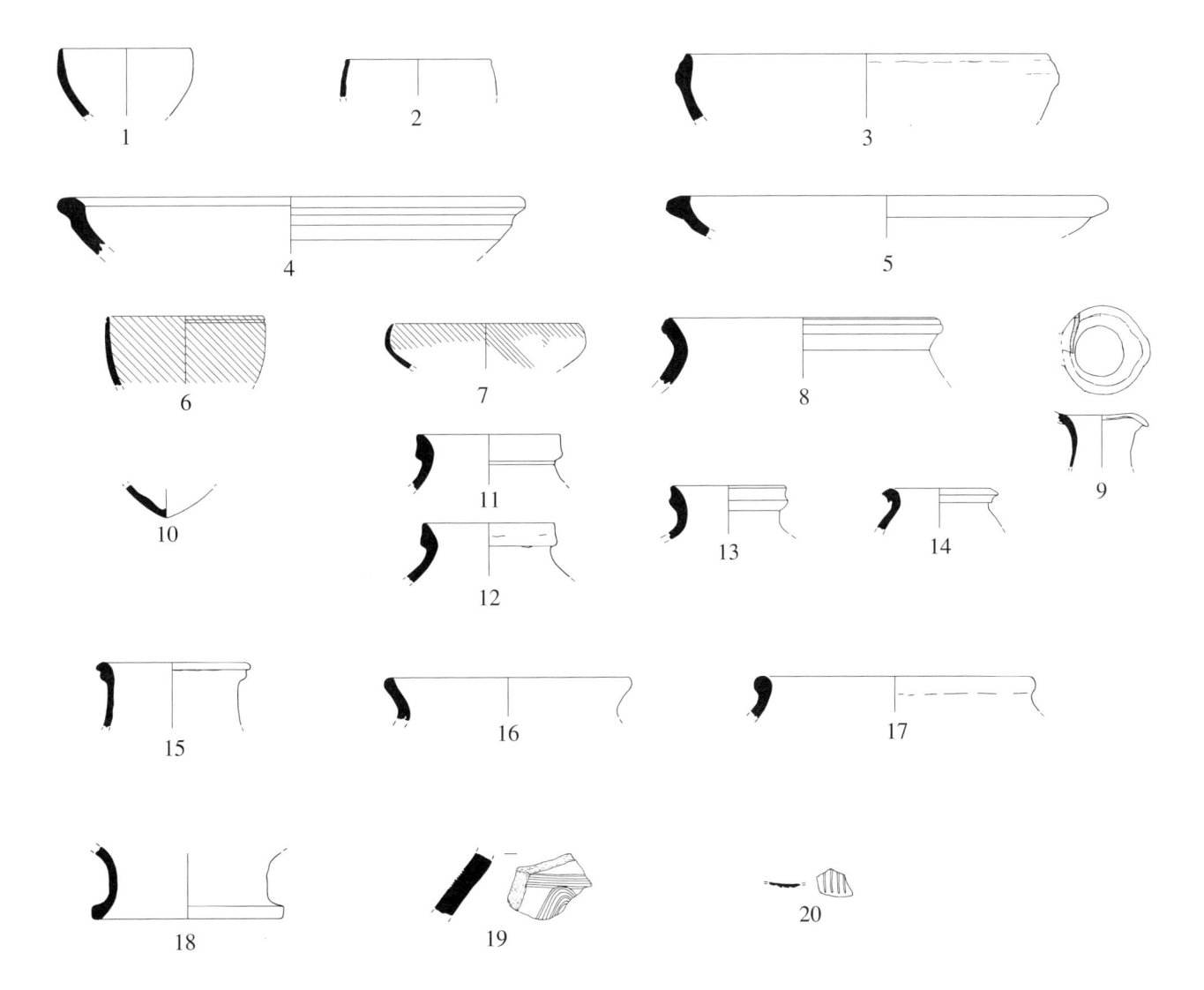

Pottery from Trench IIA (Phase 9; Period C — Hellenistic). Scale 1:5

Figure 38

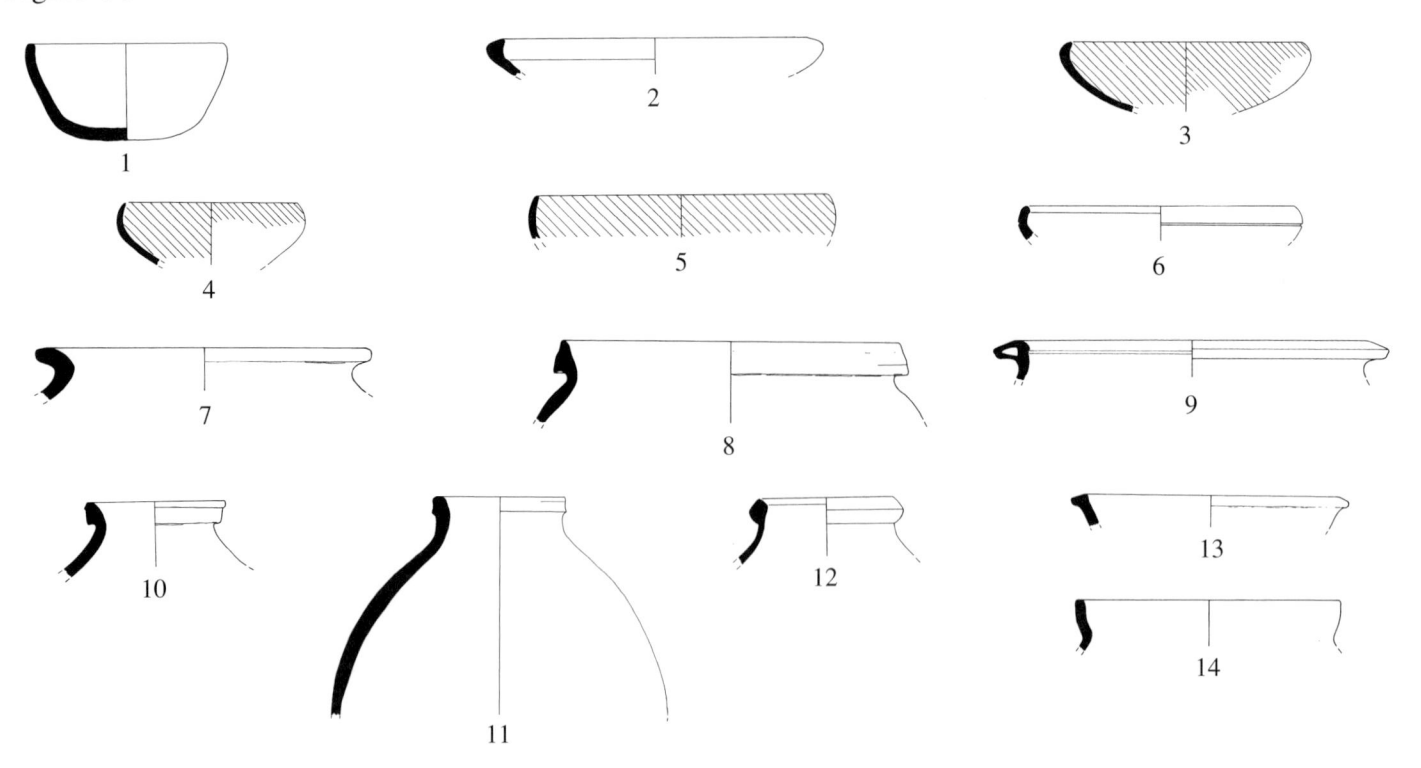

Pottery from Trench IIA, Pits 7.1, 7.2, and 7.3 (Phase 10; Period C — Hellenistic). Scale 1:5

1. H.SBR. A.II.b (SW. 261; IIA, 7.2). Fragment of complete profile. Slightly coarse buff ware with various colored lime grits, fairly evenly fired.
2. H.BR. B.III.h (TS. 20; IIA, 7.2). Small rim and upper wall segment. Fairly fine pinkish-buff ware with lime and mica grits, evenly fired. Self slip in and out.
3. H.RSB. D.II.a (TS. 83; IIA, 7.1). About 1/8 rim segment and most of wall profile. Fine pinkish-brown ware with lime and mica grits, evenly fired. Red slip in and over rim out in irregular pattern, fired black.
4. H.RSB. D.II.c (TS. 82; IIA, 7.1). Small rim segment and most of wall profile. Fine pinkish-brown ware with lime and mica grits, evenly fired. Red slip in and over rim out in irregular pattern, fired black.
5. H.RSB. D.II.d (TS. 1541; IIA, 7.2). Small rim segment. Fairly close buff ware with fine lime and mica grits, evenly fired. Remains of reddish-brown slip in and out.
6. H.BGB. B.I.d (TS. 7; IIA, 7.2). About 1/6 rim segment. Fine light grayware with mica grits, evenly fired. Burnished horizontally in and out.
7. H.JR. A.I.a (TS. 80; IIA, 7.1). About 1/8 rim and neck segment. Hard, fine grayish-buff ware with fine lime and mica grits, evenly fired. Red slip worn off.
8. H.JR. C.I.h (TS. 16; IIA, 7.2). Tureen. About 1/5 segment of rim and shoulder. Fine light pink ware with lime and mica grits, evenly fired. Cream slip in and out.
9. H.JR. E.I.a (TS. 19; IIA, 7.2). Small segment of rim and shoulder. Slightly coarse pinkish-buff ware, evenly fired. Self slip in and out.
10. H.St.J. A.I.c (TS. 84; IIA, 7.1). Complete rim and shoulder segment. Fine pinkish-buff ware with lime and gold-colored mica grits, evenly fired. Creamy-buff slip out and over rim in.
11. H.St.J. A.I.d (SW. 280; IIA, 7.2). Complete rim and portion of body. Hard, close pinkish-buff ware with gold- and silver-colored mica grits and some lime grits, evenly fired.
12. H.St.J. A.I.j (TS. 17; IIA, 7.2). About 1/3 rim, neck, and shoulder segment. Fine pink ware with lime and mica grits, evenly fired. Self slip out and over rim in.
13. H.St.J. B.II.l (TS. 29; IIA, 7.2). Small rim and neck segment. Fine buff ware with lime grits, evenly fired. Self slip in and out.
14. H.CP. B.I.a (TS. 1996; IIA, 7.2). Small segment of two joining rim fragments. Fairly coarse and gritty pinkish-brown ware, fairly evenly fired.

Other Hellenistic Type Series Examples:
Pit 7.1 — (1) H.RSJ. B.I.b (SC. 3340), (2) H.RSJ. C.I.a (SC. 3346), (3) H.Ld. 5 (SW. 183).
Pit 7.2 — (1) H.BR. A.V.c (TS. 1990), (2) H.BR. B.I.a (TS. 18), (3) H.BGB. A.I.a (TS. 21), (4) H.BGB. B.I.d (TS. 6), (5) H.SJR. A.II.c (TS. 1539), (6) H.Ld. 6 (SW.174), (7) H.Ld. 2 (TS. 1542), (8) H.Ld.1 (TS. 1543).

Other Hellenistic Study Collection Examples:
Pit 7.1 — (1) H.JR. B.I.a (SC. 148), (2) H.Jg. B.II.d (SC. 2774).
Pit 7.2 — (1) H.BR. A.III.d (SC. 2821), (2) H.BR. A.V.c (SC. 2826), (3) H.BR. (not typed, SC. 145), (4) H.RSB. B.II.c (SC. 2872), (5) H.Jg. B.II.a (SC. 2771), (6) H.St.J. A.I.c (SC. 2660), (7) H.St.J. A.I.c (SC. 2662), (8) H.St.J. A.I.e (SC. 2666), (9) H.St.J. A.I.e (SC. 2667), (10) H.St.J. B.I.d (SC. 2693), (11) H.St.J. B.I.d (SC. 2687), (12) H.BE. B.I.a (SC. 3176), (13) H.BE. B.II.a (SC. 3207), (14) H.JR.Sh. (IP [G.4] G.II.b; SC. 3250).

Figure 39

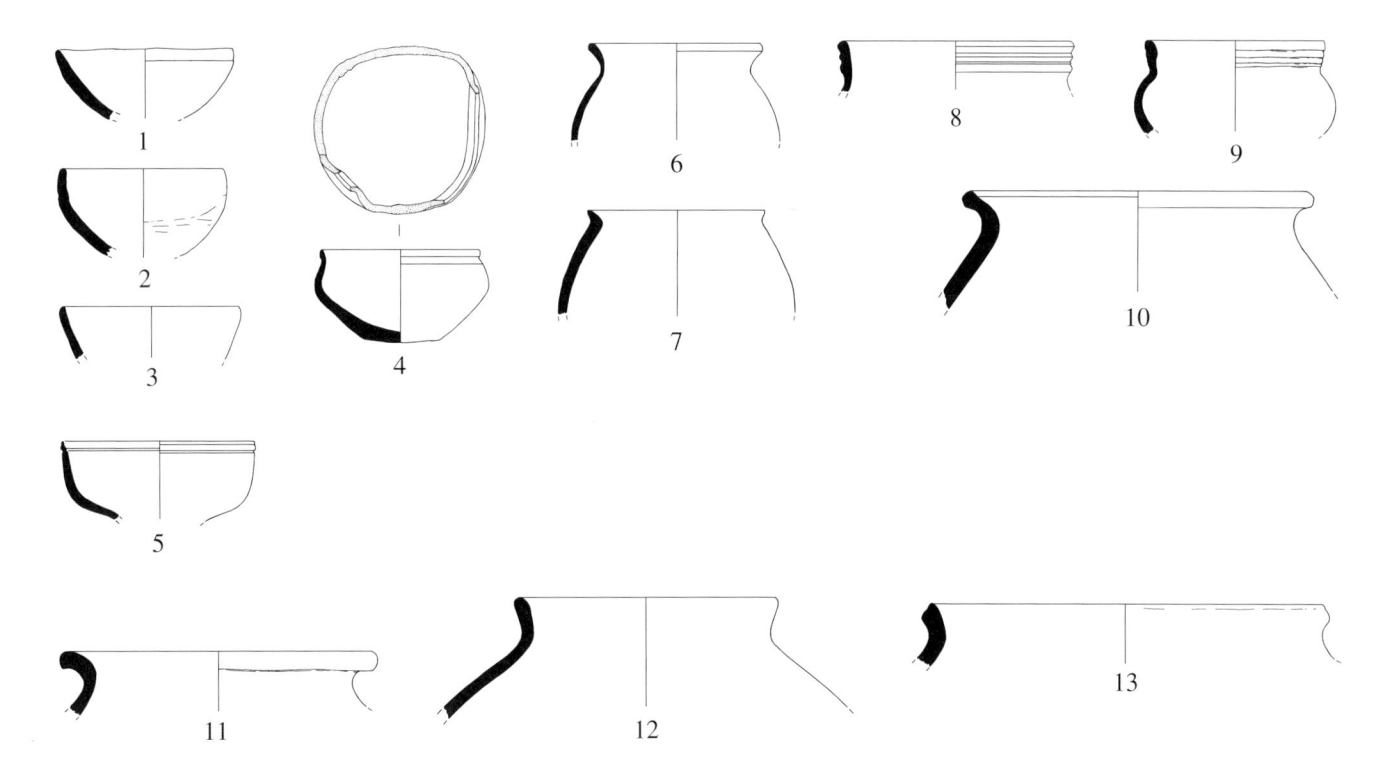

Pottery from Trench IIA, Loci Disturbed by Hellenistic Pits 7.2, 7.3, and Locus 7.12 (Phase 10;
Period C — Derived Early Bronze Age). Scale 1:5

1. SBR. C.II.b (TS. 167; IIA, 7.12). About 1/4 rim segment and most of wall profile. Fine pinkish-brown ware with mica and lime grits, evenly fired. Buff slip in and out.
2. SBR. C.III.b (SW. 258; IIA, 7.3). Small rim segment and most of wall profile. Hard, fairly fine buff ware with black and white-colored lime and mica grits, unevenly fired creamy-buff at surfaces.
3. SBR. C.IV.a (TS. 2203; IIA, 7.3). Small rim and upper wall segment. Slightly coarse pinkish-red ware, evenly fired. Creamy-buff slip out.
4. SBR. F.I.b (SW. 253; IIA, 7.3). About 1/2 rim and most of body profile, with rim pinched inward, possibly for use as a lamp. Slightly coarse greenish-buff ware with many mica and black- and white-colored lime grits, evenly fired.
5. BR. A.II.a (TS. 30; IIA, 7.2). Small rim segment with most of body profile. Slightly coarse light grayish-buff ware with lime and mica grits, evenly fired. Self slip in and out.
6. SJR. A.I.a (TS. 1986; IIA, 7.3). Small rim, neck, and upper wall segment. Slightly coarse pinkish-buff ware, fairly evenly fired. Buff slip in and out.
7. SJR. A.III.a (TS. 32; IIA, 7.2). About 1/5 rim and upper wall segment. Slightly coarse buff ware with lime and mica grits, evenly fired. Self slip in and out.
8. JR. C.I.b (TS. 163; IIA, 7.12). Small rim and neck segment. Fairly fine pinkish-brown ware, evenly fired. Buff slip out.
9. JR. C.II.b (TS. 3; IIA, 7.3). About 1/4 rim, neck and wall segment. Fairly fine, drab ware, evenly fired. Dark buff slip in and out. Traces of burning in.
10. JR. F.I.b (TS. 15; IIA, 7.2). About 1/10 rim, neck, and upper shoulder segment. Hard, fine pinkish-grayware with lime grits, evenly fired. Dark discoloration below lip of rim inside.
11. JR. J.I.c (TS. 5; IIA, 7.3). About 1/8 rim and neck segment. Fairly fine pink ware, evenly fired. Self slip in and out.
12. CP. A.III.a (TS. 1987, IIA, 7.2). Small rim, neck, and shoulder segment. Fairly coarse and gritty pinkish-brown ware, evenly fired.
13. CP. B.II.f (TS. 9; IIA, 7.3). Small rim and neck segment. Fairly coarse, very light brown ware with lime grits, evenly fired.

Another Derived Early Bronze Age Type Series Example:
    Pit 7.2 — (1) JR. G.III.a (PM. C.8; TS. 14).

Other Derived Early Bronze Age Study Collection Examples:
    Pit 7.2 — (1) SBR. B.I.b (SC. 265), (2) SBR. B.I.l (SC. 578), (3) SBR. C.II.e (SC. 689), (4) SBR. C.II.e (SC. 686), (5) SBR. C.III.a (SC. 694), (6) SJR. C.I.c (SC. 2532), (7) JR. C.I.h (SC. 2742), (8) JR. F.I.c (SC. 1205), (9) JR. F.II.a (SC. 1218), (10) JR. J.I.a (SC. 2450).
    Pit 7.3 — (1) SBR. C.II.a (SC. 679).

Figure 40. Pottery from Trench IIA, Street and Associated Remains (Phase 11; Period C — Hellenistic)

1. H.SBR. A.II.a (TS. 67; IIA, 5.7, Street). Small rim and upper wall segment. Hard, light greenish-grayware with fine lime and mica grits, evenly fired. Self slip in and out.
2. H.SBR. A.II.c (TS. 11; IIA, 7.4). About 1/6 rim and upper wall segment. Fairly fine creamy-white ware with a few lime grits, evenly fired. Self slip in and out.
3. H.BR. A.III.a (TS. 12; IIA, 7.4). About 1/10 rim and upper wall segment. Fairly fine light brown ware with a few lime grits, evenly fired. Self slip in and out.
4. H.BR. A.III.c (TS. 68; IIA, 5.7, Street). Small rim and upper wall segment. Fairly fine buff ware with lime and mica grits, evenly fired. Self slip in and out.
5. H.BR. A.III.a (TS. 70; IIA, 5.7, Street). Small rim and upper wall segment. Fairly fine pinkish-buff ware with fine lime and mica grits, evenly fired. Creamy-buff slip in and out.
6. H.BR. B.IV.a (TS. 8; IIA, 7.4). About 1/8 rim and upper wall segment. Fairly fine creamy-white ware with lime grits, evenly fired. Self slip in and out.
7. H.SJR. A.I.b (TS. 4; IIA, 7.4). About 1/6 rim, neck, and shoulder segment. Hard, fine salmon-pink ware, evenly fired. Pinkish-cream slip in and out.
8. H.JR. A.I.d (TS. 1538; IIA, 7.5). Small rim and upper shoulder segment. Slightly coarse pinkish-buff ware with lime and mica grits, fairly evenly fired. Creamy-buff slip out.
9. H.JR. B.II.a (TS. 215; IIA, 5.5). Small rim, neck, and upper shoulder segment. Slightly coarse pinkish-brown ware with lime and mica grits, evenly fired. Buff slip out.
10. H.JR. D.III.a (TS. 218; IIA, 5.5). Small rim and upper wall segment. Slightly coarse buff ware with lime and mica grits, unevenly fired pinkish at surfaces. Creamy-buff slip in and out.
11. H.Jg. B.I.a (TS. 226; IIA, 5.5). About 1/5 rim and neck segment. Slightly coarse buff ware with lime and mica grits, unevenly fired pinkish-buff out. Creamy-buff slip out.
12. H.St.J. A.I.a (TS. 219; IIA, 5.5). About 1/4 rim, neck, and shoulder segment with traces of burning out. Fairly fine drab brown ware with lime and mica grits, evenly fired. Self slip in and out.
13. H.St.J. A.I.b (TS. 220; IIA, 5.5). Small rim and neck segment. Fairly fine pinkish-brown ware with lime and mica grits, evenly fired. Pinkish-buff slip out.
14. H.St.J. A.II.e (TS. 13; IIA, 7.4). About 1/5 rim and neck segment. Fine light brown ware with micaceous grits, evenly fired. Self slip in and out.
15. H.St.J. B.II.c (TS. 217; IIA, 5.5). Small rim and neck segment. Slightly coarse pinkish-buff ware with lime and mica grits, evenly fired. Burnished buff slip in and out.
16. H.Hd. (not typed; SW. 267; IIA, 5.7, Street). Double-winged lug handle. Horizontally pierced near wall of vessel. Pinkish-buff ware with a few lime and mica grits, unevenly fired light green out.

Other Type Series Examples: (1) H.SBR. A.II.c (TS. 1533), (2) H.SBR. A.III.a (TS. 213), (3) H.BR. A.III.c (TS. 211), (4) H.BR. B.IV.a (TS. 66), (5) H.JR. A.I.b (TS. 1540), (6) H.JR. A.I.f (TS. 233), (7) H.Jg. B.I.c (TS. 216), (8) H.St.J. A.I.i (TS. 210), (9) H.PS.2 (TS. 42 = TS. 212, 252, and Tr. IIB, TS. 63).

Other Hellenistic Study Collection Examples: (1) H.RSB. C.II.a (SC. 2873), (2) H.St.J. B.II.f (SC. 2705), (3) H.CP. A.I.a (SC. 1782), (4) H.CP. B.II.a (SC. 1843).

Incised Hellenistic Pottery Sherd: (1) IP [G.1] C.IV.a (TS. 2010; see fig. 153:1).

Another Derived EBA Study Collection Example: (1) BE. F.VIII.b (SC. 1925).

Figure 40

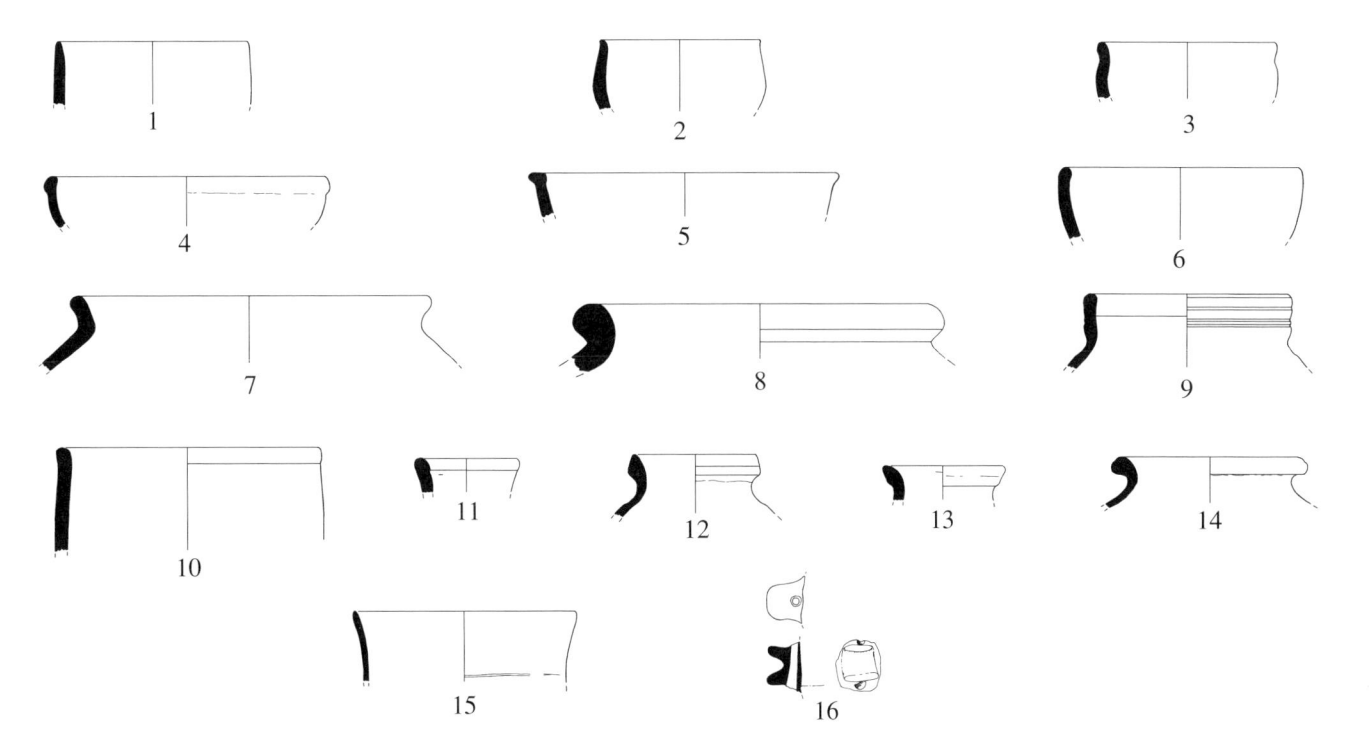

Pottery from Trench IIA, Street and Associated Remains (Phase 11; Period C — Hellenistic). Scale 1:5

Figure 41. Potttery from Trench IIA, Pit C (Phase 12; Period C — Hellenistic)

1. H.SBR. A.II.c (SW. 154; IIA, 5.3). Small rim segment and almost complete wall profile. Light buff ware, unevenly fired brown on surfaces and discolored in and out.
2. H.BR. A.I.a (TS. 1991; IIA, 5.2). Small rim and upper wall segment. Close buff ware, evenly fired. Creamy-buff slip in and out.
3. H.BR. A.V.a (TS. 59; IIA, 5.6). Small rim and upper wall segment. Slightly coarse pinkish-brown ware with lime and mica grits, evenly fired. Creamy-buff slip out.
4. H.BR. A.V.b (TS. 60; IIA, 5.2). Small rim and upper wall segment. Fairly fine grayware with lime and mica grits, evenly fired. Pinkish-cream slip out with traces of burning also outside.
5. H.BR. B.I.d (TS. 109; IIA, 5.6). Small rim and upper wall segment. Fairly fine, soft, brown ware with lime and silver-colored mica grits, unevenly fired pinkish-brown at surfaces. Pinkish-buff slip in and out.
6. H.BR. B.I.e (TS. 236; IIA, 5.2, 4.11). Small rim and upper wall segment. Slightly coarse buff ware with lime and mica grits, evenly fired. Self slip in and out.
7. H.BR. B.III.i (TS. 137; IIA, 5.2). Small rim and upper wall segment. Slightly coarse buff ware with lime and mica grits, evenly fired. Self slip in and out.
8. H.BR. B.III.i (TS. 136; IIA, 5.2, 4.11). Two small joining rim and upper wall segments. Slightly coarse dark buff ware with lime and mica grits, evenly fired. Self slip in and out.
9. H.BR. B.III.j (TS. 138; IIA, 5.2). Small rim and upper wall segment. Fairly fine pinkish-buff ware with lime and mica grits, evenly fired. Creamy-buff slip in and out.
10. H.BR. B.III.j (TS. 3027; IIA, 5.3). Small rim and upper wall segment. Fairly fine pink ware, evenly fired. Buff slip out.
11. H.BR. B.III.j (TS. 47; IIA, 5.18). Small rim and upper wall segment. Fine pinkish-brown ware with lime and mica grits, evenly fired. Self slip in and out.
12. H.BR. B.III.k (TS. 106; IIA, 5.6). Small rim and upper wall segment. Fairly fine reddish-brown ware with lime and gold-colored mica grits, evenly fired. Dark buff slip in and out.
13. H.BR. B.III.m (TS. 50; IIA, 5.2). Small rim and upper wall segment. Fairly fine pinkish-brown ware with lime and mica grits, evenly fired. Light flesh-pink colored slip in and out.
14. H.BR. C.I.b (TS. 39; IIA, 5.18). Small rim and wall segment with patch of bitumen adhering to outside wall at point of carination. Fairly coarse pink ware with lime and mica grits, evenly fired. Self slip out.
15. H.BR. C.II.b (TS. 140; IIA, 5.2). Large rim and upper wall segment. Coarse pinkish-buff ware with lime and mica grits and chaff temper, evenly fired. Self slip in and out.
—. H.RSB. B.I.b (TS. 146; IIA, 4.14). Small rim and upper wall segment. Fairly fine pinkish-brown ware with lime and mica grits, evenly fired. Reddish-brown slip in and out, but very blackened inside.

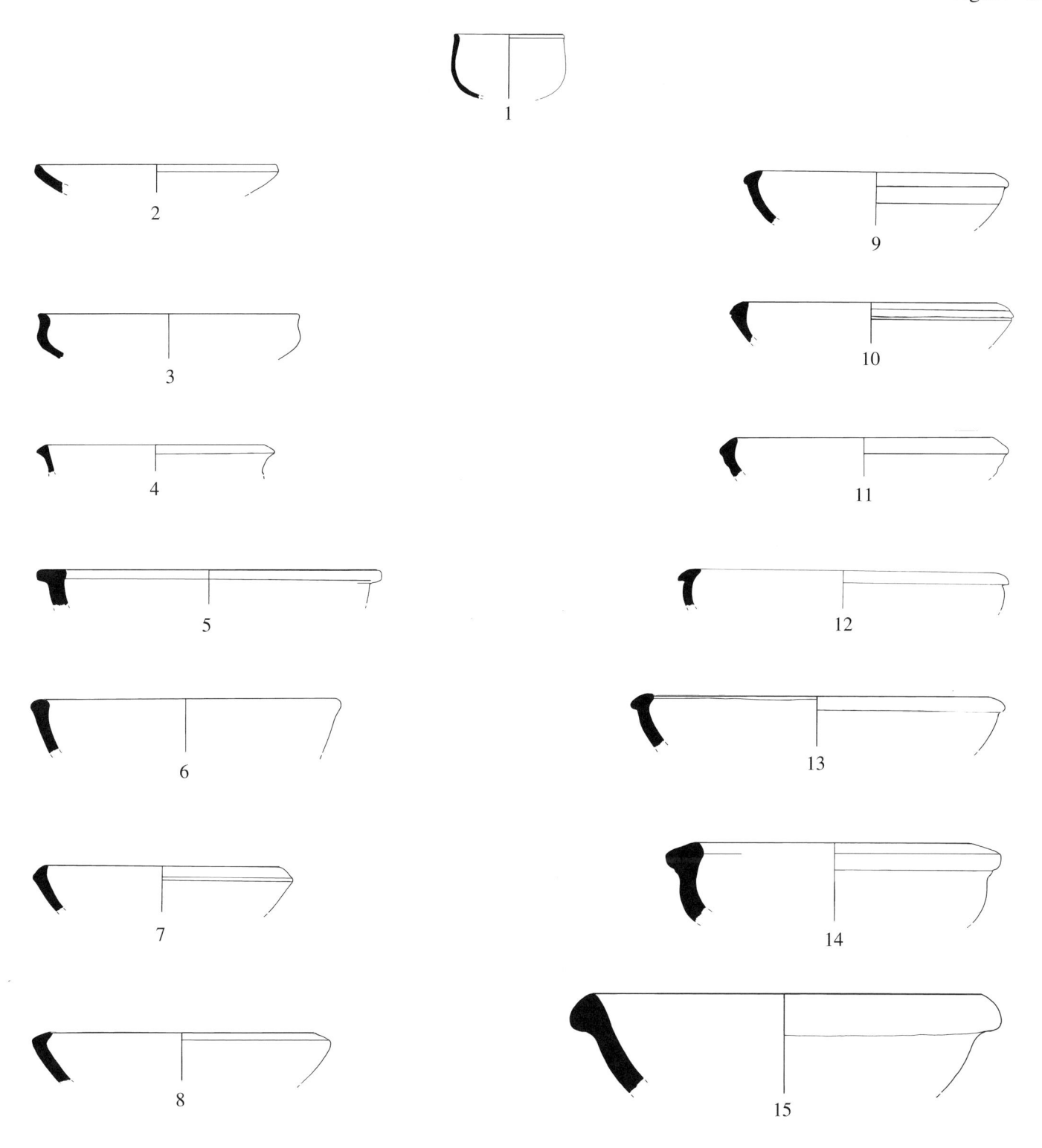

Figure 41

Pottery from Trench IIA, Pit C (Phase 12; Period C — Hellenistic). Scale 1:5

Figure 42. Pottery from Trench IIA, Pit C (Phase 12; Period C — Hellenistic)

1. H.JR. C.I.e (TS. 122; IIA, 5.3). Small rim, neck, and upper shoulder segment. Fairly close, hard, buff ware with gold-colored mica and lime grits, evenly fired. Buff self slip in and out.
2. H.JR. C.I.h (TS. 58; IIA, 5.6). Tureen. Small rim and shoulder segment. Slightly coarse buff ware with lime and mica grits, evenly fired. Creamy-buff slip out.
3. H.JR. C.I.h (TS. 38; IIA, 5.18). Tureen. About 1/8 rim, neck, and shoulder segment. Slightly coarse pinkish-brown ware with lime and mica grits, evenly fired. Buff slip in and out.
4. H.JR. D.I.d (TS. 123; IIA, 5.3). Small rim and shoulder segment. Fairly fine, hard, pink ware with mica and lime grits, evenly fired. Creamy-buff slip in and out.
5. H.JR. D.II.a (TS. 117; IIA, 5.6). Small rim, neck, and shoulder segment. Fairly fine pinkish-buff ware with lime and gold-colored mica grits, evenly fired. Creamy-buff slip out.
6. H.JR. D.II.b (TS. 43; IIA, 5.18). Small rim, neck, and shoulder segment. Slightly coarse buff ware with lime and mica grits, evenly fired. Creamy-buff slip in and out.
7. H.JR. D.II.b (TS. 134; IIA, 5.2). Small rim and neck segment. Fairly fine buff ware with lime grits, evenly fired. Buff slip out.
8. H.JR. E.III.a (TS. 57; IIA, 5.14). Fairly large rim, neck, and upper shoulder segment. Slightly coarse light brown ware with lime and mica grits, evenly fired. Creamy-buff slip in and out.
9. H.JR. E.III.a (TS. 104; IIA, 5.6). Small rim, neck, and upper shoulder segment. Coarse pinkish-brown ware with lime and mica grits, evenly fired. Greenish-buff slip in and out.
10. H.JR. E.III.a (TS. 243; IIA, 5.2). About 1/6 rim, neck, and shoulder segment. Dark pink ware with lime and mica grits, evenly fired. Cream slip in and out.
11. H.JR. E.IV.a. (TS. 132; IIA, 5.2). Jar shoulder sherd with about 1/2 of one extant vertical loop handle. Hard, fairly fine pinkish-buff ware with lime and mica grits, evenly fired.
12. H.JR. G.II.b (TS. 73; IIA, 5.18). "Dinos." Small rim and upper shoulder fragment. Fairly fine buff ware with lime and mica grits, evenly fired. Self slip in and out.
13. H.JR. G.II.b (TS. 105; IIA, 5.6). "Dinos." Small rim and upper shoulder segment. Fairly fine reddish-brown ware with lime and gold-colored mica grits, evenly fired. Dark buff slip in and out.
14. H.JR. G.II.b (TS. 153; IIA, 4.14). "Dinos." Small rim and shoulder segment. Slightly coarse buff ware with fine mica grits, evenly fired. Self slip in and out.
15. H.JR. G.II.b (TS. 3013; IIA, 4.14). Small rim and upper shoulder segment with scar just below the rim for attachment of a vertical loop handle. Slightly coarse buff ware, evenly fired. Self slip in and out.
16. H.Jg. A.I.b (TS. 115; IIA, 5.6). Small rim and neck segment. Fairly fine, soft, light brown ware with fine lime and mica grits, evenly fired. Self slip out.
—. H.Jg. B.II.a (TS. 144; IIA, 4.14, 5.2). About 1/3 rim and neck joined from two segments. Fairly fine buff ware with lime and mica grits, evenly fired. Self slip in and out.
17. H.Jg. B.II.b (TS. 102; IIA, 5.6). Small rim and neck segment with part of one vertical strap handle extant. Fine brown ware with lime and gold-colored mica grits, evenly fired. Dark buff slip in and out.
18. H.Jg. B.II.b (TS. 133; IIA, 5.2). Small rim and neck segment with possible remains of attachment of one vertical loop handle extant. Hard, fine pinkish-brown ware with lime and mica grits, evenly fired. Self slip out.
19. H.St.J. B.I.a (TS. 255; IIA, 5.2). Small rim and upper neck segment. Fairly fine buff ware with lime and mica grits, evenly fired. Self slip out.
20. H.St.J. B.II.c (TS. 241; IIA, 5.2). About 1/6 rim and neck segment. Fairly fine pinkish-buff ware with lime and mica grits, evenly fired. Buff slip out.
21. H.St.J. B.II.h (TS. 112 = TS. 246; IIA, 5.6 + 5.2). Small rim and neck segment. Slight coarse, soft, pinkish-orange ware with lime and gold-colored mica grits, evenly fired. Bitumen-like substance adhering to inside wall.
22. H.St.J. B.II.h (TS. 143 = TS. 1343; IIA, 4.14). Two joining rim and neck segments, about 1/4 of rim. Fairly fine buff ware with lime and mica grits, evenly fired. Self slip in and out.
23. H.St.J. B.II.k (TS. 107; IIA, 5.6). Small rim and upper neck segment. Slightly coarse pinkish-buff ware with lime and silver-colored mica grits, evenly fired. Creamy-buff slip out and just over the rim in.
24. H.CP. B.II.i (TS. 248; IIA, 5.2). See also pl. 278:9. Small rim and upper neck segment. Slightly coarse pinkish-brown ware with lime and mica grits, evenly fired.
25. H.ABS. C (TS. 129; IIA, 5.3). Jar wall sherd with remains of two applied bands with vertical and diagonally incised lines of decoration.

Other Hellenistic Type Series Examples: (1) H.BR. A.III.a (TS. 101), (2) H.BR. A.IV.c (TS. 100), (3) H.BR. B.I.e (TS. 235), (4) H.BR. B.I.g (TS. 113), (5) H.BR. B.III.a (TS. 111), (6) H.BR. B.III.c (TS. 131), (7) H.BR. B.III.h (TS. 135), (8) H.BR. B.III.i (TS. 1992), (9) H.BR. B.III.n (TS. 145), (10) H.BR. C.II.c (TS. 45), (11) H.BR. C.II.d (TS. 41), (12) H.BR. C.II.g (TS. 99), (13) H.BGB. A.I.b (TS. 239), (14) H.SJR. B.I.a (TS. 247), (15) H.JR. D.II.a (TS. 251), (16) H.JR. F.I.b (TS. 40), (17) H.Jg. B.II.a (TS. 144), (18) H.Jg. B.II.c (TS. 154), (19) H.Jg. B.II.d (TS. 152), (20) H.St.J. B.II.b (TS. 254), (21) H.CP. B.II.a (TS. 48), (22) H.CP. D.I.c (TS. 139), (23) H.Bt. Sp. (TS. 108), (24) H.ABS. A (TS. 237), (25) H.ABS. B (TS. 114).

Other Hellenistic Study Collection Examples: (1) H.BR. B.III.j (SC. 2834), (2) H.BR. B.III.j (SC. 2835), (3) H.BR. C.II.a (SC. 2843), (4) H.BR. C.II.d (SC. 2847), (5) H.RSB. B.II.c (SC. 2864), (6) H.RSB. C.I.a (SC. 2855), (7) H.JR. A.I.c (SC. 1189), (8) H.JR. C.I.c (SC. 2727), (9) H.JR. E.I.a (SC. 2750), (10) H.JR. E.I.b (SC. 1988), (11) H.JR. E.I.c (SC. 2803), (12) H.JR. F.II.d (SC. 1713), (13) H.JR. G.II.b (SC. 2756), (14) H.Jg. B.II.a (SC. 2757), (15) H.Jg. B.II.a (SC. 2767), (16) H.Jg. B.II.a (SC. 2766), (17) H.Jg. B.II.b (SC. 2773), (18) H.Jg. B.III.c (SC. 2779), (19) H.St.J. A.II.a (SC. 2720), (20) H.St.J. A.II.a (SC. 2721), (21) H.St.J. B.I.a (SC. 2682), (22) H.BE. A.II.a (SC. 3112), (23) H.BE. B.I.b (SC. 3238), (24) H.Hd. (SC. 3277), (25) H.SR. (SC. 3292), (26) H.BR. Sh. (IP [G.4] D.I; SC. 3252), (27) H.WPS. B (SC. 3071).

Figure 42

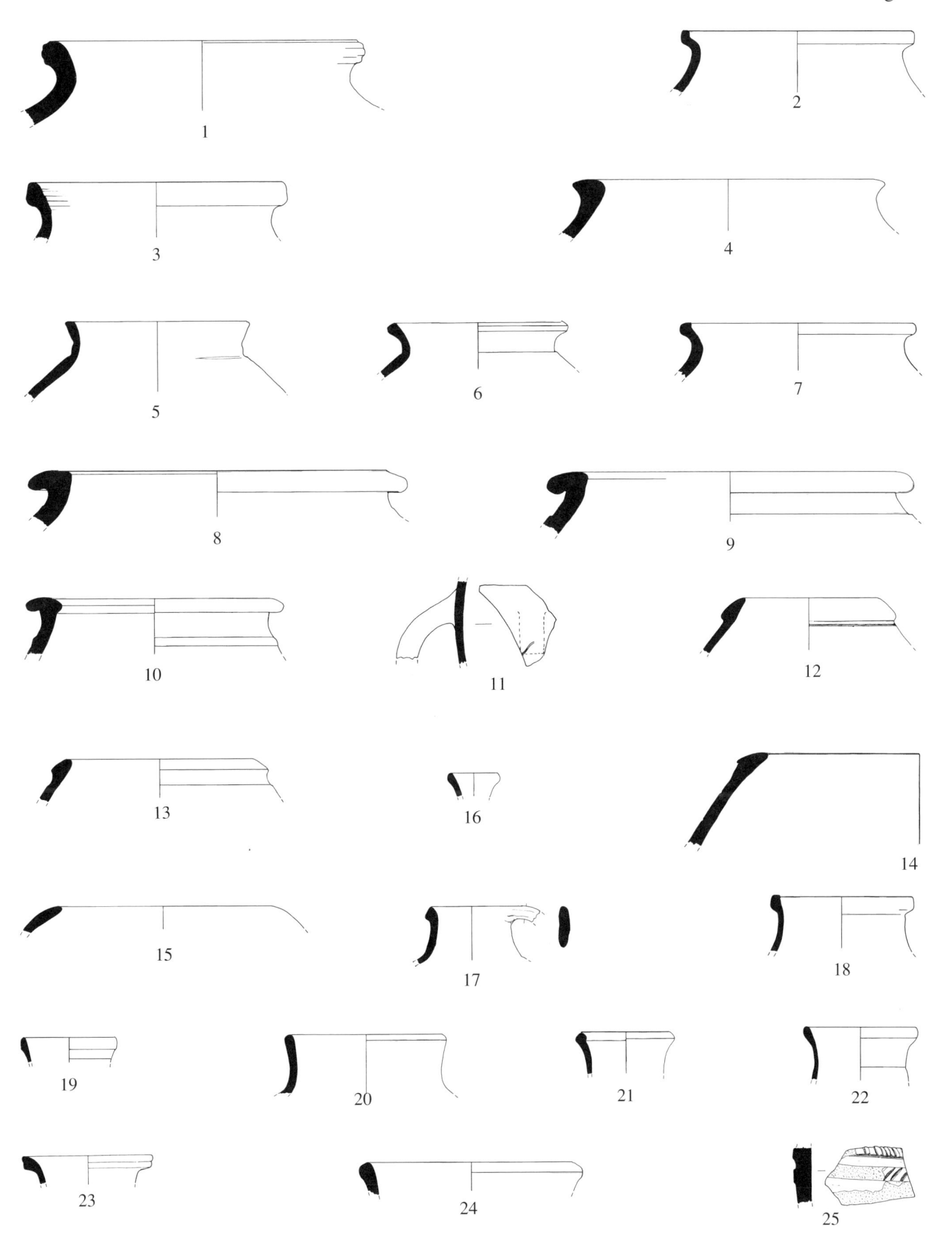

Pottery from Trench IIA, Pit C (Phase 12; Period C — Hellenistic) (*cont.*). Scale 1:5

Figure 43

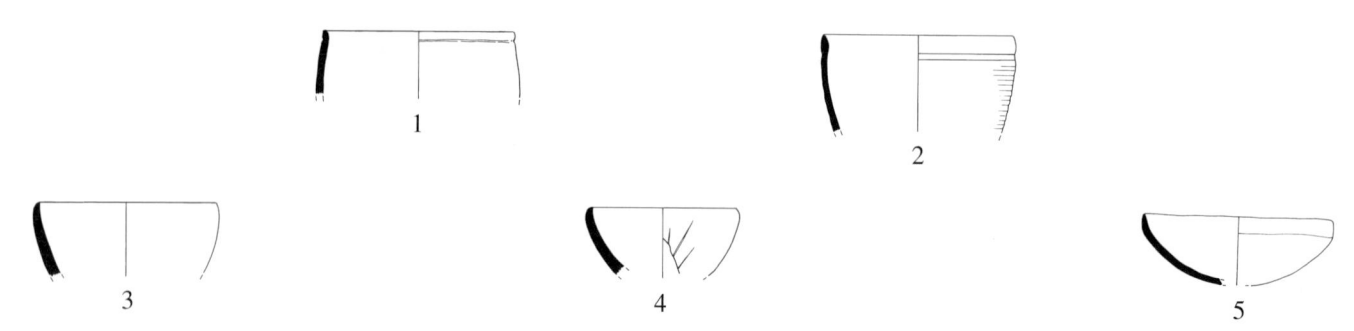

Pottery from Trench IIA, Pit C (Phase 12; Period C — Derived Early Bronze Age). Scale 1:5

1. SBR. B.I.d (TS. 65; IIA, 5.6). Small rim and upper wall segment. Slightly coarse pinkish-buff ware with mica and lime grits, evenly fired. Self slip in and out.
2. SBR. B.I.j (TS. 2518; IIA, 5.6). About 1/5 rim and most of wall profile. Slightly coarse yellow-green ware, evenly fired. Self slip in and out.
3. SBR. C.II.a (TS. 69; IIA, 5.18). Small rim and upper wall segment. Fairly fine grayish-buff ware with fine mica and lime grits, evenly fired. Greenish-buff slip in and out.
4. SBR. C.IV.a (PM. D.19; TS. 52; IIA, 5.6). Small rim and most of wall profile with remains of a tree or wheat stalk potter's mark incised on the outer wall before firing.
5. SBR. C.IV.a (TS. 242; IIA, 5.2). Small rim and most of wall profile. Slightly coarse pinkish-buff ware with lime and mica grits, evenly fired. Creamy-buff slip in and out.

Other EBA Study Collection Examples: (1) SBR. A.I.a (SC. 2781), (2) SBR. A.I.b (SC. 2787), (3) SBR. C.II.a (SC. 682), (4) BR. G.I.d (SC. 823), (5) JR. B.III.f (SC. 950), (6) JR. C.III.a (SC. 1007), (7) JR. D.V.a (SC. 1076), (8) JR. F.I.c (SC. 1196), (9) JR. J.IV.b (SC. 2373), (10) JR. K.I.d (SC. 2396), (11) JR. K.I.d (SC. 2395), (12) JR. P.II.c (SC. 1722), (13) CP. A.II.b (SC. 1801), (14) CP. A.III.b (SC. 1811), (15) CP. A.III.b (SC. 1810).

Figure 44. Pottery from Trenches IIA and IIB (Phase 13; Period C — Hellenistic)

1. H.SBR. A.II.a (TS. 141; IIA, 4.13). Small rim segment and most of wall profile. Slightly coarse pinkish-buff ware with lime and mica grits, evenly fired Self slip in and out.
2. H.BR. A.III.c (TS. 150; IIA, 4.15). Small rim and upper wall segment. Fairly fine pinkish-buff ware with lime and mica grits, evenly fired. Creamy-buff slip in and out.
3. H.BR. A.IV.b (TS. 284; IIA, 4.9). Small rim and upper wall segment. Fairly fine pink ware with lime and mica grits, evenly fired. Creamy-buff slip out.
4. H.BR. A.V.a (TS. 191; IIA, 4.12). Small rim, upper wall, and portion of lower wall segment. Fairly fine pinkish-red ware, evenly fired. Pink slip out.
5. H.BR. B.I.b (TS. 155; IIA, 4.13). Small rim and upper wall segment. Coarse green ware with many lime and mica grits, evenly fired. Self slip in and out.
6. H.BR. B.III.k (TS. 280; IIA, 4.9). Large rim and upper wall segment. Coarse ware with lime and mica grits, with gray core, unevenly fired pinkish-brown at surfaces. Very worn self slip in and out.
7. H.BR. B.III.k (TS. 282; IIA, 4.9). Large rim and upper wall segment. Fairly fine grayish-buff ware with lime and mica grits, unevenly fired pink at surfaces. Pinkish-buff slip in and out.
8. H.RSB. B.II.b (TS. 3032; IIA, 5.12). Small rim and upper wall segment. Fine brown ware, evenly fired. Red slip in and out.
9. H.RSB. C.II.a (TS. 3031; IIA, 5.1). Four joining rim segments making nearly complete diameter. Fairly fine brown ware, evenly fired. Reddish-brown slip in and out to carination on body.
10. H.RSB. D.II.d (TS. 244; IIA, 5.1). Small rim and upper wall segment. Fairly fine buff ware with lime and mica grits, evenly fired. Self slip in and out.
11. H.RSB. D.II.d (TS. 1546; IIB, 6.8, Wall B). Small rim and large portion of wall segment. Fairly soft light brown ware with fine lime and mica grits, evenly fired. Red slip in and out.
12. H.JR. A.II.d (TS. 188; IIA, 4.12). Small rim, neck, and upper shoulder segment. Fairly fine light brown ware with lime and mica grits, unevenly fired pinkish-brown at surfaces.
13. H.JR. D.I.b (TS. 273; IIA, 4.9). Small rim, neck, and shoulder segment. Fairly fine pinkish-buff ware with lime and mica grits, evenly fired. Self slip in and out.
14. H.JR. D.II.a (TS. 183; IIA, 4.9). Small rim, neck and shoulder segment. Fairly fine light tannish-buff ware with lime and mica grits, evenly fired. Creamy-tan slip out.
15. H.JR. D.II.b (TS. 2537; IIA, 4.9). About 1/8 rim and neck segment. Slightly coarse light greenish-buff ware, evenly fired. Creamy-green slip in and out.

16. H.JR. D.II.c (TS. 277; IIA, 4.9). Small rim and shoulder segment. Fairly fine light pink ware with lime and mica grits, evenly fired. Pinkish-buff slip in and out.
17. H.JR. F.I.b (H.ABS. C; TS. 182; IIA, 4.11). Small rim and upper wall segment decorated with a thickened band of clay below the rim which is incised with "stabbed" impressions. Coarse brown ware with lime and mica grits, evenly fired. Self slip out.
18. H.JR. G.II.b (TS. 270; IIA, 4.9). "Dinos." Small rim segment with a portion of one vertical loop handle extant. Fairly fine pinkish-buff ware with lime and mica grits, evenly fired. Creamy-buff slip out.

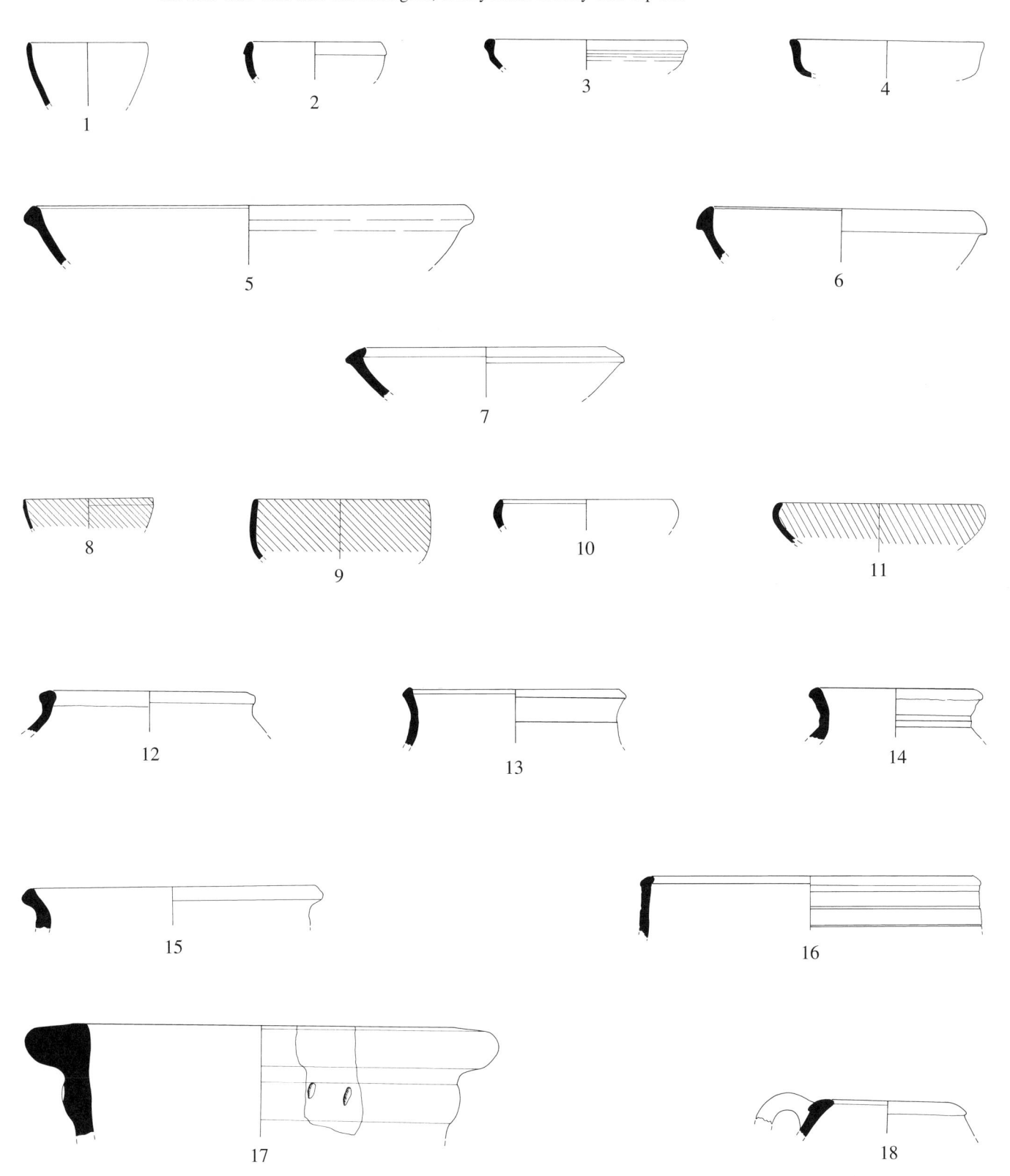

Pottery from Trenches IIA and IIB (Phase 13; Period C — Hellenistic). Scale 1:5

Figure 45. Pottery from Trenches IIA and IIB (Phase 13; Period C — Hellenistic [*cont.*] and Derived Early–Middle Bronze Age)

1. H.Jg. A.I.a (TS. 285; IIA, 4.9). Small rim and neck segment. Fine pink ware with lime and mica grits, evenly fired. Self slip in and out.
2. H.Jg. A.II.a (TS. 195; IIA, 5.1). About 1/4 rim and neck segment. Fine salmon-pink ware with lime and mica grits, evenly fired. Pinkish-buff slip out.
3. H.Jg. A.II.a (TS. 149; IIA, 4.15). About 1/3 rim and neck segment. Fine light pink ware with lime and mica grits, evenly fired. Light creamy-pink slip out.
4. H.Jg. B.I.a (TS. 190; IIA, 4.11). Small rim and neck segment with traces of a vertical loop handle attachment at rim and lip pinched in for pouring. Fairly fine pinkish-brown ware with lime and mica grits, evenly fired. Self slip out.
5. H.Jg. B.II.d (TS. 253; IIA, 5.1). Small rim and neck segment. Slightly coarse buff ware with lime and mica grits, evenly fired. Self slip out.
6. H.St.J. B.II.d (TS. 187; IIA, 4.9). Small rim and shoulder segment. Slightly coarse pinkish-buff ware with lime and mica grits, evenly fired. Creamy-buff slip out.
7. H.St.J. B.II.i (TS. 250; IIA, 1.13). About 1/4 rim, neck, and shoulder segment. Fairly fine pinkish-buff ware with lime and mica grits, evenly fired. Cream slip in and out.
8. H.BE. B.II.b (TS. 3085; IIA, 5.1). About 1/2 segment. Fairly fine pink ware, evenly fired. Light gray slip in and out.
9. H.Hd. (TS. 245; IIA, 5.1). Small segment of a strap handle of unknown vessel type. Slightly coarse buff ware with lime and mica grits, evenly fired.
10. H.Lp. (TS. 192; IIA, 4.9). Small segment of lip of lamp.
11. JR. D.V.e (TS. 275; IIA, 4.9). Derived Early–Middle Bronze Age. Small rim and upper shoulder segment. Slightly coarse buff ware with lime and mica grits, unevenly fired pinkish at surfaces. Yellow-buff slip out and just below lip of rim in.
12. CP. B.I.g (TS. 283; IIA, 4.9). Derived Early–Middle Bronze Age. Small rim and shoulder segment with triangular-shaped ledge handle attached to rim. Coarse light brown ware with many lime and mica grits, evenly fired. Wet-smoothed and horizontally burnished on outside surface.

—. H.JR.Sh. (SF. 10; Greek Ostracon; SW. 196; IIB, 6.8, Wall B). See fig. 51:15 and pl. 132a.

Other Hellenistic Type Series Examples:
  Area IIA — (1) H.SBR. A.II.a (TS. 1985), (2) H.BR. A.III.b (TS. 240), (3) H.BR. A.V.b (SW. 124), (4) H.BR. A.V.c (TS. 1990), (5) H.BR. B.I.a (TS. 18), H.BR. B.I.c (TS. 249), (6) H.RSB. C.II.a (TS. 1569), (7) H.RSB. D.II.e (SW. 116), (8) H.BGB. A.I.a (TS. 21), (9) H.BGB. B.I.d (TS. 6), (10) H.SJR. A.II.c (TS. 1539), (11) H.JR. A.I.d (TS. 238), (12) H.JR. A.II.b (TS. 274), (13) H.JR. A.II.e (TS. 142), (14) H.JR. B.I.a (TS. 148), (15) H.JR. D.I.e (TS. 184), (16) H.JR. D.I.g (TS. 180), (17) H.JR. D.II.b (TS. 1998), (18) H.JR. D.II.c (TS. 181), (19) H.Jg. B.II.a (TS. 272), (20) H.St.J. A.II.e (TS. 151), (21) H.CP. D.I.a (TS. 281), (22) H.CP. D.I.b (TS. 189), (23) H.Bt. 2 (SC. 3341), (24) H.Ld. 6 (SW. 174), (25) H.Ld. 2 (TS. 1542), (26) H.Ld. 1 (TS. 1543), (27) H.Ld. 5 (SW. 183), (28) H.Ld. 4 (TS. 1989), (29) H.Lp. 1 (SW. 122), (30) H.ABS. C (TS. 1253).
  Area IIB — (1) H.JR. A.II.d (TS. 1547).

Other Hellenistic Study Collection Examples:
  Area IIA — (1) H.BR. A.II.a (SC. 2810), (2) H.BR. A.V.c (SC. 2825), (3) H.BR. C.I.a (SC. 2846), (4) H.BR. C.II.a (SC. 2845), (5) H.BR. (not typed, SC. 147), (6) H.RSB. B.II.b (SC. 2852), (7) H.RSB. B.II.c (SC. 2863), (8) H.RSB. B.II.c (SC. 2869), (9) H.RSB. B.II.c (SC. 2871), (10) H.RSB. B.II.c (SC. 2868), (11) H.RSB. B.II.c (SC. 2861), (12) H.RSB. C.II.c (SC. 2865), (13) H.RSB. D.I.b (SC. 2877), (14) H.RSB. D.I.b (SC. 2878), (15) H.RSB. D.II.c (SC. 2889), (16) H.RSB. D.II.c (SC. 2888), (17) H.RSB. D.II.d (SC. 2897), (18) H.St.J. A.I.a (SC. 2664), (19) H.St.J. B.I.a (SC. 2612), (20) H.St.J. B.II.q (SC. 2719), (21) H.BE. C.I (SC. 3140), (22) H.PS.1 (SC. 2743), (23) H.ABS. B (SC. 3288).
  Area IIB — (1) H.JR. A.I.c (SC. 2130), (2) H.JR. A.I.e (SC. 2657); (3) H.JR. C.I.a (SC. 1724), (4) H.JR. C.I.f (SC. 2738).

Derived Early–Middle Bronze Age Incised Pottery Sherds:
  Area IIA — (1) JR.Sh. (IP [G.1] G.I.a; TS. 194; see fig. 153:2), (2) JR.Sh. (IP [G.1] B.II.a; TS. 2006, see fig. 153:3).

Derived Early–Middle Bronze Age Study Collection Examples:
  Area IIA — (1) SBR. B.I.d (SC. 285), (2) SBR. C.III.a (SC. 699), (3) SJR. B.I.c (SC. 2502), (4) JR. C.II.a (SC. 1001), (5) JR. C.V.d (SC. 1022), (6) JR. D.V.a (SC. 1069), (7) JR. D.V.b (SC. 1080), (8) JR. F.I.c (SC. 1201), (9) JR. J.I.b (SC. 2092), (10) JR. J.II.g (SC. 2146), (11) JR. J.III.t (SC. 2357), (12) JR. O.I.i (SC. 1621), (13) JR. O.II.d (SC. 1633), (14) JR. P.III.c (SC. 2465), (15) SJR.Sh. (PM. D.17; SC. 3264; see fig. 333:16).

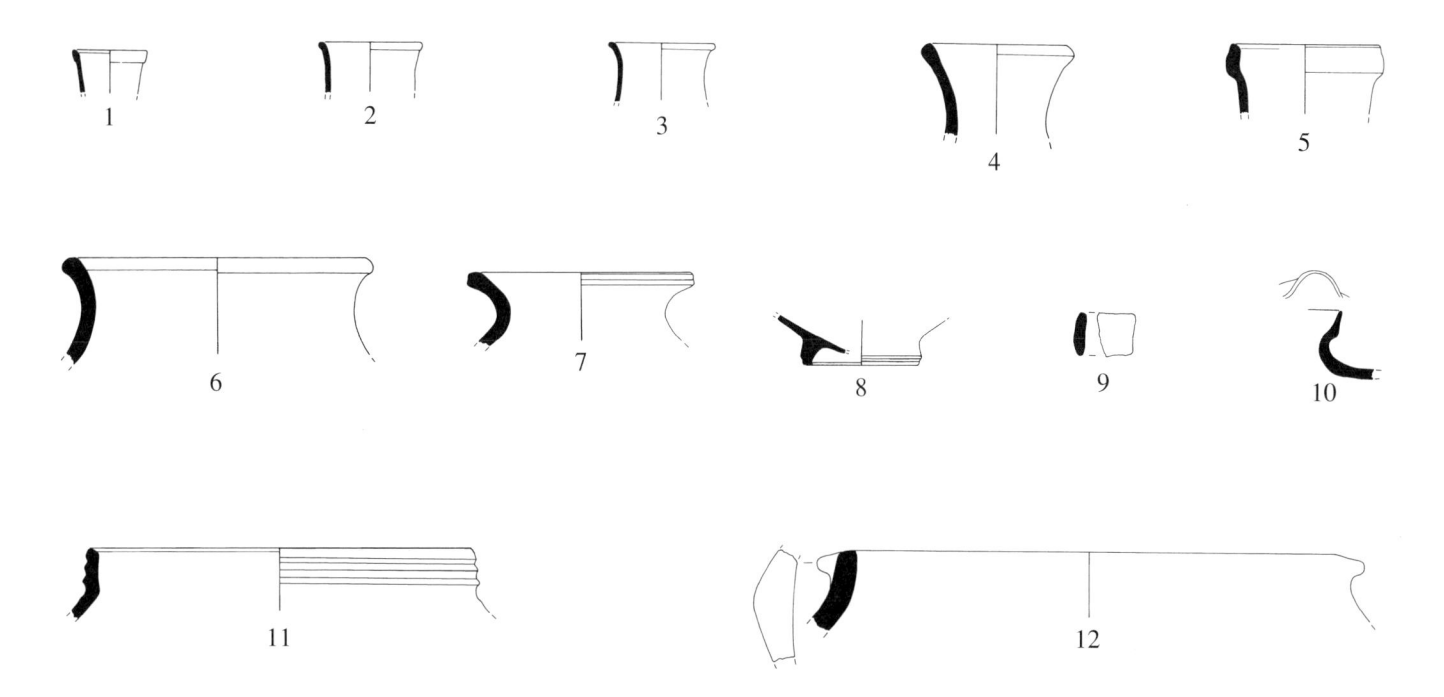

Figure 45

Pottery from Trenches IIA and IIB (Phase 13; Period C — Hellenistic [*cont.*] and Derived Early Bronze–Middle Bronze Age). Scale 1:5

Figure 46. Pottery from Trenches IIA and IIB (Phase 14; Period C — Hellenistic)

1. H.SBR. B.I.b (TS. 230; IIB, 6.5). Small rim and upper wall segment. Slightly coarse buff ware with lime grits, evenly fired. Self slip in and out.
2. H.BR. A.I.b (TS. 225; IIB, 6.5). Small rim and upper wall segment. Slightly coarse buff brown ware with lime and mica grits, evenly fired. Self slip in and out.
3. H.BR. A.III.c (TS. 232; IIB, 6.5). Small rim and upper wall segment. Fairly coarse pinkish-buff ware with lime and mica grits, evenly fired. Creamy-buff slip out.
4. H.BR. B.I.d (TS. 1470 = TS. 1480; IIA, 4.1). Two large joining rim and upper wall segments. Fairly close pinkish-buff ware with fine lime and mica grits, evenly fired. Smooth Self slip in and out.
5. H.BR. B.I.f (TS. 1482; IIA, 4.1). Small rim and upper wall segment. Hard, close pinkish-buff ware with fine lime and mica grits, evenly fired. Buff slip in and out.
6. H.BR. B.II.a (TS. 1478; IIA, 4.1). Small rim and upper wall segment. Slightly coarse pinkish-buff ware with lime and mica grits, evenly fired.
7. H.BR. B.III.i (TS. 279; IIA, 4.1). Small rim and upper wall segment. Slightly coarse pinkish-buff ware with lime and mica grits, evenly fired. Self slip in and out.
8. H.BR. B.III.i (TS. 1472; IIA, 4.1). Small rim and upper wall segment. Fairly close pinkish-buff ware with mica grits, evenly fired. Creamy-buff slip in and out.
9. H.BR. B.III.j (TS. 1476; IIA, 4.1). Small rim and upper wall segment. Fairly close pink ware, evenly fired. Self slip in and out.
10. H.BR. B.III.k (TS. 258; IIA, 1.10). Small rim and upper wall segment. Fairly fine buff ware with lime and mica grits, evenly fired. Self slip in and out.
11. H.BR. B.V.c (TS. 263; IIA, 1.10). Small rim and upper wall segment. Slightly coarse buff ware with lime and mica grits, evenly fired. Self slip in and out.
12. H.BR. C.II.a (TS. 269; IIA, 1.10). About 1/8 rim and upper wall segment with suspension hole drilled through wall before firing. Coarse buff-tan ware with lime, mica, and organic temper, evenly fired. Self slip in and out.
13. H.BR. C.II.a (TS. 28; IIB, 6.2). About 1/12 rim and upper wall segment. Fairly coarse pinkish-buff ware with lime and mica grits and chaff temper, evenly fired. Self slip in and out, very worn.
14. H.RSB. A.II.c (TS. 1571; IIA, 4.1). Large rim segment and most of wall profile. Close, dark buff ware with fine lime and mica grits, evenly fired. Reddish-brown slip in and out.
15. H.RSB. B.II.c (TS. 267; IIA, 1.10). Small rim and upper wall segment. Fine light brownish-buff ware with lime grits, evenly fired. Red slip in and out.
16. H.RSB. C.I.a (SW. 125; IIA, 4.1, 4.9). Two joining segments forming about 1/2 rim and wall of vessel. Fine, well levigated brown clay with a little mineral temper. Band of reddish-brown slip around inside and outside of rim with drips running down both sides.
17. H.RSB. C.I.a (TS. 257; IIB, 6.7). Small rim and upper wall segment. Fairly fine light brown ware with lime and mica grits, evenly fired. Reddish-brown slip fired black below rim in and out.
18. H.RSB. D.I.a (TS. 1485; IIA, 4.1). Small rim and upper wall segment. Fine pink ware, evenly fired. Red slip applied to rim in and out.
19. H.RSB. D.II.a (TS. 332; IIA, 1.8, Oven). Small rim and upper wall segment. Pinkish-buff ware, evenly fired. Reddish-brown slip around rim in and out.
20. H.RSB. D.II.a (TS. 1487; IIA, 4.1). Small rim and upper wall segment. Close pink ware with fine lime and mica grits, evenly fired. Red slip in and out.
21. H.RSB. D.II.c (SW. 128b = SC. 2886; IIA, 4.1, 4.9, 4.11 5.1). Two joining rim segments and five non-joining body sherds. Buff ware with reddish-brown slip in and around rim out with drips onto lower wall.
22. H.RSB. D.II.d (TS. 266; IIA, 1.10). Small rim and upper wall segment. Fairly fine light brown ware with lime grits, evenly fired. Red slip in and out.
23. H.RSB. D.II.d (TS. 227; IIB, 6.7). Small rim and upper wall segment. Soft, fine pink ware with lime and mica grits, evenly fired. Blackened grayish-red slip in and out.

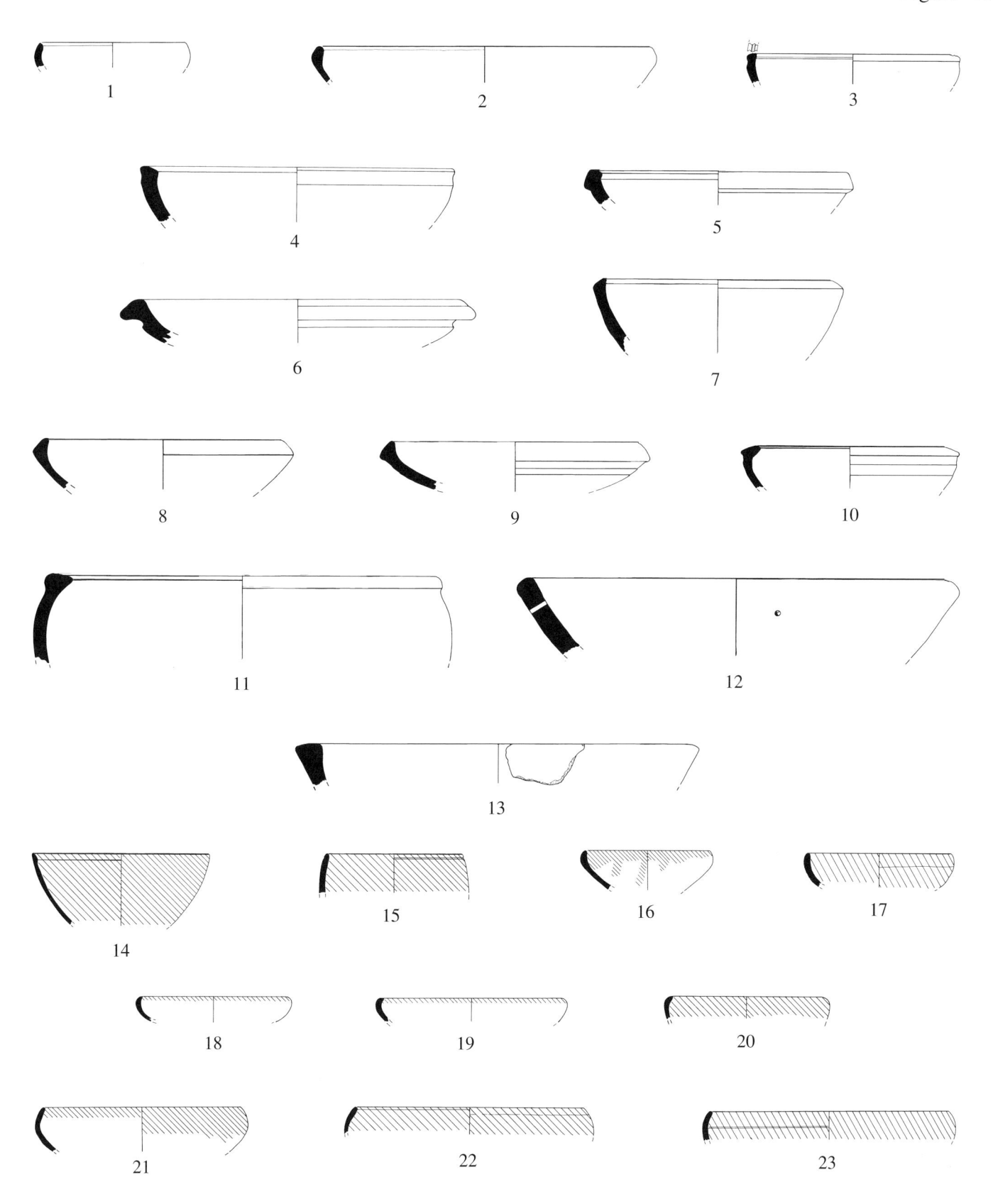

Figure 46

Pottery from Trenches IIA and IIB (Phase 14; Period C — Hellenistic). Scale 1:5.

Figure 47: Pottery from Trenches IIA and IIB (Phase 14; Period C — Hellenistic) (*cont.*)

1. H.JR. A.II.e (TS. 221; IIB, 6.5). Small rim and upper shoulder segment. Coarse greenish-grayware with lime and mica grits, evenly fired. Self slip out.
2. H.JR. A.II.f (TS. 186; IIA, 4.8). Small rim and shoulder segment. Slightly coarse grayish-buff ware, evenly fired. Self slip out.
3. H.JR. C.I.c (TS. 341; IIA, 1.8). Small rim and neck segment. Fine buff ware evenly fired.
4. H.JR. C.I.i (TS. 1479; IIA, 4.1). Small rim and shoulder segment. Slightly coarse buff ware with lime and mica grits, evenly fired. Self slip in and out.
5. H.JR. D.I.b (TS. 2235; IIB, 6.7). Small rim and upper neck segment with possible remains of a spout or mending hole at bottom edge of the preserved portion of the neck. Fairly fine pinkish-buff ware with lime and mica grits, evenly fired. Creamy-buff slip out and on top of rim.
6. H.JR. D.II.b (TS. 260; IIA, 1.10). Small rim and neck segment. Fairly fine pinkish-buff ware with lime and mica grits, evenly fired. Self slip out.
7. H.Jg. B.I.b (TS. 264; IIA, 1.10). About 1/4 rim and neck segment. Slightly coarse buff ware with lime and mica grits, evenly fired. Self slip in and out.
8. H.St.J. B.I.d (TS. 204; IIA, 4.6). Small rim and neck segment. Fairly fine buff ware with lime and mica grits, evenly fired. Creamy-buff slip in and out.
9. H.St.J. B.I.d (TS. 1486; IIA, 4.1). Small rim and shoulder segment. Fairly close pinkish-buff ware, evenly fired. Creamy-buff slip out.
10. H.St.J. B.I.d (TS. 1448; IIA, 1.5, 1.6, 1.7, Enclosure). Fairly large rim and neck segment. Fairly close pinkish-buff ware with lime and mica grits, evenly fired. Self slip in and out.
11. H.St.J. B.I.d (TS. 35 = TS. 185; IIA, 5.20, 4.10, Pit A). About 1/5 rim, neck, and upper shoulder segment. Fine pinkish-brown ware with micaceous temper, evenly fired. Creamy-buff slip out.
12. H.St.J. B.I.i (TS. 352; IIA, 1.12). Small rim and neck segment. Fine pinkish-buff ware, evenly fired.
13. H.St.J. B.II.d (TS. 1473; IIA, 4.1). Small rim and neck segment. Hard, fairly close pinkish-buff ware with fine mica grits, evenly fired. Creamy-buff slip in and out.
14. H.St.J. B.II.h (TS. 223; IIB, 6.7). About 1/4 rim and neck segment. Fairly coarse, friable pinkish-brown ware with lime and mica grits, evenly fired. Buff slip out.
15. H.St.J. B.II.i (TS. 1453; IIA, 1.12). Small rim and neck segment. Fairly close pinkish-buff ware with lime and mica grits, evenly fired. Creamy-buff slip in and out.
16. H.St.J. B.II.j (TS. 1471; IIA, 4.1). Small rim and neck segment. Fairly close pinkish-buff ware with lime and mica grits, evenly fired. Self slip in and out.
17. H.CP. A.I.a (TS. 1423; IIA, 1.5, 1.6, 1.7, Enclosure). Three small joining rim segments. Fairly fine reddish-brown ware, evenly fired.
18. H.CP. B.I.a (TS. 265; IIA, 1.10). Small rim and shoulder segment. Coarse light brown ware with mineral temper, evenly fired. Charred outside.
19. H.CP. B.II.a (TS. 328; IIA, 1.8, Oven). Small rim and neck segment. Pinkish-brown ware, evenly fired. Self slip in and out.
20. H.CP. D.I.b (TS. 271; IIA, 4.4). Small rim and upper wall segment with remains of one wide loop handle. Coarse grayish-brown ware with lime and mica grits, evenly fired.
21. H.BE. B.II.b (TS. 541; IIA, 1.8, Oven). Complete base and lower half of jar body. Fine pinkish-buff ware with mineral temper, evenly fired.
22. H.BE. B.III.b (TS. 3044; IIA, 1.10). Complete base with drainage hole manufactured in center of base before firing. Fine pink ware, evenly fired. Creamy-tan slip out.
23. H.ABS. A (TS. 1227; IIA, 1.8, Oven). Jar body sherd with two stranded rope bands applied to outside wall. Very hard, slightly coarse ware, unevenly fired buff on inside surface. Grayish-buff slip out.
24. H.ABS. B (TS. 1228; IIA, 1.8, Oven). Jar body sherd with wide applied band decorated with X-shaped incisions. Slightly coarse pink ware, evenly fired. Buff slip out.
25. H.ABS. C (TS. 1229; IIA, 1.10). Jar body sherd with applied rope-like band on the outside wall. Slightly coarse grayish-buff ware, evenly fired. Creamy-buff slip out.
26. H.JR.Sh. (PM. D.22; TS. 1247; IIA, 4.1). Jar body sherd with remains of a potter's mark on the outside wall. Slightly coarse pinkish-buff ware, evenly fired. Self slip out.
27. H.JR.Sh. (IP [G.4] G.I.a; TS. 2013; IIB, 6.6, Floor). Jar body sherd with incised decoration. Fairly fine pinkish-buff ware with lime and mica grits, evenly fired. Creamy-buff slip out.

Other Hellenistic Type Series Examples:
Area IIA — (1) H.SBR. A.I.a (TS. 1484), (2) H.SBR. B.I.b (TS. 335), (3) H.BR. A.II.b (TS. 1475), (4) H.BR. A.IV.b (TS. 259), (5) H.BR. B.IV.d (TS. 3029), (6) H.RSB. A.II.a (SW. 126), (7) H.RSB. E.II.b (TS. 1418), (8) H.RSB. E.II.c (TS. 327), (9) H.JR. A.II.c (TS. 1474), (10) H.JR. C.I.f (TS. 268), (11) H.JR. D.I.b (TS. 359), (12) H.St.J. B.I.g (TS. 337), (13) H.St.J. B.II.a (TS. 1477), (14) H.St.J. B.II.f (TS. 331), (15) H.CP. A.I.a (TS. 261).

Area IIB — (1) H.BR. B.III.j (TS. 208), (2) H.BR. B.III.m (TS. 222), (3) H.RSB. B.II.b (TS. 256), (4) H.RSB. E.I.b (TS. 200), (5) H.BGB. B.I.b (TS. 229), (6) H.JR. A.I.a (TS. 209), (7) H.JR. C.I.c (TS. 110), (8) H.JR. D.I.c (TS. 196), (9) H.JR. D.I.f (TS. 98 = TS. 362), (10) H.JR. D.III.c (TS. 234), (11) H.JR. F.II.a (SC. 1619), (12) H.JR. G.II.b (TS. 199), (13) H.Jg. B.I.d (TS. 231), (14) H.Jg. B.III.b (TS. 214), (15) H.St.J. B.I.a (TS. 198), (16) H.St.J. B.II.i (TS. 197), (17) H.CP. B.I.a (TS. 228), (18) H.BE. C.I (TS. 1393), (19) H.BE. D.I.b (SC. 3348), (20) H.BE. E.I.a (TS. 1393), (21) H.BE. E.I.c (SC. 3147), (22) H.Hd. 1 (TS. 103), (23) H.ABS. D (TS. 97).

Hellenistic Incised Pottery Sherd: Area IIA — (1) H.JR.Sh. (IP [G.4] G.I.a; TS. 2012, see fig. 153:4).

Other Hellenistic Study Collection Examples:
Area IIA — (1) H.BR. B.I.d (SC. 2829), (2) H.RSB. D.I.b (SC. 2879), (3) H.RSB. D.II.c (SC. 2886 = SW. 128b), (4) H.RSB. D.II.d (SC. 2904), (5) H.Jg. B.I.d (SC. 1920), (6) H.Jg. B.II.a (SC. 2763), (7) H.Jg. B.II.b (SC. 2758), (8) H.Jg. B.II.d (SC. 2643), (9) H.St.J. B.II.d (SC. 2702), (10) H.St.J. B.II.d (SC. 2703), (11) H.St.J. B.II.f (SC. 2708), (12) H.St.J. B.II.i (SC. 2714), (13) H.St.J. B.II.k (SC. 2717), (14) H.St.J. B.II.l (SC. 2718), (15) H.CP. A.I.a (SC. 1818), (16) H.CP. B.I.a (SC. 3067), (17) H.BE. B.I.b (SC. 3171), (18) H.BE. B.I.b (SC. 3213), (19) H.BE. B.II.b (SC. 3164), (20) H.BE. B.II.c (SC. 3195 = SW. 128d), (21) H.PS.1 (SC. 1918).

Area IIB — (1) H.BR. A.III.e (SC. 2840), (2) H.BR. B.III.j (SC. 3344), (3) H.RSB. B.II.c (SC. 2870), (4) H.Jg. B.II.b (SC. 2777, with pinched pouring lip), (5) H.St.J. B.I.d (SC. 2701), (6) H.St.J. B.II.n (SC. 984), (7) H.WPS. (SC. 3072).

Figure 47

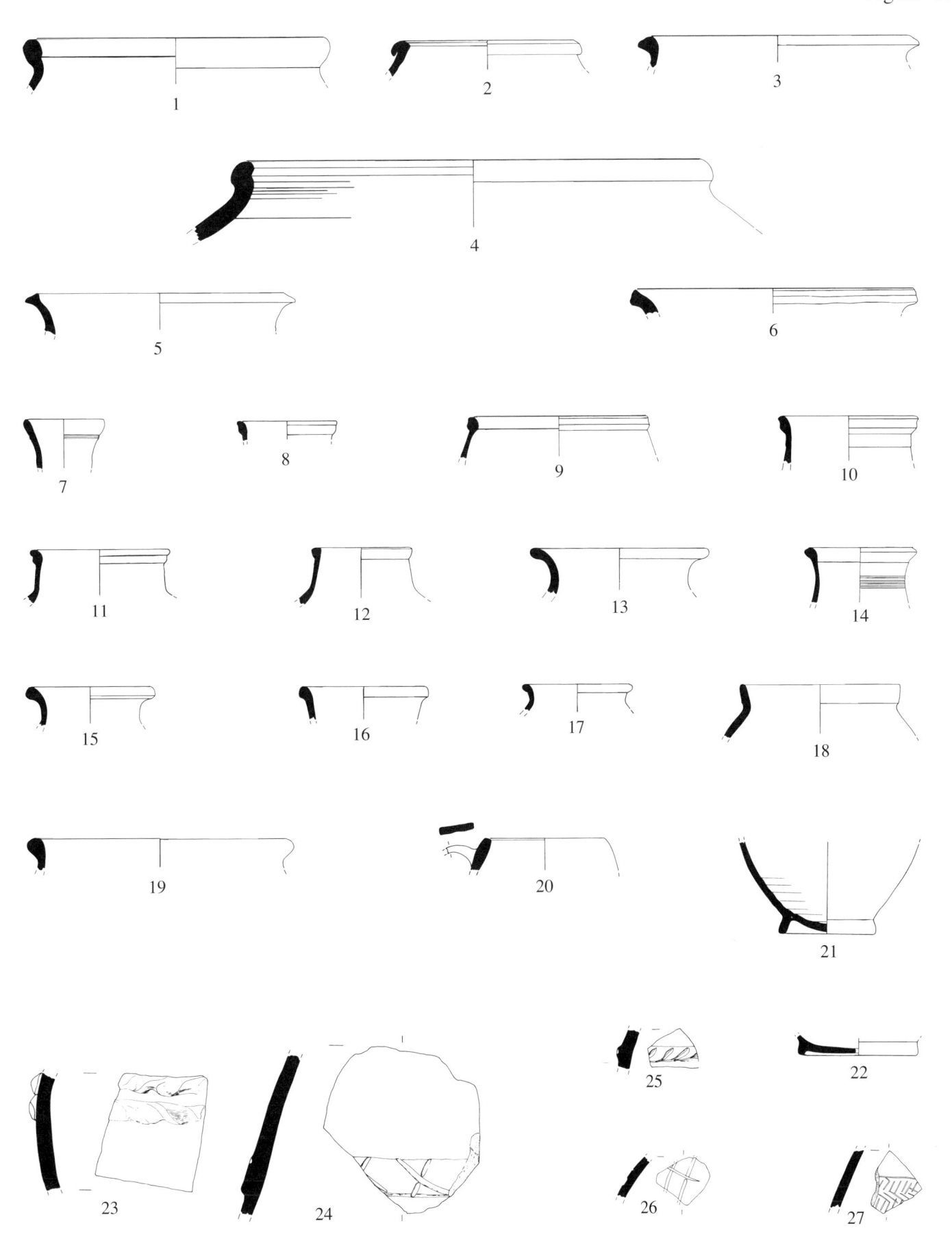

Pottery from Trenches IIA and IIB (Phase 14; Period C — Hellenistic) (*cont.*). Scale 1:5

Figure 48

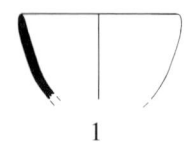

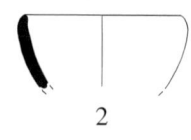

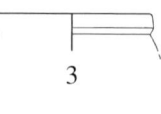

1  2  3

Figure 48. Pottery from Trench IIA (Phase 14; Period C — Derived Early Bronze Age). Scale 1:5

1. SBR. C.II.b (TS. 1481; IIA, 4.1). Small rim and most of wall profile. Fairly close buff ware with fine mica grits, evenly fired. Creamy-buff slip out.
2. SBR. C.IV.a (TS. 1483; IIA, 4.1). Small rim and upper wall segment. Fairly close buff ware, evenly fired. Self slip in and out.
3. SBR. D.I.b (TS. 350; IIA, 1.11). Small rim and shoulder segment. Fine pinkish-buff ware, evenly fired. Cream slip out.

Figure 49. Pottery from Trenches IIA and IIB (Phase 15; Period C — Hellenistic)

1. H.BR. A.III.d (TS. 348; IIA, 1.1). Small rim and upper wall segment. Fine pinkish-buff ware, evenly fired.
2. H.BR. A.IV.c (TS. 347; IIA, 1.1). Small rim and upper wall segment. Fairly fine pinkish-buff ware, evenly fired. Burnished on top of rim and on outside wall.
3. H.BR. A.IV.c (TS. 382; IIA, 1.1). Small rim and upper wall segment. Pinkish-brown ware, evenly fired. Self slip in and out.
4. H.BR. B.I.a (TS. 364; IIB, 2.3). Small rim and upper wall segment. Hard, pinkish-buff ware, evenly fired. Creamy-buff slip in and out.
5. H.BR. B.I.b (TS. 1406; IIB, 2.1). Small rim and upper wall segment. Fine pinkish-buff ware with small mica grits, evenly fired. Creamy-buff slip out.
6. H.BR. B.I.f (SC. 2841; IIB, 2.3). About 1/12 rim and upper wall segment. Fairly fine pinkish-buff ware with very fine gold- and silver-colored mica grits, evenly fired. Light self slip in and out.
7. H.BR. B.I.f (TS. 1409; IIB, 2.1). Small rim segment. Hard, grayish-buff ware with lime and mica grits, evenly fired. Buff slip in and out.
8. H.BR. B.I.f (TS. 1447; IIB, 2.4). Large rim and upper wall segment. Fairly fine pinkish-buff ware with lime and mica grits, evenly fired. Surfaces very worn.
9. H.BR. B.III.e (TS. 384; IIA, 1.1). Small rim and upper wall segment. Fine grayish-buff ware, evenly fired.
10. H.BR. B.III.f (TS. 1451; IIA, 1.2). Small rim and upper wall segment with probable suspension hole drilled through upper wall before firing. Fairly close pinkish-buff ware with lime and mica grits, evenly fired. Self slip on top of rim and outside.
11. H.BR. B.III.i (TS. 1530; IIA, 1.2). Small rim and upper wall segment. Fairly close buff ware with fine lime and mica grits, evenly fired. Self slip in and out.
12. H.BR. B.III.j (TS. 373; IIA, 1.1). Small rim and upper wall segment. Fairly coarse pinkish-buff ware, evenly fired. Self slip in and out.
13. H.BR. B.III.j (TS. 1532; IIA, 1.2). Small rim and upper wall segment. Close pinkish-buff ware with fine lime and mica grits, evenly fired. Buff slip in and out.
14. H.BR. B.III.l (TS. 1408; IIB, 2.1). Small rim and upper wall segment. Hard, fine buff ware with fine mica grits, evenly fired. Surfaces worn.
15. H.BR. B.III.m (TS. 374; IIA, 1.1). Small rim and upper wall segment. Fairly fine pinkish-buff ware, evenly fired. Creamy-buff slip in and out.
16. H.BR. B.III.m (TS. 383; IIB, 3.1). Large rim and upper wall segment. Fine pinkish-brown ware, evenly fired. Self slip in and out.
17. H.RSB. A.I.b (TS. 1459; IIB, 2.4). Small rim and wall segment. Fine buff ware with very fine lime and mica grits, evenly fired. Reddish-brown slip out and just over rim in.
18. H.RSB. A.II.b (TS. 360; IIB, 2.1). Small rim segment. Slightly coarse reddish-brown ware, evenly fired. Red slip in and out, burnished on outside wall.
19. H.RSB. A.II.c (TS. 276 = TS. 1467 and 1488; IIA, 1.8, 1.10; 1.2; 4.1). Three joining rim and upper wall segments. Close pink ware with fine lime and mica grits, evenly fired. Red slip in and out.
20. H.RSB. B.II.c (TS. 367; IIB, 2.3). Small rim and upper wall segment (ca. 12 cm diameter). Fine pinkish-brown ware, evenly fired. Red slip in and out.
21. H.RSB. B.II.c (TS. 1446; IIB, 2.12). Small rim and upper wall segment (ca. 13 cm diameter). Fairly fine pinkish ware, evenly fired. Slip worn off of inner and outer surfaces.
22. H.RSB. B.II.c (TS. 1415; IIB, 2.1). Small rim and upper wall segment. Fine light brown ware with mica grits, evenly fired. Red slip in and out.
23. H.RSB. C.I.a (TS. 365; IIB, 2.3). Small rim and upper wall segment. Fine grayware, evenly fired. Red slip fired black on inside and around outside of the rim.
24. H.RSB. C.I.a (TS. 339; IIB, 2.11). Small rim and upper wall segment. Fine light brown ware, evenly fired. Red slip in and out fired black around outside of the rim.
25. H.RSB. C.I.a (TS. 1401; IIB, 2.1). Small rim and upper wall segment. Fine light brown ware with mica grits, evenly fired. Red slip in and out.
26. H.RSB. C.I.a (TS. 1445; IIB, 2.12). Small rim and upper wall segment. Fine light pink ware with gold-colored mica grits, evenly fired. Red slip in and out.
27. H.RSB. C.II.b (TS. 1425; IIB, 2.12). Large rim and wall segment. Fairly fine light brown ware with very fine lime and mica grits, overly fired; outside burnt green with bubbled surface. Plain red slip in and out.
28. H.RSB. D.II.a (TS. 334; IIB, 2.2, Oven). Small rim and large segment of wall. Brown ware, evenly fired. Red slip in and out, fired black below rim inside and on all of outer surface.
29. H.RSB. D.II.c (TS. 1456; IIA, 1.2). Small rim and upper wall segment. Fairly fine pink ware, evenly fired. Red slip in and out.
30. H.RSB. D.II.d (TS. 1404; IIB, 2.1). Small rim and upper wall segment. Fine light brown ware with mica grits, evenly fired. Red slip worn off in and out.

Figure 49

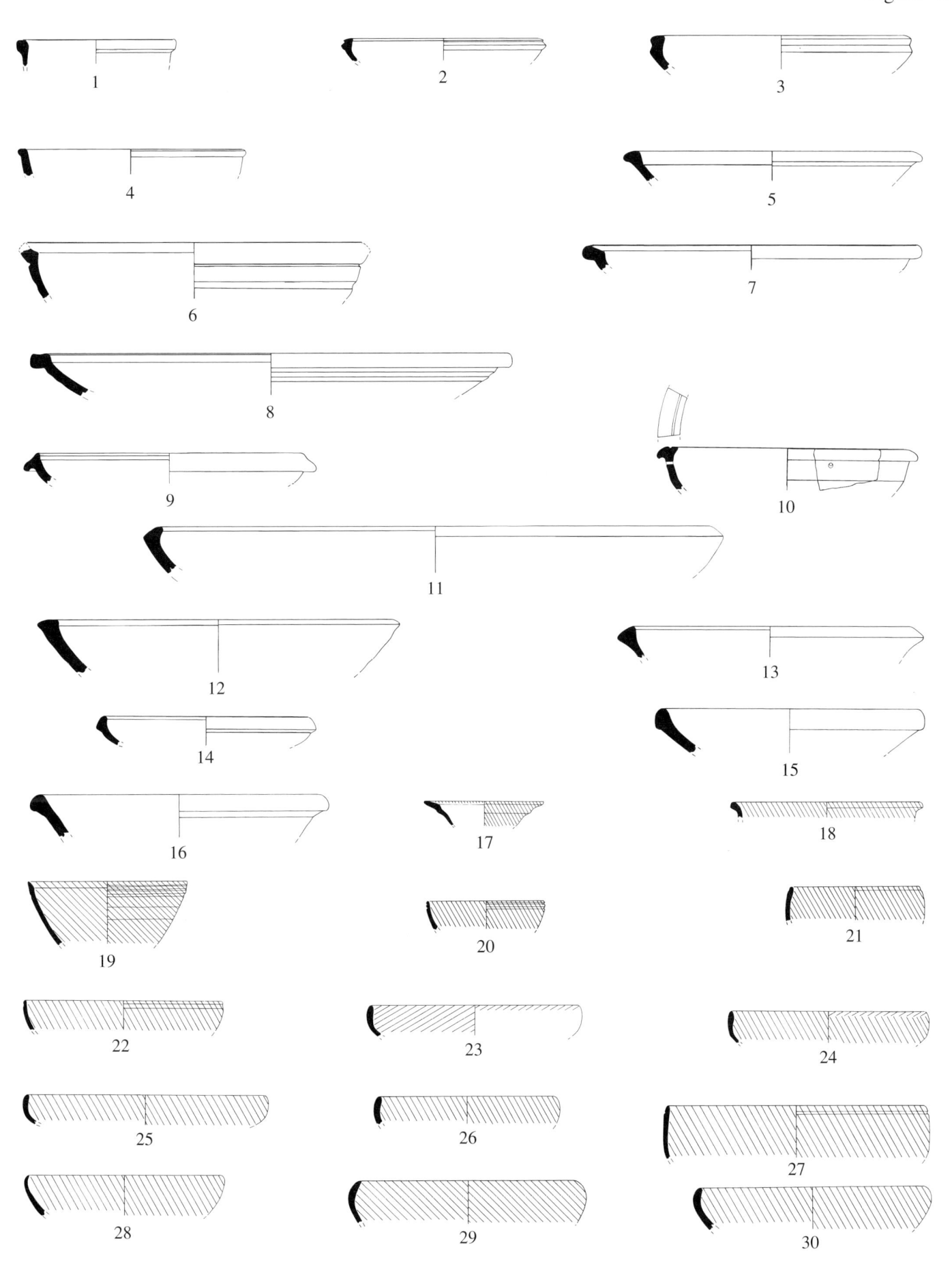

Pottery from Trenches IIA and IIB (Phase 15; Period C — Hellenistic). Scale 1:5

Figure 50. Pottery from Trenches IIA and IIB (Phase 15; Period C — Hellenistic) (*cont.*)

1. H.SJR. A.II.f (TS. 1468; IIA, 1.2). Small rim and upper neck segment. Slightly coarse ware with lime and mica grits, with gray core, unevenly fired reddish-brown at surfaces. Self slip in and out.
2. H.JR. C.I.a (TS. 1463; IIA, 1.2). Small rim and shoulder segment. Fairly coarse grayish-brown ware, evenly fired. Red slip out and over rim in.
3. H.JR. C.I.c (TS. 397; IIB, 2.1). Small rim and neck segment. Fairly fine buff ware, unevenly fired with gray core. Self buff slip in and out.
4. H.JR. E.I.a (TS. 381; IIA, 1.1). Small rim and neck segment, very worn. Fairly coarse pinkish-buff ware, evenly fired.
5. H.JR. F.II.a (SW. 14; IIA, 1.2). Small rim and neck segment with decorated band around the upper shoulder. Pinkish-buff ware with fine black mineral temper, evenly fired.
6. H.JR. F.II.b (TS. 376; IIA, 1.1). Small rim and upper shoulder segment. Fairly coarse-tempered dark buff ware, evenly fired.
7. H.JR. G.I.a (TS. 1411; IIB, 2.1). Small rim and upper shoulder segment. Fairly fine buff ware with lime and mica grits, evenly fired. Self slip in and out.
8. H.Jg. B.I.b (TS. 346; IIA, 1.1). Small rim and neck segment. Buff ware, evenly fired.
9. H.St.J. A.I.a (TS. 344; IIA, 1.1). Small rim and neck segment. Light buff ware, evenly fired.
10. H.St.J. A.I.b (TS. 1466; IIA, 1.2). Small rim and neck segment. Close buff ware, evenly fired.
11. H.St.J. A.I.e (TS. 387; IIB, 3.1). Small rim and neck segment. Fairly fine pinkish-buff ware, evenly fired. Self slip in and out.
12. H.St.J. A.I.g (TS. 379; IIA, 1.1). Small rim and neck segment. Pinkish-brown ware, evenly fired. Self slip in and out.
13. H.St.J. A.I.h (TS. 372; IIA, 1.1). Small rim and neck segment. Fairly fine light brown ware, evenly fired.
14. H.St.J. A.I.h (TS. 1413; IIB, 2.1). Small rim and neck segment. Fine pinkish-buff ware with fine lime and mica grits, evenly fired. Buff slip in and out.
15. H.St.J. A.I.m (TS. 349; IIB, 2.11). Small rim and upper neck segment. Fairly fine pinkish-buff ware, evenly fired.
16. H.St.J. A.I.m (TS. 1414 = TS. 2029; IIB, 2.1, 2.11). About 1/3 rim and upper neck segments. Fine light grayware with lime and mica grits, evenly fired. Horizontally line burnished on rim and outside wall.
17. H.St.J. B.I.b (TS. 1527; IIA, 1.2). Small rim and neck segment. Fine buff-brown ware with fine lime and mica grits, evenly fired. Light greenish-buff slip out.
—. H.St.J. B.I.g (TS. 399; IIB, 2.1) Portion of rim and upper neck segment. Brownish-buff ware evenly fired. Self slip in and out.
18. H.St.J. B.I.h (TS. 1432; IIB, 2.12). About 1/2 rim and neck segment. Hard, fairly fine greenish-grayware with fine mica grits, evenly and slightly overfired.
19. H.St.J. B.I.i (TS. 378; IIA, 1.1). Small rim and neck segment. Fine pinkish-buff ware, evenly fired.
20. H.St.J. B.I.i (TS. 385; IIA, 1.1). Small rim and neck segment. Fairly fine grayish-brown ware, evenly fired.
21. H.St.J. B.I.i (TS. 1460; IIA, 1.2). Small rim and neck segment. Fairly fine buff ware with mica grits, evenly fired.
22. H.St.J. B.I.i (TS. 1416; IIB, 2.1). Small rim and upper neck segment. Fine, light buff ware with lime and mica grits, evenly fired. Creamy-buff slip out, burnished on top of rim.
23. H.St.J. B.I.i (TS. 345; IIB, 2.2, Oven). Small rim and upper neck segment. Fairly fine buff ware, evenly fired.
24. H.St.J. B.II.c (TS. 1410; IIB, 2.1). Large rim, neck, and upper shoulder segment. Fairly fine ware with lime and mica grits, unevenly fired with gray core and pinkish-buff at surfaces. Traces of self slip out.
25. H.St.J. B.II.d (TS. 1436; IIB, 2.12). Small rim and neck segment. Fairly fine pinkish-buff ware with mica grits, evenly fired. Creamy-buff slip in and out.
26. H.St.J. B.II.g (TS. 1458; IIB, 2.4). Small rim and upper neck segment. Slightly coarse buff ware with fine lime and mica grits, evenly fired. Greenish-buff slip in and out.
—. H.St.J. B.II.g (PM. C.14; TS. 1524; IIB, 2.10). See fig. 333:4.
27. H.St.J. B.II.q (TS. 1441; IIA, 1.2). Small rim and neck segment. Fairly fine pinkish-buff ware with mica grits, evenly fired. Creamy-buff slip in and out.
28. H.CP. A.I.a (TS. 1420; IIA, 1.2). Large rim and upper wall segment with one extant vertical strap handle. Slightly coarse light brown ware with lime and mica grits, evenly fired. Self slip out.
29. H.CP. B.II.a (TS. 392; IIB, 2.1). Small rim and upper neck segment. Slightly coarse grayish-brown ware, evenly fired. Self slip in and out, very worn.
30. H.CP. B.II.a (TS. 1421; IIA, 1.2). Small rim, neck, and shoulder segment. Slightly coarse drab ware with lime and mica grits, evenly fired.
31. H.CP. E.I.b (TS. 1464; IIB, 2.4). Small rim and neck segment. Coarse grayish-brown ware with many medium lime and mica grits, evenly fired.
32. H.CP. E.I.b (TS. 391; IIB, 2.1). Large rim and neck segment. Fairly coarse and gritty light brown ware, evenly fired.
33. H.BE. A.I.a (TS. 1523; IIA, 1.1). Complete base and portion of lower wall of vessel. Fairly fine buff ware with lime and mica grits, evenly fired.
34. H.BE. A.I.b (TS. 371; IIA, 1.1). Complete base and portion of lower wall of vessel. Buff-brown ware, evenly fired.
35. H.BE. A.II.a (TS. 369; IIA, 1.1). Complete base and portion of lower wall of vessel. Buff-brown ware, evenly fired. Creamy-buff slip out.

Figure 50

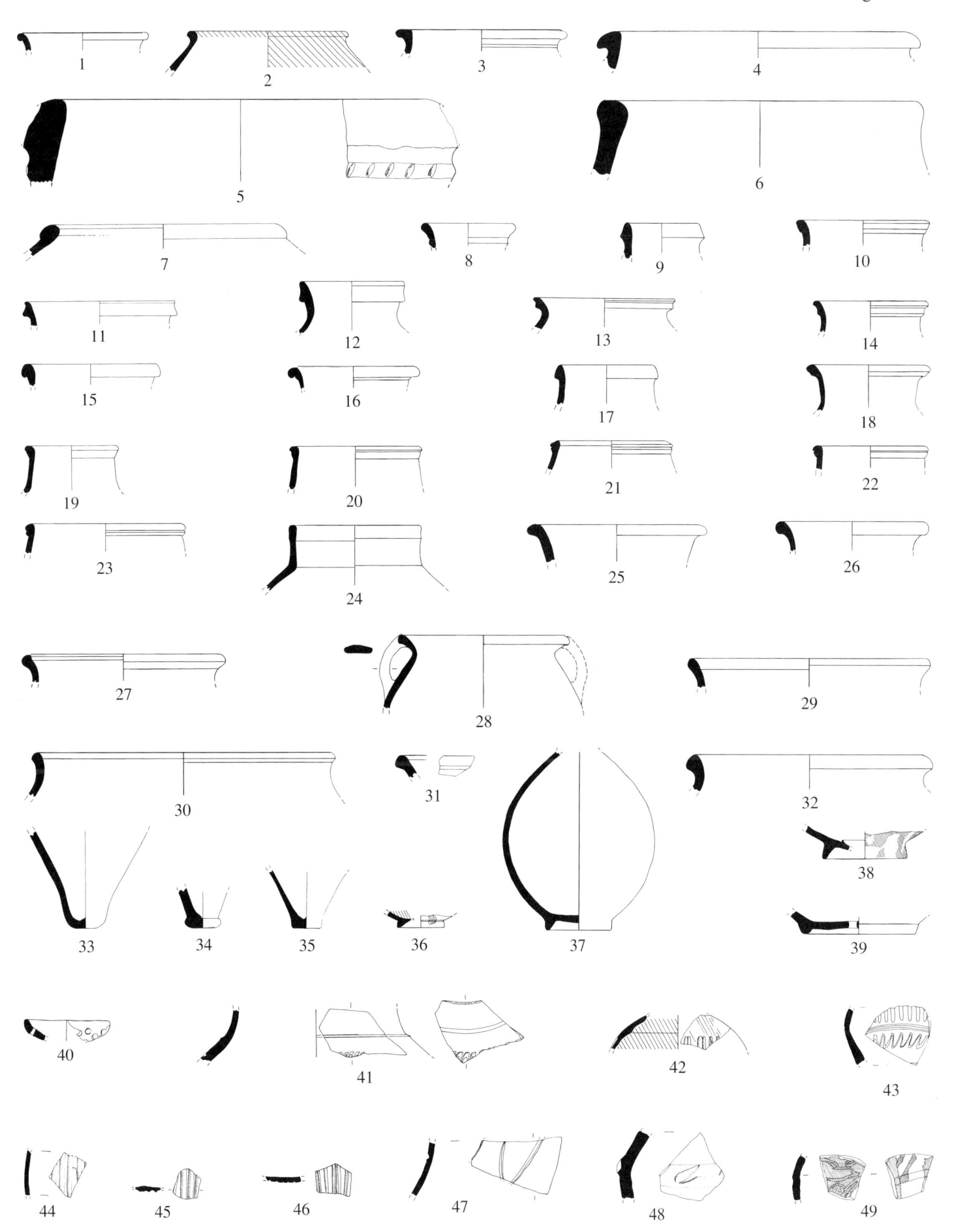

Pottery from Trenches IIA and IIB (Phase 15; Period C — Hellenistic) (*cont.*). Scale 1:5

Figure 50. Pottery from Trenches IIA and IIB (Phase 15; Period C — Hellenistic) (*cont.*)

36. H.BE. B.I.b (SC. 3211; IIB, 2.3). One half ring with fragment of lower wall attached. Fairly fine pinkish-buff ware with small lime and gold-colored mica grits, evenly fired. Remains of red slip in and red slip drip line on outside base of wall.
37. H.BE. B.II.a (SW. 130; IIA, 1.2). Complete base and most of body belonging to a jar. Fairly fine light buff ware with black- and gold-colored mineral temper, evenly fired. Greenish-buff slip out.
38. H.BE. B.II.c (TS. 3086; IIA, 1.2). About 1/5 base segment with small portion of vessel wall. Fine flesh-pink colored ware, evenly fired. Red slip in and irregularly applied outside with drip lines to bottom of the base.
39. H.BE. B.III.b (TS. 3087; IIA, 1.2). About 1/3 base segment with drainage hole manufactured slightly off-center in base before firing. Slightly coarse purple-pink ware, evenly fired.
40. H.SR. (TS. 2524; IIA, 1.1). Strainer bowl (not typed). About 1/8 rim and upper wall segment, handmade. Slightly coarse pink ware, evenly fired. Self slip in and out.
—. H.JR.Sh. (IP [G.1] C.V.a; TS. 2009, IIA, 1.2). See fig. 153:5.
—. H.Lp.1 (IP [G.4] A.I.a; TS. 353; IIB, 2.3). See pl. 340:31.
41. H.JR.Sh. (Dec.; SC. 3343; IIB, 2.1). Jar neck and upper shoulder segment with "rocker" stamp decoration outside. Slightly coarse pinkish-orange ware with many fine black lime and gold-colored mica grits, evenly fired. Creamy-pink self slip out, which was originally glazed.
42. H.JR.Sh. (Dec.; SC. 3347; IIB, 2.1). Jar shoulder and upper body sherd with remains of vertical tool-impressed decoration just below the shoulder. Hard, fairly fine pinkish-orange ware with lime and silver-colored mica grits, evenly fired. Traces of blackened red slip out and on most of inner surface.
43. H.JR.Sh. (IP [G.4] G.II.a; SW. 38; IIA, 1.1). Jar body sherd with comb-incised linear decoration and vertical tool-impressed design applied at the leather-hard stage of manufacture. Fairly fine orange ware, evenly fired.
44. H.JR.Sh. (Dec.; TS. 1225; IIB, 2.2, Oven). Jar body sherd with vertical tool-impressed decoration on outside wall. Fairly fine light grayware, evenly fired. Self slip or wash out.
45. H.JR.Sh. (Dec.; SC. 3349; IIB, 2.1). Jar body sherd with vertical tool-impressed decoration on outside wall. Fine grayish-buff ware with fine lime grits, evenly fired. Self slip in and out.
46. H.JR.Sh. (Dec.; SC. 3350; IIA, 1.2). Jar body sherd with vertical tool-impressed decoration on outside wall. Fine light creamy-pink ware with small gold-colored mica grits, unevenly fired with buff core. Vertically burnished self slip out.
47. H.JR.Sh. (IP [G.4] G.I.a; TS. 1252; IIA, 1.1). Jar shoulder fragment with remains of a design or a pot mark incised before firing. Fairly close pink ware, evenly fired. Self slip out.
—. H.JR.Sh. (IP [G.1] I.I.a; TS. 1224; IIB, 2.1). See plate 340:20.
48. H.ABS. D (TS. 1222; IIB, 2.11). Jar body sherd with decorated band around maximum girth of vessel. Fairly fine light grayish-green ware, evenly fired. Self slip in and out.
49. Isl.Sh. (SW. 24; IIB, 2.1). Derived Islamic body sherd, probably belonging to a bowl. Glazed on inside and outside surfaces; inside has a yellow background with green leaves outlined with brown; outside has drips of green and yellow glaze.

Other Type Series Examples:

Area IIA — (1) H.MBR. (SW. 143), (2) H.BR. A.III.e (TS. 1450), (3) H.BR. A.V.a (TS. 351), (4) H.BR. B.I.d (TS. 53 = TS. 370), (5) H.BR. C.II.a (TS. 1422), (6) H.RSB. B.II.a (TS. 380), (7) H.RSB. D.I.b (TS. 1469), (8) H.SJR. A.I.b (TS. 1528), (9) H.SJR. A.II.d (TS. 1461), (10) H.JR. C.I.i (TS. 1449), (11) H.JR. D.III.b (TS. 1424), (12) H.JR. E.I.a (TS. 342), (13) H.Jg. A.I.a (TS. 389), (14) H.St.J. A.I.f (TS. 1529), (15) H.BE. B.I.a (TS. 377), (16) H.PS. 2 (TS. 42 = TS. 212, 252, and IIB, TS. 363), (17) H.PS. 3 (TS. 1462).

Area IIB — (1) H.SBR. A.I.b (TS. 1417), (2) H.SBR. D.I.a (TS. 1444), (2) H.BR. A.III.d (TS. 1993), (3) H.BR. B.I.f (TS. 1465), (4) H.BR. B.III.d (TS. 1531), (5) H.BR. B.III.e (TS. 390), (6) H.BR. B.V.b (TS. 1438), (7) H.BR. C.I.b (TS. 1439), (8) H.BR. C.II.e (TS. 1525), (9) H.RSB. A.I.a (TS. 1426), (10) H.RSB. A.I.d (TS. 1442), (11) H.RSB. B.I.a (TS. 1419), (12) H.RSB. B.I.b (TS. 336), (13) H.RSB. B.II.d (TS. 394), (14) H.RSB. C.II.b (TS. 1400), (15) H.RSB. D.II.a (TS. 398), (16) H.RSB. D.II.b (TS. 333), (17) H.RSB. D.II.d (TS. 357), (18) H.RSB. E.I.a (TS. 1428), (19) H.RSJ. B.I.a (TS. 354), (20) H.RSJ. C.I.a (SC. 3346), (21) H.RSJ. C.I.a (SC. 3346), (22) H.SJR. A.I.a (TS. 308), (23) H.SJR. A.II.a (TS. 224 = TS. 388), (24) H.SJR. A.II.b (SC. 2378), (25) H.SJR. A.II.e (TS. 340), (26) H.JR. A.I.e (TS. 1452), (27) H.JR. A.II.a (SC. 2338), (28) H.JR. A.II.f (TS. 330), (29) H.JR. C.I.a (SC. 1634), (30) H.JR. C.I.b (TS. 1412), (31) H.JR. C.I.d (TS. 1430), (32) H.JR. C.I.h (TS. 1407), (33) H.JR. C.I.l (SC. 2462), (34) H.JR. D.I.a (TS. 1526 = TS. 1994), (35) H.JR. D.I.d (TS. 361), (36) H.JR. D.IV.a (SC. 2398), (37) H.JR. E.I.b (TS. 1454), (38) H.JR. F.II.e (SC. 1688), (39) H.JR. G.III.a (SC. 1261), (40) H.Jg. A.I.b (SW. 50), (41) H.Jg. B.III.a (TS. 343 = TS. 1437), (42) H.Jg. C.II.a (TS. 2028), (43) H.St.J. A.I.a (TS. 1440), (44) H.St.J. A.I.b (TS. 355), (45) H.St.J. A.I.c (TS. 329), (46) H.St.J. A.I.d (TS. 1457), (47) H.St.J. A.I.g (TS. 366), (48) H.St.J. A.I.h (TS. 1431), (49) H.St.J. A.I.m (TS. 1435), (50) H.St.J. A.II.b (TS. 1427), (51) H.St.J. A.II.d (TS. 278), (52) H.St.J. B.I.c (TS. 338), (53) H.St.J. B.I.d (TS. 1429 = TS. 2686), (54) H.St.J. B.I.i (TS. 396), (55) H.St.J. B.II.c (SW. 26), (56) H.St.J. B.II.d (TS. 1434), (57) H.St.J. B.II.g (TS. 1402), (58) H.St.J. B.II.j (TS. 1403), (59) H.CP. A.I.b (TS. 356), (60) H.CP. E.I.a (TS. 395), (61) H.CP. E.I.b (TS. 358 = TS. 386), (62) H.BE. A.I.a (TS. 455), (63) H.BE. A.II.a (TS. 1405), (64) H.BE. B.I.b (TS. 3090), (65) H.BE. B.I.c (SC. 3203), (66) H.BE. B.II.a (TS. 1223), (67) H.BE. C.I.a (SC. 3078), (68) H.BE. C.II.a (SC. 3080), (69) H.BE. D.I.a (SC. 3093), (70) H.BE. E.I.b (SC. 3135), (71) H.PS. 1 (SW. 55), (72) H.Ld. 3 (TS. 393), (73) H.ABS. E (TS. 1226).

Figure 50. Pottery from Trenches IIA and IIB (Phase 15; Period C — Hellenistic) (*cont.*)

Other Study Collection Examples:
- Area IIA — (1) H.SBR. A.II.a (SC. 2786), (2) H.SBR. A.II.a (SC. 2784), (3) H.BR. C.I.a (SC. 2926), (4) H.BR. (not typed, SC. 149), (5) H.BR. (not typed, SC. 150), (6) H.RSJ. B.I.a (SC. 2909), (7) H.JR. C.I.i (SC. 2730), (8) H.JR. D.II.a (SC. 2732), (9) H.JR. F.II.a (SC. 1628), (10) H.Jg. A.II.a (SC. 2762), (11) H.Jg. B.II.e (SC. 2775), (12) H.Jg. B.II.a (SC. 2806), (13) H.St.J. B.I.d (SC. 2692), (14) H.St.J. B.I.d (SC. 2691), (15) H.St.J. B.I.d (SC. 2690), (16) H.St.J. B.II.d (SC. 2700), (17) H.BE. B.I.b (SC. 3205), (18) H.BE. B.II.b (SC. 3206), (19) H.BE. B.II.c (SC. 3194: red slip bowl base), (20) H.ABS. B (SC. 3287).
- Area IIB — (1) H.SBR. A.II.a (SC. 2792), (2) H.BR. B.I.g (SC. 2844), (3) H.BR. B.III.i (SC. 2836), (4) H.RSB. B.II.a (SC. 2621), (5) H.RSB. B.II.b (SC. 2853), (6) H.RSB. C.I.a (SC. 2857), (7) H.RSB. C.I.a (SC. 2860), (8) H.RSB. D.I.a (SC. 2874), (9) H.RSB. D.II.a (SC. 2880), (10) H.RSB. D.II.b (SC. 2885), (11) H.RSB. D.II.c (SC. 2624), (12) H.RSB. D.II.c (SC. 2887), (13) H.RSB. D.II.d (SC. 2892), (14) H.RSB. D.II.d (SC. 2893), (15) H.RSB. D.II.d (SC. 2895), (16) H.RSB. D.II.d (SC. 2898), (17) H.RSB. D.II.d (SC. 2899), (18) H.RSB. D.II.d (SC. 2905), (19) H.RSB. D.II.e (SC. 3345), (20) H.SJR. A.II.a (SC. 2552), (21) H.JR. A.I.e (SC. 2745), (22) H.JR. C.I.h (SC. 2140), (23) H.JR. D.I.a (SC. 2735), (24) H.JR. D.I.b (SC. 1477), (25) H.JR. F.I.a (SC. 1664), (26) H.Jg. A.I.a (SC. 3058), (27) H.Jg. B.I.a (SC. 2770), (28) H.Jg. B.II.a (SC. 2790), (29) H.Jg. B.II.a (SC. 2764), (30) H.Jg. B.III.b (SC. 2761), (31) H.St.J. A.I.c (SC. 2661), (32) H.St.J. A.I.e (SC. 2672), (33) H.St.J. A.I.f (SC. 2673), (34) H.St.J. A.I.g (SC. 2674), (35) H.St.J. A.I.h (SC. 2679), (36) H.St.J. A.I.k (SC. 2942), (37) H.St.J. A.II.d (SC. 2614), (38) H.St.J. B.I.d (SC. 2688), (39) H.St.J. B.I.d (SC. 2689), (40) H.St.J. B.II.f (SC. 2707), (41) H.St.J. B.II.f (SC. 2709), (42) H.St.J. B.II.g (sc. 2711), (43) H.St.J. B.II.i (SC. 2712), (44) H.St.J. B.II.j (SC. 2715), (45) H.St.J. B.II.j (SC. 2716), (46) H.ABS. D (SC. 3290).

Other Derived EBA Study Collection Examples:
- Area IIA — (1) JR. D.V.a (SC. 1074), (2) JR. D.V.c (SC. 1093), (3) JR. D.VI.a (SC. 1105), (4) JR. H.I.g (SC. 2077), (5) SR. A.I.b (SC. 1956).
- Area IIB — (1) SBR. B.I.i (SC. 530).

Other Derived Early–Middle Bronze Age Examples:
- Area IIB — (1) JR. A.III.d (TS. 1443), (2) JR. D.VIII.a (TS. 1433), (3) JR. K.II.e (SC. 1138).

Figure 51. Miscellaneous Clay Small Finds and Greek Ostracon from Trenches IIA and IIB

1. Type SF.1a, e (SW. 178; IIA, 7.2, Pit). Phase 10 (Hellenistic; see pl. 132g). Figurine, human and animal combination. Hollow, double-molded figure of a woman astride a quadruped, possibly a camel or horse. About 1/2 portion of a central hole manufactured in the center of the back of the figure. Fine buff ware with greenish-yellow slip on all surfaces in and out.
2. Type SF.1a (SW. 142; IIB, 2.3). Phase 15 (Hellenistic). Female figurine plaque. Flat back, partially broken. Relief design in front depicts a necklace or the edge of a garment, which is positioned in a V-shape between the breasts. The breasts are shown by triangular delinations and indentations for the nipples. Fairly fine buff ware, evenly fired.
—. Type SF.1a (SW. 239; IIB, 3.1). Phase 15 (Hellenistic). Fragment of hollow-molded figure of a woman astride a quadruped, similar to SW. 178 from Phase 10 (see above). Smooth brown ware with specks of small black grits, evenly fired. Fragment with round hole in wall.
3. Type SF.1c (SW. 111; IIA, 4.11). Phase 13 (Hellenistic; see pl. 115a). Figurine, human type pillar stand with concave bell-shaped base. Fairly fine brown ware with a small amount of black lime grit temper. Light greenish-buff slip on surfaces.
4. Type SF.1c (SW. 112; IIA, 4.9). Phase 13 (Hellenistic; see pl. 115b). Figurine, human type pillar stand with traces of neck and arms extant. Friable, coarse light grayware with black and orange mineral and vegetable temper.
—. Type SF.1c (SW. 153; IIB, 6.5). Phase 14 (Hellenistic; see fig. 331:12, pl. 115i).
5. Type SF.1e (SW. 207; IIA, 8.12, Room 10). Phase 6 (EB III). Figurine, animal. Hindquarter fragment. Fairly fine buff ware with black- and silver-colored mica grits, unevenly fired with a gray core.
6. Type SF.1d (SW. 87; IIA, 4.14, Pit C). Phase 12 (Hellenistic; see pl. 115k). Figurine, dove. Head, tip of tail, and lower portion of pillar-like stand missing. Fairly fine greenish-buff ware with black mineral temper, evenly fired.
7. Type SF.1e (SW. 79; IIA, 4.14, Pit C). Phase 12 (Hellenistic; see pl. 117h). Figurine, animal. Torso fragment of a quadruped. Head, part of neck, tip of tail, and legs broken. Coarse greenish-buff ware, fairly evenly fired except for some discoloration on surface.
8. Type SF.1e (SW. 206; IIA, 4.4). Phase 14 (Hellenistic). Figurine, animal. Torso hindquarter fragment of a quadruped with tail and legs broken. Fairly fine buff ware with small black- and silver-colored mica grits, evenly fired.
9. Type SF.1d (SW. 85; IIA, 4.11). Phase 13 (Hellenistic; see pl. 115j). Figurine, animal. Head fragment of a probable ox or bull. Buff ware with black mica grits. Evenly fired.
10. Type SF.2b (SW. 215; IIA, 7.10). Phase 11 (Hellenistic). Model chariot wheel. Fairly fine brown ware with black and white lime grits and vegetable temper, unevenly fired creamy-buff at surfaces.
11. Type SF.6f (SW. 41; IIA, 1.2). Phase 15 (Hellenistic). Baton-like object, probably used as a pestle. Fine yellow ware, evenly fired.
12. Type SF.6b (SW. 210; IIA, 8.1, Pit C1). Phase 9 (Hellenistic). Spindle whorl. One half fragment. Orangish ware with small black and white grits. Cream bloom or slip on outer surfaces. Possibly reused pot sherd.
13. Type SF.6b (SW. 166; IIA, 7.2, Pit). Phase 10 (Hellenistic). Spindle whorl. Reused pot sherd. Buff ware with black mineral temper. Light greenish-yellow slip on both inner and outer surfaces.
—. Type SF.6e (SC. 154; IIA, 9.9, Room 1). Phase 1 (EB I) Tool, disk shaped. Reused pot sherd.
14. Type SF.6e (SW. 37; IIA, 1.2). Phase 15 (Hellenistic). Tool, disk shaped. Reused pot sherd. Coarse buff ware with mineral temper.
15. Type SF.10 (SW. 196; IIB, 6.8; Wall B). Phase 13 (Hellenistic). Jar shoulder sherd with Greek name Daras painted in black on the outside wall (see pl. 132a and Benoit 1976, p. 66, pl. 8:B). Slightly coarse pink ware with a white bloom and lime and mica grits, evenly fired.
16. Type SV.5 (SW. 172; IIA, 5.18, Pit C). Phase 12 (Hellenistic). Lid, disk shape. Fine polished buff ware with mineral temper, evenly fired.

Figure 51

Miscellaneous Clay Small Finds and Greek Ostracon from Trenches IIA and IIB. Scale 1:2

Figure 52. Miscellaneous Small Finds of Various Materials from Trench IIA

1. Type SF.5i (SW. 231; IIA, 5.6, Pit C). Phase 12 (Hellenistic). Iron pin or nail fragments. Heavily corroded.
2. Type SF.5c (SW. 170; IIA, 5.18, Pit C). Phase 12 (Hellenistic). Copper or bronze fibula. Complete except for attachment pin.
—. Type SF.5i (SW. 98; IIA, 4.14, Pit C). Phase 12 (Hellenistic). Iron fragment, unidentifiable. Measurments: 1.0 × 2.5 × 2.5 cm.
3. Type SF.5i (SW. 133; IIA, 5.1). Phase 13 (Hellenistic). Iron nail. Square-shaped head and shaft. Tip of shaft broken.
—. Type SF.5i (SW. 99; IIA, 4.10, Pit A). Phase 14 (Hellenistic). Iron. Blunt at one end and tapered at the other end. Measurements: length, 3.0 cm; width at maximum point, 3.5 cm, from blunt end, 2.0 cm.
—. Type SF.5c (SW. 117; IIB, 2.12). Phase 15 (Hellenistic; see fig. 331:24). Metal pin (not analyzed).
—. Type SF.5h (SW. 43; IIB, 2.1). Phase 15 (Hellenistic)(see fig. 332:6). Iron implement (not analyzed).
4. Type SF.9a (SW. 243; IIA, 8.1, Pit C1). Phase 9 (Hellenistic). Bone pin or needle. Complete. Well-incised decorative grooves and highly polished surface.
5. Type SF.11b (SW. 5; IIA, 1.2). Phase 15 (Hellenistic). Shell pendant. One half of a bivalve pierced at hinged side for stringing. Cream color with brown-colored markings.
6. Type SF.7a (SW. 96; IIA, 4.1). Phase 14 (Hellenistic). Glass handle fragment. Light colored green. Spiral-twisted shape.
7. Type SF.6g (SW. 228; IIA, 8.17, Room 12). Phase 6 (EB III). Clay ring fragment. Hard-fired grayware.
8. Type SF.3b (TS. 3152; IIA, 7.2, Pit). Phase 10 (Hellenistic). Sling stone. Limestone.
9. Type SF.3a (SW. 114; IIA, 4.8). Phase 14 (Hellenistic). Granite whetstone(?) fragment. Buff color. Highly polished surface.
10. Type SF.4a (SW. 187; IIA, 7.2, Pit). Phase 10 (Hellenistic). Greenstone amulet fragment. Very smooth with possible working marks on surface.
11. Type SF.6c (SW. 195; IIA, 7.1, Pit). Phase 10 (Hellenistic). Unbaked clay loom weight. One half extant.
12–14. Type SF.6c (SW. 191; IIA, 7.1, Pit). Phase 10 (Hellenistic). Three unbaked clay loom weights. Slightly coarse clay with pieces of charcoal, vegetable matter, and grits. Holes pierced vetically while the clay was wet.
15. Type SF.6c (SW. 341; IIA, 7.2, Pit). Phase 10 (Hellenistic). Unbaked clay loom weight. About one half segment. Blackish-brown ware with mineral grits.
16–21. Type SF.6c (TS. 3153 a–f; IIA, 7.2, Pit). Phase 10 (Hellenistic). Six unbaked clay loom weights.

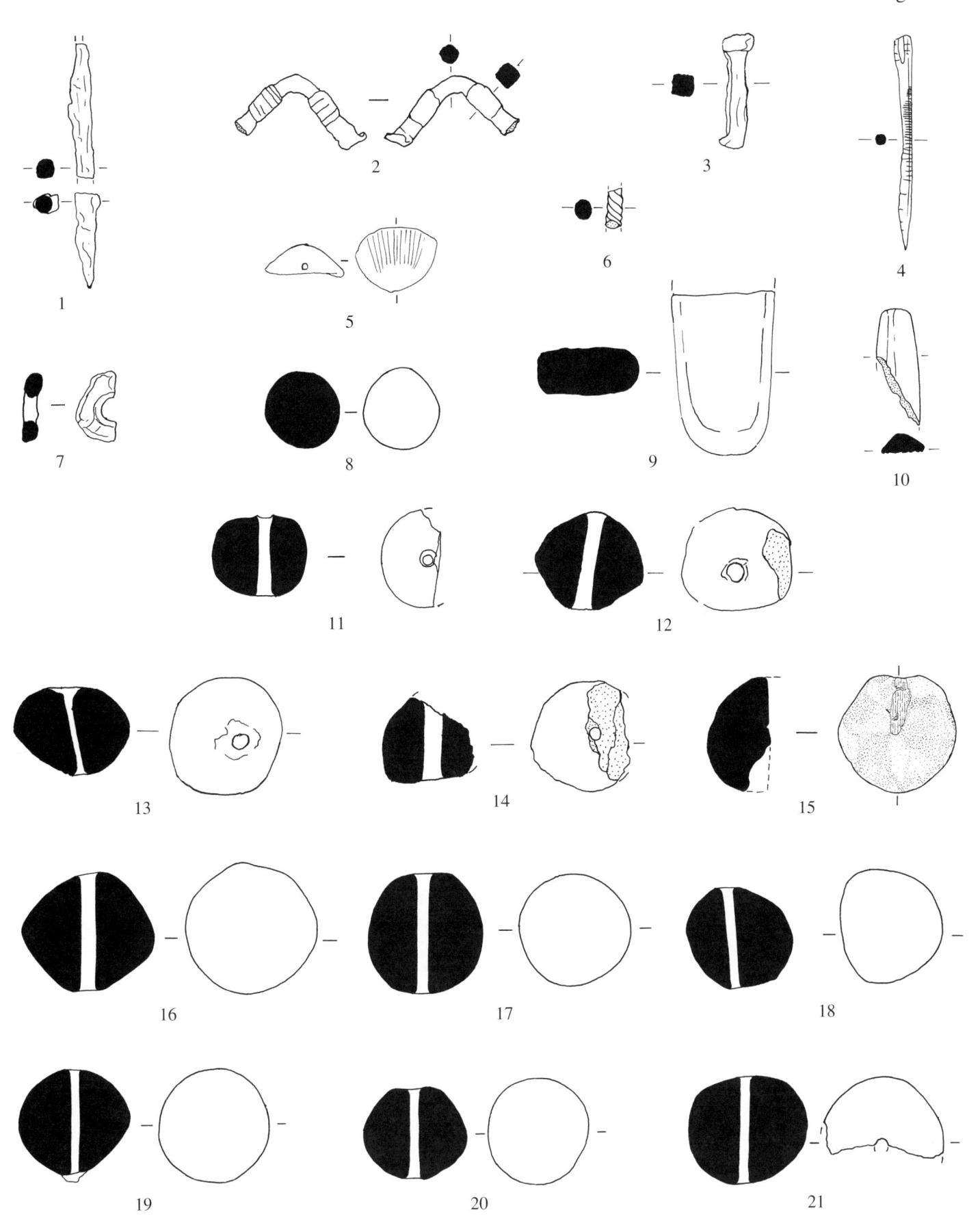

Figure 52

Miscellaneous Small Finds of Various Materials from Trench IIA. Scale 1:2

Figure 53. Miscellaneous Stone Vessels and Tools from Trench IIA

1. Type SF.3c (SW. 338; IIA, 5.9). Phase 9. Bowl rim fragment. Igneous stone. Dark brownish-black color. Fine grained.
—. Type SF.3c (SC. 3338; IIA, 5.17, Pit C). Phase 12. Bowl rim fragment. Gray basalt.
2. Type SF.3c (SW. 119; IIA, 4.14, Pit C). Phase 12. Ring base fragment of a bowl. Medium gray basalt.
3. Type SF.3c (SW. 127; IIA, 4.14, Pit C). Phase 12. Bowl rim. Very small fragment (diameter uncertain). Dark gray basalt.
4. Type SF.3c (SW. 35; IIA, 1.1). Phase 15. Bowl rim and upper wall fragment. Black basalt.
—. Type SF.3c (SC. 3339; IIA, 1.8, Oven). Phase 14. Bowl rim fragment. Green basalt.
5. Type SF.3a (SW. 56; IIA, 1.4, Room). Phase 14. Grinder fragment. Sperical shape. Dark gray granite.
6. Type SF.3a (SW. 66; IIA, 1.10). Phase 14. Grinder. Euphrates gravel stone. Light green with darker green flecks on surface.
7. Type SF.3e (SW. 78; IIA, 4.1). Phase 14. Weight(?). Talc stone. Light gray color with some iron-colored markings. Three lugs with hole pierced through near edge of one lug.
8. Type SF.3a (SW. 22; IIA, 1.2). Phase 15. Polisher fragment. Igneous stone. Brown color with black markings on the surfaces. Polished on the broad flat surfaces and rounded on the edge of the extant fragment.

Figure 53

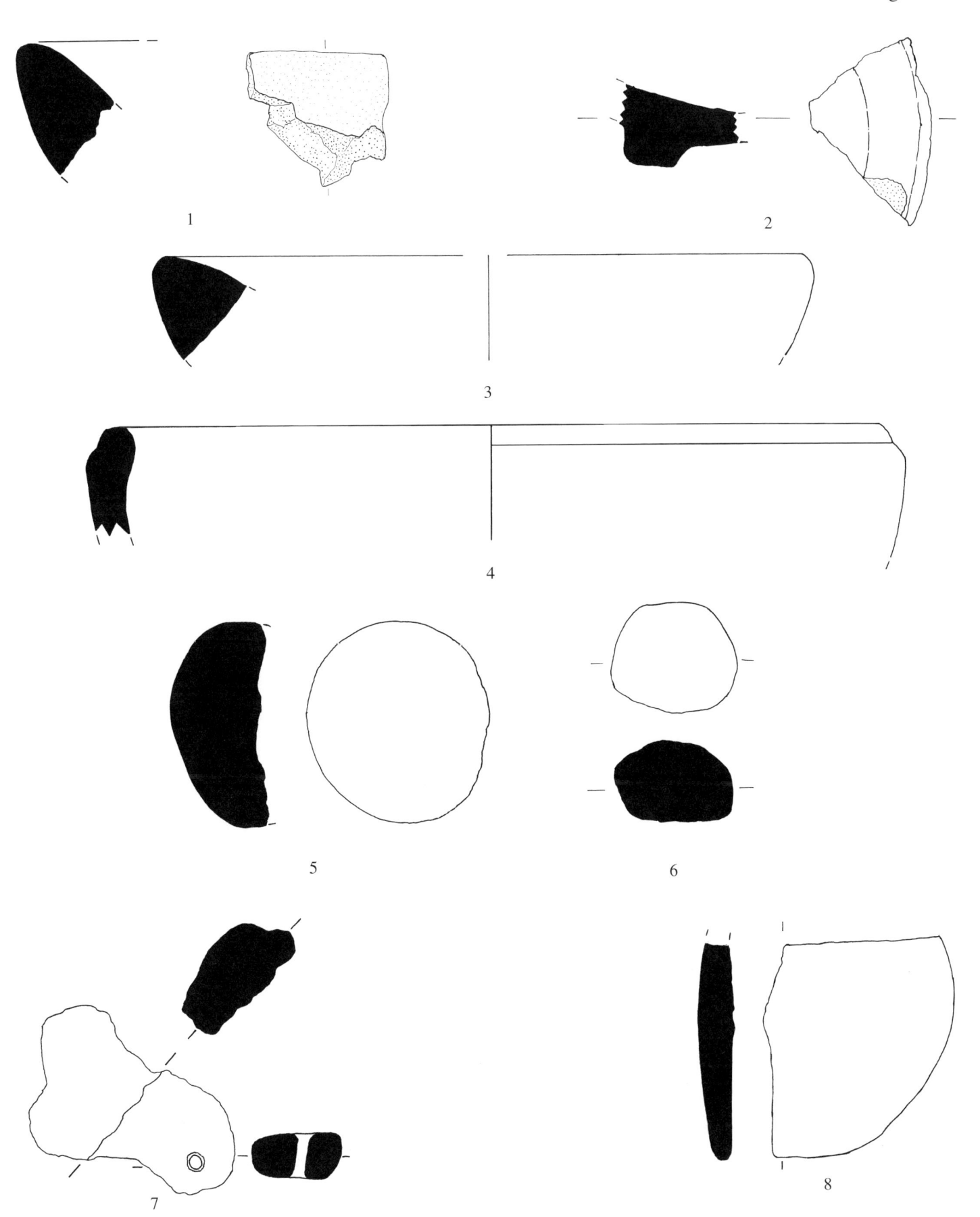

Miscellaneous Stone Vessels and Tools from Trench IIA. Scale 1:2

Figure 54. Miscellaneous Stone Vessels and Tools from Trenches IIA and IIB

1. Type SF.3a (SW. 118; IIA, 5.2, Pit C). Phase 12. Grinder. Tufa. Central fragment of original oblong shape. Dark gray color, very pitted.
2. Type SF.3a (SW. 362; IIA, 5.2, Pit C). Phase 12. Grinder. Vesicular basalt. Dark gray color. Both ends broken.
3. Type SF.3a (SW. 110; IIA, 4.11). Phase 13. Grinder. Tufa. Fragment of one end. Dark gray color, very pitted.
4. Type SF.3a (SW. 36; IIA, 1.2). Phase 15. Grinder. Granite with white inclusions. Gray color.
5. Type SF.3a (SW. 44; IIA, 1.1). Phase 15. Grinder. Granite. Dark gray color.
6. Type SF.3a (SW. 8; IIA, 1.1). Phase 15. Grinder. Sedimentary rock. Brownish-gray with white surface markings. Polished on all surfaces.
7. Type SF.3c (SW. 226; IIB, 2.2, Oven). Phase 15. Bowl. Ring base and lower wall of a basalt bowl.
8. Type SF.3a (SW. 76; IIB, 2.10). Phase 15. Pounder. Polished granite. Fragment, $3.25 \times 5.50 \times 7.00$ cm.
9. Type SF.3a (SW. 72; IIB, 2.4). Phase 15. Pounder. Polished granite. Measurements: $4.00 \times 5.70 \times 6.00$ cm.
10. Type SF.3a (SW. 74; IIB, 2.6). Phase 15. Pounder. Chert, light gray. Measurements: $5.50 \times 6.00 \times 6.50$ cm.
11. Type SF.3a (SW. 73; IIB, 2.10). Phase 15. Grinder. Basalt, dark gray. Measurements: $5.50 \times 7.50 \times 10.50$ cm.
12. Type SF.3c (SW. 75; IIB, 2.10). Phase 15. Quern. Limestone, light gray. Measurements: $6.00 \times 9.00 \times 14.50$ cm.
13. Type SF.3e (SW. 77; IIB, 2.4). Phase 15. Weight (loom or digging stick). Limestone, cream. Measurements: $3.00 \times 5.00 \times 11.00$ cm.

Figure 54

Miscellaneous Stone Vessels and Tools from Trenches IIA and IIB. Scale 1:2

# Figures 55–56

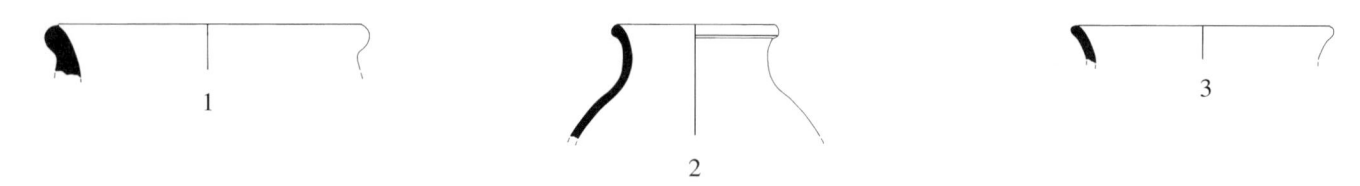

Figure 55. Pottery from Trench IVM, Sounding Below Room 7 (Phase 1A; Period J — Early Bronze Age I). Scale 1:5

1. JR. E.I.a (TS. 3001; IVM, 10.4). Small rim and neck segment. Fairly fine pink ware, evenly fired. Creamy-pink slip in and out.
2. JR. J.III.e (TS. 2660; IVM, 10.4). About 1/2 rim, neck, and shoulder segment. Fine pinkish-brown ware, evenly fired. Light pinkish-buff slip in and out.
3. CP. B.III.b (TS. 2863; IVM, 10.5). Small rim and neck segment. Slightly coarse grayish-buff ware, evenly fired. Self slip in and out, horizontally burnished out and just over rim in.
   Other Type Series Examples: (1) SBR. B.I.a (TS. 2631), (2) BR. A.I.b (TS. 2632), (3) JR. E.II.g (TS. 1731), (4) JR. F.I.b (TS. 2774), (5) CP. B.II.j (TS. 2628).

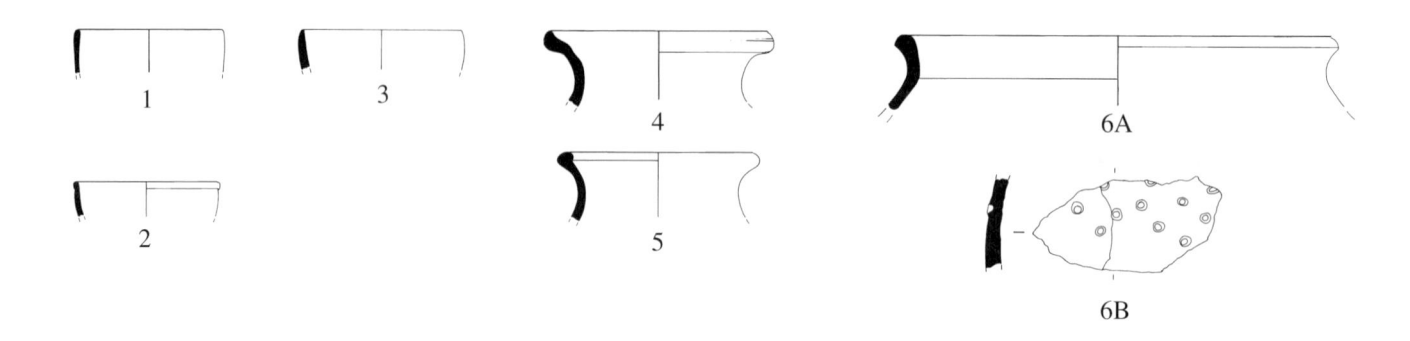

Figure 56. Pottery from Trench IVM, Sounding Below Room 7 (Phase 1B; Period H — Early Bronze Age II). Scale 1:5

1. SBR. A.I.b (TS. 2978; IVM, 10.3). Small rim and upper wall segment. Fairly fine light brown ware, evenly fired. Self slip in and out.
2. SBR. A.I.d (TS. 2976; IVM, 10.3). Small rim and upper wall segment. Slightly coarse pinkish-buff ware, evenly fired. Cream slip in and out.
3. SBR. C.III.a (TS. 2977; IVM, 10.3). Small rim and upper wall segment. Fairly fine creamy-green ware, evenly fired. Self slip in and out.
4. JR. J.III.q (TS. 2904; IVM, 10.3). Small rim and neck segment. Fairly fine pinkish-buff ware, evenly fired. Cream slip in and out.
5. JR. J.III.aa (TS. 2989; IVM, 10.3). Small rim and neck segment. Fairly fine pinkish-brown ware, evenly fired. Self slip in and out.

6A, B. CP. B.II.b (TS. 1741a, b; IVM, 10.3). Incomplete rim segments (6A) and two joining body sherds (6B) with stick-impressed holes partially incised on outer wall before firing. Medium coarse pink ware with lime and mica grits, unevenly fired. Self slip in and out. Compare "First Cooking-Pot Ware" from Amuq G (Braidwood and Braidwood, 1960, fig. 229:14).

Other Study Collection Examples: (1) JR. E.II.w (SC. 1171), (2) SV.2, Vessel Spout (SC. 3281; see fig. 170:11).

Figure 57

Area IV, Operation 6, Sounding Below Room 16 (Phase 1B; Period H — Early Bronze Age II). Scale 1:5

1. BR. D.III.a (TS. 3222; Op. 6, 19.4). About 1/12 rim and upper wall segment. Fairly fine light pink ware with gold-colored mica and lime grits, evenly fired. Creamy-pink slip in and out.
2. JR. J.III.c (TS. 3225; Op. 6, 19.4). About 1/8 rim and neck segment. Fine, close pinkish-brown ware with small black and white lime grits, evenly fired. Self slip in and out.
3. JR. O.I.a (TS. 3223; Op. 6, 19.4). About 1/10 rim and upper shoulder segment. Slightly coarse buff ware with very few visible white mica and lime grits, evenly fired. Self slip in and out.
4. BE. B.I (TS. 3460; Op. 6, 19.2). About 1/2 base with segment of lower wall of vessel. Fairly fine pinkish-brown ware with gold- and white-colored mica and lime grits, evenly fired. Self slip out.

Other Type Series Examples: (1) JR. J.IV.d (TS. 3219), (2) BE. E.I.e (TS. 3221), (3) BE. E.I.k (TS. 3224).

Other Phase 1B Study Collection Examples from Area IVB Sounding Through Town Wall: (1) SBR. B.I.g (SC. 413), (2) SBR. B.I.g (SC. 418), (3) SBR. B.I.g (SC. 420), (4) SBR. B.I.h (SC. 490), (5) BR. F.II.d (SC. 875), (6) SJR. A.III.b (SC. 2491), (7) JR. K.I.b (SC. 2388).

Figure 58

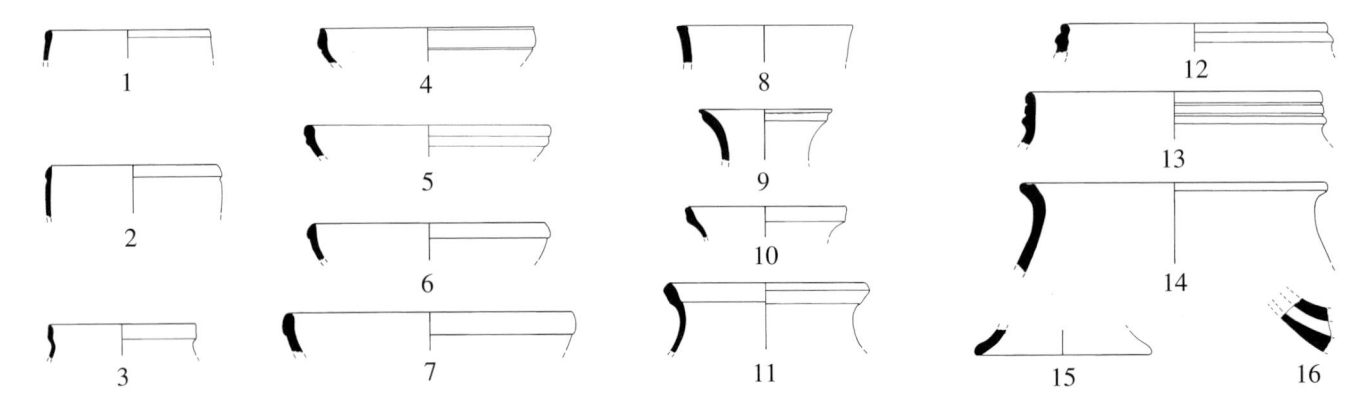

Pottery from Trench IVB, Sounding Through Town Wall Tower and Trenches IVC, D, J, M, and Z(S) (Phase 1C; Period G — Early Bronze Age III). Scale 1:5

1. SBR. B.I.e (TS. 2979; IVJ, 1.8). Small rim and upper wall segment. Fine creamy-green ware, evenly fired. Self slip in and out.
2. SBR. B.I.h (TS. 2971; IVM, 10.1). Small rim and upper wall segment. Fine buff ware, evenly fired. Cream slip in and out.
3. SBR. D.I.b (TS. 2959; IVC, 1.14b). Small rim and upper wall segment. Fairly fine creamy-buff ware, evenly fired. Self slip in and out.
4. BR. D.I.a (TS. 2946; IVD, 2.6a). Small rim and upper wall segment. Fairly fine pink ware, evenly fired. Creamy-buff slip in and out.
5. BR. D.II.a (TS. 2973; IVM, 10.1). Small rim and upper wall segment. Fine buff ware, evenly fired. Cream slip in and out.
6. BR. D.III.b (TS. 2027; IVB, 2.3). Small rim and upper wall segment. Fairly close pinkish-brown ware, evenly fired. Light pink slip out.
7. BR. E.III.d (TS. 2719; IVC, 1.14b). Small rim and upper wall segment. Fairly fine pinkish-buff ware, evenly fired. Creamy-buff slip in and out.
8. SJR. B.II.b (TS. 2970; IVM, 10.1). Small rim and upper neck segment. Fine creamy-green ware, evenly fired. Self slip in and out.
9. SJR. C.I.a (TS. 3002; IVZ(S), 5.9). About 1/3 rim and neck segment of two joining fragments. Slightly coarse buff ware, evenly fired. Cream slip in and out.
10. SJR. C.II.e (TS. 2927; IVM, 10.1). About 1/5 rim and upper neck segment. Slightly coarse pinkish-buff ware, evenly fired. Creamy-buff slip in and out.
11. SJR. C.II.s (TS. 2667; IVJ, 1.8). About 1/8 rim and neck segment. Close pinkish-brown ware, evenly fired. Creamy-buff slip out and just over rim in.
12. JR. C.I.d (TS. 2825; IVZ(S), 5.9). Small rim and upper neck segment. Slightly coarse grayware, evenly fired. Self slip in and out.
13. JR. D.I.b (TS. 2988; IVM, 10.1). Small rim and upper neck segment. Slightly coarse grayish-buff ware evenly fired. Creamy-green slip in and out.
14. JR. G.I.b (TS. 1935; IVB, 2.3). Small rim, neck, and upper shoulder segment. Slightly coarse grayish-buff ware fairly evenly fired. Self slip in and out.
15. PS. A.I.a (TS. 2981; IVJ, 1.8). Small rim and wall segment. Slightly coarse dark buff ware, evenly fired. Pink slip out.
16. SV. 2 (TS. 2714; IVC, 1.16). About 1/2 segment of a spout. Fairly fine grayish-brown ware, evenly fired. Self slip out.

Other Type Series Examples:
Area IVB — (1) BR. L.II.e (TS. 1936).
Area IVC — (1) BE. E.II.h (TS. 3049).
Area IVJ — (1) BR. O.I.c (TS. 2952), (2) JR. F.III.d (TS. 2998).
Area IVM — (1) SBR. B.I.j (TS. 2974), (2) SJR. C.I.c (TS. 2964), (3) JR. H.I.i (TS. 2815), (4) JR. H.III.c (TS. 2816), (5) JR. J.III.aa (TS. 2987), (6) JR. M.I.a (TS. 2626), (7) Ld. C.III.c (TS. 2830).
Area IVZ(S) — (1) JR. J.V.b (TS. 2692).

Other Study Collection Examples:
Area IVB — (1) SJR. A.I.a (SC. 2479), (2) JR. J.II.h (SC. 2166).
Area IVC — (1) Ld. C.III.a (SC. 1941).
Area IVD — (1) SBR. B.I.e (SC. 322).
Area IVM — (1) SBR. D.I.c (SC. 641), (2) JR. J.III.d (SC. 1374), (3) JR. J.III.q (SC. 1479), (4) JR. J.IV.a (SC. 1522), (5) BE. B.I (SC. 3105), (6) BE. E.I.a (SC. 3151).
Area IVZ(S) — (1) SBR. D.II.c (SC. 655), (2) JR. A.V.c (SC. 1980), (3) JR. J.III.ab (SC. 1517), (4) JR. B.III.e (SC. 947).

Figures 59–60

Figure 59. Pottery from Trench IVP, Operation 6, Sounding Below Courtyard Room 9 (Phase 1C; Period G — Early Bronze Age III). Scale 1:5

1. SBR. B.I.h (TS. 3214; Op. 6, 20.3). About 1/10 rim and upper wall segment. Fine, close pinkish-buff ware with no visible grits except a few small holes from which the vegetable temper was burned out during firing. Creamy-buff slip out.
2. BR. E.I.a (TS. 3212; Op. 6, 20.3). About 1/12 rim and upper wall segment. Fairly fine light brown ware with lime grits, evenly fired. Self slip in and out.
3. BR. L.III.a (TS. 3213; Op. 6, 20.3). About 1/16 rim and upper wall segment. Fine light pink ware with very few lime grits, evenly fired. Creamy-buff slip in and out.
4. JR. F.II.f (TS. 3434; Op. 6, 20.3). About 1/10 rim and neck segment. Fairly fine pinkish-buff ware with a few lime grits, evenly fired. Buff slip out.

Another Type Series Example: (1) JR. O.II.l (TS. 3211).

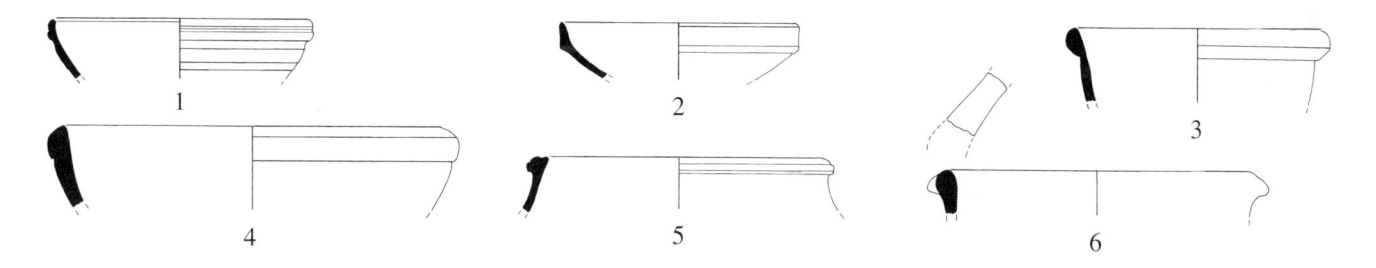

Figure 60. Pottery from Area IV, Operation 6, Sounding Below Room 16 (Phase 1C, Period G — Early Bronze Age III). Scale 1:5

1. BR. D.II.c (TS. 3471; Op. 6, 19.1). Portion of rim and upper wall segment. For ware, compare Phase 2A Type Series example from Area IVW (TS. 2744).
2. BR. D.IV.a (TS. 3474; Op. 6, 19.3). Portion of rim and upper wall segment. For ware, compare Phase 2A Type Series example from Area IVM (TS. 2639).
3. BR. E.IV.b (TS. 3475; Op. 6, 19.3). Portion of rim and upper wall segment. For ware, compare Phase 2B Type Series example from Area IVJ (TS. 1599).
4. BR. L.III.d (TS. 3472; Op. 6, 19.1). Portion of rim and upper wall segment. For ware, compare Phase 6 Type Series example from Area IIIG/H (TS. 1071).
5. JR. H.III.e (TS. 3476; Op. 6, 19.3). Portion of rim and upper shoulder segment. For ware, compare Phase 2A(a) Type Series example from Operation 7 (TS. 3509).
6. CP. C.II.b (TS. 3473; Op. 6, 19.1). Portion of rim and neck segment with remains of one triangular-shaped lug handle attached to the rim. For ware, compare Phase 2A Type Series example from Area IVJ (TS. 1590).

Figure 61

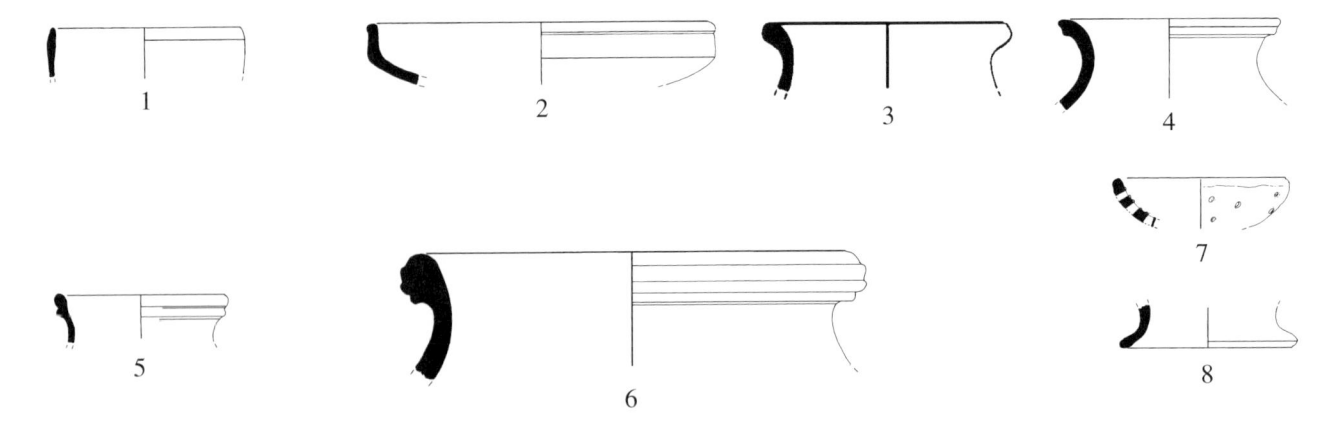

Figure 61. Pottery from Trench XA, Operation 11, Sounding Below Room 15 (Phase 1C; Period G — Early Bronze Age III). Scale 1:5

1. SBR. B.I.j (TS. 3377; Op. 11, 3.3). About 1/12 rim and upper wall segment. Fairly fine pinkish-buff ware with gold- and silver-colored mica and lime grits, evenly fired. Self slip in and out.
2. BR. E.I.a (TS. 4038; Op. 11, 3.3). About 1/12 rim and wall segment. Fairly fine buff ware with gold- and silver-colored mica and lime grits, evenly fired. Charred self slip in and out.
3. JR. J.I.c (TS. 4124; Op. 11, 3.3). About 1/8 rim and neck segment. Fairly fine pink ware with gold- and silver-colored mica and lime grits, evenly fired. Creamy-buff slip in and out.
4. JR. J.II.i (TS. 4039; Op. 11, 3.3). About 1/3 rim, neck, and shoulder segment. Fine pinkish-buff ware with small gold- and silver-colored mica and lime grits, evenly fired. Creamy-buff slip in and out.
5. JR. J.III.v (TS. 3376; Op. 11, 3.3). About 1/8 rim and neck segment. Fairly fine pinkish-buff ware with gold-colored mica and white lime grits, evenly fired. Self slip in and out.
6. JR. Q.I.b (TS. 3339; Op. 11, 3.3). About 1/10 rim and shoulder segment. Slightly coarse pinkish-buff ware with gold- and silver-colored mica and lime grits, evenly fired. Self slip in and out.
7. SR. A.I.b (TS. 3378; Op. 11, 3.3). Small segment of rim and wall. Slightly coarse pink ware with gold- and silver-colored mica and white lime grits, evenly fired. Creamy-buff slip in and out.
8. PS. A.II.a (TS. 4125; Op. 11, 3.3). Small rim and body segment. Coarse underfired light green ware with lime grits, evenly fired. Creamy-green self slip in and out.

Figure 62

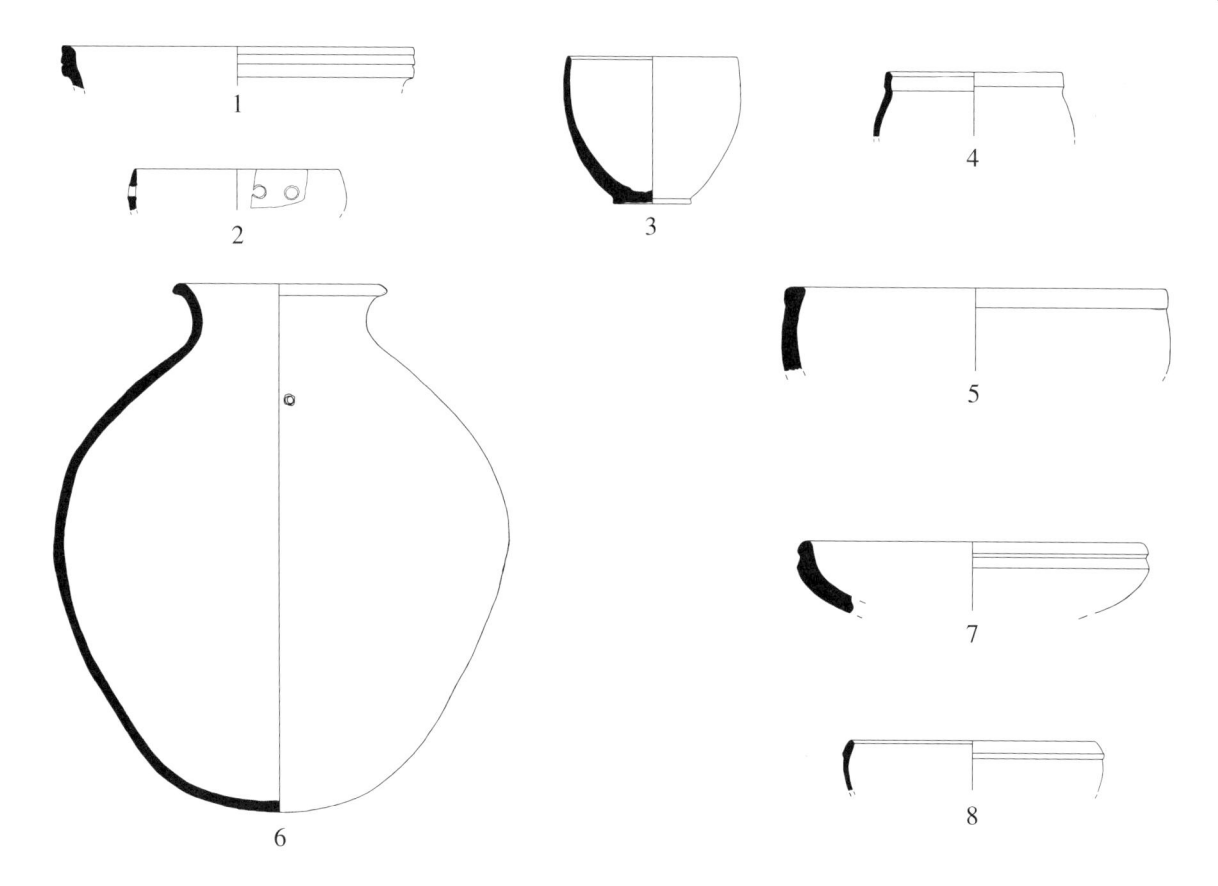

Pottery from Trenches IVA; IVB, Room 1 and Tower Foundations; and IVC, Room 7
(Phase 2A; Period F — Early Bronze Age IVa). Scale 1:5

1. JR. D.V.e (TS. 1974; IVA, 2.5). Small rim and upper neck segment. Fairly close pinkish-buff ware, evenly fired. Grayish-buff slip in and out.
2. SR. B.II.a (TS. 2428; IVA, 2.5). About 1/12 rim and upper wall segment with remains of two pierced strainer holes below rim. Slightly coarse buff-brown ware, evenly fired. Light creamy-green slip in and out.
3. SBR. A.I.b (SW. 268; IVB, 3.6, Room 1). Complete profile with 1/6 rim segment. Hard, fairly fine buff ware with some lime and mica grits, evenly fired.
4. SBR. D.I.b (TS. 2470; IVB, 3.8, Room 1). About 1/6 rim and upper wall segment. Fairly coarse light green ware, evenly fired. Self slip in and out.
5. BR. L.I.b (TS. 75; IVB, 2.2; Tower Stone Foundations). Small rim and upper wall segment. Fairly fine pink ware with lime and gold-colored mica grits, evenly fired. Creamy-buff slip in and out.
6. JR. J.III.a (SW. 293; IVB, 3.6, Room 1). Mended to near completion (1/2 rim and 2/3 body; see pl. 95b). Hard, slightly coarse pinkish-buff ware with lime and mica grits, fairly evenly fired. Creamy-buff slip out and over rim to base of neck in. One extant hole drilled into shoulder after firing may represent a mending hole.
7. BR. C.I.d (TS. 1753; IVC, 4.1= IVM, Room 7). Small rim and upper wall segment. Medium coarse pink ware with lime and mica grits, evenly fired. Cream slip in and out.
8. BR. D.VII.a (TS. 2703; IVC, 4.1 = IVM, Room 7). About 1/2 rim and upper wall segment. Fairly fine pinkish-buff ware, evenly fired. Creamy-buff slip in and out.

Other Type Series Examples:
  Area IVA — (1) SJR. B.III.c (TS. 2479).
  Area IVB — (1) JR. J.III.z (TS. 2005), (2) SR. C.I.b (TS. 1249).
  Area IVC —(1) SR. A.II.a (TS. 2432).

Other Study Collection Examples:
  Area IVA — (1) SBR. B.I.h (SC. 475).
  Area IVB, Room 1 — (1) JR. J.I.b (SC. 2104).
  Area IVC, 4.1 = IVM, Room 7 — (1) BR. A.III.b (SC. 726), (2) BR. E.III.f (SC. 762), (3) JR. A.III.a (SC. 895).
  Area IVC, Southwest of Town Wall Tower — (1) JR. G.I.c (SC. 1240), (2) JR. P.III.c (SC. 1760); Area IVC, Baulk between IVM and IVC — (1) JR. C.V.b (SC. 1012), (2) JR. J.IV.a (SC. 2372), (3) JR. P.II.s (SC. 2463).

Derived Hellenistic Type Series Example: Area IVC, Town Wall Tower — (1) H.RSB. A.I.c (TS. 1944).

Figure 63. Pottery from Trench IVE, Room 2 (Phase 2A; Period F — Early Bronze Age IVa)

1. SBR. A.I.e (TS. 1980; IVE, 1.6 = Room 2, East side of IVK). About 1/2 rim and most of wall profile. Fairly fine pinkish-brown ware, evenly fired. Self slip out.
2. JR. J.IV.c (TS. 2294; IVE, 1.6 = Room 2, East side of IVK). About 1/10 rim and upper neck segment. Slightly coarse pinkish-brown ware, evenly fired. Self slip in and out.
3. JR. O.II.m (TS. 1639; IVE, 1.6 = Room 2, East side of IVK). About 2/3 rim and shoulder with incised linear decoration on one portion of rim. Hard, very coarse grayish ware, evenly fired. Cream slip in and out.
4. JR. O.II.m (PM. D.17; SW. 662; IVE, 1.6 = Room 2, East side of IVK). Complete in situ, but not mended. Oval-shaped potter's mark incised on shoulder before firing. Coarse grayish-black ware, fairly evenly fired. Cream slip in and out.
5. FL. B.I.a (PM. E.2; SW. 273; IVE, 3.2 = Room 3, Southeast corner of IVL). Nearly complete except for one of the two vertical loop handles on opposite sides of the upper shoulder. Irregular incised potter's marks near one handle. Slightly coarse pinkish-buff ware with lime grits unevenly fired greenish-buff at surfaces.

Other Type Series Examples:
  Room 2 — (1) JR. E.I.c (TS. 2211), (2) JR. E.I.g (TS. 2777), (3) JR. P.II.e (TS. 1666 = TS. 2360), (4) JR. P.II.j (SW. 311).
  Room 3 — (1) SJR. A.II.a (SW. 263), (2) SJR. C.II.l (SW. 247), (3) JR. J.I.h (PM. D.10; SW. 733).

Other Study Collection Examples:
  Room 2 — (1) SBR. B.I.h (SC. 454), (2) SBR. B.I.j (SC. 540), (3) JR. K.II.b (SC. 1598).
  Room 3 — (1) BR. E.III.f (SC. 760).

Figure 63

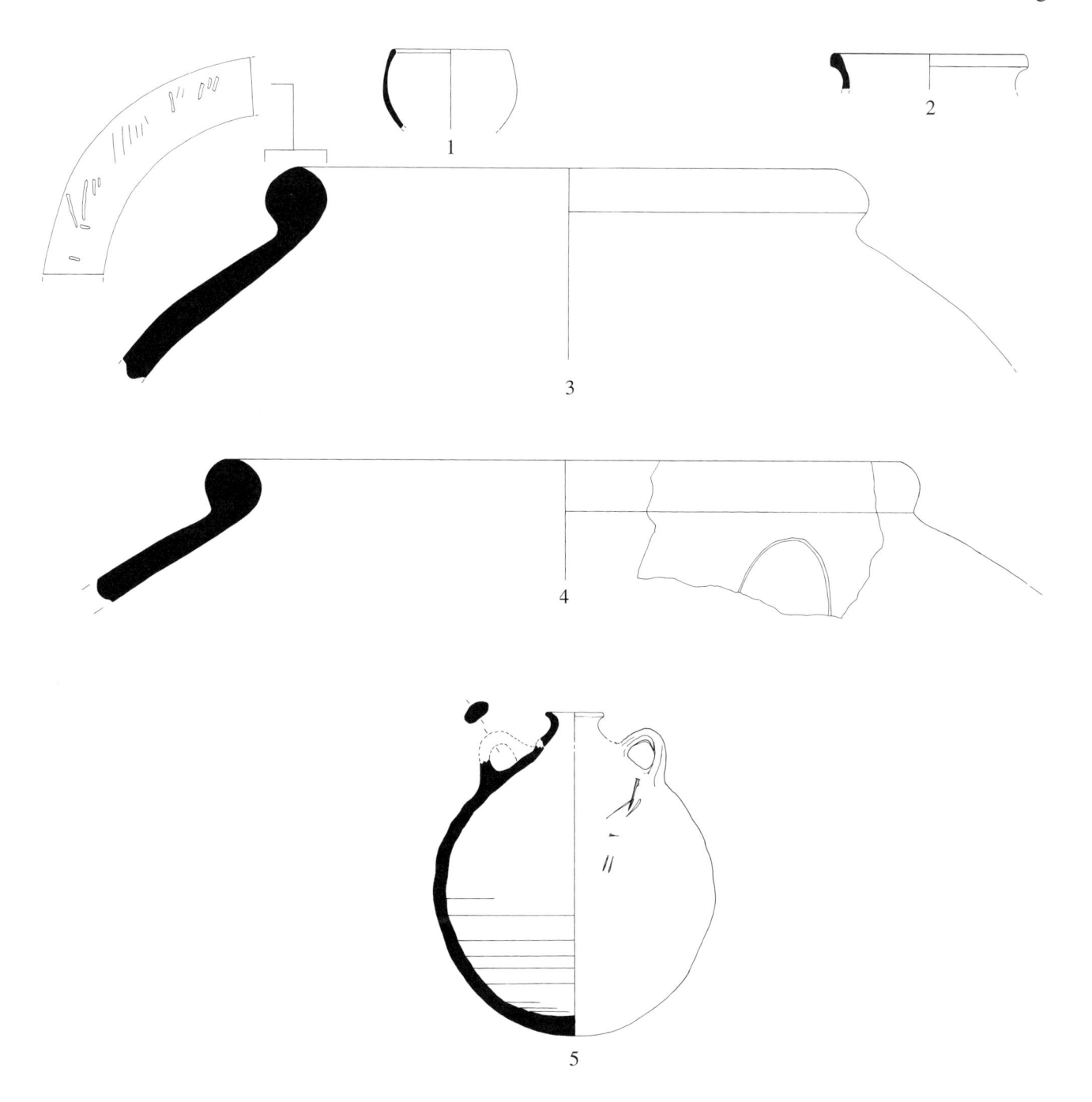

Pottery from Trench IVE, Room 2 (Phase 2A; Period F — Early Bronze Age IVa). Scale 1:5

Figure 64. Trench IVF, Room 1 and Doorway Between Rooms 1 and 8 (Phase 2A; Period F — Early Bronze Age IVa)

1. SBR. D.I.e (TS. 1631; IVF, 4.1). Nearly complete profile to base level. Fine pink ware, evenly fired. Cream slip in and out.
2. SJR. C.II.p (TS. 2783; IVF, 4.1). About 1/10 rim and upper neck segment. Fairly fine pinkish-brown ware, evenly fired. Self slip in and out. Irregular horizontal burnishing on top of rim and around inside of neck.
3. JR. E.II.k (TS. 1632; IVF, 3.1). Small rim and shoulder segment. Fairly fine buff ware, evenly fired. Light cream slip in and out.
4. JR. H.I.g (IP [G.4] F.III.a; SW. 294; IVF, 1.11, 1.12, 1.13, 4.1 = Room 1; IVM, 1.4, 1.7, 3.1, 100.13 = Room 7; and IVX, 2.4, 2.5, 2.6 = Room 7). About 1/5 rim and very many body fragments scattered among rooms 1, 7, and 14 (see pl. 93). Mended to near completion apart from missing applied heads belonging to the central figure of the eagle situated under the missing spout and the two mythical "griffin-like" animals facing the eagle on the upper body. All animal body decoration tool-incised before firing. Very hard ware with fine lime and mica grits, unevenly fired with gray core, pinkish-orange in and grayish-buff out.
5. JR. H.I.i (TS. 1629; IVF, 4.1). Large rim and upper wall segment. Medium coarse pinkish ware, evenly fired. Cream slip in and out.
6. JR. J.III.j (TS. 2997; IVF, 1.15). About 1/3 rim and neck segment. Fairly fine pink ware, evenly fired. Creamy-green slip in and out.
7. JR. J.III.m (TS. 2776; IVF, 4.1). About 1/4 rim and neck segment. Slightly coarse buff ware, evenly fired. Creamy green slip in and out.
8. JR. J.III.m (TS. 2778; IVF, 4.1). Small rim and neck segment. Hard, close buff ware, evenly fired. Creamy-green slip in and out.
9. JR. O.II.b (TS. 1623; IVF, 1.13, 3.1 + IVE, 1.6, Rooms 1, 2). Mended to complete rim and about 1/2 body. Very coarse buff ware with lime and mica grits, unevenly fired. Self slip out. (n.b. Drawing Scale 1:10).
10. JR. P.II.a (PM. C.7; SW. 666; IVF, 1.12–14, 3.1). Complete rim and shoulder with potter's mark incised on shoulder before firing (see pl. 102a). Medium coarse grayish-black ware, evenly fired. Cream slip out.
11. JR. P.II.c (TS. 1628; IVF, 1.11-13, 1.13, 3.1). Rim and shoulder mended to completion. Fairly coarse grayish ware, evenly fired. Cream slip in and out.
12. BE. E.II.d (TS. 3065; IVF, 1.15). About 1/5 base and lower portion of wall of vessel. Fairly coarse buff ware, evenly fired. Creamy-buff slip in and out.
13. JR.Sh. (PM. D.10; TS. 1586; IVF, 4.1). Segment of jar shoulder with potter's mark incised before firing (see pl. 100d). Coarse pink ware, evenly fired. Cream slip out.
14. JR.Sh. (PM. D.25; TS. 1734; IVF, 1.13). Segment of jar body with a potter's mark incised on the outside wall before firing (see pl. 100f). Medium coarse buff ware, unevenly fired. Cream slip out.
—. JR.Sh. (PM. F; TS. 3147; IVF, 1.13). Jar sherd with incomplete potter's mark incised on outside wall before firing. Ware description not available.

Other Type Series Examples: (1) BR. F.III.g (TS. 1630), (2) SJR. A.I.a (TS. 2961), (3) SJR. C.II.a (TS. 2780), (4) JR. A.V.d (TS. 2655), (5) JR. D.I.f (TS. 2743 = TS. 2984), (6) JR. O.III.e (SW. 739), (7) JR. P.III.h (TS. 1634), (8) FL. A.II.a (TS. 2563), (9) CP. A.I.e (TS. 712), (10) CP. B.II.b (TS. 649 = SW. 681 = TS. 729), (11) CP. B.II.e (TS. 648 = TS. 1625), (12) Ld. C.III.b (TS. 2672), (13) Hd. F (TS. 2782).

Other Study Collection Examples:
Room 1 — (1) SBR. A.I.b (SC. 203), (2) SBR. A.I.b (SC. 213), (3) SBR. B.I.e (SC. 321), (4) SBR. B.I.g (SC. 389), (5) SBR. B.I.g (SC. 404), (6) SBR. B.I.h (SC. 434), (7) SBR. B.I.h (SC. 444), (8) SBR. B.I.h (SC. 448), (9) SBR. B.I.j (SC. 547), (10) SBR. B (Gen. Type, SC. 12), (11) SBR. C.II.a (SC. 596), (12) BR. F.I.d (SC. 784), (13) SJR. B.I.a (SC. 2495), (14) SJR. B.I.a (SC. 2499), (15) SJR. B.II.j (SC. 660), (16) SJR. B.II.j (SC. 662), (17) SJR. C.I.h (SC. 2637), (18) JR. E.I.c (SC. 1993), (19) JR. E.II.a (SC. 2645), (20) JR. F.II.f (SC. 1225), (21) JR. G.I.c (SC. 2040), (22) SR. A.I.b (SC. 1957), (23) SR. C.I.a (SC. 1960).
Doorway Between Rooms 1 and 8 — (1) SBR. B.I.e (SC. 319), (2) SBR. B.I.g (SC. 397), (3) SBR. B.I.j (SC. 553), (4) BR. L.II.c (SC. 856), (5) JR. E.II.b (SC. 2656).

Figure 64

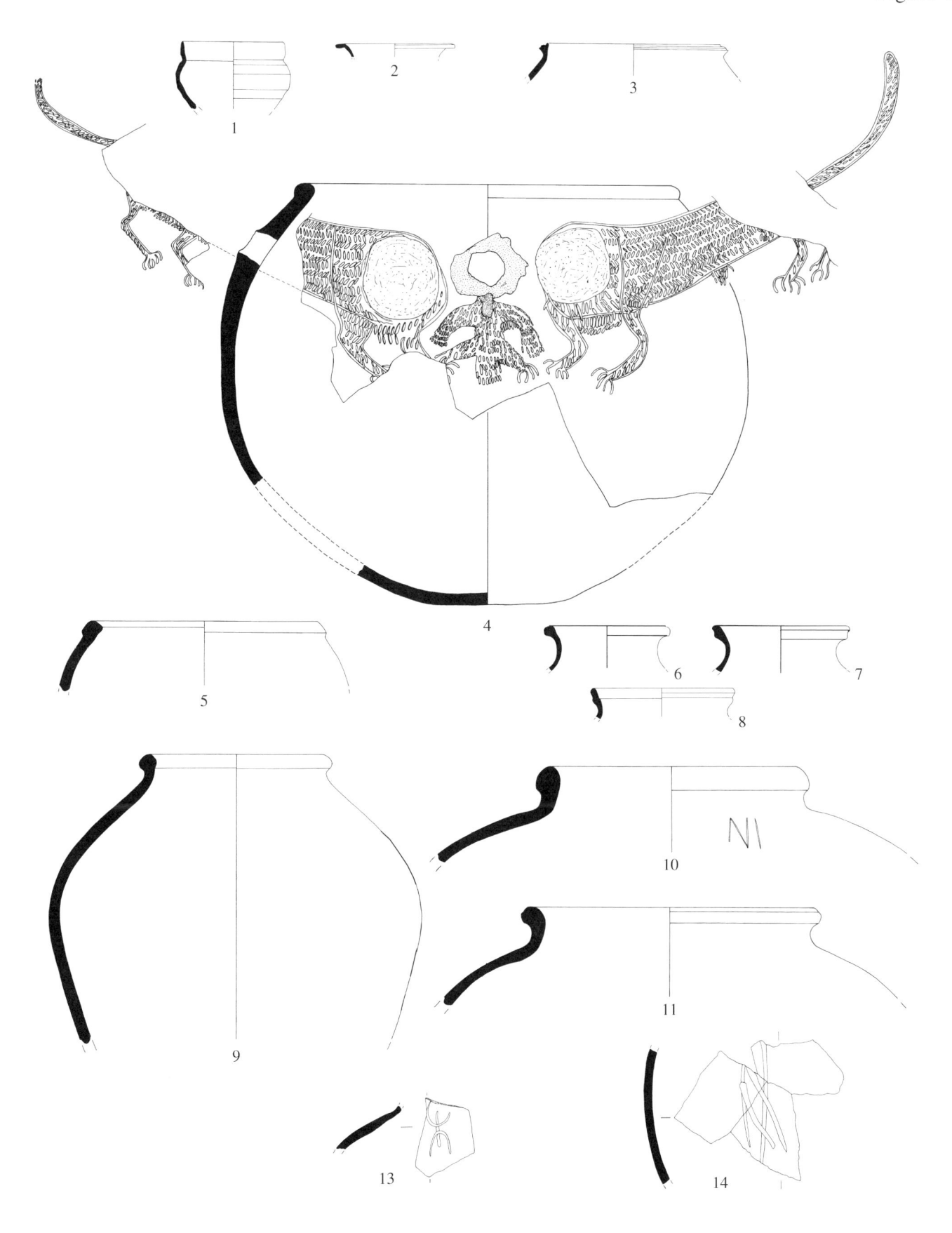

Pottery from Trench IVF, Room 1 and Doorway Between Rooms 1 and 8 (Phase 2A; Period F — Early Bronze Age IVa).
Scales (1–3, 5–8, 10–14) 1:5, (4) 1:4, and (9) 1:10

Figure 65

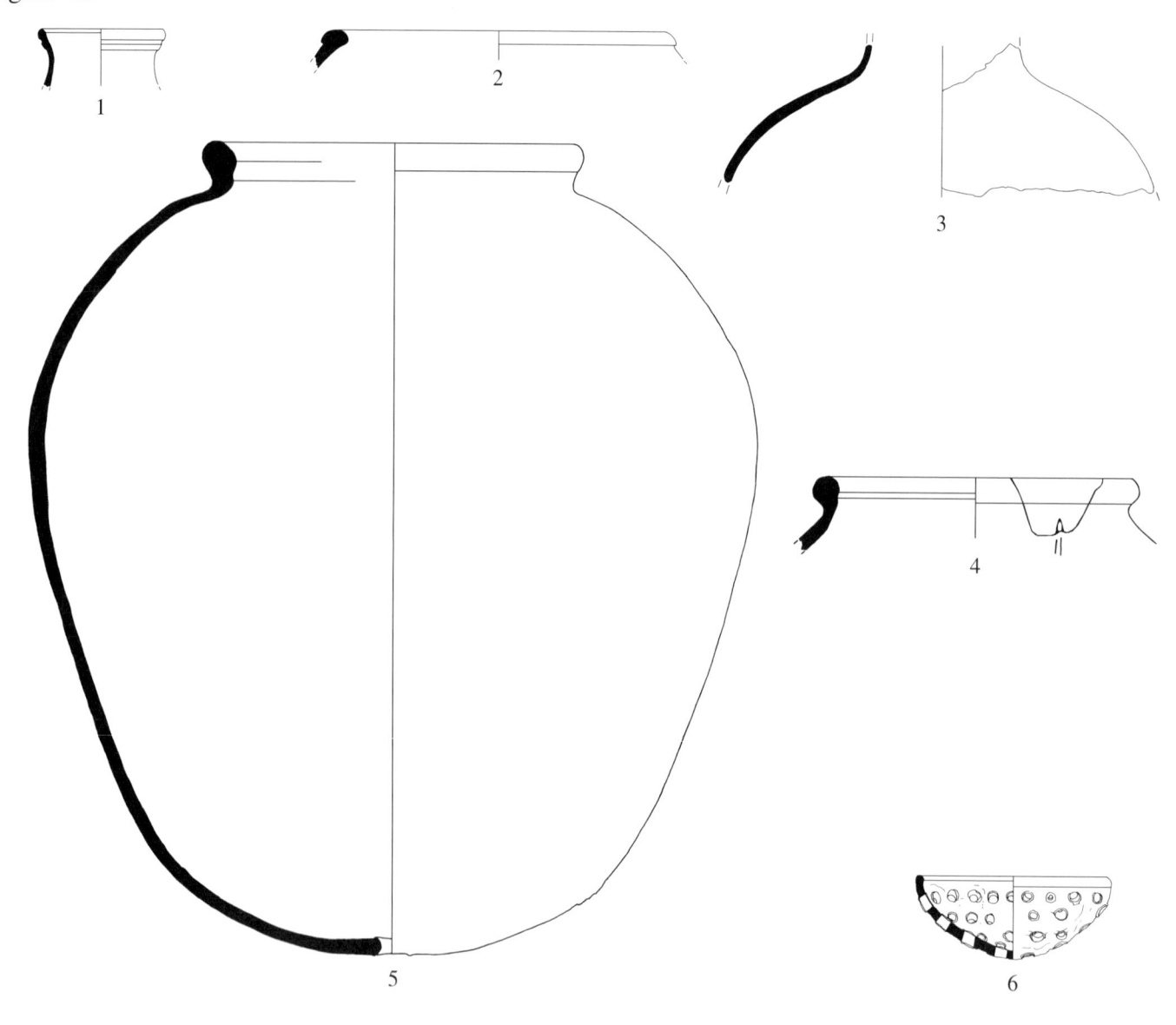

Figure 65. Pottery from Trench IVG, Northwest Corner of Room 3 (Phase 2A; Period F — Early Bronze Age IVa). Scale 1:5

1. SJR. C.II.d (TS. 2434; IVG, 1.5). About 1/4 rim and neck segment. Fairly fine pinkish-buff ware, evenly fired. Creamy-buff slip in and out.
2. JR. H.I.m (TS. 2818; IVG, 1.5). Small rim and upper shoulder segment. Slightly coarse pinkish-buff ware, evenly fired. Creamy-buff slip in and out.
3. JR. J.III.o (TS. 1771; IVG, 1.5). Large neck and shoulder segment. Slightly coarse pinkish-brown ware with lime and mica grits, unevenly fired.
4. JR. O.II.b (PM. A.5; TS. 2359; IVG, 1.5). About 1/8 rim and shoulder segment. Fairly coarse and gritty grayish-brown ware, evenly fired. Brown slip in and out. Fragmentary remains of a potter's mark vertically incised before firing.
5. JR. O.II.b (SW. 310 = TS. 444; IVG, 1.5). Mended to completion. Drainage hole 1.5 cm in diameter in base and with bitumen applied to a small area of the lower outer wall. Fairly coarse pinkish ware with lime and mica grits, evenly fired. Cream slip out.
6. SR. B.I.b (SW. 250; IVG, 1.5). Complete. Hard, tannish-buff ware with lime and gold-colored mica grits, evenly fired.
   Other Type Series Examples: (1) BR. F.V.a (TS. 2572), (2) CBR. A.I.a (SW. 381), (3) SJR. A.II.i (TS. 1956), (4) SJR. C.I.f (TS. 2314), (5) JR. F.II.f (TS. 2236), (6) JR. J.III.v (SW. 309), (7) JR. P.I.b (TS. 1642), (8) JR. P.I.d (SW. 326), (9) CP. B.I.a (SW. 308 = TS. 1949).

   Another Study Collection Example: (1) BR. F.III.d (SC. 1968).

Figure 66

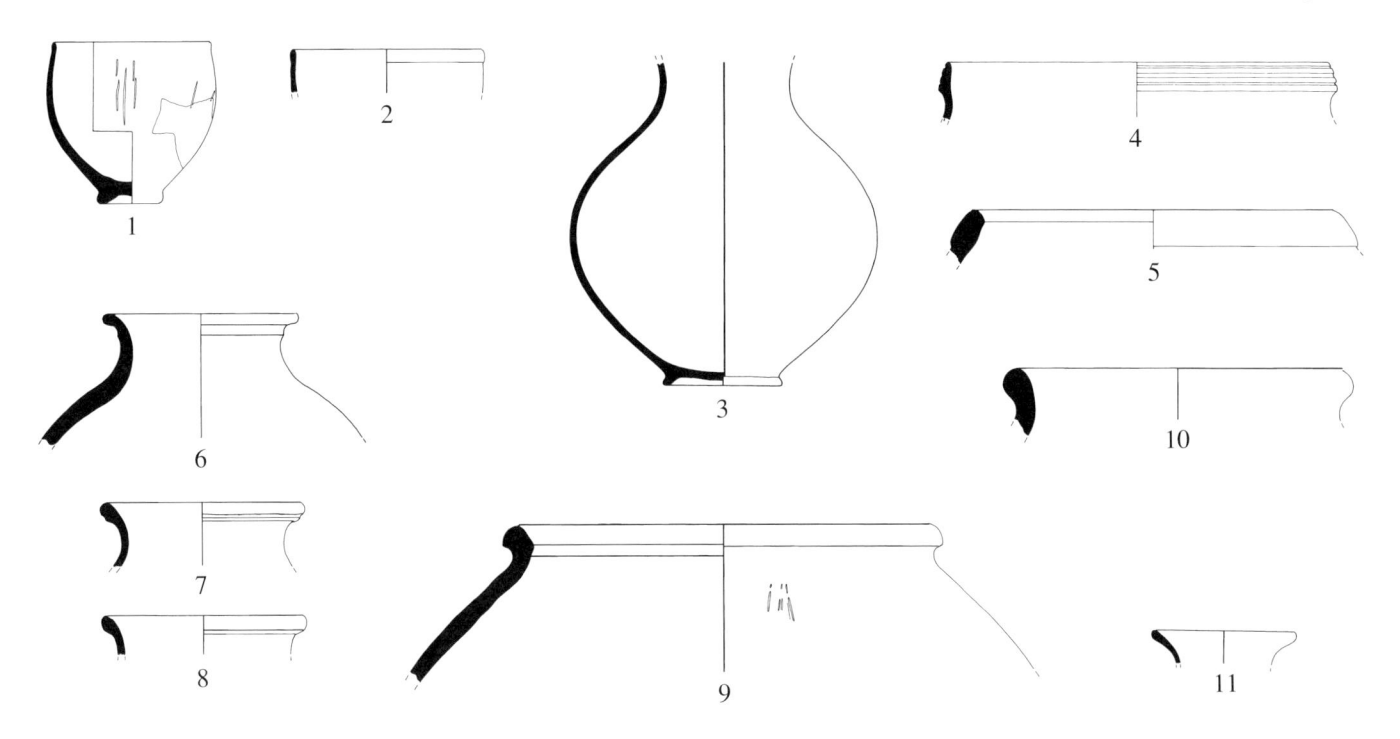

Pottery from Trench IVJ, Room 4 and Room 5 Bin (Phase 2A; Period F — Early Bronze Age IVa). Scale 1:5

1. SBR. A.I.a (PM. A.23; SW. 569; IVJ, 1.5, 2.1, Room 4). Mended to near completion with two potter's marks incised on outside wall before firing (see pl. 89b). Fairly coarse cream ware, evenly fired.
2. SBR. B.I.h (TS. 2980; IVJ, 1.6, Room 4). Small rim and upper wall segment. Fine buff ware, evenly fired. Creamy-buff slip out and creamy-green slip in.
3. SJR. C.II.i (SW. 500; IVJ, 2.1, Room 4, NE corner near door). Complete in situ except for rim. Fairly coarse brown-buff ware, evenly fired. Cream slip in and out.
4. JR. D.III.a (TS. 2897; IVJ, 2.1, Room 4, NE corner near door). Small rim and neck segment. Fairly fine buff ware, evenly fired. Creamy-buff slip in and out.
5. JR. H.I.d (TS. 3028; IVJ, 1.6, Room 4). Small rim segment. Slightly coarse ware unevenly fired with light brown core and buff at surfaces. Cream slip in and out.
6. JR. J.III.e (SW. 669; IVJ, 2.1, Room 4, NE corner near door). Mended to 1/2 segment of rim, neck, and shoulder. Fairly coarse buff ware, evenly fired. Traces of black slip near rim.
7. JR. J.III.m (TS. 2950; IVJ, 1.6, Room 4). About 1/6 rim and neck segment. Fairly fine creamy-green ware, evenly fired. Thick self slip in and out.
8. JR. J.III.ab (TS. 2953; IVJ, 1.6, Room 4). Small rim and upper neck segment. Slightly coarse buff ware, evenly fired. Creamy-buff slip in and out.
9. JR. O.II.e (PM. A.14; TS. 2792; IVJ, 1.5, 2.1, 2.3, Room 4). Mended to complete rim and shoulder with potter's mark incised on upper shoulder before firing. Slightly coarse pink ware, evenly fired. Cream slip out.
10. JR. P.II.i (TS. 2949; IVJ, 1.7, Room 4). About 1/8 rim and neck segment. Slightly coarse creamy-green ware, evenly fired. Worn self slip in and out.
11. SJR. C.I.e (TS. 2916; IVJ, 3.5, Storage Bin, Room 5). About 1/4 rim and upper neck segment. Fine greenish-buff ware, evenly fired. Creamy-green slip in and out.

Other Type Series Examples:

Room 4 — (1) SBR. B.I.e (TS. 2601 = TS. 2929), (2) BR. E.III.a (SW. 496), (3) SJR. B.II.j (SW. 497), (4) SJR. C.II.c (TS. 1143), (5) JR. E.II.k (TS. 1696), (6) JR. E.II.r (SW. 524), (7) JR. H.I.m (TS. 1593), (8) JR. H.II.f (TS. 1598), (9) JR. J.III.a (SW. 552), (10) JR. J.III.m (SW. 672), (11) JR. J.III.q (TS. 1596 = TS. 1621), (12) JR. J.III.u (TS. 2954), (13) JR. J.IV.a (SW. 649), (14) JR. L.II.a (SW. 651), (15) JR. O.II.a (SW. 624), (16) JR. O.II.e (TS. 2814), (17) JR. O.II.g (TS. 2813), (18) JR. P.II.i (SW. 650), (19) CP. A.II.a (SW. 539), (20) CP. C.II.b (TS. 1590), (21) BE. C.I (TS. 3071), (22) BE. E.I.c (TS. 1609), (23) BE. E.II.f (TS. 3041), (24) BE. E.II.j (TS. 2871), (25) BE. E.II.k (TS. 3038), (26) BE. F.II.b (SW. 675), (27) BE. F.III.b (SW. 674).

Room 5 — (1) SBR. A.I.c (SW. 568), (2) JR. E.II.f (TS. 2650), (3) JR. J.III.t (SW. 567).

Other Study Collection Examples:

Room 4 — (1) SBR. B.I.g (SC. 380), (2) SBR. B.I.h (SC. 439), (3) SBR. B.I.h (SC. 441), (4) JR. J.III.x (SC. 1500), (5) JR. K.I.a (SC. 1560), (6) JR. K.I.c (SC. 2394), (7) JR. (not typed, SC. 94), (8) CP. B.II.a (SC. 1846), (9) BE. E.I.a (SC. 3152), (10) BE. E.II.c (SC. 3199).

Room 5 — (1) SBR. B.I.b (SC. 259), (2) SBR. B.I.g (SC. 361), (3) SBR. B.I.j (SC. 535), (4) SBR. B.I.j (SC. 538), (5) BR. A.II.e (SC. 715).

Figure 67

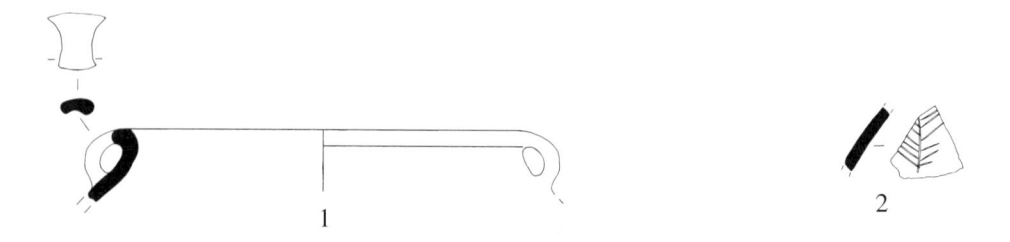

Figure 67. Pottery from Trench IVL, Room 3 (Phase 2A; Period F — Early Bronze Age IVa). Scale 1:5

1. CP. B.II.e (TS. 1727; IVL, 1.5). Rim and shoulder segment with vertical loop handle attached from rim to shoulder. Medium coarse buff ware with lime and mica grits, evenly fired. Self slip in and out.
2. JR.Sh. (IP [G.4] D.III; PM. D.19; TS. 1702; IVL, 1.5). Body sherd with tree or wheat stalk pattern incised on outer wall before firing. Hard, fairly fine, buff ware, evenly fired. Cream slip in and out.

Another Type Series Example: (1) JR. J.I.h (SW. 733).

Other Study Collection Examples: (1) SBR. B.I.p (SC. 590), (2) SBR. D.I.a (SC. 630), (3) JR. H.I.d (SC. 1265), (4) JR. J.VI.b (SC. 1557), (5) BE. E.II.i (SC. 3222).

Figure 68. Pottery from Trenches IVM, IVX, and IVC, Room 7 (Phase 2A; Period F — Early Bronze Age IVa; see also fig. 79)

1. SBR. A.I.g (TS. 2969; IVM, 100.13). About 1/8 rim and upper wall segment. Fairly fine buff ware, evenly fired. Self slip in and out.
2. SBR. B.I.e (TS. 2968; IVM, 100.13). Small rim and upper wall segment. Fine pink ware, evenly fired. Cream slip out.
3. SJR. B.II.j (SW. 519; IVM, 1.5). Mended to near completion (see pl. 91a). Fairly coarse pink ware, evenly fired. Cream slip in and out.
4. JR. E.II.m (TS. 2653; IVM, 1.6). About 1/5 rim and upper shoulder segment. Slightly coarse light pinkish-buff ware, evenly fired. Creamy-buff slip out.
5. JR. J.III.o (TS. 1713; IVM, 1.7). About 2/3 rim and shoulder segment. Medium fine buff ware, evenly fired. Grayish-green slip in and out.
6. JR. J.III.aa (TS. 2986; IVM, 1.6). Small rim and neck segment. Slightly coarse light buff ware, evenly fired. Cream slip in and out.
7. JR. J.IV.a (IP [G.1] A.II.c; TS. 1719; IVM, 1.7). Small rim, neck, and shoulder segment with horizontal comb-incised lines around upper portion of the shoulder. Fairly fine, hard, grayish ware, evenly fired. Cream slip in and out.
8. JR. L.II.a (SW. 736; IVX, 2.6 = IVM). Most of base and body mended; upper portion unexcavated. Fairly coarse buff ware, unevenly fired, green in patches out. Probable self slip out, but very heavily burned with inner surface flaking off.
9. JR. O.II.e (TS. 1715; IVM, 1.7). Complete rim and shoulder. Fairly coarse pink ware, unevenly fired. Light cream slip in and out, wheel-applied and in reserve outside.
10. JR. P.II.a (TS. 2808; IVM, 1.7). About 1/3 rim and shoulder segment. Slightly coarse grayish-buff ware, evenly fired. Creamy-green slip out.
11. CP.Ld. A.I.a (TS. 2861; IVM, 100.13). Small rim segment with deeply incised horizontal linear decoration on extant portion of the outer wall. Slightly coarse grayish-buff ware, evenly fired. Self slip in and out.
—. JR.Sh. (IP [G.4] D. III; PM. D.20; TS. 2573; IVM, 1.7). Jar sherd (see fig. 154:11 for description and plate 100e for photographic view).
—. JR.Sh. (PM. F; TS. 3115; IVM, 1.6). Jar sherd. Ware description not available.
—. JR.Sh. (PM. F; TS. 3142; IVC, 4.1). Jar sherd. Ware description not available.

Other Type Series Examples:

Room Occupation — (1) MBR. B.II.a (SW. 498), (2) SJR. C.I.a (SW. 540), (3) JR. C.I.a (SW. 477), (4) JR. H.I.e (SW. 728), (5) JR. J.I.b (TS. 2661), (6) JR. O.I.a (SW. 695), (7) FL. A.II.b (SW. 706), (8) CP. C.II.a (SW. 740), (9) CP.Ld. A.I.a (TS. 2831), (10) WPS. A.I.b (TS. 3081).

Pit 3.1 — (1) BR. A.I.a (TS. 2633), (2) JR. J.III.h (TS. 3019), (3) Ld. A.III.a (TS. 3091).

Room and Pit 3.1 — (1) BR. D.IV.a (TS. 2639).

Other Study Collection Examples:

Room Occupation — (1) SBR. B.I.a (SC. 247), (2) SBR. B.I.g (SC. 408), (3) SBR. B.I.h (SC. 446), (4) SBR. B.I.h (SC. 460), (5) SBR. B.I.j (SC. 550), (6) SBR. B.I.k (SC. 565), (7) SBR. C.III.a (SC. 611), (8) SJR. B.III.d (SC. 2531), (9) SJR. C.I.e (SC. 2549), (10) SJR. C.I.f (SC. 2556), (11) JR. J.III.h (SC. 2286), (12) JR. J.III.aa (SC. 1511), (13) JR. Q.I.b (SC. 144), (14) JR. J. (Gen. Type, SC. 107), (15) JR. (not typed, SC. 98), (16) BE. A.I (SC. 3091), (17) BE. B.I (SC. 3108).

Pit 3.1 — (1) SBR. B.I.g (SC. 410), (2) SBR. B.I.g (SC. 412), (3) SJR. C.II.q (SC. 2609), (4) JR. G.I.b (SC. 2034), (5) JR. H.I.d (SC. 1264), (6) SV.2 (SC. 3279).

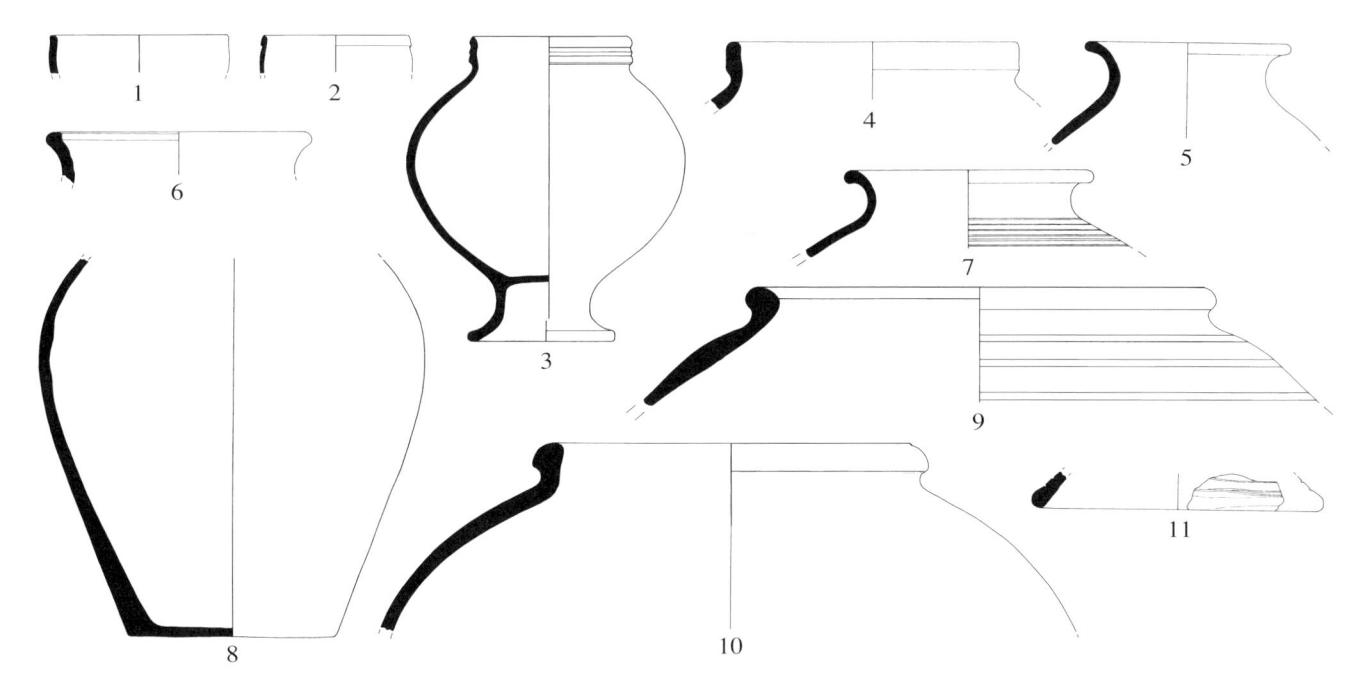

Figure 68. Pottery from Trenches IVM, IVX, and IVC, Room 7 (Phase 2A; Period F — Early Bronze Age IVa; see also fig. 79). Scale 1:5

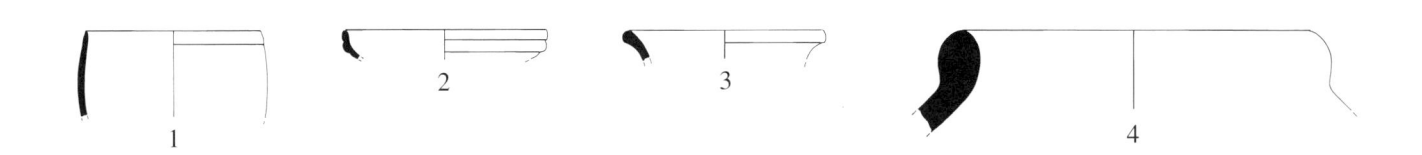

Figure 69. Pottery from Trench IVX = Northern Half of Trench IVM, Room 7 (Phase 2A; Period F — Early Bronze Age IVa). Scale 1:5

1. SBR. A.I.a (TS. 2919; IVX, 10.8). Small rim and upper wall segment. Fairly fine buff ware, evenly fired. Creamy-buff slip in and out.
2. BR. D.II.c (TS. 2957; IVX, 10.8). About 1/8 rim small portion of upper wall segment. Fine light pinkish-buff ware, evenly fired. Creamy-buff slip in and out.
3. JR. J.III.g (TS. 3003; IVX, 10.8). About 1/6 rim and upper neck segment. Fine pinkish-buff ware, evenly fired. Creamy-buff slip in and out.
4. JR. O.II.m (TS. 3011; IVX, 10.7). Small rim and upper shoulder segment. Slightly coarse pink ware, evenly fired. Cream slip in and out.
—. JR.Sh. (PM. F; TS. 3136; IVX, 10.7). Jar sherd. Ware description not available.

Other Type Series Examples: (1) JR. C.II.b (TS. 2560), (2) JR. H.I.n (TS. 2556), (3) JR. P.II.s (TS. 2996), (4) CP. B.II.f (TS. 2627), (5) BE. E.II.l (TS. 3046), (6) BE. H (TS. 3066).

Other Study Collection Examples: (1) SBR. B.I.g (SC. 409), (2) BR. F.III.b (SC. 806), (3) JR. C.V.e (SC. 1030), (4) JR. J.I.b (SC. 2093), (5) JR. J.I.b (SC. 2105), (6) JR. J.III.x (SC. 1501), (7) JR. K.I.h (SC. 1597), (8) JR. (not typed, SC. 143), (9) BE. B.I (SC. 3107).

Figure 70. Pottery from Trench IVN, Rooms 8 and 18 (Phase 2A; Period F — Early Bronze Age IVa)

1. SBR. A.I.c (TS. 2559; IVN, 5.1, Room 8). About 1/2 rim and almost complete wall profile. Fairly fine drab ware, evenly fired. Buff slip in and out.
2. SBR. A.I.g (SW. 726; IVN, 5.2, Built into wall of Room 8 bench). Complete apart from about 1/2 of rim; hole through lower wall caused by overlarge pebble included in the temper. Slightly coarse greenish-buff ware, evenly fired. Self slip out.
3. SBR. C.III.a (TS. 2616; IVN, 2.2, Room 8). About 1/10 rim and upper wall segment. Slightly coarse pink ware, evenly fired. Cream slip out.
4. SBR. D.II.a (TS. 2614; IVN, 2.3, Room 18). About 1/10 rim and upper wall segment. Fairly fine light pink ware, evenly fired. Self slip in and out.
5. BR. L.I.e (TS. 1255; IVN, 2.2, Room 8). About 1/14 rim and upper wall segment. Slightly coarse pinkish-buff ware, evenly fired. Cream slip in and out.
6. SJR. A.I.a (TS. 2827; IVN, 2.2, Room 8). About 1/5 rim and upper shoulder segment. Fairly fine buff ware, evenly fired. Self slip in and out.
7. SJR. C.II.p (TS. 2999; IVN, 4.4, Room 18). About 1/3 rim and neck segment. Fine buff ware, evenly fired. Creamy-green slip out.
8. JR. C.I.d (TS. 2736; IVN, 2.3, Room 18). Ablut 1/5 rim and upper wall segment. Slightly coarse creamy-green ware, evenly fired.
9. JR. E.II.b (TS. 2640; IVN, 2.3, Room 18). Small rim and shoulder segment. Fairly fine pinkish-buff ware, evenly fired. Creamy-green slip in and out.
10. JR. F.III.f (TS. 2769; IVN, 2.3, Room 18). Small rim and upper shoulder segment. Hard, close light grayware, unevenly fired pink out. Flesh-colored pink slip out.
11. JR. H.I.g (TS. 2907; IVN, 4.4, Room 18). Small rim and shoulder segment. Slightly coarse ware, unevenly fired with dark brown core and pink at surfaces. Creamy-green slip out.
12. JR. J.I.h (TS. 2746; IVN, 2.3, Room 18). Small rim and neck segment. Fairly fine pinkish-brown ware, evenly fired. Self slip in and out.
13. JR. J.III.m (TS. 2577; IVN, 2.2, Room 8). Two joining fragments; about 1/2 rim and neck segment. Fairly fine light pink ware, evenly fired. Creamy-buff slip in and out.
14. JR. J.III.q (TS. 2576; IVN, 4.4, Room 18). About 1/3 rim and neck segment. Fairly fine buff ware, evenly fired. Cream slip in and out.
15. JR. J.IV.a (TS. 1699; IVN, 3.1, Room 18). Large segment of rim, neck, and shoulder. Medium fine grayish ware with lime and mica grits, evenly fired. Cream slip in and out.
16. JR. O.II.b (TS. 2791; IVN, 2.3, Room 18). Complete rim and most of body, but not mended to completion. Slightly coarse grayish-brown ware, evenly fired. Self slip in and out. Interior wall vertically straw-wiped during wet-smooth stage of manufacture.
17. JR. O.II.d (TS. 2806; IVN, 2.2, Room 8). About 1/7 rim and shoulder segment. Slightly coarse pink ware, evenly fired. Creamy-pink slip out.
18. JR. O.II.f (TS. 2805; IVN, 2.3, Room 18). About 1/4 rim and shoulder segment. Hard, close buff ware, evenly fired. Creamy-green slip in and out.
19. CP. B.V.a (TS. 2853; IVN, 2.2, Room 8). About 1/14 of rim and upper neck (two joining segments). Slightly coarse gritty pinkish-brown ware, fairly evenly fired. Self slip in and out.
20. BE. E.II.d (TS. 3042; IVN, 4.4, Room 18). Small rim of base and portion of lower wall of the vessel. Slightly coarse pink ware, evenly fired. Cream slip out.
21. JR.Sh. (PM. D.24; TS. 2750; IVN, 2.3, Room 18). Jar shoulder sherd with potter's mark incised before firing. Fairly coarse grayish-buff ware, evenly fired. Wheel-applied creamy-green slip lines in reserve out.
22. JR. J.III.e (TS. 1692; IVN, 4.4, Room 18). Large neck and shoulder segment. Medium fine buff ware, evenly fired. Cream slip in and out.
—. JR.Sh. (PM. F; TS. 3122; IVN, 2.3, Room 18). Jar sherd. Ware description not available.
—. JR.Sh. (PM. F; TS. 3141; IVN, 4.4, Room 18). Jar sherd. Ware description not available.
—. JR.Sh. (PM. F; TS. 3144; IVN, 2.2, Room 8). Jar sherd. Ware description not available.

Other Type Series Examples:
Room 8 — (1) BR. F.IV.e (TS. 1754), (2) BR. L.III.h (TS. 1701), (3) JR. D.X.b (TS. 1743), (4) JR. G.I.c (TS. 1730), (5) Ld. C.III.a (TS. 1747), (6) SR. C.I.a (SW. 725), (7) BE. F.IV.a (TS. 2914), (8) ABS. B (SW. 631).
Room 18 — (1) SBR. D.I.a (TS. 1681), (2) SBR. D.I.e (TS. 1682), (3) SBR. F.I.d (TS. 1707), (4) BR. F.IV.d (TS. 2731), (5) BR. L.I.a (TS. 2915), (6) SJR. C.II.m (SW. 723), (7) SJR. D.I.c (TS. 2745), (8) JR. H.III.t (TS. 2738), (9) JR. O.III.a (TS. 2807), (10) JR. P.II.b (TS. 2804), (11) JR. P.II.c (TS. 1627 = TS. 1735), (12) CP. B.II.c (TS. 2840), (13) CP. B.III.b (TS. 2854), (14) PS. A.II.c (TS. 1745).

Other Study Collection Examples:

Room 8 — (1) SBR. B.I.a (SC. 236), (2) SBR. B.I.e (SC. 329), (3) SBR. B.I.f (SC. 344), (4) SBR. B.I.f (SC. 348), (5) SBR. B.I.g (SC. 392), (6) SBR. B.I.g (SC. 399), (7) SBR. B.I.g (SC. 422), (8) SBR. B.I.h (SC. 482), (9) BR. A.II.e (SC. 718), (10) BR. F.III.b (SC. 808), (11) BR. F.IV.b (SC. 818), (12) BR. L.I.e (SC. 835), (13) BR. L.I.e (SC. 838), (14) BR. (not typed, SC. 26), (15) SJR. C.I.a (SC. 2538), (16) SJR. C.I.a (SC. 2534), (17) JR. E.II.c (SC. 1997), (18) JR. E.II.d (SC. 1143), (19) JR. E.II.n (SC. 1157), (20) JR. G.I.b (SC. 1538), (21) JR. H.III.i (SC. 2083), (22) JR. J.II.i (SC. 2173), (23) J.III.c (SC. 2220), (24) JR. J.III.h (SC. 2294), (25) JR. J.III.k (SC. 2305), (26) JR. J.III.m (SC. 2319), (27) JR. J.III.m (SC. 2315), (28) JR. J.III.n (SC. 1498), (29) JR. J.III.x (SC. 1499), (30) JR. J.III.z (SC. 1509), (31) JR. J.IV.a (SC. 1521), (32) JR. K.I.b (SC. 1567), (33) JR. K.I.d (SC. 1585), (34) JR. K.I.g (SC. 1596), (35) JR. K.II.c (SC. 1604), (36) JR. K.II.d (SC. 1599), (37) JR. (not typed, SC. 72), (38) BE. (not typed, SC. 156).

Room 18 — (1) SBR. A.I.a (SC. 169), (2) SBR. B.I.a (SC. 243), (3) SBR. B.I.f (SC. 346), (4) SBR. B.I.f (SC. 347), (5) SBR. B.I.g (SC. 365), (6) SBR. B.I.g (SC. 379), (7) SBR. B.I.g (SC. 390), (8) SBR. B.I.g (SC. 401), (9) SBR. B.I.h (SC. 479), (10) SBR. B.I.h (SC. 510), (11) SBR. B.I.j (SC. 552), (12) SBR. B.I.q (SC. 591), (13) SBR. D.I.a (SC. 627), (14) SBR. D.I.b (SC. 635), (15) BR. F.IV.e (SC. 821), (16) BR. (not typed, SC. 27), (17) JR. J.II.g (SC. 2149), (18) JR. J.II.j (SC. 1356), (19) JR. J.III.l (SC. 2312), (20) JR. J.III.p (SC. 2351), (21) JR. J.IV.b (SC. 1523), (22) JR. O.II.k (SC. 1657), (23) CP. A.I.a (SC. 1776), (24) CP. C.I.d (SC. 1902), (25) Jg. A.I.b (SC. 1930), (26) Hd. A (SC. 3271), (27) SV.2 (SC. 3278).

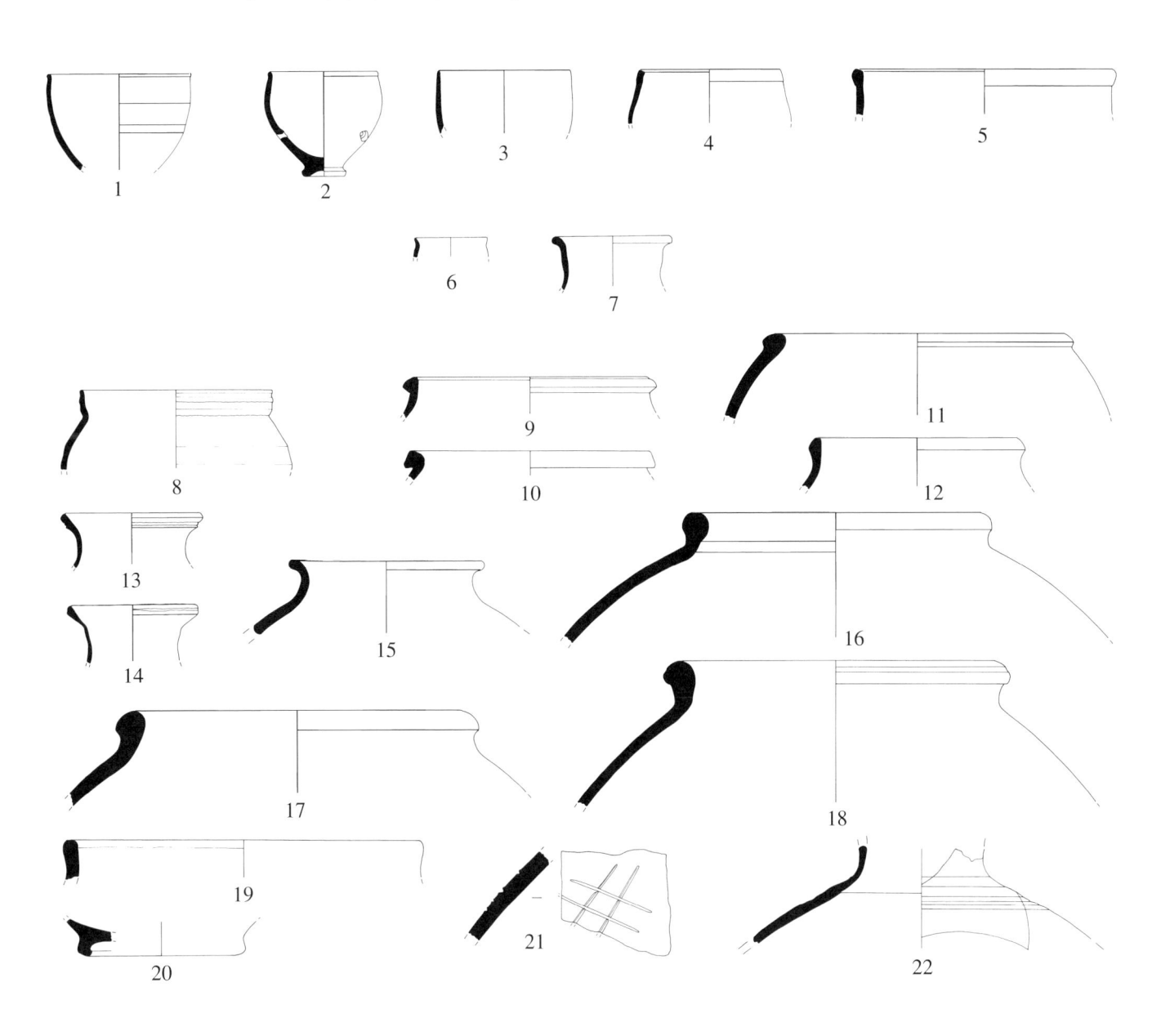

Pottery from Trench IVN, Rooms 8 and 18 (Phase 2A; Period F — Early Bronze Age IVa). Scale 1:5

Figure 71. Pottery from Trench IVN, Operation 10, Rooms 8 and 18 (Phase 2A; Period F — Early Bronze Age IVa)

1. SBR. A.I.a (TS. 4022; Op. 10, 20, Room 18). Small rim and upper wall segment. For ware, compare Phase 2A Type Series example from Area IVB (SW. 268).
2. SBR. A.I.c (TS. 4067; Op. 10, 20, Room 18). About 1/12 rim and upper wall segment. Fine light pinkish-buff ware with a few small gold- and silver-colored mica grits, evenly fired. Pale creamy-green slip in and out.
3. SBR. A.I.e (TS. 4061; Op. 10, 20, Room 18). About 1/3 rim broken in six parts and about 1/3 of body. Fairly fine light pinkish-orange ware with small gold- and silver-colored mica and lime grits, evenly fired. Self slip in and out.
4. SBR. A.I.e (TS. 4064; Op. 10, 23, Room 8, N. of bench). About 1/5 rim and upper wall segment. Very fine light pinkish-brown ware with gold- and silver-colored mica grits, evenly fired. Self slip in and out.
5. SBR. A.I.g (TS. 4062; Op. 10, 20, Room 18). Small rim (2 cm) and about 1/6 body segment. Fairly coarse greenish-buff ware with a few small black-, gold-, and silver-colored mica and lime grits, evenly fired. Creamy-green slip in and out.
6. SBR. B.I.h (TS. 4066; Op. 10, 20, Room 18). Small rim (3.5 cm) and upper wall segment. Fairly fine dark buff-brown ware with gold- and silver-colored mica and lime grits, evenly fired. Buff slip out.
7. SBR. C.II.a (TS. 3333; Op. 10, 22.3, Room 8). About 1/2 of rim and most of wall profile; base missing. For ware, compare Phase 3 Type Series example from Area IC (TS. 1042).
8. SBR. D.I.c (TS. 4025; Op. 10, 20, Room 18). Small rim and upper wall segment. For ware, compare Phase 2B Type Series example from Area IXA (TS. 1017).
9. SBR. D.I.e (TS. 4026; Op. 10, 20, Room 18). Small rim and upper wall segment. For ware, compare Phase 2A Type Series example from Area IVN (TS. 1682).
10. BR. A.I.d (TS. 4069; Op. 10, 20, Room 18). About 1/10 rim and most of wall profile. Fairly fine buff ware with gold- and silver-colored mica and lime grits, evenly fired. Creamy-buff slip in and out.
11. BR. D.I.b (TS. 3332; Op. 10, 22.3, Room 8, NE corner). Small rim and upper wall segment. For ware, compare Phase 7 example from Area IC (TS. 1083).
12. BR. K.I.b (TS. 4020; Op. 10, 20, Room 18). Small rim and upper wall segment. Hard, close, pinkish-white ware, evenly fired. Creamy-buff slip out.
13. BR. L.III.e (TS. 3335; Op. 10, 22.3, Room 8, NE corner). Small rim and upper wall segment. Slightly coarse pinkish-brown ware, evenly fired. Self slip in and out.
14. SJR. A.I.a (TS. 4071; Op. 10, 20, Room 18). About 1/12 rim and upper wall segment. Fine pinkish-orange ware with gold- and silver-colored mica grits, evenly fired. Creamy-buff slip out.
15. SJR. A.I.c (PM. D.14; TS. 3364; Op. 10, 20, Room 18). About 1/2 rim and body segment with a potter's mark incised on shoulder before firing. For ware, compare Phase 2A Type Series example from Area IIIB (TS. 158).
16. SJR. B.II.d (TS. 4032; Op. 10, 20, Room 18). Small rim, neck, and shoulder segment. For ware, compare Phase 4 Type Series example from Area IVN (TS. 1711).
17. SJR. D.I.c (TS. 4021; Op. 10, 20, Room 18). Small rim and shoulder segment. For ware, compare Phase 2A Type Series example from Area IVN (TS. 2745).
18. JR. E.I.a (TS. 3334; Op. 10, 22.3, Room 8, NE corner). Small rim and upper shoulder segment. For ware, compare Phase 5 Type Series example from Area IC (TS. 2125).
19. JR. H.I.j (TS. 4065; Op. 10, 21, Room 8, NE corner). Small rim (5 cm) and upper wall segment. Fairly coarse ware with gold- and silver-colored mica and lime grits, unevenly fired with dark brown core and pinkish-orange at surfaces. Creamy-buff slip out and on top of rim.
20. JR. H.III.j (TS. 3355; Op. 10, 20, Room 18). Small rim and upper shoulder segment. For ware, compare Phase 2B Type Series example from Area IVM (TS. 1716).
21. JR. L.I.a (TS. 3337; Op. 10, 23, Room 8, on floor midway along bench). Mended to near completion. Very hard reddish-brown ware with a few lime grits, evenly fired. Coarsely made inside with additional clay added at the juncture of the neck and shoulder to provide extra strength; the additional clay had the impressions of a potter's fingerprints fired into the clay.
22. JR. O.I.a (TS. 3331; Op. 10, 22.3, Room 8, NE corner). Small rim, neck, and upper shoulder segment. For ware, compare Phase 2A Type Series example from Area IVM (SW. 695).
23. JR. O.II.b (TS. 4019; Op. 10, 20, Room 18). Small rim and upper shoulder segment; diameter 30 cm. For ware, compare Phase 3 Type Series example from Area IVR (SW. 711).
24. WPS. B (PM. D.19; TS. 4074; Op. 10, 20, Room 8, W. side). Fragment of a windowed stand with remains of two windows with a tree or wheat stalk potter's mark incised between the windows before firing. Fairly fine light pink ware with small gold- and silver-colored mica and lime grits, evenly fired. Creamy-buff slip in and out.
25. JR.Sh. (IP [G.4] F.I; TS. 4073; Op. 10, 20, Room 8, W. side). Jar body sherd with remains of an animal's legs, incised before firing. Slightly coarse pinkish-buff ware with small gold- and silver-colored mica and lime grits, fairly evenly fired.
26. JR.Sh. (PM. A.4; TS. 4076; Op. 10, 21, Room 8, W. side). Jar sherd with remains of pot mark on shoulder, incised before firing. Slightly coarse light pinkish-orange ware with gold-colored mica and white lime grits, evenly fired. Light creamy-green slip out.

Figure 71

27. JR.Sh. (PM. E.2; TS. 4075; Op. 10, 20, Room 8, W. side). Jar sherd with remains of a potter's mark on shoulder, incised before firing. Slightly coarse reddish-brown ware with gold- and silver-colored mica and black and white lime grits, fairly evenly fired. Brownish-buff slip out.
28. SV.2 (TS. 4072; Op. 10, 20, Room 8, W side). About 1/2 fragment of a spout and segment of the wall of a vessel (cf. jar Type H.III.t, TS. 2738, pl. 250:12, to which this spout may belong). Fairly fine creamy-green ware with small gold-colored mica and white lime grits, evenly fired. Self slip in and out.
29. SV.5 (TS. 4068; Op. 10, 20, Room 8, W side). About 1/2 segment of a hollow leg of a bowl. Fairly fine pink-brown ware with gold- and silver-colored mica and lime grits, evenly fired. Self slip in and out.
30. BE. B.I (TS. 4033; Op. 10, 20, Room 18). About 1/2 base and lower wall of vessel. For ware, compare Phase 2B example from Area IVN (TS. 2768).
31. BE. F.VII (IP [G.4] G.I.a; TS. 4023; Op. 10, 20, Room 18). Fragment of vessel and pedestal-type stand with decoration on outside wall, incised before firing. For ware, compare Phase 2 Type BE. F.VIII.c example from Area IIA (TS. 526).

Other Type Series Examples:
 Room 8 — (1) JR. J.III.ae (TS. 4024), (2) JR. O.I.g (TS. 3362), (3) JR. O.I.h (TS. 4031), (4) JR. O.II.i (TS. 4030), (5) JR. P.II.k (TS. 4018), (6) JR. P.II.l (TS. 4029), (7) BE. F.I.b (TS. 4070).
 Room 18 — (1) JR. A.I.a (TS. 3363).

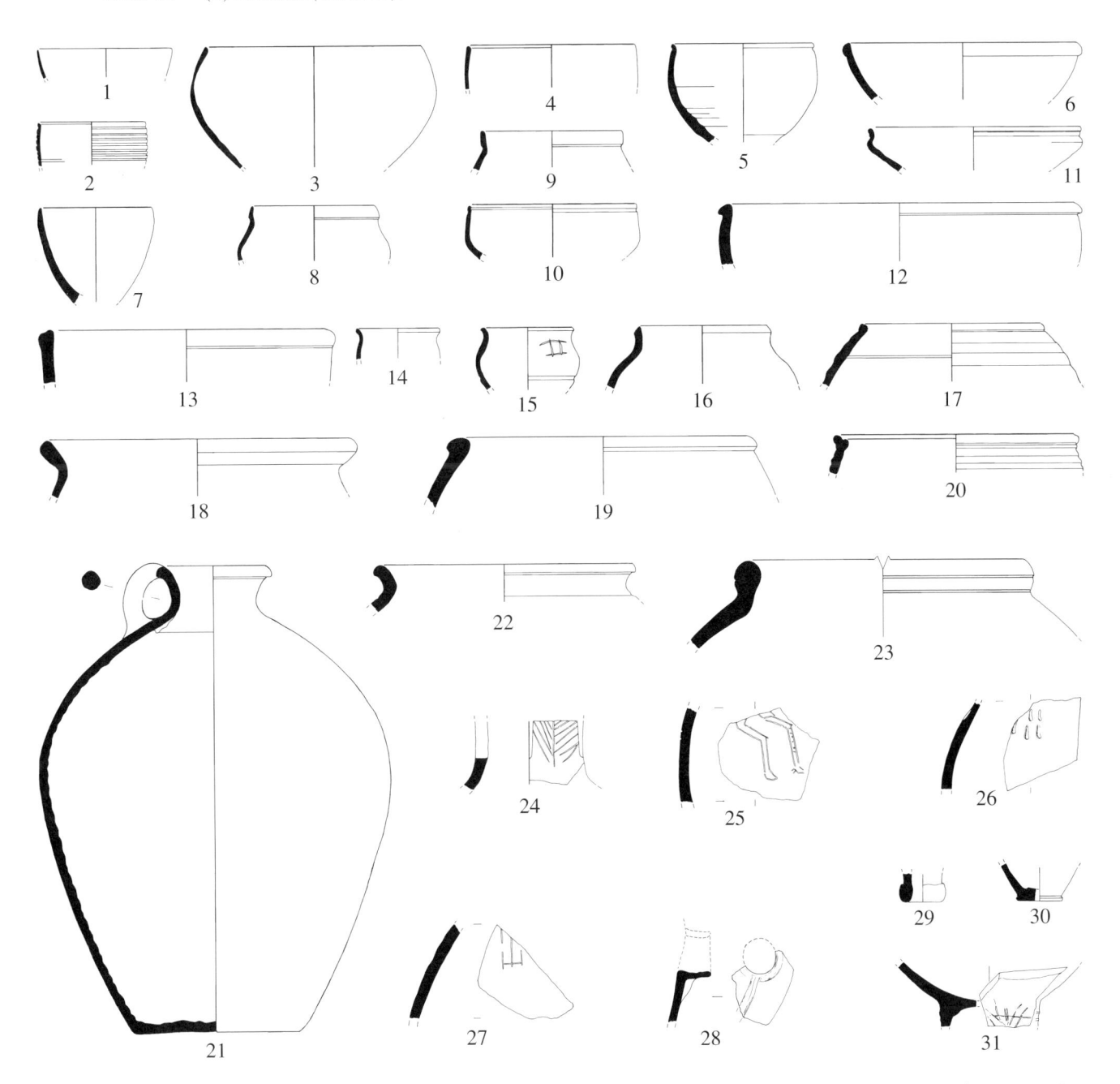

Pottery from Trench IVN, Operation 10, Rooms 8 and 18 (Phase 2A; Period F — Early Bronze Age IVa). Scale 1:5

Figure 72. Pottery from Trench IVO, Room 10 (Phase 2A; Period F — Early Bronze Age IVa)

1. SBR. A.I.e (TS. 2606; IVO, 1.3 [base], + 1.4 [rim]). Mended to near completion. Slightly coarse pinkish-brown ware, evenly fired. Self slip in and out.
2. SBR. B.I.f (TS. 2920; IVO, 1.4). About 1/5 rim and upper wall segment. Fairly fine light pink ware, evenly fired. Thick creamy-green slip on inside.
3. SBR. D.I.e (TS. 2962; IVO, 1.4). Small rim and upper wall segment. Fairly fine dark buff ware, evenly fired. Creamy-buff slip in and out.
4. BR. L.I.a (TS. 2902; IVO, 1.4). About 1/8 rim and upper wall segment. Hard, close greenish-buff ware, evenly fired. Self slip in and out.
5. BR. L.I.a (TS. 2207; IVO, 1.4). Small rim and upper wall segment. Hard, fairly close light pink ware with small white lime grits, evenly fired. Cream slip in and out.
6. SJR. C.II.k (SW. 520; IVO, 1.4). Complete in situ. Fairly coarse pinkish-buff ware, evenly fired. Gray slip in and out, burnished out on the body below the neck and on the base.
7. JR. E.II.g (PM. A.22; SW. 665; IVO, 1.3, 1.4). Large rim and shoulder segment with potter's mark incised on shoulder before firing. Medium coarse pink ware, evenly fired. Cream slip in and out.
8. JR. J.I.c (TS. 1776; IVO, 1.4). Body complete in situ, but rim missing. Fairly fine light greenish-buff ware with fine lime and mica grits, evenly fired. Wheel-applied light creamy-green slip in reserve out.
9. JR. J.I.h (TS. 3017; IVO, 1.4). Two joining rim, neck, and shoulder fragments, about 1/5 segment. Fairly fine pink ware, evenly fired. Creamy-buff slip in and out.
10. JR. J.III.e (TS. 3024; IVO, 1.3, 1.4). Two joining rim, neck, and shoulder fragments, about 1/4 segment. Slightly coarse pink ware, evenly fired. Self slip out and just over rim in.
11. JR. L.II.a (TS. 1615 = TS. 1617; IVO, 1.3, 1.4) Complete rim and neck with one loop handle and most of upper body mended. Medium fine grayish-buff ware, unevenly fired. Self slip in and out.
12. JR. O.II.b (TS. 2797; IVO, 1.3, 1.4). Seven joining rim, neck, and upper shoulder fragments, about 3/4 segment. Slightly coarse light grayware, evenly fired. Creamy-green slip in and out.
13. JR. O.II.b (TS. 2800; IVO, 1.3, 1.4). Five joining rim and shoulder fragments, about 1/2 segment. Hard, fine pinkish-buff ware, evenly fired. Creamy-buff slip in and out.
14. JR. O.II.b (TS. 3034; IVO, 1.3, 1.4). Small rim and upper shoulder segment. Coarse grayish-buff ware fairly, evenly fired. Self slip in and out with traces of burnishing on rim.
15. JR. O.II.e (PM. D.17; TS. 2794; IVO, 1.3, 1.4). Three joining rim and shoulder fragments, about 1/5 segment, with portion of potter's mark on shoulder before firing. Slightly coarse brown ware, unevenly fired reddish-brown at surfaces. Self slip out.
16. JR. O.II.g (TS. 2803; IVO, 1.4). Small rim and shoulder segment. Slightly coarse pinkish-brown ware, evenly fired. Self slip in and out.
17. JR. P.I.b (TS. 2796; IVO, 1.3, 1.4). Two joining rim and shoulder fragments, about 1/6 segment. Slightly coarse grayish-buff ware, evenly fired. Creamy-green slip in and out.
18. CP. B.II.e (TS. 2799; IVO, 1.4). Complete rim and most of upper body. Fairly coarse pinkish-brown ware, evenly fired. Self slip in and out.
19. BE. E.II.k (TS. 3039; IVO, 1.4). Complete base and most of lower body. Fairly coarse pinkish-orange ware, evenly fired. Cream slip out.
20. JR.Sh. (PM. C.11; TS. 1736; IVO, 1.4). Jar body sherd with potter's mark incised on inside of wall before firing. Medium coarse grayish ware with mica grits, evenly fired. Light green slip in and out.

Other Type Series Examples: (1) SBR. D.I.g (TS. 2598), (2) BR. F.III.a (TS. 2766), (3) BR. F.III.f (TS. 2990), (4) JR. E.II.b (TS. 2571), (5) JR. E.II.j (TS. 2789), (6) JR. H.I.g (SW. 642), (7) JR. H.III.k (TS. 2790), (8) JR. J.I.c (SW. 682), (9) JR. J.I.f (TS. 1626), (10) JR. J.II.l (SW. 664), (11) JR. J.IV.k (SW. 667), (12) JR. O.II.k (TS. 2801), (13) JR. Q.I.b (SW. 684), (14) CP. A.I.g (SW. 671), (15) BE. E.II.b (TS. 3077), (16) Hd. D.I (SW. 641).

Other Study Collection Examples: (1) SBR. B.I.d (SC. 298), (2) SBR. B.I.h (SC. 453), (3) SBR. B.I.h (SC. 520), (4) BR. L.II.c (SC. 855), (5) JR. E.I.a (SC. 76), (6) JR. E.II.d (SC. 2008), (7) JR. H, (Gen. Type SC. 40), (8) JR. J.III.e (SC. 2272), (9) JR. J.III.q (SC. 1484), (10) JR. K.II.c (SC. 1605), (11) JR. L.II.a (SC. 1609), (12) JR. J (Gen. Type, SC. 114), (13) CP. B.I.d (SC. 1825), (14) BE. E.II.i (SC. 3221).

Figure 72

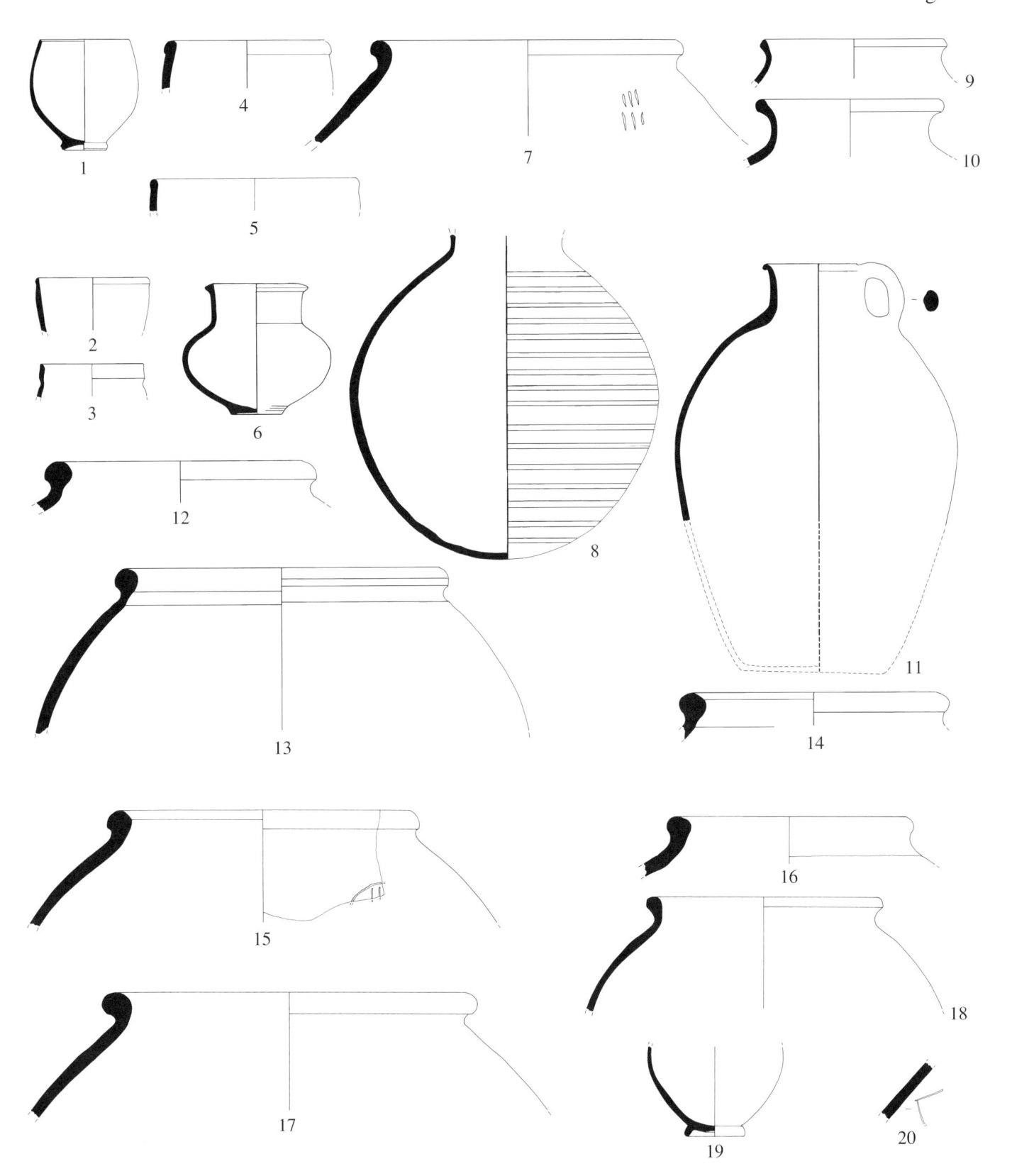

Pottery from Trench IVO, Room 10 (Phase 2A; Period F — Early Bronze Age IVa). Scale 1:5

Figure 73

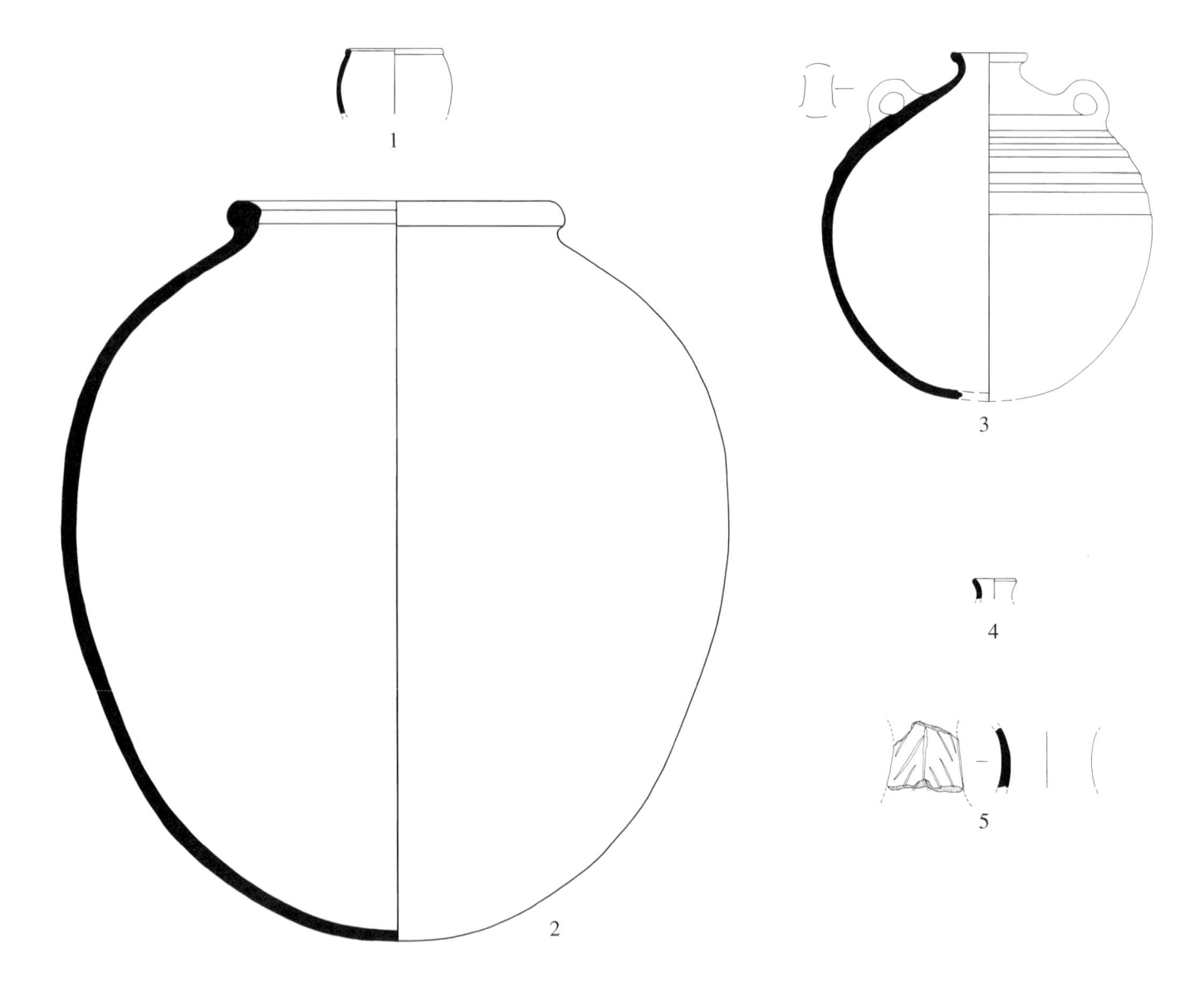

Pottery from Trench IVP, Courtyard Room 9 (Phase 2A; Period F — Early Bronze Age IVa). Scale 1:5

1. SBR. A.I.d (TS. 2917; IVP, 1.6). Four joining rim and upper wall fragments; about 2/3 segment. Fairly fine pinkish-buff ware, evenly fired. Cream slip out.
2. JR. O.II.b (SW. 737; IVP, 1.6, Inside blocked doorway on the northwest corner of Room 9). Mended to completion; heavily burned in and out. Fairly fine ware with a few lime and mica grits, unevenly fired with light green core and buff at surfaces. Fine creamy-green slip out. Wheel-applied additional slip lines in reserve at base.
3. FL. B.I.a (SW. 729; IVP, 1.6). Mended to near completion with two vertical loop handles on opposite sides of shoulder. Fairly fine close pinkish-brown ware with lime and mica grits, evenly fired. Creamy-green slip out.
4. FL. B.I.a (TS. 2947; IVP, 1.6). Complete rim and neck segment. Fine creamy-buff ware, evenly fired. Self slip in and out.
5. WPS. B (IP [G.4] D.IV; PM. D.20; TS. 2779; IVP, 1.6). Segment of body with a tree or wheat stalk potter's mark incised before firing. Hard, close pinkish-brown ware, evenly fired. Self slip in and out.

Other Type Series Examples: (1) SBR. B.I.e (TS. 2601 = TS. 2929), (2) PS. A.II.b (SW. 727).

Other Study Collection Examples: (1) SBR. B.I.g (SC. 372), (2) SBR. B.I.g (SC. 378), (3) SBR. D.I.b (SC. 634), (4) SBR. D.I.b (SC. 637), (5) SBR. D.I.b (SC. 638), (6) SJR. B.II.j (SC. 666), (7) JR. H.III.i (SC. 2084), (8) JR. J.III.c (SC. 2653), (9) PS. (not typed, SC. 55).

Figure 74

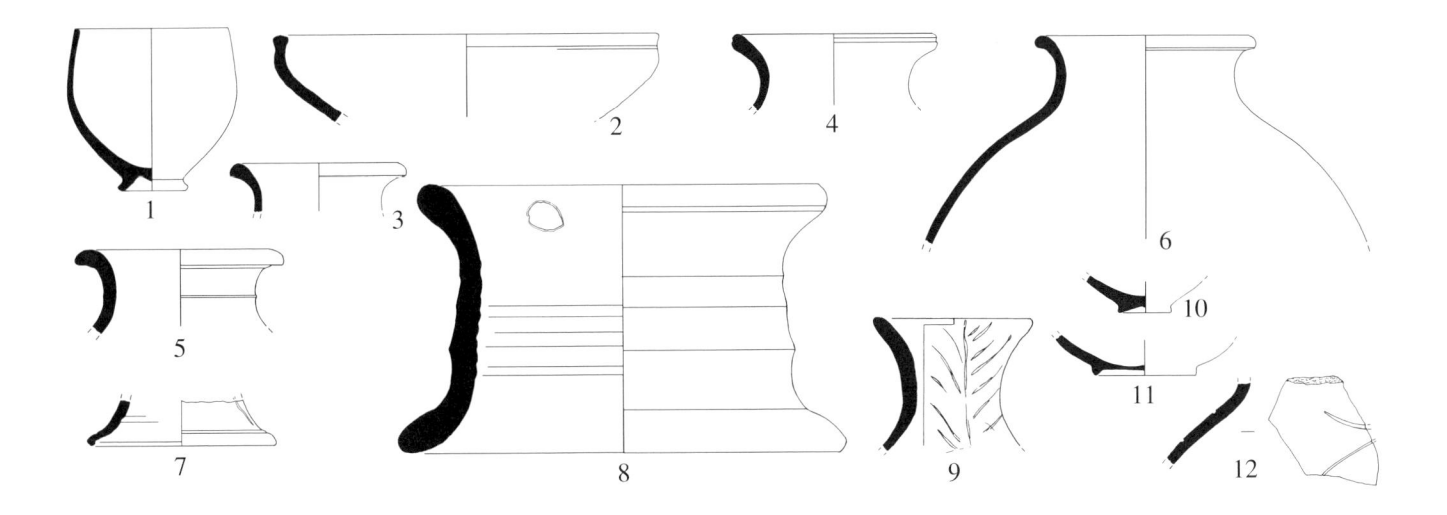

Pottery from Trench IVP, Operation 6, Courtyard Room 9 (Phase 2A; Period F — Early Bronze Age IVa). Scale 1:5

1. SBR. A.I.e (TS. 3294; Op. 6, 20.1). Complete profile with 3/4 base and small rim segment. Slightly coarse pinkish-brown ware with many gold- and silver-colored mica and fewer lime grits, evenly fired. Creamy-buff slip in and on upper wall out.
2. BR. J.I.c (TS. 3216; Op. 6, 20.1). About 1/10 segment. Fairly fine pinkish-buff ware with small gold- and white-colored mica grits, evenly fired. Cream slip in and out.
3. JR. J.III.d (TS. 4094; Op. 6, 1.24). About 1/10 rim and neck segment. Fairly fine creamy-buff ware with fine mica grits, evenly fired. Self slip in and out.
4. JR. J.III.m (TS. 4095; Op. 6, 1.24). About 1/10 rim and neck segment. Fairly fine creamy-green ware with fine lime grits, evenly fired. Self slip in and out.
5. JR. J.III.s (TS. 3459; Op. 6, 1.37). About 1/6 segment. Slightly coarse pinkish-buff ware with some white mica grits, evenly fired. Buff slip in and out.
6. JR. J.III.ab (TS. 3466; Op. 6, 1.10). Complete rim and about 1/2 shoulder and body segment. Large depression on extant part of shoulder made during firing. Fairly fine, close creamy-buff ware with small and large lime grits, evenly fired. Self slip in and out.
7. PS. A.II.c (PM. A.5; TS. 3468; Op. 6, 1.37). About 1/4 of top or bottom rim and wall segment with remains of a potter's mark incised before firing. Hard, compact pinkish-brown ware with a few fine white mica grits, evenly fired. Self buff slip in and out.
8. PS. B.I.a (PM. D.17; TS. 3351; Op. 6, 20.1). About 1/3 of top and bottom rim forming complete profile with a potter's mark incised just below the lip of one rim inside, made before firing. Slightly coarse light pink ware with gold- and white-colored mica and lime grits, evenly fired. Self slip in and out.
9. WPS. B (PM. D.19; TS. 3197 = TS. 3269 and TS. 3272; Op. 6, 1.3 + 1.17). About 2/3 rim and segments of wall profile with a tree or wheat stalk potter's mark incised on the wall before firing (see pl. 97e). Hard, fine pinkish-brown ware with very few gold-and white-colored mica grits, evenly fired. Self slip in and out.
10. BE. B.II (TS. 4096; Op. 6, 1.24). Complete base and portion of lower wall of vessel. Fine pinkish-buff ware with gold- and silver-colored mica and lime grits, evenly fired. Creamy-buff slip out.
11. BE. E.I.d (TS. 4097; Op. 6, 1.24). Complete base and portion of lower wall of vessel. Hard, fine ware with fine gold- and silver-colored mica and lime grits, unevenly fired with pinkish-brown core and gray at surfaces in and out. Self slip horizontally burnished in and out.
12. JR.Sh. (PM. B.3; TS. 4098; Op. 6, 1.24). Jar shoulder segment with portion of a potter's mark incised on the shoulder before firing. Slightly coarse pinkish-buff ware with fine gold- and silver-colored mica and white lime grits, evenly fired. Creamy-buff slip in and out.

Other Type Series Examples: (1) BR. M.I.a (TS. 3215), (2) JR. H.III.h (TS. 3295).

Figure 75

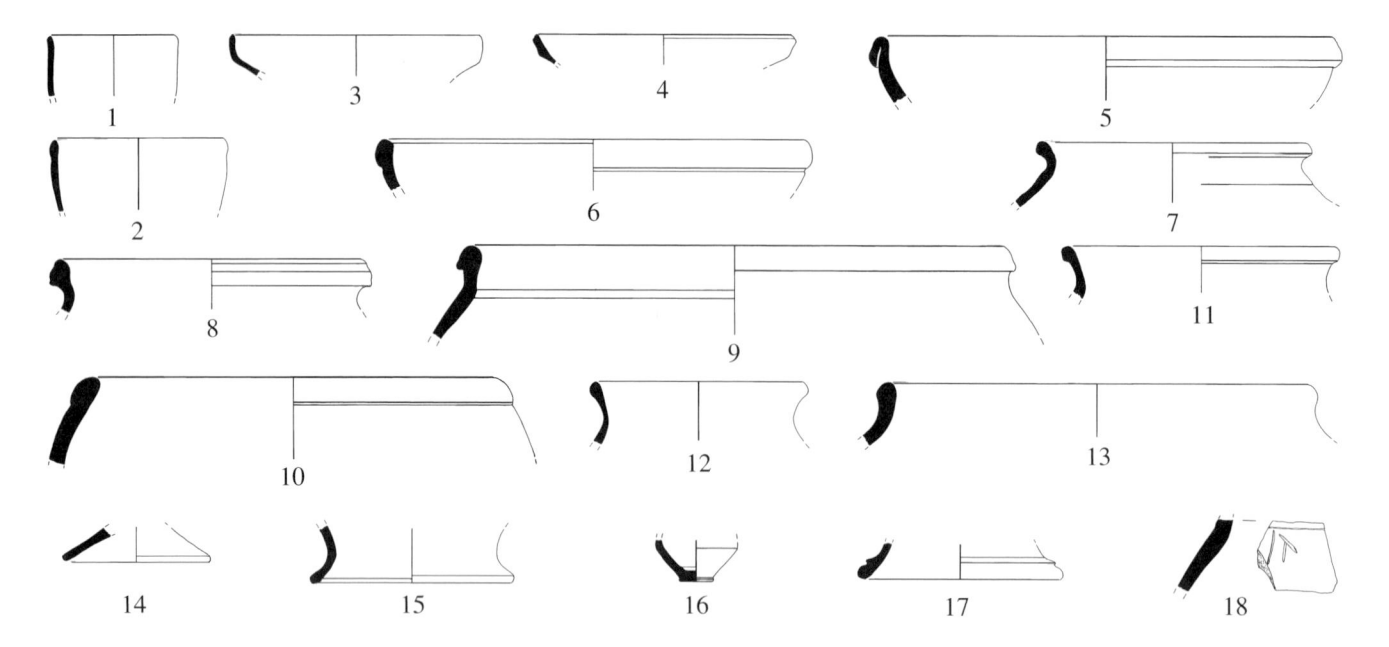

Pottery from Area IV, Operation 6, Room 16 (Phase 2A; Period F — Early Bronze Age IVa). Scale 1:5

1. SBR. A.I.b (TS. 3463; Op. 6, 18.7). About 1/8 rim and upper wall segment. Fairly fine pinkish-buff ware with small white mica grit, evenly fired. Creamy-buff slip out.
2. SBR. B.I.h (TS. 4088; Op. 6, 18.1). Small rim and upper wall segment. Fine buff ware with very fine gold- and silver-colored mica grits, evenly fired. Creamy-buff slip in and out.
3. BR. A.IV.f (TS. 3450; Op. 6, 18.7). About 1/10 rim and upper wall segment with burned patch on rim; vessel possibly used as a lamp. Fine buff ware with a few lime grits, evenly fired. Creamy-buff slip in and out.
4. BR. D.IV.a (TS. 3480; Op. 6, 18.6). Small rim and upper wall segment. For ware, compare Phase 2A Type Series example from Area IVM (TS. 2639).
5. BR. G.I.e (TS. 3453; Op. 6, 18.7). About 1/10 rim and upper wall segment with traces of burning out. Fairly fine pinkish-buff ware with white- and gold-colored mica grits, evenly fire. Cream slip in and out.
6. BR. L.III.h (TS. 3452; Op. 6, 18.7). Small rim and upper wall segment. Fairly fine buff ware with white- and gold-colored mica grits, evenly fired. Cream slip in and out.
7. JR. E.I.c (TS. 3220; Op. 6, 18.5). About 1/20 rim and shoulder segment. Slightly coarse buff ware with a few white lime grits, evenly fired. Creamy-green slip in and out.
8. JR. E.II.h (TS. 3456; Op. 6, 18.7). About 1/12 rim and neck segment. Fairly fine brownish-buff with fine lime grits, evenly fired. Cream slip in and out.
9. JR. E.II. n (TS. 3457; Op. 6, 18.7). Small rim, neck, and shoulder segment. Fine pinkish-brown ware with fine gold-colored mica grits, evenly fired. Cream slip out and just over rim in.
10. JR. H.I.a (TS. 3217; Op. 6, 18.5). About 1/20 rim and upper shoulder segment. Fairly fine pinkish-brown ware with very few visible lime grits, evenly fired. Creamy-buff slip out.
11. JR. J.III.c (TS. 3454; Op. 6, 18.7). Small rim and neck segment. Fairly fine pinkish-buff ware with lime grits, evenly fired. Self slip in and out.
12. JR. J.III.i (TS. 4089; Op. 6, 18.1). Small rim and neck segment. Fine dark buff-brown ware with fine lime grits, evenly fired. Self slip in and out.
13. CP. B.II.a (TS. 4092; Op. 6, 18.1). About 1/12 rim and neck segment. Slightly coarse pink ware with many gold- and silver-colored mica and black and white lime grits, evenly fired. Self slip in and out.
14. Ld. C.I.a (TS. 3464; Op. 6, 18.7). About 1/8 segment, but missing its knob-like handle. Hard, compact buff ware with no visible grit, evenly fired. Self slip in and out.
15. PS. A.II.a (TS. 4091; Op. 6, 18.1). About 1/8 rim and neck segment. Fine light pink ware with gold- and silver-colored mica and lime grits, evenly fired. Creamy-buff slip in and out.
16. BE. B.I (TS. 3462; Op. 6, 18.5). Complete base with portion of lower wall of vessel, string-cut from potter's wheel. Fairly fine pinkish-buff ware with a few gold-colored mica grits, evenly fired. Creamy-buff slip in and out. Partially charred on outside wall and on break of section.
17. BE. F.V.b (TS. 4090; Op. 6, 18.1). Small rim and wall segment. Fine brown ware with a few lime grits, evenly fired. Self slip in and out.
18. JR.Sh. (PM. C.19; TS. 3489; Op. 6, 18.7). Jar shoulder sherd with remains of a potter's mark incised before firing. Ware description unavailable.

Other Type Series Examples: (1) BR. P.I.a (TS. 3455), (2) JR. B.III.c (TS. 3451), (3) JR. D.IX.a (TS. 3469), (4) JR. J.III.i (TS. 3218), (5) BE. E.I.m (TS. 3465).

Figure 76

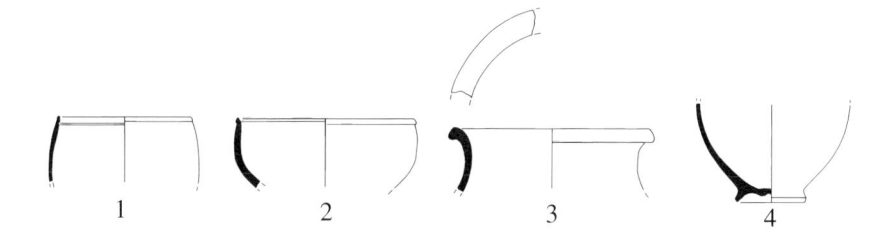

Pottery from Area IV, Operation 6, Room 17 (Phase 2A; Period F — Early Bronze Age IVa). Scale 1:5

1. SBR. A.I.c (TS. 3486; Op. 6, 17.3). Small rim and upper wall segment. For ware, compare Phase 2A Type Series example from Area IVJ (SW. 568) and Base BE. E.I.k (fig. 76:4 below), which belongs to this cup.
2. SBR. B.I.d (TS. 3487; Op. 6, 17.3). Small segment of rim and nearly complete profile of wall. For ware, compare Phase 4 Type Series example from Area IIIA (SW. 59).
3. JR. J.III.d (TS. 3488; Op. 6, 17.3). About 1/5 rim and neck segment. For ware, compare Phase 2A Type Series example from Area IVQ (TS. 3023).
4. BE. E.I.k (TS. 4093; Op. 6, 17.7). Complete base and lower half of cup, which belongs to SBR. A.I.c (fig. 76:1 above). Fairly fine pinkish-brown ware with fine gold- and silver-colored mica and lime grits, fairly evenly fired. Worn self slip in and out.

Figure 77. Pottery from Trench IVQ, Room 6 (Phase 2A; Period F — Early Bronze Age IVa)

1. JR. J.III.c (TS. 2624; IVQ, 2.4). About 1/4 rim and neck segment. Slightly coarse grayish-green ware, evenly fired. Self slip in and out.
2. JR. O.II.m (PM. A.10; SW. 639; IVQ, 1.4). Broken, but nearly complete, 1.60 m high with round base, in situ in northeast corner of room (not mended), with potter's mark incised on shoulder before firing. Coarse pink ware, evenly fired. Cream slip out.
3. JR. O.II.m (PM. A.12; SW. 643; IVQ, 1.4). Broken, but nearly complete in situ with round base (not mended), with potter's mark incised on shoulder before firing. Coarse ware, unevenly fired pink in and various shades of buff, cream, black, and green out.
4. JR. O.II.m (PM. C.5; SW. 644; IVQ, 1.4). Broken, but nearly complete in situ with round base (not mended), with potter's mark incised on shoulder before firing (see pl. 101c). Coarse pinkish-brown ware, unevenly fired with brown core and pinkish-brown at surfaces. Cream slip in and out.
5. JR. O.III.e (PM. D.1; SW. 638; IVQ, 1.4). Broken, but nearly complete in situ with round base (not mended), with potter's mark incised on shoulder before firing (see pl. 101d). Coarse pink ware, evenly fired. Cream slip out.
6. JR. O.III.e (PM. D.23; SW. 645; IVQ, 1.4). Broken, but nearly complete in situ with round base (not mended), with potter's mark incised on shoulder before firing. Fairly coarse pink ware, evenly fired. Cream slip out.
7. JR. P.II.a (PM. E.2; SW. 640; IVQ, 1.4). Broken, but nearly complete in situ with round base (not mended), with remains of potter's mark incised on shoulder before firing. Fairly coarse pinkish-brown ware, evenly fired. Creamy-buff slip in and out.
8. CP. B.II.a (TS. 1739 = TS. 2833; IVQ, 2.1 + IVH, unstratified, Room 3). Complete rim and most of body with round base (not mended). Fairly coarse pinkish-brown ware, wet-smoothed and evenly fired. Irregular horizontal burnishing out.
9. SR. C.I.a (SW. 591; IVQ, 1.6). Mended to completion. Fairly fine pink ware, evenly fired. Cream slip in and out.
10. JR.Sh. (PM. D.16; TS. 1774; IVQ, 2.4). Large fragment of jar body with remains of potter's mark incised on outside wall before firing (see pl. 101e). Fairly coarse grayish-brown ware, fairly evenly fired. Greenish-gray slip out.

Other Type Series Examples: (1) SBR. A.I.e (SW. 732), (2) JR. J.III.d (TS. 3023), (3) CP. C.I.c (SW. 680), (4) CP. C.I.f (SW. 678), (5) Bt. A.I.a (SW. 626), (6) PS. A.I.a (SW. 560), (7) PS. A.II.a (SW. 670 = TS. 2473).

Other Study Collection Examples: (1) SBR. B.I.e (SC. 659), (2) SBR. B.I.g (SC. 386), (3) SBR. B.I.h (SC. 516), (4) SBR. B.I.h (SC. 668), (5) JR. J. (Gen. Type, SC. 113), (6) CP. B.II.a (SC. 1840).

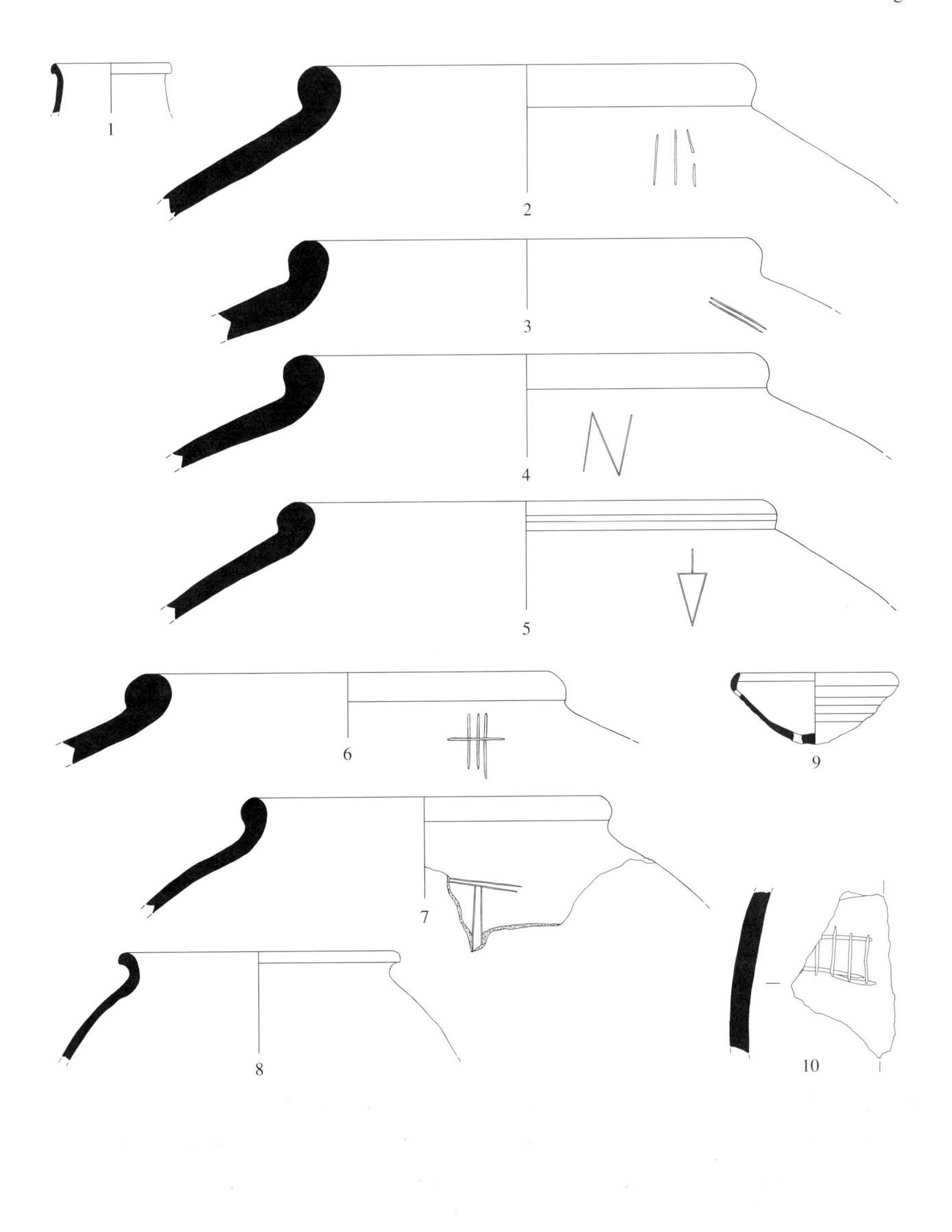

Figure 77

Pottery from Trench IVQ, Room 6 (Phase 2A; Period F — Early Bronze Age IVa). Scale 1:5

Figure 78

1

2

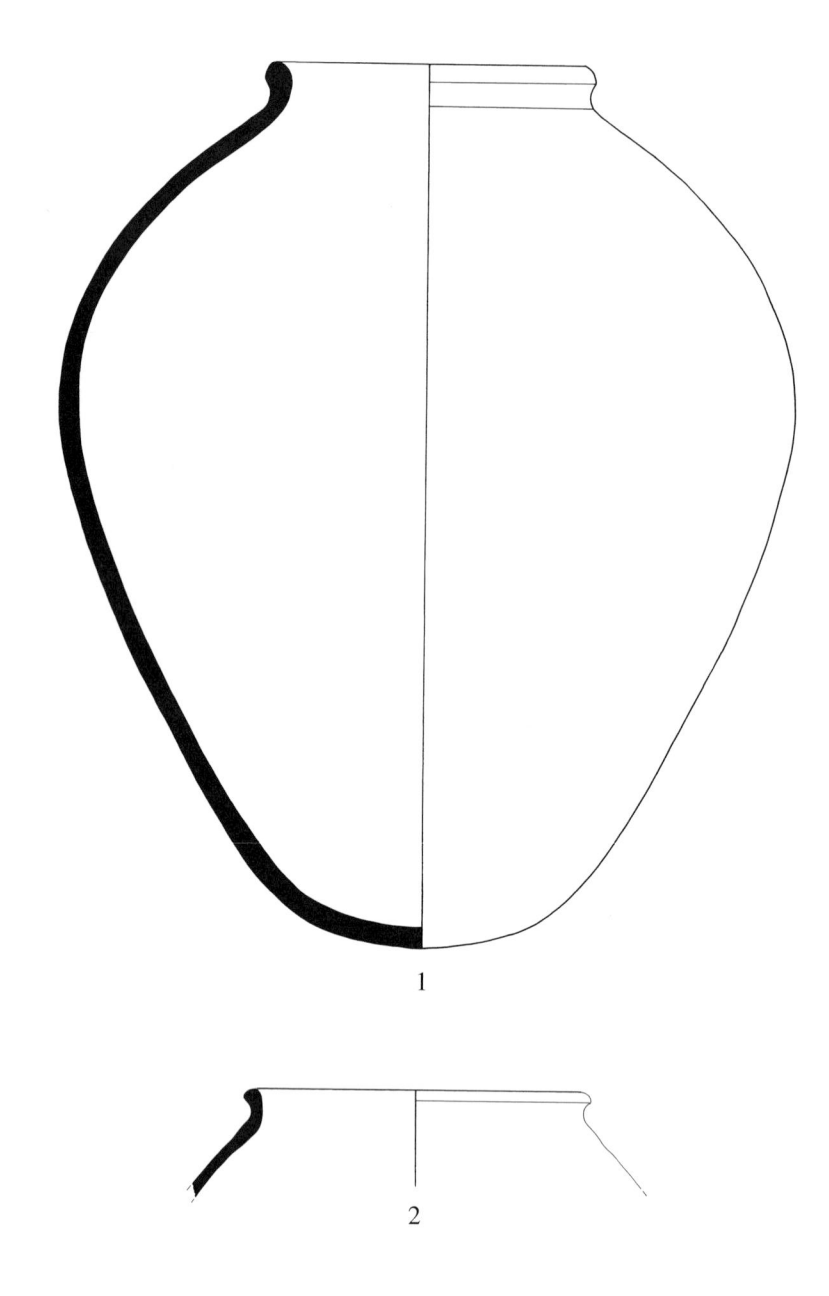

Pottery from Trenches IVR, Room 11, and IVS, Room 12 (Phase 2A; Period F — Early Bronze Age IVa). Scale 1:5

1. JR. P.II.i (SW. 738; IVS, 4.10). Mended to completion. Fairly coarse light brown ware with lime and mica grits, unevenly fired gray in patches out, pink in. Creamy-buff slip out and just over rim in.
2. CP. B.II.b (TS. 2843; IVS, 4.10). About 1/10 rim, neck, and upper wall segment. Fairly coarse and gritty grayish-brown ware, unevenly fired. Self slip in and out. Irregular burnishing out and over rim to base of neck.

   Type Series Examples: (1) JR. H.III.u (TS. 2740), (2) FL. A.II.a (SW. 722).
   Area IVR, Room 11 (Phase 2A, Period F) Early Bronze Age IVa Pottery (not illustrated here. See Type Series Example listed below).

   Type Series Example: (1) SR. A.II.d (TS. 2932).

Figure 79. Pottery from Trenches IVW, Sounding, and IVM, Room 7, Pit A (Phase 2A; Period F — Early Bronze Age IVa). Scale 1:5

1. JR. H.I.e (TS. 2742; IVW, 2.1). About 1/10 rim and upper shoulder segment. Slightly coarse salmon-pink ware, evenly fired. Cream slip out.
2. BR. G.I.c (TS. 1721; IVX=IVM, 3.1, Pit A). Small rim and upper wall segment. Coarse pink ware, evenly fired. Cream slip in and out.

Other Type Series Examples: Area IVW — (1) BR. D.II.c (TS. 2744), (2) SJR. C.II.v (TS. 1770).

Other Study Collection Examples:
    Area IVX = IVM, Pit A — (1) SBR. B.I.c (SC. 270), (2) SBR. D.I.d (SC. 647).
    Area IVW Sounding — (1) SBR. B.I.g (SC. 387), (2) BR. L.II.f (SC. 862), (3) SJR. B.II.j (SC. 664), (4) JR. H.I.d (SC. 1253), (5) JR. (not typed, SC. 133).

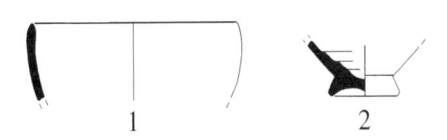

Figure 80. Pottery from Area IV, Operation 7, Room 34 (Phase 2A(a); Period F — Early Bronze Age IVa; see also figs. 143–45). Scale 1:5

1. BR. B.I.a (TS. 3534; Op. 7, 18.4). About 1/10 rim and upper wall segment. Fairly fine light pink ware with small gold-colored mica, lime grits, and vegetable temper, evenly fired. Cream slip in and out.
2. BE. E.I.c (TS. 3536; Op. 7, 18.4). Complete base and segment of lower wall of vessel. Slightly coarse orange-brown ware with gold-colored mica and lime grits, evenly fired. Self slip in and out.

Another Type Series Example: (1) JR. H.III.s (TS. 3535).

Figure 81

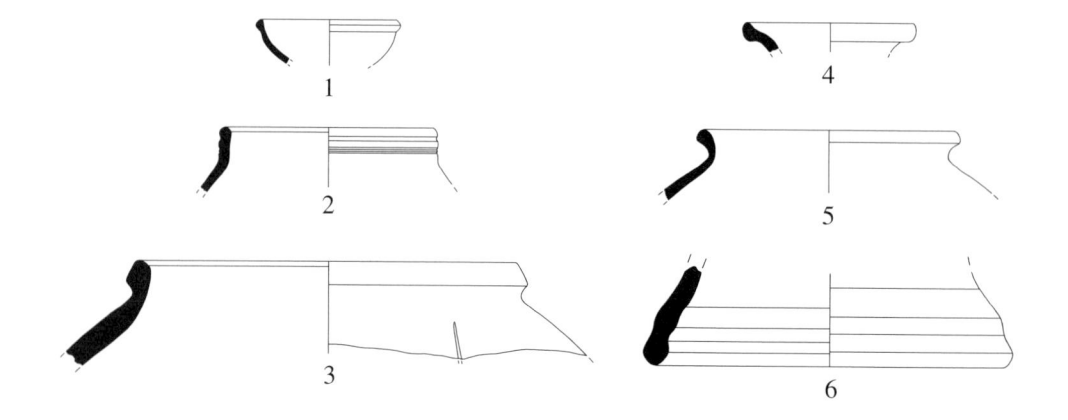

Pottery from Trenches IVZ(S) and IVZ(N1) (Phase 2A; Period F — Early Bronze Age IVa). Scale 1:5

1. BR. D.III.b (TS. 2943; IVZ(N1), 1.8). Small rim and wall segment. Fairly fine buff ware, evenly fired. Self slip in and out.
2. JR. C.III.a (TS. 2681; IVZ(S), 5.6, 5.7). About 1/5 of two joining rim and shoulder segments. Fairly coarse gritty ware, unevenly fired purplish at core. Creamy-green slip in and out.
3. JR. E.II.m (PM. A.5; TS. 3010; IVZ(S), 5.8 b, c). Two joining rim and shoulder segments with portion of a potter's mark incised on shoulder before firing. Slightly coarse pinkish-brown ware, unevenly fired light green at surfaces. Creamy-green slip in and out.
4. JR. J.III.q (TS. 2945; IVZ(S), 5.7). Small rim and neck segment. Slightly coarse and gritty pinkish-buff ware, unevenly fired pink at surfaces. Creamy-pink slip in and out.
5. CP. B.II.b (TS. 2842; IVZ(S), 5.7). About 1/8 rim and shoulder segment. Slightly coarse gritty pinkish-brown ware, evenly fired. Self slip in and out. Heavily burned outside.
6. PS. B.I.a (TS. 1732; IVZ(S), 5.6, 5.7). Incomplete segment of top or bottom of a pot stand. Medium fine grayware, evenly fired. Light green slip in and out.
—. JR.Sh. (PM. F; TS. 3109; IVZ(S), 5.6). Jar sherd. Ware description not available.
—. JR.Sh. (PM. F; TS. 3118; IVZ(S), 5.6, 5.7). Jar sherd. Ware description not available.

Other Type Series Examples:
    Area IVZ(S) — (1) JR. B.IV.f (TS. 2683), (2) JR. E.II.o (TS. 2682).
    Area IVZ(N1) — (1) JR. J.VI.b (TS. 2704).

Other Study Collection Examples:
    Area IVZ(S) — (1) SBR. A.I.a (SC. 186), (2) SBR. A.I.b (SC. 206), (3) SBR. B.I.h (SC. 443), (4) BR. F.III.c (SC. 878), (5) BR. J.I.d (SC. 828), (6) SJR. B.II.h (SC. 2514), (7) SJR. (not typed, SC. 57), (8) JR. C.I.b (SC. 992), (9) JR. D.II.a (SC. 1057), (10) JR. G.I.c (SC. 2039), (11) JR. H.I.d (SC. 1254), (12) JR. H.I.k (SC. 2449), (13) JR. J.I.c (SC. 1320), (14) JR. J.I.c (SC. 2114), (15) JR. J.III.g (SC. 2280), (16) JR. J.III.n (SC. 1448), (17) JR. J.III.q (SC. 1474), (18) JR. J.IV.j (SC. 1551), (19) JR. O.II.b (SC. 1625), (20) JR. P.II.e (SC. 1727), (21) BE. F.III.a (SC. 1908).
    Area IVZ(N1) — (1) JR. D.I.c (SC. 1050), (2) JR. D.I.d (SC. 1052).

Figure 82

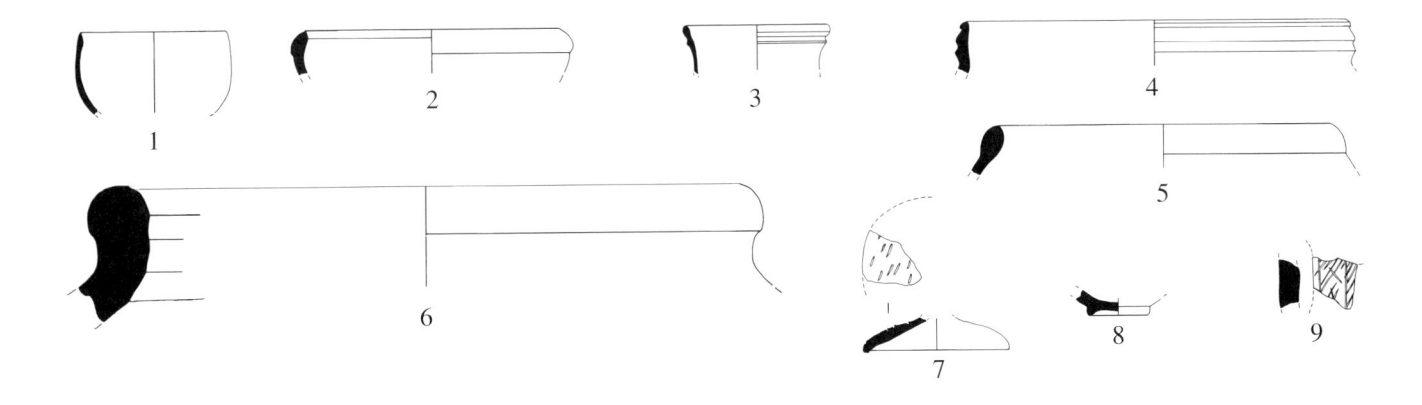

Pottery from Trench IXA (Phase 2A; Period F — Early Bronze Age IVa). Scale 1:5

1. SBR. A.I.e (TS. 2485; IXA, 1.8b). Small rim segment and most of wall profile. Slightly coarse buff-pink ware, unevenly fired buff on outer surface. Buff slip out and just over rim in.
2. BR. F.I.e (TS. 2240; IXA, 1.8b). Small rim and upper wall segment. Slightly coarse creamy-green ware, evenly fired. Self slip in and out.
3. SJR. C.II.a (TS. 1022; IXA, 1.8b). About 1/8 rim and neck segment. Fairly coarse reddish-pink ware, evenly fired. Self slip burnished in horizontal bands on outer rim and neck.
—. SJR. C.II.m (SC. 3307; IXA, 1.8b). Body sherd. Hard, fairly fine light grayware with silver-colored mica and small black and white lime grits, evenly fired. Dark gray self slip outside with irregular and vertical spaced narrow lines burnished after the slip was applied at the leather-hard stage of manufacture.
4. JR. D.III.a (TS. 1884; IXA, 1.8b). Small rim and neck segment. Fairly fine pinkish-buff ware, evenly fired. Creamy-buff slip out.
5. JR. H.I.a (TS. 1023; IXA, 1.8b). About 1/16 rim and upper shoulder segment. Fairly fine brown ware, evenly fired. Grayish-cream slip out.
6. JR. Q.II.d (TS. 1007; IXA, 1.8b). About 1/2 rim, neck, and upper shoulder segment. Fairly fine pink ware, unevenly fired with buff core. Cream slip out.
7. Ld. C.III.b (IP [G.4] G.II.a; TS. 1024; IXA, 1.8b). About 1/10 segment. Fairly coarse buff ware, evenly fired. Short decorative lines incised on top before firing.
8. BE. E.I.e (TS. 3080; IXA, 1.8b). Complete ring base. Fairly coarse pinkish-buff ware, evenly fired. Cream slip in and out.
9. WPS. A.I.a (IP [G.4] G.I.a; TS. 1885; IXA, 1.19). Segment with small portion of one side of a window in the wall of the vessel. Hard, fine pinkish-buff ware, evenly fired. Creamy-buff slip out.

Other Type Series Examples: (1) SJR. C.II.b (TS. 1892), (2) JR. C.IV.b (TS. 1882), (3) JR. D.III.a (TS. 994).

Other Study Collection Examples: (1) SBR. B.I.h (SC. 498), (2) SBR. D.I.e (SC. 652), (3) BR. F.II.a (SC. 791), (4) BR. F.II.b (SC. 801), (5) BR. L.I.e (SC. 839), (6) SJR. C.I.a (SC. 2539), (7) SJR. C.I.h (SC. 2572), (8) JR. J.II.g (SC. 2147), (9) JR. J.III.o (SC. 2341), (10) BE. E.I.f (SC. 3172).

Figure 83

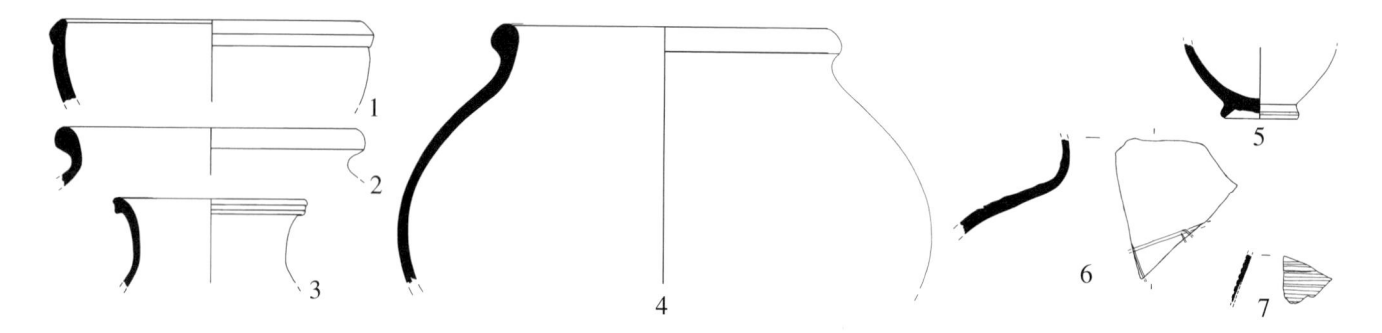

Pottery from Trench XA, Room 15 (Phase 2A; Period F — Early Bronze Age IVa). Scale 1:5

1. BR. F.III.h (TS. 2246; XA, 1.4). Small rim and upper wall segment. Fairly close pinkish-buff ware, evenly fired. Light creamy-green slip out.
2. JR. J.II.j (TS. 2353; XA, 1.4). About 1/4 rim and neck segment. Fairly fine pink ware, evenly fired. Buff slip out.
3. JR. J.III.m (TS. 1074 = TS. 1208; XA, 1.4 + 1.3). Two joining fragments, about 1/3 rim and neck segment. Medium fine creamy-buff ware, evenly fired. Self slip in and out.
4. CP. B.IV.c (TS. 2031; XA, 1.3, 1.4). Mended to nearly complete profile (round base, but no joins). Slightly coarse gritty light brown ware, evenly fired. Charred on rim and body out.
5. BE. E.I.c (TS. 3079; XA, 1.4). About 1/2 base and lower wall of vessel. Fairly fine grayish-buff ware, evenly fired. Self slip in and out.
6. JR.Sh. (PM. E.2; TS. 1267; XA, 1.4). Portion of neck and shoulder of jar with remains of a potter's mark incised on the shoulder before firing. Fairly coarse ware, unevenly fired with gray core and buff at surfaces. Creamy-green slip in and out.
7. JR.Sh. (TS. 1257; XA, 1.4). Body sherd. Fine grayware, evenly fired. Outside wall ribbed and well burnished.
—. JR.Sh. (PM. F; TS. 3120; XA, 1.4). Jar sherd. Ware description not available.

Other Type Series Examples: (1) SBR. B.I.n (TS. 1085), (2) JR. B.III.e (TS. 1050), (3) JR. C.I.b (TS. 1067), (4) JR. H.III.o (TS. 2504), (5) JR. J.III.b (TS. 1069), (6) JR. J.III.c (TS. 1075), (7) JR. K.I.a (TS. 2338).

Other Study Collection Examples: (1) SBR. A.I.a (SC. 191), (2) SBR. B.I.d (SC. 289), (3) BE. B.II (SC. 3109).

Figure 84

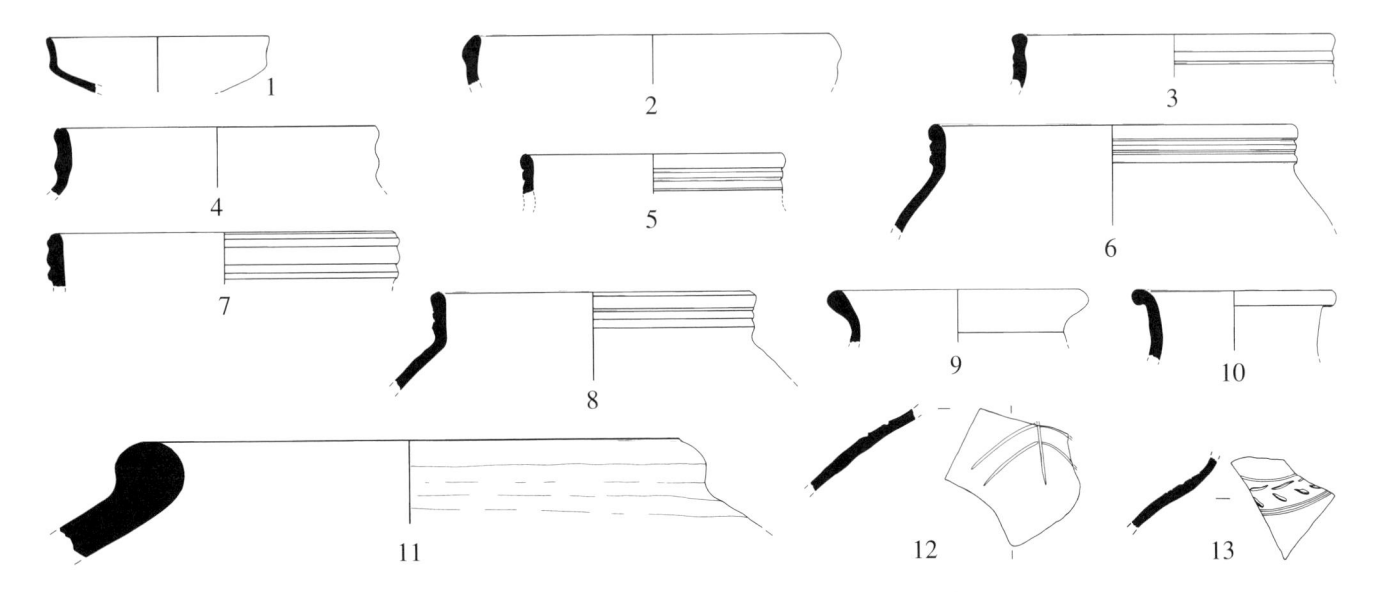

Pottery from Trench IVA (Phase 2B; Period F — Early Bronze Age IVa). Scale 1:5

1. BR. C.I.a (TS. 1924; IVA, 2.4, Street). Small rim and wall segment. Fairly fine pinkish-buff ware, evenly fired. Creamy-buff slip in and out. Iron ore-like color staining in and out.
2. BR. F.I.d (TS. 2190; IVA, 2.4, Street). Small rim and upper wall segment. Fairly close pinkish-buff ware, evenly fired. Cream slip in and out.
3. JR. B.I.a (TS. 2698; IVA, 2.3, Street). About 1/2 rim and neck segment. Hard, close pink ware, evenly fired. Creamy-yellow slip in and out.
4. JR. B.III.e (TS. 2184; IVA, 2.3, Street). Small rim and neck segment. Fairly close pink ware, evenly fired. Buff slip in and out.
5. JR. C.I.b (TS. 2187; IVA, 2.1). Small rim and neck segment. Fairly close pink ware, evenly fired. Creamy-buff slip in and out.
6. JR. D.V.d (TS. 2182; IVA, 2.1). Large rim, neck, and upper shoulder segment. Fairly close pink ware, evenly fired. Creamy-buff slip out and just over rim in.
7. JR. D.V.d (TS. 1976; IVA, 2.3, Street). Small rim and neck segment. Fairly coarse pinkish-orange ware, evenly fired. Buff slip out.
8. JR. D.V.d (TS. 2185; IVA, 2.3, Street). Large rim, neck, and upper shoulder segment. Fairly close pink ware, evenly fired. Creamy-buff slip out.
9. JR. E.I.b (TS. 2297; IVA, 2.4, Street). About 1/4 rim and neck segment. Fairly coarse buff ware, evenly fired. Creamy-buff slip in and out.
10. JR. J.III.e (TS. 2299; IVA, 2.3, Street). About 1/8 rim and neck segment. Slightly coarse grayish-buff ware, evenly fired. Light creamy-green slip in and out.
11. JR. O.II.m (TS. 2401; IVA, 2.3, Street). About 1/20 rim and upper shoulder segment. Coarse pinkish-brown ware, evenly fired. Creamy-green slip out and just over rim in.
12. JR.Sh. (PM. D.20; TS. 1942; IVA, 2.2). Shoulder sherd of jar with remains of a potter's mark incised on outside wall before firing. Fairly fine pink ware, evenly fired. Creamy-buff slip out.
13. JR.Sh. (IP [G.3] B.II.a; TS. 1948; IVA, 2.3, Street). Fragment of jar neck and shoulder with incised herringbone decoration bordered by horizontally comb-incised lines. Fine light grayware, evenly fired. Burnished self slip out.
—. JR.Sh. (PM. F; TS. 3121; IVA, 2.2). Jar sherd. Ware description not available.

Other Type Series Examples: (1) BR. A.IV.g (TS. 1930), (2) SJR. D.II.a (TS. 2014), (3) JR. J.III.k (TS. 2271), (4) JR. J.III.y (TS. 2335), (5) JR. P.II.m (TS. 603), (6) WPS. B (IP [G.4] D.IV; TS. 1183).

Other Study Collection Examples: (1) SBR. A.I.b (SC. 217), (2) SBR. A.I.f (SC. 2), (3) SBR. B.I.e (SC. 325), (4) SBR. B.I.k (SC. 561), (5) BR. L.II.b (SC. 854), (6) JR. C.II.a (SC. 1002), (7) JR. E.II.d (SC. 2014), (8) JR. J.I.b (SC. 1306), (9) JR. J.I.i (SC. 2136), (10) JR. J.II.h (SC. 2158), (11) JR. J.III.e (SC. 2252), (12) JR. J.III.e (SC. 2238), (13) JR. J.III.e (SC. 2262), (14) JR. O.II.e (SC. 1642), (15) JR. (not typed, SC. 138), (16) CP. A.II.d (SC. 1805), (17) SR. A.I.a (SC. 2639).

Figures 85–86

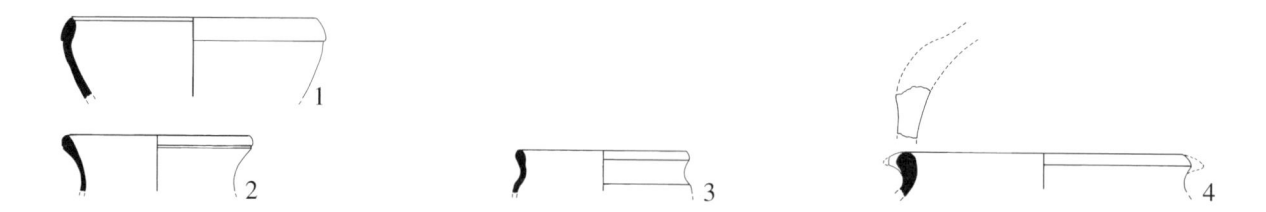

Figure 85. Pottery from Trench IVB = Southwest Corner of Trench IVF, Room 1 (Phase 2B;
Period F — Early Bronze Age IVa). Scale 1:5

1. BR. D.VII.a (TS. 2720; IVB, 3.3). Small rim and wall segment. Fairly fine buff ware, evenly fired. Creamy-buff slip in and out.
2. JR. J.III.t (TS. 2276; IVB, 3.5). About 1/4 rim and neck segment. Fairly coarse creamy-green ware, evenly fired. Self slip in and out.
3. CP. A.I.b (TS. 1972; IVB, 3.3). Small rim, neck, and upper wall segment. Fairly coarse gritty ware, unevenly fired with light gray core and light brown at surfaces.
4. CP. A.I.f (TS. 1186; IVB, 3.5). Small rim and neck segment with remains of one triangular-shaped lug handle. Slightly coarse grayish-brown ware with many lime and mica grits, fairly evenly fired.

Another Type Series Example: (1) BR. L.I.e (TS. 1926).

Other Study Collection Examples: (1) SBR. A.I.a (SC. 187), (2) SBR. A.I.b (SC. 211).

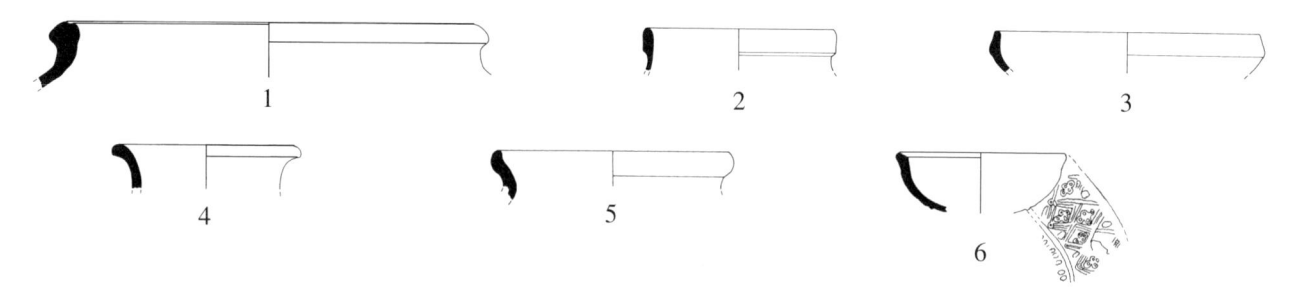

Figure 86. Pottery from Trench IVC, North and West Side of Town Wall Tower, Pit 1.6 and Room 7, and Trench IVD,
West Side of Town Wall (Phase 2B; Period F — Early Bronze Age IVa; see also fig. 154). Scale 1:5

1. JR. E.II.c (TS. 2397; IVC, 1.6, Pit). About 1/5 rim segment. Coarse ware, unevenly fired with gray core and reddish at surfaces. Thick yellow-green slip out.
2. SBR. D.I.f (TS. 2484; IVD, 3.1). About 1/8 rim and upper neck segment. Fairly fine pink ware, evenly fired. Pinkish-buff slip out.
3. BR. E.III.a (TS. 2505; IVD, 3.1). About 1/8 rim and upper wall segment. Fairly coarse pinkish-buff ware, evenly fired. Creamy-buff slip in and out.
4. JR. J.III.a (TS. 2318; IVD, 3.1). About 1/8 rim and neck segment. Fairly fine pinkish-buff ware, evenly fired. Creamy-buff slip out and just over rim in.
5. CP. A.I.h (TS. 1940; IVD, 3.1). Small rim and neck segment. Fairly coarse gritty ware, unevenly fired with light gray core and brown at surfaces.
6. Isl. Ld. (SW. 225; IVC, 1.7). Derived Islamic. About 1/6 rim of a shallow carinated bowl with mold-made decorative pattern outside. Pale greenish grayware with lime and mica grits, evenly fired. Light creamy-green at surface. Dated to about ninth–tenth century A.D.

Other Type Series Examples:
    Area IVC, Room 7 — (1) JR. J.II.d (TS. 2405), (2) JR. K.II.c (TS. 2347), (3) CP. A.I.b (TS. 326), (4) CP. A.I.f (TS. 1955), (5) CP. B.I.c (TS. 1971), (6) Jg. A.I.b (TS. 2221).
    Area IVD — (1) BR. F.II.d (TS. 2662).

Other Study Collection Examples:
    Area IVC, Room 7 — (1) SBR. B.I.h (SC. 499), (2) BR. J.I.d (SC. 827), (3) JR. B.III.e (SC. 945).
    Area IVC, Pit 1.6 — (1) SBR. B.I.h (SC. 495), (2) SJR. C.I.a (SC. 56), (3) JR. J.III.a (SC. 2210), (4) JR. J.III.e (SC. 2259), (5) JR. J.III.n (SC. 1442), (6) JR. J.III.n (SC. 1464), (7) JR. (not typed, SC. 132).
    Area IVD — (1) SR. B.II.b (SC. 1959).

Figure 87

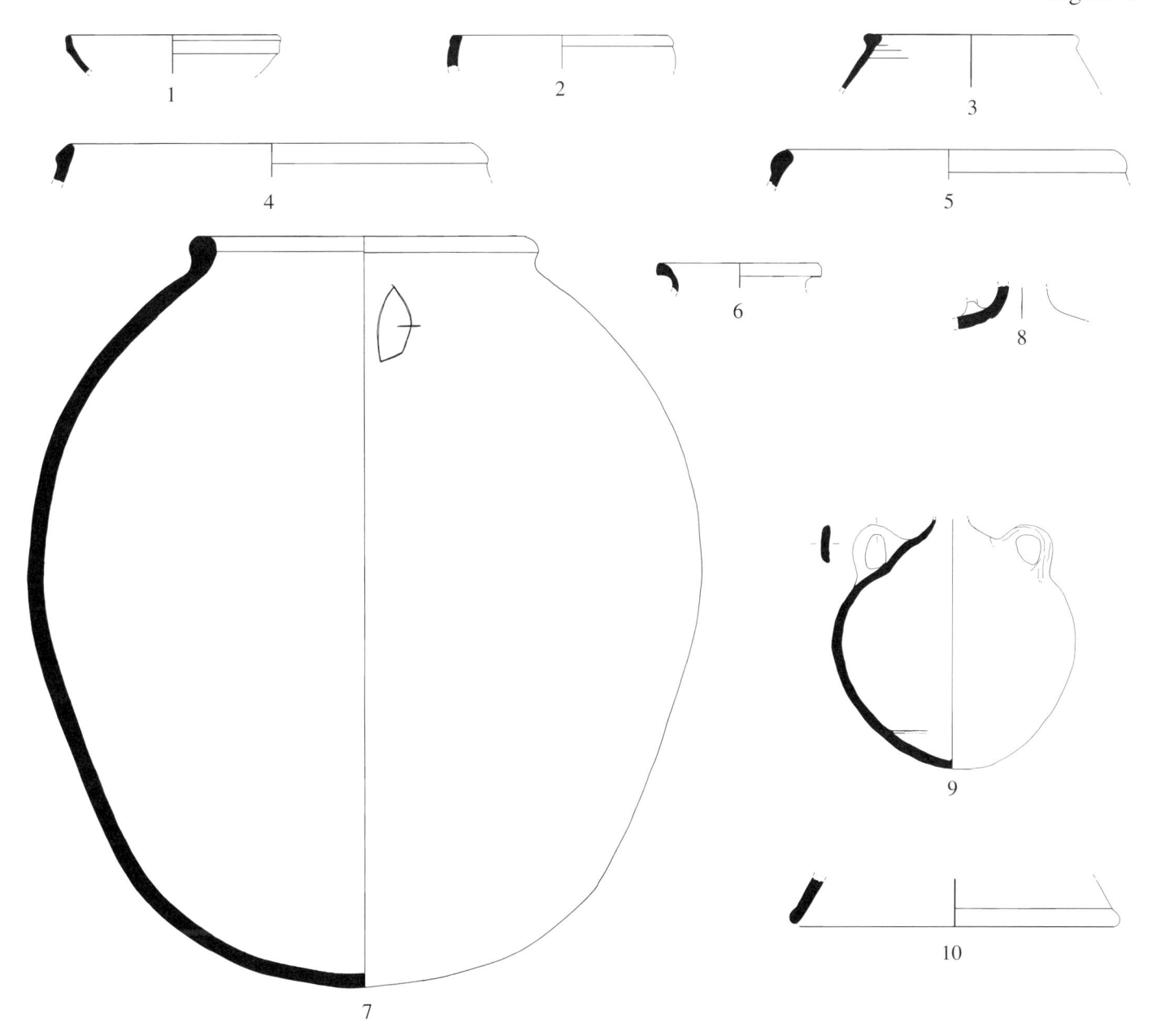

Pottery from Trench IVD, Room 2 (Phase 2B; Period F — Early Bronze Age IVa). Scale 1:5

1. BR. D.I.a (TS. 1938; IVD, 2.5). Small rim and upper wall segment. Fairly close buff ware, evenly fired. Creamy-buff slip in and out.
2. BR. L.I.b (TS. 1979; IVD, 2.5). Small rim and upper wall segment. Slightly coarse light greenish-buff ware, evenly fired. Self slip in and out.
3. SJR. D.II.b (TS. 1931; IVD, 2.5). Small rim and shoulder segment. Slightly coarse light grayish-buff ware, evenly fired. Self slip in and out.
4. JR. H.I.b (TS. 2189; IVD, 2.5). Small rim and upper shoulder segment. Hard, close pinkish-brown ware, evenly fired. Creamy-buff slip out.
5. JR. H.I.m (TS. 1968; IVD, 2.5). Small rim and upper shoulder segment. Hard, close pinkish-brown ware, evenly fired.
6. JR. J.I.c (TS. 2293; IVD, 2.5). About 1/8 rim and upper neck segment. Fairly fine buff ware, evenly fired. Creamy-buff slip out and just over rim in.
7. JR. P.II.i (PM. D.17; SW. 307; IVD, 2.4). Mended to near completion with a potter's mark incised on upper shoulder before firing. Hard, fairly coarse drab ware, unevenly fired pinkish-brown in and with pink patches out. Creamy-green slip out.
8. FL. A.I.b (TS. 1969; IVD, 2.5). Neck and shoulder segment with remains of one vertical loop handle. Hard, close pinkish-brown ware, evenly fired. Creamy-buff slip out.
9. FL. B.I.a (SW. 271; IVD, 2.5). Nearly complete body with two vertical loop handles on opposite sides of the shoulder (rim missing). Slightly coarse light green ware with lime grits, evenly fired. Lower body hand-shaved with tool before firing.
10. BE. F.II.b (TS. 1192; IVD, 2.5). Small rim and wall segment. Slight coarse pinkish-buff ware, evenly fired. Creamy-buff slip in and out.
—. JR.Sh. (PM. F; TS. 3125; IVD, 2.5). Jar sherd. Ware description not available.

Other Type Series Examples: (1) SBR. A.I.a (SW. 246), (2) SBR. A.I.g (SW. 301 = TS. 1742), (3) SJR. B.III.d (TS. 2548), (4) JR. E.II.w (TS. 2291), (5) JR. F.II.d (TS. 1933), (6) JR. J.I.d (SW. 295), (7) JR. J.I.e (SW. 292), (8) JR. J.II.h (TS. 2407), (9) JR. K.II.d (TS. 2398), (10) JR. O.II.m (SW. 368), (11) BE. F.IV.b (SW. 249).

Other Study Collection Examples: (1) SBR. A.I.a (SC. 177), (2) SBR. A.I.a (SC. 185), (3) SBR. B.I.b (SC. 4), (4) SBR. B.I.g (SC. 403), (5) SBR. B.I.h (SC. 433), (6) SBR. B.I.h (SC. 440).

Figure 88

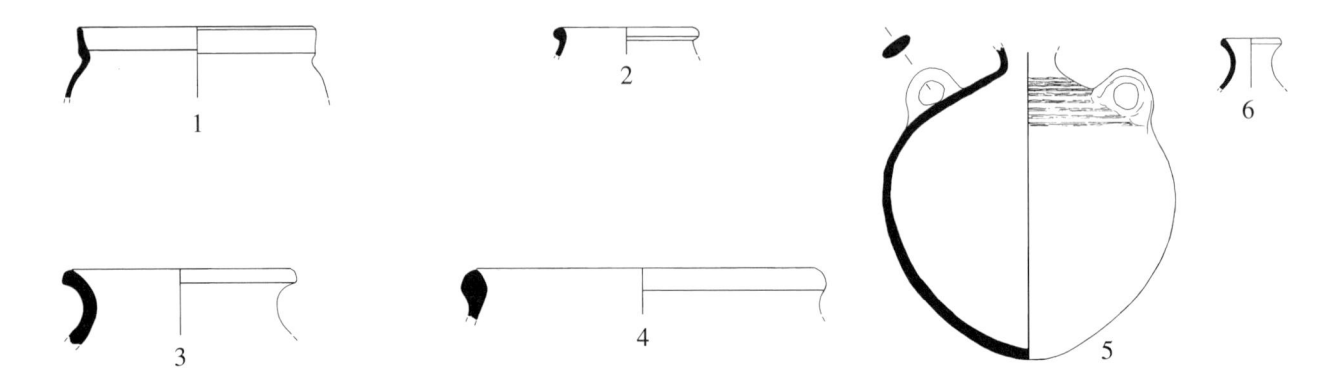

Pottery from Trench IVE, Rooms 3 and 4 (Phase 2B; Period F — Early Bronze Age IVa). Scale 1:5

1. SBR. D.I.g (TS. 1977; IVE, 1.4, Room 3). Small rim and upper wall segment. Fine close grayish-buff ware, evenly fired.
2. SJR. A.II.b (TS. 1950; IVE, 1.4, Room 3). Small rim and upper wall segment. Fine dark grayware, evenly fired. Burnished self slip out.
3. JR. J.III.g (TS. 2290; IVE, 2.1, Room 4). About 1/5 rim and neck segment. Slightly coarse pinkish ware, evenly fired. Creamy-buff slip in and out.
4. JR. P.II.d (TS. 2994; IVE, 1.4, Room 3). About 1/10 rim and neck segment. Fine creamy-green ware, evenly fired. Self slip in and out.
5. FL. B.I.a (SW. 272; IVE, 1.4, Room 3). Complete except for rim (see pl. 97a). Fairly fine buff ware with some small lime and mica grits, evenly fired. Wet-smoothed with irregular line brushing on body. Self slip with traces of burnishing marks.
6. FL. B.I.a (TS. 1185; IVE, 1.4, Room 3). Complete rim and neck. Fine, close pinkish-brown ware with lime and mica grits, evenly fired.
—. JR.Sh. (PM. F; TS. 3123; IVE, 1.4, Room 3). Jar sherd. Ware description not available.

Other Type Series Examples:
Room 3 — (1) SJR. C.II.q (TS. 2541), (2) JR. J.III.l (TS. 1958), (3) JR. P.I.a (TS. 2375), (4) BE. E.I.a (TS. 3073).

Other Study Collection Examples:
Room 3 — (1) SBR. B.I.c (SC. 275), (2) SBR. D.I.e (SC. 651), (3) BR. F.I.c (SC. 766), (4) JR. E.II.c (SC. 2004), (5) JR. J.III.o (SC. 2340), (6) JR. J.III.v (SC. 2362), (7) JR. O.II.b (SC. 2415), (8) JR. O.II.e (SC. 1643), (9) BE. E.II.c (SC. 3198), (10) BE. E.II.c (SC. 3215).
Room 4 — (1) SBR. B.I.h (SC. 489).

Figure 89

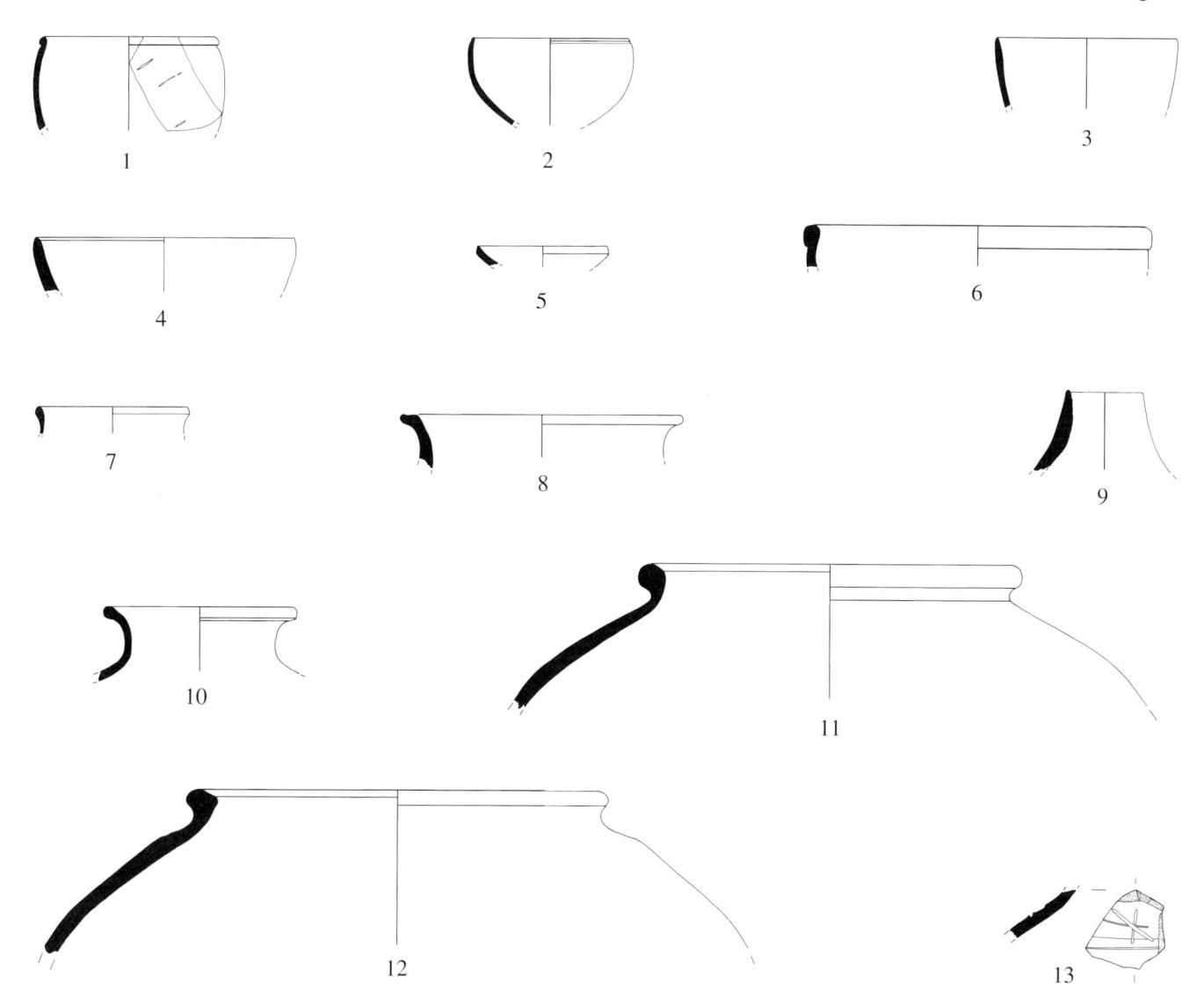

Pottery from Trench IVF, Southeast Corner of Room 1 (Phase 2B; Period F — Early Bronze Age IVa). Scale 1:5

1. SBR. A.I.d (PM. A.13; TS. 1927; IVF, 1.11). Small rim and wall segment with diagonally incised "fingernail" impressions on outside wall. Fairly fine pinkish-buff ware, evenly fired. Creamy-buff slip out and just over rim in.
2. SBR. B.I.a (TS. 2192; IVF, 1.11). Small rim segment with wall profile to base level. Slightly coarse buff ware, evenly fired. Creamy-buff slip in and out, heavily charred in.
3. SBR. C.III.a (TS. 2612; IVF, 1.14). About 1/8 rim and upper wall segment. Fine buff ware, evenly fired. Creamy-buff slip in and out.
4. BR. B.II.c (TS. 1929; IVF, 1.11). Small rim and upper wall segment. Fairly close pinkish-buff ware, evenly fired. Creamy-buff slip in and out.
5. BR. D.IV.a (TS. 1937; IVF, 1.9). Small rim and upper wall segment. Fairly close buff ware, evenly fired. Creamy-buff slip in and out.
6. BR. L.I.h (TS. 1947; IVF, 1.9). Small rim and upper wall segment. Fairly close pinkish-brown ware, evenly fired. Self slip out.
7. SJR. B.II.d (TS. 2022; IVF, 1.11). Small rim and neck segment. Fine light brown ware, evenly fired. Buff-brown slip in and out.
8. JR. G.I.b (TS. 2908; IVF, 1.14). Small rim and neck segment. Fairly fine pinkish-buff ware, evenly fired. Cream slip in and out.
9. JR. H.III.m (TS. 2652; IVF, 1.11). Small rim and neck segment. Fairly fine pink ware, evenly fired. Creamy-buff slip in and out.
10. JR. J.III.h (TS. 2266; IVF, 1.11, 1.12, 1.13). Complete rim and neck with partial shoulder. Slightly coarse grayish-buff ware, fairly evenly fired. Creamy-buff slip out and just over rim in.
11. JR. O.II.e (TS. 1537; IVF, 1.12). Complete rim and portion of shoulder mended. Slightly coarse ware with lime and mica grits, unevenly fired with gray core and pinkish-brown in. Thick creamy-buff slip out and just over rim in.
12. JR. O.II.e (TS. 1637; IVF, 1.11, 1.12, 1.13). Mended to 2/3 of rim and shoulder segment. Hard grayish ware, evenly fired. Cream slip in and out with reserved slip lines out.
13. JR.Sh. (PM. C.14; TS. 1982; IVF, 1.11). Segment of a jar shoulder with a potter's mark incised before firing. Hard, close pinkish-buff ware, evenly fired. Smooth buff slip out.

Other Type Series Examples: (1) BR. F.III.h (TS. 1633), (2) BR. F.IV.c (TS. 1928), (3) BR. L.I.c (TS. 1184), (4) BR. L.III.c (TS. 1925), (5) SJR. B.I.d (TS. 1978), (6) JR. D.II.d (2186), (7) JR. D.V.d (TS. 2183), (8) JR. F.I.e (TS. 2654), (9) JR. J.IV.j (TS. 2382), (10) JR. P.II.d (TS. 2992), (11) JR. P.III.b (TS. 1636).

Other Study Collection Examples: (1) SBR. B.I.h (SC. 508), (2) SBR. D.I.b (SC. 636), (3) BR. F.II.a (SC. 794), (4) SJR. B.I.c (SC. 2504), (5) JR. G.I.c (SC. 2045), (6) CP. A.I.b (SC. 1786), (7) BE. E.II.c (SC. 3200), (8) WPS. C (IP [G.4] D.IV; SC. 3253).

Figure 90. Pottery from Trench IVF/N, Doorway Between Rooms 1 and 8; Trench IVG, Northwest Corner of Trench IVL, Room 3; Trench IVH, Southeast Corner of Area IVL, Room 3; and Trench IVL = Central Portion, Room 3 (Phase 2B; Period F — Early Bronze Age IVa)

1. JR. E.II.d (TS. 2727; IVF/N, 5.1). About 1/4 rim, neck, and shoulder segment. Fairly coarse pinkish-orange ware, evenly fired. Creamy-green slip out.
2. JR. P.III.b (TS. 1638; IVF/N, 5.1). Two large joining rim, neck, and shoulder segments. Medium coarse pinkish ware with mica grits, evenly fired. Cream slip in and out.
3. JR.Sh. (IP [G.4] F.III.a; TS. 1733; IVF/N, 5.1). Jar body sherd with mythical-like animal decoration incised on outside wall before firing (see pl. 100a). Medium fine pink ware with a few grits, evenly fired. Buff slip in and out.
4. JR. H.III.c (TS. 2238; IVG, 1.4, Room 3). Small rim and shoulder segment. Fairly close buff ware, evenly fired. Creamy-buff slip in and out.
—. JR.Sh. (PM. F; TS. 3112; IVG, 1.4, Room 3). Jar sherd. Ware description not available.
—. JR.Sh. (IP [G.1] D.II.A; TS. 1749; IVL, 1.4, Room 3). See fig. 154:9.
5. JR. H.I.1 (TS. 1962; IVH, 1.3, Room 3). Small rim and upper shoulder segment. Fairly coarse and gritty ware, unevenly fired with gray core and pinkish-buff at surfaces. Irregular horizontally burnished self slip out.

Other Type Series Examples:
    Area IVF/N —(1) Ld. C.II.b (SC. 1939).
    Area IVG, Room 3 — (1) SBR. B.I.o (TS. 1981), (2) SBR. C.III.a (TS. 2447), (3) BR. N.II.a (TS. 2938), (4) JR. J.III.r (SW. 291).
    Area IVH, Room 3 — (1) BR. A.IV.e (TS. 1965), (2) BR. D.III.a (TS. 1973), (3) BR. D.III.b (TS. 1967), (4) JR. H.I.h (TS. 1961).

Other Study Collection Examples:
    Area IVF/N — (1) SJR. B.I.a (SC. 2492), (2) JR. E.I.e (SC. 1137), (3) JR. K.I.e (SC. 1593).
    Area IVG, Room 3 — (1) BE. A.II (SC. 3098).
    Area IVL, Room 3 — (1) SBR. B.I.h (SC. 429).

Figure 90

Pottery from Trench IVF/N, Doorway Between Rooms 1 and 8; Trench IVG, Northwest Corner of Trench IVL, Room 3;
Trench IVH, Southeast Corner of Area IVL, Room 3; and Trench IVL = Central Portion, Room 3
(Phase 2B; Period F — Early Bronze Age IVa). Scale 1:5

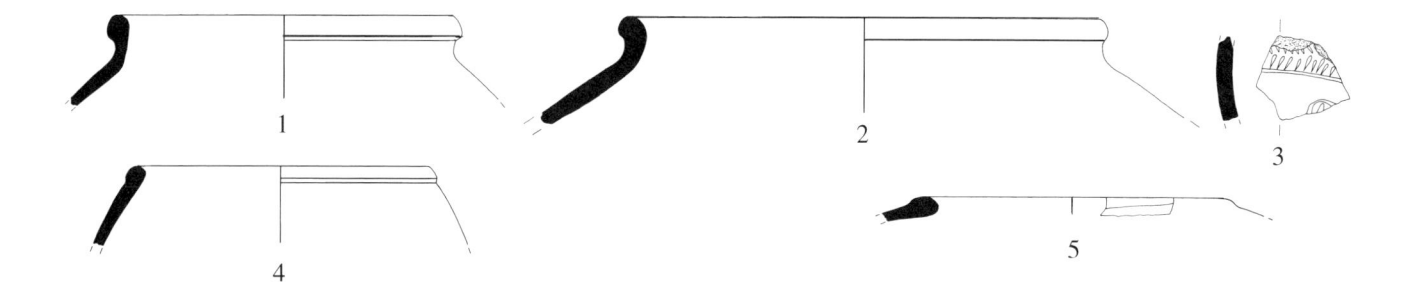

Figure 91. Pottery from Trench IVJ, Room 4 and Room 5 Bin (Phase 2B; Period F — Early Bronze Age IVa)

1. SBR. A.I.e (TS. 2926; IVJ, 1.5, Room 4). Small rim segment and most of wall profile. Fairly fine greenish-buff ware, evenly fired. Creamy-buff slip in and out.
2. SBR. B.I.c (TS. 2928; IVJ, 1.5, Room 4). About 1/5 rim and upper wall segment. Slightly coarse creamy-green ware, evenly fired. Self slip in and out.
3. BR. D.IV.a (TS. 2638; IVJ, 1.5, Room 4). About 1/5 rim and upper wall segment. Fine pinkish-brown ware, evenly fired. Creamy-buff slip in and out.
4. JR. E.II.b (TS. 3022; IVJ, 1.5, Room 4). Small rim, neck, and shoulder segment. Fairly fine buff ware, evenly fired. Cream slip in and out.
5. JR. F.I.a (TS. 3025; IVJ, 1.5, Room 4). About 1/8 rim and neck segment. Fairly coarse creamy-green ware, evenly fired. Self slip in and out.
6. JR. J.I.c (PM. C.14; TS. 1622; IVJ, 1.5, Room 4). Mended to complete rim, neck, and shoulder with a potter's mark incised on shoulder before firing. Slightly coarse and gritty pinkish-buff ware, fairly evenly fired. Self slip in and out.
7. JR. O.II.m (TS. 2811; IVJ, 1.5, Room 4). Complete rim (body not mended). Slightly coarse dark pink ware, evenly fired. Creamy-pink slip in and out.
8. JR. O.II.m (TS. 2812; IVJ, 1.5, Room 4). Complete rim (body not mended). Slightly coarse brown ware, unevenly fired pinkish at surfaces. Creamy-green slip out.
9. JR. P.II.a (PM. D.3; TS. 2788; IVJ, 1.5, Room 4). Complete rim (body not mended). Portion of a potter's mark on shoulder incised before firing. Slightly coarse pinkish-buff ware, evenly fired. Creamy-green slip in and out.
10. JR. P.II.a (PM. D.15; TS. 2810; IVJ, 1.5, Room 4). Complete rim (body not mended). Potter's mark incised on shoulder before firing (see pl. 102b). Slightly coarse pinkish-buff ware, evenly fired. Wheel-applied creamy-pink slip lines out.
11. FL. B.I.a (SW. 677; IVJ, 1.5, Room 4). Mended to near completion apart from missing rim; two vertical loop handles on opposite sides of shoulder. Slightly coarse buff ware, evenly fired. Creamy-pink slip out.
12. BE. B.II (TS. 3060; IVJ, 1.5, Room 4). Complete base and lower wall of vessel. Fine buff ware, evenly fired. Self slip in and out.
13. BE. E.I.j (TS. 3036; IVJ, 1.5, Room 4). Complete base and portion of lower wall of vessel. Fairly fine pinkish-buff ware, evenly fired. Cream slip out.
14. SV.1 (TS. 1591; IVJ, 1.5, Room 4). Funnel nearly mended to completion. Fine pink ware, evenly fired. Cream slip in and out.
—. JR.Sh. (PM. F; TS. 3117; IVJ, 1.5, Room 4). Jar sherd. Ware description not available.

Other Type Series Examples:
Room 4 — (1) SBR. A.II.c (TS. 1601), (2) BR. C.I.a (TS. 1592), (3) BR. C.I.f (TS. 1608), (4) BR. D.I.b (TS. 2637), (5) BR. D.VII.a (TS. 1607), (6) BR. E.III.h (TS. 1600), (7) BR. E.IV.b (TS. 1599), (8) BR. L.I.b (TS. 1606), (9) BR. L.I.h (TS. 1610), (10) SJR. A.I.d (SW. 455), (11) SJR. E.I.a (TS. 2646), (12) JR. L.I.a (SW. 676), (13) JR. L.II.b (SW. 637), (14) JR. O.I.i (TS. 2793), (15) JR. Q.II.a (TS. 1595), (16) JR. Q.II.e (TS. 1589), (17) FL. B.I.a (SW. 537), (18) CP. B.V.b (TS. 2848), (19) Bt. B.I (SW. 659 = SC. 3320), (20) SR. B.II.d (TS. 2934), (21) BE. E.II.c (TS. 3070), (22) BE. F.VI.a (TS. 2664).
Room 5 — (1) CP. C.II.d (TS. 2870).

Other Study Collection Examples:
Room 4 — (1) SBR. A.I.b (SC. 198), (2) SBR. A.I.b (SC. 200), (3) SBR. A.I.b (SC. 209), (4) SBR. B.I.e (SC. 332), (5) SBR. B.I.g (SC. 394), (6) SBR. B.I.h (SC. 424), (7) SBR. B.I.h (SC. 445), (8) SBR. B.I.h (SC. 456), (9) SBR. B.I.h (SC. 459), (10) SBR. B.I.h (SC. 503), (11) SBR. B.I.h (SC. 670), (12) SBR. B.I.j (SC. 533), (13) SBR. B.I.j (SC. 536), (14) SBR. B.I.j (SC. 551), (15) SBR. D.I.a (SC. 631), (16) BR. D.II.d (SC. 748), (17) BR. F.II.b (SC. 802), (18) BR. F.IV.e (SC. 879), (19) JR. G.II.c (SC. 2050), (20) JR. H.I.c (SC. 1248), (21) JR. J.III.a (SC. 1360), (22) JR. J.III.m (SC. 2451), (23) JR. J.III.t (SC. 1493), (24) JR. (not typed, SC. 92), (25) CP. B.I.c (SC. 1822), (26) SR. B.I.b (SC. 61), (27) BE. D.I (SC. 3126), (28) BE. E.I.l (SC. 3190), (29) Hd. D.I (SC. 3275).

Figure 91

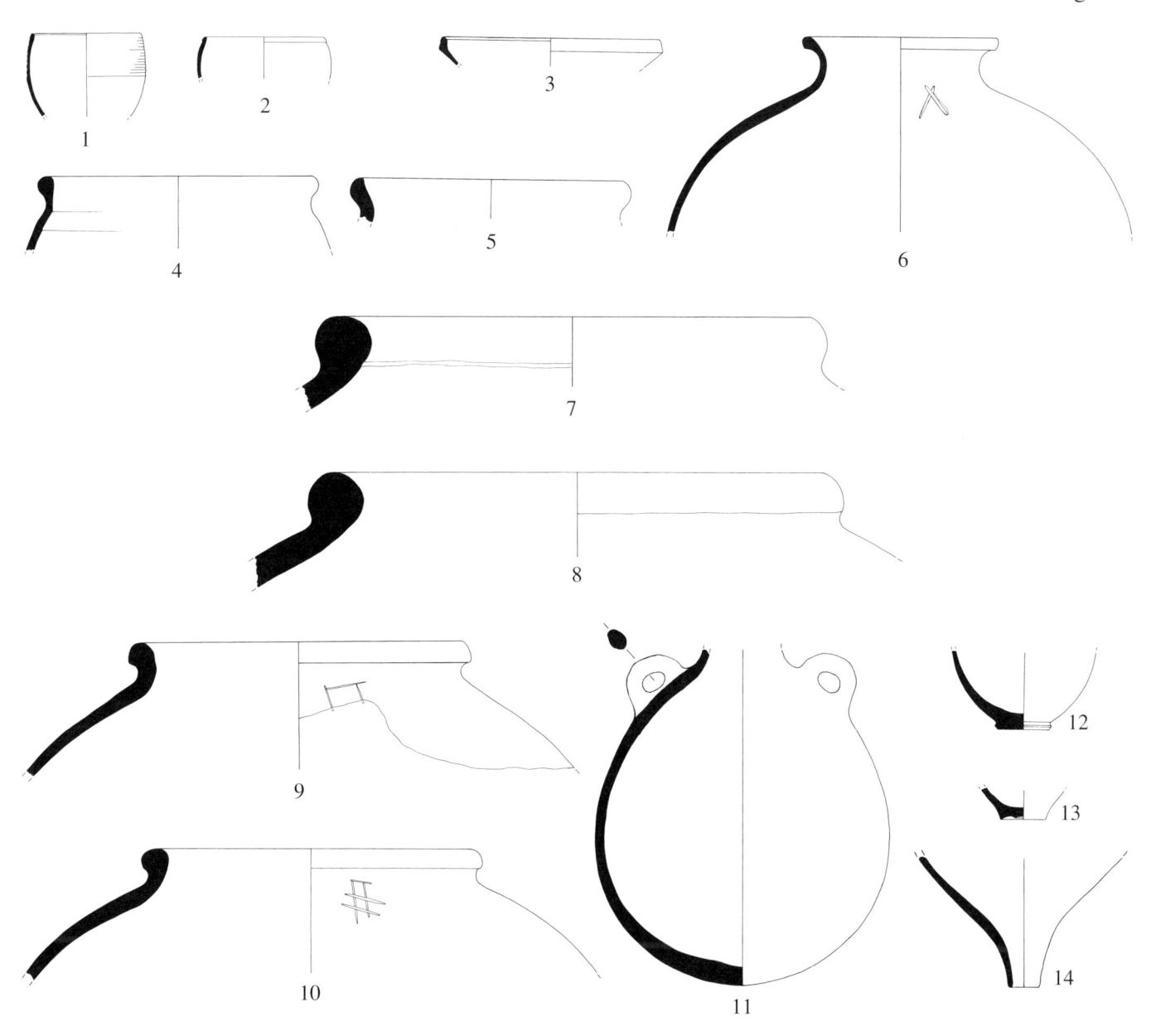

Pottery from Trench IVJ, Room 4 and Room 5 Bin (Phase 2B; Period F — Early Bronze Age IVa). Scale 1:5

Figure 92

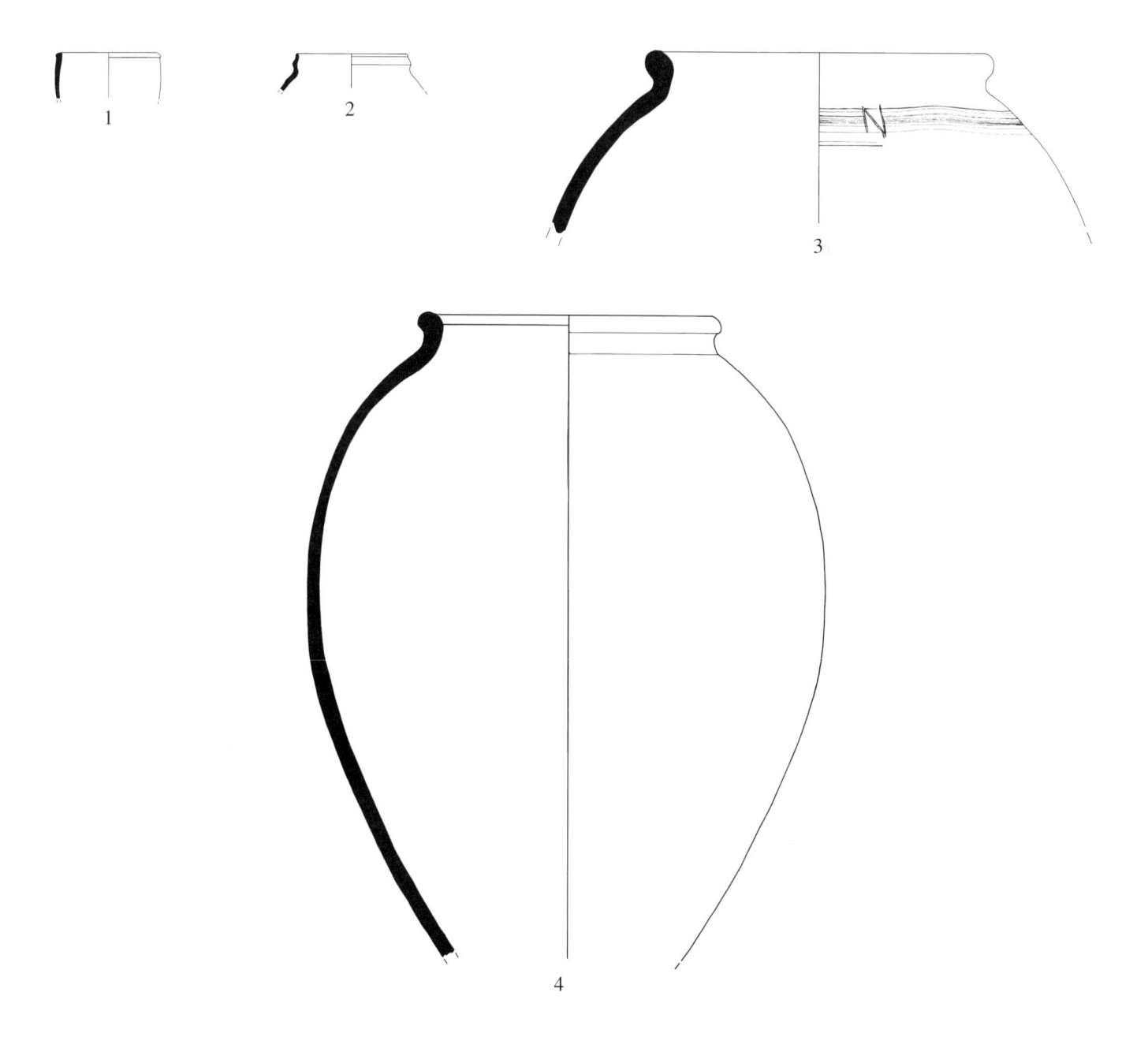

Pottery from Trench IVK, Room 2 (Phase 2B; Period F — Early Bronze Age IVa). Scale 1:5

1. SBR. B.I.f (TS. 2956; IVK, 2.4). About 1/4 rim and upper wall segment. Fairly fine dark pinkish-buff ware, evenly fired. Self slip in and out.
2. SBR. D.I.i (TS. 2634; IVK, 2.4). About 1/4 rim and shoulder segment. Fairly fine light brown ware, evenly fired. Cream slip out and just over rim in.
3. JR. P.I.b (PM. C.5; SW. 663 = SW. 698; IVK, 2.4). Complete rim and most of body, not mended to completion. Potter's mark incised on shoulder over combed linear band of decoration before firing. Medium coarse grayish ware with lime grits, evenly fired. Cream slip in and out.
4. JR. P.II.i (TS. 1772; IVK, 2.4). Complete rim and most of body mended. Medium coarse pink ware with lime and mica grits, evenly fired. Wheel-applied, reserved, slip out.

Other Type Series Examples: (1) SBR. A.I.b (SW. 382), (2) BR. A.III.b (TS. 2955), (3) SJR. B.II.c (SW. 264 = TS. 1760), (4) SJR. C.II.k (SW. 395 = TS. 1767), (5) JR. C.I.e (SW. 394), (6) JR. J.II.e (TS. 2629), (7) JR. J.III.x (TS. 2993), (8) JR. P.II.a (TS. 2562), (9) CP. C.I.b (SW. 484), (10) BE. F.VIII.c (SW. 457).

Other Study Collection Examples: (1) SBR. B.I.h (SC. 432), (2) SBR. B.I.h (SC. 2945), (3) SBR. B.I.j (SC. 549), (4) SBR. B.I.r (SC. 594), (5) SBR. B. (Gen. Type, SC. 16), (6) SJR. B.III.c (SC. 2527), (7) SJR. C.I.h (SC. 2575), (8) JR. J.III.a (SC. 2211), (9) BE. B.I (SC. 3102), (10) BE. E.II.l (SC. 3227).

Figure 93

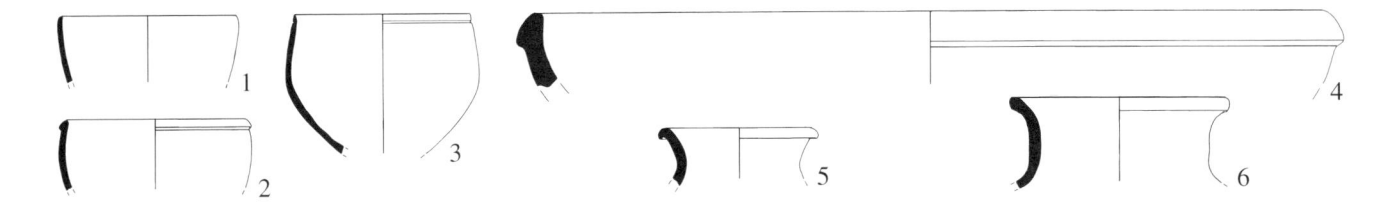

Pottery from Trenches IVM and IVC, Room 7 (Phase 2B; Period F — Early Bronze Age IVa; see also fig. 99). Scale 1:5

1. SBR. A.I.b (TS. 2983; IVM, 100.10). Small rim and upper wall segment. Fairly fine buff ware, evenly fired. Creamy-buff slip in and out.
2. SBR. B.I.f (TS. 2179; IVM, 100.8, niche in town wall). Small rim and upper wall segment. Fairly fine pinkish-buff ware, evenly fired. Self slip in and out.
3. SBR. F.I.a (TS. 2561; IVM, 100.7). About 1/4 segment of rim and complete wall profile; base missing. Fairly fine buff ware, evenly fired. Self slip in and out.
4. BR. F.IV.a (TS. 1729; IVM, 1.4). Small rim and upper wall segment. Coarse pink ware with lime grits, evenly fired. Cream slip in and out.
5. JR. J.III.a (TS. 2658; IVM, 1.4). About 1/4 rim and neck segment. Fairly fine creamy-green ware, evenly fired. Self slip in and out.
6. JR. J.III.h (TS. 3021; IVM, 1.4). Small rim and neck segment. Fairly fine creamy-green ware, evenly fired. Self slip in and out.
—. JR.Sh. (PM. F; TS. 3143; IVC, 2.1). Jar sherd. Ware description not available.

Other Type Series Examples:
    Area IVC, Room 7 — (1) SBR. B.I.p (SW. 265).
    Area IVM, Room 7 — (1) SBR. B.I.f (TS. 2555), (2) BR. E.IV.c (TS. 1640), (3) BR. F.IV.a (TS. 2985), (4) JR. H.III.g (TS. 2651), (5) JR. H.III.j (TS. 1716), (6) JR. O.II.d (TS. 1773), (7) FL. A.I.a (TS. 1720), (8) BE. E.I.f (TS. 3072).

Other Study Collection Examples:
    Area IVM, Room 7 — (1) SBR. B.I.g (SC. 391), (2) SBR. B.I.h (SC. 474), (3) SBR. C.III.b (SC. 614), (4) BR. A.II.e (SC. 712), (5) BR. A.III.b (SC. 727), (6) BR. F.III.c (SC. 877), (7) BR. (not typed, SC. 35), (8) CBR. A.II.b (SC. 3125), (9) JR. D.I.b (SC. 1040), (10) JR. H.I.d (SC. 1257), (11) JR. J.III.a (SC. 2213), (12) JR. J.III.h (SC. 2293), (13) JR. J.IV.g (SC. 1528), (14) JR. K.I.b (SC. 2391), (15) JR. O.III.c (SC. 1674), (16) CP. B.I.a (SC. 1814), (17) BE. B.II (SC. 3118).

Figures 94–95

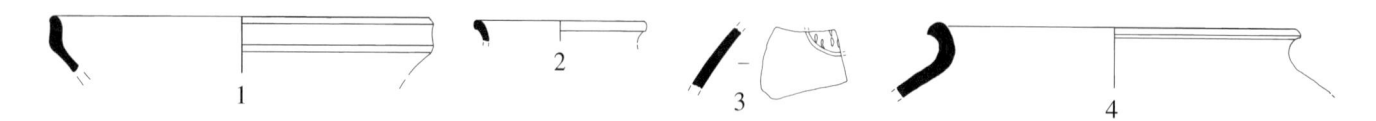

Figure 94. Pottery from Trench IVN, Room 8, and Operation 10, Northeast Corner of Room 8 (Phase 2B; Period F — Early Bronze Age IVa). Scale 1:5

1. BR. E.I.a (TS. 1744; IVN, 2.1). Small rim and upper wall segment. Slightly coarse grayish ware with mica grits, evenly fired. Pink slip in and out.
2. CP. A.I.a (TS. 2864; IVN, 2.1). About 1/8 rim and neck segment. Fairly fine dark brown ware with lime and mica grits, evenly fired. Grayish-colored slip in and out.
3. JR.Sh. (PM. D.18; TS. 2748; IVN, 2.1). Body sherd with portion of a potter's mark incised on the outside wall before firing. Slightly coarse grayish-buff ware, evenly fired. Self slip out.
4. JR. P.I.a (TS. 3361; Op. 10, 22.2). Large rim, neck, and shoulder segment. For ware, compare Phase 3 Type Series example from Area IVE (TS. 2375).
—. JR.Sh. (PM. F; TS. 3146; IVN, 2.1, Room 8). Jar sherd. Ware description not available.

Other Type Series Examples:
Area IVN, Room 8 — (1) JR. C.II.e (TS. 1698), (2) JR. H.I.d (TS. 2900), (3) JR. K.II.e (TS. 1688), (4) JR. P.II.r (TS. 1697), (5) CP. A.I.i (TS. 2838), (6) SR. A.I.a (TS. 1687), (7) BE. B.I (TS. 2768), (8) BE. E.II.i (TS. 3074), (9) Hd. E.II (TS. 2773).
Operation 10, Northeast Corner of Room 8 — (1) Ld. A.II.a (TS. 3360).

Other Study Collection Examples:
Area IVN, Room 8 — (1) SBR. A.I.a (SC. 194), (2) SBR. B.I.a (SC. 238), (3) SBR. B.I.e (SC. 311), (4) SBR. B.I.f (SC. 333), (5) SBR. B.I.l (SC. 673), (6) SBR. D.I.a (SC. 623), (7) BR. A.IV.a (SC. 872), (8) BR. G.I.c (SC. 822), (9) SJR. B.II.c (SC. 2507), (10) SJR. B.II.j (SC. 2518), (11) SJR. C.I.e (SC. 2550), (12) SJR. C.I.f (SC. 2561), (13) JR. B.II.c (SC. 930), (14) JR. E.I.c (SC. 1994), (15) JR. F.III.e (SC. 1229), (16) JR. J.I.b (SC. 1312), (17) JR. J.I.b (SC. 2106), (18) JR. J.I.c (SC. 1314), (19) JR. J.I.c (SC. 1315), (20) JR. J.II.h (SC. 2162), (21) JR. J.II.n (SC. 1358), (22) JR. J.III.a (SC. 2201), (23) JR. J.III.d (SC. 2223), (24) JR. J.III.m (SC. 1417), (25) JR. J.III.y (SC. 1504), (26) JR. J.III.y (SC. 1506), (27) JR. K.I.a (SC. 1561), (28) JR. K.I.d (SC. 1590), (29) JR. K.II.c (SC. 1606), (30) JR. O.II.d (SC. 1636), (31) CP. A.I.f (SC. 1791), (32) CP. B.IV.b (SC. 1867), (33) BE. E.II.l (SC. 3228), (34) SB. fragments (not typed, SC. 3291).

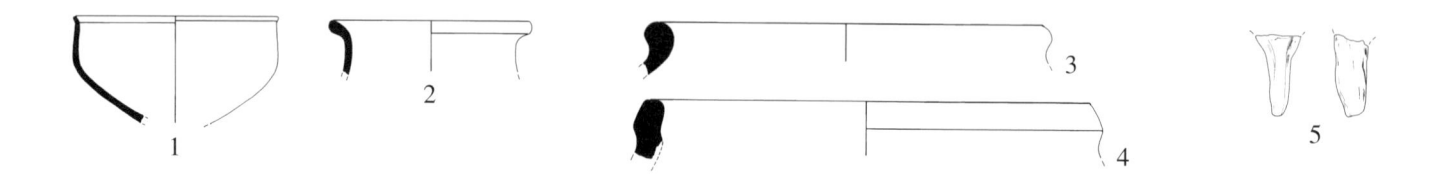

Figure 95. Pottery from Trench IVP, Courtyard Room 9 (Phase 2B; Period F — Early Bronze Age IVa). Scale 1:5

1. SBR. F.I.b (TS. 2609; IVP, 1.5). About 1/4 rim and most of wall profile. Slightly coarse grayish-buff ware, evenly fired. Self slip in and out.
2. JR. J.III.p (TS. 3020; IVP, 1.5). About 1/6 rim and neck segment. Fairly fine dark pink ware, evenly fired. Self slip in and out.
3. JR. O.I.d (TS. 2772; IVP, 1.5). Small rim and neck segment. Fairly fine light pink ware, evenly fired. Very light creamy-green slip in and out.
4. JR. O.II.h (TS. 2767; IVP, 1.5). Small rim and neck segment. Fairly coarse grayish ware, evenly fired. Self slip in and out.
5. SV.5 (TS. 1062; IVP, 1.5). Handmade leg from tripod-legged bowl. Slightly coarse pinkish-brown ware with many small gold-colored mica and lime grits, evenly fired.
—. JR.Sh. (PM. F; TS. 3114; IVP, 1.5). Jar sherd. Ware description not available.

Other Type Series Examples: (1) SBR. D.I.f (TS. 2607), (2) SBR. D.I.i (TS. 2821), (3) BR. D.I.c (TS. 2608), (4) BR. E.I.b (TS. 2589), (5) BR. E.I.c (TS. 2592), (6) BR. L.I.j (TS. 2899), (7) JR. B.VI.a (TS. 2909), (8) JR. C.I.g (TS. 2623), (9) JR. J.I.l (TS. 2764), (10) JR. K.II.b (TS. 2757), (11) JR. P.III.d (TS. 2758), (12) SR. A.II.b (TS. 2935).

Other Study Collection Examples: (1) MBR. A.I.b (SC. 2638), (2) SBR. A.I.a (SC. 190), (3) SBR. A.I.b (SC. 199), (4) SBR. A.II.b (SC. 232), (5) SBR. B.I.b (SC. 261), (6) SBR. B.I.b (SC. 262), (7) SBR. B.I.i (SC. 525), (8) SBR. B.I.l (SC. 579), (9) SBR. D.I.a (SC. 622), (10) SBR. D.I.e (SC. 8), (11) BR. F.I.b (SC. 763), (12) BR. L.I.f (SC. 845), (13) SJR. A.I.d (SC. 2631), (14) SJR. D.II.a (SC. 2628), (15) JR. C.V.c (SC. 1015), (16) JR. E.II.e (SC. 2020), (17) JR. J.III.g (SC. 2282), (18) JR. J.III.m (SC. 1418), (19) JR. J.III.m (SC. 1433), (20) JR. J.III.m (SC. 2322), (21) JR. J.III.ab (SC. 1518), (22) JR. J.V.a (SC. 1554), (23) JR. (not typed, SC. 74), (24) CP. B.V.b (SC. 1898), (25) BE. D.II (SC. 3132).

Figures 96–97

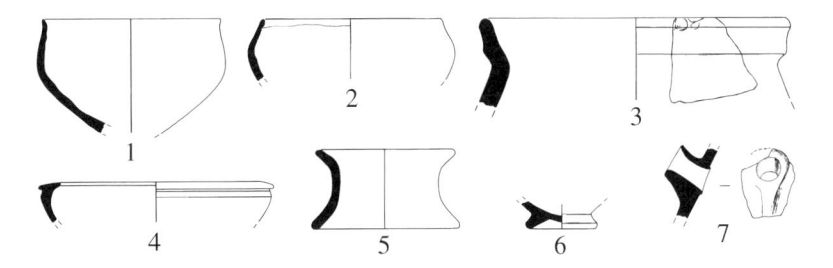

Figure 96. Pottery from Area IV, Operation 6, Courtyard Room 9 (Phase 2B; Period F — Early Bronze Age IVa). Scale 1:5

1. SBR. B.I.d (TS. 3477; Op. 6, 1.30). About 1/2 rim and wall segment; base missing. For ware, compare Phase 4 Type Series example from Area IIIA (SW. 59).
2. SBR. B.I.o (TS. 3483; Op. 6, 16.1). Small rim and upper wall segment. For ware, compare Phase 2A Type Series example from Area IVG (TS. 1981).
3. JR. B.III.a (TS. 3449; Op. 6, 1.19). Small rim and shoulder segment with remains of two extant finger indentations impressed in the rim before firing. Fairly fine pinkish-brown ware, evenly fired. Self slip in and out.
4. Lp. A.II.a (TS. 3448; Op. 6, 1.19). About 1/6 rim and upper wall segment. Fairly coarse pinkish-brown ware with lime grits, evenly fired. Self slip in and out.
5. PS. A.I.a (TS. 3273; Op. 6, 1.30). About 1/2 segment of complete profile. Fairly fine buff ware with white- and gold-colored mica grits, evenly fired. Self slip in and out.
6. BE. E.I.c (TS. 3485; Op. 6, 16.1). Small segment of base and lower wall of vessel. For ware, compare Phase 2A example from Area IVJ (TS. 1609).
7. SV.2 (TS. 3484; Op. 6, 1.19). Nearly complete spout from the shoulder of a jar. For form and ware, compare Phase 2A(a) example, JR. H.II.e, from Operation 7 (TS. 3517).

Another Type Series Example: (1) JR. A.V.a (TS. 3271).

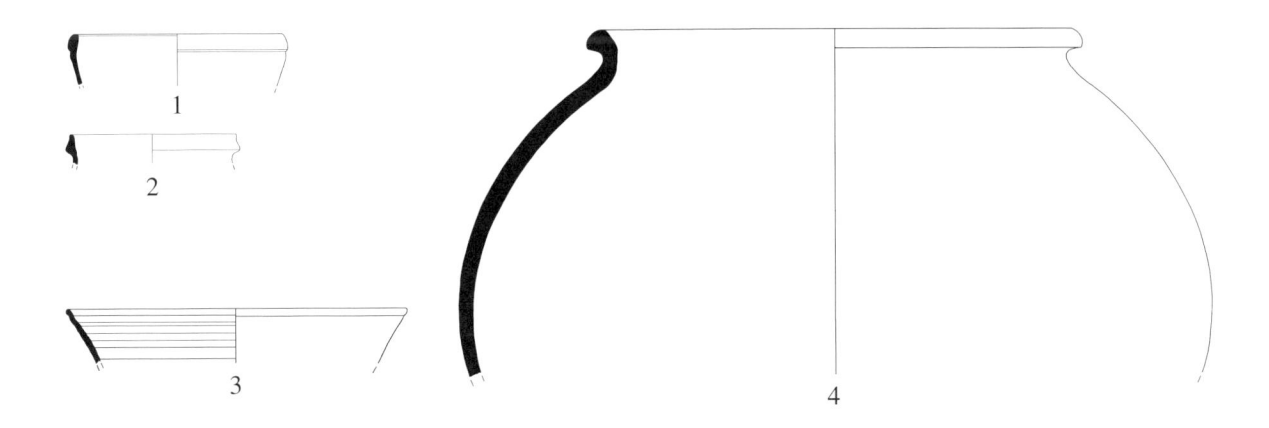

Figure 97. Pottery from Trench IVQ, Room 6 (Phase 2B; Period F — Early Bronze Age IVa). Scale 1:5

1. SBR. B.I.h (TS. 2747; IVQ, 1.4). About 1/10 rim and upper wall segment. Fine pinkish-brown ware, evenly fired. Self slip in and out. Irregular horizontal burnish lines out.
2. SBR. D.I.i (TS. 2823; IVQ, 1.4). About 1/5 rim and neck segment. Slightly coarse buff ware, evenly fired. Creamy-buff slip in and out.
3. BR. O.I.a (SW. 646; IVQ, 1.4). Small rim and upper wall segment. Fairly coarse ware, unevenly fired reddish-brown in and black out.
4. CP. B.II.d (TS. 2787; IVQ, 1.4). Mended to near completion. Fairly coarse and gritty pinkish-brown ware, evenly fired. Self slip in and out. Wet-smoothed and horizontally burnished out and just over rim in.

Another Type Series Example: (1) BE. G (TS. 2785).

Figure 98

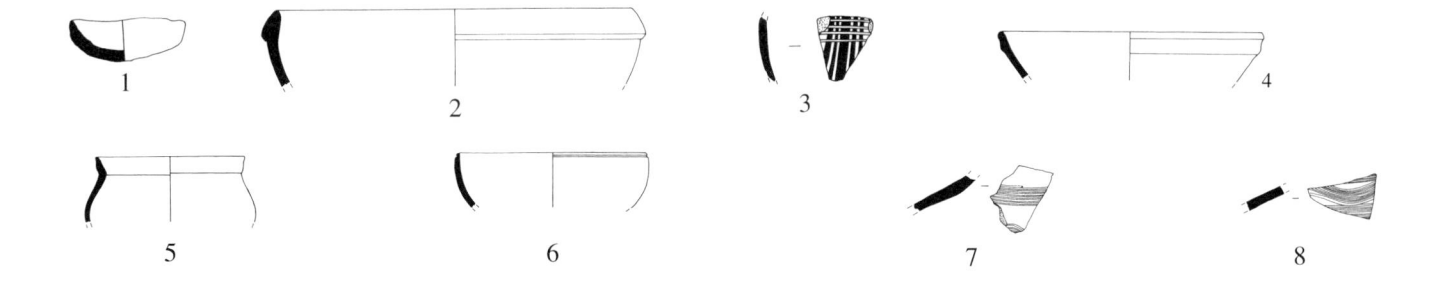

Pottery from Trench IVO, Room 11; Trench IVS, Room 13; Sounding IVW; Trench IVX, Room 14; and Sounding IVY (Phase 2B; Period F — Early Bronze Age IVa). Scale 1:5

1. CBR. A.II.a (SW. 542; IVO, 2.1). Complete, handmade crucible bowl used for metal working. Fine light brown ware, fairly evenly fired. Light grayish-buff slip in and on outside of rim.
2. BR. F.III.e (TS. 2991; IVS, 4.4). Small rim and upper wall segment. Fairly fine pink ware, evenly fired. Pinkish-buff slip in and out.
3. JR.Sh. Pt. (SW. 694; IVS, 4.4). Body sherd with pink slip out overlaid with dark red-painted checkerboard design. Fine buff ware, evenly fired.
4. BR. D.I.a (TS. 2635; IVX, 2.1). About 1/10 rim and upper wall segment. Fine pink ware, evenly fired. Light pink slip in and just over rim out.
5. SBR. D.I.d (TS. 2918; IVX, 2.2). About 1/5 rim and upper wall segment. Fairly fine buff ware, evenly fired. Creamy-buff slip in and out.
6. SBR. B.I.n (TS. 2604; IVY, 1.4). About 1/8 rim and upper wall segment. Fine grayish-pink ware, evenly fired. Creamy slip in and out.
7. JR.Sh. (IP [G.1] A.II.a; TS. 2644; IVY, 1.5) Jar shoulder sherd with comb-incised horizontal and wavy band decoration. Fairly coarse creamy-green ware, evenly fired.
8. JR.Sh. (IP [G.1] C.IV.a; TS. 2645; IVY, 1.4). Jar shoulder sherd with comb-incised horizontal and wavy band decoration. Fairly coarse creamy-green ware, evenly fired.

Other Type Series Examples:
  Area IVX — (1) SJR. B.IV.a (TS. 2829).
  Area IVY — (1) BR. D.VI.b (TS. 2605).

Other Study Collection Exampes:
  Area IVS — (1) SJR. D.I.b (SC. 2625).
  Area IVW — (1) SBR. A.I.f (SC. 230), (2) Ld. C.II.a (SC. 1936).
  Area IVX — (1) SBR. A.I.d (SC. 299), (2) SBR. B.I.e (SC. 324), (3) SBR. B.I.f (SC. 350), (4) SBR. B.I.g (SC. 388), (5) SBR. B.I.h (SC. 449), (6) SBR. B.I.h (SC. 514), (7) SBR. B.I.j (SC. 546), (8) SBR. B.I.l (SC. 581), (9) SBR. D.I.a (SC. 633), (10) SBR. D.I.a (SC. 632), (11) BR. F.I.d (SC. 874), (12) BR. L.I.e (SC. 1972), (13) BR. (not typed, SC. 47), (14) SJR. B.II.j (SC. 2520), (15) SJR. C.II.q (SC. 2607), (16) JR. D.V.a (SC. 1072), (17) JR. E.II.s (SC. 1166), (18) JR. F.III.f (SC. 1234), (19) JR. H.I.b (SC. 2062), (20) JR. K.I.b (SC. 1564), (21) JR. (not typed, SC. 84), (22) CP. A.II.a (SC. 1796), (23) BE. E.I.d (SC. 3160).
  Area IVY — (1) SBR. B.I.f (SC. 336), (2) BR. (not typed, SC. 44), (3) JR. B.V.c (SC. 955), (4) JR. E.II.m (SC. 2028), (5) JR. J.III.x (SC. 1502), (6) BE. F.III.a (SC. 1912).

Figure 99

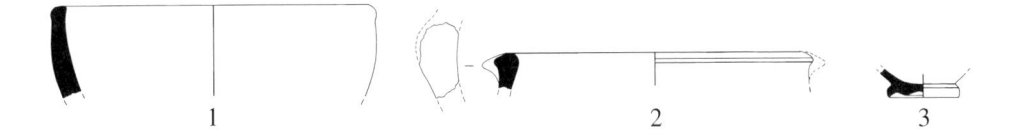

Pottery from Trench IVX = North Side of Trench IVM, Room 7 (Phase 2B; Period F — Early Bronze Age IVa). Scale 1:5

1. BR. L.I.b (TS. 2901; IVX, 2.3). Small rim and upper wall segment. Fairly fine creamy-green ware, evenly fired. Self slip in and out.
2. CP. C.II.b (TS. 2866; IVX, 2.3). Small rim segment with portion of triangular-shaped ledge handle attached to rim. Slightly coarse pinkish-buff ware, evenly fired. Self slip in and out.
3. BE. E.II.k (TS. 3037; IVX, 2.3). One half of base and small segment of lower wall of vessel. Slightly coarse pink ware, evenly fired. Creamy-buff slip out.

Other Type Series Examples: (1) JR. O.I.e (TS. 2656), (2) JR. P.III.f (TS. 1718), (3) CP.Ld. A.II.b (TS. 2566).

Other Study Collection Examples: (1) SBR. B.I.a (SC. 248), (2) SJR. B.II.d (SC. 2509),(3) JR. J.I.b (SC. 2088), (4) JR. J.I.f (SC. 2118), (5) JR. J.III.q (SC. 1478), (6) JR. P.II.d (SC. 1726), (7) JR. (not typed, SC. 139), (8) Jg. A.I.a (SC. 2946).

Figure 100. Pottery from Trench IVZ(S), (N1), and (N2), Room 21 (Phase 2B; Period F — Early Bronze Age IVa)

1. MBR. B.II.a (TS. 2948; IVZ(N1), 2.3, Room 21). Small rim and upper wall segment. Fine pinkish-brown ware, evenly fired. Self slip in and out. Smooth, even burnish in.
2. BR. A.I.e (TS. 2960; IVZ(S), 5.4). Small rim and upper wall segment. Fairly fine grayish-buff ware, evenly fired. Creamy-green slip in and out.
3. BR. E.I.a (TS. 2582; IVZ(N2), 3.4, Room 21). About 1/10 rim and most of wall profile. Slightly coarse pinkish-buff ware, evenly fired. Creamy-green slip in and out.
4. BR. E.I.a (TS. 2597; IVZ(N2), 3.5, Room 21). About 1/6 rim and upper wall segment. Slightly coarse pinkish-buff ware, evenly fired. Buff slip in and out.
5. BR. J.I.a (TS. 2594; IVZ(N1), 1.5), Small rim and upper wall segment. Slightly coarse ware, unevenly fired with grayish core and brown at surface out, light pink in. Pinkish-brown self slip out.
6. BR. L.I.c (TS. 2602; IVZ(N2), 3.4, Room 21). About 1/8 rim and upper wall segment. Hard, close dark pink ware, evenly fired. Self slip in and out.
7. JR. D.V.e (TS. 2680; IVZ(N1), 1.5). About 1/5 rim and upper wall segment. Fairly coarse light pink ware, evenly fired. Creamy-green slip in and out.
8. JR. D.X.b (TS. 2695; IVZ(S), 5.3). Small rim and neck segment. Hard, close ware, unevenly fired with gray core and pinkish-brown at surfaces. Self slip in and out.
9. JR. F.III.f (TS. 2737; IVZ(N1), 1.6). About 1/10 rim, neck, and shoulder segment. Slightly coarse pinkish-buff ware, evenly fired. Cream slip out.
10. JR. J.III.e (IP [G.1] A.I.a; TS. 2726; IVZ(N2), 3.5, Room 21). About 3/4 rim, neck, and shoulder segment with comb-incised horizontal line decoration on lower part of shoulder. Slightly coarse pinkish-buff ware, evenly fired. Cream slip in and out.
11. JR. O.II.e (TS. 3012; IVZ(N1), 2.2, Room 21). About 1/4 rim and neck segment. Slightly coarse creamy-green ware, evenly fired. Self slip in and out.
12. JR. Q.II.a (SW. 734; IVZ(N2), 3.5). About 1/2 rim and large portion of body with applied finger-impressed rope band decoration around mid-girth of vessel. Fairly coarse ware with lime and mica grits, unevenly fired buff in and gray out. Thick greenish-buff slip out and just over rim in.
13. CP. C.I.c (TS. 2837; IVZ(N1), 2.4, Room 21). Small rim and neck segment. Slightly coarse and gritty pinkish-brown ware, evenly fired. Self slip in and out, horizontally burnished.
14. Hd. E.II (TS. 2775; IVZ(N1), 1.5). Double-pierced lug handle originally situated horizontally on the shoulder of the vessel. Slightly coarse grayish-buff ware, evenly fired.
15. WPS. B (TS. 2687; IVZ(N1), 2.4, Room 21). Wall fragment with portions of two windows extant and incised horizontal line decoration. Slightly coarse pink ware, evenly fired. Pinkish-buff slip in and out.
16. JR.Sh. (PM. D.6; TS. 1694; IVZ(S), 5.3). Jar body sherd with portion of a potter's mark incised on outer surface before firing. Medium coarse pink ware with lime and mica grits, evenly fired. Light gold-colored slip in and out.
—. JR.Sh. (PM. F; TS. 3110; IVZ(N1), 2.3, Room 21). Jar sherd. Ware description not available.
—. JR.Sh. (PM. F; TS. 3134; IVZ(N1), 1.5). Jar sherd. Ware description not available.
—. JR.Sh. (PM. F; TS. 3148; IVZ(N1), 1.5). Jar sherd. Ware description not available.
—. JR.Sh. (PM. F; TS. 3140; IVZ(S), 5.4). Jar sherd. Ware description not available.

Other Type Series Examples:

Area IVZ(S) — (1) SBR. B.I.h (TS. 2702), (2) BR. A.I.d (TS. 2942), (3) BR. A.I.e (TS. 2941), (4) SJR. C.II.h (TS. 2694), (5) Lp. B.I.2 (TS. 1740), (6) SR. B.I.e (TS. 2936), (7) BE. E.II.e (TS. 3076).

Area IVZ(N1) — (1) BR. H.III.a (TS. 2685), (2) JR. D.VIII.d (TS. 3156), (3) BE. F.II.a (TS. 2679).

Area IVZ(N1), Room 21 — (1) BR. C.I.d (SW. 735), (2) JR. R.I.a (SW. 730).

Area IVZ(N2), Room 21 — (1) CP. A.II.e (TS. 2841), (2) CP. C.I.d (TS. 2817).

Other Study Collection Examples:

Area IVZ(S) — (1) SBR. B.I.i (SC. 531), (2) BR. C.I.d (SC. 741), (3) BR. L.I.e (SC. 836), (4) SJR. A.I.a (SC. 2476), (5) JR. D.I.b (SC. 1038), (6) JR. D.II.d (SC. 1060), (7) JR. D.VI.d (SC. 1112), (8) JR. E.II.d (SC. 2005), (9) JR. E.II.d (SC. 2006), (10) JR. H.II.a (SC. 2049), (11) JR. J.I.f (SC. 2119), (12) JR. J.II.m (SC. 2193), (13) JR. J.III.i (SC. 2299), (14) JR. J.III.l (SC. 2308), (15) JR. J.III.n (SC. 1453), (16) JR. J.III.o (SC. 1471), (17) JR. P.II.h (SC. 1735), (18) JR. P.II.i (SC. 1736), (19) JR. P.II.i (SC. 1740), (20) JR. (not typed, SC. 65), (21) CP. B.IV.a (SC. 1864), (22) BE. E.I.g (SC. 3178), (23) BE. E.I.g (SC. 3179), (24) BE. E.II.g (PM. C.14; SC. 3219), (25) Hd. C (SC. 3274).

Area IVZ(N1) — (1) SBR. B.I.c (SC. 281), (2) SBR. B. (Gen. Type, SC. 13), (3) BR. F.I.d (SC. 782), (4) SJR. A.II.b (SC. 2484), (5) JR. C.V.d (SC. 1023), (6) JR. D.VI.c (SC. 1111), (7) JR. D.VI.e (SC. 1114), (8) JR. J.II.k (SC. 2186), (9) JR. J.III.c (SC. 1367), (10) JR. J.III.h (SC. 2289), (11) JR. J.III.m (SC. 1415), (12) JR. J.IV.j (SC. 1548), (13)

Figure 100

JR. O.III.c (SC. 1673), (14) JR. P.II.a (SC. 1706), (15) JR. P.II.a (SC. 1711), (16) JR. P.II.d (SC. 1725), (17) JR. P.II.j (SC. 1743), (18) Ld. C.III.c (SC. 1938), (19) ABS. B (SC. 3244).

Area IVZ(N1), Room 21 — (1) SBR. B.I.g (SC. 419), (2) JR. E.II.d (SC. 1144), (3) JR. J.II.i (SC. 2168), (4) JR. K.I.d (SC. 589).

Area IVZ(N2), Room 21 — (1) BR. C.I.d (SC. 743), (2) JR. B.III.f (SC. 949), (3) JR. E.I.c (SC. 1995), (4) JR. E.II.c (SC. 1141), (5) JR. J.III.a (SC. 2206), (6) JR. J.III.m (SC. 1428), (7) JR. J.III.n (SC. 1451), (8) JR. J.III.n (SC. 1466), (9) JR. K.I.d (SC. 1588), (10) JR. O.II.a (SC. 1623), (11) JR. O.II.k (SC. 1656), (12) CP. B.I.a (SC. 1813), (13) CP. B.I.c (SC. 1821), (14) BE. D.II (SC. 3129).

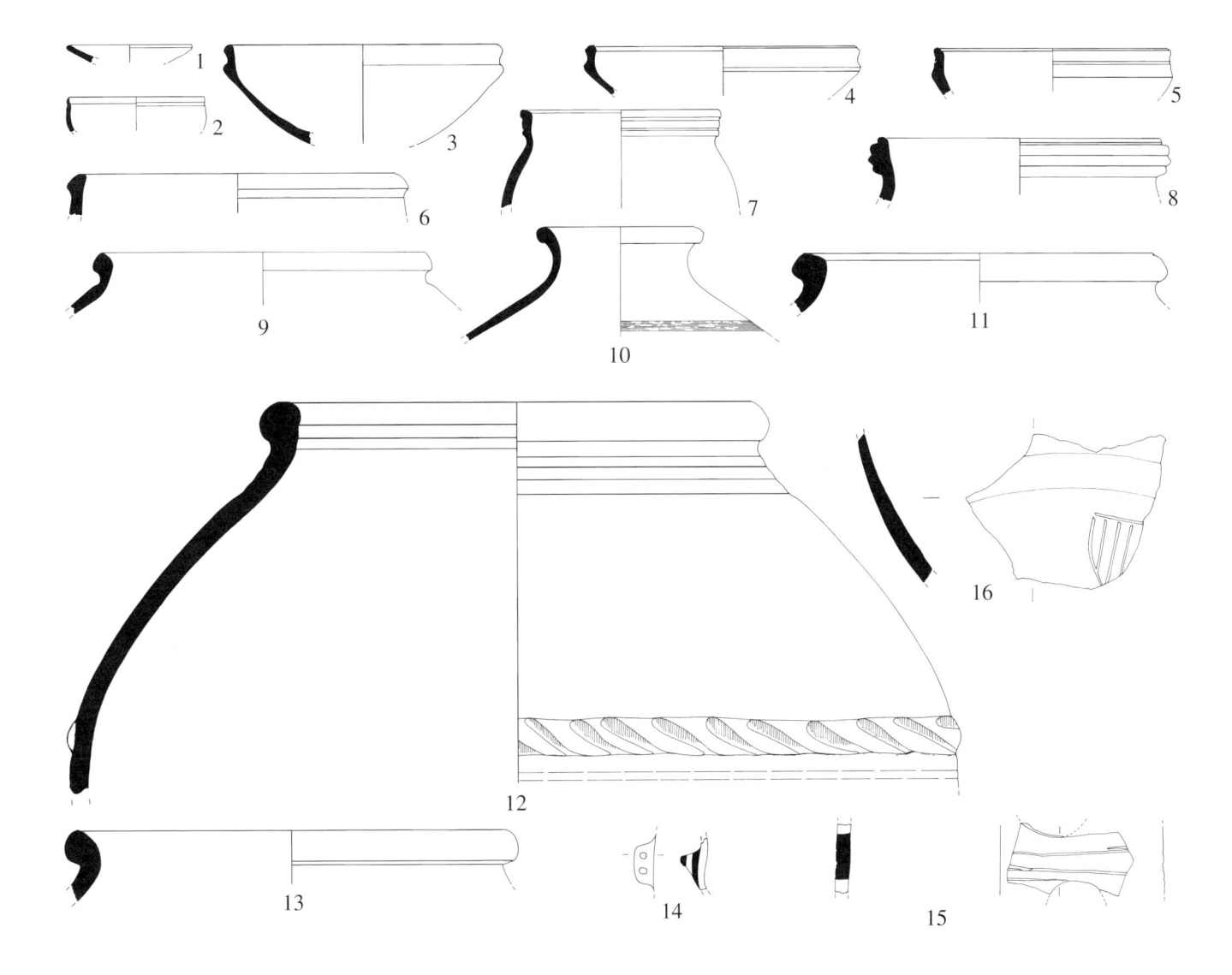

Pottery from Trench IVZ(S), (N1), and (N2), Room 21 (Phase 2B; Period F — Early Bronze Age IVa). Scale 1:5

Figure 101

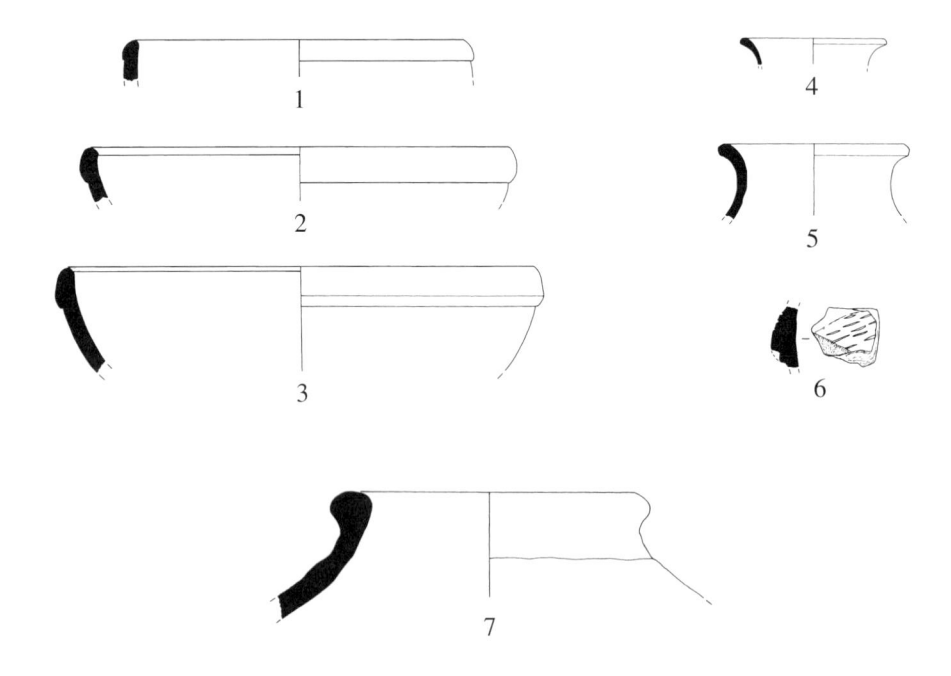

Pottery from Trenches IXA and IXB, Modern Water Barrel Pit (Phase 2B; Period F — Early Bronze Age IVa). Scale 1:5

1. BR. F.III.d (TS. 1010; IXA, 1.16). About 1/16 rim and upper wall segment. Fairly fine pinkish-buff ware, evenly fired. Creamy-buff slip out.
2. BR. F.IV.d (TS. 2424; IXA, 1.4). About 1/10 rim and upper wall segment. Fairly fine pinkish-brown ware, evenly fired. Cream slip in and out.
3. BR. F.IV.d (TS. 1033; IXA, 1.4). About 1/16 rim and most of wall profile. Fairly coarse pink ware, evenly fired. Buff slip out.
4. SJR. C.I.e (TS. 2315; IXA, 1.17). About 1/8 rim and upper neck segment. Fine pinkish-buff ware, evenly fired. Buff slip out.
5. JR. J.III.e (TS. 2278; IXA, 1.17). About 1/5 rim and neck segment. Close pinkish-brown ware, evenly fired. Buff slip in and out.
6. ABS. B (TS. 1880; IXA, 1.4). Fragment of wall of vessel with an incised band of clay on outside wall, which may be part of an appliqué animal decoration. Hard, slightly coarse light brown ware, evenly fired.
7. JR. O.II.1 (SC. 3317; IXB, Modern Water Barrel Pit). Large rim, neck and upper wall segment.

   Other Type Series Examples: (1) SBR. D.I.c (TS. 1017), (2) BR. F.III.d (TS. 2241), (3) BR. Q.II.a (TS. 1026), (4) CBR. A.II.b (SW. 551 = TS. 1891), (5) SJR. C.I.b (TS. 1013), (6) SJR. C.II.r (TS. 2543), (7) JR. K.I.e (TS. 2332).

   Other Study Collection Examples: (1) SBR. A.I.b (SC. 220), (2) SBR. B.I.k (SC. 558), (3) BR. A.II.e (SC. 717), (4) BR. K.I.b (SC. 830), (5) BR. L.III.g (SC. 886), (6) SJR. C.II.q (SC. 2608), (7) JR. B. (Gen. Type, SC. 88), (8) JR. H.I.e (SC. 1267), (9) JR. J.I.a (SC. 1298), (10) JR. J.IV.j (SC. 1550).

   Area IXB, Modern Water Barrel Pit, (Phase 2B, Period F) Early Bronze Age IVa Pottery

   Another Type Series Example: (1) CP. B.IV.b (SW. 132).

Figure 102

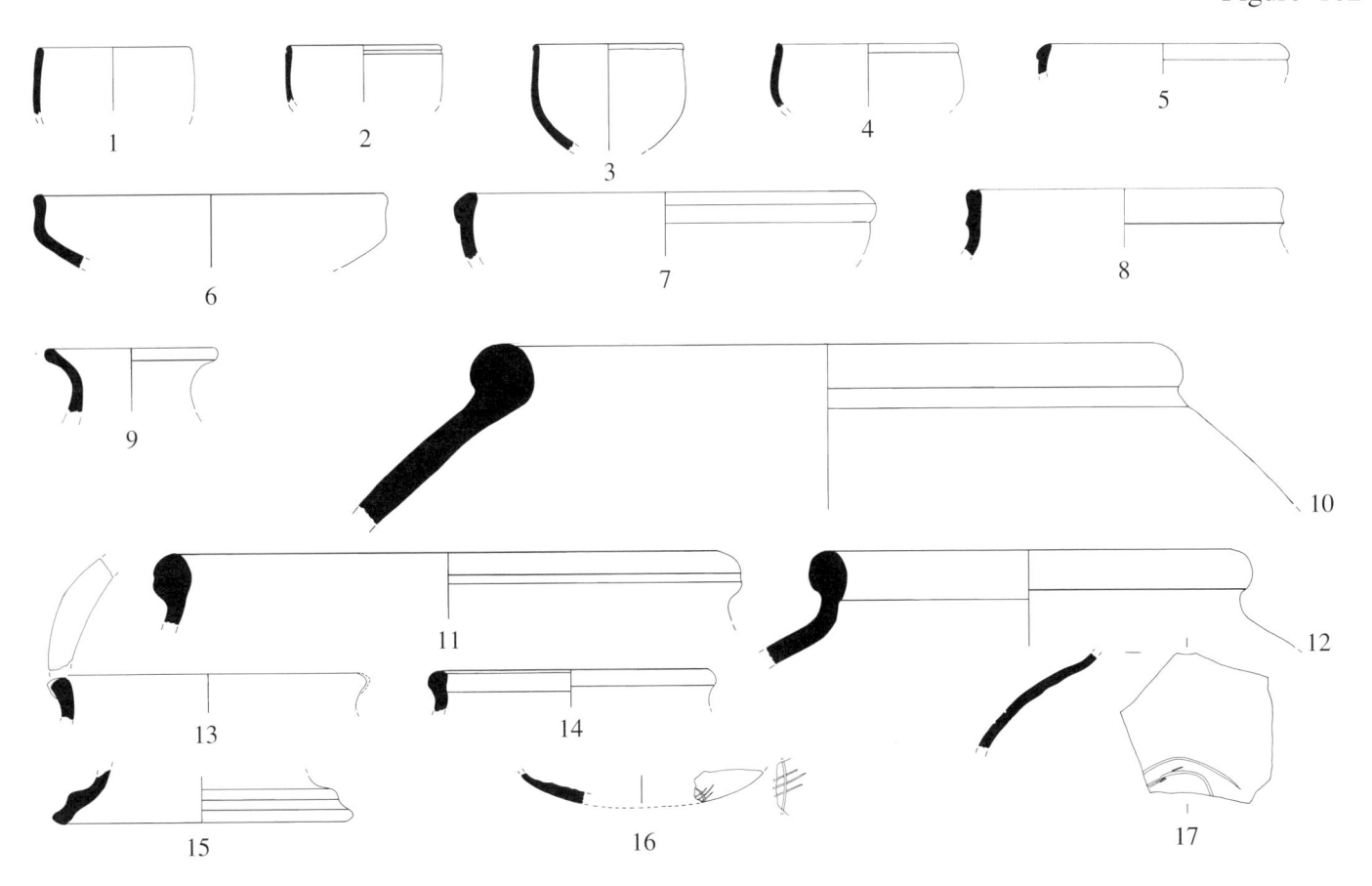

Pottery from Trench XA, Room 15 (Phase 2B; Period F — Early Bronze Age IVa). Scale 1:5

1. SBR. A.I.b (TS. 1262; XA, 1.3). Small rim and upper wall segment. Hard, close light green ware, evenly fired. Self slip in and out.
2. SBR. B.I.c (TS. 1260; XA, 1.3). Small rim and upper wall segment. Fairly fine light brown ware, evenly fired. Charred grayish-buff slip out.
3. SBR. B.I.d (TS. 938; XA, 1.3). About 1/4 rim and most of wall profile; base missing. Fairly coarse pink ware, evenly fired. Cream slip out.
4. SBR. B.I.e (TS. 1259; XA, 1.3). Small rim and upper wall segment. Slightly coarse buff ware, evenly fired. Creamy-green slip in and out.
5. BR. A.II.e (TS. 2026; XA, 1.3). Small rim and upper wall segment. Fairly close pinkish-buff ware, evenly fired. Creamy-buff slip out and just over rim in.
6. BR. E.I.a (TS. 1108; XA, 1.3). About 1/8 rim and about 1/2 of wall segment. Fairly coarse buff-brown ware with many grits, evenly fired. Cream slip in and out.
7. BR. F.IV.d (TS. 1263; XA, 1.3). Small rim and upper wall segment. Fairly coarse buff ware, evenly fired. Creamy-buff slip in and out.
8. JR. B.III.e (TS. 1872; XA, 1.3). Small rim and neck segment. Hard, fairly close pinkish-buff ware, evenly fired. Buff slip in and out.
9. JR. J.III.o (TS. 1265; XA, 1.3). Small rim and neck segment. Fairly close buff ware, evenly fired. Creamy-buff slip in and out.
10. JR. O.II.m (TS. 1077; XA, 1.3). About 1/8 rim and upper shoulder segment. Coarse pink ware, evenly fired. Cream slip in and out.
11. JR. P.II.e (TS. 1073; XA, 1.3). About 1/8 rim and neck segment. Fairly coarse pinkish-buff ware, unevenly fired with light gray core. Thick green slip out and very thin cream slip in.
12. JR. Q.II.a (TS. 1081; XA, 1.3). About 1/6 rim, neck, and upper shoulder segment. Fairly coarse brown ware, evenly fired. Cream slip in and out.
13. CP. A.I.f (TS. 2153; XA, 1.3). About 1/8 rim and neck segment with elongated triangular-shaped ledge handle attached to rim. Slightly coarse and gritty pinkish-brown ware, evenly fired.
14. CP. A.II.e (TS. 2157; XA, 1.3). Small rim and neck segment. Soft grayish-brown ware, evenly fired. Heavily blackened by fire in and out.
15. PS. B.I.b (TS. 2441; XA, 1.3). About 1/10 rim and wall segment. Hard, slightly coarse dark pink ware, evenly fired. Pinkish-buff slip out.
16. BE. A.I (PM. D.15; TS. 1258; XA, 1.3). Sherd from round base with portion of a potter's mark incised on the outside lower portion before firing. Slightly coarse pinkish-brown ware, evenly fired. Buff slip in and out.
17. JR.Sh. (PM. B.2; TS. 1207; XA, 1.3). Jar shoulder sherd with portion of a potter's mark incised on the lower part of the shoulder before firing. Slightly coarse pink ware, evenly fired. Cream slip out.

Other Type Series Examples: (1) BR. D.II.a (TS. 983), (2) BR. F.I.a (TS. 2532), (3) SJR. B.I.b (TS. 1059), (4) SJR. B.II.h (TS. 955), (5) JR. J.III.w (TS. 2292), (6) JR. J.VI.a (TS. 979), (7) JR. O.II.f (TS. 1209), (8) CP. A.I.a (TS. 2160), (9) Jg. A.I.a (TS. 2307), (10) Jg. B.I.a (TS. 2343), (11) Jg. C (TS. 1266), (12) SB. A.I.a (TS. 1210), (13) BE. D.II (TS. 1261), (14) Hd. B (TS. 1089).

Other Study Collection Examples: (1) SBR. B.I.b (SC. 263), (2) SBR. B.I.f (SC. 343), (3) SBR. B.I.h (SC. 483), (4) SBR. C.III.a (SC. 609), (5) SJR. C.I.h (SC. 2574), (6) JR. J.III.h (SC. 1405), (7) JR. J.III.u (SC. 2359), (8) SR. A.II.a (SC. 1958).

Figure 103. Pottery from Area XA, Operation 11, Rooms 19 and 20 (Phase 2B, Period F — Early Bronze Age IVa)

1. SBR. A.I.e (TS. 3383; Op. 11, 4.1, Room 20). About 1/2 rim and most of wall profile. For ware, compare Phase 2A Type Series example from Area IVQ (SW. 732).
2. SBR. B.I.i (TS. 3342; Op. 11, 5.1, Room 19). About 1/3 rim and complete wall profile; base missing. Slightly coarse buff ware with very fine silver-colored mica and lime grits, evenly fired. Creamy-buff slip in and out.
3. SBR. D.I.a (TS. 3369; Op. 11, 4.1, Room 20). Nearly complete apart from missing base. For ware, compare Phase 2A Type Series example from Area IVN (TS. 1681).
4. SBR. F.I.a (TS. 3373; Op. 11, 4.1, Room 20). About 1/12 rim and upper wall segment. Fairly fine pinkish-buff ware with fine gold- and silver-colored mica and lime grits, evenly fired. Creamy-buff slip in and out with traces of horizontal red-painted bands of decoration inside.
5. BR. C.I.a (TS. 3447; Op. 11, 5.1, Room 19). Small rim (1.5 cm) and upper wall segment. Slightly coarse buff ware with many small black and white lime grits, evenly fired. Creamy-buff slip in and out.
6. BR. F.II.d (TS. 3370; Op. 11, 4.1, Room 20). About 1/4 rim and upper wall segment. For ware, compare Phase 2A Type Series example from Area IVJ (SW. 496).
7. BR. K.I.b (TS. 3388; Op. 11, 5.1, Room 19). About 1/16 rim and upper wall segment. Slightly coarse pinkish-brown ware with gold- and silver-colored mica and lime grits, evenly fired. Creamy-buff slip in and out.
8. BR. O.I.a (TS. 3446; Op. 11, 5.1, Room 19). Small rim and upper wall segment. Fairly coarse ware with many white lime grits, unevenly fired with gray core and dark buff at surfaces. Self slip in and out, burnished with a horizontal band below the rim outside.
9. JR. D.I.b (TS. 3380; Op. 11, 4.1, Room 20). About 1/8 rim and most of body profile; base missing. Fairly fine pinkish-orange ware with small gold- and white-colored mica and a few lime grits, evenly fired. Creamy-buff slip out.
10. JR. E.II.y (TS. 3366; Op. 11, 4.1, Room 20). Small rim, neck, and shoulder segment. For ware, compare Phase 3 Type Series example with oval-shaped mouth from Areas IVS and IVY (TS. 2735 = TS. 2676).
11. JR. E.II.y (TS. 3437; Op. 11, 5.1, Room 19). About 1/6 rim and upper shoulder segment. Slightly coarse pink ware with gray and white lime and gold-colored mica grits, evenly fired. Creamy-buff slip out.
12. JR. H.II.d (TS. 3436; Op. 11, 5.1, Room 19). Small rim, neck, and shoulder segment. For ware, compare Phase 4 Type Series example from Area IVP (TS. 2763).
13. JR. J.II.i (TS. 3382; Op. 11, 4.1, Room 20). About 1/5 rim and neck segment. Fine buff ware with gold- and silver-colored mica grits, evenly fired. Buff self slip in and out.
14. JR. J.III.c (TS. 3445; Op. 11, 5.1, Room 19). About 1/4 rim, neck, and shoulder segment. Fairly fine light pinkish-buff ware with gold- and silver-colored mica and lime grits, evenly fired. Self slip in and out.
15. JR. J.IV.f (TS. 3381; Op. 11, 4.1, Room 20). Small rim and neck segment. For ware, compare Phase 8 Type Series example from Area IC (TS. 2138).
16. SR. A.II.c (TS. 3372; Op. 11, 4.1, Room 20). About 1/4 rim and wall segment with remains of two strainer holes below the rim of the vessel. For ware, compare Phase 4 example from Area IVJ (TS. 2933).
17. BE. B.II (TS. 3375; Op. 11, 4.1, Room 20). Complete base and portion of lower wall of vessel. For ware, compare Phase 3 Type Series example from Area IVL (TS. 3061).
18. BE. B.II (PM. C.14; TS. 3386; Op. 11, 5.1, Room 19). Complete base and portion of lower wall of vessel with an X-shaped potter's mark incised before firing. For ware, compare Phase 3 Type Series example from Area IVL (TS. 3061).
19. BE. E.I.c (TS. 3435; Op. 11, 5.1, Room 19). About 1/2 base and lower wall segment. Hard, fine, metallic-like, pink ware with small gold- and silver-colored mica and lime grits, evenly fired. Self slip or wash, burnished outside with horizontally spaced bands.
20. BE. E.I.d (TS. 3374; Op. 11, 4.1, Room 20). About 1/2 of a ring-type base and lower wall of the vessel. Slightly coarse buff ware, evenly fired.
21. JR.Sh. (IP [G.1] H.II.a; TS. 3385; Op. 11, 5.1, Room 19). Three jar shoulder sherds, two joining, with remains of one register bounded by comb-incised horizontal lines with zigzag lines inside. Fairly fine pink ware with lime grits, evenly fired. Creamy-buff slip in and out.
22. SV.5 (PM. D.3; TS. 3343; Op. 11, 5.1, Room 19). Portion of jug or possibly part of a model wagon. Linear decoration incised outside before firing. Fairly fine pinkish-brown ware with fine gold-colored mica and lime grits, evenly fired. Creamy-buff slip in and out.
—. JR.Sh. (PM. C.15; TS. 4190; Op. 11, 4.1, Room 20). Jar Sherd.
—. JR.Sh. (PM. C.14; TS. 4191; Op. 11, 5.1, Room 19). Jar Sherd.
—. JR.Sh. (PM. C.14; TS. 4192; Op. 11, 5.1, Room 19). Jar Sherd.
—. JR.Sh. (PM. E.2; TS. 4193; Op. 11, 4.1, Room 20). Jar Sherd.
—. JR.Sh. (PM. A.21; TS. 4194; Op. 11, 5.1, Room 19). Jar Sherd.
—. JR.Sh. (PM. A.11; TS. 4195; Op. 11, 5.1, Room 19). Jar Sherd.
—. JR.Sh. (PM. A.14; TS. 4196; Op. 11, 5.1, Room 19). Jar Sherd.

Figure 103

—. JR.Sh. (PM. E.2; TS. 4197; Op. 11, 5.1, Room 19). Jar Sherd.

Other Type Series Examples:
Room 19 — (1) JR. D.IV.a (TS. 3389), (2) JR. O.II.c (TS. 3384), (3) JR. P.I.e (TS. 3387), (4) JR. P.II.p (TS. 3365).
Room 20 — (1) SJR. C.II.o (TS. 3341), (2) JR. F.III.c (TS. 3438), (3) JR. J.II.i (TS. 3371), (4) JR. J.III.s (TS. 3368), (5) JR. O.I.f (TS. 3443), (6) JR. Q.II.c (TS. 3367), (7) JR. Q.II.d (TS. 3444), (8) CP. B.IV.c (SW. 761), (9) Bt. A.I.b (TS. 3439).

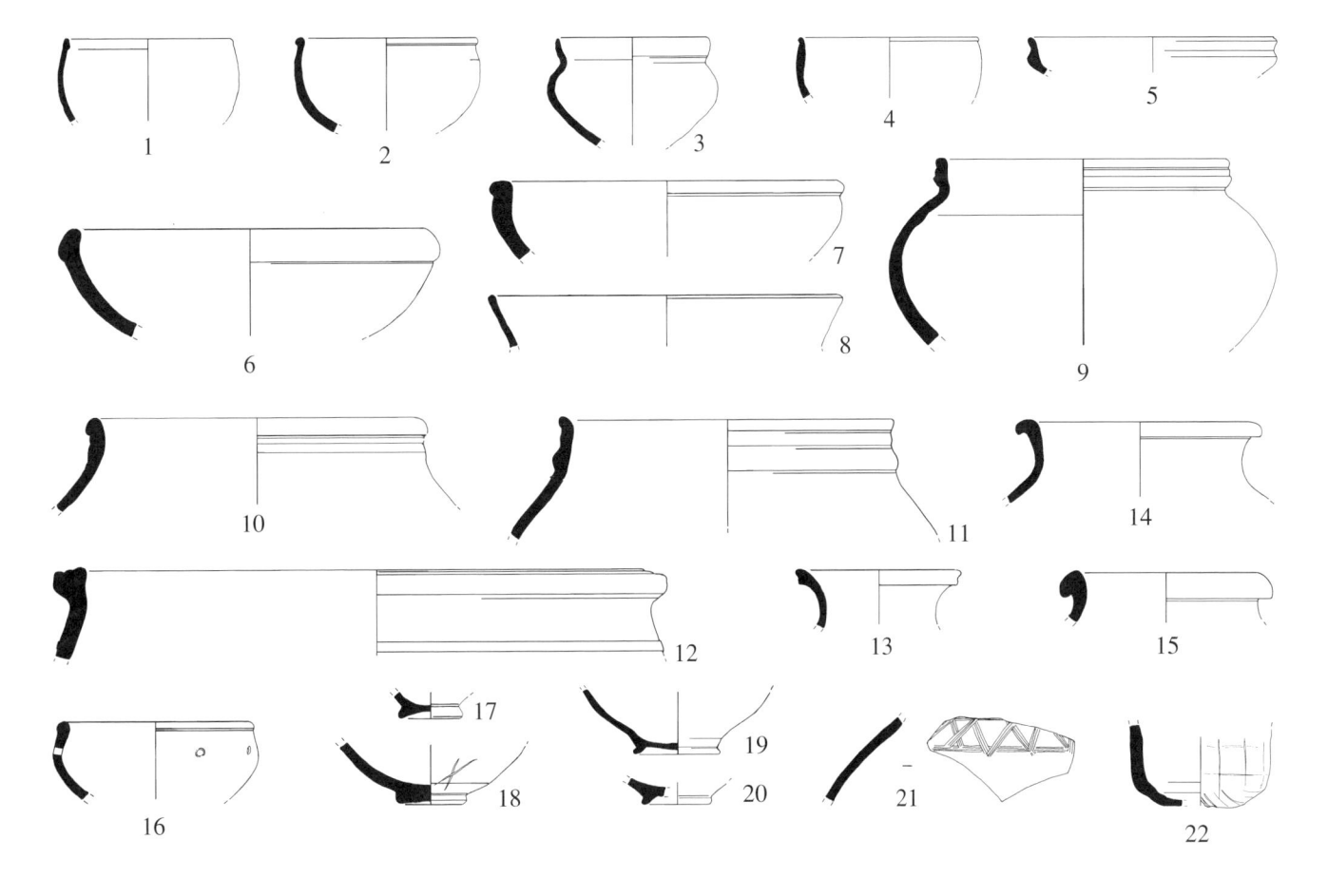

Pottery from Trench XA, Operation 11, Rooms 19 and 20 (Phase 2B; Period F — Early Bronze Age IVa). Scale 1:5

# Figures 104–05

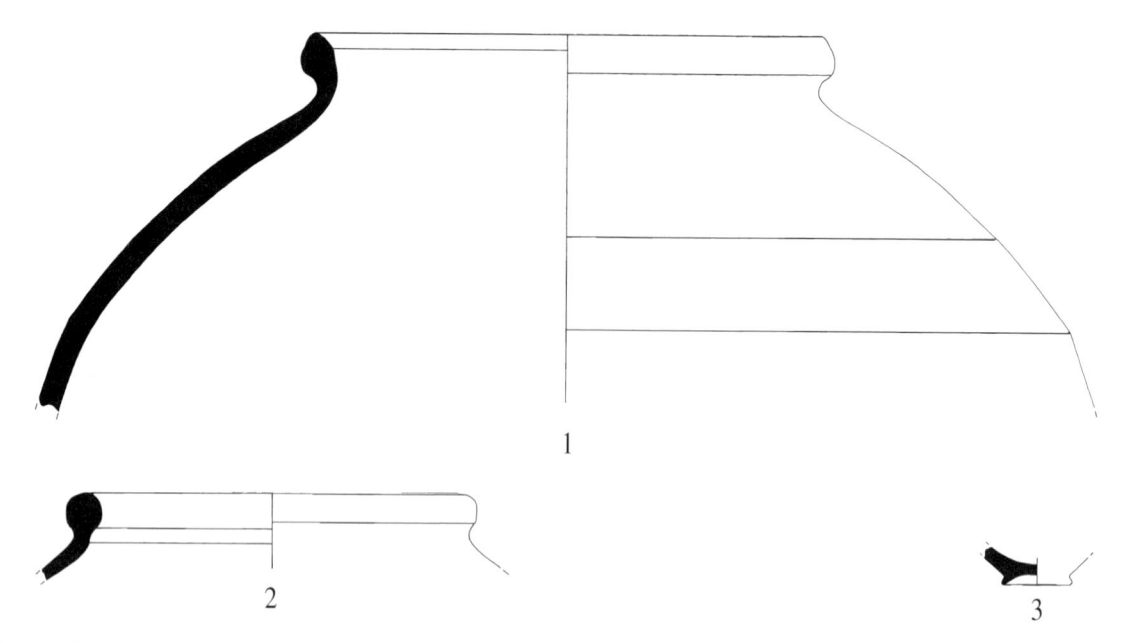

Figure 104. Pottery from Trenches IVA and IVB (= Southwest Corner of Trench IVF, Room 1A; Phase 3; Period E — Early Bronze Age IVb). Scale 1:5

1. JR. O.II.e (TS. 1683; IVA, 1.4). Large rim and shoulder segment. Medium coarse pink ware, evenly fired. Cream slip in and out.
2. JR. O.II.b (TS. 2374; IVB, 3.2). About 1/6 rim and upper shoulder segment. Fairly coarse ware, unevenly fired with gray core and pinkish-buff at surfaces. Creamy-green slip out.
3. BE. E.I.d (TS. 3078; IVB, 3.2). Complete base and lower portion of vessel wall. Fine creamy-green ware, evenly fired. Self slip in and out.

Another Type Series Example: Area IVB: (1) JR. P.II.f (TS. 2361).

Another Study Collection Example: Area IVA: (1) JR. J.III.d (SC. 2231).

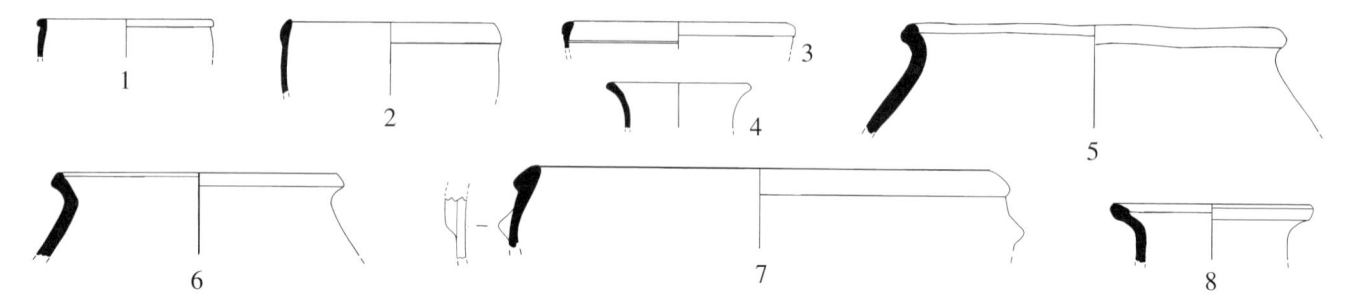

Figure 105. Pottery from Trench IVC (= Town Wall Tower; Phase 3; Period E — Early Bronze Age IVb). Scale 1:5

1. SBR. B.I.f (TS. 2030; IVC, 1.2). Small rim and upper wall segment. Slightly coarse greenish-buff ware, evenly fired. Self slip in and out.
2. SBR. B.I.h (TS. 1966; IVC, 1.2). Small rim and upper wall segment. Fine pinkish-buff ware, fairly evenly fired.
3. BR. D.VI.a (TS. 2722; IVC, 1.2). Small rim segment. Hard, close brown ware, evenly fired. Self slip in and out, horizontally burnished out.
4. SJR. C.I.e (TS. 2313; IVC, 1.2). About 1/6 rim and neck segment. Fairly fine buff ware, evenly fired. Light creamy-green slip out and just over rim in.
5. JR. F.I.c (TS. 1945; IVC, 1.2). Large rim and upper shoulder segment. Fairly coarse greenish-gray buff ware, evenly fired. Self slip in and out.
6. JR. F.I.c (TS. 1957; IVC, 1.2). Small rim and upper shoulder segment. Slightly coarse and gritty pinkish-buff ware, fairly evenly fired. Creamy-buff slip in and out.
7. JR. H.I.b (TS. 1752; IVC, 1.2). Small rim and upper wall segment with portion of a horizontal lug handle on the shoulder. Medium fine buff ware, evenly fired. Cream slip in and out.
8. JR. K.I.a (TS. 2329; IVC, 1.2). About 1/8 rim and neck segment. Fairly coarse greenish-buff ware, evenly fired. Self slip in and out.
—. JR.Sh. (PM. F; TS. 3137; IVC, 1.2). Jar sherd. Ware description not available.

Other Type Series Examples: (1) SBR. A.I.h (TS. 2024), (2) JR. P.I.c (TS. 2384).

Other Study Collection Examples: (1) SBR. A.I.a (SC. 184), (2) SBR. A.I.a (SC. 188), (3) SBR. B.I.a (SC. 242), (4) SBR. B.I.a (SC. 250), (5) SBR. B.I.g (SC. 357), (6) SBR. B.I.h (SC. 472), (7) SBR. B.I.h (SC. 473), (8) SBR. B.I.h (SC. 480), (9) SBR. B.I.h (SC. 501), (10) SBR. B.I.h (SC. 515), (11) SBR. B.I.h (SC. 521), (12) SBR. B.I.k (SC. 563), (13) SBR. B.I.l (SC. 585), (14) SBR. C.III.a (SC. 608), (15) BR. E.I.b (SC. 754), (16) BR. F.II.a (SC. 790), (17) BR. L.III.c (SC. 885), (18) SJR. B.II.d (SC. 2508), (19) SJR. C.II.q (SC. 2610), (20) JR. C.III.a (SC. 1006), (21) JR. D.X.a (SC. 1124), (22) JR. F.I.a (SC. 1186), (23) JR. G.I.b (SC. 2038), (24) JR. H.I.a (SC. 1243), (25) JR. H.I.l (SC. 1289), (26) JR. J.III.g (SC. 1391), (27) JR. J.III.h (SC. 2287), (28) JR. J.III.m (SC. 1438), (29) JR. J.III.q (SC. 1475), (30) JR. J.IV.d (SC. 2375), (31) JR. K.I.b (SC. 2390), (32) JR. O.II.f (SC. 2421), (33) JR. Q.I.a (SC. 1766), (34) CP. C.I.a (SC. 1899).

Derived Hellenistic Examples (not illustrated): (1) H.BR. A.IV.a (TS. 1932), (2) H.St.J. B.II.p (TS. 1943).

Figures 106–07

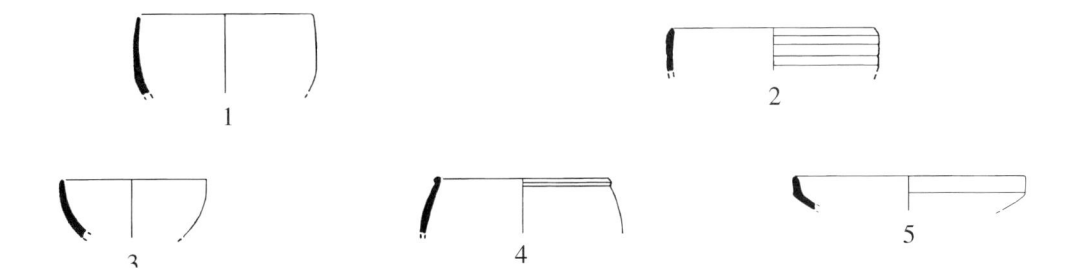

Figure 106. Pottery from Trench IVF, Room 1A (Phase 3; Period E — Early Bronze Age IVb). Scale 1:5

1. SBR. A.I.e (SC. 174; IVF, 1.5). 1/10 rim and upper wall segment. Fairly fine pinkish-brown ware with small gold- and silver-colored mica and black and white lime grits, evenly fired. Self slip in and out.
2. SBR. A.II.c (SC. 555; IVF, 1.5). 1/8 rim and upper wall segment. Fine pinkish-buff ware with a few small black and white lime grits, evenly fired. Creamy colored greenish-buff slip in and out.
3. SBR. B.I.b (SC. 618, IVF, 1.4). 1/12 rim and most of wall profile. Fairly fine pinkish-orange ware with fine gold- and silver-colored mica and lime grits, evenly fired. Self slip in and out.
4. SBR. B.I.f (SC. 341; IVF, 1.5). 1/12 rim and upper wall segment. Fairly fine pinkish-brown ware with very fine gold- and silver-colored mica and small lime grits, evenly fired. Creamy-buff slip in and out.
5. BR. D.IV.a (TS. 2718; IVF, 1.5). Small rim and upper wall segment. Fine light pink ware, evenly fired. Cream slip in and out.

Other Type Series and Study Collection Examples (see fig. 107).

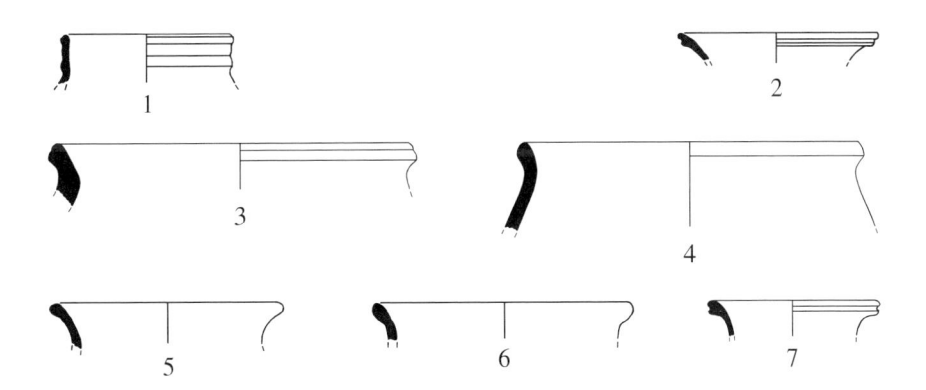

Figure 107. Pottery from Trench IVF, Room 1A (Phase 3; Period E — Early Bronze Age IVb) (*cont.*). Scale 1:5

1. SJR. B.II.j (SC. 2523; IVF, 1.5). 1/16 rim and neck segment. Fairly fine pinkish-brown ware with fine gold colored mica and white lime grits, evenly fired. Self slip in and out.
2. SJR. C.I.a (SC. 2530; IVF, 1.4). 1/12 rim and upper neck segment. Hard-fired, fairly fine greenish-buff ware with small black and white lime grits, evenly fired. Self slip in and out, horizontally burnished just below the inside of the rim.
3. JR. F.I.c (TS. 1960; IVF, 1.5). Small rim and upper shoulder segment. Hard, close buff-brown ware, evenly fired. Grayish-buff slip out.
4. JR. F.II.a (TS. 1946; IVF, 1.4). Small rim and upper shoulder segment. Fairly close buff ware, evenly fired. Creamy-buff slip out and just over rim in.
5. JR. J.I.b (SC. 2555; IVF, 1.4). About 1/8 rim and neck segment. Fine greenish-buff ware with a few black and white lime grits, evenly fired. Self slip in and out, discolored reddish-brown in patches due to earth staining.
6. JR. J.I.f (SC. 2573; IVF, 1.4). About 1/16 rim and upper neck segment. Fairly fine pinkish-buff ware with some mica and lime grits, evenly fired. Creamy-buff slip in and out.
7. JR. J.III.ad (TS. 2544; IVF, 1.4). Small rim and upper neck segment. Slightly coarse greenish-buff ware, evenly fired. Creamy-green slip in and out. Compare Phase 4 Type Series comb-incised jar from Operation 10 (TS. 3330 = TS. 3336).

Other Type Series Examples: (1) SBR. E.I.b (TS. 2471), (2) BR. E.III.b (TS. 1959), (3) JR. F.II.b (TS. 2538), (4) JR. H.I.c (TS. 1939), (5) CP. A.II.d (TS. 1941), (6) CP. B.I.d (SC. 1824).

Other Study Collection Examples: (1) SBR. A.I.a (SC. 193), (2) SBR. A.I.a (SC. 196), (3) SBR. B.I.g (SC. 395), (4) SBR. B.I.q (SC. 592), (5) SBR. C.III.a (SC. 613), (6) SJR. C.I.e (SC. 2634), (7) JR. J.III.a (SC. 2217), (8) JR. J.III.d (SC. 2221), (9) JR. K.I.g (SC. 2655), (10) JR. (not typed, SC. 123), (11) CP. C.II.b (SC. 66).

Figures 108–10

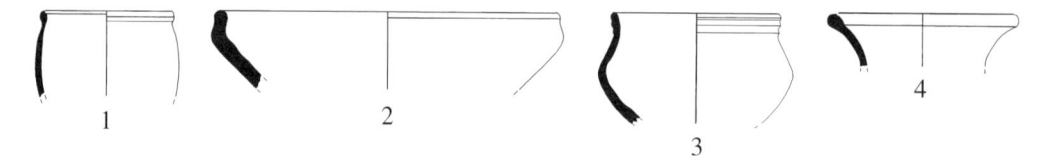

Figure 108. Pottery from Trench IVG, Room 3A (Phase 3; Period E — Early Bronze Age IVb). Scale 1:5

1. SBR. B.I.h (TS. 2451; IVG, 1.3). About 1/10 rim and upper wall segment. Slightly coarse buff ware, evenly fired. Thick self slip in and out.
2. BR. E.II.a (TS. 2939; IVG, 1.3). Small rim and upper wall segment. Slightly coarse pink ware, evenly fired. Remains of self slip in and out.
3. JR. C.II.b (SW. 255; IVG, 1.3, 1.4). About 4/5 rim and most of wall profile. Fairly fine pinkish-rose ware with various colored lime and mica grits, evenly fired. Creamy-tan slip in and out. Trace of burning on rim.
4. JR. K.I.b (TS. 2339; IVG, 1.3). About 1/12 rim and neck segment. Fine buff ware, evenly fired. Self slip in and out.
—. JR.Sh. (PM. F; TS. 3099; IVG, 1.3). Jar sherd. Ware description not available.

Other Type Series Examples: (1) BR. F.I.d (TS. 2526), (2) SJR. C.II.g (TS. 1970), (3) Ld. A.I.a (TS. 1951), (4) SR. A.II.c (SW. 257).

Other Study Collection Examples: (1) BR. L.I.b (SC. 832), (2) BE. E.I.k (SC. 3188).

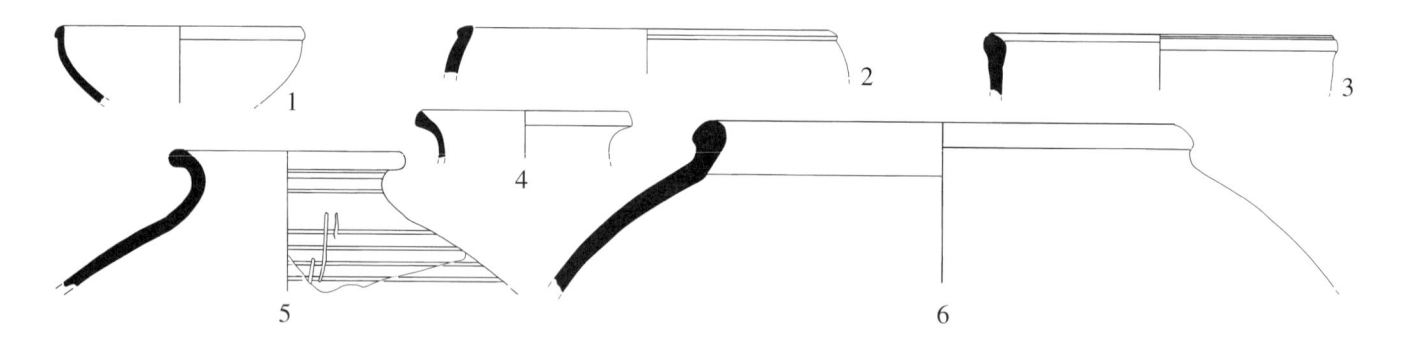

Figure 109. Pottery from Trench IVJ, Room 4A (Phase 3; Period E — Early Bronze Age IVb). Scale 1:5

1. SBR. B.I.h (TS. 1605; IVJ, 1.3 + 1.4). Small rim and wall segment. Fairly fine pinkish-buff ware, evenly fired. Self slip in and out.
2. BR. A.II.e (TS. 2931; IVJ, 1.4). Small rim and upper wall segment. Fairly fine pink ware, evenly fired. Traces of cream slip out.
3. BR. L.I.e (TS. 2951; IVJ, 1.4). Small rim and upper wall segment. Fairly fine creamy-buff ware, evenly fired. Self slip in and out.
4. JR. J.I.h (TS. 2642; IVJ, 1.3, 1.5). About 1/6 rim and neck segment. Fine creamy-green ware, evenly fired. Self slip in and out.
5. JR. J.IV.a (PM. A.8; TS. 1613; IVJ, 1.3 + 1.4). Complete, but broken in situ; only rim, neck, and upper body mended. Potter's mark on shoulder incised before firing. Medium fine pink ware, evenly fired. Wheel-applied cream slip lines in reserve around neck and body.
6. JR. P.II.a (TS. 2809; IVJ, 1.3 + 1.4). Complete in situ, but only upper portion mended. Slightly coarse pinkish-brown ware, evenly fired. Creamy-buff slip out.

Other Type Series Examples: (1) SJR. B.II.a (TS. 3004), (2) JR. E.II.a (SW. 595), (3) JR. E.II.l (TS. 1587 = TS. 1671), (4) JR. O.I.b (SW. 668).

Other Study Collection Examples: (1) SBR. B.I.h (SC. 423), (2) JR. E.II.m (SC. 1156), (3) JR. F.I.a (SC. 1182), (4) JR. J.II.m (SC. 2194), (5) JR. K.I.b (SC. 1565), (6) BE. E.I.e (SC. 3167).

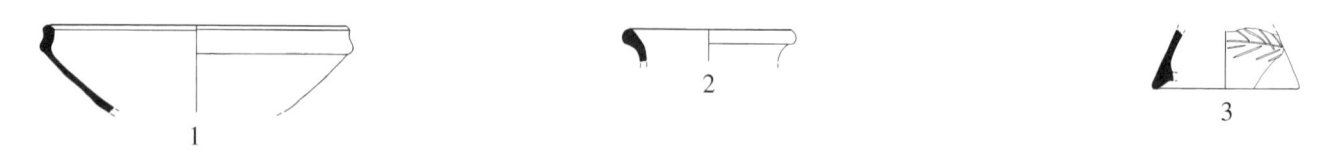

Figure 110. Pottery from Trench IVJ Bin, Room 5A (Phase 3; Period E — Early Bronze Age IVb). Scale 1:5

1. BR. C.I.a (TS. 2575; IVJ Bin, 3.2). About 1/6 rim segment and most of wall profile. Hard, fine buff ware, evenly fired. Cream slip in and out.
2. JR. J.III.e (TS. 3030; IVJ Bin, 3.2). Small rim and neck segment. Slightly coarse green ware, evenly fired. Self slip in and out.
3. Ld. C.II.b (IP [G.4] D.IV; PM. D.21; TS. 2643; IVJ Bin, 3.2). Lid segment with tree or wheat stalk potter's mark incised horizontally on outside wall before firing. Fine pink ware, evenly fired. Self slip out.

Other Study Collection Examples: (1) SBR. A.I.b (SC. 208), (2) JR. J.III.m (SC. 2324), (3) JR. K.I.e (SC. 1594), (4) BE. B.II (SC. 3121).

Figure 111

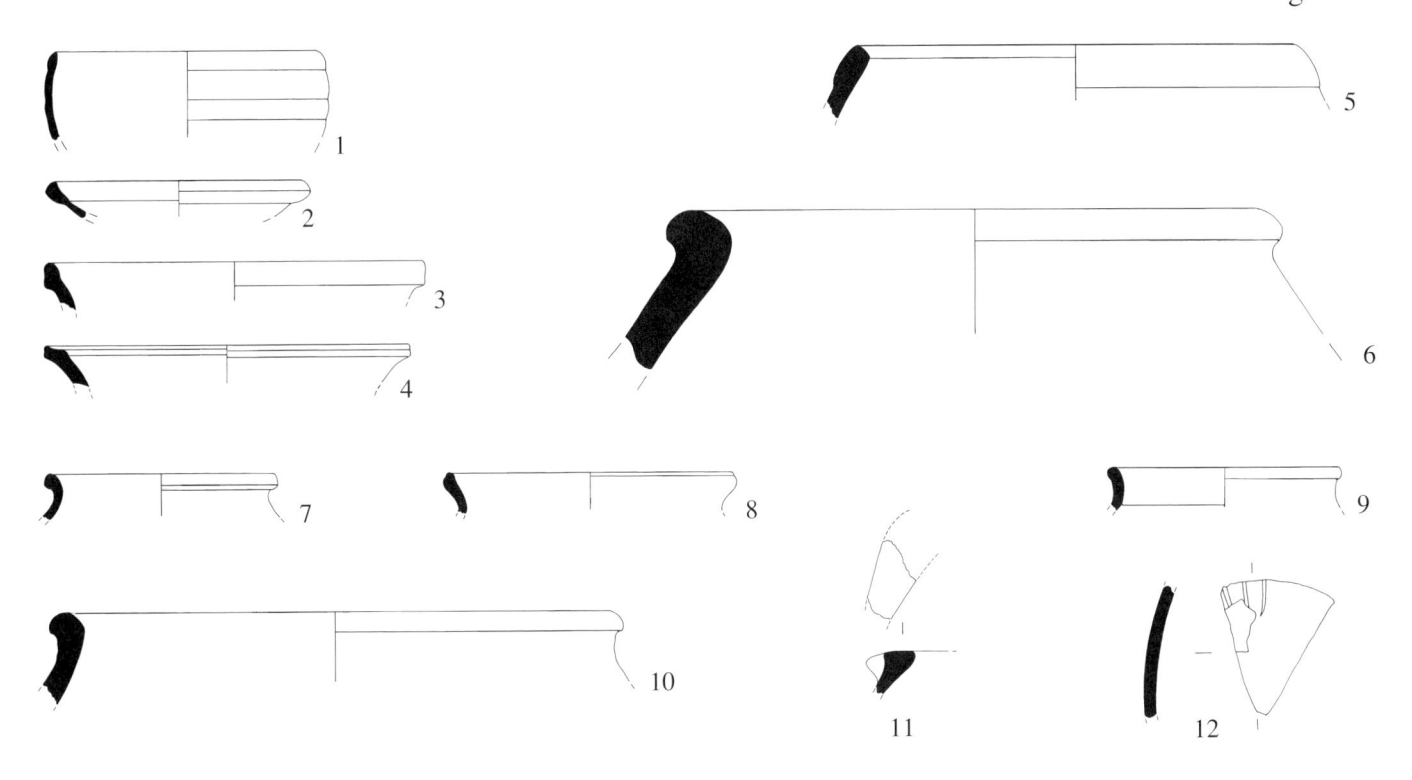

Pottery from Trench IVK, Room 2A (Phase 3; Period E — Early Bronze Age IVb). Scale 1:5

1. SBR. B.I.h (TS. 1759; IVK, 1.3). Small rim and wall segment. Hard, fine pink ware, evenly fired. Cream slip in and out.
2. BR. D.VI.b (TS. 1708; IVK, 1.3). Small rim and upper wall segment. Medium fine buff ware, evenly fired. Self slip in and out.
3. JR. E.II.n (TS. 2663; IVK, 1.3). About 1/10 rim and neck segment. Hard, fairly fine, pinkish-brown ware, evenly fired. Creamy-green slip in and out.
4. JR. G.I.c (TS. 2630; IVK, 1.3). Abour 1/10 rim and neck segment. Fairly fine creamy-green ware, evenly fired. Self slip in and out.
5. JR. H.I.d (TS. 2665; IVK, 2.3). Small rim and shoulder segment. Slightly coarse grayish-brown ware, evenly fired. Self slip in and out.
6. JR. O.I.d (TS. 1644; IVK, 1.3). Large rim and upper shoulder segment. Very coarse pink ware, evenly fired. Self slip in and out.
7. CP. A.I.b (TS. 2860; IVK, 1.3). About 1/8 rim and upper shoulder segment. Slightly coarse brown ware, evenly fired. Self slip in and out.
8. CP. A.I.h (TS. 2868; IVK, 2.3). Small rim and neck segment. Slightly coarse buff ware, evenly fired. Self slip in and out.
9. CP. B.III.b (TS. 2862; IVK, 1.3). Small rim and neck segment. Slightly coarse grayish-buff ware, evenly fired. Self slip in and out. Burnished out and just over rim in.
10. CP. C.I.b (TS. 1679; IVK, 1.3). Small rim and shoulder segment. Coarse pink ware with lime and mica grits, unevenly fired. Self slip in and out.
11. CP. C.II.b (TS. 2867; IVK, 1.3). Small rim segment with remains of triangular-shaped ledge handle attached to rim. Slightly coarse grayish-buff ware, evenly fired. Self slip in and out. Burnished in and out on surviving portions of fragment.
12. JR.Sh. (PM. A.14; TS. 1668; IVK. 2.3). Body sherd with portion of a potter's mark incised on outside wall before firing. Hard pink ware, evenly fired. Cream slip in and out.
—. JR.Sh. (PM. F; TS. 3119; IVK, 1.3). Jar sherd. Ware description not available.
—. JR.Sh. (PM. F; TS. 3126; IVK, 1.3). Jar sherd. Ware description not available.

Other Type Series Examples: (1) BR. A.II.e (TS. 1714), (2) BR. M.III.a (TS. 1675), (3) JR. E.I.e (TS. 1656), (4) JR. J.II.a (TS. 2659), (5) JR. J.IV.b (TS. 1662), (6) JR. P.III.e (TS. 1704), (7) BE. A.II (TS. 3067).

Other Study Collection Examples: (1) SBR. A.I.a (SC. 170), (2) SBR. A.I.b (SC. 202), (3) SBR. A.I.b (SC. 218), (4) SBR. B.I.a (SC. 241), (5) SBR. B.I.a (SC. 249), (6) SBR. B.I.d (SC. 300), (7) SBR. B.I.g (SC. 381), (8) SBR. B.I.g (SC. 407), (9) SBR. B.I.h (SC. 427), (10) SBR. B.I.h (SC. 438), (11) SBR. B.I.h (SC. 452), (12) SBR. B.I.h (SC. 461), (13) SBR. B.I.l (SC. 577), (14) SBR. B.I.l (SC. 672), (15) BR. L.II.b (SC. 851), (16) SJR. B.III.d (SC. 2529), (17) SJR. (not typed, SC. 99), (18) JR. G.III.a (SC. 2053), (19) JR. H.I.e (SC. 1270), (20) JR. J.III.d (SC. 1371), (21) JR. J.III.e (SC. 2250), (22) JR. J.III.i (SC. 1406), (23) JR. J.III.m (SC. 1434), (24) JR. J.III.o (SC. 2346), (25) JR. J.III.q (SC. 1482), (26) JR. J.III.q (SC. 1483), (27) JR. J.III.q (SC. 1485), (28) JR. J.III.q (SC. 1486), (29) JR. J.III.r (SC. 1489), (30) JR. J.IV.g (SC. 1530), (31) BE. E.I.d (SC. 3161), (32) BE. E.I.e (SC. 3166), (33) CP. A.I.f (SC. 3318).

Figure 112

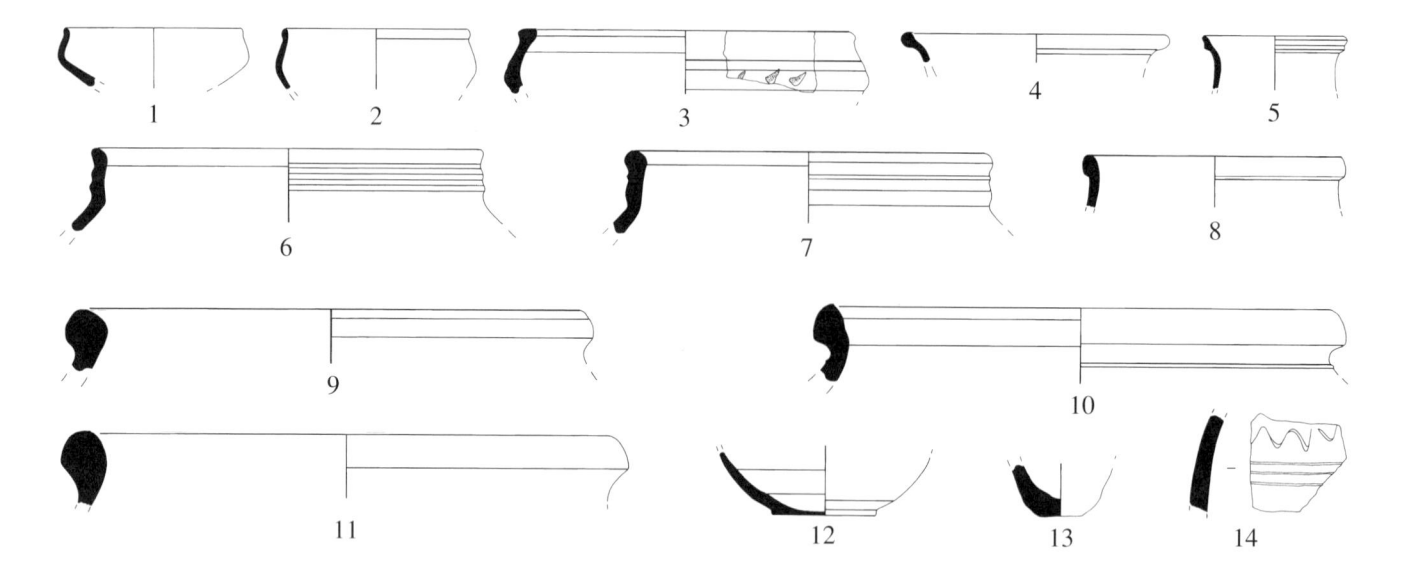

Pottery from Trench IVL, Room 3A (Phase 3; Period E — Early Bronze Age IVb). Scale 1:5

1. BR. A.IV.c (TS. 1725; IVL, 2.1). Small rim and wall segment. Fine grayish-colored ware, evenly fired. Pink slip in and out.
2. BR. A.IV.c (TS. 1755; IVL, 2.1). Small rim and wall segment. Hard, fine pink ware, evenly fired. Cream slip in and out.
3. BR. N.II.a (TS. 1728; IVL, 2.1). About 1/10 rim and upper wall segment with tool-incised wedge-shaped decoration around the girth of the vessel. Medium coarse pink ware with lime grits, unevenly fired. Cream slip in and out.
4. SJR. B.I.b (TS. 1726; IVL, 2.1). Small rim and neck segment. Dark grayware with many grits, evenly fired. Buff slip in and out.
5. SJR. C.II.c (TS. 1768; IVL, 2.1). About 1/5 rim and neck segment. Fine pink ware, evenly fired. Self slip in and out.
6. JR. D.V.e (TS. 1669; IVL, 1.3). Large rim and upper shoulder segment. Hard, pink ware with lime and mica grits, evenly fired. Cream slip in and out.
7. JR. D.V.f (TS. 1672; IVL, 2.1), Small rim and upper shoulder segment. Pink ware, evenly fired. Cream slip in and out.
8. JR. E.II.j (TS. 3016; IVL, 1.3). Small rim and neck segment. Fine light grayware, evenly fired. Self slip in and out.
9. JR. O.II.e (TS. 1657; IVL, 2.1). Small rim segment. Coarse reddish ware with lime and mica grits, evenly fired. Cream slip in and out.
10. JR. O.II.e (TS. 1678; IVL, 2.1). Small rim, neck, and upper shoulder segment. Coarse pinkish ware with lime and mica grits, unevenly fired. Cream slip in and out.
11. CP. C.I.d (TS. 2847; IVL, 2.1). Small rim segment. Fairly coarse grayish-brown ware, evenly fired. Burnished self slip in and out.
12. BE. B.I (TS. 1660; IVL, 2.1). Incomplete base and lower wall of vessel. Fairly fine pink ware with lime and mica grits, evenly fired. Cream slip in and out.
13. BE. D.II (TS. 1680; IVL, 2.1). Complete handmade base and lower wall of vessel. Grayish ware, fairly evenly fired. Self slip in and out.
14. JR.Sh. (IP [G.1] B.I.a; TS. 1655; IVL, 2.1). Jar body sherd with wavy and horizontal lines incised outside before firing (see pl. 102c). Buff ware, evenly fired. Cream slip in and out.
—. JR.Sh. (PM. F; TS. 3108; IVL, 2.1). Jar sherd. Ware description not available.
—. JR.Sh. (PM. F; TS. 3128; IVL, 2.1). Jar sherd. Ware description not available.

Other Type Series Examples: (1) SBR. F.I.c (TS. 1712), (2) BR. E.II.a (TS. 1674 = TS. 1690), (3) BR. G.I.f (TS. 2671), (4) JR. A.IV.a (TS. 1757), (5) JR. B.VI.b (TS. 1646), (6) JR. H.II.a (TS. 1764), (7) CP. B.IV.d (TS. 2852), (8) Ld. C.II.a (PM. E.2; TS. 1746), (9) BE. B.II (TS. 3061), (10) BE. E.II.d (TS. 1673), (11) ABS. A (TS. 1670), (12) ABS. A (TS. 1649).

Other Study Collection Examples: (1) SBR. B.I.b (SC. 256), (2) SBR. B.I.d (SC. 286), (3) SBR. B.I.h (SC. 476), (4) BR. F.I.d (SC. 778), (5) JR. B.II.c (SC. 929), (6) JR. B.III.f (SC. 948), (7) JR. C.V.d (SC. 1027), (8) JR. E.I.c (SC. 1992), (9) JR. E.I.e (SC. 1996), (10) JR. E.II.r (SC. 1165), (11) JR. J.I.c (SC. 2109), (12) JR. J.III.a (SC. 2215), (13) JR. J.III.d (SC. 1373), (14) JR. J.III.l (SC. 2309), (15) JR. J.III.n (SC. 1447), (16) JR. J.III.n (SC. 1461), (17) JR. K.II.e (SC. 2402), (18) JR. J. (Gen. Type, SC. 118), (19) JR. (not typed, SC. 100), (20) BE. D.II (SC. 3137).

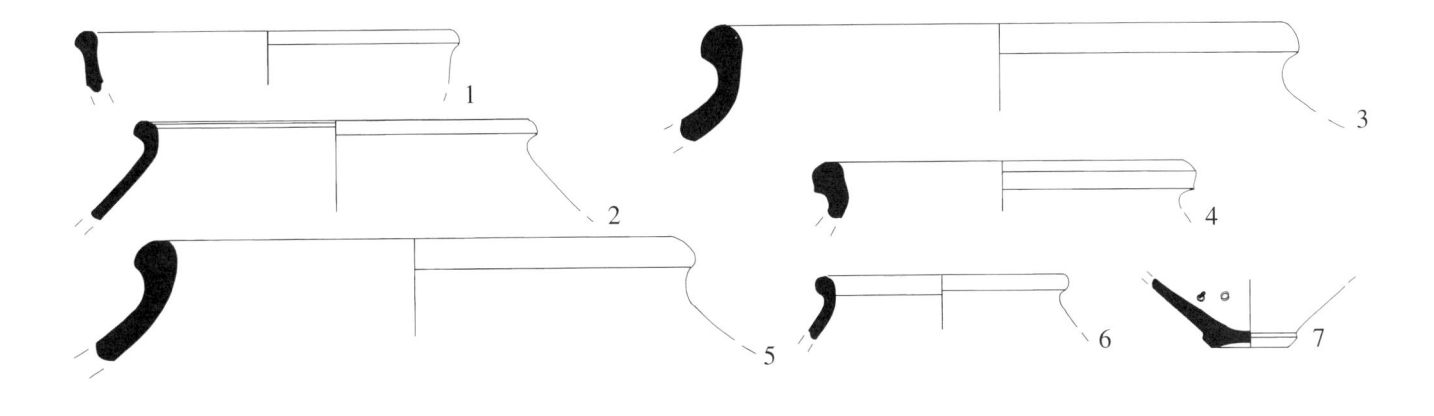

Figure 113

Figure 113. Pottery from Trench IVL/P, Pit Cutting Wall North of Door Between Rooms 3 and 9 (Phase 3; Period E — Early Bronze Age IVb). Scale 1:5

1. BR. L.III.a (TS. 1765; IVL/P, 1.3). Small rim and upper wall segment. Medium fine light pink ware, evenly fired. Cream slip in and out.
2. JR. E.II.g (TS. 1677; IVL/P, 1.3). Large rim and upper shoulder segment. Hard, pink ware, evenly fired. Cream slip in and out.
3. JR. P.II.a (TS. 1654; IVL/P, 1.3). Large rim, neck, and shoulder segment. Fairly coarse pink ware, evenly fired. Cream slip in and out.
4. JR. P.II.c (TS. 1761; IVL/P, 1.3). Small rim and neck segment. Medium coarse buff ware with lime grits, evenly fired. Cream slip in and out.
5. JR. P.III.a (TS. 1658; IVL/P, 1.3). Large rim, neck, and shoulder segment. Coarse grayish ware with lime and mica grits, unevenly fired. Cream slip in and out.
6. CP. A.II.c (TS. 1758; IVL/P, 1.3). About 1/8 rim and upper shoulder segment. Medium coarse pink ware with many mica grits, unevenly fired. Self slip in and out.
7. BE. B.II (PM. C.20; TS. 1661; IVL/P, 1.3). Complete base and segment of lower wall of vessel with a potter's mark, two circles, incised inside before firing. Hard, medium coarse pink ware with lime grits, evenly fired. Buff slip in and out.

Other Type Series Examples: (1) MBR. B.I.a (SW. 557), (2) BR. E.III.i (TS. 1722), (3) JR. D.V.f (TS. 1653), (4) JR. E.I.f (TS. 1665), (5) JR. N.II.a (TS. 1652), (6) CP. A.II.b (TS. 1647), (7) Ld. C.I.b (TS. 1762), (8) BE. A.I (TS. 1650).

Figures 114–15

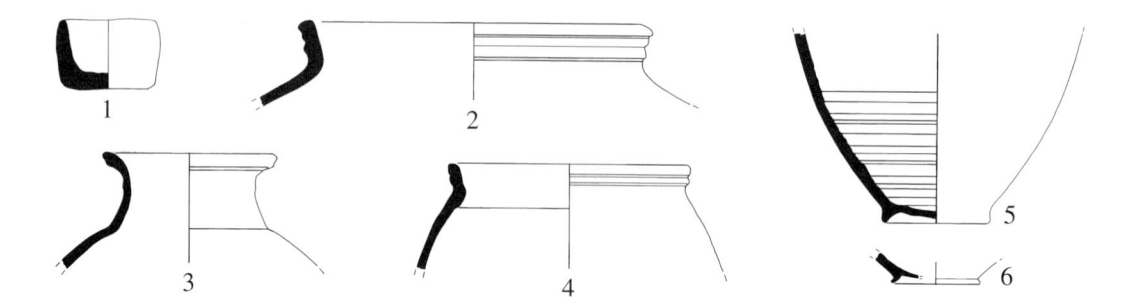

Figure 114. Pottery from Trench IVP, Operation 6, Room 22, Above Courtyard Room 9 (Phase 3; Period E — Early Bronze Age IVb). Scale 1:5

1. MBR. B.I.a (TS. 3490; Op. 6, 7.4). About 1/2 of a handmade vessel. Slightly coarse pinkish-buff ware with gold- and silver-colored mica and lime grits, fairly evenly fired. Creamy-buff slip in and out.
2. JR. D.V.d (TS. 3470; Op. 6, 7.3). About 1/8 rim and upper shoulder segment. Fairly fine pinkish-buff ware with fine white and gold-colored mica grits, evenly fired. Self slip in and out.
3. JR. J.III.n (TS. 3467; Op. 6, 7.3). About 1/6 rim, neck, and upper shoulder segment. Fairly coarse light pinkish-buff ware with many medium-sized black and white grits, evenly fired. Creamy-buff slip out.
4. JR. J.VI.a (TS. 3461; Op. 6, 7.3). About 1/10 rim and upper wall segment. Hard, close pinkish-brown ware with white- and gold-colored mica grits and a few lime inclusions, evenly fired. Self slip out.
5. BE. E.I.b (TS. 3293; Op. 6, 7.2). Complete base and about 1/2 of upper wall extant. Fine pinkish-orange ware with many gold-colored mica and a few lime grits, evenly fired. Creamy-buff slip out.
6. BE. E.I.c (TS. 3481; Op. 6, 15.1). Incomplete base and lower wall of vessel. For ware, compare Type Series example from Area IVJ (TS. 1609).

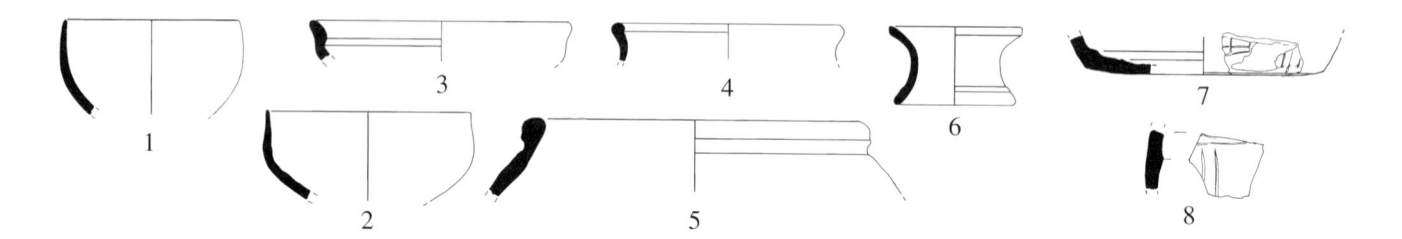

Figure 115. Area IV, Operation 6, Room 24 and Alley (Phase 3; Period E — Early Bronze Age IVb). Scale 1:5

1. SBR. A.I.b (TS. 4099; Op. 6, 4.11). Small rim segment with about 1/5 of wall of vessel. Fairly fine pinkish-buff ware with gold- and silver-colored mica and lime grits, evenly fired. Creamy-buff slip in and out.
2. SBR. A.I.g (TS. 3478; Op. 6, 14.6, Alley). About 1/3 rim and most of wall profile; base missing. For ware, compare Type Series example from Area IVD/K, Room 2 (SW. 301 = TS. 1742).
3. BR. E.I.a (TS. 3479; Op. 6, 14.5). Small rim and upper wall segment. For ware, compare Phase 4 example from Area IVP (TS. 2620).
4. JR. J.III.aa (TS. 3482; Op. 6, 14.4). Small rim and neck segment. For ware, compare Type Series example from Area IVM (TS. 2987).
5. JR. P.I.c (TS. 4100; Op. 6, 4.11). About 1/10 rim and shoulder segment with remains of horizontally painted black bands around rim and shoulder. Fine ware with gold- and silver-colored mica and lime grits, unevenly fired gray-buff in and brown-buff out. Self slip below very worn black paint out.
6. PS. A.II.a (TS. 3458; Op. 6, 14.6, Alley). Complete profile of small pot stand. For ware, compare Type Series example from Area IVQ (SW. 670 = TS. 2473).
7. BE. D.III (PM. D.14; TS. 3198; Op. 6, 14.2). About 1/2 segment with potter's mark incised on the outside wall before firing. Fairly fine buff-brown ware with gold- and white-colored mica and fine lime grits, evenly fired.
8. JR.Sh. (PM. A.6; TS. 3196; Op. 6, 14.2). Jar shoulder sherd with remains of a potter's mark incised on the outside wall before firing. Fairly fine pinkish-buff ware with white lime grits, evenly fired. Creamy-buff slip in and out.

Figure 116

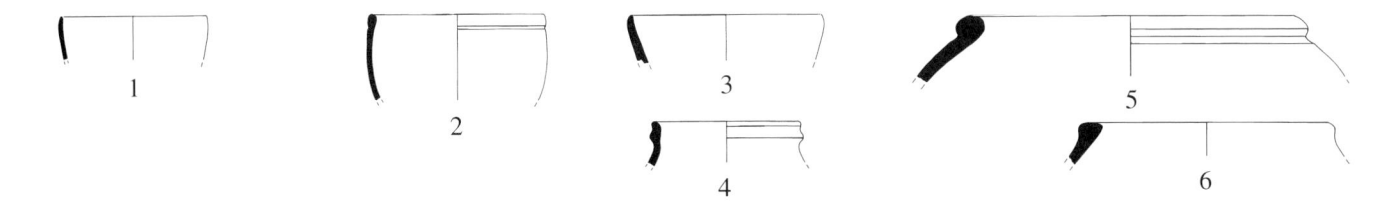

Pottery from Trench IVM, Room 7A (Phase 3; Period E — Early Bronze Age IVb). Scale 1:5

1. SBR. A.I.a (TS. 2533; IVM, 1.3). About 1/6 rim and upper wall segment. Fine flesh pink ware, evenly fired. Creamy-buff slip out.
2. SBR. B.I.h (TS. 2461; IVM, 1.3). Small rim and upper wall segment. Fairly fine buff ware, evenly fired. Creamy-gray slip in and out.
3. SBR. C.II.a (TS. 2636; IVM, 1.3). About 1/8 rim and upper wall segment. Hard, fine grayware, unevenly fired pinkish-brown at surfaces. Burned.
4. SJR. A.II.h (TS. 2438 = TS. 2513; IVM, 1.3). About 1/10 rim and upper shoulder (two joining segments). Slightly coarse buff ware, evenly fired. Creamy-buff slip in and out.
5. JR. H.I.e (TS. 2416; IVM, 1.3). About 1/10 rim and shoulder segment. Slightly coarse pink ware, evenly fired. Creamy-buff slip out and just over rim in.
6. JR. H.III.g (TS. 2417; IVM, 1.3). About 1/10 rim and upper shoulder segment. Slightly coarse pinkish-buff ware, evenly fired. Creamy-buff slip out.

Another Type Series Example: (1) SJR. A.II.h (TS. 2437).

Other Study Collection Examples: (1) SBR. B.I.a (SC. 244), (2) JR. H.I.d (SC. 1256), (3) JR. J.III.w (SC. 1497), (4) BE. B.II (SC. 3117).

Figure 117

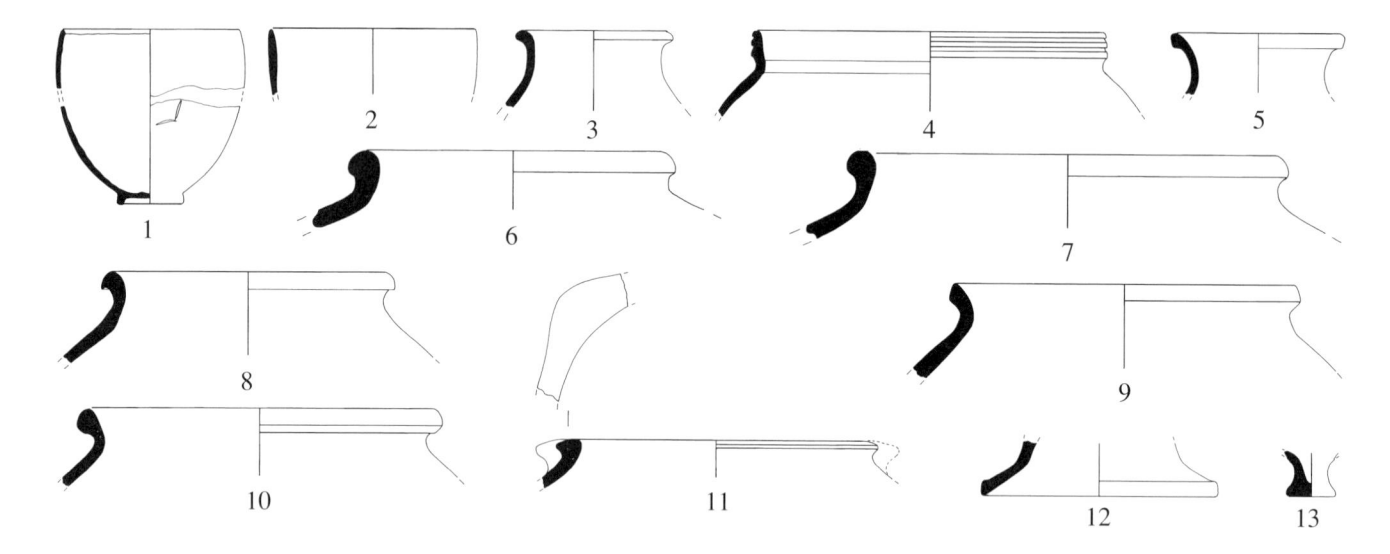

Pottery from Trench IVN, Rooms 8A/18A (Phase 3; Period E — Early Bronze Age IVb). Scale 1:5

1. SBR. A.I.e (PM. D.2; TS. 2618; IVN, 1.4, Rooms 8A/18A). About 1/6 rim, body sherds, and complete base mended to nearly complete profile; potter's mark on lower outside wall incised before firing. Slightly coarse pinkish-buff ware, evenly fired. Creamy-buff slip in and out.

2. SBR. C.III.a (TS. 2617; IVN, 1.4, Rooms 8A/18A). About 1/8 rim and upper wall segment. Fairly fine pinkish-buff ware, evenly fired. Creamy-buff slip in and out.

3. SJR. C.II.o (TS. 1738; IVN, 1.4, Rooms 8A/18A). Small rim, neck and shoulder segment. Fine buff ware, evenly fired. Self slip in and out.

4. JR. D.I.b (TS. 2903; IVN, 1.4, Rooms 8A/18A). About 1/4 rim and shoulder segment. Fairly fine pink ware, evenly fired. Buff slip out.

5. JR. J.III.h (TS. 2912; IVN, 1.4, Rooms 8A/18A). About 1/5 rim and neck segment. Close greenish-buff ware, unevenly fired pinkish at surface out. Creamy-green slip in and out.

6. JR. P.II.i (TS. 1703; IVN, 1.4, Rooms 8A/18A). Small rim, neck, and shoulder segment. Coarse pink ware, fairly evenly fired. Cream slip in and out.

7. JR. P.III.a (TS. 1709; IVN, 1.4, Rooms 8A/18A). Small rim, neck, and shoulder segment. Medium coarse grayish ware with lime grits, evenly fired. Cream slip in and out.

8. CP. A.I.f (TS. 1695; IVN, 1.4, Rooms 8A/18A). About 1/6 rim, neck, and shoulder segment. Medium coarse grayware with lime and mica grits, unevenly fired with gray core and pinkish-buff at surfaces. Pink slip in and out.

9. CP. B.I.b (TS. 2846; IVN, 1.4, Rooms 8A/18A). About 1/10 rim, neck, and shoulder segment. Coarse gritty ware, unevenly fired reddish-brown out, gray in. Self slip out and over rim in to base of neck.

10. CP. B.II.d (TS. 2849; IVN, 1.4, Rooms 8A/18A). About 1/8 rim, neck, and shoulder segment. Fairly coarse pinkish-brown ware, evenly fired. Self slip in and out.

11. CP. C.II.b (TS. 2858; IVN, 1.4, Rooms 8A/18A). About 1/6 rim and shoulder segment with triangular-shaped lug handle attached to rim. Coarse gritty dark brown ware, evenly fired. Self slip in and out. Burnished on handle, rim, and outside.

12. BE. F.IV.a (TS. 2913; IVN, 4.3, Room 18A). About 1/4 rim and wall segment. Slightly coarse pink ware, evenly fired. Creamy-green slip in and out.

13. BE. H (TS. 3092; IVN, 1.4, Rooms 8A/18A). Complete knob base and portion of lower wall. Fine grayish-brown ware, evenly fired. Self slip in and out.

Other Type Series Examples: (1) BR. D.I.a (TS. 1706), (2) JR. E.II.d (TS. 2845), (3) JR. F.III.e (TS. 2995), (4) JR. O.III.c (TS. 1685), (5) JR. P.II.q (TS. 1693), (6) CP. A.II.c (TS. 2869).

Other Study Collection Examples: (1) SBR. A.I.a (SC. 173), (2) SBR. A.I.a (SC. 189), (3) SBR. A.II.c (SC. 233), (4) SBR. A. (Gen. Type, SC. 11), (5) SBR. B.I.a (SC. 245), (6) SBR. B.I.f (SC. 351), (7) SBR. B.I.g (SC. 396), (8) SBR. B.I.g (SC. 405), (9) SBR. B.I.g (SC. 411), (10) SBR. E.I.b (SC. 656), (11) BR. F.I.d (SC. 775), (12) SJR. B.I.c (SC. 3319), (13) SJR. C.I.a (SC. 2537), (14) SJR. C.I.f (SC. 2563), (15) SJR. C.I.f (SC. 2635), (16) JR. E.II.o (SC. 1163), (17) JR. G.I.b (SC. 2036), (18) JR. J.III.f (SC. 2276), (19) JR. J.III.f (SC. 2278), (20) JR. J.III.k (SC. 2307), (21) JR. J.III.l (SC. 1413), (22) JR. J.III.m (SC. 1419), (23) JR. J.III.u (SC. 1494), (24) JR. K.I.b (SC. 1563), (25) JR. K.I.e (SC. 1592), (26) BE. H (SC. 3230).

Figure 118

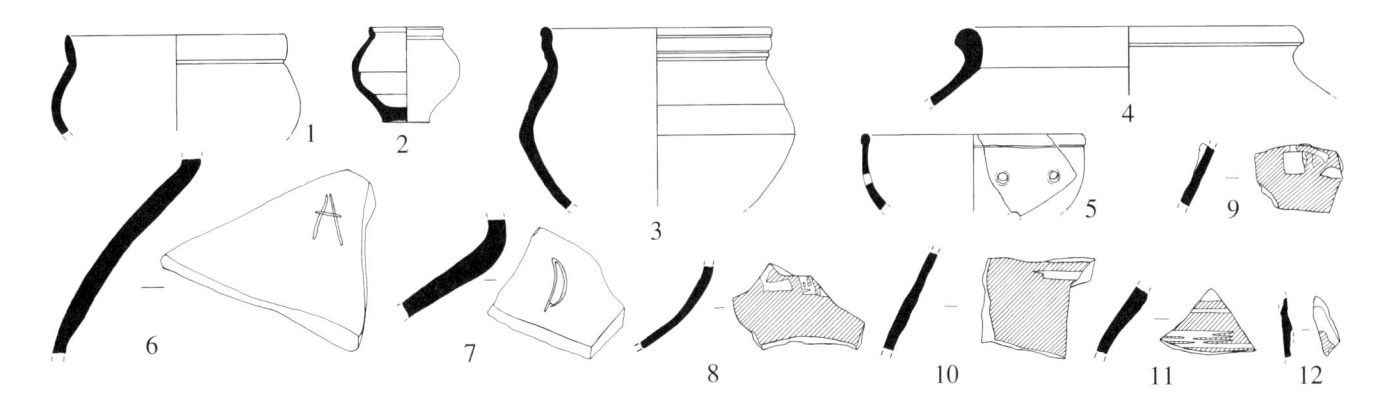

Pottery from Trench IVN, Operation 10, Northeast Corner of Room 8A (Phase 3;
Period E — Early Bronze Age IVb). Scale 1:5

1. SBR. D.I.d (TS. 4047; Op. 10, 22.1). Small rim and upper wall segment. For ware, compare Phase 6 Type Series example from Area IIIG/H (SW. 485).
2. SJR. A.I.c (TS. 3359; Op. 10, 22.1). Completely mended profile of a small jar. For ware, compare Phase 5 example from Area IVX (TS. 2826).
3. JR. C.I.e (TS. 3352; Op. 10, 22.1). Large segment of rim and wall of vessel. For ware, compare Phase 2B Type Series example from Area IVK (SW. 394).
4. JR. O.I.a (TS. 4027; Op. 10, 22.1). Small rim and upper shoulder segment. For ware, compare Phase 2A Type Series example from Area IVM (SW. 695).
5. SR. A.II.c (TS. 4028; Op. 10, 22.1). About 1/6 rim and body segment with remains of three strainer holes through the wall. For ware, compare Phase 3 Type Series example from Area IVG (SW. 257).
6. JR.Sh. (PM. C.1; TS. 3358; Op. 10, 22.1). Upper wall and shoulder segment of a jar with a potter's mark incised on the shoulder before firing. Ware description not available.
7. JR.Sh. (PM. C.2; TS. 3353; Op. 10, 22.1). Upper shoulder and neck segment of a jar with a potter's mark incised on the shoulder before firing. Ware description not available.
8. JR.Sh. Pt. (TS. 4010; Op. 10, 22.1). Shoulder and neck segment of a jar with painted red decoration. Ware description not available.
9. JR.Sh. Pt. (TS. 4012; Op. 10, 22.1). Shoulder segment of a jar with portion of a handle and with painted red decoration. Ware description not available.
10. JR.Sh. Pt. (TS. 4011; Op. 10, 22.1). Shoulder segment of a jar with painted red decoration. Ware description not available.
11. JR.Sh. Pt. (TS. 4013; Op. 10, 22.1). Shoulder segment of a jar with painted red decoration. Ware description not available.
12. JR.Sh. Pt. (TS. 4014; Op. 10, 22.1). Body sherd of a jar with painted red decoration. Ware description not available.
—. JR.Sh. Dec. (TS. 4015; Op. 10, 22.1). Body sherd of a jar with spaced horizontal and vertical bands of painted red decoration. Ware description not available.

Figure 119

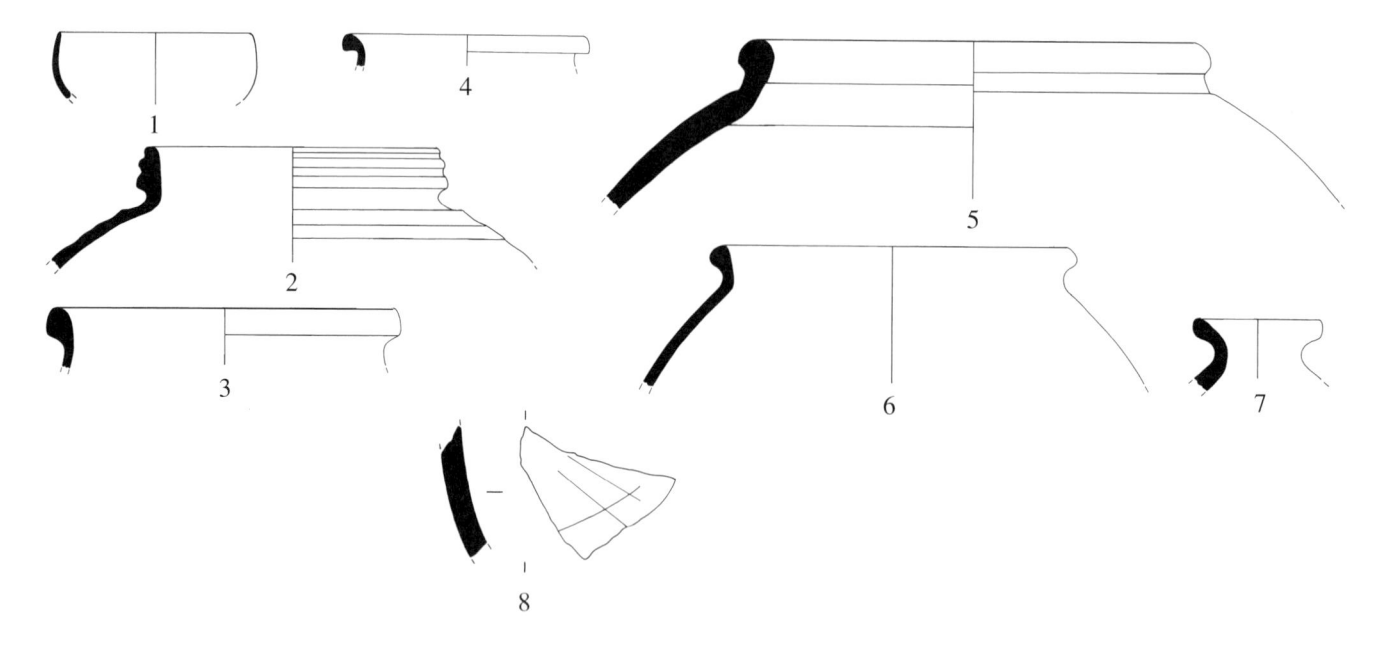

Pottery from Trench IVO, Fill Above Rooms 10A and 11 (Phase 3; Period E — Early Bronze Age IVb). Scale 1:5

1. SBR. B.I.o (TS. 1603; IVO, 1.3). Small rim and upper wall segment. Fine pink ware, evenly fired. Self slip out. Fill above Rooms 10A and 11.
2. JR. D.X.b (TS. 2574; IVO, 1.3). About 1/2 rim and shoulder segment. Slightly coarse pinkish-buff ware, evenly fired. Creamy-buff slip out. Fill above Rooms 10A and 11.
3. JR. E.II.c (TS. 2802; IVO, 1.3). About 1/4 rim and neck segment. Slightly coarse grayish-buff ware, evenly fired. Creamy-green slip in and out. Fill above Rooms 10A and 11.
4. JR. E.II.p (TS. 3009; IVO, 1.3). Small rim and neck segment. Fairly fine grayish-buff ware, evenly fired. Burnished self slip in and out. Fill above Rooms 10A and 11.
5. JR. P.II.a (TS. 2795; IVO, 1.3). About 1/5 rim, neck, and shoulder segment. Slightly coarse grayish-buff ware, evenly fired. Creamy-green slip out. Fill above Rooms 10A and 11.
6. CP. B.II.d (TS. 2835; IVO, 1.3). Segment of rim, neck, and upper body. Coarse gritty pinkish-brown ware, evenly fired. Self slip in and out. Outer surface worn and pitted. Fill above Rooms 10A and 11.
7. Jg. B.I.a (TS. 2759; IVO, 1.3). About 1/3 segment of rim, neck, and upper shoulder. Fairly fine salmon-pink ware, evenly fired. Cream slip out and over rim to base of neck in. Fill above Rooms 10A and 11.
8. JR.Sh. (PM. D.22; TS. 1611; IVO, 1.3). Body sherd with portion of potter's mark or decoration incised on outside surface before firing. Coarse pink ware with mica grits, unevenly fired. Fill above Rooms 10A and 11.

Other Type Series Examples: (1) MBR. A.I.a (SW. 483), (2) SBR. D.II.c (TS. 1614), (3) JR. D.VI.c (TS. 2622), (4) JR. Q.II.f (TS. 2798), (5) SR. B.I.b (SW. 558).

Other Study Collection Examples: (1) SBR. B.I.f (SC. 334), (2) BR. L.I.f (SC. 881), (3) SJR. D.I.c (SC. 2626), (4) SJR. D. (Gen. Type, SC. 10), (5) JR. E.I.c (SC. 1991), (6) JR. E.II.d (SC. 1148), (7) JR. F.I.a (SC. 1185), (8) JR. G.I.c (SC. 2046), (9) JR. J.I.f (SC. 1350), (10) JR. J.III.e (SC. 2260), (11) JR. J.III.e (SC. 2263), (12) CP. B.IV.b (SC. 1866), (13) BE. B.II (SC. 3111), (14) BE. E.I.j (SC. 3186), (15) BE. E.II.a (SC. 3193), (16) JR.Sh. IP. (not typed, SC. 158).

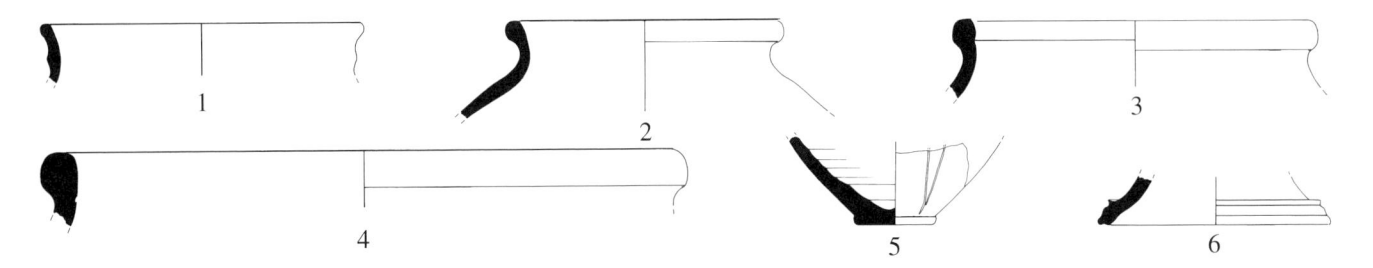

Figure 120. Pottery from Trench IVP, Room 9A (Phase 3; Period E — Early Bronze Age IVb). Scale 1:5

1. JR. B.V.b (TS. 2910; IVP, 1.4/5). Small rim and neck segment. Slightly coarse pink ware, evenly fired. Cream slip in and out.
2. JR. E.II.f (TS. 2754; IVP, 1.4). About 1/4 rim, neck, and shoulder segment. Fairly coarse pink ware, evenly fired. Light creamy-green slip out.
3. JR. K.II.d (TS. 2760; IVP, 1.4). About 1/10 rim and shoulder segment. Slightly coarse buff ware, evenly fired. Grayish-green slip in and out.
4. CP. C.I.e (TS. 2839; IVP, 1.4). About 1/8 rim and neck segment. Very coarse gritty ware, unevenly fired gray in and pinkish-brown out. Self slip in and out.
5. BE. B.II (PM. C.10; TS. 3059; IVP, 1.4). About 1/2 base and lower wall segment with portion of a potter's mark incised on the outside surface before firing. Coarse pink ware, evenly fired. Buff slip out.
6. BE. F.V.b (TS. 2688; IVP, 1.4). About 1/8 segment. Slightly coarse dark pink ware, evenly fired. Creamy-buff slip in and out.

Other Type Series Examples: (1) BR. A.I.c (TS. 2924), (2) BR. J.I.a (TS. 2581), (3) BR. M.II.a (TS. 2728), (4) JR. B.V.b (TS. 2911), (5) JR. E.II.z (TS. 2675), (6) CP. B.I.i (TS. 2836), (7) Jg. C (TS. 1604).

Other Study Collection Examples: (1) SBR. A.I.a (SC. 165), (2) SBR. A.I.b (SC. 210), (3) SBR. D.I.a (SC. 620), (4) SBR. D. (Gen. Type, SC. 15), (5) JR. A.VI.a (SC. 1974), (6) JR. B.III.d (SC. 940), (7) JR. C.VI.a (SC. 1031), (8) JR. D.V.f (SC. 1101), (9) JR. J.I.b (SC. 2098), (10) JR. J.III.d (SC. 1370), (11) JR. J.III.y (SC. 1508), (12) JR. K.I.b (SC. 1569), (13) JR. O.II.e (SC. 1641), (14) JR. (not typed, SC. 141), (15) BE. B.II (SC. 3110).

Pottery from Area IVQ, Room 6A (Phase 3, Period E — Early Bronze Age IVb) (not illustrated)

One Study Collection Example: JR. A.III.f (SC. 919; IVQ, 1.3).

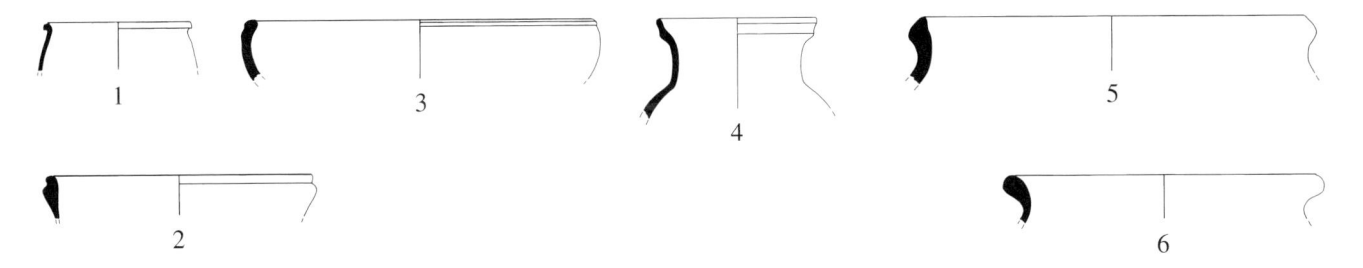

Figure 121. Pottery from Trench IVR, Rooms 11A and 12A (Phase 3; Period E — Early Bronze Age IVb). Scale 1:5

1. SBR. A.I.h (TS. 2930; IVR, 2.1, 2.2, Room 11A). Two small non-joining rim and upper wall segments. Fine reddish-brown ware, evenly fired. Buff slip out.
2. BR. C.I.d (TS. 2958; IVR, 2.4, Room 12A). Small rim and upper wall segment. Slightly coarse buff ware, evenly fired. Self slip in and out.
3. BR. D.III.b (TS. 1763; IVR, 2.4, Room 12A). Small rim and upper wall segment. Fairly fine pink ware with mica grits, evenly fired. Cream slip in and out.
4. SJR. C.II.v (TS. 3000; IVR, 2.1, Room 11A). About 1/4 rim, neck, and shoulder segment. Fairly fine buff ware, evenly fired. Creamy-green slip in and out.
5. JR. E.II.a (TS. 1667; IVR, 2.4, Room 12A). Small rim and neck segment. Slightly coarse grayish ware with mica grits, unevenly fired. Greenish slip in and out.
6. CP. B.I.a (TS. 2859; IVR, 2.2, Room 11A). About 1/6 rim and neck segment. Slightly coarse pinkish-buff ware, evenly fired. Self slip in and out. Burnished on rim and on the inside surfaces of the extant fragments.

Another Type Series Example:
Room 11A — (1) JR. O.II.b (PM. E.2; SW. 711).
Other Study Collection Examples:
Room 11A — (1) SBR. B.I.f (SC. 352), (2) SBR. D.I.a (SC. 628), (3) JR. O.I.i (SC. 1620).
Room 12A — (1) BR. F.I.d (SC. 777), (2) JR. J.III.l (SC. 1412), (3) JR. (not typed, SC. 106).

Figure 122

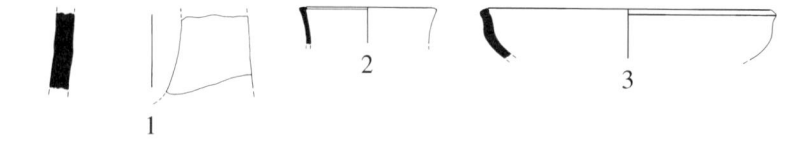

Pottery from Trench IVS, Room 12A, IVX, Room 14A, and Soundings IVW and IVY (Phase 3;
Period E — Early Bronze Age IVb). Scale 1:5

1. WPS. B (TS. 2770; IVS, 4.3, Room 12A). Small body segment with portion of one side of a window opening through the wall. Coarse grayish-buff ware, evenly fired. Light green slip in and out.
2. SJR. B.II.b (TS. 2781; IVW, 1.2). About 1/3 rim and upper neck segment. Fairly fine grayish-brown ware, evenly fired. Self slip in and out.
3. BR. J.I.a (TS. 2595; IVY, 1.3). About 1/8 rim and upper wall segment. Slightly coarse light pink ware, evenly fired. Buff slip out.
—. JR.Sh. (PM. F; TS. 3102; IVY, 1.3). Jar sherd. Ware description not available.
—. JR.Sh. (PM. F; TS. 3139; IVY, 1.3). Jar sherd. Ware description not available.

Other Type Series Examples:
  Area IVS — (1) BR. A.I.f (TS. 2944).
  Area IVS and Y — (1) SJR. B.III.f (TS. 2828), (2) JR. E.II.y (TS. 2676 = TS. 2735).
  Area IVX — (1) Ld. C.I.a (TS. 2670).

Other Study Collection Examples:
  Area IVS, Room 12A — (1) SBR. B.I.j (SC. 534), (2) SBR. B.I.l (SC. 573), (3) SBR. B.I.l (SC. 583), (4) JR. J.III.n (SC. 2335), (5) JR. J.IV.j (SC. 1542), (6) JR. O.I.d (SC. 1614), (7) BE. E.I.g (SC. 3180).
  Area IVW — (1) SBR. B.I.h (SC. 513), (2) SBR. D.I.a (SC. 269), (3) BR. E.I.b (SC. 753), (4) BR. F.II.a (SC. 798), (5) BR. L.I.f (SC. 880), (6) JR. H.I.g (SC. 1274), (7) CP. A.I.a (SC. 1784), (8) CP. B.I.a (SC. 1819).
  Area IVX, Room 14A — (1) BR. A.II.e (SC. 719), (2) JR. J.IV.e (SC. 2376).
  Area IVY — (1) BR. C.I.b (SC. 2642), (2) JR. A.V.a (SC. 913), (3) JR. B.III.a (SC. 936), (4) JR. D.VI.b (SC. 1106), (5) JR. E.II.c (SC. 1999), (6) JR. E.II.o (SC. 1162), (7) JR. J.I.b (SC. 2108), (8) JR. J.III.e (SC. 2235), (9) JR. J.III.e (SC. 2264), (10) JR. J.III.f (SC. 2274), (11) JR. J.III.o (SC. 2348), (12) JR. P.II.a (SC. 1710), (13) JR. (not typed, SC. 63), (14) CP. A.I.a (SC. 1777), (15) PS. A.II.c (SC. 1929), (16) BE. E.I.d (SC. 3163).

Figure 123

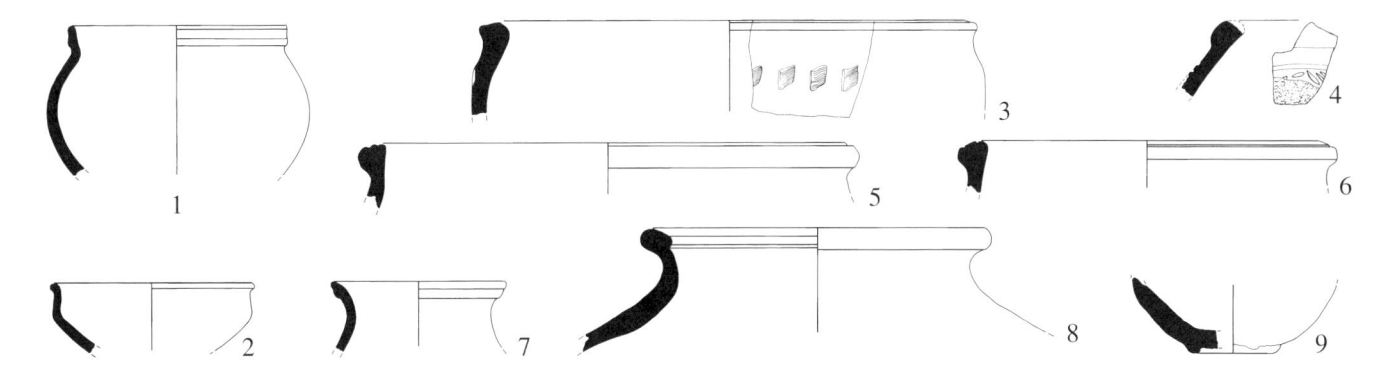

Pottery from Trench IVZ(N1), (N2), and (S) (Phase 3; Period E — Early Bronze Age IVb). Scale 1:5

1. SBR. D.I.f (TS. 2610; IVZ(N2), 3.3). About 1/6 rim segment and most of body profile. Fairly fine pink ware, evenly fired. Creamy-buff slip out.
2. BR. E.I.b (TS. 2583; IVZ(N2), 3.3). About 1/6 rim and wall segment. Fairly fine pinkish ware, evenly fired. Self slip in and out.
3. BR. N.II.a (TS. 2733; IVZ(N2), 3.3). About 1/10 rim and upper wall segment decorated on outer wall with stabs in clay made with wooden tool before firing. Slightly coarse dark pink ware, evenly fired. Buff slip in and out.
4. JR. H.I.g (IP [G.4] F.III.a; TS. 2701; IVZ(N2), 3.3). Very small segment with portion of animal design incised on outside wall before firing. Hard, slightly coarse grayish-buff ware, evenly fired. Buff slip in and out.
5. JR. H.II.a (TS. 2700; IVZ(N2), 3.3). Small rim and neck segment. Slightly coarse pink ware, evenly fired. Self slip in and out.
6. JR. H.II.a (TS. 2723; IVZ(N1), 1.4). Small rim and neck segment. Fairly coarse light brown ware, evenly fired. Pinkish-brown slip in and out.
7. JR. J.III.i (TS. 2693; IVZ(N1), 2.1). About 1/6 rim and neck segment. Fairly fine pink ware, unevenly fired with thin brown core. Creamy-pink slip in and out.
8. JR. K.II.e (TS. 2730; IVZ(N1), 2.1). Small rim, neck, and shoulder segment. Slightly coarse pinkish-buff ware, evenly fired. Cream slip out.
9. BE. J. (TS. 3035; IVZ(N2), 3.3). Small segment of base and lower wall of vessel. Fairly coarse, handmade, creamy-green ware, evenly fired. Self slip in and out.
—. JR.Sh. (PM. F; TS. 3105; IVZ(N1), 2.1). Jar sherd. Ware description not available.
—. JR.Sh. (PM. F; TS. 3111; IVZ(N2), 3.3). Jar sherd. Ware description not available.
—. JR.Sh. (PM. F; TS. 3127; IVZ(N2), 3.3). Jar sherd. Ware description not available.
—. JR.Sh. (PM. F; TS. 3103; IVZ(S), 5.2). Jar sherd. Ware description not available.
—. JR.Sh. (PM. F; TS. 3135; IVZ(S), 5.2). Jar sherd. Ware description not available.

Other Type Series Examples:
Area IVZ(N1) — (1) BR. J.II.a (TS. 2585), (2) JR. O.II.h (TS. 2732).
Area IVZ(N2) — (1) CP. C.I.g (TS. 2856), (2) Hd. G (TS. 2706).
Area IVZ(S) — (1) JR. D.VIII.a (TS. 1775).

Other Study Collection Examples:
Area IVZ(N1) —(1) SJR. C.I.a (SC. 2547), (2) JR. E.II.c (SC. 2001), (3) JR. F.III.e (SC. 1172), (4) JR. J.II.k (SC. 2183), (5) JR. J.III.e (SC. 2268), (6) JR. J.III.l (SC. 2311), (7) JR. J.III.n (SC. 1459), (8) JR. K.II.e (SC. 2401), (9) JR. P.II.s (SC. 2464), (10) JR. (not typed, SC. 140), (11) CP. A.I.a (SC. 1785).
Area IVZ(N2) — (1) BR. C.I.b (SC. 737), (2) BR. C.I.d (SC. 742), (3) BR. E.I.a (SC. 752), (4) BR. L.III.a (SC. 883), (5) JR. A.III.a (SC. 1977), (6) JR. C.V.d (SC. 1021), (7) JR. D.I.b (SC. 1044), (8) JR. D.V.a (SC. 1068), (9) JR. D.VI.e (SC. 1113), (10) JR. D.VI.e (SC. 1115), (11) JR. E.I.a (SC. 1126), (12) JR. J.I.b (SC. 1307), (13) JR. J.I.f (SC. 1349), (14) JR. J.II.l (SC. 2188), (15) JR. J.III.j (SC. 2302), (16) JR. K.I.d (SC. 1587), (17) JR. O.II.c (SC. 1627), (18) JR. O.II.h (SC. 1651), (19) JR. O.III.a (SC. 1669), (20) JR. P.II.a (SC. 1707), (21) JR. J. (Gen. Type, SC. 110).
Area IVZ(S) — (1) BR. L.I.f (SC. 840), (2) SJR. C.I.f (SC. 2567), (3) JR. F.I.c (SC. 2647), (4) JR. J.III.n (SC. 1455), (5) JR. J.III.n (SC. 1465), (6) JR. O.I.a (SC. 2452).

Figures 124–25

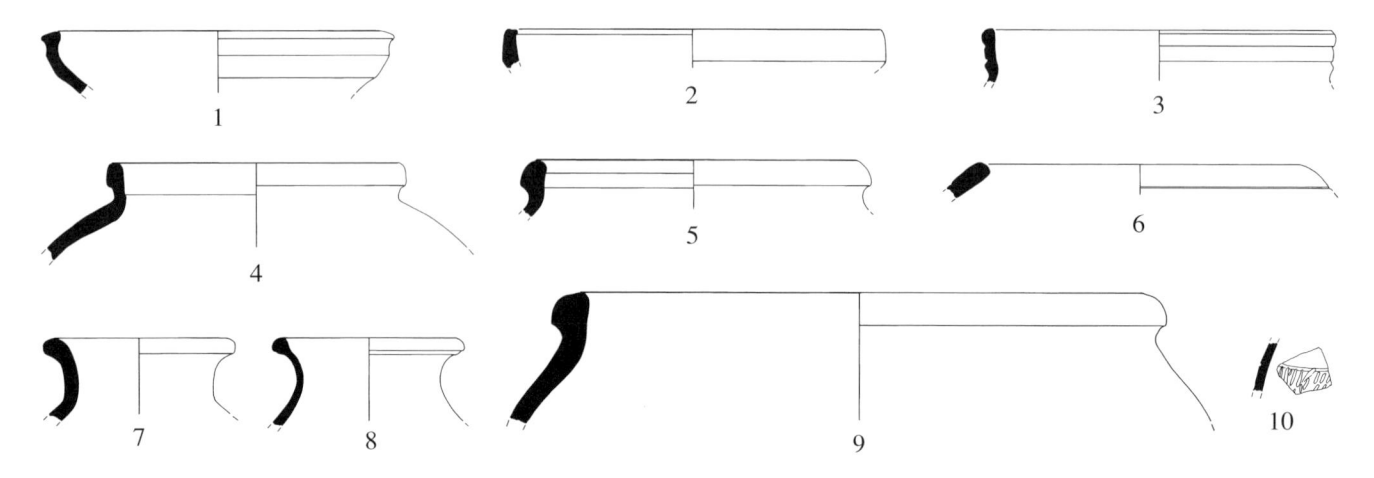

Figure 124. Pottery from Trench IXA (Phase 3; Period E — Early Bronze Age IVb). Scale 1:5

1. BR. E.I.b (TS. 1019; IXA, 1.2). About 1/8 rim and upper wall segment. Fairly coarse pink ware, evenly fired. Cream slip in and out.
2. BR. F.II.d (TS. 1888; IXA, 1.15a). Small rim and upper wall segment. Slightly coarse grayish-buff ware, evenly fired. Self slip in and out.
3. JR. D.I.c (TS. 1889; IXA, 1.15a). Small rim and neck segment. Hard, gritty, coarse brownish-buff ware, fairly evenly fired. Green slip out.
4. JR. E.II.m (TS. 1031; IXA, 1.6). About 1/6 rim, neck, and upper shoulder segment. Fairly coarse pink ware, evenly fired. Buff slip in and out.
5. JR. E.II.t (TS. 2371; IXA, 1.15a). About 1/10 rim, neck, and upper shoulder segment. Slightly coarse pink ware, evenly fired. Cream slip out.
6. JR. H.I.h (TS. 1883; IXA, 1.15a). Small rim segment. Close, hard, light grayish-green ware, evenly fired. Self slip in and out.
7. JR. J.III.e (TS. 2232; IXA, 1.15a). Small rim, neck, and upper shoulder segment. Hard, fairly fine pink ware, evenly fired. Creamy-buff slip out and over rim in.
8. JR. J.III.x (TS. 2255; IXA, 1.15a). Small rim, neck, and upper shoulder segment. Fairly coarse reddish-brown ware, evenly fired. Creamy-buff slip out and over rim in.
9. JR. P.II.m (TS. 977; IXA, 1.15a). About 1/8 rim, neck, and upper shoulder segment. Coarse pink ware with many lime and mica grits, unevenly fired with dark core. Buff slip out with traces of horizontal burnishing around neck in.
10. JR.Sh. (IP [G.4] F.III.a; TS. 923; IXA, 1.6). Jar body sherd with probable remains of an incised animal body on outside wall. Fairly coarse pinkish-buff ware. Light brown slip out.

Other Type Series Examples: (1) SJR. A.II.g (TS. 1890), (2) JR. B.III.a (TS. 1879), (3) CP. B.I.e (TS. 2249).

Other Study Collection Examples: (1) SBR. B.I.f (SC. 335), (2) BR. F.II.a (SC. 795), (3) JR. C.I.f (SC. 997), (4) JR. D.V.d (SC. 1094), (5) JR. J.II.h (SC. 2163), (6) CP. B.I.a (SC. 1812), (7) CP. B.IV.b (SC. 1871).

Figure 125. Pottery from Trench IXB, Modern Water Barrel Pit (Phase 3; Period E — Early Bronze Age IVb). Scale 1:5

1. JR. F.II.b (TS. 2621; IXB, Modern Water Barrel Pit). About 1/2 rim, neck, and upper shoulder segment. Fairly fine grayish-green ware, evenly fired. Self slip in and out. Heavily burned.
2. CP. B.II.f (TS. 4226; IXB, Modern Water Barrel Pit). Large rim, neck, and shoulder segment. Fairly coarse brown ware with lime and mica grits, evenly fired. Burnished self slip on outside surface.

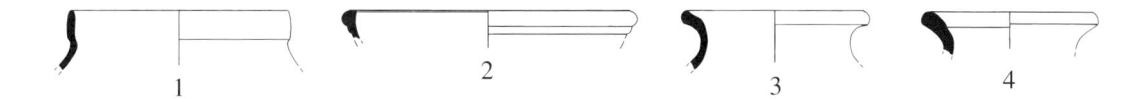

Figure 126. Pottery from Trench XA, Room 15A (Phase 3; Period E — Early Bronze Age IVb). Scale 1:5

1. SBR. D.I.e (TS. 2442; XA, 1.2). About 1/10 rim and shoulder segment. Fairly coarse yellow-buff ware, evenly fired. Self slip in and out.
2. BR. D.VI.a (TS. 1264; XA, 1.2). Small rim segment. Fairly fine pinkish-buff ware, evenly fired. Buff slip in and out.
3. JR. J.III.o (TS. 2322; XA, 1.2). About 1/6 rim and neck segment. Fairly close pinkish-buff ware, evenly fired. Creamy-green slip out and over rim to base of neck in.
4. JR. K.I.b (TS. 2342; XA, 1.2). About 1/12 rim and neck segment. Fairly fine pinkish ware, evenly fired. Creamy-yellow slip out.
—. CP.Sh. (PM. F; TS. 3113; XA, 1.2). Cooking Pot sherd. Ware description not available.
   Other Type Series Examples: (1) JR. J.I.a (TS. 2265), (2) JR. J.III.n (TS. 1066), (3) JR. K.I.d (TS. 2340), (4) JR. K.I.g (TS. 1034).
   Other Study Collection Examples: (1) SBR. B.I.h (SC. 457), (2) SBR. B.I.h (SC. 504), (3) JR. J.III.e (SC. 2261).

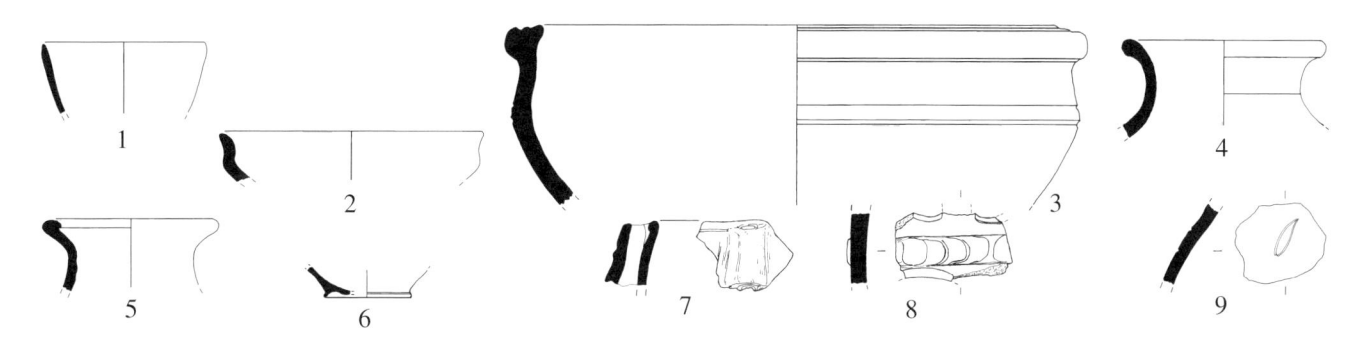

Figure 127. Pottery from Trench XA, Operation 11, Rooms 15A and 19A (Phase 3; Period E — Early Bronze Age IVb). Scale 1:5

1. SBR. C.II.a (TS. 3611; Op. 11, 3.1, Room 19A). About 1/10 rim and wall segment. Fine buff ware with a few silver-colored mica and lime grits, evenly fired. Self slip in and out.
2. BR. C.I.a (TS. 3605; Op. 11, 3.1, Room 19A). Small rim (3 cm) and upper wall segment. Slightly coarse pinkish-buff ware with gold- and silver-colored mica and lime grits, evenly fired. Creamy-green slip in and out.
3. BR. N.I.a (TS. 3379; Op. 1–2.1, Room 15A). About 1/8 rim segment and most of wall profile. Fairly fine pinkish-orange ware with gold- and white-colored mica and small lime grits, evenly fired. Buff slip out and on top of rim, possibly inside, but worn away.
4. JR. J.III.e (TS. 3442; Op. 11, 3.1, Room 19A). About 1/2 rim, neck, and shoulder segment. Fairly fine pinkish-buff ware with fine silver-colored mica and lime grits, evenly fired. Creamy greenish-buff slip in and out.
5. JR. J.III.aa (TS. 3612; Op. 11, 3.1, Room 19A). Small rim (3 cm) and neck segment. Fairly fine pink ware with gold- and silver-colored mica and lime grits, evenly fired. Creamy-buff slip out.
6. BE. E.I.j (TS. 3441; Op. 11, 3.1, Room 19A). About 1/3 base and lower wall segment. Fairly fine pinkish-buff ware with silver-colored mica and white lime grits, evenly fired. Horizontal band-burnished self slip out.
7. Hd. A (TS. 3440; Op. 11, 2.1, Room 15A). Complete, vertically pierced, barrel-type lug handle with 3 cm segment of rim. Hard, fairly fine pinkish-buff ware with fine lime grits, evenly fired. Cream slip out.
8. WPS. B (TS. 3614; Op. 11, 3.1, Room 19A). Fragment with remains of three extant windows in body; two above applied rope band decoration and one below. Slightly coarse dark buff-brown ware with fine silver-colored mica and lime grits, evenly fired. Creamy-green slip in and out.
9. JR.Sh. (PM. E.1; TS. 3606; Op. 11, 3.1, Room 19A). Jar shoulder sherd with a potter's mark incised on the shoulder before firing. Fairly fine light pinkish-brown ware with lime grits and burned out vegetable temper, evenly fired. Creamy-green slip in and out.

Another Type Series Example—Room 19A: (1) BR. N.I.a (TS. 3613).

Figure 128. Pottery from Trench IVB, Southwest Corner of Trench IVF, Room 1B; Trench IVC, Town Wall Tower; Trench IVD, Above Town Wall and Pit in Wall; Trench IVE, Room 3B; and Trench IVF, Room 1B (Phase 4; Period E — Early Bronze Age IVb); for Trench IVA, Above Street, and Trench IVG, Room 3B, Northwest End, see Type Series and Study Collection Examples

1. SBR. A.I.g (TS. 23; IVB, 1.2). About 1/4 rim and wall segment. Slightly coarse pinkish-buff ware with lime and mica grits, evenly fired. Self slip out.
2. SBR. D.I.f (TS. 1952; IVB, 1.2). Small rim and upper wall segment. Fairly fine pink ware, evenly fired. Self slip out.
3. JR. B.II.e (TS. 2514; IVB, 1.2). About 1/10 rim and shoulder segment. Hard, pinkish-buff ware, evenly fired. Buff self slip out.
4. JR. D.V.d (TS. 2515; IVB, 1.2). Small rim segment. Slightly coarse pinkish-buff ware, evenly fired. Creamy-buff slip in and out.
5. JR. J.III.m (TS. 2302; IVC, 1.1). About 1/4 rim and neck segment. Very hard, close creamy-buff ware, evenly fired. Cream slip in and out.
6. SBR. D.II.a (TS. 1766; IVD, 1.2). Small rim and upper wall segment. Fairly fine pink ware, evenly fired. Cream slip in and out.
7. BR. F.II.b (TS. 2666; IVD, 1.3). Small rim and upper wall segment. Slightly coarse grayish-buff ware, evenly fired. Creamy-green slip in and out.
8. JR. J.III.h (TS. 2281; IVD, 1.2 + IVF, 1.1). About 1/3 rim and neck segment. Fairly coarse pinkish-buff ware, evenly fired. Creamy-buff slip out and just over rim in.
9. CP. C.I.a (TS. 2252; IVD, 1.2). Small rim and neck segment with traces of possible triangular-shaped ledge handle attached to rim. Hard, slightly coarse and gritty pinkish-brown ware, evenly fired. Thick, self-burnished slip out and over rim in.
10. BR.Sh. (PM. C.14; TS. 1189; IVD, 1.2). Body sherd with portion of a potter's mark incised on outside wall before firing. Fairly close light pinkish-buff ware with lime and mica grits, evenly fired.
11. SJR. A.II.a (TS. 1934; IVE, 1.2). Small rim and shoulder segment. Slightly coarse pinkish-buff ware, evenly fired. Creamy-buff slip out.
12. JR. J.III.a (TS. 2319; IVF, 1.2, Room 1B). About 1/8 rim and upper neck segment. Fairly fine buff-brown ware, evenly fired. Grayish-buff slip in and out.
13. JR.Sh. Pt. (TS. 1624; IVF, 1.2, Room 1B). Jar body sherd with remains of two horizontal painted black bands. Fairly fine dark grayware with lime and mica grits, unevenly fired grayish-green at surfaces.

Other Type Series Examples:
Area IVA — (1) JR. A.III.f (TS. 2188).
Area IVD — (1) BR. F.II.a (TS. 1963), (2) BR. L.I.i (TS. 1923), (3) JR. K.I.c (TS. 2334).
Area IVE— (1) SJR. C.II.j (TS. 2016).
Area IVF, Room 1B — (1) BE. E.I.b (TS. 3069).
Area IVG, Room 3B — (1) JR. E.I.h (TS. 2403).

Other Study Collection Examples:
Area IVA — (1) CP. A.III.a (SC. 1809), (2) Ld. C.III.c (SC. 1943).
Area IVB — (1) SBR. A.II.a (SC. 2788), (2) SBR. B.I.j (SC. 532), (3) BR. A.II.e (SC. 711), (4) BR. A.II.e (SC. 720), (5) JR. J.II.g (SC. 2148), (6) JR. J.III.a (SC. 2202), (7) JR. J.III.m (SC. 2316), (8) JR. J.IV.a (SC. 1520), (9) JR. J.IV.g (SC. 1533), (10) JR. K.I.b (SC. 1568), (11) JR. J. (not typed, SC. 111), (12) PS. A.II.a (SC. 1928).
Area IVC — (1) SBR. B.I.j (SC. 541), (2) BR. A.II.e (SC. 724), (3) JR. J.III.n (SC. 1452), (4) JR. K.I.a (SC. 1559), (5) JR. K.I.b (SC. 1571).
Area D — (1) SBR. A.I.b (SC. 207), (2) SBR. B.I.a (SC. 246), (3) SBR. B.I.b (SC. 257), (4) SBR. B.I.h (SC. 465), (5) SBR. B.I.h (SC. 437), (6) SBR. B.I.h (SC. 506), (7) SBR. C.III.b (SC. 615), (8) BR. F.I.d (SC. 767), (9) BR. F.I.d (SC. 771), (10) BR. (not typed, SC. 19), (11) SJR. A.I.a (SC. 2480), (12) SJR. C.II.d (SC. 2588), (13) JR. D.I.c (SC. 1049), (14) JR. E.II.f (SC. 2022), (15) JR. H.I.d (SC. 1262), (16) JR. J.I.b (SC. 1310), (17) JR. J.II.h (SC. 2156), (18) JR. J.II.h (SC. 2167), (19) JR. J.II.i (SC. 2169), (20) JR. J.III.d (SC. 1369), (21) JR. J.III.e (SC. 2239), (22) JR. K.I.b (SC. 1566), (23) JR. P.I.a (SC. 1693), (24) JR. P.II.a (SC. 1708), (25) BE. E.II (SC. 1921).
Area IVF — (1) SBR. B.I.a (SC. 240), (2) SBR. B.I.g (SC. 402), (3) SBR. B.I.h (SC. 464), (4) BR. F.I.d (SC. 768), (5) BR. F.I.d (SC. 781), (6) SJR. B.I.b (SC. 2501), (7) JR. F.I.c (1207), (8) JR. J.III.q (SC. 1487), (9) JR. N.I.b (SC. 1611), (10) JR. O.II.h (SC. 1652).
Area IVG — (1) SJR. B.I.a (SC. 2498), (2) JR. J.III.o (SC. 2347), (3) BE. E.I.l (SC. 3191), (4) BE. E.II.g (SC. 3218).

Derived Hellenistic Type Series Examples: Area IVC — (1) H.BR. B.III.b (TS. 1964), (2) H.St.J. B.II.h (TS. 157).

Figure 128

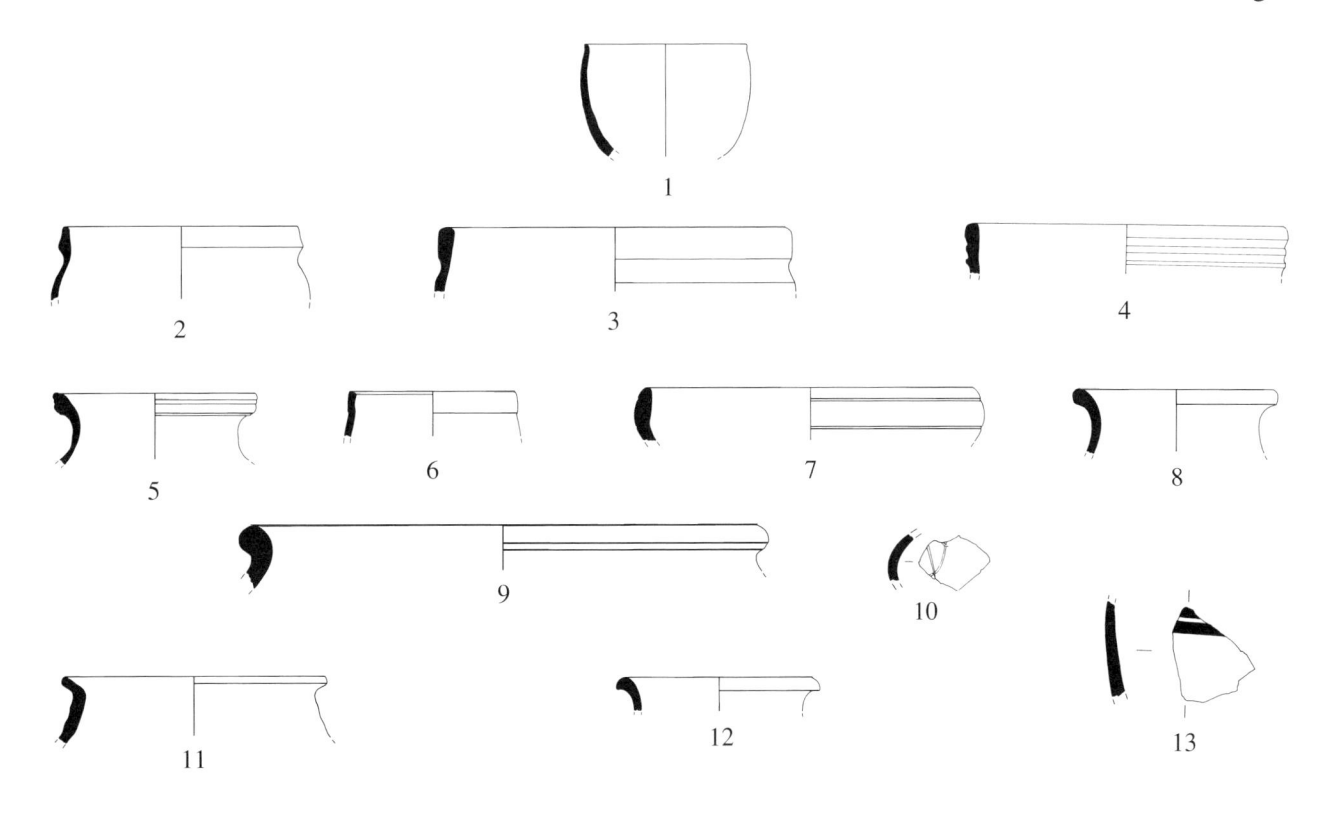

Pottery from Trench IVB, Southwest Corner of Trench IVF, Room 1B; Trench IVC, Town Wall Tower; Trench IVD, Above Town Wall and Pit in Wall; Trench IVE, Room 3B; and Trench IVF, Room 1B (Phase 4; Period E — Early Bronze Age IVb). Scale 1:5

Figures 129–30

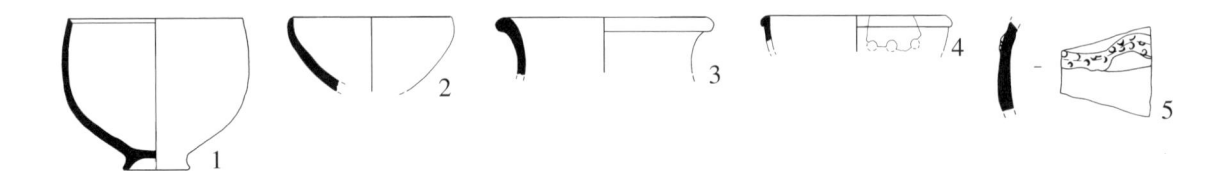

Figure 129. Pottery from Trench IVJ, Room 4B (Phase 4; Period E — Early Bronze Age IVb). Scale 1:5

1. SBR. A.I.e (SW. 673; IVJ, 1.3). Mended to near completion. Fairly fine buff ware, evenly fired. Dark self slip out.
2. SBR. C.II.a (TS. 2615; IVJ, 1.3). About 1/10 rim and most of wall profile. Fairly fine pink ware, evenly fired. Cream slip in and out.
3. JR. J.III.e (TS. 3018; IVJ, 1.3). About 1/5 rim and neck segment. Fairly fine pink ware, evenly fired. Creamy-buff slip out and on top of rim.
4. SR. A.II.c (TS. 2933; IVJ, 1.3). Small rim and upper wall segment with remains of three strainer holes pierced through upper wall. Slightly coarse pinkish-brown ware, evenly fired. Self slip in and out.
5. JR.Sh. (IP [G.4] C.I.a; TS. 1597; IVJ, 1.3). Jar body sherd with a portion of an applied, snake-like, strip of clay tool/reed-incised with small circles (see pl. 100b). Fairly fine buff ware with mica grits, evenly fired. Cream slip in and out.

Another Type Series Example: (1) BR. F.III.i (TS. 2648).

Other Study Collection Examples: (1) SBR. B.I.h (SC. 470), (2) SBR. B.I.h (SC. 478), (3) SBR. B.I.h (SC. 500), (4) BE. C.I (SC. 3123).

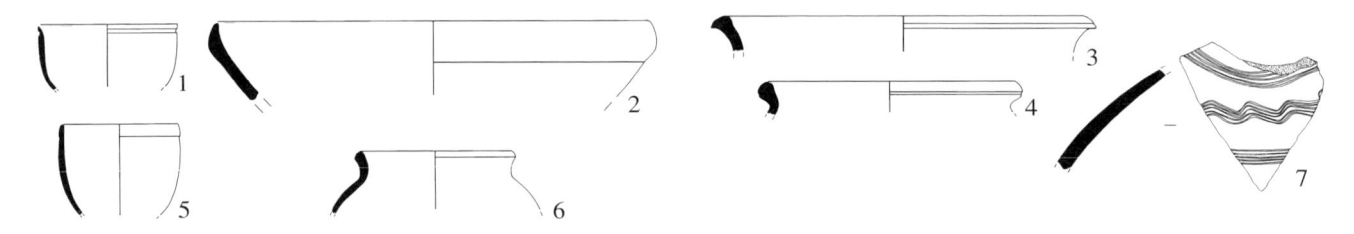

Figure 130. Pottery from Trench IVK, Room 2B; Trench IVL, Room 3B; and Trench IVM, Room 7B (Phase 4; Period E — Early Bronze Age IVb). Scale 1:5

1. SBR. B.I.d (TS. 2923; IVK, 1.2). About 1/5 rim and most of wall profile. Fairly fine light pink ware, evenly fired. Buff slip in and out.
2. BR. F.III.b (TS. 1756; IVK, 1.2). Large rim and upper wall segment. Fine pink ware, evenly fired. Cream slip in and out.
3. JR. E.I.d (TS. 2657; IVK, 1.2). About 1/12 rim and neck segment. Slightly coarse grayish-green ware, evenly fired. Self slip in and out.
4. JR. J.I.h (TS. 2669; IVK, 1.2). About 1/8 rim and neck segment. Slightly coarse ware, unevenly fired with gray core and pinkish-buff at surfaces.
5. SBR. B.I.h (TS. 2922; IVL, 1.2). About 1/4 rim and most of wall profile. Fairly fine ware, unevenly fired greenish-buff in and pinkish out. Buff slip out.
6. CP. A.I.b (TS. 2855; IVL, 1.2). About 1/5 rim and shoulder segment. Fairly coarse pinkish-buff ware, evenly fired. Self slip in and out.
7. JR.Sh. (IP [G.1] C.IV.a; TS. 1651; IVL, 1.2). Jar shoulder sherd with horizontal and wavy comb-incised bands outside (see pl. 102d). Fairly fine pink ware, evenly fired. Cream slip in and out.
—. JR.Sh. (PM. F; TS. 3124; IVK, 1.2). Jar sherd. Ware description not available.
—. JR.Sh. (PM. F; TS. 3131; IVK, 1.2). Jar sherd. Ware description not available.
—. JR.Sh. (PM. F; TS. 3116; IVL, 1.2). Jar sherd. Ware description not available.
—. JR.Sh. (PM. F; SC. 75; IVL, 1.2). Jar sherd. Ware description not available.

Other Type Series Examples:
Area IVK — (1) BR. F.I.e (TS. 2570), (2) JR. H.I.a (TS. 2906), (3) JR. O.III.b (TS. 1663).
Area IVL — (1) BR. O.I.a (TS. 1643), (2) ABS. C (TS. 1664).
Area IVM — (1) CP. C.I.a (TS. 2851).

Other Study Collection Examples:
Area IVK — (1) SBR. A.I.b (SC. 214), (2) SBR. B.I.h (SC. 467), (3) BR. A.II.e (SC. 716), (4) BR. L.II.e (SC. 861), (5) JR. C.V.a (SC. 1010), (6) JR. D.V.a (SC. 1078), (7) JR. G.I.c (SC. 2042), (8) JR. J.I.f (SC. 1351), (9) JR. J.III.ab (SC. 1516), (10) JR. K.I.b (SC. 2393), (11) BE. D.IV (SC. 3149), (12) BE. E.II.d (SC. 3210).
Area IVL — (1) SBR. B.I.c (SC. 278), (2) SJR. C.I.f (SC. 2562), (3) JR. B.IV.c (SC. 963), (4) JR. C.V.c (SC. 1014), (5) JR. E.II.d (SC. 1146), (6) JR. E.II.d (SC. 2009), (7) JR. E.II.o (SC. 1159), (8) JR. E.II.o (SC. 1160), (9) JR. E.II.o (SC. 1161), (10) JR. J.III.m (SC. 1436), (11) JR. J.III.n (SC. 1443), (12) JR. O.II.c (SC. 1629), (13) JR. P.I.e (SC. 2428), (14) JR.Sh., PM (not typed, SC. 75).
Area IVM — (1) SBR. A.I.b (SC. 204), (2) SBR. B.I.g (SC. 393), (3) SBR. B.I.j (SC. 544), (4) SJR. C.I.h (SC. 2571), (5) JR. E.II.j (SC. 1154).

Figures 131–32

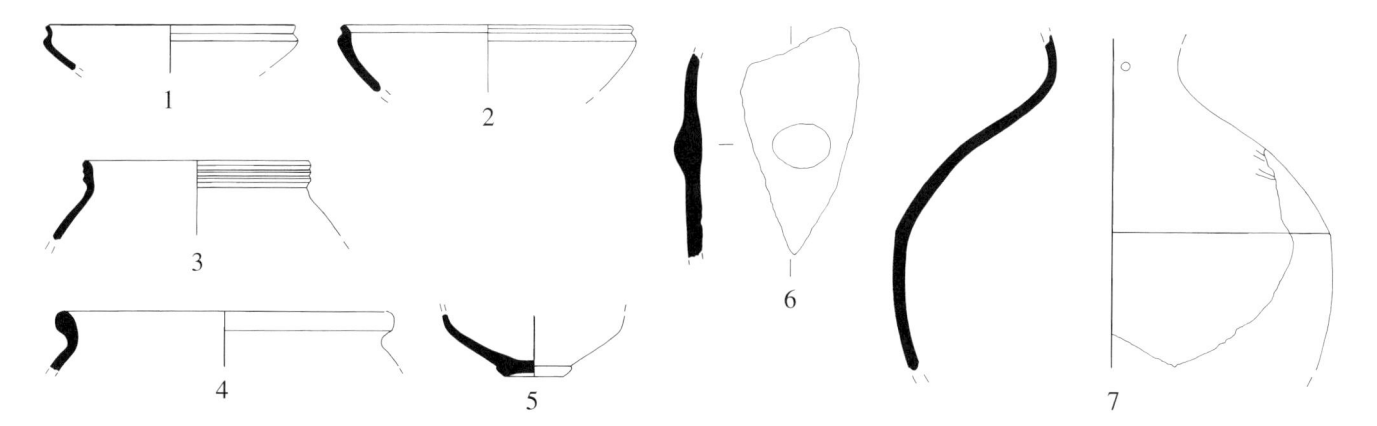

Figure 131. Pottery from Trench IVN, Rooms 8B and 18B (Phase 4; Period E — Early Bronze Age IVb). Scale 1:5

1. BR. C.I.a (TS. 1748; IVN, 1.3). Small rim and upper wall segment. Fine pink ware with lime grits, evenly fired. Cream slip in and out.
2. BR. C.I.d (TS. 1705; IVN, 1.3). Small rim and upper wall segment. Hard, medium fine pink ware, evenly fired. Cream slip in and out.
3. JR. C.II.b (TS. 1684; IVN, 1.3). About 1/3 rim and shoulder segment. Fairly fine pink ware with lime and mica grits, evenly fired. Cream slip out.
4. CP. B.II.c (TS. 2844; IVN, 1.3). About 1/4 rim and upper shoulder; two joining segments. Slightly coarse gritty pinkish-brown ware, evenly fired. Self slip in and out.
5. BE. B.II (TS. 1691; IVN, 1.3). Complete base and portion of lower wall of vessel. Medium fine pink ware, evenly fired. Cream slip in and out.
6. Hd. G (TS. 1737; IVN, 1.3). Body sherd with circular-shaped knob-like handle. Hard, grayish ware, evenly fired. Buff slip in and out.
7. JR.Sh. (PM. A.18; TS. 1717; IVN, 4.2). Neck and body segment with portion of potter's mark or decoration incised on shoulder before firing; one hole pierced through neck may be a post-fired mending hole. Medium fine pink ware with lime grits, evenly fired. Light greenish slip in and out.
—. JR.Sh. (PM. F; TS. 3132; IVN, 1.3). Jar sherd. Ware description not available.

Other Type Series Examples: (1) SJR. B.II.d (TS. 1711), (2) JR. C.I.i (TS. 2611), (3) JR. O.I.d (TS. 1777), (4) BE. D.III (TS. 1689), (5) Hd. A (TS. 1686).

Other Study Collection Examples: (1) SBR. A.I.a (SC. 166), (2) SBR. A.I.a (SC. 167), (3) SBR. A.I.a (SC. 171), (4) SBR. B.I.h (SC. 451), (5) SBR. B.I.l (SC. 576), (6) SBR. B.I.p (SC. 589), (7) BR. F.II.a (SC. 788), (8) BR. L.I.f (SC. 841).

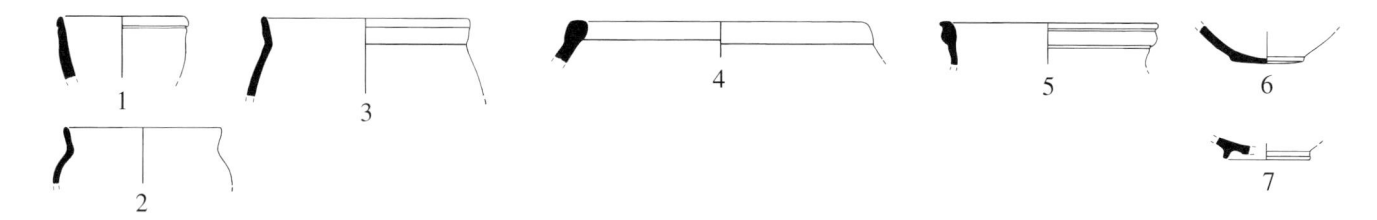

Figure 132. Pottery from Trench IVN, Operation 10, Room 8B, Northeast Corner (Phase 4; Period E–D — Early–Middle Bronze Age). Scale 1:5

1. SBR. B.I.h (TS. 4017; Op. 10, 22). Small rim and upper wall segment. For ware, compare Phase 2B Type Series example from Area IVZ(S) (TS. 2702).
2. SBR. D.I.e (TS. 4045; Op. 10, 22). Small rim and shoulder segment. For ware, compare Phase 2A Type Series example from Area IVN (TS. 1682).
3. SBR. D.I.e (TS. 4042; Op. 10, 22). Small rim and upper wall segment. For ware, compare Phase 2A example from Area IVF (TS. 1631).
4. JR. H.III.c (TS. 4043; Op. 10, 22). Small rim and upper shoulder segment. For ware, compare Phase 1C Type Series example from Area IVM (TS. 2816).
5. JR. J.III.ae (TS. 4016; Op. 10, 22). Small rim and neck segment. Ware description unavailable.
6. BE. B.I (TS. 4046; Op. 10, 22). Complete base and portion of lower wall of vessel. For ware, compare Phase 2A Type Series example from Area IVN (TS. 2768).
7. BE. E.I.j (TS. 4044; Op. 10, 22). About 1/2 base and small portion of lower wall of vessel. Ware description unavailable.

Another Type Series Example: (1) JR. J.III.ad (TS. 3330 = TS. 3336).

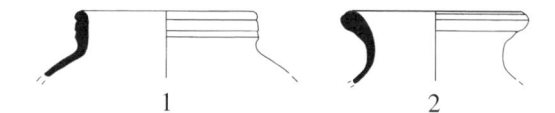

Figure 133

Figure 133. Pottery from Trench IVO, Room 10B (Phase 4; Period E — Early Bronze Age IVb). Scale 1:5

1. JR. C.V.a (TS. 1619; IVO, 1.2). Small rim and shoulder segment. Fairly fine pink ware, evenly fired. Cream slip in and out.
2. JR. J.I.f (TS. 1618; IVO, 1.2). Complete rim and neck segment. Fairly fine buff ware, evenly fired. Cream slip in and out.

Other Type Series Examples: (1) BR. E.IV.a (TS. 1588), (2) BR. R.I.a (SW. 501), (3) SJR. B.III.e (SW. 502), (4) JR. C.I.c (TS. 1616), (5) JR. C.I.h (TS. 1620), (6) JR. J.III.j (TS. 572), (7) CP. B.IV.a (TS. 2857).

Other Study Collection Examples: (1) JR. J.III.o (SC. 2344), (2) JR. J.IV.b (SC. 1524), (3) JR. J.VI.b (SC. 1556), (4) JR. N.I.b (SC. 1610), (5) Hd. B (SC. 3273).

Derived Hellenistic Type Series Example: (1) H.Jg. B.II.e (TS. 2940).

Figure 134. Pottery from Trench IVP, Room 9B (Phase 4; Period E — Early Bronze Age IVb)

1. SBR. B.I.f (TS. 2921; IVP, 1.3). About 1/5 rim and most of wall profile. Slightly coarse pinkish-brown ware, evenly fired. Traces of cream slip out.
2. BR. E.I.a (TS. 2588; IVP, 1.2). About 1/5 rim and upper wall segment. Slightly coarse greenish-buff ware, evenly fired. Creamy-green slip in and out.
3. BR. E.I.a (TS. 2620; IVP, 1.2). About 1/10 rim and most of wall profile. Coarse, gritty grayish-brown ware, evenly fired. Creamy-green slip in and out.
4. BR. E.I.b (TS. 2590; IVP, 1.2, 1.3). About 1/6 rim and upper wall segment; two non-joining fragments. Slightly coarse grayish-buff ware, evenly fired. Creamy-green slip in and out.
5. BR. E.I.b (TS. 2591; IVP, 1.2). About 1/10 rim and upper wall segment. Slightly coarse creamy-green ware, evenly fired. Self slip in and out.
6. BR. E.I.c (TS. 2593; IVP, 1.2). Small rim and upper wall segment. Fairly coarse buff ware, evenly fired. Self slip in and out.
7. JR. C.I.h (TS. 2741; IVP, 1.2). About 1/6 rim and upper shoulder segment. Slightly coarse pink ware, evenly fired. Creamy-buff slip in and out.
8. JR. C.II.a (TS. 2599; IVP, 1.2). About 1/6 rim and upper wall segment. Slightly coarse brown ware, evenly fired. Light creamy-green slip out.
9. JR. C.II.f (TS. 2749; IVP, 1.2). Small rim and shoulder segment. Fairly coarse buff ware, evenly fired. Self slip in and out.
10. JR. E.II.c (TS. 2753; IVP, 1.2). About 1/6 rim and shoulder segment. Slightly coarse pinkish-buff ware, evenly fired. Cream slip in and out.
11. JR. O.II.e (TS. 2771; IVP, 1.3). Small rim and neck segment. Slightly coarse orange ware, evenly fired. Cream slip in and out.
12. JR. P.I.a (TS. 2765; IVP, 1.2). Small rim, neck, and shoulder segment. Hard, close pink ware, evenly fired. Pinkish-buff slip in and out.
—. JR.Sh. (PM. F; TS. 3095; IVP, 1.2). Jar sherd. Ware description not available.
—. JR.Sh. (PM. F; TS. 3098; IVP, 1.2). Jar sherd. Ware description not available.
—. JR.Sh. (PM. F; TS. 3107; IVP, 1.2). Jar sherd. Ware description not available.
—. JR.Sh. (PM. F; TS. 3138; IVP, 1.2). Jar sherd. Ware description not available.

Figures 134–35

Other Type Series Examples: (1) BR. A.IV.b (TS. 2558), (2) BR. E.I.a (TS. 2587), (3) BR. L.II.d (TS. 2586), (4) BR. L.II.g (TS. 2739), (5) BR. L.II.h (TS. 2580), (6) BR. T. (TS. 2584), (7) JR. E.II.m (TS. 2755), (8) JR. H.II.d (TS. 2763), (9) JR. J.III.e (TS. 1787), (10) JR. J.IV.c (TS. 2756), (11) JR. P.III.a (TS. 2752), (12) CP. C.I.e (TS. 2834), (13) PS. B.I.b (TS. 2557 = TS. 3396).

Other Study Collection Examples: (1) SBR. B.I.b (SC. 254), (2) BR. (not typed, SC. 30), (3) SJR. B.II.j (SC. 663), (4) SJR. C.II.s (SC. 2613), (5) SJR. C.II.s (SC. 2615), (6) JR. C.II.f (SC. 1020), (7) JR. D.VI.b (SC. 1109), (8) JR. D.VIII.c (SC. 1121), (9) JR. E.II.d (SC. 2013), (10) JR. G.II.c (SC. 2051), (11) JR. H.I.f (SC. 1271), (12) JR. J.III.a (SC. 2209), (13) JR. J.III.e (SC. 2273), (14) JR. J.III.y (SC. 1507), (15) JR. J. (Gen. Type, SC. 120), (16) JR. O.II.d (SC. 1637), (17) JR. P.II.c (SC. 1723), (18) JR. P.III.a (SC. 2467), (19) JR. P.III.f (SC. 1762), (20) CP. B.IV.c (SC. 1878), (21) CP. C.I.b (SC. 1900), (22) BE. E.II.d (SC. 3209), (23) BE. F.VIII.c (SC. 1926), (24) SV.2 (SC. 3280).

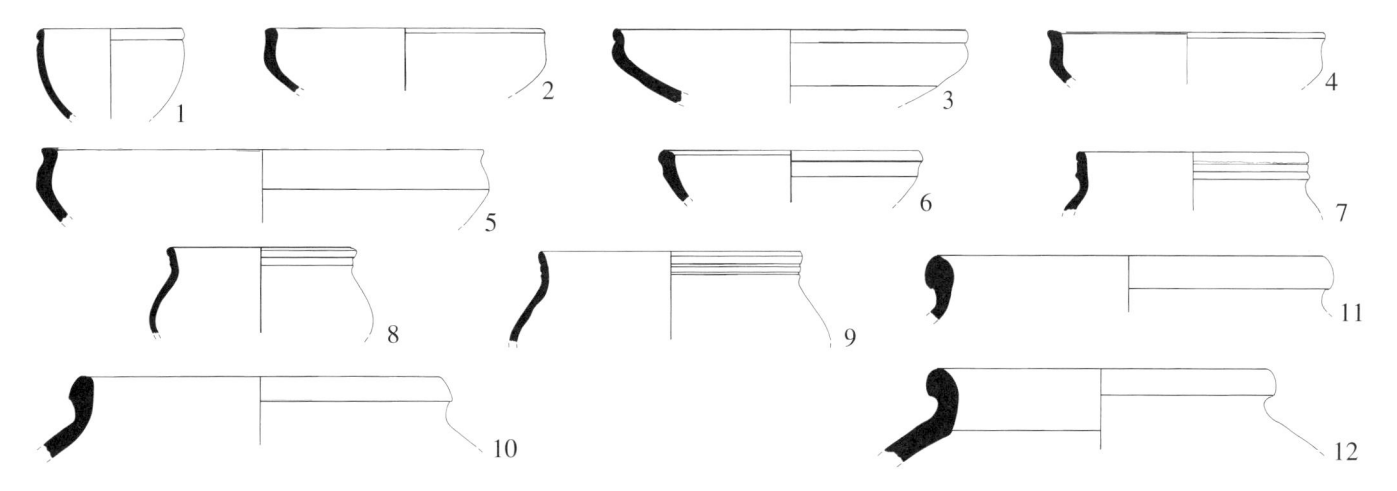

Figure 134. Pottery from Trench IVP, Room 9B (Phase 4; Period E — Early Bronze Age IVb). Scale 1:5

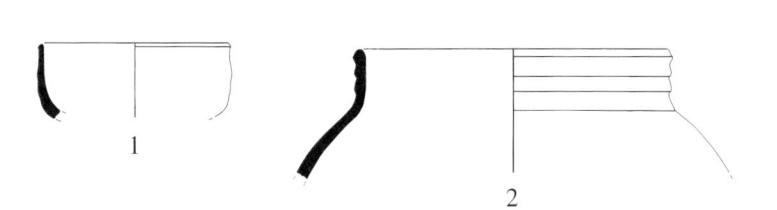

Figure 135. Pottery from Area IV, Operation 6, Room 31, Built Over Room 22 (Phase 4; Period E–D — Early–Middle Bronze Age). Scale 1:5

1. SBR. A.II.a (TS. 4086; Op. 6, 3.2). About 1/4 rim and wall segment. Fairly fine light green ware with silver-colored mica and lime grits, evenly fired. Creamy-green slip in and out.
2. JR. D.V.f (TS. 4087; Op. 6, 3.2). About 1/8 rim and shoulder segment. Fairly fine light pink ware with gold- and silver-colored mica and black and white lime grits, evenly fired. Creamy-buff slip out and on top of rim.

Figure 136. Pottery from Area IV, Operation 6, Room 32, Built Over Room 23 (Phase 4; Period E–D — Early–Middle Bronze Age)

1. SBR. A.II.c (TS. 4084; Op. 6, 3.1). About 1/2 rim and most of wall profile. Fairly fine buff ware with gold- and silver-colored mica grits, evenly fired. Creamy-buff slip in and out.
2. SBR. F.I.a (TS. 4101; Op. 6, 3.1). Small rim and most of wall profile. Slightly coarse light green ware with fine black and white grits, evenly fired. Creamy-green slip in and out.
3. BR. C.I.e (TS. 3278; Op. 6, 3.1). About 1/2 rim and nearly complete base, mended to complete profile. Slightly coarse buff ware with small gray and white grits and a few small pebbles, especially protruding from the base, evenly fired. Creamy-green slip in and out. Disk base string-cut off center to edge of base.
4. BR. C.I.e (TS. 3282; Op. 6, 3.1). Small rim and upper wall segment. For ware, compare Type Series example from Area IVJ (TS. 1594).
5. BR. E.I.a (TS. 3285; Op. 6, 3.1). Nearly mended to completion. For ware, compare Phase 4 example from Area IVP (TS. 2620).
6. BR. E.I.b (TS. 3279; Op. 6, 3.1). Small rim and most of wall profile. For ware, compare Type Series example from Area IVP (TS. 2589).
7. BR. J.I.a (TS. 4085; Op. 6, 3.1). About 1/2 rim and upper wall segment. Slightly coarse light green ware with silver-colored mica and lime grits, evenly fired. Creamy-green self slip in and out.
8. BR. J.II.a (TS. 4102; Op. 6, 3.1). About 1/10 rim and upper wall segment. Fairly fine buff ware with lime grits, evenly fired. Creamy-green slip in and out.
9. BR. M.I.a (TS. 3201; Op. 6, 3.1). About 1/20 rim and upper wall segment with tool-made decoration incised on shoulder before firing. Slightly coarse pinkish-orange ware with with small lime and mica grits, evenly fired. Creamy-buff slip in and out.
10. SJR. B.II.i (TS. 4103; Op. 6, 3.1). About 1/7 rim, neck, and shoulder segment. Fairly fine pinkish-brown ware with fine gold- and silver-colored mica and lime grits, evenly fired. Creamy-buff slip out and over rim in.
11. JR. B.I.a (TS. 3283; Op. 6, 3.1). Large rim and shoulder segment. Ware description unavailable.
12. JR. B.I.b (TS. 4104; Op. 6, 3.1). Small rim and neck segment. Hard, close buff ware with fine gold- and silver-colored mica and lime grits, evenly fired. Creamy-green slip in and out.
13. JR. B.III.b (PM. A.11; TS. 3290; Op. 6, 3.10). About 1/4 segment with fairly large portion of the body with a potter's mark incised on the shoulder before firing. Slightly coarse buff ware with very fine gold-colored mica and a few lime pebble inclusions, fairly evenly fired. Creamy-buff slip in and out.
14. JR. B.IV.c (TS. 3276; Op. 6, 3.1). Small rim and upper neck segment. For ware, compare Type Series example from Area VB (TS. 408).
15. JR. C.V.a (PM. B.3; TS. 4106; Op. 6, 3.1). About 1/4 rim, neck, and shoulder segment with portion of a potter's mark incised on shoulder before firing. Fairly fine pinkish-brown ware with gold- and silver-colored mica and lime grits, evenly fired. Creamy-green slip out.
16. JR. J.II.b (PM. A.6; TS. 3291; Op. 6, 3.16). About 1/3 rim, neck, and shoulder segment with a potter's mark incised on the shoulder before firing. Hard, slightly coarse pinkish-orange ware with small gold- and white-colored mica and medium-sized black and white lime grits, evenly fired. Self slip in and out. Inside surface below neck slightly pitted from burned out vegetable temper.
17. JR. J.III.c (TS. 4105; Op. 6, 3.1). About 1/3 rim, neck, and shoulder segment. Hard, fairly fine pinkish-brown ware with fine gold-and silver-colored mica and lime grits, evenly fired. Creamy-green slip out.
18. JR. J.III.ab (TS. 3275; Op. 6, 3.1). Small rim and neck segment. For ware, compare Type Series example from Area IC (TS. 2283).
19. Hd. B (TS. 4107; Op. 6, 3.1). Jar body sherd with wide vertically positioned loop handle. Coarse, friable reddish-brown ware with some mica and many large black and white lime grits and small pebble inclusions, fairly evenly fired.

Other Type Series Examples: (1) SBR. F.I.e (TS. 3281), (2) SJR. A.III.e (TS. 3200), (3) JR. P.III.c (TS. 3277).

Derived Islamic Sherds: (1) Isl. JR. (not typed, TS. 3274), (2) Isl. BE. (not typed, TS. 3289).

Pottery from Area IV, Operation 6, Room 33, Above Rooms 16 and 24 (Phase 4; Period E–D — Early–Middle Bronze Age)

—. SJR. C.I.a (SW. 820; Op. 6, 3.9). About 1/2 portion of a flat-based cylindrical-shaped small jar or possible a model covered wagon. Linear decoration on outside wall and base incised before firing. For photographic illustrations, see pl. 99a and compare pl. 119c, which may belong to this vessel or model. Ware description not available.

Figure 136

Pottery from Area IV, Operation 6, Room 32, Built Over Room 23 (Phase 4; Period E–D — Early–Middle Bronze Age). Scale 1:5

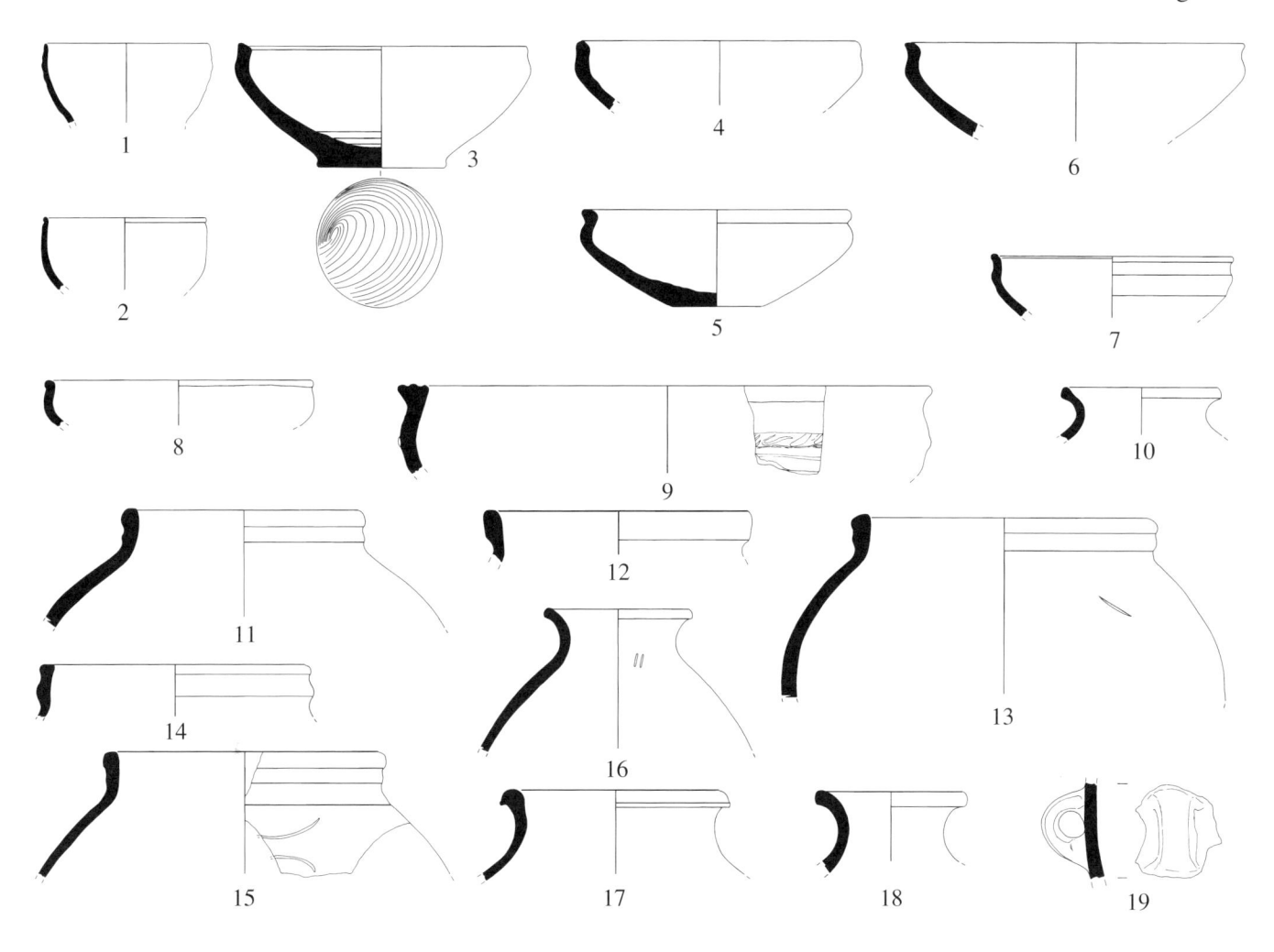

Figures 137–38

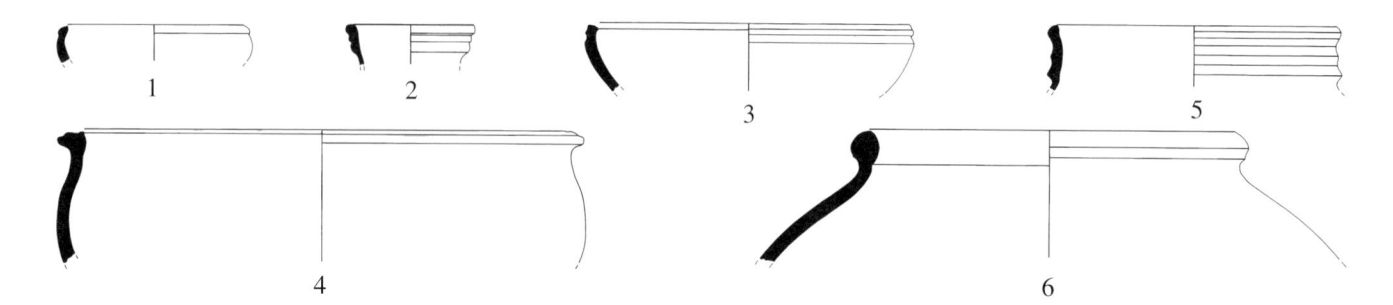

Figure 137. Trench IVQ, Room 25, and Soundings IVV, W, and Y Above and South of Operation 7 Street (Phase 4; Period E — Early Bronze Age IVb). Scale 1:5

1. BR. D.III.b (TS. 2784; IVQ, 1.2). Small rim and upper wall segment. Slightly coarse pink ware, evenly fired. Self slip in and out.
2. SJR. C.II.h (TS. 2673; IVV, 1.1). About 1/8 rim and neck segment. Hard, slightly coarse pink ware, evenly fired. Self slip in and out.
3. BR. E.II.c (TS. 2603; IVY, 1.2). About 1/10 rim and upper wall segment. Fairly coarse buff ware, evenly fired. Creamy-buff slip out.
4. BR. H.I.b (TS. 2579; IVY, 1.2). About 1/10 rim and upper wall segment. Hard, close pink ware, evenly fired. Cream slip in and on top of rim.
5. JR. D.I.c (TS. 2686; IVY, 1.2). About 1/10 rim and neck segment. Slightly coarse creamy-green ware, evenly fired. Self slip out.
6. JR. P.II.d (TS. 2729; IVY, 1.2). About 1/8 rim and shoulder segment. Slightly coarse buff ware, evenly fired. Creamy-green slip out and just over rim in.

Other Type Series Examples:
Area IVV — (1) JR. O.III.h (TS. 2677).
Area IVW — (1) BE. F.II.b (SW. 679).
Area IVY — (1) SBR. D.II.h (TS. 2625), (2) JR. B.V.f (TS. 2689).

Other Study Collection Examples:
Area IVW —(1) ABS. C (SC. 3247).
Area IVY — (1) BR. A.IV.a (SC. 1966), (2) BR. (not typed, SC. 29), (3) SJR. B.II.j (SC. 661), (4) JR. C.II.c (SC. 1005), (5) JR. D.II.d (SC. 1062), (6) JR. D.V.b (SC. 1082), (7) JR. E.II.d (SC. 2015), (8) JR. J.III.x (SC. 1503), (9) JR. J.IV.j (SC. 1545), (10) JR. P.II.n (SC. 2434), (11) JR. (not typed, SC. 77), (12) BE. E.I.g (SC. 3181), (13) BE. F.VIII.a (SC. 1924).

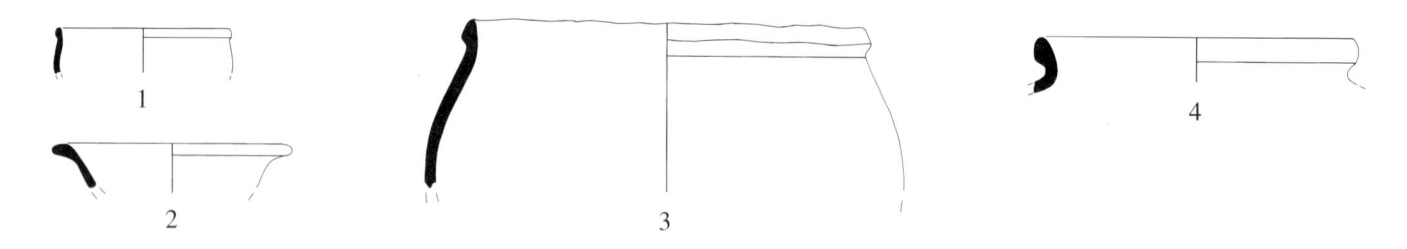

Figure 138. Pottery from Trench IVT, Sounding (Phase 4; Period E — Early Bronze Age IVb). Scale 1:5

1. SBR. B.I.d (TS. 2820; IVT, 1.2). About 1/6 rim and upper wall segment. Slightly coarse pinkish-buff ware, evenly fired. Cream slip in and out.
2. SJR. C.I.f (TS. 1659; IVT, 1.2). Small rim and upper neck segment. Fairly fine buff ware, evenly fired. Cream slip in and out.
3. JR. F.III.f (TS. 1645; IVT, 1.2). Large rim and upper wall segment. Slightly coarse and gritty grayware, evenly fired. Cream slip in and out.
4. JR. J.II.a (TS. 1602; IVT, 1.3). Small rim and shoulder segment. Medium fine pink ware, unevenly fired. Burnished self slip out and around rim in.
—. JR.Sh. (PM. F; TS. 3097; IVT, 1.2). Jar sherd. Ware description not available.

Other Study Collection Examples: (1) SBR. D.I.a (SC. 619), (2) JR. E.II.d (SC. 1147), (3) JR. J.III.b (SC. 1362), (4) JR. J.III.m (SC. 1416), (5) CP. B.III.d (SC. 1861), (6) BE. B.II (SC. 3114), (7) BE. F.IV.a (SC. 1915).

Figure 139

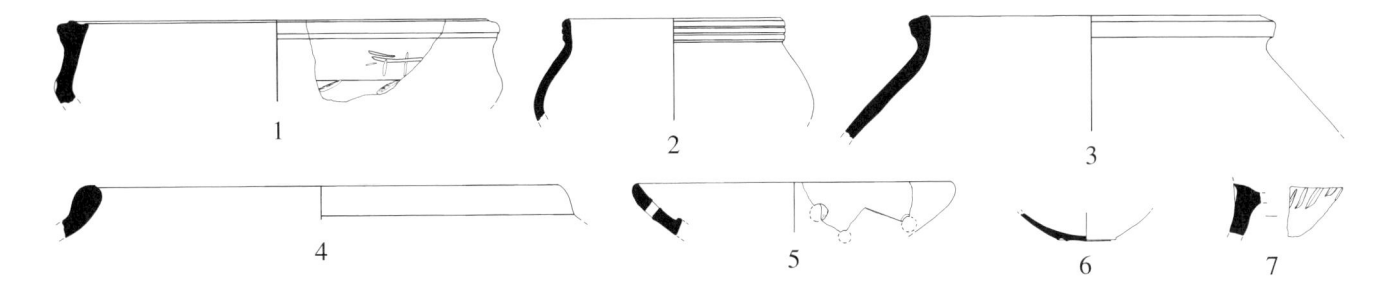

Pottery from Trench IVZ(N1), (N2), and (S) (Phase 4; Period E — Early Bronze Age IVb). Scale 1:5

1. BR. H.III.a (PM. E.2; TS. 2684; IVZ(S), 5.1). About 1/8 rim and upper wall segment with incised and impressed band decoration on outside wall and remains of a potter's mark incised on the outside wall before firing. Fairly coarse light pink ware, evenly fired. Buff slip out.
2. JR. C.I.b (TS. 2613; IVZ(N1), 1.2). About 1/6 rim and upper wall segment. Coarse buff ware, evenly fired. Creamy-buff slip in and out.
3. JR. E.II.x (TS. 2751; IVZ(N2), 3.2/3). About 1/10 rim and shoulder segment. Slightly coarse gritty brown ware, evenly fired. Buff slip in and out.
4. JR. O.III.b (TS. 2699; IVZ(N1), 1.3). Small rim segment. Hard, close buff ware, fairly evenly fired. Self slip out.
5. SR. A.I.a (TS. 2937; IVZ(N2), 3.2/3). About 1/8 rim and upper wall segment (two joining fragments) with remains of three strainer holes in wall. Slightly coarse buff ware, evenly fired. Self slip in and out.
6. BE. J (TS. 3063; IVZ(N2), 3.2/3). About 1/3 base segment and portion of lower wall of vessel. Fairly fine light red ware, evenly fired. Self slip horizontally burnished out.
7. BE. F.VIII.a (TS. 2711; IVZ(N1), 1.3). Pedestal base fragment with diagonally-impressed slash decoration at joining point between pedestal base and upper missing portion of vessel. Hard, close pink ware, evenly fired. Creamy-buff slip in and out.
—. JR.Sh. (PM. F; TS. 3096; IVZ(N2), 3.2/3). Jar sherd. Ware description not available.
—. JR.Sh. (PM. F; TS. 3140a; IVZ(N2), 3.2). Jar sherd. Ware description not available.

Other Type Series Examples:
Area IVZ(N1) — (1) SJR. D.III.b (TS. 2824), (2) CP. B.IV.h (TS. 2865), (3) SB. A.I.b (TS. 2832).

Other Study Collection Examples:
Area IVZ(N1) — (1) BR. E.I.a (SC. 751), (2) JR. B.IV.c (SC. 966), (3) JR. B.VI.b (SC. 985), (4) JR. C.V.d (SC. 1028), (5) JR. D.I.b (SC. 1042), (6) JR. G.II.c (SC. 2052), (7) JR. H.I.m (SC. 1290), (8) JR. J.I.d (SC. 2115), (9) JR. J.II.g (SC. 2151), (10) JR. J.III.m (SC. 1437), (11) JR. J.III.m (SC. 1440), (12) JR. J.III.u (SC. 2358), (13) JR. J.III.y (SC. 2366), (14) JR. O.II.h (SC. 1653), (15) JR. (not typed, SC. 136), (16) BE. F.III.a (SC. 1909).
Area IVZ(N2) — (1) BR. E.I.b (SC. 756), (2) BR. E.III.c (SC. 758), (3) BR. (not typed, SC. 39), (4) JR. J.II.i (SC. 2171), (5) JR. J.II.i (SC. 2175), (6) JR. J.II.k (SC. 2180), (7) JR. J.II.k (SC. 2181), (8) JR. J.III.b (SC. 1363), (9) JR. J.III.e (SC. 2256), (10) JR. J.III.q (SC. 1476), (11) JR. J.III.w (SC. 1496), (12) JR. J.III.ab (SC. 1513), (13) JR. P.II.f (SC. 1730), (14) SR. A.I.a (SC. 1954).
Area IVZ(S) — (1) BR. C.I.d (SC. 740), (2) BR. L.II.b (SC. 850), (3) JR. D.I.b (SC. 1037), (4) JR. F.II.c (SC. 2033), (5) JR. H.I.l (SC. 1288), (6) JR. J.I.f (SC. 1348), (7) JR. J.III.k (SC. 2304), (8) JR. O.I.a (SC. 2403), (9) JR. P.III.g (SC. 1765), (10) JR. (not typed, SC. 91), (11) BE. F.IV.b (SC. 1919), (12) BE. F.V.b (SC. 1923).

Figure 140. Pottery from Trench IXA (Phase 4; Period E–D — Early–Middle Bronze Age)

1. SBR. A.I.c (TS. 2531; IXA, 1.1). About 1/6 rim and upper wall segment. Fairly fine buff ware, evenly fired. Creamy-white slip in and out.
2. SBR. B.I.d (TS. 2966; IXA, 1.1). About 1/3 rim and most of wall profile. Fairly fine pinkish-buff ware, evenly fired. Worn self slip in and out.
3. SBR. F.I.a (TS. 950; IXA, 1.1). About 1/4 rim and most of wall profile. Rim slightly pinched inward on one side of the vessel for pouring or where vessel misfired. Fairly fine buff ware, evenly fired. Cream slip out and around rim in.
4. BR. E.I.a (TS. 936; IXA, 1.1). About 1/20 rim, neck, and upper wall segment. Fairly coarse pink ware, evenly fired. Buff slip in and out.
5. BR. E.I.a (TS. 1060; IXA, 1.1). About 1/5 rim, neck, and most of wall profile. Fairly coarse pink ware, evenly fired. Cream slip in and out.
6. BR. F.III.h (TS. 1029; IXA, 1.1). About 1/20 rim and upper wall segment. Fairly fine pink ware, evenly fired. Cream slip out.
7. SJR. C.II.t (SW. 536; IXA, 1.1). Complete except for missing rim. Hole placed through lower wall of vessel after it had been fired. Fairly coarse pink ware, evenly fired. Buff slip in and out.
8. JR. C.I.d (TS. 1954 = TS. 1975; IXA, 1.1). Large segment of rim, neck, and upper wall profile. Slightly coarse pinkish-buff ware, evenly fired. Creamy-buff slip out and over rim in.
9. JR. D.II.c (TS. 1881; IXA, 1.1). Small rim and neck segment. Hard, close pink ware, evenly fired. Self slip out.
10. JR. E.II.p (PM. F; SW. 538; IXA, 1.1). Mended to complete profile, but with only 2/3 of upper shoulder extant. One side of shoulder has two round holes with part of a potter's mark incised below before firing. Two pairs of holes in the shoulder imply they were for securing a lid onto the vessel or for suspending the vessel.
11. JR. J.III.c (TS. 2257; IXA, 1.1). Small segment of rim, neck, and upper wall. Slightly coarse pinkish-buff ware, evenly fired. Self slip in and out.
12. JR. J.IV.c (TS. 2277; IXA, 1.1). About 1/5 rim, neck, and shoulder segment with shallow, short, horizontal slashes incised around the base of the neck before firing. Fairly close buff ware, evenly fired. Self slip or wash out.
13. JR. K.I.h (TS. 1036; IXA, 1.10 —Pit A). About 1/12 rim and neck segment. Fairly fine buff ware, evenly fired. Cream slip out.
14. JR. P.II.h (TS. 940; IXA, 1.1). About 1/3 rim, neck, and upper body profile. Fairly coarse buff ware, evenly fired. Cream slip in and out.
15. JR. P.II.l (TS. 2372; IXA, 1.1). About 1/8 rim, neck, and upper shoulder segment. Slightly coarse buff ware, evenly fired. Creamy-green slip in and out.
16. CP. A.II.c (TS. 1065; IXA, 1.1). About 1/12 rim, neck, and most of body profile. Coarse brown ware with lime and mica grits, evenly fired. Self slip in and out, blackened on outside wall and lower portion of wall inside.
17. ABS. C (TS. 941; IXA, 1.1). Body sherd of large jar with applied rope-like band with a portion of an applied animal figure below it. Fairly coarse buff ware, evenly fired. Cream slip out.
18. JR.Sh. (PM. D.10; TS. 945; IXA, 1.1). Jar body sherd with an incomplete potter's mark incised on the outside wall before firing.

Other Type Series Examples:
  Bronze Age — (1) SBR. A.I.f (TS. 1021), (2) MJR. 3 (SW. 433), (3) SJR. C.I.e (SW. 461).
  Derived Hellenistic — (1) H.JR. D.III.a (TS. 1028).

Other Study Collection Examples:
  Bronze Age — (1) SBR. A.I.a (SC. 2783), (2) SBR. A.I.d (SC. 3306), (3) SBR. B.I.h (SC. 471), (4) SBR. B.I.i (SC. 528), (5) BR. A.III.c (SC. 2818), (6) BR. L.I.f (SC. 842), (7) SJR. A.II.d (SC. 2487), (8) SJR. C.I.a (SC. 2535), (9) JR. D.I.c (SC. 1047), (10) JR. J.I.b (SC. 2102), (11) JR. J.I.h (SC. 2128), (12) JR. J.I.i (SC. 2133), (13) JR. J.II.h (SC. 2165), (14) JR. J.III.e (SC. 2251), (15) JR. K.I.b (SC. 1578), (16) JR. K.I.b (SC. 1579), (17) JR. P.II.m (SC. 2433), (18) JR. (not typed, SC. 48), (19) CP. B.II.a (SC. 1837), (20) CP. B.II.a (SC. 1844), (21) CP. B.IV.b (SC. 1870), (22) CP. (not typed, SC. 67), (23) BE. A.II (SC. 3096), (24) BE. C.I (SC. 3122), (25) BE. D.III (SC. 3148), (26) BE. F.IV.a (SC. 1916).
  Derived Hellenistic — (1) H.St.J. A.I.c (SC. 2663).

Figure 140

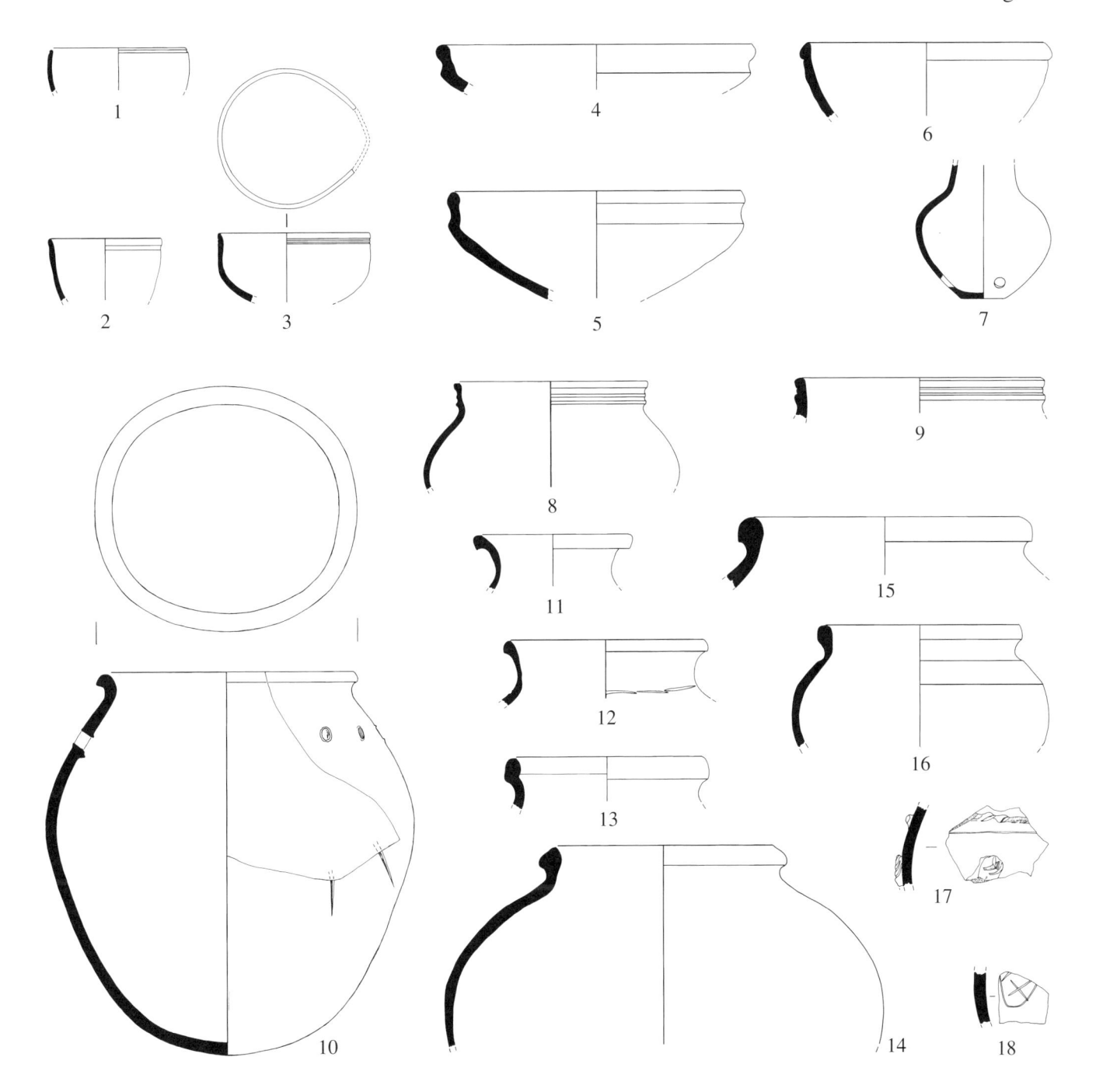

Pottery from Trench IXA (Phase 4; Period E–D — Early–Middle Bronze Age). Scale 1:5

Figure 141. Pottery from Trench XA, Above Room 15A and Operation 11, Above Rooms 19A and 20A (Phase 4; Period E–D — Early–Middle Bronze Age)

1. BR. M.II.a (TS. 790; XA, 1.1). Large rim and upper body segment with two finger-impressed rope bands around the wall of the bowl. Fairly coarse pink ware, fairly evenly fired. Cream slip out.
2. SJR. C.I.c (TS. 2478; XA, 1.1). About 1/8 rim and upper neck segment. Fairly fine buff ware, evenly fired. Self slip in and out.
3. JR. G.I.c (TS. 789; XA, 1.1). About 1/20 rim and upper neck segment. Fairly fine pink ware, evenly fired. Cream slip out.
4. JR. K.I.b (TS. 2330; XA, 1.1). About 1/10 rim, neck, and upper shoulder segment. Fairly coarse ware, unevenly fired with light green core and buff at surfaces. Creamy-green slip in and out.
5. JR. O.III.b (TS. 2164; XA, 1.1). Large segment of rim and upper shoulder. Coarse, flaky, orange-buff ware, fairly evenly fired.
6. SBR. F.I.c (TS. 3338; Op. 11, 1a, above Room 19A). About 1/4 rim and most of wall profile. Very fine grayish-green "metallic-like" ware with fine gray and white lime grits, evenly fired. Light creamy-green slip in and out with decorative pattern in reserve on upper outside wall.
7. Hd. E.II (TS. 3604; Op. 11, 1b, above Room 20A). About 1/4 neck and body segment of a small jar with one double-pierced, horizontally attached, ledge handle situated at maximum girth of vessel for suspension. Slightly coarse grayware with small silver-colored mica and lime grits, evenly fired. Burnt and very worn in and out, but with traces of burnished self slip on the outside of the neck.

Another Type Series Example from Area XA, 1.1: (1) CP. B.IV.e (TS. 899).

Other Study Collection Examples from Area XA, 1.1: (1) SBR. B.I.g (SC. 398), (2) SBR. F.I.a (SC. 657), (3) SBR. F.I.b (SC. 658), (4) BR. F.I.d (SC. 780), (5) BR. F.IV.d (SC. 820), (6) BR. L.II.b (SC. 853), (7) BR. (not typed, SC. 45), (8) SJR. A.I.a (SC. 2471), (9) SJR. A.II.d (SC. 2801), (10) SJR. C.I.a (SC. 2546), (11) SJR. C.I.f (SC. 2557), (12) SJR. C.II.t (SC. 2617), (13) JR. F.II.f (SC. 1227), (14) JR. J.III.t (SC. 2356).

Derived Hellenistic Type Series Example from Area XA, 1.1: (1) H.JR. C.I.g (TS. 1025).

Figure 141

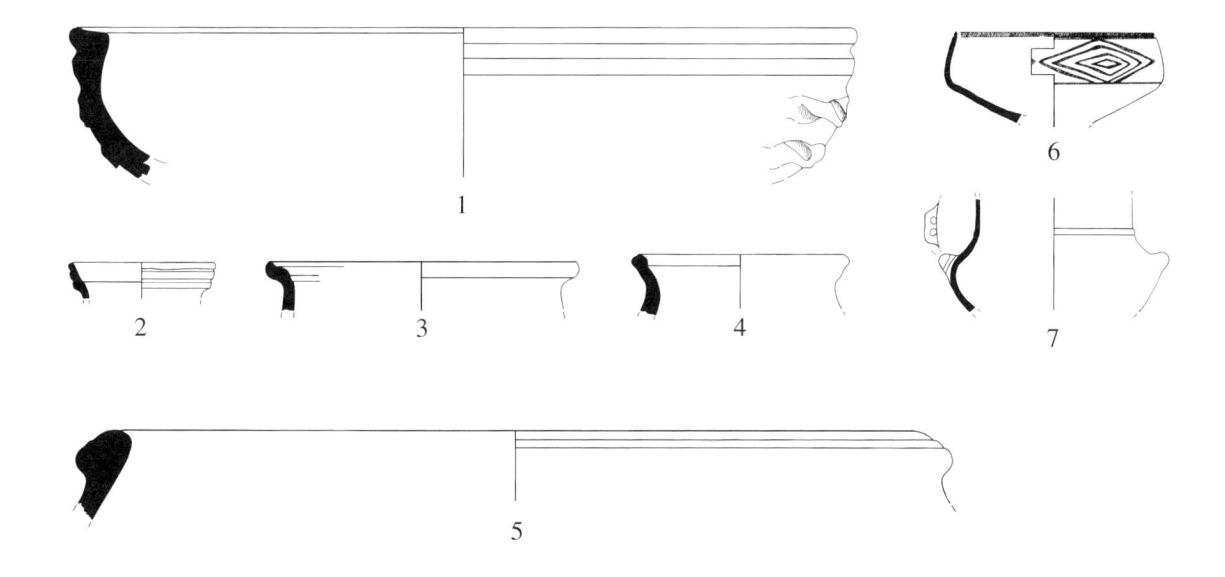

Pottery from Trench XA, Above Room 15A and Operation 11, Above Rooms 19A and 20A (Phase 4; Period E–D — Early–Middle Bronze Age). Scale 1:5

Figure 142. Pottery from Area IV, Lower and Upper Surface Layers (Phase 5; Periods E–D to D — Early–Middle Bronze Age to Middle Bronze Age I)

1. BE. F.VIII.a (TS. 2707; IVA, 1.1). Segment of pedestal base with two extant registers of diagonally incised linear decoration. Slightly coarse dark pink ware, evenly fired. Self slip in and out.
2. BR. E.III.f (TS. 2697; IVB, 1.4). About 1/12 rim and upper wall segment. Hard, close pink ware, evenly fired. Light pink slip in and out.
3. JR. E.I.d (TS. 1953; IVB, 1.1). Rim, neck, and shoulder segment. Fairly close greenish-buff ware, evenly fired. Self slip out.
4. JR. P.II.n (TS. 2696; IVB, 1.3). About 1/12 rim and upper neck segment. Slightly coarse light pink ware, evenly fired. Buff slip in and out.
5. BE. J (TS. 3064; IVB, 1.4). Incomplete ring type base and portion of lower wall of vessel. Fine pinkish-orange ware, evenly fired. Tan-colored slip irregularly burnished on outside surface.
6. SBR. A.I.a (TS. 2448; IVF, 1.1). About 1/8 rim and upper wall segment. Fairly fine light green ware, evenly fired. Creamy-green slip out.
7. JR. J.III.n (TS. 2288; IVF, 1.1). About 1/6 rim and neck segment. Slightly coarse buff-brown ware, evenly fired. Creamy-green slip out and just over rim in.
8. JR. K.I.b (TS. 2333; IVF, 1.1). About 1/6 rim and neck segment. Slightly coarse pink ware, evenly fired. Creamy-yellow slip out and just over rim in.
9. JR. O.I.d (TS. 1635; IVF, 1.1). Small rim and shoulder segment. Coarse pink ware, fairly evenly fired. Cream slip in and out.
10. JR. O.II.k (TS. 2369; IVF, 1.1). About 1/8 rim and and upper shoulder segment. Fairly coarse pink ware, evenly fired. Cream slip in and out.
11. BR. D.IV.a (TS. 2674; IVJ, 1.2). About 1/12 rim segment. Slightly coarse creamy-green ware, evenly fired. Self slip in and out.
12. BR. G.I.b (TS. 2668; IVJ, 1.2). Small rim and wall segment. Fairly coarse grayish-buff ware, evenly fired. Self slip in and out.
13. BR. G.I.d (TS. 3026; IVJ, 1.2). Small rim segment. Fairly fine pinkish-buff ware, evenly fired. Self slip in and out.
14. JR. D.V.c (TS. 1676; IVN,1.1). About 1/3 rim, neck, and shoulder segment. Medium fine buff ware, evenly fired. Cream slip out.
15. JR. E.I.a (TS. 2761; IVN, 1.1). About 1/10 rim and upper shoulder segment. Fairly close pinkish-brown ware, evenly fired. Buff slip in and out.
16. JR. E.I.a (TS. 2850; IVS, 1.2). About 1/10 rim and upper shoulder segment. Slightly coarse grayish-buff ware, evenly fired. Self slip in and out.
17. SJR. A.I.c (TS. 2826; IVX, 1.1). About 1/3 rim and shoulder segment. Slightly coarse pink ware, evenly fired. Self slip in and out.
18. JR. J.I.h (TS. 2705; IVY, 1.1). About 1/10 rim and neck segment. Fairly fine buff ware, evenly fired. Creamy-buff slip in and out.
19. BR. E.I.a (TS. 2596; IVZ(N1), 1.1). About 1/6 rim and upper wall segment. Slightly coarse pinkish-buff ware, evenly fired. Creamy-buff slip in and out.
20. BR. F.IV.a (TS. 2600; IVZ(N1), 1.1). About 1/10 rim and upper wall segment. Hard, close pink ware, evenly fired. Creamy-buff slip in and out.
21. SJR. C.II.c (TS. 2819; IVZ(N2), 3.1). About 1/4 rim and neck segment. Fairly fine light pinkish-buff ware, evenly fired. Cream slip in and out.
22. SJR. C.II.o (TS. 2963; IVZ(N2), 3.1). Two small joining rim and upper neck segments. Fine dark buff ware, evenly fired. Cream slip in and out.
23. BE. D.III (PM. D.19; SC. 3145; IVZ(N2), 3.1). About 1/4 segment of a flat base (bowl?) with the remains of a potter's mark on the lower inside wall. Hard, light pinkish-buff ware with some very fine lime and mica grits, evenly fired. Self slip in and out.
—. JR.Sh. (PM. F; TS. 3101; IVA, 1.1). Jar sherd. Ware description not available.
—. JR.Sh. (PM. F; TS. 3106; IVF, 1.1). Jar sherd. Ware description not available.

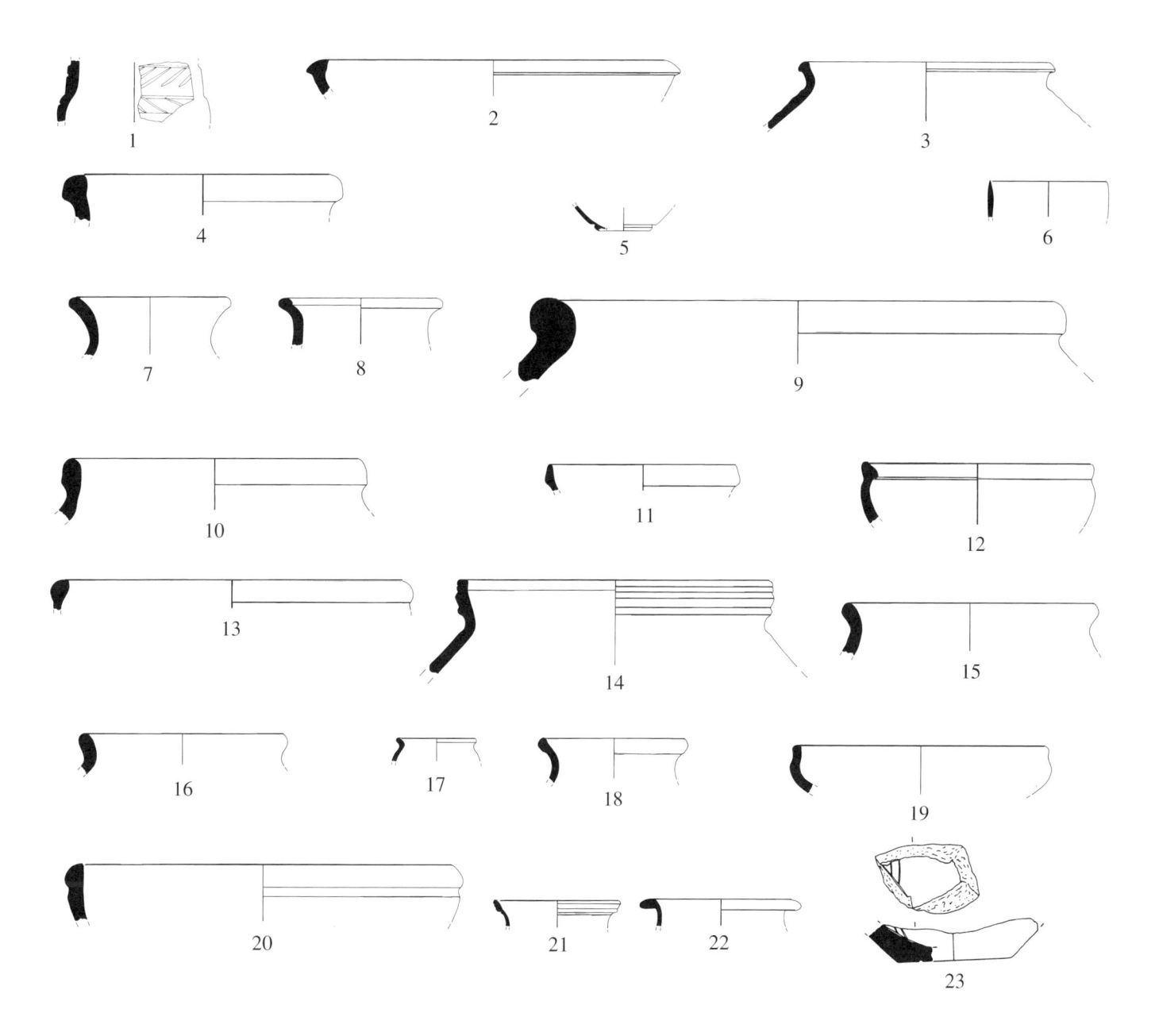

Figure 142. Pottery from Area IV, Lower and Upper Surface Layers (Phase 5; Periods E–D to D — Early–Middle Bronze Age to Middle Bronze Age I). Scale 1:5

Figure 142 (*cont.*). Pottery from Area IV, Lower and Upper Surface Layers (Phase 5; Periods E–D to D — Early–Middle Bronze Age to Middle Bronze Age I)

Other Type Series Examples:
- Area IVB — (1) BE. F.V.a (TS. 2691).
- Area IVG — (1) BR. E.III.j (TS. 2578).
- Area IVJ — (1) BR. C.I.e (TS. 1594).
- Area IVN — (1) BE. C.II (TS. 1648).
- Area IVO + R — (1) JR. E.II.x (TS. 2762).
- Area IVZ(N1) — (1) JR. F.II.a (TS. 2734).
- Area IVZ(N2) — (1) JR. D.V.c (TS. 2619), (2) JR. J.I.k (TS. 2708).

Other Study Collection Examples:
- Area IVA — (1) BR. A.II.e (SC. 710), (2) JR. A.III.a (SC. 894), (3) JR. B.IV.c (SC. 967), (4) JR. C.II.b (SC. 1016), (5) JR. E.I.e (SC. 2448), (6) JR. J.III.n (SC. 1446), (7) JR. K.I.c (SC. 1584), (8) JR. P.II.d (SC. 2461).
- Area IVB — (1) SBR. B.I.e (SC. 309), (2) SBR. B.I.f (SC. 353), (3) SBR. B.I.g (SC. 415), (4) SBR. B.I.i (SC. 526), (5) BR. A.I.d (SC. 706), (6) BR. F.I.d (SC. 769), (7) BR. F.I.d (SC. 1963), (8) SJR. A.I.a (SC. 2470), (9) SJR. C.II.k (SC. 2600), (10) JR. G.III.a (SC. 2054), (11) JR. J.I.l (SC. 2139), (12) JR. J.III.m (SC. 1439), (13) JR. J.III.m (SC. 2328), (14) SR. A.I.a (SC. 1955), (15) Ld. C.II.c (SC. 1937); Derived Hellenistic: (1) H.RSB. B.II.a (SC. 2850), (2) H.RSJ. A.I.a (SC. 2908).
- Area IVC — (1) BR. L.II.c (SC. 857), (2) JR. J.II.b (SC. 1353), (3) JR. K.I.g (SC. 1595).
- Area IVD — (1) SBR. B.I.e (SC. 323), (2) BR. F.II.a (SC. 792), (3) BE. F.III.a (SC. 1907).
- Area IVF — (1) SBR. B.I.g (SC. 373), (2) SBR. B.I.l (SC. 674), (3) SBR. D.I.a (SC. 625), (4) BR. L.II.b (SC. 847), (5) JR. B.III.a (SC. 933), (6) JR. J.II.j (SC. 2176), (7) JR. J.III.o (SC. 2349), (8) BE. E.II.d (SC. 3204), (9) BE. F.III.a (SC. 1914).
- Area IVG — (1) SBR. B.I.a (SC. 235), (2) SBR. B.I.g (SC. 370), (3) JR. C.V.b (SC. 1011), (4) JR. E.II.j (SC. 2033), (5) JR. O.III.f (SC. 2424), (6) BE. D.II (SC. 3130).
- Area IVH — (1) SBR. A.I.a (SC. 168), (2) SBR. B.I.c (SC. 277), (3) SBR. B.I.h (SC. 484), (4) BR. D.II.a (SC. 746), (5) BR. L.III.g (SC. 887), (6) SJR. D.I.c (SC. 2627), (7) JR. E.II.t (SC. 1167), (8) JR. G.I.c (SC. 2043), (9) JR. H.I.j (SC. 2078), (10) JR. J.III.m (SC. 1422), (11) JR. J.III.v (SC. 2361), (12) BE. D.II (SC. 3139), (13) BE. F.III.a (SC. 1913).
- Area IVK — (1) JR. O.II.k (SC. 2456).
- Area IVL — (1) SBR. B.I.h (SC. 462), (2) BR. L.III.c (SC. 864), (3) JR. A.III.d (SC. 1979), (4) JR. E.II.j (SC. 2024), (5) JR. J.IV.k (SC. 1552), (6) JR. K.I.d (SC. 1586), (7) JR. P.III.a (SC. 1759), (8) JR. (not typed, SC. 64).
- Area IVN — (1) SBR. B.I.a (SC. 239), (2) BR. (not typed, SC. 28), (3) SJR. C.II.k (SC. 2598), (4) SJR. D.III.b (SC. 2630), (5) JR. C.III.b (SC. 1008), (6) JR. D.II.c (SC. 1059), (7) JR. G.I.c (SC. 2041), (8) JR. H. (Gen. Type, SC. 41), (9) JR. J.II.l (SC. 2189), (10) JR. J.III.i (SC. 1407), (11) JR. J.III.m (SC. 1420), (12) JR. J.III.r (SC. 2354), (13) JR. J. (Gen. Type, SC. 108), (14) JR. P.III.a (SC. 1756).
- Area IVR — (1) JR. B.I.b (SC. 1981), (2) JR. J.I.h (SC. 2123), (3) JR. J.III.i (SC. 2297), (4) JR. J.III.o (SC. 2345).
- Area IVS — (1) SJR. B.III.e (SC. 3086), (2) JR. D.X.a (SC. 1125), (3) JR. E.I.a (SC. 1986), (4) JR. J.III.e (SC. 2241), (5) JR. J.III.m (SC. 2318), (6) JR. J.III.n (SC. 1463), (7) JR. J.III.n (SC. 2331), (8) BE. E.I.d (SC. 3162).
- Area IVX — (1) SBR. B.I.a (SC. 237), (2) SBR. B.I.h (SC. 447), (3) SBR. B.I.h (SC. 455), (4) SBR. B.I.h (SC. 468), (5) BR. D.I.a (SC. 745), (6) BR. D.II.a (SC. 747), (7) BR. D.V.a (SC. 3084), (8) BR. K.I.b (SC. 831), (9) BR. L.II.b (SC. 849), (10) BR. (not typed, SC. 32), (11) SJR. A.II.f (SC. 2489), (12) SJR. C.II.a (SC. 2577), (13) JR. B.IV.c (SC. 1985), (14) JR. B.IV.f (SC. 976), (15) JR. D.V.c (SC. 1090), (16) JR. E.I.a (SC. 1987), (17) JR. J.I.b (SC. 1305), (18) JR. J.I.b (SC. 2087), (19) JR. J.I.f (SC. 1347), (20) JR. J.I.i (SC. 2135), (21) JR. J.III.d (SC. 1378), (22) JR. J.III.n (SC. 1469), (23) JR. J.IV.g (SC. 1529), (24) CP. B.III.d (SC. 1862), (25) BE. F.V.b (SC. 1922).
- Area IVY — (1) JR. B.V.b (SC. 979), (2) JR. J.I.i (SC. 2134), (3) JR. J.III.a (SC. 2200), (4) JR. J.III.l (SC. 2313), (5) JR. J.III.m (SC. 2314), (6) JR. J.III.n (SC. 2337), (7) JR. K.I.c (SC. 1583).
- Area IVZ(N1) — (1) BR. F.II.a (SC. 796), (2) BR. K.I.b (SC. 829), (3) JR. A.II.a (SC. 891), (4) JR. A.III.a (SC. 893), (5) JR. A.III.b (SC. 896), (6) JR. A.III.c (SC. 898), (7) JR. B.III.a (SC. 934), (8) JR. C.II.b (SC. 1018), (9) JR. D.V.a (SC. 1067), (10) JR. E.I.c (SC. 1989), (11) JR. J.I.c (SC. 2111), (12) JR. J.I.i (SC. 2131), (13) JR. J.I.i (SC. 2132), (14) JR. J.III.d (SC. 1376), (15) JR. J.III.i (SC. 2295), (16) JR. J.III.m (SC. 1429), (17) JR. J.III.m (SC. 1432), (18) JR. J.III.q (SC. 1480), (19) JR. K.I.b (SC. 2387), (20) JR. O.I.f (SC. 2407), (21) JR. (not typed, SC. 60), (22) CP. B.IV.a (SC. 1863), (23) Jg. B.I.a (SC. 2759), (24) BE. H (SC. 3231), (25) ABS. A (SC. 3242).

Figure 142 (*cont.*). Pottery from Area IV, Lower and Upper Surface Layers (Phase 5; Periods E–D to D — Early–Middle Bronze Age to Middle Bronze Age I)

Area IVZ(N2) — (1) SBR. A.I.a (SC. 192), (2) SBR. B.I.e (SC. 304), (3) SBR. B.I.g (SC. 421), (4) BR. F.I.d (SC. 1964), (5) BR. L.II.a (SC. 846), (6) JR. A.III.a (SC. 1976), (7) JR. D.I.g (SC. 1054), (8) JR. D.VI.e (SC. 1118), (9) JR. E.II.m (SC. 2027), (10) JR. J.I.b (SC. 2103), (11) JR. J.III.n (SC. 1445), (12) JR. P.II.i (SC. 1739), (13) JR. P.III.f (SC. 1764), (14) Jg. A.I.b (SC. 1934), (15) BE. D.III (SC. 3145), (16) ABS. C (SC. 3246).

Derived Hellenistic Type Series Examples: (1) H.Jg. B.II.b (TS. 2712), (2) H.Lp. 2 (SW. 715).

Figure 143. Pottery from Area IV, Operation 7 (Phase 2A(a); Period F — Early Bronze Age IVa)

1. SBR. A.I.e (TS. 3569; Op. 7, 20.1, Room 36). About 1/6 rim and upper wall segment. Fairly fine pinkish-orange ware with small gold- and silver-colored mica and lime grits, evenly fired. Creamy-buff slip in and out.
2. SBR. A.II.c (TS. 3555; Op. 7, 19.1, Street). About 1/6 rim and most of wall profile. Fairly fine pinkish-orange ware with small gold- and silver-colored mica and lime grits, evenly fired. Creamy-buff slip in and out.
3. SBR. B.I.c (TS. 3548; Op. 7, 19.1, Street). About 1/10 rim and upper wall segment. Fine brownish-buff ware with gold- and silver-colored mica and lime grits, evenly fired. Self slip in and out.
4. SBR. B.I.i (TS. 3525; Op. 7, 18.1, Room 34). About 1/6 rim and upper wall segment. Fairly fine light pink ware with gold- and silver-colored mica, lime grits, and burned out vegetable temper, evenly fired. Creamy-buff slip out.
5. SBR. F.I.d (TS. 3550; Op. 7, 19.1, Street). About 1/5 rim and upper wall segment. Fine pinkish-brown ware with gold- and silver-colored mica and lime grits, evenly fired. Creamy-pink slip in and out.
6. SBR. G (TS. 3499; Op. 7, 17.2, Street). About 1/6 rim and upper wall (two non-joining segments). Fairly fine pinkish-buff ware with lime grits, evenly fired. Cream slip in and out.
7. SBR. G (TS. 3523; Op. 7, 18.1, Room 34). About 1/5 rim and upper wall segment. Hard, fine buff ware with fine black and white lime grits, and burned out vegetable temper, evenly fired. Self slip in and out.
8. BR. A.I.b (TS. 3573; Op. 7, 20.1, Room 36). About 1/12 rim and upper wall segment. Fine, light pinkish-buff ware with small lime grits, evenly fired. Self slip in and out.
9. BR. C.I.f (TS. 3580; Op. 7, 20.3, Town Wall). Small rim (3 cm) segment. Fine light pinkish-orange ware with small gold- and silver-colored mica and lime grits, evenly fired. Creamy-buff slip in and out. Horizontal line burnish in and out on extant fragment.
10. BR. D.II.d (TS. 3558; Op. 7, 19.1, Street). About 1/12 rim and wall segment. Fairly fine pinkish-buff ware with gold- and silver-colored mica and a few lime grits, evenly fired. Creamy-buff slip in and out.
11. BR. D.II.d (TS. 3562; Op. 7, 19.1, Street). Small rim and upper wall segment. Fairly fine pinkish-brown ware with gold- and silver-colored mica and black and white lime grits, evenly fired. Creamy-buff slip in and out.
12. BR. E.III.a (TS. 3547; Op. 7, 19.1, Street). Small rim (5 cm) and upper wall segment. Slightly coarse pinkish-orange ware with small gold- and silver-colored mica and lime grits, evenly fired. Creamy-buff slip in and out.
13. BR. E.III.g (TS. 3505; Op. 7, 18.1, Room 34). About 1/8 rim and upper wall segment. Hard, fine pinkish-orange ware with gold- and silver-colored mica and lime grits, evenly fired. Cream slip in and out.
14. BR. E.IV.b (TS. 3502; Op. 7, 18.1, Room 34). Small rim (4 cm) and upper wall segment. Fine pinkish-orange ware with small gold- and silver-colored mica, lime grits, and vegetable temper, evenly fired. Cream slip in and out.
15. BR. F.III.f (TS. 3506; Op. 7, 18.1, Room 34). Small rim and upper wall segment. Slightly coarse pinkish-buff ware with a few fine mica and lime grits, evenly fired. Cream slip in and out.
16. BR. F.IV.e (TS. 4178; Op. 7, 17.2, Street). About 1/10 rim and upper wall segment. Slightly coarse pinkish-brown ware with gold- and silver-colored mica and lime grits, evenly fired. Cream slip out and probably in, but inner surface very worn.
17. BR. G.I.e (TS. 3508; Op. 7, 18.1, Room 34). About 1/10 rim and upper wall segment. Hard, close pinkish-brown ware with fine gold- and silver-colored mica and white lime grits, unevenly fired light brown at surfaces. Self slip in and out. Irregular horizontal burnish on the folded-over rim and on the outer wall of the bowl below the line of the carination, which was applied at the leather-hard stage of manufacture.
18. BR. H.I.b (TS. 3545; Op. 7, 19.1, Street). Small rim (5 cm) and upper wall segment. Slightly coarse ware with fine gold- and silver-colored mica and lime grits; unevenly fired with gray core and orange-brown at surfaces. Cream slip in and out.
19. BR. J.I.b (TS. 3541 = TS. 4147; Op. 7, 19.1, Street and 7.2, Extramural). About 1/3 rim and upper wall segment (two joining and one non-joining sherds). Fairly coarse light purple-buff ware with silver-colored mica and white lime grits, evenly fired. Creamy-buff slip in and out.
20. BR. J.I.c (TS. 3556; Op. 7, 19.1, Street). Complete profile with small rim and wall segment and about 1/3 of base. Fine pinkish-orange ware with small gold- and silver-colored mica and lime grits, evenly fired. Creamy-buff slip in and out.
21. BR. L.I.a (TS. 3524; Op. 7, 18.1, Room 34). About 1/8 rim and upper wall segment. Slightly coarse pinkish-orange ware with fine gold- and silver-colored mica and lime grits, evenly fired. Cream slip out.
22. BR. L.I.a (TS. 3572; Op. 7, 20.1, Room 36). Small rim (5 cm) and upper wall segment. Hard, close pinkish-buff ware with a few gold- and silver-colored mica and lime grits, evenly fired. Cream slip in and out.
23. BR. M.III.a (TS. 3542; Op. 7, 19.1, Street). About 1/12 rim and upper wall segment. Hard, fairly fine pinkish-brown ware with gold- and silver-colored mica and small lime grits, evenly fired. Creamy-buff slip in and out.
24. BR. T (IP [G.3] A.II.a; TS. 3571; Op. 7, 20.1, Room 36). Small rim (4 cm) and upper wall segment with incised herringbone pattern decoration on top of rim. Fairly coarse brown ware with many gold- and silver-colored mica and lime grits, evenly fired. Similar to cooking pot ware. Self slip in and out.

Figure 143

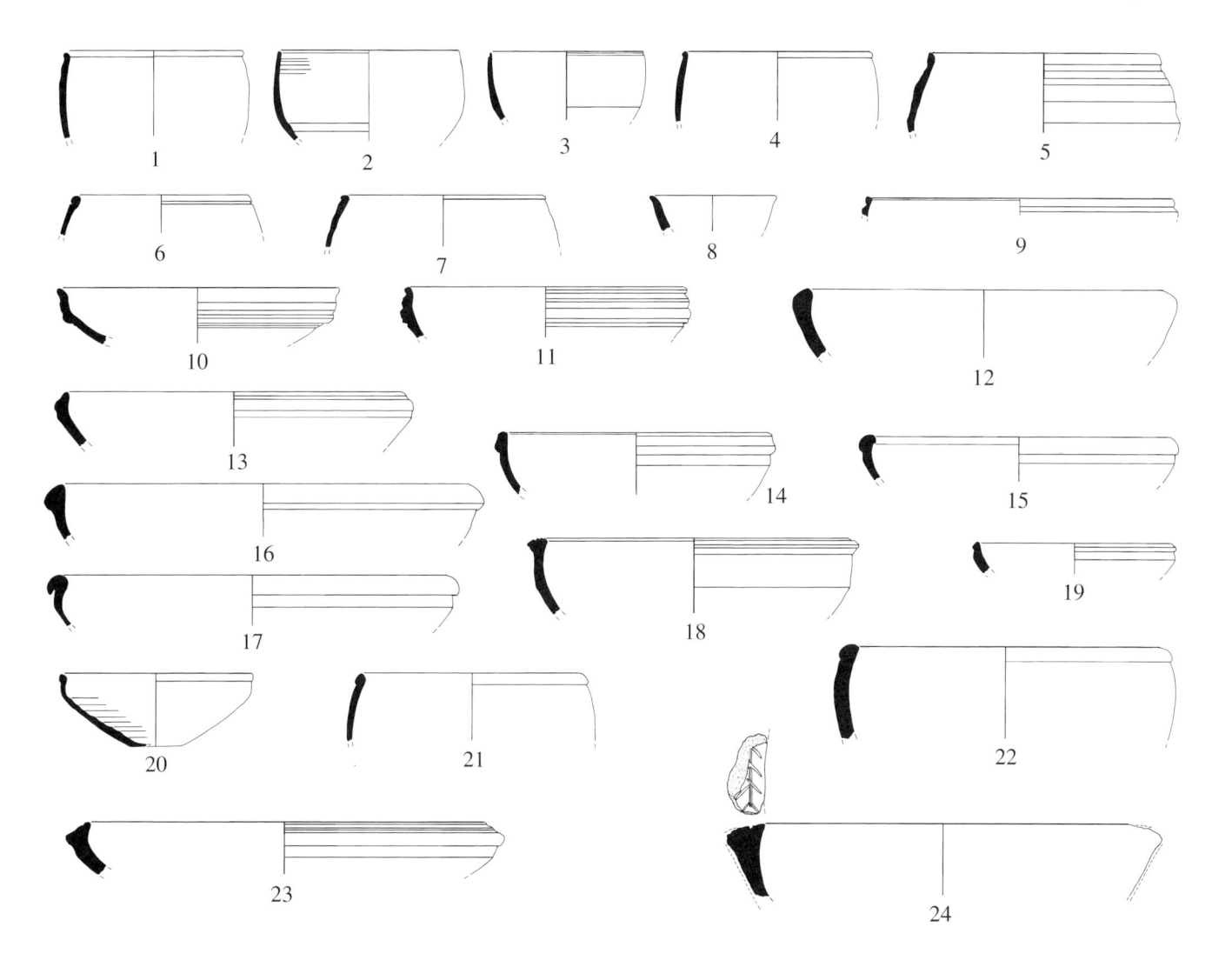

Pottery from Area IV, Operation 7 (Phase 2A(a); Period F — Early Bronze Age IVa). Scale 1:5

Figure 144. Pottery from Area IV, Operation 7 (Phase 2A(a); Period F — Early Bronze Age IVa) (*cont.*)

1. MJR. 4 (TS. 3533; Op. 7, 18.1, Room 34). About 1/3 body segment manufactured to imitate the shape of a pomegrante. Fairly fine creamy-buff ware with small lime grits, evenly fired. Cream slip out.
2. SJR. A.II.b (TS. 3570; Op. 7, 20.1, Room 36). About 1/8 rim and neck segment. Hard, fine grayware with very small silver-colored mica and lime grits, evenly fired. Self slip in and out. Irregular horizontal burnish below rim in and overall burnish on neck out.
3. SJR. A.III.a (TS. 3518; Op. 7, 18.1, Room 34). About 1/5 rim and upper wall segment. Fairly fine creamy-buff ware with lime grits and vegetable temper, evenly fired. Self slip in and out.
4. SJR. C.I.g (TS. 3561; Op. 7, 19.1, Street). About 1/6 rim and neck segment. Slightly coarse dark buff ware with many black and white lime grits, evenly fired. Creamy-green slip in and out.
5. SJR. C.II.k (TS. 3559; Op. 7, 19.1, Street). About 1/4 rim, neck, and body segment. Hard, fine light brown ware with a few very small mica and lime grits, evenly fired. Self slip in and out.
6. SJR. C.II.u (TS. 3498; Op. 7, 17.2, Street). About 1/10 rim and neck segment. Hard, fine grayware with gold- and silver-colored mica and small lime grits, evenly fired. Horizontal spaced-band burnish on edges of ribs below lip of rim out and on extant portion of the neck.
7. SJR. F (IP [G.3] B.III.a + B.IV.a; TS. 3582; Op. 7, 19.1, Street). About 1/5 rim with tool-incised linear decoration on outside wall, made before firing. Fairly fine pinkish-brown ware with lime grits, evenly fired. Cream slip in and out.
8. JR. E.I.d (TS. 3530; Op. 7, 18.1, Room 34 + 20.1, Room 36). About 3/4 rim, neck, and shoulder, consisting of seven joining segments. Fairly fine pinkish-buff ware with lime grits and vegetable temper, evenly fired. Creamy-buff slip out and just over rim in.
9. JR. F.III.g (TS. 3579; Op. 7, 20.3, Town Wall). Small rim (5 cm) and shoulder segment. Fine dark buff ware with small gold- and silver-colored mica and lime grits, evenly fired. Creamy-buff slip in and out.
10. JR. H.I.d (TS. 3575; Op. 7, 20.1, Room 36). Small rim and upper shoulder segment. Fairly coarse pinkish-orange ware with many fine gold- and silver-colored mica and black and white lime grits, evenly fired. Cream slip in and out.
11. JR. H.I.e (PM. D.22; TS. 3522; Op. 7, 18.1, Room 34). About 1/3 rim and shoulder segment with remains of a potter's mark incised on the shoulder before firing. Slightly coarse pinkish-orange ware with many gold- and silver-colored mica and lime grits, evenly fired. Cream slip out.
12. JR. H.II.e (TS. 3517; Op. 7, 18.1, Room 34). Small rim and shoulder segment with remains of a on the upper wall of the vessel. Slightly coarse pinkish-red ware with gold- and silver-colored mica and lime grits, evenly fired. Creamy-pink slip in and out.
13. JR. J.III.c (TS. 3512; Op. 7, 18.1, Room 34). About 1/4 rim and neck segment. Slightly coarse pinkish-buff ware with small gold- and silver-colored mica and lime grits, evenly fired. Creamy-buff slip in and out.
14. JR. J.III.d (TS. 3520; Op. 7, 18.1, Room 34). About 1/4 rim, neck, and shoulder segment. Fairly fine pinkish-buff ware with gold- and silver-colored mica and lime grits, evenly fired. Cream slip out and around upper portion of the neck inside.
15. JR. M.I.a (TS. 3531; Op. 7, 18.1, Room 34). Small rim and shoulder segment with complete strap handle. Hard, close buff ware with lime and vegetable temper, evenly fired. Creamy-green slip out.
16. JR. M.I.a (TS. 3567; Op. 7, 20.1, Room 36). Small rim (6 cm) and shoulder segment with complete strap handle. Fairly fine buff ware with lime and vegetable temper, evenly fired. Creamy-green slip out.

Figure 144

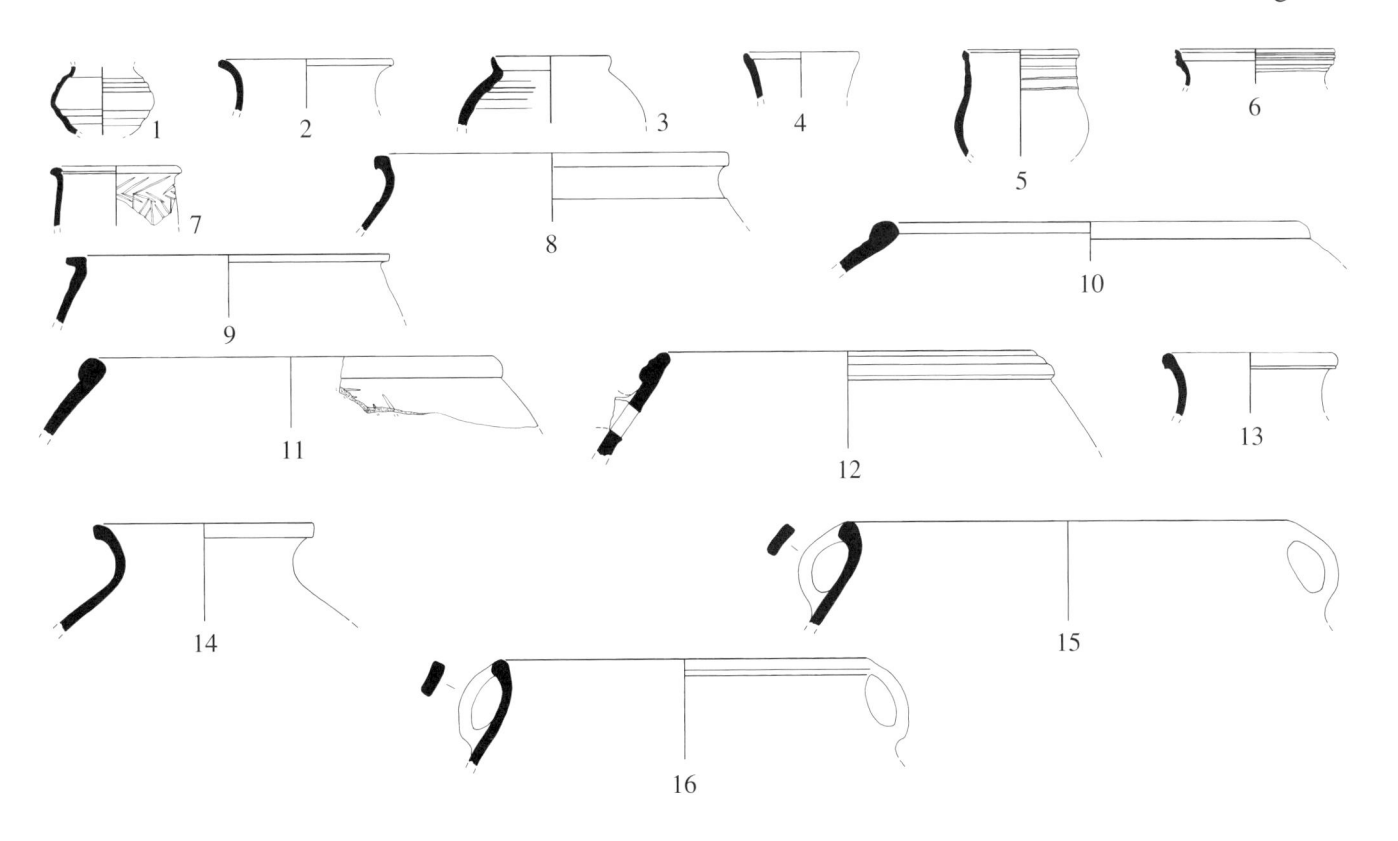

Pottery from Area IV, Operation 7 (Phase 2A(a); Period F — Early Bronze Age IVa) *(cont.)*. Scale 1:5

Figure 145. Pottery from Area IV, Operation 7 (Phase 2A(a); Period F — Early Bronze Age IVa) (*cont.*)

1. CP. A.I.f (TS. 3554; Op. 7, 19.1, Street). About 1/6 rim, neck, and shoulder segment. Fairly coarse dark pinkish-brown ware with many silver-colored mica and black and white lime grits, evenly fired. Self slip in and out. Heavily charred around the neck on both the inside and outside of the vessel.
2. CP. A.II.e (TS. 3507; Op. 7, 18.1, Room 34). About 1/8 rim and neck segment with complete triangular-shaped ledge handle attached to the rim. Slightly coarse light brown ware with many gold- and silver-colored mica and lime grits, evenly fired. Wet-smoothed and irregularly burnished at the leather-hard stage of manufacture on top of the handle and on both the inside and outside of the vessel wall.
3. CP. B.I.g (TS. 3549; Op. 7, 19.1, Street). Small rim and neck segment. Fairly coarse brown ware with many silver-colored mica and lime grits, evenly fired. Burnished self slip in and out; burnished vertically on neck out and irregular horizontal burnish on top of rim and on inside wall.
4. CP. B.II.a (TS. 3544; Op. 7, 19.1, Street). Small rim and neck segment, heavily charred on top of rim and on outside wall. Coarse pinkish-brown ware with many silver-colored mica and lime grits, evenly fired. Self slip in and out.
5. CP. B.II.b (TS. 3528; Op. 7, 18.1, Room 34). About 1/8 rim, neck, and shoulder segment. Fairly coarse dark brown ware with many translucent mica and black and white grits, evenly fired. Self slip in and out. Patch of burning of rim.
6. CP. B.II.e (TS. 3516; Op. 7, 18.1, Room 34). About 1/10 rim and shoulder segment with complete strap handle. Fairly coarse brown-buff ware with many gold- and silver-colored mica and black and white lime grits, evenly fired. Self slip in and out with traces of irregular burnish marks on top of rim and handle.
7. CP. B.II.e (TS. 3543; Op. 7, 19.1, Street). About 1/8 rim, neck, and shoulder segment, heavily charred on top of rim and on outside wall. Coarse pinkish-brown ware with many silver-colored mica and lime grits, evenly fired. Self slip in and out.
8. PS. A.II.c (TS. 3526; Op. 7, 18.1, Room 34). About 1/10 rim and portion of wall. Fairly fine pinkish-buff ware with fine gold- and silver-colored mica and a few lime grits, evenly fired. Cream slip out.
9. PS. B.I.a (TS. 3510; Op. 7, 18.1, Room 34). About 1/12 segment; complete profile; handmade. Fairly coarse pinkish-brown ware with gold- and silver-colored mica and lime grits, evenly fired. Creamy-buff slip in and out.
10. SR. A.II.b (TS. 3504; Op. 7, 18.1, Room 34). Small rim (4 cm) and upper wall segment with a portion of one pierced strainer hole extant. Fine pinkish-buff ware with small silver-colored mica and vegetable temper, evenly fired. Cream slip in and out.
11. SR. C.I.a (TS. 3519; Op. 7, 18.1, Room 34). About 1/12 rim and segment of upper wall with portions of two pierced strainer holes extant. Fine, light creamy-buff ware with gold-colored mica and a few lime grits, evenly fired. Self slip in and out.
12. BE. B.I (TS. 3529; Op. 7, 18.1, Room 34). Complete string-cut disk type base with small segment of vessel wall attached. Slightly coarse buff ware with a few white lime grits, evenly fired. Self slip in and out.
13. BE. B.I (TS. 3532; Op. 7, 18.1, Room 34). Nearly complete base with small segment of lower wall of vessel. Fine dark buff ware with lime and vegetable temper, evenly fired. Creamy-green slip in and out.
14. BE. E.I.c (TS. 3540; Op. 7, 19.1, Street). About 1/5 of base and portion of lower wall of vessel. Hard, close grayware with fine silver-colored mica and a few lime grits, evenly fired. Irregular-spaced horizontal burnish on outside wall made during leather-hard stage of manufacture.
15. BE. E.I.l (TS. 4179; Op. 7, 17.2, Street). Complete base except for chips at lip with remains of lower wall of vessel. Slightly coarse light pinkish-buff ware with many white lime and a few gold- and silver-colored mica grits, evenly fired. Self slip in and out.
16. BE. E.I.l (TS. 3546; Op. 7, 19.1, Street). Complete base and segment of lower wall of vessel. Slightly coarse greenish-grayware with very fine gold- and silver-colored mica and lime grits, evenly fired. Self slip in and out.
17. BE. F.V.a (TS. 3538; Op. 7, 19.1, Street). About 1/8 rim and segment of vessel wall. Fairly fine light pinkish-buff ware with gold- and silver-colored mica and lime grits, evenly fired. Cream slip in and out.
18. JR.Sh. (IP [G.4] F.I; TS. 3608; Op. 7, 17.2, Street). Jar sherd with portion of an animal motif incised on shoulder before firing. Fairly fine pinkish-orange ware with gold- and silver-colored mica and lime grits, evenly fired. Cream slip out.
19. JR.Sh. (IP [G.4] F.I; TS. 3609; Op. 7, 18.1, Room 34). Jar shoulder segment with portion of an animal's legs and feet incised before firing. Slightly coarse ware with many gold- and silver-colored mica and lime grits, unevenly fired with some gray core fired pinkish-orange at surfaces. Cream slip out.
20. JR.Sh. (IP [G.4] D.III; PM. D.20; TS. 3610; Op. 7, 21.1, Room 35). Jar shoulder sherd with tree or wheat stalk potter's mark incised on the outside wall before firing. Hard, close pinkish-buff ware with very fine gold- and silver-colored mica and lime grits, unevenly fired rose-pink on inner surface.
21. SV.5 (TS. 3557; Op. 7, 19.1, Street). One leg on fragment of a bowl base. Hard, close pinkish-buff ware with lime grits, evenly fired. Self slip in and out.
22. Hd. D.II (TS. 3511; Op. 7, 18.1, Room 34). Strap handle fragment. Fairly fine buff ware with lime grits, evenly fired. Cream slip.
23. JR.Sh. Pt. (TS. 4139; Op. 7, 18.1, Room 34). Fairly fine buff ware with a few silver-colored mica and many lime grits, evenly fired. Cream slip in and out. Spaced horizontal painted reddish-brown bands outside.
24. JR.Sh. Pt. (TS. 4138; Op. 7, 19.1, Street). Fairly fine buff ware with black and white lime grits, evenly fired. Cream slip in and out. Spaced horizontal painted reddish-brown bands outside.
—. JR.Sh. (PM. A.6; TS. 4200; Op. 7, 19.1, Street). Jar sherd.
—. JR.Sh. (PM. A.9; TS. 4199; Op. 7, 18.1, Room 34). Jar sherd.
—. JR.Sh. (PM. B.6; TS. 4198; Op. 7, 18.1, Room 34). Jar sherd.

Other Type Series Examples: (1) SBR. E.I.a (TS. 3539, Street), (2) SBR. G (TS. 3499, Street), (3) BR. D.VI.a (TS. 3568, Room 36), (4) BR. K.I.b (TS. 3514, Room 34), (5) JR. A.II.a (TS. 3537), (6) JR. D.VII.a (TS. 3552), (7) JR. E.II.n (TS. 3576), (8) JR. F.III.g (TS. 3503 = TS. 4166), (9) JR. H.I.f (TS. 3515), (10) JR. H.II.c (TS. 3551), (11) JR. H.III.e (TS. 3509), (12) JR. H.III.m (TS. 3553), (13) JR. H.III.y (TS. 3560), (14) JR. H.III.z (TS. 3574), (15) JR. J.II.c (TS. 3513), (16) JR. J.V.a (TS. 3500), (17) JR. N.I.a (TS. 3501), (18) Bt. A.I.b (TS. 3527), (19) BE. E.I.g (TS. 3578), (20) BE. E.I.h (TS. 3521), (21) BE. F.VIII.a (TS. 3577).

Figure 145

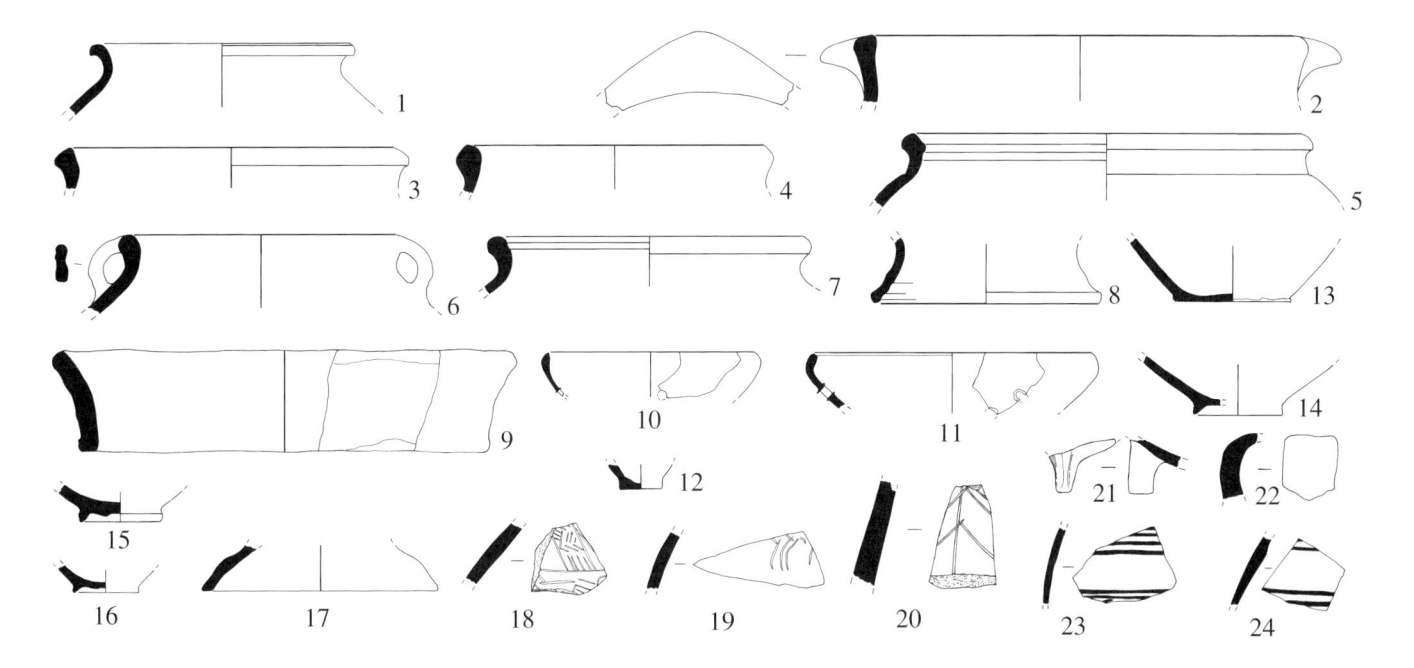

Pottery from Area IV, Operation 7 (Phase 2A(a); Period F — Early Bronze Age IVa) (*cont.*). Scale 1:5

Figure 146

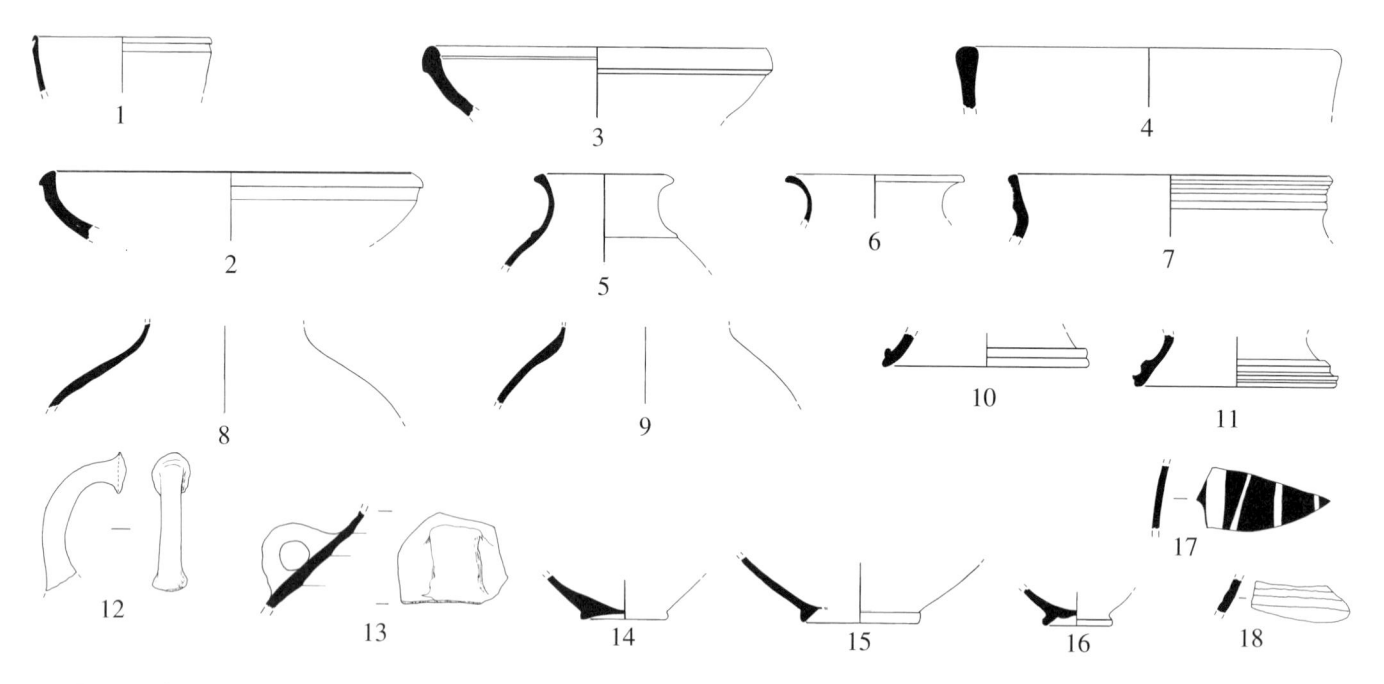

Pottery from Area IV, Operation 7 Extramural Areas (Phase 2A(b); Period F — Early Bronze Age IVa). Scale 1:5

1. SBR. B.I.q (TS. 4168; Op. 7, 13.1). About 1/10 rim and upper wall segment. Slightly coarse buff ware with a few gold- and silver-colored mica and lime grits, fairly evenly fired. Light creamy-green slip in and out.
2. BR. E.I.b (TS. 4141; Op. 7, 13.1). Small rim and upper wall segment. Slightly coarse buff ware with gold- and silver-colored mica and lime grits, evenly fired. Cream slip in and out.
3. BR. F.IV.e (TS. 4157; Op. 7, 17.1). Small rim (4.5 cm) and upper wall segment. Slightly coarse pinkish-orange ware with a few gold- and silver-colored mica and many white lime grits, evenly fired. Creamy-buff slip in and out.
4. BR. L.II.f (TS. 4180; Op. 7, 17.1). About 1/8 rim and upper wall segment. Fairly fine pinkish-buff ware with gold- and silver-colored mica and lime grits, evenly fired. Creamy-green slip out and on top of rim.
5. SJR. B.I.b (TS. 4142; Op. 7, 13.1). About 1/2 rim, neck, and shoulder segment. Fine grayware with small silver-colored mica and lime grits, evenly fired. Self slip in and out. Closely burnished self slip out and on top of rim.
6. SJR. C.I.f (TS. 3496; Op. 7, 17.1). About 1/6 rim and neck segment. Hard, fine grayish-buff ware with small gold- and silver-colored mica and a few white lime grits, evenly fired. Self slip in and out. Charred patch on rim in and out.
7. JR. D.II.c (TS. 4167; Op. 7, 13.1). Small rim (4 cm) and neck segment. Fairly fine pinkish-buff ware with a few gold-colored mica and lime grits, evenly fired. Cream slip in and out.
8. JR. J.III.o (TS. 4156; Op. 7, 17.1). Segment of lower neck and shoulder. Fine metallic-like grayish-brown ware with lime grits and vegetable temper, evenly fired. Thick creamy-green slip out.
9. JR. L.II.a (TS. 4155; Op. 7, 17.1). Segment of lower neck and shoulder. Fairly coarse "layered" ware with gray core fired pinkish-brown at surfaces; gold- and silver-colored mica with a few lime inclusions. Irregular-spaced thin lines of horizontal burnish on self slip out.
10. PS. B.I.b (TS. 4181; Op. 7, 17.1). About 1/12 rim and small wall segment. Fine light pinkish-buff ware with small gold- and silver-colored mica and lime grits, evenly fired. Cream slip in and out.
11. PS. B.I.b (TS. 4158; Op. 7, 17.1). About 1/10 rim and wall segment. Fairly fine buff ware with a few small silver-colored mica and lime grits, evenly fired. Creamy-buff slip in and out.
12. FL. A.II.a (TS. 3493; Op. 7, 17.1). Complete loop handle of a flask. Hard, fairly fine brown-buff ware with silver-colored mica and lime grits, evenly fired. Self slip.
13. Hd. D.II (TS. 3497; Op. 7, 17.1). Jar shoulder sherd with complete strap handle. Slightly coarse buff ware with a few gold- and silver-colored mica and lime grits, evenly fired. Creamy-buff slip in and out.
14. BE. B.II (TS. 4169; Op. 7, 17.1). About 1/2 base and lower wall segment of vessel. Fairly fine brownish-buff ware with gold- and silver-colored mica and small lime grits, evenly fired. Creamy-buff slip out.
15. BE. E.I.d (TS. 4183; Op. 7, 13.1). About 1/6 rim and wall segment. Hard, ringing, fairly fine pinkish-brown ware with gold- and silver-colored mica and lime grits, evenly fired. Self slip in and out. Irregular horizontal burnish on outside wall.
16. BE. E.I.k (TS. 4170; Op. 7, 17.1). Complete base profile, except for 2/3 of the lip of the rim, which was chipped off in antiquity. Slightly coarse creamy-green ware with fine lime grits, evenly fired. Self slip in and out.
17. JR.Sh. Pt. (TS. 4140; Op. 7, 17.1). Jar body sherd. Fairly fine pinkish-orange ware with very small gold- and silver-colored mica and a few lime grits, evenly fired. Buff slip with painted purple-brown decoration on top.
18. JR.Sh. Bur. (TS. 4184; Op. 7, 13.1). Small shoulder sherd. Fairly fine pinkish-red ware with many fine gold- and silver-colored mica and white lime grits, evenly fired. Irregular-spaced horizontal line burnish on self slip out.

Other Type Series Examples: (1) JR. A.III.c (TS. 3494), (2) Jg. C (TS. 3495).

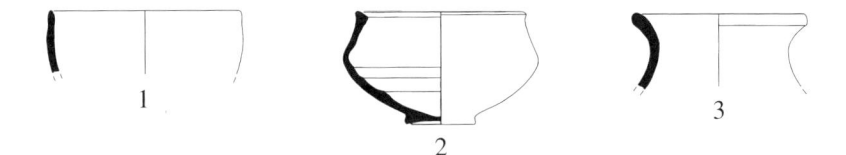

Figure 147

Pottery from Area IV, Operation 7, Room 40, Pit (Phase 2B(a); Period E — Early Bronze Age IVb). Scale 1:5

1. SBR. B.I.j (TS. 3563; Op. 7, 19.2). About 1/5 rim and upper wall segment. Fairly fine pinkish-buff ware with small gold- and silver-colored mica and lime grits, evenly fired. Creamy-buff slip in and out.
2. SBR. F.I.b (TS. 3564; Op. 7, 19.2). About 1/10 rim, complete base, and segment of wall mended to complete profile. Slightly coarse grayware with silver-colored mica and lime grits, evenly fired. Self slip in and out. Irregular horizontal burnish on outside wall.
3. SJR. B.I.a (TS. 3566; Op. 7, 19.2). About 1/3 rim and neck segment. Fairly coarse grayish-green ware with mica and lime grits, evenly fired. Thick, discolored, creamy-green slip in and out.

Another Type Series Example: (1) BE. E.I.j (TS. 3565).

Figure 148. Pottery from Area IV, Operation 7, Rooms 37–40, Courtyard, and Extramural (Phase 2B(b); Period E — Early Bronze Age IVb)

1. SBR. A.I.b (TS. 4108; Op. 7, 3.1, Courtyard). About 1/10 rim and upper wall segment. Fine buff ware with gold- and silver-colored mica and lime grits, evenly fired. Self slip in and out.
2. BR. A.I.d (TS. 4109; Op. 7, 3.1, Courtyard). Small rim and upper wall segment. Slightly coarse pinkish-buff ware with gold- and silver-colored mica and lime grits, evenly fired. Creamy-buff slip in and out.
3. BR. C.I.d (TS. 4129; Op. 7, 7.2, Extramural). About 1/12 rim and upper wall segment. Fairly fine buff-brown ware with a few small gold- and silver-colored mica and lime grits, evenly fired. Creamy-buff slip in and out.
4. BR. C.I.e (TS. 4145; Op. 7, 7.2, Extramural). Small rim and upper wall segment. Slightly coarse light pink ware with gold- and silver-colored mica and lime grits, evenly fired. Cream slip in and out.
5. BR. E.I.a (TS. 4163; Op. 7, 7.2, Extramural). About 1/10 rim and most of wall profile. Fairly coarse pinkish-buff ware with many gold- and silver-colored mica and lime grits, evenly fired. Creamy-green slip in and out.
6. BR. E.I.c (TS. 4173; Op. 7, 7.1, Room 39). About 1/12 rim and most of wall profile. Slightly coarse light pinkish-buff ware with gold-colored mica and lime grits, evenly fired. Self slip in and out.
7. BR. E.III.d (TS. 4112; Op. 7, 3.1, Courtyard). About 1/7 rim and most of wall profile. Fairly fine pinkish-buff ware with many gold- and silver-colored mica grits, evenly fired. Creamy-buff slip in and out.
8. BR. F.III.a (TS. 4111; Op. 7, 3.1, Courtyard). About 1/10 rim and upper wall segment. Hard, close pink ware with gold- and silver-colored mica and white lime grits, evenly fired. Creamy-pink slip in and out.
9. BR. F.III.g (TS. 4113; Op. 7, 3.1, Courtyard). Small rim and upper wall segment. Fairly fine pinkish-buff ware with gold- and silver-colored mica and black and white lime grits, evenly fired. Creamy-buff slip in and out.
10. BR. H.III.a (TS. 4171; Op. 7, 7.1, Room 39). Small rim (4 cm) and most of wall profile. Fairly fine light pinkish-brown ware with a few gold- and silver-colored mica and lime grits, evenly fired. Cream slip in and out.
11. BR. L.I.a (TS. 4176; Op. 7, 7.1, Room 39). Small rim and upper wall segment. Fairly fine pinkish-brown ware with a few mica and lime grits, fired pink in. Creamy-buff slip out and just over rim in.
12. BR. L.I.e (TS. 4110; Op. 7, 3.1, Courtyard). Small rim and upper wall segment. Hard, close pink ware with gold- and silver-colored mica and lime grits, evenly fired. Self slip in and out.
13. BR. L.III.b (TS. 4144; Op. 7, 7.2, Extramural). About 1/14 rim and upper wall segment. Fairly coarse ware with gold- and silver-colored mica and many lime grits, fired gray in and pinkish-brown out. Self slip in and out.
14. BR. T (TS. 4133; Op. 7, 11.1, Room 38). Small rim (5 cm) and upper wall segment. Fairly fine light pink ware with gold- and silver colored mica and lime grits, evenly fired. Creamy-pink slip in and out.
15. SJR. A.I.c (TS. 4161; Op. 7, 7.2, Extramural). About 1/5 rim and shoulder segment. Slightly coarse gray-green ware with fine lime grits, evenly fired. Self slip in and out.
16. SJR. A.III.a (TS. 4151; Op. 7, 16.1, Extramural). Small rim and upper body segment. Fine pinkish-brown ware with gold- and silver-colored mica and lime grits, evenly fired. Self slip in and out.
17. SJR. A.III.c (TS. 4175; Op. 7, 7.1, Room 39). Small rim (3.5 cm) and shoulder segment. Fairly fine light pinkish-brown ware with gold- and silver-colored mica and lime grits, evenly fired. Creamy-buff slip in and out.
18. SJR. B.III.f (TS. 4132; Op. 7, 11.1, Room 38). About 1/3 rim and neck segment. Fairly fine brownish-grayware with gold- and silver-colored mica and lime grits, evenly fired. Self slip in and out. Irregular horizontal and vertical spaced line burnish on the outside of the neck.
19. JR. C.I.g (TS. 4118; Op. 7, 7.1, Room 39). Small rim and neck segment. Fairly fine pinkish-buff ware with fine lime grits, evenly fired. Creamy-buff slip in and out.
20. JR. C.VI.a (TS. 4152; Op. 7, 16.1, Extramural). About 1/10 rim and neck segment. Slightly coarse greenish-buff ware with black and white lime grits, evenly fired. Creamy-green slip in and out.
21. JR. D.V.d (TS. 4159; Op. 7, 7.1, Room 39). About 1/16 rim and small shoulder segment. Slightly coarse light pink ware with gold- and silver-colored mica and lime grits, evenly fired. Creamy-green slip in and out.
22. JR. D.VI.c (TS. 4172; Op. 7, 7.1, Room 39). About 1/10 rim and upper shoulder segment. Hard, fairly fine reddish-brown ware with many gold- and silver-colored mica and lime grits, evenly fired. Buff slip in and out. Partially charred outside.
23. JR. E.II.e (TS. 4122; Op. 7, 7.1, Room 39). About 1/8 rim and upper shoulder segment. Slightly coarse buff ware with fine gold- and silver-colored mica and lime grits, evenly fired. Creamy-buff slip in and out.
24. JR. H.I.j (TS. 4119; Op. 7, 7.1, Room 39). Small rim and upper shoulder segment. Fairly fine pinkish-buff ware with fine gold- and silver-colored mica and lime grits, evenly fired. Creamy-buff slip in and out.
25. JR. J.I.a (TS. 4160; Op. 7, 7.2, Extramural). About 1/8 rim and neck segment. Fine light pinkish-brown ware with many gold-colored mica and some lime grits, evenly fired. Self slip in and out.

Figure 148

Pottery from Area IV, Operation 7, Rooms 37–40, Courtyard, and Extramural (Phase 2B(b); Period E — Early Bronze Age IVb). Scale 1:5

Figure 148 (*cont.*). Pottery from Area IV, Operation 7, Rooms 37–40, Courtyard, and Extramural (Phase 2B(b); Period E — Early Bronze Age IVb)

26. JR. J.III.c (TS. 4120; Op. 7, 7.1, Room 39). About 1/2 rim, neck, and shoulder segment. Slightly coarse pinkish-buff ware with gold- and silver-colored mica and lime grits, evenly fired. Creamy-buff slip in and out.
27. JR. J.III.k (TS. 4146; Op. 7, 7.2, Extramural). About 1/8 rim, neck, and shoulder segment. Slightly coarse light pinkish-orange ware with gold- and silver-colored mica and lime grits, unevenly fired with some gray core. Creamy-green slip out and over rim interior.
28. JR. O.II.f (TS. 4123; Op. 7, 7.1, Room 39). About 1/16 rim and neck segment. Hard, close pinkish-brown ware with gold- and silver-colored mica and lime grits, evenly fired. Creamy-buff slip out; inside surface flaked off.
29. JR. O.II.h (TS. 4137; Op. 7, 7.1, Room 39). Small rim (4 cm) and neck segment. Slightly coarse light pink ware with a few mica and black and white lime grits, evenly fired. Thick cream slip in and out.
30. JR. P.II.a (TS. 4121; Op. 7, 7.1, Room 39). About 1/12 rim, neck, and shoulder segment. Slighly coarse pinkish-brown ware with fine gold- and silver-colored mica and lime grits, evenly fired. Creamy-buff slip in and out.
31. JR. S (TS. 4164; Op. 7, 7.2, Extramural). Small rim and upper wall segment. Slightly coarse pinkish-brown ware with many gold- and silver-colored mica and a few lime grits, evenly fired. Cream slip in and out.
32. FL. B.I.a (TS. 4148; Op. 7, 7.2, Extramural). About 1/4 rim and upper shoulder segment. Fine light buff ware with mica and lime grits, evenly fired. Self slip in and out. Soil stained reddish-brown in and out.
33. Bt. A.I.b (TS. 4149; Op. 7, 7.1, Room 39). Complete rim and portion of neck. Fine grayware with silver-colored mica and fine lime grits, evenly fired. Self slip in and out. Closely-spaced horizontal burnish on neck out and around flange of rim inside.
34. Lp. A.II.a.1 (TS. 3309; Op. 7, 4.7, Room 40). About 1/4 rim and upper wall segment. Fairly fine pinkish-buff ware with small gold- and silver-colored mica and lime grits, evenly fired. Creamy-buff slip in and out.
35. Ld. C.III.b (TS. 4177; Op. 7, 7.1, Room 39). About 1/12 rim and wall segment. Fine light pink ware with gold- and silver-colored mica and lime grits, evenly fired. Self slip in and out.
36. PS. B.I.b (TS. 4162; Op. 7, 7.2, Extramural). Small rim (4 cm) and wall segment. Fairly coarse buff ware with lime grits, evenly fired. Creamy-buff slip in and out.
37. BE. F.III.a (TS. 4117; Op. 7, 7.1, Room 39). Small segment. Fine buff ware with gold- and silver-colored mica and some lime grits, evenly fired. Self slip in and out.
38. BE. F.IV.a (TS. 4182; Op. 7, 15.1, Extramural). About 1/2 rim and wall segment. Fine light pink ware with a few gold-colored mica and small lime grits, evenly fired. Creamy-buff slip in and out.
39. BE. F.IV.b (TS. 3307; Op. 7, 4.7, Room 40). Segment with finger-impressed rope band applied around join of stand and vessel attached to the top. Hard, fairly fine pinkish-buff ware evenly fired. Self slip in and out.
40. BE. F.V.a (TS. 4174; Op. 7, 7.1, Room 39). Small rim and wall segment. Slightly coarse pinkish-buff ware with a few mica and lime grits, evenly fired. Creamy-green slip in and out.
41. BE. F.VIII.a (TS. 4165; Op. 7, 7.2, Extramural). Segment with complete incised rope band between pedestal base and lower portion of the vessel wall attached above it. Fairly coarse pinkish-brown ware with gold- and silver-colored mica and lime grits, evenly fired. Buff slip in and out.
42. JR.Sh. (IP [G.4] A.IV.a; TS. 3199; Op. 7, 11.1, Room 38). Shoulder and girth fragment with cylinder seal-impressed linear herringbone pattern in two bands. Slightly coarse dark grayware with gold- and silver-colored mica and lime grits, evenly fired. The wall below the impressed design is completely burnished.
43. BR.Sh. (PM. D.14; TS. 3305; Op. 7, 2.3, Room 37). Bowl body segment with a potter's mark incised just above the base on the outside wall before firing. Fairly fine pinkish-orange ware with gold- and silver-colored mica and lime grits, evenly fired. Self slip in and out.
44. JR.Sh. (IP [G.4] G.I.a; TS. 3607; Op. 7, 11.1, Room 38). Jar shoulder fragment with portions of geometric designs on two registers, incised before firing. Slightly coarse pinkish-buff ware with gold-colored mica and lime grits, evenly fired. Dark buff self slip in and out.
45. JR.Sh. (IP [G.3] B.III.a; TS. 3304; Op. 7, 2.3, Room 37). Jar shoulder sherd with diagonal short lines incised in two registers before firing. Slightly coarse grayware with silver-colored mica and lime grits, evenly fired. Self slip in and out. Irregular horizontal burnish on extant wall below incised registers.
46. JR.Sh. (IP [G.3] B.III.a; TS. 4153; Op. 7, 7.2, Extramural). Jar shoulder sherd with diagonal short lines incised in two registers before firing. Fairly coarse pinkish-brown ware with many lime grits, evenly fired. Creamy-green slip out.

Other Type Series Examples: Room 37— (1) MBR. D.II.a (SW. 810), Room 40— (1) BR. A.II.g (TS. 3310), (2) JR. D.VIII.f (TS. 3308).

Figure 149

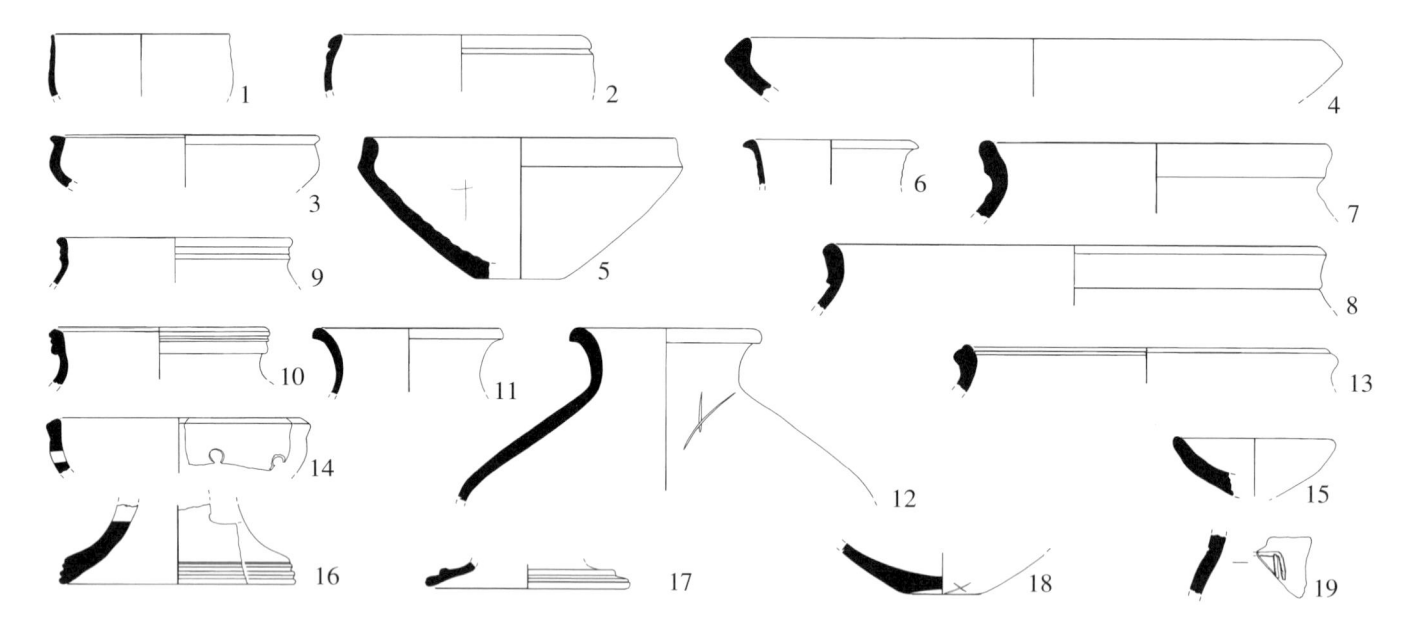

Pottery from Area IV, Operation 7, Courtyard, and Extramural (Phase 3; Period E — Early Bronze Age IVb). Scale 1:5

1. SBR. A.II.c (TS. 4114; Op. 7, 4.1). About 1/8 rim and upper wall segment. Fairly fine pinkish-buff ware with gold- and silver-colored mica and black and white lime grits, evenly fired. Creamy-buff slip in and out.
2. BR. A.II.e (TS. 4127; Op. 7, 10.1). About 1/10 rim and upper wall segment. Slightly coarse greenish-buff ware with black and white lime grits, evenly fired. Creamy-green slip in and out.
3. BR. E.I.b (TS. 4128; Op. 7, 10.1). About 1/10 rim and upper wall segment. Slightly coarse light pinkish-brown ware with lime grits, evenly fired. Creamy-buff slip in and out.
4. BR. E.III.a (TS. 4126; Op. 7, 10.1). About 1/14 rim and upper wall segment. Slightly coarse pinkish-buff ware with a few silver-colored mica and lime grits, evenly fired. Creamy-green slip in and out.
5. BR. E.III.h (PM. C.14; TS. 3306; Op. 7, 4.1). About 1/5 segment of nearly complete profile with remains of a potter's mark incised on the inside wall before firing. Fairly coarse pinkish-buff ware with black and white lime grits, evenly fired. Creamy-buff slip in and out.
6. SJR. C.II.k (TS. 4134; Op. 7, 9.1). About 1/5 rim and neck segment. Fine pinkish-brown ware with small white lime grits, evenly fired. Self slip in and out. Irregular-spaced horizontal line burnish out on neck, on top of rim, and on extant portion of the inside of the neck.
7. JR. A.II.a (TS. 4082; Op. 7, 4.1). About 1/6 rim, neck, and shoulder segment. Fairly fine, close, buff ware with gold- and silver-colored mica and lime grits, evenly fired. Buff slip in and out.
8. JR. B.III.d (TS. 4150; Op. 7, 10.1). About 1/16 rim and shoulder segment. Slightly coarse pinkish-buff ware with gold- and silver-colored mica and small lime grits, evenly fired. Creamy-buff slip out.
9. JR. C.II.d (TS. 4080 = TS. 4115; Op. 7, 4.1). About 1/10 rim and shoulder segment. Fairly fine pinkish-buff ware with gold- and silver-colored mica and lime grits, evenly fired. Creamy-buff slip in and out.
10. JR. C.V.e (TS. 4131; Op. 7, 10.1). About 1/4 rim, neck, and upper shoulder segment. Fairly fine pinkish-buff ware with gold- and silver-colored mica and lime grits, evenly fired. Cream slip out and on top of rim.
11. JR. J.II.g (TS. 4081; Op. 7, 4.1). About 1/5 rim and neck segment. Slightly coarse, hard, greenish-grayware with lime grits, evenly fired. Grayish-green self slip in and out.
12. JR. J.III.a (PM. C.14; TS. 3302; Op. 7, 2.1, Extramural). About 2/3 rim, neck, and shoulder segment with a potter's mark incised on the shoulder before firing. For ware, compare Phase 2A Type Series example from Area IVJ (SW. 552).
13. CP. B.II.f (TS. 4116; Op. 7, 4.1). Small rim and neck segment. Slightly coarse light brown ware with many silver-colored mica and black and white lime grits, evenly fired. Self slip in and out.
14. SR. B.I.a (TS. 4136; Op. 7, 9.1). About 1/8 rim and upper wall segment with remains of two pierced strainer holes in the wall. Slightly coarse light pink ware with gold- and silver-colored mica and lime grits, evenly fired. Creamy-buff slip in and out.
15. CBR. A.II.a (TS. 4135; Op. 7, 9.1). About 1/12 rim and most of wall profile. Handmade. Fairly coarse pinkish-brown ware with many small gold- and silver-colored mica and lime grits, evenly fired. Buff slip in and out.
16. WPS. C (TS. 4143; Op. 7, 10.1). About 1/4 rim and wall segment with small portion of window in the wall. Slightly coarse pinkish-brown ware with lime grits, evenly fired. Cream slip in and out.
17. Ld. C.III.c (TS. 4083; Op. 7, 4.1). Small segment. Fairly fine pinkish-buff ware with fine gold-colored mica and lime grits, evenly fired. Self slip in and out.

Figure 150

18. BE. C.I (PM. C.14; TS. 3301; Op. 7, Surf. 2). About 1/2 base and lower wall of vessel with a potter's mark incised on outside wall before firing. Slightly coarse pinkish-buff ware with gold- and silver-colored mica and lime grits, evenly fired. Self slip in and out.
19. JR.Sh. (IP [G.4] F.I; PM. C.4; TS. 4154; Op. 7, 10.1). Jar shoulder fragment with portion of a potter's mark incised on the shoulder before firing. Fairly fine light pink ware with a few small gold-colored mica and lime grits, evenly fired. Creamy-green slip in and out.

Another Type Series Example: (1) JR. O.III.g (TS. 3303).

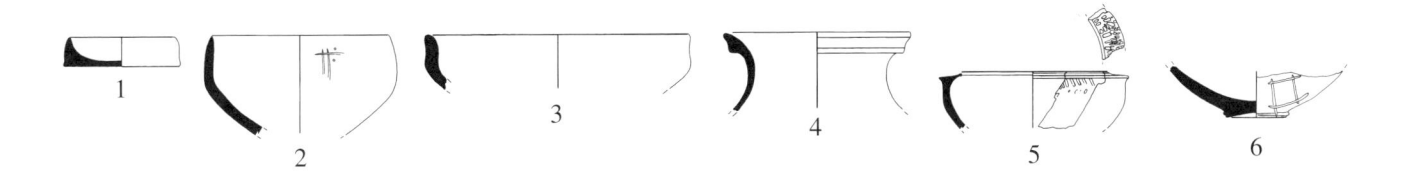

Pottery from Area IV, Operation 7 (Phase 4; Period E–D — Early–Middle Bronze Age). Scale 1:5

1. MBR. B.I.a (TS. 3298; Op. 7, Surf. 1.1). About 1/2 segment of complete profile. Fairly fine yellow-buff ware with gold- and silver-colored mica and lime grits, evenly fired. Self slip in and out.
2. SBR. B.I.o (PM. D.23; TS. 3299; Op. 7, Surf. 1.1). Segments, about 1/4 rim, mended to complete wall profile with complete potter's mark incised on the upper outside wall. Fairly coarse pinkish-buff ware with gold- and silver-colored mica and gray and white lime grits, evenly fired. Light creamy-green slip in and out.
3. BR. E.III.h (TS. 4077; Op. 7, Surf. 1.1). Small rim (2.5 cm) and upper wall segment. Slightly coarse dark buff ware with gold- and silver-colored mica and lime grits, evenly fired. Buff slip in and out.
4. JR. J.III.m (TS. 4078; Op. 7, Surf. 1.1). About 1/3 rim, neck, and upper shoulder segment. Fairly fine light pink ware with gold- and silver-colored mica and lime grits, evenly fired. Buff slip in and out.
5. Lp. A.II.a.1 (IP [G.4]) A.III.a; TS. 3297; Op. 7, Surf. 1.1). Small rim and upper wall segment. Irregular tool-stabbed design on top of the rim and one band of an incised pattern below the rim on the outside wall. Fairly fine grayware with fine silver-colored mica and small white lime grits, evenly fired.
6. BE. B.II (PM. D.14; TS. 4079; Op. 7, Surf. 1.1). Complete base and lower wall of vessel with a potter's mark incised outside before firing. Slightly coarse pinkish-brown ware with gold- and silver-colored mica and lime grits, evenly fired. Buff slip out; inside surface worn away.

Other Type Series Examples: (1) MBR. D.I.a (TS. 3300), (2) BE. F.V.b (TS. 3311).

Figure 151. Pottery from Area IV, Operation 8, Room 29 (Phase 3; Period E — Early Bronze Age IVb)

1. SBR. F.I.a (TS. 3595; Op. 8, 3.3). About 1/10 rim and most of wall profile. Slightly coarse buff ware with gold-colored mica and lime grits, evenly fired. Cream slip in and out.
2. SBR. G (TS. 3326; Op. 8, 3.2). About 1/2 segment of complete profile. Fairly coarse pinkish-buff ware with lime and mica grits, evenly fired. Cream slip in and out.
3. SBR. G (PM. C.14; TS. 3345; Op. 8, 3.4). About 1/6 rim and 1/2 base mended to complete profile with X-shaped potter's mark incised on outer wall before firing. Slightly coarse buff ware with gray and white lime grits, evenly fired. Creamy-buff slip in and out.
4. BR. K.I.b (TS. 3597; Op. 8, 3.3). About 1/12 rim and upper wall segment. Fairly fine grayware with very small silver-colored mica and lime grits, evenly fired. Self slip in and out. Irregular-spaced horizontal band burnish on outside wall, top of rim, and on inside wall.
5. BR. K.I.b (TS. 4009; Op. 8, 3.3). Small rim and upper wall segment. For ware, compare similar example above (TS. 3597, fig. 151:4).
6. SJR. A.I.a (TS. 3593; Op. 8, 3.2). About 1/8 rim and upper shoulder segment. Fairly fine pinkish-orange ware with gold- and silver-colored mica and a few lime grits, evenly fired. Creamy-buff slip out.
7. SJR. A.III.a (TS. 3594; Op. 8, 3.2). About 1/8 rim and upper wall segment. Slightly coarse pinkish-buff ware with a few small gold- and silver-colored mica and lime grits, evenly fired. Creamy-buff slip in and out.
8. SJR. B.I.a (TS. 3327; Op. 8, 3.2). About 1/2 rim, neck, and shoulder segment. Fairly coarse buff ware with lime and a few mica grits, evenly fired. Probable self slip, but much worn.
9. JR. C.II.a (TS. 3596; Op. 8, 3.3). Small rim (4.5 cm) and upper shoulder segment. Fairly fine pinkish-orange ware with gold colored mica and lime grits, evenly fired. Self slip in and out.
10. JR. D.I.e (TS. 3600; Op. 8, 3.4). Large rim, neck, and upper wall segment. For ware, compare Phase 5 Type Series example from Area IIIC (TS. 460).
11. JR. S (TS. 4005; Op. 8, 3.4). Most of body and 1/2 segment of shoulder with large piece of bitumen used to patch a hole in the wall of the vessel. Slightly coarse buff ware with black and white lime and fine gold-colored grits, fairly evenly fired. Creamy-buff slip out.
12. FL. B.I.a (TS. 3601; Op. 8, 3.4). Complete rim and neck segment with small portion of shoulder. Fine pinkish-buff ware with black and white lime and vegetable temper, evenly fired. Creamy-buff slip in and out.
13. CP. A.II.c (TS. 3599; Op. 8, 3.3). About 1/7 rim, neck, and shoulder segment. Coarse brown ware with very many translucent mica and black and white lime grits, evenly fired. Self slip in and out; heavily burned on shoulder and neck and on inside wall.
14. SR. A.I.b (TS. 3195; Op. 8, 3.3). Nearly complete. Coarse, handmade unevenly shaped rim. Fine pink ware with very small gold-colored mica grits, evenly fired. Self slip in and out.
15. PS. B.I.b (TS. 4008; Op. 8, 3.3). Small rim and wall segment. For ware, compare Phase 4 Type Series example from Area IVP (TS. 2557 = TS. 3396).
16. BE. D.III (PM. C.13; TS. 4006; Op. 8, 3.3). About 3/4 segment with a potter's mark incised on the inside wall before firing. Hard, pinkish-orange ware with gold- and white-colored mica and lime grits, evenly fired. Creamy-buff slip out.
17. BE. E.I.f (TS. 3602; Op. 8, 3.4). Complete base and about 1/4 segment of lower wall of vessel. Slightly coarse buff ware with a few small gold- and silver-colored mica and lime grits, and vegetable temper, evenly fired. Self slip in and out.

Other Type Series Examples: (1) JR. C.VI.a (TS. 3598), (2) JR. Q.II.b (TS. 4007).

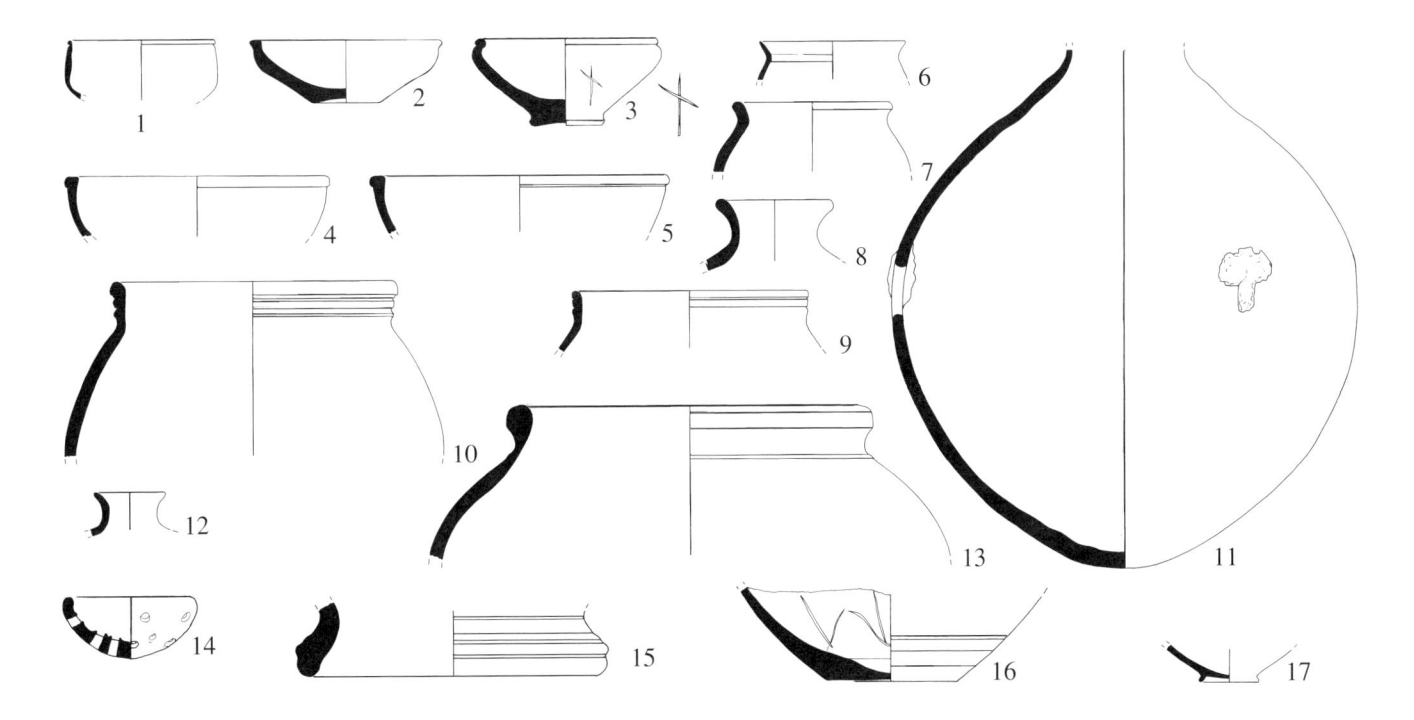

Figure 151

Pottery from Area IV, Operation 8, Room 29 (Phase 3; Period E — Early Bronze Age IVb). Scale 1:5

Figure 152. Pottery from Area IV, Operation 8, Room 29A (Phase 4; Period E–D — Early–Middle Bronze Age)

1. SBR. A.I.b (PM. C.8; TS. 3344; Op. 8, 2.1). About 1/4 rim and 1/2 base mended to complete profile with P-shaped potter's mark incised on outer wall before firing; off center string-cut base. Fine pink ware with gold- and white-colored mica grits, evenly fired. Creamy-buff slip in and outside to just above the base.
2. SBR. A.I.c (TS. 3587; Op. 8, 2.1). About 1/5 rim and upper wall segment. Fairly fine pinkish-orange ware with gold-colored mica and lime grits, evenly fired. Creamy-buff slip in and out.
3. SBR. B.I.a (TS. 3319; Op. 8, 1.1). About 1/8 rim and most of wall profile. Fairly fine pinkish-buff ware with gold-colored mica and lime grits, evenly fired. Cream slip in and out.
4. SBR. B.I.p (TS. 3315; Op. 8, Surf. 1.1). About 1/3 rim, wall, and base forming complete profile. Fairly coarse creamy-green ware with small silver-colored mica and black and white lime grits, evenly fired. Self slip in and out.
5. SBR. F.I.b (TS. 3586; Op. 8, 2.1). About 1/10 rim and most of wall profile. Slightly coarse buff ware with a few silver-colored mica and many black and white lime grits, evenly fired. Creamy-buff slip in and out.
6. BR. E.I.a (TS. 3584; Op. 8, 2.1). Small rim (5 cm) and upper wall segment. Fairly fine light pinkish-buff ware with gold- and silver-colored mica and lime grits, evenly fired. Creamy-buff slip in and out.
7. BR. E.I.b (PM. C.10; TS. 3328; Op. 8, 2.1). Complete string-cut base with body and 1/3 segment of rim with remains of a potter's mark incised on the inside base before firing. Fairly fine pinkish-brown ware with gold- and silver-colored mica and small lime grits, evenly fired. Self slip in and to carination below rim out.
8. BR. E.I.b (TS. 3591; Op. 8, 2.1). Small rim (3 cm) and upper wall segment. Slightly coarse buff ware with gold- and silver-colored mica and lime grits, evenly fired. Creamy-buff slip in and out.
9. BR. H.I.b (TS. 3286 = TS. 3603; Op. 8, 1.1). About 1/6 rim and upper wall segment. Slightly coarse pinkish-orange ware with small gold- and silver-colored mica and black and white lime grits, evenly fired. Creamy-buff slip in and out.
10. BR. L.I.b (TS. 3585; Op. 8, 2.1). About 1/12 rim and upper wall segment. Slightly coarse greenish-buff ware with a few small gold-colored mica and lime grits, evenly fired. Self slip in and out.
11. BR. L.I.d (TS. 3583; Op. 8, 2.1). About 1/3 rim and wall segment. Slightly coarse pinkish-buff ware with gold-colored mica and black and white lime grits, fairly evenly fired. Creamy-green slip out and on top of rim.
12. SJR. A.III.d (TS. 3320; Op. 8, 1.1). About 1/5 rim and shoulder segment. Fairly coarse light pink ware with gold-colored mica and lime grits, evenly fired. Cream slip out.
13. JR. A.III.d (TS. 3322; Op. 8, 1.1). About 1/10 rim and neck segment. Fairly fine pinkish-brown ware with small gold- and silver-colored mica and lime grits, evenly fired. Creamy-pink slip in and out.
14. JR. H.II.d (TS. 3588; Op. 8, 2.1). About 1/12 rim and neck segment. Fairly fine pinkish-buff ware with lime grits, evenly fired. Creamy-green slip in and out.
15. JR. H.III.g (TS. 3592; Op. 8, 2.1). About 1/10 rim and shoulder segment. Slightly coarse buff ware with some translucent mica and black and white lime grits, evenly fired. Creamy-green slip in and out.
16. JR. J.III.a (TS. 3589; Op. 8, 2.1). About 1/5 rim and neck segment. Fairly fine grayware with silver-colored mica and lime grits, evenly fired. Very worn self slip in and out with traces of burnish on outside neck and on top of rim.
17. JR. J.III.b (TS. 3314; Op. 8, Surf. 1.1). About 2/3 rim and neck segment. Fairly fine brownish-buff ware with small silver-colored mica and lime grits, evenly fired. Creamy-green slip in and out.
18. JR. J.III.h (TS. 3325; Op. 8, 1.1). About 1/8 rim and neck segment. Fairly fine light pink ware with gold- and silver-colored mica and lime grits, evenly fired. Creamy-buff slip out and over rim in to mid neck.
19. JR. J.III.ad (TS. 3321; Op. 8, 1.1). About 1/3 rim and neck segment. Slightly coarse pinkish-buff ware with gold- and silver-colored mica, lime, and vegetable temper, evenly fired. Creamy-buff slip in and out.
20. JR. P.II.a (TS. 3317; Op. 8, 1.1). Small rim, neck, and shoulder segment. For ware, compare Type Series example from Area IVK (TS. 2562).
21. CP. B.II.l (TS. 3324; Op. 8, 1.1). Small rim and upper shoulder segment. Ware description not available.
22. WPS. B (TS. 3318; Op. 8, 1.1). Small rim (4 cm) and portion of wall with applied band decoration and part of one side of a window in the wall. Slightly coarse creamy-green ware with small lime grits, evenly fired. Self slip in and out.
—. JR.Sh. (PM. D.10; TS. 4201; Op. 8, 2.1). Jar sherd. Ware description not available.

Other Type Series Examples: (1) JR. C.IV.a (TS. 3590), (2) JR. E.II.u (TS. 3316), (3) JR. P.III.g (TS. 3323).

Figures 152–53

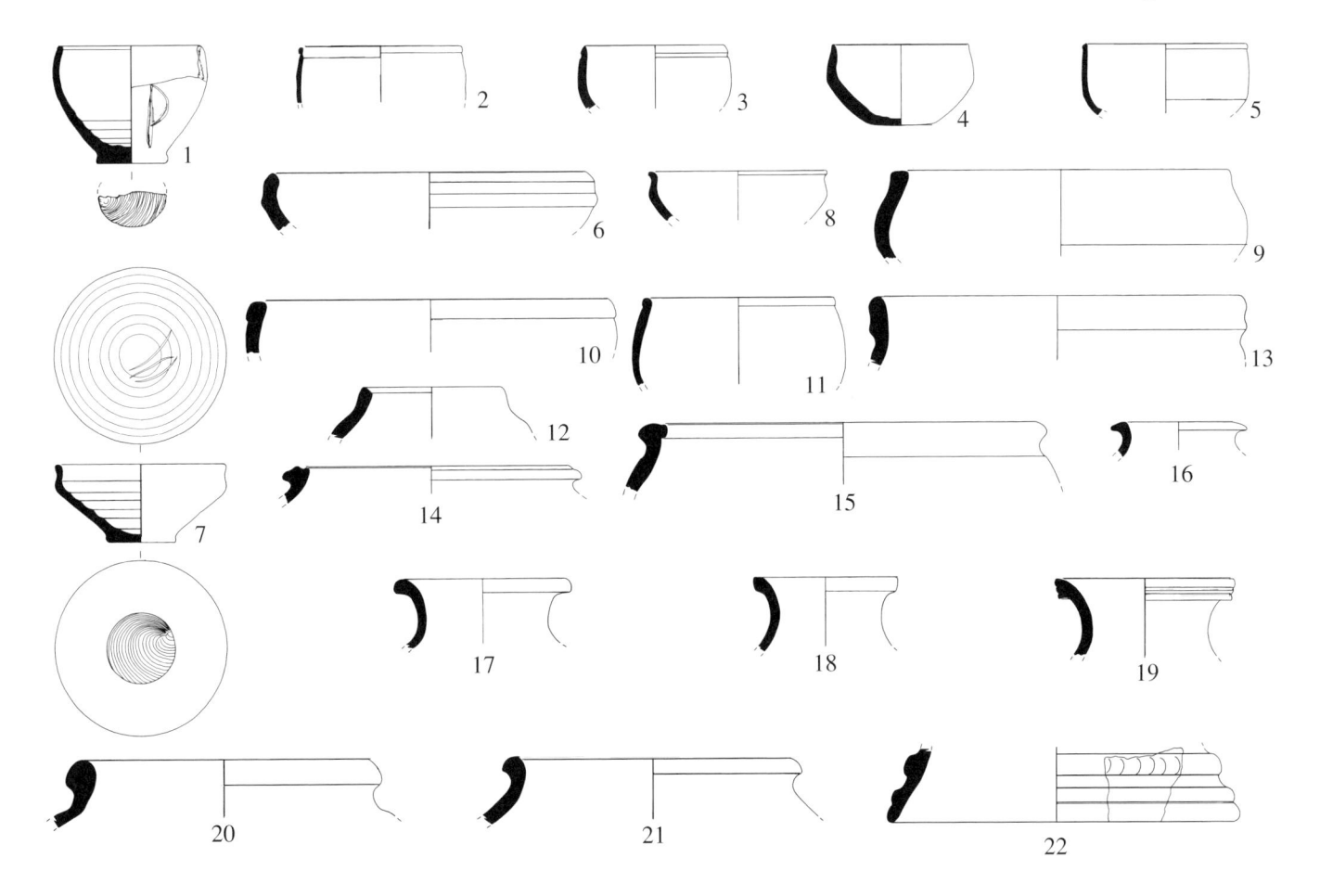

Figure 152. Pottery from Area IV, Operation 8, Room 29A (Phase 4; Period E–D — Early–Middle Bronze Age).
Scale 1:5

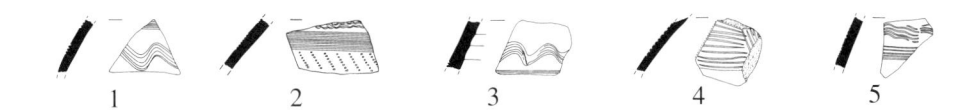

Figure 153. Miscellaneous Incised Pottery Sherds from Area IIA (Phases 11, 13, 14, and 15; Period C — Hellenistic).
Scale 1:5

1. H.JR.Sh. (IP [G.1] C.IV.a; TS. 2010; IIA, 5.5). Phase 11. Jar shoulder sherd with comb-incised decoration on the outside wall. Slightly coarse ware, unevenly fired pink at core and buff on surfaces.
2. H.JR.Sh. (IP [G.1] G.I.a; TS. 194; IIA, 4.9). Phase 13. Jar shoulder sherd with comb-incised decoration and small impressed circles on the outside wall. Slightly coarse buff ware, evenly fired. Creamy-buff slip out.
3. H.JR.Sh. (IP [G.1] B.II.a; TS. 2006; IIA, 4.9). Phase 13. Jar shoulder sherd with comb-incised decoration on the outside wall. Fairly close pinkish-buff ware, evenly fired.
4. H.JR.Sh. (IP [G.4] G.I.a; TS. 2012; IIA, 1.5–7). Phase 14. Jar shoulder sherd with linear decoration incised on the outside wall before firing. Fairly fine pinkish-buff ware, evenly fired. Creamy-buff slip in and out.
5. H.JR.Sh. (IP [G.1] C.V.a; TS. 2009; IIA, 1.2). Phase 15. Jar shoulder sherd with comb-incised decoration on the outside wall. Slightly coarse pinkish-buff ware, evenly fired.

Figure 154. Area IV (Phases 2A, 2B, 3, 4, and 5; Periods F to E–D) Early Bronze Age IVa to Early–Middle Bronze Age, Miscellaneous Incised Pottery Sherds, Potters' Marks, and an Applied-band Sherd

1. JR.Sh. (IP [G.2] A.III.a; TS. 2721; IVB, 1.2, Room 1B). Phase 4 (EB IVb). Jar shoulder sherd with linear decoration incised on the outside wall before firing. Fairly fine light pink ware, evenly fired. Creamy-buff slip in and out.
2. JR.Sh. (IP [G.3] B.III.a; TS. 2713; IVC, 1.2, TW Tower). Phase 3 (EB IVb). Jar shoulder sherd with linear decoration incised on the outside wall before firing. Hard, close pinkish-brown ware, evenly fired. Creamy-buff slip out.
3. JR.Sh. (PM. B.5; TS. 1724; IVC, 1.6, Pit, NE Tower). Phase 2B (EB IVa). Portion of flat base and lower wall of a jar with an "eye-shaped" potter's mark incised on the outside wall before firing. Medium coarse buff ware, evenly fired. Cream slip out.
4. JR.Sh. (IP [G.4] D.III; PM. D.20; TS. 1188; IVC, 1.6). Phase 2B (EB IVa). Jar shoulder sherd with a portion of a tree or wheat stalk potter's mark incised on the outside wall before firing. Slightly coarse pinkish-buff ware with lime and mica grits, evenly fired. Creamy-buff slip out.
5. JR.Sh. (IP [G.1] H.II.a; TS. 2008; IVC, 1.6, Pit, NE Tower). Phase 2B (EB IVa). Small shoulder fragment of a jar with remains of comb-incised decoration on the outside wall. Slightly coarse pinkish-buff ware, evenly fired.
6. JR.Sh. (IP [G.4] E.I; SW. 627; IVC, 4.1, Room 7). Phase 2A (EB IVa). Body sherd of a probable jar with remains of a "warrior's" torso holding a spear in the left hand (see pl. 99b). Kilt-like clothing is represented with incised waistband and a fringe as well as short vertical incisions on the portion of the chest that is preserved. Fairly coarse pinkish-buff ware. Cream slip out.
7. ABS. A (TS. 1723; IVG, 1.5, Room 3). Phase 2A (EB IVa). Jar body sherd with an applied and incised rope-like band round the outside of the vessel. Coarse pink ware, evenly fired. Traces of burning on lower end of the sherd.
8. JR.Sh. (IP [G.4] B.I.a; TS. 2569; IVJ, 2.1, Room 4). Phase 2A (EB IVa). Jar shoulder sherd with a linear design and impressed circles incised on the outside wall of the vessel before firing. Slightly coarse pink ware, evenly fired. Self slip out.
9. JR.Sh. (IP [G.1] D.II.a; TS. 1749; IVL, 1.4, Room 3). Phase 2B (EB IVa). Body sherd with comb-incised straight and wavy bands of decoration. Medium fine pink ware with lime and mica grits unevenly fired. Cream slip out.
10. JR.Sh. (IP [G.4] F.III.a; SW. 629; IVM, 1.4, Room 7). Phase 2B (EB IVa). Jar body sherd with portion of an unidentifiable animal incised on the outside wall of the vessel before firing (compare decoration on the "cauldron"-like jar SW. 294, fig. 64:4). Fairly fine pink ware, evenly fired.
11. JR.Sh. (IP [G.4] D.III; PM. D.20; TS. 2573; IVM, 1.7, Room 7). Phase 2A (EB IVa). Jar shoulder sherd with tree or wheat stalk potter's mark incised on the outside wall of the vessel before firing (see pl. 100e). Fairly fine greenish-buff ware, evenly fired. Slip out out.
12. JR.Sh. (IP [G.4] F.I; TS. 1641; IVN, 1.1). Phase 5 (EB–MB). Jar shoulder sherd with remains of a quadruped (onager?) and horizontal lines incised on the outside wall of the vessel before firing. Slightly coarse pinkish-buff ware, evenly fired. Cream slip in and out.
13. JR.Sh. (IP [G.4] F.I; SW. 630; IVN, 2.1, Room 8). Phase 2B (EB IVa). Jar body sherd with the hindquarter remains of a quadruped (horse?) incised on the outside wall of the vessel before firing (see pl. 99c). Fairly coarse pink ware, unevenly fired with a lighter core. Cream slip out and buff slip in.
14. JR.Sh. (IP [G.1] C.V.a; TS. 2568; IVO, 1.3, Fill). Phase 3 (EB IVb). Jar shoulder sherd with comb-incised linear decoration. Fairly fine buff ware, evenly fired. Creamy-buff slip out.
15. JR.Sh. (IP [G.1] C.IV.a; TS. 2567; IVP, 1.4, Room 9A). Phase 3 (EB IVb). Jar shoulder sherd with comb-incised linear decoration. Hard, slightly coarse grayish-buff ware, evenly fired. Salt encrusted on all edges.
16. JR.Sh. (PM. E.2; TS. 2678; IVP, 1.4, Room 9A). Phase 3 (EB IVb). Jar shoulder sherd with a potter's mark incised before firing. Slightly coarse pinkish-buff ware, evenly fired. Buff slip in and out.
17. JR.Sh. (IP [G.3] B.II.a; TS. 2641; IVP, Unstratified). Small jar shoulder sherd with a band of herringbone decoration incised at the base of the neck before firing. Fairly fine grayware, evenly fired. Self slip horizontally burnished on outside wall.
18. JR.Sh. (IP [G.4] C.II.a; TS. 2565; IVZ(S), 5.6, 5.7). Phase 2A (EB IVa). Jar body sherds with remains of an animal's feet applied on the outside wall of the vessel. Hard, close pinkish-buff ware, evenly fired. Cream slip out.
19. JR.Sh. (IP [G.1] C.V.a; TS. 2724; IVZ(N1), 1.1). Phase 5 (EB–MB). Jar shoulder sherd with comb-incised linear decoration. Fairly fine pink ware, evenly fired. Self slip out.
20. JR.Sh. (IP [G.1] D.II.a; TS. 2717; IVZ(N1), 1.2). Phase 4 (EB IVb). Jar shoulder sherd with comb-incised linear decoration on outside wall. Slightly coarse buff ware, evenly fired. Creamy-buff slip out.
21. JR.Sh. (IP [G.1] B.II.a; TS. 2709; IVZ(N2), 3.1). Phase 5 (EB IVb). Jar shoulder sherd with comb-incised linear decoration on outside wall. Slightly coarse buff ware, evenly fired. Self slip in and out.
22. JR.Sh. (IP [G.2] B.I.a; TS. 2564; IVZ(S), 5.2, 5.3). Phases 3/2B (EB IVa-IVb). Jar shoulder sherds with registers of linear decoration on outside wall incised before firing. Hard, close buff ware, evenly fired. Creamy-buff slip out.
23. JR.Sh. (IP [G.1] A.II.a; TS. 2716; IVZ(N2), 3.3). Phase 3 (EB IVb). Jar shoulder sherd with comb-incised decoration on outside wall. Fairly fine pinkish-buff ware, evenly fired. Cream slip out.
24. JR.Sh. (IP [G.1] D.II.a; TS. 2715; IVZ(N2), 3.3). Phase 3 (EB IVb). Jar should sherd with comb-incised decoration on outside wall. Hard, close pinkish-brown ware, evenly fired. Creamy-buff slip out.
25. JR.Sh. (IP [G.1] A.II.a; TS. 2725; IVZ(N2), 3.4, Room 21). Phase 2B (EB IVa). Jar shoulder sherd with comb-incised decoration on outside wall. Slightly coarse buff ware, evenly fired. Self slip out.
26. JR.Sh. (IP [G.2] C; TS. 2647; IVX, 1.1). Phase 5 (EB–MB). Small jar shoulder sherd with linear decoration incised on outside wall before firing. Fairly fine light pink ware, evenly fired. Creamy-buff slip out.

Figure 154

Area IV (Phases 2A, 2B, 3, 4, and 5; Periods F to E–D) Early Bronze Age IVa to Early–Middle Bronze Age, Miscellaneous Incised Pottery Sherds, Potters' Marks, and Applied-band Sherds. Scale 1:5

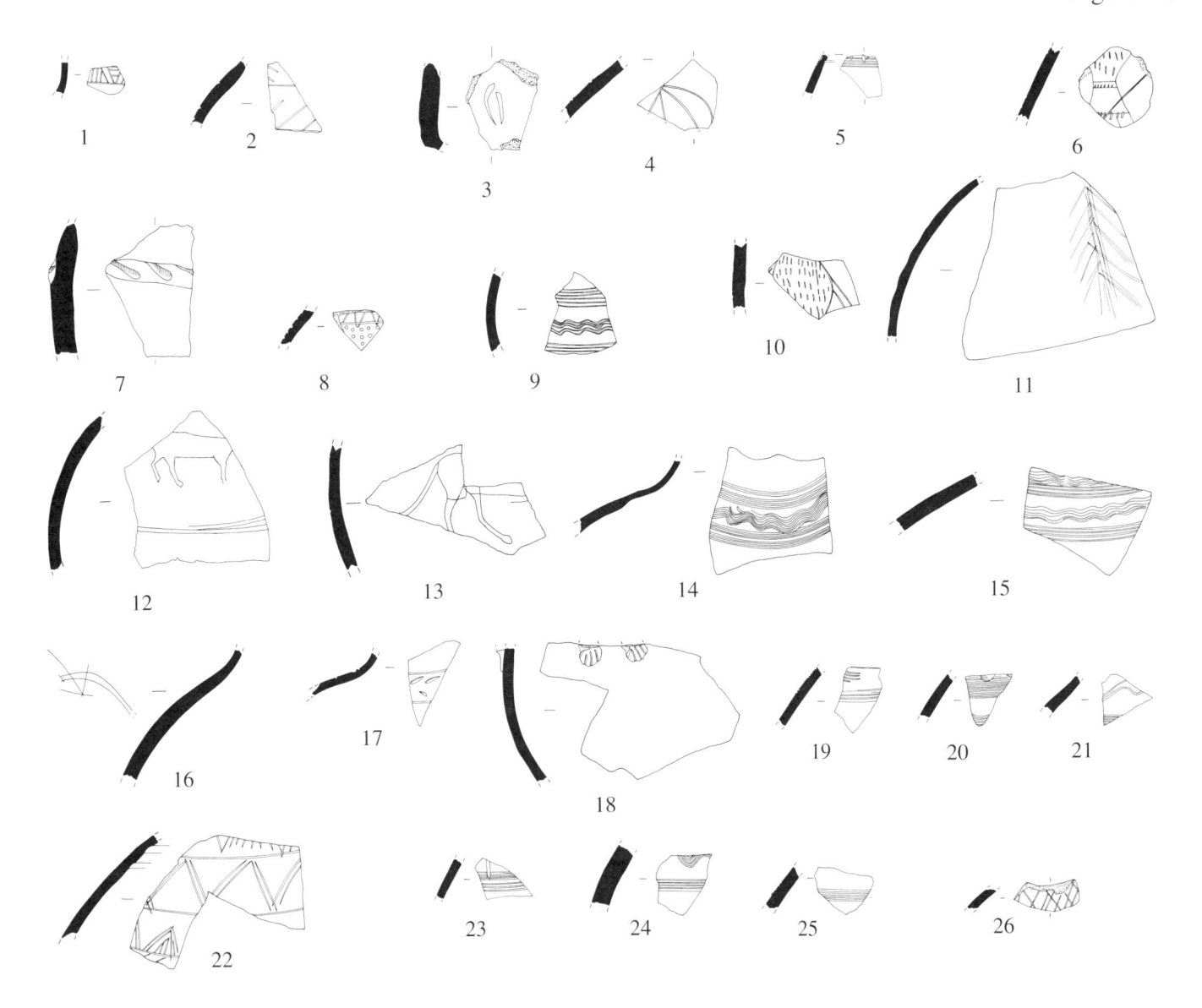

Figure 155. Human Figurines from Area IV (Phases 2–3; Periods F and E — Early Bronze Age IVa and Early Bronze Age IVb)

1. Type SF.1c (SW. 241; IVD, 2.6a, Below Room 2). Phase 1C. (EB IVa). Probable fragment of a female figurine. Very worn neck and upper torso extant. Hard pinkish-buff ware with mica and lime grits, unevenly fired tan at surfaces.
2. Type SF.1a (SW. 318; IVG, Unstratified, Room 3). Phase 2A (EB IVa) on comparative analysis (see pl. 108a). Female. Head and neck. Head has appliqué socketed eyes and ear ornaments depicted in the clay. One single-stranded appliqué necklace positioned around the front and sides of the neck. Very fine buff ware with little grit temper.
3. Type SF.1a (SW. 383; IVF, 3.1, Room 1). Phase 2A (EB IVa; see pl. 109b). Female. Neck and upper torso extant. Appliqué incised stranded necklace positioned around the front and sides of neck. Left hand rests on flat breast. Fairly fine pink ware with some small grit. Cream slip covers all surfaces.
4. Type SF.1a (SW. 714; IVX, 10.7 = IVM, Room 7). Phase 2A (EB IVa; see pl. 110a). Female. Neck, upper torso, and portion of pillar-type stand extant. Single appliqué incised necklace with traces of reddish paint. Bitumen applied at the neck was probably used to reattach head after breakage in antiquity. Medium fine pink ware, evenly fired.
5. Type SF.1a (FN. 171; Op. 10, 20, Room 18). Phase 2A (EB IVa). Female. Upper torso with vestigial arms extant. Single appliqué incised necklace. Hard, fine light grayish-green ware with no trace of grit. Cream slip covers all surfaces.
—. Type SF.1a (FN. 141; Op. 6, 20.1, Room 9). Phase 2A (EB IVa). Female. Upper torso fragment with two-stranded appliqué necklace and remains of one hand on the breast. Fairly fine buff ware with lime and gold-colored mica grits, evenly fired. Self slip covers all surfaces.
6. Type SF.1c (SW. 481; IVJ, 1.5, Room 4). Phase 2B (EB IVa; see pl. 115h). Female or male. Pillar-type torso fragment. Fairly coarse pinkish-buff ware, unevenly fired with a darker core. Cream slip covers all surfaces.
7. Type SF.1c (FN. 110; Op. 6, 1.7, Room 9). Phase 2A (EB IVa). Pillar-type human figurine stand fragment. Fairly coarse green ware with some lime grits, evenly fired.
8. Type SF.1c (FN. 96; Op. 7, 19.1, Gateway Street). Phase 2A(a) (EB IVa). Female. Neck, upper torso with vestigial arms, and pillar-type stand extant.
9. Type SF.1c (TS. 3581; Op. 7, 21.1, Room 35). Phase 2A(a) (EB IVa). Pillar-type human figurine stand fragment with concave bell-shaped base.
10. Type SF.1c (SW. 319; IVE, 1.4 = IVL, Room 3). Phase 2B (EB IVa). Pillar-type human figurine stand fragment with slightly concave bell-shaped base. Fairly coarse buff ware, evenly fired.
11. Type SF.1c (SW. 548; IVP, 1.5, Room 9). Phase 2B (EB IVa; see pl. 115f). Pillar-type human figurine stand fragment with slightly concave bell-shaped base. Fine pink ware, evenly fired. Cream slip covers all surfaces.
12. Type SF.1a (SW. 814; Op. 7, 7.1, Room 39). Phase 2B(b) (EB IVb; see pl. 108c). Female. Head and neck extant.
13. Type SF.1a (SW. 836; Op. 7, 7.1, Room 39). Phase 2B(b) (EB IVb; see pl. 110c). Female. Neck, upper torso with vestigial arms, and portion of pillar-type stand. Single appliqué incised necklace with three incised triangular-shaped patterns on the front of the figure which represents clothing and incised strands emanating from the head and neck onto the back, which represent hair.

Figure 155

Human Figurines from Area IV (Phases 2–3; Periods F and E — Early Bronze Age IVa and Early Bronze Age IVb).
Scale 1:2

Figure 156. Human Figurines from Area IV (Phases 2–4; Periods F, E, and E–D — Early Bronze Age IVa, Early Bronze Age IVb, and Early–Middle Bronze Age)

1. Type SF.1c (FN. 68; Op. 7, 3.1, Courtyard south of Room 37). Phase 2B(b) (EB IVb). Female figurine. Torso fragment with stump of left arm and portion of a bell-shaped pillar-type stand. Slightly coarse pinkish-brown ware with fine gray and white lime grits, evenly fired. Burnished self slip covers all surfaces.
2. Type SF.1c (FN. 113; Op. 7, 3.1, Courtyard south of Room 37). Phase 2B(b) (EB IVb). Pillar-type human figurine stand fragment with concave bell-shaped base. Fairly fine light pink ware with small black and white lime grits, evenly fired. Cream slip covers all surfaces.
3. Type SF.1c (TS. 4130; Op. 7, 7.2; West side of Wall 5.3, Room 39). Phase 2B(b) (EB IVb). Pillar-type human figurine stand fragment with concave bell-shaped base. Fairly coarse grayish-buff ware with black and white lime grits, evenly fired. Handmade with hand-burned surfaces.
—. Type SF.1c (SW. 815; Op. 7, 4.7; East of Wall 4.6, Room 40). Phase 2B(b) (EB IVb; see pl. 111d). Pillar-type human figurine stand fragment.
4. Type SF.1a (SW. 390; IVC, 1.2; Town Wall Tower). Phase 3 (EB IVb). Female. Upper torso with multiple-stranded appliqué incised necklace and both arms resting on flat breast area. Fairly fine pink ware, cream slip covers all surfaces.
—. Type SF.1c (TS. 1700; IVK, 1.3, Room 2A). Phase 3 (EB IVb). Pillar-type human figurine stand fragment. Medium fine buff ware with mica grits, evenly fired. Self slip covers all surfaces.
—. Type SF.1c (SC. 3331; IVN, 2.2, Room 8). Phase 2A (EB IVa). Female or male human pillar-type torso fragment, 0.8 cm thick × 3.0 cm high. Fine buff ware with small white lime grits, evenly fired. Self slip on surfaces; heavily burned on one surface and on upper part of broken section indicating either deliberate or accidental breakage at some stage before being burned.
5. Type SF.1a (SW. 556; IVL/P, 1.3, Pit). Phase 3 (EB IVb; see pl. 111a). Female. Left side torso fragment of a coil-made human figurine. One half of incised triangle represents pubic area which is incised with dots. Fairly coarse pink ware, unevenly fired with a lighter colored core.
6. Type SF.1a (SW. 434; IVN, 1.4, Room 8A/18A). Phase 3 (EB IVb). Female. Upper torso fragment with both hands originally held upright on breast; only the left hand is preserved. Lines representing one or more strands of a necklace are both incised and impressed around the front portion of the neck. Fairly fine pink ware. Cream slip covers all surfaces.
7. Type SF.1a (SW. 765; Op. 7, 4.1; SE quadrant C, Courtyard/work area). Phase 3 (EB IVb; see pl. 111c). Female. Head, left shoulder, and base of pillar-type stand missing. One strand appliqué and incised necklace is situated around the front of the neck and on the shoulders. Fairly fine creamy-buff ware with some lime grits, evenly fired. Self slip covers all surfaces.
8. Type SF.1a (SW. 766; Op. 7, 10.1; NW quadrant A, Courtyard/work area). Phase 3 (EB IVb; see pl. 109a). Female. Head and neck fragment with incised appliqué button-type eyes. Slightly coarse and gritty buff ware, evenly fired. Cream slip covers all surfaces.
—. Type SF.1a (FN. 45; Op. 7, 10.1; NW quadrant A, Courtyard/work area). Phase 3 (EB IVb; see pl. 111b). Female. Head and base of pillar-type stand missing. Both hands are held against the breast. Fairly fine pinkish-buff ware with small black, gold, and white micaceous grits, evenly fired. Self slip covers all surfaces.
9. Type SF.1c (FN. 107; Op. 7, 9.1; Southwest quadrant C, paved courtyard/work area). Phase 3 (EB IVb). Pillar-type human figurine stand fragment with slightly concave bell-shaped base. Slightly coarse light pink ware with lime and gold-colored mica grits, evenly fired. Self slip covers all surfaces.
10. Type SF.1c (TS. 2180; IVN, 1.4, Room 8A/18A). Phase 3 (EB IVb). Female or male human pillar-type torso fragment with slightly concave bell-shaped base. Fairly fine pinkish-buff ware, evenly fired. Creamy-buff slip covers all surfaces.
11. Type SF.1c (FN. 174; Op. 6, 14.6; Alley between Rooms 24 and 27). Phase 3 (EB IVb). Pillar-type human figurine stand fragment with concave bell-shaped base. Slightly coarse buff ware with black and white lime grits, evenly fired. Creamy-buff slip covers all surfaces.
—. Type SF.1a (FN. 14; Op. 6, 12.2, Room 26). Phase 3 (EB IVb). Female. Human pillar-type torso fragment, 6.4 cm high and 4.5 cm wide at the beginning of the shoulders.
12. Type SF.1a (TS. 3292; Op. 6, 3.16, Room 32). Phase 4 (EB–MB; see pl. 108b). Female. Head and neck fragment with appliqué button-type eyes and impressed headdress; remains of an appliqué necklace exant at the front of the base of the neck.
13. Type SF.1a (SW. 811; Op. 6, 3.16, Room 32). Phase 4 (EB–MB; see pl. 110b). Female. Head and base of pillar-type torso missing. Both hands clutch the breasts. An incised one-stranded necklace is applied to the front of the neck and just over the front edge of the shoulders.
—. Type SF.1a (FN. 132; Op. 7, Surface 1). Phase 4 (EB–MB). Female. Head and left arm broken off. Right hand is folded onto the right shoulder. The pillar-type stand is bell-shaped at the base. Fairly fine pinkish-buff ware, evenly fired.
14. Type SF.1c (FN. 34; Op. 6, 3.16, Room 32). Phase 4 (EB–MB). Pillar-type human figurine stand fragment with concave bell-shaped base. Fairly fine grayish-buff ware with lime grits, evenly fired. Self slip covers all surfaces.
—. Type SF.1c (SC. 3332; IVP, 1.2, Room 9B). Phase 4 (EB IVb). Base of pillar-type human figurine stand fragment with concave bell shape, 5.5 cm diameter. Fairly coarse pinkish-buff ware with gold-colored mica and black and white lime grits, evenly fired. Creamy-green slip on surfaces. Heavily salt-encrusted on outside surfaces (not underside of bell shape) and on break of the pillar, 3 cm in diameter.

Figure 156

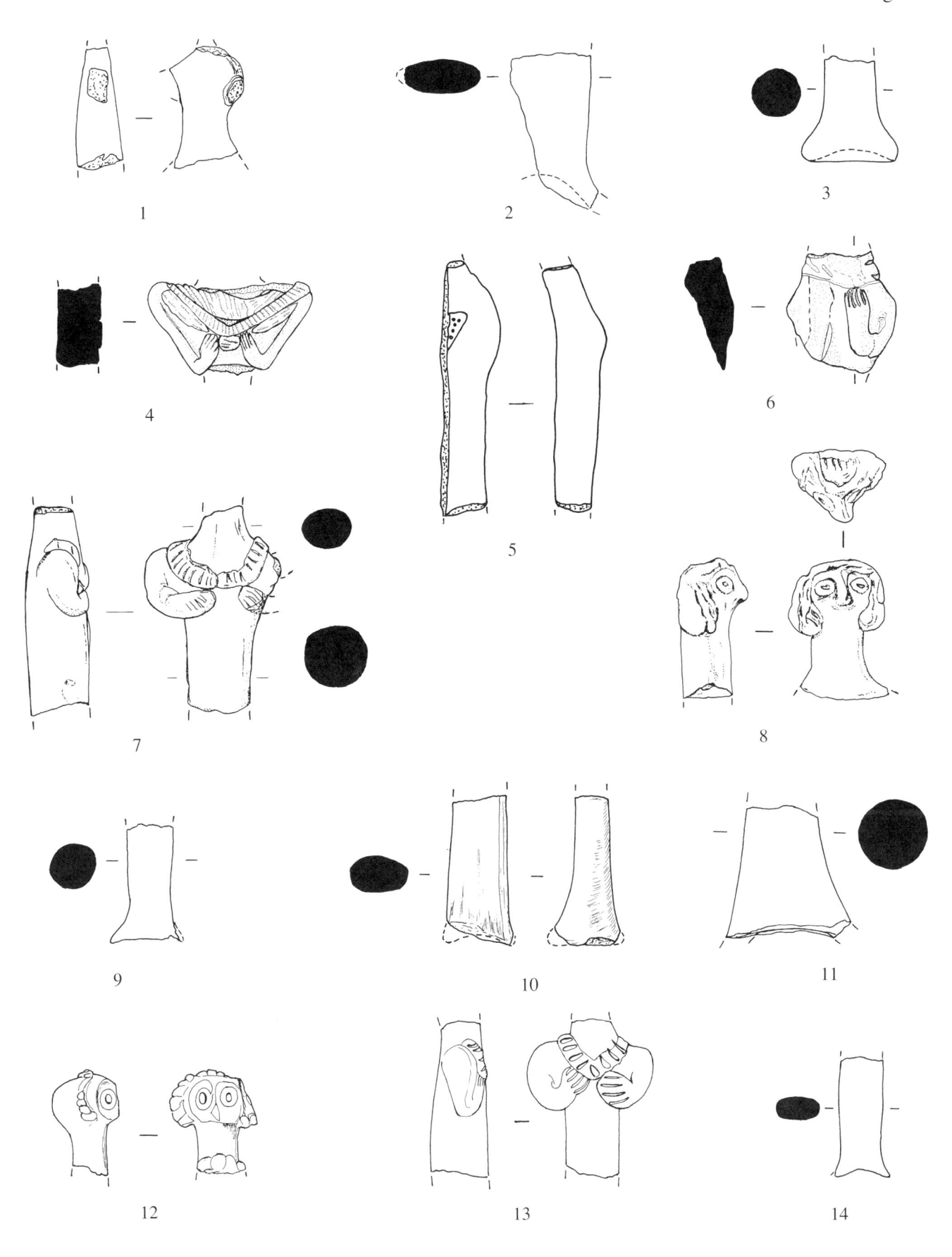

1
2
3
4
5
6
7
8
9
10
11
12
13
14

Human Figurines from Area IV (Phases 2–4; Periods F, E, and E–D — Early Bronze Age IVa, Early Bronze Age IVb, and Early–Middle Bronze Age). Scale 1:2

Figure 157. Animal Figurines from Area IV (Phases 2–4; Periods F and E — Early Bronze Age IVa and Early Bronze Age IVb)

1. Type SF.1d (SW. 396; IVF, 4.1, Room 1). Phase 2A (EB IVa; see pl. 116b). Horse head fragment with appliqué button-like impressed eyes and incised nostrils and mouth. Fine pinkish-buff ware, unevenly fired with a light brown core. Thin cream slip on all unbroken surfaces.
2. Type SF.1d (SW. 386; IVL, 2.1, Room 3A). Phase 3 (EB IVb). Sheep head fragment with incised linear decoration. Tips of ears and nose broken. Hard, fine dark grayware, evenly fired.
3. Type SF.1d (SW. 518; IVL, 2.1, Room 3A). Phase 3 (EB IVb; see pl. 117g). Bovine-like head fragment. Tips of ears broken and nostrils chipped. Handmade, unfired brown ware.
4. Type SF.1d (SW. 713; IVP, 2.1, Room 9). Phase 2A (EB IVa; see pl. 117f). Sheep or goat-like head fragment. Ears broken off. Fine buff ware, evenly fired. Self slip on unbroken surfaces.
5. Type SF.1e (SW. 712; IVX, 10.7 = IVM, Room 7). Phase 2A (EB IVa; see pl. 117l). Torso fragment of unknown quadruped type. Fine buff ware, evenly fired. Self slip on unbroken surfaces.
6. Type SF.1d (SW. 770; Op. 10, 22.3 = NE corner of IVN, Room 8). Phase 2A (EB IVa; see pl. 116a). Horse. Complete except for lower portions of the legs, two pieces of the applied forelock beside the left ear, and the tip of the tail. The horse has a long mane to the base of its neck which lies flat on both sides of neck that indicates a domesticated horse; it also has a bushy tail and a complete set of male genitals. One hole bored through the muzzle was made before firing. Fairly fine light greenish-buff ware with lime and mica grits, evenly fired. Self slip on unbroken surfaces.
—. Type SF.1e (FN. 155; Op. 6, 1.3, Room 9). Phase 2A (EB IVa). Three unbaked animal figurine fragments of unidentifiable quadruped types. Coarse grayish-buff ware with small black pebbles and other lime grit temper.
7. Type SF.1d (FN. 126; Op. 7, 20.1, Room 36). Phase 2A(a) (EB IVa). Horse head fragment with rudimentary mane. Tip of muzzle and left ear broken off. Fairly fine buff ware with fine black and white lime grits, evenly fired.
8. Type SF.1e (SW. 731; IVZ(N2), 3.5, Room 21). Phase 2B (EB IVa). Torso fragment of unknown quadruped type. Hard, fairly fine pinkish-buff ware with mica grits, evenly fired. Smooth creamy-buff slip on unbroken surfaces.
9. Type SF.1d (SW. 232; IVE, 1.3, Room 3A). Phase 3 (EB IVb; see pl. 117e). Bovine-like head and forequarter fragment. Tip of snout, ears, and front legs broken off. Hard, fairly fine pinkish-tinged buff ware with lime and mica grits, unevenly fired light creamy-green on outer surface.
10. Type SF.1d (SW. 592; IVD, 1.3). Phase 4 (EB IVb; see pl. 118a). Sheep or goat-like hindquarter fragment. Lower portions of hind legs broken off. Fairly fine pinkish-buff ware. Cream slip on unbroken surfaces.
11. Type SF.1d (SW. 208; IVD, 1.2). Phase 4 (EB IVb). Bovine-like head and forequarter fragment. Ears partially broken and front legs missing. Fairly fine brown ware, evenly fired.
12. Type SF.1d (SW. 230; IVC, 1.2; Town Wall tower). Phase 3 (EB IVb). Bovine-like head and forequarter fragment. Both ears broken off. Pink-tinged buff ware, unevenly fire grayish at surface.

Figure 157

1  2  3  4  5  6  7  8  9  10  11  12

Animal Figurines from Area IV (Phases 2–4; Periods F and E — Early Bronze Age IVa and Early Bronze Age IVb).
Scale 1:2

Figure 158. Animal Figurines from Area IV (Phases 2–5; Periods F to E–D — Early Bronze Age IVa to Early Bronze–Middle Bronze Age)

1. Type SF.1e (SW. 387; IVC, 1.2; Town Wall Tower). Phase 3 (EB IVb; see pl. 118b). Torso fragment of unknown quadruped type. Three incisions on the middle left side of the back made before firing. Fine pinkish-buff ware, evenly fired. Cream slip on unbroken surfaces.
2. Type SF.1d (SW. 570; IVB, 1.2, Room 1B). Phase 4 (EB IVb). Bovine head fragment. Tips of ears or horns broken off. Fairly coarse pink ware, evenly fired. Cream slip on unbroken surfaces.
3. Type SF.1e (SW. 685; IVR, 2.1, Room 11A). Phase 3 (EB IVb). Torso fragment of unknown quadruped type. Fairly fine buff ware, evenly fired.
4. Type SF.1d (SW. 523; IVQ, 1.2, Room 25). Phase 4 (EB IVb). Horse(?). Forequarter fragment with tips of ears and forelegs broken off. The mouth and nostrils are indicated by incisions made into the clay before firing. Fairly fine creamy-buff ware, evenly fired.
5. Type SF.1d (SW. 418; IVN, 1.1; Topsoil). Phase 5 (EB–MB; see pl. 117d). Forequarter fragment of a bovine. Fine pinkish-buff ware, evenly fired. Creamy-green slip on unbroken surfaces.
6. Type SF.1d (SW. 555; IVP, unstratified, Room 9). Probably Phase 2B (EB IVa; see pl. 116c). Bovine head with incised nostrils, appliqué and indented eyes, and an incised design on the forehead extending to eye level. The body was originally hollow, which may indicate that this head belonged to a zoomorphic type of vessel. Fine pink ware, evenly fired. Cream slip on outer surface.
7. Type SF.1d (FN. 30; Op. 6, 1.2, Room 9). Phase 2A. (EB IVa). Horse(?). Forequarter fragment with most of head and front legs broken. Indented, tool-punched. circular holes extend from lower portion of the front of the neck and along the central portion of the stomach. Fairly fine pinkish-buff ware with mica grits, evenly fired. Self slip on unbroken surfaces.

Figure 158

Animal Figurines from Area IV (Phases 2–5; Periods F to E–D — Early Bronze Age IVa to Early Bronze–Middle Bronze Age). Scale 1:2

Figure 159. Model Chariots and Wheels from Area IV (Phases 1C–4; Periods G–E — Early Bronze Age III to Early Bronze Age IVb)

1. Type SF.2a (SW. 522; XA, 1.3, Room 15). Phase 2B (EB IVa; see pl. 119a). Model chariot fragment. Front portion with one half section of horizontal wheel axle hole and diagonally positioned hole for harness shaft. Coarse pink ware, evenly fired. Cream slip on all surfaces.
2. Type SF.2a (SW. 393; IVK, 1.3, Room 2A). Phase 3 (EB IVb; see pl. 119b). Model chariot fragment. Front portion with horizontal wheel axle hole and diagonally positioned hole for harness shaft. Fine creamy-buff ware, evenly fired. Traces of pink slip on surfaces. Diamond pattern seal-rolled impression on front and tool-incised linear lines of decoration on the front and right side.
3. Type SF.2a (SW. 842; Op. 6, 3.1, Room 32). Phase 4 (EB–MB; see pl. 119c). Model chariot fragment. Rear portion with horizontally applied bar of clay. Left leg with axle hole extant. Tool-incised linear decoration on extant portion of back and left side.
—. Type SF.2b (FN. 158; Op. 6, 20.2; sndg. below Room 9). Phase 1C (EB III). Model chariot wheel with wide hub.
4. Type SF.2b (SW. 392; IVK, 2.4, Room 2). Phase 2A (EB IVa; see pl. 119d). Model chariot wheel. Fine brown ware, unevenly fired with lighter brown core. Buff slip on outer surfaces.
5. Type SF.2b (SW. 475; IVN, 2.2, Room 8). Phase 2A (EB IVa; see pl. 119e). Model chariot wheel. Fine light grayware, evenly fired.
6. Type SF.2b (SW. 625; IVQ, 1.6, Room 6). Phase 2A (EB IVa). Model chariot wheel fragment. Fairly coarse pinkish-buff ware.
7. Type SF.2b (TS. 4063; Op. 10, 20; = IVN, Room 18). Phase 2A (EB IVa). About 1/2 segment of model chariot wheel with wide hub. Fairly fine buff ware with a few small silver-colored mica and lime grits, evenly fired. Self slip on outer surfaces.
—. Type SF.2b (FN. 122; Op. 6, 1.30, Room 9). Phase 2B (EB IVa). Model chariot wheel fragment.
8. Type SF.2b (SW. 547; XA, 1.3, Room 15). Phase 2B (EB IVa; see pl. 119g). Model chariot wheel fragment. Fine greenish-buff ware, evenly fired.
9. Type SF.2b (SW. 549; XA, 1.3, Room 15). Phase 2B (EB IVa; see pl. 120a). Complete model chariot wheel. Fairly fine creamy-buff ware, evenly fired.
10. Type SF.2b (SW. 233; IVG, 1.3, Room 3A). Phase 3 (EB IVb). About 1/2 of a model chariot wheel with edge chipped. Pinkish-buff ware with lime and micaceous grits, unevenly fired green at surfaces.
11. Type SF.2b (SW. 444; IVN, 1.4, Room 8A/18A). Phase 3 (EB IVb). About 1/5 segment of model chariot wheel. Fine buff-white ware.
12. Type SF.2b (FN. 167; Op. 10, 22.1, Room 8A). Phase 3 (EB IVb). Nearly complete model chariot wheel, except for chipping on portions of the outer edge.

Figure 159

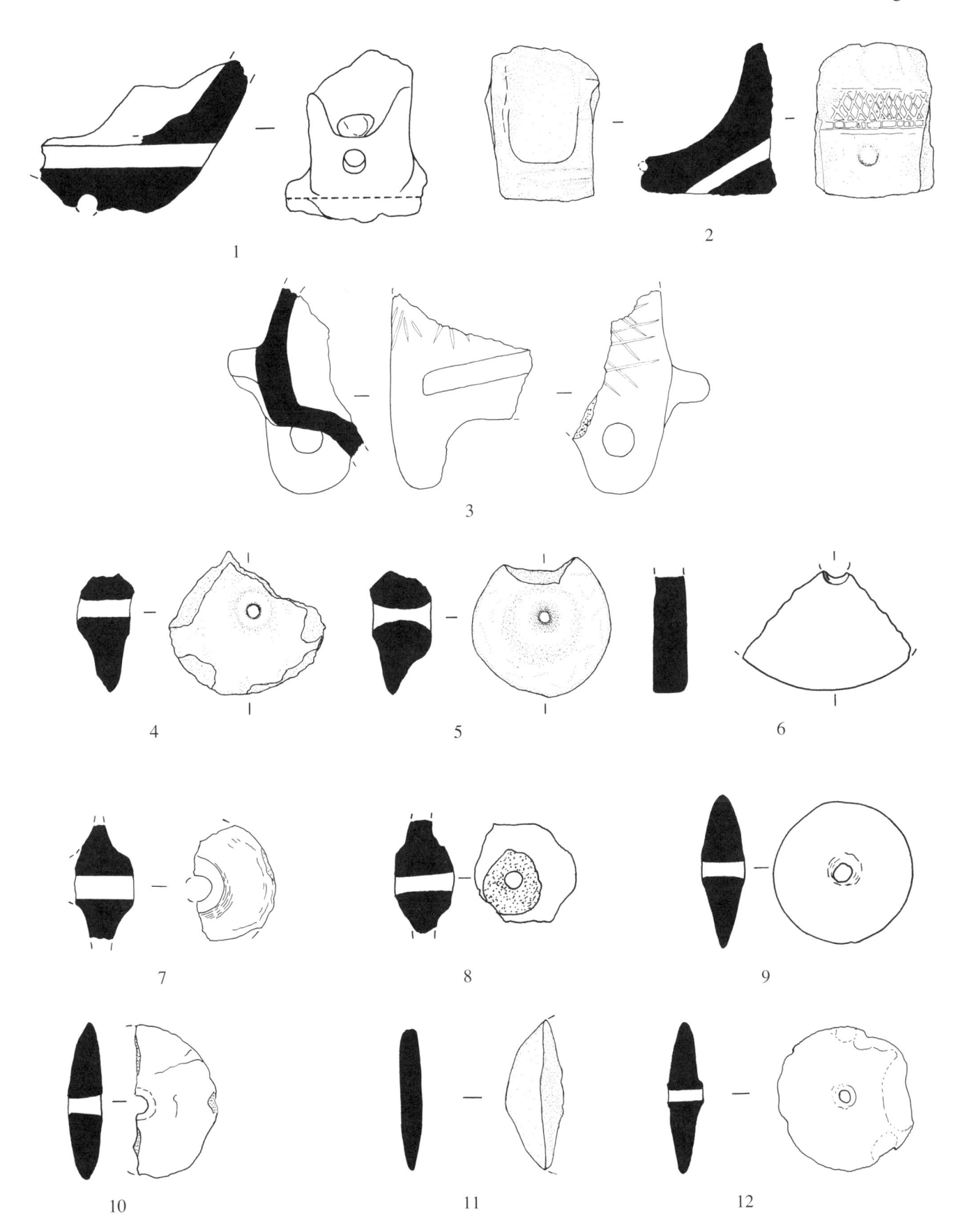

Model Chariots and Wheels from Area IV (Phases 1C–4; Periods G–E — Early Bronze Age III to Early Bronze Age IVb).
Scale 1:2

Figure 160. Miscellaneous Clay Objects from Area IV (Phases 2A–4; Periods F to E–D — Early Bronze Age IVa to Early–Middle Bronze Age)

1. Type SF.6f (SW. 270; IVB, 2.2, Room 1). Phase 2A (EB IVa). Pestle or other unknown type of clay tool. Hard, slightly coarse buff ware with lime and mica grits, unevenly fired creamy-green at surfaces. Handmade.
2. Type SF.6d (SW. 660; IVM, 1.5, Room 7). Phase 2A (EB IVa; see pl. 120b). Unfired clay mold fragment with only a portion of the receiver channel extant.
3. Type SV.4 (SW. 384; IVC, 2.1 = IVM, Room 7). Phase 2B (EB IVa). Clay stopper. Fairly fine brown ware partially fired gray.
—. Type SF.6g (SC. 3314; IVM, 1.4, Room 7). Phase 2B (EB IVa). Reused sherd smoothing tool; triangular shaped, 3 × 4 cm at broadest points. Very worn and smoothed from use on all edges. Fairly fine buff ware with fine mica and lime grits, evenly fired. Self slip in and out, but very worn.
4. Type SF.6g (SW. 553; IVL/P, 1.3 baulk; later pit which cut through the northern segment of the wall dividing rooms 3 and 9). Phase 3 (EB IVb; see pl. 120c). Offering stand. Fairly fine pink ware, evenly fired. Unevenly applied cream slip on surfaces.
5. Type SF.6g (SW. 441; IVN, 1.4, Room 8A/18A). Phase 3 (EB IVb). Unknown object broken on three sides. Fine buff ware. Incised linear decoration.
6. Type SF.6g (SW. 478; IVN, 1.4, Room 8A/18A). Phase 3 (EB IVb). Small sphere with single incised mark on surface. Soft and fine white-buff ware.
7. Type SF.6f (FN. 27; Op. 6, 3.1, Room 32). Phase 4 (EB–MB). Cone-shaped object which may be a small pestle.
8. Type SF.6g (FN. 119; Op. 8, 1.1, Room 29A). Phase 4 (EB–MB). Clay smoothing tool (possibly a spatula or handle).
9. Type SF.6g (TS. 2710; IVZ(N1), 1.2). Phase 4 (EB IVb). 2/3 fragment of a plaque-like object (school tablet?). Fairly coarse grayish-buff ware, evenly fired. Self slip on surfaces.
10. Type SF.6a.4 (TS. 3150a; IVB, 3.3; in debris of Town Wall). Phase 2B (EB IVa). Sling bullet (elongated biconical). Handmade and baked.
11. Type SF.6a.1 (TS. 3150b; IVB, 3.3; in debris of Town Wall). Phase 2B (EB IVa). Sling bullet (point-ended ellipsoid). Handmade and baked.
12. Type SF.6a.1 (TS. 3150c; IVB, 3.3; in debris of Town Wall). Phase 2B (EB IVa). Sling bullet (point-ended ellipsoid). Handmade and baked.
13. Type SF.6a.7 (TS. 3151a; IVB, 3.2; in debris of Town Wall). Phase 2B (EB IVa). Sling bullet (flat on one end). Handmade and baked.
14. Type SF.6a.3 (TS. 3151b; IVB, 3.2; in debris of Town Wall). Phase 2B (EB IVa). Sling bullet (biconical). Handmade and baked.
15. Type SF.6a.1 (TS. 3151c; IVB, 3.2; in debris of Town Wall). Phase 2B (EB IVa). Sling bullet (point-ended ellipsoid). Handmade and baked.
16. Type SF.6a.8 (TS. 3151d; IVB, 3.2; in debris of Town Wall). Phase 2B (EB IVa). Sling bullet (round). Handmade and baked.
17. Type SF.6a.3 (TS. 3151e; IVB, 3.2; in debris of Town Wall). Phase 2B (EB IVa). Sling bullet (biconical). Handmade and baked.
18. Type SF.6a.2 (TS. 3151f; IVB, 3.2; in debris of Town Wall). Phase 2B (EB IVa). Sling bullet (flat-ended ellipsoid). Handmade and baked.
19. Type SF.6a.1 (TS. 3151g; IVB, 3.2; in debris of Town Wall). Phase 2B (EB IVa). Sling bullet (point-ended ellipsoid). Handmade and baked.
20. Type SF.6a.7 (TS. 3151h; IVB, 3.2; in debris of Town Wall). Phase 2B (EB IVa). Sling bullet (flat on one or both ends). Handmade and baked.
—. Type SF.6e (SC. 153; IVZ(S), 5.7). Phase 2A (EB IVa). Reworked sherd disk used as a tool.
—. Type SF.6e (SC. 3283; IVP, 1.4). Phase 3 (EB IVb). Reworked sherd disk used as a tool. Slightly coarse ware with lime and gold-colored mica grits, unevenly fired with gray core firing pinkish-orange at surfaces. Outside surface painted with two horizontal bands (maximum width unknown) of red paint with a 2 cm width of self slip in reserve between the two bands.

Figure 160

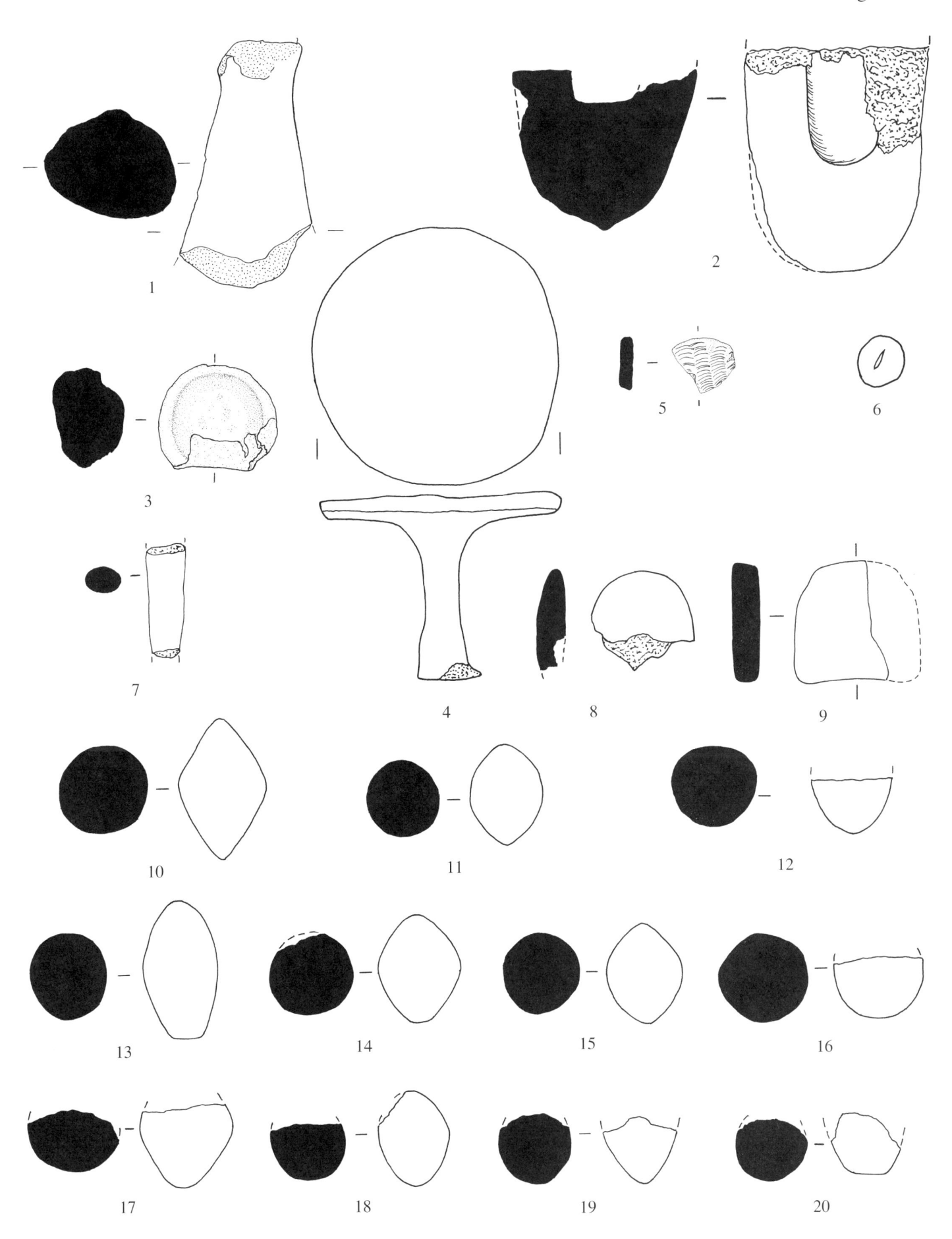

Miscellaneous Clay Objects from Area IV (Phases 2A–4; Periods F to E–D — Early Bronze Age IVa to Early Bronze–Middle Bronze Age). Scale 1:2

Figure 161. Metal Objects from Area IV (Phases 2A–3; Periods F and E — Early Bronze Age IVa and Early Bronze Age IVb)

1. Type SF.5a (SW. 234; IVK, 2.5, Room 2). Phase 2B (EB IVa; see pl. 121a). Tongs (copper/bronze?, not analyzed). Nearly complete, but one arm broken away. Heavily corroded.
2. Type SF.5b (SW. 598; IVJ, 2.1, Room 4). Phase 2A (EB IVa; see pl. 121b). Collar fitting (copper) for the neck of a pottery vessel. See Appendix 6.
3. Type SF.5c (SW. 619; IVJ, 2.1, Room 4). Phase 2A (EB IVa; see pl. 121c). Pin (copper/bronze?, not analyzed) with mushroom-shaped head; incomplete shaft.
4. Type SF.5c (SW. 604; IVJ, 2.1, Room 4). Phase 2A (EB IVa). Pin (copper/bronze?, not analyzed) with mushroom-shaped head and eyelet hole through upper portion of the incomplete shaft.
5. Type SF.5c (SW. 618; IVJ, 2.1, Room 4). Phase 2A (EB IVa). Pin (copper) with mushroom-shaped head and small portion of upper shaft extant. See Appendix 6.
6. Type SF.5c (SW. 633; IVJ, 2.1, Room 4). Phase 2A (EB IVa). Pin (copper/bronze?, not analyzed) tapered at both ends.
7. Type SF.5c (SW. 620; IVJ, 1.5, Room 4). Phase 2B (EB IVa). Pin (copper/bronze?, not analyzed) square in section and tapered at both ends.
8. Type SF.5c (SW. 632; IVJ, 1.5, Room 4). Phase 2B (EB IVa). Pin (copper/bronze?, not analyzed) tapered at both ends.
9. Type SF.5c (SW. 623; IVJ, 2.1, Room 4). Phase 2A (EB IVa). Pin (copper/bronze?, not analyzed). Four broken shaft segments of one or more examples.
10. Type SF.5c (SW. 605; IVM, 1.5, Room 7). Phase 2A (EB IVa). Pin (copper/bronze?, not analyzed) shaft fragment.
11. Type SF.5d (SW. 720; IVN, 2.3, Room 18). Phase 2A (EB IVa; see pl. 121e). Hasp (copper/bronze?, not analyzed). Complete; corroded over much of the surface. Found in situ inside complete gray-burnished small jar, Type C.II.m (SW. 723).
12. Type SF.5d (SW. 721; IVN, 2.3, Room 18). Phase 2A (EB IVa; see pl. 121f). Hasp (copper/bronze?, not analyzed). Complete; corroded over much of the surface. Found 30 cm from the gray-burnished jar, SW. 723, from which it was most likely thrown when the vessel fell to the floor.
—. Type SF.5c (FN. 202; Op. 7, 17.1; Extramural). Phase 2A(b) (EB IVa). Pin, shaft fragment (copper). See *Appendix 6*.
—. Type SF.5h (FN. 203; Op. 7, 18.1, Room 34). Phase 2A(a) (EB IVa). Blade fragment (arsenical bronze). See *Appendix 6*.
—. Type SF.5c (FN. 204; Op. 8, 3.3, Room 29). Phase 3 (EB IVb). Pin fragment (arsenical copper). See *Appendix 6*.
—. Type SF.5c (FN. 200; Op. 6, 4.3, Room 23). Phase 3 (EB IVb). Pin fragment (copper). See *Appendix 6*.
—. Type SF.5h (FN. 201; Op. 6, 4.7, Room 23, Oven). Phase 3 (EB IVb). Blade fragment (arsenical copper). See *Appendix 6*.

Figure 161

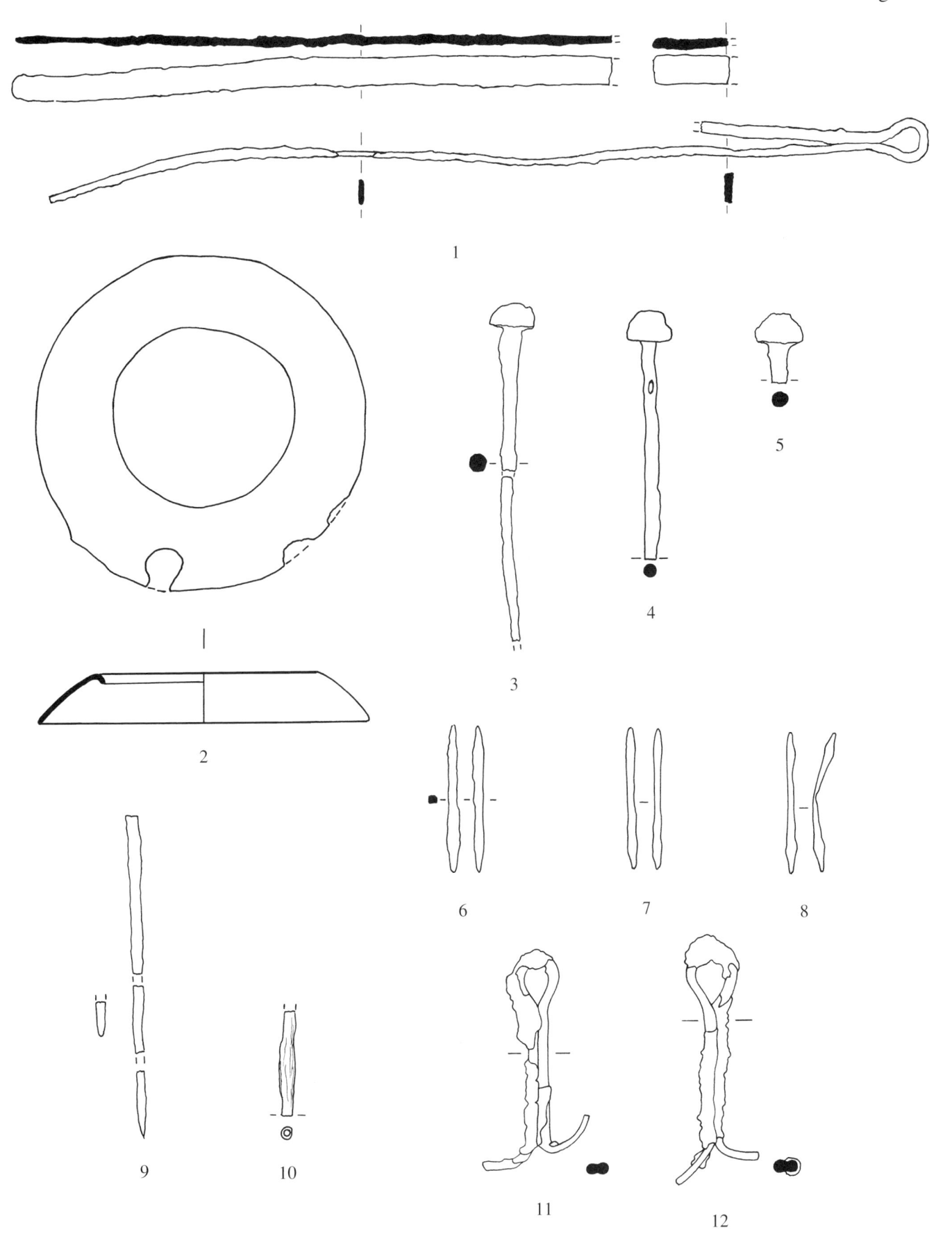

Metal Objects from Area IV (Phases 2A–3; Periods F and E — Early Bronze Age IVa and Early Bronze Age IVb).
Scale 1:2

Figure 162. Metal Objects from Area IV (Phases 2A–4; Periods F to E–D — Early Bronze Age IVa to Early Bronze–Middle Bronze Age)

1. Type SF.5c (FN. 185; Op. 10, 20 = IVN, Room 18). Phase 2A (EB IVa). Pin (arsenical copper). Incomplete shaft with bent-over head. See *Appendix 6*.
2. Type SF.5i (SW. 621; IVO, 1.4, Room 10). Phase 2A (EB IVa). Flattened strip of wire (copper/bronze?, not analyzed). Incomplete and bent into a loop.
3. Type SF.5b (SW. 513; IVO, 1.4, Room 10). Phase 2A (EB IVa). Fitting (silver). Seven pieces of unknown type of fitting with five punched holes in larger dome-shaped piece. Small area of replaced textile near the bottom edge of the dome-shaped piece.
4. Type SF.5c (SW. 634; XA, 1.4, Room 15). Phase 2A (EB IVa). Pin (copper). Shaft fragment. See *Appendix 6*.
5. Type SF.5i (SW. 600; IVL, 1.4, Room 3). Phase 2B (EB IVa). Lump (copper). Indistinguishable piece of probable slag. See *Appendix 6*.
6. Type SF.5c (FN. 184; Op. 11, 4.1, Room 20). Phase 2B (EB IVa). Pin shaft fragment (arsenical copper). See *Appendix 6*.
7. Type SF.5c (SW. 771; Op. 11, 4.1, Room 20). Phase 2B (EB IVa). Pin. Complete wtih mushroom-shaped head and eyelet hole in upper shaft (arsenical copper). See *Appendix 6*.
8. Type SF.5e (FN. 180; Op. 11, 4.1, Room 20). Phase 2B (EB IVa). Amulet. Frog-shaped. Complete (lead). See *Appendix 6*.
9. Type SF.5f (FN. 182; Op. 11, 5.1, Room 19). Phase 2B (EB IVa). Bracelet. Three fragments; incomplete (copper). See *Appendix 6*.
10. Type SF.5h (FN. 181; Op. 11, 5.1, Room 19). Phase 2B (EB IVa). Lump. Possibly an ax (arsenical copper). See *Appendix 6*.
—. Type SF.5i (FN. 205; Op. 11, 4.1, Room 20). Phase 2B (EB IVa). Lumps (arsenical copper). See *Appendix 6*.
11. Type SF.5c (SW. 601; IVM, 1.3, Room 7A). Phase 3 (EB IVb). Pin (copper/bronze?, not analyzed). Fragment with club-shaped head and eyelet hole in upper shaft.
—. Type SF.5c (SW. 635; IVN, 4.3, Room 18A). Phase 3 (EB IVb). Pin(s; copper). Many small fragments, non-mendable. See *Appendix 6*.
12. Type SF.5c (SW. 802; Op. 7, Surf. 2, Courtyard). Phase 3 (EB IVb; see pl. 121d). Pin (copper/bronze?, not analyzed). Incomplete shaft fragment.
13. Type SF.5f (FN. 178; Op. 8, 2.1, Room 29A). Phase 4 (EB–MB). Ring. Non-joining ring segment (lead). See *Appendix 6*.
14. Type SF.5i (SW. 321; XA, 1.1, above Room 15A). Phase 4 (EB–MB). Fitting (zinc). Indistinguishable. See *Appendix 6*.
15. Type SF.5h (SW. 606; IVL, 4.1, Room 3B). Phase 4 (EB IVb; see pl. 121f). Toilet implement (copper/bronze?, not analyzed). Flat strip with point missing and hole through upper broad end.
—. Type SF.5c (FN. 69; Op. 6, 3.1, Room 32). Phase 4 (EB–MB). Pin (copper/bronze?, not analyzed). Fragment of shaft.
—. Type SF.5g (FN. 177; Op. 6, 3.1, Room 32). Phase 4 (EB–MB). Awl (arsenical copper). See *Appendix 6*.

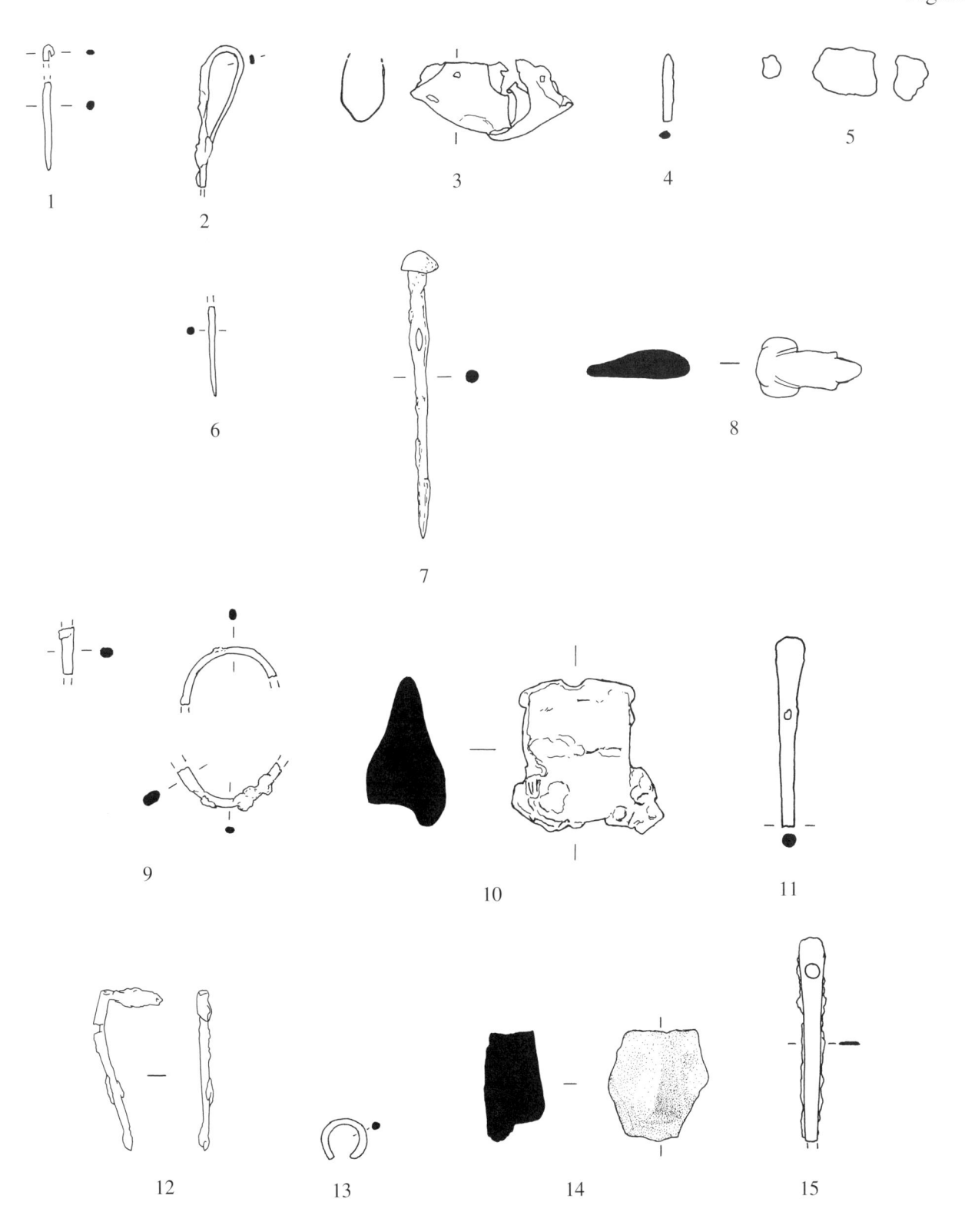

Figure 162

Metal Objects from Area IV (Phases 2A–4; Periods F to E–D — Early Bronze Age IVa to Early Bronze–Middle Bronze Age). Scale 1:2

Figure 163. Stone Objects from Area IV (Phases 1C–2B; Periods G and F — Early Bronze Age III and Early Bronze Age IVa)

1. Type SF.3f (SW. 767; Op. 11, 3.3 = Area XA, Pre-Room 15). Phase 1C (EB III; see pl. 123a). Pivot stone for potter's wheel. Vesicular black basalt with some accretions of limestone. Circular-shaped base with cone-shaped central dome. Surface surrounding the dome and radiating 2 cm from the base of the dome is very highly polished from use.
2. Type SF.3e and SF.10 (SW. 585; IVL, 1.5, Room 3). Phase 2A (EB IVa; see pl. 123b). Limestone weight inscribed with cuneiform designating it a one mana weight. (See full description in Holland 1975, pp. 75–76).
3. Type SF.3e (SW. 469; IVJ, 1.5, Room 4). Phase 2B (EB IVa). Cylindrical dark brown igneous stone likely used for a weight, but not inscribed.
4. Type SF.3f (SW. 647; IVL, in stone footing of wall dividing the Southwest corner of Room 3 and the NE corner of Room 4). Phase 2A (EB IVa; see pl. 123d). Cylinder seal. Limestone chipped at one end and very heavily worn. Slight indentations at each end for insertion into some type of clip.
—. Type SF.3a (SW. 361; IVB, 2.2, Town Wall Tower, Stone Foundations). Phase 2A (EB IVa). Grinding stone, 7.0 × 13.5 × 18.5 cm. Dark gray vesicular basalt. Parabolic in plan and semicircular in section with one flat, slightly chipped face.
—. Type SF.3a (SW. 473; IVJ, 1.5, Room 4). Phase 2A (EB IVa). Creamy-brown stone. Small triangular pebble. Measurements: 3 × 3 × 3 cm on all sides.
—. Type SF.3a (SW. 470; IVJ, 2.1, Room 4). Phase 2A (EB IVa). Rubbing or burnishing stone. Goethite nodule. Reddish-brown color. Length, 3 cm.
—. Type SF.3a (SW. 610; IVJ, 3.5, Room 5). Phase 2A (EB IVa). Rubbing stone. Smooth, flattened river stone. Measurements: 2 × 7 × 8 cm.
—. Type SF.3a (SW. 374; IVK, 2.4, Room 2). Phase 2A (EB IVa). Whetstone. Igneous stone. Gray-brown color. Well-rounded, elongate shape. Measurements: 3.0 × 6.5 × 14.0 cm.
—. Type SF.3a (SW. 613; IVL, 1.5, Room 3). Phase 2A (EB IVa). Rubbing or burnishing stone. Goethite nodule with polished beveled edges. Measurements: 1 cm in diameter, 2 cm in length.
—. Type SF.3a (SW. 577; IVO, 1.4, Room 10). Phase 2A (EB IVa). Rubbing stone. Dark gray color. Smooth rounded Euphrates cobble. Measurements: 5 × 8 × 16 cm.
5. Type SF.3c (SW. 471; IVN, 2.2, Room 8). Phase 2A (EB IVa; see pl. 123e). Bowl. Light yellow alabaster with engraved decoration on top of extant rim and around the outside wall of the vessel just below the rim.
6. Type SF.3f (SW. 530; IVN, 2.2, Room 8). Phase 2A (EB IVa). Counter. Complete white alabaster counter with cylindrical hole drilled through the long axis. Five circular impressions inscribed into both sides of the rectangular-shaped piece.
7. Type SF.3f (SW. 544; IVO, 1.4, Room 10). Phase 2A (EB IVa). Counter. Incomplete white alabaster with cylindrical hole drilled through the long axis. Three of probably five circular impressions inscribed into both sides of the original rectangular-shaped piece.
—. Type SF.3f (FN. 168; Op. 10, 20, Room 18). Phase 2A (EB IVa). Incense burner(?). White limestone, crudely worked.
8. Type SF.3a (TS. 4185; IVE, 1.6 = NE corner of IVK, Room 2). Phase 2A (EB IVa). Large sphere-shaped tool (hematite).
9. Type SF.3a (TS. 4186; IVJ, 2.1, Room 4). Phase 2A (EB IVa). One small sphere-shaped tool and one oblong-shaped tool (hematite).
10. Type SF.3a (TS. 4187; IVJ, 1.5, Room 4). Phase 2B (EB IVa). Two tools (hematite).
11. Type SF.3c (SW. 545; XA, 1.3, Room 15). Phase 2B (EB IVa). Miniature circular bowl constructed from white chalky limestone. Lip of rim damaged in antiquity.

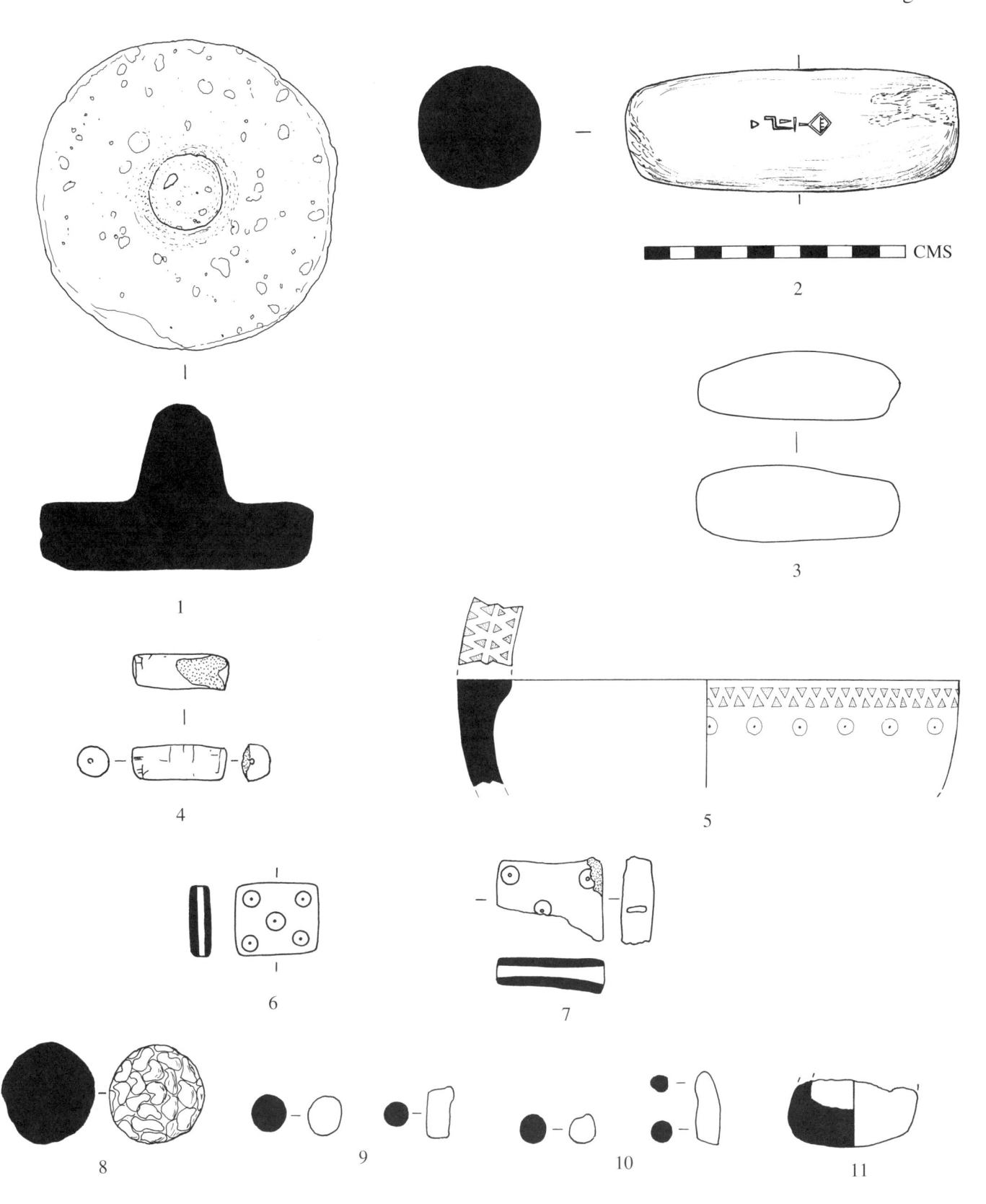

Figure 163

Stone Objects from Area IV (Phases 1C–2B; Periods G and F — Early Bronze Age III and Early Bronze Age IVa). Scale 1:2

Figure 164. Stone Objects from Area IV (Phases 2B(b) (EBIVb)–5; Periods F to E–D — Early Bronze Age IVb to Early Bronze–
Middle Bronze Age)

1. Type SF.3c (SW. 832; Op. 7, 2.3, Room 37). Phase 2B(b) (EB IVb). Bowl. Fine gray limestone.
2. Type SF.3a (SW. 465; IVJ, 1.3, Room 4B). Phase 4 (EB IVa). Burnishing stone fragment; barrel-shaped with metal concretion (possibly manganese). Reddish-black on exterior surface.
3. Type SF.3f (FN. 118; Op. 7, 10.1, NW quadrant A, Courtyard/work area). Phase 3 (EB IVb). Triangular-shaped stone inlay or gaming piece. Chalky white gypsum-like stone.
4. Type SF.3e (FN. 52; Op. 6, 4.9, Room 23). Phase 3 (EB IVb). Stone loom weight (1/2 segment).
—. Type SF.3e (FN. 125; Op. 6, 4.9, Room 23). Phase 3 (EB IVb; see pl. 126b). Loom weight. Gray limestone drilled in funnel-shaped pattern from opposing sides of the stone.
—. Type SF.3e (FN. 129; Op. 6, 4.7, Room 23). Phase 3 (EB IVb). Fishnet weight. Limestone river gravel stone with natural hole.
5. Type SF.3f (SW. 833; Op. 6, 3.1, Room 32). Phase 4 (EB–MB; see pl. 124c). One half of a stone mold used for casting metal jewelry. Hard dark black basalt-like stone, well polished on the outer surface.
6. Type SF.3c (SW. 804; Op. 6, 3.19, Room 32). Phase 4 (EB–MB; see pl. 125a). Limestone cosmetic container.
7. Type SF.3e (SW. 822; Op. 7, Surf. 1, SE quadrant C). Phase 4 (EB–MB; see pl. 125b). Limestone fishnet weight or loom weight. Well made with wedge-shaped groove cut into the middle surface of the polished stone on the long axis.
8. Type SF.3c (SW. 527; IVO, 1.1, topsoil). Phase 5 (EB–MB). Stone bowl fragment. Section of wall made from translucent white alabaster.
9. Type SF.3a (SW. 242; IVC, 1.2, Town Wall Tower). Phase 3 (EB IVb). Stone ax fragment. Mottled greenish-brown volcanic stone, broken at both ends.
—. Type SF.3a (FN. 173; Op. 11, 5.1, Room 19). Phase 2B (EB IVa). Polisher. Black basalt. Oval-shaped in section; measurements, 5.5 × 16.5 cm.
—. Type SF.3a (FN. 172; Op. 11, 5.1, Room 19). Phase 2B (EB IVa). Polisher. Black basalt. Cucumber-shaped and round in midsection; measurements, 2.0 × 9.5 cm.

Figure 164

Stone Objects from Area IV (Phases 2B–5; Periods F to E–D — Early Bronze Age IVb to Early Bronze–Middle Bronze Age). Scale 1:2

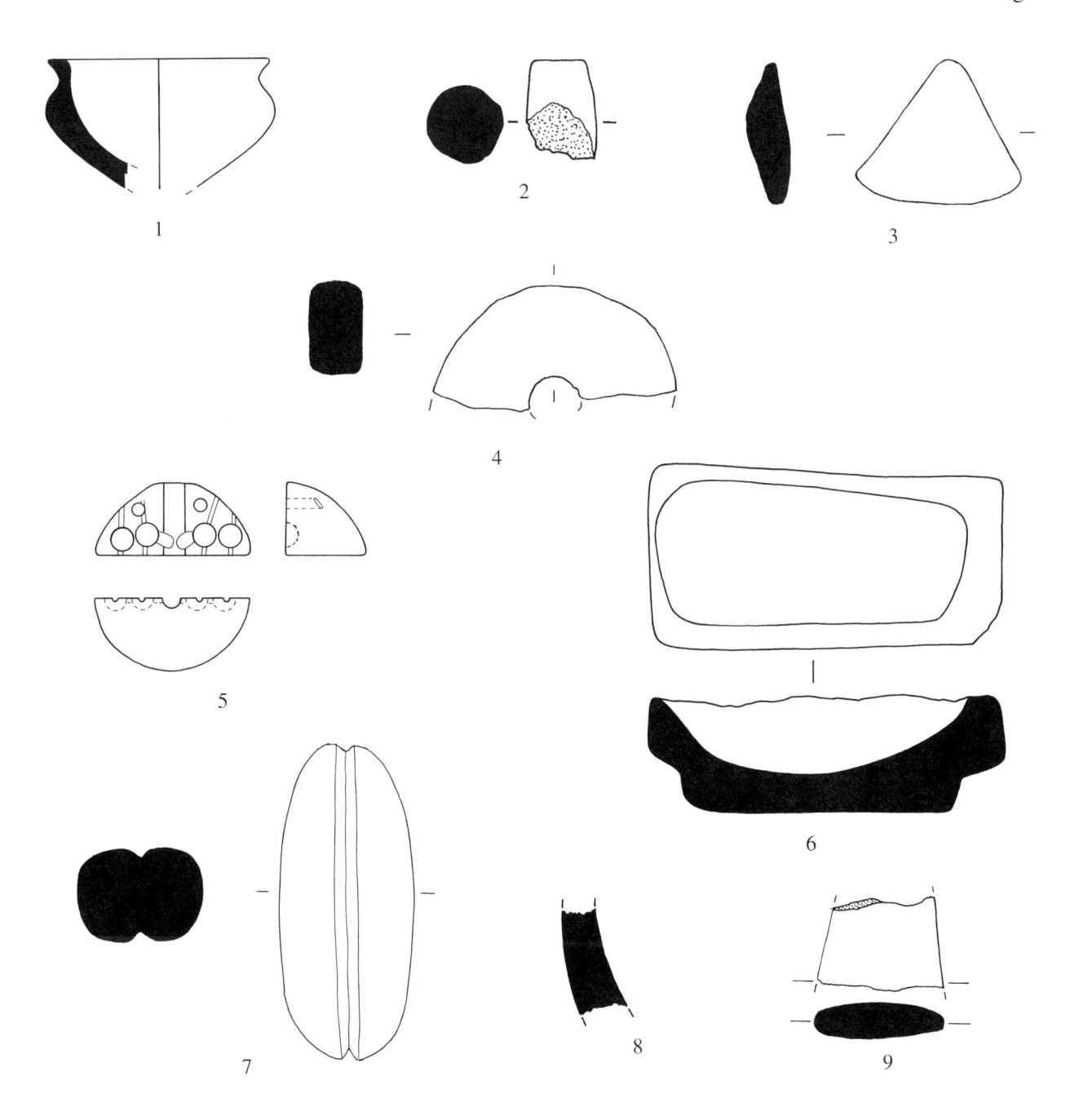

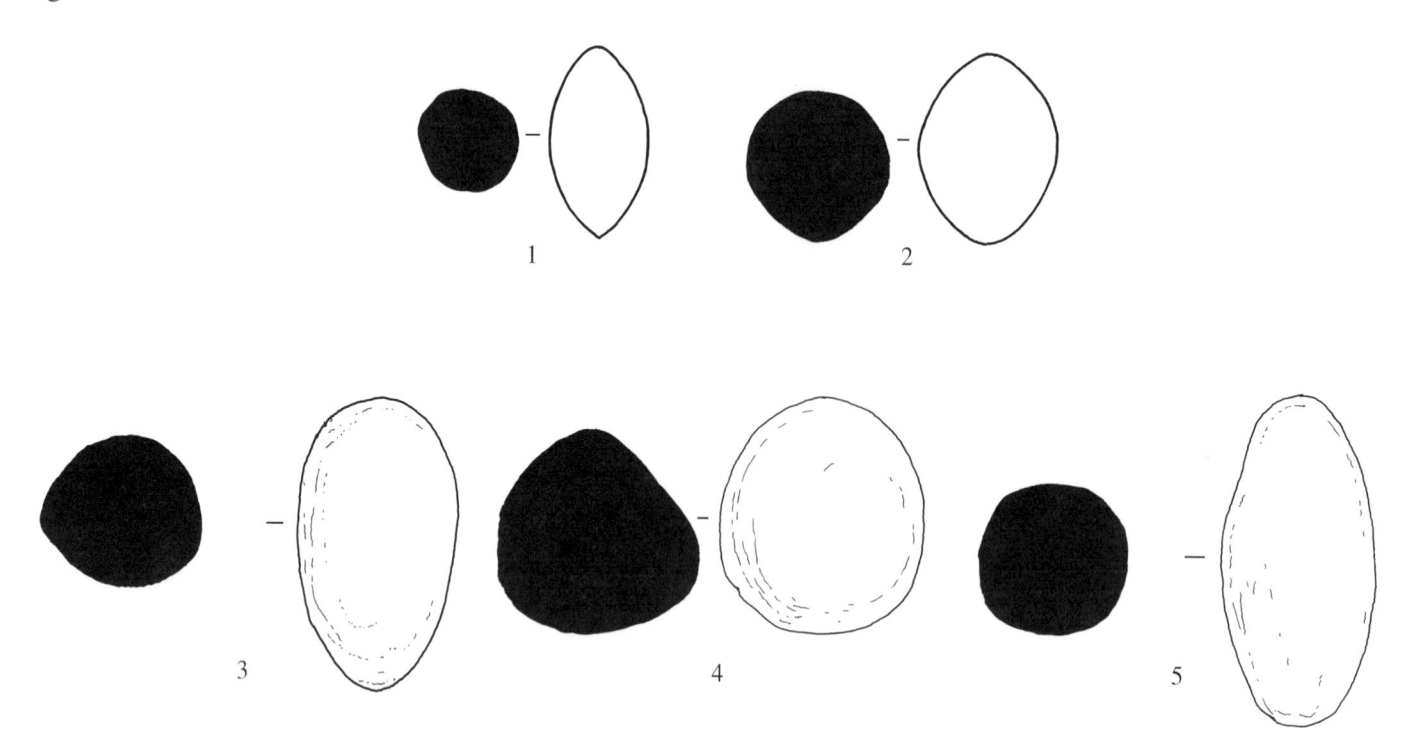

Figure 165

Figure 165. Clay Sling Bullets from Area IVK, Room 2A (Phase 3; Period E — Early Bronze Age IVb). Scale 1:2

1. Type SF.6a.1 (SW. 420a; IVK, 1.3). Phase 3. (Point-Ended Ellipsoid). Baked-clay sling bullet.
2. Type SF.6a.2 (SW. 420b; IVK, 1.3). Phase 3. (Flat-Ended Ellipsoid). Baked-clay sling bullet.
3. Type SF.6a.3 (SW. 420c; IVK, 1.3). Phase 3. (Biconical). Baked-clay sling bullet.
4. Type SF.6a.8 (SW. 420d; IVK, 1.3). Phase 3. (Round). Baked-clay sling bullet.
5. Type SF.6a.4 (SW. 420e; IVK, 1.3). Phase 3. (Elongated Biconical). Baked-clay sling bullet.

Figure 166. Clay Sling Bullets from Area IV, Room 2A (Phase 3; Period E — Early Bronze Age IVb; see pl. 120c)

1–7. Type SF.6a.1 (SW. 420 f–l; IVK, 1.3). Phase 3. (Point-ended Ellipsoid). Baked-clay sling bullets.
8–10. Type SF.6a.2 (SW. 420 m–o; IVK, 1.3). Phase 3. (Flat-ended Ellipsoid). Baked-clay sling bullets.
11–16. Type SF.6a.3 (SW. 420 p–u; IVK, 1.3). Phase 3. (Biconical). Baked-clay sling bullets.
17–20. Type SF.6a.4 (SW. 420 v–y; IVK, 1.3). Phase 3. (Elongated Biconical). Baked-clay sling bullets.
21–25. Type SF.6a.5 (SW. 420 z–dd; IVK, 1.3). Phase 3. (Knob-like on One End). Baked-clay sling bullets.
26–28. Type SF.6a.6 (SW. 420 ee–gg; IVK, 1.3). Phase 3. (Slightly Pointed on One Side). Baked-clay sling bullets.
29–31. Type SF.6a.7 (SW. 420 hh–jj; IVK, 1.3). Phase 3. (Flat on One or Both Ends). Baked-clay sling bullets.

Figure 166

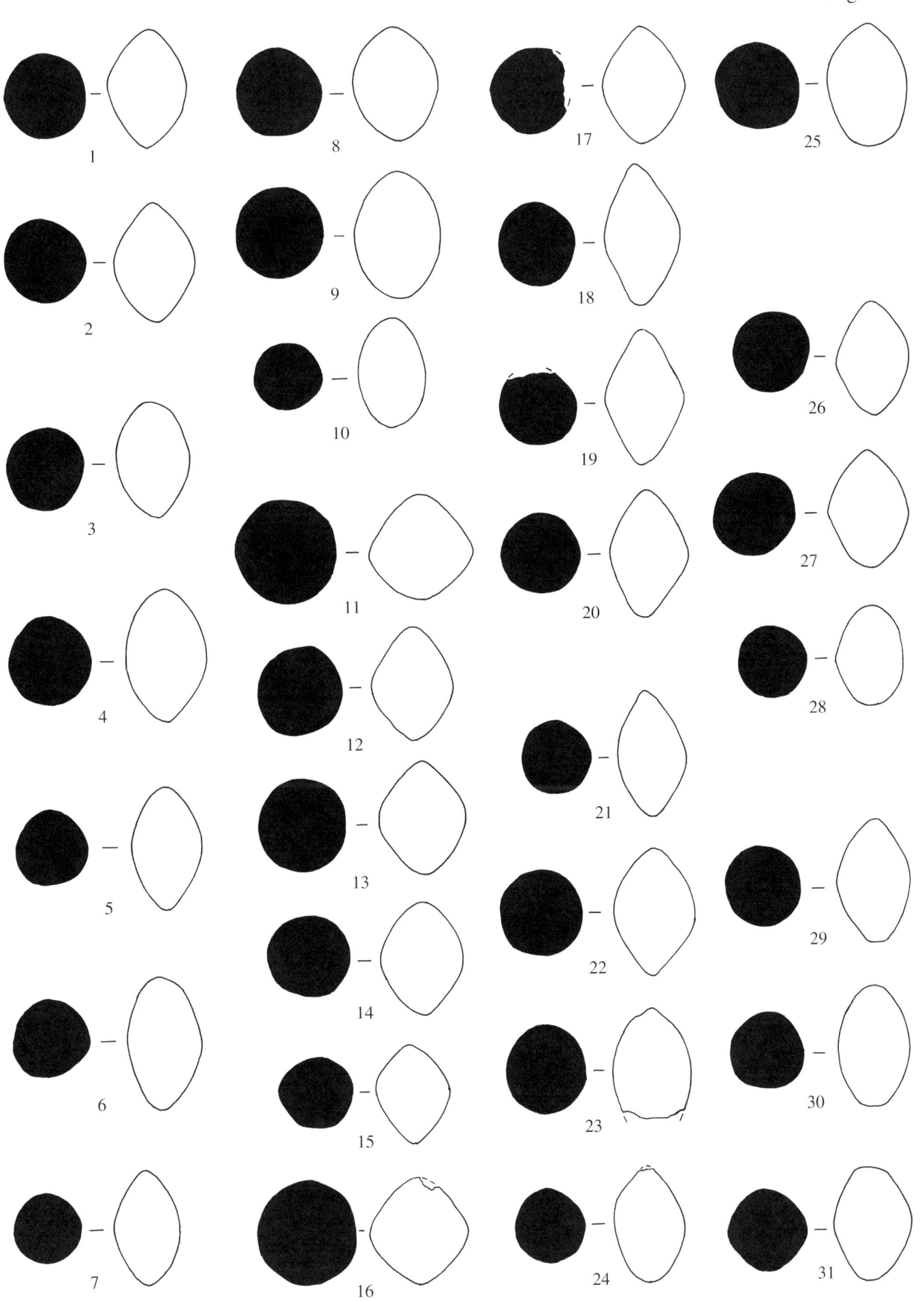

Clay Sling Bullets from Area IV, Room 2A (Phase 3; Period E — Early Bronze Age IVb). Scale 1:2

Figure 167

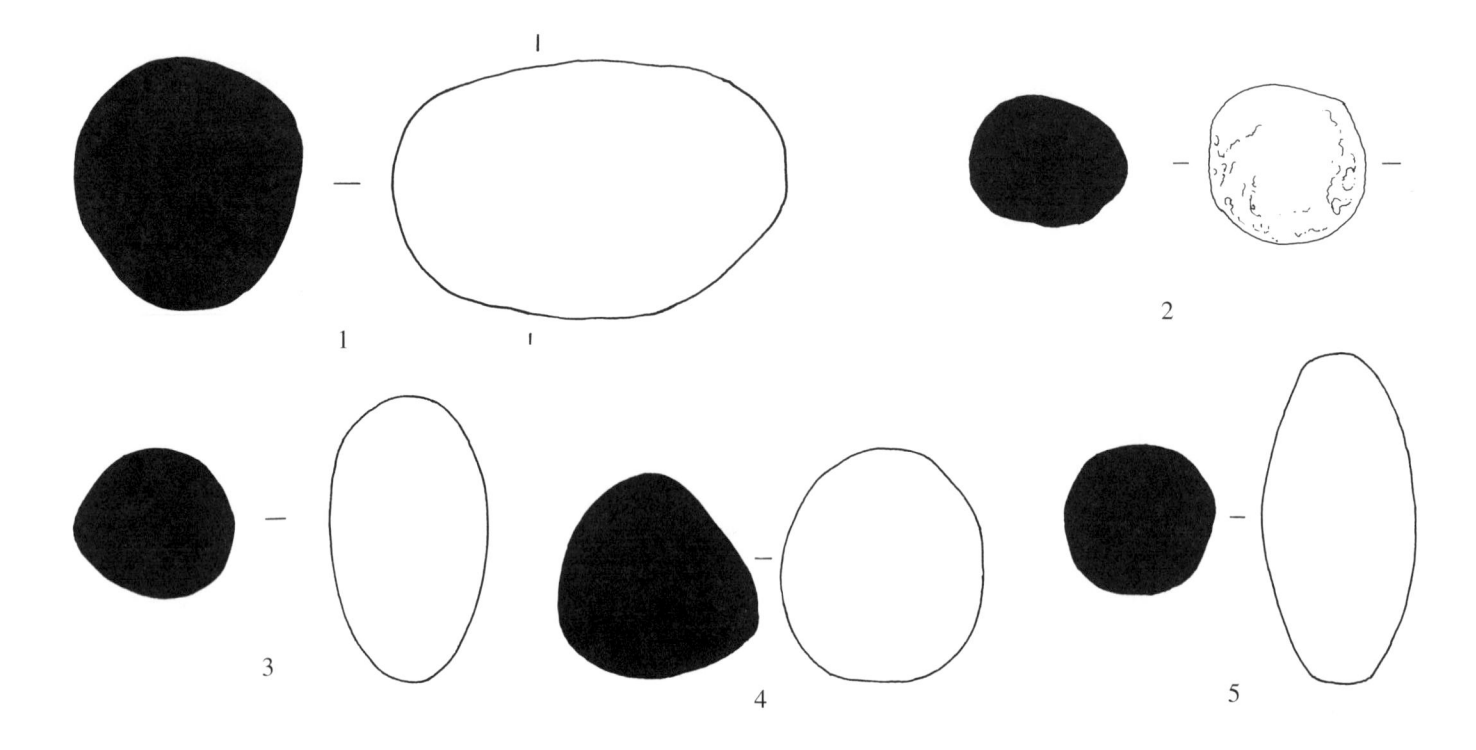

Stone Pestle/Pounder Tool and Stone Sling Bullets from Area IV (Phases 2A–3; Periods F and E — Early Bronze Age IVa and Early Bronze Age IVb). Scale 1:2

1. Type SF.3a (SW. 699; IVM, 2.6, Room 7). Phase 2A (EB IVa). Pestle/pounder. Fine-grained reddish igneous rock interspersed with fine creamy lines. Smooth on all surfaces.
2. Type SF.3b (TS. 3329; Op. 10, 20 = IVN, Room 18). Phase 2A (EB IVa). Stone sling bullet.
3. Type SF.3b (TS. 3179; Op. 11, 4.1, Room 20). Phase 2B (EB IVa). Stone sling bullet.
4. Type SF.3b (TS. 3340; Op. 11, 4.1, Room 20). Phase 2B (EB IVa). Stone sling bullet.
5. Type SF.3b (SW. 769; Op. 11, 4.1, Room 20). Phase 2B (EB IVa). Stone sling bullet.
—. Type SF.3b (FN. 186; Op. 11, 4.1, Room 20). Phase 2B (EB IVa). Sling stone. Gray limestone. Measurement: 5 × 6 cm.
—. Type SF.3b (SW. 466; IVN, 1.4, Room 8A/18A). Phase 3 (EB IVb). Stone sling bullet. Flattened spheroid-shaped stone, brown in color.

Figure 168

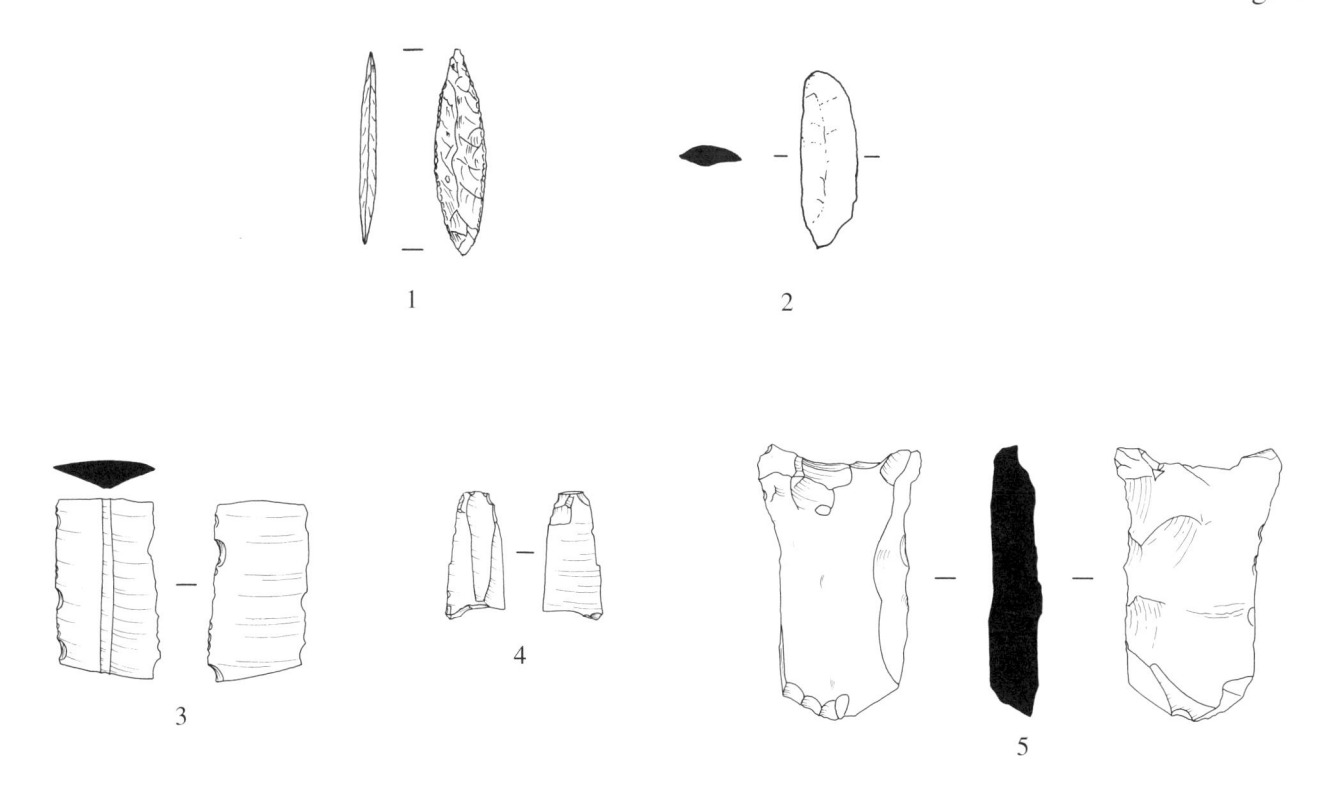

Flint Tools and Weapons from Area IV (Phases 1C–2B; Periods G and F — Early Bronze Age III and Early Bronze Age IVa). Scale 1:2

1. Type SF.12b (SW. 593; IVM, 1.7, Room 7). Phase 2A (EB IVa; see pl. 124a). Arrowhead. Finely manufactured willow-shaped flint point.
2. Type SF.12a (TS. 3270a; Op. 6, 1.30, Room 9). Phase 2B (EB IVa). Scraping tool.
3. Type SF.12a (TS. 3270b; Op. 6, 1.30, Room 9). Phase 2B (EB IVa). Incomplete sickle-like blade. Triangular in section.
4. Type SF.12a (TS. 3270c; Op. 6, 1.30, Room 9). Phase 2B (EB IVa). Boring tool. Tip and part of shaft broken.
5. Type SF.12a (TS. 3174; Op. 11, 5.1, Room 19). Phase 2B (EB IVa). Scraping tool. Complete.
—. Type SF.12a (SC. 163; IVZ(S), 5.9a). Phase 1C (EB III). Scraping tool. Complete.

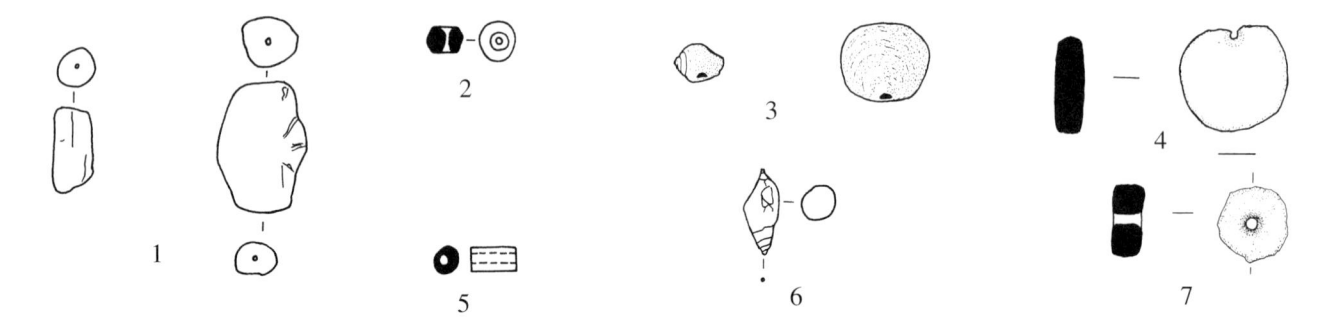

Figure 169

Figure 169. Beads and Pendants from Area IV (Phases 2A–4; Periods F to E–D — Early Bronze Age IVa to Early–Middle Bronze Age). Scale 1:2

1. Type SF.4b (SW. 653; IVJ, 1.5, Room 4). Phase 2B (EB IVa). Two beads. Hematite globules, roughly barrel shaped, pierced with longitudinal holes for stringing.
2. Type SF.4b (SW. 529; IVJ, 2.1, Room 4). Phase 2A (EB IVa). Bead. Obsidian. Bevel shaped with central stringing hole bored from two sides.
3. Type SF.4c (SW. 354; IVK, 2.4, Room 2). Phase 2B (EB IVa). Two pendants. Shell. Pink-colored seashells pierced for stringing at smaller hinged edge.
—. Type SF.4c (SW. 823; Op. 6, 3.9, Room 33). Phase 4 (EB–MB; see pl. 124b). Worked shell pendant with suspension hole drilled on one curved broad side; inside decorated with shallow drilled circular impressions.
4. Type SF.4c (SW. 399; IVL, 2.1, Room 3A). Phase 3 (EB IVb). Pendant. Clay. Outer portion of drilled hole for stringing broken off. Very fine, soft, creamy-white fired ware.
5. Type SF.4b (SW. 515; IVO, 1.4, Room 10). Phase 2A (EB IVa). Bead. Bone. Cylindrical shaped with longitudinal drilled hole for stringing.
—. Type SF.4c (FN. 145; Op. 7, 19.1; Gateway street). Phase 2A(a) (EB IVa). Pendant. Shell. Bivalve.
6. Type SF.4b (SW. 594; XA, 1.3, Room 15). Phase 2B (EB IVa). Bead. Snail shell with drilled hole near one end for stringing.
—. Type SF.9a (FN. 108; Op. 6, 14.6, Room 24). Phase 3 (EB IVb). Tool? Fragment of worked bone.
7. Type SF.4b (SW. 482; XA, 1.1, above Room 15A). Phase 4 (EB–MB). Bead. Clay. Fine white ware.


Figure 170. Miscellaneous Vessels and Objects from Area IV (Phases 1B, 2A–5; Periods H, F, E, and E–D — Early Bronze Age II, Early Bronze Age IVa, Early Bronze Age IVb, and Early–Middle Bronze Age)

1. Type SV.5 (SW. 342; IVE, 1.6 = NE corner of IVK, Room 2). Phase 2A (EB IVa). Windowed incense or pedestal stand fragment. Remains of two windows extant. Coarse pink ware with lime and mica grits, evenly fired. Creamy-buff slip on all surfaces.
—. Type SF.6e (FN. 82; Op. 6, 17.3, Room 17). Phase 2A (EB IVa). A possible clay counter; disk shaped.
—. Type SF.6b (FN. 156; Op. 7, 19.1, Gateway street). Phase 2A(a) (EB IVa). Clay spindle whorl. Diameter, 6.4 cm; thickness, 1.2 cm at center; central stringing hole, 9 mm diameter. Hard grayish-buff ware with white and gray lime grits, evenly fired. Heavily chipped at the edges.
2. Type SF.6b (SW. 218; IVB, 3.3, Room 1). Phase 2B (EB IVa). Clay spindle whorl. Fairly fine brown ware with lime grits and some vegetable temper.
—. Type SF.8c (FN. 136; Op. 6, 1.30, Room 9). Phase 2B (EB IVa). Plaster sealing. Ball-shaped with string impressions on the surfaces.
3. Type SF.6b (SW. 211; IVC, 1.2; Town Wall Tower). Phase 3 (EB IVb). Clay spindle whorl. About 1/2 segment of a reused pot sherd cut with uneven circumference.
—. Type SF.6b (FN. 144; Op. 7, Surf. 1.1; Topsoil). Phase 4 (EB–MB). Clay spindle whorl. Diameter, 4.7 cm; pierced hole in center, 4 mm. Fine pink ware.
4. Type SV.5 (SW. 457a; IVK, 2.4, Room 2). Phase 2B (EB IVa). Tripod footed bowl or jar, incomplete. Unbaked, handmade, heavily straw-tempered *libn* ware with thick coat of plaster covering surfaces inside and outside.
5 a, b. Type 6g (SW. 648; IVJ/O, 3.2, east–west baulk, Room 5). Phase 2B (EB IVa; see pl. 128b). Two unfired handmade, heavily straw-tempered *libn* ware, conical-shaped, objects with cylindrical-shaped hollows in center of each object.

Figure 170

6. Type SF.2c (SW. 521; XA, 1.3, Room 15). Phase 2B (EB IVa; see pl. 120d). Model house or compartment vessel. Fairly coarse pink ware with cream slip in and out.
7. Type SV.5 (PM. C.14; SW. 768; Op. 11, 5.1, Room 19). Phase 2B. Footed mortar with incised cross shape on underside. Very coarse grayish-brown ware with many lime and mica inclusions, fairly evenly fired. Creamy-green slip on all surfaces.
8. Type SV.3 (IP [G.4] F. II; SW. 655; IVN, 4.3, Room 8A). Phase 3 (EB IVb; see pl. 103a and *Chapter 7, Incised Pottery Typology* catalogue for parallels). Zoomorphic-shaped vessel with bird-like head and neck spout, pouring holes through both the beak and the eyes; and with incised linear decoration extended down the neck onto the surviving portion of the body of the vessel. Fairly coarse green ware, evenly fired.
—. Type SV.5 (FN. 127; Op. 6, 14.1, Room 24). Phase 3 (EB IVb). Clay vessel. Fragment of unidentifiable form.
9. Type SV.2 (TS. 1751; IVN, 1.1; Topsoil). Phase 5 (EB–MB). Spout fragment. Medium fine pink ware, evenly fired.
10. Type SF.6d (TS. 3094; IVS, 1.2; Surface soil near gateway through town wall). Phase 5 (EB–MB). Mold for bread. Fairly coarse pinkish-brown ware, evenly fired. Heavy lime encrustation on all surfaces.
11. Type SV.2 (SC. 3281; IVM, 10.3, Below Room 7). Phase 1B (EB II). Pottery vessel spout. Fairly fine buff ware with very small lime and mica grits, evenly fired. Self slip out.
12. Type SV.2 (SC. 3279; IVM, 3.1, Room 7, Pit A). Phase 2A (EB IVa). Pottery vessel spout. Slightly coarse pinkish-buff ware with small lime and mica grits, evenly fired. Creamy-buff slip in and out.
13. Type SV.2 (SC. 3278; IVN, 4.4, Room 18). Phase 2A (EB IVa). Pottery vessel spout. Slightly coarse pinkish-buff ware with medium-sized lime and small mica grits, evenly fired. Self slip in and out.
14. Type SV.2 (SC. 3280; IVP, 1.2, Room 9B). Phase 4 (EB IVb). Pottery vessel spout or leg of vessel. Fairly coarse grayish-buff ware with many black and white lime grits, evenly fired. Self slip in and out.
—. Type SF.6d (SW. 596; IVQ, Unstratified). Unfired clay object with bowl-like impression; possibly a fragment of a crucible bowl.

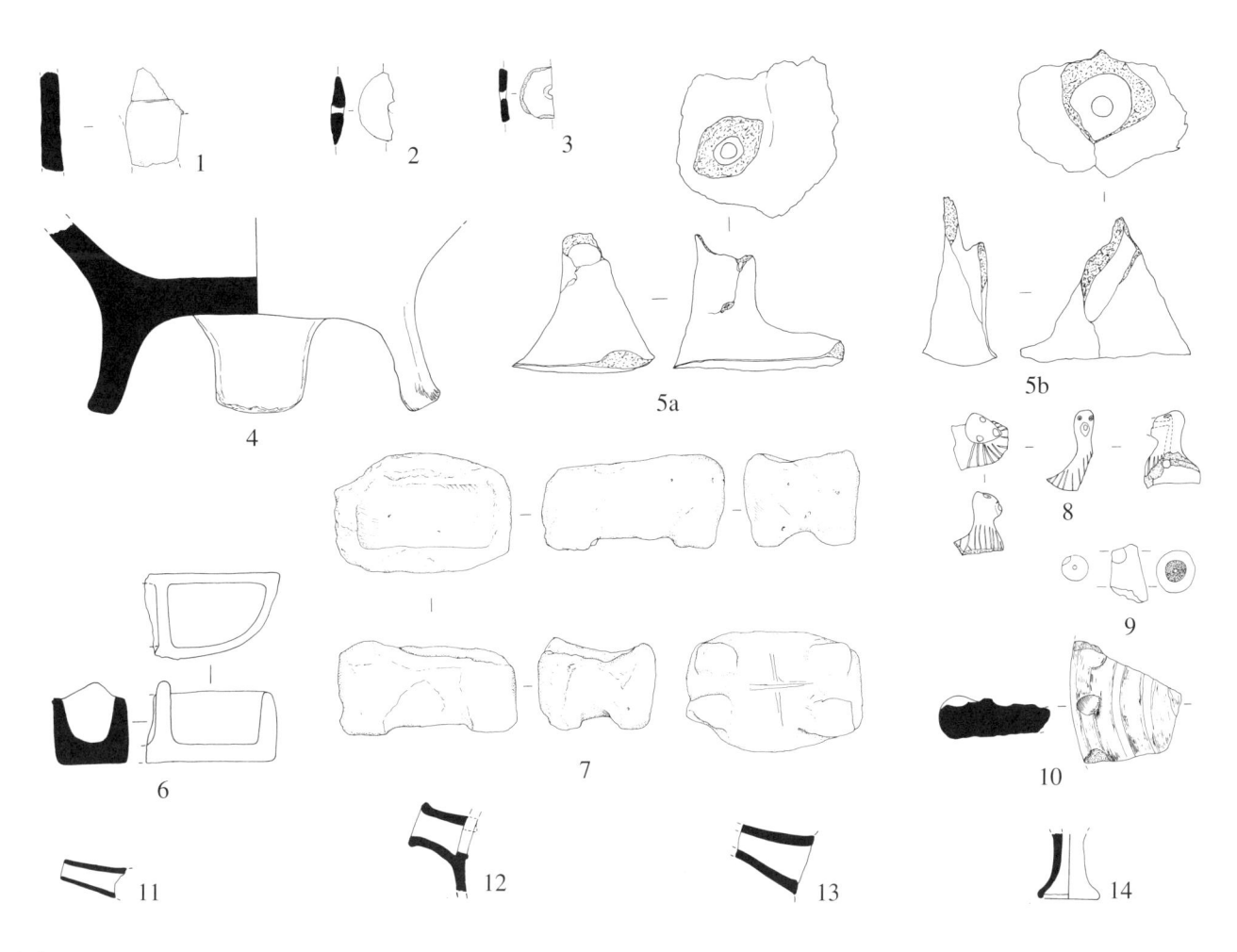

Miscellaneous Vessels and Objects from Area IV (Phases 1B, 2A–5; Periods H, F, E, and E–D — Early Bronze Age II, Early Bronze Age IVa, Early Bronze Age IVb, and Early–Middle Bronze Age). Scale 1:2

Figure 171. Stone Mortars, Type SF.3a, from Area IV (Phases 2A–4; Periods F to E–D — Early Bronze Age IVa to Early–Middle Bronze Age)

1. Type SF.3c (SW. 222; IVB, 2.2, Tower, Stone Fndts.). Phase 2A (EB IVa). Mortar. Limestone fragment with very pitted surfaces and traces of burning in the surviving portion of the bowl.
2. Type SF.3c (SW. 221; IVB, 2.2, Tower, Stone Fndts.). Phase 2A (EB IVa). Mortar. Limestone fragment with very pitted surfaces. Two working bowl depressions, one large and one small, on opposing sides of the vessel.
3. Type SF.3c (SW. 364; IVB, 2.2, Tower, Stone Fndts.). Phase 2A (EB IVa). Mortar. Very porous dark gray vesicular basalt.
4. Type SF.3c (SW. 353; IVA, 2.3; Street). Phase 2B (EB IVa). Mortar. Limestone with two similar-sized working bowl depressions on opposing sides of the vessel.
—. Type SF.3c (SW. 407; IVA, 2.4; Street). Phase 2B (EB IVa). Mortar. Limestone. Cream color. Rounded on lower surface; upper surface flat with bowl-like depression. Measurements: $6.5 \times 13.0 \times 15.0$ cm.
5. Type SF.3c (SW. 164; IVC, 1.2; Town Wall Tower). Phase 3 (EB IVb). Mortar. Cream-colored limestone, irregularly shaped.
6. Type SF.3c (SW. 700; IVM, 3.1, Room 7, Pit A). Phase 2A (EB IVa). Mortar fragment. Grayish-black lump of basalt with a very rough and pitted surface surrounding the bowl area.
7. Type SF.3c (SW. 821; Op. 6, 3.1, Room 32). Phase 4 (EB–MB; see pl. 126c). Four-footed mortar. Gray basalt.

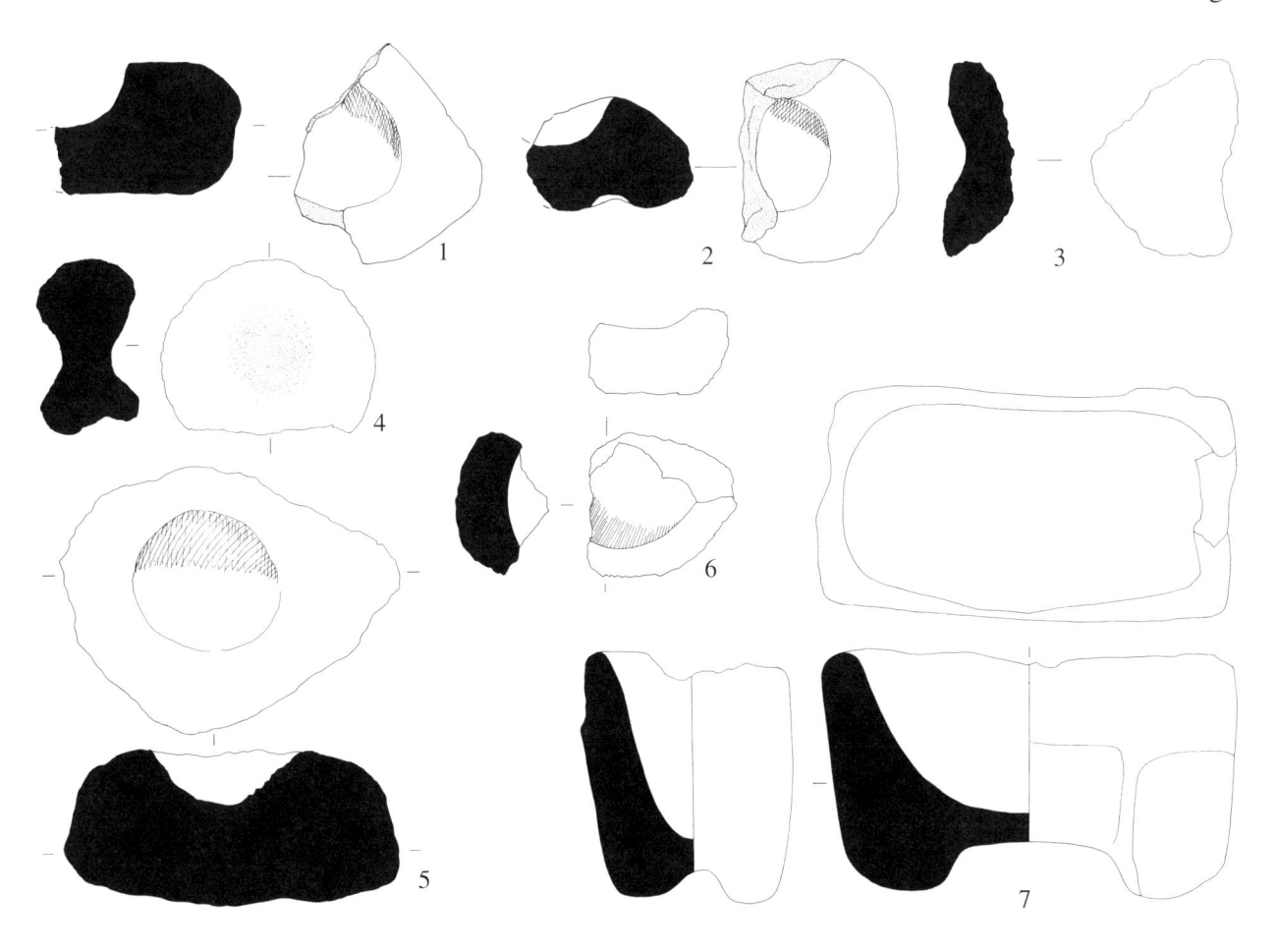

Figure 171

Stone Mortars, Type SF.3a, from Area IV (Phases 2A–4; Periods F to E–D — Early Bronze Age IVa to Early–Middle Bronze Age). Scale 1:5

Figure 172. Grinding Stones, Type SF.3a, from Area IV (Phases 2A–4; Periods F to E–D — Early Bronze Age IVa to Early–Middle Bronze Age)

—. Type SF.3a (SW. 212; IVB, 2.2, Room 1). Phase 2A (EB IVa). Basalt-trachyte fragment. Semi-ovoid and broken at each end. Measurements: length, 14.6 cm; maximum height, 8.1 cm; and width, 6.0 cm.
1. Type SF.3a (SW. 335; IVD, 2.4, Room 2). Phase 2B (EB IVa). Volcanic igneous rock. Dark brownish-black with reddish colored area.
2. Type SF.3a (SW. 351; IVF, 1.13, Room 1). Phase 2A (EB IVa). Grayish-pink limestone. Elongate and elliptical with one end broken.
—. Type SF.3a (SW. 609; IVJ, 3.5, Room 5, Bin). Phase 2A (EB IVa). Basalt. Small fragment, 8 cm long.
—. Type SF.3a (SW. 371; IVK, 2.4, Room 2). Phase 2B (EB IVa). Limestone, pock-marked and cream colored. Elongate, elliptical, and parabolic in section. Measurements: $5.5 \times 11.0 \times 21.0$ cm.
—. Type SF.3a (SW. 724; IVX, 10.7 = IVM, Room 7). Phase 2A (EB IVa). Basalt, coarse pitted surfaces and charcoal colored. Both ends broken. Roughly rectangular shape. Measurements: $16.5 \times 21.8$ cm.
3. Type SF.3a (TS. 3168; Op. 10, 23, Room 8). Phase 2A (EB IVa). Limestone. Tips of both ends broken.
4. Type SF.3a (TS. 3169; Op. 10, 23, Room 8). Phase 2A (EB IVa). Limestone. Major portion of one end broken and small segment of other end chipped.
—. Type SF.3a (TS. 1769; IVP, 1.6, Room 9). Phase 2A (EB IVa). Basalt. Flat on lower grinding surface and semi-circular on top. Hole bored through for secondary use as a pivot stone(?). Measurements: $11.0 \times 15.5$ cm.
—. Type SF.3a (SW. 701; IVQ, 1.4, Room 6). Phase 2A (EB IVa). Limestone. Cream colored. Flat on lower grinding surface and semi-circular on top. One end vertical and the other end tapered. Measurements: $10.6 \times 10.9$ cm.
—. Type SF.3a (SW. 705; IVR, 2.5, Room 12A). Phase 2A (EB IVa). Igneous rock, fine-grained, reddish color. One end vertical, other end tapered to rounded point. Flat on lower grinding surface; upper surface also flat with small depression near vertical end for thumb grip(?). Measurements: $7.4 \times 10.5$ cm.
—. Type SF.3a (SW. 707; IVS, 4.10, Room 12). Phase 2A (EB IVa). Basalt, charcoal gray color. Flat on lower grinding surface and semi-circular on top.
—. Type SF.3a (SW. 709; IVS, 4.10, Room 12). Phase 2A (EB IVa). Igneous rock, fine-grained, charcoal black color. Oblong with rounded ends. Lower grinding surface and one end worn.
—. Type SF.3a (SW. 710; IVS, 4.10, Room 12). Phase 2A (EB IVa). Igneous rock, fine-grained, charcoal to reddish color. Almost ovoid shape, one end broken transversely; lower grinding surface flat.
—. Type SF.3a (SW. 689; IVW, 2.1). Phase 2A (EB IVa). Limestone. Cream color. Flat on lower grinding surface and semi-circular on top. One end vertical and the other end tapered to a point. Measurements: $5.2 \times 9.9 \times 19.5$ cm.
—. Type SF.3a (SW. 691; IVW, 2.1). Phase 2A (EB IVa). Limestone. Cream color. Flat on lower grinding surface and on sides and top. One end vertical and the other end tapered. Measurements: $8.0 \times 11.7 \times 16.1$ cm.
—. Type SF.3a (SW. 690; IVW, 2.1). Phase 2A (EB IVa). Basalt. Black color. Flat on lower grinding surface and semi-circular on top. One end vertical and the other end tapered. Measurements: $6.9 \times 12.2 \times 15.0$ cm.
—. Type SF.3a (SW. 582; XA, 1.4, Room 15). Phase 2A (EB IVa). Limestone. Elliptical shaped. Measurements: $6 \times 10 \times 15$ cm.
—. Type SF.3a (SW. 583; XA, 1.4, Room 15). Phase 2A (EB IVa). Limestone. About 1/2 of elliptical shaped fragment. Measurements: $6 \times 10 \times 17$ cm.
—. Type SF.3a (SW. 587; XA, 1.4, Room 15). Phase 2A (EB IVa). Limestone. Complete, elliptical shaped. Grinding surface has large hole in surface. Measurements: $8 \times 14 \times 30$ cm.
—. Type SF.3a (SW. 574; IVP, 1.5, Room 9). Phase 2B (EB IVa). Limestone. Complete, elliptical shaped. Measurements: $5 \times 13 \times 35$ cm.
—. Type SF.3a (SW. 573; IVP, 1.5, Room 9). Phase 2B (EB IVa). Limestone. Complete, elliptical shaped. Measurements: $6 \times 12 \times 33$ cm.
—. Type SF.3a (SW. 563; IVP, 1.5, Room 9). Phase 2B (EB IVa). Basalt, vesicular. Dark gray color. Fragment with both ends broken. Elliptical-shaped. Measurements: $5 \times 8 \times 10$ cm.
—. Type SF.3a (SW. 702; IVS, 4.2, Room 12A). Phase 3 (EB IVb). Limestone. Cream color. Flat on lower grinding surface and rounded on top. One end vertical and the other end rough and uneven. Measurements: $9.2 \times 13.0$ cm.
—. Type SF.3a (SW. 703; IVS, 4.2, Room 12A). Phase 3 (EB IVb). Limestone. Pinkish color. Flat on lower grinding surface with triangular-shaped section. Both ends vertical. Measurements: $11.6 \times 12.2$ cm.
—. Type SF.3a (SW. 692; IVW, 1.4). Phase 2B (EB IVa). Limestone. Cream color. Flat on lower grinding surface and rounded on top. One end vertical and the other end slightly rounded. Measurements: $6.0 \times 11.6 \times 10.3$ cm.
—. Type SF.3a (SW. 717; IVZ(N1), 1.5). Phase 2B (EB IVa). Basalt, black. Flat on lower grinding surface and rounded on top. Both ends broken vertically. Very rough pitted surfaces. Measurements: $11.6 \times 14.0$ cm.
—. Type SF.3a (SW. 716; IVZ(N1), 1.5). Phase 2B (EB IVa). Igneous rock, fine-grained. Dark gray color. Flat on both upper and lower surfaces, almost square in shape with one corner rounded and the other three corners rectangular-shaped. Measurements: $1.5 \times 5.3 \times 5.5$ cm.
—. Type SF.3a (SW. 718; IVZ(S), 5.3). Phase 2B (EB IVa). Igneous rock, fine-grained. Light gray color. Flat on lower grinding surface and rounded on top. One end rounded and the other end tapered. Slightly pitted.
—. Type SF.3a (SW. 584; XA, 1.3, Room 15). Phase 2B (EB IVa). Limestone. Elliptical shaped. Fragment. Measurements: $5 \times 12 \times 14$ cm.
5. Type SF.3a (TS. 3171; Op. 11, 4.1, Room 20). Phase 2B (EB IVa). Limestone. Cream color. Flat on lower grinding surface and semi-circular on top. Fairly rough and pitted.
6. Type SF.3a (TS. 3170; Op. 11, 4.1, Room 20). Phase 2B (EB IVa). Limestone. Cream color. Flat on lower grinding surface and semi-circular on top except on one end, which is sharply cut away for securing a firm hold with one hand on the grinder.
—. Type SF.3a (SW. 719; IVZ(N1), 2.1). Phase 3 (EB IVb). Basalt. Black color and very rough and pitted. Flat on lower grinding surface and rounded on top. One end tapered to rounded point and the other end vertically broken. Measurements: $12.2 \times 13.6$ cm.
—. Type SF.3a (SW. 656; IVD, 1.3). Phase 4 (EB IVb). Basalt. Black color. Fragment. Measurements: $4.5 \times 8.5 \times 9.0$ cm.
—. Type SF.3a (SW. 704; IVQ, 3.1, Room 6A). Phase 3 (EB IVb). Limestone. Cream color. Flat on lower grinding surface with a slight depression. Upper surface ovoid with a thin veneer layer of flint. Both sides diagonal. One end vertical and the other end rounded.
7. Type SF.3a (SW. 683; IVW, 1.5). Phase 3 (EB IVb). Limestone. Cream color. Flat on lower grinding surface and semi-circular on top. One end rounded and the other end broken off transversely. Very pitted. Measurements: $9 \times 11 \times 22$ cm.
8. Type SF.3a (TS. 1612; IVW, 1.3). Phase 3 (EB IVb). Limestone. Cream color. Flat on lower grinding surface and rounded on top. One end tapered to rounded point and the other end transversely broken.
—. Type SF.3a (SW. 492; XA, 1.1, above Room 15A). Phase 4 (EB–MB). Limestone. Elliptical-shaped fragment. Measurements: $6 \times 12 \times 25$ cm.
—. Type SF.3a (SW. 708; IVZ(S), 5.1). Phase 4 (EB IVb). Basalt. Charcoal gray color. Flat on lower grinding surface and rougly-shaped rectangular section. Rough and pitted.

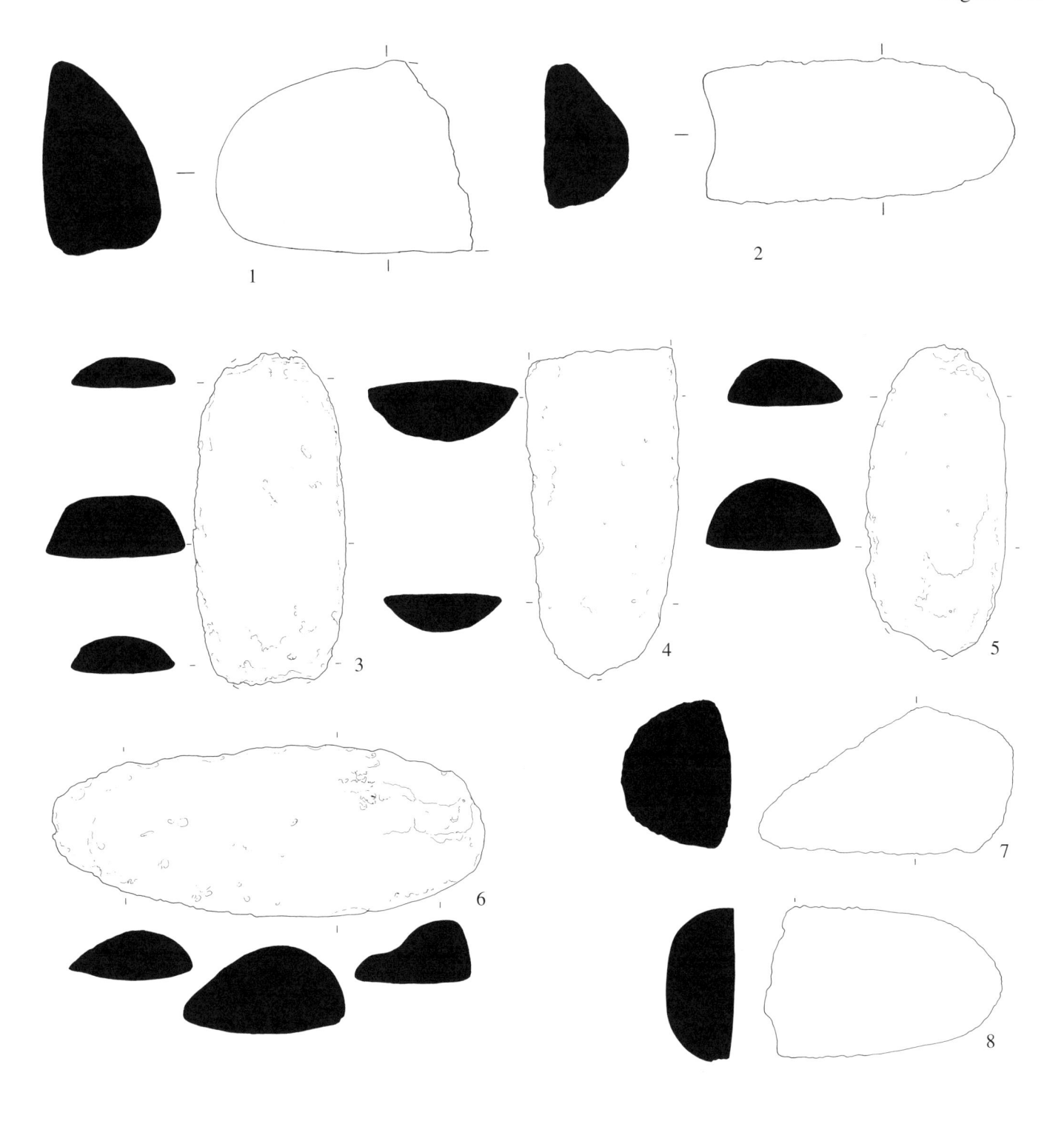

Figure 172

Grinding Stones, Type SF.3a, from Area IV (Phases 2A–4; Periods F to E–D — Early Bronze Age IVa to Early–Middle Bronze Age). Scale 1:5

Figure 173

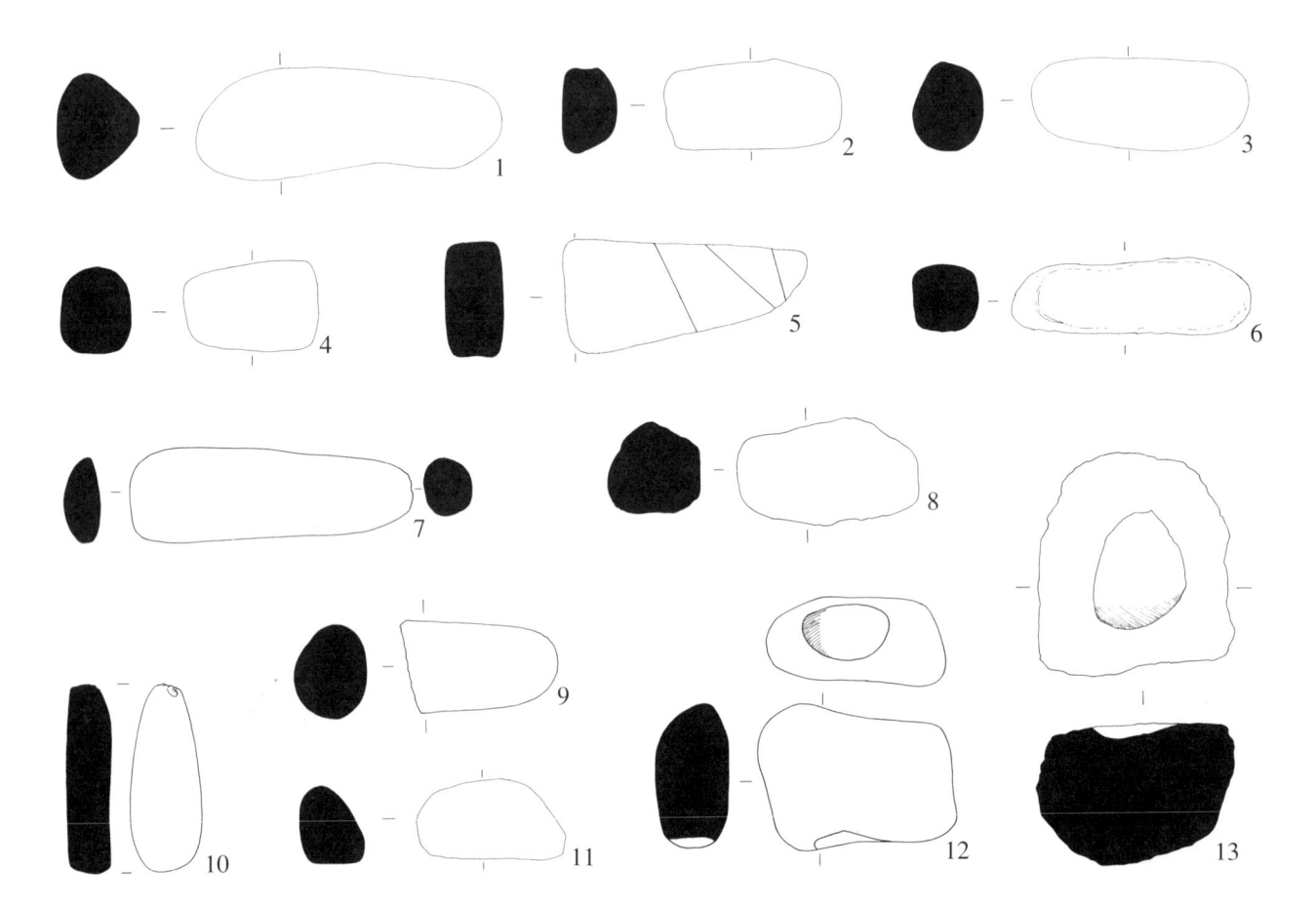

Stone Pounders and Grinder/Pounder Tools, Type SF.3a, from Area IV (Phases 2A–5; Periods F to E–D — Early Bronze Age IVa to Early–Middle Bronze Age). Scale 1:5

1. Type SF.3a (SW. 333; IVD, 2.4, Room 2). Phase 2B (EB IVa). Pounder. Igneous rock with medium-sized feldspar crystal, fine-grained.
2. Type SF.3a (SW. 336; IVD, 2.5, Room 2). Phase 2B (EB IVa). Pounder. Igneous rock. Greenish, medium grained with weathered reddish-brown outer skin. One end broken.
—. Type SF.3a (SW. 408; IVF, 1.11–13, Room 1). Phase 2B (EB IVa). Pounder. Igneous rock. Grayish-brown. Rectangular in section with rounded edges. Measurements: 5.5 × 9.0 × 12.0 cm.
3. Type SF.3a (SW. 337; IVF, 1.12, Room 1). Phase 2B (EB IVa). Pounder. Igneous rock. Dark gray and veined.
4. Type SF.3a (SW. 411; IVF, 3.1, Room 1). Phase 2A (EB IVa). Pounder. Igneous rock. Fine-grained, dark gray color.
—. Type SF.3a (SW. 430; IVF, 4.1, Room 1). Phase 2A (EB IVa). Pounder. Igneous rock. Dark gray color. Elongate shape with well rounded and abraded edges on both ends. Measurements: 5 × 6 × 11 cm.
—. Type SF.3a (SW. 431; IVF, 4.1, Room 1). Phase 2A (EB IVa). Pounder. Igneous rock. Gray color. Slightly tapered with roughly rectangular cross section. One end broken, broad end abraded and chipped. Measurements: 5 × 10 × 12 cm.
5. Type SF.3a (SW. 332; IVG, 1.5, Room 3). Phase 2A (EB IVa). Pounder. Chert with fine thin veins. Dark brown color.
—. Type SF.3a (SW. 571; IVJ, 1.5, Room 4). Phase 2B (EB IVa). Pounder. Limestone fragment. Elliptical shape. Measurements: 6 × 10 × 17 cm.
6. Type SF.3a (TS. 3176; Op. 6, 18.3, Room 16). Phase 2A (EB IVa). Pounder. Limestone.
—. Type SF.3a (SW. 612; IVP, 1.6, Room 9). Phase 2A (EB IVa). Pounder. Euphrates cobble. Measurements: 5 × 8 × 12 cm.
—. Type SF.3a (SW. 615; IVQ, 1.6, Room 6). Phase 2A (EB IVa). Pounder. Euphrates cobble. Dark brown color. Elongate shape very worn and chipped at both ends. Measurements: 4 × 7 × 17 cm.
7. Type SF.3a (SW. 616; IVQ, 1.6, Room 6). Phase 2A (EB IVa). Pounder. Euphrates cobble. Elongate shape, apparently worn from use into a rounded triangular cross section. Utilized at both ends. Measurements: 4 × 6 × 20 cm.
8. Type SF.3a (SW. 687; IVX, 2.2, Room 14). Phase 2B (EB IVa). Pounder. Basalt. Black color. Corners and edges well smoothed. Measurements: 6.7 × 7.7 × 12.7 cm.
—. Type SF.3a (SW. 661; IVO, 1.3, Room 10A). Phase 3 (EB IVb). Pounder. Igneous rock. Greenish-gray color. Elongate shape, abraded at the larger blunt end.
—. Type SF.3a (SW. 562; IVQ, 1.4, Room 6). Phase 2B (EB IVa). Pounder. Euphrates pebble. Elongate, cylindrical shape. Measurements: 4.0 × 12.5 cm.
9. Type SF.3a (SW. 697; IVS, 4.3, Room 12A). Phase 3 (EB IVb). Pounder. Basalt. Grayish-black color. Rounded at one end and broken transversely at the other end.
—. Type SF.3a (SW. 526; XA, 1.2, Room 15A). Phase 3 (EB IVb). Pounder. Fragment of igneous rock. Dark gray.
10. Type SF.3a (SW. 805; Op. 6, 3.16, Room 32). Phase 4 (EB–MB; see pl. 126a). Pounder. Limestone.
11. Type SF.3a (SW. 358; IVG, Unstratified topsoil). Phase 5 (EB–MB). Pounder. Igneous stone. Bluish-gray color.
12. Type SF.3a (SW. 693; IVQ, 1.4, Room 6). Phase 2A (EB IVa). Grinder/Pounder Tool. Igneous stone. Dark red color. Measurements: 6.1 × 8.2 × 13.4 cm.
13. Type SF.3a (SW. 688; IVY, 1.1, debris over street). Phase 5 (EB–MB). Grinder/Pounder Tool. Limestone. Cream color. Measurements: 8.5 × 14.1 × 14.8 cm.

Figure 174

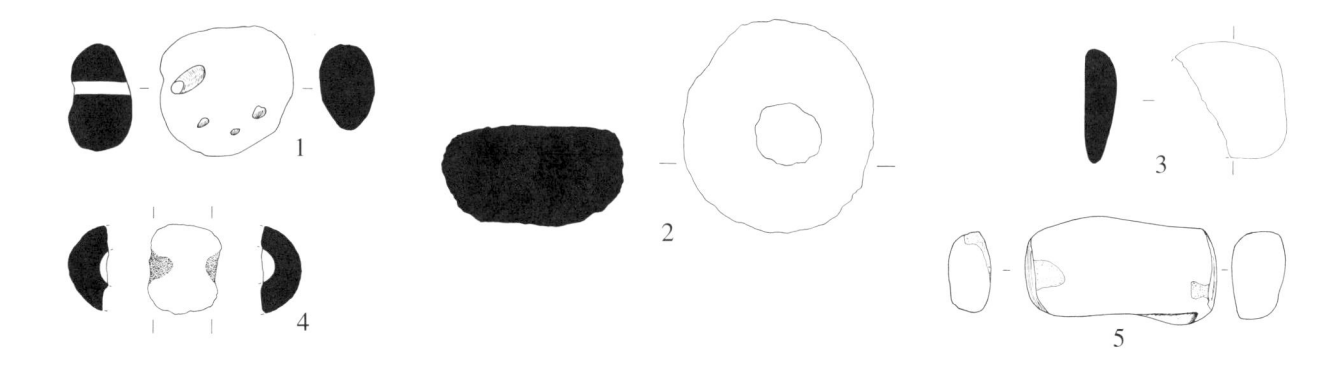

Stone Weights and Miscellaneous Stone Objects from Area IV (Phases 1C–5; Periods G to E–D — Early Bronze Age III to Early–Middle Bronze Age). Scale 1:5

1. Type SF.3e (SW. 576; IVQ, 1.6, Room 6). Phase 2A (EB IVa). Weight (Digging Stick?). Natural limestone. Gray color. One hole pierced through near the edge. Measurements: 5 × 8 × 9 cm.
2. Type SF.3e (SW. 686; IVQ, 2.3, Room 6). Phase 2B (EB IVa). Weight (Digging Stick). Limestone. Gray color. Heavily pitted. Hole bored from two sides.
—. Type SF.3e (SW. 468; IVN, 1.4, Room 8A/18A). Phase 3 (EB IVb). Loom weight. Vesicular basalt. Dark gray color. One half of a ring shape. Measurements: external diameter, 6.5 cm; internal diameter, 2.0 cm.
3. Type SF.3a (SW. 355; IVE, 3.2 = IVL, Room 3). Phase 2A (EB IVa). Polisher. Tabular-shaped fragment. Polished, reddish-brown color. Fine-grained stone.
—. Type SF.3a (FN. 112; Op. 6, 18.7, Room 16). Phase 2A (EB IVa). Sphere-shaped rubbing stone. Chalky limestone. One half segment.
—. Type SF.3f (FN. 161; Op. 7, 20.1, Room 36). Phase 2A(a) (EB IVa). White limestone disk. Measurements: 2.6 × 7.0 mm.
—. Type SF.3a (FN. 160; Op. 7, 21.1, Room 35). Phase 2A(a) (EB IVa). Sphere-shaped rubbing stone. Gray limestone. Measurement: 2.5 cm in diameter.
—. Type SF.3e (FN. 139; Op. 6, 20.2, Pre-Room 9). Phase 1C (EB III). Weight. Pyrite. Cylindrical shape.
—. Type SF.3a (FN. 53; Op. 6, 1.19, Room 9). Phase 2B (EB IVa). Sphere-shaped rubbing stone. White limestone. Measurement: 3.5 cm in diameter.
—. Type SF.3e (FN. 164; Op. 6, 1.30, Room 9). Phase 2B (EB IVa). Weight. Chalky limestone. Groove, 2 cm wide, cut around the circumference. Measurements: 2.0 × 2.2 cm.
—. Type SF.3f (FN. 121; Op. 6, 1.30, Room 9). Phase 2B (EB IVa). Disk. Chalky limestone. Measurements: 2 cm thick × 7 cm diameter.
—. Type SF.3a (FN. 101; Op. 7, 2.3, Room 37). Phase 2B(b) (EB IVb). Rubbing or burnishing stone. Pyrite. Cylindrical shape.
—. Type SF.3a (FN. 71; Op. 7, 4.7, East of Wall 4.6, Room 40). Phase 2B(b) (EB IVb). Unidentified.
4. Type SF.3e (SW. 696; IVY, 1.3, debris above gateway street). Phase 3 (EB IVb). Loom weight. Igneous stone. Grayish-black color. One half extant. Central hole drilled in funnel-like shape from two sides, but not completely through the object.
5. Type SF.3a (SW. 617; IVB–D Extension, Surface soil). Phase 5 (EB–MB). Pounder. Igneous stone. Bluish-black color.
—. Type SF.3d (SW. 511; IVJ, 1.5, Room 4). Phase 2B (EB IVa). Door socket. Vesicular basalt. Dark gray color. Oval shape with deep socket hole. Measurements: 7 × 12 × 14 cm with 4 cm socket diameter.
—. Type SF.3d (SW. 505; IVO, 1.4, Room 10). Phase 2A (EB IVa). Door socket. Limestone. Rectangular shape with smooth surfaces. Measurements: 8 × 10 × 24 cm with 9 cm socket diameter.
—. Type SF.3d (SW. 572; IVJ, 3.2, Bin, Room 5A). Phase 3 (EB IVb). Door socket. Vesicular basalt. Gray color. Circular shape. Measurements: 8 × 16 cm with 4 to 5 cm socket diameter.
—. Type SF.3d (SW. 589; IVF, 1.2, Room 1B). Phase 4 (EB IVb). Door socket. Limestone. Battered fragment. Measurements: 9 × 13 × 20 cm.

Figure 175. Various Small Finds from Area IXA (Phases 2A–4; Periods F to E–D — Early Bronze Age IVa to Early–Middle Bronze Age)

1. Type SF.1a (SW. 504; IXA, 1.1). Phase 4 (EB–MB). Female figurine head with applied button-like eyes, appliqué earrings indented in centers, and short incised stroke decoration for hair on back and sides of head and also as decoration on forehead and bridge of nose. Fairly fine pink ware, evenly fired. Cream slip on all outer surfaces.
2. Type SF.1c (SW. 479; IXA, 1.8b). Phase 2A (EB IVa; see pl. 105e). Upper torso fragment of a female figurine. One shoulder extant with a portion of one arm. Unfired buff clay.
3. Type SF.1d (SW. 436; IXA, 1.4). Phase 2B (EB IVa; see pl. 118c). Animal figurine fragment. Head and horn on right side of the head extant. Fairly fine pinkish-buff ware, evenly fired. Greenish-buff slip on all surfaces.
4. Type SF.1f (SW. 458; IXA, 1.8b). Phase 2A (EB IVa; see pl. 127a, b). Complete profile of an animal-shaped toy designed for wheels and hole through snout for pulling; probably a bull or ram. Left side and legs missing and most of right horn missing. Coarse pink ware, evenly fired. Cream slip over most of outside surfaces.
5. Type SF.2b (SW. 439; IXA, 1.1). Phase 4 (EB–MB). Complete model chariot wheel. Fine pinkish-buff ware, evenly fired.
6. Type SF.6b (TS. 1893; IXA, 1.1). Phase 4 (EB–MB). Reused sherd spindle whorl. Hole drilled from both sides of sherd before firing indicates that this sherd may have come from the base of a jar with a deliberately manufactered drainage hole. Fairly fine pinkish-buff ware, evenly fired. Light creamy-pink slip out.
7. Type SF.5c (SW. 608; IXA, 1.13). Phase 3 (EB IVb). Fragment of a metal pin shaft with little corrosion (copper/bronze?, not analyzed).
—. Type SF.5c (SW. 636; IXA, 1.19). Phase 2A (EB IVa). Six metal pin fragments (copper). See *Appendix 6*.
8. Type SF.3c (SW. 448; IXA, 1.1). Phase 4 (EB–MB; see pl. 127c). Stone mortar. Cream-colored limestone. Deep elliptical inner depression and three short and flat carved feet (two on one end and one on the other end).
—. Type SF.3a (SW. 579; IXA, 1.15a). Phase 3 (EB IVb). Grinding stone fragment. Vesicular basalt.
—. Type SF.3a (SW. 495; IXA, 1.6). Phase 3 (EB IVb). Grinding stone fragment. Elongate limestone, 8 × 10 × 14 cm.
—. Type SF.3a (SW. 490; IXA, 1.6). Phase 3 (EB IVb). Grinding stone with 1/3 of one end missing. High quality limestone, 5 × 10 × 20 cm.
—. Type SF.3c (SW. 449; IXA, 1.2). Phase 3 (EB IVb). Mortar. Irregular-shaped lump of limestone with shallow circular depression in one face and a slight elongate depression in the opposite face. 8 × 13 × 15 cm.
—. Type SF.3a (SW. 510; IXA, 1.6). Phase 3 (EB IVb). Pounder fragment. Igneous rock broken at one end and heavily chipped at the other end. About 3 × 5 × 12 cm.
—. Type SF.3a (SW. 578; IXA, 1.1). Phase 4 (EB–MB). Grinding stone fragment. Elliptical limestone, 6 × 13 × 13 cm.
—. Type SF.3a (SW. 575; IXA, 1.1). Phase 4 (EB–MB). Grinding stone. About half of an elliptical-shaped limestone grinder, 5.5 × 13.0 × 14.0 cm.
—. Type SF.3a (SW. 427; IXA, 1.1). Phase 4 (EB–MB). Pounder. Laminated stone. Hard and elongate with roughly square cross section with rounded edges. No conspicuous sign of abrasion. 4 × 6 × 16 cm.

Figure 175

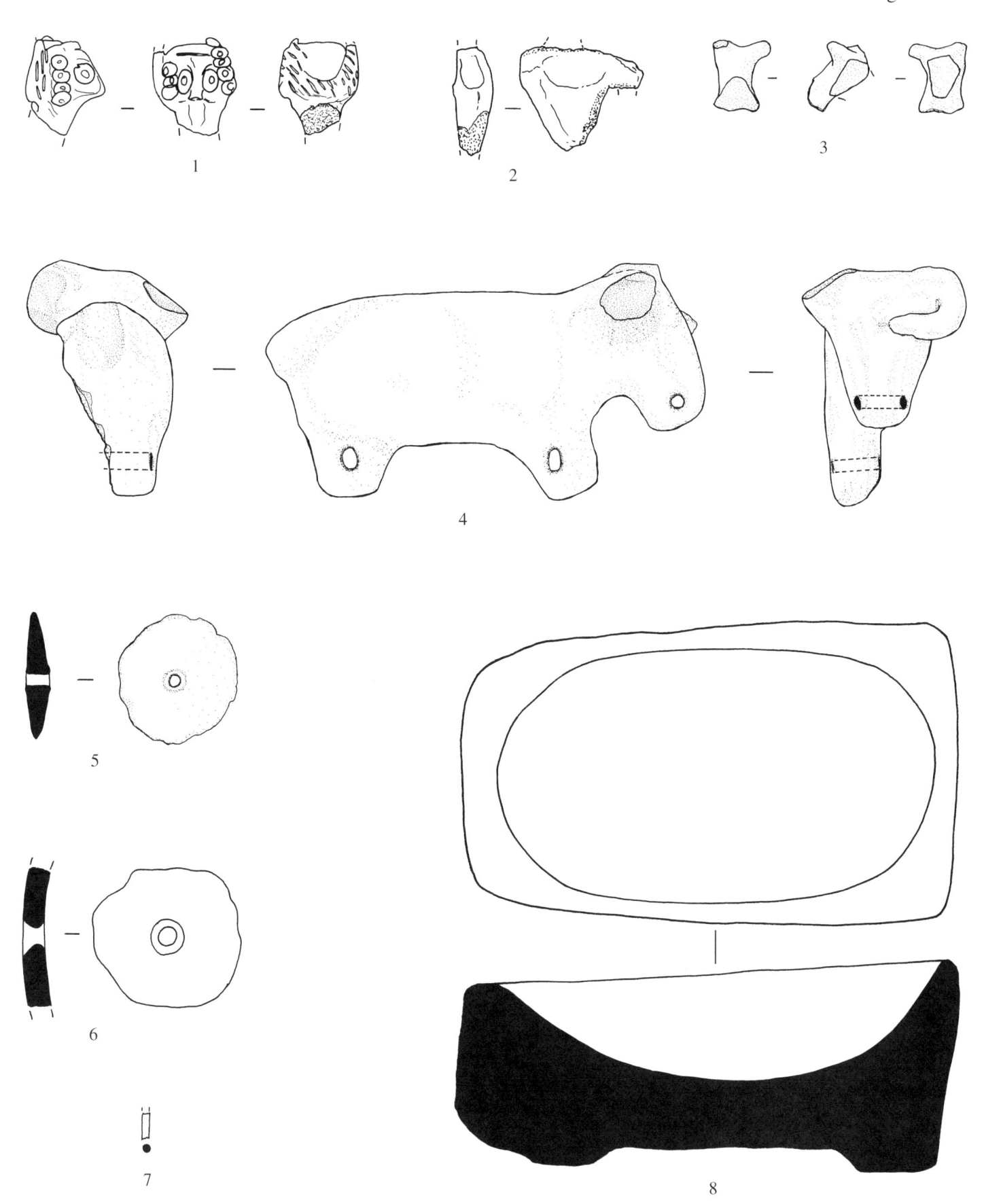

Various Small Finds from Area IXA (Phases 2A–4; Periods F to E–D — Early Bronze Age IVa to Early–Middle Bronze Age). Scale 1:2

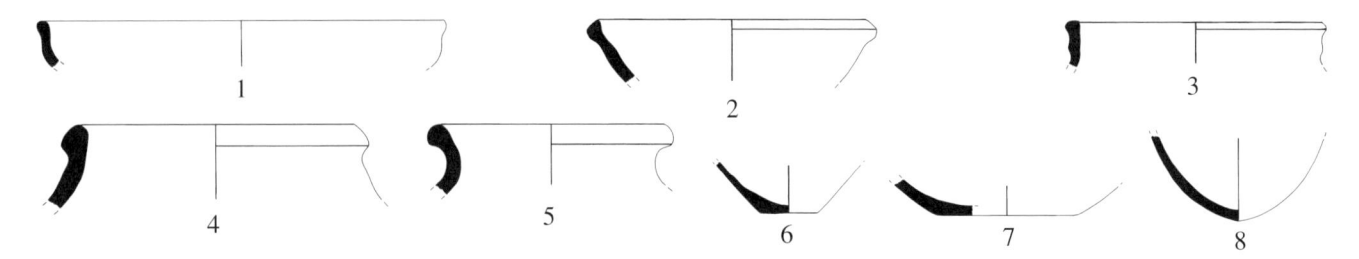

Figure 176

Figure 176. Pottery from Area IIIA, Rooms 4A and 4B (Phase 3; Period F — Early Bronze Age IVa). Scale 1:5.

1. BR. C.I.b (TS. 1793; IIIA, 4.5, Room 4B). Slightly coarse purple-pink ware, evenly fired. Creamy-buff slip in and out.
2. BR. D.VI.b (TS. 1806; IIIA, 4.5, Room 4B). Slightly coarse ware, unevenly fired pink at core and buff at surfaces. Creamy-buff slip in and out.
3. JR. A.III.d (TS. 1913; IIIA, 4.5, Room 4B). Slightly coarse pinkish-buff ware, evenly fired. Creamy-buff slip in and out.
4. JR. H.III.h (TS. 543; IIIA, 4.4, Room 4A). Coarse pink ware with lime and mica grit, evenly fired. Cream slip out.
5. JR. J.II.j (TS. 2354; IIIA, 4.4, Room 4A). Slightly coarse pink ware, evenly fired Buff slip out and over rim in to base of neck.
6. BE. D.II (TS. 3054; IIIA, 4.4, Room 4A). Slightly coarse pinkish-orange ware, evenly fired. Cream slip out.
7. BE. D.III (TS. 1784; IIIA, 4.4, Room 4A). Slightly coarse light grayware, evenly fired. Self slip, burnished out.
8. BE. G (TS. 3052; IIIA, 4.5, Room 4B). Slightly coarse ware, unevenly fired pinkish-buff out and grayish-brown in. Self slip in.

Other Type Series Examples:
  Room 4A — (1) SJR. D.III.a (TS. 1800).
  Room 4B — (1) SBR. A.II.b (SW. 64).

Other Study Collection Examples:
  Room 4A — (1) JR. J.III.ab (SC. 1514), (2) JR. J. (Gen. Type, SC. 119), (3) CP. B.I.i (SC. 1835), (4) CP. C.I.f (SC. 1904), (5) BE. E.I.d (SC. 3159).
  Room 4B — (1) SBR. B.I.h (SC. 496), (2) BR. F.II.a (SC. 789), (3) BR. F.II.c (SC. 805), (4) SJR. C.I.a (SC. 2542), (5) JR. E.II.c (SC. 2000), (6) JR. F.II.e (SC. 1222), (7) JR. (not typed, SC. 102), (8) JR. (not typed, SC. 124), (9) CP. B.I.d (SC. 1828).

Figure 177. Pottery from Area IIIA, Rooms 8A, 8B, and 11 (Phase 4; Period E — Early Bronze Age IVb)

1. SBR. B.I.c (SW. 88; IIIA, 1.4, Room 11). Fairly fine buff ware with black mineral temper, evenly fired.
2. SBR. B.I.d (SW. 58; IIIA, 1.4, Room 11). Fairly fine buff ware, evenly fired.
3. SBR. D.II.c (TS. 1921; IIIA, 4.1, Room 8B). Slightly coarse buff ware, evenly fired. Creamy-buff slip in and out. Charred inside.
4. SBR. D.II.c (TS. 2466; IIIA, 4.1, 4.3, Room 8B). Slightly coarse pink ware, evenly fired. Creamy-buff slip out.
5. SBR. F.I.b (TS. 1205; IIIA, 1.4, 4.1, Rooms 11 and 8B). Fairly fine grayware with fine lime and mica grits, evenly fired. Self slip in and out. Remains of one horizontally positioned lug handle, with two vertically pierced stringing holes, at maximum girth of the upper wall of bowl.
6. BR. E.III.c (TS. 1194 = TS. 1781; IIIA, 1.4, Room 11 and IIIC, 4.6). Fairly fine pinkish-buff ware with fine lime and mica grits, evenly fired. Creamy-buff slip out.
7. SJR. B.II.c (TS. 1786; IIIA, 4.2/3, Rooms 8A/8B). Fine light grayware, evenly fired. Plain self slip in and burnished out.
8. SJR. B.IV.b (TS. 1350; IIIA, 4.1, Room 8B). Body fragment. Slightly coarse pinkish-buff ware, evenly fired.
9. JR. A.II.a (TS. 1810 = TS. 1869; IIIA, 1.4, Room 11). Slightly coarse buff ware, evenly fired. Self slip out.
10. JR. A.IV.a (TS. 1897; IIIA, 4.2/3, Rooms 8A/8B). Slightly coarse pinkish-buff ware, evenly fired. Creamy-buff slip in and out. Charred out and just over rim in.
11. JR. B.III.b (TS. 1898; IIIA, 4.1, Room 8B). Slightly coarse pinkish-buff ware, evenly fired. Creamy-buff slip out and over rim in.
12. JR. B.III.d (PM. C.17; SW. 296 = SW. 322 = TS. 1878; IIIA, 1.4, Room 11 and IIIC, 4.7, Courtyard Room 11A). Slightly coarse pinkish-buff ware with lime and mica grits, fairly evenly fired. Creamy-green slip out and over rim to base of neck in. Potter's mark incised on shoulder before firing.
13. JR. C.I.a (TS. 1858; IIIA, 4.1, Room 8B). Fairly fine pinkish-buff ware, evenly fired. Creamy-green slip in and out.
14. JR. C.II.a (SW. 80; IIIA, 1.4, Room 11). Fairly fine brown ware with black mineral temper, evenly fired.
15. JR. D.II.c (TS. 1835; IIIA, 1.4, Room 11). Fairly fine pinkish-buff ware, evenly fired. Self slip in and out.
16. JR. D.V.c (TS. 1827; IIIA, 4.1, Room 8B). Slightly coarse rose-pink ware, evenly fired. Self slip in and out.
17. JR. D.V.c (TS. 1831; IIIA, 1.4, 4.1, Room 11 and 8B). Slightly coarse pinkish-buff ware, evenly fired. Creamy-buff slip in and out.
18. JR. D.V.d (TS. 1272; IIIA, 1.4, 4.1, Rooms 11 and 8B). Fairly fine buff ware, evenly fired. Self slip out.
19. JR. D.V.e (PM. C.10; SW. 313; IIIA, 1.4, Room 11). Fairly coarse buff ware with very gritty mineral temper, evenly fired. Incomplete potter's mark incised on shoulder before firing.
20. JR. E.II.n (TS. 2412; IIIA, 4.1, 4.2/3, Room 8A/8B). Fairly coarse grayish-buff ware, evenly fired. Brownish-buff slip in and out.
21. JR. H.I.f (TS. 545; IIIA, 4.1, Room 8B). Fairly coarse grayish-buff ware, evenly fired. Self slip in and out.

Figure 177

22. JR. J.I.c (SW. 323; IIIA, 1.4, Room 11). Fairly coarse buff ware with some lime and mica grits, evenly fired. Cream slip in and out.
23. JR. J.III.e (PM. C.12; TS. 1813; IIIA, 4.1, Room 8B). Fine metallic-like grayware, evenly fired. Remains of buff slip out and over rim in. Incomplete potter's mark incised on shoulder before firing.
24. JR. J.III.e (TS. 2282; IIIA, 4.1, Room 8B). Fairly coarse buff ware, evenly fired. Creamy-green slip in and out.
25. JR. J.III.e (TS. 2300; IIIA, 1.4, Room 11). Slightly coarse pinkish-buff ware, evenly fired. Creamy-green slip in and out.
26. JR. J.III.n (TS. 525; IIIA, 4.2, Room 8A). Coarse pink ware, evenly fired. Cream slip out.
27. JR. O.III.b (PM. A.3; TS. 606; IIIA, 1.4, Room 11). Coarse brown ware, evenly fired. Cream slip in and out. Potter's mark impressed with blunt tool on shoulder before firing.

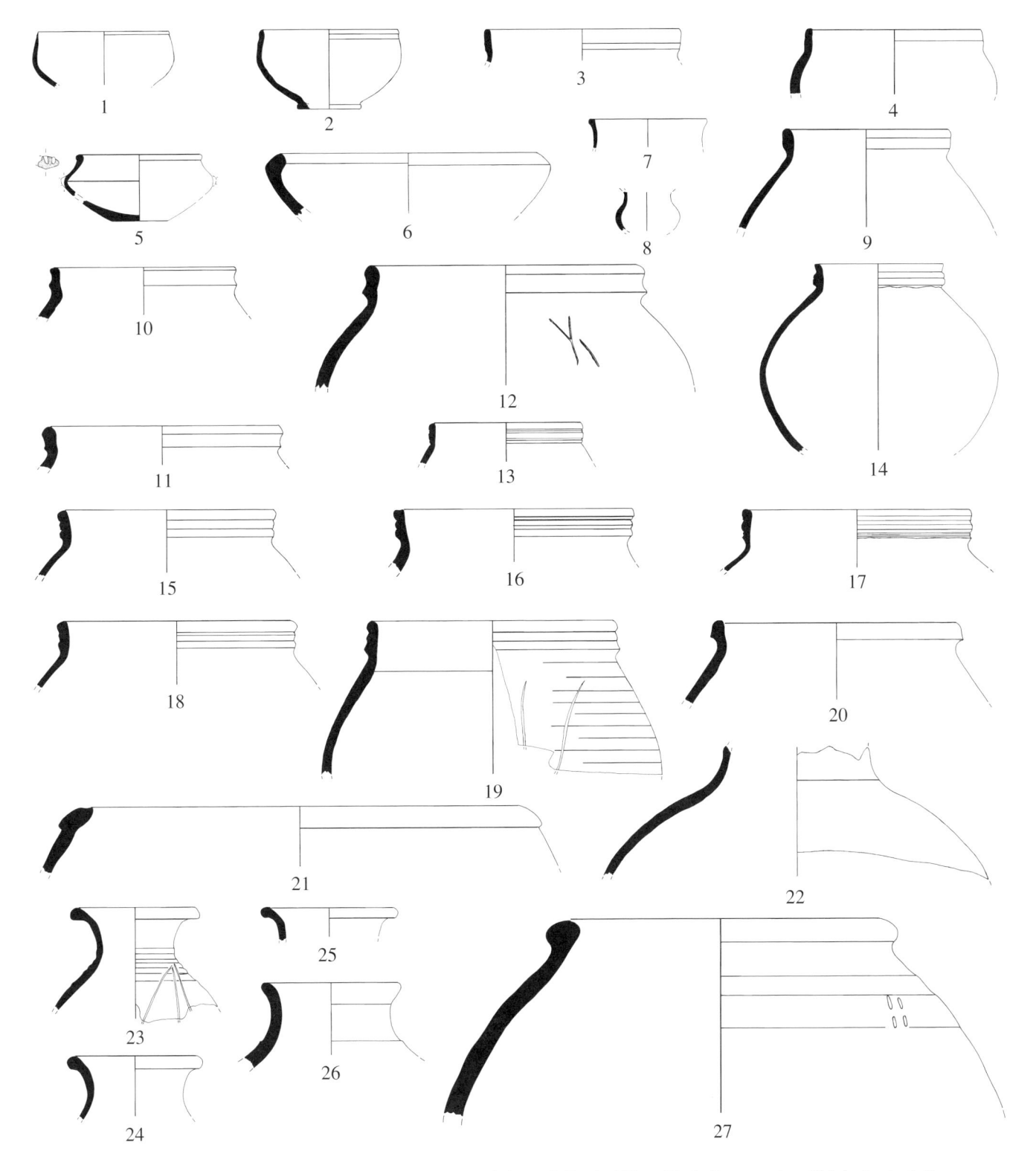

Pottery from Area IIIA, Rooms 8A, 8B, and 11 (Phase 4; Period E — Early Bronze Age IVb). Scale 1:5

Figure 178. Pottery from Trench IIIA, Rooms 8A, 8B, and 11 (Phase 4; Period E — Early Bronze Age IVb Pottery) (*cont.*)

1. JR. P.II.e (TS. 2356; IIIA, 4.1, Room 8B). Fairly coarse pink ware, evenly fired. Creamy-green slip in and out.
2. JR. P.II.n (TS. 1802; IIIA, 4.2/3, Rooms 8A/8B). Fairly coarse and gritty pinkish-buff ware, evenly fired.
3. CP. A.II.c (TS. 2251; IIIA, 4.1, Room 8B). Fairly coarse and gritty buff-brown ware, evenly fired. Irregular self slip, burnished out and around rim in.
4. CP. C.I.d (TS. 524; IIIA, 1.4, Room 11). Coarse pink ware with lime and mica grits, evenly fired. Brown slip in and out.
5. Jg. C (TS. 485; IIIA, 4.1, Room 8B). Fairly coarse pink ware, evenly fired.
6. SR. A.I.b (TS. 2431; IIIA, 4.2/3, Rooms 8A/8B). Slightly coarse pink ware, evenly fired. Pinkish-white slip in and out. Hand-made.
7. BE. A.II (SW. 290; IIIA, 1.4, 4.1, Rooms 11 and 8B). Fairly fine pink ware with various colored lime grits, evenly and hard fired. Drainage hole in center of base.
8. BE. A.II (SW. 329; IIIA, 1.4, Room 11). Fairly fine light brownish-buff ware, evenly fired. Drainage hole in center of base.
9. BE. B.I (TS. 1782; IIIA, 4.1, Room 8B). Fine light grayware, evenly fired. Self gray-black slip, ring-burnished on wall inside and outside and spiral-burnished on base.
10. BE. C.I (PM. B.2; TS. 484; IIIA, 1.4, Room 11). Coarse brown ware with much gritty mineral temper. Cream slip out. Potter's mark incised on inside of the base before firing.
11. BE. D.I (TS. 3051; IIIA, 4.1, Room 8B). Slightly coarse dark pink ware, evenly fired. Self slip in and cream slip out.
12. BE. D.III (TS. 3055; IIIA, 4.1, Room 8B). Fairly coarse pinkish-buff ware, evenly fired. Thick self slip in, cream slip out. Lower wall of vessel and just above the inside of the base vertically finger-smoothed at leather-hard stage of manufacture. Remains of bitumen inside.
13. BE. E.I.c (TS. 1783; IIIA, 4.2/3, Rooms 8A/8B). Fairly fine light grayware, evenly fired. Surface worn, but possible traces of ring burnish on self slip.
14. BE. E.I.d (TS. 1785; IIIA, 4.2/3, Rooms 8A/8B). Slightly coarse light grayware, evenly fired. Bluish-gray self slip in and out.
—. BE. F.IV.a (SW. 109a; IIIA, 4.1, Room 8b). Coarse brown ware with fine black and white mineral temper. Light greenish-buff slip in and out. Heavily iron-stained outside.
15. BE. F.IV.a (SW. 109b; IIIA, 1.4, Room 11). Coarse brown ware with fine black and white mineral temper. Light greenish-buff slip in and out.
16. JR.Sh. (IP [G.1] C.IV.a; TS. 1780; IIIA, 4.2/3, Rooms 8A/8B). Slightly coarse pink ware, evenly fired. Creamy-buff slip out. Comb-incised horizontal and wavy bands applied to shoulder before firing.
17. JR.Sh. (PM. D.26; TS. 1778; IIIA, 4.2/3, Rooms 8A/8B). Slightly coarse pink ware, evenly fired. Creamy-buff slip out. Potter's mark incised on outside wall before firing.
18. JR.Sh. (PM. D.12; TS. 1779; IIIA, 4.1, Room 8B). Fine pinkish-brown ware, evenly fired. Buff slip out. Potter's mark incised on outside wall before firing.

Other Type Series Examples:

Room 8A — (1) BR. C.I.b (TS. 1791), (2) CBR. A.II.a (PM. C.10; SW. 121).

Room 8B — (1) SBR. D.II.a (TS. 1268), (2) JR. B.IV.d (TS. 1790), (3) JR. D.V.g (TS. 1822).

Rooms 8A/8B — (1) JR. B.V.a (TS. 1875), (2) JR. D.VI.d (TS. 1832).

Room 11 — (1) SBR. B.I.d (SW. 59), (2) BR. C.I.c (TS. 1797), (3) SJR. C.II.d (SW. 102), (4) SJR. C.II.t (SW. 25 = TS. 2480), (5) JR. O.II.j (TS. 443), (6) SR. B.I.c (TS. 2425), (7) SR. B.I.d (TS. 2427).

Rooms 8A and 11 — (1) ABS. C (TS. 1812).

Rooms 8B and 11 —(1) SR. B.II.b (TS. 2430), (2) BE. F.III.a (SW. 279 = TS. 1798).

Other Study Collection Examples:

Room 8A — (1) SBR. B.I.g (SC. 375), (2) SBR. B.I.k (SC. 559), (3) JR. J.III.e (SC. 1379).

Room 8B — (1) SBR. B.I.g (SC. 359), (2) SBR. B.I.i (SC. 522), (3) SBR. D.I.d (SC. 645), (4) BR. B.I.a (SC. 2641), (5) BR. L.III.d (SC. 1961), (6) JR. J.I.c (SC. 1319), (7) JR. J.I.d (SC. 1325), (8) JR. J.I.f (SC. 1337), (9) JR. J.III.d (SC. 1372), (10) JR. O.II.e (SC. 2420), (11) JR. P.II.k (SC. 2432), (12) JR. J. (Gen. Type, SC. 116), (13) JR. (not typed, SC. 127), (14) JR. (not typed, SC. 134), (15) JR. (not typed, SC. 142), (16) CP. A.II.e (SC. 1807), (17) CP. B.IV.d (SC. 1891), (18) SR. (sherds, not typed, SC. 62), (19) BE. C.I (SC. 1910).

Room 8A/8B — (1) JR. J.I.a (SC. 1297), (2) JR. J.II.d (SC. 2142), (3) JR. J.III.d (SC. 2232), (4) JR. J.III.e (SC. 2253), (5) JR. J.III.m (SC. 1423), (6) JR. O.III.g (SC. 1689), (7) CP. B.I.b (SC. 1820), (8) CP. B.II.i (SC. 1858), (9) CP. B.II.i (SC. 1857).

Room 11 — (1) SBR. A.I.c (SC. 223), (2) SBR. B.I.d (SC. 284), (3) SBR. B.I.d (SC. 287), (4) SBR. B.I.d (SC. 296), (5) SBR. B.I.l (SC. 582), (6) JR. J.I.b (SC. 1313), (7) JR. P.II.k (SC. 1745), (8) JR. J. (Gen. Type, SC. 112), (9) CP. A.I.a (SC. 1779), (10) CP. B.II.i (SC. 1854).

Figure 178

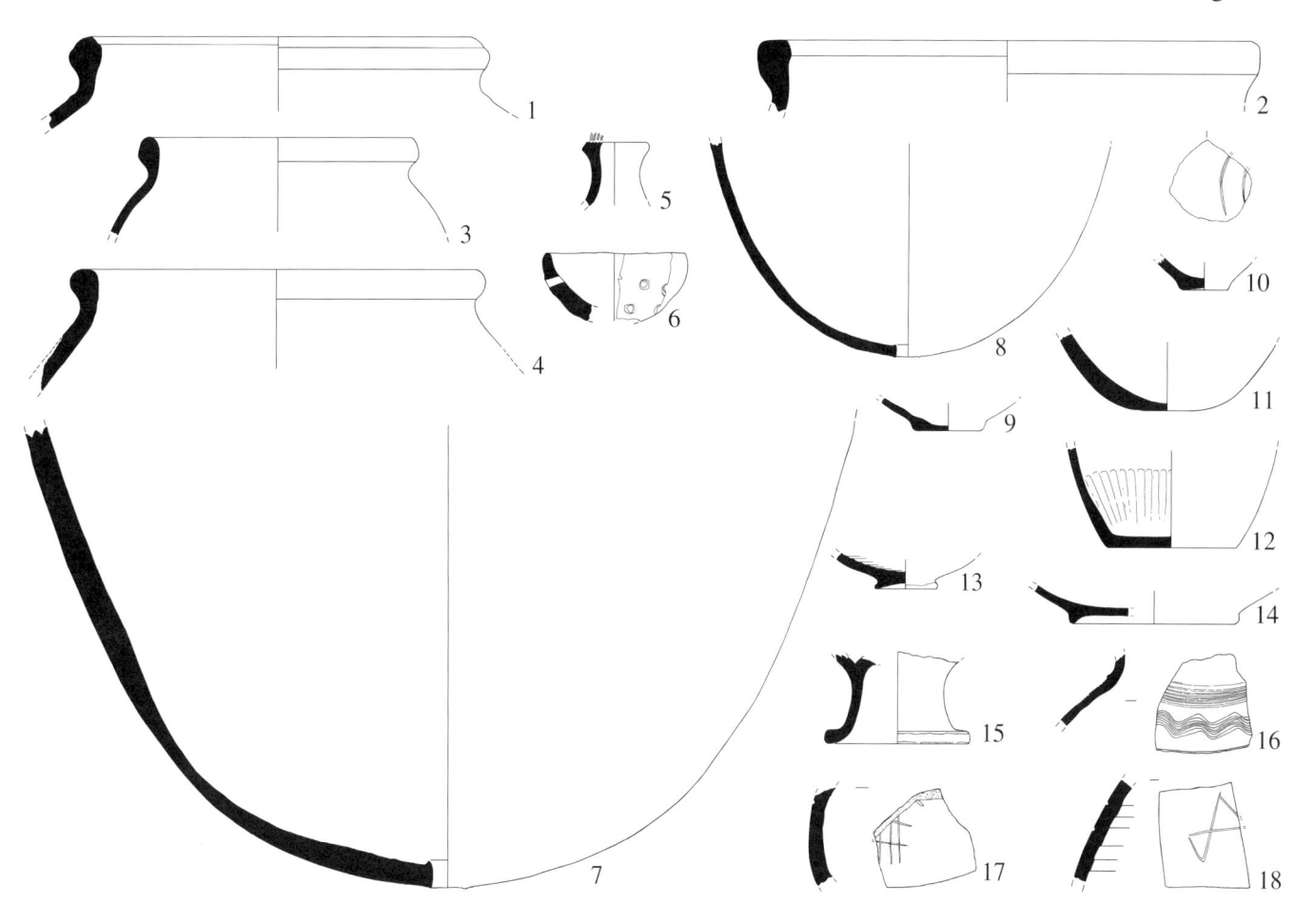

Pottery from Trench IIIA, Rooms 8A, 8B, and 11 (Phase 4; Period E — Early Bronze Age IVb Pottery) (*cont.*). Scale 1:5

Figure 179. Pottery from Trench IIIA (Phase 5; Period E — Early Bronze Age IVb)

1. SBR. B.I.k (TS. 647; IIIA, 1.3). Fairly coarse buff-grayware, evenly fired. Greenish-buff slip in and out.
2. SJR. A.II.f (TS. 517; IIIA, 1.3). Fairly fine pinkish-buff ware, evenly fired. Brown slip in and out.
3. JR. B.IV.c (TS. 1896; IIIA, 1.3). Slightly coarse pinkish-buff ware, evenly fired. Self slip in and out.
4. JR. J.III.d (SW. 306; IIIA, 1.3). Fairly gritty black ware, hard and evenly fired. Green slip in and out.
5. JR. J.III.z (TS. 534; IIIA, 1.3). Fairly coarse pink ware, evenly fired. Cream slip in and out.
6. JR. O.II.i (TS. 2549; IIIA, 1.3 and IIIB, 3.2, Room 7). Slightly coarse pinkish-buff ware with lime and mica grits, evenly fired. Creamy greenish-buff slip in and out.
7. JR. P.II.a (PM. B.2; SW. 328; IIIA, 1.3). Fairly coarse light brown-buff ware, evenly fired. Cream slip out. Potter's mark incised on shoulder before firing.
8. JR. P.II.c (SW. 288; IIIA, 1.3, 1.4, Room 11). Very hard-fired pinkish-grayware with lime and mica grits, evenly fired. Creamy-green slip in and out.
9. JR. Q.II.b (SW. 330; IIIA, 1.3). Coarse pink ware with lime and mica grits, evenly fired. Cream slip out.
10. CP. B.I.i (TS. 2245; IIIA, 1.3). Fairly coarse grayish ware, evenly fired.
11. BE. A.I (PM. C.2; TS. 3053; IIIA, 1.3). Slightly coarse pinkish-buff ware, evenly fired. Self slip in and cream slip out. Potter's mark incised on lower outside wall before firing.
12. BE. F.VIII.a (SW. 104; IIIA, 1.3). Coarse reddish-brown ware with black- and gold-colored mica and lime grits, evenly fired. Yellow-buff slip out.
13. JR.Sh. (PM. C.14; TS. 530; IIIA, 1.3). Coarse buff ware with small mineral temper, unevenly fired with gray core. Cream slip out. Potter's mark incised on outside wall before firing.

Other Type Series Examples: (1) BR. J.I.d (TS. 481 = TS. 514), (2) SR. B.I.a (SW. 21).

Other Study Collection Examples: (1) SBR. B.I.m (SC. 586), (2) SBR. D.I.b (SC. 639), (3) BR. C.I.b (SC. 739), (4) BR. G.I.f (SC. 826), (5) BR. H.I.a (SC. 1970), (6) JR. J.I.c (SC. 1317), (7) JR. J.I.f (SC. 1335), (8) JR. J.I.g (SC. 2121), (9) JR. J.III.m (SC. 1431), (10) BE. E.I.e (SC. 3169).

Figure 179

Pottery from Trench IIIA (Phase 5; Period E — Early Bronze Age IVb). Scale 1:5

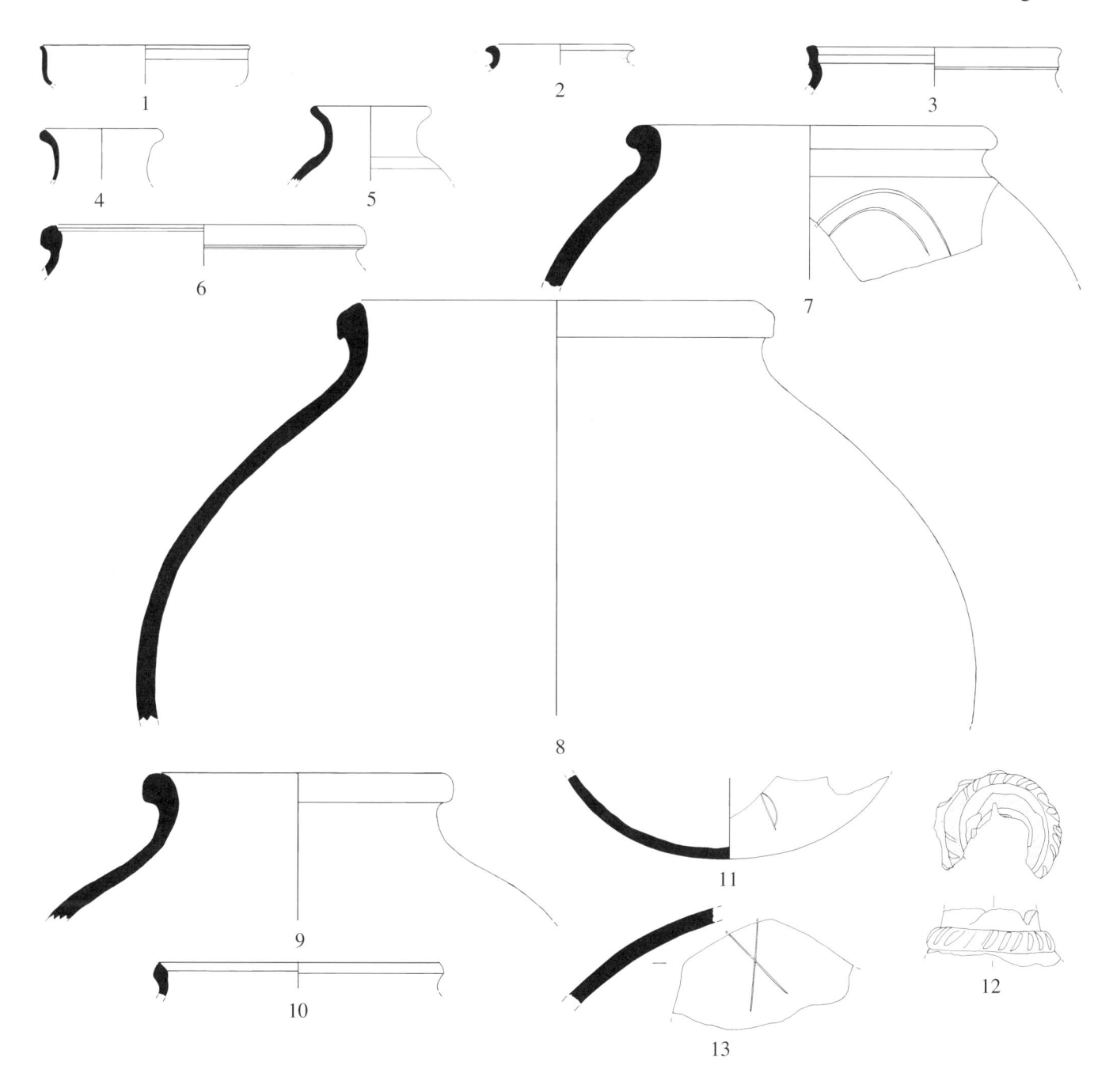

Figures 180–81

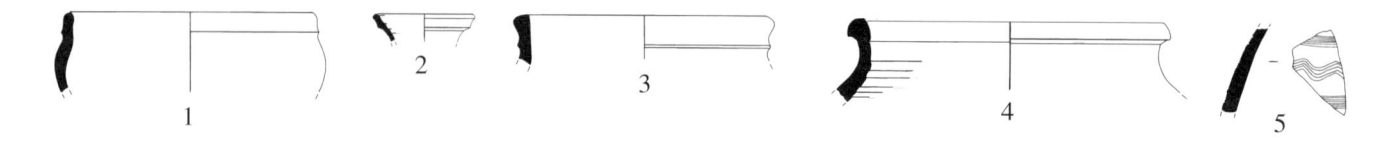

Figure 180. Pottery in Trench IIIA (Phase 6; Period E–D — Early–Middle Bronze Age). Scale 1:5

1. SBR. D.II.c (TS. 1916; IIIA, 1.2). Slightly coarse pinkish-buff ware, evenly fired. Creamy-buff slip in and out.
2. SJR. B.III.a (TS. 2446; IIIA, 1.2). Fine pink ware, evenly fired. Creamy-yellow slip in and out.
3. JR. A.III.d (TS. 1901; IIIA, 1.2). Slightly coarse light pinkish-buff ware, evenly fired. Self slip out.
4. JR. K.II.c (TS. 2327; IIIA, 1.2). Slightly coarse light pinkish-buff ware, evenly fired. Creamy-buff slip out and over rim in.
5. JR.Sh. (IP [G.1] C.IV.a; TS. 1811; IIIA, 1.2). Slightly coarse buff ware, evenly fired. Self slip out.
—. JR.Sh. (PM. F; TS. 3133; IIIA, 1.2). Jar sherd. Ware description not available.

Another Type Series Example: (1) JR. B.III.b (TS. 1899).

Other Study Collection Examples: (1) SBR. B.I.h (SC. 458), (2) BR. A.I.a (SC. 21), (3) SJR. C.II.g (SC. 2591), (4) JR. J.III.m (SC. 1435), (5) JR. P.II.a (SC. 1703), (6) CP. B.I.d (SC. 1830), (7) CP. B.II.a (SC. 1842), (8) CP. B.IV.b (SC. 1874), (9) CP. B.IV.c (SC. 1883), (10) CP. C.I.b (SC. 1901).

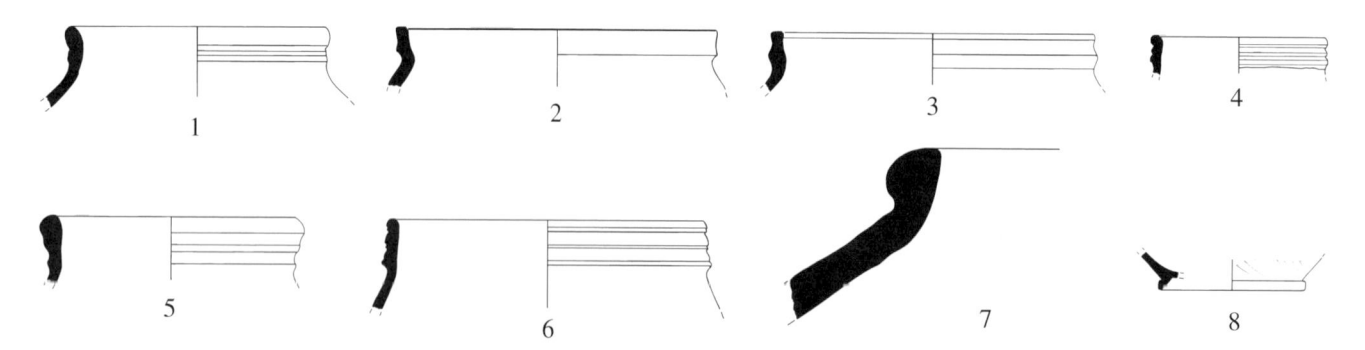

Figure 181. Pottery from Trench IIIA (Phase 7; Period D — Middle Bronze Age I). Scale 1:5

1. JR. A.V.c (TS. 1910; IIIA, 1.1). Slightly coarse pinkish-buff ware, evenly fired. Creamy-buff slip in and out.
2. JR. B.III.c (TS. 1906; IIIA, 1.1). Fairly fine buff ware, evenly fired.
3. JR. B.IV.c (TS. 1895; IIIA, 1.1). Slightly coarse grayish-buff ware, evenly fired. Pinkish-buff slip in and out.
4. JR. C.I.h (TS. 1865; IIIA, 1.1). Slightly coarse pinkish-buff ware, evenly fired. Buff slip in and out.
5. JR. C.V.b (TS. 1861; IIIA, 1.1). Fairly coarse buff ware, evenly fired. Creamy-buff slip in and out.
6. JR. D.I.b (TS. 1820; IIIA, 1.1). Slightly coarse light pink ware, evenly fired. Creamy-yellow slip out.
7. JR. P.III.f (TS. 433; IIIA, 1.1). Coarse pink ware with lime and mica grits, unevenly fired with brown-gray core. Cream slip in and out.
8. BE. E.II.e (TS. 1801; IIIA, 1.1). Fairly fine light brown ware, evenly fired. Self slip, obliquely burnished above the base on extant outside portion of lower wall of the vessel.

Other Type Series Examples:
    Bronze Age — (1) SBR. D.II.d (TS. 1809), (2) JR. B.II.a (TS. 1795), (3) JR. B.II.b (TS. 3155).
    Hellenistic — (1) H.BE. A.I.b (TS. 1803).

Other Study Collection Examples:
    Bronze Age — (1) SJR. B.II.h (SC. 2515), (2) JR. E.II.d (SC. 2016), (3) JR. J.I.f (SC. 1343), (4) JR. J.II.h (SC. 2155), (5) JR. J.III.b (SC. 2218), (6) JR. J.III.h (SC. 1401), (7) JR. J.III.j (SC. 2301), (8) JR. J.III.m (SC. 1441), (9) JR. J.IV.h (SC. 2380), (10) JR. J.IV.j (SC. 1541), (11) JR. O.II.a (SC. 2414), (12) JR. O.II.c (SC. 1630), (13) JR. O.II.e (SC. 1639), (14) JR. O.II.h (SC. 1654), (15) JR. O.III.f (SC. 1684), (16) JR. P.II.a (SC. 1709), (17) JR. P.II.r (SC. 2438), (18) CP. A.I.a (SC. 1780), (19) CP. B.II.a (SC. 1838), (20) BE. E.I.b (SC. 3153), (21) WPS. C (SC. 1949).

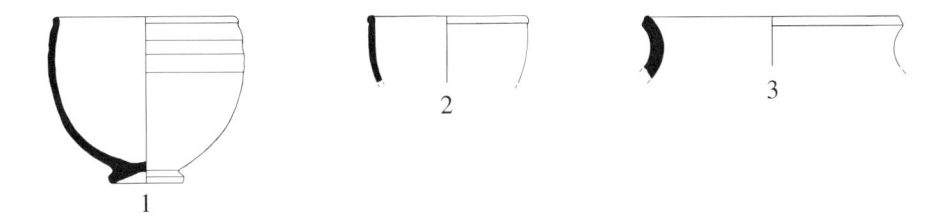

Figure 182. Pottery from Trench IIIB (Phase 1B; Period G — Early Bronze Age III). Scale 1:5

1. SBR. A.I.d (SW. 248; IIIB, 2.15). Medium fine pinkish-buff ware with fine gold-colored mica and lime grits, evenly fired.
2. SBR. B.I.f (TS. 463; IIIB, 2.15). Slightly coarse creamy-buff ware, evenly fired.
3. JR. J.II.m (TS. 464; IIIB, 2.15). Fairly coarse pinkish-buff ware, evenly fired. Cream slip out.

Another Study Collection Example: (1) JR. J.II.g (SC. 2144).

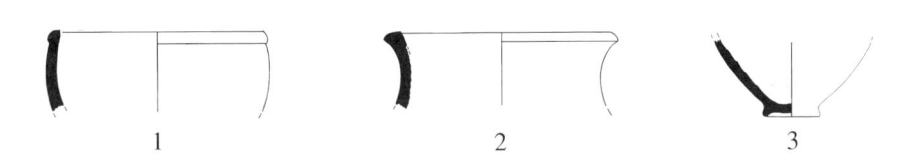

Figure 183. Pottery from Trench IIIB (Phases 1C and 2; Periods G and F — Early Bronze Age III and Early Bronze Age IVa). Scale 1:5

1. SBR. B.I.h (TS. 2025; IIIB, 2.11; Phase 1C). Fairly fine pinkish-buff ware, evenly fired. Self slip out.
2. JR. J.IV.d (TS. 498; IIIB, 2.11; Phase 1C). Fairly fine pink ware with mica grits, evenly fired.
3. BE. E.I.k (TS. 515; IIIB, 2.10, Room 1A, Phase 2). Fairly fine pinkish-buff ware, evenly fired.

Other Type Series Examples:
Phase 1C — (1) SJR. A.I.c (TS. 158), (2) SJR. A.II.b (TS. 2020), (3) SJR. B.II.g (TS. 2316).
Phase 2, Room 1A— (1) SBR. A.I.d (SW. 245).

Other Study Collection Examples:
Phase 1C — (1) SBR. A.I.b (SC. 219), (2) SBR. B.I.g (SC. 377), (3) SBR. C.III.a (SC. 602), (4) SJR. A.I.a (SC. 2478), (5) JR. G.I.c (SC. 1239), (6) CP. B.III.a (SC. 1859).
Phase 2, Room 1A — (1) SBR. B.I.g (SC. 400), (2) SBR. B.I.g (SC. 414).

Figure 184

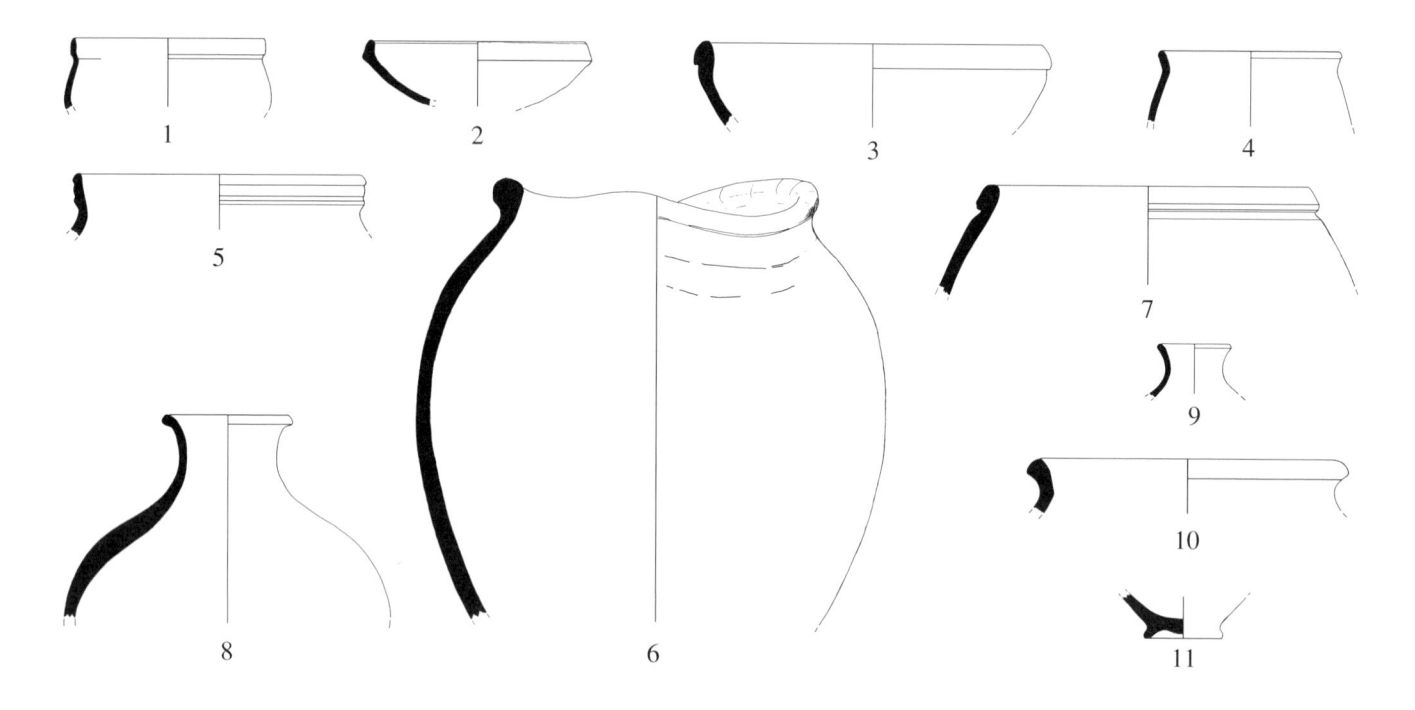

Pottery from Trench Area IIIB, Rooms 1A/B and 1B (Phase 3; Period F — Early Bronze Age IVa). Scale 1:5

1. SBR. D.I.e (TS. 643; IIIB, 2.9, Room 1B). Fairly coarse buff ware, evenly fired. Yellow-buff slip out.
2. BR. D.I.a (TS. 193; IIIB, 2.9, 2.10, Room 1A/B). Ware description not available.
3. BR. G.I.e (TS. 506; IIIB, 2.4, Room 1B). Very coarse pink ware with lime grits, unevenly fired with light brown out. Cream slip out.
4. SJR. A.I.a (TS. 480; IIIB, 2.5, Room 1B). Fairly coarse buff ware, evenly fired. Cream slip in and out.
5. JR. C.II.a (TS. 1837; IIIB, 2.4, Room 1B). Fairly fine grayish-buff ware, evenly fired. Heavily charred on outside surface.
6. JR. E.II.s (SW. 289; IIIB, 2.5, 2.9, Room 1A/B). Hard, fairly fine ware with fine lime grits, unevenly fired green out and brownish-gray in. Thick greenish-brown slip out. Rim and upper body warped during firing.
7. JR. H.I.e (TS. 1382; IIIB, 2.9, Room 1B). Slightly coarse pinkish-brown ware, evenly fired. Buff slip in and out. Heavily charred.
8. JR. J.III.e (SW. 276; IIIB, 2.5, 2.9, Room 1A/B). Fairly fine creamy-buff ware with a few mica and lime grits, evenly fired. Very smooth self slip out.
9. FL. B.I.a (TS. 1391; IIIB, 2.9, Room 1B). Fine pinkish-red ware, evenly fired. Thick self slip in and out.
10. CP. B.II.d (TS. 462; IIIB, 2.9, Room 1B). Coarse dark grayware with lime and mica grits, evenly fired. Brownish-buff slip in and out.
11. BE. E.II.i (TS. 448; IIIB, 2.4, Room 1B). Fairly fine light brown ware with mica grits, evenly fired.

Other Type Series Examples:
    Room 1B — (1) BR. A.II.a (TS. 1387), (2) BR. L.III.e (TS. 1386), (3) SJR. C.II.f (TS. 1388), (4) CP. B.II.d (SW. 284).

Other Study Collection Examples:
    Room 1B — (1) SBR. A.I.f (SC. 227), (2) SBR. B.I.e (SC. 318), (3) SBR. B.I.g (SC. 5), (4) BR. L.I.f (SC. 843), (5) JR. J.III.f (SC. 1386), (6) JR. J.IV.g (SC. 1534), (7) CP. A.I.a (SC. 1781).

Figure 185

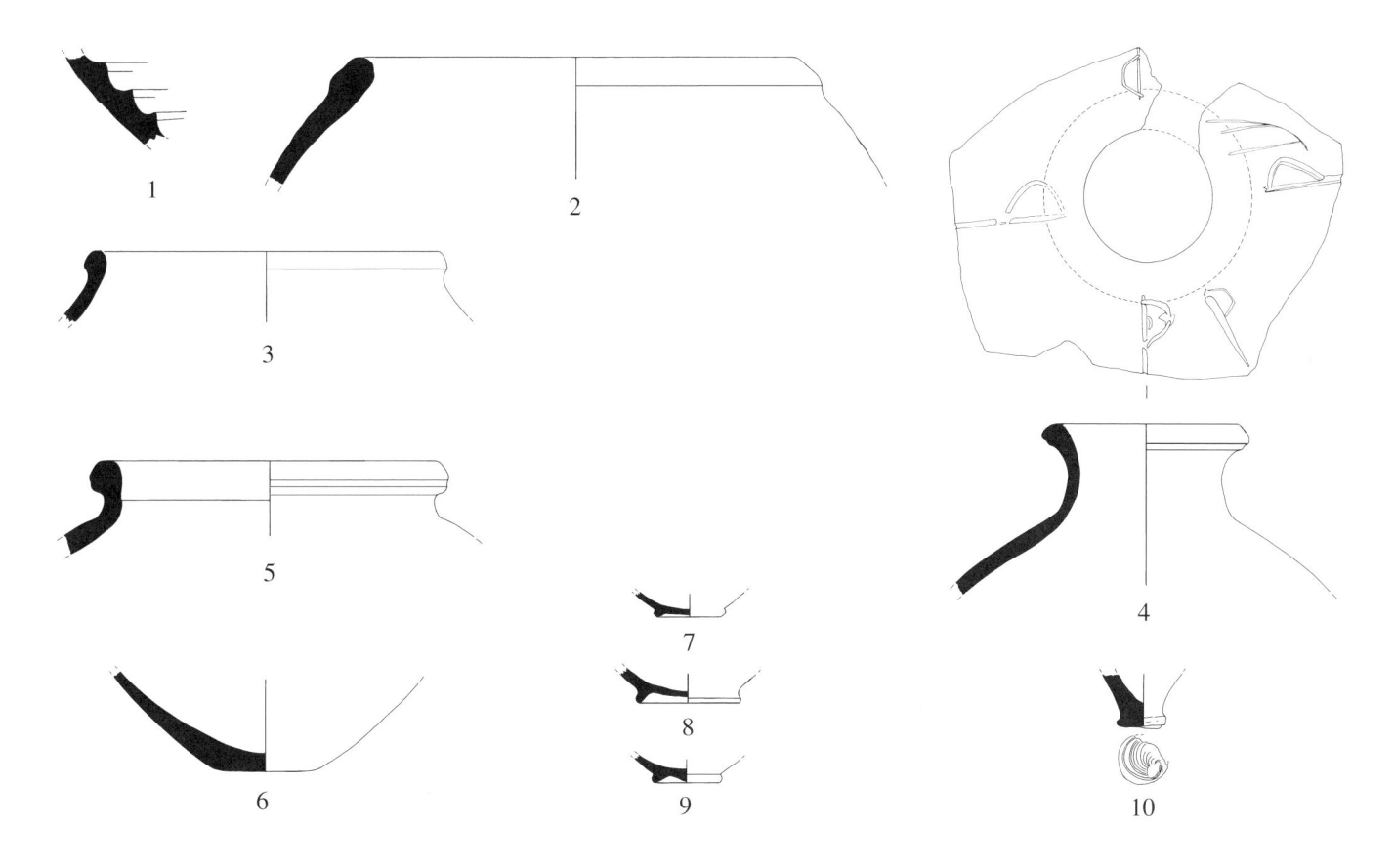

Pottery from Trench IIIB, Rooms 6 and 7 (Phase 4; Period E — Early Bronze Age IVb). Scale 1:5

1. BR. R.II.a (TS. 467; IIIB, 3.2, Room 7). Coarse pink ware with lime and mica grits, unevenly fired with light brown core. Cream slip out.
2. JR. H.I.k (TS. 1384; IIIB, 2.3, Room 6). Slightly coarse pinkish-buff ware, fairly evenly fired. Creamy-buff slip out and over rim in.
3. JR. H.III.h (TS. 1385; IIIB, 2.3, Room 6). Slightly coarse buff ware, evenly fired. Ceamy-green slip in and out.
4. JR. J.III.s (PM. C.8 and C.15; SW. 131 = TS. 1173; IIIB, 3.2, Room 7 = IIID, 5.4, Room 12). Coarse buff ware with black- and gold-colored mineral temper, evenly fired. Light greenish-buff slip out and just over rim in. Potter's marks incised around the shoulder after the slip was applied.
5. JR. P.II.c (TS. 2357; IIIB, 2.3, Room 6). Slightly coarse pinkish-buff ware, evenly fired. Buff slip out and over rim in.
6. BE. D.III (TS. 3050; IIIB, 3.2, Room 7). Slightly coarse pink ware, evenly fired. Cream slip out.
7. BE. E.I.i (TS. 458; IIIB, 2.3, Room 6). Fairly coarse light brown ware, evenly fired.
8. BE. E.II.h (TS. 496; IIIB, 2.3, Room 6). Fairly coarse pink ware, evenly fired. Brown slip out and pink slip in.
9. BE. E.II.i (TS. 482; IIIB, 2.3, Room 6). Fine buff ware, evenly fired.
10. BE. H (TS. 527; IIIB, 3.2, Room 7). Fairly coarse ware, unevenly fired pink and brown on surfaces in and out. Cream slip in and out. String-cut base.

Other Type Series Examples:
   Room 6 —(1) BR. L.III.b (TS. 501), (2) JR. C.V.b (TS. 1390), (3) JR. D.X.a (TS. 469), (4) JR. J.I.i (TS. 2295), (5) JR. J.IV.h (TS. 492).
   Room 7 — (1) JR. B.V.d (TS. 431), (2) Hd. E.I.a (TS. 557).

Other Study Collection Examples:
   Room 6 —(1) SBR. A.I.e (SC. 226), (2) SBR. B.I.b (SC. 266), (3) SBR. B.I.f (SC. 339), (4) BR. (not typed, SC. 52), (5) JR. E.I.c (SC. 1136), (6) JR. E.II.j (SC. 1152), (7) JR. J.I.b (SC. 1301), (8) JR. J.III.n (SC. 1444), (9) JR. J.III.z (SC. 1510), (10) JR. P.II.i (SC. 1742), (11) CP. B.II.i (SC. 1855), (12) BE. A.II (SC. 3100), (13) BE. E.I.g (SC. 3177), BE. E.II.d (SC. 3208), (14) BE. E.II.f (SC. 3216).
   Room 7 — (1) BR. L.III.c (SC. 863), (2) JR. E.II.d (SC. 2012).

Figure 186

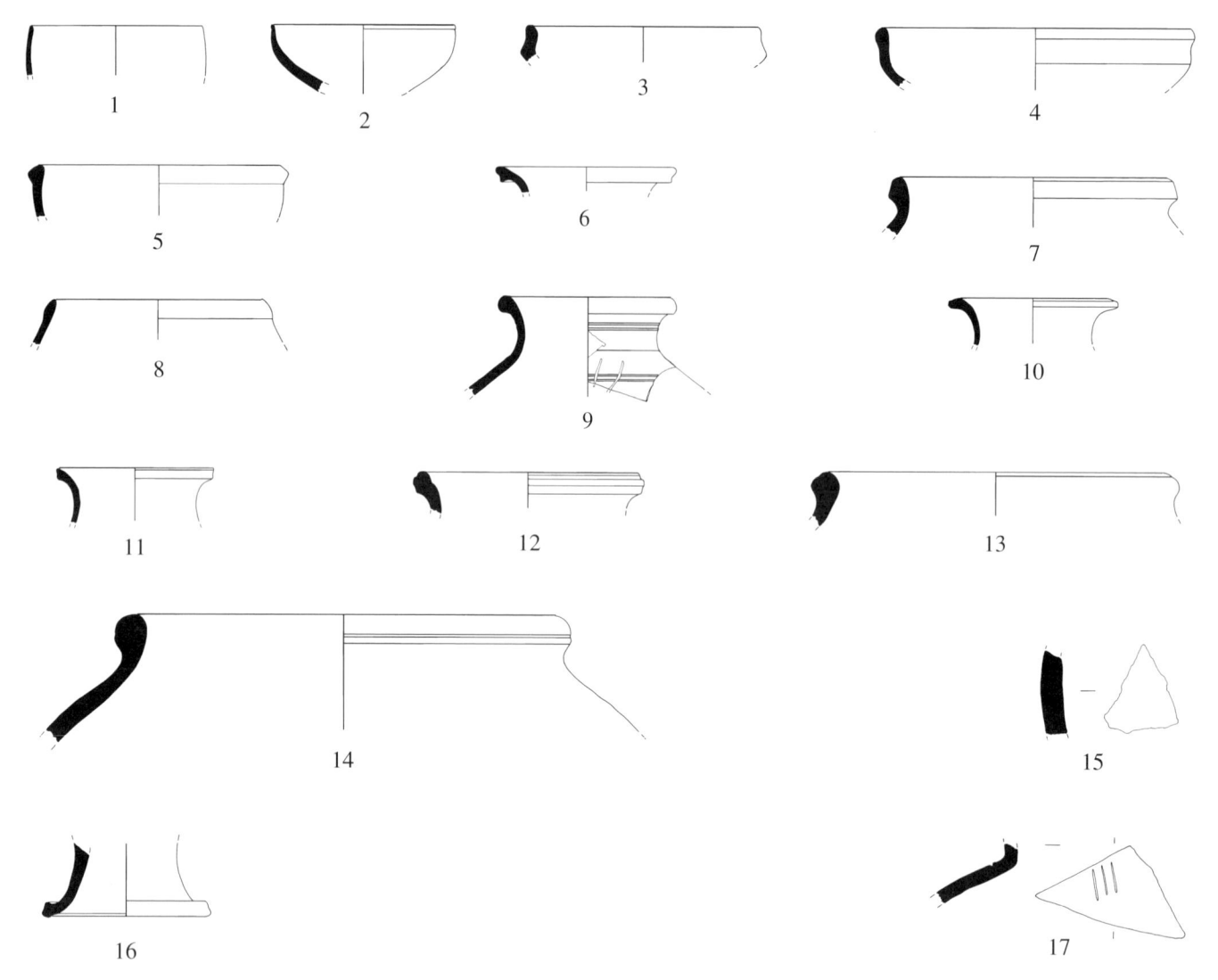

Pottery from Trench IIIB (Phase 5; Period E — Early Bronze Age IVb). Scale 1:5

1. SBR. A.I.a (TS. 656; IIIB, 2.2). Fairly fine pink ware, evenly fired. Cream slip out.
2. SBR. B.I.c (TS. 461; IIIB, 4.1, 4.2, Pit). Fairly coarse pinkish-buff ware, evenly fired. Cream slip in and out.
3. BR. C.I.b (TS. 1876; IIIB, 3.1). Slightly coarse pinkish-buff ware, evenly fired. Self slip in and out.
4. BR. E.I.a (TS. 500; IIIB, 2.2). Coarse pinkish-buff ware, evenly fired.
5. BR. L.II.d (TS. 1805; IIIB, 2.2). Slightly coarse buff ware, evenly fired. Creamy-yellow slip out.
6. SJR. C.I.a (TS. 2308; IIIB, 2.2). Slightly coarse buff ware, evenly fired. Light creamy-green slip out and over rim in. Traces of charring out.
7. JR. E.II.n (TS. 2409; IIIB, 2.2). Fairly fine pink ware, evenly fired. Buff slip out.
8. JR. H.I.a (TS. 1808; IIIB, 2.2). Slightly coarse grayish-buff ware, evenly fired. Self slip in and out.
9. JR. J.III.g (PM. A.6; TS. 1381; IIIB, 4.1, Pit). Fairly fine pink ware, evenly fired. Buff slip out and over rim to base of neck in. Incomplete potter's mark incised on shoulder before firing.
10. JR. J.III.l (TS. 2264; IIIB, 4.2, Pit). Slightly coarse buff ware, evenly fired. Light creamy-green slip in and out.
11. JR. J.III.m (TS. 2306; IIIB, 3.1). Slightly coarse pinkish-buff ware, evenly fired. Creamy-buff slip out and over rim in.
12. JR. J.VI.a (TS. 1389; IIIB, 4.2, Pit). Fine light grayware, unevenly fired reddish-brown at surfaces.
13. JR. O.II.a (TS. 2380; IIIB, 2.2). Fairly coarse buff ware, evenly fired. Light creamy-green slip in and out.
14. JR. P.II.b (TS. 2387; IIIB, 3.1). Slightly coarse pinkish-buff ware, evenly fired. Buff slip out and over rim in.
15. BR.Sh. (Tool; SW. 357; IIIB, 3.1). Fine dark grayware with many fine grits, evenly fired. Broken sherd roughly triangularly shaped for use as a tool.
16. BE. F.V.b (TS. 1383; IIIB, 4.1, Pit). Slightly coarse pinkish-buff ware, evenly fired. Creamy-buff slip in and out.
17. JR.Sh. (PM. A.14; TS. 1807; IIIB, 2.2). Fine pink ware, evenly fired. Buff slip out with creamy-buff slip rings in reserve out. Potter's mark incised on shoulder before firing.

Other Type Series Examples: (1) BR. J.I.b (TS. 505), (2) SJR. A.II.c (TS. 1799), (3) JR. B.IV.g (TS. 1306), (4) JR. D.VIII.b (TS. 1834).

Other Study Collection Examples: (1) SBR. B.I.g (SC. 356), (2) SBR. B.I.m (SC. 588), (3) BR. F.III.d (SC. 813), (4) JR. B.V.d (SC. 980), (5) JR. E.I.c (SC. 1134), (6) JR. H.I.a (SC. 2058), (7) JR. J.I.b (SC. 1303), (8) JR. J.I.f (SC. 1338), (9) JR. J.I.f (SC. 1340), (10) JR. J.III.a (SC. 2203), (11) JR. J.III.g (SC. 2283), (12) JR. J.III.aa (SC. 2367), (13) JR. O.III.c (SC. 1678), (14) CP. B.II.a (SC. 1845), (15) Hd. D.II (SC. 3276).

Figures 187–88

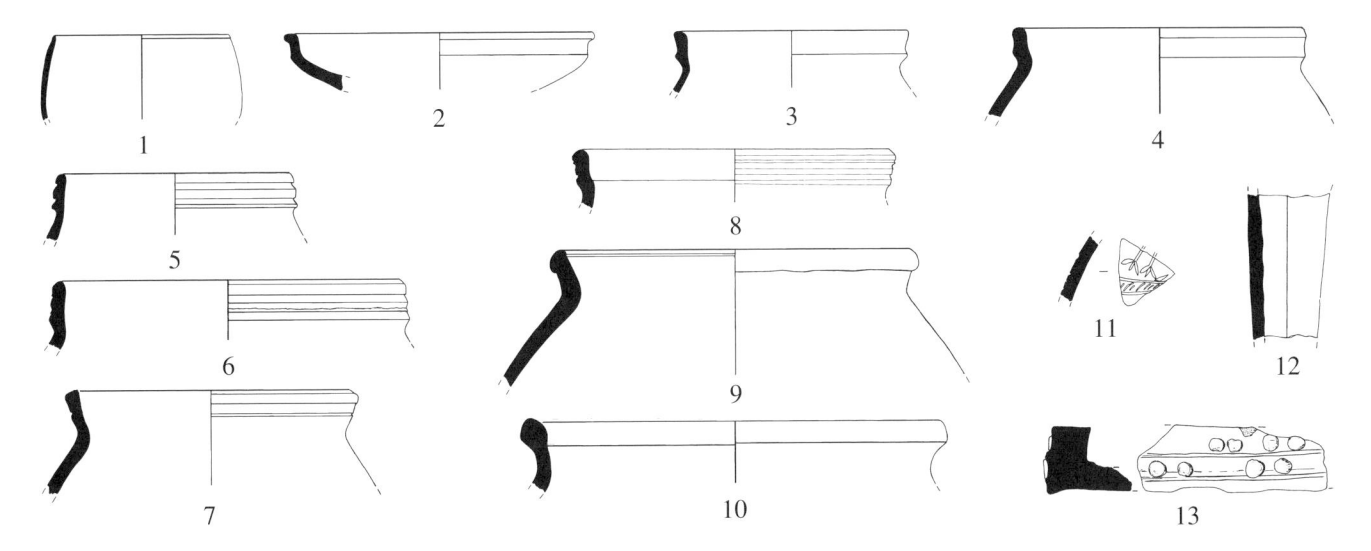

Figure 187. Pottery from Trench IIIB (Phase 6; Period E–D — Early–Middle Bronze Age). Scale 1:5

1. SBR. A.I.c (TS. 2516; IIIB, 1.6). Slightly coarse pinkish-buff ware, evenly fired. Cream slip out and remains in.
2. BR. E.I.b (TS. 1792; IIIB, 1.6). Fairly coarse pinkish-buff ware, evenly fired. Creamy-buff slip out.
3. JR. A.III.c (TS. 1877; IIIB, 1.6). Slightly coarse buff ware, evenly fired. Self slip in and out.
4. JR. A.IV.a (TS. 1894; IIIB, 1.6 and IIID, 4.8, 5.2). Slightly coarse grayish-buff ware, evenly fired. Self slip in and out.
5. JR. C.III.a (TS. 1816; IIIB, 1.6). Slightly coarse pinkish-buff ware, evenly fired. Creamy-buff slip in and out.
6. JR. D.V.d (TS. 1842; IIIB, 1.6). Fairly coarse and gritty buff ware, evenly fired. Creamy-buff slip in and out.
7. JR. D.VI.c (TS. 1907; IIIB, 1.6). Fairly fine, hard, pink ware, evenly fired. Creamy-buff slip out.
8. JR. D.VII.a (TS. 1849; IIIB, 1.6). Slightly coarse pinkish-buff ware, evenly fired. Creamy-buff slip out. Charred inside.
9. JR. F.II.b (TS. 2198; IIIB, 1.6). Fairly fine pinkish-buff ware, unevenly fired with light gray core. Creamy-buff slip in and out.
10. JR. K.II.b (TS. 2390; IIIB, 1.6). Fairly coarse pinkish-buff ware, evenly fired. Creamy-buff slip in and out.
11. JR.Sh. (IP [G.4] F.II; TS. 1789; IIIB, 1.6). Slightly coarse pinkish-buff ware, evenly fired. Self slip out. Remains of incised stylistic animal legs above a possible tail of a second figure.
—. JR.Sh. (PM. F; TS. 3104; IIIB, 1.6). Jar sherd. Ware description not available.
12. SV.1 (TS. 494; IIIB, 1.6). Fragment of a funnel-shaped object or pipe. Fairly fine buff ware, evenly fired. Cream slip in and out.
13. SV.5 (TS. 529; IIIB, 1.6). Fragment of a model house or box-shaped vessel. Coarse pinkish-brown ware, evenly fired. Creamy-buff slip in and out. Appliqué "buttons" on outside surface.

Other Type Series Examples: (1) JR. A.II.b (TS. 1794), (2) JR. A.V.c (TS. 1903), (3) JR. B.IV.a (TS. 1796), (4) JR. B.VI.c (TS. 1874).

Other Study Collection Examples: (1) SBR. B.I.g (SC. 384), (2) SBR. B.I.i (SC. 524), (3) SBR. B.I.r (SC. 593), (4) SBR. D.I.d (SC. 642), (5) BR. (not typed, SC. 53), (6) SJR. A.I.a (SC. 2474), (7) JR. J.I.b (SC. 2091), (8) JR. J.I.h (SC. 2127), (9) JR. J.II.g (SC. 2154), (10) JR. P.II.k (SC. 1747), (11) JR. (not typed, SC. 121), (12) CP. A.II.b (SC. 1800), (13) BE. D.II (SC. 3128).

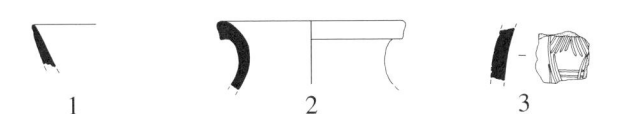

Figure 188. Pottery from Trench IIIB (Phase 7; Period D — Middle Bronze Age I). Scale 1:5

1. SBR. E.I.a (TS. 1804; IIIB, 1.5). Very small rim segment; diameter of bowl indeterminable. Fairly fine pinkish-buff ware, evenly fired. Creamy-buff slip in and out.
2. JR. J.III.m (TS. 2301; IIIB, 1.5). Slightly coarse pinkish-buff ware, evenly fired. Creamy-green slip out and over rim in to base of neck.
3. JR.Sh. (IP [G.4] E.I; TS. 1788; IIIB, 1.5). Slightly coarse pink ware, evenly fired. Buff slip out. Portion of a human figure incised on outside wall of a vessel with incised lines representing clothing.

Other Study Collection Examples: (1) SBR. B.I.m (SC. 587), (2) JR. E.I.e (SC. 2447), (3) JR. E.II.c (SC. 2002), (4) JR. H.II.a (SC. 2047), (5) JR. H.III.f (SC. 2081).

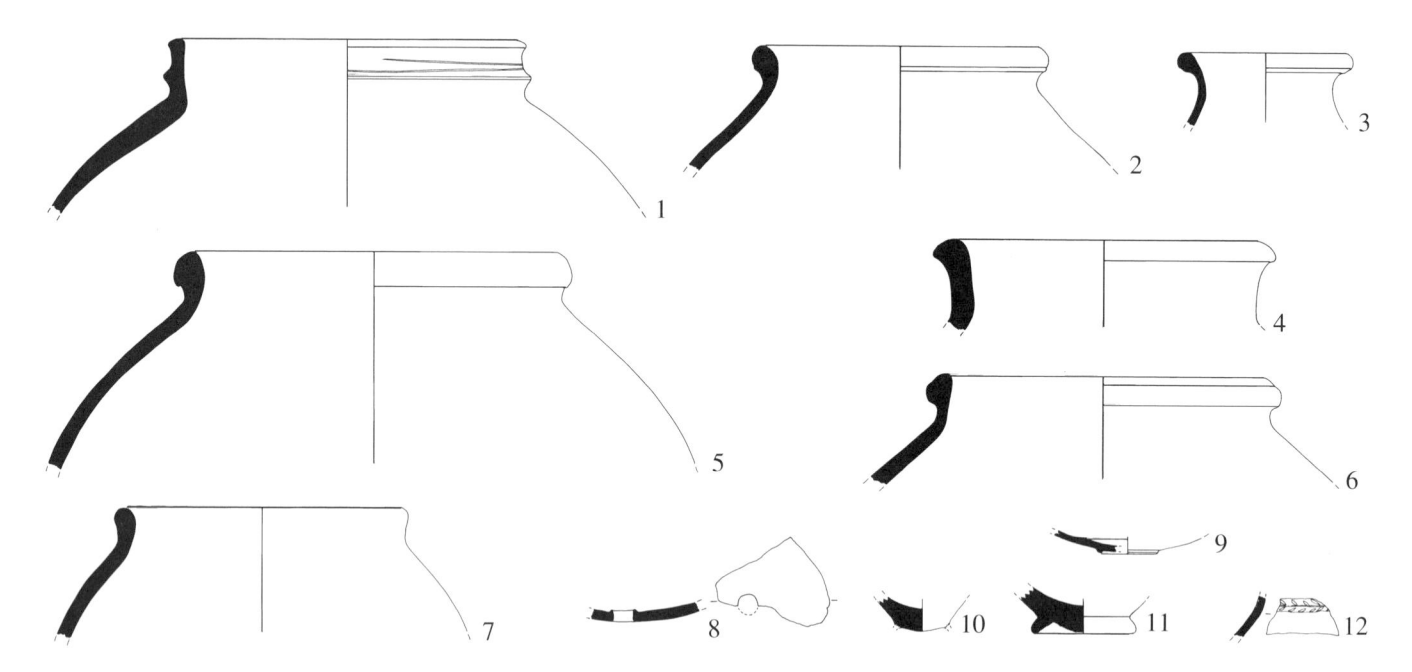

Figure 189

Figure 189. Pottery from Trench IIIC, Room 9 (Phase 4; Period E — Early Bronze Age IVb). Scale 1:5

1. JR. B.IV.f (TS. 441; IIIC, 4.10). Fairly coarse pink ware, unevenly fired with brownish-gray core.
2. JR. E.II.f (TS. 450; IIIC, 4.10). Fairly coarse pinkish-buff ware, evenly fired. Cream slip in and out.
3. JR. J.III.j (TS. 2256; IIIC, 4.10). Slightly coarse light buff ware, evenly fired. Thick creamy-buff slip in and out.
4. JR. J.IV.i (TS. 472; IIIC, 4.10). Coarse pink ware with lime and mica grits, unevenly fired buff at surfaces. Cream slip out.
5. JR. P.II.a (SW. 331; IIIC, 4.10). Coarse, gritty, light brown ware, evenly fired. Cream slip out.
6. JR. P.II.h (TS. 2355; IIIC, 4.10). Fairly coarse buff ware, unevenly fired pink on inner surface. Creamy-buff slip out.
7. CP. B.II.a (TS. 3007; IIIC, 4.10). Fairly coarse and gritty brown ware, evenly fired. Self slip, horizontally burnished out and around inner rim.
8. BE. A.II (TS. 1371; IIIC, 4.10). Fairly fine pinkish-brown ware, evenly fired. Creamy-buff slip out. One half of drainage hole extant.
9. BE. E.I.f (TS. 1369; IIIC, 4.10). Hard, fine gray, "metallic-like" ware, evenly fired. Self slip, radially burnished inside and horizontally outside.
10. BE. E.II.i (TS. 445; IIIC, 4.10). Coarse gritty pinkish-buff ware, evenly fired.
11. BE. E.II.i (TS. 510; IIIC, 4.10). Coarse pink ware, evenly fired. Buff slip in and out.
12. JR.Sh. (IP [G.3] B.I.a; TS. 511; IIIC, 4.10). Fairly coarse grayware, evenly fired. Jar shoulder sherd with impressed herringbone decoration.
—. JR.Sh. (PM. F; TS. 3129; IIIC, 4.10). Jar sherd. Ware description not available.

Other Type Series Examples: (1) SBR. B.I.k (TS. 475), (2) BR. A.II.b (TS. 437), (3) BR. A.IV.c (SW. 148), (4) JR. C.V.a (SW. 325), (5) JR. E.I.b (TS. 1374).

Other Study Collection Examples: (1) SBR. A.I.c (SC. 221), (2) JR. J.I.d (SC. 1323), (3) JR. J.II.k (SC. 2184), (4) JR. J.III.j (SC. 1411), (5) JR. O.II.f (SC. 1646), (6) JR. O.II.m (SC. 1666), (7) CP. B.I.d (SC. 1827).

Figure 190. Pottery from Trench IIIC, Rooms 19A and 19C (Phase 5; Period E — Early Bronze Age IVb)

1. SBR. B.I.a (SW. 317; IIIC, 4.9, Room 19A). Fine, hard, light brown ware, evenly fired. Cream slip out. Base string-cut from potter's wheel.
2. SBR. B.I.d (TS. 508; IIIC, 4.9, Room 19A). Fairly coarse pink ware, evenly fired. Cream slip in and out.
3. BR. E.I.b (TS. 483; IIIC, 4.9, Room 19A). Coarse and gritty pinkish-buff ware, evenly fired.
4. BR. F.III.e (TS. 489; IIIC, 4.9, Room 19A). Fairly fine pink ware, evenly fired. Buff slip in and out.
5. BR. L.I.c (TS. 479; IIIC, 4.9, Room 19A). Coarse pink ware with lime and mica grits, evenly fired. Cream slip in and out.
6. JR. A.I.a (TS. 1920; IIIC, 4.9, Room 19A). Slightly coarse light grayware, fairly evenly fired. Grayish-buff slip in and out.
7. JR. C.II.a (TS. 1917; IIIC, 4.9, Room 19A). Slightly coarse pinkish-buff ware, evenly fired. Creamy-buff slip in and out.
8. JR. C.II.b (TS. 476; IIIC, 4.9, Room 19A). Fairly coarse greenish-buff ware, evenly fired. Light green slip out.
9. JR. C.III.a (TS. 1828; IIIC, 4.9, Room 19A). Fairly fine pinkish-buff ware, evenly fired. Creamy-buff slip in and out.
10. JR. F.II.d (TS. 459; IIIC, 4.9, Room 19A). Fairly fine pink ware, evenly fired. Cream slip in and out.
11. JR. J.I.a (TS. 503; IIIC, 4.9, Room 19A). Fairly coarse pinkish-buff ware, evenly fired. Cream slip in and out.
12. JR. J.III.e (TS. 435; IIIC, 4.9, Room 19A). Fairly coarse creamy-buff ware, evenly fired.
13. JR. O.I.a (TS. 2379; IIIC, 4.11, Room 19C). Fairly coarse buff ware, evenly fired. Self slip out.
14. JR. O.II.a (TS. 2363; IIIC, 4.9, Room 19A). Fairly coarse buff ware, evenly fired. Creamy-green slip in and out.
15. JR. Q.I.a (TS. 495; IIIC, 4.9, Room 19A). Coarse pink ware, unevenly fired with light brown core. Cream slip in and out.
16. CP. B.IV.h (TS. 2244; IIIC, 4.9, Room 19A). Fairly coarse and gritty pinkish-brown ware, evenly fired. Self slip, horizontally burnished on rim and vertically on neck out.
17. BE. A.II (TS. 1372; IIIC, 4.9, Room 19A). Slightly coarse creamy-buff ware, evenly fired. Self slip burnished in and out. Rivet mending hole in base, drilled from both sides of vessel.
18. BE. B.II (PM. C.10; TS. 3057; IIIC, 4.9, Room 19A). Fairly coarse pinkish-orange ware, evenly fired. Cream slip in and out. Remains of a potter's mark incised on outside wall before firing.
19. BE. D.II (TS. 473; IIIC, 4.9, Room 19A). Fairly coarse pink ware with lime and mica grits, evenly fired. Cream slip out.
20. BE. D.II (PM. C.14; TS. 1392; IIIC, 4.9, Room 19A). Slightly coarse pinkish-buff ware, evenly fired. Remains of a potter's mark incised on outside wall before firing.

Figure 190

21. BE. D.III (TS. 1269; IIIC, 4.9, Room 19A). Slightly coarse buff ware, evenly fired. Self slip out.
22. BE. D.III (PM. C.14; TS. 1395; IIIC, 4.9, Room 19A). Fairly coarse pink ware, evenly fired. Creamy-green slip in and out. Remains of a potter's mark incised on outside wall before firing.
23. BE. E.I.d (TS. 477; IIIC, 4.9, Room 19A). Fairly coarse buff ware, evenly fired. Drainage hole in center of base.
24. BE. E.II.k (TS. 468; IIIC, 4.9, Room 19A). Coarse pink ware with lime and mica grits, evenly fired.
25. BE. H (TS. 1368; IIIC, 4.11, Room 19C). Slightly coarse light pink ware, evenly fired. Creamy-buff slip out. Base string-cut from potter's wheel.
—. JR.Sh. (PM. F; TS. 3100; IIIC, 4.9, Room 19A). Jar sherd. Ware description not available.
26. JR.Sh. (PM. A.17; TS. 1397; IIIC, 4.9, Room 19A). Slight coarse pinkish-buff ware, evenly fired. Creamy-buff slip out. Remains of a potter's mark incised on outside wall before firing.
27. JR.Sh. (PM. D.22; TS. 1398; IIIC, 4.9, Room 19A). Fairly fine pinkish-brown ware, evenly fired. Creamy-buff slip out. Remains of a potter's mark incised on outside wall before firing.
28a, b. JR.Sh. (PM. D.15 and A.6; TS. 1399a, b; IIIC, 4.9, Room 19A). Two jar sherds with remains of potter's marks incised on outside walls before firing. Slightly coarse pinkish-buff ware, evenly fired. Creamy-buff slip out.
29. JR.Sh. (PM. A.6; TS. 1396; IIIC, 4.9, Room 19A). Slightly coarse ware, unevenly fired with light gray core and buff at surfaces. Creamy-green slip in and out. Jar shoulder sherd with potter's mark incised on outside wall before firing.
30. JR.Sh. (PM. C.8; TS. 1394; IIIC, 4.9, Room 19A). Slightly coarse pink ware, evenly fired. Creamy-buff slip out. Jar sherd with portion of a potter's mark incised on outside wall before firing.

Other Type Series Examples:
Room 19A — (1) BR. Q.I.b (TS. 2464), (2) JR. C.I.d (TS. 1277), (3) JR. C.II.c (TS. 1844), (4) JR. C.V.d (TS. 490), (5) JR. D.I.e (TS. 460), (6) JR. D.VI.a (TS. 1274), (7) JR. D.VIII.e (TS. 1845), (8) Lp. A.II.a (IP [G.4] A.IV.a; SW. 145), (9) BE. F.VIII.b (TS. 544).

Other Study Collection Examples:
Room 19A — (1) SBR. A.I.a (SC. 195), (2) SBR. B.I.l (SC. 671), (3) SBR. D.I.d (SC. 644), (4) JR. E.I.c (SC. 1135), (5) JR. J.I.f (SC. 1345), (6) JR. J.II.j (SC. 2177), (7) JR. J.II.k (SC. 2179), (8) JR. J.III.a (SC. 2205), (9) JR. J.III.c (SC. 1368), (10) JR. J.III.e (SC. 2258), (11) JR. J.III.o (SC. 2343), (12) JR. O.III.c (SC. 1677), (13) JR. P.II.k (SC. 1748), (14) JR. (not typed, SC. 130), (15) CP. B.I.d (SC. 1829), (16) CP. B.IV.g (SC. 1895), (17) BE. E.I.b (SC. 3154), (18) BE. E.II.h (SC. 3220), (19) BE. F.VIII.b (SC. 3083).
Room 19C — (1) JR. J.I.d (SC. 1326).

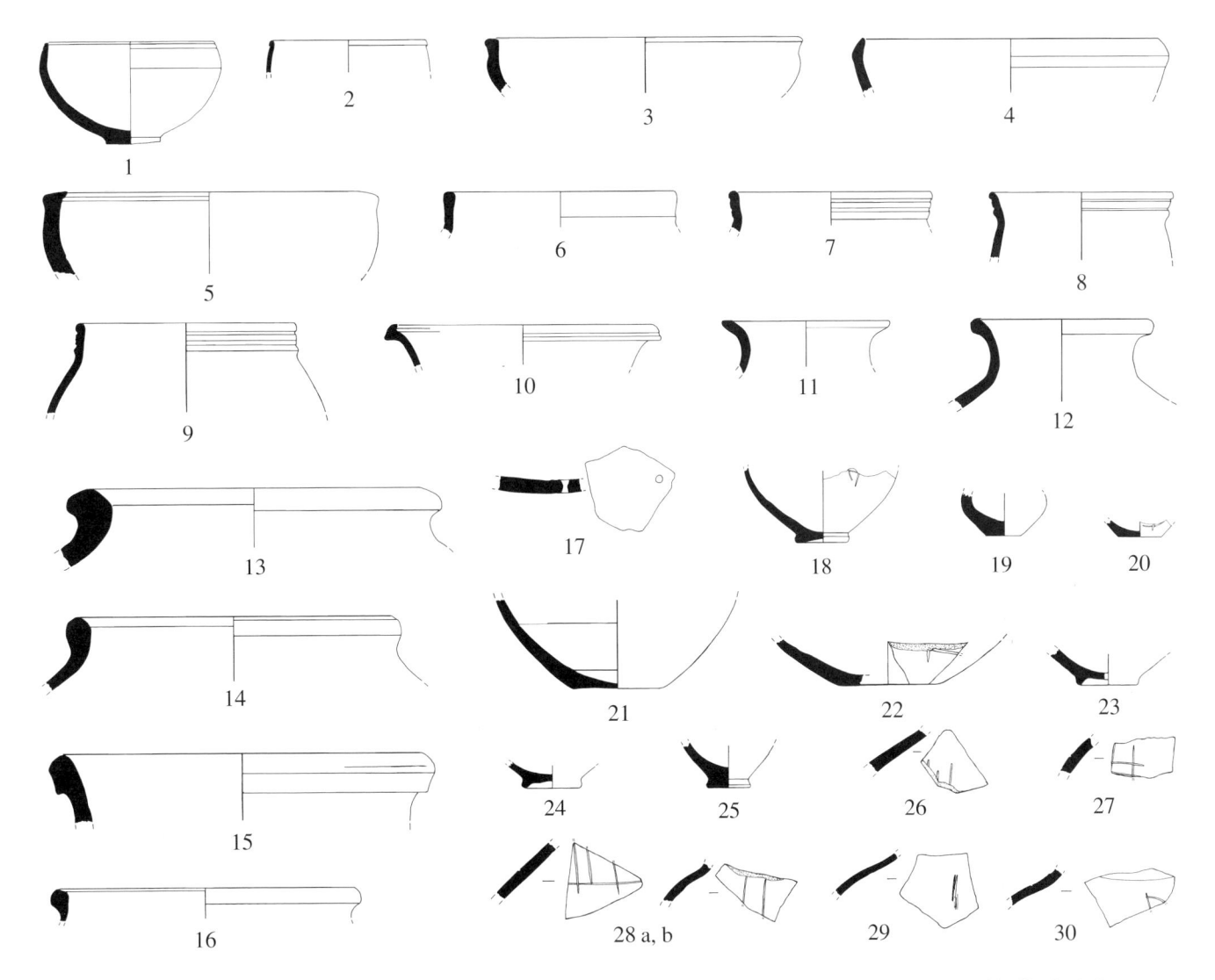

Pottery from Trench IIIC, Rooms 19A and 19C (Phase 5; Period E — Early Bronze Age IVb). Scale 1:5

Figure 191

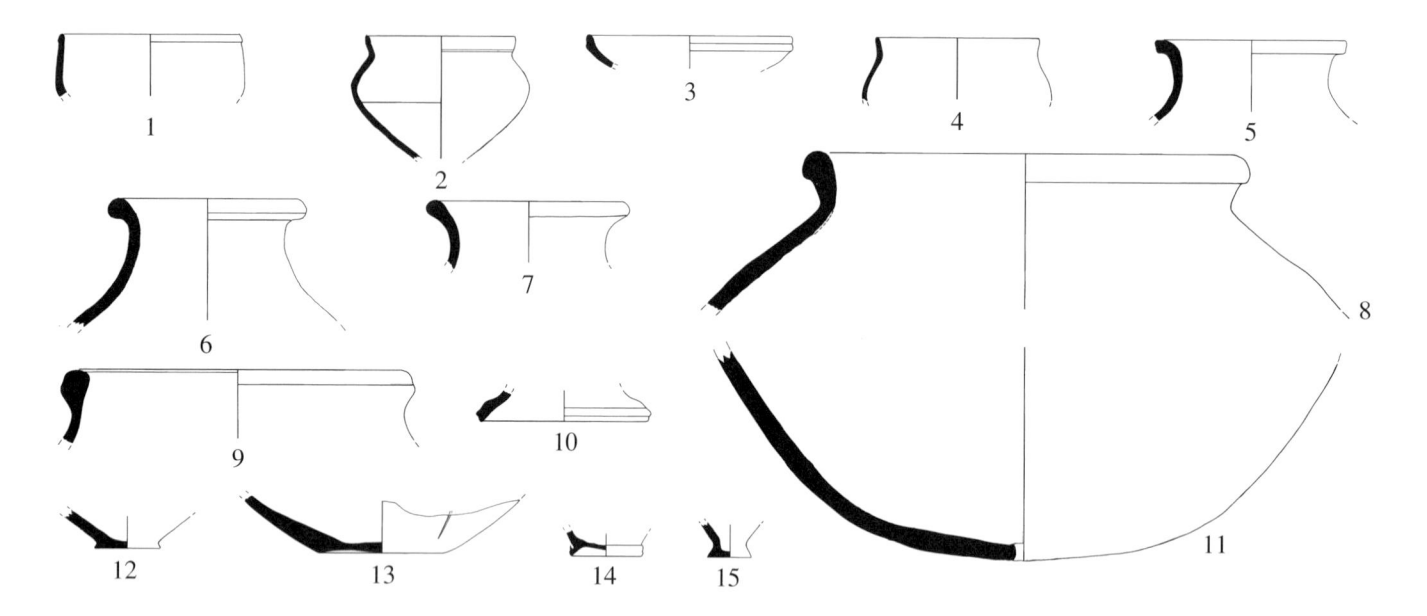

Pottery from Trench IIIC (Phase 6; Period E–D — Early–Middle Bronze Age). Scale 1:5

1. SBR. B.I.g (TS. 3154; IIIC, 4.7). Slightly coarse and gritty buff ware, evenly fired. Self slip in and out.
2. SBR. D.I.a (SW. 314; IIIC, 4.7). Fine, hard, buff ware with a few grits, evenly fired. Traces of red slip in, on rim and part of body out.
3. BR. D.I.a (TS. 1376; IIIC, 4.7). Fairly fine buff ware, evenly fired. Creamy-buff slip in and out.
4. SJR. A.I.a (TS. 2023; IIIC, 4.7). Slightly coarse greenish-buff ware, evenly fired. Self slip in and out.
5. JR. J.III.d (TS. 471; IIIC, 4.7). Fairly fine pink ware, evenly fired. Cream slip in and out.
6. JR. J.III.e (SW. 315; IIIC, 4.7). Fairly fine buff ware, evenly fired.
7. JR. J.III.n (TS. 2287; IIIC, 4.7). Fairly coarse pinkish-buff ware, evenly fired. Thick cream slip in and out.
8. JR. P.I.a (TS. 605; IIIC, 4.7, IIIA, 1.3, and IIID, 5.3). Coarse pink ware, evenly fired. Cream slip out.
9. JR. P.II.n (TS. 2386; IIIC, 4.7, 4.9). Fairly fine buff ware, evenly fired. Self slip in and out.
10. Ld. C.III.c (TS. 1370; IIIC, 4.7). Slightly coarse brownish-buff ware, evenly fired. Self slip in and out.
11. BE. A.II (SW. 179; IIIC, 4.7). Light buff ware with much brown and black and some red temper, evenly fired. Traces of yellow-green slip in and more heavily applied outside with traces of iron staining. Drainage hole in center of base.
12. BE. B.I (TS. 478; IIIC, 4.7). Fairly coarse buff ware, evenly fired. Base string-cut from potter's wheel.
13. BE. C.II (PM. A.11; SW. 108; IIIC, 4.7). Coarse brown ware with black- and gold-colored mineral temper. Light buff slip in and out; concentric rings of reserve slip inside. Remains of a potter's mark incised on outside wall before firing.
14. BE. E.I.a (TS. 1377; IIIC, 4.7). Fine light grayish-buff ware, evenly fired. Self slip in and out.
15. BE. H (TS. 470; IIIC, 4.7). Fairly fine pinkish-buff ware, evenly fired. Cream slip in and out.

Other Type Series Examples: (1) BR. A.II.c (TS. 1196), (2) BR. A.II.d (TS. 502), (3) BR. E.II.b (TS. 1375), (4) BR. E.III.d (TS. 1238), (5) SJR. F (IP [G.2] B.I.a; TS. 513 = TS. 531), (6) JR. A.III.b (TS. 596), (7) JR. B.IV.b (TS. 1373), (8) JR. C.III.c (TS. 1276).

Other Study Collection Examples: (1) SBR. A.I.d (SC. 290), (2) SBR. B.I.a (SC. 3), (3) SBR. B.I.c (SC. 279), (4) SBR. B.I.g (SC. 360), (5) BR. L.II.c (SC. 859), (6) JR. J.III.a (SC. 1361), (7) CP. A.I.d (SC. 1788), (8) CP. B.I.f (SC. 1831), (9) CP. B.IV.e (SC. 1893), (10) CP. (not typed, SC. 71), (11) BE. D.II (SC. 3127).

Figure 192

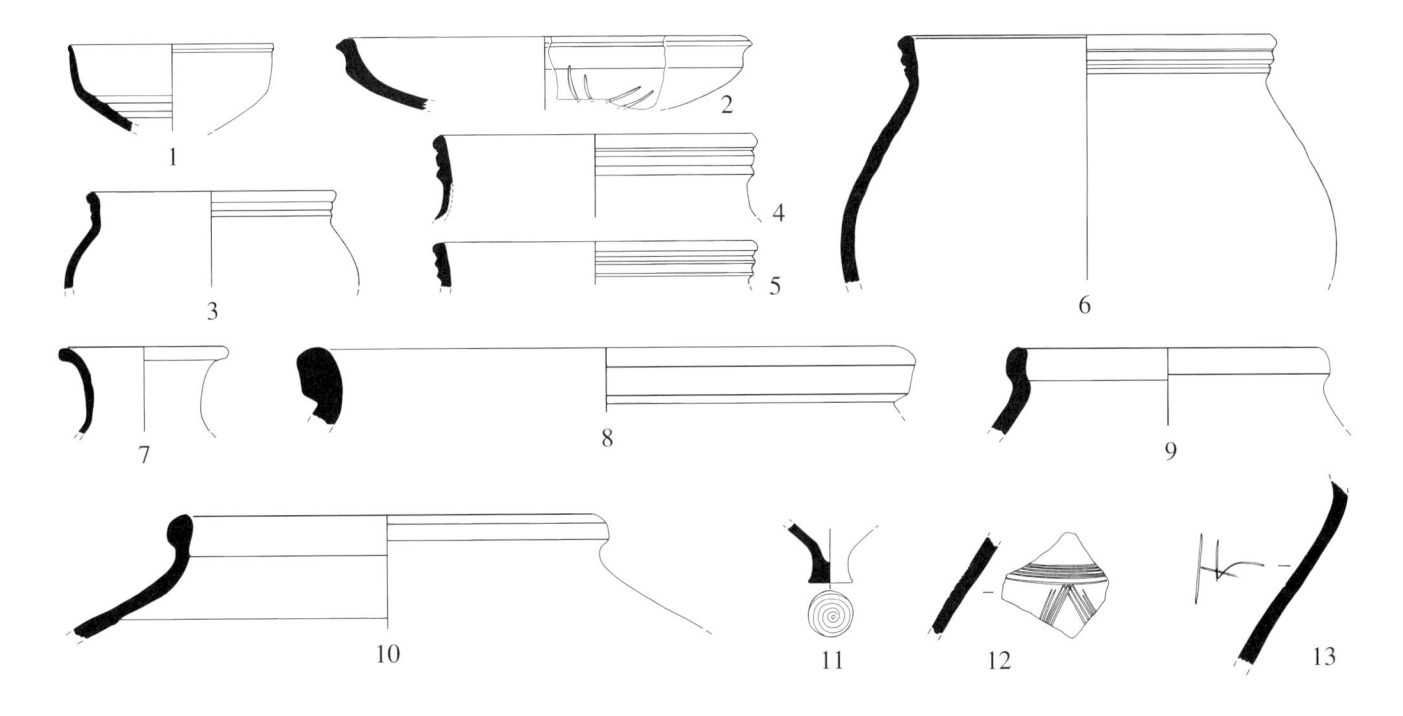

Pottery from Trench IIIC (Phase 7; Period D — Middle Bronze Age I). Scale 1:5

1. SBR. F.I.a (TS. 2196; IIIC, 4.6). Slightly coarse pink ware, evenly fired. Creamy-buff slip in and out.
2. BR. E.I.b (PM. B.2; TS. 451 = TS. 1367; IIIC, 4.6, 4.7 and IIIC, 4.7). Slightly coarse pinkish-buff ware, evenly fired. Self slip in and out. Potter's mark or decoration incised on outside wall before firing.
3. JR. C.II.a (TS. 1273; IIIC, 4.6). Fairly fine light pink ware, evenly fired. Creamy-buff slip out and over rim in.
4. JR. D.I.c (TS. 1270 = SW. 180; IIIC, 4.6 and IIID, 5.3). Slightly coarse pinkish-orange ware, evenly fired. Inner surface of neck broken away due to corrosive effect of original contents.
5. JR. D.II.a (TS. 1864; IIIC, 4.6). Fairly coarse pinkish-buff ware, evenly fired. Creamy-green slip in and out.
6. JR. D.VI.c (TS. 1833; IIIC, 4.6. 4.7. 4.10). Slightly coarse pinkish-buff ware, evenly fired. Creamy-buff slip out.
7. JR. J.III.e (TS. 446; IIIC, 4.6). Fine buff ware, unevenly fired with black core. Cream slip in and out.
8. JR. O.I.h (TS. 2408; IIIC, 4.6). Coarse ware, unevenly fired with grayish core and pink at surfaces. Creamy-yellow slip out.
9. JR. O.II.h (TS. 2392; IIIC, 4.6). Coarse brownish-buff ware, evenly fired. Self slip out.
10. JR. P.II.f (TS. 2362; IIIC, 4.6). Fairly coarse pinkish-buff ware, evenly fired. Buff slip in and out.
11. BE. H (TS. 2195; IIIC, 4.6). Fairly fine buff ware, evenly fired. Self slip in and out. Base string-cut from potter's wheel.
12. JR.Sh. (IP [G.1] H.III.a; TS. 1256; IIIC, 4.6). Slightly coarse and gritty buff ware, evenly fired. Creamy-buff slip in and out. Comb-incised decoration on jar shoulder.
—. JR.Sh. (PM. F; TS. 3130; IIIC, 4.6). Jar sherd. Ware description not available.
—. JR.Sh. (PM. F; TS. 3145; IIIC, 4.6). Jar sherd. Ware description not available.
13. JR.Sh. (PM. E.2; TS. 575; IIIC, 4.6). Coarse brown ware, evenly fired. Cream slip in and out. Potter's mark incised on jar shoulder before firing.

Other Type Series Examples: (1) SJR. B.I.c (SW. 129 = TS. 1378), (2) JR. B.II.c (TS. 1344), (3) JR. B.II.d (TS. 1275 = TS. 1380), (4) JR. B.III.f (TS. 1900), (5) JR. C.VI.b (TS. 1843), (6) JR. D.I.a (TS. 1852), (7) JR. D.II.c (TS. 1271).

Other Study Collection Examples: (1) SBR. B.I.e (SC. 303), (2) SBR. B.I.e (SC. 308), (3) JR. E.I.c (SC. 1133), (4) JR. E.II.j (SC. 2025), (5) JR. F.I.d (SC. 1211), (6) JR. J.I.b (SC. 1309), (7) JR. J.I.b (SC. 2094), (8) JR. J.I.b (SC. 2107), (9) JR. J.III.a (SC. 2199), (10) JR. J.III.h (SC. 2291), (11) JR. J.III.o (SC. 2339), (12) JR. J.III.o (SC. 2342), (13) JR. J.IV.j (SC. 1543), (14) JR. O.II.a (SC. 2413), (15) JR. O.II.d (SC. 2454), (16) JR. O.II.m (SC. 1662), (17) JR. O.III.f (SC. 1687), (18) JR. O.III.g (SC. 2425), (19) JR. P.II.a (SC. 1699), (20) JR. P.II.l (SC. 1750), (21) JR. (not typed, SC. 131), (22) BE. G (SC. 3232), (23) WPS. C (SC. 1946), (24) WPS. (not typed, SC. 155).

Figure 193. Pottery from Trench IIID, Rooms 11A, 12, and 13 (Phase 4; Period E — Early Bronze Age IVb)

1. MBR. A.II.a (TS. 2426; IIID, 6.1, Room 13). Coarse buff ware, fairly evenly fired. Self slip in and out. Handmade.
2. SBR. B.I.g (TS. 1206; IIID, 5.4, Room 12). Fairly coarse pinkish-buff ware with lime and mica grits, evenly fired. Creamy-buff slip in and out.
3. JR. B.II.c (TS. 1338; IIID, 5.4, Room 12). Slightly coarse pinkish-brown ware, evenly fired. Creamy-buff slip out.
4. JR. D.I.b (TS. 1824; IIID, 5.4, Room 12). Fine grayish-buff ware, evenly fired. Self slip in and out.
5. JR. E.II.d (SW. 277; IIID, 5.4, Room 12). Slightly coarse pinkish-buff ware with small lime and mica grits, unevenly fired creamy-buff at surfaces.
6. JR. J.III.a (TS. 2267; IIID, 6.1, Room 13). Fairly coarse pink ware, evenly fired. Light creamy-green slip out, buff in.
7. JR. J.III.g (TS. 521; IIID, 5.4, Room 12). Fairly coarse pinkish-buff ware, evenly fired. Cream slip out.
8. JR. J.III.i (TS. 1348; IIID, 5.4, Room 12). Slightly coarse brown ware, evenly fired. Creamy-green slip out.
9. JR. O.II.b (SW. 278; IIID, 5.4, Room 12). Slightly coarse pinkish-buff ware with lime and mica grits, evenly fired. Greenish-buff slip out with polished reserved slip rings.
10. JR. O.III.a (SW. 287; IIID, 5.4, Room 12). Hard, fairly coarse ware with various colored lime grits, unevenly fired with gray core and light brown at surfaces. Thick greenish slip in and out.
11. JR. O.III.b (TS. 1347; IIID, 5.4, Room 12). Fairly coarse brownish-buff ware, evenly fired. Creamy-green slip in and out.
12. JR. P.II.a (TS. 604; IIID, 5.5, Courtyard Room 11A). Fairly coarse pink ware, evenly fired. Thin buff slip out.
13. JR. P.II.g (TS. 1202; IIID, 5.4, Room 12). Slightly coarse light brown ware with fine lime and mica grits, evenly fired. Creamy-green slip rings in reserve.

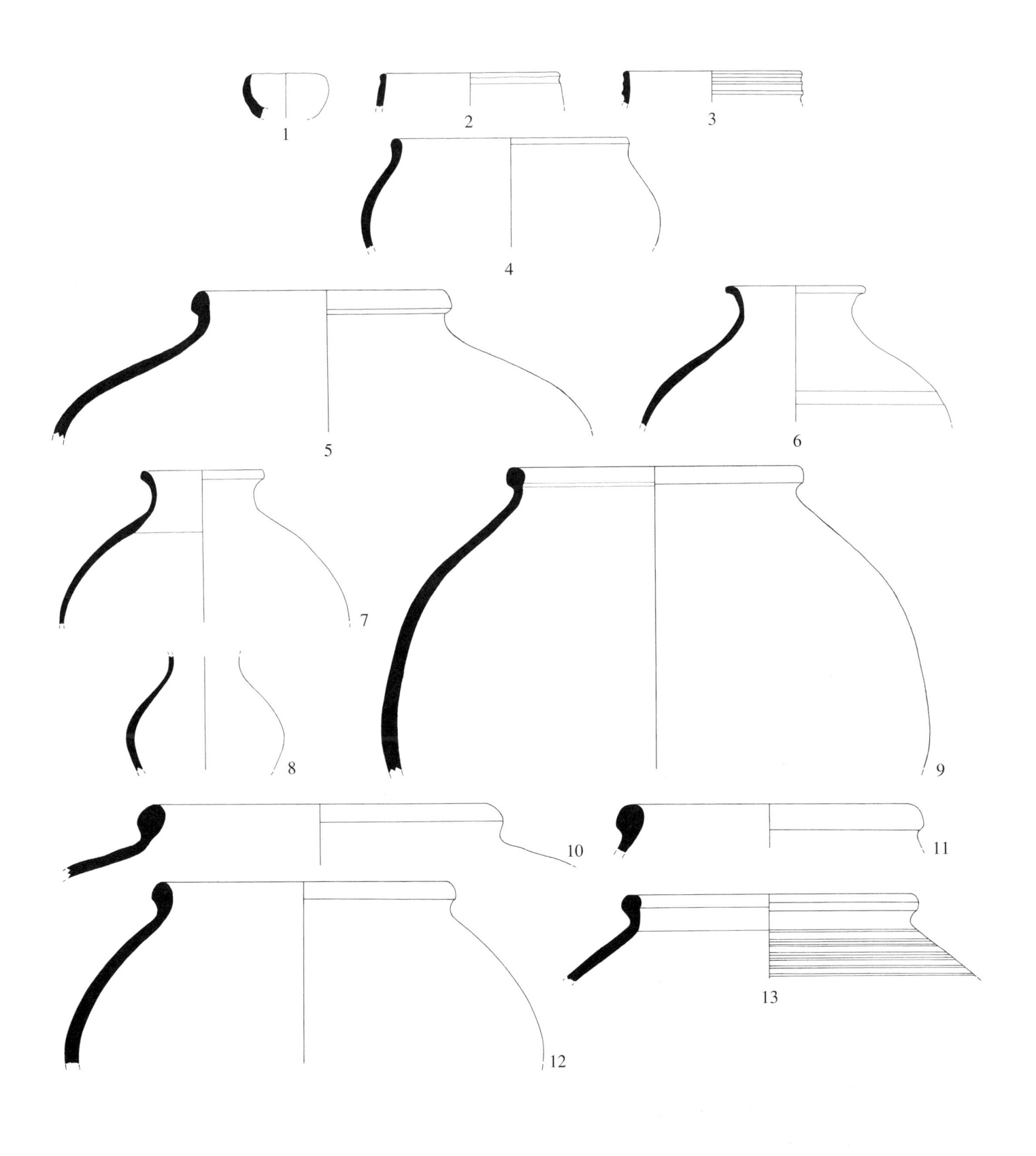

Figure 193

Pottery from Trench IIID, Rooms 11A, 12, and 13 (Phase 4; Period E — Early Bronze Age IVb). Scale 1:5

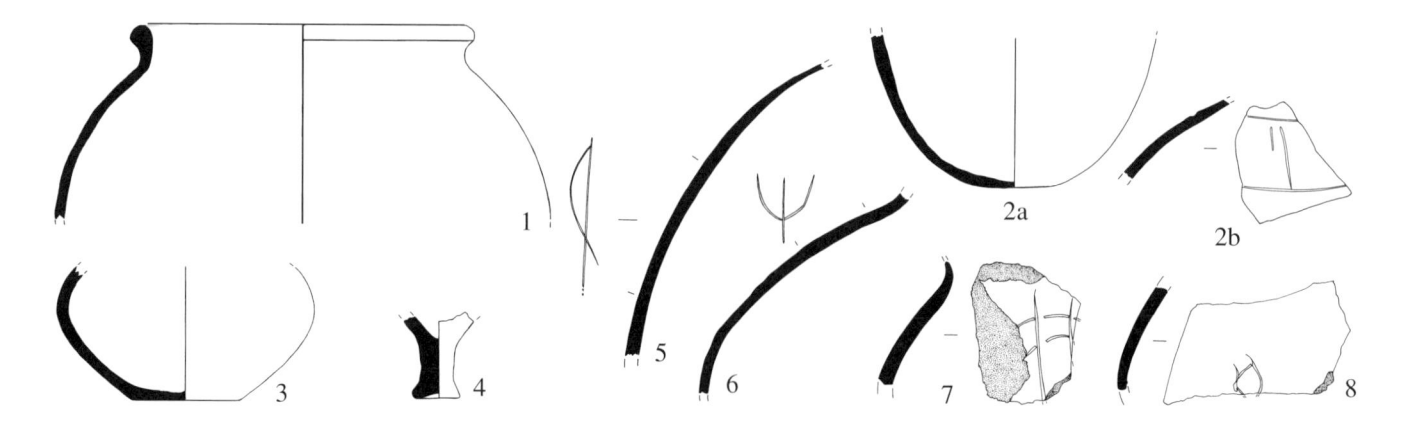

Figure 194

Figure 194. Pottery from Trench IIID, Rooms 11A, 12, and 13 (Phase 4; Period E — Early Bronze Age IVb) (*cont.*).
Scale 1:5

1. CP. B.IV.d (SW. 176; IIID, 5.4, Room 12). Coarse brown ware with much white-colored mica temper. Inside wet-smoothed; body handmade.
2a, b. BE. D.I + JR.Sh. (PM. A.7; TS. 1379; IIID, 5.4, Room 12). Slightly coarse pinkish-brown ware, evenly fired. Self slip in and out. Jar base fragment and non-joining shoulder sherd with a potter's mark incised outside before firing.
3. BE. D.III (SW. 324; IIID, 5.4, Room 12). Fairly fine dark grayware, unevenly fired with light gray core.
4. BE. H (TS. 1204; IIID, 6.1, Room 13). Fairly fine pinkish-buff ware, evenly fired. Self slip out.
5. JR.Sh. (PM. C.9; TS. 598; IIID, 5.4, Room 12). Jar shoulder sherd with potter's mark incised on outside wall before firing. Fairly coarse pink ware, evenly fired. Cream slip out.
6. JR.Sh. (PM. D.29; TS. 599; IIID, 5.4, Room 12). Jar shoulder sherd with potter's mark incised on outside wall before firing. Fairly coarse pink ware. Cream slip out.
7. JR.Sh. (PM. D.11; TS. 1172; IIID, 5.4, Room 12). Jar shoulder sherd with portion of a potter's mark incised on outside wall before firing. Fine pinkish buff ware with lime and mica grits, evenly fired. Thin buffish-colored slip in and out.
8. JR.Sh. (PM. D.17; TS. 1174; IIID, 5.4, Room 12). Jar shoulder sherd with portion of a potter's mark incised on outside wall before firing. Fine buff ware with lime and mica grits, evenly fired. Creamy-buff slip out.

Other Type Series Examples:
  Room 12 — (1) BR. A.IV.f (TS. 1349), (2) BR. F.III.e (TS. 2191), (3) BR. G.I.e (TS. 1244).
  Room 13 — (1) BR. P.I.b (TS. 595).

Other Study Collection Examples:
  Rooms 11A and 12 — (1) JR. J.I.f (SC. 1334), (2) CP. B.IV.b (SC. 3324).
  Room 12 — (1) SBR. B.I.c (SC. 268), (2) SBR. B.I.g (SC. 355), (3) SBR. B.I.k (SC. 556), (4) SBR. B.I.l (SC. 570), (5) BR. F.I.d (SC. 783), (6) JR. E.II.d (SC. 2011), (7) JR. J.I.b (SC. 2101), (8) JR. J.III.o (SC. 1472), (9) JR. (not typed, SC. 135), (10) CP. B.II.a (SC. 3323).
  Room 13 — (1) SBR. B.I.d (SC. 283), (2) BR. (not typed, SC. 38).

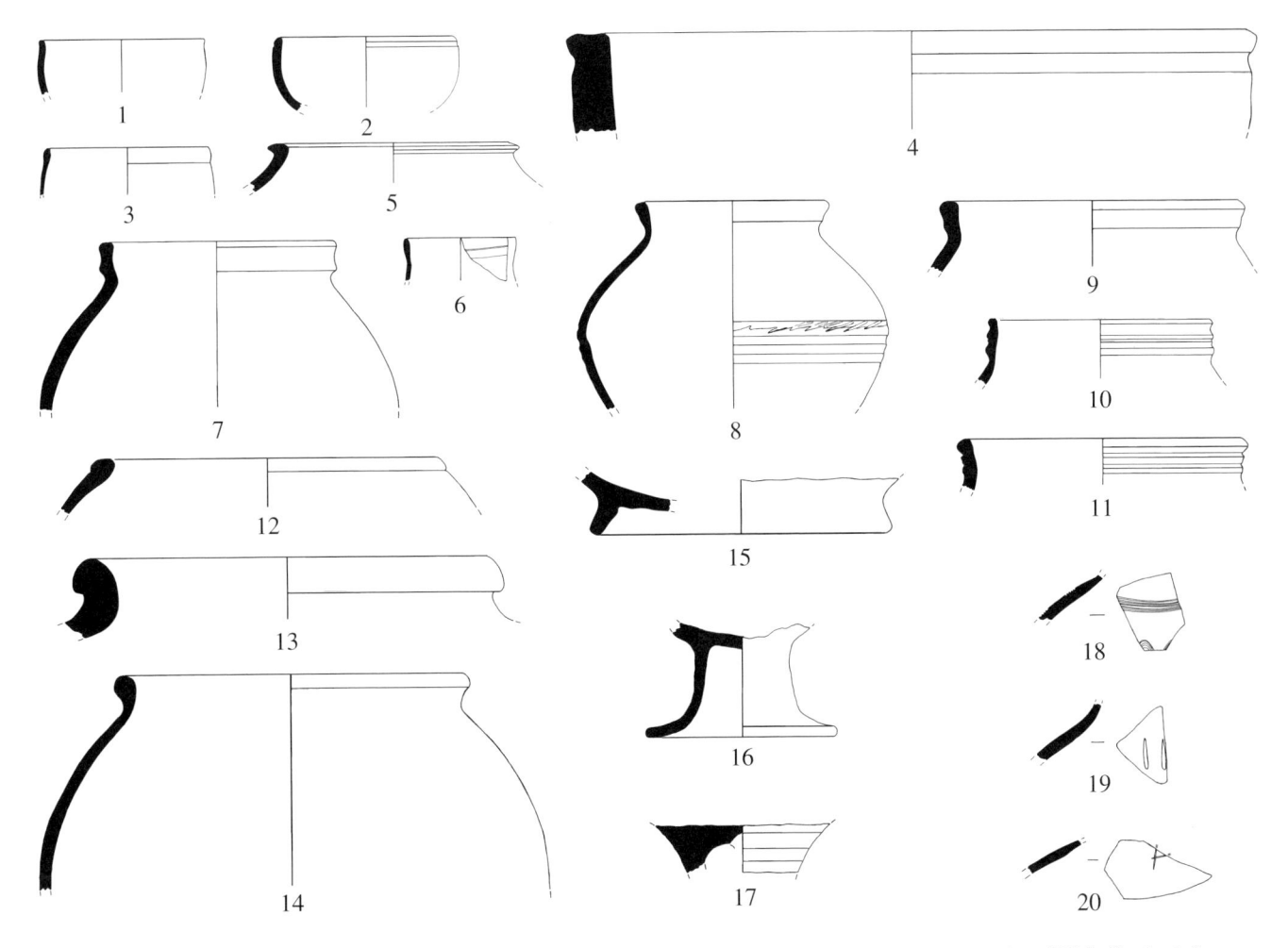

Figure 195. Pottery from Trench IIID, Rooms 20/21 (Phase 5; Period E — Early Bronze Age IVb). Scale 1:5

1. SBR. A.I.g (TS. 1365; IIID, 5.3). Fairly fine buff ware, evenly fired. Traces of self slip out.
2. SBR. B.I.c (TS. 1355; IIID, 5.3). Slightly coarse pinkish-brown ware, evenly fired. Light creamy-green slip in and out.
3. SBR. B.I.j (TS. 1360; IIID, 5.3). Fine pinkish-buff ware, evenly fired. Creamy-buff slip in and out.
4. BR. T (TS. 1352; IIID, 5.3). Coarse pinkish-colored ware with chaff temper, evenly fired. Light creamy-green slip in and out.
5. SJR. A.II.f (TS. 1358; IIID, 5.3). Fairly fine pink ware, evenly fired. Creamy-yellow slip out and on top of rim.
6. SJR. B.II.a (TS. 1364; IIID, 5.3). Slightly coarse brown ware, evenly fired. Self slip in and out.
7. JR. A.IV.a (TS. 1088; IIID, 5.3). Fairly coarse pink ware, evenly fired. Cream slip in and out.
8. JR. A.V.a (TS. 1337 = TS. 1346; IIID, 5.4 (Phase 4, Room 12) and IIID, 5.3 (Phase 5, Rooms 20/21). Slightly coarse buff ware, evenly fired. Creamy-buff slip out. Tool-gouged decorated band around central girth of vessel.
9. JR. B.V.c (TS. 1908; IIID, 5.3). Slight coarse pinkish-buff ware, evenly fired. Light creamy-green slip in and out.
10. JR. C.I.d (TS. 1823; IIID, 5.3). Hard, grayish-buff ware, evenly fired. Light creamy-green slip in and out.
11. JR. D.VI.d (TS. 1848; IIID, 5.3). Slightly coarse pinkish-buff ware, evenly fired. Creamy-green slip in and out.
12. JR. H.I.g (TS. 1354; IIID, 5.3). Slightly coarse pink ware, evenly fired. Creamy-green slip out and over rim in.
13. JR. O.I.f (TS. 2378; IIID, 5.3). Fairly coarse pink ware, evenly fired. Light green slip out.
14. CP. B.IV.c (SW. 175; IIID, 5.3). Coarse brown ware, evenly fired. Heavily charred outside.
15. BE. E.II.b (TS. 1351; IIID, 5.3). Slightly coarse pinkish-buff ware, evenly fired. Creamy-yellow slip out.
16. BE. F.III.b (SW. 147; IIID, 5.3). Fairly fine buff ware with some fine temper and some large black grits. Light greenish-buff slip in and out.
17. BE. F.VII (TS. 1353; IIID, 5.3). Fairly coarse pink ware, evenly fired. Traces of pinkish-buff slip out.
18. JR.Sh. (IP [G.1] C.II.a; TS. 1363; IIID, 5.3). Slightly coarse pinkish-buff ware, evenly fired. Creamy-buff slip out.
19. JR.Sh. (PM. A.6; TS. 1359; IIID, 5.3). Fairly fine pink ware, evenly fired. Creamy-buff slip out. Jar shoulder sherd with remains of a potter's mark incised on outside wall before firing.
20. JR.Sh. (PM. C.14; TS. 1362; IIID, 5.3). Slightly coarse pinkish-buff ware, evenly fired. Creamy-buff slip in and out. Jar shoulder sherd with remains of a potter's mark incised on outside wall before firing.

Other Type Series Examples: (1) MBR. B.I.b (TS. 1241), (2) SBR. B.I.q (TS. 1361), (3) SBR. D.I.h (TS. 1245), (4) SBR. D.II.b (TS. 1922), (5) SBR. D.II.e (TS. 1357), (6) SBR. F.I.b (SW. 149), (7) BR. E.III.c (TS. 1197), (8) BR. M.I.b (SW. 275), (9) JR. A.V.b (TS. 1356), (10) JR. J.II.j (PM. D.10; SW. 285).

Other Study Collection Examples: (1) JR. J.I.f (SC. 2117), (2) JR. J.III.b (SC. 1364), (3) JR. J.III.e (SC. 2244), (4) JR. J.III.n (SC. 2336), (5) JR. J.IV.j (SC. 2383), (6) JR. O.II.m (SC. 1667), (7) JR. O.III.h (SC. 2426), (8) CP. B.I.d (SC. 1823), (9) Ld. A.III.a (SC. 3087).

Figures 196–97

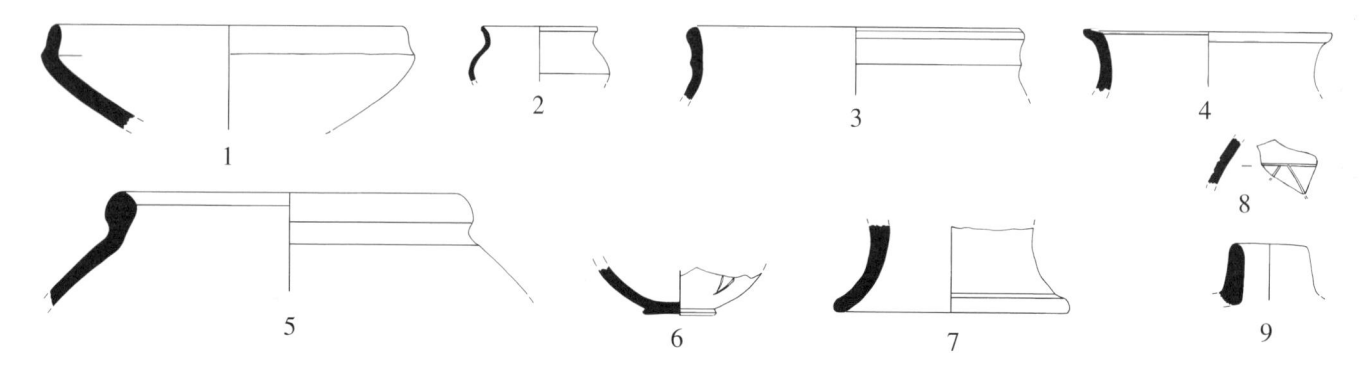

Figure 196. Pottery from Trench IIID (Phase 6; Period E–D — Early–Middle Bronze Age). Scale 1:5

1. BR. E.II.a (TS. 582 = TS. 591; IIID, 5.2). Coarse creamy-buff ware, evenly fired. Lower wall inside horizontally finger-impressed during manufacture.
2. SJR. A.I.a (TS. 2017; IIID, 5.2). Fairly fine pinkish-buff ware, evenly fired. Creamy-buff slip in and out.
3. JR. B.V.a (TS. 1871; IIID, 5.2). Fairly fine pinkish-buff ware, evenly fired. Self slip in and out.
4. JR. G.I.c (TS. 1340; IIID, 5.2). Hard, fine creamy-yellow ware, evenly fired. Self slip in and out. Traces of irregular horizontal burnishing in and out.
5. JR. P.III.d (TS. 2365; IIID, 5.2, 5.4, Room 12). Slightly coarse pinkish-buff ware, evenly fired. Buff slip out.
6. BE. B.II (PM. C.10; TS. 1171; IIID, 5.2). Fairly fine buff ware with lime and mica grits, evenly fired. Portion of a potter's mark incised on lower outer wall before firing.
7. BE. F.I.b (TS. 1243; IIID, 5.2). Slightly coarse pink ware, evenly fired. Buff slip in and out.
8. JR.Sh. (IP (G.2] A.I.a; TS. 1341; IIID, 5.1). Slightly coarse brownish buff ware, evenly fired. Creamy-buff slip out.
9. SV.2 (TS. 597; IIID, 5.2). Spout. Fairly coarse pinkish-buff ware, evenly fired. Cream slip in and out.

Other Type Series Examples: (1) SJR. C.II.n (TS. 143 = TS. 1343), (2) JR. A.III.e (TS. 1867), (3) JR. C.III.d (TS. 1862), (4) JR. D.I.c (TS. 1829).

Other Study Collection Examples: (1) SBR. B.I.l (SC. 575), (2) BR. N.I.a (SC. 866), (3) SJR. B.I.a (SC. 2497), (4) JR. E.I.c (SC. 1130), (5) JR. E.II.j (SC. 2026), (6) JR. E.II.v (SC. 1168), (7) JR. J.III.a (SC. 1359), (8) JR. J.III.e (SC. 2234), (9) JR. J.III.e (SC. 2248), (10) JR. J.III.h (SC. 1398), (11) JR. J.IV.j (SC. 2382), (12) JR. P.I.c (SC. 1695), (13) CP. B.II.a (SC. 1847), (14) CP. B.IV.d (SC. 1886), (15) CP. B.IV.d (SC. 1887), (16) BE. E.II.j (SC. 3225).

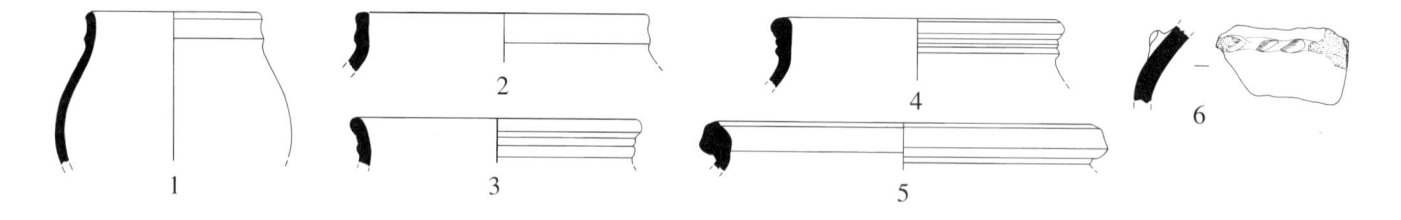

Figure 197. Pottery from Trench IIID (Phase 7; Period D — Middle Bronze Age I). Scale 1:5

1. JR. A.III.a (TS. 594; IIID, 4.8, 5.2). Fairly coarse pink ware, evenly fired. Cream slip out.
2. JR. B.IV.c (TS. 1911; IIID, 4.8). Slightly coarse pinkish-buff ware, evenly fired. Creamy-buff slip out.
3. JR. C.VI.a (TS. 1846; IIID, 4.8). Fairly fine pinkish-buff ware, evenly fired. Self slip in.
4. JR. D.V.b (TS. 1836; IIID, 4.8). Fairly fine buff ware, evenly fired. Creamy-buff slip in and out.
5. JR. O.II.i (TS. 1345; IIID, 4.8). Slightly coarse pinkish-buff ware, evenly fired. Creamy-buff slip out and over rim in.
6. ABS. A (TS. 1342; IIID, 4.8). Fairly coarse greenish-buff ware, evenly fired. Self slip in and out.

Other Type Series Examples: (1) JR. A.III.d (TS. 1904), (2) JR. B.I.b (TS. 601), (3) JR. B.V.c (TS. 1339).

Other Study Collection Examples: (1) BR. E.III.c (SC. 759), (2) JR. F.I.a (SC. 1190), (3) JR. J.I.b (SC. 1304), (4) JR. J.III.d (SC. 2233), (5) JR. J.III.m (SC. 1426), (6) JR. P.I.c (SC. 1696), (7) JR. P.II.h (SC. 1734), (8) JR. (not typed, SC. 122), (9) Jg. A.I.b (SC. 1935).

Figure 198

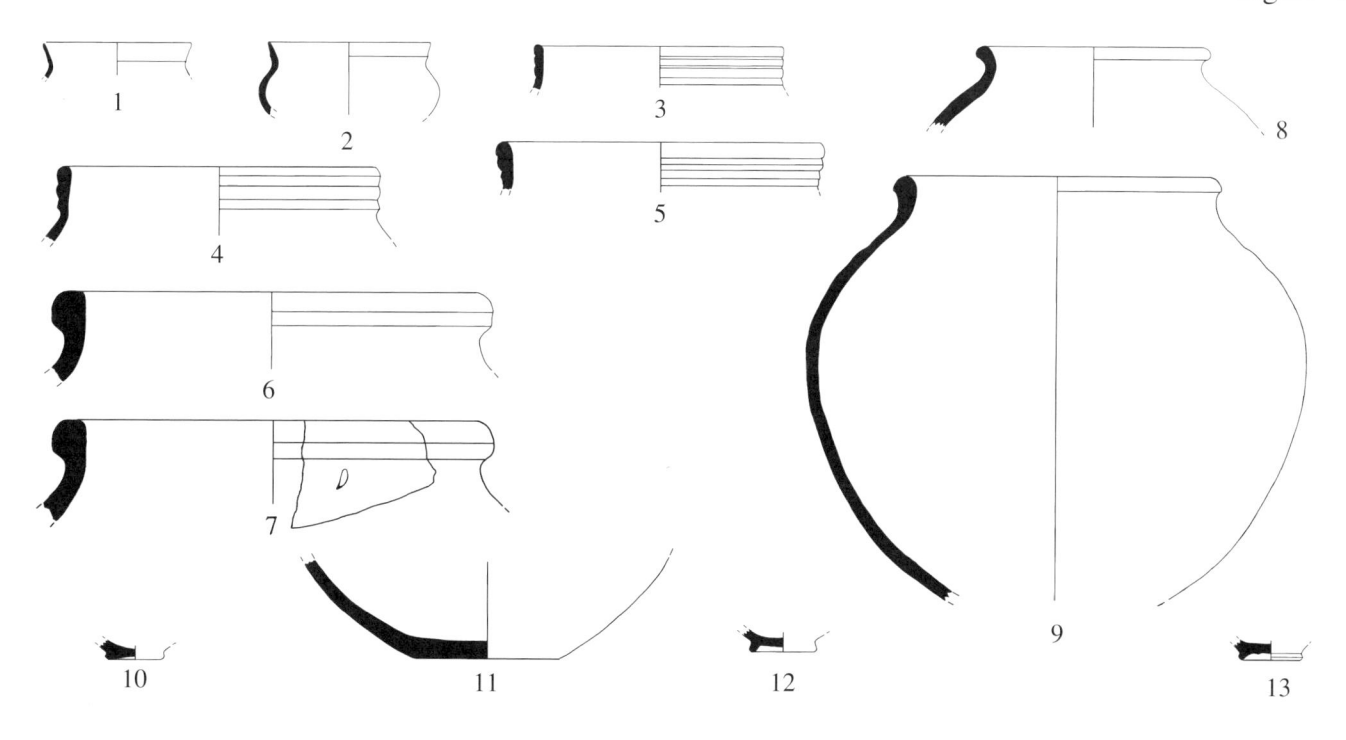

Pottery from Trench IIIE, Room 5 (Phase 4; Period E — Early Bronze Age IVb). Scale 1:5

1. SBR. D.I.d (TS. 465; IIIE, 3.2). Fairly coarse and crumbly greenish-buff ware, fairly evenly fired.
2. SBR. D.I.d (TS. 466; IIIE, 3.2). Fairly coarse creamy-buff ware, evenly fired.
3. JR. C.I.a (TS. 1838; IIIE, 3.2). Slightly coarse pinkish-buff ware, evenly fired. Buff slip in and out.
4. JR. D.V.c (TS. 1305; IIIE, 3.2). Slightly coarse light pinkish-brown ware, evenly fired. Creamy-buff slip out.
5. JR. D.VI.b (TS. 454; IIIE, 3.2). Fairly coarse pinkish-buff ware, evenly fired.
6. JR. P.II.m (TS. 452; IIIE, 3.2). Fairly coarse pink ware, unevenly fired with light brown core.
7. JR. P.II.m (PM. A.5; TS. 486; IIIE, 3.2). Jar rim, neck, and shoulder segment with a potter's mark incised on the upper shoulder before firing. Coarse pink ware with lime and mica grits, unevenly fired with buff core. Cream slip out.
8. CP. A.I.a (TS. 457; IIIE, 3.3). Coarse pink ware with much lime and mica grit, evenly fired. Blackened in and out from kiln reduction.
9. CP. B.IV.b (SW. 286; IIIE, 3.3). Very friable, coarse, gritty, brown ware with many lime and mica grits, evenly fired.
10. BE. B.II (TS. 504; IIIE, 3.3). Coarse gray-brown ware with many grits, evenly fired. Greenish-colored slip in. Base string-cut from potter's wheel.
11. BE. D.III (TS. 442; IIIE, 3.3). Coarse pinkish-buff ware, evenly fired. Creamy-buff slip in and out.
12. BE. E.I.d (TS. 487; IIIE, 3.2). Fairly coarse pink ware, evenly fired. Cream slip in.
13. BE. E.II.k (TS. 453; IIIE, 3.3). Fairly fine pink ware, evenly fired. Cream slip out.
    Other Type Series Examples: (1) SBR. B.I.c (SW. 327), (2) BR. J.I.c (SW. 182 = TS. 493), (3) Hd. C (TS. 497).
    Other Study Collection Examples: (1) SBR. A.I.g (SC. 231), (2) SBR. B.I.c (SCV. 272), (3) BR. A.II.e (SC. 870), (4) JR. E.I.c (SC. 1132), (5) JR. J.III.e (SC. 2254), (6) JR. J.III.r (SC. 1491), (7) JR. (not typed, SC. 126), (8) CP. A.I.i (SC. 1795).

Figures 199–200

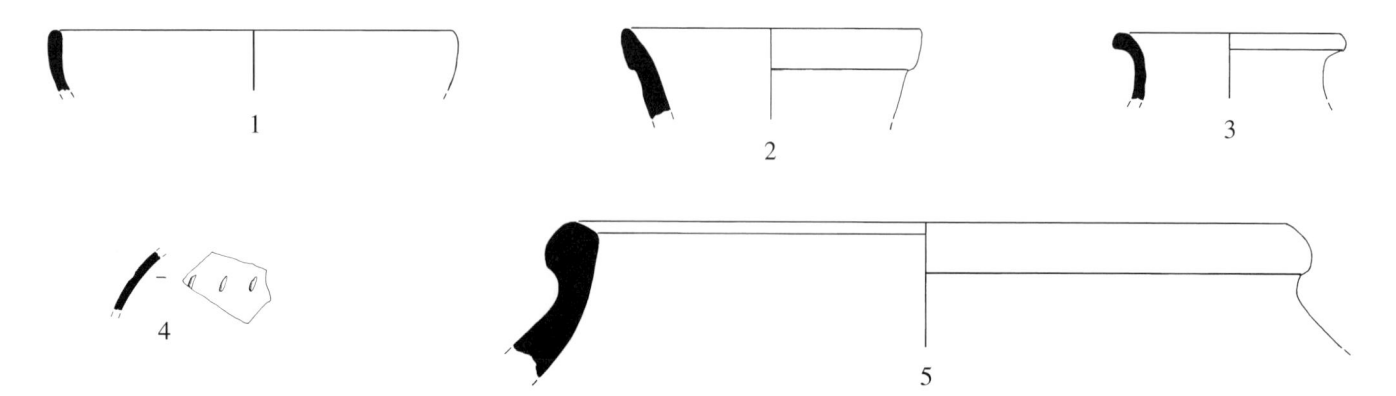

Figure 199. Pottery from Trench IIIE, Room 15 and Courtyard Room 14 (Phase 5; Period E — Early Bronze Age IVb). Scale 1:5

1. BR. A.IV.f (TS. 4227; IIIE, 3.1, Room 15). Slightly coarse pinkish-buff ware with lime and very fine gold- and silver-colored mica grits, evenly fired. Self slip in and out. Outer surface abraded away.
2. JR. B.III.a (SC. 1982; IIIE, 3.1, Room 15). Slightly coarse greenish-grayware with fine lime and gold-colored mica grits, evenly fired. Creamy-colored slip in and out. Heavily salt-encrusted outside.
3. JR. J.I.d (SC. 1331; IIIE, 3.1, Room 15). Fairly coarse pinkish-orange ware with many fine black and white lime grits and medium-sized gold-colored mica grits, evenly fired. Thick self slip out and inside to base of existing fragment.
4. JR.Sh. (IP [G.4] B.III.a; TS. 1316; IIIE, 3.1, Room 15). Slightly coarse pinkish-brown ware, evenly fired. Creamy-green slip out. Decorated with tool-impressed jab marks on outside wall.
5. JR. P.II.p (SC. 2436; IIIE, 1.2, Courtyard Room 14). Fairly coarse dark buff ware with fine lime grits and very small gold- and silver-colored mica grits, evenly fired. Horizontally reserved creamy-buff slip bands on outside and continuous on inside surviving portion of vessel. Rim completed by folding one half of the rim thickness inside of the vessel.

Other Type Series Examples: Room 15 — (1) BR. L.I.d (TS. 456 = TS. 1203), (2) JR. C.V.c (TS. 1307).

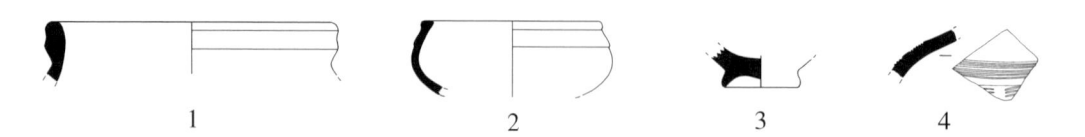

Figure 200. Pottery from Trench IIIE (Phase 6/7; Period E–D — Early–Middle Bronze Age). Scale 1:5

1. JR. B.III.b (TS. 1912; IIIE, 1.1). Slightly coarse pinkish-buff ware, evenly fired. Creamy-buff slip in and out.
2. Lp. B.I (TS. 499; IIIE, 1.1). Fairly coarse light grayware, evenly fired.
3. BE. E.II.i (TS. 491; IIIE, 1.1). Coarse pink ware, evenly fired. Cream slip in.
4. JR.Sh. (IP [G.1] F.I.a; TS. 1314; IIIE, 1.1). Slightly coarse buff ware, evenly fired. Creamy-green slip in and out.

Another Type Series Example: (1) JR. D.II.b (TS. 507).

Other Study Collection Examples: (1) BR. A.II.e (SC. 714), (2) BR. D.VIII.a (SC. 750), (3) JR. B.II.c (SC. 931), (4) JR. J.III.h (SC. 1402), (5) JR. (not typed, SC. 105).

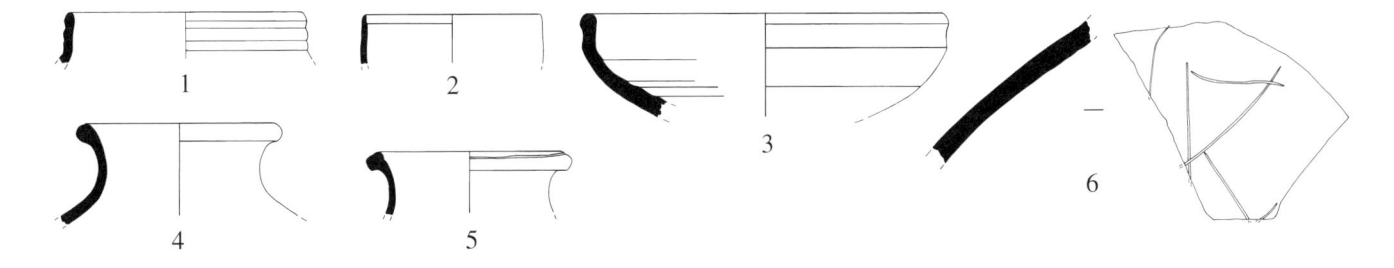

Figure 201. Pottery from Trench IIIF, Room 16, Floors, and Alley (Phases 3 and 4; Periods F and E — Early Bronze Age IVa and Early Bronze Age IVb). Scale 1:5

1. JR. C.III.b (TS. 1847; IIIF, 2.3, Floors; Phase 3). Slightly coarse pinkish-buff ware, evenly fired. Creamy-buff slip out.
2. SBR. A.I.a (TS. 2194; IIIF, 3.2, Room 16; Phase 4). Slightly coarse pink ware, evenly fired. Possible self slip in and out, but very worn.
3. BR. E.I.a (TS. 1302; IIIF, 3.1, Room 16; Phase 4). Slightly coarse buff ware, evenly fired. Self slip in and out.
4. JR. J.III.e (TS. 2272; IIIF, 3.1, Room 16; Phase 4). Fairly coarse pinkish-brown ware, evenly fired. Creamy-green slip out and over rim to base of neck in.
5. JR. J.III.k (TS. 2261; IIIF, 3.1, Room 16; Phase 4). Fairly fine buff ware, evenly fired. Creamy-buff slip out and over rim in.
6. JR.Sh. (PM. D.13; TS. 1237; IIIF, 3.1, Room 16; Phase 4). Slightly coarse pink ware, unevenly fired buff at surfaces. Self slip in and out. Jar shoulder sherd with remains of a potter's mark incised on outside wall before firing.

Other Type Series Examples:
   Phase 4, Room 16 — (1) BR. G.I.a (TS. 602), (2) CP. A.I.d (TS. 1239).
   Phase 4, Alley — (1) JR. C.V.e (TS. 1819), (2) JR. D.VII.b (TS. 1840).

Other Study Collection Examples:
   Phase 3, Floors — (1) JR. E.I.c (SC. 1131), (2) JR. K.I.b (SC. 1577), (3) JR. (not typed, SC. 109).
   Phase 4, Alley — (1) JR. P.II.m (SC. 1752).
   Phase 4, Room 16 — (1) SBR. B.I.c (SC. 274), (2) SBR. B.I.e (SC. 310), (3) BR. (not typed, SC. 37), (4) CP. B.I.i (SC. 1836).

Figure 202

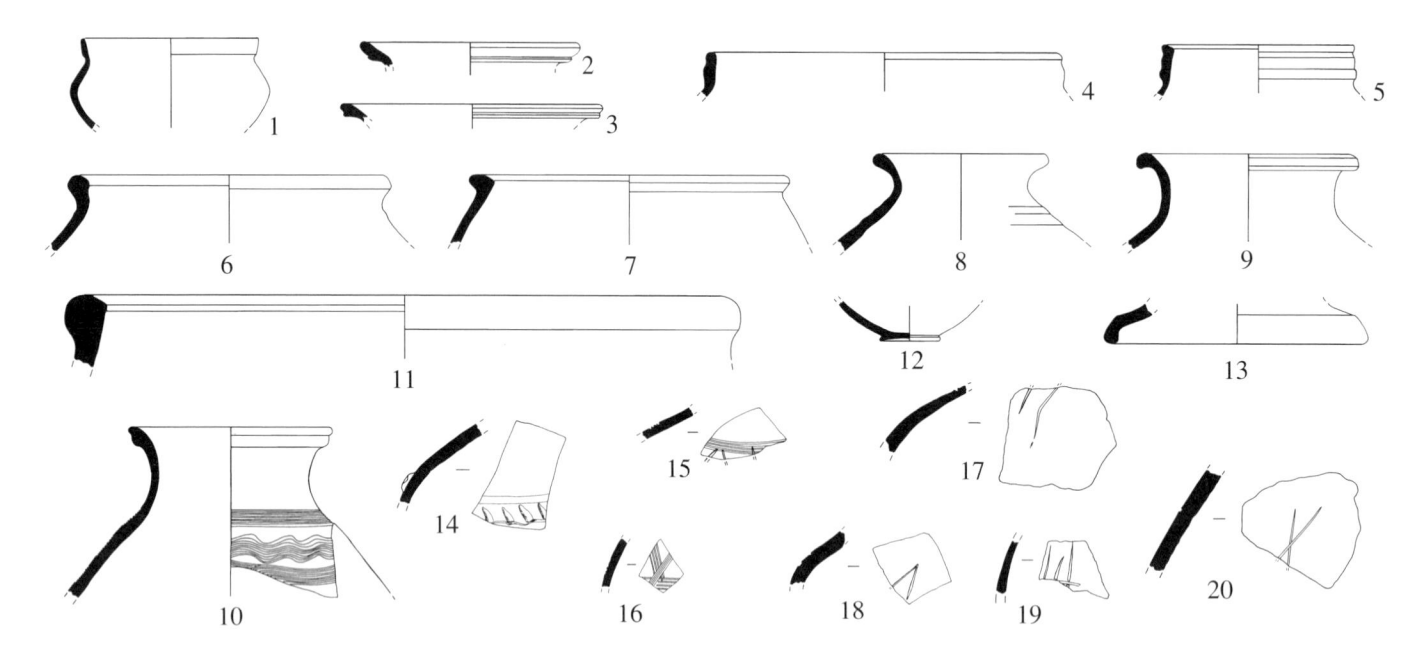

Pottery from Trench IIIF (Phase 5; Period E — Early Bronze Age IVb). Scale 1:5

1. SBR. D.I.a (TS. 1309; IIIF, 1.2). Slightly coarse buff ware, evenly fired. Self slip in and out.
2. SJR. B.III.d (TS. 1242; IIIF, 1.2). Hard, fine buff ware, evenly fired. Self slip in and out.
3. SJR. C.I.a (TS. 1336; IIIF, 2.1). Slightly coarse pinkish-buff ware, evenly fired. Creamy-green slip in and out.
4. JR. B.I.a (TS. 1915; IIIF, 1.2). Fairly fine pinkish-buff ware, evenly fired. Creamy-buff slip out.
5. JR. C.I.e (TS. 1863; IIIF, 1.2). Slightly coarse buff ware, evenly fired. Creamy-buff slip out and over rim in.
6. JR. E.I.h (TS. 2391; IIIF, 2.1). Fairly coarse pink ware, evenly fired. Buff-yellow slip out.
7. JR. H.III.j (TS. 1366; IIIF, 1.2). Hard, fine pinkish-buff ware, evenly fired. Creamy-buff slip out and on top of rim.
8. JR. J.I.b (TS. 2286; IIIF, 2.1). Fairly fine pinkish-buff ware, evenly fired. Creamy-buff slip out and over rim in.
9. JR. J.III.k (TS. 2260; IIIF, 1.2). Slightly coarse buff ware, evenly fired. Light creamy-green slip in and out.
10. JR. J.III.ad (IP [G.1] D.II.a; TS. 1216; IIIF, 1.2, 2.1). Slightly coarse pinkish-buff ware, evenly fired. Light greenish slip in and out. Horizontal and wavy band-combed decoration on shoulder.
11. JR. O.III.c (TS. 2389; IIIF, 2.1). Fairly coarse pink ware, evenly fired. Self slip in and out.
12. BE. B.II (TS. 1230; IIIF, 1.2). Fine light grayware, evenly fired. Irregular stroke burnishing on self slip out.
13. BE. F.V.a (TS. 1191; IIIF, 2.1). Fairly fine pinkish-buff ware, evenly fired. Creamy-buff slip in and out.
14. ABS. C (TS. 1279; IIIF, 2.1). Fairly fine pinkish-buff ware, evenly fired. Creamy-buff slip out.
15. JR.Sh. (IP [G.1] H.II.a; TS. 1300; IIIF, 1.2). Slightly coarse pink ware, evenly fired.
16. JR.Sh. (IP [G.1] H.II.a; TS. 2011; IIIF, 1.2). Slightly coarse pinkish-buff ware, evenly fired. Self slip out.
17. JR.Sh. (PM. A.13; TS. 1321; IIIF, 1.2). Slightly coarse creamy-buff ware, fairly evenly fired. Self slip in and out. Jar shoulder sherd with remains of a potter's mark incised on outside wall before firing.
18. JR.Sh. (PM. C.11; TS. 1315; IIIF, 1.2). Slightly coarse pinkish-buff ware, evenly fired. Creamy-green slip out. Jar shoulder sherd with remains of a potter's mark incised on outside wall after slip applied.
19. JR.Sh. (PM. D.23; TS. 1178; IIIF, 1.2). Fairly fine buff ware with lime and mica grits, evenly fired. Jar shoulder sherd with remains of a potter's mark incised on outside wall before firing.
20. JR.Sh. (PM. C.14; TS. 1176; IIIF, 1.2). Hard, fairly fine buff ware, evenly fired. Jar shoulder sherd with remains of a potter's mark incised on outside wall before firing.

Other Type Series Examples: (1) MBR. A.II.a (SW. 262), (2) SBR. B.I.g (TS. 2019), (3) BR. E.III.e (TS. 1301), (4) JR. A.III.a (TS. 1905), (5) JR. D.I.d (TS. 1855), (6) Lp. B.I.1 (SW. 343).

Other Study Collection Examples: (1) SBR. A.I.b (SC. 216), (2) SBR. B.I.h (SC. 511), (3) SBR. B.I.h (SC. 512), (4) BR. (not typed, SC. 46), (5) SJR. (not typed, SC. 96), (6) JR. E.II.d (SC. 2010), (7) JR. E.II.d (SC. 2017), (8) JR. J.I.d (SC. 1321), (9) JR. J.I.d (SC. 1324), (10) JR. J.I.f (SC. 1342), (11) JR. J.I.f (SC. 1344), (12) JR. J.III.a (SC. 2216), (13) JR. J.III.e (SC. 2243), (14) JR. J.IV.d (SC. 1526), (15) JR. J.IV.j (SC. 1547), (16) JR. P.II.a (SC. 2459), (17) JR. (not typed, SC. 82), (18) JR. (not typed, SC. 103), (19) CP. B.IV.b (SC. 1869), (20) BE. A.I (SC. 3088), (21) BE. J (SC. 3237).

Figure 203

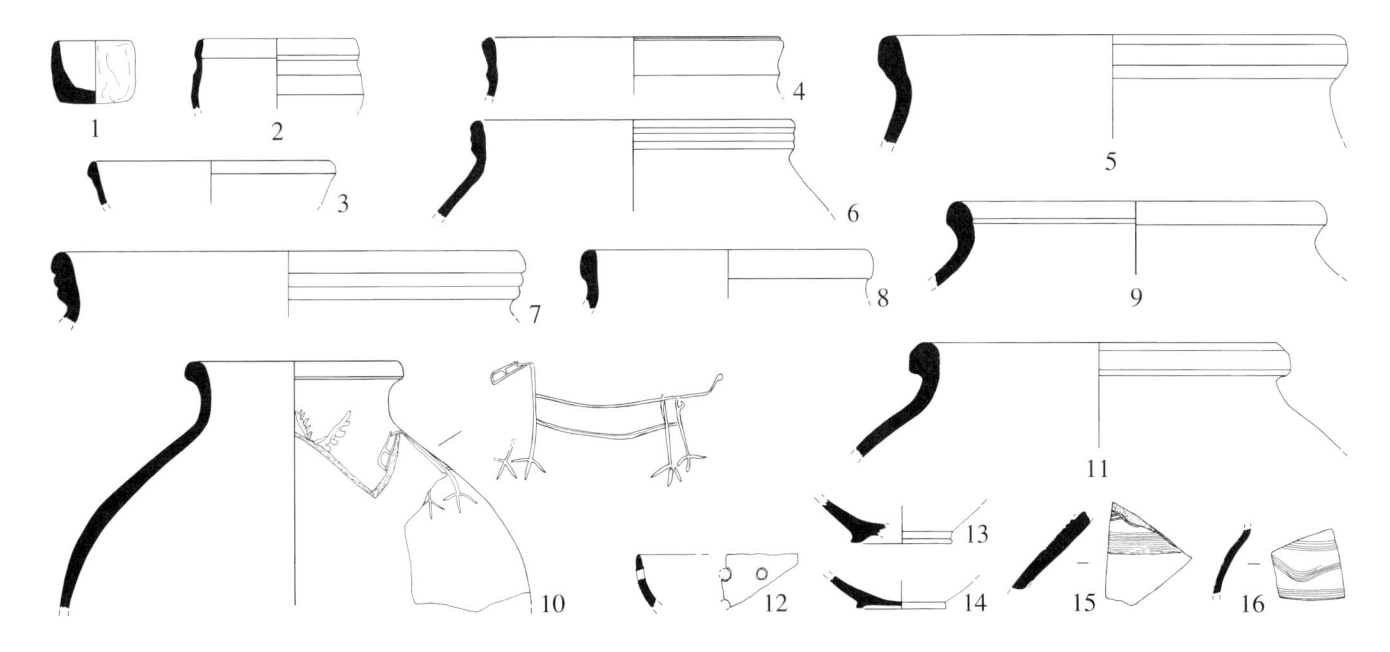

Pottery from Trench IIIF (Phase 6/7, Period E–D — Early–Middle Bronze Age). Scale 1:5

1. MBR. B.I.a (SW. 266; IIIF, 1.1). Coarse ware, unevenly fired with brownish-black core and greenish-buff at surfaces. Many lime grits. Handmade.
2. SBR. D.I.c (TS. 1319; IIIF, 1.1). Fine pink ware, evenly fired. Creamy colored slip out.
3. BR. L.III.c (TS. 2015; IIIE, 1.1). Fairly fine pinkish-buff ware, evenly fired. Creamy-buff slip out.
4. JR. B.V.a (TS. 1870; IIIF, 1.1). Fairly fine pinkish-buff ware, evenly fired. Creamy-buff slip out.
5. JR. B.V.d (TS. 2368; IIIF, 1.1). Fairly coarse grayish-buff ware, evenly fired. Buff slip in and out.
6. JR. D.V.d (TS. 1830; IIIF, 1.1). Fairly coarse and gritty ware, unevenly fired with gray core and grayish-brown at surfaces. Traces of dark green slip in and out.
7. JR. D.VI.a (TS. 1195; IIIF, 1.1). Fairly fine pinkish-buff ware with fine lime and mica grits, evenly fired. Creamy-buff slip in and out.
8. JR. E.II.m (TS. 2492; IIIF, 1.1). Slightly coarse pinkish-brown ware, evenly fired. Buff slip out.
9. JR. E.II.u (TS. 2373; IIIF, 1.1 and IIIG/H, 1.5, Phase 4, Room 17). Fairly coarse pinkish-buff ware, evenly fired. Creamy-green slip out.
10. JR. J.III.j (IP [G.4] F.I; SW. 269 = TS. 1179; IIIF, 1.1). Fine salmon-pink ware with lime and mica grits, evenly fired. Creamy-buff slip out. Stylized animals incised around shoulder before firing.
11. JR. P.II.c (TS. 713 = TS. 2376; IIIG/H, 1.5 and IIIF, 1.1, Phase 4, Room 17). Hard, fine pink ware, evenly fired. Self slip out.
12. SR. C.I.b (SW. 320; IIIF, 1.1). Hard, fine cream ware, evenly fired.
13. BE. E.I.b (TS. 1317; IIIF, 1.1). Fairly fine tan-colored ware, evenly fired. Self slip out.
14. BE. E.I.d (TS. 1318; IIIF, 1.1). Slightly coarse light grayware, evenly fired. Self slip, burnished in and out.
15. JR.Sh. (IP [G.1] B.II.a; TS. 1326; IIIF, 1.1). Hard, gritty, fairly coarse light green ware, evenly fired. Comb-incised decoration on shoulder.
16. JR.Sh. (IP [G.1] C.III.a; TS. 1278; IIIF, 1.1). Fairly fine pinkish-buff ware, evenly fired. Creamy-buff slip out. Comb-incised decoration on shoulder.

Other Type Series Examples:
Bronze Age — (1) BR. E.II.c (TS. 1304), (2) JR. C.II.d (TS. 1854), (3) JR. D.II.a (TS. 1850), (4) JR. D.III.c (TS. 1853).
Derived Hellenistic Period — (1) H.BGB. A.I.d (TS. 1190); Derived Roman Period — (1) R.BR. D.II.a (TS. 1320).

Other Study Collection Examples:
Bronze Age — (1) SBR. B.I.g (SC. 366), (2) SBR. B.I.l (SC. 580), (3) SBR. B.I.l (SC. 676), (4) SBR. D.I.e (SC. 648), (5) BR. A.I.e (SC. 707), (6) BR. E.I.b (SC. 757), (7) SJR. B.II.j (SC. 665), (8) JR. D.V.c (SC. 1086), (9) JR. E.II.c (SC. 1998), (10) JR. H.I.k (SC. 1281), (11) JR. H.I.k (SC. 1282), (12) JR. J.I.d (SC. 1328), (13) JR. J.III.e (SC. 2270), (14) JR. P.II.a (SC. 1702), (15) JR. P.III.a (SC. 1758), (16) JR. P.III.c (SC. 1761), (17) CP. B.IV.c (SC. 1877), (18) BE. B.I (SC. 3076).

Figure 204

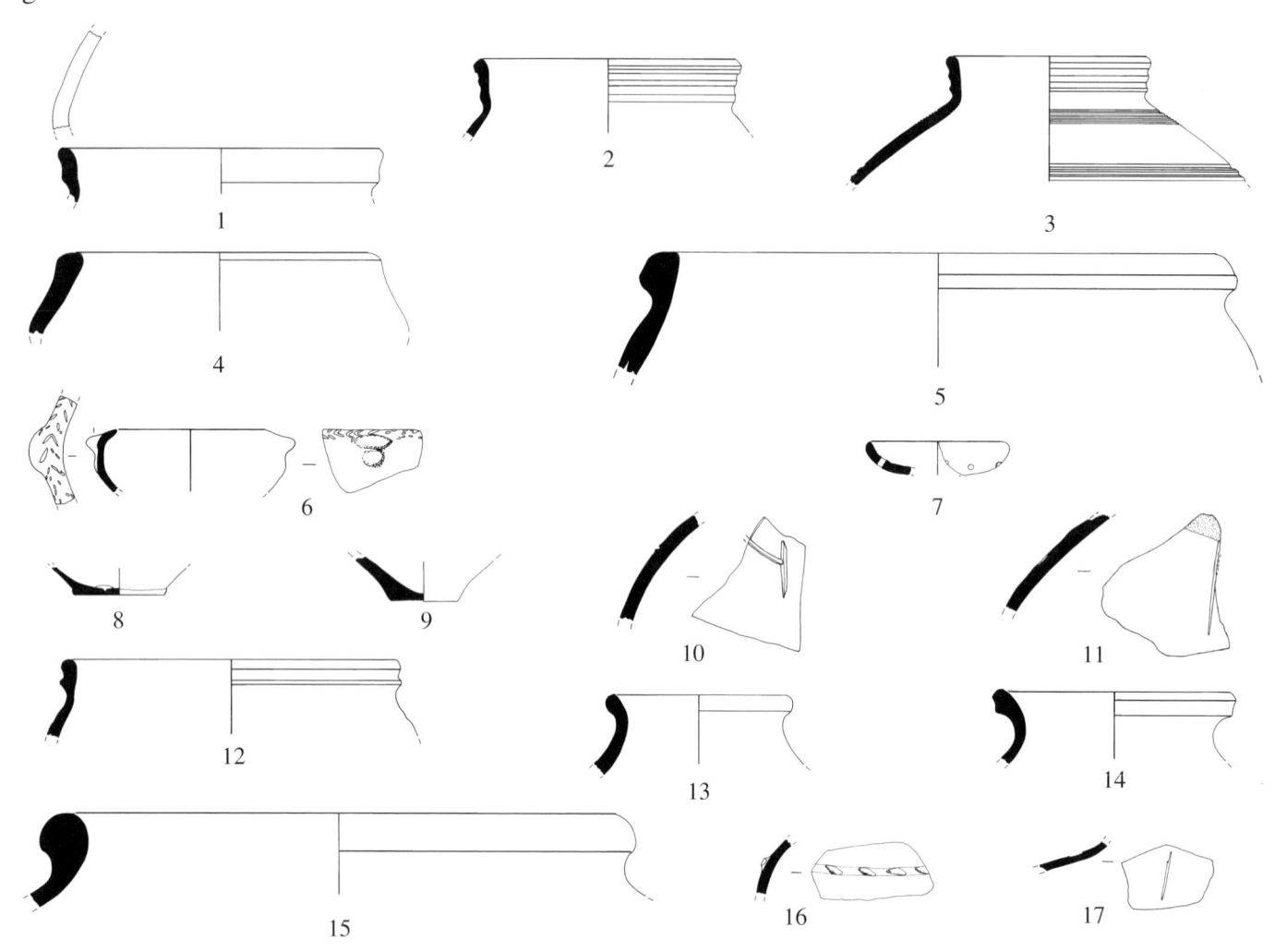

Pottery from Trench IIIG (Phases 4 and 5; Period E — Early Bronze Age IVb). Scale 1:5

1. JR. B.III.f (TS. 1909; IIIG, 3.1, Room 18; Phase 4). Fairly fine pink ware, evenly fired. Creamy-buff slip out and over rim in.
2. JR. D.II.c (TS. 1841; IIIG, 3.1, Room 18; Phase 4). Slightly coarse pinkish-buff ware, evenly fired. Creamy-buff slip out and over rim in.
3. JR. D.II.d (IP [G.1] A.II.c; TS. 580; IIIG, 3.1, Room 18, Phase 4; and IIIH, 1.1). Coarse pink ware, evenly fired. Horizontal comb-incised lines on shoulder.
4. JR. H.III.g (TS. 1282; IIIG, 3.1, Room 18; Phase 4). Slightly coarse ware, unevenly fired with light gray core and pink at surfaces. Creamy-buff slip out.
5. CP. C.I.e (TS. 1303; IIIG, 3.1, Room 18; Phase 4). Slightly coarse and gritty pinkish-brown ware, unevenly fired grayish-brown out. Thick self slip in and out.
6. Lp. A.II.a (IP [G.3] A.I.a; TS. 1193; IIIG, 3.1, Room 18; Phase 4). Fairly fine grayware with fine lime and mica grits, evenly fired. Incised herringbone pattern on top of rim filled in with white gypsum-like substance.
7. SR. A.I.b (TS. 2193; IIIG, 3.1, Room 18; Phase 4). Fairly fine dark brown ware, evenly fired. Blackened in and over rim out. Handmade.
8. BE. B.I (TS. 3040; IIIG, 3.1, Room 18; Phase 4). Fine flesh-colored pink ware, evenly fired. Cream slip out.
9. BE. C.I (TS. 1240; IIIG, 3.1, Room 18; Phase 4). Fairly fine buff ware, evenly fired. Self slip in and out.
10. JR.Sh. (PM. C.15; TS. 1322; IIIG, 3.1, Room 18; Phase 4). Hard, fine pink ware, evenly fired. Buff slip out. Jar shoulder sherd with remains of a potter's mark incised on outside wall before firing.
11. JR.Sh. (PM. A.24; TS. 1323; IIIG, 3.1, Room 18; Phase 4). Slightly coarse and gritty light brown ware, evenly fired. Self slip out. Jar shoulder sherd with remains of a potter's mark incised on outside wall before firing.
12. JR. B.IV.a (TS. 1902; IIIG, 2.1, Room 22A; Phase 5). Slightly coarse dark pink ware, evenly fired. Buff slip in and out.
13. JR. J.I.i (TS. 2296; IIIG, 2.1, Room 22A; Phase 5). Fairly coarse pink ware, evenly fired. Creamy-green slip out.
14. JR. J.II.i (TS. 2199; IIIG. 2.1, Room 22A; Phase 5). Slightly coarse grayish-buff ware, evenly fired. Thick grayish-green slip in and out.
15. JR. P.II.o (TS. 2402; IIIG, 2.1, Room 22A; Phase 5). Slightly coarse pink ware, evenly fired. Creamy-green slip out and over rim in.
16. ABS. C (TS. 1246; IIIG, 2.1, Room 22A; Phase 5). Fairly fine pink ware, evenly fired. Creamy-buff slip out.
17. JR.Sh. (PM. A.5; TS. 1325; IIIG, 2.1, Room 22A; Phase 5). Fairly fine pink ware, evenly fired. Creamy-buff slip out. Jar shoulder sherd with a potter's mark incised on outside wall before firing.

Other Type Series Examples:

Phase 4, Room 18 — (1) MJR. 2 (SW. 185), (2) JR. B.IV.e (TS. 600), (3) Lp. A.II.a (IP [G.4] A.III.a; SW. 190).

Other Study Collection Examples:

Phase 4, Room 18 — (1) BR. L.II.b (SC. 852), (2) JR. J.I.f (SC. 1339), (3) CP. B.IV.c (SC. 1879), (4) CP. B.IV.g (SC. 1896), (5) BE. E.I.i (SC. 3184).
Phase 5, Room 22A — (1) JR. J.I.c (SC. 1316), (2) JR. O.III.b (SC. 1670), (3) BE. F.VIII.b (SC. 3081), (4) WPS. C (SC. 1947).

Figure 205

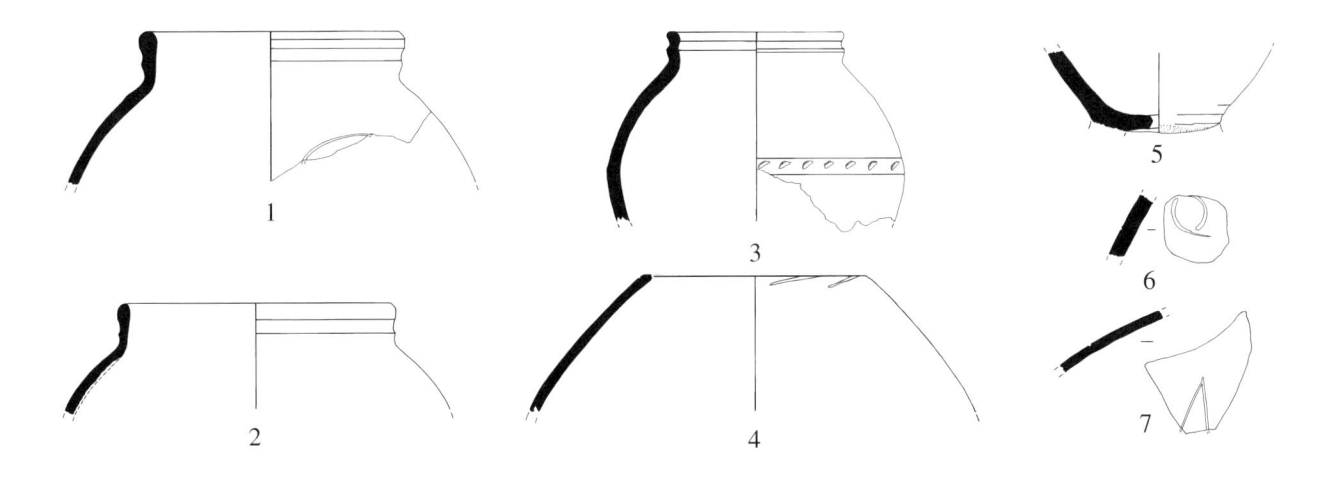

Pottery from Trench IIIG Extramural (Phase 6/7; Period E–D — Early–Middle Bronze Age). Scale 1:5

1. JR. A.III.b (PM. F; TS. 1310; IIIG, 1.1, Extramural + 3.1, Phase 4, Room 18). Slightly coarse pinkish-buff ware, evenly fired. Creamy-green slip out. Extant portion of a potter's mark incised on the shoulder before firing.
2. JR. A.III.b (PM. F; TS. 1311; IIIG, 1.1). Large rim, neck, and shoulder segment plus one non-joining body sherd with an incomplete, vertical line potter's mark incised on outside surface before firing. Slightly coarse pinkish-brown ware, evenly fired. Creamy-green slip out and over rim in.
3. JR. A.IV.a (SW. 316; IIIG, 1.1). Fairly coarse buff ware, unevenly fired. Tool-impressed decoration around maximum girth of the body wall.
4. JR. H.III.n (TS. 1201; IIIG, 1.1). Fine pinkish-buff ware, evenly fired. Creamy-buff slip out. Diagonally incised decoration around outside rim of the vessel.
5. BE. F.VIII.c (TS. 552; IIIG, 1.1). Coarse brown ware, evenly fired. Cream slip out. Drainage hole in base.
6. JR.Sh. (PM. B.4; TS. 1175; IIIG, 1.1). Fairly fine buff ware with fine lime and mica grits, evenly fired. Self slip out. Jar shoulder sherd with remains of a potter's mark incised on outside wall before firing.
7. JR.Sh. (PM. C.11; TS. 1324; IIIG, 1.1). Fairly fine pinkish-buff ware, evenly fired. Creamy-buff slip out. Jar shoulder sherd with remains of a potter's mark incised on outside wall before firing.

Another Type Series Example: (1) SJR. A.II.d (TS. 1308).

Other Study Collection Examples: (1) SBR. B.I.d (SC. 288), (2) JR. H.I.h (SC. 1276), (3) JR. (not typed, SC. 129).

Figure 206. Pottery from Trench IIIG/H (Phases 1C and 2; Periods G and F — Early Bronze Age III and Early Bronze Age IVa)

1. JR. D.X.b (TS. 1099; IIIG/H, 1.11; Phase 1C, Pit; Period G). Fairly coarse buff ware, unevenly fired with light gray core. Cream slip out.
2. CP. A.II.b (TS. 1087; IIIG/H, 1.11; Phase 1C, Pit; Period G). Coarse brown-grayware, fairly evenly fired. Brown self slip in and out. Partially blackened on extant portions outside.
3. BE. E.II.l (TS. 2535; IIIG/H, 1.11; Phase 1C, Pit; Period G). Slightly coarse pinkish-buff ware, evenly fired. Self slip out.
4. JR.Sh. (PM. C.11; TS. 1136; IIIG/H, 1.11; Phase 1C, Pit; Period G). Fairly coarse pink ware. Creamy-buff slip out. Jar shoulder sherd with potter's mark incised on outside wall before firing.
5. SBR. D.I.a (TS. 1051; IIIG/H, 1.10; Phase 2, Room 2B; Period F). Fairly coarse pinkish-buff ware, evenly fired. Cream slip out and over rim in.
6. SBR. D.I.e (TS. 1053; IIIG/H, 1.8b, Phase 2, Room 2A; Period F). Fairly coarse pinkisk-buff ware, evenly fired. Cream slip in and out.
7. BR. A.IV.f (TS. 1047; IIIG/H, 1.10; Phase 2, Room 2B; Period F). Fairly coarse pink ware, evenly fired. Cream slip out.
8. JR. H.I.e (TS. 1049; IIIG/H, 1.10; Phase 2, Room 2B; Period F). Fairly coarse pink ware, evenly fired. Cream slip out.
9. JR. H.I.g (PM. A.14; TS. 1254; IIIG/H, 1.8b; Phase 2, Room 2A; Period F). Potter's mark incised on outside shoulder before firing. Slightly coarse and gritty pinkish-brown ware, evenly fired. Creamy-buff slip out.
10. JR. H.I.k (TS. 1233; IIIG/H, 1.10; Phase 2, Room 2B; Period F). Slightly coarse pinkish-buff ware, unevenly fired. Creamy-buff slip out and over rim in.
11. JR. J.I.l (TS. 3083; IIIG/H, 1.10; Phase 2, Room 2B; Period F). Hard, fine grayish-buff ware, unevenly fired pinkish-buff out. Cream slip below rim out.
12. JR. J.III.m (TS. 2303; IIIG/H, 1.10; Phase 2, Room 2B; Period F). Slightly coarse buff ware, evenly fired. Cream slip in and out.
13. JR. K.I.b (TS. 2328; IIIG/H, 1.8b; Phase 2, Room 2A; Period F). Fairly coarse greenish-buff ware, evenly fired. Creamy-buff slip out and on top of rim.
14. JR. O.I.f (TS. 1234; IIIG/H, 1.10; Phase 2, Room 2B; Period F). Hard, fine pinkish-brown ware, evenly fired.
15. JR. P.III.c (TS. 1235; IIIG/H, 1.10; Phase 2, Room 2B; Period F). Slightly coarse pink ware, evenly fired. Creamy-buff slip in and out.
16. CP. A.I.e (TS. 1152; IIIG/H, 1.8b; Phase 2, Room 2A; Period F). Coarse pinkish-brown ware, evenly fired. Buff-brown slip, irregularly burnished in and out.
17. BE. E.II.e (TS. 1135; IIIG/H, 1.8b; Phase 2, Room 2A; Period F). Fairly fine pink ware, evenly fired. Cream slip out.

Other Type Series Examples:
Phase 2, Room 2A — (1) SBR. D.I.b (TS. 1096).
Phase 2, Room 2B — (1) BR. D.II.b (TS. 1046), (2) BR. H.I.a (TS. 1232), (3) SJR. A.II.f (TS. 1048), (4) ABS. B (TS. 1070).

Other Study Collection Examples:
Phase 1C, Pit — (1) SBR. A.I.a (SC. 175), (2) SBR. A.I.d (SC. 224), (3) SBR. B.I.h (SC. 430).
Phase 2, Room 2B — (1) BE. B.I (SC. 3101).

Figure 206

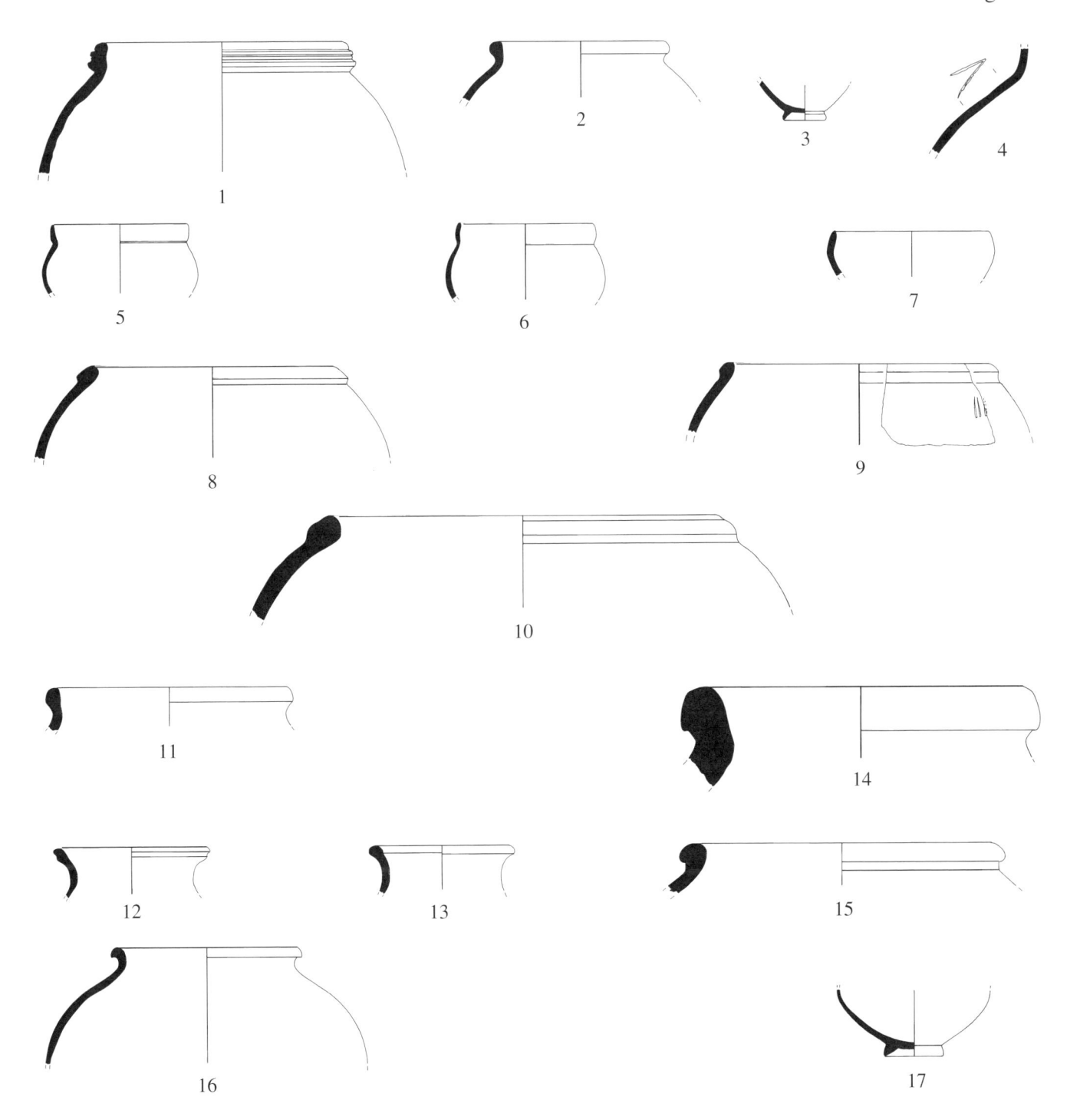

Pottery from Trench IIIG/H (Phases 1C and 2; Periods G and F — Early Bronze Age III and Early Bronze Age IVa).
Scale 1:5

Figure 207. Pottery from Trench IIIG/H, Rooms 3A and 3B (Phase 3; Period F — Early Bronze Age IVa)

1. SBR. A.I.a (TS. 2523; IIIG/H, 1.9, Room 3B). Fine buff ware, fairly evenly fired. Yellow-buff slip out.
2. SBR. A.I.d (TS. 1120; IIIG/H, 1.8a, Room 3A). Fairly coarse gray-brown ware. Cream slip out.
3. SBR. A.I.e (TS. 2517; IIIG/H, 1.8a, Room 3A). Fairly fine pinkish-brown ware, evenly fired. Self slip out and over rim in.
4. SBR. B.I.d (TS. 905; IIIG/H, 1.9, Room 3B). Fairly coarse pink ware, evenly fired.
5. SBR. D.I.a (TS. 1131; IIIG/H, 1.9, Room 3B). Fairly coarse pink ware, evenly fired. Cream slip out.
6. CBR. A.I.a (SW. 462; IIIG/H, 1.9, Room 3B). Unfired tempered brown *libn*. Handmade. Blackened in and out.
7. JR. E.II.d (TS. 3082; IIIG/H, 1.8a, Room 3A). Fairly coarse ware, unevenly fired rosy-pink in and buff out. Creamy-green slip out.
8. JR. E.II.g (TS. 972; IIIG/H, 1.9, Room 3B). Fairly fine pinkish-buff ware, evenly fired. Grayish-cream slip out. Blackened in and out.
9. JR. H.III.a (TS. 2237; IIIG/H, 1.9, Room 3B). Slightly coarse pinkish-rose colored ware, evenly fired. Creamy-buff slip out.
10. JR. H.III.y (variant; TS. 1072; IIIG/H, 1.9, Room 3B). Fairly coarse pink ware with straw temper, unevenly fired with gray core. Cream slip out.
11. JR. J.III.i (TS. 824; IIIG/H, 1.9, Room 3B). Fairly coarse buff ware, evenly fired.
12. JR. J.III.m (TS. 2305; IIIG/H, 1.9, Room 3B). Fairly coarse creamy-buff ware, evenly fired. Self slip in and out.
13. JR. J.III.o (TS. 1149; IIIG/H, 1.8a, Room 3A). Fairly coarse pinkish-buff ware, evenly fired. Cream slip in and out.
14. JR. P.II.k (TS. 1095; IIIG/H, 1.8a, Room 3A). Fairly coarse cream ware, unevenly fired with gray core.
15. JR. Q.I.b (TS. 837; IIIG/H, 1.9, Room 3B). Fairly fine buff ware, unevenly fired with darker core.
16. CP. B.II.b (TS. 1145; IIIG/H, 1.8a, Room 3A). Fairly coarse pinkish-brown ware, evenly fired. Self slip, irregularly burnished in and out.
17. CP. C.I.b (TS. 2250; IIIG/H, 1.8a, Room 3A). Slightly coarse and gritty pinkish-brown ware, evenly fired. Self slip, irregularly burnished out and over rim in.
18. CP. Ld. A.II.b (TS. 1016; IIIG/H, 1.9, Room 3B). Coarse brown ware, evenly fired. Self slip, burnished out; inner face worn off. Blackened out.
19. BE. E.I.a (TS. 2171; IIIG/H, 1.8a, Room 3A). Slightly coarse greenish-buff ware, evenly fired. Self slip out. Very worn in.
20. BE. E.I.e (TS. 838; IIIG/H, 1.9, Room 3B). Fairly coarse pink ware, evenly fired. Cream slip in and out.
21. BE. E.I.i (TS. 1231; IIIG/H, 1.8a, Room 3A). Fine pinkish-brown ware, fairly evenly fired.
22. BE. E.I.j (TS. 1148; IIIG/H, 1.8a, Room 3A). Fairly coarse pink ware, evenly fired. Blackened in and out.
23. BE. E.II.j (TS. 1147; IIIG/H, 1.8a, Room 3A). Fairly coarse pink ware, evenly fired. Cream slip out.
24. BE. G (TS. 833; IIIG/H, 1.9, Room 3B). Very fine dark grayware, evenly fired. Self slip, burnished black out.

Other Type Series Examples:
Room 3A — (1) SBR. B.I.l (TS. 1213), (2) BR. E.III.f (TS. 1146), (3) FL. A.I.b (TS. 1236).
Room 3B — (1) BR. D.VI.c (TS. 1055), (2) BR. J.II.b (TS. 865), (3) CP. B.II.l (TS. 2253).

Other Study Collection Examples:
Room 3A — (1) SBR. B.I.c (SC. 267), (2) SBR. B.I.l (SC. 571), (3) JR. L.II.a (SC. 1608), (4) BE. E.II.a (SC. 3192), (5) BE. J (SC. 3240).
Room 3B — (1) SBR. B.I.j (SC. 542), (2) BE. B.II (SC. 3113), (3) SB. B (SC. 3294).

Figure 207

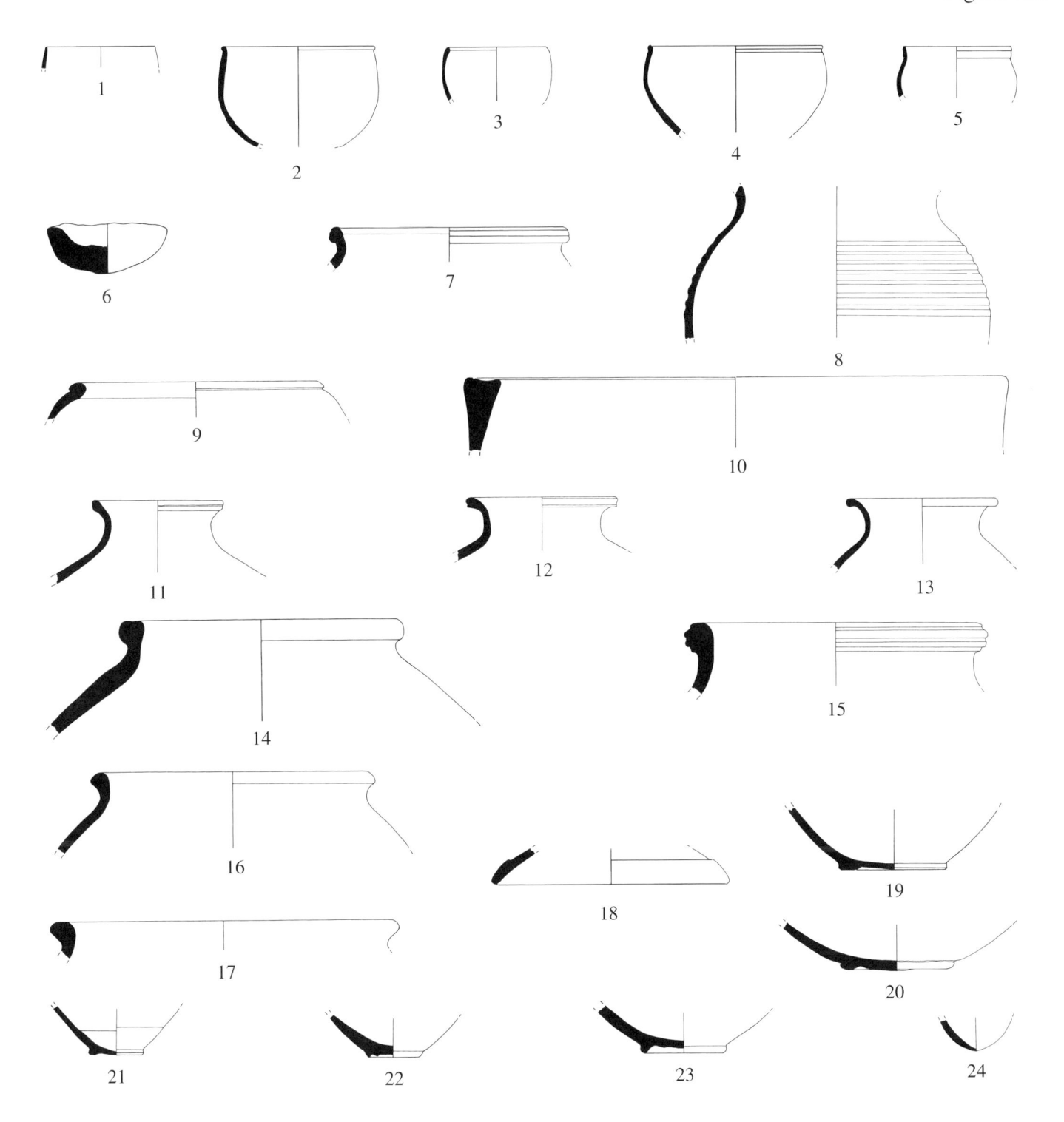

Pottery from Trench IIIG/H, Rooms 3A and 3B (Phase 3; Period F — Early Bronze Age IVa). Scale 1:5

Figure 208. Pottery from Trench IIIG/H, Rooms 17, 17A, and 18 (Phase 4; Period E — Early Bronze Age IVb)

1. SBR. A.I.a (TS. 1080; IIIG/H, 1.6, Room 17A). Fairly coarse pink ware, evenly fired. Cream slip out.
2. SBR. B.I.c (TS. 671; IIIG/H, 1.7, Room 18). Fairly coarse light brown ware, evenly fired. Cream slip out.
3. SBR. B.I.e (TS. 1291; IIIG/H, 1.5, Room 17, 1.8a, Room 3A, Phase 3). Slightly coarse pinkish-buff ware, fairly evenly fired. Creamy-buff slip in (wheel-applied rings in reserve) and covering all of wall outside.
4. SBR. D.I.d (TS. 996; IIIG/H, 1.6, Room 17A). Fairly fine greenish-cream ware, evenly fired. Blackened in and out.
5. BR. A.II.e (TS. 1284; IIIG/H, 1.7, Room 18). Hard, fine pinkish-brown ware, unevenly fired.
6. BR. J.II.a (TS. 717; IIIG/H, 1.5, Room 17). Fairly coarse pink ware, evenly fired. Cream slip applied thickly in and thinly out.
7. BR. L.I.d (TS. 2469; IIIG/H, 1.7, Room 18). Fairly coarse pinkish-brown ware, evenly fired. Self slip in and out.
8. BR. L.II.a (TS. 708; IIIG/H, 1.7, Room 18). Fairly coarse pink ware with lime and mica grits, unevenly fired with light brown core.
9. CBR. A.II.a (TS. 633; IIIG/H, 1.6, Room 17A). Fairly coarse pink ware, unevenly fired with darker core. Cream slip in and out. Handmade.
10. SJR. C.I.a (TS. 1004; IIIG/H, 1.7, Room 18). Fairly coarse pink ware, evenly fired. Creamy-buff slip in and out.
11. JR. C.I.d (TS. 1821; IIIG/H, 1.7, Room 18). Slightly coarse pinkish-buff ware, evenly fired. Creamy-green slip out.
12. JR. C.V.b (TS. 1857; IIIG/H, 1.5, Room 17). Hard, fine ware, unevenly fired with light gray core and brownish-buff at surfaces. Creamy-green slip in and out
13. JR. D.IX.a (TS. 670; IIIG/H, 1.7, Room 18). Fairly coarse pink ware, evenly fired. Cream slip in and out.
14. JR. G.I.c (TS. 1076; IIIG/H, 1.5, Room 17). Fairly coarse pink ware, evenly fired. Cream slip in and out.
15. JR. H.I.i (TS. 1296; IIIG/H, 1.6, Room 17A). Slightly coarse light pink ware, evenly fired. Creamy-buff slip out and on top of rim.
16. JR. J.I.k (TS. 1056; IIIG/H, 1.5, Room 17). Fine creamy-green ware, evenly fired.
17. JR. J.III.h (TS. 1298; IIIG/H, 1.6, Room 17A). Fairly fine light pink ware, evenly fired. Creamy-buff slip in and out.
18. JR. O.III.b (TS. 1299; IIIG/H, 1.6, Room 17A). Fairly coarse pinkish-buff ware, evenly fired. Self slip in and out.
19. JR. P.II.d (TS. 915; IIIG/H, 1.7, Room 18). Fairly coarse greenish-cream ware, evenly fired.
20. JR. P.III.c (TS. 1297; IIIG/H, 1.7, Room 18). Hard, fine pink ware, evenly fired. Buff slip in and out.
21. CP. B.II.d (TS. 707; IIIG/H, 1.7, Room 18). Very coarse pink ware with large lime and mica grits, unevenly fired with irregular black core. Buff slip out.
22. CP. B.IV.c (SW. 421; IIIG/H, 1.6, Room 17A). Complete in situ with infant burial. Soft, coarse brown ware with large lime and mica grits, unevenly fired. Blackened on surfaces in and out.
23. BE. B.II (PM. C.6; TS. 761; IIIG/H, 1.5, Room 17). Fairly coarse pink ware, evenly fired. Remains of a potter's mark incised on the outside wall before firing.
24. BE. C.II (TS. 669; IIIG/H, 1.7, Room 18). Coarse creamy-buff ware, evenly fired. Buff slip out.
25. BE. D.I (TS. 3045; IIIG/H, 1.5, Room 17, 1.8a, Room 3A, Phase 3). Fairly fine pink ware, unevenly fired with brown core in patches. Cream slip out.
26. BE. D.II (TS. 2534; IIIG/H, 1.6, Room 17A). Fine creamy-buff ware, evenly fired. Self slip in and out.
27. BE. D.III (TS. 3056; IIIG/H, 1.6, Room 17A). Slightly coarse ware, unevenly fired pink out and buff in. Thick self slip in and cream slip out.
28. JR.Sh. (PM. D.3; TS. 1293; IIIG/H, 1.5, Room 17). Hard, fairly fine pinkish-buff ware, evenly fired. Creamy-buff slip out. Remains of a potter's mark incised on outside wall before firing.
29. Bt.Sh. (Burnished; TS. 1214; IIIG/H, 1.6, Room 17A). Sherd from small bottle. Fine grayware, evenly fired. Self slip, horizontally burnished with irregularly-spaced bands.

Other Type Series Examples:

Room 17 — (1) JR. J.IV.e (TS. 731).

Room 17A — (1) BR. F.IV.b (TS. 1009), (2) SJR. B.II.i (TS. 2325), (3) SJR. C.II.e (TS. 971), (4) JR. D.VIII.c (TS. 1295).

Room 18 — (1) BR. A.IV.a (TS. 746), (2) SJR. C.II.i (SW. 10 = TS. 848), (3) SJR. A.I.b (TS. 672), (4) SJR. B.I.a (TS. 710), (5) Bt. A.I.b (TS. 1142).

Other Study Collection Examples:

Room 17 — (1) SJR. C.I.f (SC. 2554), (2) JR. J.I.b (SC. 1311).

Room 17A — (1) SBR. A.I.a (SC. 181), (2) SBR. B.I.e (SC. 326), (3) SBR. (not typed, SC. 20), (4) SJR. B.II.j (SC. 2517), (5) JR. J.II.n (SC. 2196), (6) CP. A.I.a (SC. 1775), (7) Jg. A.I.b (SC. 1931).

Room 18 — (1) SBR. B.I.l (SC. 675), (2) SBR. D.I.a (SC. 624), (3) JR. J.III.c (SC. 1365), (4) CP. B.I.f (SC. 1833), (5) BE. D.II (SC. 3131).

Figure 208

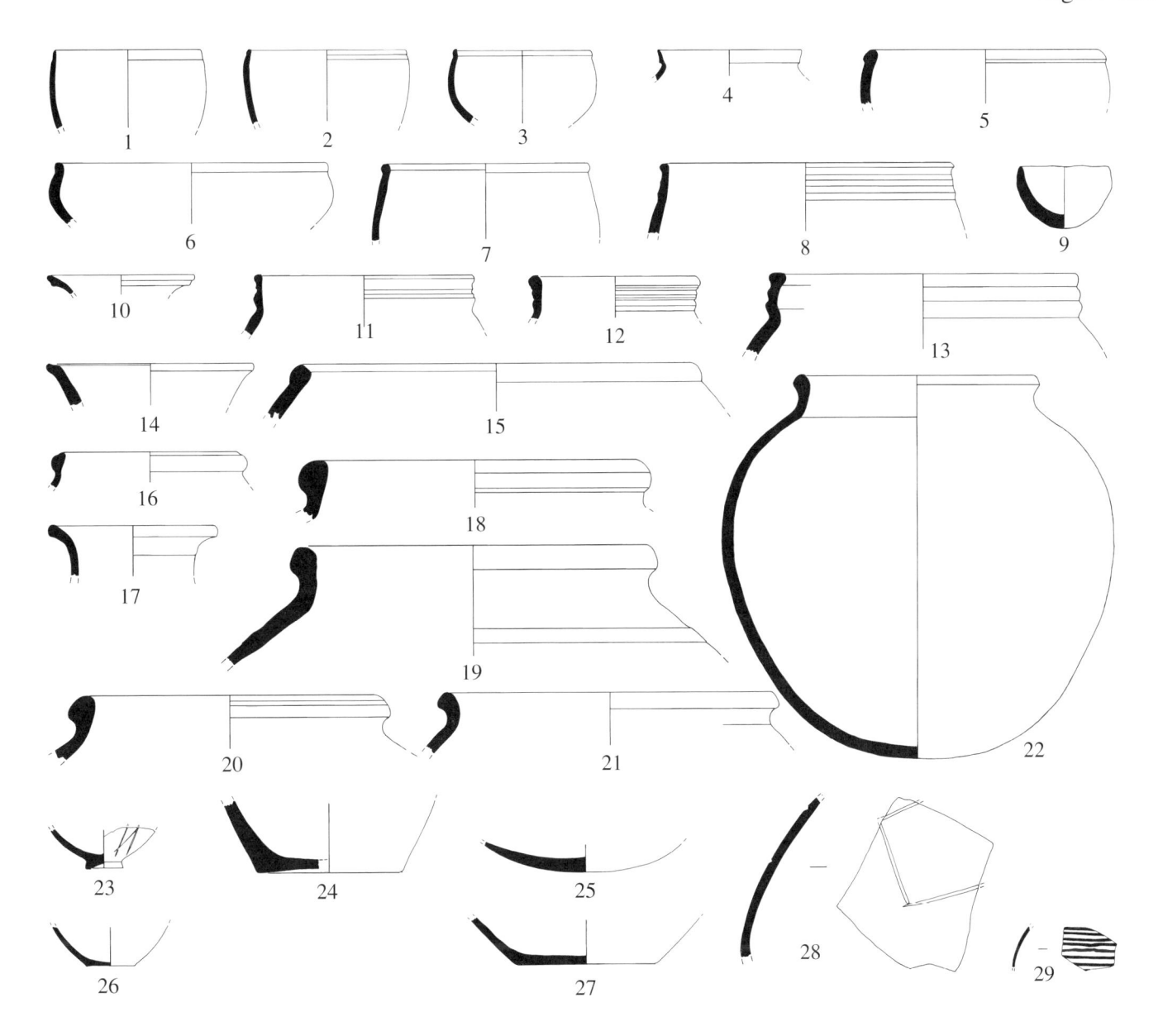

Pottery from Trench IIIG/H, Rooms 17, 17A, and 18 (Phase 4; Period E — Early Bronze Age IVb). Scale 1:5

Figure 209. Pottery from Trench IIIG/H, Rooms 22A, 22B, and 22A/B Extramural (Phase 5;
Period E — Early Bronze Age IVb)

1. SBR. A.I.a (TS. 813; IIIG/H, 1.4, Rooms 22A/B Extramural). Fine brown ware, evenly fired. Buff slip in and out.
2. SBR. B.I.c (PM. D.14; TS. 993; IIIG/H, 1.4, Rooms 22A/B Extramural). Fairly coarse pink ware, evenly fired. Cream slip out and on upper wall in. Remains of a potter's mark incised on the lower outside wall before firing.
3. SBR. B.I.l (TS. 1000; IIIG/H, 1.4, Rooms 22A/B Extramural). Fairly coarse cream ware, evenly fired.
4. SBR. D.I.d (TS. 1141; IIIG/H, 1.4, Rooms 22A/B Extramural). Fairly coarse buff ware, evenly fired. Cream slip in and out.
5. BR. A.IV.f (TS. 981; IIIG/H, 1.3, Room 22A). Fairly coarse buff ware, evenly fired. Pink slip on outside upper upper of vessel.
6. BR. F.III.a (TS. 2465; IIIG/H, 1.4, Rooms 22A/B Extramural). Fairly fine pinkish-buff ware, evenly fired. Creamy-buff slip out.
7. BR. F.III.g (TS. 984; IIIG/H, 1.3, Room 22A). Fairly coarse yellow-buff ware, evenly fired. Greenish-cream slip in and out.
8. BR. F.III.g (TS. 1003; IIIG/H, 1.3, Room 22A). Fairly fine pink ware, evenly fired. Thick buff slip on outside of rim only.
9. BR. F.IV.d (TS. 1290; IIIG/H, 1.3, Room 22A). Hard, fine pink ware, fairly evenly fired. Self slip in and out.
10. BR. J.I.a (TS. 679 = TS. 684; IIIG/H, 1.3, Room 22A). Fairly coarse pink ware, evenly fired. Very thin traces of cream slip out.
11. BR. L.III.c (TS. 989; IIIG/H, 1.4, Rooms 22A/B Extramural). Fairly fine pink ware, evenly fired. Creamy-buff slip in and out.
12. BR. P.I.a (TS. 902; IIIG/H, 1.4, Rooms 22A/B Extramural). Fairly coarse pink ware, evenly fired. Buff slip out.
13. SJR. B.I.c (TS. 812; IIIG/H, 1.4, Rooms 22A/B Extramural). Fairly coarse pink ware, evenly fired. Cream slip in and out.
14. JR. A.III.b (IP [G.1] A.I.b; TS. 886; IIIG/H, 1.2, Room 22B). Fairly fine pink ware, evenly fired. Light cream slip in and out. Horizontal comb-incised lines on shoulder.
15. JR. B.III.c (TS. 1873; IIIG/H, 1.3, Room 22A). Fairly fine pinkish-buff ware, evenly fired. Creamy-buff slip out.
16. JR. B.V.b (TS. 896; IIIG/H, 1.3-1.5, Room 22A). Fairly coarse greenish-buff ware, unevenly fired with brownish-gray core. Self slip out.
17. JR. B.V.b (TS. 912; IIIG/H, 1.2, Room 22B, and 1.4, Rooms 22A/B Extramural). Fairly coarse pink ware, evenly fired. Buff slip out.
18. JR. B.IV.e (TS. 1918; IIIG/H, 1.4, Rooms 22A/B Extramural). Fairly fine dark pink ware, evenly fired. Pinkish-buff slip in and out. Remains of a spout or mending hole on extant portion of shoulder.
19. JR. C.I.g (TS. 1856; IIIG/H, 1.3, Room 22A). Slightly coarse pinkish-brown ware, evenly fired. Creamy-green slip in and out.
20. JR. C.II.b (TS. 831; IIIG/H, 1.4, Rooms 22A/B Extramural). Fairly coarse pinkish-buff ware, evenly fired. Cream slip in and out.
21. JR. C.II.b (TS. 998; IIIG/H, 1.4, Rooms 22A/B Extramural). Fairly fine pinkish-buff ware, evenly fired. Cream slip in and out.
22. JR. C.V.e (TS. 1815; IIIG/H, 1.3-1.5, Room 22A). Slightly coarse grayish-buff ware, evenly fired. Self slip in and out.
23. JR. D.IV.a (TS. 1814 = TS. 1817; IIIG/H, 1.4, Rooms 22A/B Extramural). Fairly fine pinkish-buff ware, evenly fired. Creamy-buff slip out.
24. JR. D.V.d (TS. 1851; IIIG/H, 1.3, Room 22A). Hard, fine grayish-buff ware, unevenly fired pink at surface out. Creamy-buff slip out.
25. JR. E.I.a (TS. 2394; IIIG/H, 1.4, Rooms 22A/B Extramural). Fairly coarse creamy-buff ware, evenly fired. Thick self slip in and out.
26. JR. E.II.m (TS. 1868; IIIG/H, 1.3, Room 22A). Hard, fine pinkish-brown ware, evenly fired. Creamy-buff slip out.
27. JR. F.II.b (TS. 2231; IIIG/H, 1.3, Room 22A). Slightly coarse light grayish-green ware, evenly fired. Self slip in and out.
28. JR. J.III.a (TS. 2263; IIIG/H, 1.4, Rooms 22A/B Extramural). Fairly fine pink ware, evenly fired. Creamy-buff slip on rim and out.
29. JR. J.III.i (TS. 560; IIIG/H, 1.3, Room 22A). Fairly coarse pink ware, evenly fired. Cream slip in and out.
30. JR. J.III.i (PM. C.16; TS. 1312; IIIG/H, 1.3, Room 22A). Slightly coarse pinkish-buff ware, evenly fired. Creamy-buff slip out and over rim in. Remains of a potter's mark incised on shoulder before firing.
31. JR. J.III.o (TS. 2284; IIIG/H, 1.4, Rooms 22A/B Extramural). Fairly coarse grayish-buff ware, evenly fired. Plain creamy-green slip in and in reserve out.
32. JR. J.VI.b (TS. 1887; IIIG/H, 1.3, Room 22A). Slightly coarse brownish-buff ware, evenly fired. Self slip in and out.
33. JR. K.II.c (TS. 2400; IIIG/H, 1.4, Rooms 22A/B Extramural). Slightly coarse pink ware, evenly fired. Self slip out and over rim in.
34. JR. Q.II.c (TS. 913; IIIG/H, 1.2, Room 22B). Coarse pink ware, evenly fired. Cream slip in and out.
35. CP. B.II.a (TS. 887; IIIG/H, 1.2, Room 22B). Coarse pinkish-tan ware with lime and mica grits, evenly fired. Self slip in and out.
36. BE. B.I (TS. 893; IIIG/H, 1.3 and IIIG, 2.1, Room 22A). Fairly coarse ware, unevenly fired pink in and cream out.
37. BE. B.I (TS. 1294; IIIG/H, 1.4, Rooms 22A/B Extramural), Slightly coarse pinkish-buff ware, fairly evenly fired. Buff slip out.
38. BE. B.II (TS. 3058; IIIG/H, 1.3, Room 22A). Fine reddish-pink ware, evenly fired. Cream slip out.
39. BE. C.I (TS. 898; IIIG/H, 1.3, Room 22A). Fairly fine pinkish-buff ware, evenly fired.
40. BE. C.II (TS. 911; IIIG/H, 1.4, Rooms 22A/B, Extramural, and 1.5, Room 17). Fine grayware, evenly fired. Self slip, burnished out.
41. BE. E.II.i (TS. 688; IIIG/H, 1.3, Room 22A). Fairly fine pink ware, evenly fired. Buff slip out.
42. BE. E.II.l (TS. 3048; IIIG/H, 1.4, Rooms 22A/B Extramural). Fairly coarse ware, unevenly fired purple-pink in and green out. Thick creamy-green slip out.
43. BE. F.VIII.a (TS. 921; IIIG/H, 1.3, Room 22A). Fairly coarse pink ware, evenly fired. Cream slip in and out. Diagonally incised decoration out.

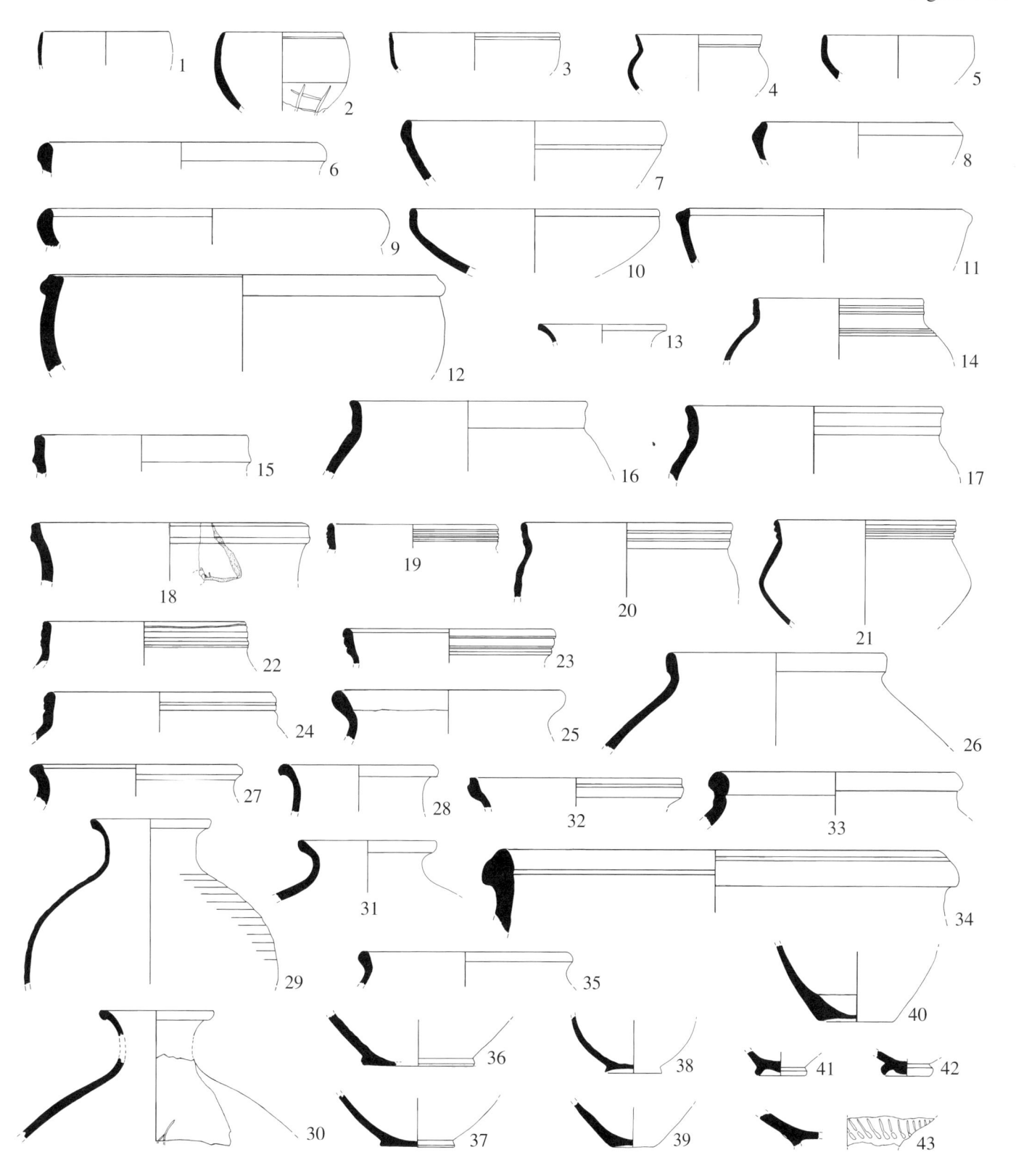

Figure 209

Pottery from Trench IIIG/H, Rooms 22A, 22B, and 22A/B Extramural (Phase 5; Period E — Early Bronze Age IVb).
Scale 1:5

Figure 210. Pottery from Trench IIIG/H, Rooms 22A, 22B, and Rooms 22A/B Extramural (Phase 5;
Period E — Early Bronze Age IVb) (*cont.*)

1. JR.Sh. (IP [G.1] C.I.a; TS. 868; IIIG/H, 1.4, Rooms 22A/B Extramural). Fairly fine light brown ware with a few lime and mica grits, evenly fired. Comb-incised horizontal and wavy-line decoration around shoulder. Traces of burnishing below incised decoration. Reed- or wood-shaved bands at maximum girth as on an example from Tell Mardikh (Ebla) (Matthiae 1964, pl. 40:1).
2. JR.Sh. (IP [G.4] F.I; TS. 1285; IIIG/H, 1.4, Rooms 22A/B Extramural). Fairly coarse buff ware, evenly fired. Creamy-buff slip in and out.
3. JR.Sh. (PM. C.10; TS. 1286; IIIG/H, 1.3, Room 22A). Hard, slightly coarse pink ware, evenly fired. Buff slip in and out. Remains of a potter's mark incised on shoulder before firing.
4. JR.Sh. (PM. D.3; TS. 1289; IIIG/H, 1.4, Rooms 22A/B Extramural). Slightly coarse pinkish-buff ware, evenly fired. Creamy-buff slip in and out. Remains of a potter's mark incised on shoulder before firing.

Other Type Series Examples:

Room 22A — (1) SBR. D.I.d (SW. 485), (2) SBR. D.III.a (TS. 779 = TS. 995), (3) BR. F.II.b (TS. 1292), (4) BR. O.I.b (TS. 700), (5) SJR. B.II.b (TS. 1212), (6) SJR. B.II.f (TS. 2018), (7) JR. C.III.b (TS. 1839), (8) JR. D.V.a (TS. 1826), (9) JR. E.I.d (TS. 2262), (10) CP. Ld. A.II.c (TS. 488).

Room 22B — (1) JR. A.VI.a (PM. A.11; TS. 890).

Room 22A/B Extramural — (1) SBR. F.I.a (PM. D.15; TS.571), (2) BR. A.III.a (TS. 832), (3) BR. D.V.a (TS. 888), (4) BR. L.III.d (TS. 1071), (5) JR. D.V.h (TS. 914), (6) JR. D.VI.b (TS. 1818), (7) JR. H.III.d (TS. 992), (8) JR. J.II.f (TS. 2404), (9) CP. B.I.g (TS. 967).

Other Study Collection Examples:

Room 22A — (1) SBR. A.I.a (SC. 1), (2) SBR. B.I.d (SC. 282), (3) SBR. D.I.a (SC. 626), (4) SJR. B.II.h (SC. 2516), (5) SJR. C.II.c (SC. 2582), (6) JR. E.II.c (SC. 1142), (7) JR. H.III.i (SC. 1295), (8) JR. J.I.f (SC. 1336), (9) JR. J.III.d (SC. 1377), (10) JR. J.III.n (SC. 1456), (11) JR. P.II.i (SC. 1737), (12) BE. D.III (SC. 3143), (13) BE. E.I.h (SC. 3183).

Room 22B — (1) SBR. A.I.d (SC. 294), (2) SBR. B.I.k (SC. 568), (3) SBR. B.I.k (SC. 560), (4) CP. A.I.a (SC. 1774).

Room 22A/B Extramural — (1) SBR. B.I.h (SC. 487), (2) SBR. D.I.d (SC. 643), (3) SBR. D.I.d (SC. 646), (4) BR. F.I.d (SC. 779), (5) BR. F.II.c (SC. 804), (6) JR. J.I.f (SC. 1346), (7) JR. J. (Gen. Type, SC. 104), (8) JR. P.II.k (SC. 1746), (9) JR. (not typed, SC. 73), (10) CP. B.IV.b (SC. 1865), (11) BE. D.III (SC. 3144), (12) CP. (not typed, SC. 70).

Figure 210

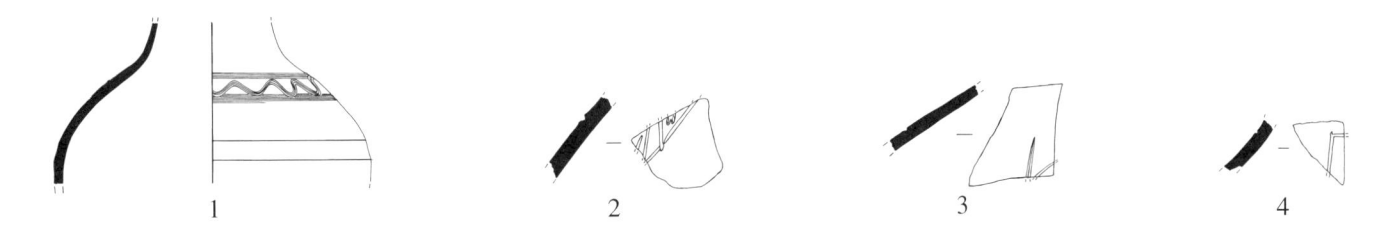

Pottery from Trench IIIG/H, Rooms 22A, 22B, and Rooms 22A/B Extramural (Phase 5; Period E — Early Bronze Age IVb) (*cont.*). Scale 1:5

Figure 211. Pottery from Trench IIIG/H, Rooms 23, 24, and Extramural Courtyard (Phases 6 and 7A; Periods E–D and D — Early–Middle Bronze Age and Middle Bronze Age I)

1. SBR. D.I.e (TS. 668; IIIG/H, 1.1, Courtyard; Phase 6). Fairly fine creamy-tan ware, evenly fired. Cream slip out.
2. BR. F.III.f (TS. 797; IIIG/H, 1.1, Courtyard; Phase 6). Fairly coarse pink ware, evenly fired. Buff slip out.
3. SJR. A.II.b (TS. 2021; IIIG/H, 1.1, Courtyard; Phase 6). Slightly coarse buff ware, evenly fired. Self slip in and out.
4. SJR. B.II.j (TS. 2472; IIIG/H, 1.1, Courtyard; Phase 6). Fine buff ware, evenly fired. Self slip in and out.
5. JR. C.I.h (TS. 1860; IIIG, 1.1, Courtyard; Phase 6). Slightly coarse buff ware, evenly fired. Creamy-buff slip out.
6. JR. C.V.d (TS. 1866; IIIG/H, 1.1, Courtyard; Phase 6). Hard, fine pinkish-brown ware, evenly fired. Buff slip out.
7. JR. F.III.f (TS. 720; IIIG/H, 1.1, Courtyard; Phase 6). Fairly fine greenish-buff ware, evenly fired. Light greenish-cream slip out.
8. JR. J.II.n (TS. 2493; IIIG/H, 1.1, Courtyard; Phase 6). Hard, fine flesh-colored pink ware, evenly fired. Cream slip out and on top of rim.
9. JR. J.VI.a (TS. 808; IIIG/H, 1.1, Courtyard; Phase 6). Fairly fine pink ware, evenly fired. Buff slip in and out.
10. JR. K.I.a (TS. 784; IIIG/H, 1.1, Courtyard; Phase 6). Fairly coarse buff ware, evenly fired. Cream slip in and out.
11. JR. O.II.m (TS. 767; IIIG/H, 1.1, Courtyard; Phase 6). Fairly fine pink ware, evenly fired. Cream slip out.
12. JR. P.II.b (TS. 735 = TS. 736; IIIG/H, 1.1, Courtyard; Phase 6). Coarse buff ware, evenly fired. Pink slip out.
13. JR.Sh. (IP [G.2] A.IV.a; TS. 1280; IIIG/H, 1.1, Courtyard; Phase 6). Fine buff ware, evenly fired. Smooth self wash out.
14. JR.Sh. (PM. B.1; TS. 1287; IIIG/H, 1.1, Courtyard; Phase 6). Slightly coarse pink ware, evenly fired. Buff slip in and out. Remains of a potter's mark incised on outside wall before firing.
15. JR. A.IV.a (TS. 1914; IIIG/H, 1a, Room 23; Phase 7A). Fairly coarse pinkish-buff ware, evenly fired. Creamy-buff slip out. Inside surface worn away.
16. JR. D.V.b (TS. 660 = TS. 1061; IIIG/H, 1a, Room 23; Phase 7A). Coarse greenish-buff ware, evenly fired.
17. JR. D.VI.b (TS. 1859; IIIG/H, 1b, Room 24; Phase 7A). Fairly fine pinkish-buff ware, evenly fired. Creamy-buff slip in and out.
18. JR. H.I.a (TS. 919; IIIG/H, 1a, Room 23; Phase 7A). Fairly fine buff ware, evenly fired. Cream slip out.
19. JR. J.III.c (TS. 2258; IIIG/H, 1a, Room 23; Phase 7A). Hard, fine grayish-buff "metallic-like" ware, evenly fired. Greenish-buff slip in and out.
20. JR. J.III.e (TS. 657; IIIG/H, 1b, Room 24; Phase 7A). Fairly fine pink ware, evenly fired. Cream slip out.
21. JR. J.III.t (TS. 2348; IIIG/H, 1a, Room 23; Phase 7A). Coarse green ware, evenly fired. Self slip out.
22. JR. O.III.f (TS. 663 = TS. 799; IIIG/H, 1b, Room 24; Phase 7A). Coarse pink ware, evenly fired. Cream slip in and out. Finger-impressed decoration on applied band around outside wall.
23. JR. Q.II.c (TS. 662; IIIG/H, 1a, Room 23; Phase 7A). Fairly coarse pink ware, unevenly fired with light brown core. Cream slip out.
24. CP. B.IV.c (PM. A.6; TS. 666; IIIG/H, 1a, Room 23; Phase 7A). Very coarse brown ware with large lime and mica grits, evenly fired. Self slip in and out. Remains of a potter's mark incised on shoulder before firing.
25. CP. B.IV.d (TS. 805; IIIG/H, 1a, Room 23; Phase 7A). Coarse pink ware with large lime and mica grits, evenly fired. Self slip, burnished out.
26. PS. B.I.b (TS. 667; IIIG/H, 1a, Room 23, Phase 7A). Fairly coarse ware, unevenly fired pink and buff on surfaces. Cream slip in and out.
27. BE. B.I (PM. C.5; TS. 1091; IIIG/H, 1a, Room 23; Phase 7A). Fairly coarse pink ware, evenly fired. Cream slip out. Potter's mark incised on lower wall out near base before firing.
28. BE. B.I (PM. C.3; TS. 642; IIIG/H, 1a, Room 23; Phase 7A). Coarse buff ware, evenly fired. Potter's mark incised on inside wall near base before firing. Base string-cut from potter's wheel.
29. BE. E.I.j (TS. 917; IIIG/H, 1b, Room 24; Phase 7A). Fairly fine pink ware, evenly fired. Lightly burnished cream slip out.
30. BE. F.II.b (SW. 367; IIIG/H, 1b, Room 24; Phase 7A). Coarse grayish-buff gritty ware, evenly fired. Greenish slip in and out.
31. JR.Sh. (IP [G.4] D.III; PM. D.19; TS. 1138; IIIG/H, 1a, Room 23; Phase 7A). Fairly fine pink ware, evenly fired. Cream slip out. Tree or wheat stalk potter's mark incised on outside wall before firing.

Other Type Series Examples:

Phase 6, Courtyard — (1) BR. G.I.d (TS. 766), (2) SJR. D.II.b (TS. 787), (3) JR. K.I.h (TS. 2229).

Phase 7A, Room 23: Bronze Age — (1) JR. B.III.d (TS. 661 = TS. 821), (2) JR. D.III.b (TS. 1825), (3) JR. D.VII.c (TS. 665); Roman Period — (1) R.BR. C.II.a (TS. 1327).

Other Study Collection Examples:

Phase 6, Courtyard — (1) SBR. A.I.b (SC. 205), (2) SBR. B.I.f (SC. 337), (3) SBR. B.I.f (SC. 342), (4) SBR. B.I.j (SC. 554), (5) BR. A.II.e (SC. 725), (6) BR. F.I.d (SC. 776), (7) SJR. A.I.a (SC. 2477), (8) JR. J.III.d (SC. 1375), (9) JR. J.III.o (SC. 2350), (10) JR. J.IV.j (SC. 1549), (11) JR. O.III.e (SC. 2423), (12) Ld. C.III.a (SC. 1942), (13) BE. J (SC. 3234), (14) WPS. C (SC. 1953).

Phase 7A, Room 23 — (1) SBR. B.I.d (SC. 295), (2) SBR. B.I.h (SC. 481), (3) BR. F.IV.a (SC. 815), (4) BR. L.I.i (SC. 882), (5) SJR. C.I.c (SC. 2533), (6) JR. C.V.d (SC. 1025), (7) JR. D.V.f (SC. 1103), (8) JR. E.I.h (SC. 1139), (9) JR. J.I.a (SC. 1296), (10) JR. J.I.d (SC. 1333), (11) JR. (not typed, SC. 93).

Phase 7A, Room 24 — (1) SBR. B.I.h (SC. 486), (2) SBR. B.I.h (SC. 505), (3) SBR. B.I.i (SC. 523), (4) SBR. B.I.k (SC. 557), (5) SBR. D.I.e (SC. 650), (6) SJR. C.I.f (SC. 2570), (7) JR. D.V.f (SC. 1104), (8) JR. E.I.b (SC. 1127), (9) JR. J.I.c (SC. 2110), (10) JR. J.I.d (SC. 1327), (11) JR. J.I.f (SC. 1341), (12) JR. J.III.r (SC. 1492), (13) JR. P.III.a (SC. 1757), (14) CP. A.II.c (SC. 1802), (15) CP. B.II.d (SC. 1850), (16) CP. B.IV.b (SC. 1873).

Figure 211

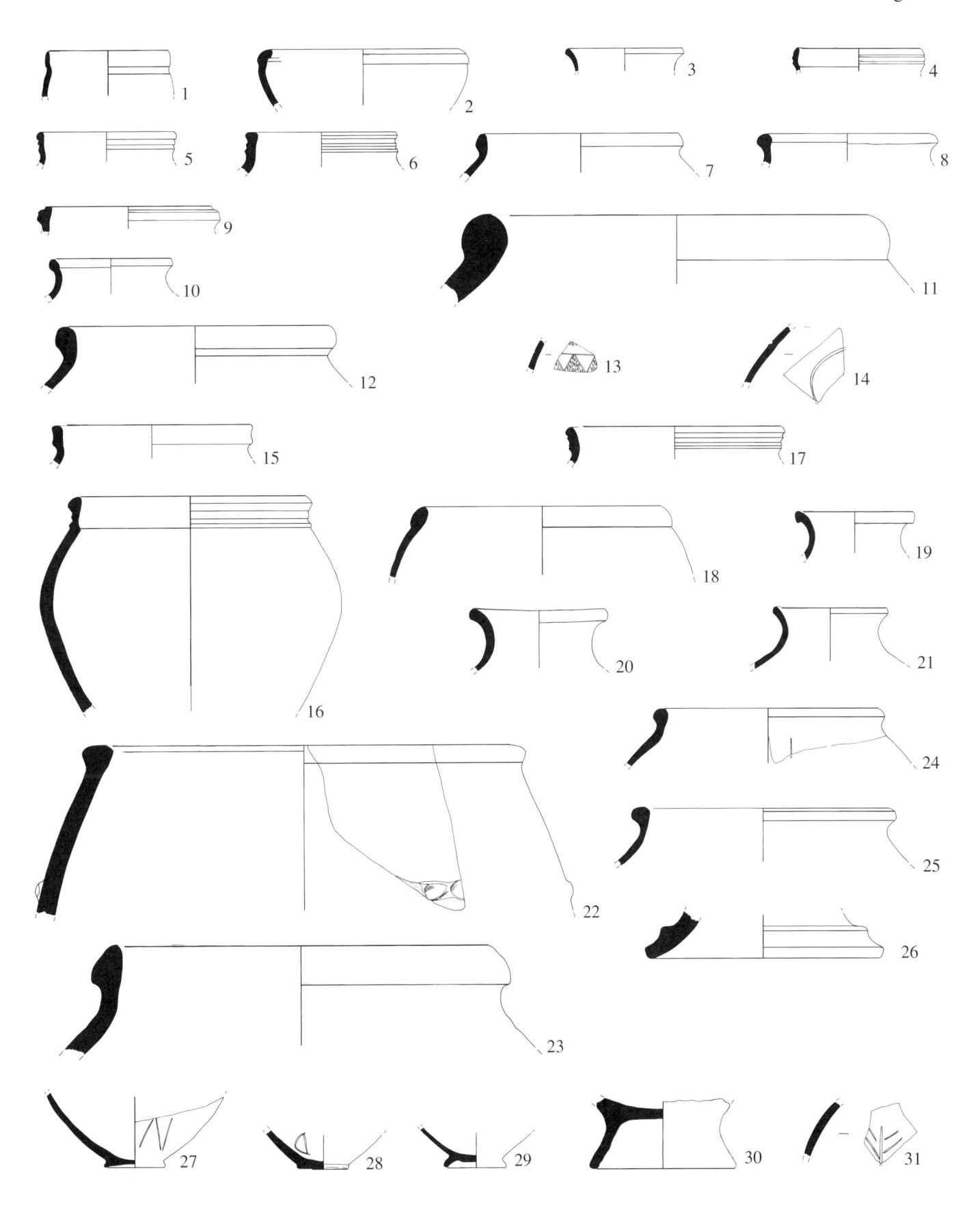

Pottery from Trench IIIG/H, Rooms 23, 24, and Extramural Courtyard (Phases 6 and 7A; Periods E–D and D — Early–Middle Bronze Age and Middle Bronze Age I). Scale 1:5

Figures 212–13

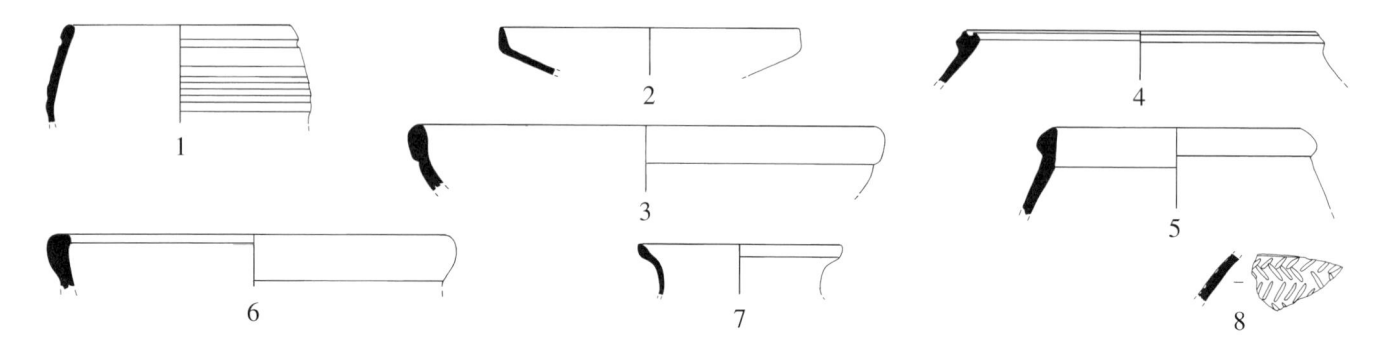

Figure 212. Pottery from Trench IIIH, Town Wall Debris (Phase 5; Period E — Early Bronze Age IVb). Scale 1:5

1. SBR. B.I.h (TS. 1281; IIIH, 1.2). Slightly coarse buff ware, evenly fired. Self slip in and out.
2. BR. D.IV.a (TS. 22; IIIH, 1.2). Fine pinkish-brown ware with lime and mica grits, evenly fired.
3. BR. F.II.a (TS. 1288; IIIH, 1.2). Hard, fine pinkish-brown ware, unevenly fired. Self slip in and out.
4. JR. H.III.e (TS. 1198 = TS. 1283; IIIH, 1.2). Fairly fine pinkish-buff ware with small lime and mica grit temper, fairly evenly fired. Creamy-buff slip out.
5. JR. H.III.k (TS. 2406; IIIH, 1.2). Slightly coarse grayish-buff ware, fairly evenly fired. Thick creamy-green slip out.
6. JR. P.II.g (TS. 1200; IIIH, 1.2). Fairly fine pinkish-buff ware with fine lime and mica grits, evenly fired. Creamy-buff slip in and out.
7. PS. A.II.c (TS. 2443; IIIH, 1.2). Fairly fine buff ware, evenly fired. Self slip in and out.
8. JR.Sh. (IP [G.4] F.III.a; TS. 763; IIIH, 1.2). Fairly fine reddish-colored ware, evenly fired. Remains of a mythological-type animal torso incised on outside wall. (Compare JR. H.I.g (SW. 294) from Area IV, fig. 64:4).

Another Type Series Example: (1) BR. F.I.c (TS. 2487).

Other Study Collection Examples: (1) SBR. A.I.a (SC. 178), (2) SBR. A.I.f (SC. 229), (3) SBR. B.I.h (SC. 509), (4) SBR. B.I.h (SC. 518), (5) SBR. B.I.j (SC. 543), (6) SBR. D.I.a (SC. 620), (7) JR. H.I.d (SC. 1263), (8) JR. J.III.f (SC. 1388), (9) JR. J.III.g (SC. 1392), (10) JR. J.III.i (SC. 1408), (11) JR. J.VI.b (SC. 2384), (12) CP. B.II.b (SC. 1848), (13) BE. F.VIII.b (SC. 3082), (14) BE. J (SC. 3239).

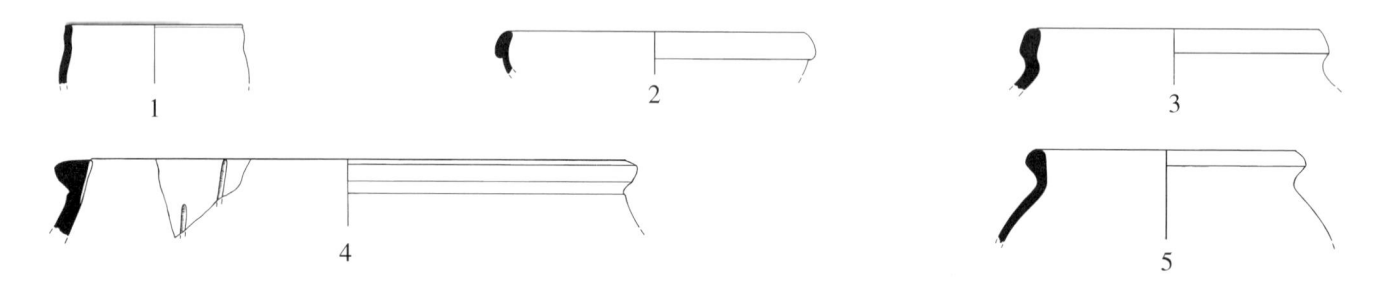

Figure 213. Pottery from Trench IIIH (Phase 6/7; Period E–D — Early–Middle Bronze Age). Scale 1:5

1. SBR. D.II.a (TS. 2477; IIIH, 1.1). Fairly fine flesh-colored pink ware, evenly fired. Cream slip out and just over rim in.
2. BR. F.I.d (TS. 2521; IIIH, 1.1). Hard, fine grayware, unevenly fired brown at surfaces. Self slip, horizontally burnished on rim and outside wall. Traces of charring out.
3. JR. B.II.b (TS. 3006; IIIH, 1.1). Slightly coarse creamy-green ware, evenly fired. Self slip in and out.
4. JR. H.III.q (PM. A.7; TS. 2149; IIIH, 1.1). Hard, fairly fine buff ware, evenly fired. Self slip in and out. Remains of a potter's mark incised on the upper inside wall before firing.
5. CP. A.II.b (TS. 2151; IIIH, 1.1). Slightly coarse and gritty pinkish-brown ware, fairly evenly fired. Self slip in and out.
—. Hd. A (TS. 4189; IIIH, 1.1). Fragment of a lug handle on a jar body sherd. Fairly coarse pink ware with many fine lime and mica grits, evenly fired. Cream slip in and out.

Other Type Series Examples: (1) BR. D.II.d (TS. 1199), (2) SJR. D.II.c (TS. 2136).

Other Study Collection Examples: (1) SBR. B.I.b (SC. 260), (2) BR. F.II.b (SC. 803), (3) BR. L.II.c (SC. 858), (4) BR. Q.I.a (SC. 868), (5) SJR. B.III.d (SC. 2528), (6) JR. H.I.d (SC. 1258), (7) JR. J.III.r (SC. 1490), (8) JR. (not typed, SC. 54), (9) JR. (not typed, SC. 78), (10) JR. (not typed, SC. 83), (11) CP. B.IV.c (SC. 1882).

Figures 214–15

Figure 214. Pottery from Trench IIIJ (Phase 3; Period F — Early Bronze Age IVa). Scale 1:5

1. SBR. A.I.g (TS. 786; IIIJ, 1.3). Fairly coarse buff ware, evenly fired. Cream slip out.
2. BR. F.IV.d (TS. 725; IIIJ, 1.3). Fairly coarse pinkish-buff ware, unevenly fired with buff core. Creamy-buff slip in and out.
3. JR. H.I.a (TS. 1144; IIIJ, 1.3). Fairly fine pink ware, evenly fired. Buff slip in and out. Small rim and shoulder segment with one horizontal ledge handle extant.
4. JR. J.III.o (TS. 750; IIIJ, 1.3). Fairly fine creamy-buff ware, evenly fired.

Other Study Collection Examples: (1) SBR. B.I.f (SC. 340), (2) SBR. B.I.h (SC. 426), (3) SBR. B.I.k (SC. 564), (4) BR. F.I.d (SC. 772), (5) BR. (not typed, SC. 51), (6) JR. F.I.a (SC. 2031), (7) JR. J.III.a (SC. 2212).

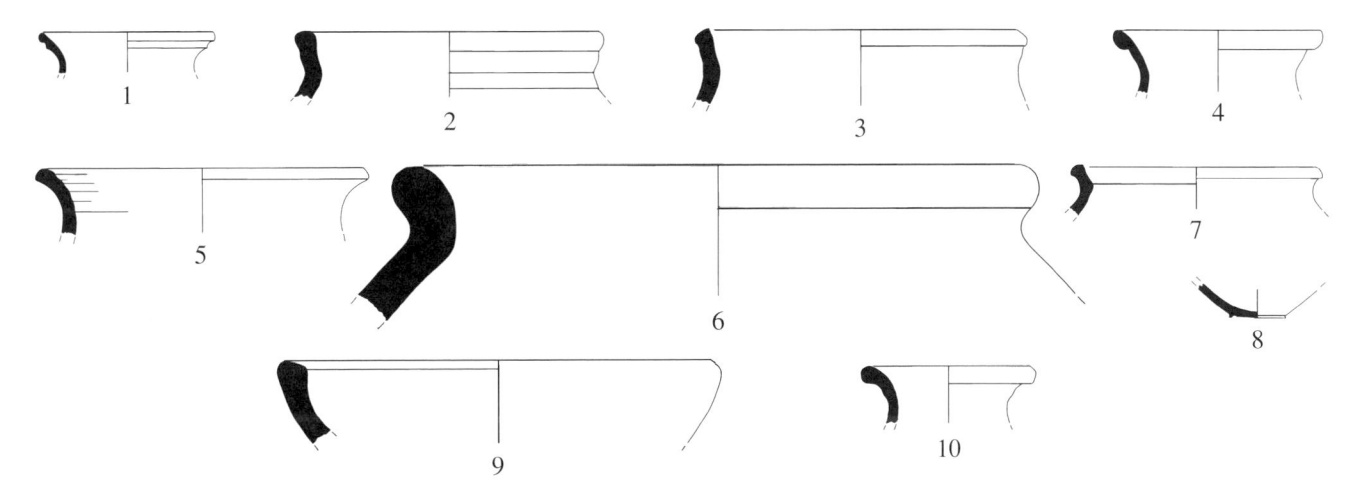

Figure 215. Pottery from Trench IIIJ (Phases 4 and 5, Period E — Early Bronze Age IVb). Scale 1:5

1. SJR. C.II.d (TS. 2435; IIIJ, 1.2, 1.3; Phase 4). Fairly fine pinkish-buff ware, evenly fired. Creamy-buff slip in and out.
2. JR. B.V.c (TS. 722; IIIJ, 1.2; Phase 4). Fairly coarse pink ware, evenly fired. Pinkish-buff slip out.
3. JR. F.II.a (TS. 773; IIIJ, 1.2; Phase 4). Fairly coarse creamy-buff ware, evenly fired.
4. JR. J.III.r (TS. 728; IIIJ, 1.2; Phase 4). Fairly fine buff ware, evenly fired. Cream slip in and out.
5. JR. J.IV.g (TS. 730; IIIJ, 1.2; Phase 4). Fairly coarse buff ware, evenly fired. Cream slip out and thin creamy wash over dark brown slip in.
6. JR. O.I.d (TS. 676; IIIJ, 1.2, 1.3; Phase 4). Fairly coarse pink ware, unevenly fired with dark core. Traces of cream slip out.
7. CP. A.I.i (TS. 778; IIIJ, 1.2; Phase 4). Very coarse brown ware with lime and mica grits, evenly fired. Blackened outside.
8. BE. E.I.j (TS. 1331; IIIJ, 1.2; Phase 4). Fine pinkish-buff ware, evenly fired. Self slip out.
9. BR. L.III.g (TS. 4228; IIIJ, 1.1; Phase 5). Fairly coarse pinkish-brown ware with fine lime and gold- and silver-colored mica grits and considerable burned out straw and vegetable temper on surfaces and inside, evenly fired. Traces of self slip in and out.
10. JR. F.II.e (SC. 1223; IIIJ, 1.1; Phase 5). Fine, hard-fired, grayish-buff ware with very fine lime and silver-colored mica grits, evenly fired. Creamy-buff slip in and out.

Other Type Series Examples:
Phase 4 — (1) BR. L.III.a (TS. 675), (2) JR. F.III.f (TS. 724), (3) PS. B.I.a (TS. 733).

Other Study Collection Examples:
Phase 4 — (1) SBR. B.I.h (SC. 463), (2) SBR. B.I.h (SC. 507), (3) SBR. D.I.e (SC. 649), (4) BR. (not typed, SC. 36), (5) JR. F.I.a (SC. 1187), (6) JR. J.III.i (SC. 1409).

Figures 216–18

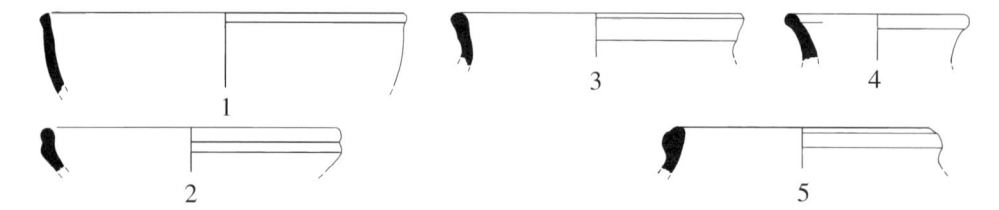

Figure 216. Pottery from Trench IIIJ (Phase 6/7; Period E–D — Early–Middle Bronze Age). Scale 1:5

1. BR. A.III.b (TS. 696; IIIJ, 1). Fairly coarse buff ware, evenly fired. Cream slip in and out.
2. BR. J.I.b (TS. 697; IIIJ, 1). Fairly coarse pink ware, evenly fired. Buff slip out.
3. JR. A.V.a (TS. 1919; IIIJ, 1). Slightly coarse pinkish-buff ware, evenly fired. Creamy-buff slip in and out.
4. JR. J.I.j (TS. 677; IIIJ, 1). Fine pink ware, evenly fired. Tan slip out.
5. JR. J.I.k (TS. 1886; IIIJ, 1). Hard, fine grayish-buff ware, evenly fired. Self slip in and out.

Another Type Series Example: Derived Hellenistic Period — (1) H.JR. C.I.k (TS. 1332).

Other Study Collection Examples: (1) BR. F.III.b (SC. 876), (2) SJR. C.I.f (SC. 2559), (3) SJR. C.I.f (SC. 2560), (4) SJR. C.II.f (SC. 2590), (5) JR. C.I.a (SC. 989), (6) JR. E.II.d (SC. 2018), (7) JR. F.II.e (SC. 1223), (8) JR. K.I.b (SC. 1573), (9) JR. P.II.a (SC. 1701).

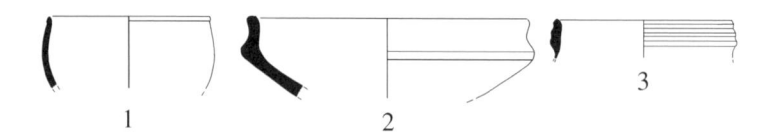

Figure 217. Pottery from Trench IIIK (Phase 6/7; Period E–D — Early–Middle Bronze Age). Scale 1:5

1. SBR. B.I.d (TS. 739; IIIK, 1.1). Fairly coarse reddish-buff ware, evenly fired.
2. BR. E.I.a (TS. 748; IIIK, 1.1). Fairly coarse pink ware, evenly fired.
3. JR. C.I.e (TS. 1330; IIIK, 1.1). Fairly fine buff ware, evenly fired. Self slip out.

Other Study Collection Examples: (1) JR. J.I.a (SC. 2085), (2) JR. J.III.e (SC. 2249), (3) JR. J.III.e (SC. 2267), (4) JR. J.III.h (SC. 1404), (5) JR. J.III.l (SC. 2310), (6) JR. K.I.a (SC. 1558), (7) JR. O.III.c (SC. 1676), (8) JR. O.III.e (SC. 1683), (9) BE. B.II (SC. 3077).

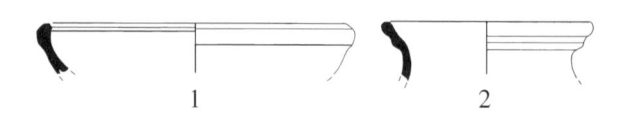

Figure 218. Pottery from Trench IIIL, Walls 1 and 2 (Phase 5; Period E — Early Bronze Age IVb). Scale 1:5

1. BR. D.VI.b (TS. 1329; IIIL, 1.2). Fine greenish-buff ware, evenly fired. Self slip, irregularly burnished out and on top of rim.
2. SJR. C.II.d (TS. 723; IIIL, 1.2). Fairly coarse buff ware, evenly fired. Cream slip in and out.

Another Type Series Example: (1) JR. E.II.e (TS. 719).

Another Study Collection Example: (1) JR. J.IV.e (SC. 1527).

Figures 219–20

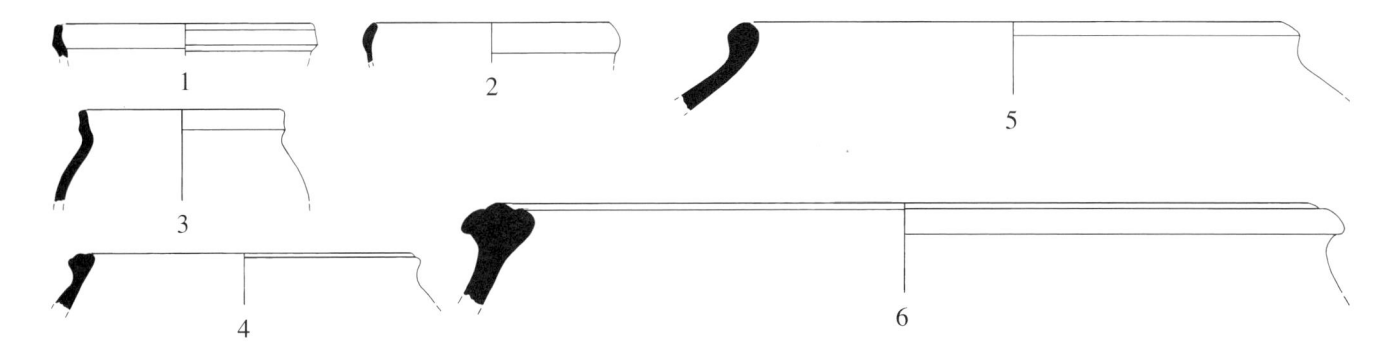

Figure 219. Pottery from Trench IIIL (Phase 6/7; Period E–D — Early–Middle Bronze Age). Scale 1:5

1. SBR. D.I.e (TS. 1335; IIIL, 1.1). Fairly fine pinkish-brown ware, evenly fired. Creamy-buff slip in and out.
2. BR. F.I.d (TS. 1334; IIIL, 1.1). Fine grayish-brown ware, evenly fired. Off-white slip out.
3. JR. A.III.a (TS. 1328; IIIL, 1.1). Slightly coarse buff ware, evenly fired. Creamy-green slip out.
4. JR. H.II.a (TS. 843; IIIL, 1.1). Fairly coarse pink ware, evenly fired. Cream slip in and out.
5. JR. O.II.d (TS. 858; IIIL, 1.1). Coarse greenish-buff ware, evenly fired.
6. JR. O.III.g (TS. 909; IIIL, 1.1). Fairly coarse pink ware, unevenly fired with buff core. Cream slip out and just over rim in.

Other Type Series Examples: (1) BR. N.II.c (TS. 846), (2) JR. B.V.e (TS. 1052), (3) JR. C.I.f (TS. 1333).

Other Study Collection Examples: (1) SBR. B.I.b (SC. 264), (2) SBR. B.I.h (SC. 488), (3) BR. A.II.e (SC. 871), (4) BR. A.IV.g (SC. 731), (5) JR. C.I.a (SC. 988), (6) JR. J.III.f (SC. 1385), (7) JR. J.III.h (SC. 1403), (8) JR. J.III.ab (SC. 1515), (9) JR. J.IV.a (SC. 2370), (10) JR. J.IV.j (SC. 1544), (11) JR. P.II.o (SC. 2435), (12) WPS. B (SC. 1951).

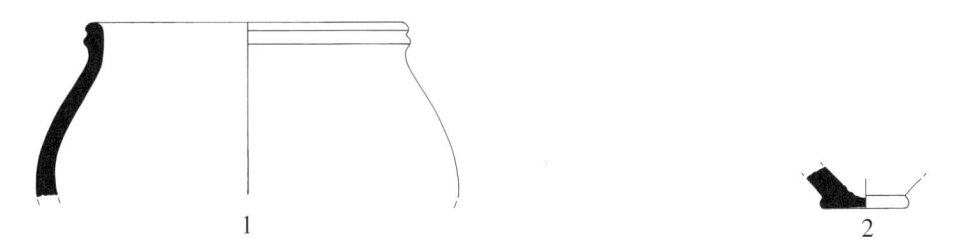

Figure 220. Pottery from Area III, Unstratified Early Bronze Age. Scale 1:5

1. JR. B.IV.a (TS. 1094; IIID, Unstratified). Fairly coarse cream ware, evenly fired. Partially blackened out.
—. JR. J.III.c (PM. C.11; TS. 628; Unstratified). See fig. 333:3.
2. BE. B.II (TS. 1132; IIIA and IIIC, Unstratified). Two segments. Fairly coarse pinkish-cream ware, evenly fired. Cream slip in and out.

Another Type Series Example: (1) JR. F.II.c (TS. 1093).

Figure 221. Human Figurines, Types SF.1a and SF.1c, from Area III (Phases 3–7A; Periods F to D — Early Bronze Age IVa to Middle Bronze Age I)

1. Type SF.1a (SW. 46; IIIA, 4.4, Room 4A). Phase 3 (EB IVa; see pl. 104c). Coarse buff ware, evenly fired. Female, head and upper torso fragment. High, cylindrical-shaped headdress with incised coiffure surrounding the top of the head, extending on both sides of the neck to shoulder length, and broad plait-like strand on the back to shoulder-blade level. Donut-shaped appliqué eyes. Short arms with clay pinched off just below the underarm level and with pierced holes through both arms at the point of the armpits. Incised and applied decoration on the chest in the shape of a disk positioned just above a crescent-shaped piece of clay.
2. Type SF.1a (SW. 152; IIIC, 4.10, Room 9). Phase 4 (EB IVb). Very hard buff ware with much black mineral temper. Light yellow-green slip covers all surfaces. Female. Head probably broken and rejoined to torso in antiquity as the transverse cut surface of the neck is covered with a black, bitumen-like, substance, which extends irregularly up the neck (compare a similar type of repair on the two-headed figurine from Area IIIG/H, SW. 476, fig. 221:7, pl. 106a). The hair also comes up in a beak over the forehead and down behind the ears; it is indicated by short parallel incisions in the clay. The solid eyebrows meet in a point above the nose and continue around to join the incised, donut-shaped, earrings. The appliqué disk-shaped eyes were pierced conically through into the head after their application.
3. Type SF.1c (SW. 223; IIIE, 3.1, Room 15). Phase 5 (EB IVb; see pl. 105a). Hard, fine grayish-green ware with lime grit, evenly fired. Buff slip on front of figure. Female. Head and lower portion of plaque-like torso stand broken. Appliqué and incised necklace positioned around the neck and top of shoulders. Rudimentary arms pinched from the shoulders and partially incised with a vertical hole from the top. Compare Braidwood and Braidwood 1960: fig. 368:4 from the Amuq Second Mixed Range.
4. Type SF.1a (SW. 192; IIIB, 4.1, Pit). Phase 5 (EB IVb; see pl. 104b). Fairly fine orange ware, evenly fired. Buff slip. Female? Headdress in the shape of a miniature basin; possibly made for holding a liquid or dry material such as incense or ochre. Headdress, nose, and ears formed from a single piece of clay; eyes and earrings applied as pellets and then incised with holes, as is the bottom of the headdress.
5. Type SF.1a (SW. 135; IIID, 5.3, Rooms 20/21). Phase 5 (EB IVb; see pl. 104a). Coarse light grayware with black temper, evenly fired. Female. Appliqué donut-shaped eyes. Small holes diagonally incised on each side of the neck do not extend to back of neck.
6. Type SF.1a (SW. 546; IIIG/H, 1.5, Room 17). Phase 4 (EB IVb; see pl. 104d). Fine buff ware, evenly fired. Cream slip on exterior surfaces. Female. Head, neck, and shoulder fragment. High headdress or crown broken at the top is decorated with short diagonally impressed incisions. Appliqué donut-shaped eyes. Double-stranded and incised necklace applied on chest at base of the front side of the neck and on top of the shoulders.
7. Type SF.1c (SW. 476; IIIG/H, 1.5, Room 17). Phase 4 (EB IVb; see pl. 106a). Fairly coarse brown ware, evenly fired. Cream slip applied over all surfaces. Two-headed figure applied to the narrow end of a four-legged basin (compare pl. 107 showing a complete unprovienced figure from a private collection). Heads broken off and probably repaired in antiquity as there are remains of bitumen on the right-side head and down the shoulder on the back. Applied and incised necklaces extend around the front and to the shoulder of both necks. The arms are rudimentary and pinched out of the clay from the shoulders. Three shallow holes are incised into each side of the joint torso, which is divided by a thinly incised vertical line down the center of the figure to the top of the broken clay, which originally supported the missing horizontally positioned footed basin.
8. Type SF.1c (SW. 366; IIIG/H, 1a, Room 23). Phase 7A (MB I; see pl. 106b). Fairly fine pink ware, evenly fired. Cream slip on front and back surfaces. Female neck and torso fragment. Remains of a bun-shaped and incised coiffure on the base and back of the neck. Double-stranded and incised necklace applied on chest at base of the front side of the neck and on top of the shoulders. Remains of the right lower arm and hand applied at the base of the necklace.
9. Type SF.1c (SW. 401; IIIG/H, 1.1, Courtyard). Phase 6 (EB–MB; see pl. 105b). Fine creamy-buff ware, evenly fired. Female neck and torso fragment. Remains of a bun-shaped and incised coiffure on the base and back of the neck extending to the base of the shoulder blade. Remains of an incised single-stranded necklace around the chest and just over the top of the shoulders, with a second incised strand applied over the right shoulder. The surviving right arm is rudimentary and diagonnaly incised with a shallow hole. Shallow incised holes in a circular pattern from base of front side of neck to top of necklace. Short, horizontally-incised lines on the torso just below the necklace as well as a rough half-moon shape.
10. Type SF.1c (SW. 344; IIIA, 4.4, Room 4A). Phase 3 (EB IVa). Human figurine pillar-shaped torso fragment. Fine light pinkish-brown ware, evenly fired. Brownish-buff slip.
11. Type SF.1c (TS. 2181; IIIG/H, 1.8a, Room 3A). Phase 3 (EB IVa). Human figurine plaque-shaped torso fragment. Fairly fine pink ware, evenly fired. Buff slip, burnished vertically on both flat sides.
12. Type SF.1c (SW. 200; IIIB, 4.1, Pit). Phase 5 (EB IVb; see pl. 115c). Human figurine pillar-shaped torso fragment with bell-shaped base, concave at bottom. Buff ware with small black and white grits, evenly fired.
13. Type SF.1c (SW. 42; IIIB, 2.2). Phase 5 (EB IVb; see pl. 115g). Human figurine rectangular-shaped torso fragment with concave bell-shaped base. Grayish-buff ware, fairly evenly fired.
14. Type SF.1c (SW. 402; IIIG/H, 1a, Room 23). Phase 7A (MB I; see pl. 115b). Human figurine pillar-shaped torso fragment with bell-shaped base, concave at bottom. Fine pink ware, evenly fired. Buff slip.
15. Type SF.1c (SW. 141; IIIC, 4.6). Phase 7 (MB I; see pl. 115d). Human figurine pillar-shaped torso fragment with bell-shaped base, concave at bottom. Coarse light buff ware with black grits, evenly fired.
—. Type SF.1c (SC. 3270; IIIB, 2.3, Room 6). Phase 4 (EB IVb). Human figurine pillar-shaped torso fragment with bell-shaped base, concave at bottom. Fine pinkish-buff ware with very small silver-colored mica grits, evenly fired. Creamy-buff slip on surfaces.

Figure 221

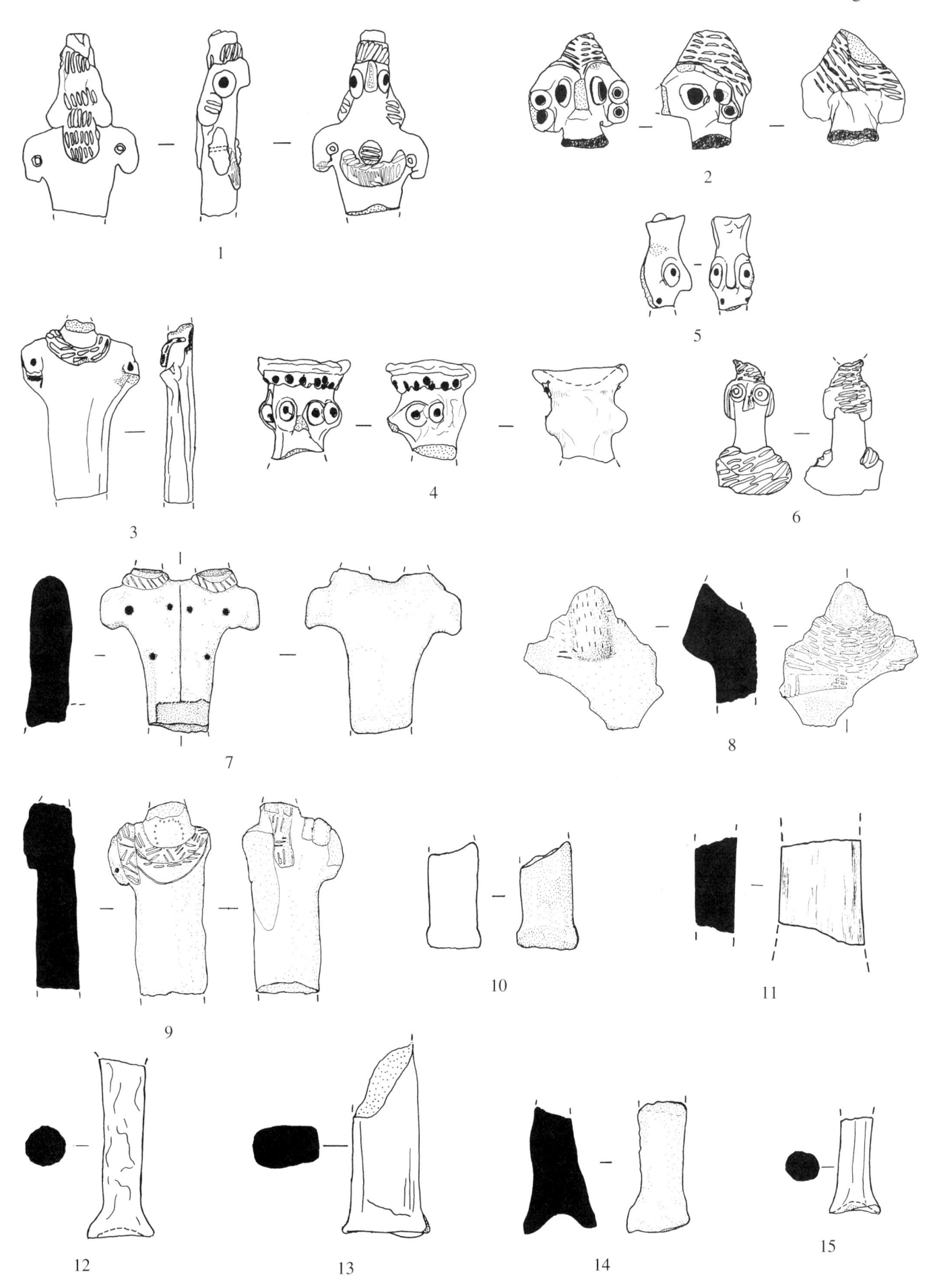

Human Figurines, Types SF.1a and SF.1c, from Area III (Phases 3–7A; Periods F to D — Early Bronze Age IVa to Middle Bronze Age I). Scale 1:2

Figure 222. Animal Figurines, Model Chariots, Model Wheels, and Miscellaneous Clay Objects from Area III (Phases 3–6/7; Periods F, E, and E–D — Early Bronze Age IVa, Early Bronze Age IVb, and Early–Middle Bronze Age)

1. Type SF.1d (SW. 51; IIIA, 4.4, Room 4A). Phase 3 (EB IVa; see pl. 117a). Animal figurine. Tips of ears, right side of muzzle, and bottom of legs broken in antiquity. Brown ware with black mineral temper, evenly fired.
2. Type SF.1e (SW. 48; IIIA, 4.1, Room 8B). Phase 4 (EB IVb; see pl. 117i). Animal torso fragment. Head and legs broken in antiquity. Fine, well levigated, light brown ware, evenly fired.
3. Type SF.1d (SW. 204; IIIF, 3.1, Room 16). Phase 4 (EB IVb; see pl. 117b). Animal forequarter fragment. Buff ware, evenly fired.
4. Type SF.1d (SW. 93; IIIC, 4.7). Phase 6 (EB–MB; see pl. 117c). Animal head, neck, and upper shoulder fragment. Coarse greenish-buff ware, evenly fired.
5. Type SF.1d (SW. 83; IIIA, 1.2, Floor sealing Phase 5 occupation). Phase 6 (EB–MB; see pl. 117m). Bird figurine fragment. Fairly fine grayware with black mineral temper, evenly fired. Remains of tail and pillar-type stand upon which the bird rested. Herringbone-style incised decoration on top represents the tail feathers of the bird.
6. Type SF.2a (SW. 445; IIIG/H, 1.9, Room 3B). Phase 3 (EB IVa). Model chariot fragment. Remains of wheel axle hole and hole for shaft pole. Fairly coarse creamish-buff ware, evenly fired.
7. Type SF.2a (SW. 312; IIID, 5.2, Debris sealing Phase 5 Room 21). Phase 6 (EB–MB). Model chariot fragment. Remains of wheel axle hole. Buff ware, fairly evenly fired.
8. Type SF.2b (SW. 213; IIIB, 2.9, Room 1B). Phase 3 (EB IVa). Model chariot wheel fragment. Light brown ware with mineral grit and vegetable temper, burned out during firing leaving surface very pitted.
9. Type SF.2b (SW. 397; IIIG/H, 1.2, Room 22B). Phase 5 (EB IVb). Model chariot wheel fragment with complete axle hole. Fairly fine pink ware, unevenly fired with gray core.
10. Type SF.2d (SW. 259; IIIE, 3.2, Room 5). Phase 4 (EB IVb). Model chair or bed (compare figurine with attached basin, pl. 107) or miniature container. Very hard, pinkish-buff ware with lime and mica grits, unevenly fired grayish-brown at surfaces. Handmade.
11. Type SF.6b (SW. 171; IIIB, 2.3, Room 6). Phase 4. (EB IVb). Pottery spindle whorl made from broken sherd. Hole bored from both faces of sherd. Buff ware, evenly fired. Light yellow-buff slip convex, outer surface.
12. Type SF.6b (SW. 229; IIID, 5.4, Room 12). Phase 4 (EB IVb). Pottery spindle whorl. Pinkish-buff ware with lime and mica grits, evenly fired.
13. Type SF.6b (TS. 1313; IIIF, 1.1). Phase 6/7 (EB–MB). Pottery spindle whorl made from broken sherd. Hole bored from both faces of sherd. Slightly coarse grayish-buff ware, evenly fired. Self slip on both surfaces.
14. Type SV.2 (SW. 442; IIIG/H, 1.9, Room 3B). Phase 3 (EB IVa). Pottery spout, broken on narrow end. Fairly fine pink ware, evenly fired. Cream slip on outside surface.
15. Type SF.6g (TS. 1137; IIIG/H, 1.9, Room 3B). Phase 3 (EB IVa). Fragment of a pottery plaque-shaped flat object incised with oval-shaped impressions. Possibly an exercise tablet (compare Hilprecht 1903, p. 405, which is described as a pre-Sargonid child's writing tablet said to come from the Fire Necropolis).
—. Type SF.6a.1 and 6a.2 (SW. 652; IIIG/H, 1.8a, Room 3A). Phase 3 (EB IVa). Two clay sling bullets. Type SF.6a.1, Flat-ended ellipsoid, 3 cm wide by 4 cm long; Type SF.6a.2, Point-ended ellipsoid, 2.5 cm wide by 5.5 cm long. Fairly fine buff ware, unfired.
—. Type SF.6e (SC. 3282; IIIB, 2.9, Room 1B). Phase 3 (EB IVa). Disk. Reworked jar sherd possibly used as a lid. Fine buff ware with silver- and gold-colored mica grits, evenly fired.

Figure 222

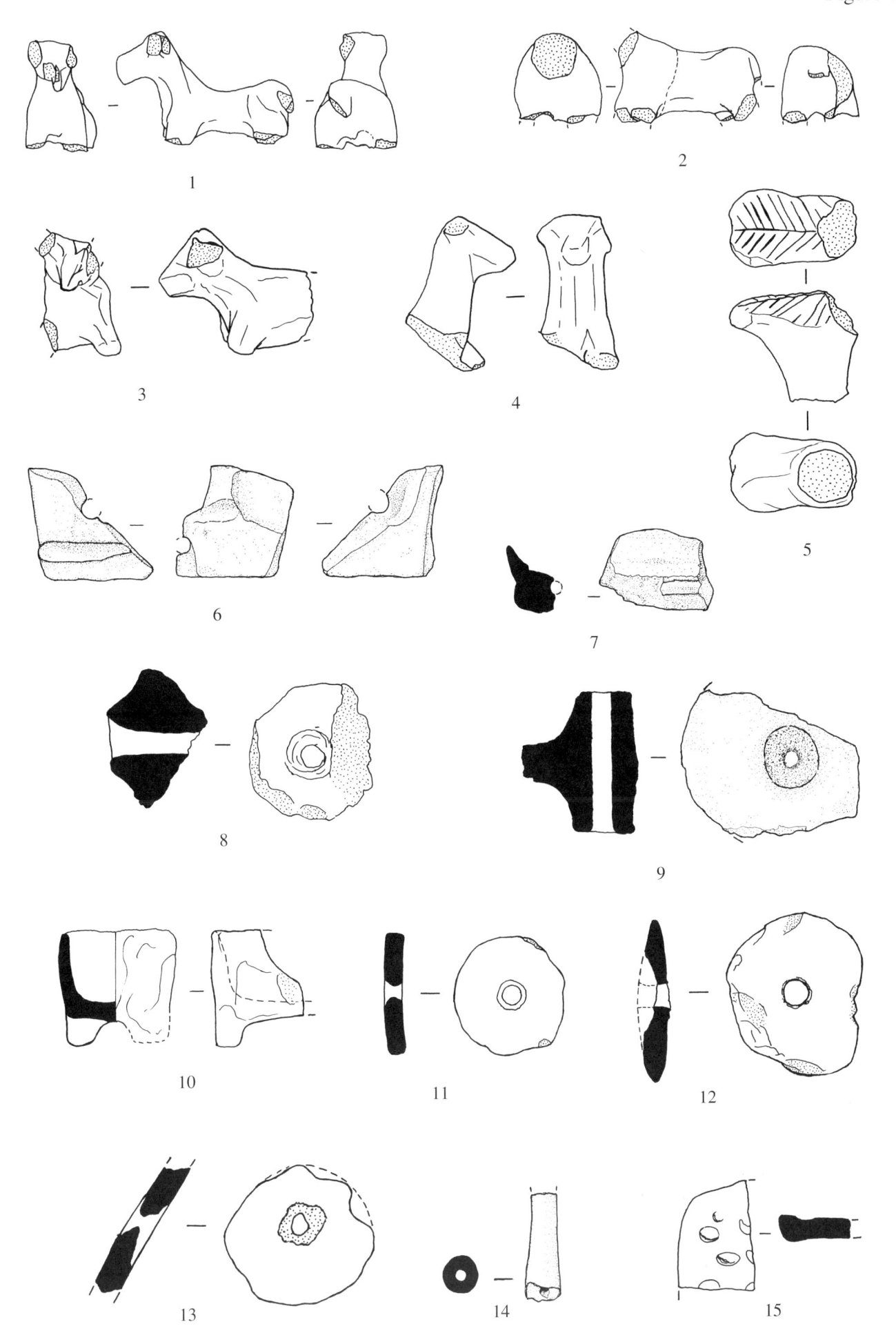

Animal Figurines, Model Chariots, Model Wheels, and Miscellaneous Clay Objects from Area III (Phases 3–6/7; Periods F, E, and E–D — Early Bronze Age IVa, Early Bronze Age IVb, and Early–Middle Bronze Age). Scale 1:2

Figure 223

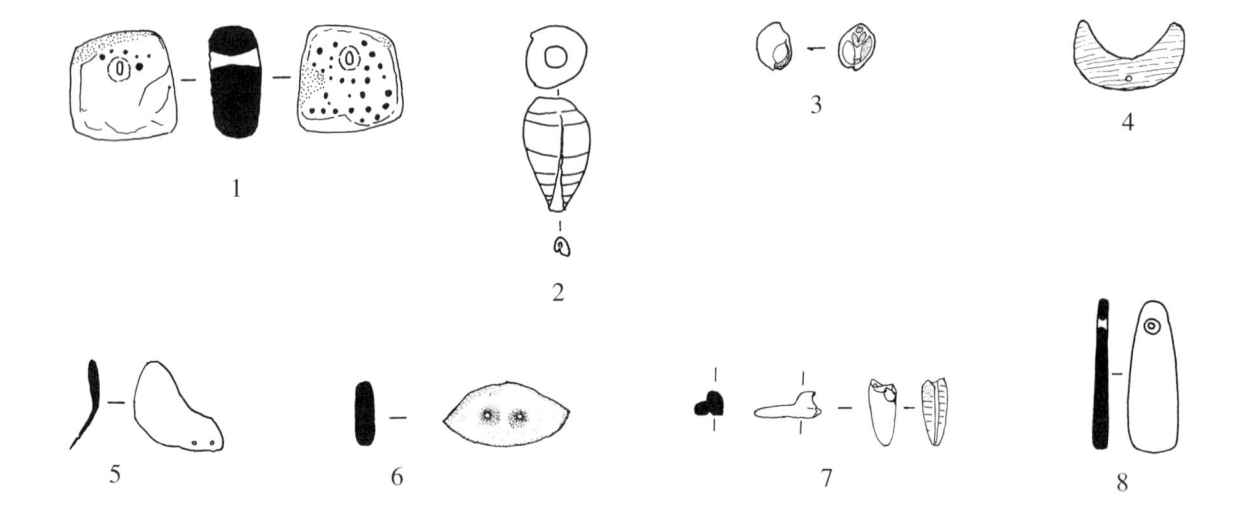

Beads and Pendants from Area III (Phases 3–6; Periods F, E, and E–D — Early Bronze Age IVa, Early Bronze Age IVb, and Early–Middle Bronze Age). Scale 1:2

1. Type SF.4c (SW. 146; IIIC, 4.9, Room 19A). Phase 5 (EB IVb). Clay pendant with suspension hole pierced through the narrow end. Decorated with small indented holes on both broad surfaces. Light buff ware with black temper, evenly fired.
2. Type SF.4c (SW. 554; IIIG/H, 1.9, Room 3B). Phase 3 (EB IVa). Snail shell pendant. Hole pierced through broad end for suspension.
3. Type SF.4c (SW. 400; IIIG/H, 1.2, Room 22B). Phase 5 (EB IVb). Seashell pendant with natural hole on one end.
4. Type SF.4c (SW. 391; IIIG/H, 1.2, Room 22B). Phase 5 (EB IVb). Seashell pendant cut into a crescent shape and pierced with a suspension hole.
5. Type SF.4c (SW. 70; IIIA, 1.1). Phase 7 (MB I). Seashell pendant cut into quarter-moon shape and pierced with two small suspension holes at one end.
—. Type SF.4c (SW. 443; IIIG/H, 1.1, Courtyard). Phase 6 (EB–MB). Pendant. Natural seashell.
6. Type SF.4b (SW. 467; IIIG/H, 1.5, Room 17). Phase 4. (EB IVb). Bead or button. White chalk-like limestone. Two holes drilled through center of oval-shaped object.
7. Type SF.4b (SW. 189; IIIF, 2.1, Debris). Phase 5 (EB IVb). Bead. Granite-like, dark green stone. Incomplete with traces of a suspension hole bored through its width.
8. Type SF.4c (SW. 543; IIIG/H, 1.9, Room 3B). Phase 3 (EB IVa). Pendant. Reddish-colored, slate-like, stone. Suspension hole drilled through the narrow end.

Figure 224

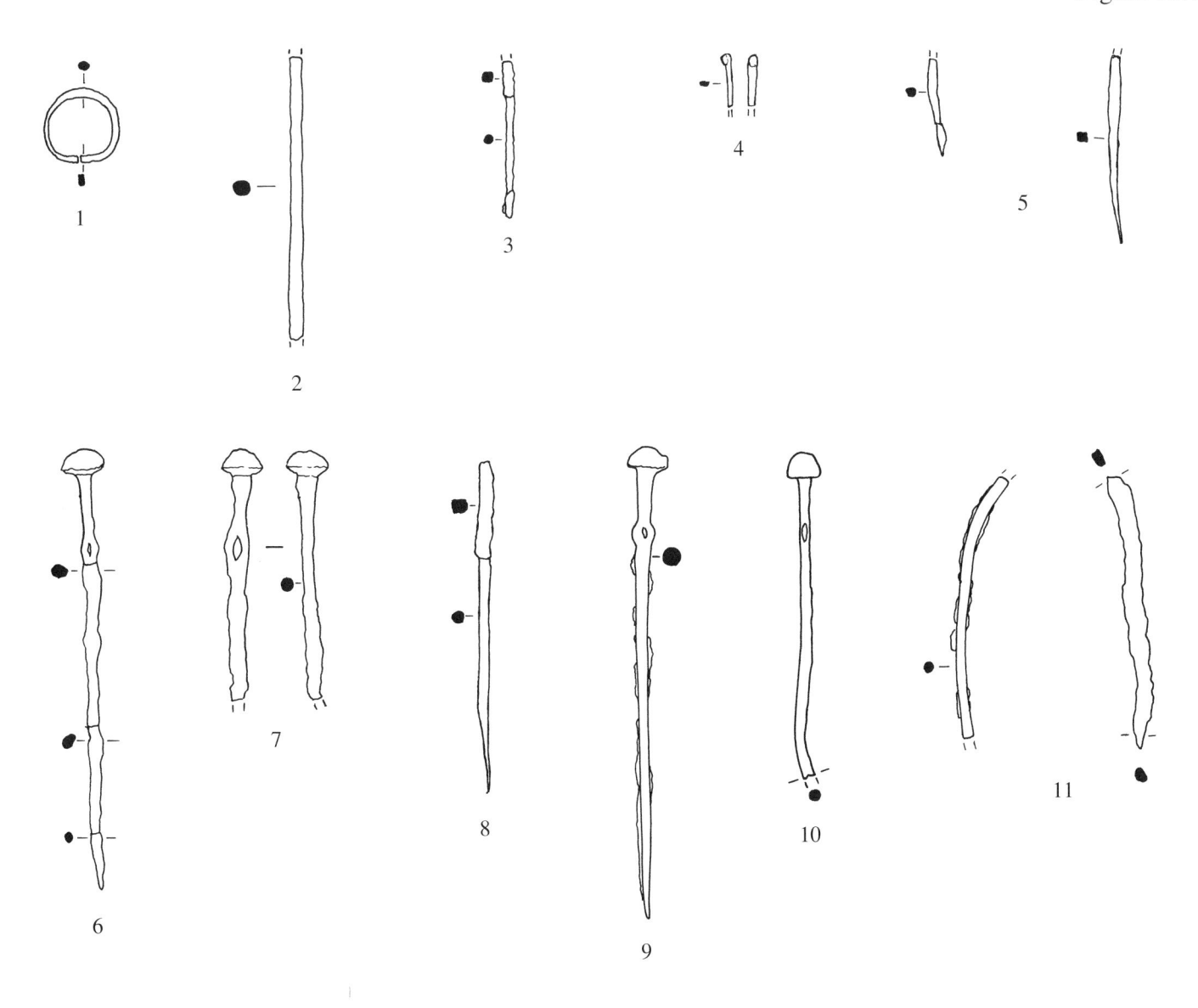

Metal Objects from Area III (Phases 4–6; Periods E and E–D — Early Bronze Age IVb and Early Bronze–Middle Bronze Age). Scale 1:2

1. Type SF.5f (SW. 2; IIIA, 1.2). Phase 6 (EB–MB). Metal ring (copper/bronze?, not analyzed). Ends meet without overlapping and are slightly flattened.
2. Type SF.5i (SW. 61; IIIA, Unstratified). Metal rod (iron, not analyzed).
3. Type SF.5c (SW. 68; IIIA, 4.1, Room 8B). Phase 4 (EB IVb). Metal pin (copper/bronze?, not analyzed), incomplete.
4. Type SF.5c (SW. 134; IIIC, 4.10, Room 9). Phase 4 (EB IVb). Metal pin (copper/bronze?, not analyzed), fragment.
5. Type SF.5c (SW. 165a, b; IIIF, 1.2). Phase 5. (EB IVb). Metal pin (copper/bronze?, not analyzed), fragments.
6. Type SF.5c (SW. 167; IIIG, 2.1, Room 22A). Phase 5 (EB IVb). Metal pin (copper/bronze?, not analyzed), with mushroom-shaped head and shaft hole. Complete.
7. Type SF.5c (SW. 184; IIIG, 3.1, Room 18). Phase 4 (EB IVb). Metal pin (copper/bronze?, not analyzed), with mushroom-shaped head and shaft hole. Pointed end missing.
8. Type SF.5c (SW. 168; IIIG, 3.1, Room 18). Phase 4 (EB IVb). Metal pin (copper/bronze?, not analyzed), shaft fragment.
9. Type SF.5c (SW. 602; IIIG/H, 1.7, Room 18). Phase 4 (EB IVb). Metal pin (copper/bronze?, not analyzed), with mushroom-shaped head and shaft hole. Broken in antiquity, but complete when mended. Break at section indicates the pin was made from three wires twisted together.
10. Type SF.5c (SW. 603; IIIG/H, 1.7, Room 18). Phase 4 (EB IVb). Metal pin (copper/bronze?, not analyzed), with mushroom-shaped head and shaft hole. Pointed tip missing.
11. Type SF.5c (SW. 607a, b; IIIG/H, 1.1, Courtyard). Phase 6 (EB–MB). Two incomplete metal pin shafts (copper/bronze?, not analyzed).

Figure 225

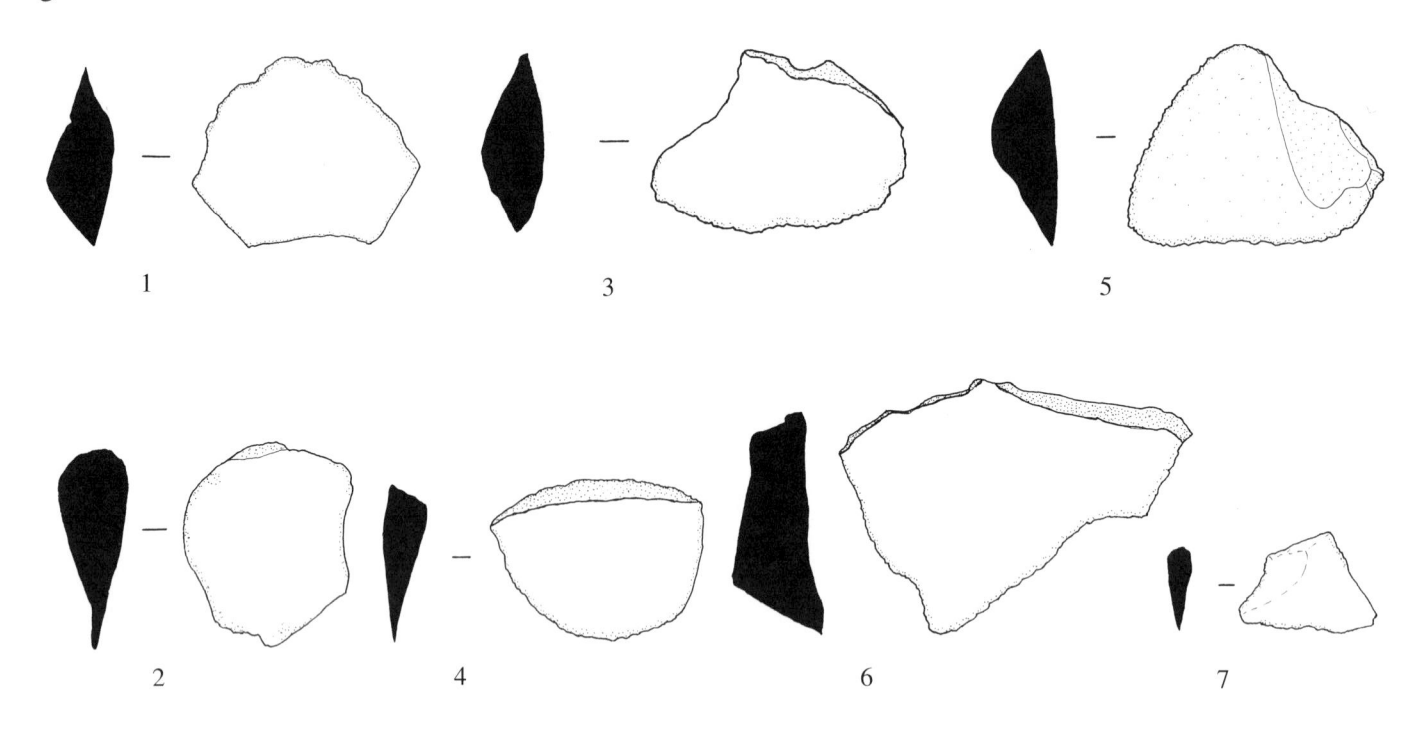

Flint Tools from Area III (Phases 3, 4, 6, and 7B; Periods F to D — Early Bronze Age IVb to Middle Bronze Age I).
Scale 1:2

1. Type SF.12a (SW. 435; IIIG/H, 1.8a, Room 3A). Phase 3 (EB IVa). Scraper.
2. Type SF.12a (SW. 403; IIIJ, 1.2). Phase 4 (EB IVb). Scraper.
3. Type SF.12a (SW. 419; IIIG/H, 1.6, Room 17A). Phase 4 (EB IVb). Scraper.
4. Type SF.12a (SW. 437; IIIG/H, 1.7, Room 18). Phase 4 (EB IVb). Scraper.
5. Type SF.12a (SW. 348; IIIG/H, 1a, Room 23 Extramural). Phase 7B (MB I). Scraper.
6. Type SF.12a (SW. 398; IIIG/H, 1.1, Courtyard). Phase 6 (EB–MB). Scraper.
7. Type SF.12a (SW. 404; IIIG/H, 1.1, Courtyard). Phase 6 (EB–MB). Scraper.

Figure 226

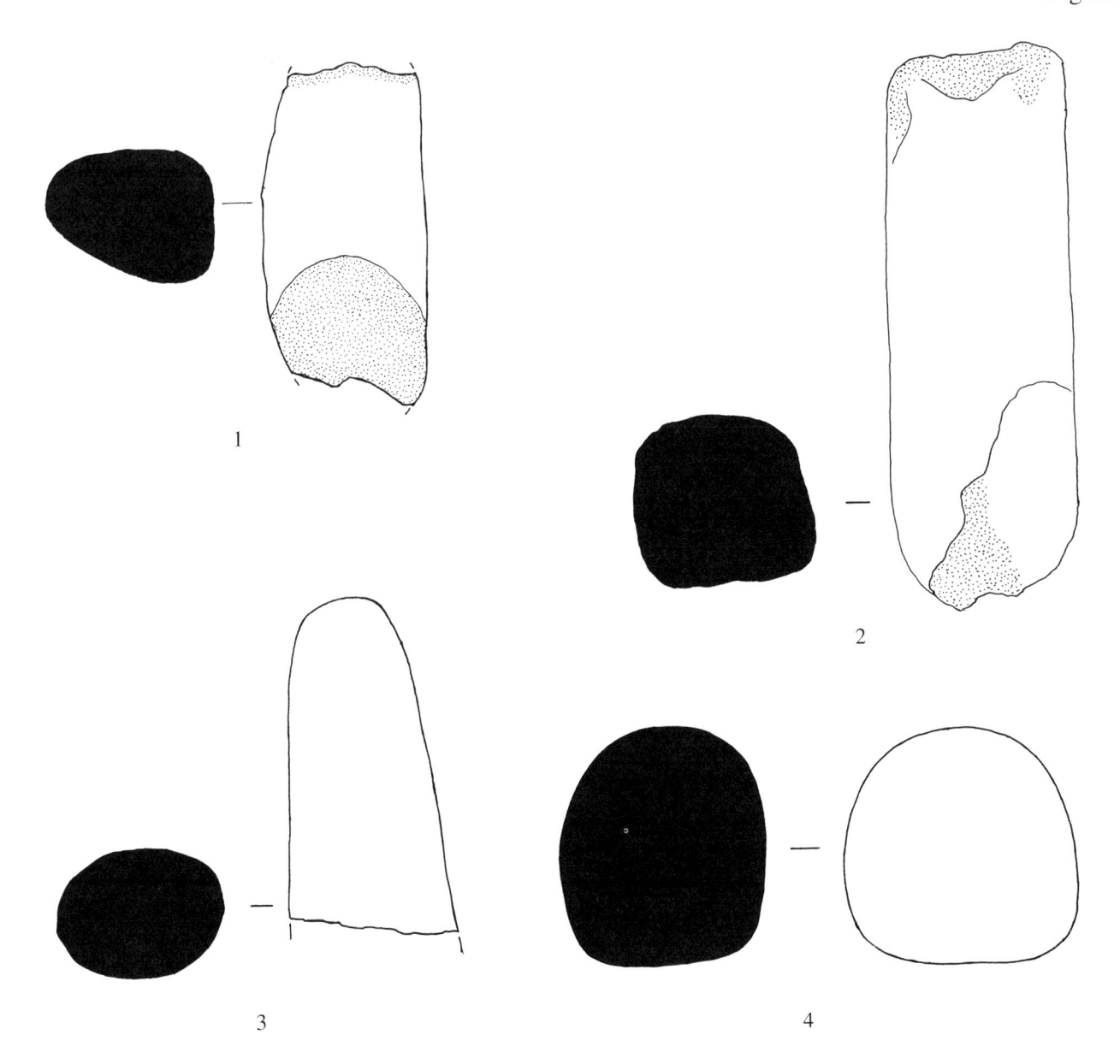

Stone Pestles and Pounders from Area III (Phases 1B, 2–4, 6–7A; Periods G to D — Early Bronze Age III to Middle Bronze Age I). Scale 1:2

1. Type SF.3a (SW. 359; IIIB, 2.15). Phase 1B (EB III). Pestle, broken at each end. Fine-grained greenish igneous stone.
2. Type SF.3a (SW. 360; IIIB, 2.10, Room 1A). Phase 2 (EB IVa). Pestle, slightly broken at each end. Fine-grained greenish-gray igneous stone with outer brown surface.
3. Type SF.3a (SW. 352; IIIA, 4.4, Room 4A). Phase 3 (EB IVa). Pestle, broken at broad end. Medium-coarse–grained igneous stone speckled white, greenish-gray, and buff.
—. Type SF.3a (SW. 425; IIIG/H, 1.7, Room 18). Phase 4 (EB IVb). Pounder with two flattened ends (7 × 9 × 18 cm), complete. Heavy, dark gray-brown igneous stone.
4. Type SF.3a (SW. 334; IIID, 5.1, Debris over Room 20). Phase 6 (EB–MB). Pounder with one flattened face, complete. Medium-coarse–grained gray igneous stone.
—. Type SF.3a (SW. 416; IIIG/H, 1a, Room 23). Phase 7A (MB I). Pounder, roughly square in cross section, complete (4 × 4 × 9 cm). Fine-grained gray igneous stone.
—. Type SF.3a (SW. 414; IIIG/H, 1a, Room 23). Phase 7A (MB I). Pounder, elongated and well rounded, complete (3.0 × 6.5 × 13.0 cm). Coarse-grained greenish-gray igneous stone.

Figure 227. Stone Mortars and Grinder from Area III (Phase 4; Period E — Early Bronze Age IVb)

1a. Type SF.3c (SW. 349a; IIID, 5.4, Room 12). Phase 4. (See pl. 128a). Mortar, nearly complete. White limestone.
1b. Type SF.3a (SW. 349b; IIID, 5.4, Room 12). Phase 4. Grinder. One end broken. White limestone.
2. Type SF.3c (SW. 139; IIIC, 4.10, Room 9). Phase 4. Mortar with one end broken. Cream-colored limestone.
3. Type SF.3c (SW. 413; IIIJ, 1.2). Phase 4. Mortar, broken at edges. Cream-colored limestone.
4. Type SF.3c (SW. 373; IIIJ, 1.2). Phase 4. Mortar, broken on one end. Dark gray vesicular basalt.

Figure 227

Stone Mortars and Grinder from Area III (Phase 4; Period E — Early Bronze Age IVb). Scale 1:5

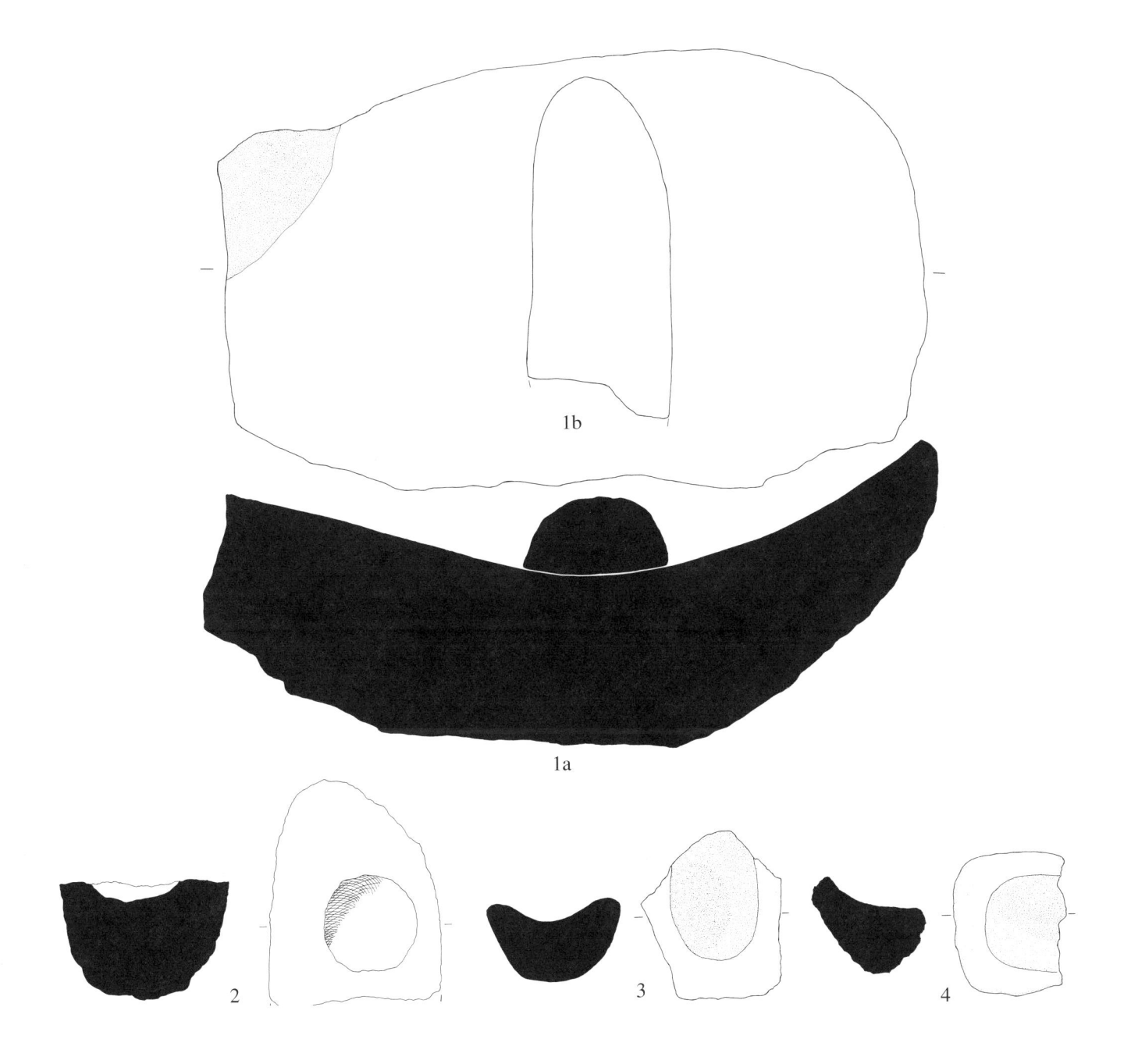

Figure 228. Stone Grinders from Area III (Phases 1C and 3–7A; Periods G to D — Early Bronze Age III to Middle Bronze Age I)

1. Type SF.3a (SW. 363; IIIB, 2.9, Room 1B). Phase 3 (EB IVa). Grinder, broken at one end. Cream-colored limestone, well weathered and slightly pock marked.
2. Type SF.3a (SW. 409; IIIB, 2.9, Room 1B). Phase 3 (EB IVa). Grinder, complete except for tip at one end. Cream-colored limestone.
—. Type SF.3a (SW. 588; IIIG/H, 1.11, Pit). Phase 1C (EB III). Grinder, incomplete. Elliptical-shaped vesicular basalt (10 cm long).
3. Type SF.3a (SW. 45; IIIA, 1.4, Room 11). Phase 4 (EB IVb). Grinder, complete. Cream limestone.
4. Type SF.3a (SW. 136; IIIC, 4.10, Room 9). Phase 4 (EB IVb). Grinder, broken at one end. Cream limestone.
5. Type SF.3a (SW. 140; IIIC, 4.10, Room 9). Phase 4 (EB IVb). Grinder, partially broken at one end. Dark gray tufa, very pitted.
6. Type SF.3a (SW. 138; IIIC, 4.9, Room 19A). Phase 5 (EB IVb). Grinder, broken at one end. Cream limestone, very round surfaces.
7. Type SF.3a (SW. 137; IIIC, 4.9, Room 19A). Phase 5 (EB IVb). Grinder, broken at one end. Cream limestone. Very pitted surface with two irregular-shaped holes on flat side.
—. Type SF.3a (SW. 144; IIIC, 4.9, Room 19A). Phase 5 (EB IVb). Grinder, broken at an approximately 40 degree angle from one end ($3.5 \times 3.5 \times 9.0$ cm). Light gray limestone with light brown incrustation on surfaces.
8. Type SF.3a (SW. 158; IIIG, 3.1, Room 18). Phase 4 (EB IVb). Grinder. Complete except for chips off one end. Cream limestone.
—. Type SF.3a (SW. 432; IIIG/H, 1.7, Room 18). Phase 4 (EB IVb). Grinder, roughly rectangular with asymmetric parabolic section. Cream-colored limestone. Complete ($8 \times 13 \times 14$ cm).
—. Type SF.3a (SW. 453; IIIG/H, 1.7, Room 18). Phase 4 (EB IVb). Grinder. Portion of elliptical-shaped cream limestone.
—. Type SF.3a (SW. 581; IIIG/H, 1.5, Room 17). Phase 4 (EB IVb). Grinder. Large elliptical grinding stone recut with a circular depression in the grinding face for use as a mortar or door socket. Complete ($11 \times 13 \times 36$ cm).
—. Type SF.3a (SW. 590; IIIG/H, 1.7, Room 18). Phase 4 (EB IVb). Grinders. Elliptical limestone. Seven examples, four complete ($5 \times 14 \times 40$ cm; $6 \times 15 \times 32$ cm; $6 \times 11 \times 34$ cm; and $4 \times 13 \times 29$ cm) and three half portions ($10 \times 14 \times 20$ cm; $7 \times 15 \times 23$ cm; and $11 \times 14 \times 20$ cm).
—. Type SF.3a (SW. 658; IIIG/H, 1.7, Room 18). Phase 4 (EB IVb). Grinder. Incomplete fragment ($5.5 \times 11.0 \times 18.0$ cm). Sandy stone with upper half of non-grinding surface composed of concreted pebbles.
—. Type SF.3a (SW. 451; IIIG/H, 1.3, Room 22A). Phase 5 (EB IVb). Grinder. Half of an ellipical, cream-colored limestone. Grinding face moderately pitted ($5 \times 12 \times 15$ cm).
—. Type SF.3a (SW. 454; IIIG/H, 1.3, Room 22A). Phase 5 (EB IVb). Grinder. Portion of elongate rectangular limestone ($3 \times 11 \times 19$ cm).
—. Type SF.3a (SW. 561; IIIG/H, 1.3, Room 22A). Phase 5 (EB IVb). Grinder. Fragment of elliptical dark gray vesicular basalt ($7 \times 12 \times 13$ cm).
—. Type SF.3a (SW. 564; IIIG/H, 1.3, Room 22A). Phase 5 (EB IVb). Grinder. Portion of elongate cream-colored limestone with shallow parabolic cross section ($4.5 \times 11.0 \times 20.0$ cm).
—. Type SF.3a (SW. 565; IIIG/H, 1.3, Room 22A). Phase 5 (EB IVb). Grinder. Portion of elliptical dark gray vesicular basalt ($5 \times 10 \times 14$ cm).
—. Type SF.3a (SW. 566; IIIG/H, 1.3, Room 22A). Phase 5 (EB IVb). Grinder. Portion of elliptical coarse pock-marked limestone ($7.5 \times 10.0 \times 14.0$ cm).
—. Type SF.3a (SW. 580; IIIG/H, 1.3, Room 22A). Phase 5 (EB IVb). Grinder. Portion of elliptical limestone ($5.5 \times 10.0 \times 13.0$ cm).
9. Type SF.3a (SW. 370; IIIG/H, 1b, Room 24). Phase 7A (MB I). Grinder. Cream-colored limestone. Broken at one end and chipped on one side.
10. Type SF.3a (SW. 380; IIIG/H, 1b, Room 24). Phase 7A (MB I). Grinder. Cream-colored limestone. Complete.
11. Type SF.3a (SW. 157; IIIH, 1.1; Extramural). Phase 6/7 (EB–MB). Grinder. Cream-colored limestone. Chipped on one side of one end.
—. Type SF.3a (SW. 161; IIIH, 1.1; Extramural). Phase 6/7 (EB–MB). Grinder. Dark gray, pitted, tufa. Incomplete. Shape similar to SW. 157 above.
—. Type SF.3a (SW. 350; IIIG/H, 1b, Room 24). Phase 7A (MB I). Grinder. Dark gray vesicular basalt. Complete ($8 \times 14 \times 42$ cm).
—. Type SF.3a (SW. 369; IIIG/H, 1b, Room 24). Phase 7A (MB I). Grinder. Dark gray vesicular basalt. Incomplete ($8 \times 12.5 \times 13$ cm).
—. Type SF.3a (SW. 372; IIIG/H, 1b, Room 24). Phase 7A (MB I). Grinder. Cream-colored limestone with small pock marks on outer surfaces. One large and irregular-shaped depression on flattened grinding face, possibly used as a mortar. Incomplete with one third of one end broken away ($3.0 \times 9.0 \times 15.5$ cm).
—. Type SF.3a (SW. 375; IIIG/H, 1b, Room 24). Phase 7A (MB I). Grinder. Cream-colored limestone, coarsely pock marked. Parabolic in cross section with flattened grinding face. Incomplete with one quarter missing at one end ($6 \times 14 \times 24$ cm).
—. Type SF.3a (SW. 376; IIIG/H, 1b, Room 24). Phase 7A (MB I). Grinder. Cream-colored limestone. Irregular asymmetric cross section with flat grinding face. Incomplete, broken at both ends ($7.5 \times 13.5 \times 11.0$ cm).
—. Type SF.3a (SW. 377; IIIG/H, 1b, Room 24). Phase 7A (MB I). Grinder. Cream-colored, pock-marked limestone. Elliptical with parabolic cross section and flat grinding face. Incomplete, about one third of one end missing ($7.0 \times 12.5 \times 23.5$ cm).
—. Type SF.3a (SW. 378; IIIG/H, 1b, Room 24). Phase 7A (MB I). Grinder. Cream-colored, pock-marked limestone. Rectangular in plan and roughly parabolic in section with flat grinding face and one long shallow groove. Incomplete ($6.5 \times 13.5 \times 18.0$ cm).
—. Type SF.3a (SW. 410; IIIG/H, 1a, Room 23). Phase 7A (MB I). Grinder. Cream-colored limestone. Almost rectangular in plan and semi-circular in section. Incomplete, about one half extant ($4 \times 9 \times 12$ cm).
—. Type SF.3a (SW. 426; IIIG/H, 1a, Room 23). Phase 7A (MB I). Grinder. Cream-colored limestone. Asymmetric parabolic cross section with flat, slightly pitted, grinding face. Incomplete portion ($6 \times 14 \times 13$ cm).
—. Type SF.3a (SW. 452; IIIG/H, 1.1, Courtyard). Phase 6 (EB–MB). Grinder. Cream-colored limestone. Roughly square portion with parabolic cross section and flat grinding face. Incomplete ($7 \times 12 \times 16$ cm).
12. Type SF.3a (SW. 159; IIIF, 1.1). Phase 6/7 (EB–MB). Grinder. Cream-colored limestone. One end broken.
—. Type SF.3a (SW. 412; IIIJ, 1). Phase 6/7 (EB–MB). Grinder. Cream-colored limestone. Elliptical fragment, semi-circular in section with flat, moderately pitted, grinding face. Incomplete ($5 \times 10 \times 10$ cm).
—. Type SF.3a (SW. 494; IIIK, 1.1). Phase 6/7 (EB–MB). Grinder. Cream-colored limestone. Elliptical fragment ($7 \times 16 \times 25$ cm).
—. Type SF.3a (SW. 533; IIIK, 1.1). Phase 6/7 (EB–MB). Grinder. Gray vesicular basalt. Incomplete fragment (7 cm long).
—. Type SF.3a (SW. 534; IIIL, 1.1). Phase 6/7 (EB–MB). Grinder. Gray vesicular basalt. Incomplete fragment.

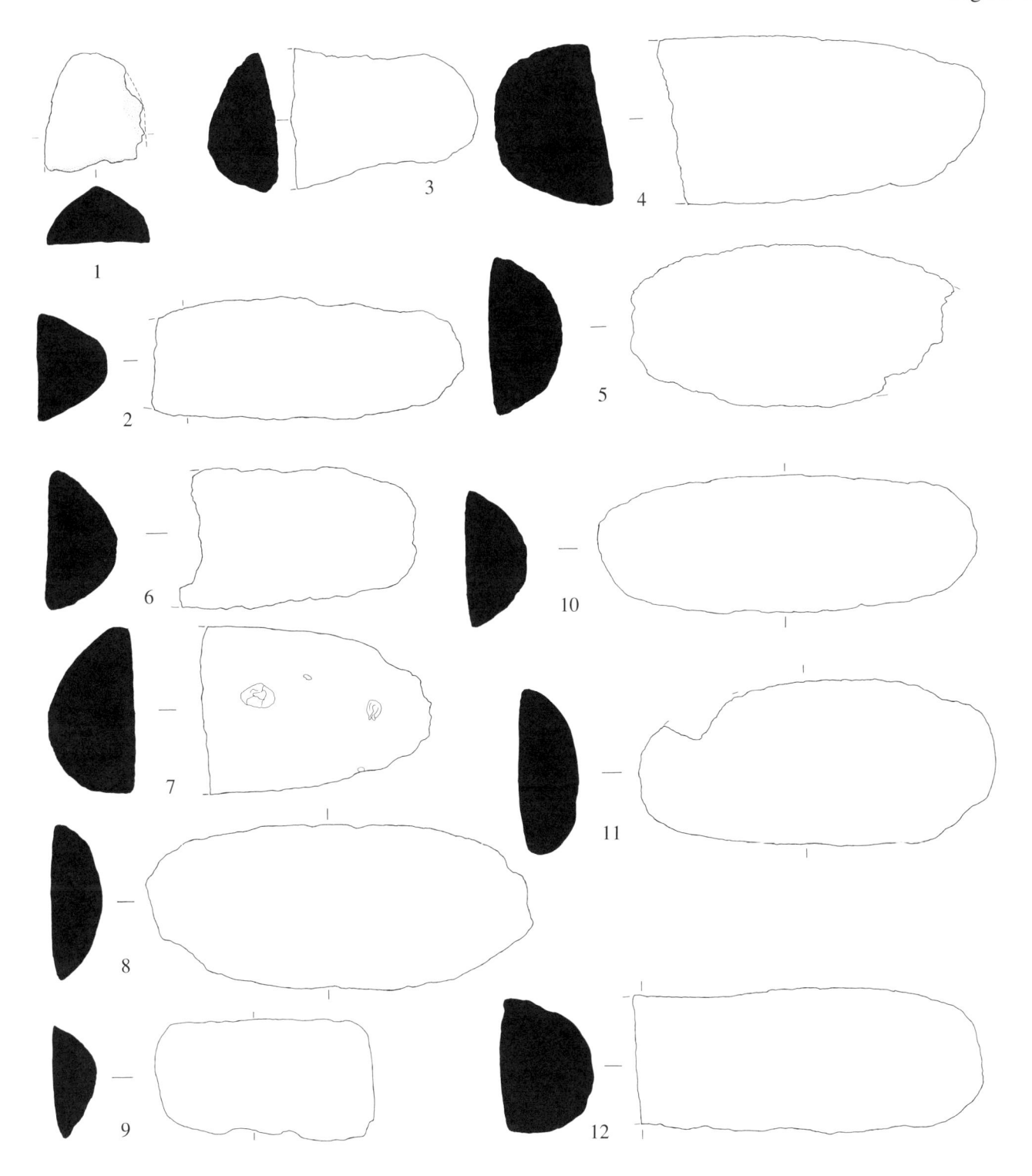

Figure 228

Stone Grinders from Area III (Phases 1C and 3–7A; Periods G to D — Early Bronze Age III to Middle Bronze Age I). Scale 1:5

Figure 229. Miscellaneous Stone Vessels and Objects from Area III (Phases 1C and 4–7; Periods G, E, E–D, and D — Early Bronze Age III, Early Bronze Age IVb, Early–Middle Bronze Age, and Middle Bronze Age I)

1. Type SF.3c (SW. 339; IIIC, 4.9, Rooms 19A). Phase 5 (EB IVb). Bowl fragment. Gray and red medium-grained igneous stone.
2. Type SF.3c (SW. 340; IIIA, 1.1). Phase 7 (MB I). Bowl fragment. Quartzite with a red outer skin and a greenish-gray interior.
3. Type SV.4 (SW. 186; IIIF, 1.2, Debris). Phase 5 (EB IVb). Jar drainage hole stopper. Limestone.
4. Type SV.4 (SW. 198; IIIG, 3.1, Room 18). Phase 4 (EB IVb). Jar drainage hole stopper. Limestone.
5. Type SF.3f (SW. 23; IIIB, 2.2). Phase 5 (EB IVb). Lid. Black stone, highly polished on surfaces.
—. Type SF.3a (SW. 472; IIIG/H, 1.9, Room 3B). Phase 3 (EB IVa). Polisher. Flattened river stone with rounded, water-worn edges (Diameter, 6.5 cm).
—. Type SF.3a (SW. 406; IIIG/H, 1a, Room 23). Phase 7A (MB I). Rubbing stone. Euphrates pebble with one flattened face and asymmetric in cross section ($2 \times 3 \times 6$ cm).
—. Type SF.3f (SW. 415; IIIJ, 1.2). Phase 4 (EB IVb). Whetstone. Flattened fragment of Euphrates pebble ($2 \times 6 \times 9$ cm).
6. Type SF.3a (SW. 224; IIIF, 1.1). Phase 6/7 (EB–MB). Scraper. Water-smoothed Euphrates stone. Brown wedge-shaped stone broken at narrow, handle end.
7. Type SF.3a (SW. 151; IIID, 5.5, Room 11A). Phase 4 (EB IVb). Scraper. Light gray chert. Worked around most of edge for cutting or scraping.
8. Type SF.3a (SW. 345; IIIF, 1.2, Debris). Phase 5 (EB IVb). Scraper. Fine-grained igneous rock.
—. Type SF.3a (SW. 464; IIIG/H, 1.7, Room 18). Phase 4 (EB IVb). Scraper. Dark gray basalt fragment (6 cm long).
9. Type SF.3b (SW. 11; IIIB, 1.6, above Room 7). Phase 6 (EB–MB). Sling bullet. Brown with dark red streaks and many white flecks on surface. Hand polished or waterworn Euphrates pebble.
10. Type SF.3f (SW. 69; IIIA, 4.5, Room 4B). Phase 3 (EB IVa). Spindle whorl. Gray granite with white inclusions. About one half extant.
11. Type SF.3e (SW. 283; IIIF, 1.2, Debris). Phase 5 (EB IVb). Digging stick weight. Cream limestone. Hole bored from both sides.
12. Type SF.3d (SW. 422; IIIA, 4.2, Room 8A). Phase 4 (EB IVb). Door socket. Cream-colored limestone.
—. Type SF.3d (SW. 506; IIIK, 1.1). Phase 6/7 (EB–MB). Door socket. Dark gray vesicular basalt penetrated in center with a 5 cm wide socket hole.
13. Type SF.3e (SW. 163; IIIG, 3.1, Room 18). Phase 4 (EB IVb). Anchor weight. Gray basalt. Hole at top of one broad side cut from both sides.
14. Type SF.3e (SW. 244; IIIB, 2.13). Phase 1C (EB III). Weight. Gray basalt pierced longitudinally. Broken at both ends.
15. Type SF.3e (SW. 188; IIIE, 3.1, Room 15). Phase 4 (EB IVb). Weight or macehead. Hard, whitish stone with a soap-like texture. Fragment broken at narrow end. Drilled hole in center of broad end incomplete and remains of a hole in the broken section of the narrow end.
16. Type SF.3e (SW. 199; IIIF, 1.2, Debris). Phase 5 (EB IVb). Loom weight. Hard limestone with chalky deposits on the surfaces. Incomplete. Central hole drilled from both sides.

Figure 229

Miscellaneous Stone Vessels and Objects from Area III (Phases 1C and 4–7; Periods G, E, E–D, and D — Early Bronze Age III, Early Bronze Age IVb, Early–Middle Bronze Age, and Middle Bronze Age I). Scale 1:5

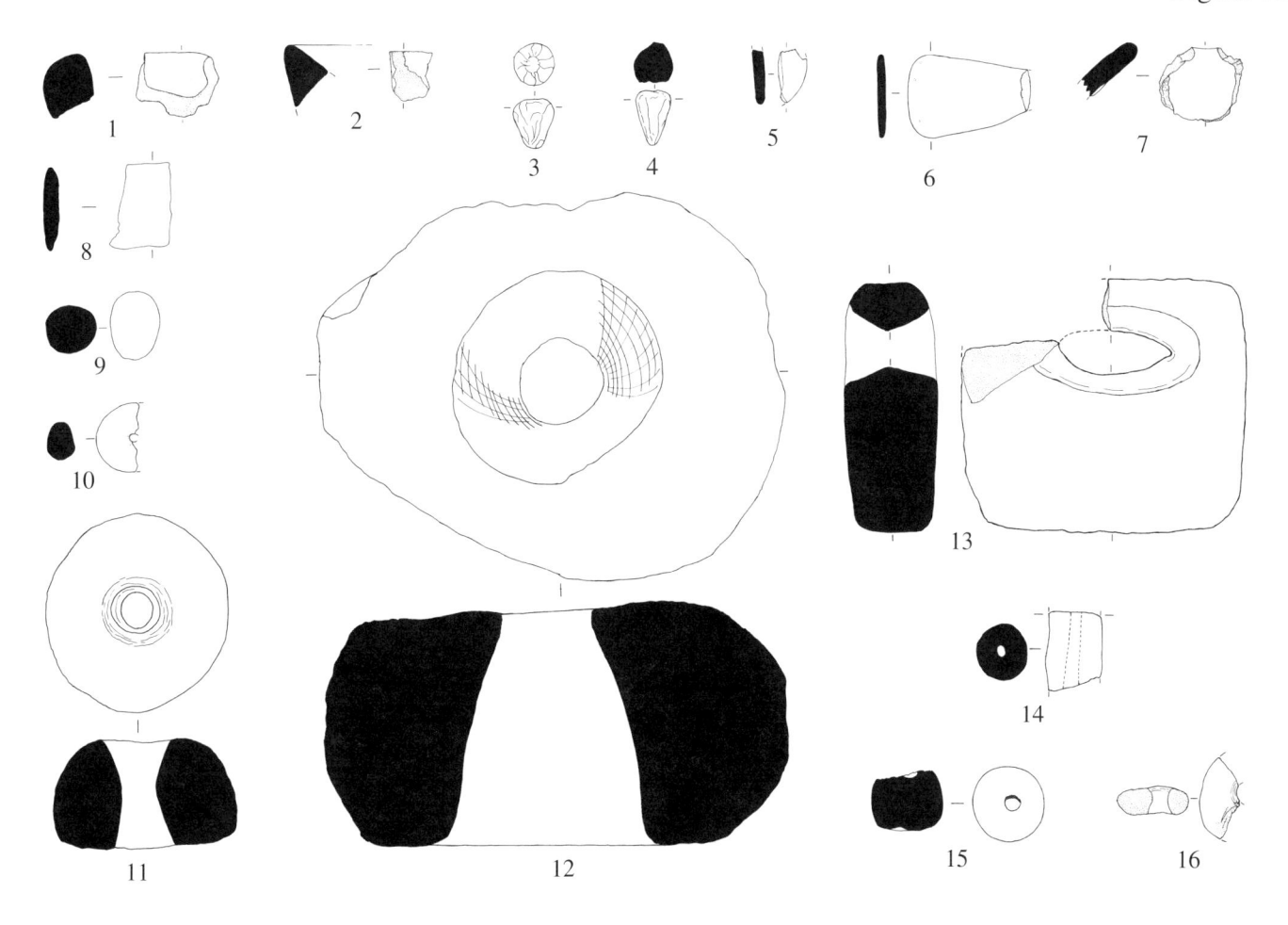

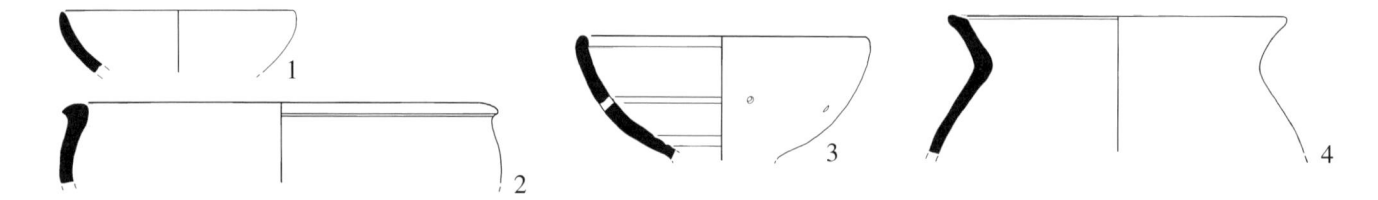

Figure 230

Figure 230. Pottery from Operation 5 (Phase 1; Period H — Early Bronze Age II). Scale 1:5

1. SBR. C.II.d (TS. 3839; Op. 5, 32.8). Small rim and most of wall profile; base missing. Ware description not available.
2. BR. N.II.a (TS. 3206; Op. 5, 32.8). Large rim and upper wall segment. Ware description not available.
3. SR. B.I.b (TS. 3202; Op. 5, 32.8). Small rim and most of wall profile; base missing. Two strainer holes extant in wall of the preserved fragment. Ware description not available.
4. JR. G.I.c (TS. 3268; Op. 5, 32.8). Large rim, neck, and upper shoulder segment. Ware description not available.

Figure 231

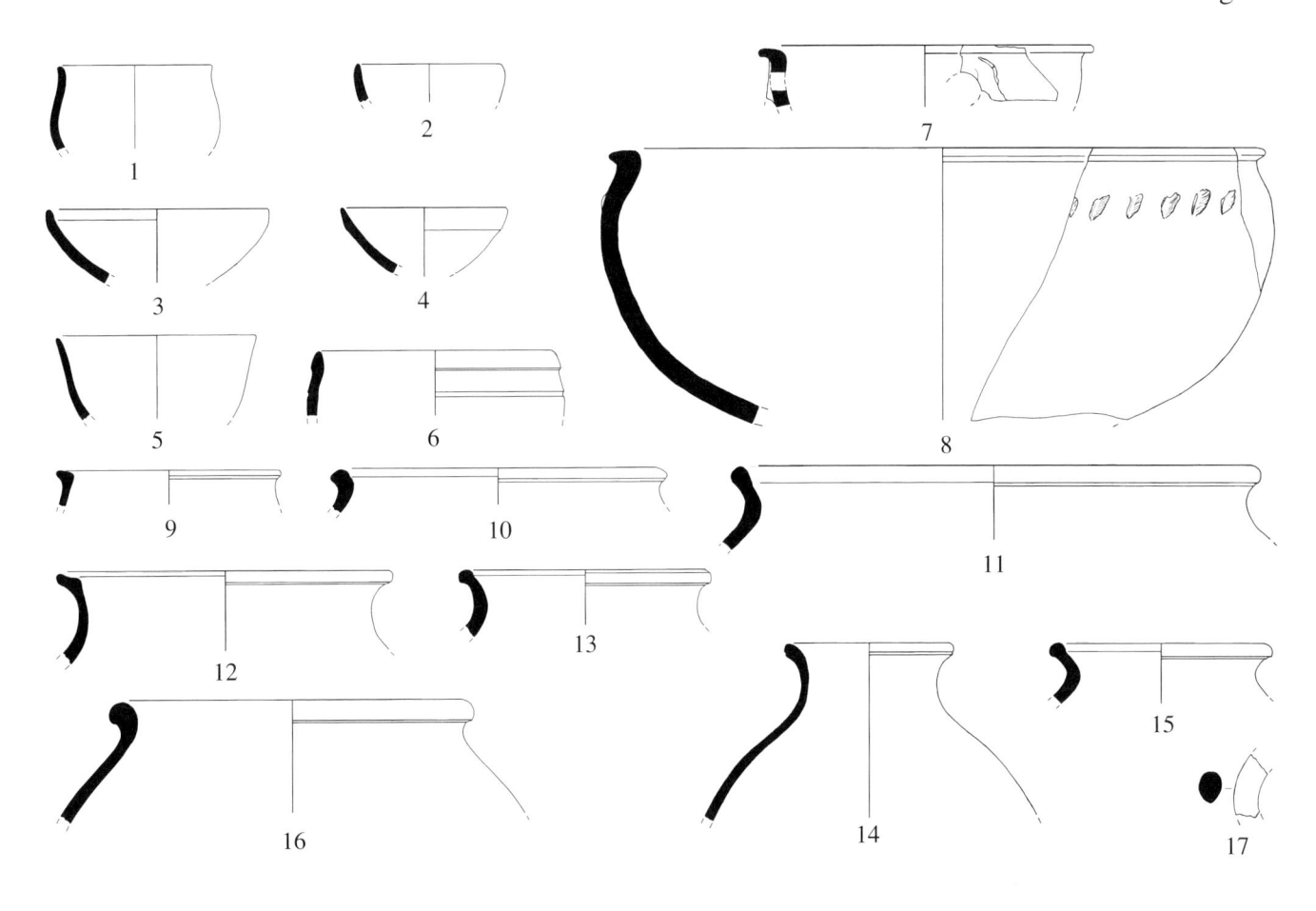

Pottery from Operation 5 (Phase 2; Period G — Early Bronze Age III). Scale 1:5

1. SBR. A.I.h (TS. 4035; Op. 5, 32.1). Small rim and nearly complete body profile; base missing. Ware description not available.
2. SBR. C.II.a (TS. 3965; Op. 5, 32.1). Small rim and upper wall segment. Ware description not available.
3. SBR. C.II.d (TS. 3263; Op. 5, 32.1). Small rim and most of body profile; base missing. Ware description not available.
4. SBR. C.II.d (TS. 3265; Op. 5, 32.1). Small rim and most of body profile; base missing. Ware description not available.
5. BR. A.III.a (TS. 3186; Op. 5, 32.1). Small rim and most of body profile; base missing. Ware description not available.
6. BR. D.VII.a (TS. 4034; Op. 5, 32.1). Small rim and upper wall segment. Ware description not available.
7. BR. N.II.a (TS. 3210; Op. 5, 32.1). About 1/12 rim and upper wall segment with remains of a spout in the upper wall of the vessel. Ware description not available.
8. BR. N.II.a (TS. 3267; Op. 5, 32.1). About 1/12 rim and most of wall profile. Tool-impressed stab marks in horizontal line on upper wall for decoration. Ware description not available.
9. SJR. A.II.a (TS. 3835; Op. 5, 32.1). Small rim and upper shoulder segment. Ware description not available.
10. JR. E.II.l (TS. 3834; Op. 5, 32.1). Small rim and neck segment. Ware description not available.
11. JR. F.I.c (TS. 3209; Op. 5, 32.1). Small rim, neck, and upper shoulder segment. Ware description not available.
12. JR. G.I.c (TS. 3831; Op. 5, 32.1). Large rim, neck, and upper shoulder segment. Ware description not available.
13. JR. J.I.j (TS. 3960; Op. 5, 32.1). Small rim, neck, and upper shoulder segment. Ware description not available.
14. JR. J.III.n (TS. 3266; Op. 5, 32.1). Small rim, neck, and complete shoulder profile. Ware description not available.
15. JR. K.I.a (TS. 3264; Op. 5, 32.1). Small rim, neck, and upper shoulder segment. Ware description not available.
16. JR. P.I.a (TS. 3830; Op. 5, 32.1). Large rim, neck, and upper shoulder segment. Ware description not available.
17. Hd. B (TS. 4059; Op. 5, 32.1). Incomplete round strap handle. Ware description not available.

Other Type Series Examples: (1) JR. F.I.d (TS. 3390), (2) JR. G.II.a (TS. 4040), (3) JR. G.II.b (TS. 3187), (4) JR. J.I.j (TS. 3958), (5) JR. J.II.m (TS. 3825).

Figure 232. Pottery from Operation 5 (Phase 3; Period G — Early Bronze Age III)

1. SBR. A.II.c (TS. 3996; Op. 5, 15.2). Small rim and upper wall of cup. Ware description not available.
2. SBR. B.I.c (TS. 3837; Op. 5, 30.10). Small rim and upper wall of cup. Ware description not available.
3. SBR. B.I.h (TS. 3998; Op. 5, 15.5). Small rim and upper wall of cup. Ware description not available.
4. SBR. B.I.o (TS. 3203; Op. 5, 30.5). Large rim and most of wall profile; base missing. Ware description not available.
5. BR. A.II.d (TS. 4001; Op. 5, 15.8). Small rim and upper wall segment. Ware description not available.
6. BR. D.I.a (TS. 3881; Op. 5, 15.6). Small rim and upper wall segment. Ware description not available.
7. BR. D.VII.a (TS. 3993; Op. 5, 15.8). Small rim and upper wall segment. Ware description not available.
8. BR. F.IV.d (TS. 3207; Op. 5, 30.6). Large rim and upper wall segment. Ware description not available.
9. SJR. A.III.a (TS. 3751; Op. 5, 17.5 = 20.2). Small rim, neck, and upper shoulder segment. Ware description not available.
10. SJR. D.I.a (TS. 3892; Op. 5, 15.3). Small rim and upper shoulder segment. Ware description not available.
11. SJR. D.I.a (TS. 3962; Op. 5, 30.10). Small rim and upper shoulder segment. Ware description not available.
12. JR. F.II.a (TS. 3743; Op. 5, 15.6). Large rim, neck, and upper shoulder segment. Ware description not available.
13. JR. F.II.b (TS. 3772; Op. 5, 17.5 = 20.2). Large rim, neck, and upper shoulder segment. Ware description not available.
14. JR. G.III.a (PM. D.17; TS. 3248; Op. 5, 15.6). Large rim, neck, and shoulder segment with incomplete potter's mark incised on outside shoulder before firing. Ware description not available.
15. JR. H.III.u (TS. 3963; Op. 5, 30.10). Small rim and upper shoulder segment. Ware description not available.
16. JR. J.III.c (TS. 3826; Op. 5, 30.6). Small rim and neck segment. Ware description not available.
17. JR. J.III.j (TS. 3205; Op. 5, 30.5). Small rim and neck segment. Ware description not available.
18. JR. J.VI.a (TS. 3719; Op. 5, 17.5 = 20.2). Small rim, neck, and upper shoulder segment. Ware description not available.
19. JR. P.II.a (TS. 3997; Op. 5, 15.3). Large rim, neck, and upper shoulder segment. Ware description not available.
20. JR. Q.II.a (TS. 3774; Op. 5, 30.8). Large rim, neck, and upper shoulder segment. Ware description not available.
21. PS. B.I.b (TS. 3180; Op. 5, 30.?). Small rim segment and small portion of wall of a pot stand. Ware description not available.
22. PS. B.I.b (TS. 3189; Op. 5, 30.9). About 1/12 rim and portion of wall of a pot stand decorated with checkerboard-type incisions. Ware description not available.
23. BE. B.II (TS. 3882; Op. 5, 15.6). Complete disk base with concave depression on the bottom. Ware description not available.
24. BE. E.I.d (TS. 3961; Op. 5, 30.8). Complete ring base and portion of lower wall of vessel. Ware description not available.
25. BE. E.I.d (TS. 4048; Op. 5, 15.7). Incomplete ring base and portion of lower wall of vessel. Ware description not available.
26. BE. E.I.l (TS. 3838; Op. 5, 30.10). Complete ring base and portion of lower wall of vessel. Ware description not available.
27. JR.Sh. + Stub of Handle (PM. A.4; TS. 3740; Op. 5, 15.6). Large body sherd from a one- or two-handled jar with a potter's mark incised on the outer wall before firing. Ware description not available.
—. JR.Sh. (PM. A.5; TS. 4203; Op. 5, 15.5). Jar body sherd with a potter's mark consisting of a single incision, 3 cm long and 3 mm wide. Ware description not available.
28. JR.Hd. B (TS. 3883; Op. 5, 15.6). Jar body sherd with remains of a wide and thick vertical strap handle. Ware description not available.
29. SJR.Sh. Pt. (TS. 3884; Op. 5, 15.6). Small jar neck and shoulder fragment painted with a black slip-like decoration. Ware description not available.

Other Type Series Examples: (1) JR. O.III.d (TS. 3208), (2) BE. E.I.i (TS. 3895).

Figure 232

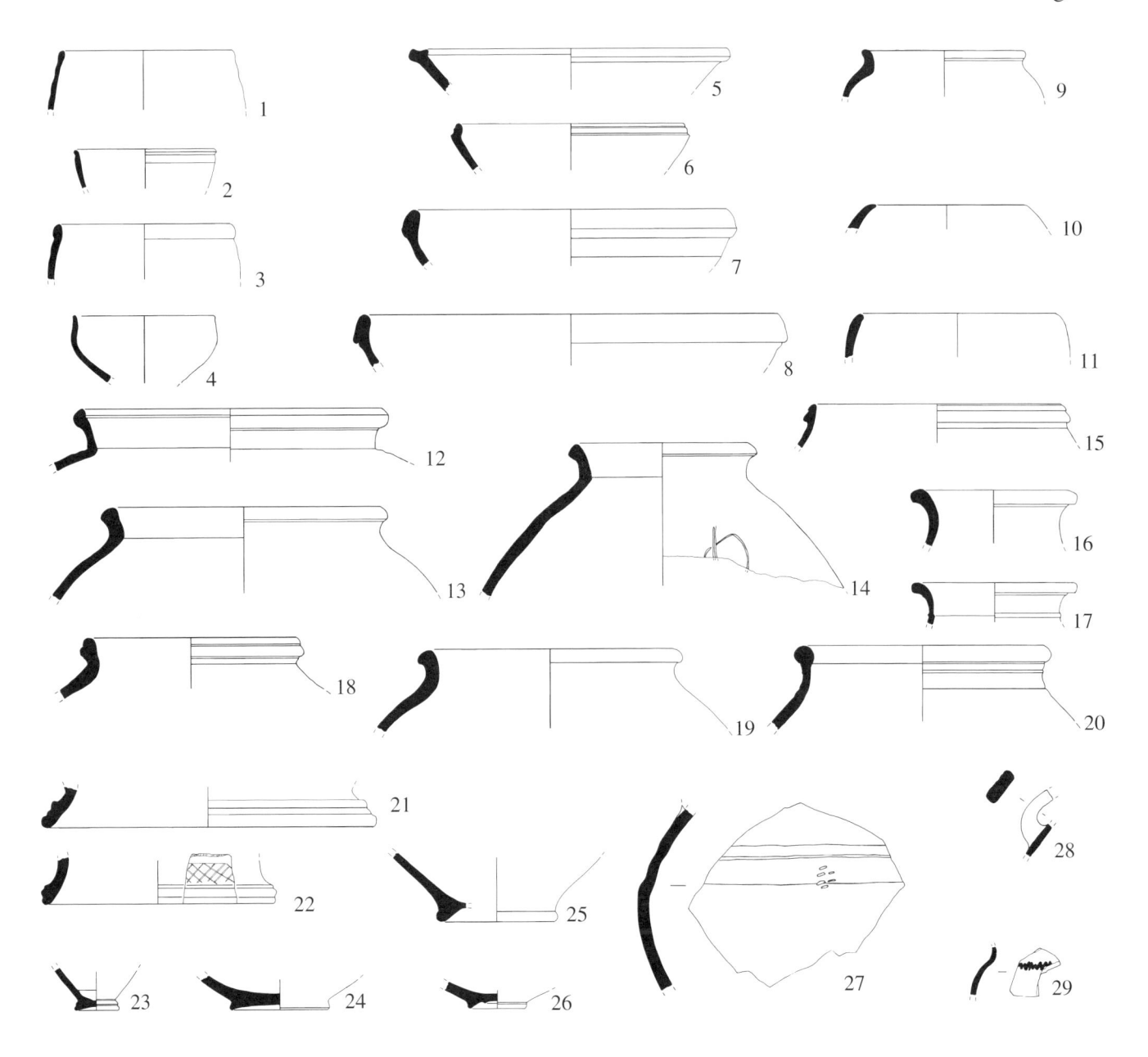

Pottery from Operation 5 (Phase 3; Period G — Early Bronze Age III). Scale 1:5

Figure 233

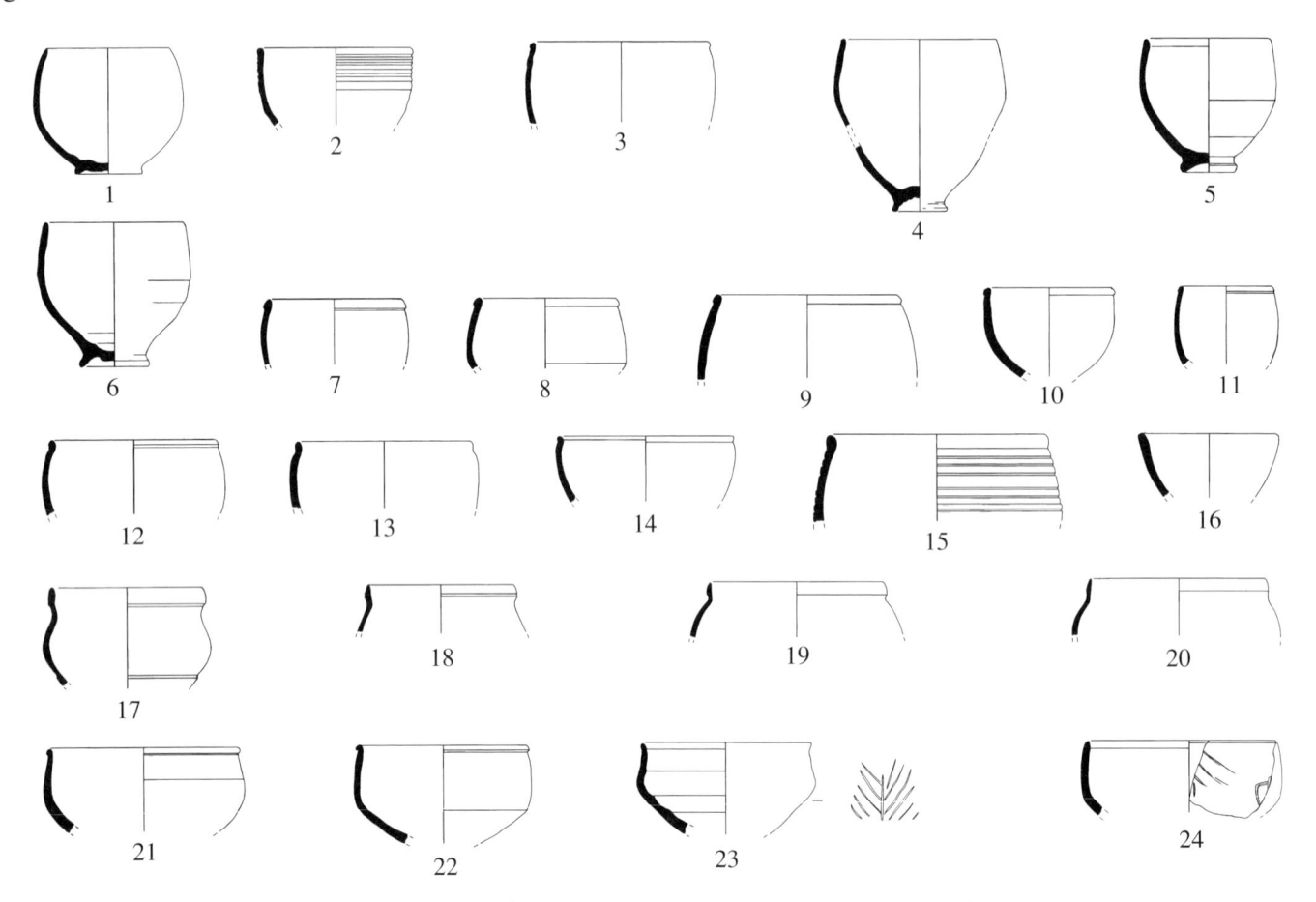

Pottery from Operation 5 (Phase 4; Period F — Early Bronze Age IVa). Scale 1:5

1. SBR. A.I.a (TS. 3246; Op. 5, 14.2). Small rim segment with complete profile of wall and base. Slightly coarse buff ware with white and gray lime grits, evenly fired. Self slip in and out.
2. SBR. A.I.c (TS. 3641; Op. 5, 17.1). Small segment of rim and nearly complete profile of body wall preserved. Horizontal wheelmade lines on outside wall. Ware description not available.
3. SBR. A.I.c (TS. 3929; Op. 5, 11.5). Small rim and upper portion of wall segment. Ware description not available.
4. SBR. A.I.d (TS. 3257; Op. 5, 17.4). Nearly complete profile of a cup with deep ring base. Ware description not available.
5. SBR. A.I.e (SW. 764; Op. 5, 14.6). Complete cup with splayed ring base. Ware description not available.
6. SBR. A.II.c (TS. 3258; Op. 5, 18.2). Complete base and about 1/8 rim segment mended to complete profile. Splayed ring base with projected disk inside the ring. Slightly coarse pinkish-buff ware with medium quantity of black and white lime and small gold-colored mica grits, evenly fired. Creamy-green slip out.
7. SBR. B.I.d (TS. 3724; Op. 5, 18.4). Small rim and upper wall segment. Ware description not available.
8. SBR. B.I.d (TS. 3887; Op. 5, 17.1). Small rim, upper wall, and upper portion of lower wall extant. Ware description not available.
9. SBR. B.I.d (TS. 3784; Op. 5, 14.5). Small rim and upper wall segment. Ware description not available.
10. SBR. B.I.d (TS. 3888; Op. 5, 17.1). Small rim and most of wall profile extant. Ware description not available.
11. SBR. B.I.h (TS. 3761; Op. 5, 17.4). Small rim and most of wall profile extant. Ware description not available.
12. SBR. B.I.i (TS. 3755; Op. 5, 18.2). Small rim and upper wall segment. Ware description not available.
13. SBR. B.I.i (TS. 3968; Op. 5, 13.4). Small rim and upper wall segment. Ware description not available.
14. SBR. B.I.i (TS. 4002; Op. 5, 13.7). Small rim and upper wall segment. Ware description not available.
15. SBR. B.I.j (TS. 3822; Op. 5, 13.7). Small rim and upper wall segment with wheelmade horizontal lines on outside wall. Ware description not available.
16. SBR. C.II.c (TS. 3783; Op. 5, 14.5). Small rim and most of wall profile extant. Ware description not available.
17. SBR. D.I.b (TS. 3260; Op. 5, 18.5). Nearly complete rim and body profile of vessel; base missing. Ware description not available.
18. SBR. D.I.c (TS. 3244; Op. 5, 13.5). Small rim and upper shoulder segment. Ware description not available.
19. SBR. D.I.c (TS. 3938; Op. 5, 11.2). Small rim and upper shoulder segment. Ware description not available.
20. SBR. D.I.c (TS. 3942; Op. 5, 11.2). Small rim and upper shoulder segment. Ware description not available.
21. SBR. F.I.a (TS. 3723; Op. 5, 18.6). About 1/3 rim and most of wall profile; base missing. Ware description not available.
22. SBR. F.I.a (TS. 3769; Op. 5, 13.4). About 1/2 rim and most of wall profile; base missing. Ware description not available.
23. SBR. F.I.b (IP [G.4] D.I; PM. D.19; TS. 3717; Op. 5, 18.5). About 2/3 rim and most of wall profile; base missing. Nearly complete pot mark on outside wall. Ware description not available.
24. SBR. F.I.c (IP [G.4] D.II; PM. D.20 and PM. D.3; TS. 3985; Op. 5, 14.6). About 1/6 rim and most of wall profile; base missing. Two incomplete potter's marks incised on outside wall before firing. Ware description not available.

Figure 234

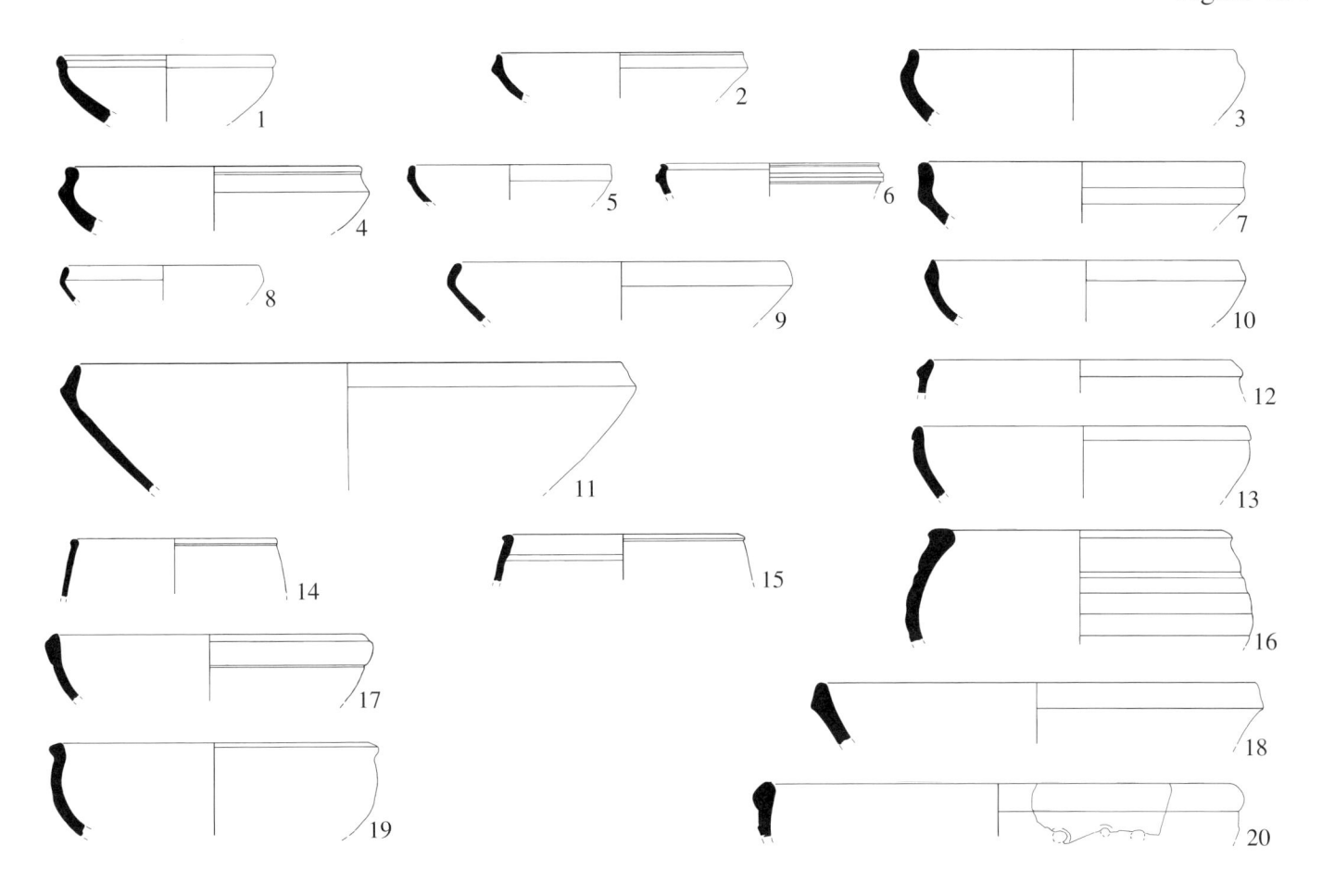

Pottery from Operation 5 (Phase 4, Period F) Early Bronze Age IVa (*cont.*). Scale 1:5

1. BR. A.IV.d (TS. 3989; Op. 5, 13.7). About 1/3 rim and most of wall profile. Ware description not available.
2. BR. C.I.a (TS. 3994; Op. 5, 13.5). Small rim and upper wall segment. Ware description not available.
3. BR. C.I.e (TS. 3722; Op. 5, 18.6). Small rim and upper wall segment. Ware description not available.
4. BR. C.I.e (TS. 3749; Op. 5, 18.2). Small rim and upper wall segment. Ware description not available.
5. BR. D.I.a (TS. 3893; Op. 5, 13.5). Small rim and upper wall segment. Ware description not available.
6. BR. D.II.d (TS. 3752; Op. 5, 17.4). Small rim and upper wall segment. Ware description not available.
7. BR. E.I.a (TS. 3785; Op. 5, 14.5). Small rim and upper wall segment. Ware description not available.
8. BR. E.II.c (TS. 3995; Op. 5, 13.5). Small rim and upper wall segment. Ware description not available.
9. BR. E.III.c (TS. 3889; Op. 5, 13.5). Small rim and upper wall segment. Ware description not available.
10. BR. E.III.d (TS. 3747; Op. 5, 17.4). Small rim and upper wall segment. Ware description not available.
11. BR. F.IV.c (TS. 3911; Op. 5, 11.2 + 3). Large rim and most of wall profile; base missing. Ware description not available.
12. BR. F.IV.c (TS. 4004; Op. 5, 13.7). Small rim and upper wall segment. Ware description not available.
13. BR. G.I.e (TS. 3986; Op. 5, 14.6). Small rim and upper wall segment. Ware description not available.
14. BR. L.I.d (TS. 3725; Op. 5, 18.4). Small rim and upper wall segment. Ware description not available.
15. BR. L.I.d (TS. 3757; Op. 5, 17.4). Small rim and upper wall segment. Ware description not available.
16. BR. L.I.i (TS. 3945; Op. 5, 13.3). About 1/3 rim and upper wall segment. Ware description not available.
17. BR. L.III.d (TS. 3758; Op. 5, 18.2). Small rim and upper wall segment. Ware description not available.
18. BR. L.III.e (TS. 3988; Op. 5, 14.2). Small rim and upper wall segment. Ware description not available.
19. BR. N.II.a (TS. 3972; Op. 5, 11.7). Large rim and most of wall profile; base missing. Ware description not available.
20. BR. Q.I.a (TS. 3245; Op. 5, 13.5). About 1/8 rim and upper wall segment. Three extant holes manufactured in extant portion of the upper wall before firing; possibly compare JR. E.II.p (SW. 538) from Area IXA (fig. 140:10). Ware description not available.

Figure 235. Pottery from Operation 5 (Phase 4; Period F — Early Bronze Age IVa) (*cont.*)

1. SJR. A.I.a (PM. D.3; TS. 3894; Op. 5, 14.6). Small rim, neck, and upper shoulder segment with incomplete potter's mark incised on the shoulder before firing. Ware description not available.
2. JR. A.II.a (TS. 3640; Op. 5, 17.1). Small rim and upper wall segment. Ware description not available.
3. JR. A.II.a (TS. 3750; Op. 5, 18.2). Small rim and upper wall segment. Ware description not available.
4. JR. C.I.d (TS. 3242; Op. 5, 13.2). About 1/3 rim and most of body profile; base missing. Ware description not available.
5. JR. C.V.a (TS. 3241; Op. 5, 11.2). One half rim; nearly complete profile except for pedestal base. Slighly coarse pinkish-red ware with many fine black and white lime and white mica grits, evenly fired. Creamy-buff slip out. Fingernail-impressed decoration between connection of vessel body and pedestal-type stand.
6. JR. D.I.f (TS. 3657; Op. 5, 14.5). Small rim and upper wall segment. Ware description not available.
7. JR. D.V.a (TS. 3727; Op. 5, 18.6). About 1/3 rim and shoulder segment. Hard, fairly fine pinkish-buff ware with very few gold-colored mica and lime grits, evenly fired. Creamy-buff slip out and just over rim in.
8. JR. D.VI.c (TS. 3728; Op. 5, 18.6). About 1/4 segment. Fairly fine pinkish-buff ware with a few small white lime and gold-colored mica grits, evenly fired. Creamy-buff slip out and to base of collar over the rim in.
9. JR. H.III.u (TS. 3973; Op. 5, 13.7). Small rim and upper shoulder segment. Ware description not available.
10. JR. H.III.x (PM. A.8; TS. 3977; Op. 5, 13.3). About 1/6 rim and shoulder segment. Incomplete potter's mark incised on the shoulder before firing. Ware description not available.
11. JR. J.I.a (TS. 3954; Op. 5, 14.5). Small rim, neck, and upper shoulder segment. Ware description not available.
12. JR. J.II.c (TS. 3718; Op. 5, 17.4). Small rim, neck, and shoulder segment. Metallic-like ware. Ware description not available.
13. JR. J.II.i (TS. 3721; Op. 5, 18.6). Small rim and neck segment. Ware description not available.
14. JR. J.II.i (TS. 3756; Op. 5, 17.4). Small rim and neck segment. Ware description not available.
15. JR. J.III.c (TS. 3775; Op. 5, 11.3). About 1/2 rim, neck, and upper body profile. Ware description not available.
16. JR. J.III.c (TS. 4037; Op. 5, 17.1). About 1/2 rim, neck, and upper body profile. Ware description not available.
17. JR. J.III.g (TS. 3967; Op. 5, 13.2). Small rim, neck, and upper shoulder segment. Ware description not available.
18. JR. J.III.j (PM. A.6; TS. 3249; Op. 5, 17.1). About 2/3 rim and body profile. Incomplete potter's mark at base of neck, incised before firing. Ware description not available.
19. JR. J.III.m (TS. 3966; Op. 5, 13.1). About 1/2 rim and neck segment. Ware description not available.
20. JR. J.III.s (TS. 3720; Op. 5, 18.6). About 1/3 rim, neck, and upper shoulder segment. Ware description not available.
21. JR. J.III.s (TS. 4051; Op. 5, 18.6). Small rim and neck segment. Ware description not available.
22. JR. J.III.u (TS. 3748; Op. 5, 17.2). Small rim and neck segment. Ware description not available.
23. JR. J.III.w (TS. 3634; Op. 5, 17.1). About 1/2 rim and neck segment. Decorated in with black slip and out with black slip over rim and with three reserved bands around the lower part of the neck. Ware description not available.
24. JR. J.VI.a (TS. 3760; Op. 5, 17.4). Small rim and neck segment. Ware description not available.
25. JR. O.I.a (TS. 3944; Op. 5, 18.4). Small rim and shoulder segment. Ware description not available.
26. JR. O.I.b (TS. 3946; Op. 5, 17.4). Small rim and neck segment. Ware description not available.
27. JR. O.I.c (TS. 3920; Op. 5, 11.5). Small rim and shoulder segment. Ware description not available.
28. JR. O.II.e (TS. 3947; Op. 5, 18.4). Small rim and neck segment. Ware description not available.
29. JR. S (TS. 3844; Op. 5, 14.7). Small rim and upper shoulder segment. Ware description not available.

Figure 235

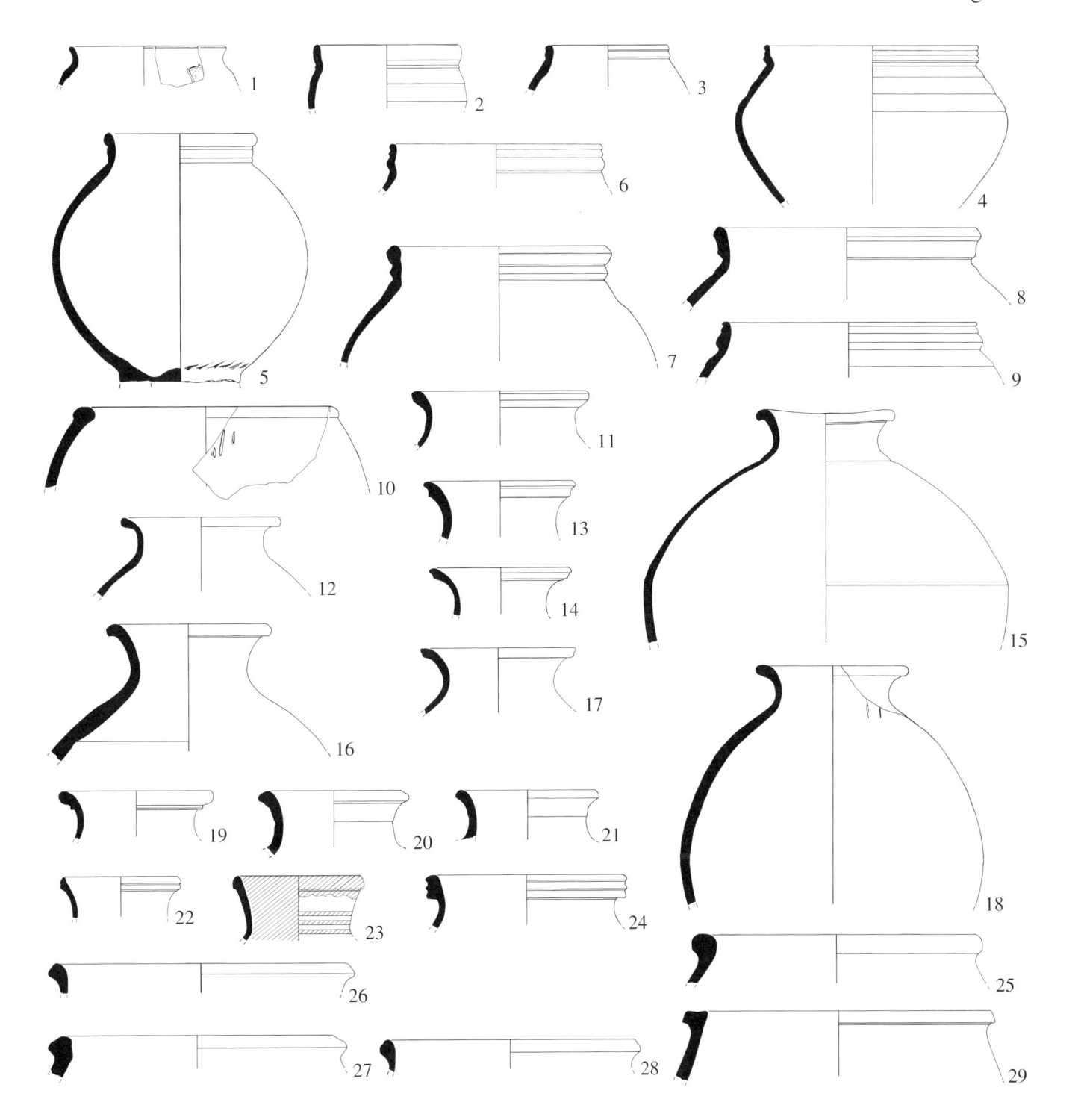

Pottery from Operation 5 (Phase 4; Period F — Early Bronze Age IVa) (*cont.*). Scale 1:5

Figure 236

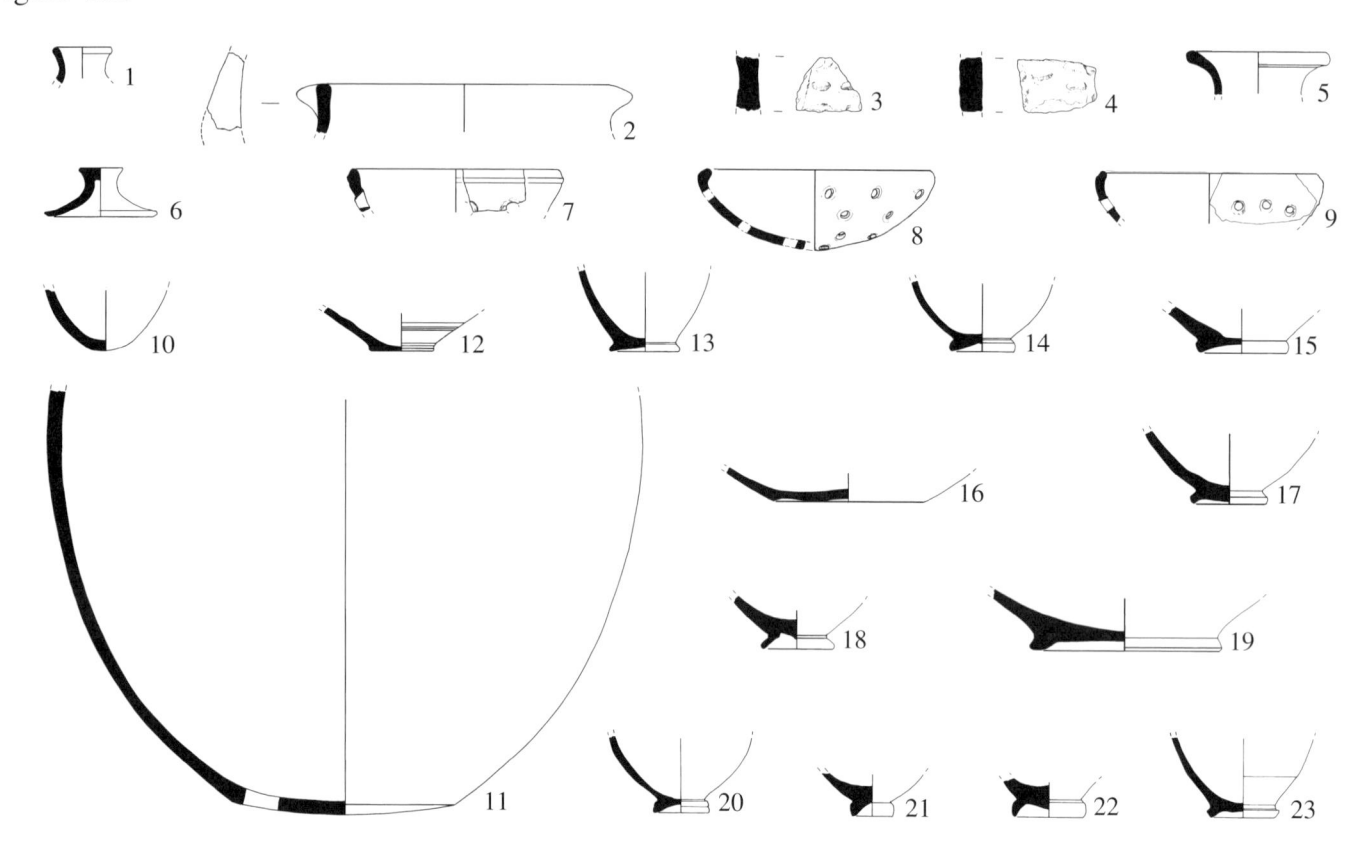

Pottery from Operation 5 (Phase 4; Period F — Early Bronze Age IVa) (*cont.*). Scale 1:5

1. FL. B.I.a (TS. 3787; Op. 5, 14.5). About 1/2 rim and neck segment of a probable two-handled flask. Ware description not available.
2. CP. A.II.e (TS. 4049; Op. 5, 13.5). Small segment of rim with remains of a triangular-shaped lug handle adjoining the top outside of the rim and the upper wall of the cooking pot. Ware description not available.
3. CP. Sh. Dec. (TS. 3915; Op. 5, 11.5). Cooking pot sherd with tool-impressed gouges in outer wall surface. Ware description not available.
4. CP. Sh. Dec. (TS. 3916; Op. 5, 11.5). Cooking pot sherd with tool-impressed gouges in outer wall surface. Ware description not available.
5. Jg. B.I.a (TS. 3759; Op. 5, 18.2). Small rim and neck segment. Ware description not available.
6. Ld. C.I.b (TS. 3247; Op. 5, 14.2). Nearly complete lid. Ware description not available.
7. SR. A.II.b (TS. 3931; Op. 5, 11.5). About 1/8 rim and upper wall segment of a strainer bowl with two extant strainer holes in the upper part of the vessel wall. Ware description not available.
8. SR. B.II.d (TS. 3259; Op. 5, 18.2). Nearly complete strainer bowl. Ware description not available.
9. SR. B.II.d (TS. 3943; Op. 5, 11.2). About 1/6 rim and upper wall segment of a strainer bowl with three extant strainer holes in the upper part of the vessel wall. Ware description not available.
10. BE. A.I (TS. 3992; Op. 5, 13.2). Complete base with lower portion of vessel wall. Ware description not available.
11. BE. A.II (TS. 3853; Op. 5, 11.2). Complete base and lower half of large storage jar. Man-made drainage hole positioned at edge of fairly flat base 2.5 cm in diameter. Fairly coarse pinkish-purple ware with black- and white- and gold-colored mica grits, evenly fired. Creamy-colored slip out.
12. BE. B.I (TS. 3937; Op. 5, 11.2). Complete disk base and lower wall of vessel. Ware description not available.
13. BE. B.II (TS. 3845; Op. 5, 13.6). Complete concave disk base and lower wall of vessel. Ware description not available.
14. BE. B.II (TS. 3847; Op. 5, 13.7). Complete splayed-out disk base and lower wall of vessel. Ware description not available.
15. BE. B.II (TS. 3974; Op. 5, 13.7). Complete splayed-out disk base and lower wall of vessel. Ware description not available.
16. BE. C.II (TS. 3795; Op. 5, 14.3). Complete concave base and lower wall of vessel. Ware description not available.
17. BE. E.I.c (TS. 3969; Op. 5, 13.2). Complete ring base and lower wall of vessel. Ware description not available.
18. BE. E.I.c (TS. 3999; Op. 5, 14.4). Complete ring base and lower wall of vessel. Ware description not available.
19. BE. E.I.e (TS. 3987; Op. 5, 13.3). Complete splayed-out ring base and lower wall of vessel. Fairly fine pinkish-buff ware with small lime and gold-colored mica grits, evenly fired. Cream slip out.
20. BE. E.I.g (TS. 3846; Op. 5, 13.7). Complete ring base and lower wall of vessel. Ware description not available.
21. BE. E.I.g (TS. 3976; Op. 5, 11.7). Complete ring base and lower wall of vessel. Ware description not available.
22. BE. E.I.i (TS. 3975; Op. 5, 13.4). Complete ring base and lower wall of vessel. Ware description not available.
23. BE. E.I.l (TS. 3741; Op. 5, 17.1). Complete ring base and about one half lower wall segment. Ware description not available.

Figure 237

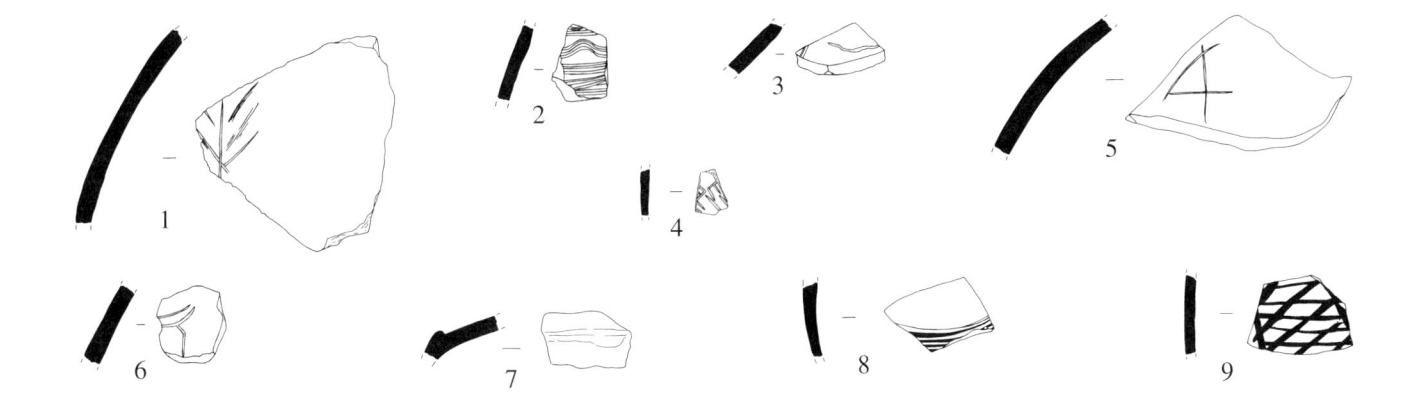

Pottery from Operation 5 (Phase 4; Period F — Early Bronze Age IVa) (*cont.*). Scale 1:5

1. JR.Sh. (IP [G.4] D.III; PM. D.19; TS. 3971; Op. 5, 13.3). Large fragment of a jar body sherd with an incomplete potter's mark incised on the outside wall before firing. Ware description not available.
2. JR.Sh. (IP [G.1] D.II.a; TS. 3731; Op. 5, 18.6). Jar body sherd with horizontal and wavy comb-incised linear bands on the outside wall. Ware description not available.
3. JR.Sh. (PM. E.2; TS. 3729; Op. 5, 18.6). Jar shoulder sherd with irregular and incomplete potter's mark incised on the outside wall before firing. Ware description not available.
4. JR.Sh. (IP [G.4] F.III.b (TS. 4003; Op. 5, 14.5). Small jar body sherd with incised strokes on outside wall, possibly part of an animal design. Ware description not available.
5. JR.Sh. (PM. C.1; TS. 3793; Op. 5, 14.5). Large jar shoulder sherd with a complete potter's mark incised on outside wall before firing. Ware description not available.
—. JR.Sh. (PM. D.14; TS. 4202; Op. 5, 11.7). Jar body sherd with an incomplete potter's mark incised on outside wall before firing. Ware description not available.
—. JR.Sh. (PM. D.22; TS. 4204; Op. 5, 18.4). Jar body sherd with an incomplete potter's mark incised on outside wall before firing. Ware description not available.
6. JR.Sh. (PM. E.2; TS. 3730; Op. 5, 18.6). Jar body sherd with an incomplete potter's mark incised on outside wall before firing. Ware description not available.
7. JR. Hd. A. (TS. 3823; Op. 5, 13.6). Jar shoulder sherd with applied horizontal lug handle. Ware description not available.
8. JR.Sh. Pt. (TS. 3970; Op. 5, 13.5). Jar body sherd decorated outside with black painted horizontal lines. Ware description not available.
9. JR.Sh. Pt. (TS. 3935; Op. 5, 11.3). Jar body sherd with burnished red surface overpainted with a black net-like pattern. Ware description not available.

Other Type Series Examples: (1) JR. D.VII.d (TS. 3250), (2) JR. D.VII.e (TS. 3841), (3) JR. E.II.p (TS. 3885), (4) JR. H.I.j (TS. 3959), (5) JR. H.I.k (TS. 3734), (6) JR. H.II.e (TS. 3347), (7) JR. H.III.a (TS. 3262), (8) JR. H.III.l (TS. 3642), (9) JR. H.III.q (TS. 3716), (10) JR. H.III.v (TS. 3261), (11) JR. H.III.w (TS. 3350 = TS. 3983), (12) JR. H.III.x (TS. 3243), (13) JR. J.III.f (TS. 3754), (14) JR. K.II.a (TS. 3726), (15) JR. P.II.o (TS. 3879), (16) PS. B.I.b (TS. 3251), (17) PS. B.I.b (TS. 3349 = TS. 3982), (18) BE. D.IV (TS. 3991), (19) BE. E.I.d (TS. 3742), (20) BE. E.I.l (TS. 3851), (21) Hd. E.I.b (TS. 3491).

Figure 238. Pottery from Operation 5, Pit 17.3 (Phase 4; Period F — Early Bronze Age IVa)

1. SBR. B.I.i (TS. 3621; Op. 5, 17.3). Small rim and upper wall segment. Ware description not available.
2. SBR. D.I.h (TS. 3252; Op. 5, 17.3). About 1/4 rim segment and all of lower body and base complete. Slightly coarse buff ware with many lime and a few small gold-colored mica grits, evenly fired. Creamy-green slip out and possibly in (ware very worn below shoulder inside).
3. SBR. D.I.h (TS. 3620; Op. 5, 17.3). Small rim and neck segment. Ware description not available.
4. BR. A.IV.a (TS. 3618; Op. 5, 17.3). Small rim and most of wall profile; base missing. Ware description not available.
5. BR. A.IV.b (TS. 3765; Op. 5, 17.3). Small rim and most of wall profile; base missing. Ware description not available.
6. BR. E.I.a (TS. 3622; Op. 5, 17.3). Small rim and upper wall segment. Ware description not available.
7. BR. E.I.a (TS. 3627; Op. 5, 17.3). Small rim and most of wall profile; base missing. Ware description not available.
8. BR. E.I.a (TS. 3629; Op. 5, 17.3). Small rim and most of wall profile; base missing. Ware description not available.
9. BR. E.II.a (TS. 3625; Op. 5, 17.3). Small rim and upper wall below carination extant. Ware description not available.
10. BR. E.III.a (TS. 3630; Op. 5, 17.3). Large rim and upper wall segment. Ware description not available.

Figure 238

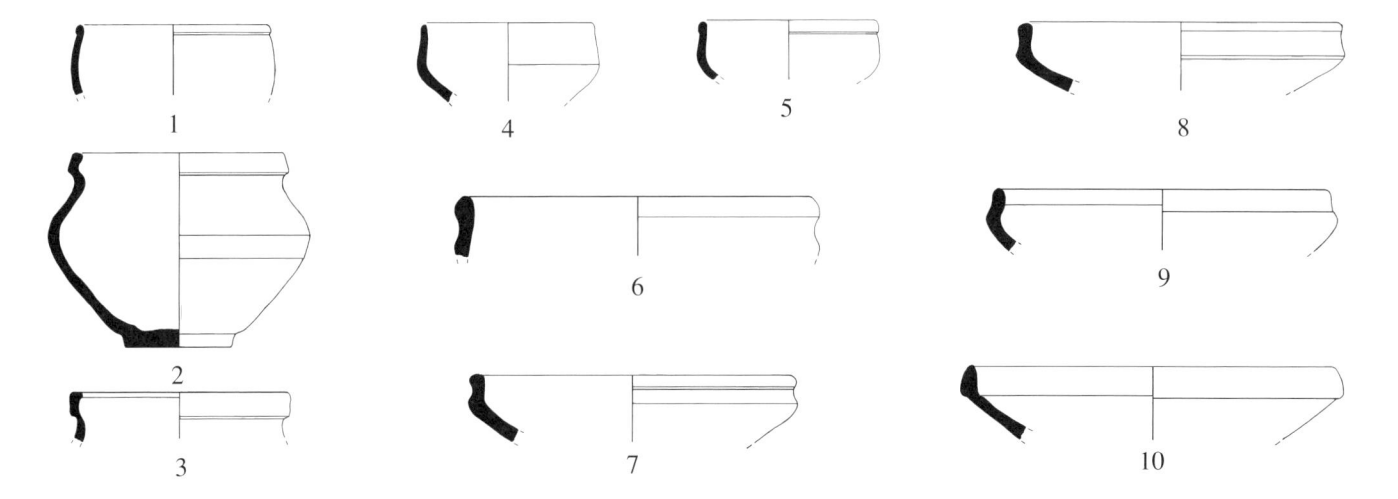

Pottery from Operation 5, Pit 17.3 (Phase 4; Period F — Early Bronze Age IVa). Scale 1:5

Figure 239. Pottery from Operation 5, Pit 17.3 (Phase 4; Period F — Early Bronze Age IVa) (*cont.*)

1. SJR. A.II.b (TS. 4057; Op. 5, 17.3). Small rim and neck segment. Ware description not available.
2. SJR. B.I.c (TS. 3637; Op. 5, 17.3). Small rim and neck segment. Ware description not available.
3. SJR. B.III.a (TS. 4054; Op. 5, 17.3). Small rim and neck segment. Ware description not available.
4. SJR. C.I.c (TS. 4052; Op. 5, 17.3). Small rim and neck segment. Ware description not available.
5. SJR. C.II.o (TS. 4056; Op. 5, 17.3). Small rim and neck segment. Ware description not available.
6. SJR. C.II.p (SW. 762; Op. 5, 17.3). Metallic-ware small jar mended to completion. Red painted horizontal bands around upper half of the body. Ware description not available.
7. JR. A.IV.a (TS. 3256; Op. 5, 17.3). Large rim, neck, and upper shoulder segment. Ware description not available.
8. JR. A.IV.a (TS. 3626; Op. 5, 17.3). Small rim, neck, and upper shoulder segment. Ware description not available.
9. JR. A.IV.a (TS. 3633; Op. 5, 17.3). Small rim, neck, and upper shoulder segment. Ware description not available.
10. JR. A.IV.a (TS. 3636; Op. 5, 17.3). Small rim, neck, and upper shoulder segment. Ware description not available.
11. JR. B.IV.c (TS. 3635; Op. 5, 17.3). About 1/4 rim segment. Slightly coarse pink ware with lime and mica grits, evenly fired. Cream slip out.
12. JR. B.IV.c (TS. 3948; Op. 5, 17.3). Large rim, neck, and about 1/2 of upper body wall extant. Ware description not available.
13. JR. C.II.a (TS. 3763; Op. 5, 17.3). Small rim, neck, and nearly complete wall profile; base missing. Ware description not available.
14. JR. C.II.f (SW. 763; Op. 5, 17.3). Mended to near completion with full profile. Ware description not available.
15. JR. E.II.p (IP [G.1] C.V.a; TS. 3639; Op. 5, 17.3). About 1/12 rim and shoulder segment with comb-incised horizontal and wavy line decoration on shoulder. Ware description not available.
16. JR. J.I.c (TS. 4053; Op. 5, 17.3). Small rim and neck segment. Ware description not available.
17. JR. J.III.b (TS. 3254; Op. 5, 17.3). Jar with concave flat base mended to near completion; central portion of base missing. Ware description not available.
18. JR. J.III.n (TS. 3619; Op. 5, 17.3). About 1/2 rim, neck, and upper wall of body extant. Ware description not available.
19. JR. J.III.s (TS. 3762; Op. 5, 17.3). Small rim and neck segment. Ware description not available.
20. JR. J.VI.a (TS. 3617; Op. 5, 17.3). Small rim, neck, and upper shoulder segment. Ware description not available.
21. JR. N.II.a (TS. 3255; Op. 5, 17.3). About 1/3 rim, neck, and upper body segment with remains of a spout just below the neck of the vessel. Ware description not available.
22. JR. P.I.a (TS. 3253; Op. 5, 17.3). About 1/3 rim segment. Slightly coarse pink ware with a few lime and many gold-colored mica grits, evenly fired. Creamy colored slip out and over rim in to base of neck.
23. JR. P.II.p (TS. 3638; Op. 5, 17.3). Large rim and neck segment. Ware description not available.
24. JR. Q.I.a (TS. 3631; Op. 5, 17.3). About 1/10 rim and neck segment. Ware description not available.
25. CP. B.II.a (PM. C.14; TS. 3715; Op. 5, 17.3). About 1/5 segment of rim and body. Fairly coarse brown ware with white mica and small limestone pebble grits, unevenly fired gray in patches in and out. Self slip in and out, but not burnished. Irregularly charred in and out. Potter's mark incised on shoulder before firing.
26. SR. A.II.c (TS. 4050; Op. 5, 17.3). About 1/6 rim and upper wall of strainer bowl with one strainer hole extant in wall. Ware description not available.
27. BE. C.I (TS. 3850; Op. 5, 17.3). Complete concave base and lower portion of body wall. Fairly coarse grayware with lime grits, evenly fired. Self slip out.
28. BE. D.III (TS. 3849; Op. 5, 17.3). Incomplete flat base with segment of lower wall of vessel. Ware description not available.
29. BE. F.III.a (TS. 4055; Op. 5, 17.3). Small rim and wall segment of a base of a pedestal-type stand. Ware description not available.
30. JR.Sh. (PM. D.5; TS. 3628; Op. 5, 17.3). Jar body sherd with an incomplete potter's mark incised before firing. Ware description not available.
31. JR.Sh. (IP [G.1] D.I.c; TS. 3623; Op. 5, 17.3). Jar neck and shoulder sherd with horizontal and wavy line comb-incised decoration on shoulder. Ware description not available.
32. JR.Sh. (IP [G.1] A.II.c; TS. 3764; Op. 5, 17.3). Jar neck and shoulder sherd with one band of horizontal comb-incised lines extant on lower portion of shoulder. Ware description not available.

Other Type Series Examples: (1) JR. B.I.a (TS. 3615), (2) JR. E.II.s (TS. 3616), (3) JR. E.II.t (TS. 3852), (4) JR. H.III.p (TS. 3624), (5) JR. O.III.f (TS. 3632), (6) BE. D.I (TS. 4036).

Figure 239

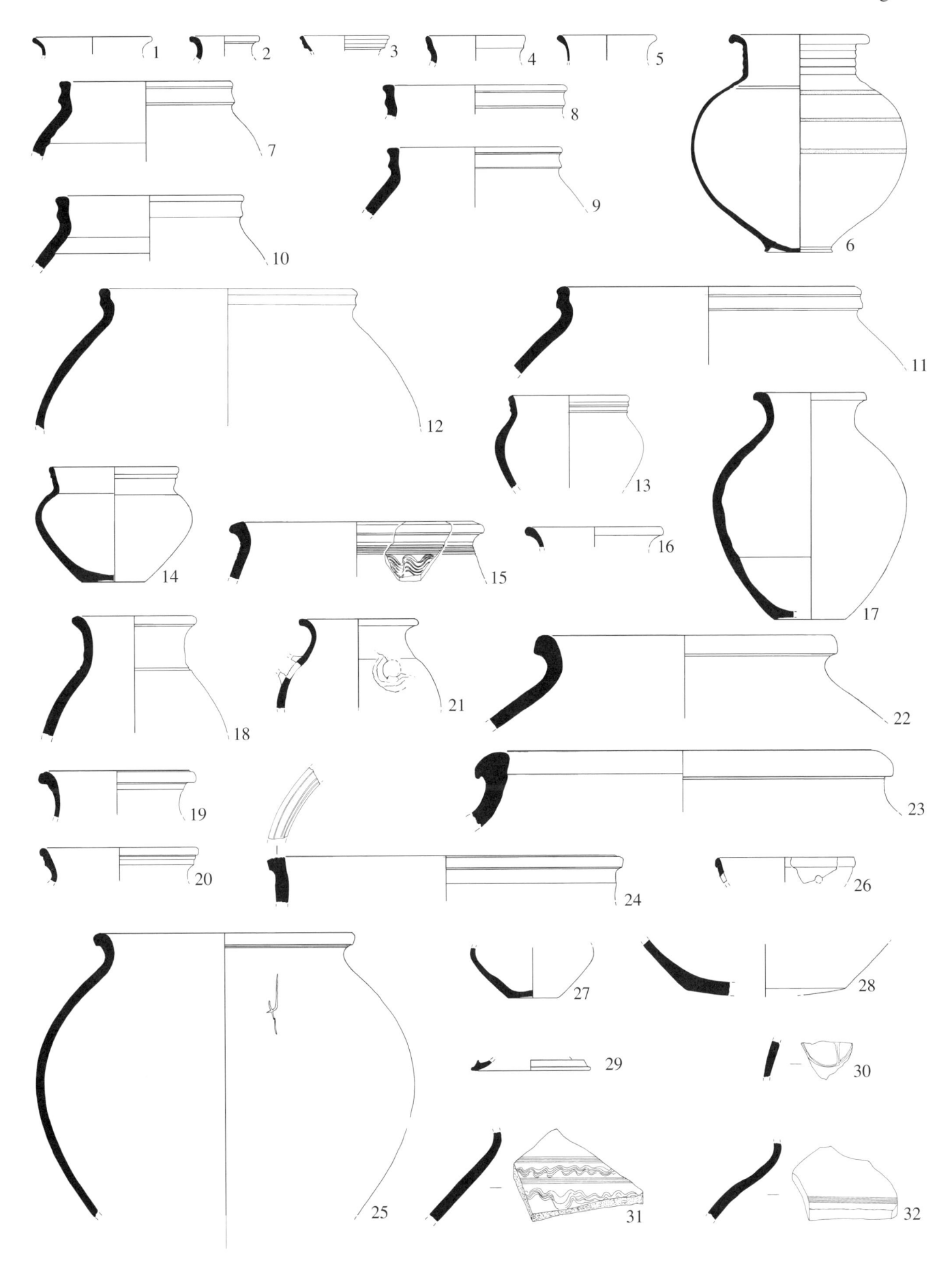

Pottery from Operation 5, Pit 17.3 (Phase 4; Period F — Early Bronze Age IVa) (*cont.*). Scale 1:5

Figure 240. Pottery from Operation 5 (Phase 5; Period B — Early Roman)

1. R.BR. A.II.a (TS. 3814; Op. 5, 9.3). Small rim and upper wall segment. Ware description not available.
2. R.BR. B.I.b (IP [G.1] K.I.a; TS. 3773; Op. 5, 29.1). Large rim and wall segment with a comb-incised wavy band of decoration on top of the rim. Ware description not available.
3. R.BR. B.I.b (IP [G.1] K.I.a; TS. 3809; Op. 5, 9.3). About 1/10 rim and upper wall segment with a comb-incised wavy band of decoration on top of the rim. Ware description not available.
4. R.BR. C.II.f (TS. 3699; Op. 5, 9.7). Small rim and upper wall segment. Ware description not available.
5. R.BR. D.I.a (TS. 3644; Op. 5, 10.4). Small rim and upper wall segment Ware description not available.
6. R.BR. D.III.a (TS. 3941; Op. 5, 11.8). Small rim and upper wall segment. Ware description not available.
7. R.BR. D.III.b (TS. 3204; Op. 5, 29.2). Large rim and most of wall profile segment. Ware description not available.
8. R.JR. A.I.c (TS. 3771; Op. 5, 29.1). Small rim and neck segment. Ware description not available.
9. R.JR. B.I.a (TS. 3918; Op. 5, 10.2). Small rim and neck segment. Ware description not available.
10. R.JR. B.I.b (PM. A.1; TS. 3705; Op. 5, 9.5). About 1/6 rim and neck segment with a potter's mark cut into the top of the rim before firing. Ware description not available.
11. R.JR. B.I.d (TS. 3820; Op. 5, 9.3). Small rim and upper neck segment. Ware description not available.
—. R.JR.C.I.d (TS. 3816; Op. 5, 9.3). Small rim and upper neck segment. Ware description not available.
12. R.HMJ. A.I.b (TS. 3804; Op. 5, 9.3). Small rim and upper shoulder segment. Ware description not available.
13. R.HMJ. A.II.c (TS. 3694; Op. 5, 9.8). Small rim, neck, and upper shoulder segment. Ware description not available.
14. R.HMJ. A.II.d (TS. 3710; Op. 5, 9.7). Large rim, neck, and upper shoulder segment. Ware description not available.
15. R.HMJ. B.II.c (TS. 3810; Op. 5, 9.3). Small rim, neck, and upper shoulder segment. Ware description not available.
16. R.HMJ. B.II.c (TS. 3811; Op. 5, 9.3). Small rim, neck, and upper shoulder segment with one applied button-like knob handle extant on shoulder. Ware description not available.
17. R.St.J. A.I.a (TS. 3739; Op. 5, 9.11). Large rim and upper shoulder segment. Ware description not available.

Figure 240

Pottery from Operation 5 (Phase 5; Period B — Early Roman). Scale 1:5

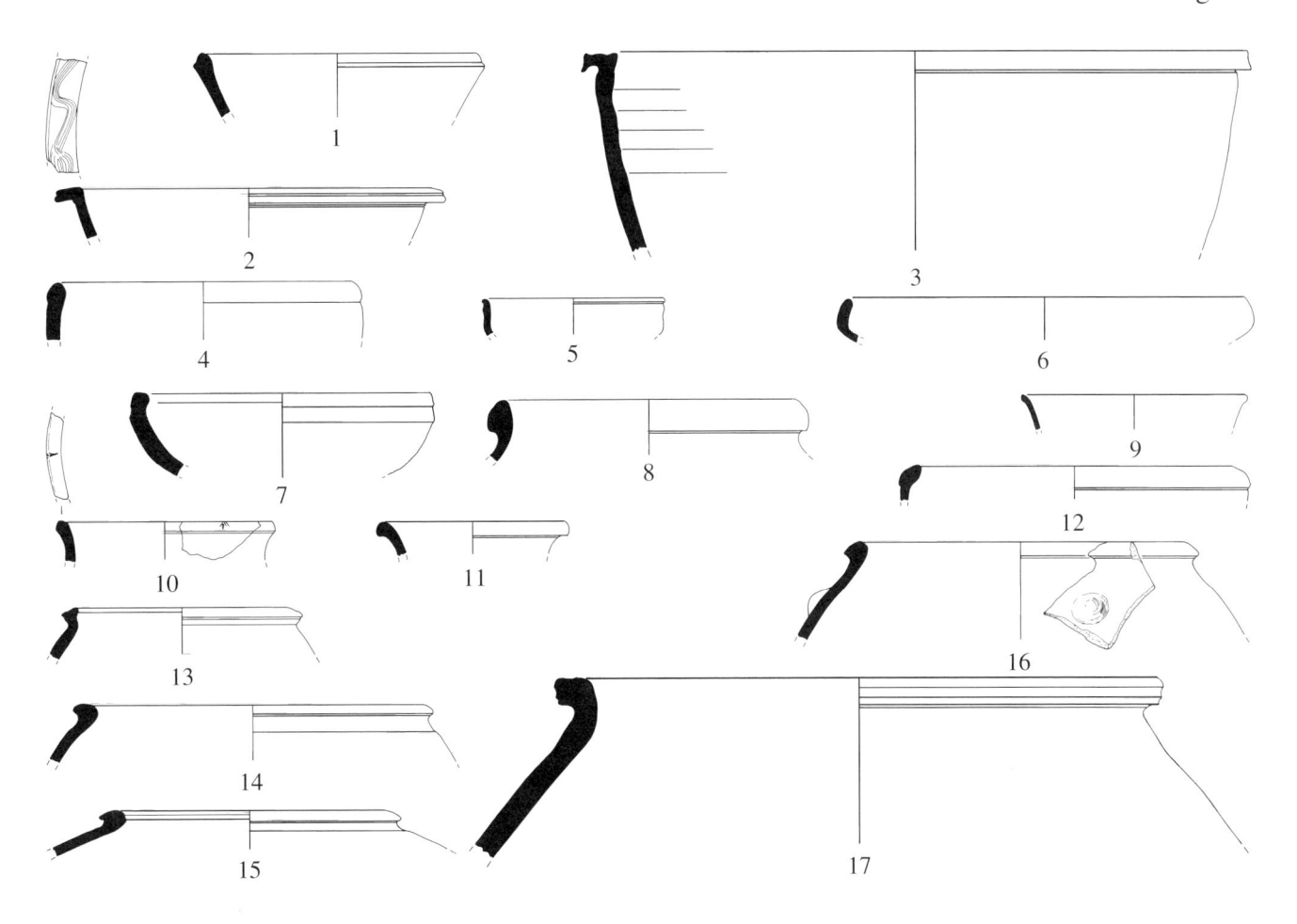

Figure 241. Pottery from Operation 5 (Phase 5; Period B — Early Roman [*cont.*] and Derived Early Bronze Age)

1. R.Jg. B.II.b (TS. 3813; Op. 5, 9.3). About 1/5 rim and neck segment with scar of a vertical loop or strap handle attachment just below the top of the rim outside. Ware description not available.
2. R.Jg. B.II.c (TS. 3766; Op. 5, 10.3). About 2/3 rim and neck with complete vertical strap handle; remains of the pinched portion of the rim for pouring. Fairly fine pink ware with lime grits and silver-colored mica grit, evenly fired. Ware description not available.
3. R.Jg. B.II.c (TS. 3768; Op. 5, 10.3). About 1/3 rim, neck, and upper half of shoulder with complete vertical strap handle; irregular-shaped rim probably pinched for pouring. Fairly fine pinkish-orange ware with lime and white-colored mica grits, evenly fired. Self slip out. Slash on lower outside of the handle may represent a potter's mark. Ware description not available.
4. R.Jg. B.II.c (TS. 3824; Op. 5, 12.1). Pouring lip and neck segment of jug. Ware description not available.
5. R.Jg. B.II.g (TS. 3821; Op. 5, 9.3). Small rim and neck segment. Ware description not available.
6. R.CP. A.IV.b (TS. 3812; Op. 5, 9.3). Small rim, neck, and upper shoulder segment. Ware description not available.
7. R.CP. B.I.b (TS. 3711; Op. 5, 9.5). Small rim and neck segment. Ware description not available.
8. R.PS. 4 (IP [G.4] G.I.a; TS. 3978; Op. 5, 12.1). About 1/12 segment of the rim and wall of a pot or pedestal stand decorated with irregular incised lines on the outside wall. Ware description not available.
9. R.Ld. 3 (TS. 3840; Op. 5, 29.2). Fragment of a lid, possibly belonging to a cooking pot. Ware description not available.
10. R.BE. A.I.a (TS. 3807; Op. 5, 9.3). Complete stump-type base, small segment of lower body of vessel. Ware description not available.
11. R.BE. A.I.a (TS. 3910; Op. 5, 10.2). Complete stump-type base and lower portion of body. Ware description not available.
12. R.BR.Sh. (TS. 3706; Op. 5, 9.8). Bowl sherd with marked carination of the body. Ware description not available.
13. R.JR.Sh. (IP [G.4] G.I.a; TS. 3683; Op. 5, 9.6). Jar body sherd with remains of two types of incised decoration on the outside wall. Ware description not available.
14. R.JR.Sh. (IP [G.4] D.III; PM D.20; TS. 3687; Op. 5, 9.9). Jar shoulder segment with remains of incised decoration on the outside wall.
15. R.JR.Sh. (IP [G.1] D.I.a; TS. 3770; Op. 5, 9.2). Large segment of a jar with horizontal and wavy comb-incised decoration and remains of stumps of one vertical loop or strap handle. Ware description not available.
16. R.JR.Sh. (IP [G.4] G.I.a; TS. 3917; Op. 5, 10.2). Jar body sherd with irregular incised linear decoration outside. Ware description not available.
17. R.JR.Sh. Dec. (TS. 3817; Op. 5, 9.3). Jar body sherd with wedge-shaped impressed decoration above comb-incised horizontal band of lines. Ware description not available.
18. R.JR.Hd. (TS. 3904; Op. 5, 10.2). Portion of a loop handle, probably belonging to a cooking pot. Ware description not available.
19. R.JR.Hd. (TS. 3819; Op. 5, 9.3). Fragment of a loop handle, squarish in section. Ware description not available.
20. R.Jg.Hd. (TS. 3767; Op. 5, 10.3). Complete vertical loop handle, probably belonging to a jar. Ware description not available.
21. R.JR.Hd. (TS. 3745; Op. 5, 9.4). Jar shoulder and wall fragment with remains of a wide vertical strap handle (possibly part of TS. 3744 below). Ware description not available.
22. R.JR.Hd. (TS. 3744; Op. 5, 9.4). Jar shoulder and wall fragment with remains of a wide vertical strap handle (possibly part of TS. 3745 above). Ware description not available.
23. JR.Sh. (PM. B.5; TS. 3873; Op. 5, 9.5). Derived Early Bronze Age sherd. Jar body sherd with remains of an incomplete potter's mark incised before firing. Ware description not available.
24. JR.Sh. (PM. D.5; TS. 3712; Op. 5, 9.9). Derived Early Bronze Age sherd. Jar body sherd with remains of an incomplete potter's mark incised before firing. Ware description not available.
25. JR.Sh. (PM. D.10; TS. 3928; Op. 5, 10.3). Derived Early Bronze Age sherd. Jar body sherd with remains of an incomplete potter's mark incised before firing. Ware description not available.
26. JR.Sh. (IP [G.4] D.III; PM. D.19; TS. 3693; Op. 5, 9.12). Derived Early Bronze Age sherd. Jar body sherd with a tree or wheat stalk potter's mark incised outside before firing. Ware description not available.
27. JR.Sh. (PM. D.22; TS. 3871; Op. 5, 9.6). Derived Early Bronze Age sherd. Jar body sherd with remains of an incomplete potter's mark incised before firing. Ware description not available.
28. JR.Sh. (PM. E.2; TS. 3939; Op. 5, 10.3). Derived Early Bronze Age sherd. Jar body sherd with remains of an incomplete potter's mark incised before firing. Ware description not available.

Other Type Series Examples:

Roman — (1) R.BR. A.II.f (TS. 3805), (2) R.BR. A.II.g (TS. 3902), (3) R.BR. B.I.f (TS. 3940), (4) R.BR. C.I.d (TS. 3984), (5) R.BR. C.II.d (TS. 3890), (6) R.BR. C.II.f (TS. 3348), (7) R.BR. D.I.a (TS. 3193), (8) R.BR. D.II.b (TS. 3836), (9) R.BR. D.II.b (TS. 3927), (10) R.BR. D.II.c (TS. 3806), (11) R.BR. D.II.d (TS. 3190), (12) R.BR. D.II.e (TS. 3737), (13) R.BR. D.III.b (TS. 3808), (14) R.BR. E.I.a (TS. 3933), (15) R.BR. E.I.b (TS. 4000), (16) R.BR. E.II.a (TS. 3877), (17) R.BR. E.II.b (TS. 3869), (18) R.SJR. A.I.b (TS. 3713), (19) R.SJR. B.I.a (TS. 3891), (20) R.JR. A.I.e (TS. 3645), (21) R.JR. A.I.f (TS. 3818), (22) R.JR. B.I.a (TS. 3923), (23) R.JR. B.I.b (TS. 3919), (24) R.JR.

Figure 241

B.I.d (TS. 3827), (25) R.JR. B.II.b (TS. 3714), (26) R.JR. B.II.c (TS. 3870), (27) R.JR. C.II.a (TS. 3930), (28) R.HMJ. A.II.g (TS. 3704); (29) R.HMJ. A.II.h (TS. 3909), (30) R.St.J. A.I.c (TS. 3815), (31) R.St.J. A.II.a (TS. 3646), (32) R.St.J. B.I.a (TS. 3647), (33) R.St.J. B.II.a (TS. 3648), (34) R.St.J. B.II.b (TS. 3880), (35) R.St.J. C.I.a (TS. 3746), (36) R.Jg. B.II.r (TS. 3980), (37) R.CP. B.I.a (TS. 3777), (38) R.Bt. A.I.b (TS. 3932), (39) R.Bt. B.I.b (TS. 3194), (40) R.PS. 4 (TS. 3708), (41) R.BE. A.I (TS. 3899), (42) R.BE. B.I.a (TS. 3689), (43) R.BE. B.II.a (TS. 3913), (44) R.BE. B.II.b (TS. 3701).

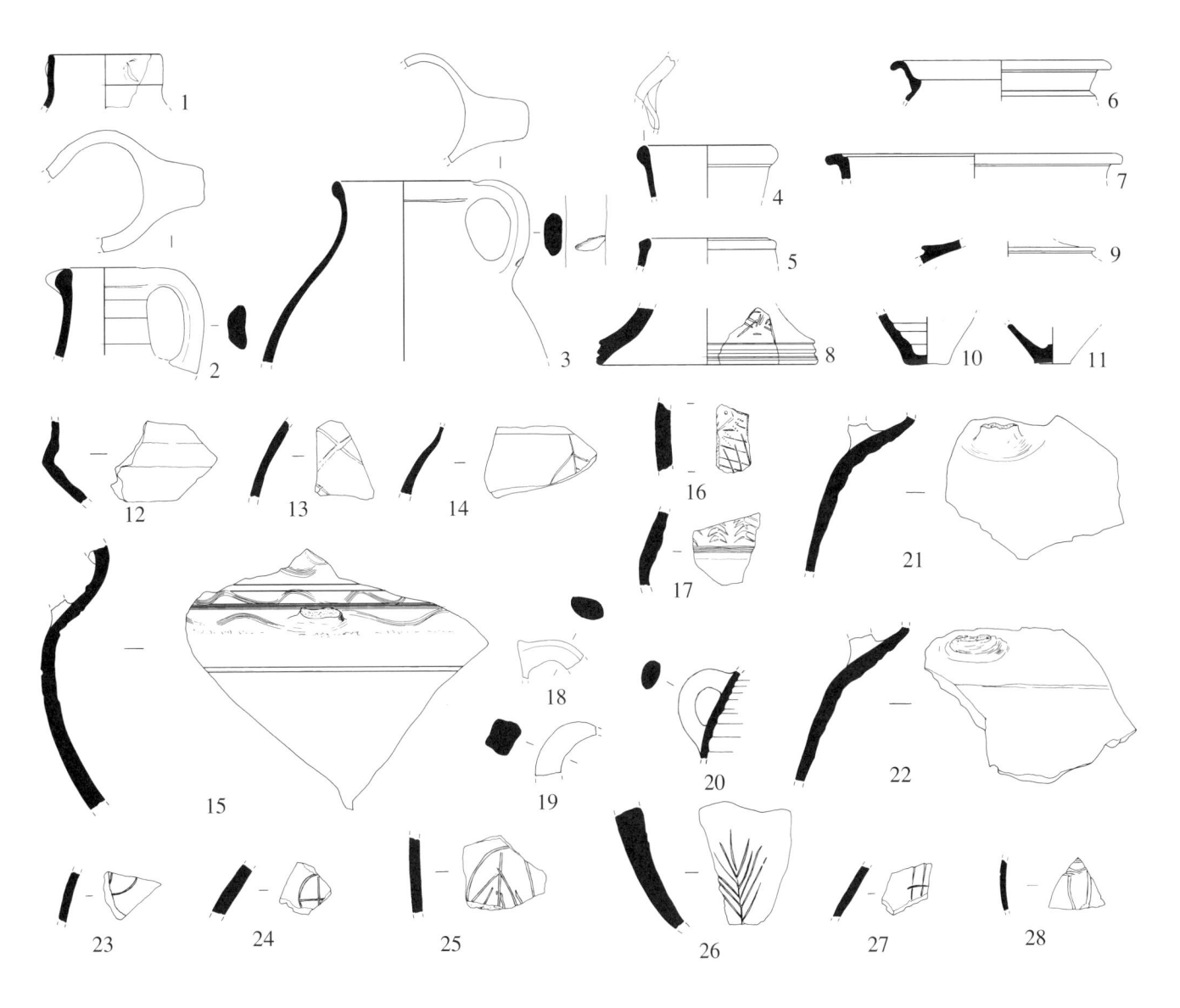

Pottery from Operation 5 (Phase 5; Period B — Early Roman [*cont.*] and Derived Early Bronze Age). Scale 1:5

Figure 242

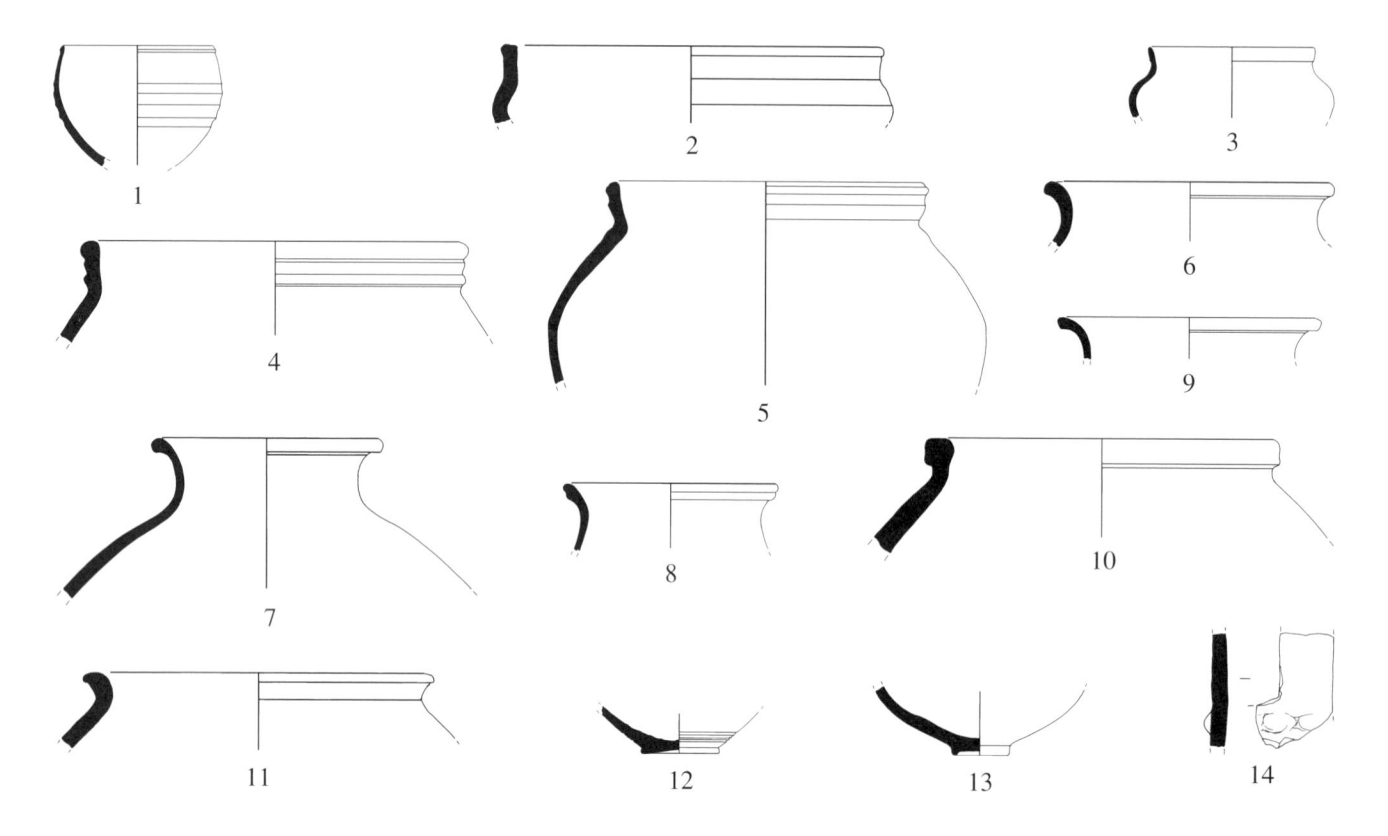

Pottery from Operation 5 (Phase 5; Period B — Derived Early Bronze Age). Scale 1:5

1. SBR. A.I.d (TS. 3903; Op. 5, 9.12). Nearly complete rim and body profile of a cup without the base. Ware description not available.
2. BR. N.I.a (TS. 3191; Op. 5, 9.11). Large rim, neck, and upper portion of lower wall extant. Ware description not available.
3. SJR. A.I.a (TS. 3829; Op. 5, 31.2). Small rim, neck, and upper wall segment. Ware description not available.
4. JR. D.V.a (TS. 3842; Op. 5, 10.5). Large rim and shoulder segment. Ware description not available.
5. JR. D.VII.a (TS. 3736; Op. 5, 10.5). Large rim, neck, shoulder, and upper part of lower wall extant. Ware description not available.
6. JR. J.II.j (TS. 3692; Op. 5, 9.7). Small rim, neck, and upper shoulder segment. Ware description not available.
7. JR. J.III.c (TS. 3738; Op. 5, 9.11). About 1/2 rim, neck, and shoulder extant. Ware description not available.
8. JR. J.III.m (TS. 3906; Op. 5, 9.12). Small rim and neck segment. Ware description not available.
9. JR. J.III.ab (TS. 3828; Op. 5, 29.2). Small rim and upper part of neck extant. Ware description not available.
10. JR. P.II.c (TS. 3926; Op. 5, 9.12). Large rim, neck, and shoulder segment. Ware description not available.
11. JR. S (TS. 3192; Op. 5, 9.11). Small rim, neck, and upper shoulder segment. Ware description not available.
12. BE. B.II (TS. 3905; Op. 5, 9.12). Complete concave disk base and lower wall of vessel extant with horizontal wheelmade lines visible on outside lower wall. Ware description not available.
13. BE. E.I.d (TS. 3643; Op. 5, 10.5). Complete ring base and lower part of vessel wall extant. Ware description not available.
14. WPS. A.I.a (TS. 3676; Op. 5, 9.6). Fragment of the wall of a windowed pedestal-type pot stand or brazier with remains of an applied horizontal rope-like band type of decoration below the window. Ware description not available.
—. JR.Sh. (PM. C.1; TS. 4205; Op. 5, 29.1). Jar body sherd with a potter's mark incised on the outside wall before firing. Ware description not available.

Another Type Series Example:
Early Bronze Age — (1) BE. E.I.k (TS. 3900).

Figure 243

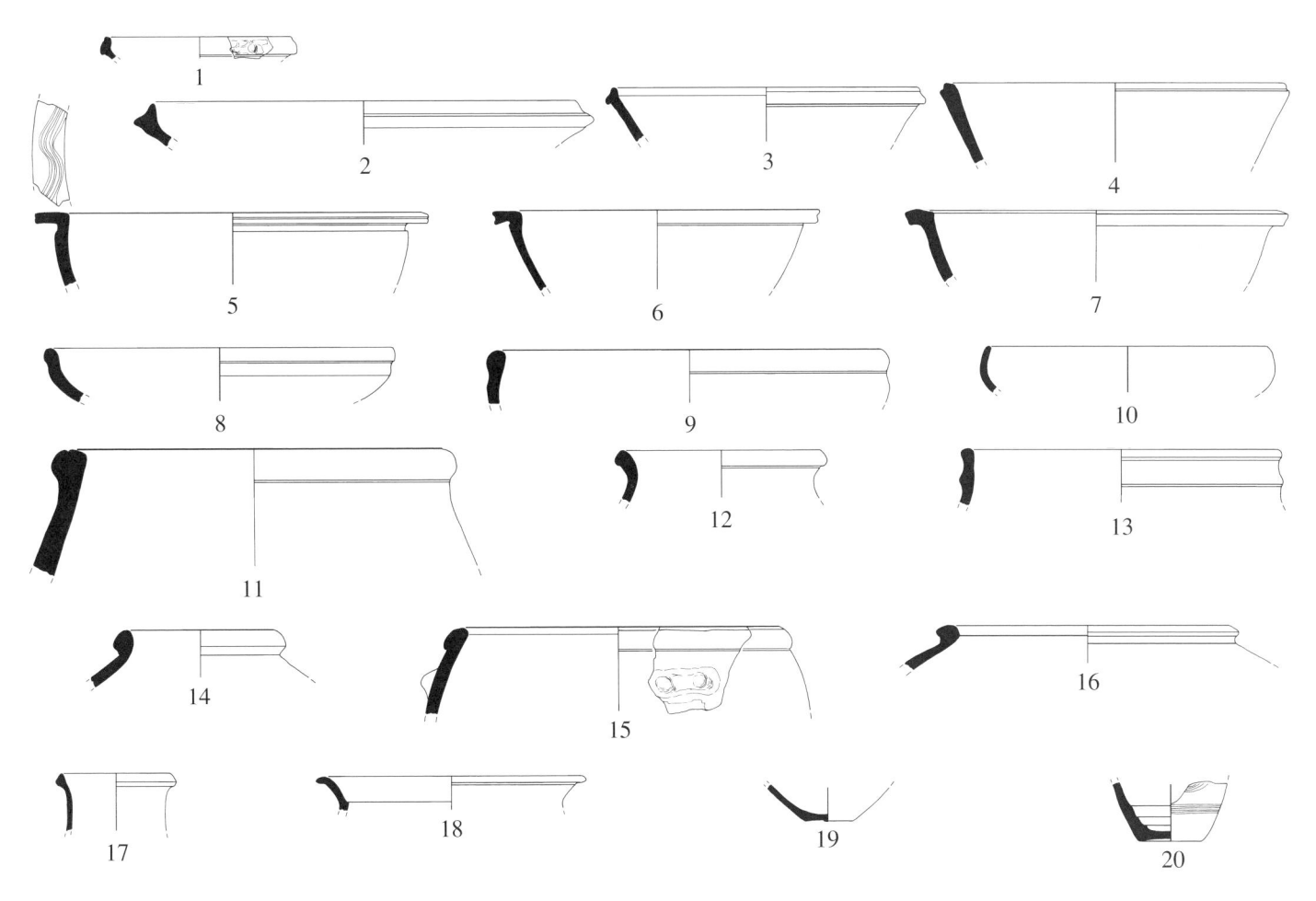

Pottery from Operation 5 (Phase 6; Period B — Late Roman). Scale 1:5

1. R.BR. A.I.d (TS. 3671; Op. 5, 6.4). Small rim and upper wall segment. Irregular punctate decoration around outside of rim. Ware description not available.
2. R.BR. A.II.a (TS. 3703; Op. 5, 6.7). Small rim and upper wall segment. Ware description not available.
3. R.BR. A.II.a (TS. 3866; Op. 5, 6.8). Small rim and upper wall segment. Ware description not available.
4. R.BR. A.II.a (TS. 3867; Op. 5, 6.5). Small rim segment with about 2/3 of vessel wall. Ware description not available.
5. R.BR. B.I.b (IP [G.1] K.I.a; TS. 3668; Op. 5, 8.1). About 1/10 rim and upper wall segment. Wavy comb-incised decoration on top of rim. Ware description not available.
6. R.BR. B.I.b (TS. 3673; Op. 5, 8.1). Small rim segment with about 2/3 of vessel wall. Ware description not available.
7. R.BR. B.I.b (TS. 3921; Op. 5, 10.1). Small rim segment and about 2/3 of vessel wall. Ware description not available.
8. R.BR. D.II.a (TS. 3690; Op. 5, 6.10. Small rim segment and about 1/2 of vessel wall. Ware description not available.
9. R.BR. D.II.a (TS. 3697; Op. 5, 6.3). Small rim segment and upper portion of slightly carinated wall. Ware description not available.
10. R.BR. D.III.a (TS. 3696; Op. 5, 8.2). Small rim segment and upper portion of curved wall. Ware description not available.
11. R.JR. A.I.c (TS. 3672; Op. 5, 8.1). Large rim, neck, and upper shoulder segment. Ware description not available.
12. R.JR. B.I.c (TS. 3695; Op. 5, 8.5). Small rim, neck, and upper shoulder segment. Ware description not available.
13. R.JR. B.II.a (TS. 3682; Op. 5, 6.3). Small rim and neck segment. Ware description not available.
14. R.HMJ. A.II.f (TS. 3664; Op. 5, 8.1). Small rim and upper shoulder segment. Ware description not available.
15. R.HMJ. B.II.a (TS. 3872; Op. 5, 6.2). About 1/10 rim and shoulder segment with double-lugged handle on the upper portion of the shoulder. Ware description not available.
16. R.HMJ. B.II.c (TS. 3925 = TS. 3951; Op. 5, 10.1). Small rim, upright neck, and upper shoulder segment. Ware description not available.
17. R.Jg. B.II.c (TS. 3936; Op. 5, 10.1). About 1/3 rim and neck segment. Ware description not available.
18. R.CP. A.IV.b (TS. 3875; Op. 5, 8.2). Small rim and neck segment with remains of top of shoulder. Ware description not available.
19. R.BE. A.I.a (TS. 3665; Op. 5, 8.1). Complete base with portion of lower wall of vessel. Ware description not available.
20. R.BE. A.I.a (IP [G.1] C.I.a; TS. 3666; Op. 5, 8.1). Complete base with most of lower wall of vessel attached. Spiral-shaped incised decoration on outside wall above horizontal comb-incised lines. Ware description not available.

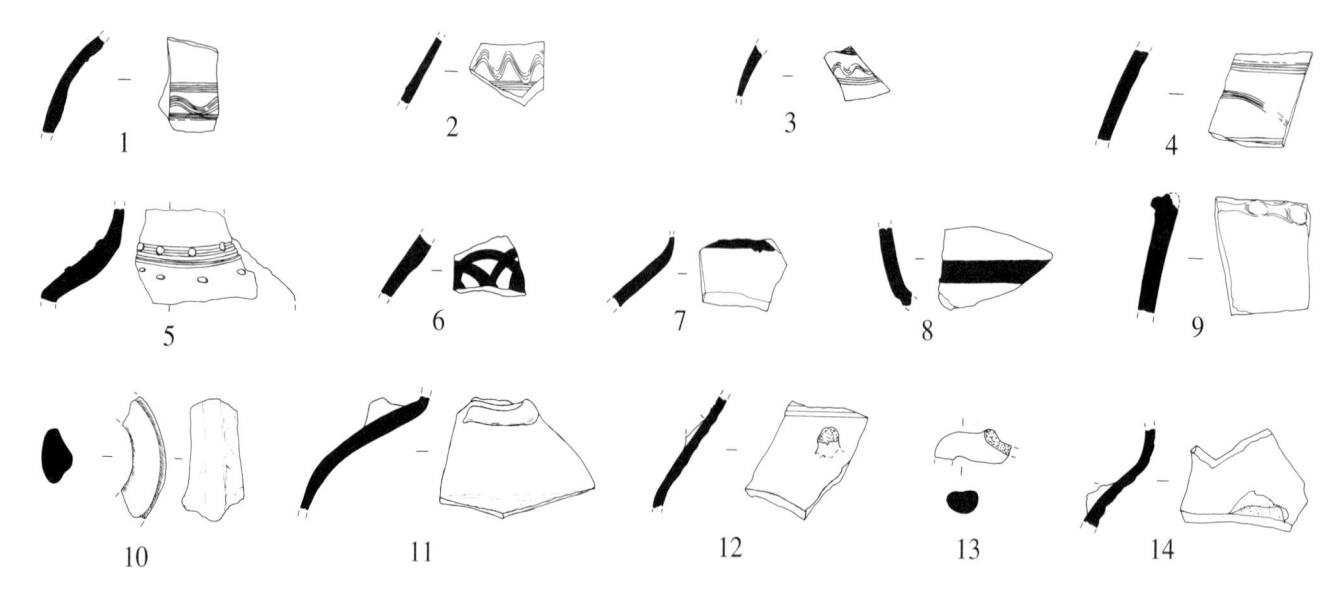

Figure 244

Figure 244. Pottery from Operation 5 (Phase 6; Period B — Late Roman) (*cont.*). Scale 1:5

1. R.JR.Sh. (IP [G.1] C.I.a; TS. 3691; Op. 5, 6.1). Jar sherd with comb-incised wavy line decoration between two horizontal bands of comb-incised lines. Ware description not available.
2. R.JR.Sh. (IP [G.1] B.II.a; TS. 3868; Op. 5, 8.2). Jar sherd with remains of comb-incised wavy line decoration above one horizontal band of comb-incised lines. Ware description not available.
3. R.JR.Sh. (IP [G.1] C.II.a; TS. 3896; Op. 5, 16.1). Jar sherd with comb-incised wavy line decoration between two horizontal bands of comb-incised lines. Ware description not available.
4. R.JR.Sh. (IP [G.1] C.III.a; TS. 3990; Op. 5, 16.1). Jar sherd with remains of a comb-incised broad arched design between two horizontal bands of comb-incised lines. Ware description not available.
5. R.JR.Sh. (IP [G.1] A.II.b; TS. 3912; Op. 5, 10.1). Jar neck and shoulder segment with comb-incised horizontal lines at juncture of neck and shoulder overlaid with applied "buttons" of clay, which also are applied on the shoulder below the comb-incised band. Ware description not available.
6. R.JR.Sh. Pt. (TS. 3670; Op. 5, 6.4). Jar sherd decorated with interlocking circles painted orange-brown. Ware description not available.
7. R.JR.Sh. Pt. (TS. 3801; Op. 5, 8.1). Jar neck and upper shoulder fragment decorated with a horizontal band painted orange-brown. Ware description not available.
8. R.JR.Sh. Pt. (TS. 3802; Op. 5, 8.1). Jar sherd decorated on the body with a horizontal band painted orange-brown. Ware description not available.
9. R.ABS. A (TS. 3865; Op. 5, 6.5). Jar sherd with remains of an applied horizontal rope-like band decorated with a potter's thumb-indented impressions at spaced intervals around the band. Ware description not available.
10. R.CP. Hd. (TS. 3979; Op. 5, 16.1). Portion of a Roman cooking pot handle. Ware description not available.
11. R.JR. Hd. (TS. 3832; Op. 5, 8.5). Jar shoulder fragment with remains of a rough horizontal ledge handle, unevenly applied. Ware description not available.
12. R.JR. Hd. (TS. 3709; Op. 5, 8.4). Jar shoulder fragment with remains of a vertical loop handle. Ware description not available.
13. R.Jg. Hd. (TS. 3674; Op. 5, 8.1). Vertical loop handle, probably belonging to a jug. Ware description not available.
14. R.JR. Hd. (TS. 3685; Op. 5, 8.1). Jar neck and shoulder segment with remains of a vertical loop handle on the shoulder. Ware description not available.

Other Type Series Examples:
Roman — (1) R.MBR (TS. 3803), (2) R.BR. A.II.d (TS. 3698), (3) R.BR. A.II.e (TS. 3799), (4) R.BR. C.II.e (TS. 3800), (5) R.BR. D.III.a (TS. 3702), (6) R.JR. A.I.d (TS. 3860), (7) R.JR. B.I.c (TS. 3859), (8) R.JR. C.II.b (TS. 3663), (9) R.JR. C.II.c (TS. 3700), (10) R.Jg. A.II.a (TS. 3669), (11) R.CP. A.IV.b (TS. 3240), (12) R.Lp. 3 (TS. 3677), (13) R.Lp. 6 (TS. 3876), (14) R.PS. 5 (TS. 3707).

Figure 245. Pottery from Operation 5 (Phase 6; Period B — Derived Early Bronze Age)

1. SBR. C.II.a (TS. 3684; Op. 5, 6.1). Large segment of a small bowl with most of body profile.
2. BR. D.II.a (TS. 3864; Op. 5, 8.3). Small rim and upper wall segment.
3. SR. B.I.e (TS. 3688; Op. 5, 8.3). Small rim and body segment of a strainer bowl with one hole extant.
4. PS. A.I.a (TS. 3907; Op. 5, 9.14). Complete profile of a small pot stand.
5. BE. B.II (TS. 3901; Op. 5, 9.15). Complete base and about 1/2 of body of a cup-like vessel preserved.
6. BE. D.II (TS. 3922; Op. 5, 9.15). Complete base and portion of lower wall of vessel preserved.

Another Type Series Example:
Early Bronze Age — (1) BE. E.I.j (TS. 3898).

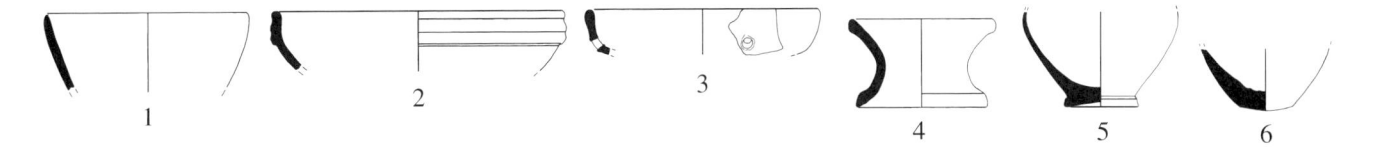

Figure 245. Pottery from Operation 5 (Phase 6; Period B — Derived Early Bronze Age). Scale 1:5

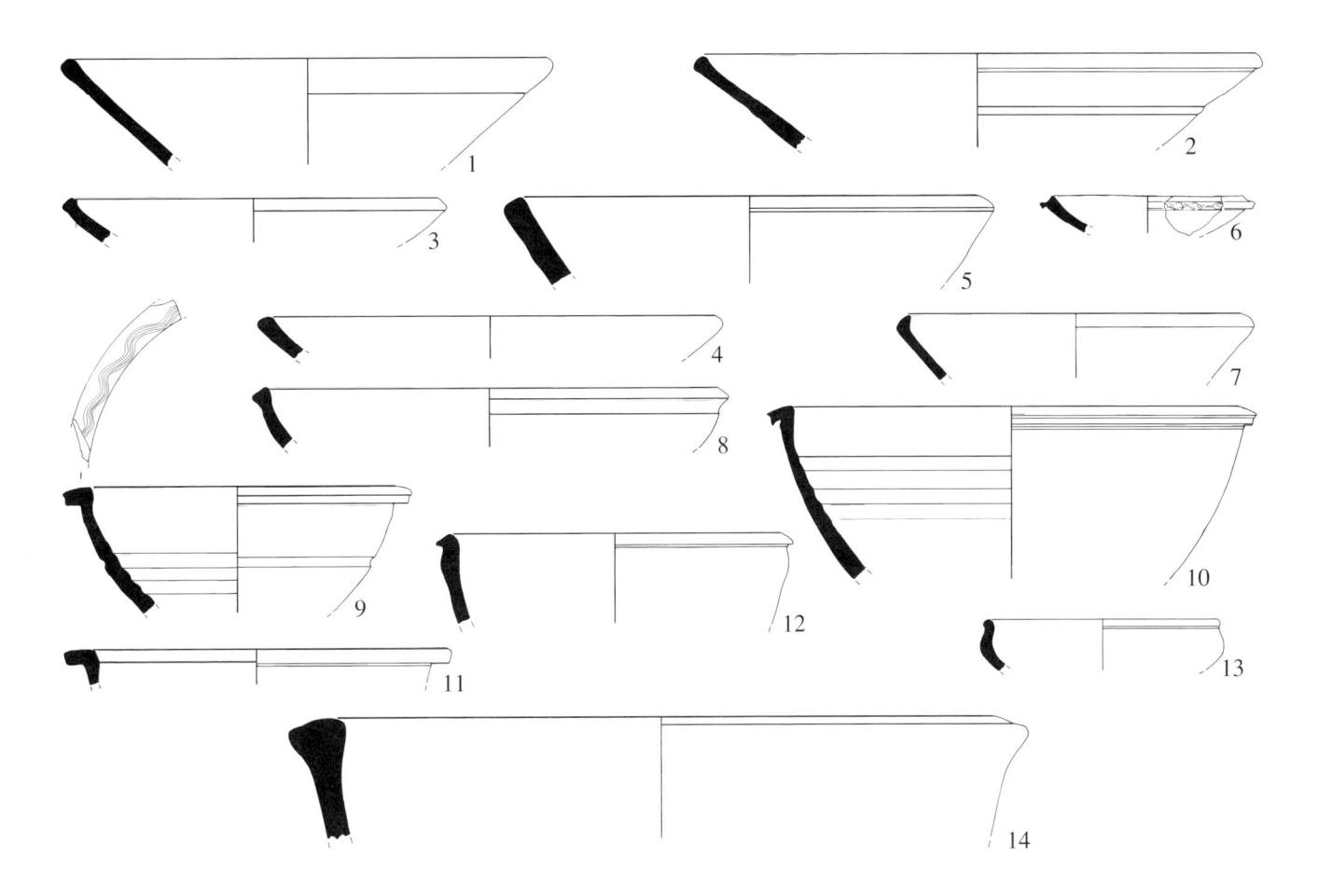

Figure 246. Pottery from Operation 5 (Phase 7, Period B — Late Roman). Scale 1:5

1. R.BR. A.I.a (TS. 3789 = TS. 3790; Op. 5, 4.2). Large portion of rim and most of wall segment. Ware description not available.
2. R.BR. A.I.a (TS. 4041; Op. 5, 4.3). Large portion of rim and most of wall segment. Ware description not available.
3. R.BR. A.I.b (TS. 3952; Op. 5, 4.2). Small rim and upper wall segment. Ware description not available.
4. R.BR. A.I.b (TS. 3678; Op. 5, 5.3). Small rim and upper wall segment. Ware description not available.
5. R.BR. A.I.b (TS. 3735; Op. 5, 4.4). Small rim segment with about 1/2 of vessel wall. Ware description not available.
6. R.BR. A.I.d (TS. 3686; Op. 5, 5.2). Small rim and upper wall segment with piecrust-like molding just below rim outside. Ware description not available.
7. R.BR. A.II.d (TS. 3953; Op. 5,2, 3.3). Small rim and upper wall segment. Ware description not available.
8. R.BR. A.II.g (TS. 3226; Op. 5, 2, 3.1). Small rim and upper wall segment. Ware description not available.
9. R.BR. B.I.b (IP [G.1] K.I.a; TS. 3230; Op. 5, 3.3). About 1/8 rim and most of wall segment. Comb-incised wavy line decoration on top of rim. Ware description not available.
10. R.BR. B.I.b (TS. 3231; Op. 5, 3.3). Large segment of rim and most of wall profile. Ware description not available.
11. R.BR. B.I.b (TS. 3679; Op. 5, 5.3). Small rim and upper wall segment. Ware description not available.
12. R.BR. B.I.e (TS. 3861; Op. 5, 5.1). Small rim segment and about 2/3 of vessel wall. Ware description not available.
13. R.BR. D.II.a (TS. 3662; Op. 5, 4.3). Small rim segment with upper portion of carinated wall. Ware description not available.
14. R.BR. E.II.c (TS. 3791; Op. 5, 3.1). Small segment of rim and upper wall. Ware description not available.

Figure 247. Pottery from Operation 5 (Phase 7; Period B — Late Roman) (*cont.*). Scale 1:5

1. R.JR. A.I.b (TS. 3346; Op. 5, 4.1). Small segment of rim and upper wall. Ware description not available.
2. R.JR. B.I.d (TS. 3955; Op. 5, 1.1). Small rim and neck segment. Ware description not available.
3. R.JR. B.I.f (TS. 3649; Op. 5, 4.4). Small rim and shoulder segment. Ware description not available.
4. R.JR. C.I.c (TS. 3957: Op. 5, 1, 4.1). Small rim and neck segment. Ware description not available.
5. R.JR. C.II.b (TS. 3732; Op. 5, 4.1). Small rim, neck, and shoulder segment. Ware description not available.
6. R.JR. C.II.b (TS. 3956; Op. 5, 2, 3.3). Small rim, neck, and upper shoulder segment. Ware description not available.
7. R.HMJ. A.II.d (TS. 3776; Op. 5, 3.2). Small rim and upper shoulder segment. Ware description not available.
8. R.Jg. A.I.b (TS. 3778; Op. 5, 3.3). Portion of rim and neck with attached vertical loop handle. Ware description not available.
9. R.Jg. B.II.g (TS. 3782; Op. 5, 4.2). Small portion of rim and upper neck with attached vertical loop handle. Ware description not available.
10. R.Jg.B.II.i (TS. 3863; Op. 5, 5.2). About 1/2 of rim, neck, and shoulder segment with complete loop handle attached. Ware description not available.
11. R.Jg. B.II.o (TS. 3780; Op. 5, 1.1). Small rim and upper neck segment. Ware description not available.
12. R.Jg. B.II.o (TS. 3796; Op. 5, 2, 3.1). Small rim and upper neck segment with attached vertical loop handle. Ware description not available.
13. R.Jg. C.I.f (TS. 3653; Op. 5, 4.1). Small rim and upper neck segment. Ware description not available.
14. R.Jg. C.I.f (TS. 3779; Op. 5, 4.2). Small rim and upper neck segment with attached vertical loop handle. Ware description not available.
15. R.BE. B.II.b (TS. 3794; Op. 5, 4.1). Complete profile of base and segment of lower wall of vessel. Ware description not available.
16. R.Sp. (TS. 3654; Op. 5, 4.1). About 1/2 segment of a jar spout. Ware description not available.
17. R.ABS. C (TS. 3650; Op. 5, 4.1). Body sherd of a large jar with applied rope-like band decorated with diagonally scored incisions. Ware description not available.
18. R.JR.Sh. (IP [G.1] C.VI.a; TS. 3229; Op. 5, 3.3). Shoulder sherd of a jar decorated with horizontal and wavy comb-incised lines. Ware description not available.
19. R.JR.Sh. (IP [G.1] D.I.b; TS. 3660; Op. 5, 2, 3.1). Small shoulder segment of a jar with comb-incised decoration. Ware description not available.
20. R.JR.Sh. (IP [G.1] C.IV.a; TS. 3788; Op. 5, 4.3). Small shoulder segment of a jar with comb-incised decoration. Ware description not available.
21. R.JR.Sh. (IP [G.3] B.IV.a; TS. 3185; Op. 5, 4.1). Jar wall sherd decorated with vertically incised columns in herringbone style. Ware description not available.
22. R.JR.Sh. (IP [G.4] A.V.a; TS. 3656; Op. 5, 4.1). Jar shoulder sherd decorated with incised checkerboard-like lines. Ware description not available.
23. R.JR.Sh. (IP [G.4] B.IV.a; TS. 3797; Op. 5, 4.3). Jar neck and shoulder sherd decorated with various linear patterns. Ware description not available.
24. R.JR.Sh. (IP [G.1] F.I.a; TS. 3680; Op. 5, 5.3). Jar shoulder sherd with vertical columns of fingernail-impressed decoration. Ware description not available.
25. R.JR.Sh. Pt. (TS. 3798; Op. 5, 2, 3.6). Jar shoulder sherd irregularly decorated with painted patterns. (Key to drawing: solid black equals dark brown paint and diagonal spaced lines equal orange-brown paint.) Ware description not available.
26. R.JR.Sh. Pt. (TS. 3733; Op. 5, 4.2). Jar shoulder sherd decorated with interconnecting half-moon or circular bands of orange-brown paint. Ware description not available.

Other Type Series Examples:
   Roman — (1) R.BR. A.I.e (TS. 3681), (2) R.BR. A.I.f (TS. 3652), (3) R.BR. B.I.g (TS. 3874), (4) R.BR. B.I.h (TS. 3235), (5) R.BR. E.II.c (TS. 3854), (6) R.BR. E.II.d (TS. 3792), (7) R.SJR. B.I.b (TS. 3950), (8) R.JR. A.I.g (TS. 3949), (9) R.JR. C.I.b (TS. 3964), (10) R.JR. C.II.d (TS. 3659), (11) R.JR. C.II.e (TS. 3651), (12) R.Bt. B.I.d (TS. 3786), (13) R.Jg. C.I.c (TS. 3675), (14) R.Jg. C.I.d (TS. 3658), (15) R.Jg. C.I.e (TS. 3661), (16) R.Jg. C.I.f (TS. 3781), (17) R.CP. B.II.b (TS. 3234), (18) R.PS.3 (TS. 3855), (19) R.BE. B.II.b (TS. 3857).
   Derived Early Bronze Age — (1) SR. B.II.a (TS. 3858).
   Derived Early–Middle Bronze Age — (1) BE. F.VIII.a (TS. 3675).

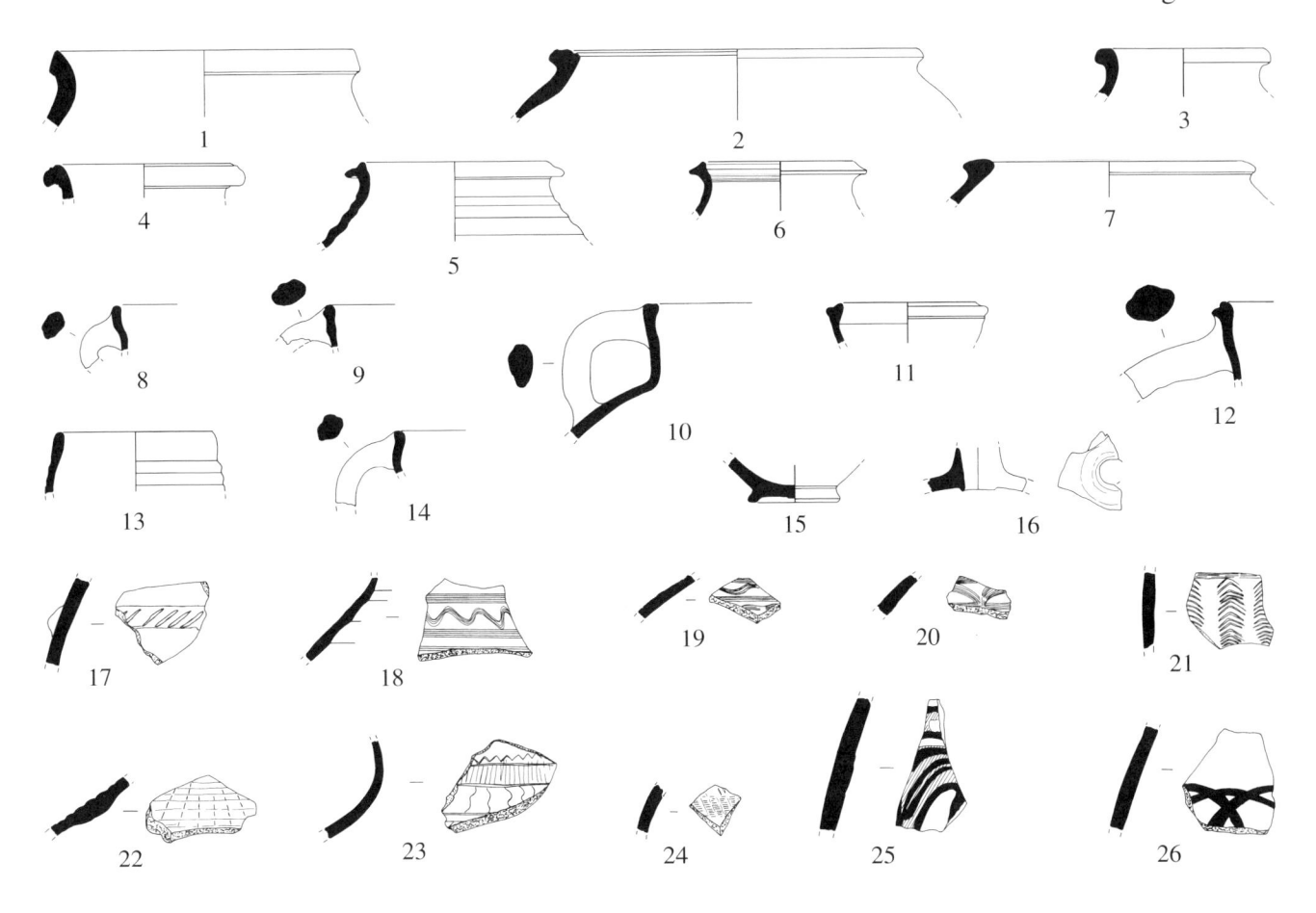

Figure 247. Pottery from Operation 5 (Phase 7; Period B — Late Roman) (*cont.*). Scale 1:5

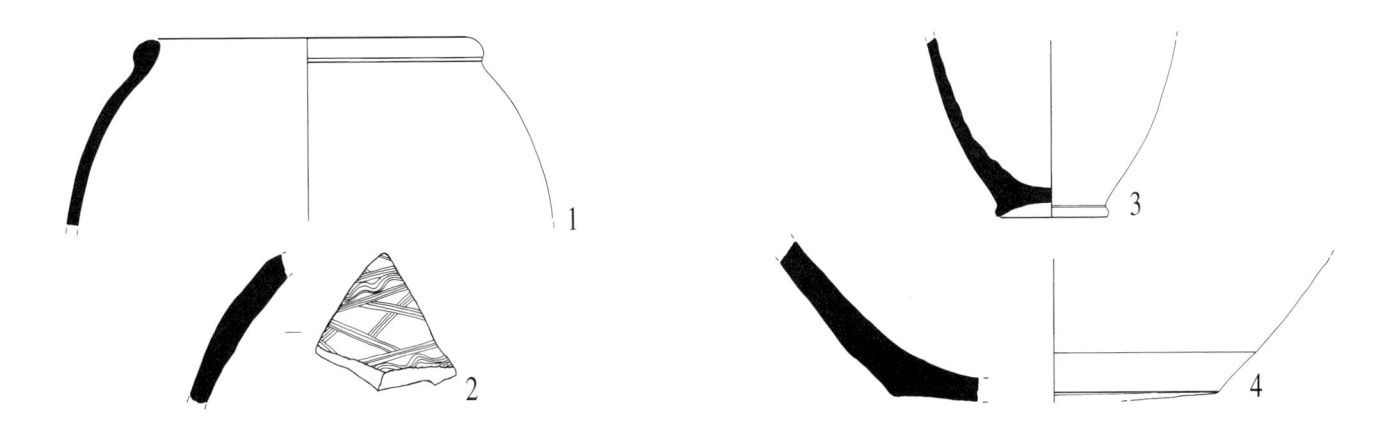

Figure 248. Pottery from Operation 5 (Unstratified; Roman and Early Bronze Age). Scale 1:5

1. R.HMJ. B.II.a (TS. 3843; Op. 5). Large rim, neck, and upper body segment. Ware description not available.
2. JR.Sh. (IP [G.1] L.I.a; TS. 3753; Op. 5). Jar shoulder sherd decoration with miscellaneous comb-incised diagonal, horizontal, and wavy bands of lines. Ware description not available.
3. BE. E.I.b (TS. 3878; Op. 5). Complete ring base and most of lower wall profile of the vessel. Ware description not available.
4. R.BE. A.II.a (TS. 3848; Op. 5). Large segment of an incomplete flat base and lower wall of vessel. Ware description not available.

Figure 249. Figurines, Model Chariot, and Model Chariot Wheel from Operation 5 (Phases 2 and 4–7; Periods G, F, and B — Early Bronze Age III, Early Bronze Age IVa, and Roman)

1. Type SF.1a (SW. 835; Op. 5, 18.4). Phase 4 (EB IVa; see pl. 112). Female figurine. Head and upper torso fragment with both arms positioned at the breasts. Ware description not available.
2. Type SF.1b (SW. 817; Op. 5, 10.1). Phase 6 (Roman, Derived EB; see pl. 113b). Male figurine head and neck fragment. Conical-shaped head or headdress. Ware description not available.
3. Type SF.1c (FN. 13; Op. 5, 16.1). Phase 6 (Roman, Derived EB; see pl. 113a). Female figurine upper torso fragment with triple-stranded necklace. Ware description not available.
4. Type SF.1a (FN. 175; Op. 5, 32.1). Phase 2 (EB III; see pl. 114a). Female figurine upper torso fragment (originally with two heads). Heads, right arm, part of left arm, and lower section of the pillar stand missing. Fine pinkish-brown ware with gray and white lime and small gold-colored mica grits, evenly fired. The single-stranded necklace is applied just over the shoulders onto the upper back of the figure and has an attached pendant-like object over the chest and stomach area in front, which possibly represents another figure (perhaps a child) that may indicate this figurine was used as a type of amulet requiring a double blessing.
5. Type SF.1c (TS. 3934; Op. 5, 11.2). Phase 4 (EB IVa). Human figurine pillar stand fragment. Ware description not available.
6. Type SF.1c (TS. 3924; Op. 5, 11.2). Phase 4 (EB IVa). Human figurine pillar stand fragment. Ware description not available.
7. Type SF.1c (TS. 3667; Op. 5, 8.1). Phase 6 (Roman). Human figurine pillar stand fragment. Ware description not available.
—. Type SF.1c (FN. 149; Op. 5, 17.3, Pit). Phase 4 (EB IVa; see pl. 114b). Human figurine pillar stand fragment. Ware description not available.
—. Type SF.1d (FN. 24; Op. 5, 13.2). Phase 4 (EB IVa; see pl. 114c). Model horse figurine; head and neck fragment. Ware description not available.
8. Type SF.1d (SW. 826; Op. 5, 4.1). Phase 7 (Roman, Derived EB; see pl. 118f). Clay lion's head with appliqué and incised decoration. Broken off at base of neck from some form of larger clay vessel. Possibly compare the cauldron from Area IVF (fig. 64:4; pl. 93). Ware description not available.
—. Type SF.1e (FN. 16; Op. 5, 12.1). Phase 5 (Roman). Animal figurine torso. Unidentifiable. 5.5 cm long with only stubs of legs present. Ware description not available.
9. Type SF.2a (SW. 841; Op. 5, 18.6, Pit). Phase 4 (EB IVa). Model chariot fragment. Front and side portions decorated with incised upside down tree or wheat patterns. Ware description not available.
10. Type SF.2b (FN. 81; Op. 5, 10.5). Phase 5 (Roman). Model chariot wheel with a very wide cone-shaped hub projections on both sides. About 1/2 fragment with ends of hubs broken. Ware description not available.

Figure 249

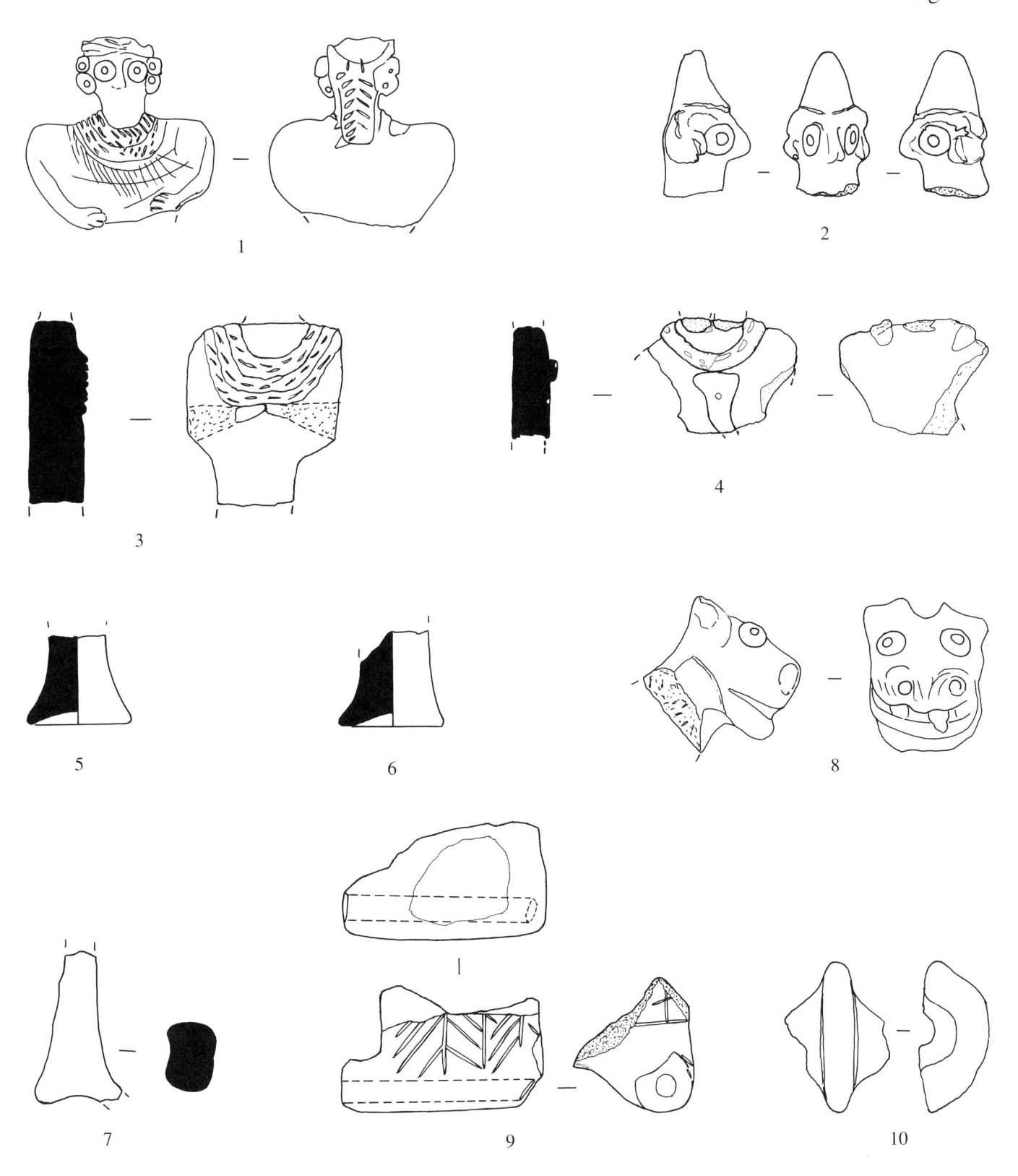

Figurines, Model Chariot, and Model Chariot Wheel from Operation 5 (Phases 2 and 4–7; Periods G, F, and B — Early Bronze Age III, Early Bronze Age IVa, and Roman). Scale 1:2

Figure 250. Stone Objects from Operation 5 (Phases 2 and 4–7; Periods G, F, and B — Early Bronze Age III, Early Bronze Age IVa, and Roman)

1. Type SF.3a (TS. 3177; Op. 5, 17.3, Pit). Phase 4 (EB IVa). Grinder.
2. Type SF.3a (TS. 3178; Op. 5, 32.5). Phase 2 (EB III). Polishing tool.
3. Type SF.3c (TS. 3233; Op. 5, 4.4). Phase 7 (Roman). About 2/3 of a mortar.
4. Type SF.3d (TS. 3172; Op. 5, 1.1). Phase 7 (Roman). Nearly 1/2 of a door socket stone.
5. Type SF.3f (TS. 3239; Op. 5, 10.1). Phase 6 (Roman). Spindle whorl. Complete with central hole drilled from both broad sides.
6. Type SF.3f (FN. 116; Op. 5, 6.8, Pit). Phase 6 (Roman). Rubbing tool. Chalky limestone sphere worn flat on the used surface.
7. Type SF.3f (SW. 830; Op. 5, 9.12). Phase 5 (Roman; see pl. 122b). Weapon mold. Gray limestone. Used for manufacture of metal blade with blunt tang, incomplete mold.
—. Type SF.3f (FN. 18; Op. 5, 9.12). Phase 5 (Roman). Limestone sphere, probably used as a rubbing or smoothing tool. 1.6 cm in diameter.

Figure 250

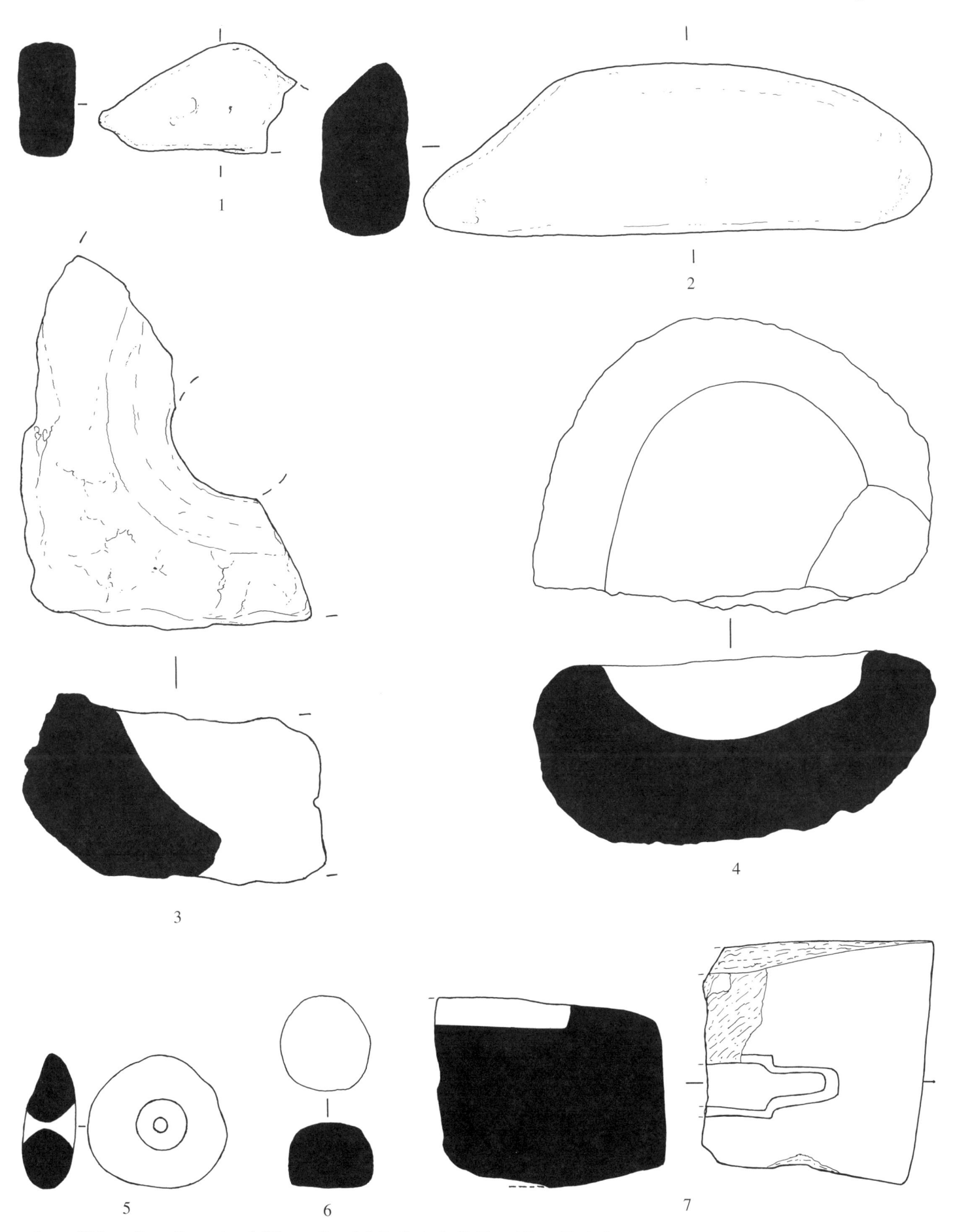

Stone Objects from Operation 5 (Phases 2 and 4–7; Periods G, F, and B — Early Bronze Age III, Early Bronze Age IVa, and Roman). Scale 1:2

Figure 251

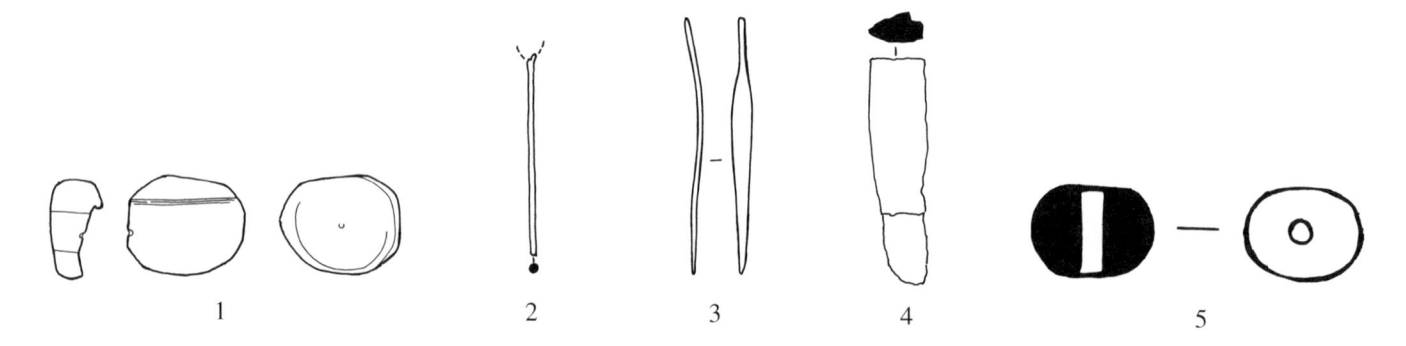

1　　　　　　　2　　　3　　　4　　　　5

Bone, Metal, and Stone Objects from Operation 5 (Phases 3–7; Periods G, F, and B — Early Bronze Age III, Early Bronze Age IVa, and Roman). Scales 1:2 (1–4) and 2:1 (5)

1. Type SF.9a (SW. 843; Op. 5, 17.3, Pit). Phase 4 (EB IVa). Bone bead or pendant. Unfinished stringing hole through long axis. Highly polished with linear incised decoration on broad surfaces and one end.
—. Type SF.9a (FN. 20; Op. 5, 10.1). Phase 6 (Roman). Bone bead or pendant. Obelisk shape, 1.5 cm long and 0.6 cm at base.
—. Type SF.5c (FN. 199; Op. 5, 15.6). Phase 3 (EB III). Metal pin fragment (arsenical copper). See *Appendix 6*.
2. Type SF.5c (FN. 179; Op. 5, 18.6, Pit). Phase 4 (EB IVa). Metal pin shaft. Both ends missing (arsenical copper). See *Appendix 6*.
—. Type SF.5c (FN. 194; Op. 5, 10.3). Phase 5 (Roman, Derived EB). Metal pin shaft fragment (copper). See *Appendix 6*.
—. Type SF.5c (FN. 196; Op. 5, 9.12). Phase 5 (Roman, Derived EB). Metal pin head (tin bronze). See *Appendix 6*.
3. Type SF.5g (SW. 801; Op. 5, Baulk scraping, 10 and 11). Phase 5 (Roman or Derived EB; see pl. 122a). Metal spatula (copper/bronze?, not analyzed).
—. Type SF.5g (FN. 197; Op. 5, 9.3). Phase 5 (Roman). Metal spatula head (brass). See *Appendix 6*.
4. Type SF.5h (FN. 176; Op. 5, 2.1). Phase 7 (Roman). Metal knife blade fragment (iron). See *Appendix 6*.
—. Type SF.5h (FN. 198; Op. 5, 18.6, Pit). Phase 4 (EB IVa). Metal blade fragment (arsenical copper). See *Appendix 6*.
—. Type SF.5h (FN. 193; Op. 5, 6.6). Phase 6 (Roman). Lump of metal (iron). See *Appendix 6*.
—. Type SF.5i (FN. 195; Op. 5, 15.3). Phase 3 (EB III). Lump of metal (copper). See *Appendix 6*.
5. Type SF.4b (SW. 844; Op. 5, 17.3, Pit). Phase 4 (EB IVa). Bead. Glazed quartz. Approximately spherical, 6.1 mm long and 8.6 mm in diameter. (scale of drawing 2:1; See Vandiver, Fenn, and Holland 1992: 519–25 and fig. 1 for a detailed description of this bead.)

Figure 252. Miscellaneous Clay Objects from Operation 5 (Phases 2, 4, 5, and 7; Periods G, F, and B — Early Bronze Age III, Early Bronze Age IVa, and Roman)

1. Type SF.6b (TS. 4058; Op. 5, 32.1). Phase 2 (EB III). Clay spindle whorl manufactured from a broken vessel sherd. Ware description not available.
—. Type SF.6b (TS. 3182; Op. 5, 32.1). Phase 2 (EB III). Clay spindle whorl. Ware description not available.
—. Type SF.6b (FN. 47; Op. 5, 10.5). Phase 5 (Roman). Clay spindle whorl. 5.6 cm diameter, 5 mm hole drilled in center. Ware description not available.
—. Type SF.6b (FN. 143; Op. 5, 18.5). Phase 4 (EB IVa). Clay spindle whorl manufactured from a broken vessel sherd. 3.0 × 3.5 cm diameter, 6 mm hole drilled in center from both sides, center of hole 1 mm wide. Fine buff ware. Ware description not available.
—. Type SF.6b (FN. 142; Op. 5, 18.6, Pit). Phase 4 (EB IVa). Clay spindle whorl. One half measuring 2.0 × 3.5 cm diameter, 1.5 cm hole drilled in center from both sides, center of hole 8 mm wide. Ware description not available.
2. Type SF.6d (TS. 3886; Op. 5, 17.1). Phase 4 (EB IVa). Pottery bread mold fragment or for some other baking or cooking use. Ware description not available.
—. Type SF.6g (FN. 163; Op. 5, 14.2). Phase 4 (EB IVa). Clay object of indeterminate shape, incompletely pierced. Ware description not available.
3. Type SF.6g (FN. 169; Op. 5, 32.1). Phase 2 (EB III; see pl. 114d). Miniature clay mortar associated with wall painting and possibly used to hold and/or mix the paint used for the wall painting. Ware description not available.
4. Type SF.6g (FN. 170; Op. 5, 32.1). Phase 2 (EB III; see pl. 114d). Miniature clay mortar found in association with FN. 169 above. Ware description not available.

Figure 252

5. Type SF.6g (TS. 3908; Op. 5, 11. 2). Phase 4 (EB IVa). Base of small "offering" table or miniature container. Ware description not available.
6. Type SF.6g (TS. 3914; Op. 5, 11.1). Phase 5 (Roman). Sherd reused as a work tool for smoothing or rubbing. Ware description not available.
7. Type SF.6g (TS. 3862; Op. 5, 5.2). Phase 7 (Roman). Manufactured clay tool, handle, or spatula-like object, incomplete. Ware description not available.

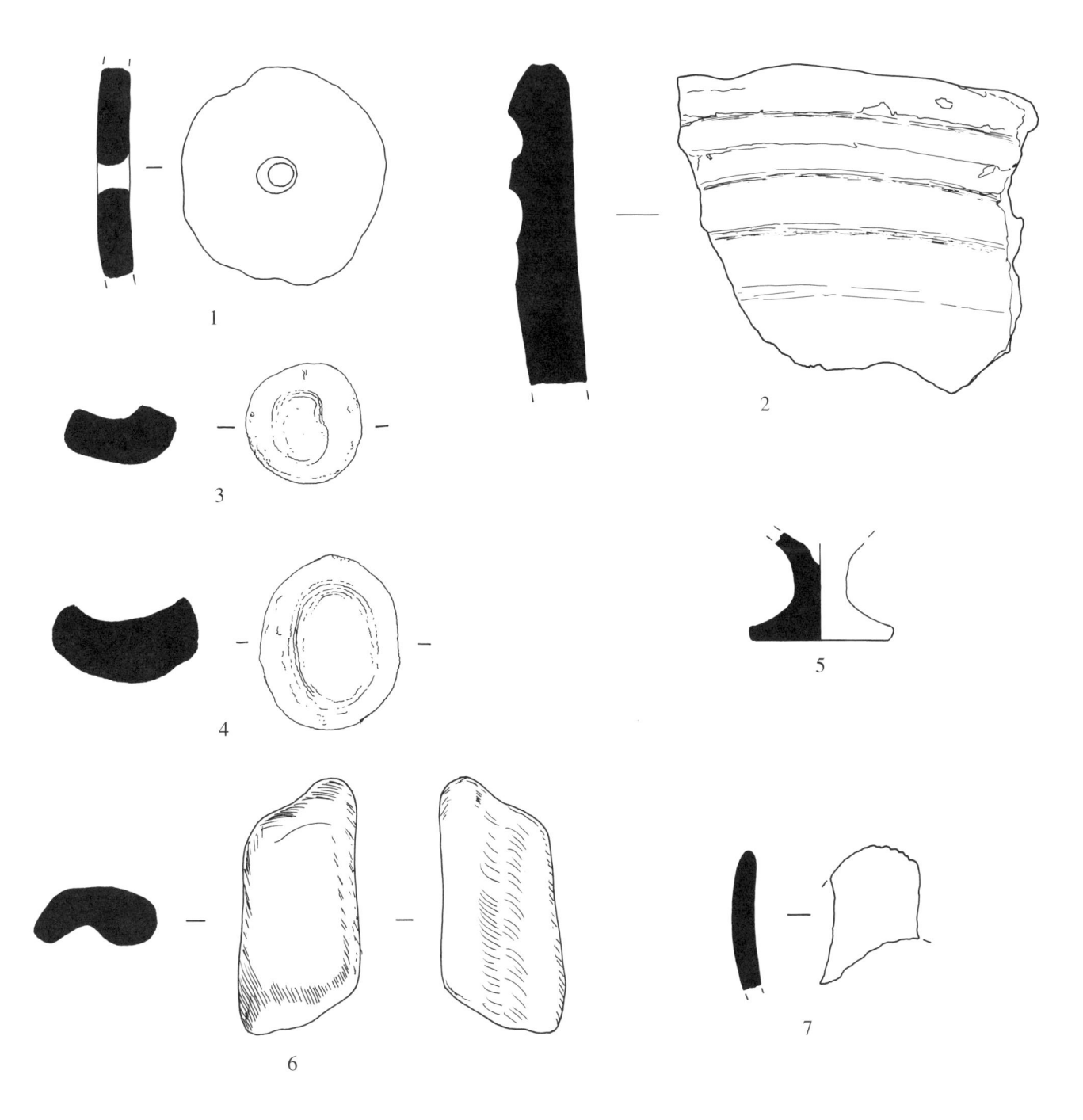

Miscellaneous Clay Objects from Operation 5 (Phases 2, 4, 5, and 7; Periods G, F, and B — Early Bronze Age III, Early Bronze Age IVa, and Roman). Scale 1:2

Figure 253. Glass, Flint, and Special Clay Vessels or Objects from Operation 5 (Phases 4–7; Periods F and B — Early Bronze Age IVa and Roman)

1. Type SF.7b (TS. 3228; Op. 5, 3.2). Phase 7 (Roman). Glass bracelet fragment.
2. Type SF.7b (TS. 3232; Op. 5, 3.3). Phase 7 (Roman). Glass bracelet fragment.
3. Type SF.7b (FN. 104; Op. 5, 5.1). Phase 7 (Roman). Glass ring fragment. Brownish color.
4. Type SF.7a (TS. 3237; Op. 5, 5.1). Phase 7 (Roman). Glass vessel fragment.
5. Type SF.7a (TS. 3238; Op. 5, 8.1). Phase 6 (Roman). Glass jar fragment.
6. Type SF.7a (TS. 3227; Op. 5, 3.2). Phase 7 (Roman). Glass vessel base.
—. Type SF.11b (FN. 146; Op. 5, 17.3, Pit). Phase 4 (EB IVa). Mother-of-pearl shell fragment.
7. Type SF.12a (TS. 3236; Op. 5, 5.1). Phase 7 (Roman). Flint scraper.
8. Type SV.4 (TS. 3856; Op. 5, 5.1). Phase 7 (Roman). Clay bottle stopper. Ware description not available.
9. Type SV.5 (TS. 3833; Op. 5, 11.2). Phase 4 (EB IVa). Clay miniature incense alter. Ware description not available.
10. Type SV.5 (TS. 3981; Op. 5, 12.1). Phase 5 (Roman). Clay object or vessel of indeterminate use. Ware description not available.
11. Type SV.5 (TS. 3897; Op. 5, 13.6). Phase 4 (EB IVa). Clay object or vessel of indeterminate use. Ware description not available.

Figure 253

Glass, Flint, and Special Clay Vessels or Objects from Operation 5 (Phases 4–7; Periods F and B — Early Bronze Age IVa and Roman). Scale 1:2

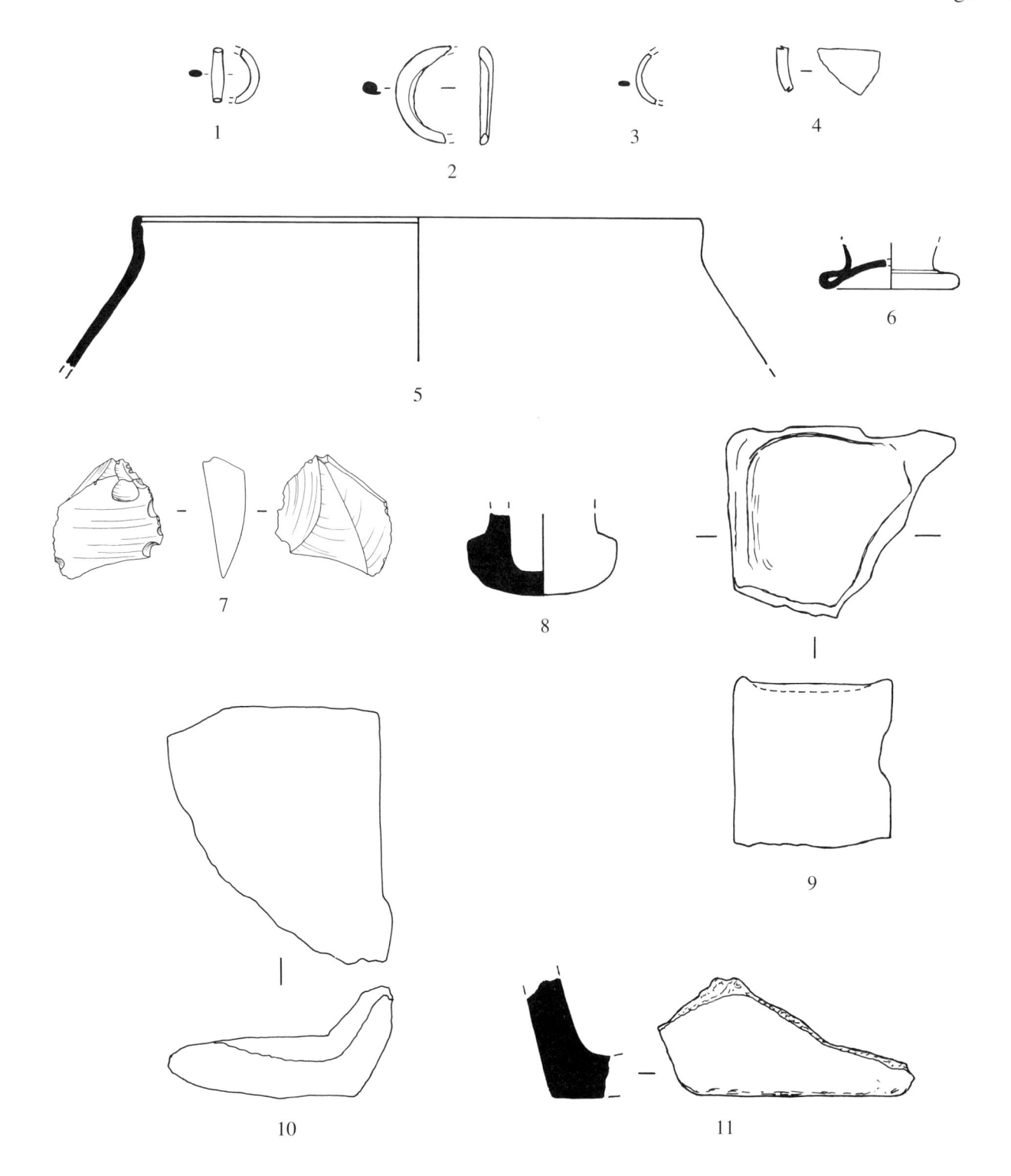

Figure 254

Wall Painting Fragment, WP.92.38, Depicting a Bovine with Suckling Calf Standing on a Mountainside from Operation 5 (Phase 2; Period G — Early Bronze Age III; for photograph, see pl. 130)

Figure 255

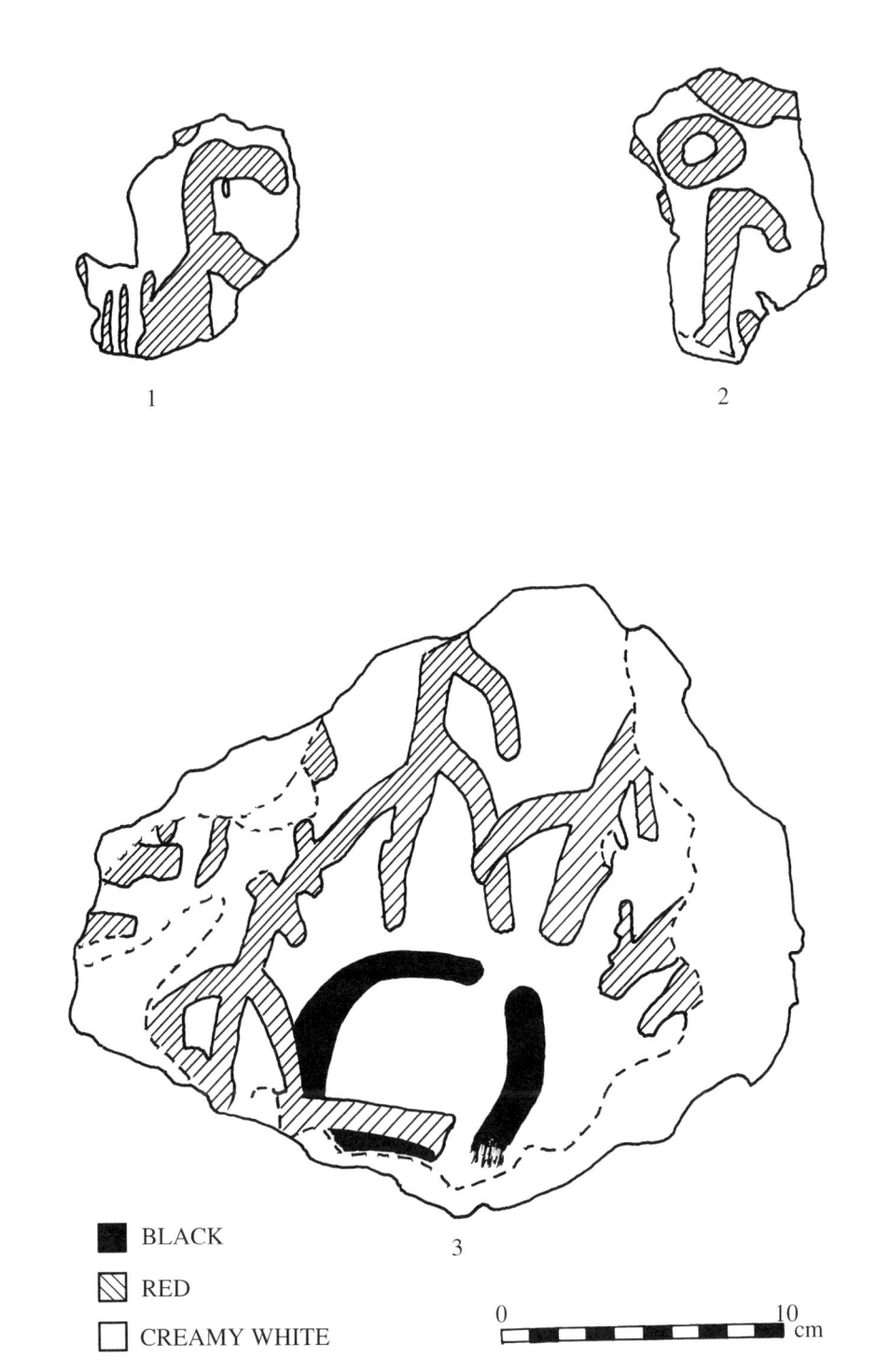

- BLACK
- RED
- CREAMY WHITE

0 — 10 cm

Wall Painting Fragments Depicting Stylized Human Figures from Operation 5 (Phase 2; Period G — Early Bronze Age III)

1. WP.92.63 (Op. 5, 32.5). Phase 2.
2. WP.92.71 (Op. 5, 32.5). Phase 2.
3. WP.92.61 (Op. 5, 32.5). Phase 2 (see pl. 131a).

Figure 256

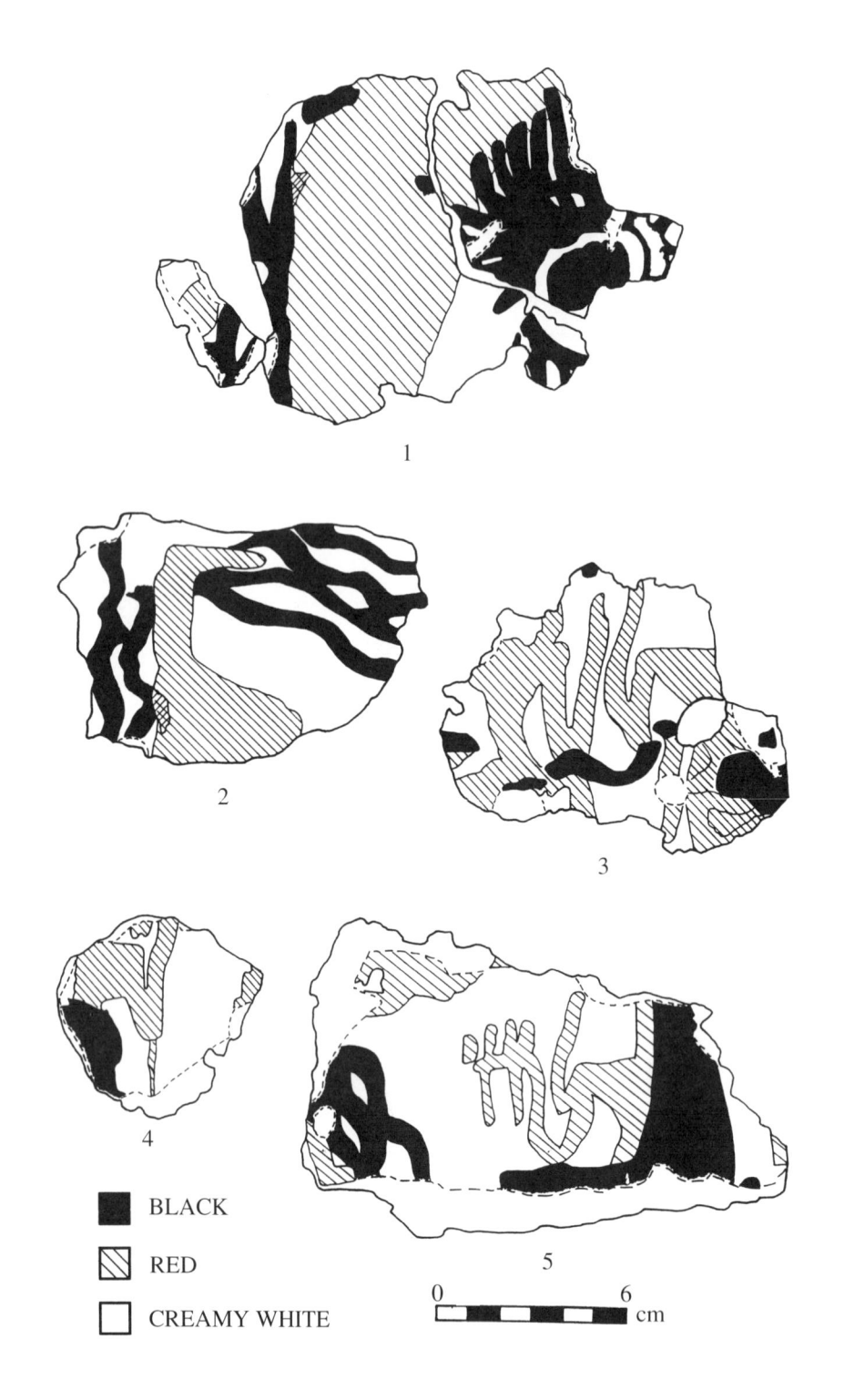

BLACK
RED
CREAMY WHITE

0  6 cm

Wall Painting Fragments Depicting Stylized Human Figures from Operation 5 (Phase 2; Period G — Early Bronze Age III)

1. WP.91.7 (Op. 5, 32.5). Phase 2.
2. WP.92.73 (Op. 5, 32.5). Phase 2.
3. WP.91.42 (Op. 5, 32.5). Phase 2.
4. WP.91.5 (Op. 5, 32.5). Phase 2.
5. WP.92.23 (Op. 5, 32.5). Phase 2.

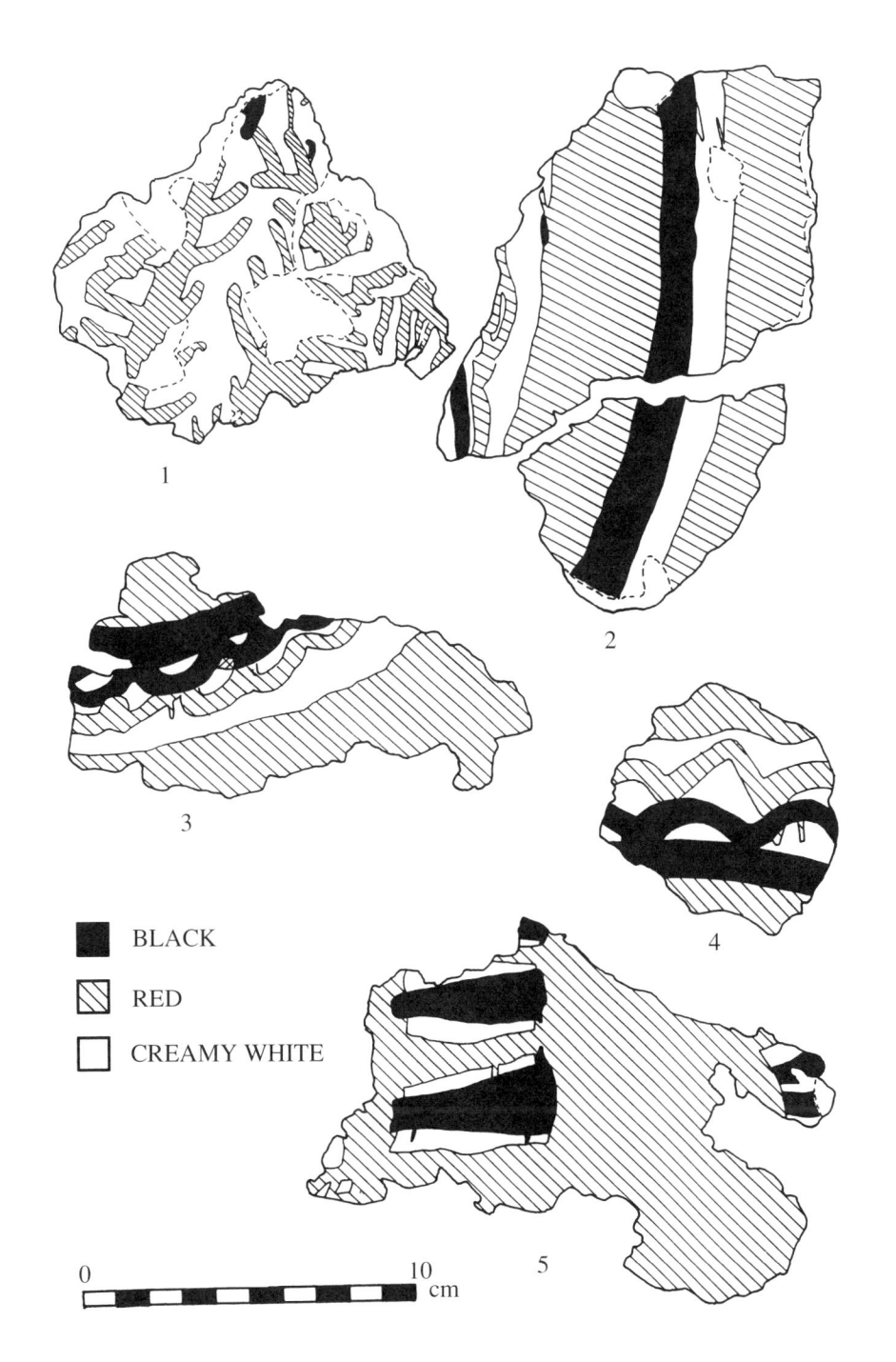

Figure 257

Wall Painting Fragments Depicting Geometric Patterns from Operation 5 (Phase 2; Period G — Early Bronze Age III)

1. WP.91.9 (Op. 5, 32.5). Phase 2.
2. WP.91.25 (Op. 5, 32.5). Phase 2.
3. WP.92.74a (Op. 5, 32.5). Phase 2 (pl. 131b).
4. WP.92.74b (Op. 5, 32.5). Phase 2 (pl. 131b).
5. WP.91.1 (Op. 5, 32.5). Phase 2.

Figure 258

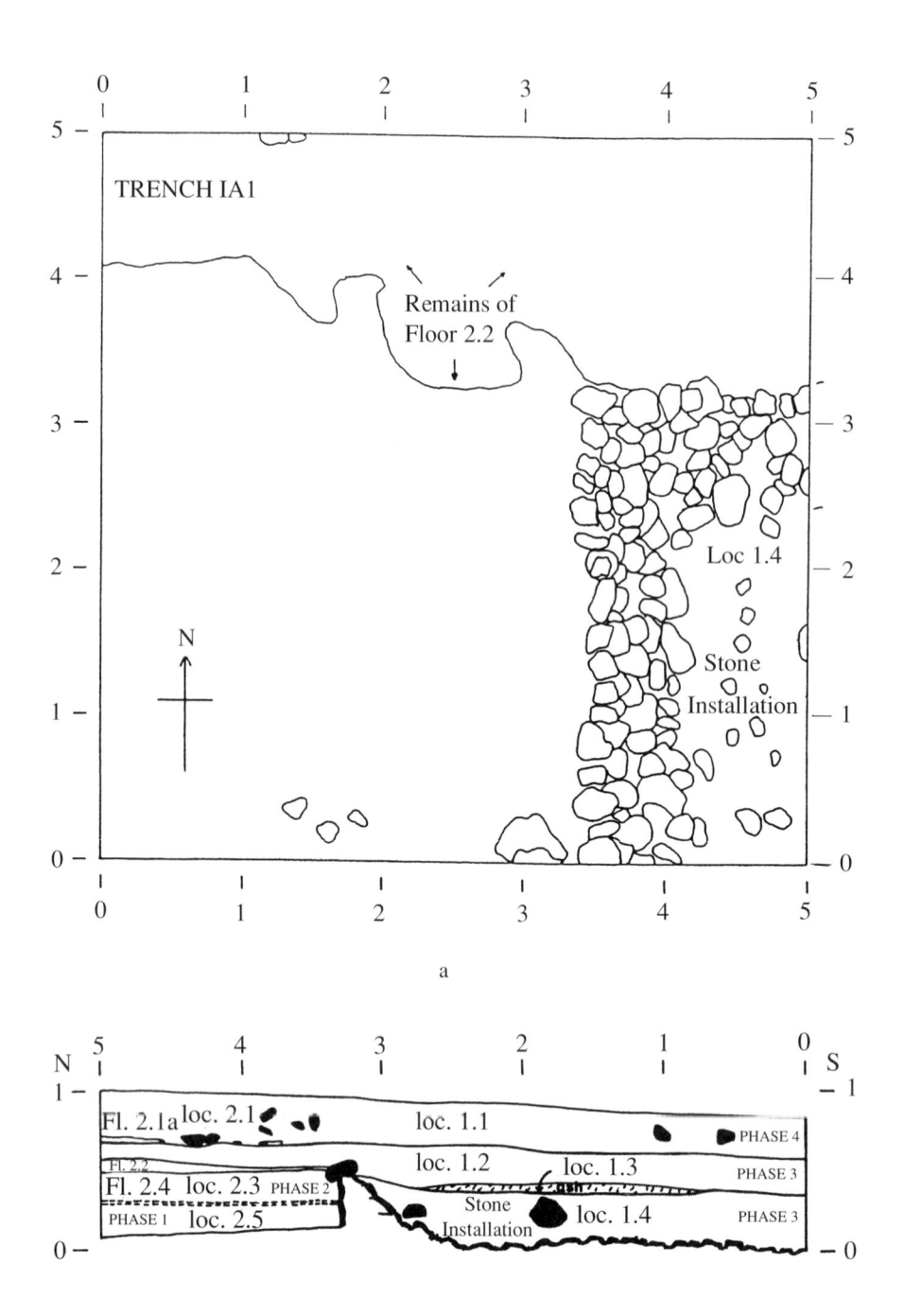

(*a*) Plan and (*b*) East Section of Trench IA1. Scale 1:50

Figure 259

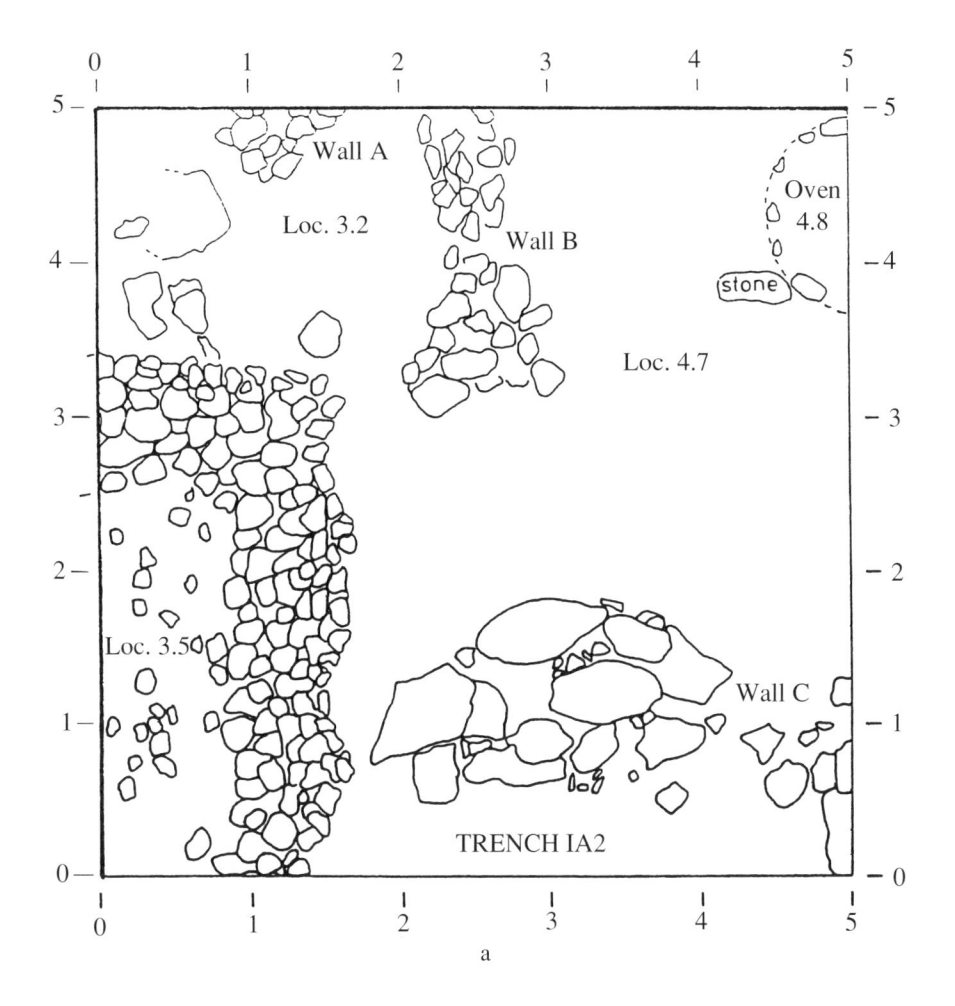

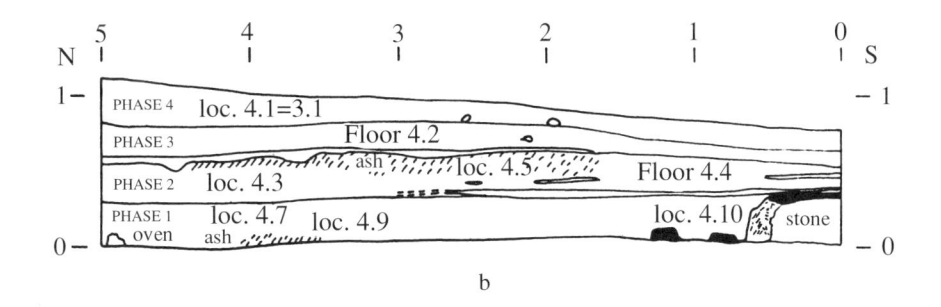

(*a*) Plan and (*b*) East Section of Trench IA2. Scale 1:50

Figure 260. Pottery from Trenches IA1 and IA2 (Phase 1, Period B — Derived Early Bronze Age and Roman)

1. BR. N.II.b (TS. 632; IA1, 2.5). About 1/8 rim and 2/3 of wall segment. Fairly coarse pink ware, evenly fired. Cream slip in and out.
2. SJR. C.II.e (TS. 646; IA2, 4.7). About 1/10 rim and neck segment. Fairly fine brown-grayware, unevenly fired with a gray core.
3. JR. B.V.b (TS. 2074; IA1, 2.5). Large segment of rim and shoulder. Fairly coarse pinkish-buff ware, evenly fired. Creamy-green slip in and out. Inner surface very worn.
4. JR. G.I.c (TS. 639; IA2, 4.7). About 1/12 rim and neck segment. Fairly fine pinkish-buff ware, evenly fired. Cream slip out.
5. CP. A.I.c (TS. 2155; IA1, 2.5). Small rim and neck segment with remains of a folded-over triangular-shaped ledge handle at the rim. Slightly coarse grayish-black ware fired brown at surfaces.
6. JR.Sh. (IP [G.3] B.III.a; TS. 592; IA1, 2.5). Fragment of a jar shoulder with a herringbone-incised decoration inside parallel horizontally incised lines. Fairly fine grayware, evenly fired.
7. R.BR. D.II.a (TS. 2089; IA1, 2.5). Small rim and wall segment. Slightly coarse grayish-buff ware, evenly fired. Self slip in and out.
8. R.BR. D.II.f (TS. 2511; IA2, 4.7). About 1/10 rim and wall segment. Coarse and gritty green ware, underfired. Self slip in and out.
9. R.JR. A.I.c (TS. 436; IA1, 2.5). About 1/6 rim and upper shoulder segment. Coarse buff ware, evenly fired. Cream slip in and out.
10. R.Jg. B.II.g (TS. 2132; IA1, 2.5). Small rim and neck segment. Fairly fine buff ware, evenly fired. Creamy-buff slip in and out.
11. R.JR.Sh. (IP [G.4] D.III.b; TS. 2036; IA1, 2.5). Large jar sherd with combed wavy and horizontal bands on the shoulder. Fairly coarse pink ware, evenly fired. Creamy-buff slip out.

Trench IA1:

Other Type Series Examples:

Derived Early Bronze Age — (1) CP. B.IV.f (TS. 2158).
Roman — (1) R.JR. C.I.d (TS. 4060), (2) R.HMJ. A.II.d (TS. 2083), (3) R.HMJ. B.II.d (TS. 432).
Roman Unillustrated Example: (1) SBR. B.I.c (TS. 574 = Tr. IIA, TS. 147, Misassigned).

Another Potter's Mark Example: Derived Early Bronze Age — (1) JR.Sh. (PM. C.11; SC. 3268), see fig. 333:10.

Other Study Collection Examples:

Derived Early Bronze Age — (1) SBR. A.I.d (SC. 3438), (2) SBR. B.I.i (SC. 3439), (3) SBR. C.II.c (SC. 3440), (4) SBR. A.I.d (SC. 3441), (5) SBR. F.I.b (variant, SC. 3467), (6) BR. (not typed, SC. 31), (7) BR. F.IV.d (SC. 819), (8) SJR. C.II.h (SC. 2592), (9) JR. B.III.a (SC. 1984), (10) JR. B.III.e (SC. 946), (11) JR. B.V.a (SC. 977), (12) JR. C.II.a (SC. 1000), (13) JR. D.V.a (SC. 1077), (14) JR. D.V.c (SC. 1085), (15) JR. H.I.e (SC. 1268), (16) JR. H.I.g (SC. 2076), (17) JR. J.II.l (SC. 2191), (18) JR. J.III.d (SC. 2227), (19) JR. J.III.e (SC. 2246), (20) JR. J.III.i (SC. 2298), (21) JR. J.III.n (SC. 1449), (22) JR. O.II.a (SC. 1622), (23) JR. P.II.a (SC. 1705), (24) JR. P.II.c (SC. 1720), (25) JR. P.III.f (SC. 1763), (26) BE. E.II.g (SC. 3217), (27) JR.Sh. (IP [G.3] Gen.; SC. 3254).
Roman — (1) R.Jg. B.II.q (SC. 3029).

Trench IA2:

Another Type Series Example: Roman — (1) R.BR. C.I.a (PM. A.6; TS. 1519).

Other Study Collection Examples:

Derived Early Bronze Age — (1) SBR. B.I.f (SC. 3447), (2) SBR. B.I.h (SC. 3446), (3)SBR. B.I.i (variant, SC. 3448), (4) JR. A.III.f (SC. 918), (5) JR. D.VIII.b (SC. 1120), (6) JR. J.III.a (SC. 2208).
Roman — (1) R.Jg. B.II.e (SC. 2778).

Figure 260

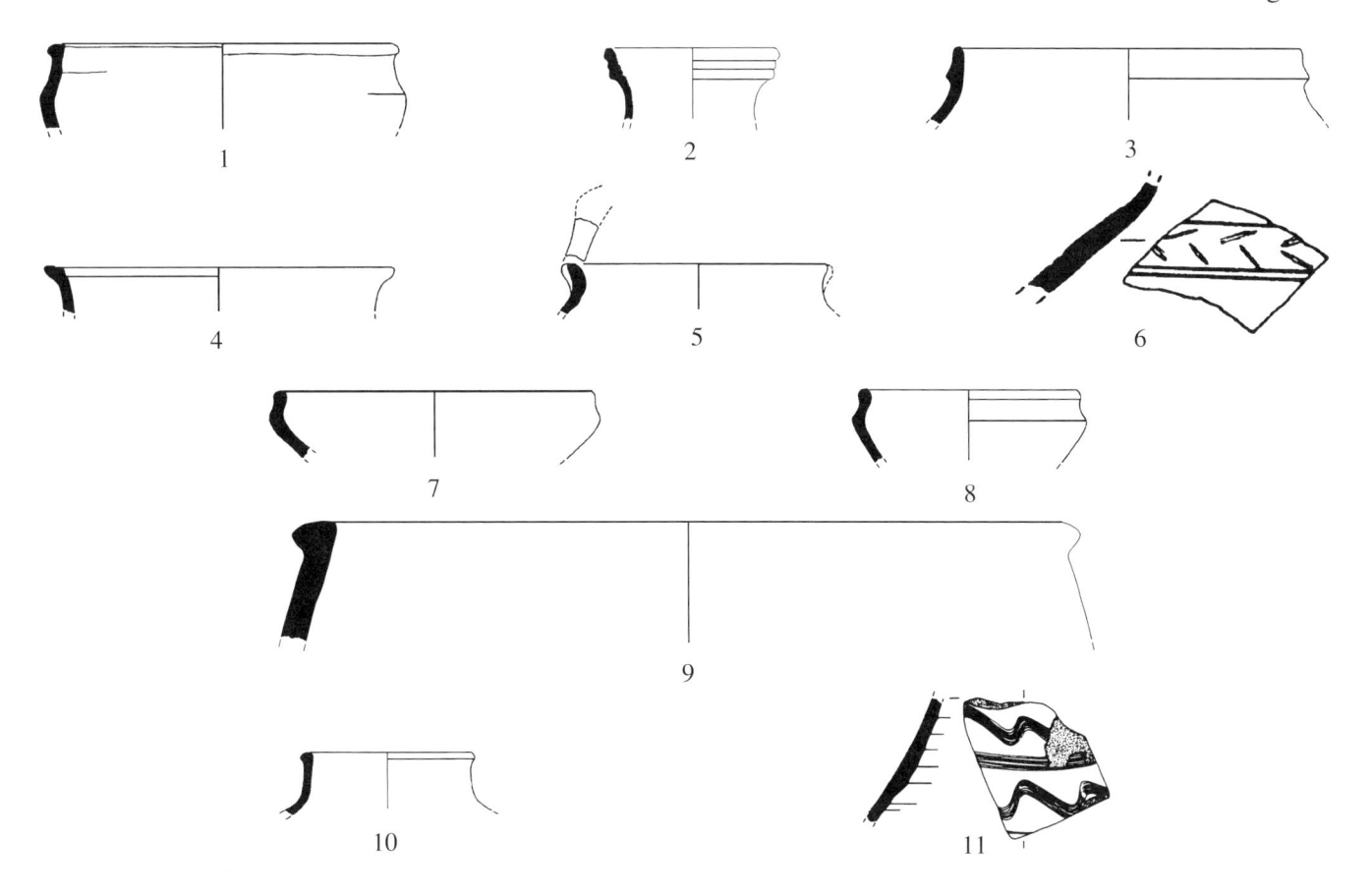

Pottery from Trenches IA1 and IA2 (Phase 1, Period B — Derived Early Bronze Age and Roman). Scale 1:5

Figure 261. Pottery from Trenches IA1 and IA2 (Phase 2; Period B — Derived Early Bronze Age, Roman, and Hellenistic)

1. SR. B.II.b (TS. 2433; IA1, 2.3). Derived EB-type strainer bowl. About 1/10 rim and upper wall segment. Fairly fine buff ware, evenly fired. Self slip in and out.
2. R.SBR. A.II.a (TS. 368; IA1, 2.3). Roman red-slip small bowl. Small rim and upper wall segment. Fine buff ware, evenly fired. Red slip in and out.
3. R.SBR. A.II.a (TS. 298; IA1, 2.3). Roman red-slip small bowl. Small rim and upper wall segment. Fairly fine pinkish-brown ware with small lime and mica grits, evenly fired. Red slip in and out.
4. R.BR. A.I.a (TS. 1499; IA2, 4.3). Small rim and wall segment. Hard, fairly fine buff ware, evenly fired. Self slip irregularly burnished in and out.
5. R.BR. A.II.b (TS. 1495; IA1, 2.4a). Small rim and upper wall segment. Slightly coarse pinkish-brown ware with lime and mica grits, evenly fired. Pinkish-buff slip out.
6. R.BR. B.I.b (TS. 288; IA1, 2.3). Small rim and upper wall segment. Slightly coarse pinkish-buff ware with lime and mica grits, evenly fired. Yellow-buff slip in and out. Square channel on inner side of top of rim.
7. R.BR. B.I.e (TS. 306; IA1, 2.3). Small rim and upper wall segment. Buff ware, evenly fired.
8. R.BR. B.I.f (TS. 302; IA1, 2.3). Small rim segment with remains of upper wall with a portion of a hole drilled through the wall after the vessel was fired, which may be a mending hole. Buff ware, evenly fired.
9. R.BR. D.II.a (TS. 309; IA1, 2.3). Small rim and wall segment. Hard-fired, light grayware, evenly fired.
10. R.BR. D.II.b (TS. 2110; IA2, 4.3). Large rim and wall segment. Slightly coarse pink ware, evenly fired. Buff slip in and out.
11. R.JR. A.I.b (TS. 1503; IA2, 4.3). Small rim and upper shoulder segment. Fine buff ware, evenly fired. Self slip in and out.
12. R.JR. C.II.d (TS. 1489; IA1, 2.4a). Small rim and neck segment. Hard-fired, fairly fine light pink ware with lime and mica grits, evenly fired. Yellow-buff slip in and out.
13. R.HMJ. B.II.a (TS. 294; IA1, 2.4). Small rim and shoulder segment. Slightly coarse buff ware with lime grits, evenly fired. Self slip in and out.
14. R.CP. B.II.a (TS. 1491; IA1, 2.4a). Large rim, neck, and upper shoulder segment. Fairly coarse ware with many lime and mica grits, unevenly fired with a light gray core and light brown at surfaces.
15. R.Bt. B.I.c (TS. 654; IA2, 4.3). About 1/6 rim and neck segment. Fairly coarse pink ware with grayish-black slip on inside of rim and on outside of extant fragment.
16. R.BE. B.II.b (TS. 635; IA2, 4.4). About 1/24 of rim of base. Fairly fine pink ware, burnished to a tan color in and out.
17. R.JR.Sh. (IP [G.1] B.II.b; TS. 1217; IA1, 2.4a). Jar shoulder segment with combed and incised decoration on outer wall. Slightly coarse creamy-buff ware, evenly fired. Self slip in and out.
18. R.JR.Sh. (IP [G.1] D.I.b; TS. 1219; IA1, 2.4a). Jar shoulder segment with combed wavy and horizontal bands of decoration. Slightly coarse creamy-buff ware, evenly fired. Self slip in and out.
19. R.JR.Sh. (IP [G.4] D.III; PM. D.20; TS. 533; IA2, 4.3). Jar shoulder segment with incised linear decoration. Fairly coarse pinkish-buff ware, evenly fired. Cream slip in and out.
—. SF.10. (SW. 105; IA2, 4.4). See fig. 28:8. Jar shoulder sherd inscribed with part of an Aramaic inscription.
20. R.Jg.Hd. (SW. 54; IA2, 4.3). Fragment of a spiral-twisted handle from a Roman jug. Compare the Type Series example on Roman jug type R.Jg. B.II.q (pl. 333:19). Pinkish-buff ware, evenly fired.

Trench IA1:

Other Type Series Examples:

Derived Hellenistic — (1) H.RSB. B.II.c (TS. 310), (2) H.St.J. A.I.j (TS. 303).

Roman — (1) R.SBR. A.IVa (SC. 2927), (2) R.BR. B.I.d (TS. 301), (3) R.BR. B.I.e (TS. 290), (4) R.BR. D.II.h (TS. 1496), (5) R.HMJ. B.II.e (TS. 289), (6) R.Jg. B.II.d (TS. 296).

Other Study Collection Examples:

Derived Early Bronze Age — (1) SBR. C.II.e (SC. 3437), (2) SJR. A.I.c (variant, SC. 3491), (3) JR. A.I.d (SC. 2699), (4) JR. A.V.a (SC. 912), (5) JR. B.IV.c (SC. 995), (6) JR. D.III.c (SC. 1065), (7) JR. F.I.a (SC. 2032), (8) JR. F.I.f (variant, SC. 3507), (9) JR. J.III.c (SC. 3506), (10) JR. O.III.d (SC. 1681), (11) JR. P.II.a (SC. 2430), (12) JR. P.III.c (SC. 2466), (13) CP. A.III.a (SC. 1808).

Roman — (1) R.Jg. A.II.a (SC. 2951), (2) R.Jg. A.II.b (SC. 2956), (3) R.Jg. A.II.c (SC. 3064), (4) R.Jg. B.II.o (SC. 3016), (5) R.CP. A.III.a (variant, SC. 3526).

Trench IA2:

Other Type Series Examples:

Roman — (1) R.MBR. 1 (TS. 438), (2) R.BR. A.I.g (TS. 1490), (3) R.BR. B.I.a (TS. 1515), (4) R.BR. C.II.b (TS. 621), (5) R.BR. C.III.a (SC. 2925), (6) R.BR. D.II.g (TS. 551), (7) R.JR. A.I.b (TS. 293), (8) R.JR. A.I.c (TS. 1492), (9) R.HMJ.

Figure 261

C.I.b (TS. 2086), (10) R.CP. A.II.a (TS. 447), (11) R.Jg. B.III.c (SC. 3019), (12) R.CP. A.II.b (SC. 3051), (13) R.Lp. 1 (SW. 53).

Other Study Collection Examples:
  Derived Early Bronze Age — (1) SBR. A.I.a (SC. 2782), (2) SBR. A.I.d (SC. 3445), (3) SBR. B (Gen. Type, SC. 22), (4) SBR. G (variant, SC. 2695), (5) BR. A.III.a (SC. 2813), (6) BR. B.III.m (SC. 2838), (7) BR. C.I.b (SC. 735), (8) BR. F.IV.a (SC. 816), (9) BR. G.I.e (SC. 825), (10) BR. (not typed, SC. 34), (11) SJR. B.I.c (SC. 2503), (12) SJR. B.II.b (SC. 2506), (13) SJR. C.I.f (SC. 2569), (14) SJR. C.II.b (SC. 2580), (15) SJR. C.II.r (SC. 2611), (16) SJR. C.II.u (SC. 2618), (17) JR. B.III.e (SC. 3470), (18) JR. C.I.f (SC. 998), (19) JR. C.II.a (SC. 3512), (20) JR. D.I.a (SC. 1033), (21) JR. D.II.d (SC. 1061), (22) JR. D.V.a (SC. 1071), (23) JR. D.V.a (SC. 3471), (24) JR. D.VIII.a (SC. 1119), (25) JR. F.I.c (SC. 1199), (26) JR. F.I.c (SC. 2649), (27) JR. F.III.f (SC. 1232), (28) JR. H.I.e (SC. 2071), (29) JR. H.I.g (SC. 1272), (30) JR. H.I.k (SC. 2079), (31) JR. J.III.x (SC. 2365), (32) JR. J.IV.g (SC. 2379), (33) JR. K.I.b (SC. 1575), (34) JR. K.II.d (SC. 1771), (35) JR. O.II.f (SC. 1644), (36) JR. O.II.j (SC. 2455), (37) JR. O.III.c (SC. 1671), (38) JR. P.I.a (SC. 1692), (39) JR. J (Gen. Type, SC. 117), (40) CP. B.IV.f (SC. 1894), (41) BE. E.I.f (SC. 3155), (42) BE. E.I.j.1 (SC. 3202).
  Roman — (1) R.SBR. A.II.a (variant, SC. 2876), (2) R.BR. B.I.d (variant, SC. 3472), (3) R.BR. B.I.e (SC. 2924), (4) R.Jg. B.I.b (SC. 2959), (5) R.Jg. B.II.c (SC. 2973), (6) R.Jg. B.II.e (SC. 2987), (7) R.Jg. B.II.g (SC. 2991), (8) R.Jg. B.II.i (SC. 2995), (9) R.Jg. B.II.k (SC. 3010), (10) R.Jg. B.II.o (SC. 3015), (11) R.Jg. B.II.o (SC. 3023), (12) R.HMJ. A.II.e (SC. 2941), (13) R.HMJ. B.I.a (SC. 3042), (14) R.CP. A.I.b (SC. 3054), (15) R.CP. A.I.b (SC. 3056).

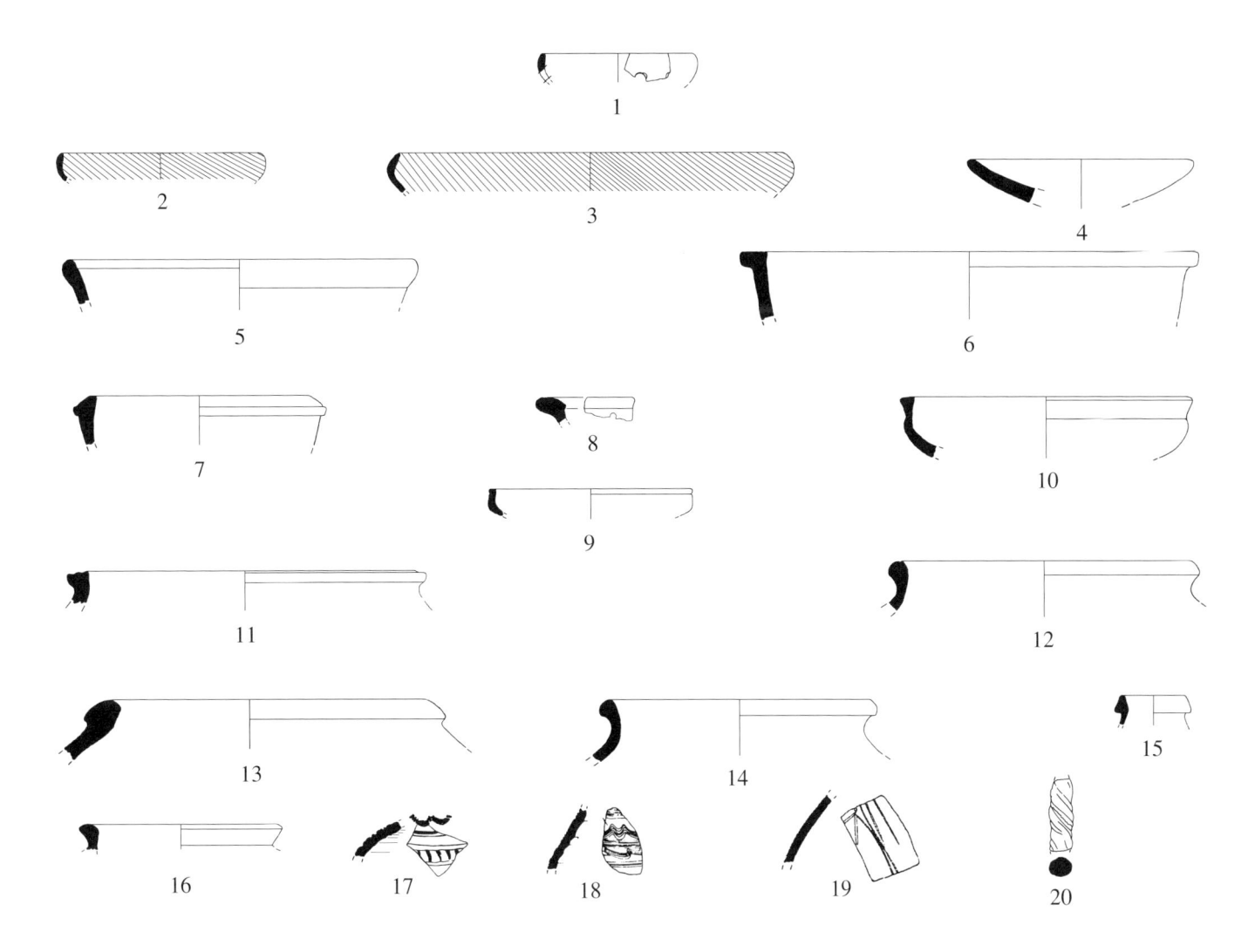

Pottery from Trenches IA1 and IA2 (Phase 2; Period B — Derived Early Bronze Age, Roman, and Hellenistic). Scale 1:5

Figure 262. Pottery from Trenches IA1 and IA2 (Phase 3; Period B — Derived Early Bronze Age and Roman)

1. R.BR. A.II.a (SC. 2916; IA2, 3.4). Small rim and upper wall segment. Slightly coarse pinkish-buff ware with lime and mica grit, evenly fired. Creamy-buff slip in and out.
2. R.BR. B.I.b (IP [G.1] K.I.b; TS. 2119; IA1, 1.3). Small rim and upper wall fragment with combed-incised decoration on top of the rim. Slightly coarse pinkish-buff ware, evenly fired. Buff slip in and out.
3. R.BR. D.III.b (TS. 1507; IA1, 1.3). Small rim and upper wall segment. Fairly fine buff ware with lime and mica grits, evenly fired. Creamy-buff slip out.
4. R.JR. B.I.c (TS. 1493; IA1, 1.3). Large rim, neck, and upper shoulder segment. Fairly fine buff ware with lime and mica grits, evenly fired. Self slip in and out.
5. R.JR. B.I.d (TS. 1502; IA1, 1.3). Small rim and neck segment. Fine buff ware with lime and mica grits, evenly fired. Self slip in and out.
6. R.JR. B.II.a (TS. 2224; IA2, 3.3). Small rim and neck segment. Slightly coarse pinkish-buff ware, evenly fired. Self slip in and out.
7. R.JR. B.II.a (TS. 1511; IA1, 1.3). Small rim and neck segment. Slightly coarse pinkish-buff ware with lime and mica grits, evenly fired.
8. R.JR. B.II.a (TS. 1505; IA1, 1.2). Large rim, neck, and upper shoulder segment. Fine buff ware with small lime and mica grits, evenly fired. Creamy-buff slip out.
9. R.HMJ. B.II.c (TS. 2084; IA2, 3.4). Large rim and shoulder segment. Fairly coarse pinkish-buff ware, unevenly fired gray in patch outside. Self slip irregularly burnished outside.
10. R.Jg. B.II.a (TS. 455; IA2, 3.4). About 1/4 rim and neck segment. Coarse pinkish-buff ware, evenly fired. Cream slip in and out.
11. R.CP. A.V.a (TS. 3015; IA2, 3.3). Small rim, neck, and upper shoulder segment. Fairly fine pinkish-red ware, evenly fired. Black slip out.

Trench IA1:

Other Type Series Examples:

Roman — (1) R.MBR. 2 (TS. 1509), (2) R.BR. A.II.h (TS. 1494), (3) R.JR. A.I.a (TS. 1497), (4) R.HMJ. B.I.b (TS. 1504), (5) R.Jg. A.II.c (SW. 40), (6) R.Jg. B.II.g (TS. 1501), (7) R.Jg. B.II.h (TS. 1498), (8) R.Jg. B.II.i (TS. 1506), (9) R.Jg. B.II.m (TS. 1512), (10) R.Bt. B.I.c (TS. 3159), (11) R.Ld. 1 (TS. 1508), (12) R.BE. C.I.a (TS. 2094).

Other Study Collection Examples:

Derived Early Bronze Age — (1) SBR. C.II.d (SC. 3436), (2) BR. L.I.e (SC. 837), (3) JR. B.IV.a (SC. 953), (4) JR. D.VI.b (SC. 1107), (5) JR. E.II.m (SC. 1155), (6) JR. F.I.a (SC. 1194), (7) JR. P.II.i (SC. 2431), (8) BE. E.II.d (SC. 3201).

Roman — (1) R.BR. C.II.a (variant, SC. 3513), (2) R.BR. D.I.b (SC. 3468), (3) R.BR. D.II.h (SC. 3379), (4) R.JR. A.I.g (SC. 2723), (5) R.JR. B.I.d (SC. 2704), (6) R.Jg. A.II.b (SC. 2955), (7) R.Jg. B.II.b (SC. 2968), (8) R.Jg. B.II.e (SC. 2988), (9) RJg. B.II.h (SC. 2992), (10) R.Jg. B.II.j (SC. 3004), (11) R.Jg. B.II.k (SC. 2694), (12) R.Jg. B.II.q (spiral twisted handle; SC. 3373), (13) R.CP. A.III.a (variant, SC. 3525).

Trench IA2:

Other Type Series Examples:

Roman — (1) R.SBR. A.I.a (TS. 2445), (2) R.SBR. A.II.a (TS. 652), (3) R.Jg. B.II.l (TS. 439).

Other Study Collection Examples:

Derived Early Bronze Age — (1) SBR. A.II.b (SC. 2791), (2) BR. B.I.a (SC. 2827), (3) BR. F.I.b (SC. 764), (4) SJR. A.I.a (SC. 2472), (5) JR. E.II.d (SC. 2007), (6) JR. K.II.b (SC. 2400), (7) JR. O.II.a (SC. 1624), (8) JR. P.II.a (SC. 2429), (9) BE. B.I (variant, SC. 3133), (10) BE. E.I.a (SC. 3175), (11) SF.8d (tabun oven fragments, SC. 3793).

Roman — (1) R.SBR. A.I.a (SC. 3510), (2) R.BR. A.I.d (SC. 2911), (3) R.BR. A.II.a (SC. 2914), (4) R.BR. C.I.a (variant, SC. 3443), (5) R.JR. A.I.a (SC. 2940), (6) R.Jg. B.II.b (SC. 2963), (7) R.Jg. B.II.f (SC. 2989), (8) R.Jg. B.II.i (SC. 2998), (9) R.Jg. B.II.l (SC. 3012), (10) R.Jg. B.II.q (SC. 3030), (11) R.HMJ. B.II.a (SC. 3043), (12) R.CP. rim fragment (not typed, SC. 152).

Figure 262

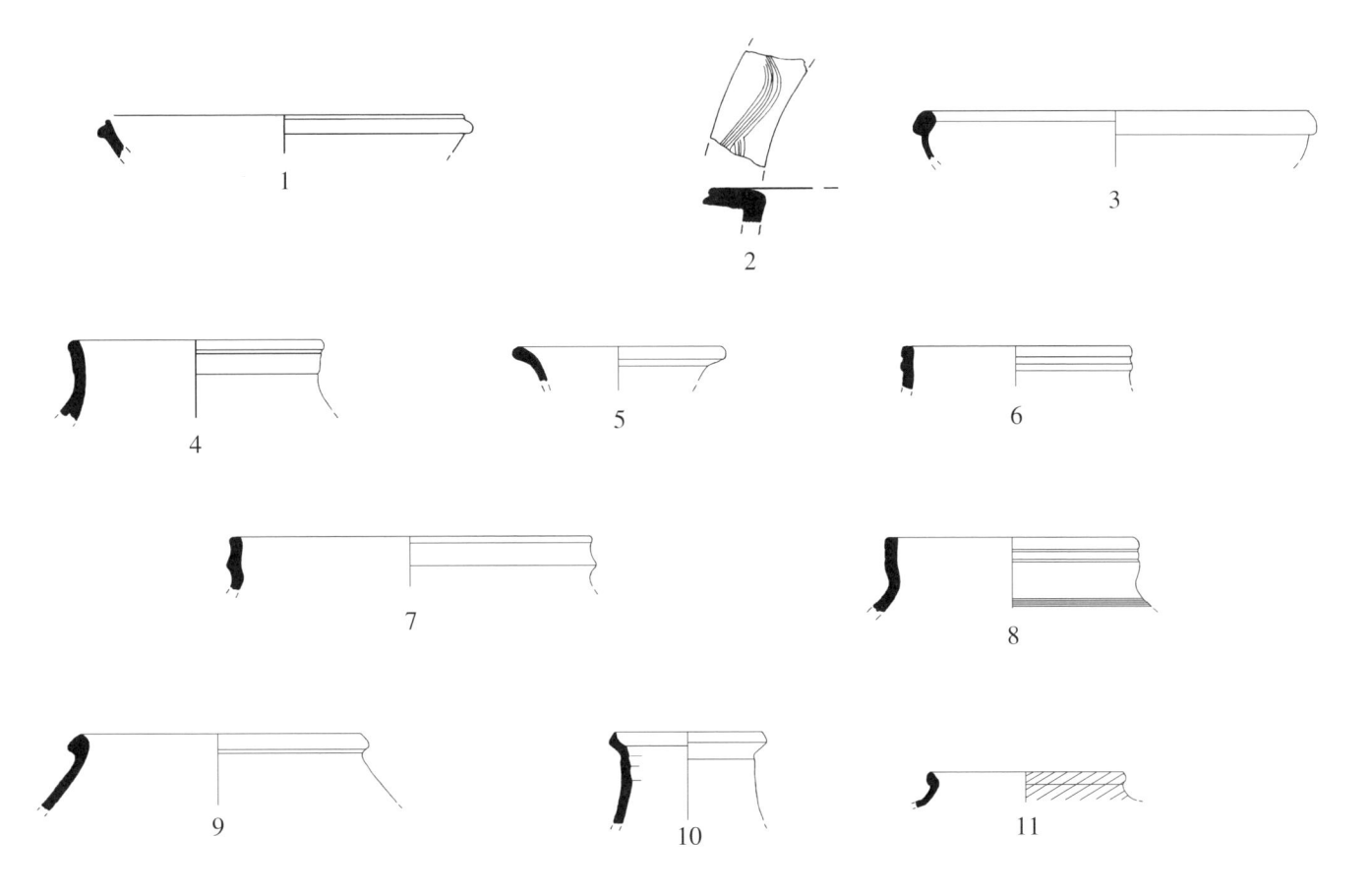

Pottery from Trenches IA1 and IA2 (Phase 3; Period B — Derived Early Bronze Age and Roman). Scale 1:5

Figure 263. Pottery from Trenches IA1 and IA2 (Phase 4; Period B — Derived Early Bronze Age and Roman)

1. R.BR. A.II.a (TS. 1514; IA2, 3.1). Small rim and upper wall segment. Slightly coarse pinkish-buff ware, evenly fired. Creamy-buff slip in and out.
2. R.BR. A.II.h (TS. 1510; IA2, 3.1). Large rim and wall segment. Fairly fine pinkish-buff ware, evenly fired. Smooth self slip in and out.
3. R.BR. B.I.b (IP [G.1] K.I.a; TS. 532; IA2, 3.1). About 1/8 rim and upper wall segment with combed wavy band decoration on top of the rim. Fairly coarse pink ware, evenly fired. Light brown slip in and out.
4. R.SJR. A.I.b (SC. 2680; IA2, 3.1). About 1.5 cm length of rim and neck segment. Slightly coarse light grayware with lime inclusions, evenly fired. Worn creamy-green slip out.
5. R.JR. B.I.a (TS. 262; IA1, 1.1). Small rim and neck segment. Ware description unavailable.
6. R.JR. B.I.d (TS. 305; IA2, 4.1). Small rim and neck segment. Pinkish-buff ware, evenly fired. Buff slip out.
—. R.JR. C.II.b (TS. 1517; IA2, 3.1). Small rim and upper neck segment. Fairly fine buff ware with fine lime and mica grits, evenly fired. Creamy-buff slip in and out.
7. R.HMJ. B.II.a (TS. 299; IA2, 4.1). Small rim and upper shoulder segment. Slightly coarse pinkish-buff ware with lime and mica grits, evenly fired. Creamy-buff slip out.
8. R.HMJ. B.II.a (SC. 1291; IA2, 4.1). About 1/2 rim and upper shoulder segment. Slighly coarse pinkish-orange ware with lime and mica grits, evenly fired. Worn buff slip in and out.
9. R.St.J. A.II.a (TS. 287; IA2, 4.1). Small rim and neck segment. Hard-fired, fairly fine pinkish-buff ware with lime and mica grits, evenly fired. Creamy-buff slip out.
10. R.Jg. B.II.c (TS. 297; IA2, 4.1). Small rim and neck segment. Fairly fine pinkish-brown ware with lime and mica grits, evenly fired. Pinkish-buff slip out.
11. R.Jg. B.II.o (TS. 307; IA2, 4.1). Small rim and neck segment. Fairly fine brown ware, evenly fired.
12. R.CP. A.II.a (TS. 1518; IA2, 3.1). Two joining small rim segments. Hard-fired, fine dark reddish-brown, brittle, ware with fine lime and mica grits, evenly fired.
13. R.CP. A.III.a (TS. 2140; IA2, 3.1). Small rim and neck segment. Slightly coarse orange ware, unevenly fired dark red in and purple-red out.
14. R.CP. A.V.a (TS. 2141; IA2, 3.1). Small rim and neck segment. Slightly coarse orange ware, evenly fired. Red slip in; surface horizontally burnished outside.
15. R.CP. A.V.a (TS. 2139; IA2, 3.1). Small rim, neck, and upper shoulder segment. Fairly coarse orange ware, evenly fired. Red slip in and out.
16. R.JR.Sh. (IP [G.1] A.II.a; TS. 1218; IA2, 3.1). Jar shoulder sherd comb incised on outside wall. Fairly fine grayish-green ware, evenly fired. Traces of black paint or bitumen on outside wall.
17. R.JR.Sh. (IP [G.1] C.IV.a; TS. 1221; IA2, 3.1). Jar shoulder sherd with horizontal and wavy comb-incised decoration on outside wall. Fine pink ware, evenly fired. Creamy-buff slip out.
18. R.JR.Sh. (IP [G.1] D.I.a; TS. 1220; IA2, 3.1). Jar shoulder sherd with horizontal and wavy comb-incised decoration on outside wall. Slightly coarse buff ware, evenly fired. Self slip in and out.
19. R.JR.Sh. (IP [G.1] D.III.a; TS. 2103; IA1, 1.1). Jar shoulder sherd with horizontal and wavy comb-incised decoration on outside wall. Slightly coarse pinkish-buff ware, evenly fired. Buff slip out.
20. R.JR.Sh. (IP [G.2] A.III.a; TS. 474; IA2, 3.1). Jar shoulder sherd with groups of diagonally incised line decoration on outside wall. Coarse pink ware with lime and mica grits. Buff slip out.
21. WPS. A.I.a (SC. 1948; IA1, 1.1). Derived Early Bronze Age. One portion of wall and left side of one window opening extant. Very hard unevenly fired ware with dark gray core fired greenish-buff at surfaces; small lime and mica inclusions.

Trench IA1:

Other Type Series Examples:
Roman — (1) R.BR. A.II.c (TS. 623), (2) R.JR. B.II.d (TS. 434), (3) R.Jg. B.II.j (TS. 518), (4) R.Jg. C.I.b (TS. 440).

Other Study Collection Examples:
Derived Early Bronze Age — (1) SBR. A.I.d (SC. 3435), (2) SBR. B.I.b (SC. 3432), (3) SBR. B.I.r (variant, SC. 3433), (4) SJR. B.II.j (SC. 2524), (5) JR. A.III.f (SC. 920), (6) JR. B.IV.a (SC. 952), (7) JR. D.V.e (SC. 1100), (8) JR. F.III.f (SC. 1235), (9) JR. J.III.m (SC. 2329), (10) JR. J.III.aa (SC. 2368), (11) JR. O.II.f (SC. 1648), (12) JR. P.II.a (SC. 1712), (13) JR. P.II.l (SC. 1751).
Roman — (1) R.SBR. A.I.a (SC. 3434), (2) R.BR. A.II.a (SC. 2913), (3) R.JR. B.I.c (variant, SC. 3505), (4) R.Jg. B.I.a (SC. 2958), (5) R.Jg. B.II.b (SC. 2965), (6) R.Jg. B.II.c (SC. 2972), (7) R.Jg. B.II.c (SC. 2982), (8) R.Jg. B.II.d (SC. 2983), (9) R.Jg. B.II.h (SC. 2993), (10) R.Jg. B.II.h (SC. 2994), (11) R.Jg. B.II.i (SC. 2996), (12) R.Jg. B.II.i (SC. 2997).

Trench IA2:

Other Type Series Examples:
Roman — (1) R.MBR.5 (SC. 3469), (2) R.SBR. A.III.b (SC. 3444), (3) R.BR. A.I.a (TS. 1516), (4) R.BR. B.I.b (TS. 286), (5) R.BR. C.I.b (TS. 1521), (6) R.BR. E.I.c (TS. 1500), (7) R.Jg. A.III.b (TS. 540), (8) R.Jg. B.II.a (TS. 291), (9) R.HMJ. A.I.b (TS. 1513), (10) R.HMJ. B.II.f (SC. 3044), (11) R.Jg. A.III.a (SC. 2949), (12) R.Jg. B.I.b (TS. 1520), (13) R.Jg. B.II.n (TS. 300), (14) R.CP. A.IV.c (SC. 3069), (15) R.CP. A.V.a (TS. 449), (16) R.Bt. C.I.a (TS. 1522), (17) R.BE. A.I.b (SC. 3229).

Other Study Collection Examples:
Derived Early Bronze Age — (1) BR. A.I.a (SC. 2807), (2) BR. A.III.a (SC. 2814), (3) BR. A.III.c (SC. 2819), (4) BR. (not typed, SC. 24), (5) BR. (not typed, SC. 43), (6) JR. A.II.a (SC. 892), (7) JR. C.II.a (SC. 1004), (8) JR. C.V.b (SC. 1013), (9) JR. C.II.b (SC. 1019),

(10) JR. D.I.b (SC. 1039), (11) JR. D.II.b (SC. 2734), (12) JR. D.III.c (SC. 1066), (13) JR. F.I.a (SC. 1192), (14) JR. F.I.e (SC. 2652), (15) JR. H.I.a (SC. 2056), (16) JR. H.I.c. (SC. 2065), (17) JR. H.I.d (SC. 2070), (18) JR. H.I.e (SC. 1269), (19) JR. H.I.k (SC. 1283), (20) JR. H.I.k (SC. 2080), (21) JR. J.III.e (SC. 2237), (22) JR. K.I.b (SC. 1562), (23) JR. K.I.b (SC. 1576), (24) JR. P.II.a (SC. 1704), (25) JR. P.III.a (SC. 2440).

Roman — (1) R.SBR. A.I.a (SC. 3442), (2) R.SBR. A.II.a (SC. 2867), (3) R.BR. A.I.e (variant, SC. 3508), (4) R.BR. B.I.b (SC. 2920), (5) R.BR. B.I.e (SC. 2923), (6) R.BR. C.II.c (SC. 2931), (7) R.BR. D.II.a (SC. 2937), (8) R.BR. D.II.a (SC. 3473), (9) R.SJR. B.I.a (SC. 3492), (10) R.JR. B.I.d (SC. 2696), (11) R.JR. B.I.a (SC. 2698), (12) R.JR. B.I.f (SC. 2713), (13) R.JR. C.II.d (SC. 2939), (14) R.HMJ. A.II.b (SC. 3509), (15) R.Jg. B.II.b (SC. 2967), (16) R.Jg. B.II.c (SC. 2970), (17) R.Jg. B.II.c (SC. 2975), (18) R.Jg. B.II.d (SC. 2984), (19) R.Jg. B.II.i (SC. 2999), (20) R.Jg. B.II.i (SC. 3001), (21) R.Jg. B.II.j (SC. 3002), (22) R.Jg. B.II.j (SC. 3003), (23) R.Jg. B.II.j (SC. 3005), (24) R.Jg. B.II.j (SC. 3006), (25) R.Jg. B.II.j (SC. 3007), (26) R.Jg. B.II.k (SC. 3008), (27) R.Jg. B.II.k (SC. 3009), (28) R.Jg. B.II.o (SC. 3022), (29) R.Jg. B.II.o (SC. 3380), (30) R.Jg. B.II.o (variant, SC. 3381), (31) R.Jg. B.II.p (SC. 3382), (32) R.Jg. B.II.p (variant, SC. 3383), (33) R.Jg. B.II.q (SC. 3031), (34) R.Jg. C.I.a (SC. 3325), (35) R.CP. A.I.b (SC. 3052), (36) R.CP. A.I.b (SC. 3053), (37) R.CP. A.IV.a (SC. 3527), (38) R.CP. A.V.a (SC. 3062), (39) R.PS.1 (variant, SC. 3511), (40) R.PS.2 (SC. 3074), (41) R.PS.3 (variant, SC. 2830), (42) R.BE. A.II (SC. 3235).

Another Intrusive Sherd: Islamic Period — (1) Isl.BR.Sh. (SC. 3774); dated to the 9th c. A.D.; bowl sherd with green glaze on inner surface (identified as "splash ware"), which was drilled through with a 4 mm diameter hole and probably reused as a pendant.

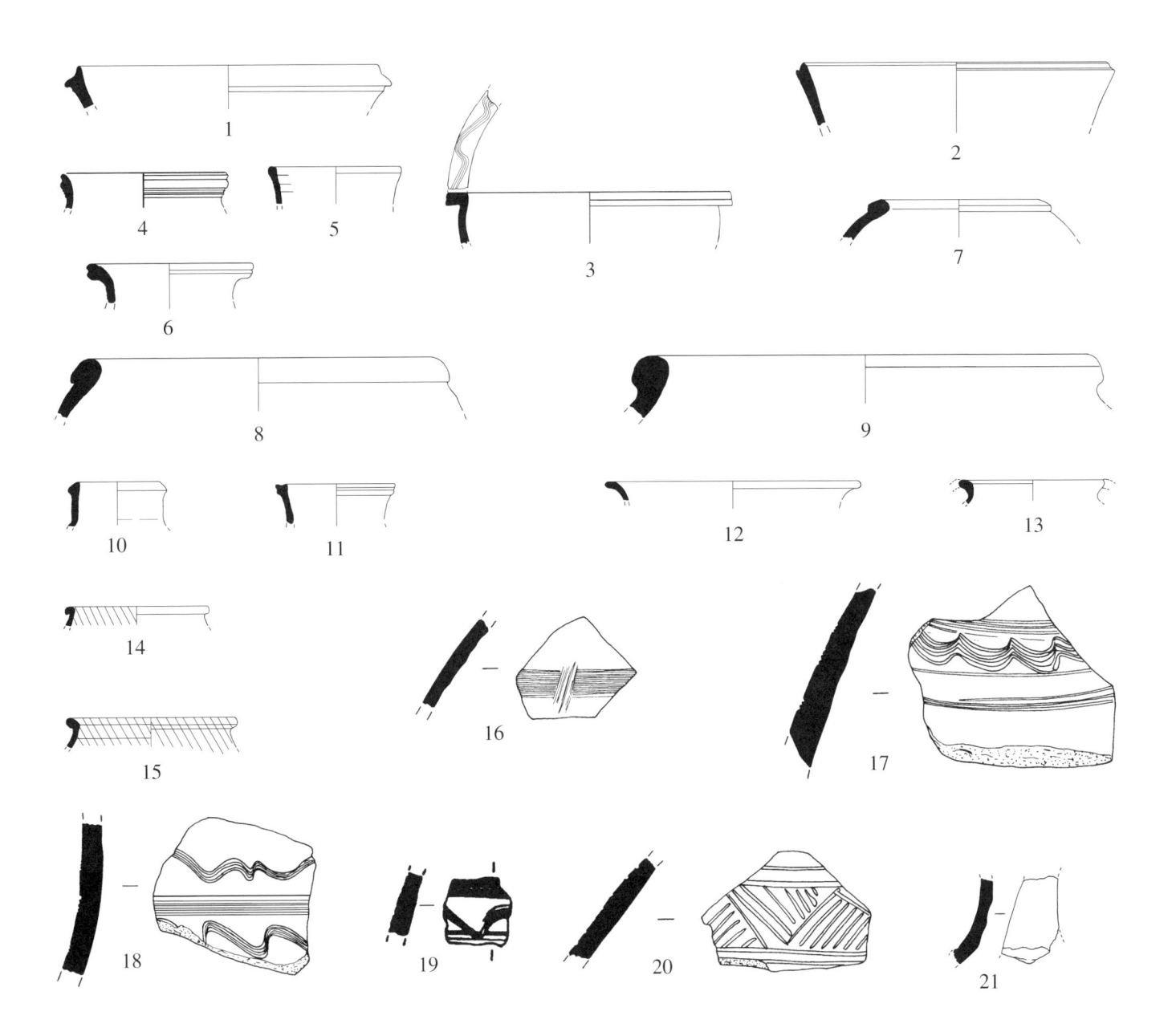

Pottery from Trenches IA1 and IA2 (Phase 4; Period B — Derived Early Bronze Age and Roman). Scales 1–15, 21 (1:5), 16–20 (1:2)

Figure 264

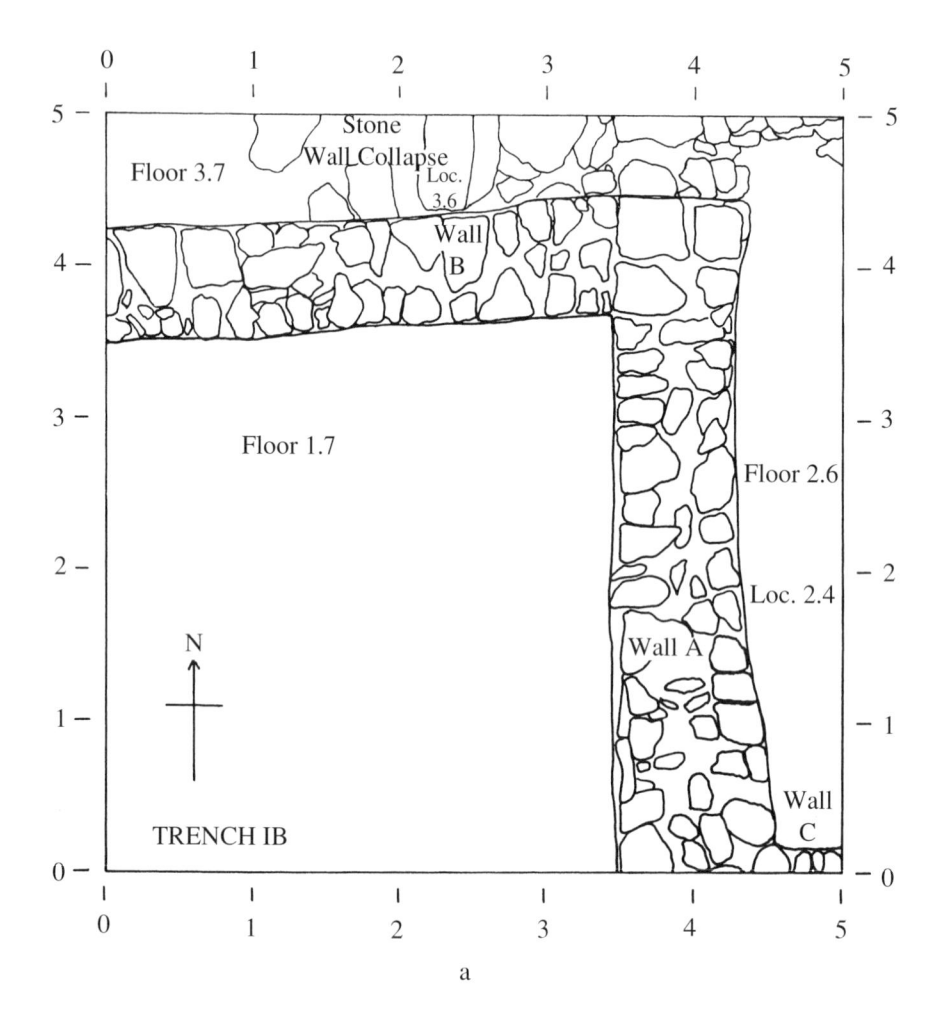

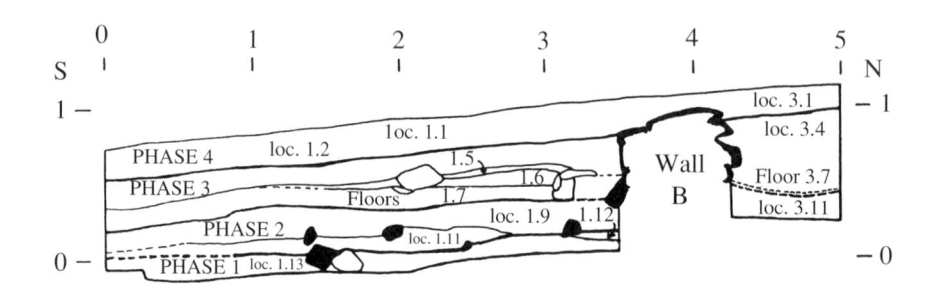

(*a*) Plan and (*b*) West Section of Trench IB. Scale 1:50

Figure 265. Pottery from Trench IB (Phases 2 to 4, Period B — Derived Early Bronze Age and Roman)

1. R.JR. B.I.c (TS. 2068 = TS. 2072; IB, 1.10 and IC, 1.5). Phase 2 and Phase 9. Two joining rim and upper shoulder segments from Trenches IB and IC. Slightly coarse pink ware, evenly fired. Creamy-buff slip out and over rim in.
2. R.PS. 4 (TS. 2111; IB, 2.9). Phase 2. Large rim and portion of wall of a pot stand. Slightly coarse pinkish-buff ware, evenly fired. Traces of self slip burnished in and out.
3. R.JR.Sh. Pt. (SC. 3531; IB, 1.11). Phase 2. Bowl or jar rim sherd painted with an irregular red pattern on the outside and with a red slip on the inside. Fairly fine ware with a few very small lime and mica inclusions, unevenly fired with a gray core and pinkish-buff at surfaces.
4. SBR. B.I.d (TS. 2150; IB, 1.7). Phase 3. Small rim and upper wall segment from an intrusive EB cup. Fairly fine pinkish-brown ware, evenly fired. Dark buff slip out.
5. R.BR. A.II.a (TS. 620; IB, 2.5). Phase 3. About 1/20 rim and upper wall segment. Fairly coarse buff ware, evenly fired.
6. R.BR. D.II.d (TS. 2512; IB, 1.7). Phase 3. Small rim and upper wall segment. Hard-fired, slightly coarse pink ware, evenly fired. Self slip in and out.
7. R.JR. A.I.b (TS. 608; IB, 2.5). Phase 3. About 1/20 rim and upper shoulder segment. Coarse pinkish-grayware. Cream slip in and out.
8. R.JR. C.I.b (TS. 2345; IB, 2.6). Phase 3. About 1/8 rim and neck segment. Slightly coarse brown-buff ware, evenly fired. Buff slip out and on top of rim.
9. R.HMJ. B.II.a (TS. 615; IB, 1.7). Phase 3. Portion of a loop handle from a holemouth jar, Type R.HMJ. B.II.a, with a vertically positioned channel in the middle of the outside of the handle. Fairly coarse pink ware covered with cream slip.
10. R.HMJ. B.II.a (TS. 2080; IB, 1.6). Phase 3. Small rim and shoulder segment. Hard-fired, fine pink ware, evenly fired. Buff slip out and just over the rim in.
11. R.St.J. A.II.a (TS. 536; IB, 1.7). Phase 3. About 1/8 rim, neck, and upper shoulder segment. Coarse pink ware, unevenly fired with gray core in rim. Cream slip in and out.
12. R.CP. A.IV.b (TS. 3014; IB, 1.6). Phase 3. About 1/6 rim, neck, and upper shoulder segment. Slightly gritty, brittle, red ware, evenly fired. Dark purple slip outside.
13. R.JR.Sh. (IP [G.1] A.II.b; TS. 2057; IB, 1.6). Phase 3. Large fragment of a jar neck and shoulder with remains of a loop handle; horizontal comb incised decoration on outside wall. Slightly coarse buff ware, fired pink at surface outside. Pinkish-buff slip out.
14. R.JR.Sh. (IP [G.2] A.VI.a; TS. 613; IB, 2.6). Phase 3. Jar shoulder sherd with incised decoration on outside wall. Fairly coarse pink ware. Self slip out.
15. R.SV.5 (TS. 640; IB, 2.4). Phase 3. About 1/3 fragment of a vessel base with remains of one cone-shaped foot. Fairly fine ware, unevenly fired from pink to gray in and out. Cream slip in and out.
16. R.BR. A.II.g (TS. 2502; IB, 3.1). Phase 4. Small rim and upper wall segment. Fine light brown ware, unevenly fired with pink patches on the outside. Cream slip out.
17. R.BR. D.II.e (TS. 2495; IB, 1.2). Phase 4. About 1/10 rim and wall segment. Hard-fired, fine pink ware, evenly fired. Self slip out.
18. R.HMJ. B.II.a (TS. 586; IB, 3.1). Phase 4. About 1/6 rim and shoulder segment. Fairly fine brown ware. Thick red slip on outside of vessel; rim blackened on the top.
19. R.JR.Sh. (PM. C.12; TS. 611; IB, 1.2). Phase 4. Jar shoulder sherd with remains of a pot mark incised on the outside wall before the vessel was fired. Fairly fine cream ware.

Other Type Series Examples:

Phase 1:
Derived Early Bronze Age — (1) SJR. A.II.e (TS. 2102).

Phase 2:
Early Bronze Age — (1) BR. R.II.a (SW. 177).

Phase 3:
Early Bronze Age — (1) MJR. 1 (SW. 86), (2) JR. D.VI.e (TS. 512).

Roman — (1) R.SBR. A.III.a (TS. 2146), (1) R.BR. A.I.i (PM. C.15; SC. 2934), (3) R.BR. A.III.a (SC. 2828), (4) R.BR. B.I.i (SC. 3516), (5) R.BR. C.II.c (TS. 295), (6) R.BR. C.III.b (SC. 3518), (7) R.SJR. C.I.b (SC. 3517), (8) R.HMJ. A.II.a (TS. 2079), (9) R.HMJ. A.II.c (TS. 3164), (10) R.HMJ. B.II.a (TS. 2061), (11) R.HMJ. C.I.a (TS. 617), (12) R.Jg. B.I.a (TS. 2344), (13) R. Jg. B.II.a (TS. 618), (14) R.Jg. B.II.c (SW. 103), (15) R.Jg. B.II.o (TS. 651), (16) R.CP. A.I.b (SC. 3050), (17) R.CP. A.IV.a (SW. 156), (18) R.Ld. 2 (SW. 81), (19) R.Lp. 4 (SW. 155), (20) R.PS. 1 (SW. 62), (21) R.PS. 2 (SW. 63).

Figure 265 (*cont.*). Pottery from Trench IB (Phases 2 to 4, Period B — Derived Early Bronze Age and Roman)

Phase 4:

Roman — (1) R.SBR. A.IV.b (SC. 3475), (2) R.BR. A.I.b (TS. 577), (3) RBR. A.II.a (TS. 638), (4) R.HMJ. A.II.e (TS. 2076), (5) R.HMJ. B.II.c (TS. 589), (6) R.Jg. B.III.a (SC. 2599), (7) R.Jg. B.III.b (SC. 2981), (8) R.Bt. B.I.a (TS. 2107).

Other Study Collection Examples:

Phase 1:

Derived Early Bronze Age — (1) SBR. A.I.d (SC. 3456), (2) BR. F.I.b (SC. 765), (3) SJR. B.III.a (SC. 2526), (4) JR. A.II.a (SC. 890), (5) JR. A.III.c (SC. 902), (6) JR. B.V.c (SC. 958), (7) JR. C.III.b (SC. 1009), (8) JR. D.I.d (SC. 1051), (9) JR. J.I.b (SC. 2090), (10) JR. J.I.d (SC. 2116), (11) JR. O.III.b (SC. 2457), (12) CP. B.IV.b (SC. 1872), (13) CP. C.I.e (SC. 1903), (14) Ld. C.III.a (SC. 1940).

Roman — (1) R.Jg. B.II.c (SC. 2980).

Phase 2:

Derived Early Bronze Age — (1) SBR. B.I.a (SC. 3455), (2) BR. D.IV.a (SC. 749), (3) BR. F.III.d (SC. 810), (4) JR. D.I.a (SC. 1036), (5) JR. E.II.i (SC. 1150), (6) JR. H.II.e (SC. 1294), (7) JR. J.I.h (SC. 1352), (8) JR. J.III.e (SC. 2266), (9) JR. J.III.n (SC. 2333), (10) JR. O.III.h (SC. 1691), (11) JR. P.II.e (SC. 1728), (12) BE. B.I (SC. 3104), (13) BE. D.II (SC. 3136), (14) BE. E.I.c (SC. 3157).

Phase 3:

Derived Early Bronze Age — (1) SBR. A.I.d (SC. 3452), (2) SBR. B.I.h (SC. 3451), (3) BR. A.I.d (SC. 3454), (4) BR. F.IV.a (SC. 817), (5) BR. N.II.b (SC. 3326), (6) SJR. B.II.g (SC. 2511), (7) SJR. C.II.b (SC. 2579), (8) JR. A.III.b (SC. 897), (9) JR. A.IV.a (SC. 924), (10) JR. B.III.e (SC. 943), (11) JR. B.IV.c (SC. 960), (12) JR. D.I.b (SC. 1045), (13) JR. D.I.c (SC. 1046), (14) JR. D.I.g (SC. 1053), (15) JR. D.II.a (SC. 1055), (16) JR. D.II.c (SC. 1058), (17) JR. D.V.a (SC. 1075), (18) JR. G.I.c (SC. 1237), (19) JR. H.I.b (SC. 2063), (20) JR. H.I.b (SC. 2064), (21) JR. J.I.i (SC. 2138), (22) JR. J.II.g (SC. 2150), (23) JR. J.II.l (SC. 2192), (24) JR. J.III.n (SC. 1467), (25) JR. O.I.h (SC. 2409), (26) JR. O.II.a (SC. 2410), (27) JR. O.II.c (SC. 2416), (28) JR. O.II.l (SC. 1661), (29) JR. P.II.b (SC. 1715), (30) JR. P.II.c (SC. 1721), (31) CP. B.I.g (SC. 1834), (32) CP. B.II.a (SC. 1839), (33) CP. B.IV.c (SC. 1881), (34) BE. E.II.i (SC. 3223).

Roman — (1) R.SBR. A.III.a (SC. 3387), (2) R.HMJ. A.II.e (SC. 3034), (3) R.HMJ. B.I.a (SC. 3040), (4) R.Jg. A.I.b (SC. 2947), (5) R.Jg. A.I.b (SC. 3453), (6) R.Jg. B.II.b (SC. 2966), (7) R.Jg. B.II.g (SC. 3386), (8) R.CP. A.I.b (SC. 3050), (9) R.CP. A.I.b (SC. 3057), (10) R.CP. A.IV.a (SC. 3530), (11) R.CP. A.IV.b (SC. 3529), (12) R.CP. A.V.a (SC. 3528), (13) R.CP. B.III.a (SC. 3370), (14) R.Bt. C.I.a (variant, SC. 3065).

Phase 4:

Derived Early Bronze Age — (1) SBR. A.I.e (SC. 3457), (2) SBR. B.I.q (SC. 3450), (3) SBR. C.II.a (SC. 3449), (4) SJR. A.II.b (SC. 3493), (5) SJR. B.III.a (SC. 2525), (6) SJR. C.I.a (SC. 2536), (7) SJR. C.I.a (SC. 2544), (8) SJR. C.II.d (SC. 2587), (9) JR. A.III.c (SC. 901), (10) JR. C.II.a (SC. 999), (11) JR. C.V.e (SC. 1029), (12) JR. D.VI.e (SC. 1116), (13) JR. H.I.b (SC. 2060), (14) JR. H.I.d (SC. 2067), (15) JR. H.I.e (SC. 2072), (16) JR. H.I.g (SC. 1275), (17) JR. J.I.d (SC. 1332), (18) JR. J.IV.c (SC. 1525), (19) Ld. C.III.b (variant, SC. 3474), (20) BE. E.I.j (SC. 3187).

Roman — (1) R.BR. A.I.d (without dec.; SC. 3477), (2) R.BR. A.I.h (smaller ex.; SC. 3476), (3) R.BR. B.I.b (SC. 2921), (4) R.BR. C.II.a (variant, SC. 3514), (5) R.BR. C.II.c (variant; SC. 2933), (6) R.BR. C.II.f (SC. 3515), (7) R.HMJ. A.II.d (SC. 3037), (8) R.HMJ. A.II.d (SC. 3041), (9) R.HMJ. B.II.a (SC. 3048), (10) R.Jg. B.II.b (SC. 2964), (11) R.Jg. B.II.c (variant, SC. 3384), (12) R.Jg. B.II.d (SC. 3385), (13) R.Jg. B.II.g (SC. 2979), (14) R.Jg. B.II.i (SC. 3000), (15) R.Jg. B.II.o (SC. 3021), (16) R.CP. A.I.b (SC. 3055).

Figure 265

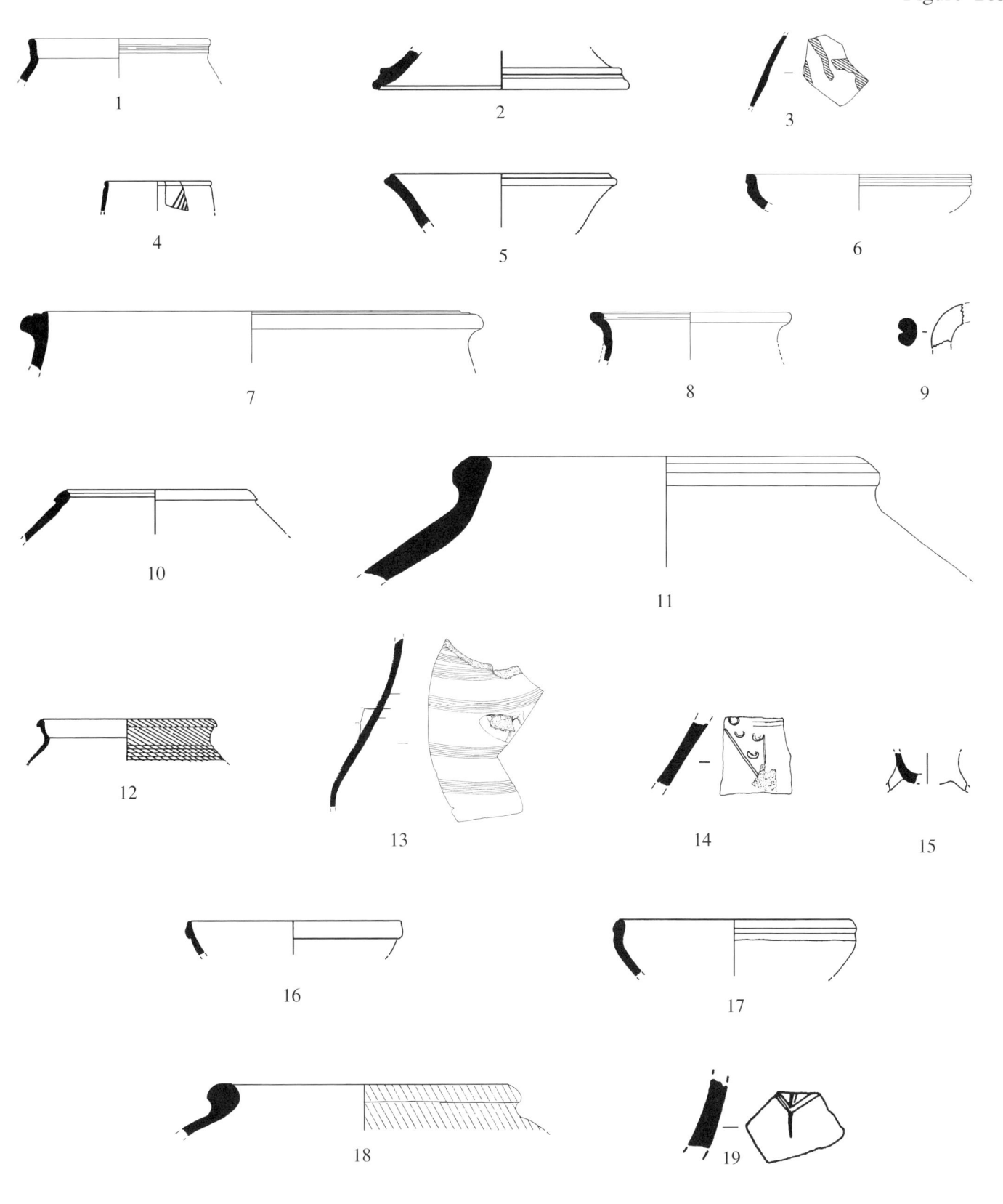

Pottery from Trench IB (Phases 2 to 4, Period B — Derived Early Bronze Age and Roman). Scales 1–13, 15–18 (1:5), 14, 19 (1:2)

Figure 266

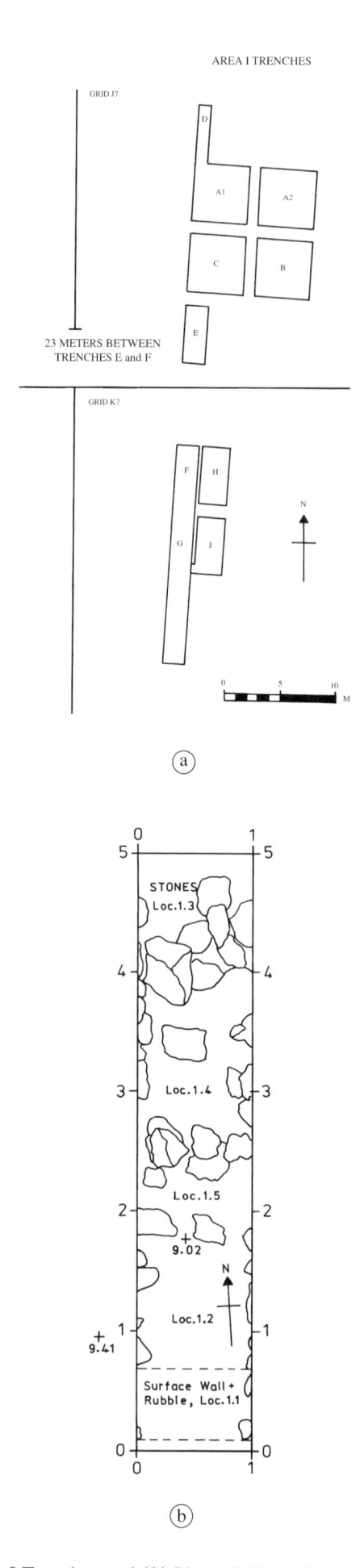

(*a*) Plan of Area I Trenches and (*b*) Phase 2 Plan of Trench ID. Scale 1:50

Figure 267

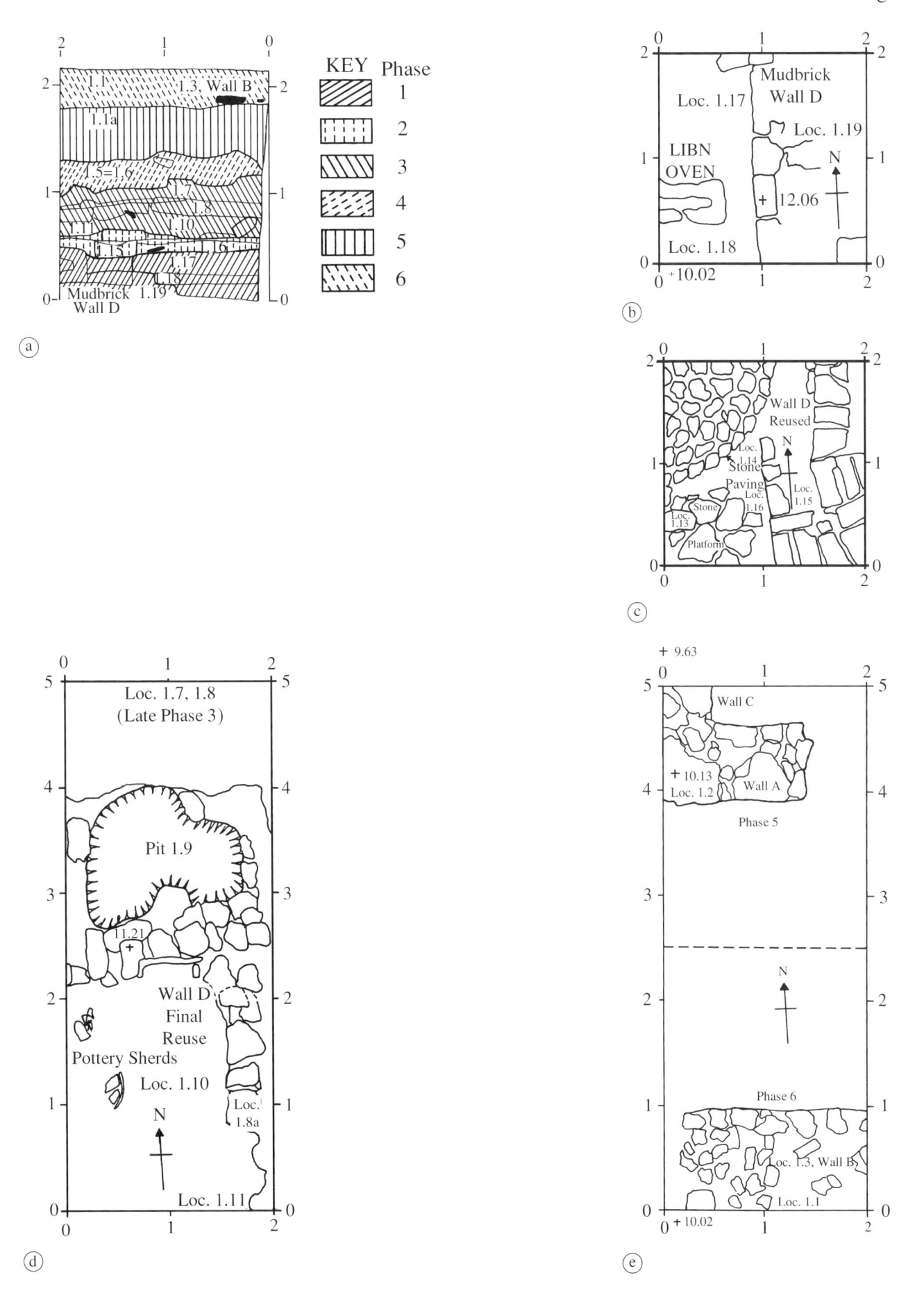

(*a*) South Section and Key to Phase Hatching of Trench IE Sections; (*b*) Trench IE, Phase 1 Plan; (*c*) Trench IE, Phase 2 Plan; (*d*) Trench IE, Phases 3 and 4 (Pit 1.9) Plan; and (*e*) Trench IE, Phases 5 and 6 Plan. Scale 1:50

Figure 268

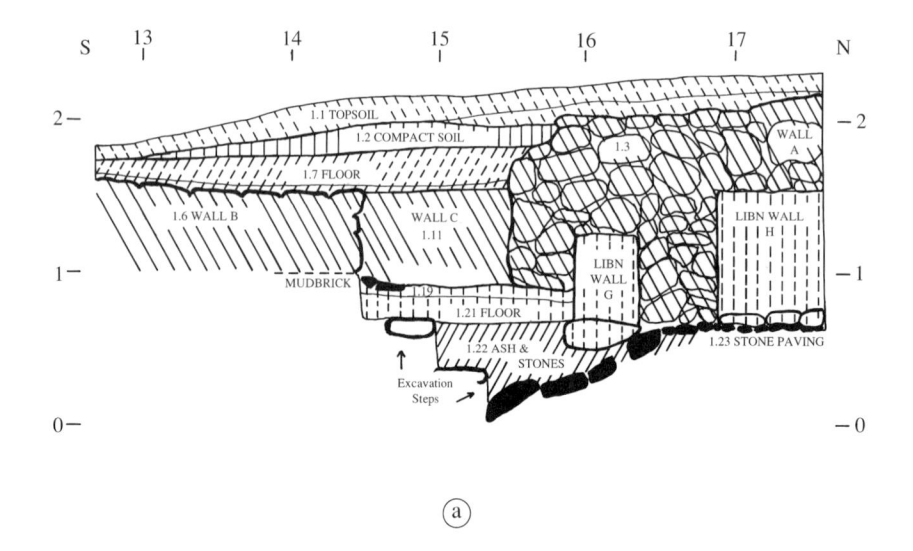

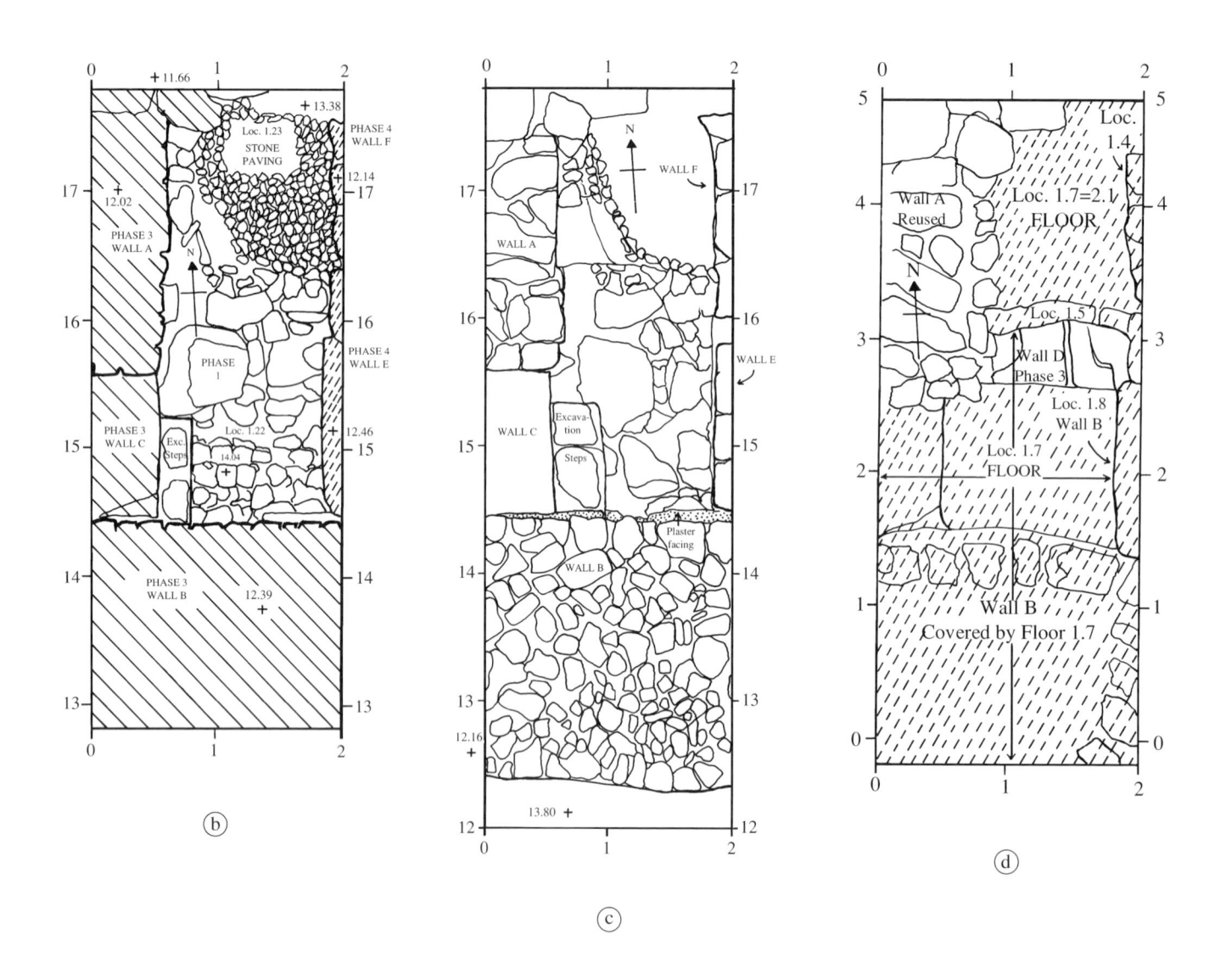

(*a*) Trench IF, West Section; (*b*) Trench IF, Phases 1, 3, and 4 Plan; (*c*) Trench IF, Phase 3 Plan; and (*d*) Trench IF, Phase 4 Plan. Scale 1:50

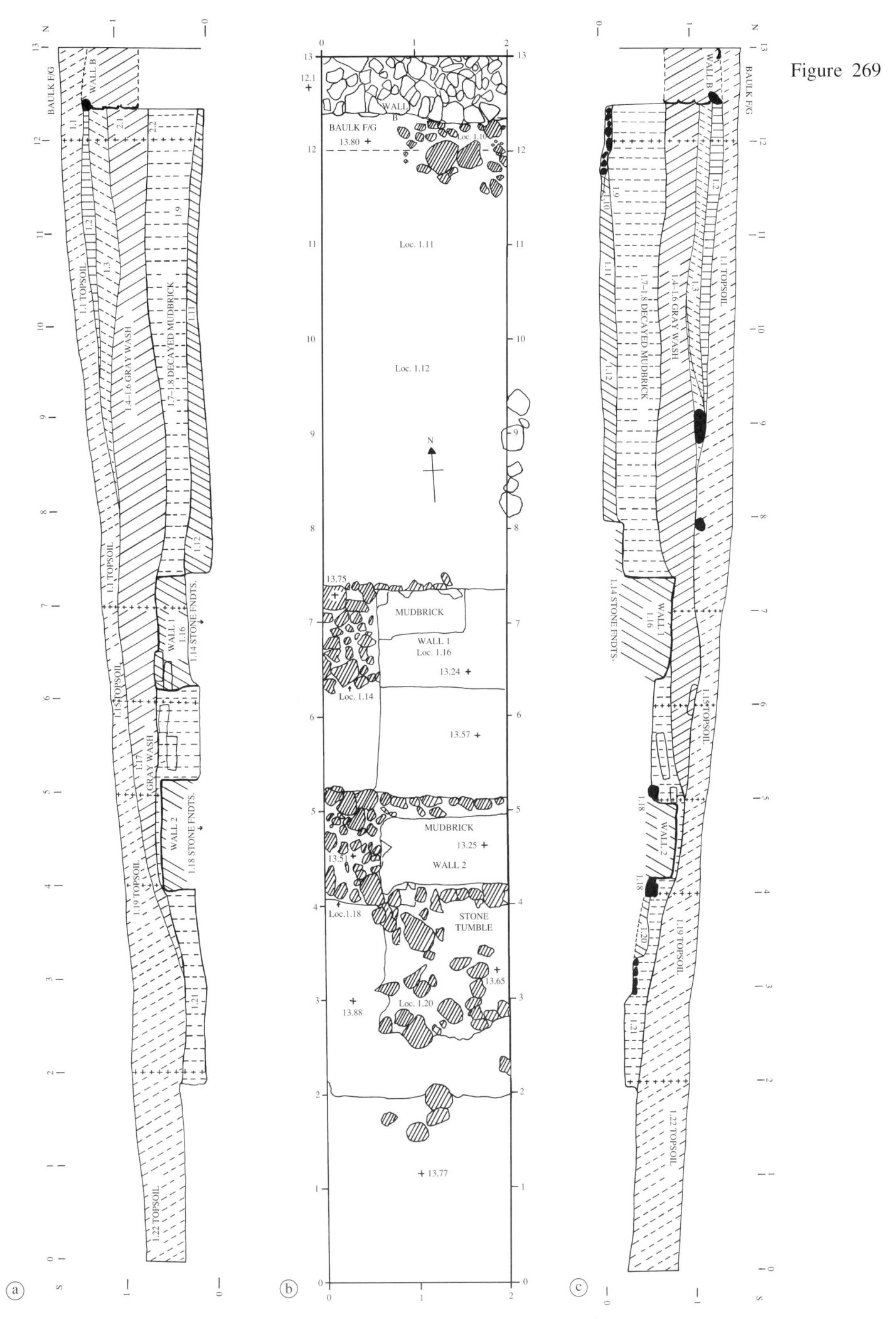

Figure 269. (*a*) Trench IG, West Section; (*b*) Trench IG, Phases 1–4 Plan; and (*c*) Trench IG, East Section. Scale 1:50

Figure 270

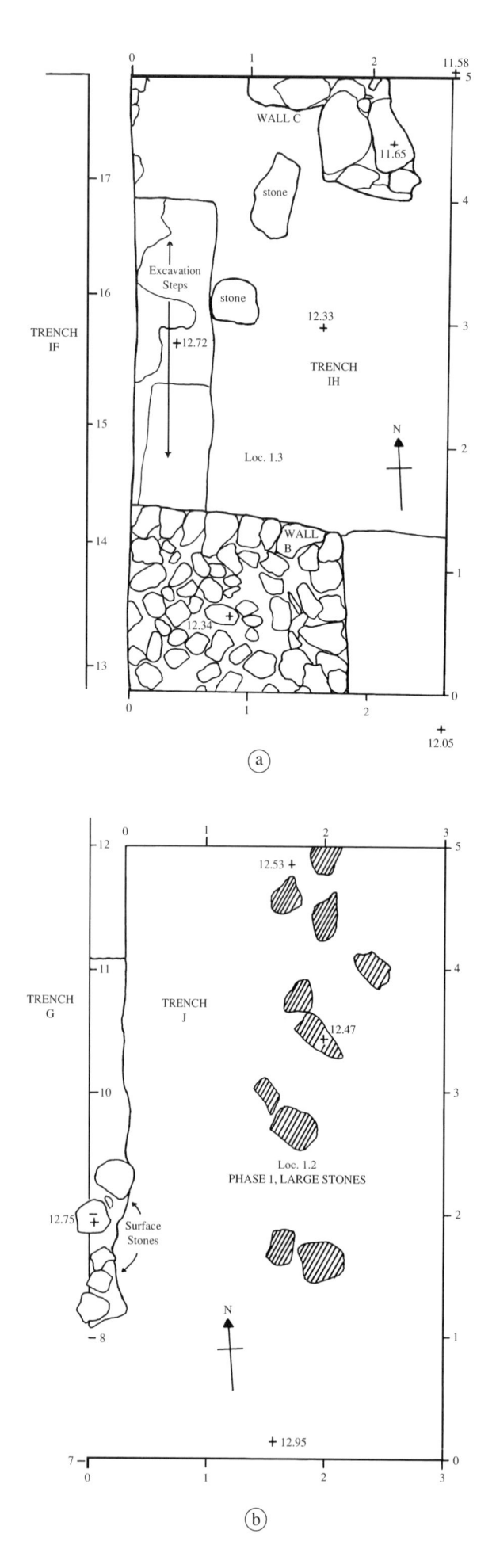

(*a*) Trench IH, Phases 1 and 2 Plan, and (*b*) Trench IJ, Phase 1 Plan. Scale 1:50

Figure 271. (*a*) Trench IE, Phase 1, and (*b*) Trench IF, Phase 1

Figure 272

a

b

(*a*) Trench IF, Phases 1–3, and (*b*) Trench IF, Phases 1–6

Figure 273

(*a*) Trench IG, Phases 1–6 (North View); (*b*) Trench IG, Phases 1–6 (South View); and (*c*) Trenches IH and IJ, Phases 1–2 (South View)

Figure 274

Pottery from Trench ID (Phase 2; Period B — Derived Early Bronze Age and Roman). Scale 1:5

1. SBR. D.I.d (TS. 2228; ID, 1.3). Small rim and upper wall segment. Slightly coarse buff ware, evenly fired. Creamy-green slip in and out.
2. SJR. B.II.j (TS. 2975; ID, 1.1). Small rim and neck segment. Fairly fine light pink ware, evenly fired. Self slip in and out.
3. JR. O.II.a (TS. 2366; ID, 1.3). About 1/12 rim and shoulder segment. Fairly coarse pinkish-brown ware, evenly fired. Creamy-green slip out and over rim in.
4. JR.Sh. (IP [G.4] Gen.; SC. 3255; ID, 1.1). Jar body sherd with incised tree or wheat stalk pattern on inside wall. Slightly coarse pinkish-buff ware with lime grits, evenly fired. Self slip in and out.

Other Type Series Examples: Roman — (1) R.BR. A.I.c (TS. 614), (2) R.CP. A.III.a (TS. 626).

Other Study Collection Examples:
  Derived Early Bronze Age — (1) SBR. B.I.e (SC. 3458), (2) SJR. C.II.a (SC. 1932), (3) JR. A.III.f (SC. 2747), (4) JR. B.IV.c (SC. 972), (5) JR. F.III.f (SC. 1230).
  Roman — (1) R.BR. A.II.a (SC. 2912), (2) R.BR. D.II.a (SC. 2935), (3) R.Jg. B.II.b (SC. 2969), (4) R.HMJ. A.I.b (SC. 3033), (5) R.CP. A.V.a (SC. 3059).

Figure 275

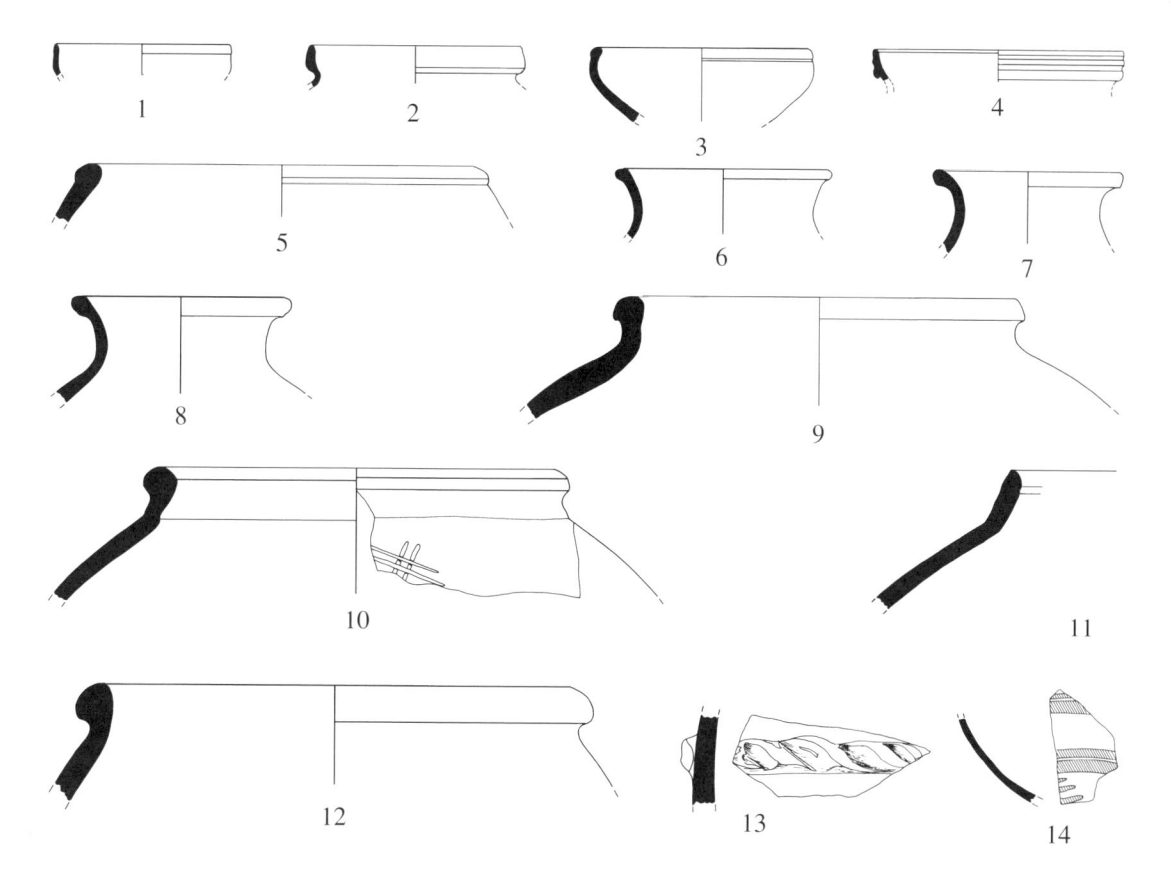

Pottery from Trench IE (Phase 1; Period F — Early Bronze Age IVa). Scale 1:5

1. SBR. B.I.a (TS. 863; IE, 1.25). About 1/6 rim and upper wall segment. Fine buff ware. Cream slip out.
2. SBR. D.II.c (TS. 1082; IE, 1.26). About 1/10 rim and neck segment. Fairly coarse pink ware with a gray core, unevenly fired. Brown slip out.
3. BR. A.II.c (TS. 850; IE, 1.25). About 1/4 rim and wall segment. Fairly coarse creamy-buff ware. Cream slip in and out.
4. SJR. C.I.c (TS. 2520; IE, 1.25). About 1/10 rim segment. Fairly fine light pinkish-buff ware, evenly fired. Cream slip out and just over rim in.
5. JR. H.I.e (TS. 2047; IE, 1.19). Small rim and upper shoulder segment. Slightly coarse pinkish-buff ware, evenly fired. Self slip in and out.
6. JR. J.III.a (TS. 2310; IE, 1.25). About 1/4 rim and neck segment. Fairly fine brown ware unevenly fired reddish-brown at outside surface. Creamy-buff slip out.
7. JR. J.III.h (TS. 2279; IE, 1.25). About 1/6 rim and neck segment. Slightly coarse pinkish-buff ware, evenly fired. Creamy-green slip in and out.
8. JR. J.III.j (TS. 2254; IE, 1.25). Section of rim, neck, and upper shoulder. Fairly coarse light brown ware, evenly fired. Thick creamy-buff slip out and over rim to base of neck inside.
9. JR. P.II.j (TS. 1092; IE, 1.26). About 1/8 rim, neck, and shoulder segment. Fairly coarse brown ware, unevenly fired with gray core. Creamy-buff slip in and out.
10. JR. P.III.e (PM. D.24; TS. 535; IE, 1.18). About 1/4 rim, neck, and shoulder segment with a portion of a pot mark on the shoulder. Coarse pink ware, unevenly fired. Cream slip out.
11. JR. S (Misc.; TS. 548; IE, 1.18). Very small part of rim with neck and shoulder segment. Potter's finger-smoothing impressions on inside of shoulder. Coarse brown ware, unevenly fired with lighter core. Cream slip in and out.
12. CP. C.I.c (TS. 876 = TS. 2096; IE, 1.25 and 8.1). About 1/2 rim and upper shoulder segment. Coarse pink ware with many lime and mica grit inclusions. Self slip burnished in and out.
13. ABS. A.2 (TS. 910; IE, 1.25). Large jar body sherd with applied rope pattern on outside wall. Fairly coarse creamy-buff ware with cream slip out and light pink slip in.
14. JR.Sh. Pt. (TS. 593; IE, 1.18). Bowl or jar body sherd with irregular horizontal painted red bands on the outside wall. Fairly coarse buff ware, evenly fired.

Another Type Series Example: (1) BR. F.III.b (TS. 2046).

Other Study Collection Examples: (1) SBR. B.I.h (SC. 363), (2) BR. F.II.a (SC. 786), (3) SJR. C.I.f (SC. 2564), (4) SJR. C.I.f (SC. 2568), (5) JR. J.II.q (SC. 1354), (6) JR. J.III.p (SC. 2226), (7) CP. (not typed, SC. 69), (8) CP. C.I.g (SC. 1905).

Figure 276

Pottery from Trench IE (Phase 2; Period E — Early Bronze Age IVb). Scale 1:5

1. SBR. B.I.f (TS. 2972; IE, 1.16). Small rim and upper wall segment. Fine creamy-green ware, evenly fired. Self slip in and out.
2. JR. H.I.a (SC. 1244; IE, 1.16). About 1/12 rim and upper wall segment. Fairly fine pinkish-buff ware with small lime grits, evenly fired. Self slip in and out.
3. JR. P.II.j (SC. 1717; IE, 1.16). About 1/12 rim, neck, and upper shoulder segment. Slightly coarse ware with small lime grit inclusions, unevenly fired grayish-green in and buff out. Creamy-green slip in and out.
   Other Study Collection Examples: (1) SBR. B.I.h (SC. 477), (2) SJR. C.I.e (SC. 3501), (3) SJR. C.II.v (SC. 2585), (4) JR. (not typed, SC. 125).

Figure 277

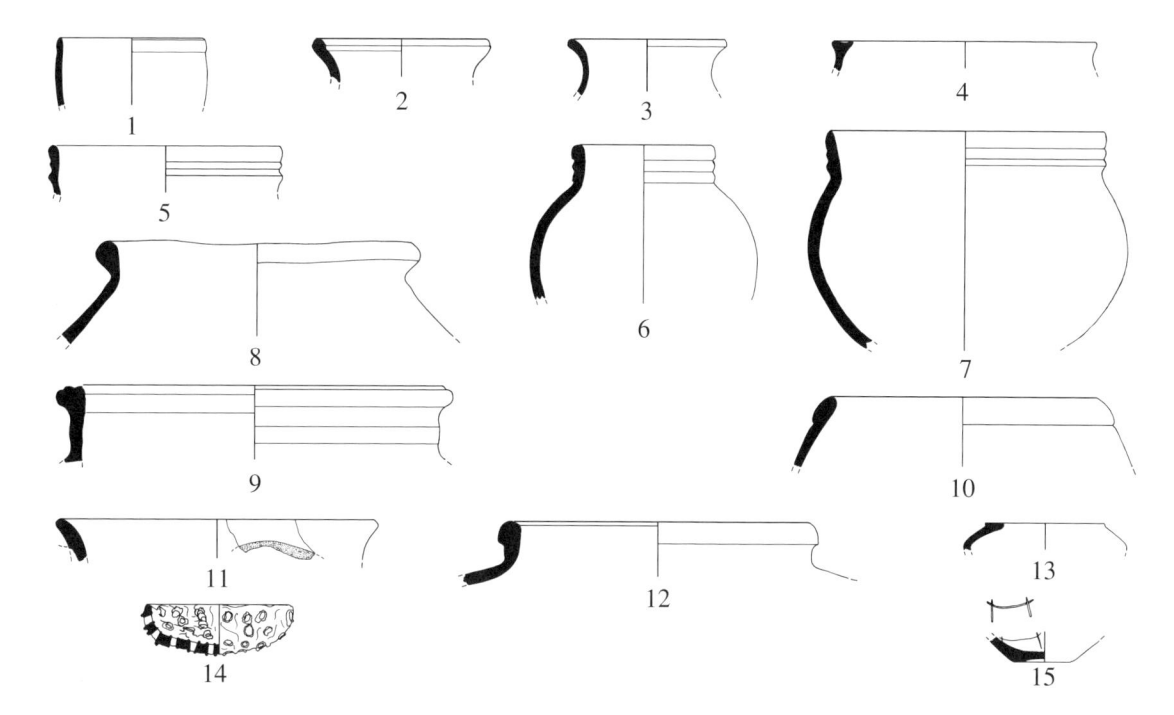

Pottery from Trench IE (Phase 3; Period E — Early Bronze Age IVb). Scale 1:5

1. SBR. B.I.h (TS. 2967; IE, 1.8). Small rim and upper wall segment. Fairly fine buff ware, evenly fired. Cream slip out.
2. SJR. B.I.b (TS. 2090; IE, 1.8). Small rim and neck segment. Fairly fine buff ware, evenly fired. Light creamy-green slip in and out.
3. SJR. C.I.f (TS. 2044; IE, 1.8, 1.10). Two small joining rim and neck segments. Slightly coarse buff ware, evenly fired. Self slip in and out.
4. SJR. D.II.c (TS. 2066; IE, 1.10). Small rim and neck segment. Fairly fine grayish-buff ware, evenly fired. Self slip on top of rim and out.
5. JR. A.III.b (SC. 2522; IE, 1.10). About 1/4 rim and upper neck segment. Slightly coarse pinkish-rose ware with small lime and mica grit inclusions, evenly fired. Creamy-buff slip in and out.
6. JR. C.V.a (SW. 256; IE, 1.10). Small portions of rim and wall of vessel. Fairly coarse grayish-brown ware with many gray and white lime inclusions, evenly fired.
7. JR. D.II.d (SW. 281; IE, 1.10). About 1/4 rim and wall of vessel. Hard-fired, fairly fine pinkish-brown ware with some lime inclusions, evenly fired. Creamy-buff slip out and over rim in.
8. JR. E.I.b (TS. 2043; IE, 1.10). Small rim and shoulder segment. Slightly coarse buff ware, evenly fired. Light greenish-buff slip out and over rim in.
9. JR. E.II.1 (TS. 2063; IE, 1.10). Small rim and neck segment. Hard-fired, fine pinkish-brown ware, evenly fired. Creamy-buff slip in and out.
10. JR. H.I.d (TS. 2085; IE, 1.8). Small rim and upper shoulder segment. Hard-fired, fine dark pink ware, evenly fired. Thick cream slip out.
11. JR. N.I.a (TS. 2352; IE, 1.8). About 1/10 rim and upper wall segment with traces of a spout attached. Fairly fine pinkish-buff ware, evenly fired. Light creamy-green slip out.
12. JR. P.II.f (SC. 1640; IE, 1.8). About 1/4 rim, neck, and upper shoulder segment. Slightly coarse pinkish-buff ware with small lime and mica inclusions and some vegetable temper, unevenly fired. Creamy-buff slip in and out.
13. Lp. B.1 (TS. 664; IE, 1.7). About 1/20 of rim and upper wall segment. Fairly fine dark brown ware. Partially burnished on top of rim and traces of charring in and out.
14. SR. A.I.a (SW. 254; IE, 1.10). About 2/3 rim with body mended to near completion. Slightly coarse pinkish-brown ware with some fine lime and mica inclusions, fairly evenly fired.
15. BE. C.I (PM. D.14; TS. 546; IE, 1.10). Complete base with segment of lower wall with remains of a potter's mark on the inside. Coarse pink ware with lime and mica inclusions, evenly fired. Cream slip out and thinly applied inside.

Other Type Series Examples: (1) SBR. A.II.a (SW. 251), (2) JR. B.II.e (TS. 2042), (3) JR. C.III.e (TS. 2225), (4) Lp. A.I.a (SW. 194).

Other Study Collection Examples: (1) BR. (not typed, SC. 33), (2) SJR. B.I.a (SC. 2493), (3) SJR. C.II.e (SC. 3462), (4) JR. J.III.d (SC. 1396), (5) JR. P.II.c (SC. 1631), (6) CP. A.I.e (SC. 1790), (7) JR.Sh. (PM. C.11; SC. 3265); see fig. 333:12, (8) JR.BE.Sh. (PM. D.6; SC. 3258); see fig. 333:11.

Figure 278. Pottery from Trenches IC (Phase 4 = IE Loci 1.40, 1.41, Period H — EBII) and IE (Phase 4; Period E — EBIVb)

1. SBR. A.I.a (IP [G.4] D.II; PM. D.20; TS. 819; IE, 1.41). About 1/10 rim and upper wall segment with potter's mark incised on the outside wall before firing. Slightly coarse creamy-buff ware, evenly fired. Self slip in and out.
2. SBR. A.I.c (TS. 1041; IE, 1.40). About 1/16 rim and wall segment. Fairly coarse cream ware, evenly fired.
3. SBR. B.I.d (TS. 2460; IE, 1.41). About 1/8 rim and upper wall segment. Pinkish-buff ware, evenly fired. Pinkish-buff self slip out.
4. SBR. B.I.f (TS. 817; IE, 1.41). About 1/12 rim and upper wall segment. Fairly coarse buff ware, evenly fired. Cream slip out.
5. SBR. B.I.g (SC. 371; IE, 1.5). About 1/4 rim and upper wall segment. Fairly fine dark buff ware with small lime and mica inclusions, evenly fired. Self slip in and out.
6. SBR. C.II.a (SC. 598; IE, 1.40). About 1/12 rim and upper wall segment. Fairly fine buff ware with small lime and mica inclusions, evenly fired. Creamy-buff self slip in and out.
7. SBR. D.I.d (TS. 818; IE, 1.41). About 1/16 rim and upper shoulder segment. Fairly fine pink ware, evenly fired. Buff slip in and out.
8. SBR. E.I.c (TS. 816; IE, 1.41). About 1/16 rim and upper wall segment. Fairly coarse pink ware, evenly fired.
9. BR. B.II.a (TS. 835; IE, 1.41). About 1/20 rim and upper wall segment. Fairly coarse pinkish-buff ware, evenly fired. Cream slip in and out.
10. BR. D.I.a (TS. 785; IE, 1.40). About 1/16 rim and upper wall segment. Fairly coarse pink ware, evenly fired. Light cream slip out.
11. BR. F.I.b (TS. 2550; IE, 1.40). Small rim and upper wall segment. Fine grayish-buff ware, unevenly fired pinkish at surface out. Creamy-buff slip in and out.
12. BR. F.IV.c (TS. 744; IE, 1.40). About 1/24 rim and upper wall segment. Fairly fine ware, unevenly fired buff and cream. Cream slip in and out.
13. BR. H.III.a (SC. 1293. IE, 1.6). Small rim and upper shoulder segment. Very hard-fired light grayish-buff ware with small lime and mica grits, evenly fired. Light creamy-green slip in and out.
14. BR. L.I.f (SC. 844; IE, 1.41). About 1/14 rim and upper wall segment. Fairly fine light pink ware with small lime and mica inclusions, evenly fired. Creamy-pink self slip in and out.
15. SJR. B.I.a (TS. 849; IE, 1.41). About 1/10 rim and upper neck segment. Fairly fine pinkish-buff ware, evenly fired. Cream slip in and out.
16. JR. E.I.c (SC. 1129; IE, 1.41). About 1/11 rim and neck segment. Fairly fine light pinkish-buff ware with small lime inclusions, evenly fired. Creamy-buff slip in and out.
17. JR. E.II.b (TS. 749; IE, 1.40). About 1/8 rim and shoulder segment. Fairly coarse pink ware, evenly fired. Creamy-buff slip in and out.
18. JR. E.II.d (TS. 2247; IE, 1.5). Small rim, neck, and shoulder segment. Hard-fired, fine dark brown ware, evenly fired. Creamy-buff slip out.
19. JR. E.II.i (TS. 2399; IE, 1.41). About 1/5 rim and neck segment. Slightly coarse greenish-buff ware, evenly fired. Self slip in and out.
20. JR. F.I.a (SC. 1177; IE, 1.40). About 1/10 rim , neck, and upper shoulder segment. Slightly coarse light pink ware with small lime and mica inclusions, evenly fired. Creamy-buff slip in and out.
21. JR. F.I.d (SC. 1221; IE, 1.40). About 1/14 rim, neck, and upper shoulder segment. Fairly fine dark pinkish-buff ware with lime and mica inclusions, evenly fired. Creamy-buff slip out and to base of neck in.
22. JR. G.I.c (TS. 758; IE, 1.40). About 1/40 rim and neck segment. Fairly fine pinkish-buff ware, evenly fired. Cream slip out.
23. JR. H.I.i (TS. 755; IE, 1.40). About 1/20 rim and upper shoulder segment. Coarse pinkish-brown ware, evenly fired. Creamy-green slip in and out.
24. JR. H.II.a (SC. 523; IE, 1.6). About 1/12 rim and upper shoulder segment with two grooved channels on top of rim. Fairly coarse brown ware, evenly fired. Cream slip out.
25. JR. J.II.h (SC. 2159; IE, 1.40). About 1/16 rim and neck segment. Fairly fine pinkish-buff ware with small lime and mica inclusions, evenly fired. Creamy-buff slip in and out.
26. JR. J.II.k (SC. 1357; IE, 1.41). About 1/16 rim and upper neck segment. Slightly coarse light pinkish-buff ware with small lime and mica inclusions, evenly fired. Yellow-buff slip in and out.
27. JR. J.III.d (SC. 2230; IE, 1.40). About 1/8 rim and neck segment. Slightly coarse pinkish-brown ware with many lime and a few mica inclusions, evenly fired. Buff slip in and out.
28. JR. J.III.e (SC. 2242; IE, 1.41). About 1/7 rim, neck, and upper shoulder segment. Fairly fine pinkish-buff ware with small lime and mica inclusions, evenly fired. Light creamy-green slip in and out.
29. JR. J.III.f (TS. 856; IE, 1.41). About 1/6 rim, neck, and upper shoulder segment. Fairly coarse buff ware with lime inclusions, unevenly fired with a darker core.
30. JR. J.III.j (TS. 2269; IE, 1.40). About 1/6 rim, neck, and upper shoulder segment. Slightly coarse buff ware, evenly fired. Creamy-buff slip in and out.
31. JR. J.III.k (SC. 2306; IE, 1.40). About 1/12 rim and upper neck segment. Slightly coarse pinkish-buff ware with small lime and mica inclusions, evenly fired. Creamy-buff slip out and on surviving inside wall.
32. JR. J.III.p (PM A.1; SC. 1393; IE, 1.6). About 1/5 rim and neck segment with a potter's mark on the outside edge of the rim. Slightly coarse pinkish-buff ware with lime and mica inclusions, evenly fired. Self slip in and out. For similar potter's mark compare Type Series base BE. F.I.b (TS. 4070), pl. 294:2.
33. JR. O.II.g (TS. 716; IE, 1.40). About 1/20 rim and upper shoulder segment. Fairly coarse pink ware, evenly fired. Greenish-gray slip out.
34. JR. P.II.1 (TS. 2385; IE, 1.40). About 1/12 rim and upper shoulder segment. Slightly coarse pinkish-buff ware, unevenly fired. Creamy-green slip out.
35. JR.Sh. (IP [G.4] F.III.a; TS. 2175; IE, 1.40). Jar shoulder segment with portion of an incised "mythological"-type creature. Slightly coarse gritty pinkish-brown ware, evenly fired. Creamy-buff slip out.
36. CP. A.I.a (TS. 908; IE, 1.41). About 1/5 rim, neck, and shoulder segment. Coarse brown ware, evenly fired. Blackened on the outside surface.
37. CP. A.I.b (TS. 809; IE, 1.40 and 1.41). About 1/12 rim, neck, and upper shoulder segment. Coarse brown ware with lime and mica inclusions, evenly fired. Irregularly burnished on the outside.
38. CP.Sh. (cf. CP. B.II.b; SC. 3539; IE, 1.40). Cooking pot wall fragment with tool-stabbed decoration on the outside wall. Coarse orange-brown ware with many black and white limestone grits and some decayed vegetable temper, evenly fired. The outer surface is horizontally straw wiped and the inner surface has a highly burnished self slip.
39. BE. B.II (SC. 3120; IE, 1.41). About 1/2 of a concave-type disk base from a small bowl or cup. Fine pinkish-red ware with many small mica and a few lime grit inclusions, evenly fired. Self slip in and out.
40. BE. E.I.c (TS. 745; IE, 1.40). About 1/3 of a concave-type ring base. Fairly coarse pinkish-buff ware, evenly fired. Cream slip out.
41. BE. E.I.f (SC. 3173; IE, 1.41). Nearly complete ring-type base and about 1/3 lower wall of a small jar. Slightly coarse light pink ware with lime and mica inclusions, evenly fired. Traces of cream slip on the outside wall in an irregular line above the base.
42. BE. F.II.a (SC. 1906; IE, 1.5). About 1/9 rim and complete profile of the pedestal-type base stand. Slightly coarse brownish-buff ware with many lime and mica inclusions, unevenly fired with a gray core. Self slip in and out.

Other Type Series Examples: (1) BR. B.II.e (TS. 2457), (2) BR. H.II.a (PM. D.3; TS. 550), (2) JR. C.II.f (TS. 2218), (3) JR. E.II.i (TS. 752), (4) JR. M.II.a (TS. 737), (5) JR.Sh. (IP [G.1] C.II.b; TS. 2038); see pl. 340:5, (6) JR.Sh. (IP [G.1] D.I.c; TS. 2033); see pl. 340:16, (7) BE. F.VII (TS. 738).

Other Study Collection Examples: (1) SBR. B.I.c (SC. 271), (2) BR. E.III.c (SC. 3522), (3) BR. N.II.b (SC. 2075), (4) BR. (not typed, SC. 23), (5) JR. B.III.b (SC. 905 = SC. 983), (6) JR. B.IV.b (SC. 922), (7) JR. B.IV.c (SC. 971), (8) JR. B.IV.d (SC. 900), (9) JR. C.I.b (SC. 991), (10) JR. D.IV.a (SC. 1122), (11) JR. D.VI.b (SC. 1083), (12) JR. E.II.w (SC. 2160), (13) JR. E.II.z (SC. 3035), (14) JR. J.III.k (SC. 2325), (15) JR. J.III.p (SC. 2170), (16) JR. J.IV.g (SC. 1414), (17) JR. O.III.f (SC. 2458), (18) JR. P.I.d (SC. 2439), (19) JR. P.III.c (SC. 1754), (20) JR. (not typed, SC. 50), (21) JR. (not typed, SC. 79), (22) JR. (not typed, SC. 90), (23) CP. A.I.a (SC. 1880), (24) CP. B.II.k (SC. 1789), (25) BE. F.V.b (SC. 3376).

Figure 278

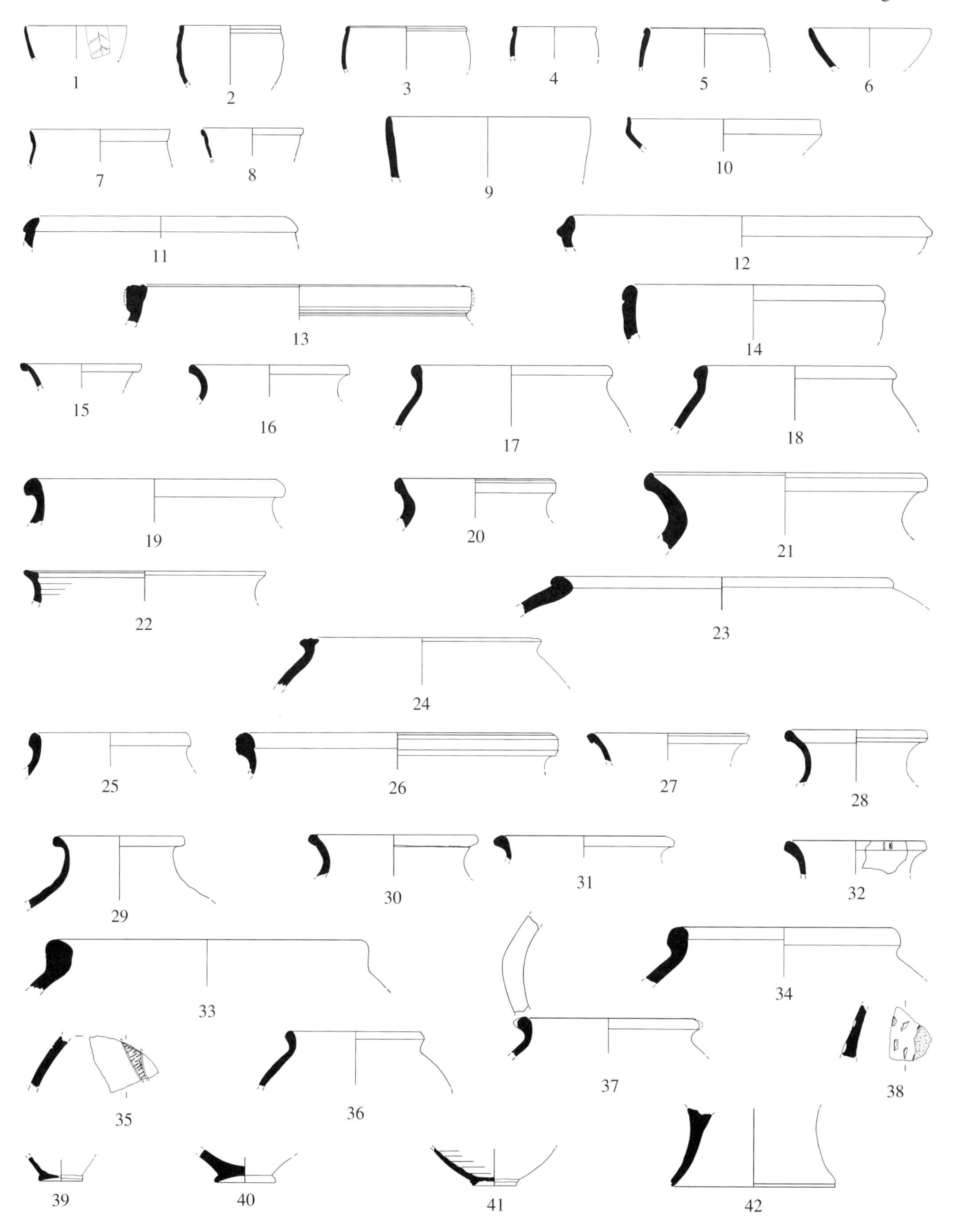

Pottery from Trench IE (Phase 4; Period E — Early Bronze Age IVb). Scale 1:5

Figure 279

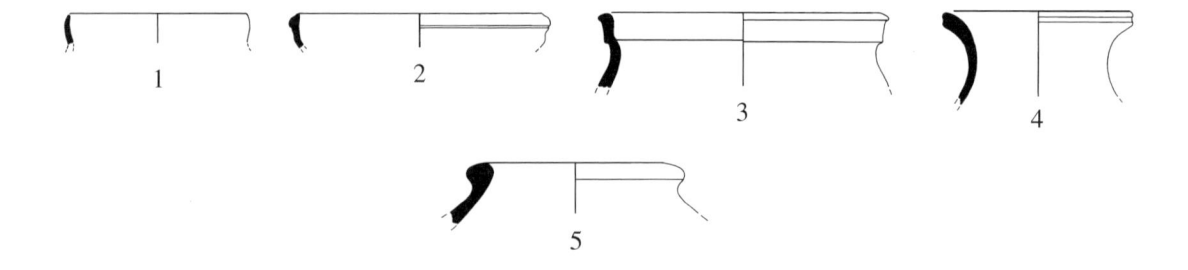

Pottery from Trench IE (Phase 5; Period E–D — Early–Middle Bronze Age and Roman). Scale 1:5

1. SBR. D.I.e (SC. 3461; IE, 1.1a). About 1/20 rim segment. Fairly fine buff ware with small lime and mica inclusions, evenly fired. Self slip in and out.
2. BR. A.III.b (SC. 2823; IE, 1.1a). About 1/20 rim and upper wall segment. Slightly coarse pinkish-buff ware with small lime and mica inclusions, evenly fired. Self slip in and out.
3. JR. B.IV.f (SC. 968; IE, 1.1a). About 1/10 rim and upper shoulder segment. Slightly coarse pinkish-brown ware with small lime and mica inclusions, fairly evenly fired. Creamy-buff slip in and out.
4. JR. J.III.g (SC. 2284; IE, 1.1a). About 1/4 rim and neck segment. Slightly coarse pinkish-buff ware with small lime and mica inclusions, evenly fired. Creamy-buff slip in and out.
5. R.HMJ. B.II.a (TS. 519; IE, 1.1a). Small rim and upper shoulder segment. Fairly coarse pink ware, unevenly fired with pinkish-buff core at rim. Self slip in and out.

Other Type Series Examples: Roman — (1) R.JR.Sh. (IP [G.1] C.V.a; TS. 2037), see pl. 340:7, (2) R.BR. D.II.f (TS. 2500), (3) R.HMJ. B.I.c (TS. 2065).

Other Study Collection Examples: Early–Middle Bronze Age — (1) JR. B.II.c (SC. 962), (2) JR. C.V.a (SC. 1073), (3) JR. D.V.d (SC.1089), (4) JR. J.I.c (SC. 3397), (5) JR. J.IV.i (SC. 1539), (6) JR. O.III.b (SC. 1668).

Figure 280

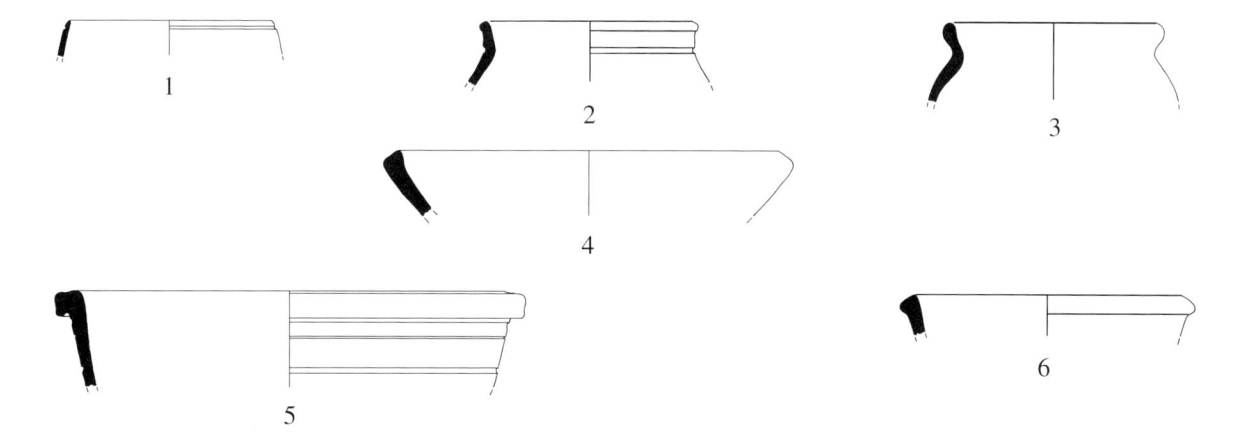

Pottery from Trench IE (Phase 6; Period B — Derived Early–Middle Bronze Age and Roman). Scale 1:5

1. SBR. A.I.d (SC. 269; IE, 1.1). About 1/12 rim and upper wall segment. Fairly fine pinkish-buff ware with small lime and mica inclusions, evenly fired. Self slip in and out.
2. JR. A.V.d (SC. 923; IE, 1.1). About 1/12 rim and upper shoulder segment. Slightly coarse creamy-green ware with small lime inclusions, evenly fired. Self slip in and out.
3. CP. A.I.a (SC. 1773; IE, 1.1). About 1/10 rim and upper shoulder segment. Coarse pinkish-brown ware with many lime and mica inclusions, evenly fired. Self slip in and out.
4. R.BR. A.II.d (SC. 2833; IE, 1.1). About 1/24 rim and upper wall segment. Slight coarse dark pinkish-buff with with small lime inclusions, evenly fired. Self buff slip in and out.
5. R.BR. C.II.c (SC. 2928; IE, 1.1). About 1/22 rim and upper wall segment. Fairly coarse buff ware with lime and mica inclusions and decayed vegetable temper, evenly fired. Thick buff slip in and out.
6. R.JR. C.I.b (TS. 509; IE, 1.1). About 1/24 rim and upper neck segment. Fairly coarse pink ware, evenly fired. Buff slip out.

Other Type Series Examples: Roman — (1) R.BR. C.II.g (SC. 3327), (2) R.Jg. A.I.b (TS. 3157), (3) R.BE. B.I.b (TS. 538).

Other Study Collection Examples:
Derived Early Bronze Age — (1) SBR. A.I.d (SC. 3459), (2) BR. A.I.b (SC. 3460), (3) BR. A.IV.d (SC. 3478), (4) JR. A.IV.a (SC. 909), (5) JR. A.V.c (SC. 3396), (6) JR. B.VI.c (SC. 986), (7) JR. J.III.b (SC. 2204), (8) JR. J.III.p (SC. 2269), (9) JR. K.I.b (SC. 1536), (10) JR. K.I.c (SC. 1572), (11) JR. K.I.e (SC. 2386), (12) CP. A.I.b (SC. 1885), (13) WPS. A.I.a (SC. 1945).
Roman — (1) R.BR. A.II.e (SC. 3521), (2) R.Jg. B.II.a (SC. 2962), (3) R.CP.Sh. A.IV.b (SC. 3538), (4) R.Jg.Hd. (SC. 3371).

Figure 281

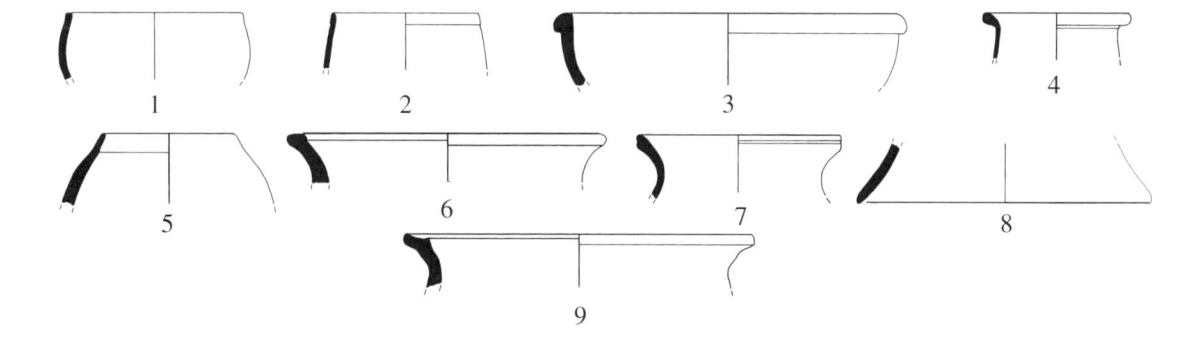

Pottery from Trench IF (Phases 1 and 2; Periods F and E — Early Bronze Age IVa and Early Bronze Age IVb).
Scale 1:5

1. SBR. A.I.g (TS. 2455; IF, 1.22). Phase 1. About 1/5 rim and upper wall segment. Fairly fine pinkish-buff ware, evenly fired. Self slip out and to just below rim in.
2. SBR. B.I.e (TS. 2463; IF, 1.22). Phase 1. About 1/6 rim and upper wall segment. Fairly fine light greenish-buff ware, evenly fired. Light creamy-green slip in and out.
3. BR. K.I.b (TS. 2488; IF, 1.22). Phase 1. Small rim and upper wall segment. Hard-fired, flesh-pink colored ware, evenly fired. Creamy-buff slip out.
4. SJR. C.II.p (TS. 634; IF, 1.22). Phase 1. About 1/4 rim and neck segment. Fairly fine pinkish-buff ware, with unevenly fired pink core.
5. SJR. E.I.a (TS. 2439; IF, 1.22). Phase 1. About 1/8 rim and shoulder segment. Fairly coarse yellow-buff ware with straw temper, evenly fired. Cream slip out.
6. JR. F.I.b (TS. 2539; IF, 1.22). Phase 1. About 1/12 rim and neck segment. Slightly coarse buff ware, evenly fired. Self slip in and out.
7. JR. J.III.m (TS. 3005; IF, 1.22). Phase 1. About 1/6 rim and neck segment. Fine salmon-pink ware, evenly fired. Creamy-pink slip in and out.
8. BE. F.I.a (TS. 2486; IF, 1.22). Phase 1. Small pedestal-type base rim and wall segment. Coarse, gritty, grayware, unevenly fired pink on outside surface.
9. JR. G.I.c (TS. 585; IF, 1.19). Phase 2. About 1/24 rim and neck segment. Fairly fine buff ware, evenly fired. Cream slip in and out.

Other Type Series Examples:
Phase 1 — (1) SJR. C.II.s (TS. 2546), (2) JR.Sh. (IP [G.4] D.III; PM. D.20; SW. 217), see fig. 333:7.
Phase 2 — (1) JR. C.III.a (TS. 118), (2) CP. B.I.f (SW. 298 = TS. 555).

Other Study Collection Examples:
Phase 1 — (1) BR. F.III.d (SC. 1965), (2) SJR. C.I.a (SC. 3504), (3) JR. O.III.a (SC. 1658), (4) CP. B.I.a (SC. 1816).
Phase 2 — (1) SBR. C.II.a (SC. 610).

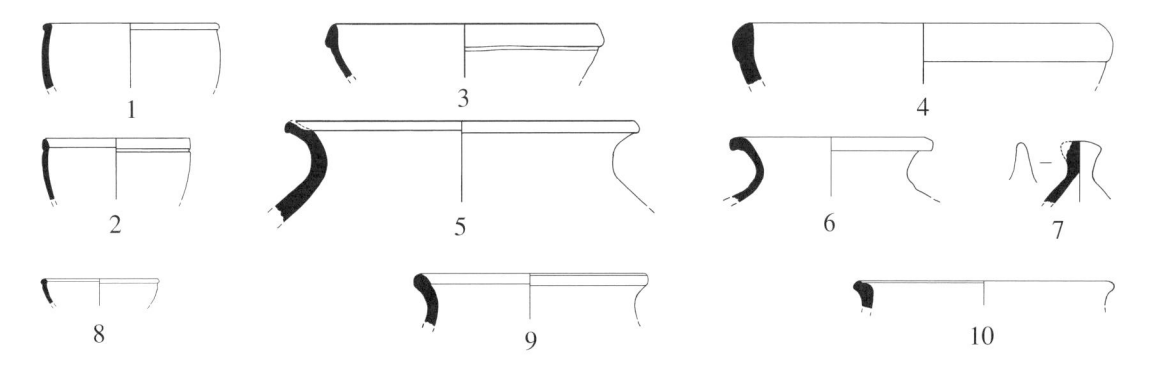

Figure 282. Pottery from Trench IF (Phases 3 and 4; Period E — Early Bronze Age IVb). Scale 1:5

1. SBR. B.I.f (TS. 2454; IF, 1.16). Phase 3. About 1/5 rim and upper wall segment. Fairly fine pinkish-brown ware, evenly fired. Self slip in and out.
2. SBR. B.I.h (TS. 2064; IF, 1.18) Phase 3. Small rim and upper wall segment. Fairly fine light pink ware, evenly fired. Creamy-white slip in and out.
3. BR. D.III.b (TS. 2075; IF, 1.14). Phase 3. Hard-fired, fine pink ware, evenly fired. Self slip in and out.
4. BR. F.II.d (TS. 2045; IF, 1.17). Phase 3. Small rim and upper wall segment. Slightly coarse grayish-buff ware, evenly fired. Greenish-buff slip in and out.
5. JR. G.I.c (SC. 1236; IF, 1.12). Phase 3. About 1/34 rim, neck, and upper shoulder segment. Slightly coarse pinkish-buff ware with a few small lime inclusions, evenly fired. Light creamy-green slip in and out.
6. JR. J.III.p (TS. 156; IF, 1.16). Phase 3. About 1/2 rim, neck and upper shoulder segment. Fairly fine pinkish-buff ware with lime and mica inclusions, evenly fired. Greenish-buff slip in and out.
7. Ld. A.II.a (TS. 565; IF, 1.13). Phase 3. Nearly complete knob-type lid handle with a portion of the wall of the lid attached. Fairly fine buff ware, evenly fired. Cream slip in and out.
8. SBR. B.I.m (SC. 3463; IF, 1.7). Phase 4. About 1/20 rim and upper wall segment. Fine dark buff ware with small lime and mica inclusions, evenly fired. Self slip in and out.
9. JR. J.I.j (TS. 2077; IF, 1.7). Phase 4. Small rim and neck segment. Hard-fired, buff ware, evenly fired. Creamy-green slip out and over rim in.
10. CP. A.II.b (SC. 1797; IF, 1.7). Phase 4. About 1/22 rim and upper neck segment. Fairly coarse brown ware with lime and mica grits, and decayed vegetable inclusions. evenly fired. Worn self slip in and out.

Other Type Series Examples: Phase 3 — (1) BR. L.III.g (TS. 2062), (2) JR. C.IV.c (TS. 2039).

Other Study Collection Examples: Phase 3 — (1) SBR. A.I.b (SC. 215), (2) SBR. B.I.e (SC. 306), (3) SBR. B.I.e (SC. 328), (4) SBR. B.I.h (SC. 435), (5) SBR. B.I.i (SC. 436), (6) SBR. B.I.k (SC. 385), (7) SBR. D.I.c (SC. 316), (8) SJR. C.I.h (SC. 2174), (9) SJR. (not typed, SC. 95), (10) JR. H.I.d (SC. 1260), (11) JR. J.I.c (SC. 3399), (12) JR. K.I.b (SC. 2392), (13) JR. K.II.c (SC. 1602), (14) CP. A.I.h (SC. 1794), (15) BE. E.II.e (SC. 3168).

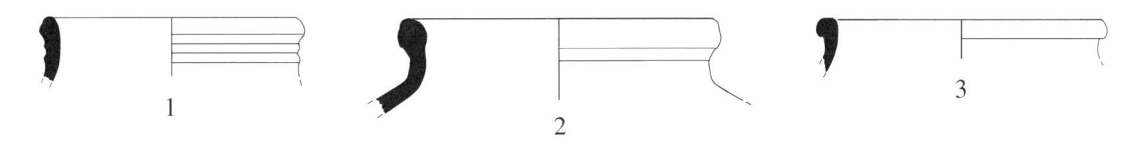

Figure 283. Pottery from Trench IF (Phase 5; Period E–D — Early–Middle Bronze Age). Scale 1:5

1. JR. C.V.a (SC. 1081; IF, 1.2). About 1/10 rim and neck segment. Slightly coarse pinkish-buff ware with lime and mica inclusions, evenly fired. Creamy-buff slip in and out.
2. JR. P.II.a (SC. 1700 = SC. 2381; IF,1.2). Two joining sherds, about 1/5 rim, neck, and upper shoulder segments. Slightly coarse pinkish-orange ware with many fine mica grits and a few lime inclusions, evenly fired. Creamy-buff slip out and over rim and neck inside, very worn.
3. CP. A.II.c (TS. 2067; IF, 1.2). Small rim and neck segment. Slightly coarse, gritty, grayish-brown ware, fairly evenly fired.

Another Study Collection Example: (1) BE. E.I.h (SC. 3182).

Figures 284–85

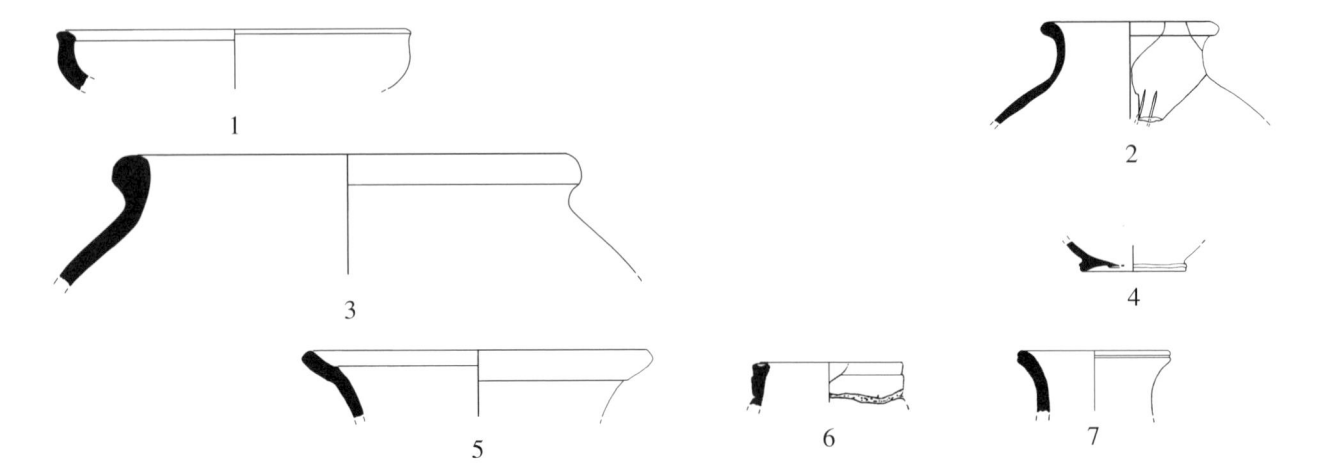

Figure 284. Pottery from Trench IF (Phase 6; Period B — Derived Early–Middle Bronze Age and Roman). Scale 1:5

1. BR. C.I.b (TS. 2498; IF, 1.1). Two joining pieces, about 1/8 rim and upper wall segment. Fairly coarse gritty buff-brown ware, evenly fired. Self slip in and out.
2. JR. J.III.k (PM. A.6; SC. 3398; IF, 1.1). About 1/24 rim, neck, and upper shoulder segment with remains of a portion of a potter's mark on outside wall. Fairly fine pinkish-buff ware with small lime and mica inclusions, evenly fired. Buff self slip in and out.
3. JR. P.II.m (TS. 2388; IF, 1.1). About 1/6 rim and shoulder segment. Slightly coarse pink ware, evenly fired. Creamy-buff slip out and over rim in.
4. BE. E.II.j (SC. 3226; IF, 1.1). About 1/4 segment of a base with the lower portion of the vessel wall attached. Fairly fine buff ware with many small gold-colored mica grits, unevenly fired orange-buff at surfaces.
5. R.BR. A.I.f (SC. 3328; IF, 1.1). About 1/20 rim and upper wall segment. Fairly fine orange-buff ware with many lime and mica inclusions, evenly fired. Self slip in and out.
6. R.Jg. B.II.n ([variant] PM. F; SC. 3014; IF, 1.1). About 1/4 rim and neck fragment. Slightly course grayish-buff ware with many gold-colored mica inclusions. Creamy-buff slip in and out.
7. R.Jg. C.I.q (TS. 559; IF, 1.1). About 1/20 rim and neck segment. Fairly coarse brownish-buff ware, evenly fired. Cream slip in and out.

Other Type Series Examples: Derived Early Bronze Age — (1) JR.Sh. (IP [G.1] J.II.a; TS. 2035).

Other Study Collection Examples:
    Derived Early Bronze Age — (1) SBR. A.I.h (SC. 566), (2) BR. C.I.b (SC. 2936), (3) SJR. B.I.c (SC. 3400), (4) SJR. B.II.j (SC. 2521), (5) JR. D.I.c (SC. 1048), (6) JR. D.V. c (SC. 1092), (7) JR. H.I.e (SC. 1278), (8) JR. O.III.b (SC. 1682).
    Roman — (1) R.Jg. B.II.n (variant; PM. F; SC. 3014), (2) R.Jg. B.II.i (SC. 2944), (3) R.Lp. spout fragment with red slip outside (SC. 3543).

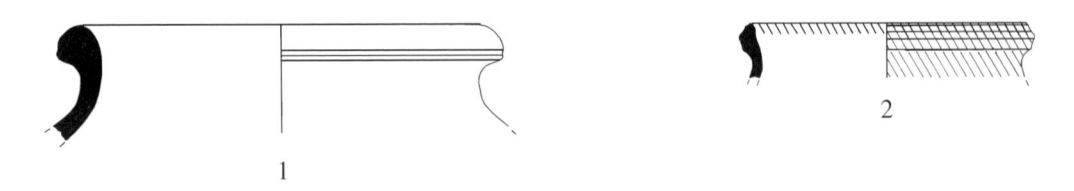

Figure 285. Pottery from Trench IF/G (Phases 2, 3, and 6; Periods E and B — Early Bronze Age IVb, Derived Early–Middle Bronze Age, and Roman). Scale 1:5

1. JR. O.I.h (TS. 867; IF/G, 2.2). Phase 2. About 1/8 rim, neck, and upper shoulder segment. Fairly coarse pink ware, evenly fired. Cream slip out.
2. R.JR. C.I.c (TS. 803; IF/G, 1.1). Phase 6. About 1/12 rim and neck segment. Fairly coarse brown ware. Thick red slip out and just over rim inside.

Other Study Collection Examples:
    Early Bronze Age — Phase 2: (1) JR. J.II.j (SC. 2178). Phase 3: (1) JR. H.I.e (SC. 2068).
    Derived Early Bronze Age — Phase 6: (1) JR. F.III.f (SC. 1233), (2) JR. J.IV.c (SC. 2281).

Figure 286. Pottery from Trench IG (Phase 1; Period F — Early Bronze Age IVa). Scale 1:5

1. SBR. B.I.h (TS. 2481; IG, 1.20). About 1/10 rim and upper wall segment. Fairly fine buff ware, evenly fired. Cream slip out.
2. SJR. C.II.p (TS. 810; IG, 1.12). About 1/8 rim and upper neck segment. Fairly fine pinkish-buff ware, unevenly fired buff core.
3. JR.Sh. (cf. JR. E.II.g, pl. 242:7; SC. 3355; IG, 1.11). About 1/12 neck and shoulder segment of a storage-type jar with deeply incised comb-type ribbing on the upper portion of the shoulder. Slightly coarse pinkish-buff ware with lime and mica inclusions, evenly fired. Self slip in and out.

Another Type Series Example: (1) SJR. B.III.b (TS. 811).

Other Study Collection Examples: (1) SJR. B.I.d (SC. 1933), (2) JR. J.III.i (SC. 2229), (3) JR. J.III.p (SC. 1473), (4) CP. B.IV.c (SC. 1889).

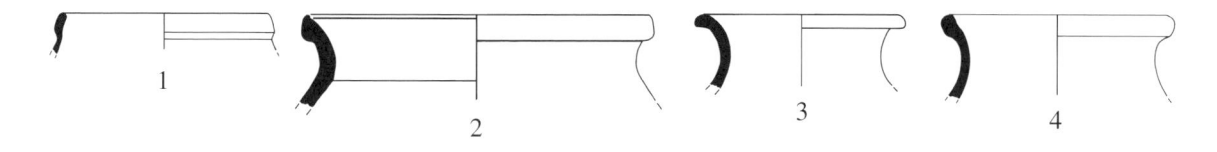

Figure 287. Pottery from Trench IG (Phase 2; Period E — Early Bronze Age IVb). Scale 1:5

1. SBR. D.II.c (TS. 2059; IG, 1.7). Small rim and upper wall segment. Fairly fine pink ware, evenly fired. Self slip out.
2. JR. F.II.c (SC. 1220; IG, 1.7). About 1/12 rim, neck, and upper shoulder segment. Slightly coarse buff ware with lime and mica inclusions, evenly fired. Creamy-buff slip out and just over rim in.
3. JR. J.III.a (TS. 839; IG, 1.7). About 1/8 rim and neck segment. Fairly coarse pinkish-buff ware, evenly fired. Cream slip in and out.
4. JR. J.III.u (TS. 2275; IG, 1.7). About 1/5 rim and neck segment. Slightly coarse greenish-buff ware, evenly fired. Creamy-green slip in and out.

Other Study Collection Examples: (1) SBR. B.I.d (SC. 376), (2) BR. (not typed, SC. 42), (3) CP. A.I.f (SC. 1792).

Figure 288

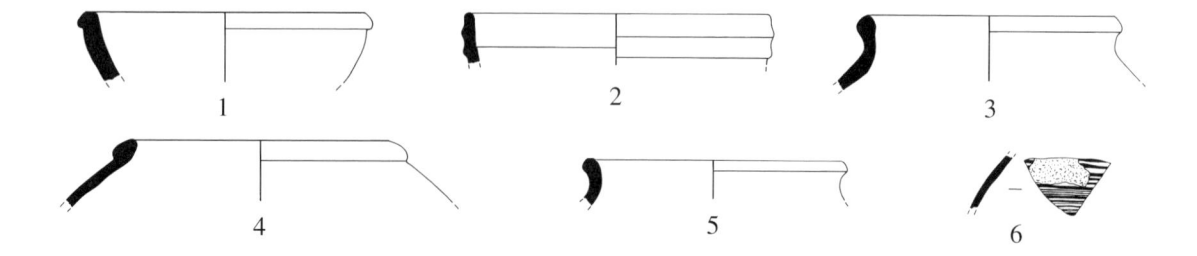

Pottery from Trench IG (Phase 3; Period E — Early Bronze Age IVb). Scale 1:5

1. BR. F.III.c (TS. 920; IG, 1.17). About 1/36 rim and upper wall segment. Fairly coarse buff ware, unevenly fired with pink in the core. Cream slip out.
2. JR. D.III.b (TS. 2041; IG, 1.6). Small rim segment. Hard-fired, fine grayish-buff ware, evenly fired. Greenish-buff slip in and out.
3. JR. E.II.d (TS. 2048; IG, 1.5). Small rim, neck, and upper shoulder segment. Fairly fine pink ware, evenly fired. Creamy-buff slip out and over rim in.
4. JR. H.I.a (TS. 2082; IG, 1.6). Small rim and upper shoulder segment. Hard-fired, fairly fine pinkish-buff ware, evenly fired. Buff slip out.
5. JR. J.II.e (TS. 2040; IG, 1.6). Small rim and neck segment. Fairly fine pink ware, evenly fired.
6. JR.Sh. Pt. (SC. 3541; IG, 1.5). Small shoulder sherd from a small type jar. Slightly coarse brownish-buff ware with small lime and mica inclusions, evenly fired. Horizontally applied black painted lines in reserve on the outside wall.

Other Study Collection Examples: (1) JR. H.I.h (SC. 2059), (2) JR. J.III.d (SC. 2225).

Figure 289

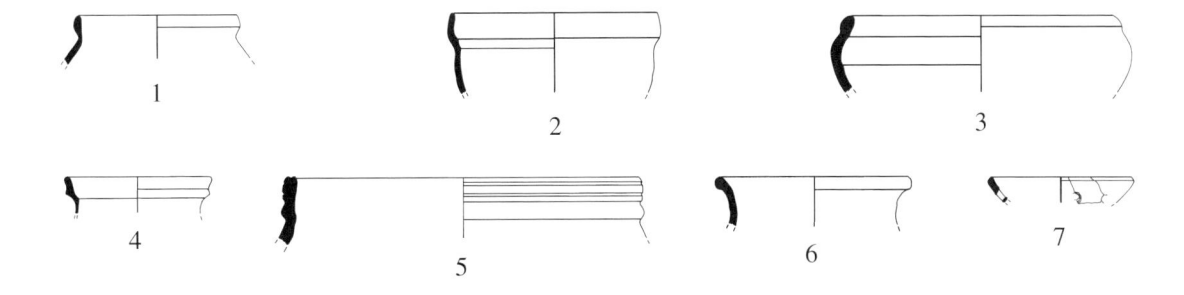

Pottery from Trench IG (Phase 4; Period E — Early Bronze Age IVb and Derived Roman). Scale 1:5

1. SBR. D.I.c (TS 2226; IG, 1.3). Small rim and upper shoulder segment. Fairly fine buff ware, evenly fired. Creamy-green slip out.
2. SBR. D.I.e (TS. 2099; IG, 1.3). Small rim and upper wall segment. Fairly fine buff ware, evenly fired. Self slip in and out.
3. BR. E.II.c (TS. 2073; IG, 1.3). Small rim and upper wall segment. Slightly coarse dark pink ware, evenly fired. Creamy-buff slip out.
4. SJR. C.II.a (SC. 2576; IG, 1.3). About 1/9 rim and upper neck segment. Fine light pinkish-brown ware with small lime and mica inclusions, evenly fired. Self slip irregularly line-burnished horizontally on the outside surface and around the inside of the rim.
5. JR. D.VIII.b (TS. 2204; IG, 1.3). Small rim and upper shoulder segment. Fairly fine dark buff ware, evenly fired. Creamy-green slip out.
6. JR. J.III.g (TS. 561; IG, 1.3). About 1/6 rim and neck segment. Fairly fine pinkish-buff ware, evenly fired. Greenish-buff slip in and out.
7. SR. A.II.b (TS. 2456; IG, 1.3). Small segment of rim and upper wall with remains of two strainer holes. Fine light pink ware, evenly fired. Self slip in and out.

Other Type Series Examples: Derived Roman — (1) R.JR. B.I.f (TS. 616), (2) R.JR. C.I.a (TS. 573).

Other Study Collection Examples:
  Early Bronze Age — (1) SBR. A.I.a (SC. 183), (2) SBR. A.I.d (SC. 383), (3) SBR. B.I.c (SC. 349), (4) SBR. B.I.d (SC. 251), (5) SBR. B.I.h (SC. 305), (6) SBR. B.I.h (SC. 428), (7) SBR. B.I.h (SC. 492), (8) SBR. B.I.i (SC. 314), (9) BR. E.II.c (SC. 3481), (10) BR. F.IV.a (SC. 811), (11) SJR. B.I.a (SC. 3503), (12) SJR. C.I.f (SC. 2566), (13) JR. F.I.a (SC. 1191), (14) JR. H (Gen. Type, SC. 49), (15) JR. J.I.c (SC. 1329), (16) JR. J.I.c (SC. 2651), (17) JR. J.II.l (SC. 2003), (18) JR. J.III.a (SC. 1231), (19) JR. J.III.f (SC. 1400), (20) JR. P.II.f (SC. 1738), (21) CP. B.II.a (SC. 1817), (22) BE. E.I.c (SC. 3174), (23) WPS. A.I.a (SC. 1468).
  Derived Roman — (1) R.Jg. B.II.b (SC. 2948), (2) R.Jg. B.II.e (SC. 2986), (3) R.Jg. B.II.r (SC. 3540), (4) R.CP., rim (not typed, SC. 151).

Figure 290. Pottery from Trench IG (Phase 6; Period B — Derived Early Bronze Age, Early–Middle Bronze Age, and Roman)

1. SBR. B.I.h (TS. 978; IG, 1.19). About 1/8 rim and upper wall segment. Fairly fine pink ware, evenly fired. Thin buff slip out.
2. SBR. B.I.h (TS. 2982; IG, 1.22). About 1/6 rim and upper wall segment. Fairly fine pinkish-buff ware, evenly fired. Creamy-buff slip in and out.
3. BR. A.II.d (TS. 973; IG, 1.19). About 1/24 rim and upper wall segment. Fairly fine pink ware, unevenly fired buff on inner half of the cross section. Cream slip on the outside upper part of the body.
4. BR. L.I.d (TS. 2208; IG, 1.19). Small rim and upper wall segment. Slightly coarse pink ware, evenly fired. Buff slip in and out.
5. SJR. A.I.a (TS. 2217; IG, 1.15). Small rim and shoulder segment. Fairly coarse ware, unevenly fired light green out and yellow-buff in.
6. SJR. C.II.i (TS. 1020; IG, 1.19). About 1/2 rim and upper neck segment. Fairly coarse pink ware, evenly fired. Cream slip out.
7. JR. D.V.e (SC. 1099; IG, 1.1). About 1/14 rim segment. Slightly coarse pinkish-orange ware with lime and mica inclusions, evenly fired. Pinkish-buff slip in and out.
8. JR. H.II.d (PM. E.2; TS. 970; IG, 1.19). About 1/16 rim and upper shoulder segment with remains of a potter's mark on upper part of the inside wall. Fairly coarse buff ware, evenly fired. Cream slip out.
9. JR. J.III.aa (TS. 2331; IG, 1.1). About 1/12 rim, neck, and upper shoulder segment. Very hard-fired, fine grayish-buff ware, evenly fired. Light green slip out.
10. BE. E.I.b (TS. 3068; IG, 1.1). About 1/3 of a ring base and lower wall segment. Fairly fine light pink ware, evenly fired. Self slip in and out.
11. BE. E.I.h (TS. 3167; IG, 1.19). Complete ring base profile. Fairly coarse ware with grit inclusions, evenly fired. Cream slip in and out.
12. BE. E.I.k.1 (TS. 932; IG, 1.15). Complete ring base with lower wall of the vessel. Fairly coarse buff ware, evenly fired. Cream slip in and partially out.
13. R.BR. A.I.d (TS. 991; IG, 1.19). About 1/7 rim and upper wall segment with piecrust-like molding below the outside of the rim. Fairly coarse pink ware, evenly fired. Some cream slip out.
14. R.BR. A.II.d (TS. 3161; IG, 1.15). Small rim and upper wall segment. Fairly fine buff ware, evenly fired. Creamy-buff slip in and out.
15. RBR. B.I.b (SC. 3085; IG, 1.1). About 1/18 rim and upper wall segment. Slightly coarse pinkish-orange ware with small lime and mica inclusions, evenly fired. Creamy self slip in and out.
16. R.BR. C.II.c (SC. 2929; IG, 1.1). About 1/16 rim and upper wall segment. Fairly fine orange-pink ware with small lime and mica inclusions, evenly fired. Self slip in and out.
17. R.HMJ. B.II.a (SC. 3046 = SC. 3047; IG, 1.1). About 1/4 rim (two non-joining sherds) and upper shoulder segments. Slightly coarse pinkish-orange ware with lime and mica inclusions, evenly fired. Creamy self slip out.
18. R.Jg. B.II.o (varient; SC. 2952; IG, 1.19). Small rim and upper neck segment. Fairly coarse buff-brown ware with lime grits, evenly fired. Possible self slip, but very worn sherd.
19. R.CP. A.II.a (TS. 1012; IG, 1.19). About 1/24 rim and neck segment. Fairly coarse reddish ware, evenly fired. Dark brown slip on outside wall.
20. R.SV.5 (TS. 553; IG, 1.1). About 1/2 segment of a pipe-shaped stand with a ribbed wall. Coarse pink ware, evenly fired. Buff slip out.
21. R.Bt. B.I.d (SC. 3401; IG, 1.1). About 1/4 rim and neck segment. Slightly coarse pinkish-orange ware with small lime inclusions, evenly fired. Creamy self slip out and over rim in.

Other Type Series Examples:

Derived Early Bronze Age — (1) BR. A.II.f (TS. 2069), (2) SJR. C.I.d (TS. 982), (3) JR.Sh. (IP [G.4] B.I.a; TS. 2034), see pl. 340:33.

Roman — (1) R.BR. A.I.d (TS. 637), (2) R.BR. A.I.h (TS. 2078), (3) R.BR. A.II.b (TS. 969), (4) R.BR. B.I.c (TS. 629), (5) R.HMJ. A.II.b (TS. 3162), (6) R.Jg. A.I.a (TS. 645), (7) R.Jg. B.II.p (TS. 3158), (8) R.Jg. B.II.q (TS. 1054), (9) R.BE. B.I.c (SC. 3189).

Other Study Collection Examples:

Derived Early Bronze Age — (1) SBR. A.I.d (SC. 3464), (2) SBR. A.I.d (SC. 3465), (3) SBR. A.I.e (SC. 252), (4) SBR. A.I.e (SC. 3466), (5) SBR. B.I.b (SC. 2789), (6) SBR. B.I.d (SC. 291), (7) SBR. B.I.f (SC. 320), (8) SBR. B.I.h (SC. 307), (9) SBR. B.I.h (SC. 425), (10) SBR. B.I.h (SC. 442), (11) SBR. B.I.h (SC. 466), (12) SBR. B.I.h (SC. 485), (13) SBR. C.II.a (SC. 616), (14) BR. A.I.e (SC. 708), (15) BR. C.I.d (SC. 2938), (16) SJR. A.II.b (SC. 2482), (17) SJR. C.I.a (SC. 2543), (18) SJR. C.II.b (SC. 2586), (19) SJR. C.II.g (SC. 1430), (20) JR. A.III.d (SC. 914), (21) JR. A.III.d (SC. 921), (22) JR. A.III.d (SC. 935), (23) JR. A.III.f (SC. 917), (24) JR. B.I.b (SC. 937), (25) JR. B.IV.b (SC. 973), (26) JR. B.IV.c (SC. 2746), (27) JR. B.VI.c (SC. 981), (28) JR. C.II.a (SC. 990), (29) JR. E.II.d (SC. 3523), (30) JR. G.I.b (SC. 3480), (31) JR. H.I.a (SC. 1273), (32) JR. H.I.d (SC. 1266), (33) JR. H.I.j

(SC. 1246), (34) JR. H.III.b (SC. 2364), (35) JR. H.III.s (SC. 2066), (36) JR. J.I.c (SC. 2112), (37) JR. J.I.f (SC. 1570), (38) JR. J.II.l (SC. 1457), (39) JR. J.III.l (SC. 2214), (40) JR. J.V.b (SC. 888), (41) JR. K.II.d (SC. 1601), (42) JR. O.II.l (SC. 2406), (43) JR. P.II.i (SC. 1632), (44) JR. P.II.l (SC. 1744), (45) JR. P.II.q (SC. 2437), (46) JR. Q.II.a (SC. 1733), (47) CP. C.I.a (SC. 1875), (48) BE. F.IV.a (SC. 1128), (49) Bt. A.I.b.3 (SC. 3544).

Roman — (1) R.BR. C.I.b (SC. 3402), (2) R.BR. D.I.a (SC. 3479), (3) R.JR. A.I.b (SC. 2445), (4) R.JR. A.I.g (SC. 1603), (5) R.HMJ. A.I.a (SC. 3039), (6) R.HMJ. A.II.g (SC. 3502), (7) R.Jg. B.II.c (SC. 2977), (8) R.Jg. B.II.f (SC. 3367), (9) R.Jg. B.II.l (SC. 3013), (10) R.Jg. B.II.o (variant, SC. 2952), (11) R.Jg. B.II.o (SC. 3020), (12) R.Jg. B.II.p (SC. 3024), (13) R.Jg. B.II.p (SC. 3025), (14) R.CP. A.IV.b (SC. 3542), (15) R.CP. B.III.a (SC. 1860).

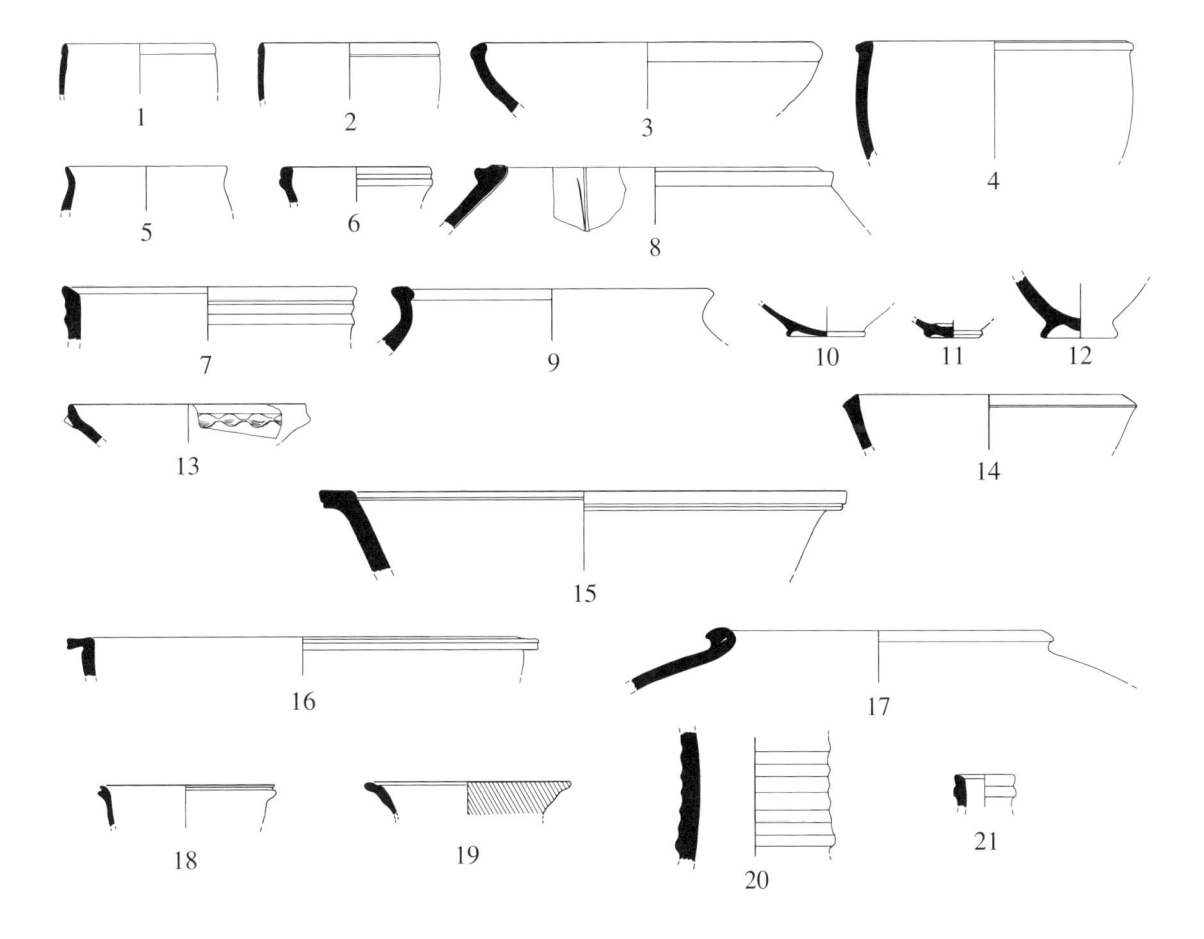

Pottery from Trench IG (Phase 6; Period B — Derived Early Bronze Age, Early–Middle Bronze Age, and Roman). Scale 1:5

Figures 291–92

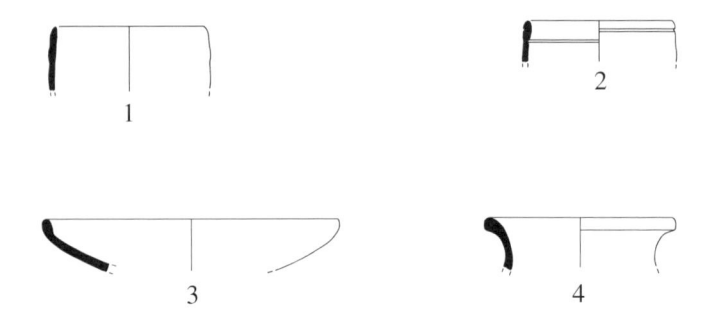

Figure 291. Pottery from Trench IH (Phase 2; Period B — Derived Early Bronze Age, Early–Middle Bronze Age, and Roman). Scale 1:5

1. SBR. B.I.j (SC. 545; IH, 1.2). Derived Early Bronze Age. About 1/22 rim and upper wall segment. Fine creamy-green buff ware without any visible inclusions, evenly fired. Self slip in and out.
2. SBR. B.I.k (SC. 367; IH, 1.2). Derived Early–Middle Bronze Age. About 1/9 rim and upper wall segment. Slightly coarse buff ware with small black and white lime inclusions, evenly fired. Creamy-green slip in and out.
3. R.BR. A.I.b (TS. 2032; IH, 1.2). Small rim and wall segment. Fairly fine pinkish-brown ware, evenly fired. Remains of tannish-buff slip in and out.
4. R.JR. B.I.d (TS. 2321; IH, 1.2). About 1/8 rim and neck segment. Fairly coarse pinkish-buff ware, evenly fired. Creamy-buff slip in and out.

Another Type Series Example: Roman — (1) R.Jg. B.II.k (TS. 933).

Another Study Collection Example: Roman — (1) R.Jg. A.II.c (SC. 2976).

Figure 292. Pottery from Trench IJ (Phase 1; Period E–D — Early–Middle Bronze Age). Scale 1:5

1. JR. B.III.a (TS. 954; IJ, 1.2). About 1/44 rim and neck segment. Fairly fine pink ware, unevenly fired with gray core. Cream slip in and out.
2. JR. B.V.f (TS. 947; IJ, 1.2). About 1/4 rim and neck segment. Fairly coarse buff ware, unevenly fired with darker colored core. Cream slip in and out.

Other Study Collection Examples: (1) SBR. A.I.d (SC. 225), (2) JR. A.III.e (SC. 908), (3) JR. B.VI.c (SC. 957), (4) JR. J.I.a (SC. 2125), (5) JR. J.III.h (SC. 2300).

Figure 293

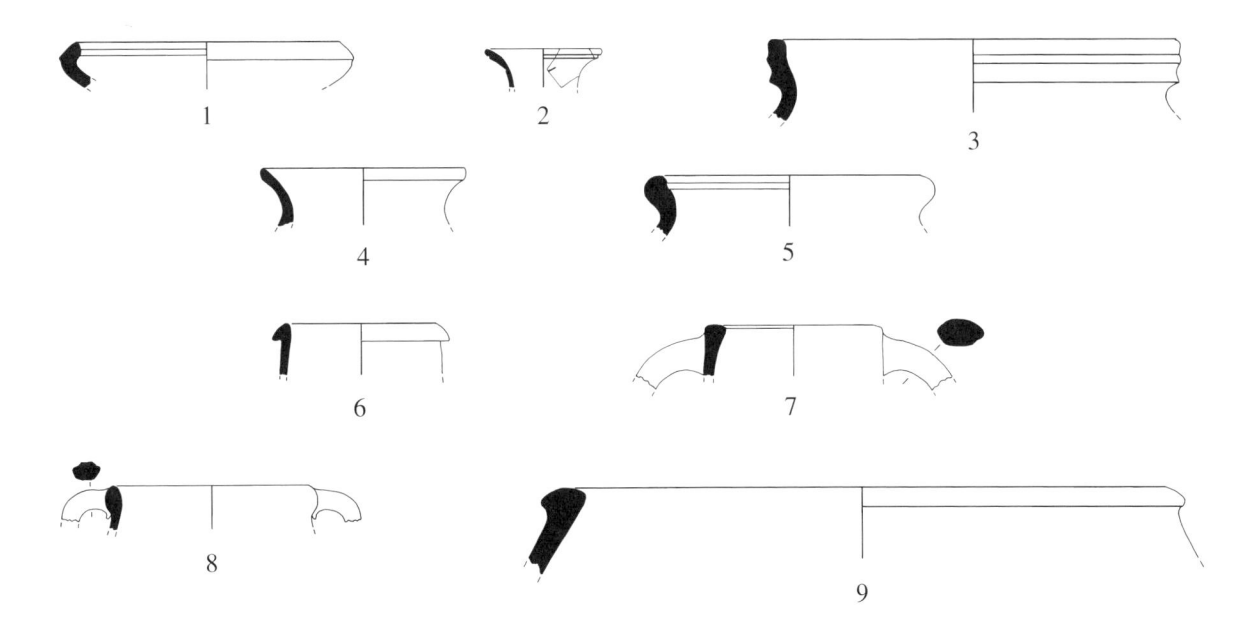

Pottery from Trench IJ (Phase 2; Period B — Derived Early–Middle Bronze Age and Roman). Scale 1:5

1. BR. D.VII.a (TS. 2476; IJ, 1.1). Derived Early–Middle Bronze Age. Small rim and upper wall segment. Fairly coarse pinkish-buff ware, evenly fired. Creamy-buff slip in and out.
2. SJR. B.II.g (PM. F; SC. 2473; IJ, 1.1). Derived Early–Middle Bronze Age. About 1/10 rim and neck segment with remains of a potter's mark on the outside of the upper neck. Fine light pinkish-buff ware with a few small lime and mica inclusions, evenly fired. Self slip in and out.
3. JR. D.VI.c (SC. 1087; IJ, 1.1). Derived Early–Middle Bronze Age. About 1/12 rim and neck segment. Fairly coarse creamy-green ware with small black and white lime inclusions, evenly fired. Self slip in and out.
4. JR. J.III.t (TS. 2349; IJ, 1.1). Derived Early–Middle Bronze Age. About 1/8 rim and neck segment. Fairly fine buff-brown ware, evenly fired. Light creamy green slip in and out.
5. JR. K.I.h (SC. 2399; IJ, 1.1). Derived Early–Middle Bronze Age. About 1/15 rim and neck segment. Fairly coarse pinkish-orange ware with lime inclusions, evenly fired. Self slip on extant surfaces.
6. R.Jg. B.II.c (SC. 2974; IJ, 1.1). About 1/10 rim and upper neck segment. Slightly coarse light greenish-buff ware with lime inclusions, evenly fired. Self slip in and out.
7. R.Jg. B.II.h (SC. 2985; IJ, 1.1). About 1/9 rim and upper neck segment with 1/2 of a loop handle attached. Coarse creamy-yellow ware with lime inclusions, fairly evenly fired. Self slip on handle and surviving portion of the inside of the neck.
8. R.Jg. B.II.i (SC. 2971; IJ, 1.1). About 1/16 rim and upper neck segment with about 1/3 of a loop handle attached. Fairly fine pinkish-buff ware with a few lime inclusions, evenly fired. Creamy-buff slip on extant surfaces in and out.
9. R.HMJ. B.II.c (variant; SC. 1686; IJ, 1.1). About 1/22 rim and upper shoulder segment. Fairly coarse brownish-buff ware with lime inclusions, evenly fired. No extant trace of slip.

Other Type Series Examples:
Derived Early–Middle Bronze Age — (1) JR.Sh. (IP [G.4] C.I.b; TS. 1139), see pl. 340:34.
Roman — (1) R.HMJ. B.I.a (TS. 3163), (2) R.HMJ. B.II.b (TS. 942), (3) R.BE. B.I.d (SC. 3158).

Other Study Collection Examples:
Derived Early–Middle Bronze Age — (1) BR. F.III.b (SC. 2824), (2) BR. F.IV.a (SC. 799), (3) JR. E.II.i (SC. 1151), (4) JR. H.I.k (SC. 1279), (5) JR. H.III.g (SC. 2669), (6) JR. J.III.e (SC. 1383), (7) JR. J.III.f (SC. 2277), (8) JR. J.III.g (SC. 2224), (9) JR. J.III.m (SC. 2317), (10) JR. J.IV.g (SC. 1531), (11) JR. K.I.a (SC. 1535).
Roman — (1) R.BR. A.II.c (SC. 2961), (2) R.BR. B.I.g (variant, SC. 3524), (3) R.Jg. B.II.o (SC. 3017), (4) R.Jg. B.II.p (variant, SC. 3018).

Other Unstratified Examples from Area I:
Early Bronze Age — (1) JR. P.II.k (SC. 1749).
Roman — (1) R.HMJ. A.II.b (SC. 3061), (2) R.CP. A.III.a (TS. 292), (3) R.CP. A.V.a (TS. 304), (4) R.CP. A.V.a (SC. 3061).

Figure 294. Glass and Stone Small Finds from Trench IA1 (Phases 1–3; Period B — Roman)

1. SF.7a (SW. 6; IA1, 2.5). Phase 1. Roman glass handle fragment with lower portion flattened for juncture with the wall of the vessel. Light green glass. Extant length 2.75 cm.
2. SF.3a (SW. 17; IA1, 2.3). Phase 2. Roman disk-shaped polishing stone. Brown stone partially broken on the edge and with a rough surface on one side. Diameter 2.5 cm.
3. SF.3a (SW. 19; IA1, 2.3). Phase 2. Roman polishing stone fragment. Brown stone with fine black specks. Extant measurements 2.3 × 3.0 cm.
4. SF.3a (SW. 18; IA1, 2.3). Phase 2. Roman polishing stone fragment. Buff-colored stone. One side is very rough and other side is highly polished. Extant measurements 3.3 × 4.0 cm.
5. SF.3a (SW. 15; IA1, 2.3). Phase 2. Roman polishing stone fragment. Brown stone with white surface flecks. Extant measurements 2.2 × 5.0 × 8.0 cm.
6. SF.3a (SW. 16; IA1, 2.3). Phase 2. Roman pounding stone. Yellow mudstone. Extant measurements 6.6 × 12.0 cm.
7. SF.3a (SW. 27; IA1, 1.2). Phase 3. Roman grinding stone fragment. Black basalt. Extant measurements 12.4 × 13.8 cm.
8. SF.3a (SW. 29; IA1, 1.2). Phase 3. Roman grinding stone fragment. Cream limestone. Extant measurements 10.8 × 12.6 cm.

Figure 294

Glass and Stone Small Finds from Trench IA1 (Phases 1–3; Period B — Roman). Scale 1:2

Figure 295. Stone and Pottery Small Finds from Trench IA1 (Phase 3; Period B — Late Roman)

1. SF.3a (SW. 30; IA1, 1.2). Phase 3. Roman grinding stone fragment. Cream limestone. Extant measurements 7.8 × 10.2 cm.
2. SF.3a (SW. 31; IA1, 1.2). Phase 3. Roman grinding stone fragment. Cream limestone. Extant measurements 6.0 × 7.8 cm.
3. SF.3a (SW. 28; IA1, 1.3). Phase 3. Roman grinding stone fragment. Cream limestone. Extant measurements 12.6 × 16.0 cm.
4. SF.6e (SW. 33; IA1, 1.3). Phase 3. Roman pottery disk made from a sherd of coarse dark grayware with mineral inclusions. Extant measurements 4.0 × 5.5 cm.
5. SF.3c (SW. 34; IA1, 1.3). Phase 3. Roman stone mortar fragment. Brown stone. Extant measurements 4.6 × 5.4 cm.
6. SF.3c (SW. 32; IA1, 1.3). Phase 3. Roman stone bowl rim fragment (diameter uncertain). Cream limestone. Extant measurements 7.0 × 7.2 cm.

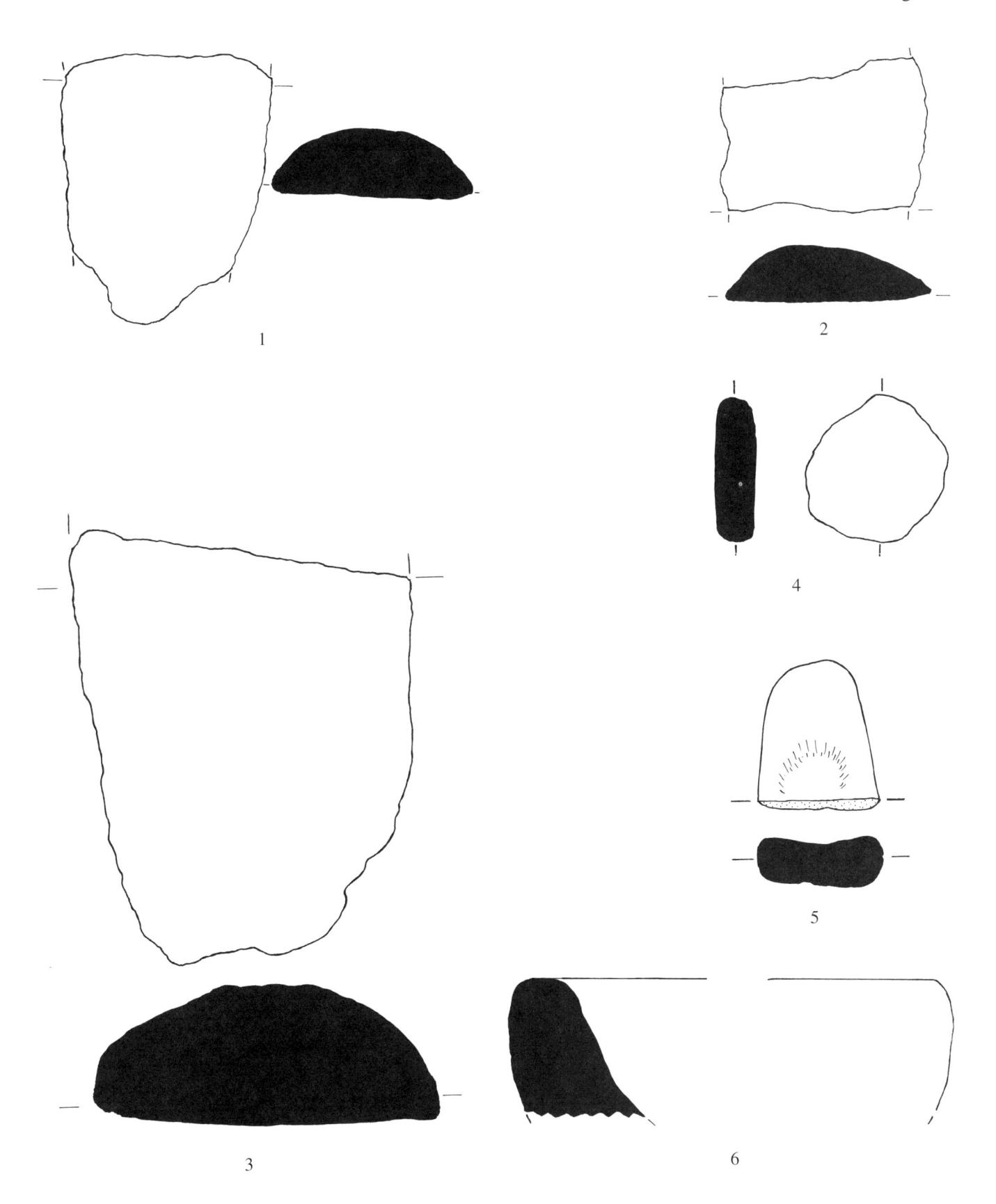

Figure 295

Stone and Pottery Small Finds from Trench IA1 (Phase 3; Period B — Late Roman). Scale 1:2

Figure 296. Glass, Pottery, and Stone Small Finds from Trench IA2 (Phases 1–4; Period B — Early and Late Roman)

1. SF.6e (SW. 169; IA2, 5.2). Phase 1. Roman pottery disk made from a probable jar sherd of orange-buff ware with black and gold mineral inclusions; light yellow slip on outside surface. Stringing hole in center of the disk was bored from both sides but not completed. Extant measurements, 1.4 cm thickness, 6.0 cm diameter.
2. SF.1c (SW. 106; IA2, 4.3) Phase 2. Roman pillar-type human figurine torso fragment incised on one broad side with a possible arm and hand extending into a crescent moon-shaped design. Coarse brown ware with black mineral temper and yellowish-buff slip. Extant measurements, thickness 2.7 cm at wider end and 2.5 cm at shorter end; maximum length 4.5 cm, maximum width 4.9 cm tapered to 4.75 cm.
3. SF.3a (SW. 100; IA2, 3.4). Phase 3. Roman grinding stone fragment. Tufa, dark gray stone. Extant measurements, $5.0 \times 8.0 \times 13.5$ cm.
—. SF.3a (SW. 101; IA2, 5.1). Phase 1. Roman grinding stone fragment. Tufa, dark gray stone with pitted surface. Extant measurements, $5 \times 7 \times 7$ cm.
4. SF.6b (SW. 39; IA2, 3.3). Phase 3. Roman clay spindle whorl fragment with hole pierced in the center. Coarse light buff ware. Extant measurements, $3 \times 5$ cm.
5. SF.7b (SW. 20; IA2, 3.3). Phase 3. Roman glass ring. Black glass slightly weathered. Extant measurements, diameter 1.8 cm.
6. SF.3a (SW. 9; IA2, 3.1). Phase 4. Roman rubbing stone fragment. Dark gray granite. Extant measurements, height 4 cm and width 4 cm.
7. SF.3a (SW. 89; IA2, 3.1). Phase 4. Roman grinding stone fragment. Cream limestone. Extant measurements, $6.5 \times 10.5 \times 13.5$ cm.
8. SF.3a (SW. 90; IA2, 3.1). Phase 4. Roman grinding stone fragment. Dark gray basalt or tufa. Extant measurements, $6.5 \times 10.0 \times 10.5$ cm.

Figure 296

Glass, Pottery, and Stone Small Finds from Trench IA2 (Phases 1–4; Period B — Early and Late Roman). Scale 1:2

Figure 297. Glass, Metal, Pottery, and Stone Small Finds from Trench IB (Phases 2–4; Period B — Early and Late Roman)

1. SF.3c (SW. 150; IB, 1.11). Phase 2. Roman mortar fragment. Polished light brown granite with 0.4 cm deep grinding surface.
2. SF.3a (SW. 92; IB, 1.6). Phase 3 floor. Roman pounding stone, chipped and broken at both ends. Polished dark gray granite with white inclusions, stained brown on the surface. Extant measurements, 4.5 × 6.5 × 13.5 cm.
3. SF.3a (SW. 91; IB, 1.6) Phase 3 floor. Roman grinding stone with a flat knob on top and concave below. Dark gray basalt. Extant measurements, diameter of knob, 6.5 cm; diameter of base, 11.0 cm; and height, 6.5 cm.
4. SF.6b (SW. 95; IB, 2.5). Phase 3. Roman pottery spindle whorl fragment. Soft brown ware, evenly fired with black surface discoloration. Extant measurements, radius 3.0 cm and thickness at center 2.5 cm.
5. SF.7a (SW. 97a; IB, 2.3). Phase 4. Roman glass bowl fragment. Weathered to iridescent light gray. Extant measurements, 0.3 × 2.5 × 3.0 cm.
6. SF.7a (SW. 97b; IB, 2.3). Phase 4. Roman glass bowl fragment. Weathered to iridescent light gray. Extant measurements, 0.2 × 1.3 × 1.6 cm.
—. SF.7a (SW. 57; IB, 1.1). Phase 4. Roman glass handle fragment with a twist in the glass. Colorless glass with pale brown surface weathering giving a brown tint to the glass. Extant measurements, 1.0 × 2.3 cm.
—. SF.5j (SW. 238; IB, 1.2). Phase 4. Roman coin. Decayed and indecipherable.

Figure 297

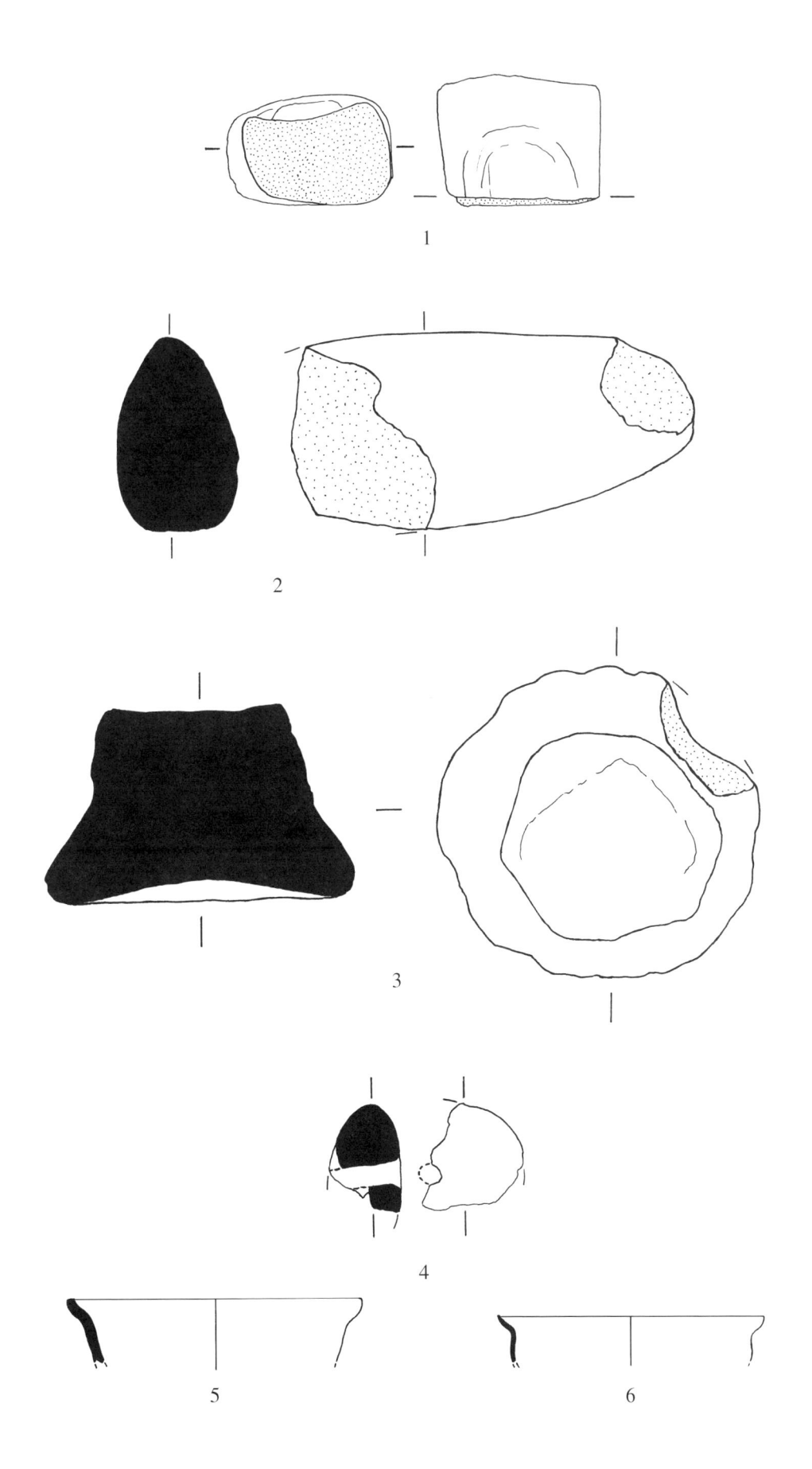

Glass, Metal, Pottery, and Stone Small Finds from Trench IB (Phases 2–4; Period B — Early and Late Roman). Scale 1:2

Figure 298. Pottery and Stone Small Finds from Trenches ID, E, F, H, and J (Phases 2–3 and 5–6; Periods E, E–D, and B — Early Bronze Age, Early–Middle Bronze Age, and Late Roman)

1. SF.7a (SW. 173; ID, 1.4). Phase 2. Late Roman glass handle fragment. Dark gray. Extant measurements, length, 2.6 cm; width at join with vessel, 2.2 cm; and width of handle, 0.7 cm.
2. SF.3a (SW. 181; IE, 1.10). Phase 3. Early Bronze pounder fragment. Dark gray granite with white flecks. Extant measurements, 4.3 × 6.8 × 10.0 cm.
3. SF.3a (SW. 365; IF, 1.19). Phase 2. Early Bronze grinding stone fragment, broken at both ends. Dark gray vesicular basalt. Extant measurements, 6 × 20 × 26 cm.
4. SF.3f (SW. 197; IF, 1.2). Phase 5. Early–Middle Bronze stone palette. Black granite. Extant measurements, length, 13.2 cm; width, 8.0 cm; and thickness, 0.6 cm.
—. SF.1c (SC. 161; IF, 1.1). Phase 6. Late Roman human figurine pillar stand fragment.
—. SF.3a (SW. 525; IH, 1.2). Phase 2. Late Roman grinding stone fragment. Dark gray vesicular basalt. Extant measurements, about 7 cm long.
—. SF.1c (SW. 388; IJ, 1.1). Phase 2. Late Roman human figurine pillar stand fragment. Fairly coarse pink ware with cream slip. See fig. 331:11.

Figure 298

Pottery and Stone Small Finds from Trenches ID, E, F, H, and J (Phases 2–3 and 5–6; Periods E, E–D, and B — Early Bronze Age, Early–Middle Bronze Age, and Late Roman). Scale 1:2

Figure 299

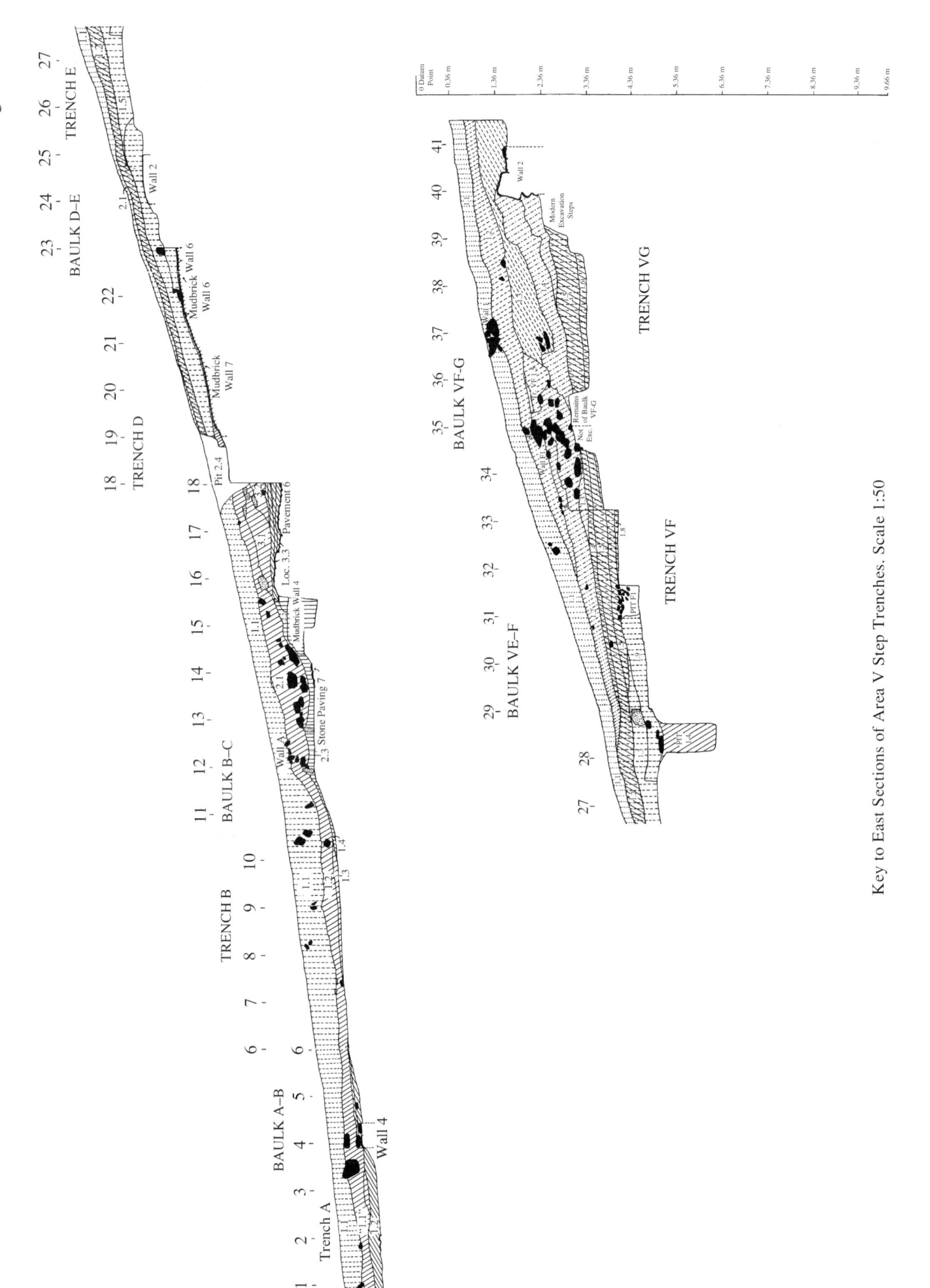

Key to East Sections of Area V Step Trenches. Scale 1:50

Figure 300

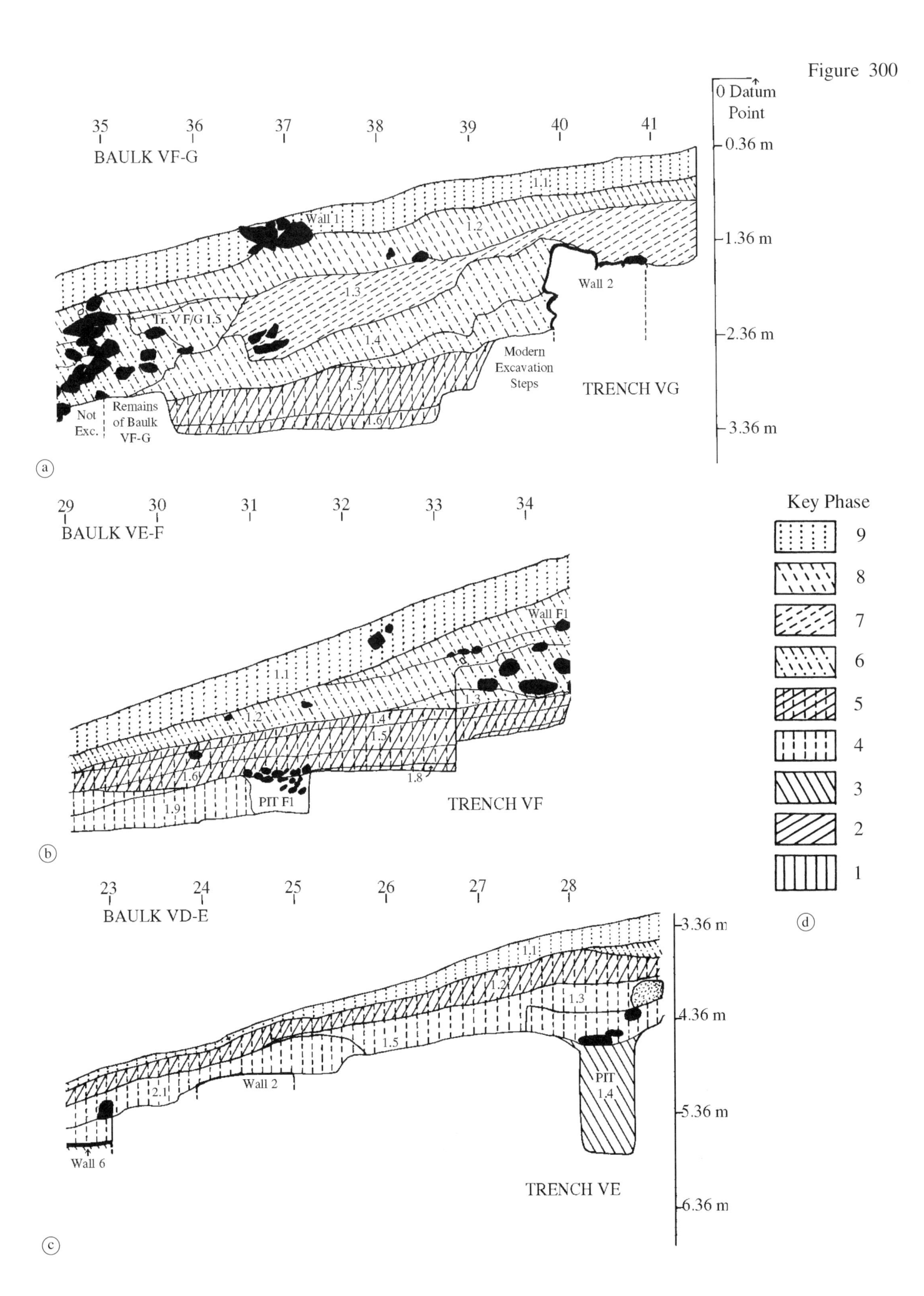

East Sections of Trenches (*a*) VG, (*b*) VF, and (*c*) VE with (*d*) Key to Hatching of Phases 1–9. Scale 1:50

Figure 301

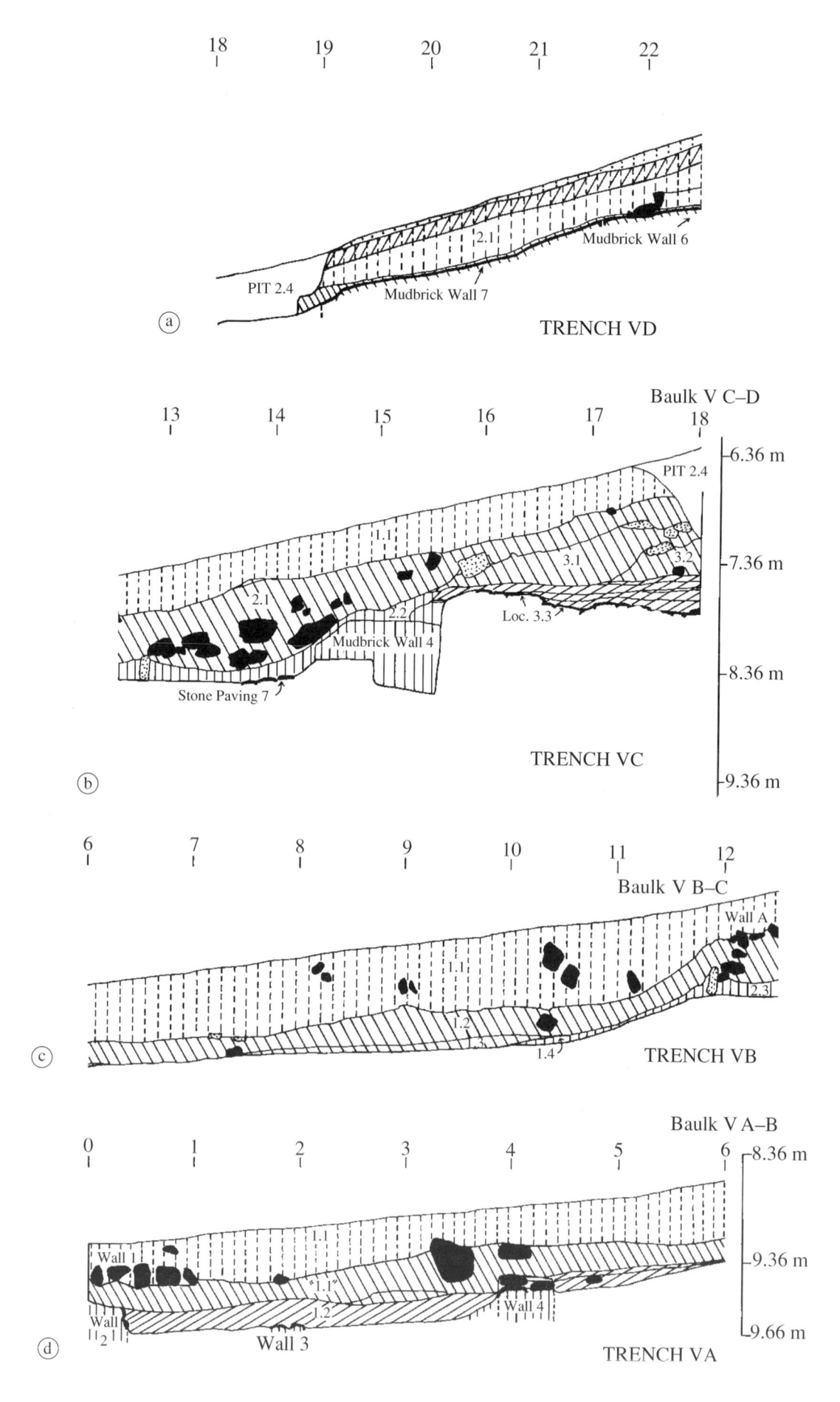

East Sections of Trenches (*a*) VD, (*b*) VC, (*c*) VB, and (*d*) VA. Scale 1:50

Figure 302

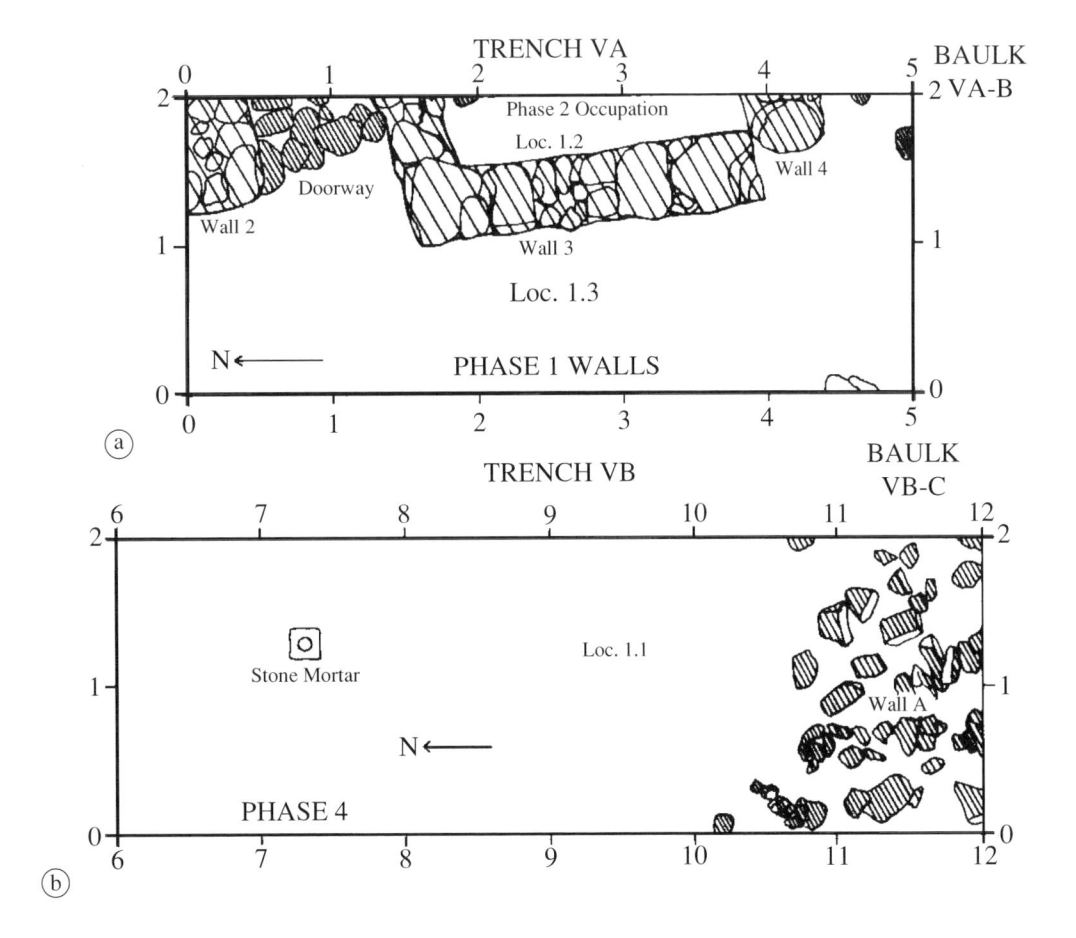

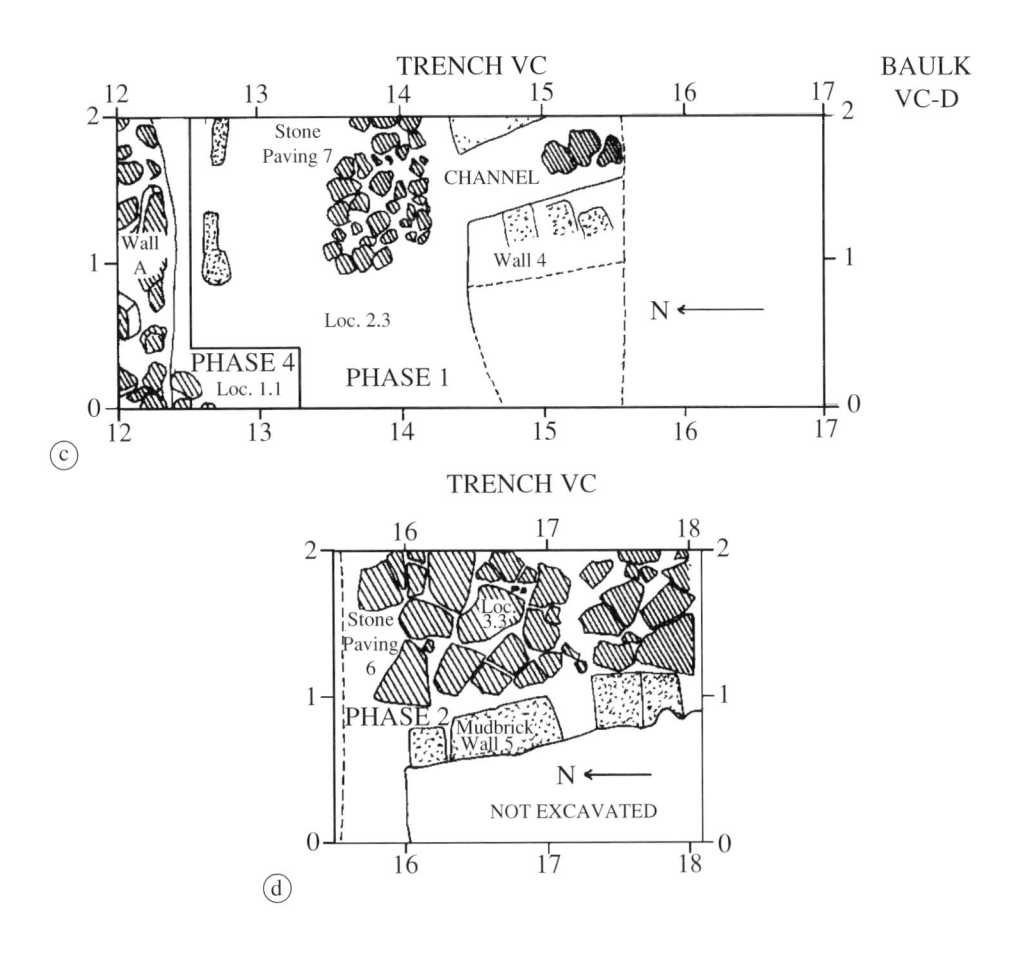

Plans of Trenches (*a*) VA (Phase 1), (*b*) VB (Phase 4), (*c*) VC (Phases 1 and 4), and (*d*) VC (Phase 2). Scale 1:50

Figure 303

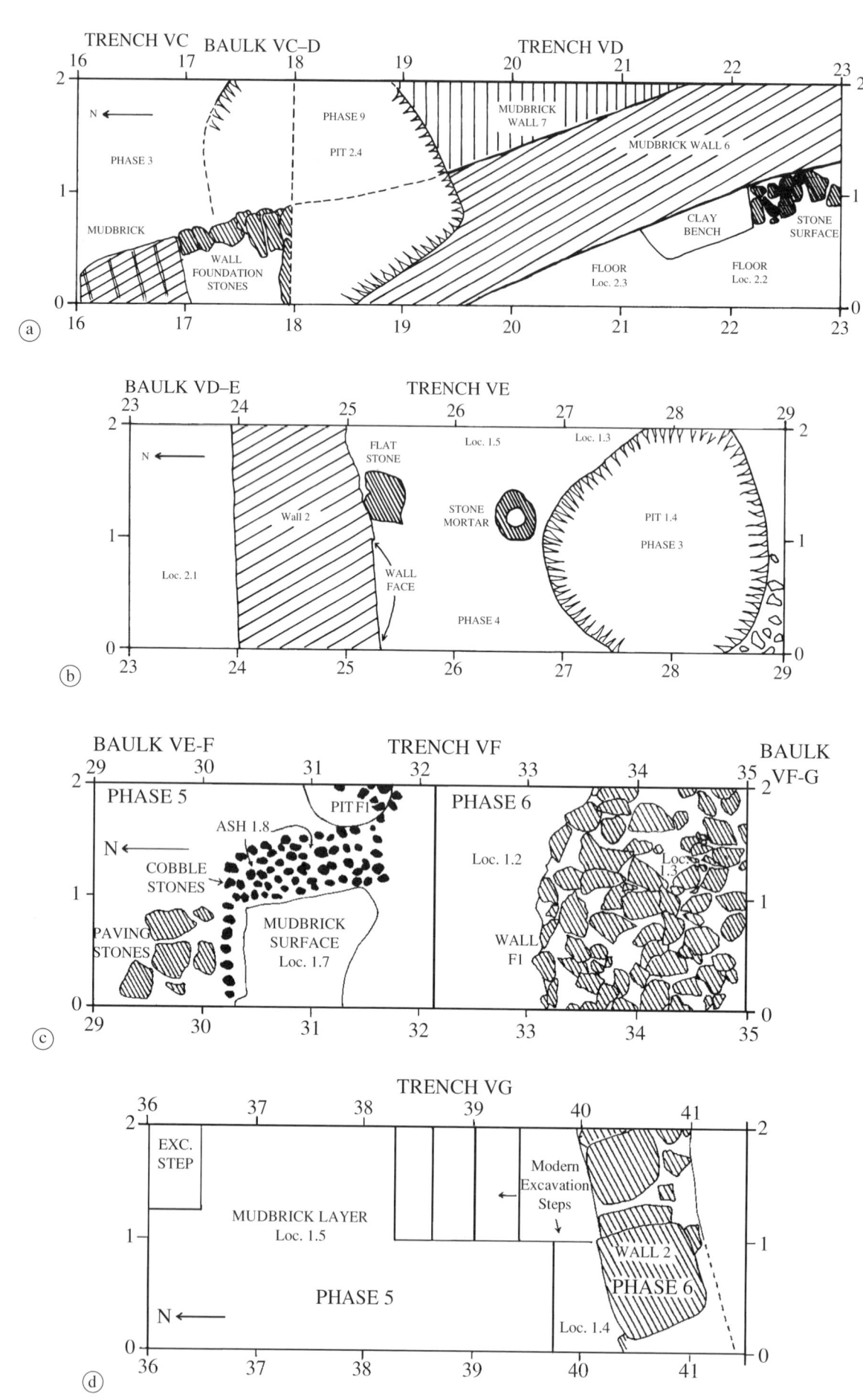

Plans of Trenches (*a*) VD (Phase 3), (*b*) VE (Phases 3 and 4), (*c*) VF (Phases 5 and 6), and (*d*) VG (Phases 5 and 6).

Figure 304

Highest, Southern Portion of Trenches VE, VF, and VG. Stone Mortar from Trench VE in situ at Bottom Left Foreground

Figure 305

Lowest, Northern Portion of Trenches VD, VC, VB, and VA

Figure 306

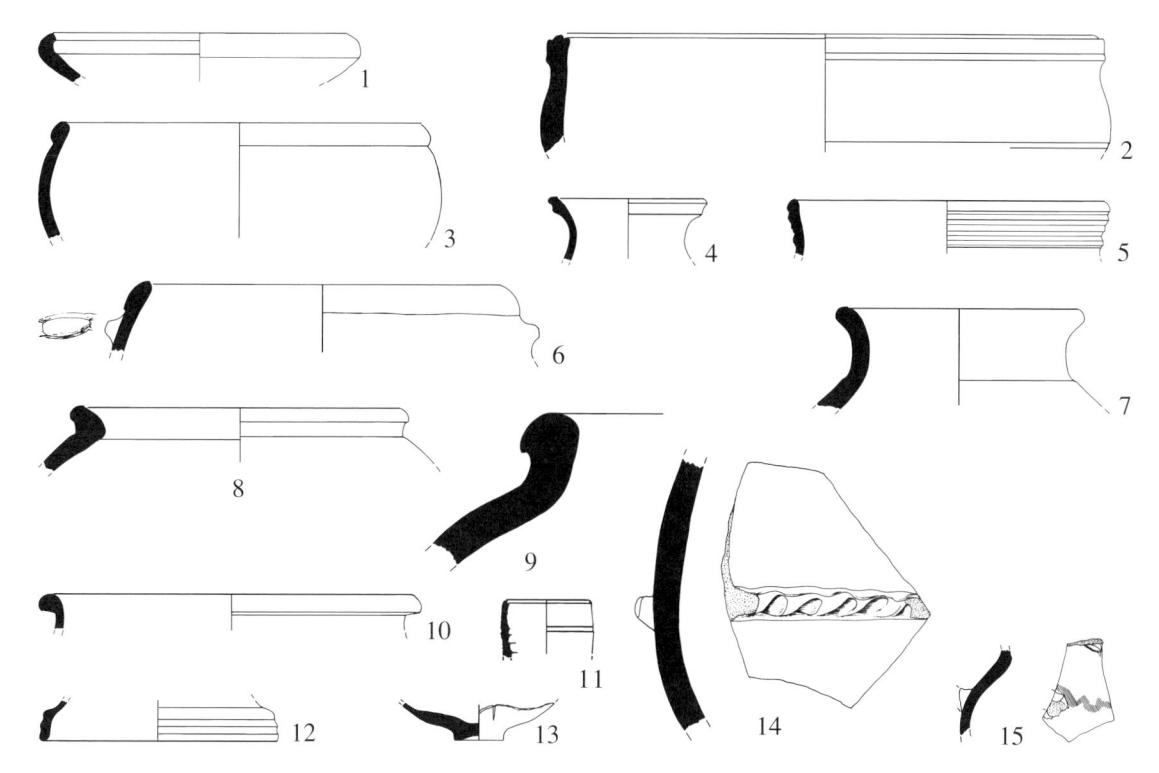

Pottery from Trench VA (Phase 3; Period E — Early Bronze Age IVb). Scale 1:5

1. BR. B.II.c (TS. 1040; VA, 1.1). About 1/16 rim and upper wall segment. Fairly coarse pink ware, evenly fired. Cream slip out.
2. BR. H.III.a (TS. 429; VA, 1.1). About 1/12 rim and upper wall segment. Coarse light brown ware, evenly fired. Cream slip in and out.
3. BR. L.III.h (TS. 411; VA, 1.1). About 1/6 rim and upper wall segment. Fairly fine pink ware, unevenly fired with light brown core. Light brownish-buff slip in and out.
4. SJR. C.I.a (TS. 2304; VA, 1.1). About 1/3 rim and neck segment. Very hard fired, salmon-pink ware, evenly fired. Creamy-yellow slip in and out.
5. JR. D.V.g (TS. 2206; VA, 1.1). Small rim and neck segment. Slightly coarse buff ware, evenly fired. Creamy-buff slip out.
6. JR. H.I.d (TS. 414; VA, 1.1). About 1/10 rim and upper shoulder segment with an applied small ledge handle, Type Hd. E.I.a (cf. pl. 297:5). Fairly coarse light brown ware, evenly fired. Cream slip out.
7. JR. J.III.e (TS. 2285; VA, 1.1). About 1/4 rim, neck, and upper shoulder segment. Fairly coarse buff ware, evenly fired. Self slip out and just over rim in.
8. JR. O.I.a (TS. 2351; VA, 1.1). About 1/8 rim and upper shoulder segment. Hard-fired, fairly fine grayware, unevenly fired pink in patches on rim and inside. Self slip wet-smoothed by hand on the outer wall.
9. JR. P.II.p (TS. 430; VA, 1.1). Small rim, neck, and upper shoulder segment. Very coarse pinkish colored ware with lime and mica inclusions, unevenly fired with light brownish-gray core. Cream slip in and out. Impressions of straw-wiped slip on outside surface.
10. CP. A.I.e (TS. 949; VA, 1.1). About 1/12 rim and upper neck segment. Coarse pinkish-brown ware, evenly fired. Buff slip in and out.
11. Jg. (misc. type; TS. 2120; VA, 1.1). Small neck segment. Very hard buff ware, evenly fired.
12. PS. B.I.b (TS. 2519; VA, 1.1). About 1/10 rim and upper neck segment. Fairly fine flesh-pink ware, evenly fired. Cream slip out and on top of rim.
13. BE. B.II (PM. A.5; SC. 3115; VA, 1.1). Nearly complete concave disk-type base with remains of a potter's mark on the lower outside wall. Hard pinkish-buff ware with small black and white lime inclusions, evenly fired. Creamy-green slip in and out.
14. ABS. A (TS. 412; VA, 1.1). Large jar body sherd with a thumb-impressed appliqué rope pattern at maximum girth of the outside wall. Coarse pink ware with lime and mica inclusions, evenly fired. Light brownish-tan slip out.
15. JR.Sh. Pt. (TS. 423; VA, 1.1). Upper body sherd from a small jar with remains of the bottom portion of a loop handle (cf. handle type Hd.B, pl. 297:2) at the base of the shoulder along with a red painted wavy line. Fairly coarse light brown ware, evenly fired. Cream slip out.

Other Type Series Examples: (1) BR. B.II.b (TS. 428), (2) SJR. C.III.a (TS. 939), (3) JR.Sh. (IP [G.1] D.II.a; TS. 2166), (4) JR.Sh. (IP [G.1] J.I.a; TS. 2142), (5) JR.Sh. (IP [G.3] B.III.a; TS. 425).

Other Pot Mark Examples: (1) JR.Sh. (PM. C.18 + D.30; TS. 2137), see fig. 333:8, (2) SJR.Sh. (PM. D.3; SC. 3261), see fig. 333:17.

Other Study Collection Examples: (1) SBR. A.I.d (SC. 3403), (2) SBR. D.I.b (SC. 7), (3) BR. B.II.a (SC. 2831), (4) SJR. A.II.c (SC. 2800), (5) SJR. C.II.d (SC. 2584), (6) SJR. C.II.o (SC. 2604), (7) JR. A.II.d (SC. 2726), (8) JR. A.II.d (SC. 2737), (9) JR. A.III.c (SC. 899), (10) JR. A.III.f (SC. 916), (11) JR. B.II.c (SC. 928), (12) JR. B.III.d (SC. 941), (13) JR. B.VI.b (SC. 982), (14) JR. C.I.c (SC. 2741), (15) JR. D.I.a (SC. 1034), (16) JR. E.II.o (SC. 2029), (17) JR. E.III.a (SC. 2753), (18) JR. F.I.a (SC. 1173), (19) JR. F.I.d (SC. 1212), (20) JR. J.I.d (SC. 1330), (21) JR. J.III.a (SC. 2207), (22) JR. J.III.f (SC. 2710), (23) JR. J.III.h (SC. 1397), (24) JR. J.III.m (SC. 1421), (25) JR. J.III.m (SC. 2321), (26) JR. J.III.q (SC.1488), (27) JR. J.IV.g (SC. 2377), (28) JR. J (Gen. Type, SC. 115), (29) JR. O.I.i (SC. 2453), (30) JR. O.II.b (SC. 1626), (31) JR. P.II.b (SC. 1716), (32) JR. P.II.f (SC. 1732), (33) JR. P.III.a (SC. 2441), (34) JR. P.III.f (SC. 2468), (35) JR. Q.III.a (SC. 2446), (36) CP. B.II.a (SC. 1841), (37) CP. (not typed, SC. 68), (38) Jg. B.II.a (SC. 2768), (39) BE. E.II.d (SC. 3214), (40) ABS. C (SC. 3289).

Figures 307–08

Figure 307. Pottery from Trench VA (Phase 4; Period C — Hellenistic). Scale 1:5

1. H.Jg. B.III.a (TS. 966; VA, 1.1). About 1/8 rim and neck segment. Fairly coarse tan ware, evenly fired.
2. H.St.J. B.I.d (TS. 424; VA, 1.1). About 1/2 rim and neck segment. Fairly fine pink ware with lime inclusions, unevenly fired with a light brown core. Cream slip in and out.
3. H.CP. C.I.b (TS. 965; VA, 1.1). About 1/8 rim and neck segment. Coarse pinkish-brown ware with very large lime inclusions and some mica grit, evenly fired.

Other Type Series Examples: (1) H.BR. B.II.c (TS. 959), (2) H.RSB. A.II.c (TS. 2145), (3) H.RSB. E.II.a (TS. 426), (4) H.RSJ. A.I.a (TS. 1084), (5) H.Jg. B.I.e (TS. 946), (6) H.St.J. B.I.b (TS. 422), (7) H.CP. E.I.c (TS. 961).

Other Study Collection Examples: (1) H.RSB. D.II.d (SC. 2890), (2) H.RSB. D.II.d (SC. 2902), (3) H.St.J. B.II.l (SC. 3359).

Figure 308. Pottery from Area V, Trench Baulk A/B (Phases 2–4; Periods E and C — Early Bronze Age IVb and Hellenistic). Scale 1:5

1. H.JR.Sh. (IP [G.4] F.III.a; TS. 1037; VA/B, unstratified). Jar body sherd with framed incised lines on outside surface. Fairly coarse pink ware, evenly fired. Cream slip out; inner surface decayed.
2. H.BR. C.I.a (TS. 1035; VA/B, unstratified). About 1/8 rim, wall, and base segment. Fairly coarse creamy-buff ware, evenly fired. Handmade.

Other Type Series Examples:
 Hellenistic — (1) H.St.J. A.I.e (TS. 1032), (2) H.St.J. B.II.o (TS. 1038).

Other Study Collection Examples:
 Early Bronze Age — (1) SBR. E.I.c (SC. 3404), (2) BR. A.IV.e (SC. 729), (3) BR. A.IV.e (SC. 730), (4) JR. B.IV.f (SC. 959), (5) JR. J.I.a (SC. 1299), (6) JR. J.III.p (SC. 2255), (7) CP. A.II.c (SC. 1803), (8) BE. D.II (PM. A.5 + C.14; SC. 3134).
 Hellenistic — (1) H.RSB. D.II.d (SC. 2785), (2) H.Jg. B.II.b (SC. 3363), (3) H.St.J. B.I.d (SC. 2670).

Figure 309

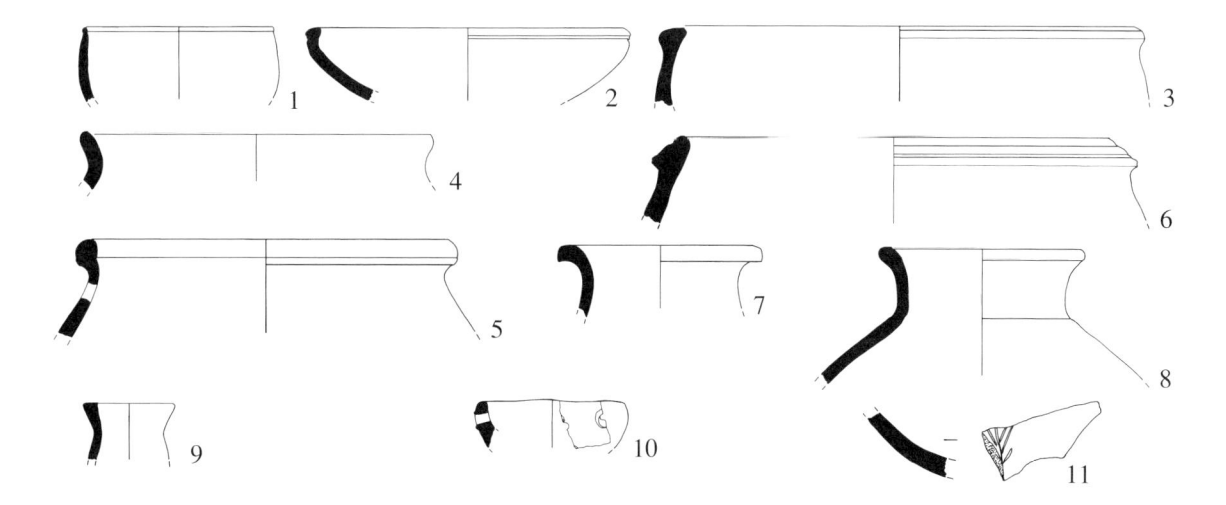

Pottery from Trench VB (Phase 3; Period E — Early Bronze Age IVb and Derived Hellenistic). Scale 1:5

1. SBR. B.I.i (TS. 400; VB, 1.2). About 1/10 rim and upper wall segment. Fairly fine pinkish-buff ware, evenly fired. Cream slip in and out.
2. BR. A.IV.e (TS. 2105; VB, 1.2). Two small rim segments, non-joining. Slightly coarse buff ware, evenly fired. Creamy-buff slip in and out.
3. BR. L.I.c (TS. 2123; VB, 1.2). Small rim and shoulder segment. Fairly coarse pinkish-buff ware, evenly fired. Buff slip in and out.
4. JR. E.I.a (TS. 2116; VB, 1.2). Small rim, neck, and upper shoulder segment. Very hard fired, light grayish-green ware, evenly fired. Worn surfaces probably originally self slipped.
5. JR. E.II.v (TS. 2411; VB, 1.2). About 1/8 rim and upper shoulder segment. Fairly coarse light pinkish-buff ware, evenly fired. Creamy-buff slip in and out.
6. JR. H.II.e (TS. 406; VB, 1.2). About 1/8 rim and upper shoulder segment. Fairly coarse pink ware with lime and mica inclusions, evenly fired. Light brownish-buff slip out.
7. JR. J.III.b (TS. 2270;VB, 1.2). About 1/4 rim and neck segment. Slightly coarse creamy-buff ware, evenly fired. Self slip in and out.
8. JR. J.III.s (TS. 2130; VB, 1.2). Small rim, neck, and upper shoulder segment. Slightly coarse buff ware, evenly fired. Self slip in and out.
9. Jg. C.5 (TS. 421; VB, 1.2). About 1/2 rim and neck segment. Fairly coarse pinkish-buff ware, evenly fired. Cream slip in and out.
10. SR. A.I.b (TS. 2429;VB, 1.2). About 1/12 rim and upper wall segment. Handmade, fairly coarse pink ware, evenly fired. Buff slip in and out.
11. BE. A.I (IP [G.4] D.IV; PM. D.21; TS 410; VB, 1.2). Base fragment from a probable bowl with remains of a potter's mark incised on the inside surface before firing. Coarse light brown ware, evenly fired. Cream slip in and out.

Other Type Series Examples:
Early Bronze Age — (1) JR. B.IV.c (TS. 408), (2) JR.Sh. (IP [G.1] C.V.a; TS. 2168), see pl. 340:9.
Derived Hellenistic — (1) H.Jg. B.I.b (TS. 416), (2) H.BE. B.III.b (TS. 405).

Another Potter's Mark Example:
Early Bronze Age — (1) JR.Sh (PM. D.3; SC. 3260), see fig. 333:19.

Other Study Collection Examples:
Early Bronze Age — (1) SBR. C.II.a (SC. 234), (2) BR. A.II.e (SC. 722), (3) JR. A.III.d (SC. 907), (4) JR. A.VI.a (SC. 954), (5) JR. B.III.e (SC. 944), (6) JR. B.VI.a (SC. 1110), (7) JR. D.VI.d (SC. 1026), (8) JR. D.VIII.b (SC. 1070), (9) JR. D.X.a (SC. 1123), (10) JR. J.I.a (SC. 1302), (11) JR. J.I.c (SC. 2245), (12) JR. J.I.c (SC. 2257), (13) JR. J.II.d (SC. 2187), (14) JR. J.II.g (SC. 2153), (15) JR. J.II.i (SC. 1425), (16) JR. J.III.b (SC. 2219), (17) JR. J.III.h (SC. 2296), (18) JR. J.III.n (SC. 2190), (19) JR. J.III.ab (SC. 1512), (20) JR. K.I.b (SC. 2389), (21) JR. O.III.f (SC. 2408), (22) JR. (not typed, SC. 128), (23) CP. B.IV.b (SC. 1868).
Derived Hellenistic — (1) H.JR. E.I.b (SC. 2751).

Figure 310

1  2  3

Figure 310. Pottery from Trench VB (Phase 4; Period C — Hellenistic and Derived Early Bronze Age IVb). Scale 1:5

1. H.BR. B.I.f (TS. 2117; VB, 1.1). Small rim and upper shoulder segment. Fine pinkish-orange ware, evenly fired.
2. BR. L.III.g (TS. 2115; VB, 1.1). Small rim and upper wall segment. Slightly coarse pinkish-buff ware, evenly fired. Creamy-buff slip out.
3. JR.Sh. (IP [G.1] C.II.a; SC. 3354; VB, 1.1) Jar neck and shoulder segment with comb-incised decoration on upper portion of shoulder. Fairly fine pinkish-buff ware with lime and mica inclusions, evenly fired. Creamy-green slip out.

Other Type Series Examples:

Hellenistic — (1) H.RSB. E.III.a (TS. 402), (2) H.JR. A.II.g (TS. 2234), (3) H.JR. G.III.b (TS. 409), (4) H.CP. C.I.b (TS. 960 = TS. 1133), (5) Ld. B.I.a (SW. 216).

Other Potter's Mark Examples:

Derived Early Bronze Age — (1) JR.Sh. (PM. D.14; SC. 3259), see fig. 333:18, (2) JR.Sh. (PM. D.28; SC. 3251), see fig. 333:23.

Other Study Collection Examples:

Hellenistic — (1) H.BR. C.II.b (SC. 2443), (2) H.RSB. C.I.a (SC. 2856), (3) H.RSB. E.II.a (SC. 2728), (4) H.JR. A.II.a (SC. 2736), (5) H.St.J. A.I.e (SC. 2671), (6) H.St.J. A.I.i (SC. 2665), (7) H.St.J. B.I.h (SC. 2804), (8) H.BE. B.II.c (3212).

Derived Early Bronze Age — (1) SBR. A.I.d (SC. 3405), (2) BR. H.I.b (SC. 1971), (3) JR. D.VI.a (SC. 1003), (4) JR. E.II.p (SC. 1164), (5) JR. J.I.b (SC. 1318), (6) JR. J.II.k (SC. 2182), (7) JR. J.IV.e (SC. 1179), (8) JR. P.I.b (SC. 2427).

Figure 311. Pottery from Trench VC (Phase 3; Periods F and E — Early Bronze Age IVa, Early Bronze Age IVb, and Derived Hellenistic)

1. SBR. B.I.a (TS. 1150; VC, 3.2). About 1/10 rim and wall segment. Fine pink ware, evenly fired.
2. SBR. B.I.h (TS. 1112; VC, 2.1). About 1/12 rim and upper wall segment. Fairly coarse cream ware, evenly fired.
3. SBR. C.II.a (TS. 2501; VC, 3.1). About 1/12 rim and wall segment. Hard-fired, flesh-pink ware, evenly fired. Creamy-buff slip out.
4. BR. A.II.e (PM. A.12; SC. 869; VC, 3.1). One centimeter of rim and upper wall segment with remains of a potter's mark incised on the outside wall before firing. Slightly coarse pinkish-orange ware with a few lime grits, evenly fired. Creamy-buff slip out.
5. BR. B.II.a (TS. 1155; VC, 3.2). About 1/20 rim segment. Fairly coarse pink ware, evenly fired. Light cream slip in and out.
6. BR. F.III.h (TS. 2527; VC, 3.1). About 1/6 rim and upper wall segment. Slightly coarse buff-yellow ware, evenly fired. Creamy-buff slip out.
7. BR. L.I.f (TS. 1122; VC, 3.1). About 1/10 rim and upper wall segment. Fairly coarse buff ware, unevenly fired with a cream core. Cream slip in and out.
8. SJR. A.II.b (TS. 1161; VC, 3.2). About 1/8 rim and neck segment. Fairly fine pink ware, evenly fired. Buff slip out.
9. SJR. C.II.o (TS. 1119; VC, 2.1). About 1/8 rim and neck segment. Fairly fine pink ware, evenly fired. Cream slip in and out.
10. JR. E.II.b (TS. 1118; VC, 3.1). About 1/8 rim and shoulder segment. Fairly fine pink ware, evenly fired. Cream slip out.
11. JR. E.II.q (variant; TS. 1100; VC, 3.1). About 1/4 rim, neck, and shoulder segment. Fairly coarse pink ware, evenly fired. Cream slip out.
12. JR. F.I.f (TS. 1103; VC, 2.1). About 1/12 rim and upper shoulder segment. Fairly coarse cream ware, evenly fired.
13. JR. F.II.e (TS. 1105; VC, 3.1). About 1/12 rim and upper shoulder segment. Fairly coarse light cream ware, unevenly fired with a darker core.
14. JR. G.I.b (TS. 1124; VC, 3.1). About 1/16 rim and neck segment. Fairly fine pink ware, evenly fired. Light cream slip in and out.
15. JR. J.I.e (PM. B.8; TS. 2098; VC, 2.1). About 1/4 rim, neck, and upper shoulder segment with remains of a potter's mark at the base of the neck, incised before firing. Fairly fine pinkish-buff ware, evenly fired. Creamy-buff slip out.

Figure 311

16. JR. J.III.c (TS. 1110; VC, 2.1). About 1/12 rim and neck segment. Fairly fine ware, unevenly fired pink in and buff out. Cream slip out.
17. JR. J.III.d (TS. 1104; VC, 2.1). About 1/3 rim, neck, and upper shoulder segment. Fairly coarse cream ware, evenly fired. Largely blackened by fire outside and traces inside.
18. JR. J.III.k (TS. 1114; VC, 2.1). About 1/6 rim, neck, and upper shoulder segment. Fairly coarse pink ware, evenly fired. Cream slip out.
19. CP. B.I.b (TS. 1130; VC, 3.1). About 1/16 rim and upper neck segment. Coarse brown ware, evenly fired.
20. CP. B.II.k (TS. 1116; VC, 2.1). About 1/16 rim and neck segment. Coarse brown ware, evenly fired. Light brown slip out.
21. Bt. A.I.b.2 (TS. 1106; VC, 2.1). About 1/2 neck and body segment. Fairly coarse buff ware, evenly fired. Cream slip in and out.

Other Type Series Examples:
    Early Bronze Age — (1) BR. B.II.c (TS. 1153), (2) JR. J.IV.g (TS. 1111), (3) JR. E.II.v (TS. 2381).
    Derived Hellenistic — (1) H.BR. B.I.b (TS. 1113), (2) H.JR. G.I.b (TS. 1115), (3) H.BE. B.II.b (TS. 1117).

Other Study Collection Examples:
    Early Bronze Age — (1) SBR. B.I.f (SC. 382), (2) SBR. C.IV.a (SC. 605), (3) SBR. D.I.h (SC. 653), (4) SBR. D.II.d (SC. 723), (5) BR. F.I.d (SC. 774), (6) BR. L.II.b (SC. 1973), (7) SJR. C.II.p (SC. 2605), (8) JR. C.II.c (SC. 1079), (9) JR. C.III.b (SC. 2519), (10) JR. C (Gen. Type, SC. 85), (11) JR. D.VI.b (SC. 1064), (12) JR. E.II.n (SC. 1158), (13) JR. E.II.w (SC. 1170), (14) JR. F (Gen. Type, SC. 80), (15) JR. H.I.b (SC. 1284), (16) JR. H.I.b (SC. 1287), (17) JR. J.II.c (SC. 2622), (18) JR. J.IV.b (SC. 2330), (19) JR. K.II.e (SC. 1553), (20) JR. O.II.f (variant type, SC. 1768), (21) JR. P.II.b (SC. 1718), (22) JR. P.II.m (SC. 1679), (23) JR. P.III.f (SC. 1680), (24) CP. B.IV.a (SC. 3068), (25) BE. E.I.k (SC. 3224).
    Derived Hellenistic — (1) H.RSB.Sh. (SC. 3545), (2) H.Jg. B.II.e (variant, SC. 2597).

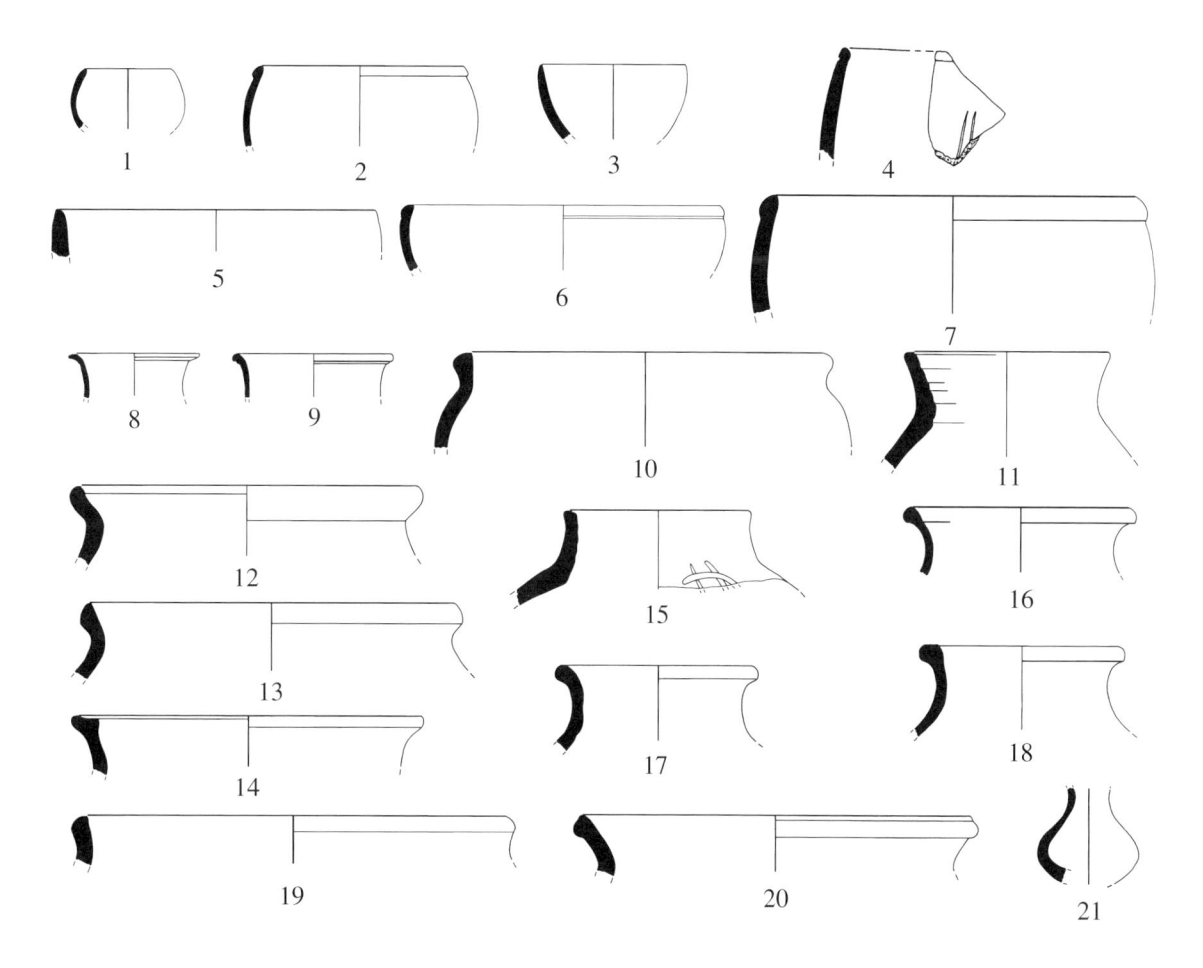

Pottery from Trench VC (Phase 3; Periods F and E — Early Bronze Age IVa, Early Bronze Age IVb, and Derived Hellenistic). Scale 1:5

Figures 312–13

Figure 312. Pottery from Trench VC (Phase 4; Period C — Hellenistic and Derived Early Bronze Age IVb). Scale 1:5

1. BR. C.I.g (TS. 857; VC, 1.1). About 1/32 rim and upper wall segment. Fairly coarse buff ware, evenly fired. Cream slip out.
2. JR. A.III.d (TS. 870; VC, 1.1). About 1/12 rim and upper shoulder segment. Fairly coarse pink ware, evenly fired. Creamy-buff slip out.
3. JR.Sh. (IP [G.1] H.II.a; TS. 2134; VC, 1.1). Jar sherd with incised or combed decoration on the outside wall. Slightly coarse pinkish-buff ware, even fired. Light creamy-green slip out.

Other Type Series Examples:

Derived Early Bronze Age — (1) BR. C.I.h (TS. 958), (2) JR.Sh (IP [G.2] A.V.a; TS. 2135).

Hellenistic — (1) H.BR. B.V.a (TS. 2147), (2) H.RSB. D.I.a (TS. 956), (3) H.BGB. B.I.a (TS. 895), (4) H.BGB. B.I.c (TS. 827), (5) H.JR. A.I.c (TS. 2095), (6) H.StJ. B.II.q (TS. 957), (7) H.BE. B.III.a (TS. 3043).

Other Study Collection Examples:

Derived Early Bronze Age — (1) SBR. A.I.d (SC. 3408), (2) SBR. A.I.e (SC. 3409), (3) SBR. B.I.d (SC. 2809), (4) SBR. B.I.i (SC. 3407), (5) SBR. B.I.r (SC. 595), (6) SBR. C.IV.a (SC. 604), (7) SBR. E.I.c (SC. 3406), (8) BR. A.III.a (SC. 2808), (9) SJR. A.II.b (SC. 2483), (10) SJR. A.II.b (SC. 2797), (11) SJR. C.I.f (SC. 2558), (12) SJR. C.II.t (SC. 2603), (13) JR. B.III.f (SC. 1975), (14) JR. C.I.e (SC. 995), (15) JR. J.I.b (SC. 2099), (16) JR. J.II.b (SC. 2332), (17) JR. J.II.e (SC. 2143), (18) JR. J.III.n (SC. 1462), (19) JR. K.I.f (SC. 2197).

Hellenistic — (1) H.BR. B.III.j (SC. 2837), (2) H.RSB. D.I.a (SC. 2875), (3) H.RSB. D.II.a (SC. 2882), (4) H.RSB. D.II.a (SC. 2884), (5) H.RSB. D.II.d (SC. 2896), (6) H.SJR. A.I.b (SC. 3364), (7) H.JR. E.III.a (variant, SC. 2754), (8) H.StJ. B.I.b (SC. 2683).

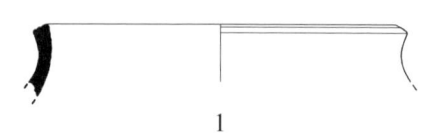

Figure 313. Pottery from Trench VD (Phase 4; Period E — Early Bronze Age IVb). Scale 1:5

1. CP. B.I.h (TS. 1102 = TS. 2152; VD, 2.1). Two joining rim, neck, and upper shoulder segments. Fairly coarse reddish-brown ware with many lime and mica inclusions, unevenly fired orange-buff in patches outside (also see Type Series pl. 277:8).

Figures 314–15

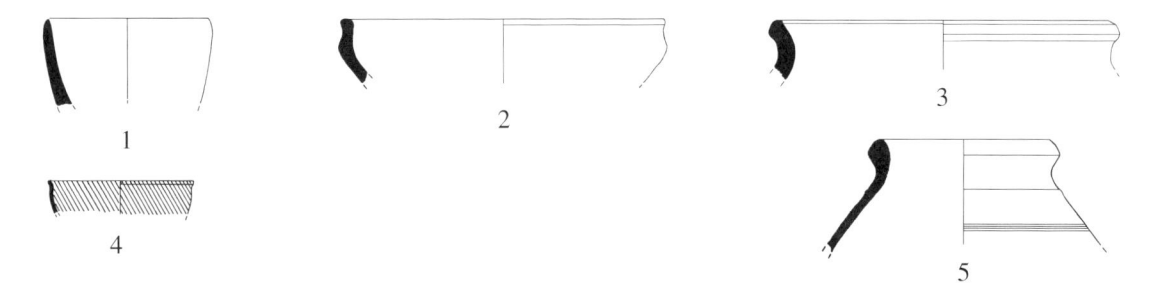

Figure 314. Pottery from Trench VD (Phase 5; Period C — Hellenistic and Derived Early Bronze Age IVb). Scale 1:5

1. SBR. C.II.c (TS. 2100; VD, 1.1). Small rim and upper wall segment. Fairly fine buff ware, evenly fired. Light creamy-green slip in and out.
2. BR. C.I.b (TS. 2113; VD, 1.1). Small rim and carinated upper shoulder segment. Slightly coarse pink ware, evenly fired. Buff slip in and out.
3. JR. F.II.e (TS. 2114; VD, 1.1). Small rim, neck, and upper shoulder segment. Fairly fine buff ware, evenly fired. Self slip out and over rim in.
4. H.RSB. E.I.a (TS. 3033; VD, 1.1). Small rim and upper wall segment. Fine pinkish-brown ware, evenly fired. Red slip in and out.
5. H.St.J. A.I.a (TS. 2092; VD, 1.1). Small rim, neck, and shoulder segment with comb-incised lines on upper shoulder. Fairly coarse pink ware, evenly fired. Creamy-buff slip out.

Other Type Series Examples:

Hellenistic — (1) H.SBR. A.II.b (TS. 2112), (2) H.BR. B.V.c (TS. 2093), (3) H.JR. E.I.b (IP [G.1] C.VI.b; TS. 2124), see pl. 340:11.

Other Study Colllection Examples:

Derived Early Bronze Age — (1) SBR. B.I.b (SC. 258), (2) BR. C.I.b (SC. 736), (3) BR. E.III.i (SC. 3032), (4) SJR. C.I.a (SC. 2320), (5) SJR. C.I.a (SC. 2540), (6) SJR. C.II.a (SC. 2578), (7) JR. E.II.w (SC. 2161), (8) JR. F.I.b (SC. 1206), (9) JR. J.I.e (SC. 2334), (10) JR. O.II.f (SC. 1647).

Hellenistic — (1) H.SBR. A.I.a (SC. 3410), (2) H.BR. B.III.h (SC. 884), (3) H.RSB. C.I.a (SC. 2854), (4) H.RSB. C.I.a (SC. 2859), (5) H.RSB. C.II.a (SC. 2858), (6) H.RSB. D.II.d (SC. 2901), (7) H.RSJ. A.I.a (SC. 2907), (8) H.RSJ. Sh. (SC. 3546), (9) H.JR. A.I.c (SC. 3362), (10) H.JR. D.I.b (SC. 2729), (11) H.JR. E.I.b (SC. 2752), (12) H.St.J. A.I.g (SC. 2677), (13) H.St.J. A.I.h (SC. 2678), (14) H.BE. E.I.b (SC. 3124), (15) H.PS. 2 (SC. 3073), (16) H.PS. 3 (SC. 3075).

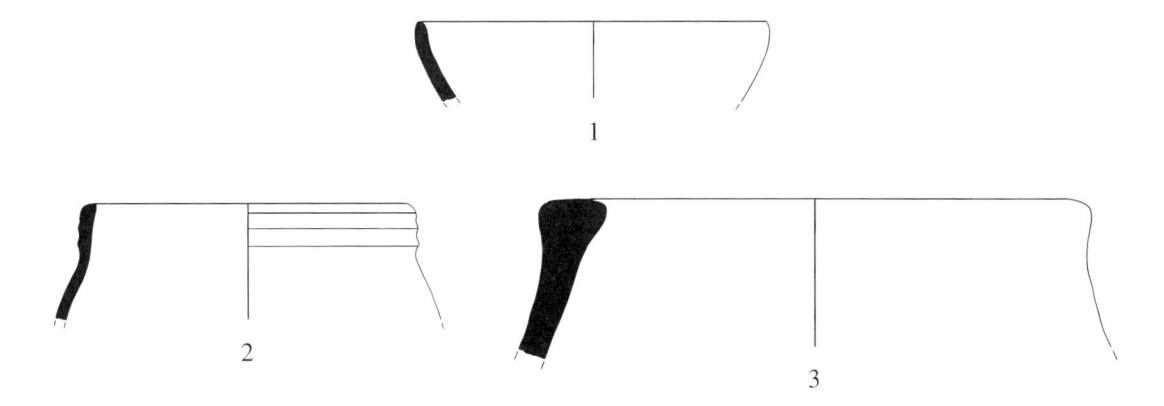

Figure 315. Pottery from Trench VD from the Bottom of Hellenistic Pit 2.4 (Phase 9; Period C — Derived Early Bronze Age II–III and Early Bronze Age IVb). Scale 1:5

1. BR. B.II.a (TS. 1128; VD, 2.4). About 1/16 rim and upper wall segment. Fairly coarse pink ware, evenly fired. Cream slip in and out.
2. JR. D.IX.a (TS. 1125; VD, 2.4). About 1/16 rim and upper shoulder segment. Fairly coarse brown ware, evenly fired. Cream slip in and out.
3. JR. R.II.a (TS. 1101; VD, 2.4). About 1/10 rim and upper shoulder segment. Very coarse pinkish-brown ware with straw temper, fairly evenly fired. Cream slip in and out.

Another Study Collection Example: (1) JR. J.V.a (variant, SC. 3358).

Figure 316

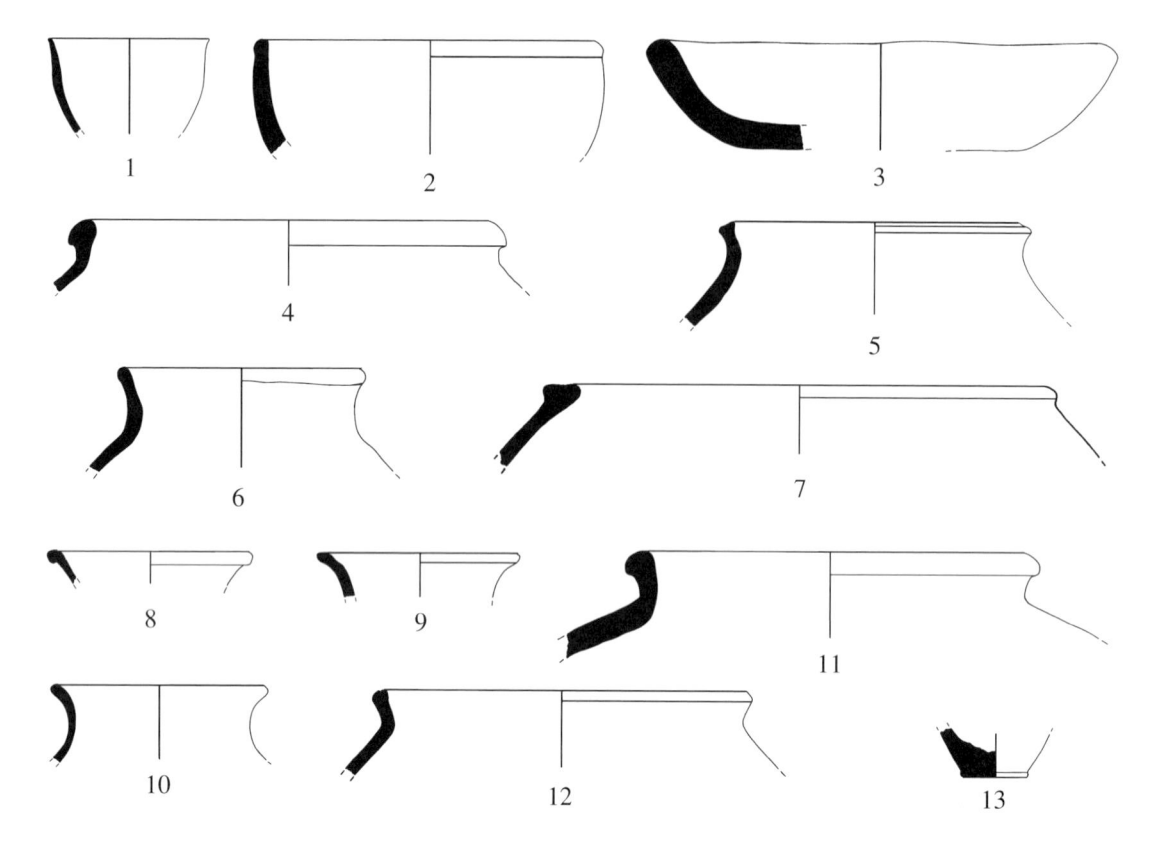

Pottery from Trench VE (Phase 3 Pit; Periods G and F — Mixed Early Bronze Age II, Early Bronze Age III, and Early Bronze Age IVa). Scale 1:5

1. SBR. A.I.h (TS. 1151; VE, 1.4). About 1/2 rim and wall segment. Fine buff ware, unevenly fired with dark brown core. Greenish-cream slip in and out.
2. BR. L.I.f (TS. 1162; VE, 1.4). About 1/8 rim and upper wall segment. Fairly coarse cream ware, evenly fired.
3. BR. L.III.g (variant; TS. 1168; VE, 1.4). About 1/12 rim, wall, and part of flat base segment. Fairly coarse buff ware, evenly fired. Greenish-cream slip in and out.
4. JR. E.II.b (TS. 1107; VE, 1.4). About 1/12 rim, neck, and upper shoulder segment. Fairly fine buff ware, unevenly fired with a black core. Greenish slip in and out.
5. JR. G.I.b (TS. 1160; VE, 1.4). Small rim, neck, and shoulder segment. Fairly fine pink ware, evenly fired. Cream slip out.
6. JR. G.II.b (TS. 1157; VE, 1.4). About 1/4 rim, neck, and upper shoulder segment. Fairly coarse pinkish-buff ware, evenly fired.
7. JR. H.I.l (TS. 1164; VE, 1.4). About 1/16 rim and upper shoulder segment. Fairly coarse buff ware, evenly fired. Cream slip in and out.
8. JR. J.III.f (TS. 935; VE, 1.4). About 1/8 rim and upper neck segment. Fine pinkish-buff ware, evenly fired. Cream slip in and out
9. JR. J.III.o (TS. 1166; VE, 1.4). About 1/8 rim and upper neck segment. Fairly coarse pink ware, evenly fired. Light cream slip out.
10. JR. J.III.z (TS. 2309; VE, 1.4). About 1/3 rim, neck, and upper shoulder segment. Slightly coarse pinkish-buff ware, evenly fired. Creamy-buff slip out.
11. JR. P.I.a (TS. 1158; VE, 1.4). About 1/12 rim, neck, and upper shoulder segment. Fairly coarse greenish-cream ware, evenly fired.
12. CP. B.III.c (TS. 1134; VE, 1.4). About 1/6 rim, neck, and upper shoulder segment. Coarse pinkish-brown ware with lime and mica inclusions, unevenly fired grayish-brown in and out. Light brown slip out.
13. BE. D.II (TS. 1121; VE, 1.4). About 3/4 segment of flat base and lower wall of vessel. Fairly coarse buff ware, evenly fired. Cream slip out.
—. BE.D.III (PM.A.6; TS. 1165, VE, 1.4). See fig. 333:5.

Other Type Series Examples: (1) BR. F.III.c (TS. 2529), (2) SJR. D.I.b (TS. 1167), (3) JR. G.I.a (TS. 1159), (4) CP. B.V.a (TS. 1156 = TS. 1163), (5) Bt. A.I.b.3 (TS. 1211), (6) JR.Sh. (IP [G.1] B.II.a; TS. 2170), see pl. 340:4.

Other Study Collection Examples: (1) SBR. A.I.e (SC. 3414), (2) SBR. B.I.k (SC. 567), (3) SJR. C.II.p (SC. 2606), (4) JR. D.I.d (SC. 1056), (5) JR. F.I.a (SC. 2646), (6) JR. F.I.c (SC. 1195), (7) JR. F.I.e (SC. 1213), (8) JR. O.I.d (SC. 1616), (9) JR. O.II.d (SC. 1612), (10) CP. B.II.d (SC. 1849), (11) Bt. B.I (SC. 3547), neck and shoulder segment, (12) Bt. Sh. (SC. 3554), "eggshell"-type ware, (13) BE. A.I (SC. 3092).

Figure 317

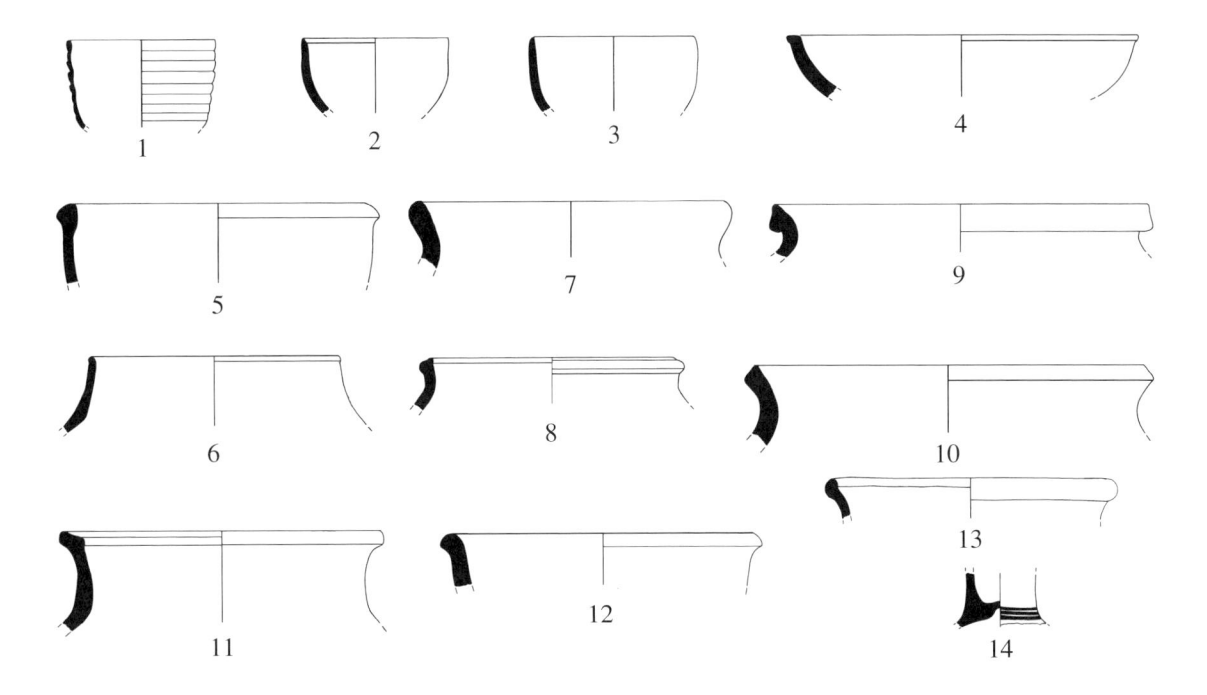

Pottery from Trench VE (Phase 4; Period E — Early Bronze Age IVb). Scale 1:5

1. SBR. A.I.c (TS. 1002; VE, 1.3). About 1/16 of a cup rim and most of the ribbed-type wall profile. Fairly fine brown ware, evenly fired.
2. SBR. A.I.h (TS. 2215; VE, 1.3). Small rim and most of wall segment. Slightly coarse ware, unevenly fired light green out and buff-yellow in.
3. SBR. C.II.c (TS. 2106; VE, 1.3). Small rim and most of wall segment. Fairly fine pink ware, evenly fired. Buff slip out.
4. BR. A.I.f (larger variant; TS. 2212; VE, 1.3). Small rim and upper wall segment. Slightly coarse pinkish-buff ware, evenly fired. Creamy-green slip in and out.
5. BR. L.II.d (TS. 2528; VE, 1.3). About 1/8 rim and upper wall segment. Slightly coarse buff ware, evenly fired. Self slip in and out.
6. SJR. B.II.f (larger variant; TS. 2133; VE, 1.3). Small rim, neck, and upper shoulder segment. Fairly coarse grayish-drab ware, evenly fired. Self slip in and out.
7. JR. E.I.a (TS. 2551; VE, 1.3). Small rim and neck segment. Slightly coarse light brown ware, evenly fired. Self slip in and out.
8. JR. E.II.a (TS. 2143; VE, 2.1). Small rim, neck, and upper shoulder segment. Slightly coarse pinkish-buff ware, evenly fired. Creamy-buff slip in and out.
9. JR. E.II.n (variant; TS. 2475; VE, 1.3). Small rim and neck segment. Slightly coarse pinkish-brown ware, evenly fired. Self slip out.
10. JR. F.II.a (TS. 2230; VE, 1.3). Small rim and neck segment. Slightly coarse light pink ware, evenly fired. Creamy-buff slip out.
11. JR. G.I.c (TS. 1001; VE, 1.3). About 1/12 rim, neck, and upper shoulder segment. Fairly coarse cream ware, evenly fired.
12. JR. J.IV.i (TS. 1011; VE, 1.3). About 1/16 rim and neck segment. Fairly coarse pinkish-buff ware, evenly fired. Buff slip out.
13. CP. A.I.h (TS. 2162; VE, 1.3). Small rim and neck segment. Underfired, fairly coarse buff-brown ware with lime inclusions, evenly fired.
14. BE. F.VII (TS. 1140; VE, 1.3). About 1/2 of a pedestal-type base with horizontally painted red lines outside. Fairly fine pinkish-buff ware, unevenly fired with a brown core.

Other Type Series Examples: (1) SBR. B.I.b (TS. 2131), (2) CP. C.II.c (TS. 976).

Other Study Collection Examples: (1) SBR. A (Gen. Type, SC. 14), (2) SBR. B.I.g (SC. 3413), (3) SJR. B.II.c (SC. 2594), (4) BR. B.II.e (SC. 2839), (5) JR. E.II.c (SC. 1140), (6) JR. F.I.c (SC. 1204), (7) JR. G.I.c (SC. 1241), (8) JR. J.I.c (SC. 1308), (9) BE. F.IV.a (SC. 1917), (10) Bt.Sh. (SC. 3553), "eggshell"-type ware.

Figure 318

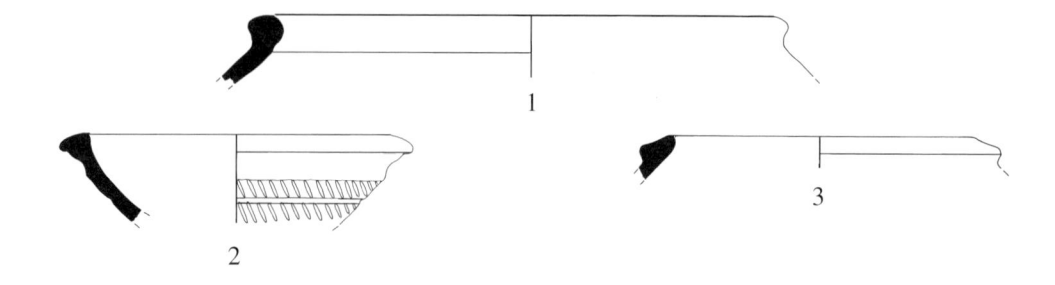

Pottery from Trench VE (Phase 5; Period C — Hellenistic and Derived Early Bronze Age IVb). Scale 1:5

1. JR. O.II.b (TS. 2395; VE, 1.2). About 1/6 rim and upper shoulder segment. Slightly coarse pink ware, evenly fired. Pinkish-buff slip out.
2. H.BR. B.II.a (TS. 1006; VE, 1.2). About 1/16 rim and wall segment with with two bands of shallow diagonal impressions on the outside wall. Fairly coarse pink ware, evenly fired. Buff slip in and out.
3. H.JR. G.II.a (TS. 990; VE, 1.2). About 1/16 rim segment. Fairly coarse greenish-buff ware, evenly fired.

Other Type Series Examples:
Derived Early Bronze Age — (1) JR. D.V.e (TS. 2223).
Hellenistic — (1) H.BR. A.I.a (TS. 974), (2) H.BR. C.II.b (TS. 986), (3) H.RSB. A.I.d (TS. 988), "Festoon" type ware, (4) H.JR. F.I.a (TS. 975).

Other Study Collection Examples:
Derived Early Bronze Age — (1) SJR. A.II.c (SC. 2486), (2) SJR. C.II.j (SC. 2593), (3) SJR. C.II.j (SC. 2595), (4) SJR. B.II.k (SC. 2760), (5) JR. F.II.a (SC.1197), (6) JR. H.III.w (SC. 2021), (7) JR. O.III.h (SC. 1690).
Hellenistic — (1) H.SBR. A.II.b (SC. 3412), (2) H.BR. B.II.a (SC. 3360), (3) H.JR. C.I.f (SC. 1618), (4) H.Jg. B.I.b (SC. 2765), (5) H.St.J. B.I.c (SC. 2684), (6) H.St.J. B.I.d (SC. 1427).

Figure 319

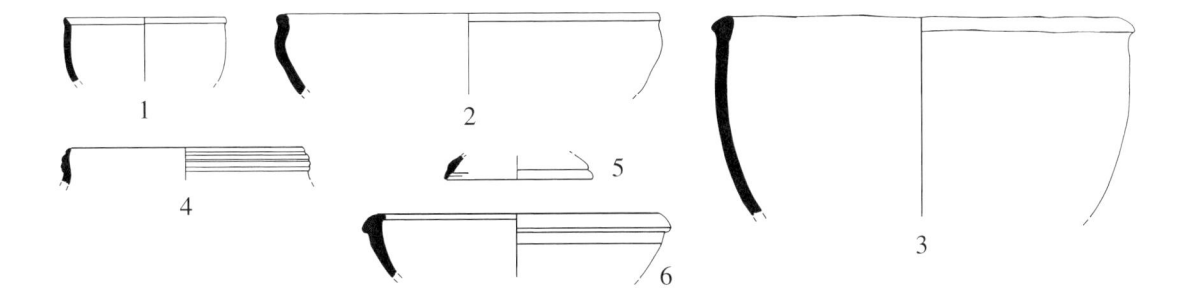

Pottery from Trench VE (Phase 9; Period C — Hellenistic and Derived Early Bronze Age IVb). Scale 1:5

1. SBR. A.I.h (TS. 2118; VE, 1.1). Small rim and most of wall segment. Fairly coarse dark buff ware, evenly fired.
2. BR. C.I.e (TS. 2127; VE, 1.1). Small rim and carinated wall segment. Coarse pink ware, evenly fired. Light pinkish-buff slip out.
3. BR. L.I.c (TS. 1030; VE, 1.1). About 1/8 rim and most of wall segment. Fairly fine pink ware, evenly fired. Cream slip in and out.
4. JR. C.IV.c (TS. 872; VE, 1.1). About 1/12 rim segment. Fairly fine ware, unevenly fired pink out and cream in. Light cream slip out.
5. Ld. C.II.b (TS. 1018; VE, 1.1). About 1/8 rim and upper wall segment. Fairly fine buff ware, evenly fired. Cream slip in and out.
6. H.BR. B.III.k (TS. 953; VE, 1.1). About 1/16 rim and upper wall segment. Fairly coarse pink ware, unevenly fired with a darker core.

Other Type Series Examples:
    Derived Early Bronze Age — (1) SJR. A.III.b (TS. 881).
    Hellenistic — (1) H.BR. B.II.a (TS. 948), (2) H.BR. B.III.k (TS. 855), (3) H.BR. B.III.l (TS. 964), (4) H.SJR. A.II.f (SC. 2326), (5) H.JR. C.I.e (TS. 963), (6) H.JR. E.I.c (TS. 934), (7) H.JR. F.II.c (TS. 907), (8) H.Jg. B.I.a (TS. 937), (9) H.BE. C.II.b (TS. 943).

Other Study Collection Examples:
    Derived Early Bronze Age — (1) BR. A.IV.a (SC. 738), (2) BR. D.V.a (SC. 2820), (3) SJR. A.II.b (SC. 2512), (4) SJR. C.II.q (SC. 2279), (5) JR. C.II.b (SC. 1017), (6) JR. F.I.c (SC. 1202), 7) JR. F.I.c (SC. 2055), (8) JR. J.I.i (SC. 2137), (9) JR. P.II.e (SC. 2417), (10) ABS. A (SC. 3286).
    Hellenistic — (1) H.SBR. A.II.b (SC. 3411), (2) H.BR. A.IV.b (SC. 2822), (3) H.RSB. C.I.a (SC. 2793), (4) H.RSB. D.II.d (SC. 2900), (5) H.SJR. A.II.c (SC. 2798), (6) H.JR. D.II.c (SC. 2749), (7) H.St.J. A.I.g (SC. 2676), (8) H.St.J. B.I.c (SC. 2685), (9) H.St.J. B.I.h (SC. 2805), (10) H.CP. E.I.c (SC. 3070), (11) H.Ld. 5 (SC. 2725).

Figures 320–21

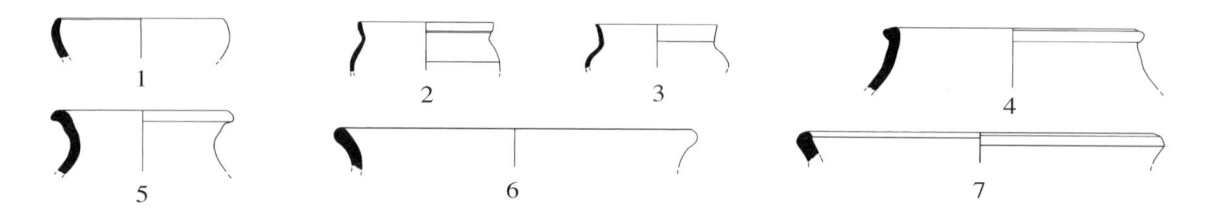

Figure 320. Pottery from Trench VF (Phase 4; Period E — Early Bronze Age IVb). Scale 1:5

1. SBR. C.II.c (TS. 1129; VF, 1.9). About 1/16 rim and upper wall segment. Fairly coarse pink ware, evenly fired. Cream slip in and out.
2. SBR. D.I.a (TS. 2216; VF, 1.9). Small rim and upper wall segment. Fairly fine pinkish-brown ware, evenly fired. Self slip in and out.
3. SBR. D.I.d (TS. 931; VF, 1.9). About 1/16 rim and shoulder segment. Fairly fine cream ware, evenly fired.
4. JR. H.III.l (TS. 2491; VF, 1.9). Small rim, neck, and upper shoulder segment. Fairly coarse yellow-buff ware, evenly fired. Creamy-green slip in and out.
5. JR. J.III.p (TS. 1126; VF, 1.9). Small rim, neck, and upper shoulder segment. Fairly coarse pink ware, evenly fired. Cream slip in and out.
6. CP. B.II.i (TS. 2154; VF, 1.9). Small rim and neck segment. Slightly coarse reddish-brown ware with lime inclusions, evenly fired.
7. CP. B.II.i (TS. 2159; VF, 1.9). Small rim and upper neck segment. Slightly coarse soft light brown ware with lime inclusions, evenly fired.

Another Type Series Example: Early Bronze Age — (1) BR. K.I.a (TS. 1097).

Other Study Collection Examples:
Early Bronze Age — (1) SJR. C.II.v (SC. 2589), (2) SJR. (not typed, SC. 59), (3) JR. A.III.f (SC. 951), (4) JR. F.I.e (SC. 1200), (5) JR. P.II.i (SC. 1741), (6) Bt.Sh. (SC. 3555), "eggshell"-type ware.
Derived Hellenistic Sherds — (1) H.RSB. D.II.a (SC. 2881), (2) H.RSB. D.II.a (SC. 2883).

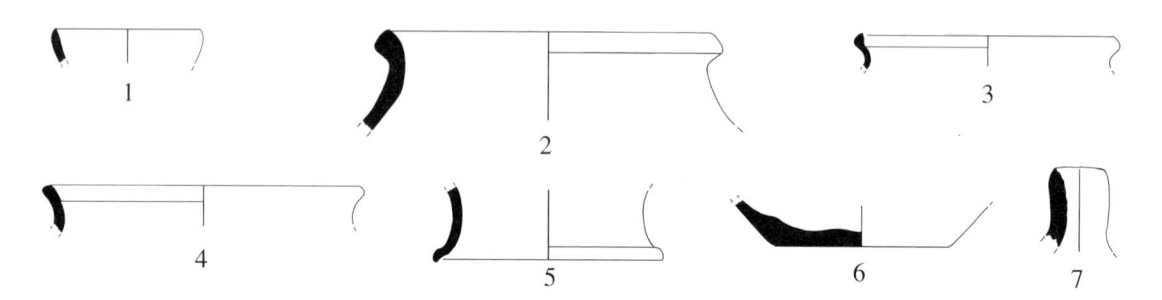

Figure 321. Pottery from Trench VF (Phase 5; Period E — Early Bronze Age IVb). Scale 1:5

1. SBR. C.I.a (TS. 2144; VF, 1.4). Small rim and upper wall segment. Fairly fine buff ware, evenly fired. Light creamy-green slip in and out.
2. JR. E.II.p (TS. 2121; VF, 1.5). Small rim and neck segment. Hard-fired, light creamy-green ware, evenly fired. Self slip in and out.
3. JR. F.II.d (TS. 1127; VF, 1.7). About 1/16 rim and neck segment. Fairly coarse brown ware, evenly fired. Pinkish-buff slip out.
4. CP. B.III.c (TS. 2156; VF, 1.8). Small rim and neck segment. Soft, well-levigated ware, unevenly fired with light gray core fired light brown at surfaces.
5. PS. A.II.c (TS. 1109; VF, 1.4). About 1/8 rim and neck segment. Fairly fine pink ware, evenly fired. Thin cream slip out.
6. BE. D.III (TS. 1154; VF, 1.8). About 1/6 base and lower wall segment. Fairly coarse creamy-buff ware, evenly fired. Cream slip out.
7. SV.2 (SW. 480; VF, 1.5). Nearly complete spout. Coarse brown ware with lime and mica inclusions, unevenly fired. Blackened in and partially out.

Another Type Series Example: Derived Hellenistic — (1) H.CP. C.I.a (TS. 904).

Another Potter's Mark Example: Early Bronze Age — (1) JR. B.III.b (PM. C.11; TS. 2128), see fig. 333:2.

Other Study Collection Examples: Early Bronze Age — (1) SBR. B.I.d (SC. 2817), (2) CP. B.V.a (SC. 1897).

Figure 322

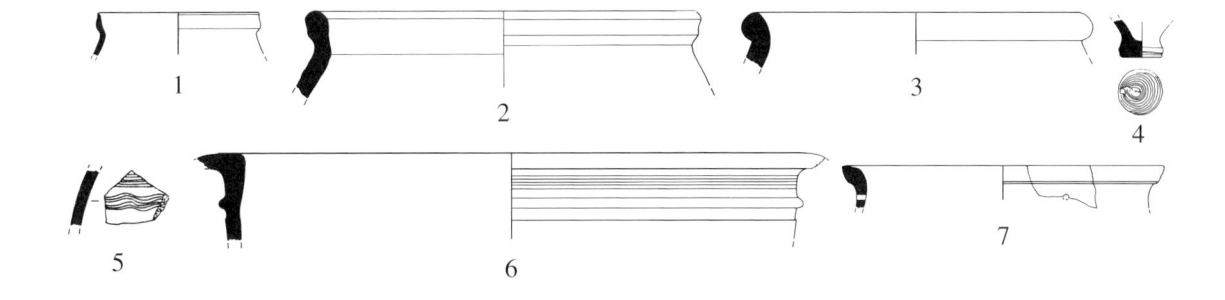

Pottery from Trench VF (Phase 6; Period E — Early Bronze Age IVb and Derived Hellenistic). Scale 1:5

1. SBR. D.I.c (TS. 2525; VF, 1.3). About 1/8 rim and upper shoulder segment. Fairly fine buff ware, evenly fired. Self slip in and out.
2. JR. B.V.d (TS. 897; VF, 1.3). About 1/10 rim and upper shoulder segment. Fairly coarse buff ware, evenly fired. Greenish-cream slip in and out.
3. CP. C.I.c (TS. 807; VF, 1.3). About 1/28 rim and upper shoulder segment. Coarse pink ware with many lime and mica inclusions, evenly fired. Burnished self slip in and out.
4. BE. H (TS. 892; VF, 1.3). Complete knob-type base, string cut from potter's wheel, and lower portion of wall of the vessel. Fairly fine buff ware, evenly fired. Cream slip in and out.
5. JR.Sh. (IP [G.1] Gen.; SC. 3249; VF, 1.3). Jar shoulder sherd with remains of one horizontal and one wavy comb-incised band. Fairly coarse buff ware with black and white lime grits, evenly fired. Self buff slip in and out.
6. H.JR. E.II.a (TS. 795; VF, 1.3). About 1/16 rim and upper wall segment with a coiled band around the upper portion of the neck. Fairly coarse pink ware, evenly fired. Buff slip in and out.
7. H.St.J. B.II.l (TS. 926; VF, 1.3). About 1/12 rim and upper neck segment with a hole pierced through the upper part of the neck before firing. Fairly coarse pink ware, unevenly fired with a buff core.

Other Type Series Examples:
Early Bronze Age — (1) JR.Sh. (IP [G.4] D.III; PM. D.19; TS. 2169), see fig. 333:9.
Derived Hellenistic — (1) H.BR. B.II.d (TS. 793).

Other Study Collection Examples:
Early Bronze Age — (1) SBR. B.I.b (SC. 3418), (2) SBR. B.I.d (SC. 2816), (3) SBR. B.I.d (SC. 3417), (4) SBR. B.I.h (SC. 3416), (5) SBR. C.II.a (SC. 3357), (6) SBR. C.II.a (SC. 612), (7) BR. A.IV.d (SC. 3415), (8) SJR. A.II.h (SC. 2490), (9) SJR. B.II.h (SC. 2658), (10) JR. C.I.e (SC. 2620), (11) JR. F.I.f (SC. 1209), (12) JR. G.I.b (SC. 2037), (13) JR. J.I.g (SC. 2122), (14) JR. J.III.ab (SC. 2275), (15) JR. J.III.ae (SC. 2744), (16) JR. P.I.b (SC. 1694), (17) JR. P.I.d (SC. 1697), (18) JR. P.III.a (SC. 2030), (19) CP. A.I.a (SC. 1783), (20) CP. A.II.a (SC. 1798), (21) CP. B.I.b (SC. 1778), (22) PS. A.I.a (SC. 3027), (23) JR.Sh. Pt. (SC. 3548), one black painted band on outside wall.

Figure 323

Pottery from Trench VF (Phase 9; Period C — Hellenistic and Derived Early Bronze Age IVb). Scale 1:5

1. H.RSB. A.II.c (TS. 403; VF, 1.1). Very small rim, 2.8 cm, and upper wall segment. Fine orange ware, evenly painted. Red-painted slip out and just over rim in.
2. H.RSB. B.II.c (SC. 2862; VF, 1.1). About 1/12 rim and upper wall segment. Remains of one red-painted band on the inner wall. Fine buff ware with a few gold-colored mica grits, evenly fired. Self slip applied before painted decoration was added.
3. H.RSB. C.I.a (TS. 417; VF, 1.1). About 1/20 rim and upper wall segment. Fine pinkish-tan ware, evenly fired. Red painted slip in and to just below top of rim out.
4. H.JR. C.I.d (TS. 2097; VF, 1.1). About 1/16 rim, neck, and upper shoulder segment. Fairly fine pink ware, evenly fired. Buff slip out.
5. H.ABS. C (TS. 407; VF, 1.1). Large jar body sherd with two tool-impressed applied rope-like bands around the girth of the vessel. Fairly coarse light brown ware, evenly fired. Cream slip in and out.

Other Type Series Examples:
  Hellenistic — (1) H.SBR. B.I.a (TS. 404), (2) H.RSB. C.I.a (TS. 401), (3) H.St.J. A.I.n (TS. 2087), (4) H.St.J. B.I.e (TS. 413).
  Derived Early Bronze Age — (5) JR.Sh. (IP [G.1] C.VI.b; TS. 2165), see pl. 340:12.

Another Potter's Mark Example: Derived Early Bronze Age— (1) JR.Sh. (PM. B.2; SC. 3266), see fig. 333:20.

Other Study Collection Examples:
  Hellenistic — (1) H.BR. C.II.b (SC. 1685), (2) H.RSB. A.II.a (SC. 2848), (3) H.RSB. D.II.d (SC. 2891), (4) H.St.J. A.I.d (SC. 2668), (5) H.St.J. A.I.i (SC. 2681), (6) H.CP. E.I.b (SC. 3066).
  Derived Early Bronze Age — (1) BR. E.I.a (SC. 3361), (2) SJR. A.II.b (SC. 2799), (3) SJR. B.II.d (SC. 2842), (4) JR. C.IV.c (SC. 2739), (5) JR. E.II.i (SC. 2444), (6) JR. F.II.d (SC. 1226), (7) JR. F.III.c (SC. 2185), (8) JR. P.I.b (SC. 2422), (9) JR. P.II.b (SC. 2460), (10) BE. J, Misc. (SC. 3236), with a 1 cm drainage hole in center of the base.

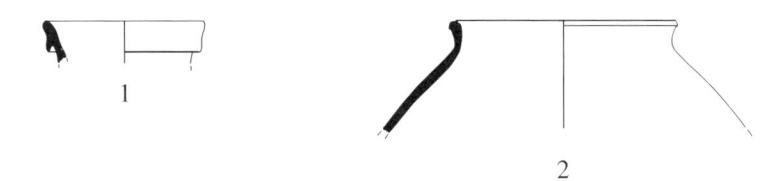

Figure 324. Pottery from Area V, Trench Baulk F/G (Phases 8 and 9; Period C — Hellenistic and Derived Early Bronze IVb). Scale 1:5

1. H.St.J. A.I.g (TS. 874; VF/G, 1.1). Phase 9. Small rim and upper neck segment. Fairly fine pink ware, evenly fired. Cream slip in and out.
2. H.CP. A.I.a (variant; TS. 877; VF/G, 1.1). Phase 9. About 1/10 rim, neck, and shoulder segment. Coarse red ware, evenly fired.

Other Type Series Examples:
Derived Early Bronze Age — Phase 9: (1) SJR. B.IV.b (TS. 864), (2) JR.Sh. (IP [G.1] H.III.a; TS. 2070), see pl. 340:19.
Hellenistic — Phase 9: (1) H.BR. B.III.g (TS. 883); Phase 8 — (2) H.JR. F.II.b (TS. 796).

Another Potter's Mark Example:
Derived Early Brone Age — Phase 9: (1) JR.BE.Sh. (PM. D.4; SC. 3257), see fig. 333:21.

Other Study Collection Examples:
Hellenistic — Phase 9: (1) H.SBR. A.II.b (SC. 3419), (2) H.BR. B.III.e (SC. 2832), (3) H.RSB. D.II.d (SC. 2894), (4) H.RSB. D.II.d (SC. 3420), (5) H.RSB. D.II.e (SC. 2906).

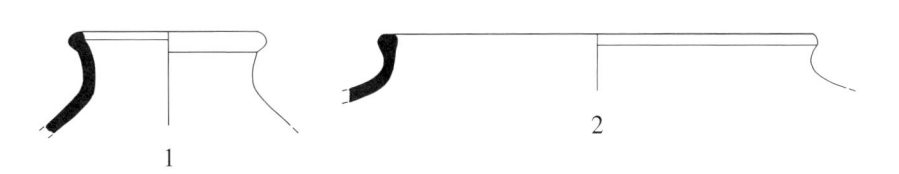

Figure 325. Pottery from Trench VG (Phase 5; Period F — Early Bronze Age IVa). Scale 1:5

1. JR. J.III.x (TS. 862; VG, 1.6). About 1/4 rim, neck, and upper shoulder segment. Fairly coarse pink ware, evenly fired. Cream slip out.
2. CP. B.V.b (TS. 861; VG, 1.6). About 1/20 rim, neck, and upper shoulder segment. Coarse dark brown ware with large lime and mica inclusions, evenly fired. Brownish-buff slip in and out. Blackened out.

Other Study Collection Examples: (1) BR. L.III.d (SC. 773), (2) SR. C.I.a (body fragment; SC. 3293).

Figure 326

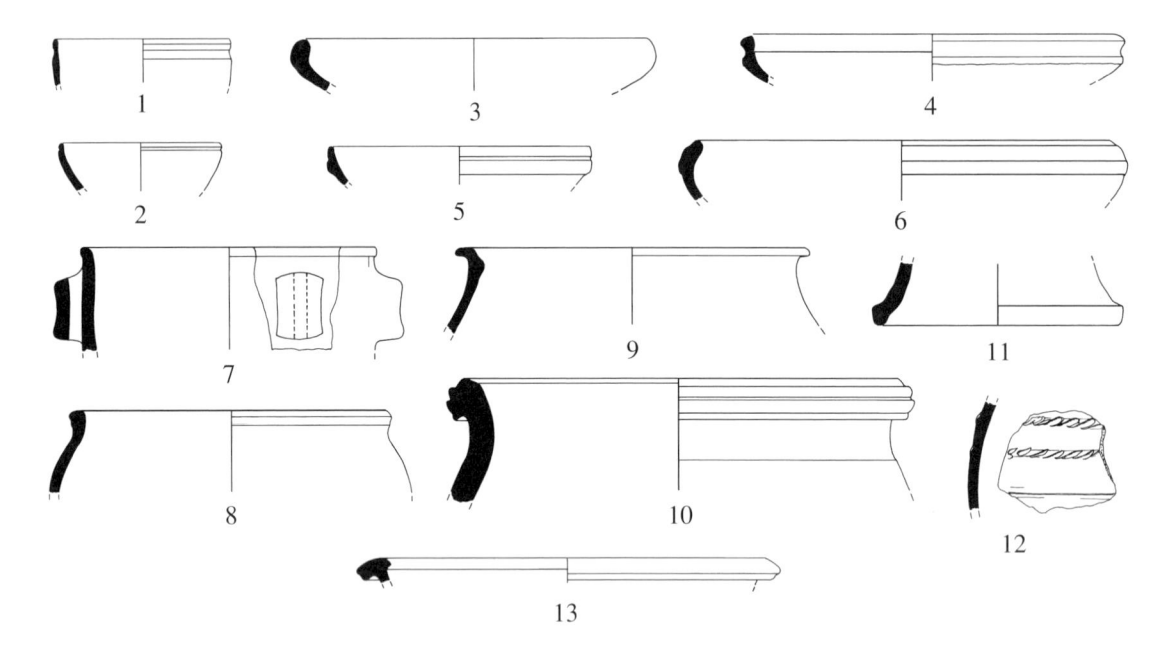

Pottery from Trench VG (Phase 6; Period E — Early Bronze Age IVb and Derived Hellenistic). Scale 1:5

1. SBR. B.I.d (TS. 930; VG, 1.4). About 1/12 rim and upper wall segment. Fairly coarse pink ware, evenly fired. Traces of cream slip in.
2. SBR. B.I.q (TS. 2214; VG, 1.4). Small rim and upper wall segment. Fine pinkish-buff ware, evenly fired. No visible slip.
3. BR. A.II.a (TS. 903; VG, 1.4). About 1/20 rim and upper wall segment. Fairly coarse pinkish-buff ware, evenly fired. Cream slip in and out.
4. BR. C.I.d (TS. 944; VG, 1.4). About 1/20 rim and upper wall segment. Fairly coarse pink ware, evenly fired. Cream slip in and out.
5. BR. D.II.c (TS. 2148; VG, 1.4). Small rim and upper wall segment. Fairly fine orange ware, evenly fired. Buff slip in and out.
6. BR. E.III.g (TS. 968; VG, 1.4). About 1/36 rim and upper wall segment. Fine pink ware, unevenly fired with a buff core in the rim. Cream slip out.
7. BR. L.II.h (Hd. C; TS. 842; VG, 1.4). Small rim and upper wall segment with a pierced vertical lug handle. Fine, hard, evenly fired buff ware. Creamy-buff slip in and out.
8. JR. E.II.B (TS. 980; VG, 1.4). About 1/24 rim and shoulder segment. Fairly coarse buff ware, evenly fired.
9. JR. F.III.g (TS. 854; VG, 1.4). Small rim and upper shoulder segment. Fairly coarse pink ware, evenly fired. Cream slip out and just over rim in.
10. JR. Q.I.b (TS. 823; VG, 1.4). Small rim, neck, and upper shoulder segment. Coarse pink ware, unevenly fired with a thick brown core. Buff slip out.
11. BE. F.IV.a (TS. 2336; VG, 1.4). About 1/10 rim and about 1/2 of wall of a pedestal-type base. Fairly coarse buff ware, evenly fired. Light creamy-green slip in and out.
12. ABS. C (TS. 878; VG, 1.4). Jar body sherd with two horizontal bands with tool-impressed decoration. Coarse reddish-brown ware, unevenly fired with brown core. Traces of burnishing on the inside wall.
13. H.JR. E.I.b (TS. 1015; VG, 1.4). Small rim segment. Fairly coarse pink ware, evenly fired. Cream slip in and out.

Other Type Series Examples:
Early Bronze Age — (1) JR. Q.II.b (IP [G.1] A.I.a; TS. 985), see pl. 340:1, (2) JR.Sh. (IP [G.1] C.V.a; TS. 2167), see pl. 340:8.
Derived Hellenistic — (1) H.JR. E.I.b (IP (G.1 C.VI.a; TS. 916 = TS. 1044), see pl. 340:10, (2) H.BR. B.II.b (TS. 1008), (3) H.St.J. A.I.k (TS. 900), (4) H.St.J. B.I.f (TS. 879), (5) H.St.J. B.I.h (TS. 866).

Another Potter's Mark: Early Bronze Age — (1) JR.Sh. (PM. D.17; SC. 3269), see fig. 333:22.

Other Study Collection Examples:
Early Bronze Age — (1) SBR. A.I.d (SC. 406), (2) SBR. A.I.d (SC. 537), (3) SBR. A.I.d (SC. 3427), (4) SBR. B.I.b (SC. 255), (5) SBR. B.I.e (SC. 3429), (6) SBR. B.I.h (SC. 450), (7) SBR. B.I.h (SC. 519), (8) SBR. B.I.h (SC. 3424), (9) SBR. B.I.h (SC. 3428), (10) SBR. B.I.i (SC. 3426), (11) BR. C.I.d (SC. 709), (12) BR. D.V.a (SC. 3425), (13) BR. F.III.a (SC. 1969), (14) SJR. C.I.b (SC. 2619), (15) JR. B.I.a (variant, SC. 2740), (16) JR. B.IV.f (SC. 965), (17) JR. F.I.a (SC. 1184), (18) JR. F.I.c (SC. 1180), (19) JR. H.I.l (SC. 2629), (20) JR. J.I.a (SC. 2796), (21) JR. J.I.b (SC. 2100), (22) JR. J.I.j (SC. 2500), (23) JR. J.II.d (SC. 2288), (24) JR. J.III.b (SC. 3365), (25) JR. J.III.d (SC. 2290), (26) JR. J.III.h (SC. 1366), (27) JR. J.III.p (SC. 2632), (28) JR. J.III.s (SC. 3366), (29) JR. J.III.w (SC. 2363), (30) JR. J.III.y (SC. 1505), (31) JR. J.III.z (SC. 2198), (32) JR. J.III.ab (SC. 2327), (33) JR. J.IV.d (SC. 2247), (34) JR. K.I.b (SC. 2794), (35) JR. O.I.h (SC. 2405), (36) JR. O.II.e (SC. 1638), (37) JR. O.III.f (SC. 2418), (38) JR. P.II.f (SC. 1675), (39) JR. P.II.s (SC. 1755), (40) JR.Sh. (SC. 3549), horizontally reserved cream slip outside, (41) JR.Sh. Dec. (SC. 3550), diagonally incised tool-made impressions on the shoulder, (42) JR.Sh. Dec. (not typed, SC. 157), (43) BE. D.IV (SC. 3146), (44) BE. E.II.f (SC. 3197), (45) BE. F.V.a (SC. 3079), (46) BE. J (Misc.; SC. 3233), pointed small jar base, flattened 1 cm on outside center.
Derived Hellenistic — (1) H.BR. B.V.b (variant, SC. 2141), (2) H.JR. D.I.b (SC. 2374), (3) H.RSB. Sh. Pt. (SC. 3551), (4) H.JR.Sh. Dec. (SC. 3552), horizontally black-painted linear decoration on outside surface.

Figures 327–29

Figure 327. Pottery from Trench VG (Phase 7; Period E — Early Bronze Age IVb and Derived Hellenistic). Scale 1:5

1. JR. F.I.a (TS. 852; VG, 1.3). About 1/20 rim and upper shoulder segment. Fairly coarse brown ware, evenly fired. Cream slip out and thinly applied in.
2. JR. J.II.i (TS. 2542; VG, 1.3). About 1.6 rim and neck segment. Slightly coarse pinkish-buff ware, evenly fired. Creamy-buff slip in and out.
3. H.BR. B.III.i (TS. 884; VG, 1.3). About 1/28 rim and upper wall segment. Fairly coarse pink ware, evenly fired. Creamy-buff slip in and out.

Other Incised Type Series Examples:
Early Bronze Age — (1) JR.Sh. (IP [G.1] C.VI.b; TS. 2161), see pl. 340:13.
Derived Hellenistic — (1) JR.Sh. (IP [G.2] B.II.a; TS. 880), see pl. 340:28.

Other Study Collection Examples:
Early Bronze Age — (1) SBR. A.I.d (SC. 3423), (2) SBR. A.I.e (SC. 548), (3) SBR. A.I.e (SC. 3422), (4) SBR. B.I.c (SC. 280), (5) SBR. B.I.c (SC. 572), (6) SBR. B.I.l (SC. 574), (7) SBR. G (Gen. Type, SC. 2815), (8) BR. F.I.d (SC. 770), (9) BR. G.I.d (SC. 824), (10) JR. H.I.a (SC. 1242), (11) JR. J.I.a (SC. 2086), (12) JR. J.I.b (SC. 2097), (13) JR. J.I.f (SC. 2795), (14) JR. J.II.b (SC. 2089), (15) JR. J.II.h (SC. 2164), (16) JR. J.III.e (SC. 2265), (17) JR. J.III.m (SC. 2323), (18) JR. O.I.h (SC. 1635), (19) JR. P.I.b (SC. 1714), (20) JR. P.III.g (SC. 1770), (21) JR. (not typed, SC. 137).

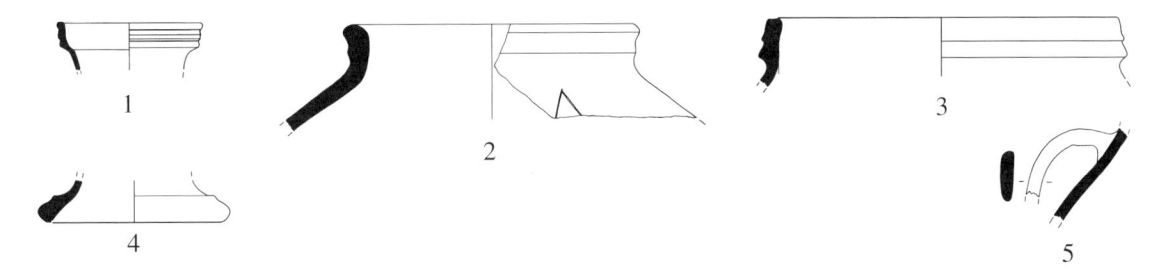

Figure 328. Pottery from Trench VG (Phase 8; Period E — Early Bronze Age IVb Pottery and Derived Hellenistic). Scale 1:5

1. SJR. C.II.u (TS. 894; VG, 1.2). About 1/12 rim and upper neck segment. Fairly fine pink ware, evenly fired. Cream slip in and out.
2. JR. B.III.b (PM. C.11; TS. 869; VG, 1.2). About 1/12 rim and upper shoulder segment with the remains of a potter's mark. Fairly coarse pink ware, evenly fired. Cream slip out.
3. JR. B.V.f (TS. 834; VG, 1.2). About 1/28 rim and neck segment. Fairly coarse pink ware, evenly fired. Cream slip in and out.
4. BE. F.V.a (TS. 847; VG, 1.2). About 1/4 rim and lower wall segment. Fairly coarse brown ware, evenly fired. Cream slip in and out.
5. H.CP. D.I.b + H.Hd.2 (TS. 851; VG, 1.2). Cooking pot shoulder segment with 2/3 portion of a broad strap handle. Fairly coarse pink ware, evenly fired.

Other Type Series Examples: Hellenistic — (1) H.JR. E.II.a (TS. 836), (2) H.St.J. A.II.a (TS. 853), (3) H.BE. B.II.c (TS. 3047).

Other Study Collection Examples: Early Bronze Age — (1) SBR. A.I.c (SC. 3421), (2) SBR. C.II.a (SC. 601), (3) JR. J.I.a (SC. 2271), (4) CP. B.IV.e (SC. 1892).

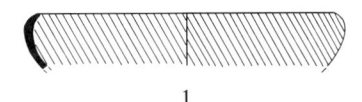

Figure 329. Pottery from Trench VG (Phase 9; Period C — Hellenistic). Scale 1:5

1. H.RSB. D.II.a (TS. 829; VG, 1.1). Small rim and upper wall segment. Fine pink ware, evenly fired. Red applied slip in and out.

Figure 330. Small Finds from Area V Step Trenches (Phases 3–7, 9; Periods E and C — Early Bronze Age IVb and Hellenistic)

1. SF.1c (TS. 427; VA, 1.1; Phase 3, Period E). Early Bronze human pillar-type figurine stand with slight bell-shaped, flat, bottom; upper portion not found. Coarse pink ware with lime and mica inclusions, evenly fired.
—. SF.1c (SW. 214; VB, 1.2; Phase 3, Period E). Early Bronze Age. Human figurine base fragment (see fig. 331:14).
—. SF.3c (SW. 586; VC, 2.1; Phase 3, Period E). Early Bronze Age. Stone mortar fragment. Elliptical-shaped limestone. Extant measurements, 10 × 15 × 23 cm. Mortar depth, 5 cm.
—. SF.5i (SW. 614; VE, 1.4; Phase 3, Period G). Early Bronze Age. Lump of dark reddish-brown iron-stained material. Compound of iron that formed an irregular mass. Extant measurements, 7 cm long.
—. SF.1a (SW. 516; VA/B baulk, 1.1; Phase 4, Period C). Derived Early Bronze Age. Human figurine head (see fig. 331:1).
—. SF.1c (SW. 541; VA/B baulk, 1.1; Phase 4, Period C). Derived Early Bronze Age. Human figurine pillar-type stand fragment (see fig. 331:13).
—. SF.1e (SC. 162; VC, 1.1; Phase 4, Period C). Animal figurine hindquarter fragment.
2. SF.3a (SW. 160; VA, 1.1; Phase 4, Period C). Grinding stone fragment. Cream limestone. Extant measurements, 6.0 × 10.5 × 14.0 cm.
3. SF.3a (SW. 162; VA, 1.1; Phase 4, Period C). Grinding stone fragment. Dark gray tufa. Extant measurements, 6.0 × 12.5 × 13.0 cm.
—. SF.3a (SW. 486; VC, 1.11; Phase 4, Period C). Grinding stone fragment. Off-white limestone with a parabolic cross section, broken at both ends. Flat grinding face has suffered heavy wear. Extant measurements, 7 × 13 × 22 cm.
4. SF.4c (SW. 559; VD, 2.1; Phase 4, Period E). Clay pendant cut from a sherd, pierced in the center, and incised with two lines, one on each side of the stringing hole. Coarse brown ware with large lime and mica inclusions, evenly fired. Surface with the incisions highly burnished.
5. SF.6b (TS. 2163; VD, 2.1; Phase 4, Period E). Clay spindle whorl probably cut from the base of a small jar with a hole drilled from both sides of the sherd. Slightly coarse orange ware, evenly fired.
—. SF.1d (SW. 517; VE, 1.2; Phase 5, Period C). Animal figurine head fragment (see fig. 331:17).
—. SF.3a (SW. 487; VF, 1.6; Phase 5, Period E). Grinding stone fragment. Limestone. Oval in section and missing one third of one side. The flat grinding face is pitted by abundant small holes. Extant measurements, 7 × 12 × 17 cm.
6. SF.3f (SW. 532; VF, 1.6; Phase 5, Period E). Stone spindle whorl fragment. Soft off-white chalk-like limestone. Extant measurements, diameter 4.5 cm.
7. SV.5 (SW. 220; VD, 1.1; Phase 5, Period C). Clay pipe bowl fragment. Brown ware with a polished surface and with black and white lime inclusions and burned out vegetable temper, unevenly fired with a gray core.
8. SF.1c (SC. 3313; VG, 1.4; Phase 6, Period E). Human figurine pillar-type stand fragment with a flattened, oval-shaped body. Vertically tool shaved on one broad side. Fairly fine creamy-green ware with small lime grits, evenly fired. Self slip.
—. SF.1c (SW. 440; VF, 1.3; Phase 6, Period E). Human figurine pillar-type body fragment (see fig. 331:15).
9. SF.4a (SC. 3316; VF, 1.3; Phase 6, Period E). Clay amulet in the shape of a bent human arm and hand. Fine pinkish-brown ware with small mica grits, evenly fired. Self slip.
—. SF.3a (SW. 599; VF, 1.3; Phase 6, Period E). Metal wire fragment (see fig. 331:22).
—. SF.3a (SW. 507; VF/G, 1.3). Phase 7. Hellenistic. Grinding stone fragment. Dark gray vesicular basalt. Extant measurements, 5 × 6 × 13 cm.
—. SF.3a (SW. 488; VE, 1.1; Phase 9, Period C). Grinding stone fragment. Limestone with one half elliptical shape. Extant measurements, 5 × 13 × 18 cm.
—. SF.3a (SW. 489; VE, 1.1; Phase 9, Period C). Grinding stone fragment. Limestone with one half elliptical shape, missing fragments at both ends. Extant measurements, 6 × 12 × 16 cm.
—. SF.3a (SW. 491; VE, 1.1; Phase 9, Period C). Grinding stone fragment. Limestone with a fairly coarsely pitted grinding face. Extant measurements, 6 × 11 × 13 cm.
—. SF.3a (SW. 508; VE, 1.1; Phase 9, Period C). Grinding stone fragment. Limestone with only the finely pitted grinding face preserved. Extant measurements, 5 × 7 × 12 cm.
—. SF.3a (SW. 509; VE, 1.1; Phase 9, Period C). Grinding stone fragment. Limestone with a shallow cross section. Extant measurements, 2.5 × 7.0 × 9.0 cm.
—. SF.3c (SW. 493; VE, 1.1; Phase 9, Period C). Stone mortar fragment. Square-shaped limestone with a roughly parabolic cross section. Extant measurements, 6 × 9 × 11 cm.
—. SF.3e (SW. 654; VD, 2.4; Phase 9, Period C). Stone loom weight fragment. About one third of a donut-shaped stone.
10. SF.3f (SW. 209; VF, 1.1; Phase 9, Period C). Stone sling bullet. Limestone with an uneven and pitted surface. Extant measurements, maximum diameter 2.2 cm.
—. SF.3f (SW. 528; VE, 1.1; Phase 9, Period C). Fossil. Fragment of a fossilized body whorl of a gastropod(?). Probably derived from the local limestone; forms three-fourth of a circle. Most likely utilized, but function unknown. Extant measurements, diameter 3.5 cm.
—. SF.5h (SW. 628; VF/G, 1.1; Phase 9, Period C). Iron knife blade fragment (see fig. 332:7).
11. SF.5h (TS. 3149; VF, 1.1; Phase 9, Period C). Iron knife blade fragment with blade tip and upper shank broken off.

Figure 330

Small Finds from Area V Step Trenches (Phases 3–7, 9; Periods E and C — Early Bronze Age IVb and Hellenistic).
Scale 1:2

Figure 331. Miscellaneous Small Finds from Area I, Trench IIB, Area V, and Trench VIA (Early Bronze Age, Early–Middle Bronze Age, and Hellenistic/Roman)

1. Type SF.1a (SW. 516; VA/B, 1.1; Phase 4, Period C, Derived Bronze Age). Head of a female figurine with socket-like eyes and ear decoration. Impressed arrow-like pattern represents hair on front and back of the head. Portion of an appliqué and incised necklace on the right shoulder, not joining on the back of the neck. Fairly coarse dark gray-brown ware, evenly fired. Greenish-buff slip on all surfaces.
2. Type SF.1a (SW. 13; IA2, 3.1; Phase 4, Period B, Derived Bronze Age). Female figurine upper torso fragment with hand-pinched nose and hands holding the breasts. Two incised "suspender-like" lines from shoulders to base of back. Coarse light buff ware, evenly fired.
3. Type SF.1a (SW. 1; IA1, 2.1; Phase 4, Period B, Derived Bronze Age). Female figurine torso fragment with head and lower parts of legs missing. Pronounced buttocks. Incised appliqué necklace around front of neck. Hands support the breasts. Fairly coarse greenish-buff clay, evenly fired.
4. Type SF.1a (SW. 389; VIA, 3.1a; Phase 5, Period E–D; see pl. 105c). Female figurine upper torso fragment without its head. Right arm broken and left hand holding breast. Fairly fine pink ware, unevenly fired with light brown core. Traces of cream slip on left elbow.
5. Type SF.1a (SW. 67; IB, 2.6; Phase 3, Period B, Derived Bronze Age). Female figurine upper torso fragment without its head. Appliqué and incised necklace around front of neck. Both hands hold the breasts. Coarse buff ware, evenly fired.
6. Type SF.1a (SW. 385; VIA, 3.1; Phase 5, Period E–D; see pl. 105d). Female figurine upper torso fragment without its head. Right hand holding breast and left arm missing. Fairly coarse cream-buff ware, evenly fired.
—. Type SF.7a (SW. 347; VIA, 1.1; Phase 5, Period E–D, Derived Hellenistic/Roman). Glass fragment. 1 mm thick, 1.5 cm long, 1.0 cm wide.
7. Type SF.1c (SW. 113a; IA2, 3.1; Phase 4, Period B, Derived Bronze Age). Human pillar-type figurine stand fragment with bell-shaped base. Coarse light buff ware with large black lime grits, evenly fired.
8. Type SF.1c (SW. 113b; IA2, 3.1; Phase 4, Period B, Derived Bronze Age). Human pillar-type figurine stand fragment with bell-shaped base. Slightly coarse brown ware with black lime and gold-colored mica grits, evenly fired. Light buff slip on surfaces.
9. Type SF.1c (SW. 47; IA2, 4.3; Phase 2, Period B, Derived Bronze Age). Human pillar-type figurine stand fragment with bell-shaped base. Fine brown ware, evenly fired.
10. Type SF.1c (SW. 94; IB, 1.2; Phase 4, Period B). Human pillar-type figurine stand fragment with slightly spread concave base.
11. Type SF.1c (SW. 388; IJ, 1.1; Phase 2, Period B). Human pillar-type figurine stand fragment with bell-shaped base. Fairly coarse pink ware, evenly fired. Cream slip on surfaces.
12. Type SF.1c (SW. 153; IIB, 6.5; Phase 14, Period C). Human figurine torso fragment with stubs of legs extant. Fine orange-brown ware with black and gold-colored mineral temper, evenly fired (see pl. 155i).
13. Type SF.1c (SW. 541; VA/B, 1.1; Phase 4, Period C, Derived EB–MB). Human figurine torso fragment with long vertically incised lines on the back and indented circular holes on the front, which may represent the pubic area. Fairly fine grayish-buff ware, evenly fired.
14. Type SF.1c (SW. 214; VB, 1.2; Phase 3, Period E). Human pillar-type figurine stand fragment with bell-shaped base. Slightly coarse pinkish-buff ware with small black grits and burned out vegetable temper, fairly evenly fired.
15. Type SF.1c (SW. 440; VF, 1.3; Phase 6, Period E). Human pillar-type figurine stand fragment. Fairly coarse pink ware, evenly fired. Cream slip on surfaces.
16. Type SF.1d (SW. 12; IA2, 3.1; Phase 4, Period B). Animal figurine head fragment with one ear missing. Indented holes for eyes and very rudimentary snout. Coarse light yellow ware, evenly fired.
17. Type SF.1d (SW. 517; VE, 1.2; Phase 5, Period C, Derived Bronze Age). Animal figurine head fragment with both ears missing. Fairly coarse pink ware, evenly fired. Buff slip on surfaces.
18. Type SF.2b (SW. 71; IB, 2.6; Phase 3, Period B, Derived Bronze Age). Model chariot wheel with pronounced hub extending from both sides of the wheel. Fairly fine buff ware with black temper, evenly fired. Iron-colored stains on surface.
19. Type SF.2b (SW. 405; VIA, 3.1a; Phase 5, Period E–D). Model chariot wheel with slightly extended hub on both sides. Mottled with remains of bitumen. Fairly fine pinkish-buff ware, evenly fired. Cream slip on surfaces.
20. Type SF.12b (SW. 120; IB, 1.7; Phase 3, Period B, Derived Bronze Age). Flint arrowhead. Dark gray flint, leaf shape, fine retouch along both edges, and tip of point broken.
21. Type SF.5i (SW. 3; IA2, 3.1; Phase 4, Period B). Metal rim of small cup or bowl (copper/bronze?, not analyzed). Vertical rim folded inward. Maximum thickness 3 cm.
22. Type SF.5i (SW. 599; VF, 1.3; Phase 6, Period E). Metal wire fragment with solid core (lead). See *Appendix 6*.
23. Type SF.4d (SW. 514; VIA, 3.1a; Phase 5, Period E–D). Metal bracelet (silver?, not analyzed). Broken, but complete bracelet with a serpent-shaped head at one end.
24. Type SF.5c (SW. 117; IIB, 2.12; Phase 15, Period C). Metal pin (copper/bronze?, not analyzed). Pin with wedge-shaped top and chipped point. Two parallel horizontal rings at base of wedge-shaped top, a bulbous section, and two more parallel horizontal rings at base of bulbous section.
25. Type SF.5h (SW. 512; VIA, 3.1a; Phase 5, Period E–D, probably derived Hellenistic, Roman, or later). Metal knife blade (iron) with rivet at broad end with small remains of wood and traces of leather along the shaft.

Figure 331

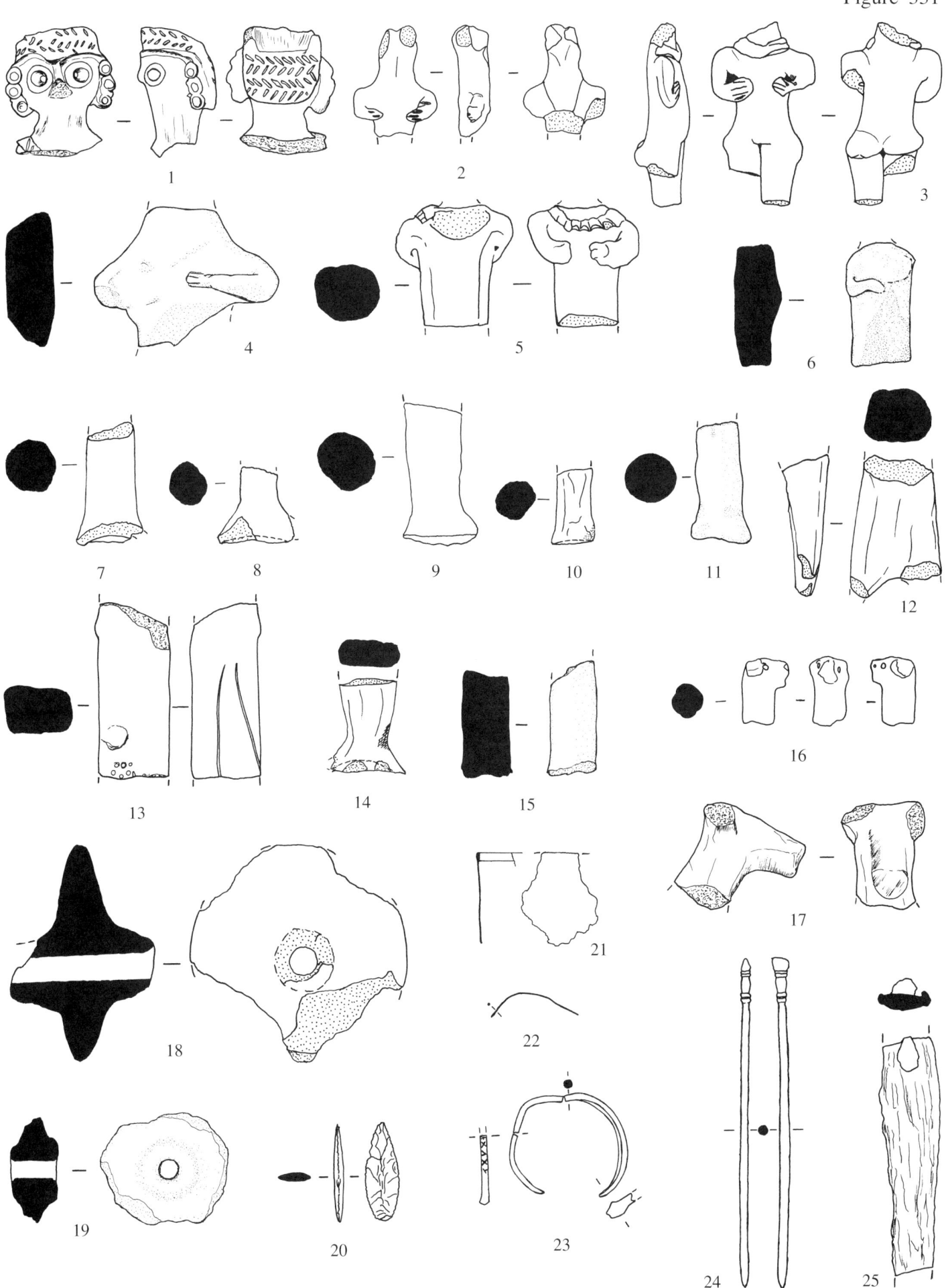

Miscellaneous Small Finds from Area I, Trench IIB, Area V, and Trench VIA (Early Bronze Age, Early–Middle Bronze Age, and Hellenistic/Roman). Scale 1:2

Figure 332. Miscellaneous Small Finds from Area I, Trench IIB, Areas V, VI, VII, and VIII, and Surface (Early Bronze Age IVa–Roman)

1. Type SF.5i (SW. 4; IA1, 2.3; Phase 2, Period B). Iron nail with missing head. Exterior heavily corroded.
2. Type SF.5i (SW. 7; IA1, 2.4a; Phase 2, Period B). Iron nail fragment.
3. Type SF.5c (SW. 52; IA2, 4.3; Phase 2, Period B). Iron pin fragment. Heavily corroded and broken into two fragments.
4. Type SF.5i (SW. 65; IB, 1.2; Phase 4, Period B). Iron nail fragment with bent point. Heavily corroded.
5. Type SF.5i (SW. 82; IB, 1.6; Phase 3, Period B). Iron nail fragment. Heavily corroded.
6. Type SF.5h (SW. 43; IIB, 2.1; Phase 15, Period C). Iron implement. Thin bar, rectangular in section. Heavily corroded.
7. Type SF.5h (SW. 628; VF/G, 1.1; Phase 9, Period C). Iron knife blade fragment.
8. Type SF.5i (SW. 622; XIA, 1.2; Phase 3, Period B). Leaded bronze strip fragment.
9. Type SF.3f (SW. 356; VIIA, 2.4; Phase 2, Period E). Stone tool (scraper) or weapon broken at each end. Fine dark gray grained igneous rock with cross section resembling aerofoil.
—. Type SF.3a (SW. 463; VIIA, 4.4; Phase 2, Period E). Stone rubbing tool. Measurement: 5.00 cm long. Dark gray basalt fragment.
10. Type SF.3b (SW. 446; VIA, 3.7; Phase 1, Period F). Stone sling bullet.
11. Type SF.6a (SW. 438; VIA, 3.4; Phase 3, Period E). Clay sling bullet.
—. Type SF.3a (SW. 423; VIA, 3.5; Phase 2, Period F). Grinding stone fragment. Measurements: 7.00 × 11.00 × 16.00 cm. Cream-colored limestone with an elliptical plan and a parabolic cross section. The grinding face is flat and heavily pitted.
—. Type SF.3c (SW. 428; VIA, 3.4; Phase 3, Period E). Stone mortar fragment. Measurements: 8.00 × 11.00 × 15.00 cm. Cream-colored limestone with parabolic cross section. Mortar depression is irregular in outline and has a rough grinding face.
—. Type SF.3a (SW. 429; VIA, 3.1a; Phase 5, Period E–D). Grinding stone fragment. Measurements: 7.00 × 12.00 × 18.00 cm. Cream-colored limestone. Roughly rectangular in shape with a semi-circular section and with a flat and very pitted grinding face.
12. Type SF.2a (TS. 2177; Area VIII, Surface; Bronze Age). Model chariot fragment. Hard, fairly coarse buff ware, evenly fired.
13. Type SF.1a (FN. 12; Lower Town Surface; Bronze Age). Human figurine head and neck fragment. Pillar-like "crown" on top of head. Nose and ears pinched out from clay and two shallow incisions made in the clay to represent the eyes. Fine, well levigated, pinkish-buff ware, evenly fired.
14. Type SF.1a (SW. 825; Op. 4, Surface; Bronze Age). Human figurine head and neck fragment. High pillar-like "crown," with applied and incised band of clay on front half, on top of head. Nose and ears pinched out from the clay. Eyes represented by two applied and incised disks of clay.
15. Type SF.1a (SW. 203; Tell Surface; Bronze Age). Human figurine head and neck fragment with protrusion of clay at back of head, which may represent remains of a "bun-shaped' hairdress. Nose fairly well molded with applied and incised disks of clay for the eyes. Fine, buff ware, evenly fired.
16. Type SF.1c (FN. 187; Lower Town Surface; Bronze Age). Headless, seated human figurine torso, possibly originally attached to another object (cf. fig. 221:7). Possibly also used as an amulet as half of a string hole remains at the top center of the chest instead of a head. The stump-like arms are chipped off and two shallow reed-made impressions are in the breast area.
17. Type SF.1c (FN. 188; Lower Town Surface; Bronze Age). Human pillar-type figurine fragment with remains of the right arm extended downward and the left arm upraised.
18. Type SF.1c (FN. 189; 1973 Modern Loo Pit on SW side of main Tell south of Area IV; Bronze Age). Human figurine neck and upper torso fragment with hands nearly joined on front of the body. Two applied and incised strips of clay are attached across the front of the chest and four narrow incised lined on the upper back may represent attachments to hold the front clothing in place.
19. Type SF.1c (SW. 752; Tell Surface; Bronze Age). Human figurine torso fragment with upraised arms. The purpose of the attached clay on front of the torso is unknown.
20. Type SF.1d (FN. 190; Lower Town Surface; Bronze Age). Animal figurine forequarter fragment; probably bovine.
21. Type SF.1e (FN. 191; Lower Town Surface; Bronze Age). Animal figurine hindquarter fragment of unknown type of quadruped.
22. Type SF.1e (FN. 192; Lower Town Surface; Bronze Age). Animal figurine hindquarter fragment; probably a sheep with a wide short tail intact.

Figure 332

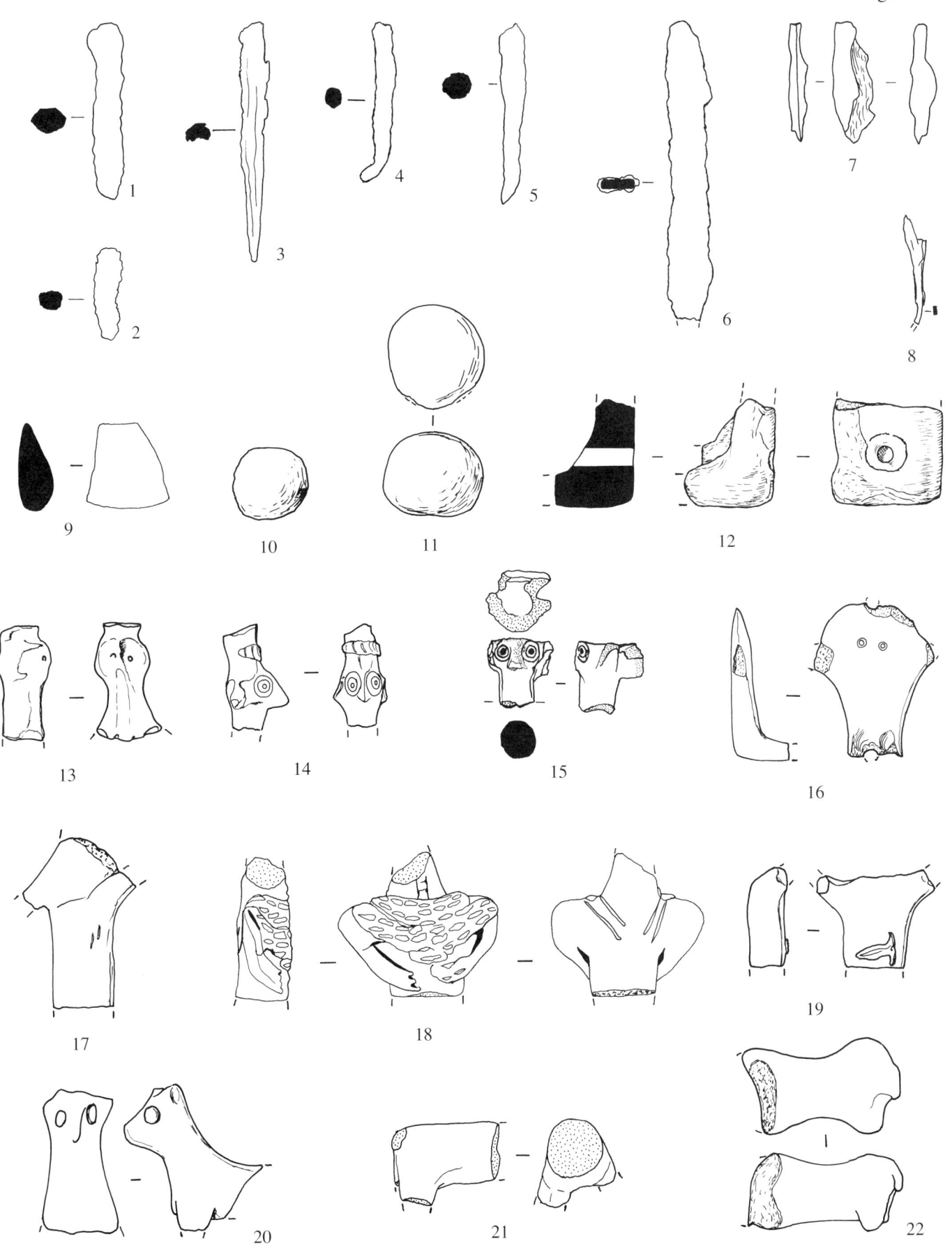

Miscellaneous Small Finds from Area I, Trench IIB, Areas V, VI, VII, and VIII, and Surface (Early Bronze Age IVa–Roman). Scale 1:2

Figure 333. Potters' Marks on Miscellaneous Vessels and Sherds from Areas I, II, III, IV, and V

1. Ld. C.II.a (PM. E.2; TS. 1746; IVL, 1.3, Room 3A; Phase 3, Period E). Lid (see pl. 236:8) or possibly a small bowl with remains of a potter's mark outside. Fairly fine pink ware, evenly fired.
2. JR. B.III.b (PM. C.11; TS. 2128; VF, 1.4; Phase 5, Period E). Small rim and upper shoulder segment with an incomplete potter's mark incised on the shoulder before firing. Slightly coarse pinkish-buff ware, evenly fired. Creamy-buff slip in and out.
3. JR. J.III.c (PM. C.11; TS. 628; Area III, unstratified). Not phased (Bronze Age). Large rim, neck, and shoulder segment with a complete potter's mark incised on the shoulder before firing.
4. JR. J.III.e (PM. C.14; TS. 1524; IIB, 2.10; Phase 15, Period C, Derived Bronze Age). Small rim, neck, and upper shoulder segment with an almost complete X-shaped potter's mark incised at junction of neck and shoulder before firing. Fairly fine pinkish-buff ware with lime and mica grits, evenly fired. Creamy-buff slip out and just over rim in.
5. BE. D.III (PM. A.6; TS. 1165; VE, 1.4; Phase 3 Pit, Period G). About 1/2 of a flat base and lower wall of vessel with a complete potter's mark incised on lower inside wall before firing. Fairly coarse pink ware, evenly fired. Cream slip in.
6. JR.Sh. (IP [G.4] D.III; PM. D.20; TS. 533; IA2, 4.3; Phase 2, Period B, Derived Bronze Age). Jar body sherd with an incomplete potter's mark incised on the outside wall before firing. Fairly coarse pinkish-buff ware, evenly fired. Cream slip in and out.
7. JR.Sh. (IP [G.4] D.III; PM. D.20; SW. 217; IF, 1.22; Phase 1, Period F). Jar body sherd with an incomplete potter's mark incised on the outside wall before firing. Slightly coarse greenish ware, unevenly fired with a yellowish core. Black and white lime grits and burned out vegetable temper.
8. JR.Sh. (PM. C.18 + D.30; TS. 2137; VA, "1.1"; Phase 3, Period E). Jar body sherd with incomplete potter's marks incised on the outside wall before firing. Fairly coarse pink ware, evenly fired. Creamy-buff slip out.
9. JR.Sh. (IP. (G.4) D.III; PM. D.19; TS. 2169; VF, 1.3; Phase 6, Period E). Jar body sherd with an incomplete incised tree or wheat stalk pattern or a potter's mark incised on the outside wall before firing. Slightly coarse light greenish-grayware, evenly fired. Self slip in and out.
10. JR.Sh. (PM. C.11; SC. 3268; IA1, 2.5; Phase 1, Period B, Derived Bronze Age). Jar shoulder sherd with an incomplete potter's mark incised outside before firing. Fairly fine pinkish-buff ware with gold- and silver-colored mica and lime grits, evenly fired. Creamy-buff slip in and out.
11. JR. BE.Sh. (PM. D.6; SC. 3258; IE, 1.8; Phase 3, Period E). Jar base sherd with an incomplete potter's mark incised outside before firing. Fairly fine pinkish-brown ware with many gold- and silver-colored mica and some lime grit, unevenly fired light buff and pinkish-brown outside. Self slip in and out.
12. JR.Sh. (PM. C.11; SC. 3265; IE, 1.8; Phase 3, Period E). Jar shoulder sherd with a complete potter's mark incised outside before firing. Slightly coarse rose-pink ware with a few silver-colored mica and black and white lime grits, fairly evenly fired. Thick creamy-buff slip out.
13. SJR.Sh. (PM. E.2; SC. 3263; IIA, 9.3, Room 8; Phase 4, Period H). Small jar shoulder sherd with an incomplete reed-made potter's mark incised outside before firing. Fine ware with vegetable temper, no visible grit, unevenly fired with gray core and light greenish-buff coloring at surfaces. Smooth self slip out.
14. JR.Sh. (PM. C.14; SC. 3267; IIA, 8.18, Pit E; Phase 5, Period H). Jar shoulder sherd with an incomplete potter's mark incised outside before firing. Slightly coarse ware with many white lime grits and some fine gold-colored mica inclusions, unevenly fired buff out and pinkish-rose in. Remains of creamy-buff slip out.
15. JR.Sh. (PM. D.17; SC. 3262; IIA, 5.13; Phase 8, Period G). Jar shoulder sherd with a nearly complete potter's mark incised outside before firing. Fairly coarse grayish-buff ware with fine gold- and silver-colored mica grits, evenly fired. Cream slip out, soil-stained reddish-brown on all surfaces.
16. SJR.Sh. (PM. D.17; SC. 3264; IIA, 4.13; Phase 13, Period C). Small jar shoulder sherd with an incomplete potter's mark incised outside before firing. Fairly fine pinkish-buff ware with lime and vegetable temper, evenly fired. Creamy-buff slip out.
17. SJR.Sh. (PM. D.3; SC. 3261; VA, "1.1"; Phase 3, Period E). Small jar shoulder sherd with an incomplete potter's mark incised outside before firing. Slightly coarse pink ware with lime and vegetable temper, evenly fired. Buff slip out.
18. JR.Sh. (PM. D.14; SC. 3259; VB, 1.1; Phase 4, Period C, Derived Bronze Age). Jar shoulder sherd with a nearly complete potter's mark incised outside before firing. Slightly coarse pinkish-buff ware with lime grits, evenly fired.
19. JR.Sh. (PM. D.3; SC. 3260; VB, 1.2; Phase 3, Period E). Jar shoulder sherd with a nearly complete potter's mark incised outside before firing. Fairly coarse pinkish-orange ware with lime and a few visible small mica grits, evenly fired. Creamy-green slip out.
20. JR.Sh. (PM. B.2; SC. 3266; VF, 1.1; Phase 9, Period C, Derived Bronze Age). Jar shoulder sherd with about one half of a potter's mark incised outside before firing. Slightly coarse pink ware with a considerable number of both small and large lime grits, evenly fired. Biege-colored self slip in and out.
21. JR. BE.Sh. (PM. D.4; SC. 3257; VF/G, 1.1; Phase 9, Period C, Derived Bronze Age). Jar shoulder sherd with a nearly complete potter's mark incised outside before firing. Fairly fine dark pinkish-brown ware with many gold- and silver-colored mica grits and vegetable temper, evenly fired. Creamy-buff slip out.
22. JR.Sh. (PM. D.17; SC. 3269; VG, 1.4; Phase 6, Period E). Jar shoulder sherd with an incomplete potter's mark shallowly incised outside before firing. Fairly fine pinkish-buff ware with fine lime grit temper, evenly fired. Creamy-green slip out.
23. JR.Sh. (PM. D.28; SC. 3251; VB, 1.1; Phase 4, Period C, Derived Bronze Age). Jar body sherd with a triangular-shaped potter's mark incised on the outside wall before firing. Salmon-pink ware with gold-colored mica grits, evenly fired. Self slip in and out.

Figure 333

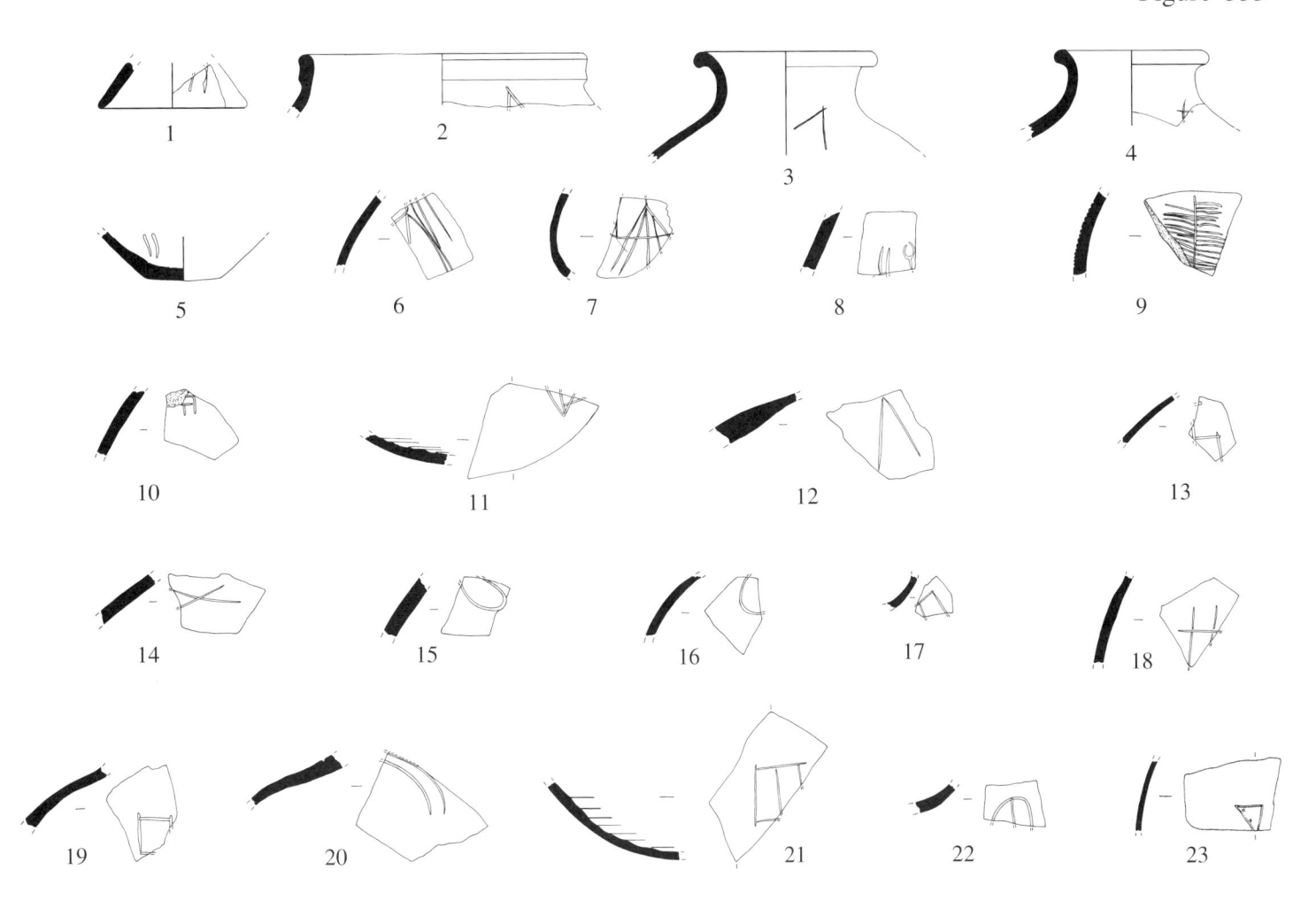

Potters' Marks on Miscellaneous Vessels and Sherds from Areas I, II, III, IV, and V. Scale 1:5

Figure 334. Selected Pottery from the Western Sector of the Lower Town, Operation 4 (Phase 1; Period F — Early Bronze Age IVa)

1. SBR. A.I.d (TS. 3423; Op. 4, 22.1). Small rim and upper wall segment. Ware description not available.
2. SBR. A.I.d (TS. 3424; Op. 4, 22.1). About 1/2 rim and upper wall segment. Ware description not available.
3. SBR. A.I.e (TS. 3408; Op. 4, 36.1). About 1/5 rim and complete wall profile; base missing. Fairly fine pink ware with small lime and gold-colored mica grits, unevenly fired gray at core. Cream slip from lip of rim to 6 cm below on outside wall.
4. SBR. B.I.b (TS. 3428; Op. 4, 32). About 1/3 rim and most of wall profile; base missing. Ware description not available.
5. BR. A.I.f (TS. 3411; Op. 4, 35). About 1/8 rim and upper wall segment. Ware description not available.
6. BR. E.III.a (TS. 3425; Op. 4, 22.1). Nearly complete profile of a bowl with a low ring base. Ware description not available.
7. BR. E.IV.b (TS. 3421; Op. 4, 22.1). About 1/4 rim and upper wall segment. Ware description not available.
8. BR. H.I.a (TS. 3429; Op. 4, 22.1). Small segment of rim and upper wall. Ware description not available.
9. BR. L.I.a (TS. 3417; Op. 4, 32.3). About 1/3 rim and upper wall segment. Ware description not available.
10. BR. L.I.a (TS. 3420; Op. 4, 22.1). Small rim and upper wall segment. Ware description not available.
11. BR. L.I.a (TS. 3426; Op. 4, 32). About 1/2 rim and considerable portion of wall profile. Ware description not available.
12. SJR. B.IV.b (SW. 831; Op. 4, 33.1). Complete small jar. Ware description not available.
13. SJR. C.II.o (SW. 838; Op. 4, 32). Complete small jar. Ware description not available.
14. JR. E.II.g (TS. 3422; Op. 4, 22.1). Segment of rim and upper shoulder of a jar. Ware description not available.
15. JR. O.I.d (TS. 3409; Op. 4, 23.1). Segment of rim and top of shoulder of a large jar. Ware description not available.
16. CP. A.I.b (TS. 3416; Op. 4, 32.3). About 1/6 rim and upper shoulder of a cooking pot with a triangular-shaped handle attached to the top outer side of the rim. Ware description not available.

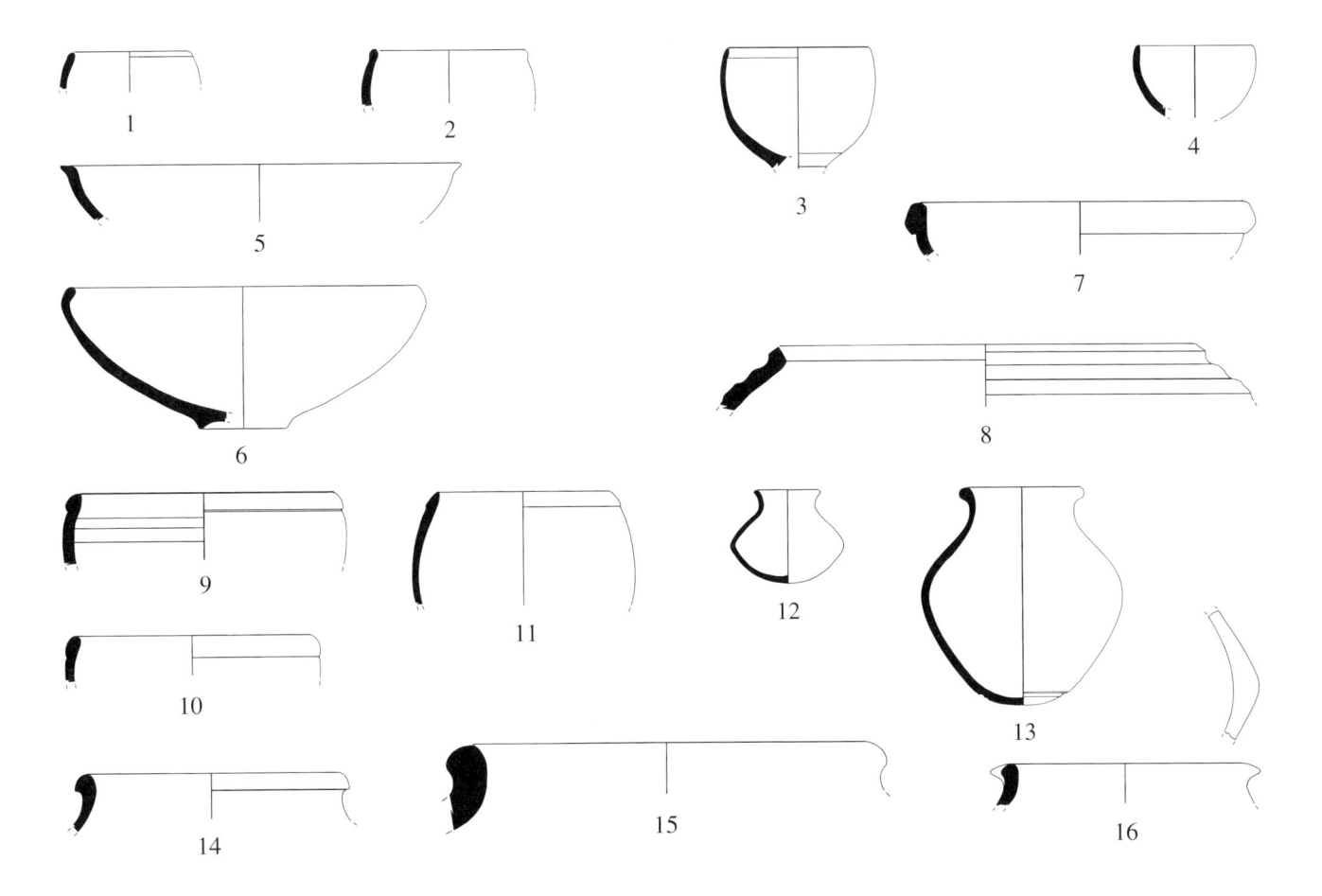

Figure 334

Selected Pottery from the Western Sector of the Lower Town, Operation 4 (Phase 1; Period F — Early Bronze Age IVa).
Scale 1:5

Figure 335. Selected Pottery from the Western Sector of the Lower Town, Operation 4 (Phase 2; Period F — Early Bronze Age IVa)

1. SBR. A.I.c (TS. 3404; Op. 4, 5.4). Nearly complete small bowl/cup with concave disk base. Ware description not available.
2. SBR. A.I.e (TS. 3412; Op. 4, 7.1). About 1/2 rim and all of the body extant. A potter's mark, Type A. 11, was incised on the lower outside wall before firing. Fairly coarse buff ware with lime and mica grits, evenly fired. Light creamy-green slip in and out (inside heavily salt encrusted).
3. SBR. A.I.e (TS. 3414; Op. 4, 17.1). Small rim segment and most of wall profile. Ware description not available.
4. BR. E.II.b (TS. 3413; Op. 4, 17.1). About 1/5 rim and upper wall segment. Ware description not available.
5. BR. F.IV.c (TS. 3284; Op. 4, 3.1). Small rim and upper wall segment. Ware description not available.
6. SJR. A.II.f (TS. 3394; Op. 4, 7.1). Three-footed small jar reconstructed from many broken fragments found in situ. About 1/4 rim, 1/2 body, and all three legs recovered. Fairly fine buff ware, unevenly fired pink at patches in the core. Fine white lime and gold-colored mica grits fired mostly buff at surfaces. Self creamy-buff slip in and out. Irregular and unevenly scored lines cover all of the interior of the vessel beginning between 6 and 7 cm below the rim. The flat base was string-cut from the potter's wheel and the three legs were added by hand (cf. one similar leg found in Area IVP, Room 9, Phase 2B, fig. 84:5). Some clay at the tops of the legs covers the edge of the flat base. The decoration around the shoulder of the vessel consists of fairly deep (ca. 3 mm) tool-incised crisscross lines.
7. SJR. B.IV.b (TS. 3419; Op. 4, 18). About 2/3 rim and most of wall profile. Ware description not available.
8. JR. H.I.n (TS. 3430; Op. 4, 13.1). About 1/6 rim and shoulder segment of a large jar with impressed decoration outside representing myth-like beasts (cf. similar decorative technique used on Jar JR. H.I.g [SW. 294; fig. 64:4] from the Area IV building in the inner town of Tell es-Sweyhat). Ware description not available.
9. JR. J.III.f (TS. 3287; Op. 4, 3.1). Small rim and neck segment. Ware description not available.
10. JR. K.II.b (TS. 3280; Op. 4, 3.1). Small rim, neck, and upper shoulder segment. Ware description not available.
11. JR. Q.I.b (TS. 3288; Op. 4, 3.1). Small rim and neck segment. Ware description not available.
12. Bt. A.I.b (TS. 3405; Op. 4, 13.2). Complete rim and neck segment. Coarse grayware with fine lime and mica grits, evenly fired. Very friable due to burning in antiquity. Ware description not available.
13. CP.Hd. E.I.b (TS. 3415; Op. 4, 2). Fragment of a cooking pot body sherd with portion of a thick, triangular-shaped ledge handle attached to the outer wall of the vessel (cf. CP. C.I.b, SW. 484, from Area IVK, Room 2, pl. 281:2). Ware description not available.
14. CP.Hd. E.I.b (TS. 3492; Op. 4, 5.4). Fragment of a cooking pot body sherd with a complete triangular-shaped ledge handle attached to the outer wall of the vessel. Coarse pinkish-brown ware with many medium-sized silver-colored mica and white lime grits, evenly fired. Traces of burnishing on self slip on inside wall opposite the ledge handle.
15. Type SV.3 (SW. 840; Op. 4, Surface, Lower Town, 3.00 m east of Operation 4). Fragment of a zoomorphic vessel with a boar's head. See pl. 103:c and compare the similar type from Area I, Trench C (pl. 103:b). Ware description not available.

Figure 335

Selected Pottery from the Western Sector of the Lower Town, Operation 4 (Phase 2; Period F — Early Bronze Age IVa).
Scale 1:5

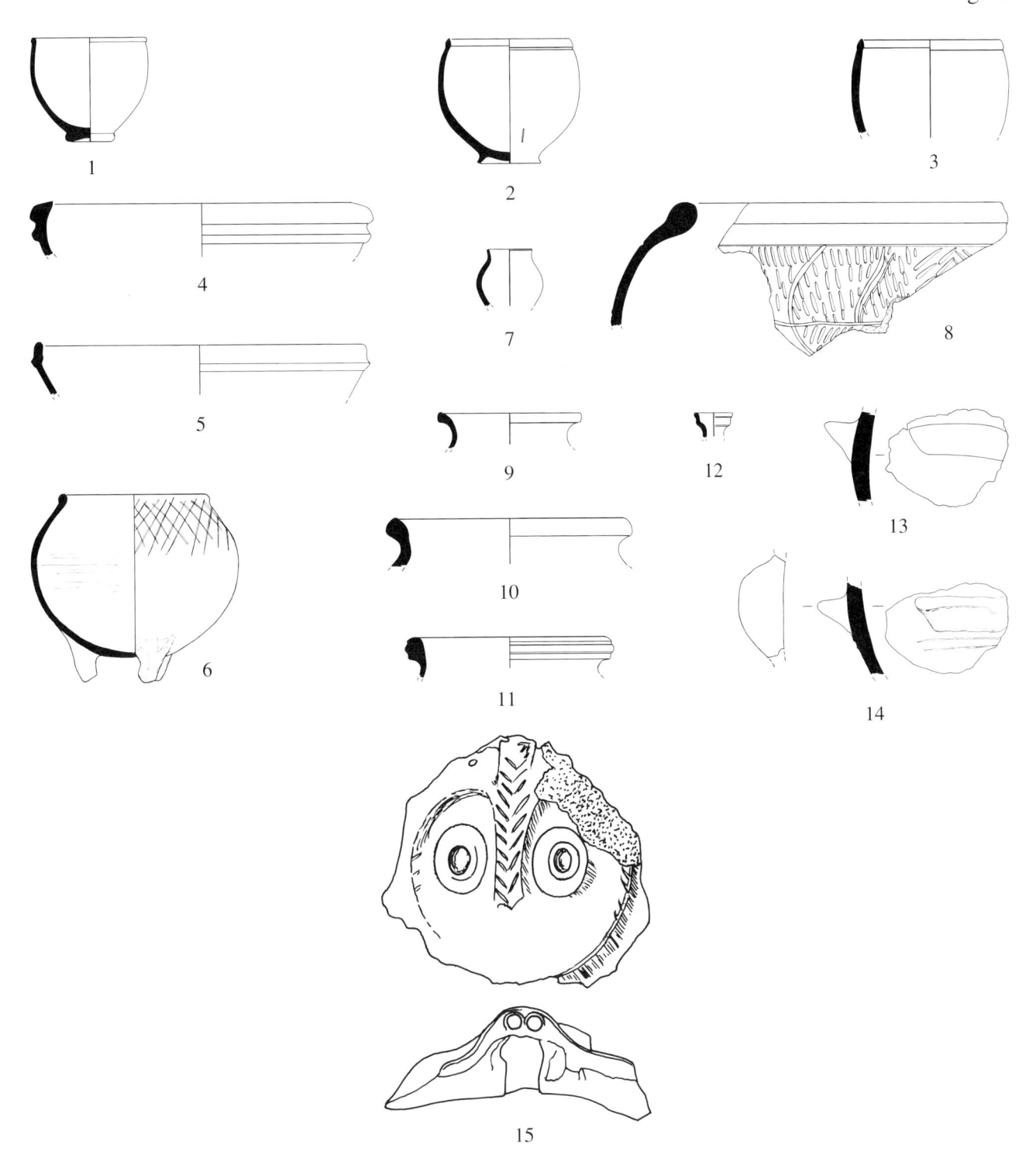

Plate 1

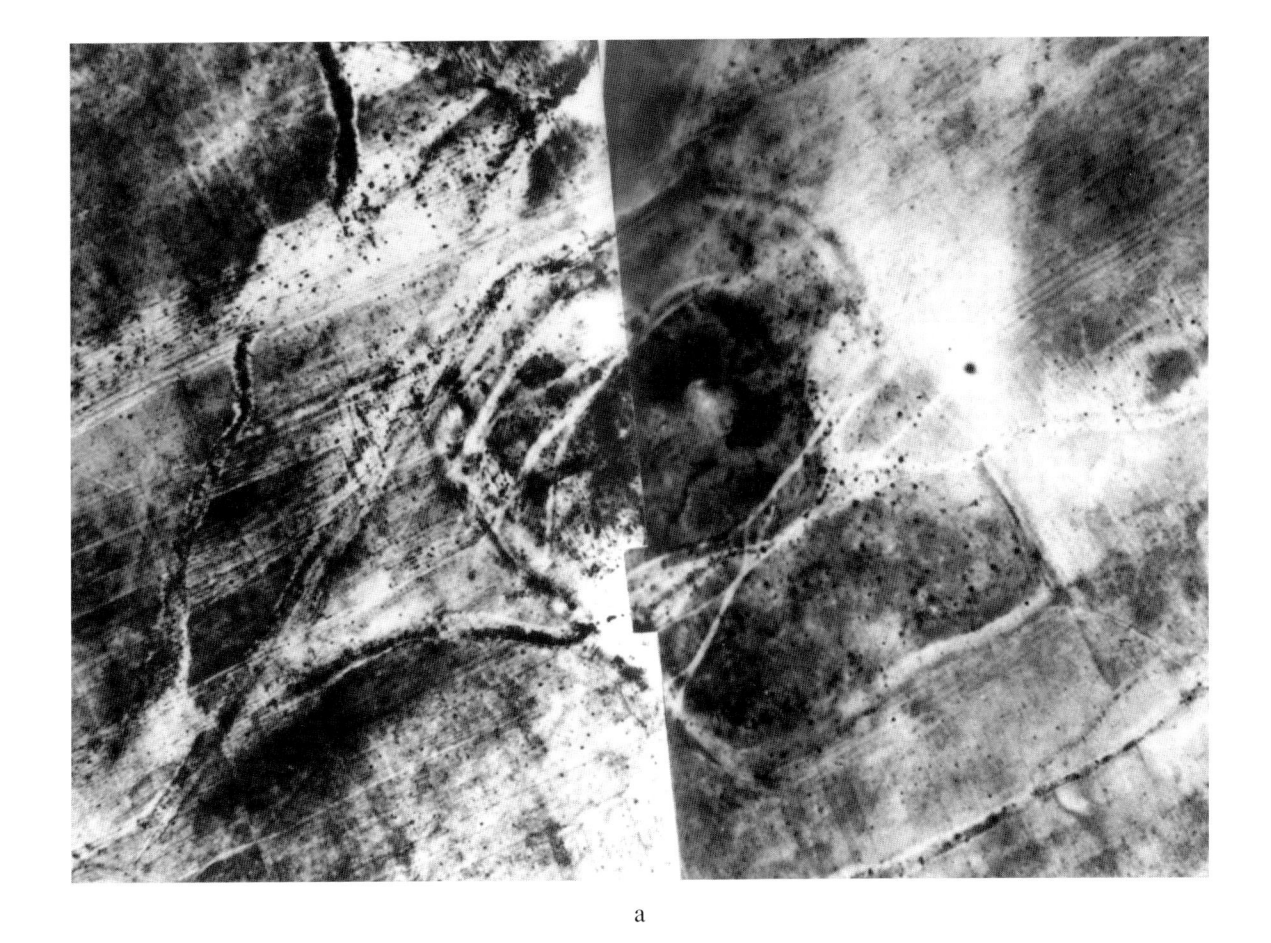

(*a*) Aerial View (ca. mid-1960s) of Tell es-Sweyhat and (*b*) View of the Central Mound from the Southwest with Uppermost Bluffs Surrounding the Sweyhat Plain East of the Mound

Plate 2

(*a*) View of the Central Mound from the Southwest Showing Area IV on the Extreme Left, Area I in the Center, and Lower Town in the Foreground; (*b*) Aerial View of Khirbet Dhiman, an Islamic Site Southwest of Tell es-Sweyhat; and (*c*) Aerial view of Khirbet al-Hamrah, an Islamic Site Northeast of Tell es-Sweyhat

Plate 3

(*a*) General North View of Trench VIA, Surface Stone Foundations, Wall 1, and (*b*) General East View of Trench VIA, Phase 5, Mudbrick Wall Remains

Plate 4

(*a*) General View of Trench VIA, Southeast End of the Area Investigated with Inner City Mound in the Background to the Northwest, and (*b*) Close-up View of Trench VIA, Phase 3, Wall 6 Stone Foundations, and Phase 1, Mudbrick Wall 5 and South Portion of the West Section

Plate 5

(*a*) Trench VIA, Phase 1 Wall 5 (center right), with Excavated Pit for a Cooking Pot (CP. B.IV.b, fig. 12:1) in Right Lower Foreground, and (*b*) Close-up View of Trench VIA, Top of Wall 6 Stone Foundations and Remains of Mudbrick Superstructure in the East Section

Plate 6

(*a*) General View of Trench VIIB to Left and Trench VIIA to Right Viewed Toward the Euphrates River and Jebel Aruda in Far Left Background, and (*b*) Close-up West View of Trench VIIA, Stone Foundations for Phase 4, Wall 1, in Foreground, and Wall 3 Against the North Section

Plate 7

(*a*) Close-up of Trench VIIA, Phase 4 Wall 1 Stone Foundations and Partial Excavation of Phase 3 Occupation Below (West View), and (*b*) General East View of Trench VIIA, Phases 3, 4, and 5 Occupation Levels

Plate 8

(*a*) General North View of Trench VIIIB Across Northern Portion of Outer Defensive Wall and Trench VIIIA Across Southern Portion of Defensive Wall in Foreground, and (*b*) Close-up View of Trench VIIIA, Buttress Wall 3 North of Wall 1

Plate 9

(*a*) South View from Trench VIIIB Toward Trench VIIIA, Phase 1, Wall 1, and (*b*) Trench VIIIA, Phases 1 and 2, Occupation Levels Between Walls 1 and 2 Viewed to the North

Plate 10

(*a*) Close-up South View of Trench VIIIA, Buttress Wall 3 and Phase 2, Occupation Levels to the Right, and
(*b*) Trench VIIIA, Phases 1, 2, and 3, Occupation Levels Viewed to the East

Plate 11

(*a*) General North View of Trench VIIIB from Trench VIIIA with Stone Wall 4 in Far Background, and (*b*) Close-up South View of Stone Wall 4 with Trench VIIIA in Background Below Level of the Landrover

Plate 12

a

b

(*a*) General Southeastern View of Trench XIB and Surface Stone Enclosure Walls on the Central Mound with Nefilah Village in the Distant Background, and (*b*) Close-up Southeastern View of Trench XIA, Locus 1.3 Stone Wall Foundations

Plate 13

a

b

(*a*) Trench IC, Pit B at Base of Deep Sounding Through the Western Half of the 5.00 × 5.00 m Square (East View), and (*b*) Trench IC, Upper Surviving Course of Mudbrick Wall D (Northwest View)

Plate 14

(*a*) South End of Trench IC, West Section Showing Remains of Mudbrick Wall D (West View), and (*b*) Trench IC, North End of the West Section Showing Remains of Mudbrick Wall D and Top of Pit A (West View)

Plate 15

(*a*) Trench IC, Stone Foundations of the Latest Excavated Walls A and B with Trench IB in Background (East View), and (*b*) Trench IC, Stone Foundations of the Latest Excavated Walls A and B (North View)

Plate 16

*a*

*b*

(*a*) Trench IIA, Close-up View of the 5.00 × 5.00 m Square after Removal of the Topsoil (Northwest View), and (*b*) General View of Trench IIA, Deep Sounding, West End with 3 m High Access Ladder Showing Lowest Undercut Phases 1 and 2 (Southwest View)

Plate 17

(*a*) General View of Trench IIA, Deep Sounding, East End Showing Phases 1, 2, and 3 in the Lowest Levels (East View), and (*b*) Trench IIA, Deep Sounding, West Section Showing Successive Rebuilding of Walls B and Y During Phases 1 to 4 (West View)

Plate 18

a

b

(*a*) Trench IIA, Deep Sounding, Phase 3, Stone Foundations for Wall Y (Southwest View), and (*b*) Trench IIA, Deep Sounding, Phase 6, Room 9 Walls and Doorway (East View)

Plate 19

(*a*) Trench IIA, Deep Sounding, Phase 10, Pit 7.2 (South View), and (*b*) Trench IIA, Deep Sounding, Phase 11, Hellenistic Stone-paved Street and Stone Collapse (Southeast View)

Plate 20

a

b

(*a*) Trench IIA, Deep Sounding, Phase 11, Hellenistic Stone-paved Street and Top Western Edge of Pit C (Northwest View), and (*b*) Trench IIA, East Quadrant of Square, Phase 12, Hellenistic Pit C in East Section (East View)

Plate 21

(*a*) Trench IIA, Deep Sounding, Phase 13, Hellenistic Pit B in South Section (South View), and (*b*) Trench IIA, Latest Surviving Occupation Level with Architecture, Phase 14, Hellenistic Room and Enclosures (Southwest View)

Plate 22

a

b

(*a*) General View of Area IV from the Outer Town (Southeast View) and (*b*) Aerial Kite View of Area IV and Operations 1, 2, 6, 7, and 8, Photographed during the 1991 Excavations by Anwar Ghafour (Aleppo National Museum)

Plate 23

(*a*) General View of Trenches IVC, B, and D Showing Mudbrick Fortification Tower and Inner City Town Wall (East View), and (*b*) Trench IVC, Stone Foundations Under Western Side of Mudbrick Fortification Tower (East View)

Plate 24

a

b

(*a*) Trench IVB, Sounding in Mudbrick Fortification Tower Showing Stone Foundations (East View), and (*b*) Trench IVD, Pit Cut into Town Wall in Foreground and East Section Showing Collapsed Wall Mudbricks into Trench IVK, Room 2 (East View)

Plate 25

a

b

(*a*) Trench IVB, East Section Showing East–West Wall Between Trench IVF, Room 1, and Trench IVK, Room 2 (East View), and (*b*) Trench IVF, Room 1, Phases 2A and 2B, East Wall Connecting Room 1, and Trench IVN, Room 8 (East View)

Plate 26. (*a*) Trench IVF, Room 1, Phase 2A, Floor and East Wall North of Central Door (East View), and (*b*) Trench IVF, Room 1, Phase 2A, Floor and East Wall South of Central Door with Upturned Stone Door Socket (East View)

Plate 27

Trenches IVF and IVN, Rooms 1 and 8, Completely Excavated Doorway Showing Paving Stones in Front of Unexcavated Workbench in Room 8 (Southeast View)

Plate 28

(*a*) Trenches IVF and IVM, Phase 2B, Doorway Connecting Rooms 1 and 7 (North View), and (*b*) Trench IVF, Room 1, Phase 2A, Niche in Eastern Side of Town Wall and Stone Door Socket on the Floor (West View)

Plate 29

a

b

(*a*) Trenches IVJ, K, L, and Q, Rooms 2–6, Phase 2A, General View Showing Partially Excavated Storage Bin (Room 5) in Foreground, Rooms 4 and 6 in Midground, and North Walls of Rooms 2 and 3 Shown Behind and to the Right of the Vertical Foot Scale in the Background (North View); and (*b*) Trenches IVL and IVP, Rooms 3 and 9, General View Showing Partially Excavated Rooms (North View)

Plate 30. (*a*) View of Trench IVJ, Room 4, Phase 2A, Stone-built Bench Constructed Against Inner Face of Town Wall (West View), and (*b*) Trench IVJ, Room 4, Phase 2B: Pottery in situ on Clay Platform Between Town Wall and Buttress (North View)

Plate 31. (*a*) Trench IVJ, Room 4, Phase 2A, Door Between Rooms 4 and 2 with Buttress to the Left of the Door (North View), and (*b*) Trench IVJ, Room 4, Phase 2A, Floor and Remaining Plaster Coating on East Wall of Room (East View)

Plate 32

(a) Trench IVJ, Room 4, Phase 2A, Northeast Corner of Room with Jar (JR. E.II.r; SW. 524; pls. 92c, 243:10) in Doorway and Small Jar (SJR. C.II.i; fig. 66:3) in Northeast Corner (East View); and (b) Trench IVJ, Room 4, Phase 2A, South Side of Room with Pottery Vessels in situ (East View)

Plate 33

Trench IVJ, Room 4, Phase 2A, South Side of Room with Pottery Vessels in situ (South View)

Plate 34

(*a*) Trench IVJ, Storage Bin, Room 5, Phase 2A, Jar (JR. J.III.t; SW. 567; pls. 95c, 254:1) and Cup (SBR. A.I.c; SW. 568; pl. 205:3) in situ on Floor (East View), and (*b*) Trench IVJ, Storage Bin, Room 5, and Trench IVO, Room 10 to Right of the South Wall (East View)

Plate 35

a

b

Plate 35. (*a*) Trench IVK, Room 2, Phase 2A, Stone-built Bench Constructed Against Inner Face of Town Wall (West View), and (*b*) Trench IVK, Room 2, Phase 2B, General View of Floor in Northeastern Sector of Room with Pottery in situ and Trench IVD Sounding into Phase 2A in Foreground (Northeast View)

Plate 36

a

b

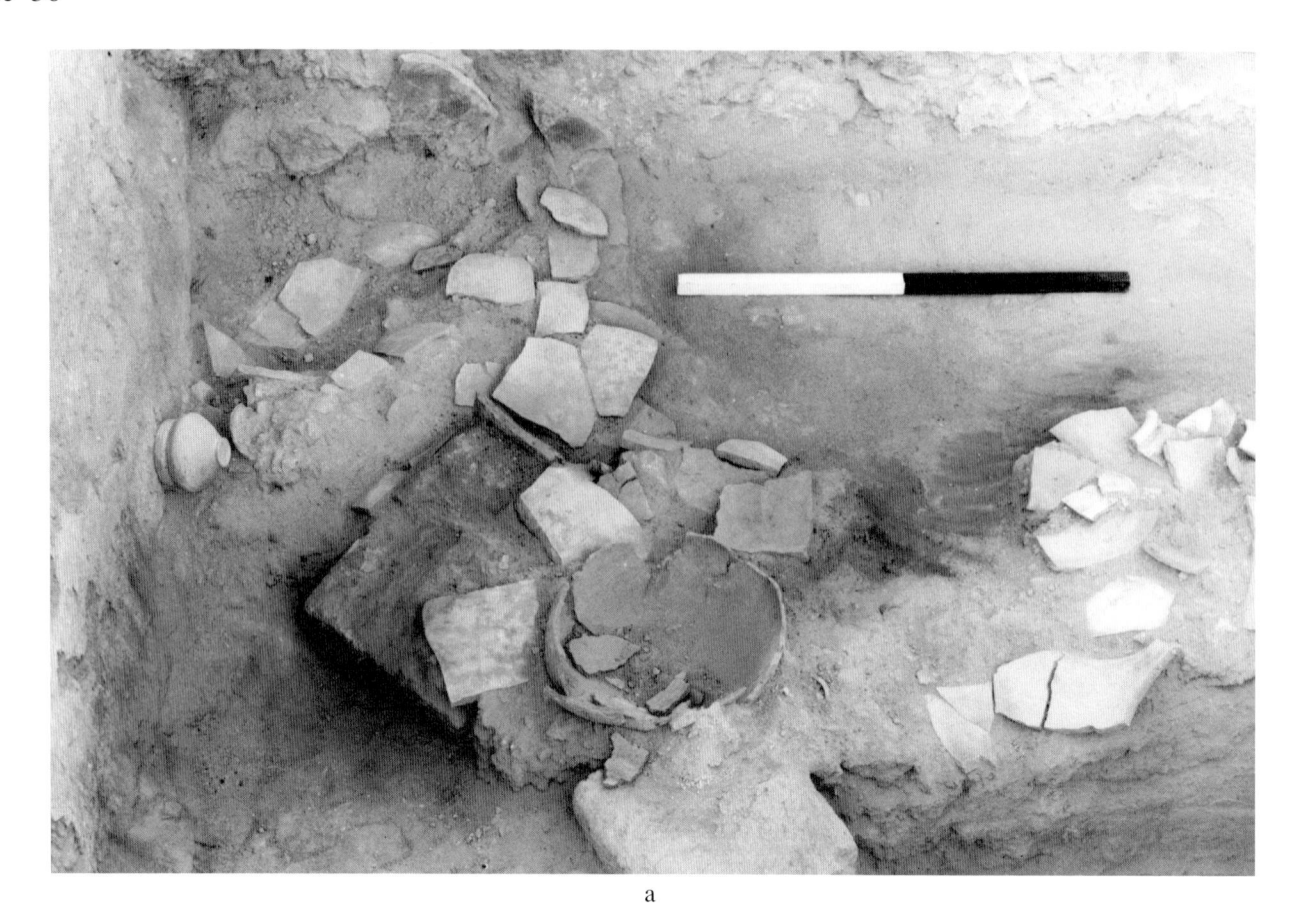

(*a*) Trench IVK, Room 2, Phase 2B, Close-up View of Floor in Northeastern Sector of Room with Mudbricks Used as Working Surfaces (East View), and (*b*) Trench IVL, Room 3, Buttress Supporting Western Wall North of the Doorway (West View)

Plate 37

(*a*) Trench IVL, Room 3, Plaster-covered Workbench in Northeast Corner of Room, Wall Niche Above and Left of Bench, and a Phase 3 Pit Cut through a Portion of the East Wall to the Right (North View), and (*b*) Trench IVL, Room 3, Unexcavated Door in Center of East Wall Showing Position of Northern Doorjamb and Posthole (East View)

Plate 38

Trenches IVM and X, Room 7, Sounding in Western Side of Room Showing North Section of Phases 1A, 1B (Cooking Pot [TS. 1741a–b; fig. 56:6] to right of meter pole), and 1C; North Half of Trench IVX in Upper Background (North View)

Plate 39

a

b

(*a*) Trench IVM, Room 7, Large Niche in Western Wall (eastern face of Town Wall) of Room (West View), and (*b*) Trench IVM, Room 7, Phase 1A, Pit C Cut into Bedrock (South View)

Plate 40

(*a*) Trench IVM, Room 7, Southeast Quadrant of Room Showing Threshold of Doorway into Trench IVN, Room 8 (East View, scale pole in feet), and (*b*) Trench IVM, Room 7, Southeast Quadrant of Room Showing Phase 2A Pit A in Right Foreground (East View)

Plate 41

(*a*) Trench IVN, Room 18, View of Partially Excavated North Side of Arch and Adjoining Bench at Lower Left with Remains of South Side of Arch Extending Out from the South Section Behind the Meter Pole to the Right (East View), and (*b*) Trench IVN, Rooms 8 and 18, General View of the South Section Showing Remains of the Mudbrick-built Arch at the Far Left with Collapsed Mudbricks from the Eastern Wall Over the Arch and into the Western Sector of the Rooms (South View, scale pole in feet)

Plate 42

*a*

*b*

(*a*) Trench IVN, Rooms 8 and 18, General View of the North Section Showing the Collapsed Mudbricks from the Eastern Wall Over the Arch and into the Western Sector of the Rooms (modern access steps cut into the ancient debris depicted to the right of the foot scale pole), and (*b*) Trench IVN, Room 18, Lower Courses of the North Side of the Arch and Bench in the Center of Room 18 (East View)

Plate 43

(*a*) Trench IVN, Room 18, South Side of Arch and Doorway into Trench IVP, Room 9 (South View), and (*b*) Trench IVN (Operation 10), Rooms 18 and 8, Jar Support Hole in Floor of Southeast Corner of Room 18, Stone Foundations of Southern Half of Arch, Doorway into Room 9, and Workbench Against Southern Wall of Room 8 Excavated During the 1992 Season (South View)

Plate 44

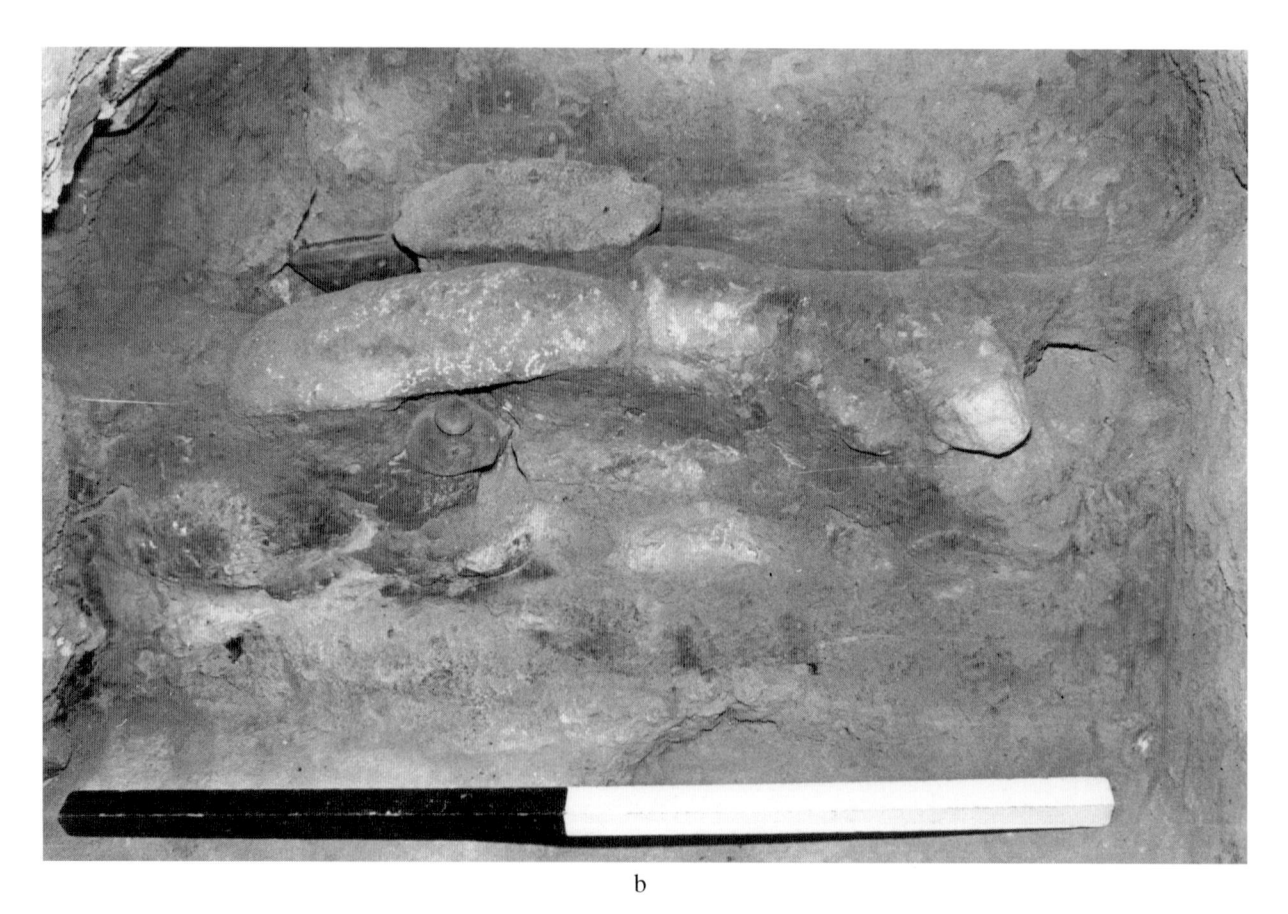

(*a*) Trench IVN (Operation 10), Room 18 in Foreground and Western Portion of Room 8 in Background Showing Completely Excavated Workbench along the Base of the Southern Wall to the Left (West View), and (*b*) Trench IVN, Room 8, Western End of the Workbench Excavated in 1975 with Stone Grinders and Strainer Bowl (SR. C.I.a, SW. 725, pl. 290:16) in situ (South View)

Plate 45

(*a*) Trench IVN, Room 8, Close-up of Central Portion of Workbench and Numerous Plastered Floor Surfaces with Large Flat Paving Stones in Front and Vessel Support Holes in the Floor (South View), and (*b*) Trench IVN (Operation 10), Room 18, General View Showing Completely Excavated Room (East View)

Plate 46

(*a*) Trench IVN (Operation 10), Room 8, General View Showing Base of Northern Side of Arch and Doorway to the Right into Room 8 (North View), and (*b*) Trench IVN (Operation 10), Room 18, Close-up View of Northeastern Doorway Partially Blocked with Stones and One Half of a Grinding Stone on the Right-hand Side of the Base of the Arch (North View)

Plate 47

Trench IVN (Operation 10), Sounding Northeast of Room 18, Stone Foundations and Remains of Mudbrick Superstructure of East–West Wall Likely Constructed on Top of the North, Unexcavated, Wall of Room 8 (North View)

Plate 48

a

b

(*a*) Trench IVQ, Room 6, General View of South Side of Room Showing Phase 2A Bench and Working Platform, Phase 2B Destruction, and Phase 3 Stone Foundations Built on Top of the Southern Wall of Room 6 (South View), and
(*b*) Trench IVQ, Room 6, Close-up View of the Phase 3 Foundation Trench for the Stones Supporting the Mudbrick Wall Constructed on Top of the Southern Wall of Room 6 in Use During Phases 2A and 2B (Southeast View)

Plate 49

a

b

(*a*) Trench IVQ, Room 6, Stone Door Socket in situ on Phase 2A Floor (South View), and
(*b*) Trench IVQ, Room 6, Phase 2A Pottery Vessels in situ on the Floor (Southeast View)

Plate 50

a

b

(*a*) Trench IVO, Room 10, General View of East Wall of the Room Showing Unexcavated Doorway in the Middle (East View, scale pole in feet), and (*b*) Trench IVR, Room 11A, Phase 3 Type Series Jar (JR. O.II.b, SW. 711, pl. 263:2) in situ in the Southwest Side of the Room (North View)

Plate 51

*a*

*b*

(*a*) Trench IVP, Room 9, Western End of Room Showing Unexcavated Central Doorway to Right of Scale Pole and North Side of Western Wall Destroyed by Later Pit; South End of Western Wall Removed During Excavation of Trench IVH (West View, scale pole in feet), and (*b*) Trench IVP, Room 9, Northwest Corner of Room Showing the Phase 2A Doorway into Room 18 Blocked and Plastered during Phase 2B and Unexcavated Square Niche to Right of Meter Pole (North View)

Plate 52

(*a*) Trench IVP, Room 9, Northwest Corner of Room Showing the Blocked and Partially Excavated Phase 2A Doorway into Room 18 (North View), and (*b*) Trench IVP, Room 9, Northwest Corner of Room Showing Full Extent of the Phase 2A Doorway ino Room 18 Blocked on the South with a Large Jar (JR. O.II.b, SW. 737; fig. 73:2) and Mudbricks (North View)

Plate 53

Area IV (Operation 6), Courtyard Room 9, General View of the Phase 2B Oven (Southeast View)

Plate 54

*a*

*b*

(*a*) Area IV (Operation 6), Rooms 16 and 17, General View Upon Completion of Excavation (Southeast View) and (*b*) Area IV (Operation 6) Rooms 16 and 17, Close-up View Showing Stone Foundations of Phase 3 Mudbrick Walls in the Foreground with the Excavator, Emma Murray, Sitting on the Surviving Portion of the Phases 2A and 2B Wall (Northwest View)

Plate 55

(*a*) Area IV (Operation 6), Room 16, General View Showing the Phase 2A Room with Bench against the Western Wall and the Sounding into Phases 1B and 1C (North View), and (*b*) Area IV (Operation 6), General View Showing the Buttress in Courtyard Room 9 at the Center Right and the Operation 2 Trench on the Right with the Inner Town Ring Road (North View)

Plate 56

(*a*) Area IV (Operation 6), General View North Showing Partial Collapse of the Fill in the Unexcavated Northeast Doorway of Room 9 (North View), and (*b*) Area IV (Operation 6), Close-up View Showing the Buttress (center right) and Partial Collapse of the Fill in the Unexcavated Northeast Doorway of Room 9 (in center background, left of the Draughtsman, John Ellsworth) (Northwest View)

Plate 57

Area IV (Operation 7). General View of 10.00 × 10.00 m Square with Phase 2B Architectural Remains on the Left Side and Phase 2A Architectural Remains on the Right Side (West View, scale pole in feet)

Plate 58

a

b

(*a*) Area IV (Operation 7), General View of 10.00 × 10.00 m Square with Phase 2A Architectural Remains on the Left Side and Phase 2B Remains on the Right Side (East View, scale pole in feet), and (*b*) Area IV (Operation 7), General View of 10.00 × 10.00 m Square with Partially Excavated Town Wall, Upper Left, and Partially Excavated Phases 2A, B, and 3 in Upper Background (North View, scale pole in feet)

Plate 59

(*a*) Trench IXA, Phase 4, Pottery in situ (South View), and (*b*) Trench IXA, Phase 4, Pottery in situ (West View)

Plate 60

(*a*) Trench IXA, General East View of Trench (scale pole in feet), and (*b*) Trench IXA, Close-up View of East End of Trench (scale poles in meters)

Plate 61

(*a*) Trench IXA, General West View of Trench (scale pole in feet), and (*b*) Trench IXA, Close-up View of West End of Trench (scale poles in meters)

Plate 62

(*a*) Trench IXA, General South View of Phase 2A Stone Foundations for Walls 6 and 8 and Wall 7 and Phase 4 Pit A in the South Section (scale pole in feet), and (*b*) Trench IXA, Close-up View of West Side of Pit A and Wall 7 Stone Foundations Extending into the South Section (scale pole in feet)

Plate 63

(*a*) Trench XA, Room 15, Inner Mudbrick Face of Phase 2A Town Wall with Stone Foundations of Later Phase 3 Wall on Top and Room 15 in the Foreground (West View), and (*b*) Trench XA, Room 15, Southern Mudbrick Wall of Room 15 Shown Obliquely in the South Section with its Stone Foundations in the Foreground after the Removal of the Mudbrick Superstructure (South View)

Plate 64

(*a*) Trench XA, Room 15, Close-up of the Stone Foundations for the South and West Mudbrick Walls 3 and 2 (South View), and (*b*) Trench XA (Operation 11), General View of Enlarged North Side of Trench XA During 1992 Showing the Remains of Mudbrick Wall 3 at Far Right (Northeast View)

Plate 65

(*a*) Trench XA (Operation 11), General View of Operation 11 Showing Partially Excavated Phase 2B Room 20 at Far Left and Room 17 to the Right of the North–South Wall Topped with Phase 3 Wall Foundation Stones (South View), and (*b*) Trench XA (Operation 11), General Central Eastern View Showing Sounding into Phases 2A and 1C to the Left of Wall 3 (East View)

Plate 66

a

b

(*a*) Trench XA (Operation 11), Close-up of the Sounding into Phases 2A and 1C (Northeast View), and (*b*) Trench XA (Operation 11), Phase 3 Stone Basin in situ with Phase 4 Wall Foundation Stones in Foreground (East View)

Plate 67

(*a*) Trench IVZ(S), Phase 3, Wall with Flat Stone Threshold and Pottery in situ on Floor (West View), and
(*b*) Trench IVZ(N1): Phase 2B Wall C at Left and Phase 2A Stone Wall Foundations at Right (South View)

Plate 68

a

b

(*a*) Trench IVZ(N2), Phase 3, Portion of Room 21 with Stone Wall Foundations and Threshold in Foreground and Some Pottery Vessels in situ (Southeast View), and (*b*) South Sector of the Central Mound Showing the Stone Foundations of the Roman Period Buildings Protruding from the Modern Surface Soil (South View)

Plate 69

(*a*) Area III, General View from Top of Central Mound (Northeast View), and (*b*) Area III, General View of Squares A–E at Right Foreground and Step Trench, Area V, at Left Foreground (North View)

Plate 70

a

b

(*a*) Trench IIIA, Phase 3, Wall 5 (South View), and (*b*) Trench IIIA, Phase 4, Walls 1 and 2 Showing Door and Socket Stone (South View)

Plate 71

*a*

*b*

(*a*) Trench IIIB, Phase 3, Destruction Levels Above the Phase 2B Occupation Shown in the Western Part of the North Section (North View), and (*b*) Trench IIIB, Phase 3, Destruction Levels Above the Phase 2B Occupation Shown in the Eastern Part of the North Section (North View)

Plate 72

(*a*) Trench IIIB, Phase 2B, Stone Foundations for Wall 3 (West View), and
(*b*) Trench IIIB, Phase 5, Stones on Top of Storage Pit (West View)

Plate 73

(*a*) Trench IIIB, Phase 4, Wall 1 (Southeast View), and (*b*) Trench IIIB, Phase 5, Close-up View of Hearth Attached to Wall 1 (Southeast View)

Plate 74

(*a*) Trench IIIC, Phase 4, Walls 13 and 15 (Foreground Left), 14 (Center), and Wall 8A, Below Phase 5 Wall 8B (Right Background) (South View), and (*b*) Trench IIIC, General View of Phases 4 and 5 Walls (West View)

Plate 75

*a*

*b*

(*a*) Trench IIID, Stone Foundations of Phase 5 Walls 1, 2, and 4 (Northwest View), and (*b*) Trench IIID, Stone Foundations of Phase 4 Walls 7 (Left) and 8 (Central Background) and Phase 5 Walls 1 and 2 (Southeast View)

Plate 76

a

b

Plate 76. (*a*) Trench IIID, Pottery and Stone Objects in situ on Phase 4, Floor 5.6, Bounded by Walls 7 and 8 (Northwest View), and (*b*) Trench IIID, General View of Phase 4, Floor 5.6, After Removal of the Finds (Northwest View)

Plate 77

(*a*) Trench IIIG/H, Close-up View of Plastered Face of Phase 3 Wall P in Courtyard Room 1 (Southeast View), and
(*b*) Trench IIIG/H, Close-up View from Above Storage Pit 1.11 of Phase 3 in Courtyard Room 1

Plate 78

a

b

(*a*) Trench IIIG/H, Phase 4, Room 17A, Cooking Pot in situ (CP. B.IV.c, SW. 421, fig. 208:22) with a Child Burial Inside in situ (East View), and (*b*) Trench IIIG/H, Stone Working Surface on North Side of Phase 5, Room 3 (North View)

Plate 79

(*a*) Trench IIIG/H, General View of Phase 6 Stone Wall Foundations (South View), and (*b*) Trench IIIG/H, General View of Phase 7, Walls E and F (South View)

Plate 80

(*a*) Trench IIIG/H, Phase 6, Courtyard Locus 1.4 Showing Burned Patch in Vicinity of a Flint Deposit (West View), and (*b*) Trench IIIL, Stone Foundations of Phase 5, Wall 1 (Foreground) and Wall 2 (Background Right; East View)

Plate 81

(*a*) Operation 5, General North View of Quadrant D, Phases 3, 4 (Pits 17.3 and 18.6), and 5 in Right Foreground and Quadrant C, Phase 3, Roman Pit and Phase 4, Wall 13.1 in Background, and (*b*) Operation 5, General South View of Quadrant C, Phase 4, Floors in Foreground and Quadrant D, Phase 4, Pits 18.6 and 17.3, in Background

Plate 82

a

b

(*a*) Operation 5, Close-up North View of Quadrant D, Phase 5, Wall 19.2 in Right Foreground, and Phase 4, Pits 17.3 and 18.6, in Background, and (*b*) Operation 5, Close-up West View of Phase 4, Pits 18.6, in Foreground, and 17.3, in Background (*a*) Operation 5, General West View of Quadrant C, Phase 4, Wall 13.1, Cut by Roman Pit 14.9, and (*b*) Operation 5, General Northeast View of Quadrant C, Phase 2, Surviving Top of Mudbrick Wall 21.2 with Buttress A in Center of Photograph

Plate 84

(*a*) Operation 5, General East View of Quadrant C, Phase 2, Mudbrick Wall 21.2 After Clearance of Fallen Wall Painting Fragments from the Face of the Wall and Buttress C; and (*b*) Operation 5, Close-up View of North Top of Wall 21.2 with Unpainted Eastern Plaster Face of the Wall in situ in the Northeast Corner of Quadrant C

Plate 85

a

b

(*a*) Operation 5, Close-up East View of Quadrant C, Phase 2, Floor Between Buttresses A and B of Wall 21.2, and
(*b*) Operation 5, Close-up South View of Phase 1 Sounding in Southwest Corner of Quadrant C with Top of Jar
(JR. F.I.d, TS. 3390, pl. 244:4) in situ at Floor Level

Plate 86

(*a*) Operation 5, Close-up East View of Quadrant C, Phase 2, Buttress A with Topmost Surviving Layer of Wall Painting Fragments in situ, and (*b*) Operation 5, Close-up South View of Quadrant C, Phase 2, North Face of Buttress A with Wall Painting Fragments Under Consolidation for Removal from the Soil

Plate 87

a

b

(*a*) Operation 5, Close-up South View of Quadrant C, Phase 2, Wall Painting Fragments in situ with Reused Jar Sherd Spindle Whorl (TS. 4058, fig. 252:1), and (*b*) Operation 5, Close-up East View of Quadrant C, Phase 2, Buttress A to Right with Wall Painting Fragment WP.92.61 (pl. 131a) in Foreground

Plate 88

a

b

(*a*) Operation 5, General West View of Quadrant C, West Section Showing Phase 5, Pit 11.8, Cutting Through the Phase 4 Occupation Levels and Floor 13.7, and (*b*) Operation 5, General West View of Quadrant C, Phase 2, Floor 32.5, Showing Mudbrick Offering or Working Platforms in situ on the Floor

Plate 89

Bronze Age Pottery Types. Miniature Bowl: (*a*) MBR. A.I.a (SW. 483, pl. 204:1), Top and Side Views; Small Bowls: (*b*) SBR. A.I.a (SW. 569, fig. 66:1), (*c*) SBR. A.I.b (SW. 382, pl. 205:2); and Bowls: (*d*) BR. E.III.a (SW. 496, pl. 214:7), and (*e*) BR. R.I.a (SW. 501, pl. 222:1)

Plate 90

Bronze Age Pottery Type. Crucible Bowl: CBR. A.I.a (SW. 381, pl. 223:1)

Plate 91

Bronze Age Pottery Types. Small Jars: (*a*) SJR. B.II.j (SW. 519, fig. 68:3), (*b*) SJR. C.II.d (SW. 102, pl. 226:12), and (*c*) SJR. C.II.i (SW. 10 = TS. 848, pl. 226:17)

Plate 92

Bronze Age Pottery Types. Small Jars: (*a*) SJR. C.II.k (SW. 395 = TS. 1767, pl. 226:19), (*b*) SJR. C.II.m (SW. 723, pl. 226:21); and Jar: (*c*) JR. E.II.r (SW. 524, pl. 243:10)

Plate 93

a

b

Bronze Age Pottery Type. Jar: JR. H.I.g (SW. 294, fig. 64:4) — (*a*) General View and (*b*) Close-up View of Eagle under the Hole of the Missing Spout

Plate 94

Bronze Age Pottery Type. Jar: JR. J.I.e (SW. 292, pl. 251:5)

Plate 95

Bronze Age Pottery Types. Jars: (*a*) JR. J.I.h (SW. 733, pl. 251:8), (*b*) JR. J.III.a (SW. 293, fig. 62:6), (*c*) JR. J.III.t (SW. 567, pls. 34a, 254:1), and (*d*) JR. J.III.v (SW. 309, pl. 254:3)

Plate 96

Bronze Age Pottery Types. Jars: (*a*) JR. J.IV.a (SW. 649, pl. 255:1), (*b*) JR. L.I.a (SW. 676, pl. 259:1), (*c*) JR. L.II.a (SW. 651, pl. 259:2), and (*d*) JR. O.II.a (SW. 624, pl. 263:1)

Plate 97

Bronze Age Pottery Types. Flasks: (*a*) FL. A.II.a (SW. 722, pl. 274:3), (*b*) FL. A.II.b (SW. 706, pl. 274:5), (*c*) FL. B.I.a (SW. 272, fig. 88:5), Pot Stand: (*d*) PS. A.I.a (SW. 560, pl. 289:1), and Windowed Pot or Pedestal Stand: (*e*) WPS. B (TS. 3197 = TS. 3269, fig. 74:9)

Plate 98

Bronze Age Pottery Types. Strainer Bowls: (*a*) SR. B.I.b (SW. 558, pl. 290:8), (*b*) SR. C.I.a (SW. 725, pl. 290:16) and Cooking Pots: (*c*) Reconstruction of Cooking Pot SW. 539 (*d*) CP. A.II.a (SW. 539, pl. 276:1), and (*e*) CP. B.IV.c (SW. 761, pl. 280:3)

Plate 99

side view

side view

a

base view

b

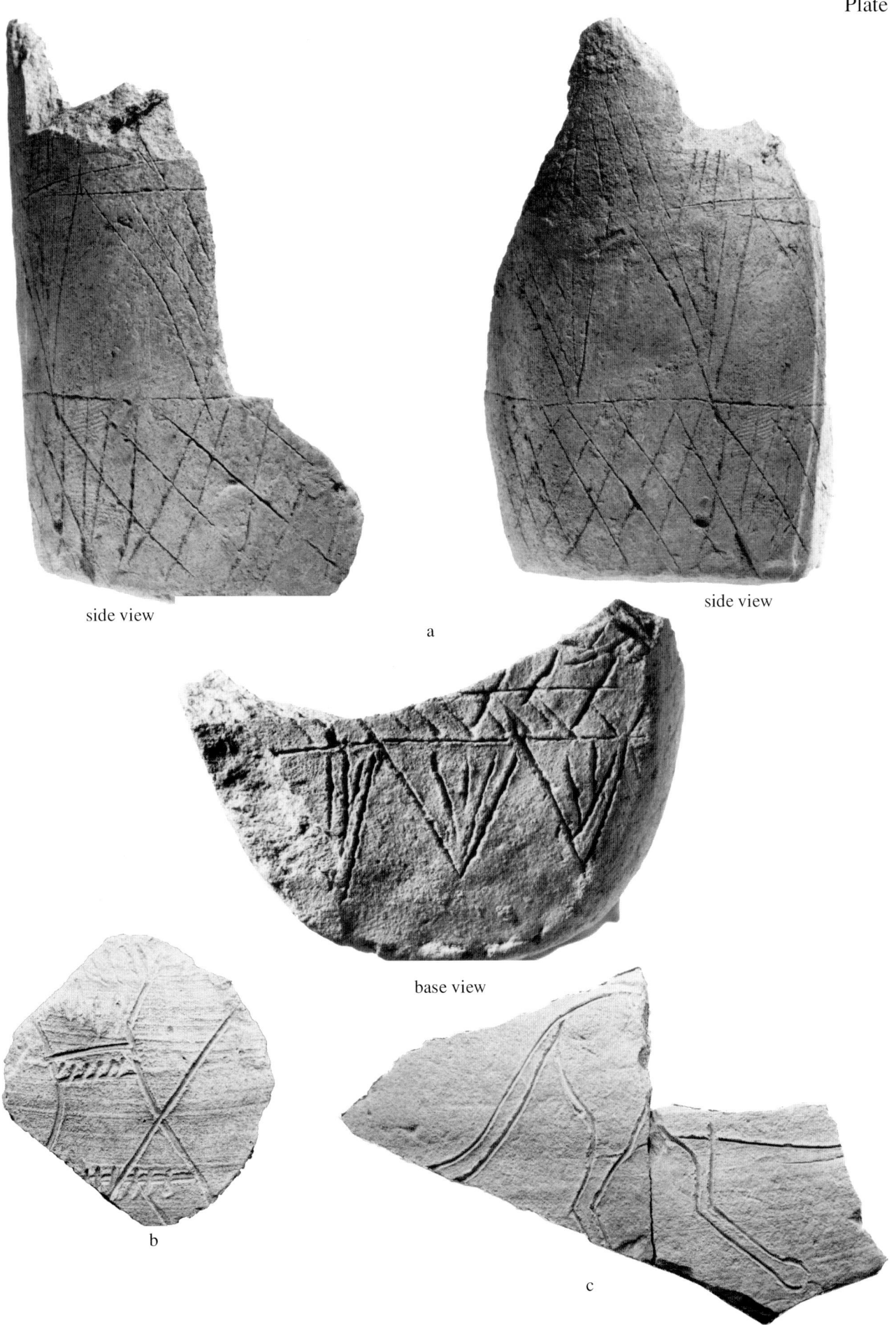

c

Bronze Age Pottery, Miscellaneous. Small Jar or Covered Model Wagon: (*a*) SJR. C.I.a (SW. 820, fig. 136 text, cf. pl. 119c) and Incised Jar Sherds: (*b*) Incised "Warrior" (SW. 627, fig. 154:6), (*c*) Incised "Horse" (SW. 630, fig. 154:13)

Plate 100

Bronze Age Pottery. Rim and Body Sherds with Miscellaneous Decoration and Potters' Marks:
(*a*) Mythical-type Incised Animals (TS. 1733, fig. 90:3), (*b*) Applied Snake-like Rope Band (TS. 1597, fig. 129:5),
(*c*) Incised Floral Decoration, Bowl BR. L.I.h (TS. 1610, pl. 219:8), (*d*) Potter's Mark on Jar Sherd (TS. 1586, fig. 64:13), (*e*) Tree or Wheat Stalk Pattern on Jar Sherd (TS. 2573, fig. 154:11), and (*f*) Potter's Mark on Jar Sherd (TS. 1734, fig. 64:14)

Plate 101

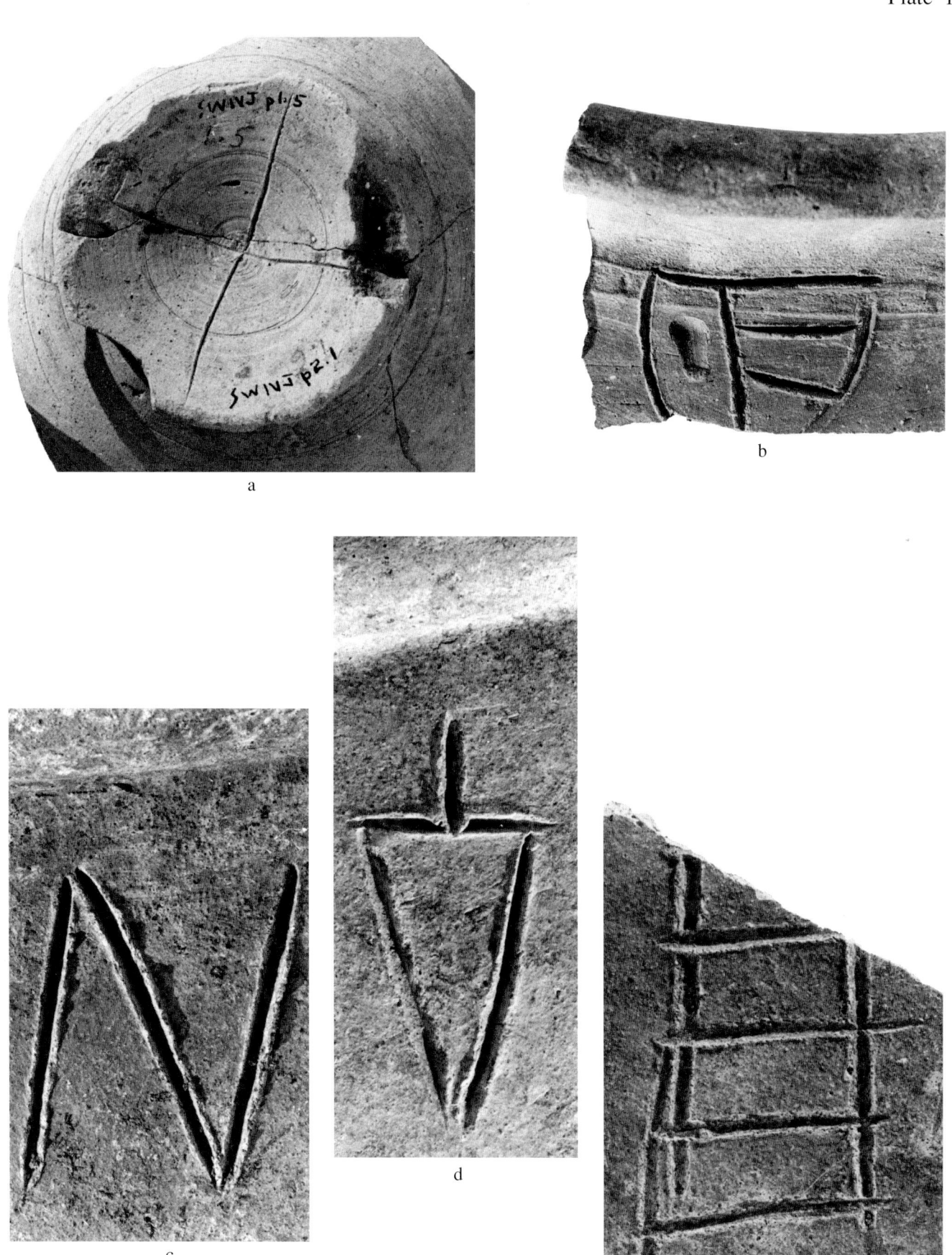

Bronze Age Pottery. Types with Incised Potters' Marks: (*a*) Jar Base BE. E.I.c [PM. C.14] (TS. 1609, pl. 292:3), (*b*) Jar JR. O.I.a [PM. D.6] (SW. 695, pl. 261), (*c*) Jar JR. O.II.m [PM. C.5] (SW. 644, fig. 77:4), (*d*) Jar JR. O.III.e [PM. D.1] (SW. 638, fig. 77:5), and (*e*) Jar Sherd, JR. Sh. [PM. D.17] (TS. 1774, fig. 77:10)

Plate 102

Bronze Age Pottery. Jar Types with Incised Potters' Marks and Comb-incised Decoration: (*a*) JR. P.II.a [PM. C.7] (SW. 666, fig. 64:10), (*b*) JR. P.II.a [PM. D.15] (TS. 2810, fig. 91:10), (*c*) Jar Sherd, JR. Sh. (IP [G.1] B.I.a) (TS. 1655, fig. 112:14), and (*d*) Jar Sherd, JR. Sh. (IP [G.1] C.IV.a) (TS. 1651, fig. 130:7)

Plate 103

Bronze Age Vessels. Zoomorphic Clay Figures, Type SV.3: (*a*) SW. 655 (IVN, fig. 170:8), Vessel Fragment with Bird-like Spout, Right Side and Frontal Views, (*b*) SW. 460 (IC, fig. 28:2), Boar's Head, Front of Head and Nostril Views; and (*c*) SW. 840 (Operation 4, fig. 335: 15), Boar's Head, Front of Head and Nostril Views

Plate 104

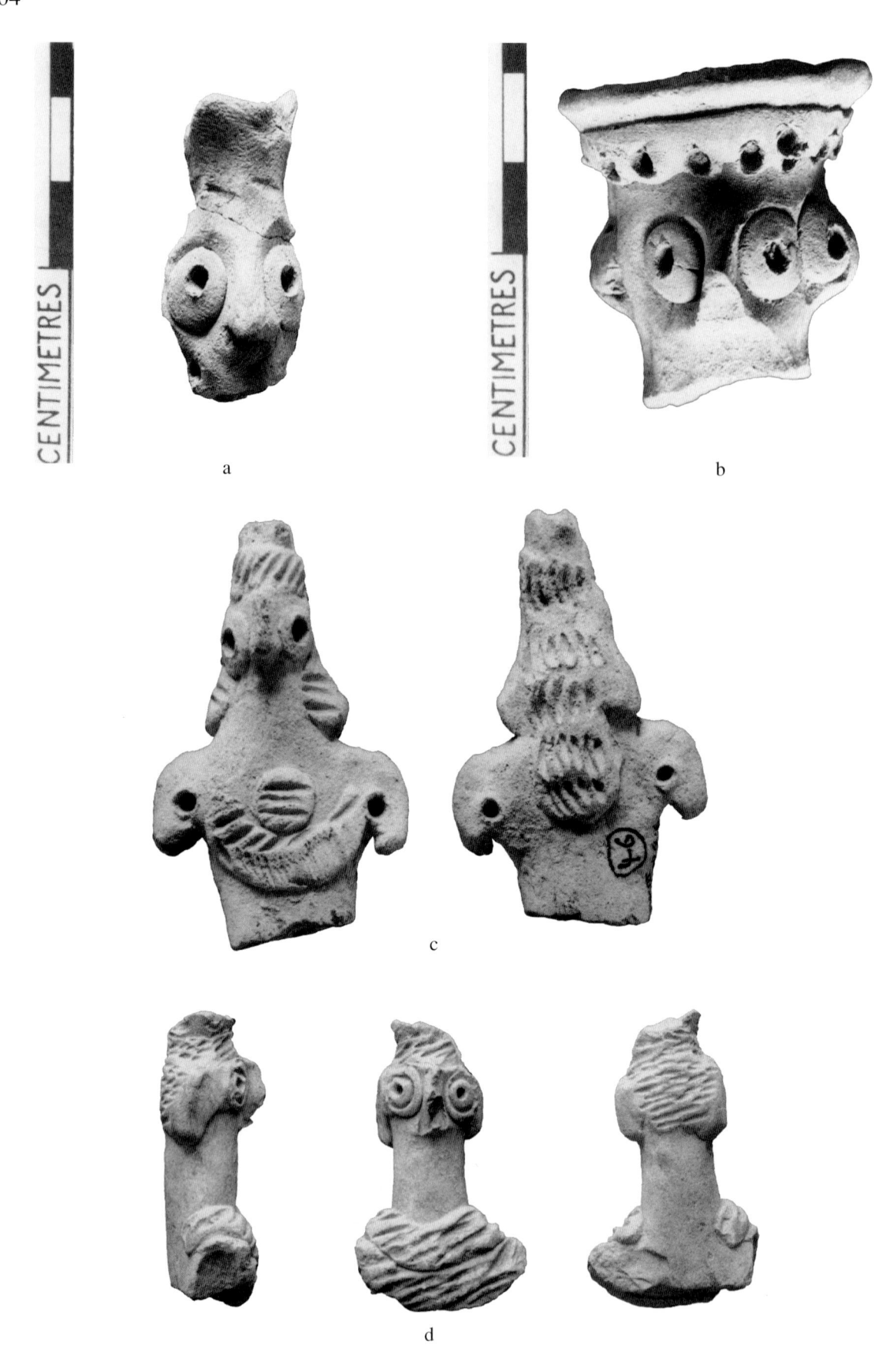

Bronze Age Figurines (Area III). Clay Human Female, Type SF.1a: (*a*) SW. 135 (IIID, fig. 221:5), (*b*) SW. 192 (IIIB, fig. 221:4), (*c*) SW. 46 (IIIA, fig. 221:1), Front and Back Views, and (*d*) SW. 546 (IIIG/H, fig. 221:6), Right Side, Front, and Back Views

Plate 105

Bronze Age Figurines (Areas III, VI, and IX). Clay Human Female, Type SF.1c: (*a*) SW. 223 (IIIE, fig. 221:3), (*b*) SW. 401 (IIIG/H, fig. 221:9), Front and Back Views, (*c*) SW. 389 (VIA, fig. 258:4), (*d*) SW. 385 (VIA, fig. 258:6), and (*e*) SW. 479 (IXA, fig. 175:2)

Plate 106

a

b

Bronze Age Figurines (Area III). Clay Human Female, Type SF.1c: (*a*) SW. 476 (IIIG/H, fig. 221:7), Front and Back Views, and (*b*) SW. 366 (IIIG/H, fig. 221:8), Front, Left Side, and Back Views

Plate 107

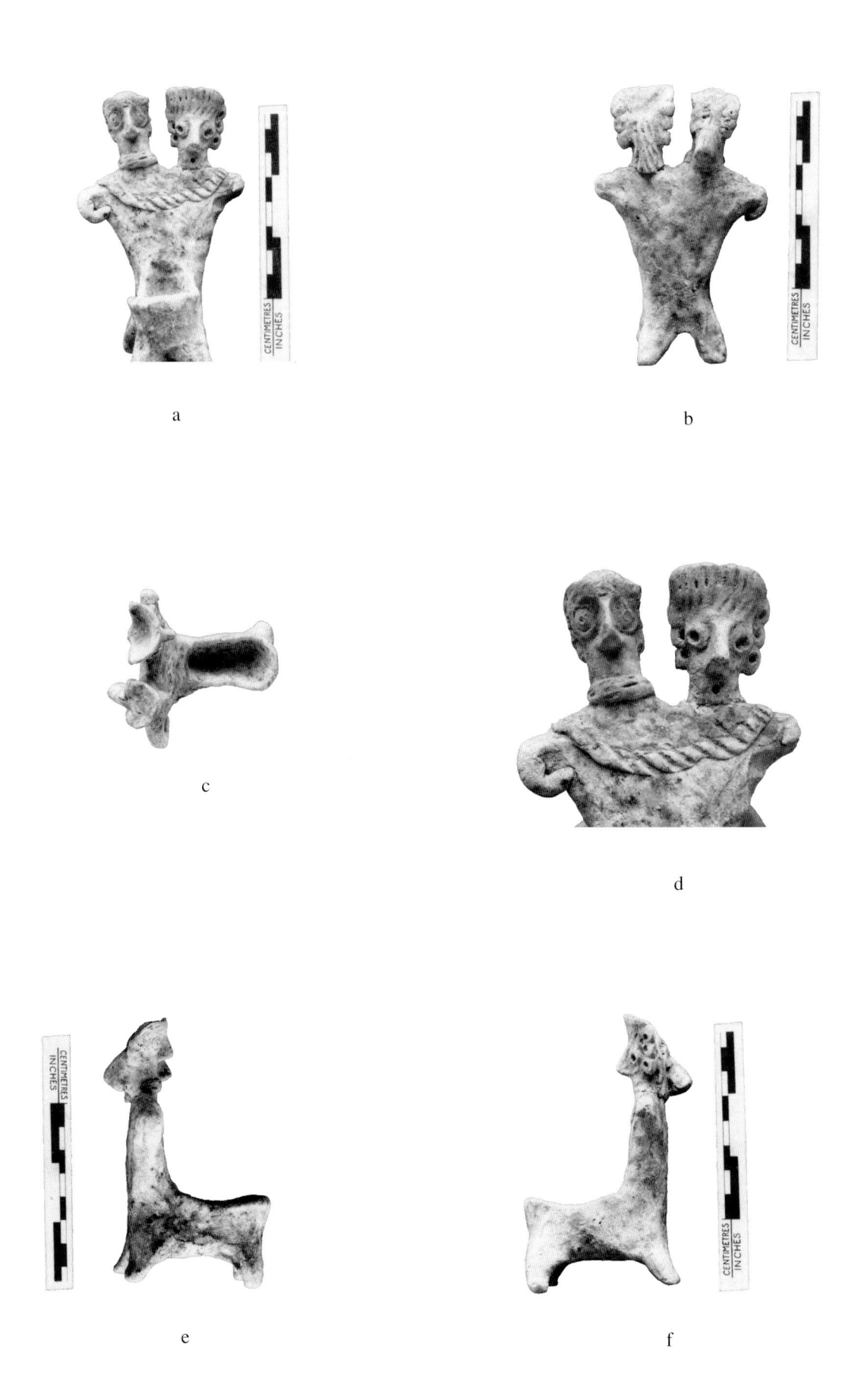

Bronze Age Figurine (Unknown Provenance). Two-headed Human Attached to Four-legged Basin: (*a*) Front, (*b*) Back, (*c*) Top, (*d*) Frontal Detail of Heads, (*e*) Right Side, and (*f*) Left Side

Plate 108

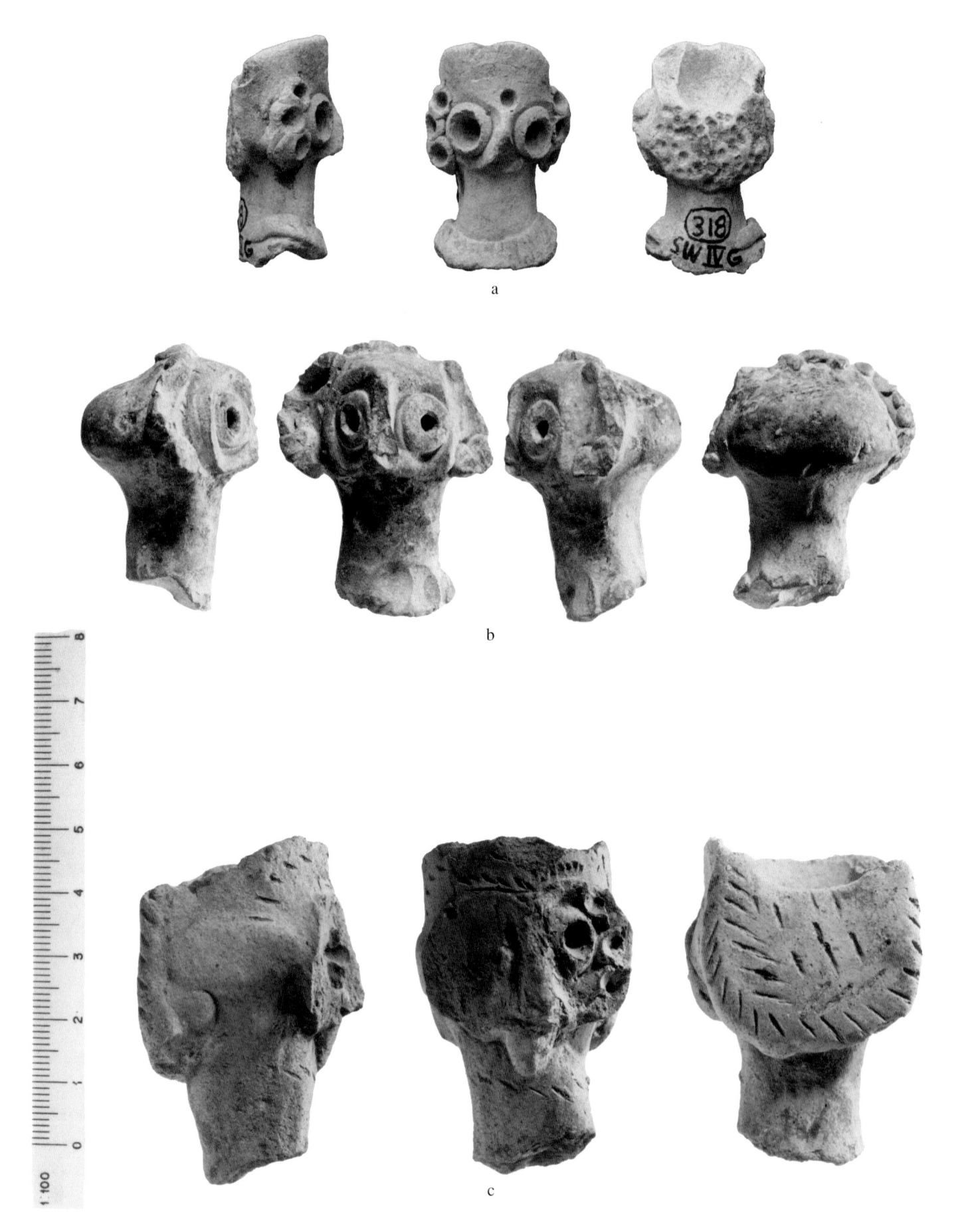

Bronze Age Figurines (Area IV). Clay Human Female, Type SF.1a: (*a*) SW. 318 (IVG, Unstratified, fig. 155:2), Right Side, Front, and Back Views; (*b*) TS. 3292 (Operation 6, fig. 156:12), Right Side, Front, Left Side, and Back Views; and (*c*) SW. 814 (Operation 7, fig. 155:12), Right Side, Front, and Back Views

Plate 109

Bronze Age Figurines (Area IV). Clay Human Female, Type SF.1a: (*a*) SW. 766 (Operation 7, fig. 156:8), Top of Head, Right Side, Front, Left Side, and Back Views; and (*b*) SW. 383 (IVF, fig. 155:3), Front and Back Views

Plate 110

a

b

c

Bronze Age Figurines (Area IV). Clay Human Female, Type SF.1a: (*a*) SW. 714 (IVX, fig. 155:4); (*b*) SW. 811 (Operation 6, fig. 156:13), Front and Back Views; and (*c*) SW. 836 (Operation 7, fig. 155:13), Front and Back Views

Plate 111

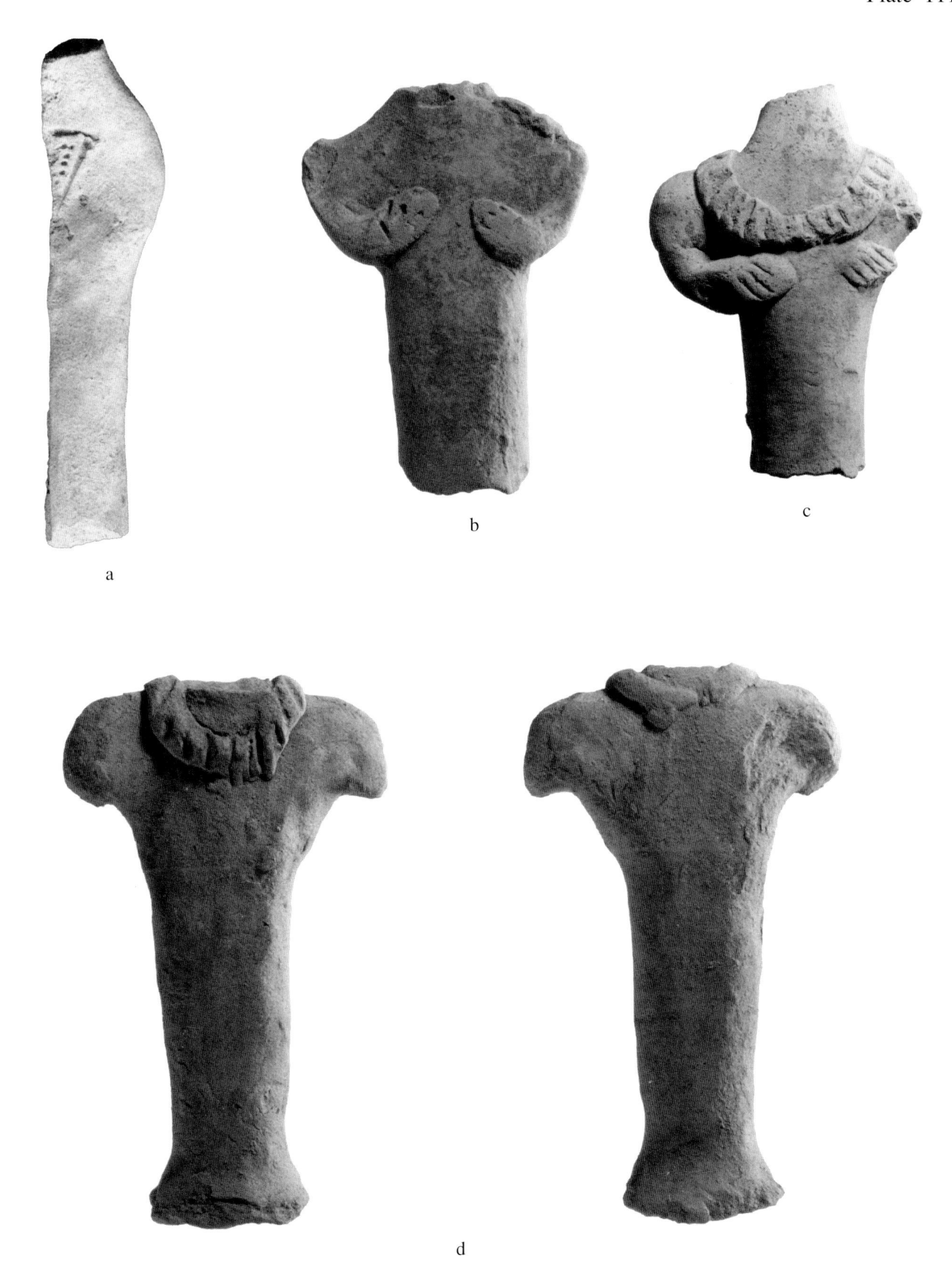

Bronze Age Figurines (Area IV). Clay Human Female, Types SF.1a and 1c: (*a*) Type SF.1a (SW. 556, IVL/P Baulk, fig. 156:5), (*b*) Type SF.1a (FN. 45, Operation 7, fig. 156 Text), (*c*) Type SF.1a (SW. 765, Operation 7, fig. 156:7), and (*d*) Type SF.1c (SW. 815, Operation 7, fig. 156 Text), Front and Back Views

Plate 112

a

b

Bronze Age Figurine (Operation 5). Clay Human Female, Type SF.1a: (*a–b*) SW. 835 (fig. 249:1), Front and Back Views

Plate 113

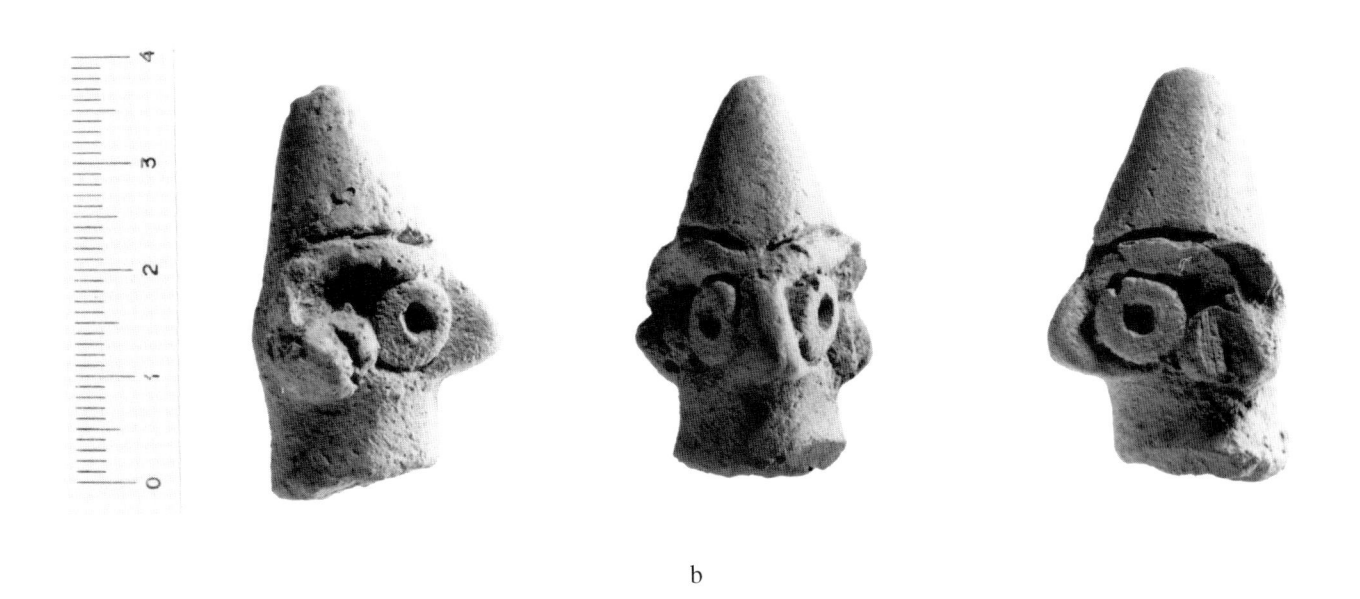

Bronze Age Figurines (Operation 5). Clay Human Figurine, Types SF.1c and 1b: (*a*) Type SF.1c, Female Torso Fragment (FN.13, fig. 249:3); and (*b*) Type SF.1b, Male Head Fragment (SW. 817, fig. 249:2), Right Side, Front, and Left Side Views

Plate 114

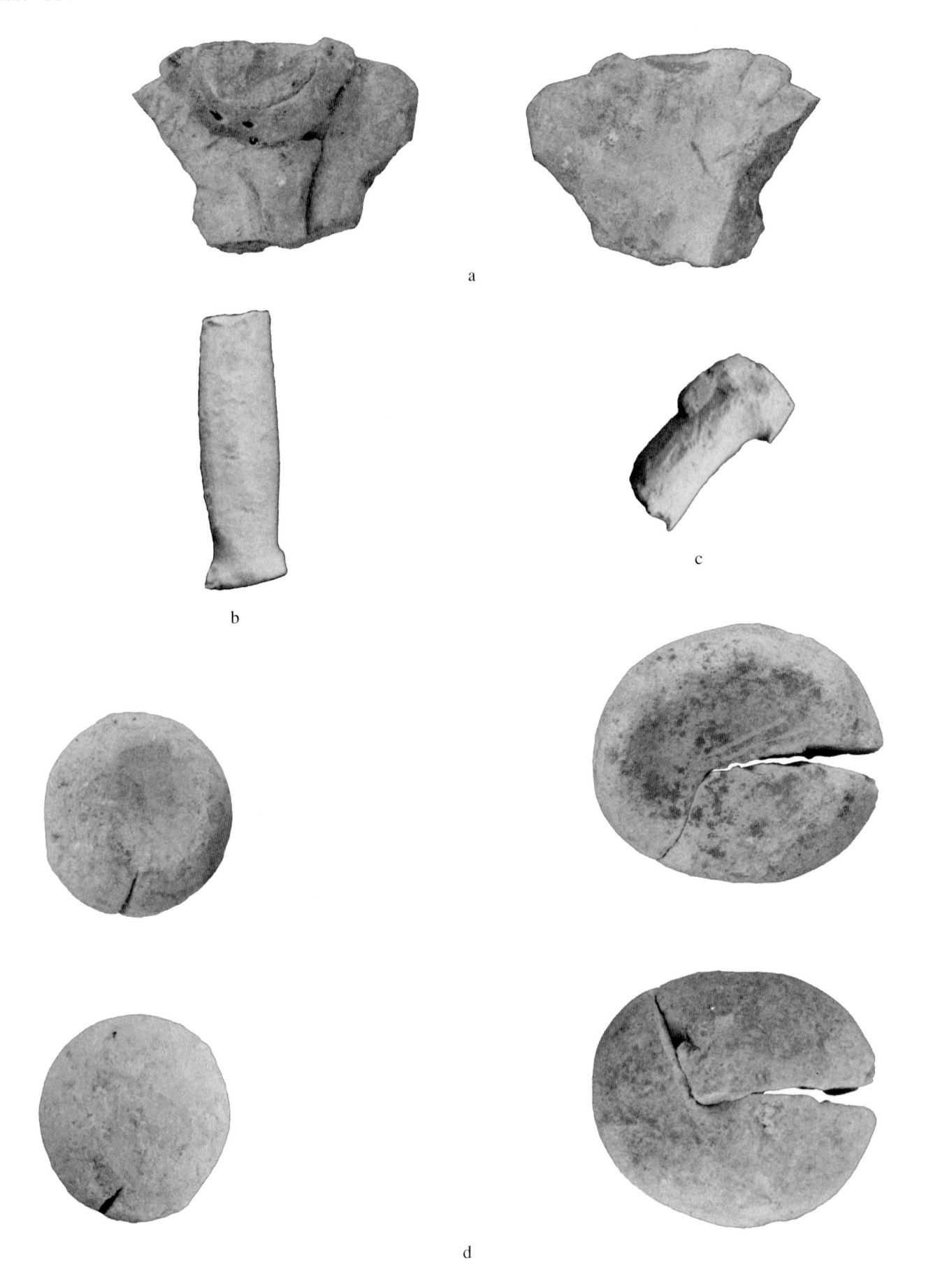

Bronze Age Figurines and Miniature Mortars (Operation 5). Clay Figurines: (*a*) Type SF.1c, Human Female Figurine (FN. 175, fig. 249:4), Front and Back Views; (*b*) Type SF.1c, Human Figurine Pillar Stand (FN. 149, fig. 249 Text); (*c*) Type SF.1d, Model Horse Figurine Fragment (FN. 24, fig. 249 Text); and Miniature Mortars: (*d*) Type SF.6g, Two Clay Mortars (FN. 169 and FN. 170, fig. 252:3, 4), Top and Bottom Views

Plate 115

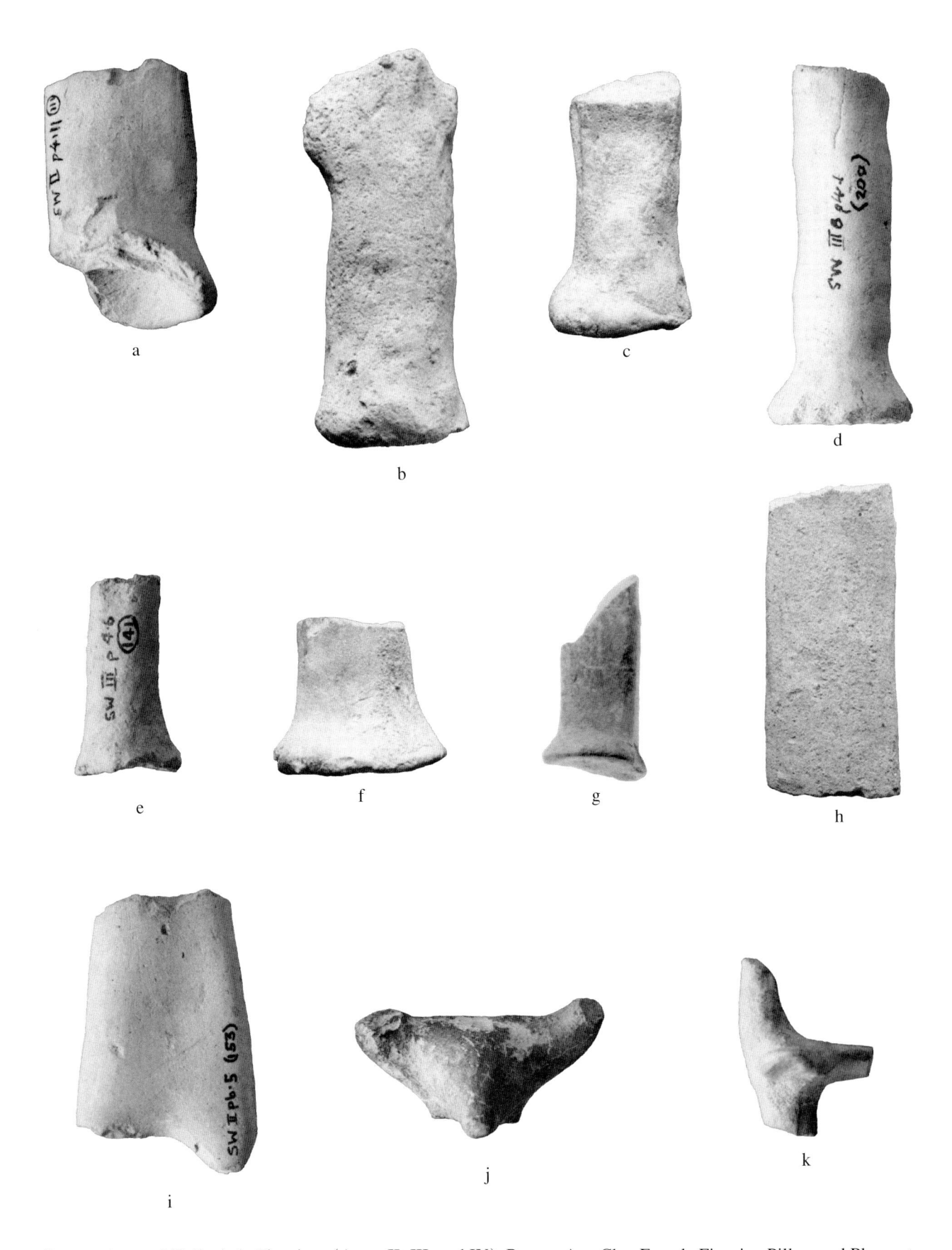

Bronze Age and Hellenistic Figurines (Areas II, III, and IV). Bronze Age Clay Female Figurine Pillar- and Plaque-type Stands: (*a*) Type SF.1c (SW. 111, IIA, fig. 51:3), (*b*) Type SF.1c (SW. 112, IIA, fig. 51:4), (*c*) Type SF.1c (SW. 402, IIIG/H, fig. 221:14), (*d*) Type SF.1c (SW. 200, IIIB, fig. 221:12), (*e*) Type SF.1c (SW. 141, IIIC, fig. 221:15), (*f*) Type SF.1c (SW. 548, IVP, fig. 155:11), (*g*) Type SF.1c (SW. 42, IIIB, fig. 221:13), (*h*) Type SF.1c (SW. 481, IVJ, fig. 155:6); Hellenistic Figurines: (*i*) Type SF.1c, Human Figurine Torso (SW. 153, IIB, fig. 258:12), (*j*) Type SF.1d, Model Bull's Head (SW. 85, IIA, fig. 51:9), and (*k*) Type SF.1d, Dove Figurine (SW. 87, IIA, fig. 51:6)

Plate 116

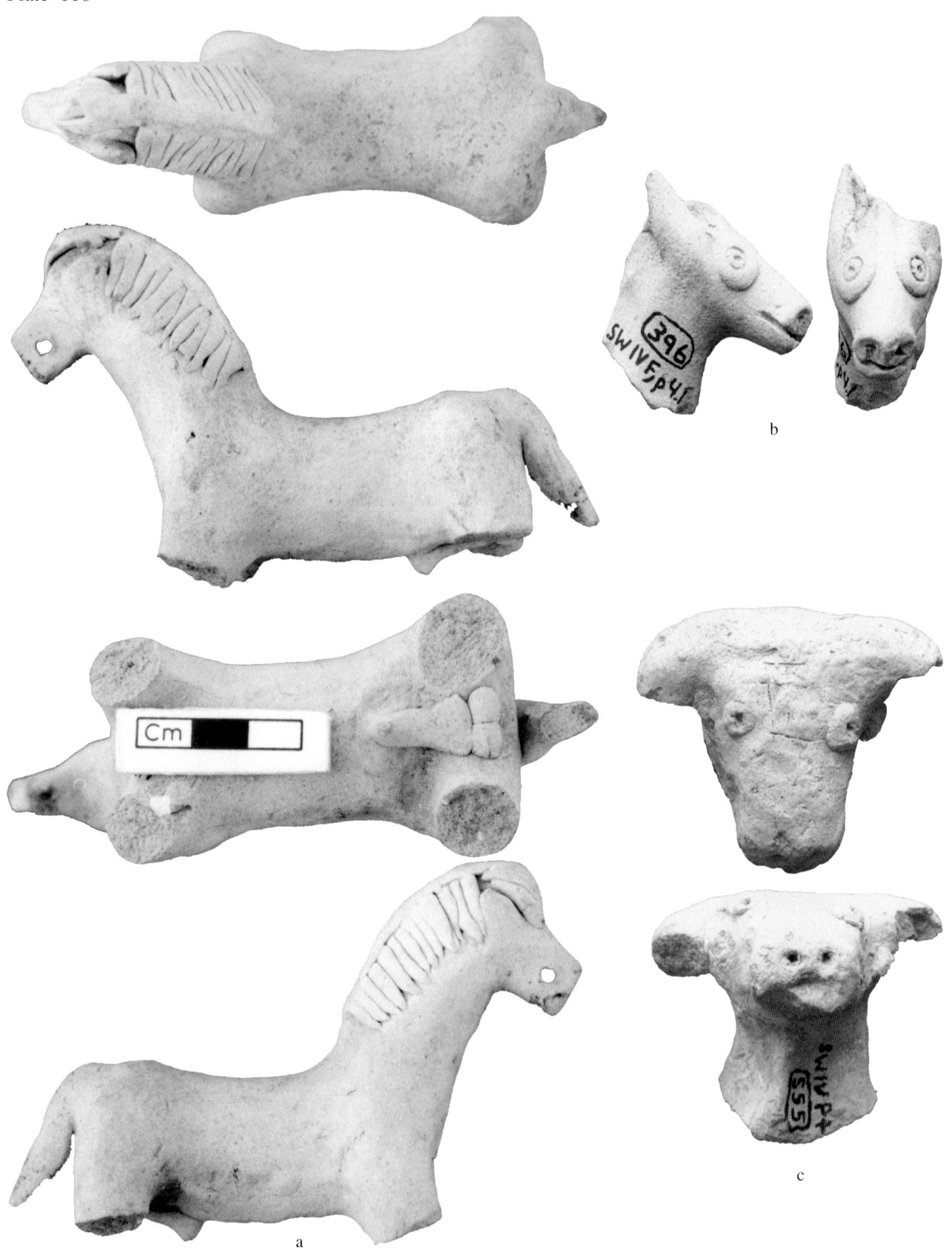

Bronze Age Clay Animal Figurines (Area IV and Operation 10). Type SF.1d: (*a*) Horse (SW. 770, Operation 10, fig. 157:6), Top, Left Side, Underside, and Right Side Views; (*b*) Horse or Onager Head (SW. 396, IVF, fig. 157:1), Right Side and Front Views; and (*c*) Bovine Head (SW. 555, IVP, Unstratified, fig. 158:6), Top of Head and Snout Views

Plate 117

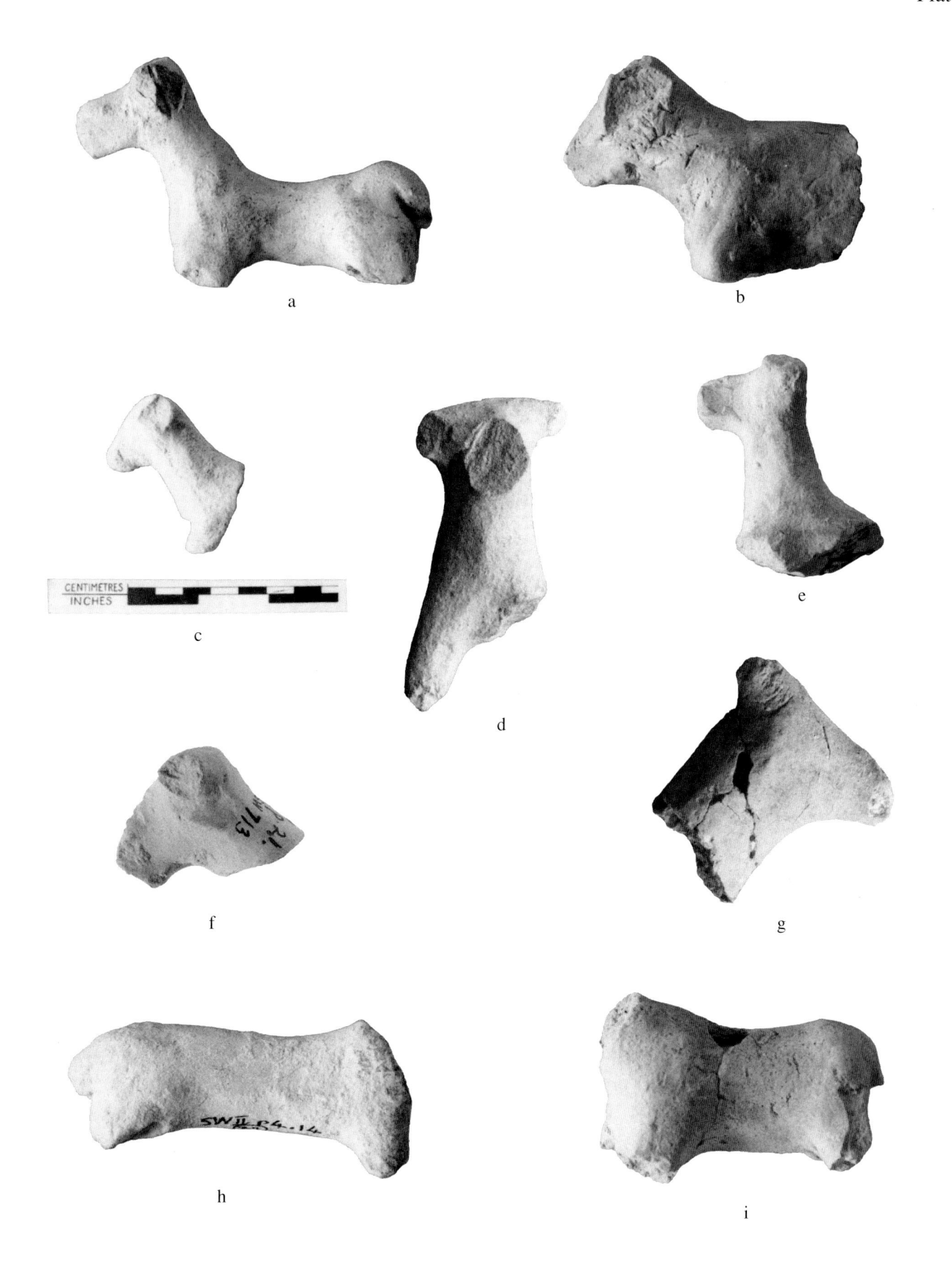

Bronze Age Clay Animal Figurines (Areas II, III, and IV): (*a*) Type SF.1d (SW. 51, IIIA, fig. 222:1), (*b*) Type SF.1d (SW. 204, IIIF, fig. 222:3), (*c*) Type SF.1d (SW. 93, IIIC, fig. 222:4), (*d*) Type SF.1d (SW. 418, IVN, fig. 158:5), (*e*) Type SF.1d (SW. 232, IVE, fig. 157:9), (*f*) Type SF.1d (SW. 713, IVP, fig. 157:4), (*g*) Type SF.1d (SW. 518, IVL, fig. 157:3), (*h*) Type SF.1e (SW. 79, IIA, fig. 51:7), and (*i*) Type SF.1e (SW. 48, IIIA, fig. 222:2)

Plate 118

a

b

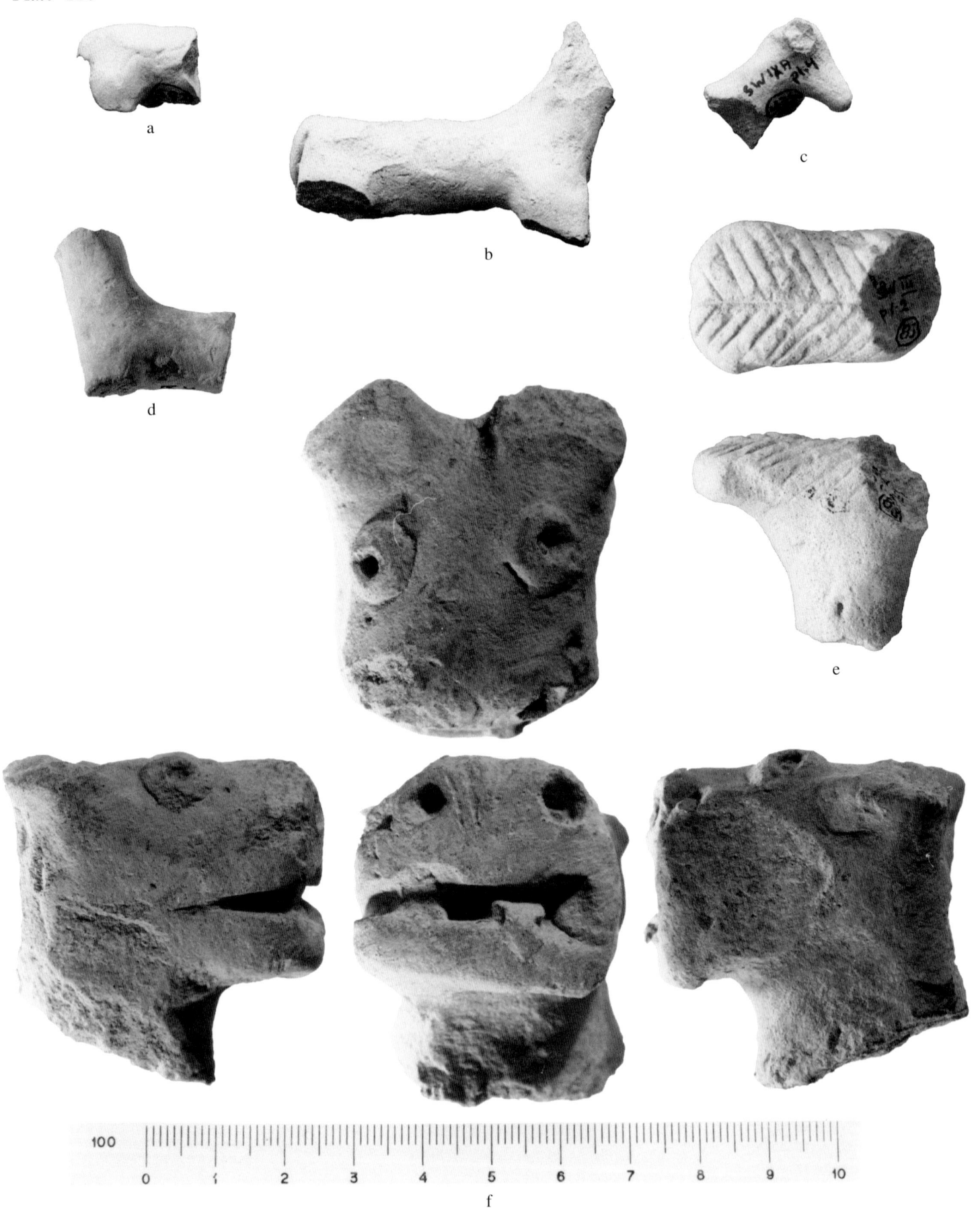

c

d

e

f

Bronze Age Clay Animal Figurines (Areas III, IV, IX, and Operation 5): (*a*) Type SF.1d (SW. 592, IVD, fig. 157:10), (*b*) Type SF.1e (SW. 387, IVC, fig. 158:1), (*c*) Type SF.1d (SW. 436, IXA, fig. 175:3), (*d*) Type SF.1e (SW. 712, IVM, fig. 157:5), (*e*) Type SF.1d (SW. 83, IIIA, fig. 222:5), Top and Right Side Views, and (*f*) Type SF.1d (SW. 826, Operation 5, fig. 249:8), Eyes, Forehead, and Ears (Top), Right Side, Front Mouth, and Left Side Views

Plate 119

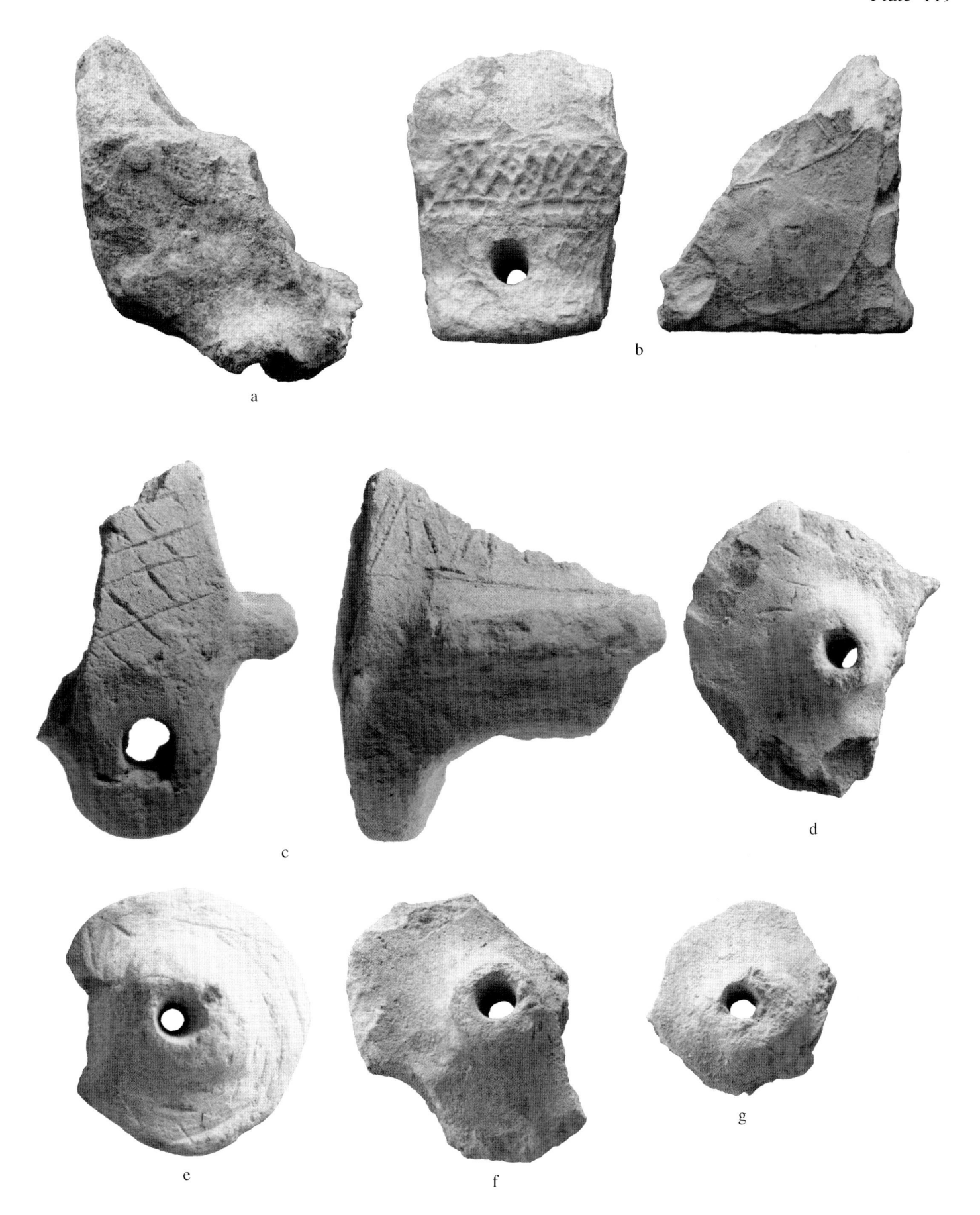

Bronze Age Clay Model Chariots and Model Wheels (Areas IC, IV, X, and Operation 6). Model Chariots, Type SF.2a: (*a*) SW. 522 (XA, fig. 159:1), Left Side View; (*b*) SW. 393 (IVK, fig. 159:2), Front and Right Side Views; (*c*) SW. 842 (Operation 6, fig. 159:3), Right Side and Front Views; and Model Wheels, Type SF.2b: (*d*) SW. 392 (IVK, fig. 159:4), (*e*) SW. 475 (IVN, fig. 159:5), (*f*) SW. 459 (IC, fig. 28:3), and (*g*) SW. 547 (XA, fig. 159:8)

Plate 120

420a  420b  420c  420d  420e

Bronze Age Clay Model Wheel and Miscellaneous Objects (Areas IV and X): (*a*) Model Wheel, Type SF.2b (SW. 549, XA, fig. 159:9); (*b*) Unfired Mold Fragment, Type SF.6d (SW. 660, IVM, fig. 160:2); (*c*) Offering Stand, Type SF.6g (SW. 553, IVL/P, Baulk, fig. 160:4); (*d*) Compartment Vessel or Model House, Type SF.2c (SW. 521, XA, fig. 170:6), Top and Oblique Side Views; and (*e*) Unbaked Sling Bullets, Types SF.6a.1–4, 8 (SW. 420a–e, IVK, fig. 165:1–5)

Plate 121

Bronze Age Metal Objects (Area IV Rooms and Operation 7): Type SF.5 (*a*) Tongs, Type SF.5a (SW. 234, IVK, fig. 161:1), (*b*) Collar for Pottery Jar, Type SF.5b (SW. 598, IVJ, fig. 161:2), (*c*) Toilet Knife, Type SF.5h (SW. 606, IVL, fig. 162:15), (*d*) Mushroom-headed Pin Type with Eyelet Hole, Type SF.5c (SW. 619, IVJ, fig. 161:3), (*e*) Lynch Pin, Type SF.5d (SW. 720, IVN, fig. 161:11), (*f*) Lynch Pin, Type SF.5d (SW. 721, IVN., fig. 161:12), and (*g*) Pin Shaft, Type SF.5c (SW. 802, Operation 7, fig. 162:12)

Plate 122

Roman Period Metal and Stone Objects and Coins (Operation 5 and Area I). (*a*) Bronze Spatula, Type SF.5g (SW. 801, Operation 5, fig. 251:3), (*b*) Stone Tool or Weapon Mold, Type SF.3f (SW. 830, Operation 5, fig. 250:7); and (*c, d*) Roman Coins, Type SF.5j (SW. 235, SW. 236, Area IA2, fig. 28 Text), Obverse and Reverse Views

Plate 123

Bronze Age Stone Objects (Area IV Rooms and Operation 11): (*a*) Limestone Cylinder Seal and Plaster-rolled Impression of Its Decoration, Type SF. 3f (SW. 647, IVL, fig. 163:4), (*b*) One Mana Cuneiform Inscribed Stone Weight, Types SF. 3e and SF. 10 (SW. 585, IVL, fig. 163:2), (*c*) Plaster Impression of One Mana Cuneiform Inscribed Weight, (*d*) Stone Pivot or Potter's Wheel, Type SF. 3f (SW. 767, Operation 11, fig. 163:1), and (*e*) Limestone Bowl with Engraved Decoration, Type SF. 3c (SW. 471, IVN, fig. 163:5)

Plate 124

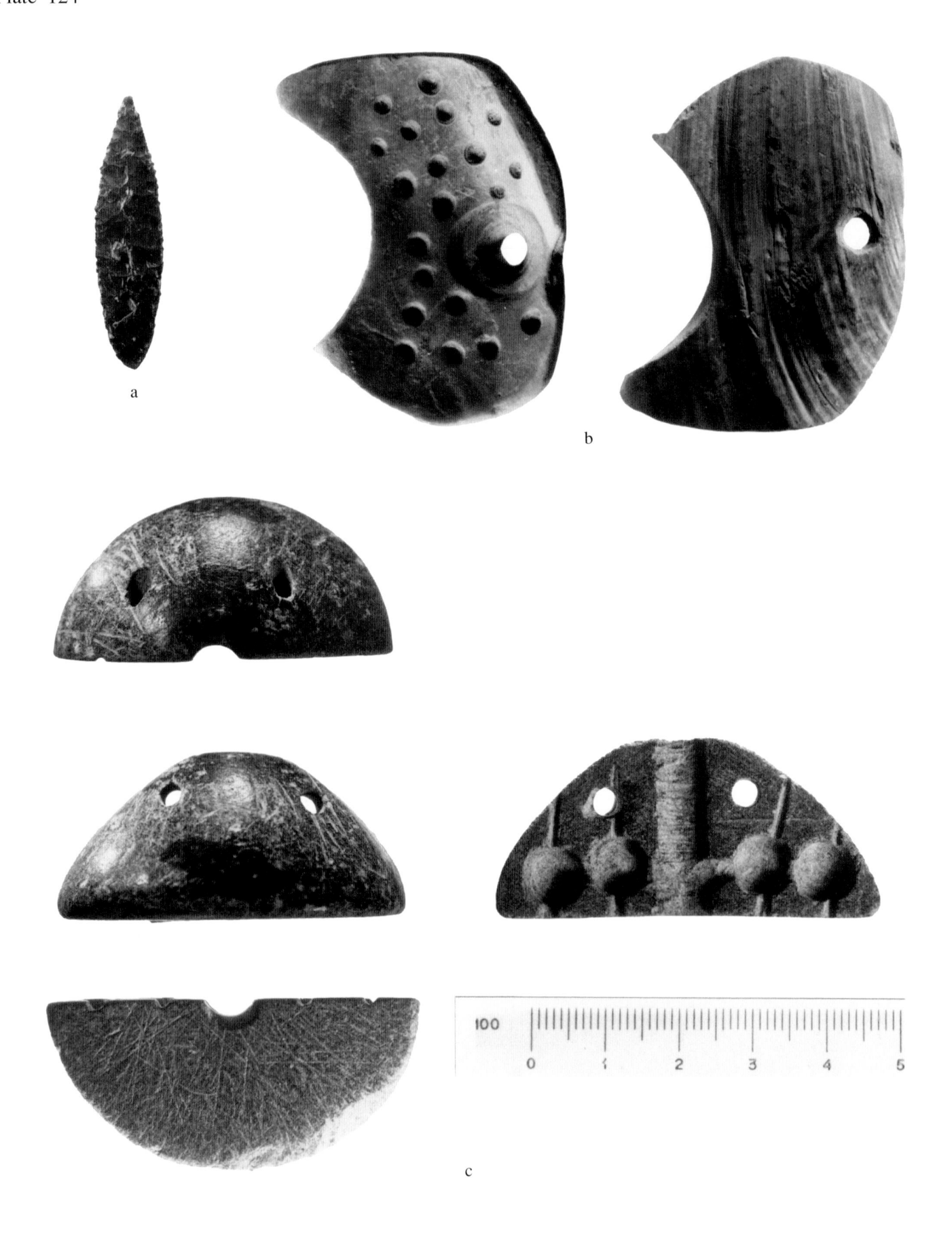

Bronze Age Miscellaneous Objects (Area IV and Operation 6 Rooms): (*a*) Flint Arrowhead, Type SF.12b (SW. 593, IVM, fig. 168:1); (*b*) Shell Pendant, Type SF.4c (SW. 823, Operation 6, fig. 169 Text), Inside Decorated and Outside Views; and (*c*) Stone Jewelry Mold, Type SF.3f (SW. 833, Operation 6, fig. 164:5), Top, Outside, Bottom, and Inside Views

Plate 125

Bronze Age Stone Objects (Operations 6 and 7 Rooms): (*a*) Cosmetic Tray, Type SF.3c (SW. 804, Operation 6, fig. 164:6), Top and Side Views; and (*b*) Fishing Net Weight or Loom Weight, Type SF.3e (SW. 822, Operation 7, fig. 164:7), Obverse and Reverse Views

Plate 126

Bronze Age Stone Objects (Operation 6 Rooms): (*a*) Pounding Tool, Type SF.3a (SW. 805, Operation 6, fig. 173:10), Broad and Flat Side Views; (*b*) Loom Weight, Type SF.3e (FN. 125, Operation 6, fig. 164 text), Obverse and Reverse Views; (*c*) Footed Mortar, Type SF.3c (SW. 821, Operation 6, fig. 171:7)

Plate 127

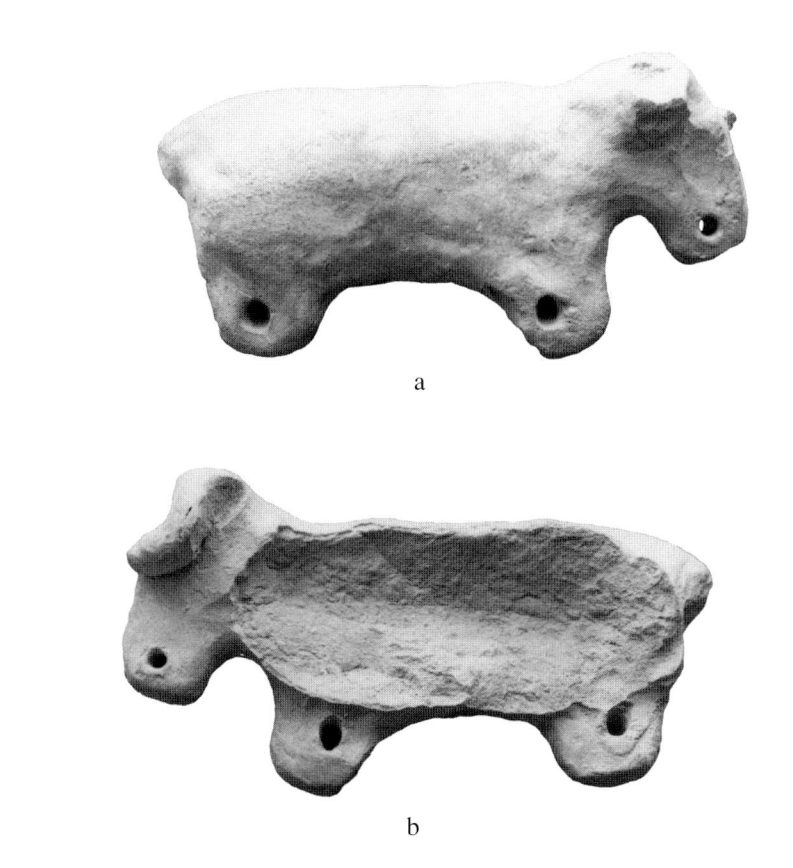

Bronze Age Objects (Area IXA). Clay Animal Pull-toy, Type SF.1f (SW. 458, fig. 175:4): (*a*) Right-hand Side, Complete, (*b*) Left-hand Side, Incomplete, and (*c*) Three-footed Limestone Mortar, Type SF.3c (SW. 448, fig. 175:8)

Plate 128

a

b

Bronze Age Stone and Clay Objects (Areas III, IV): (*a*) Mortar, Type SF.3c, with Grinder, Type SF.3a, Found in situ (SW. 349a, b; IIID, fig. 227:1a, b), and (b) Two Unfired Clay Objects, Type SF.6g (SW. 648, IVJ/O Baulk, fig. 170:5a, b)

Plate 129

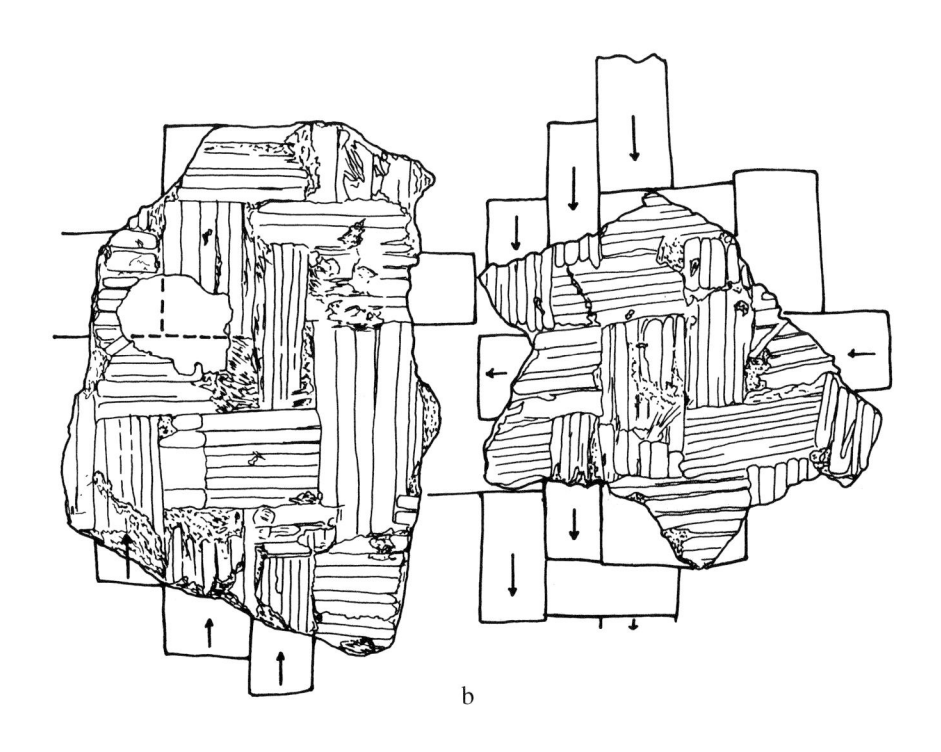

Bronze Age Mat Impressions on Fallen Roof *Libn* (IVQ, Room 6, Phase 2B): (*a*) Photograph of Two Segments, and (*b*) Line Drawing Showing Mat Impressions and Pattern of Weaving on the Two Segments (by Donald Whitcomb)

Plate 130

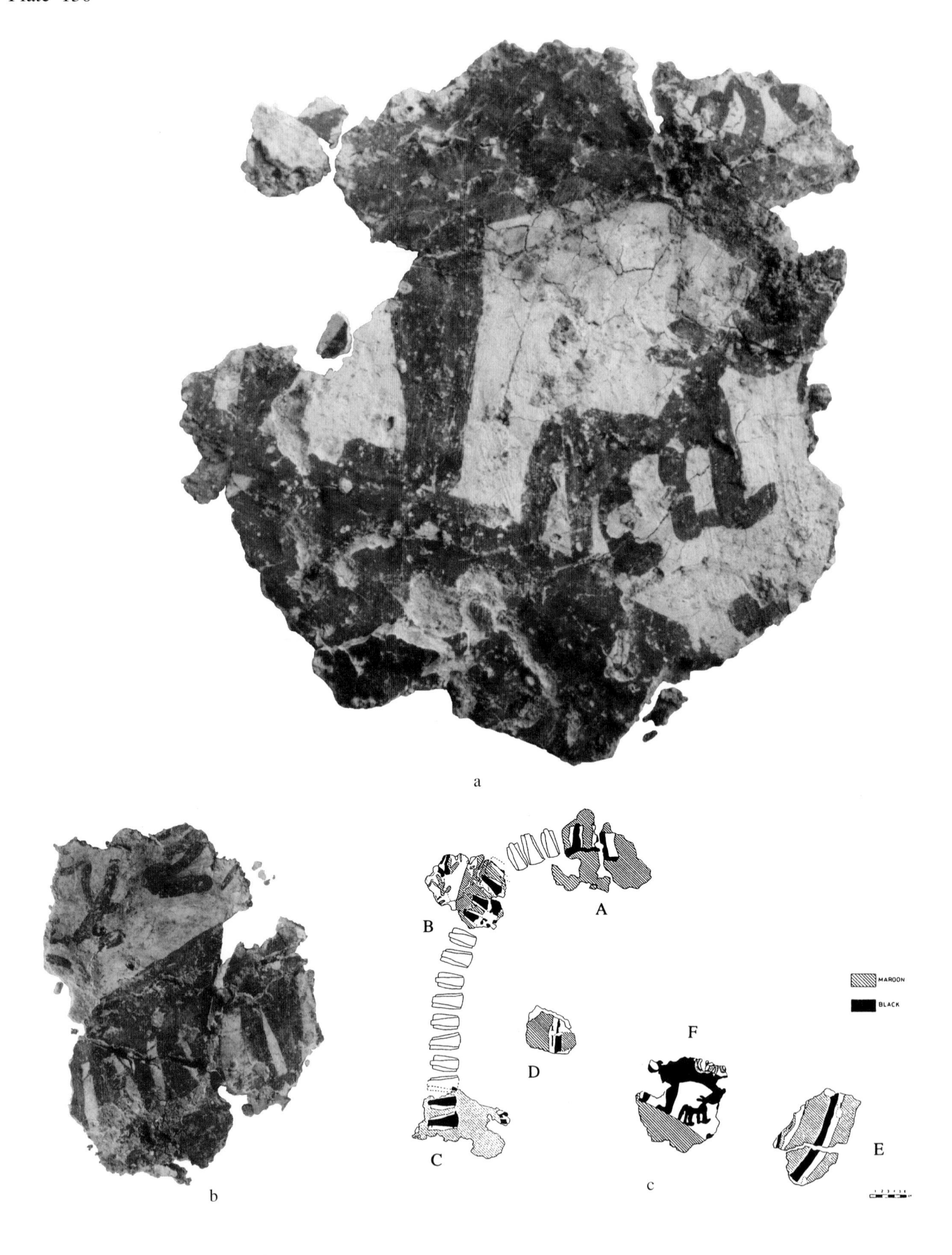

Wall Painting Fragments (Operation 5): (*a*) WP. 92.38 (fig. 254), Photograph Showing a Bovine with Suckling Calf Standing on a Mountainside, (*b*) WP. 91.18, Photograph Showing Border and Tree Pattern, and (*c*) Possible Reconstruction of Part of One Painting

Plate 131

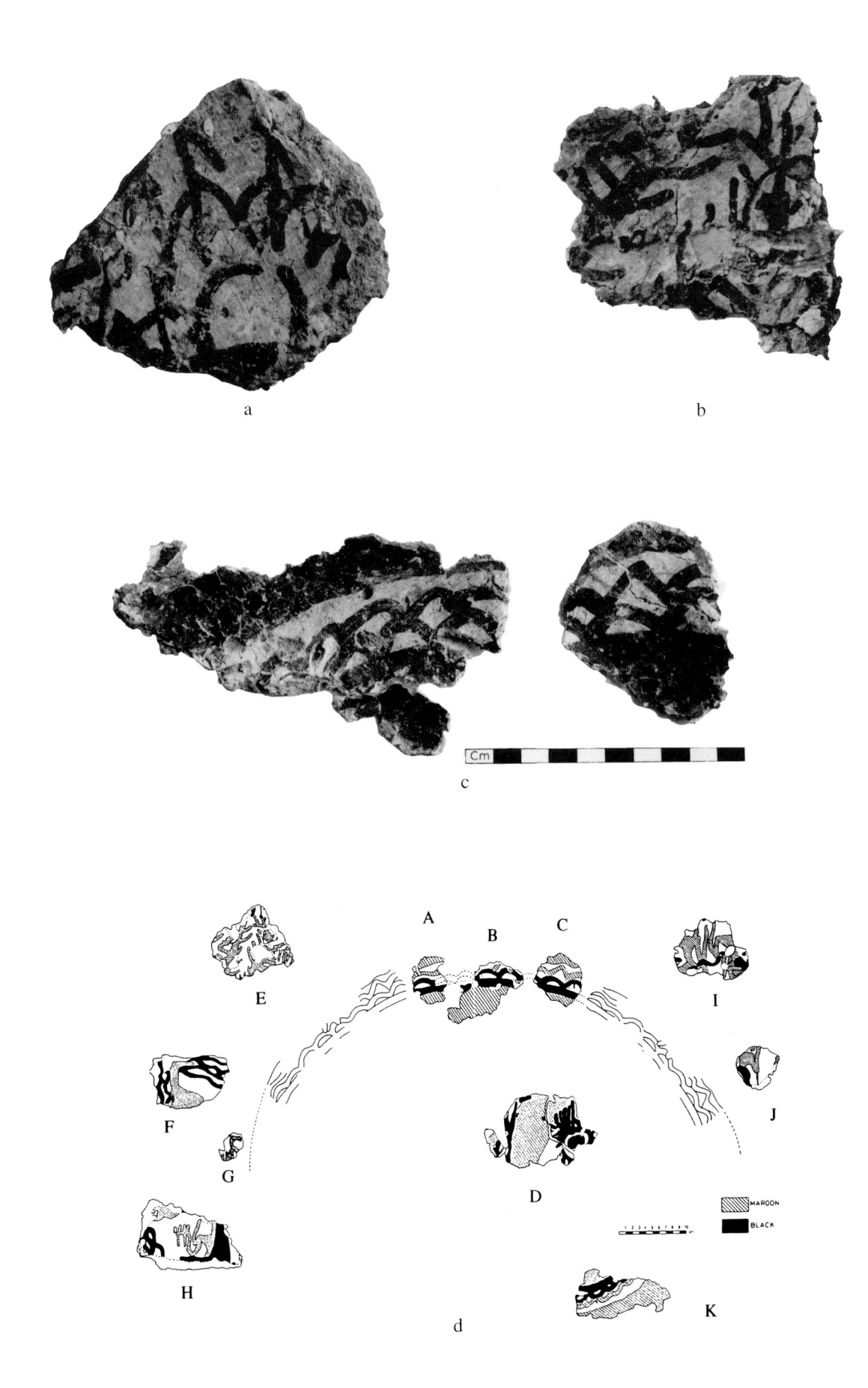

Wall Painting Fragments Depicting Human and Geometric Designs (Operation 5): (*a*) WP. 92.61 (fig. 255c), Photograph Showing Human Figures, (*b*) WP.91.9 (fig. 257:1), Photograph Showing Tree Branches, (*c*) WP. 92.74a and WP. 92.74b (fig. 257:3, 4), Photograph Showing Border Patterns, and (*d*) Possible Reconstruction of Part of a Second Painting

Plate 132

Hellenistic and Roman Finds (Areas I, II, and 1972 Survey of Romala; see fig. 9 Text): (*a*) Greek Ostracon (SW. 196, IIB, fig. 51:15), (*b*) Aramaic Inscription (SW. 105, IA2, fig. 28:8), (*c*) Geometric Stamp Seal Impression (Romala Survey), (*d*) Stamped Jar Handle (Romala Survey), (*e*) Male Human Figurine (Romala Survey), (*f*) Female Plaque-type Figurine (Romala Survey), and (*g*) Hollow-molded Figure of a Female Riding a Horse or Camel (SW. 178, IIA, fig. 51:1)

Plate 133

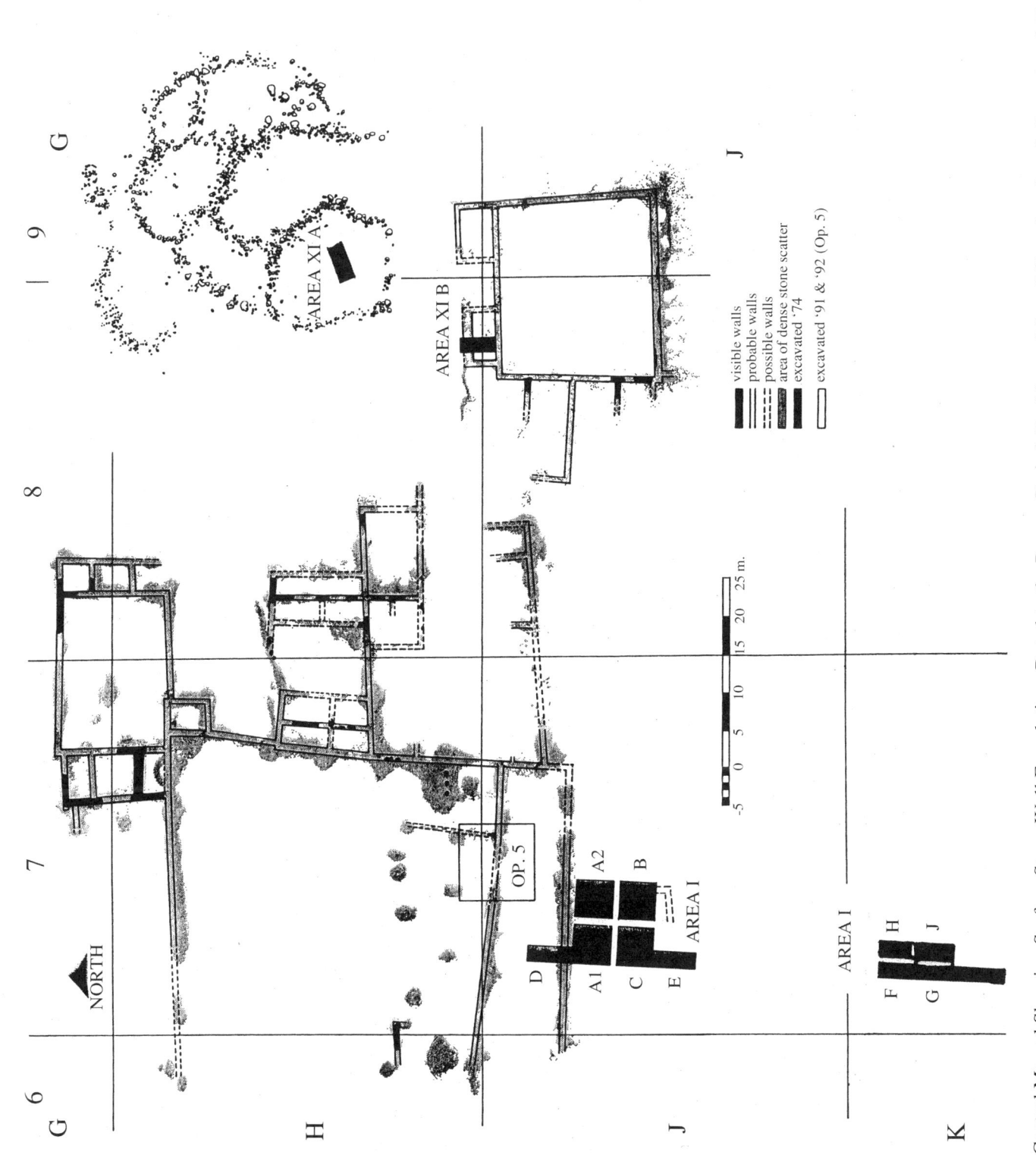

Plan of South Slope of Central Mound Showing Surface Stone Wall Foundations Dated to the Roman Period, Positions of Area I Trenches A to J, Operation 5, Trench XIB Sounding, and Later Surface Stone Enclosure Walls on the Lower Southeast Portion of the Tell with Position of Sounding XIA

Plate 134

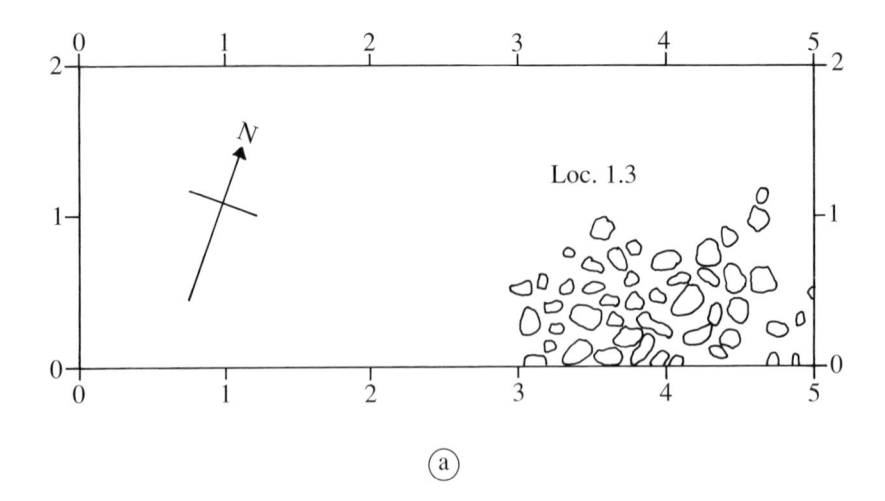

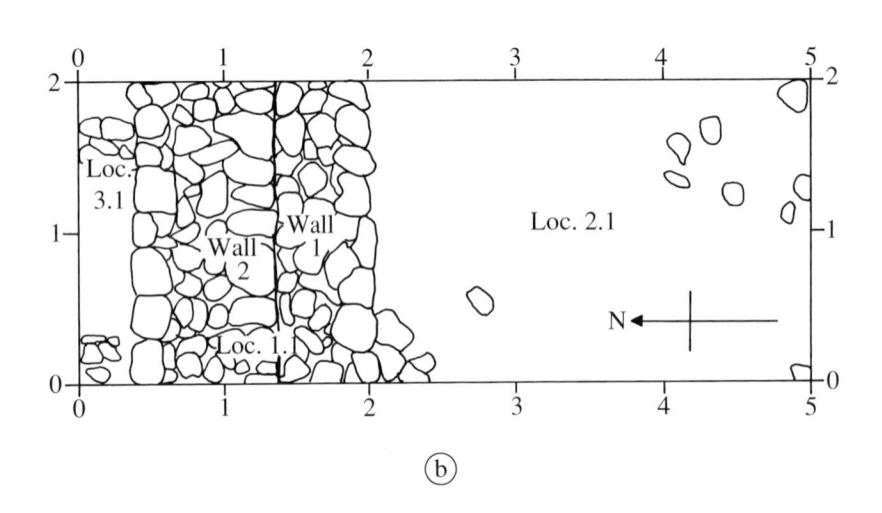

(*a*) Plan of Trench XIA, Phase 2, and (*b*) Plan of Trench XIB, Phases 1 and 2. Scale 1:50

Plate 135

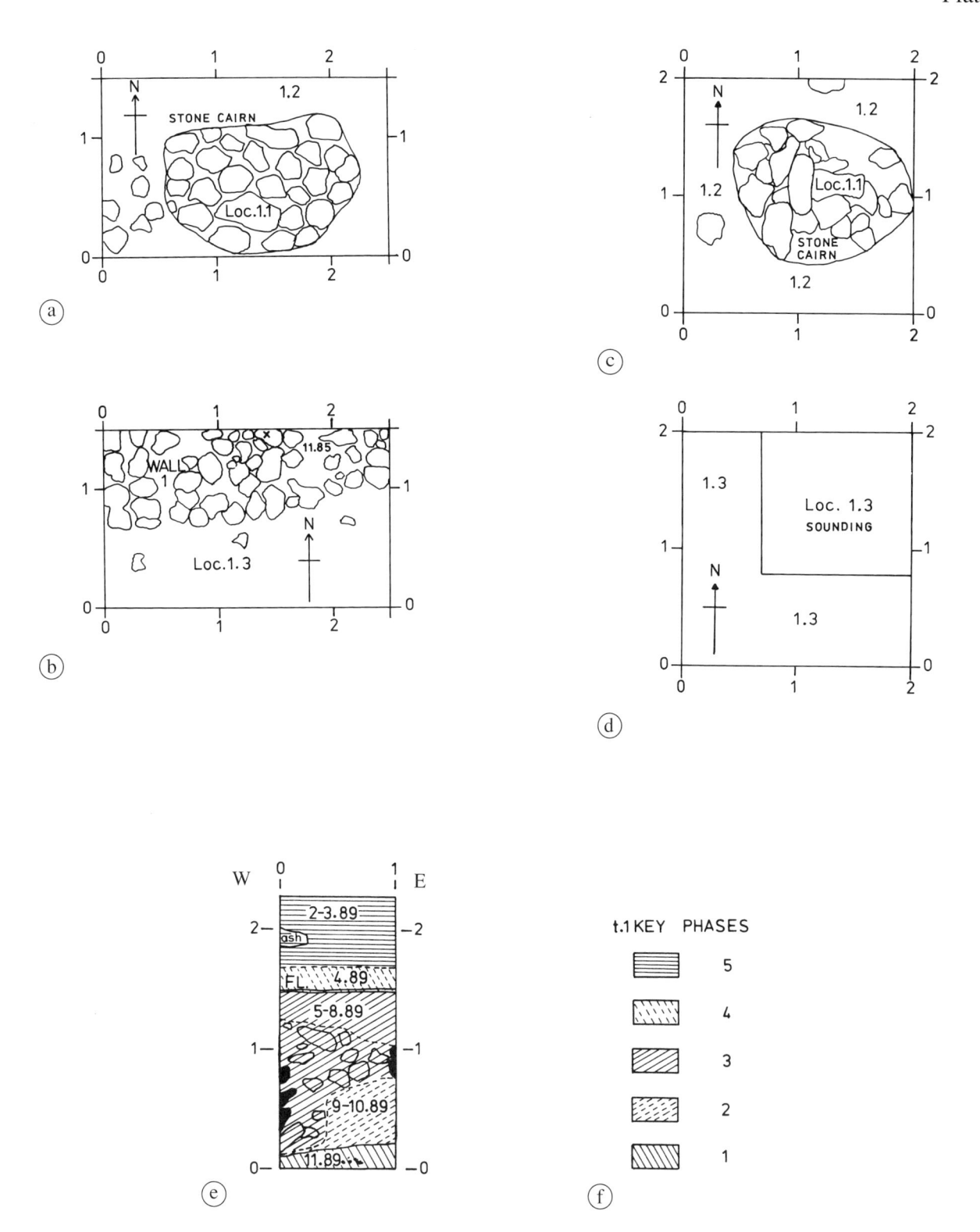

Plate 135. Lower Town and Outer Fortification Soundings: (*a*) S.1, Phase 3 Plan; (*b*) S.1, Phase 2 Plan; (*c*) S.2, Phase 2 Plan; (*d*) S.2, Phase 1 Plan; (*e*) t.1, North Section, Phases 1–5; and (*f*) t.1, Key to Hatching of Phases on North Section. Scale 1:50

Plate 136

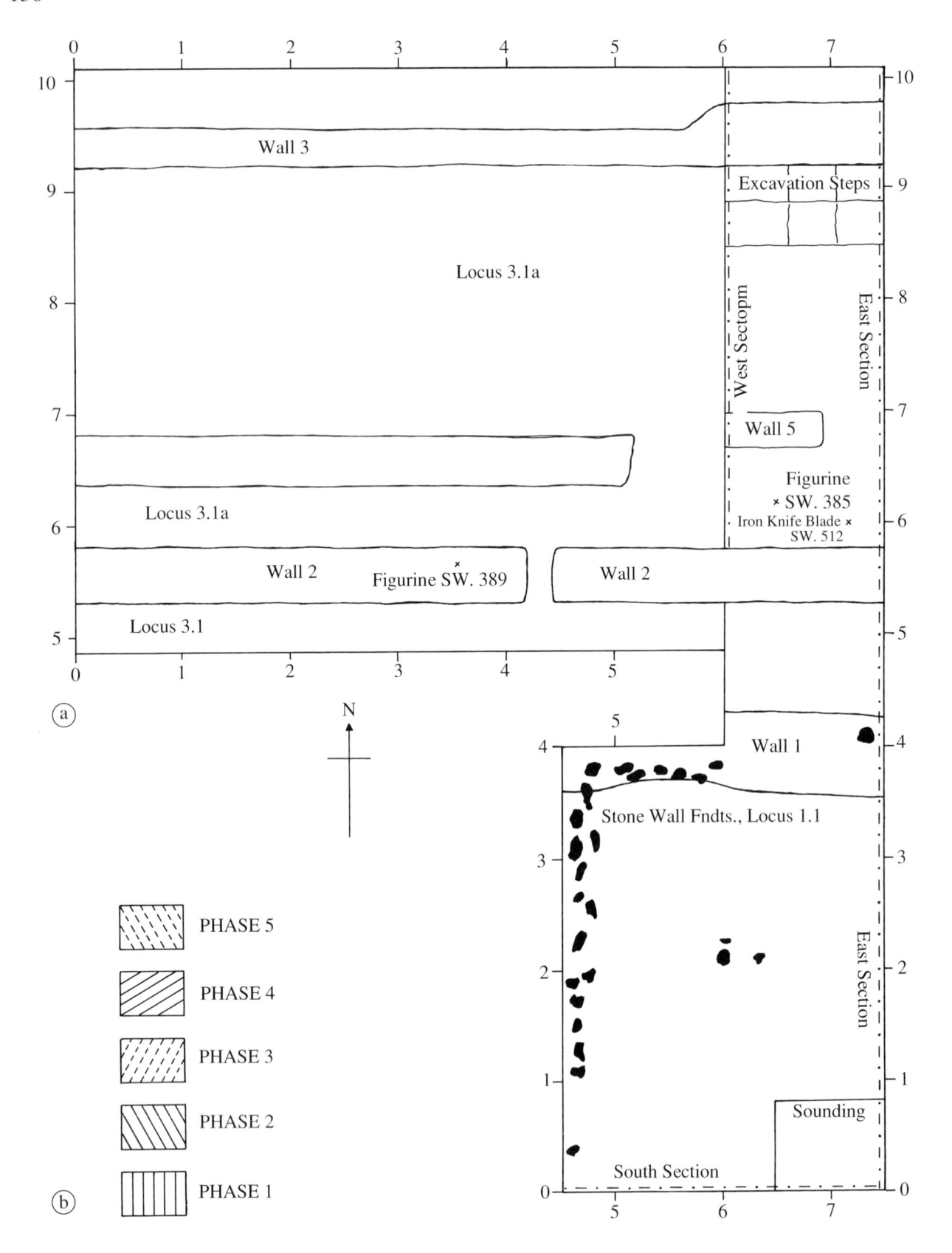

(*a*) Key to Plans and Positions of Sections of Trench VIA and (*b*) Key to Hatching of Phases on Section Drawings of Trench VIA. Scale 1:50

Plate 137

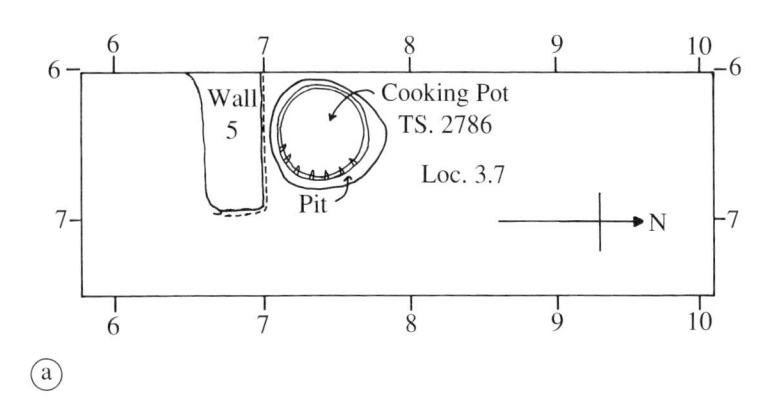

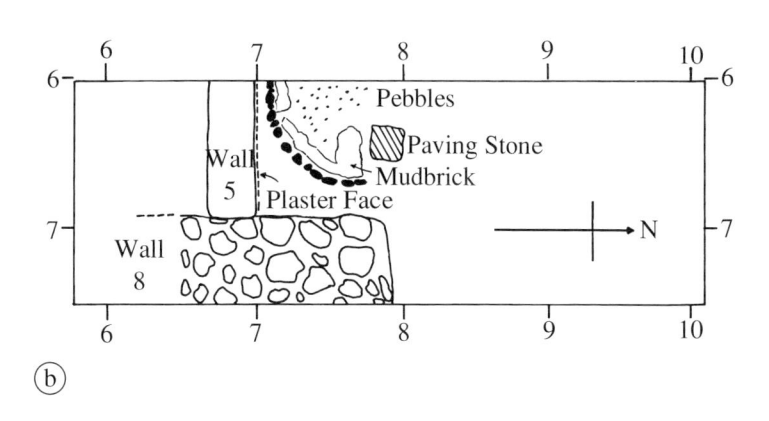

(*a*) Plan of Trench VIA, Phase 1, and (*b*) Plan of Trench VIA, Phase 2. Scale 1:50

Plate 138

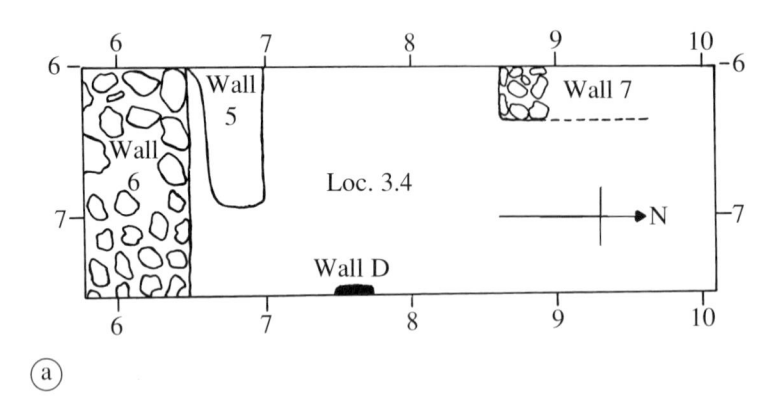

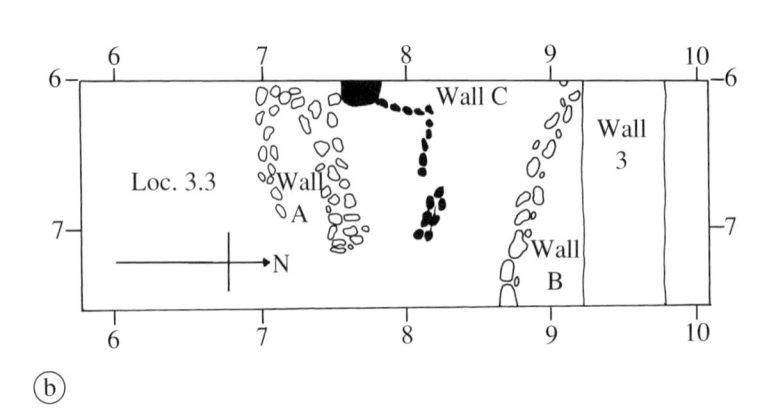

(*a*) Plan of Trench VIA, Phase 3, and (*b*) Plan of Trench VIA, Phase 4. Scale 1:50

Plate 139

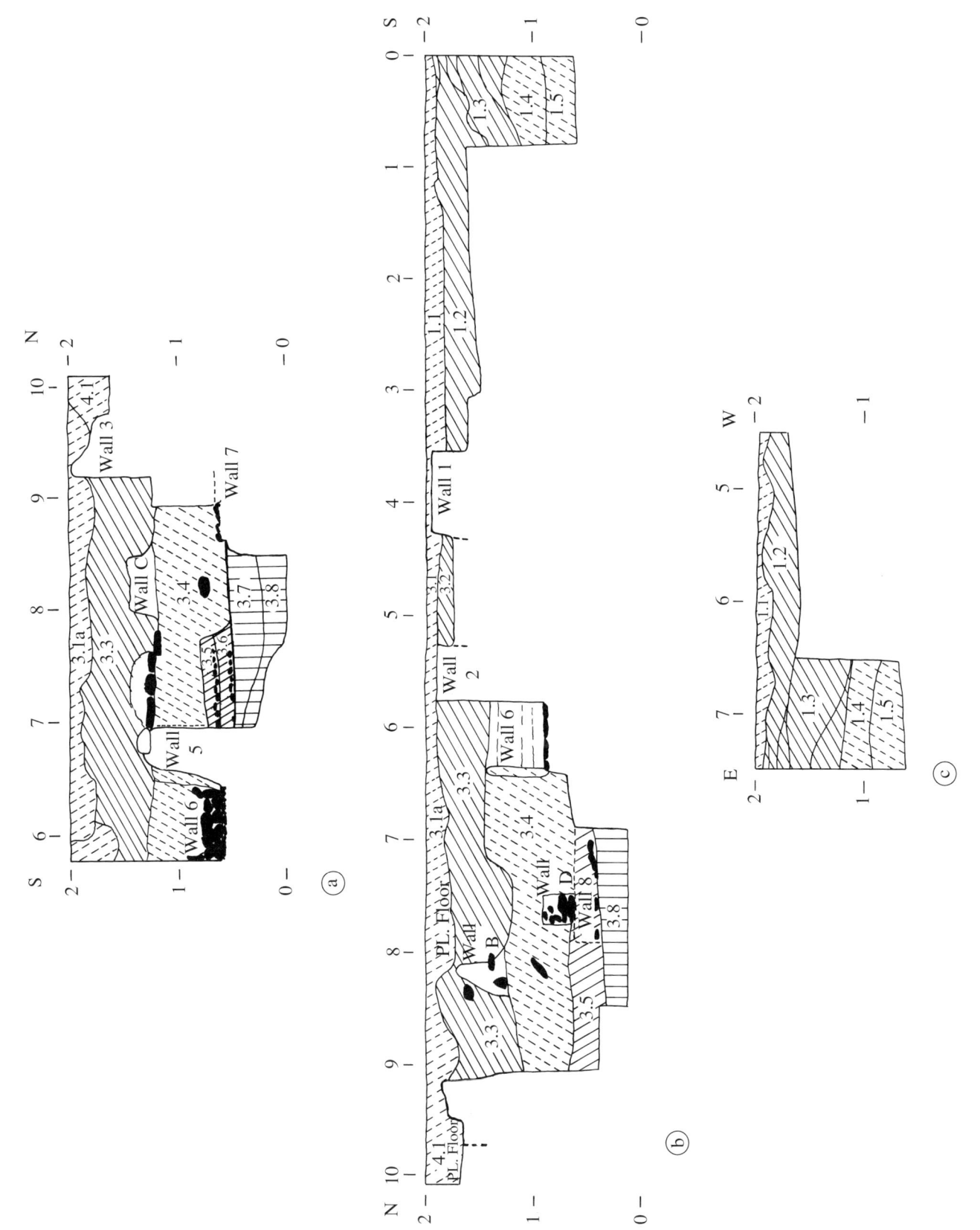

(*a*) Trench VIA, West Section, (*b*) Trench VIA, East Section, and (*c*) Trench VIA, South Section. Scale 1:50

Plate 140

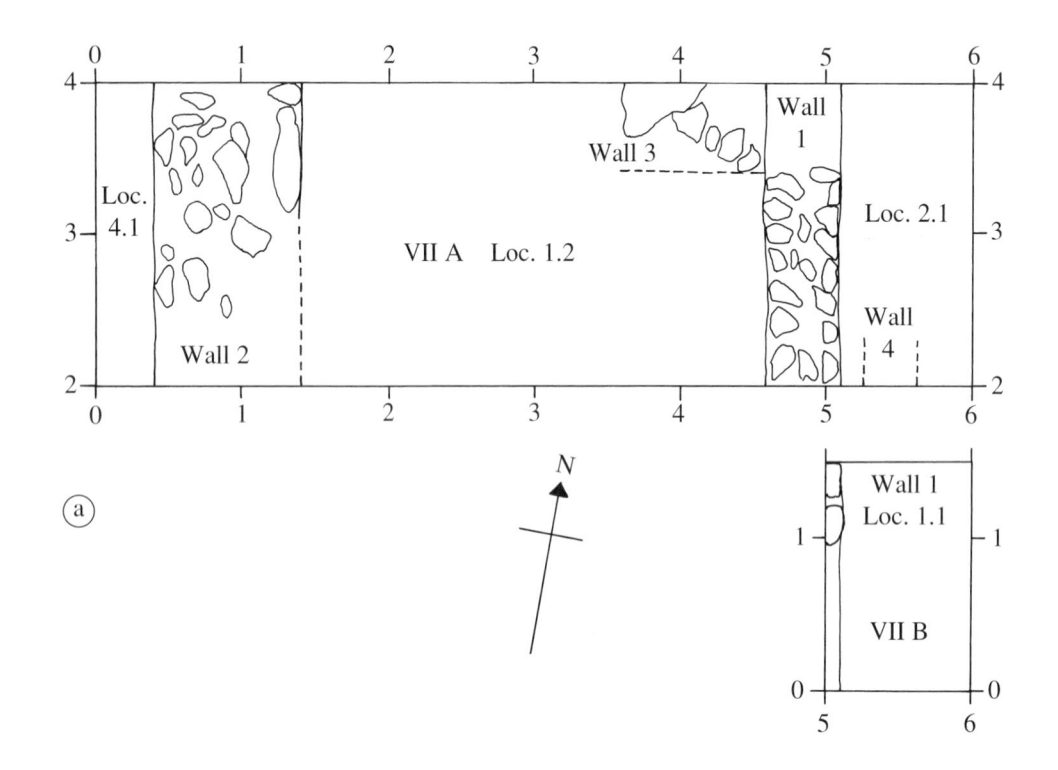

(*a*) Plan of Trenches VIIA and B and (*b*) Key to Hatching of Phases on Section Drawings of Trench VIIA.
Scale 1:50

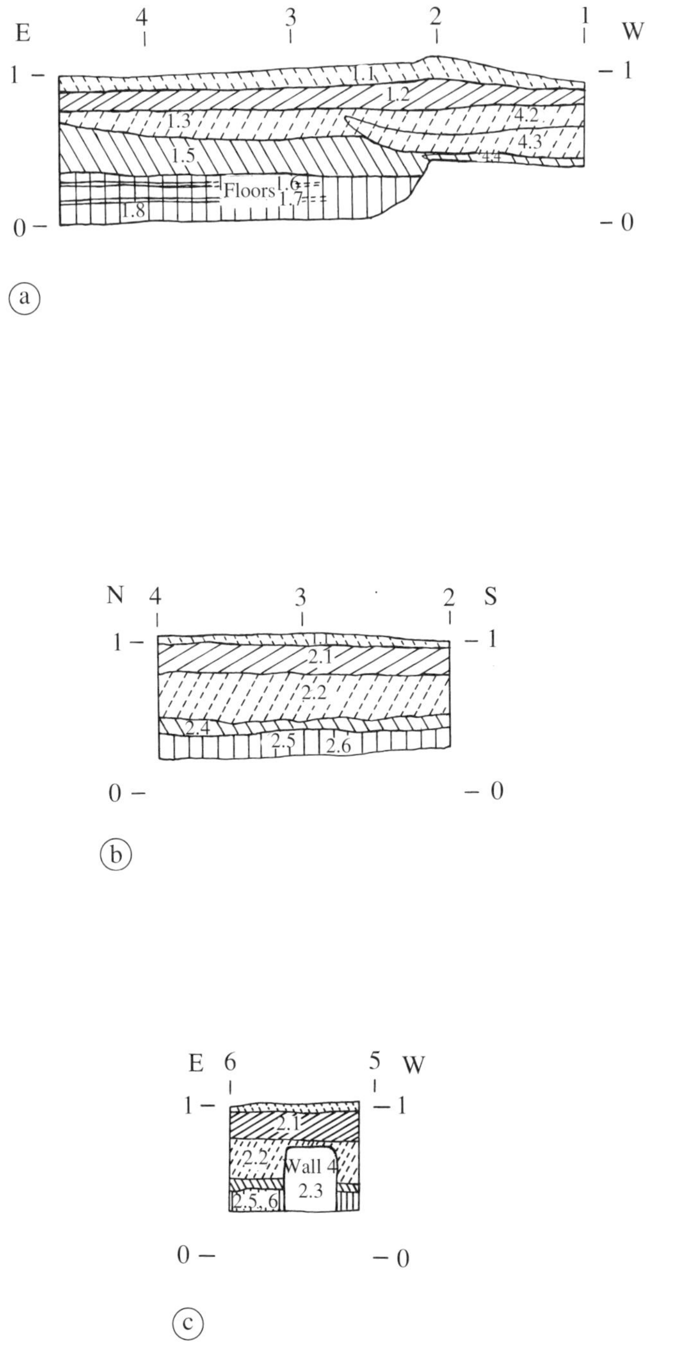

(*a*) Trench VIIA, South Section, (*b*) Trench VIIA, East Section, and (*c*) Trench VIIA, Southeast Section. Scale 1:50

Plate 142

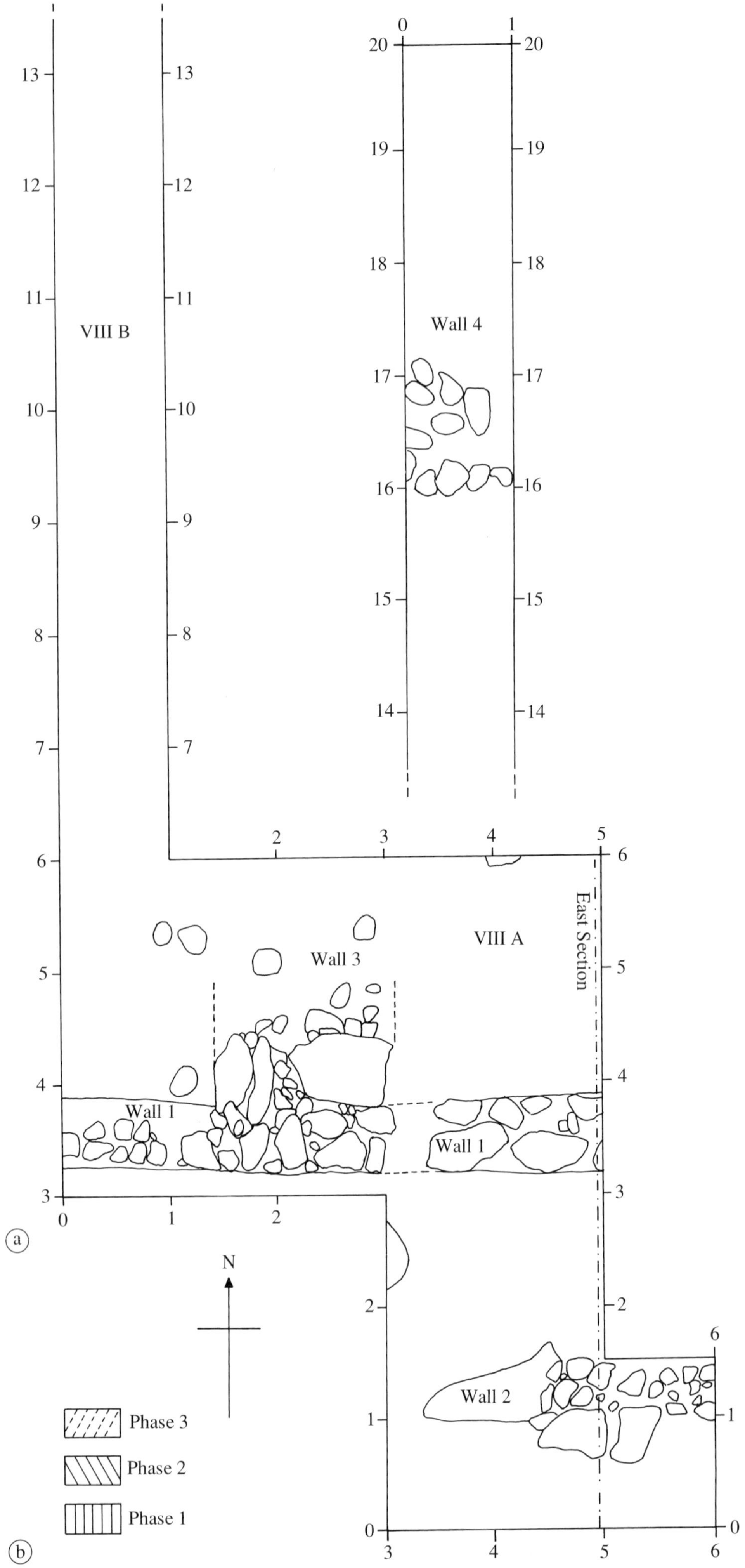

(a) Plan of Trenches VIIIA and B and (b) Key to Hatching of Phases on Section Drawings of Trenches VIIIA and B. Scale

Plate 143

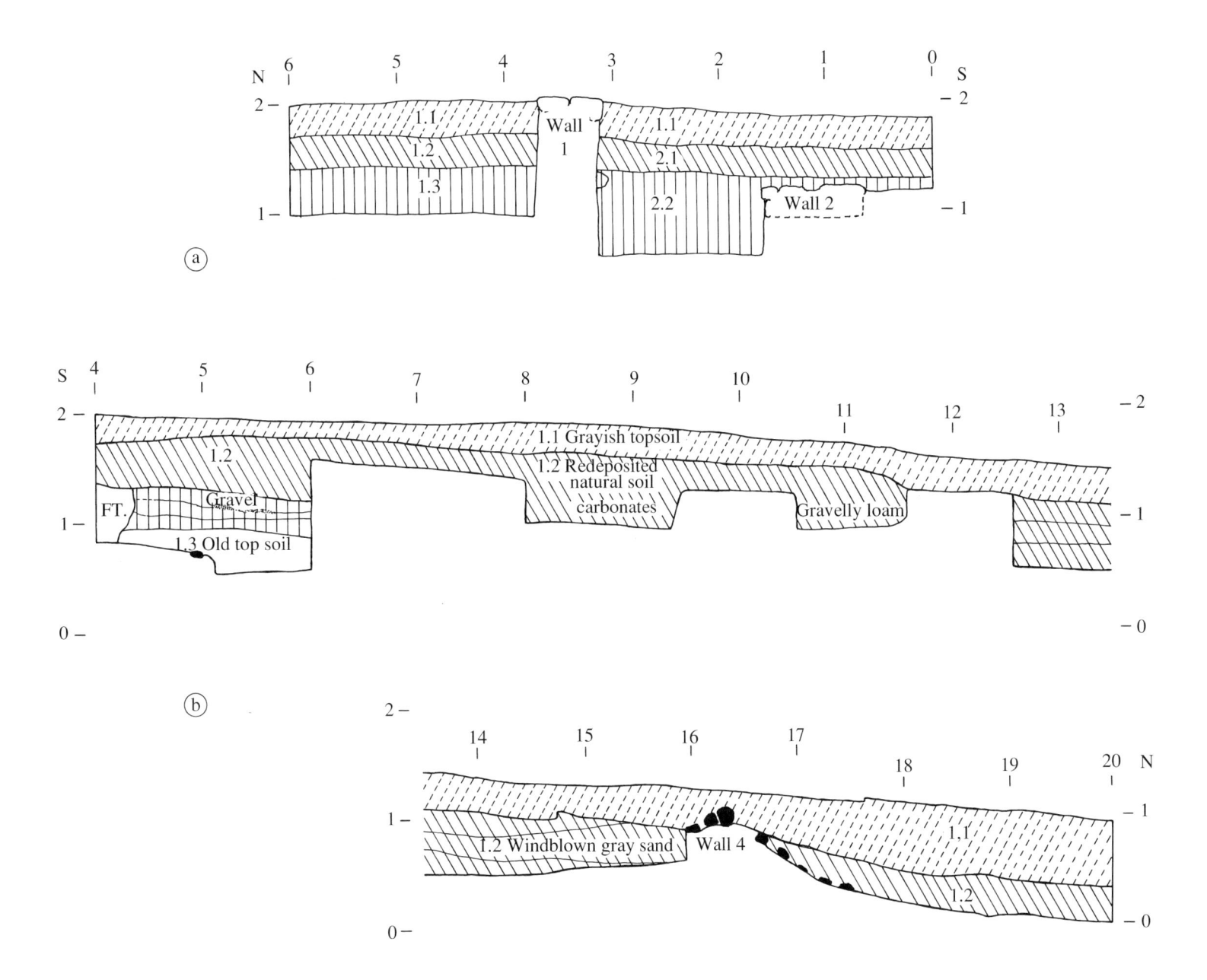

(*a*) Trench VIIIA, East Section, and (*b*) Trench VIIIB, West Section. Scale 1:50

Plate 144

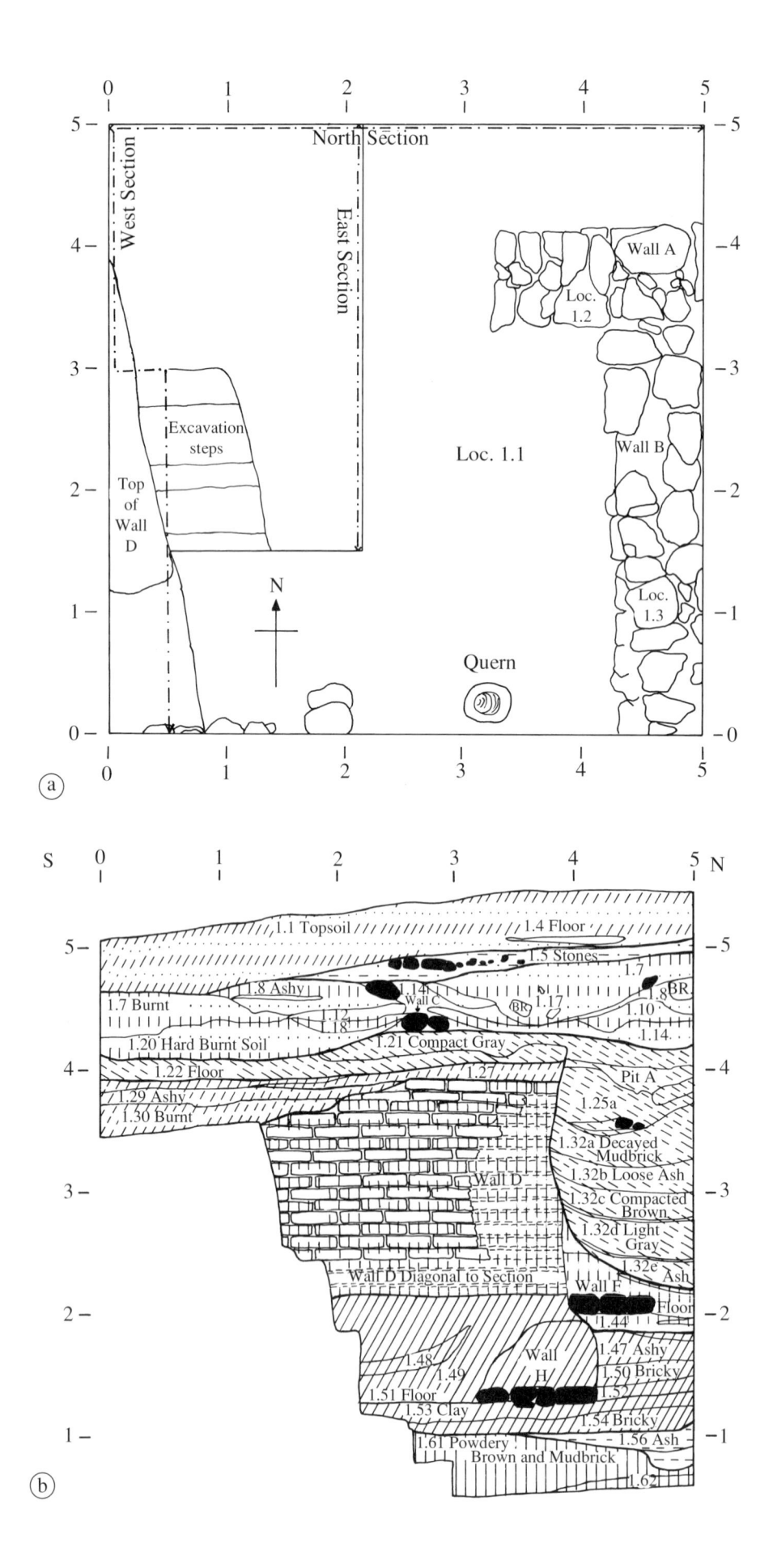

(*a*) Key to Plan and Sections of Trench IC and (*b*) Trench IC, West Section. Scale 1:50

Plate 145

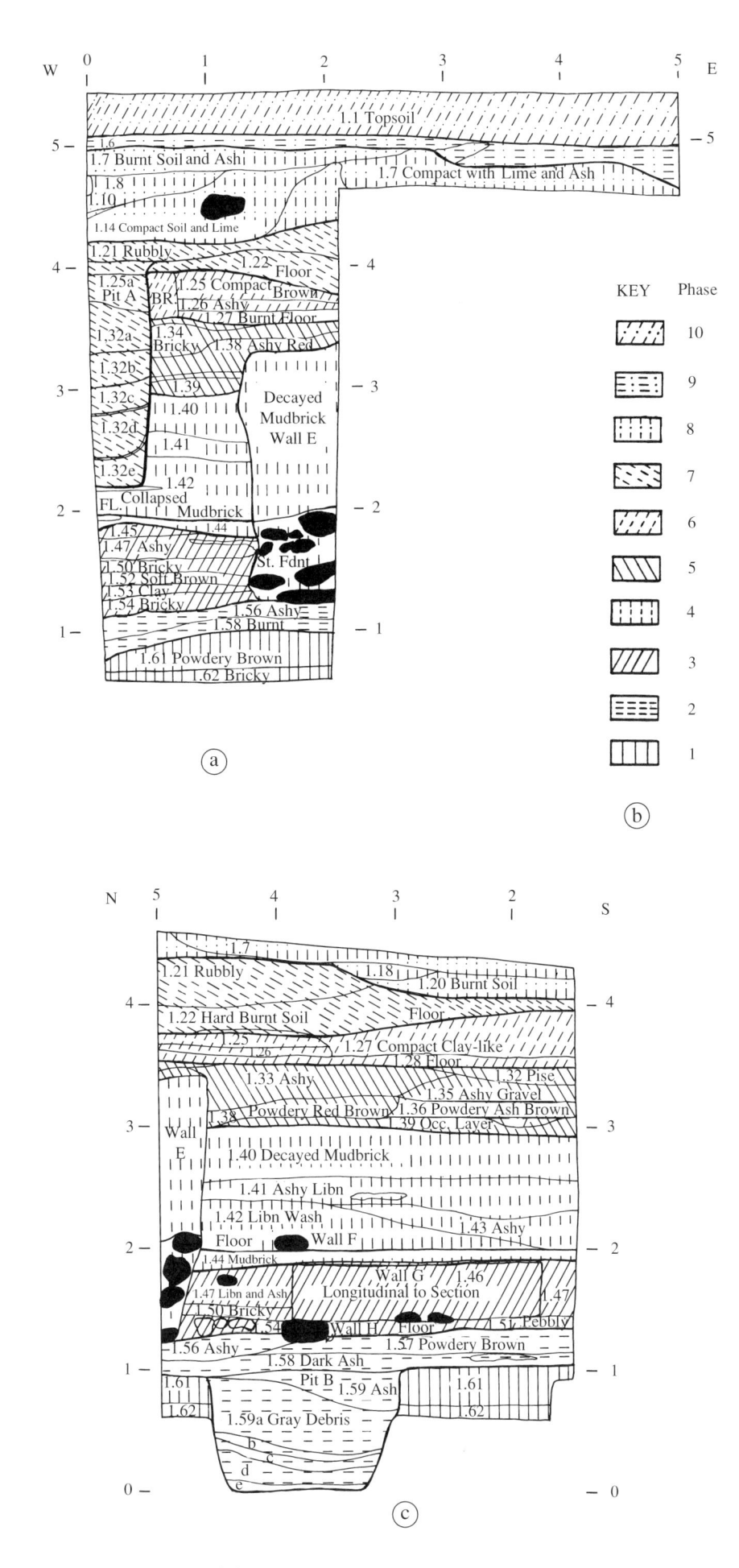

(*a*) Trench IC, North Section, (*b*) Key to Hatching of Phases on Section Drawings of Trench IC, and (*c*) Trench IC, East Section. Scale 1:50

Plate 146

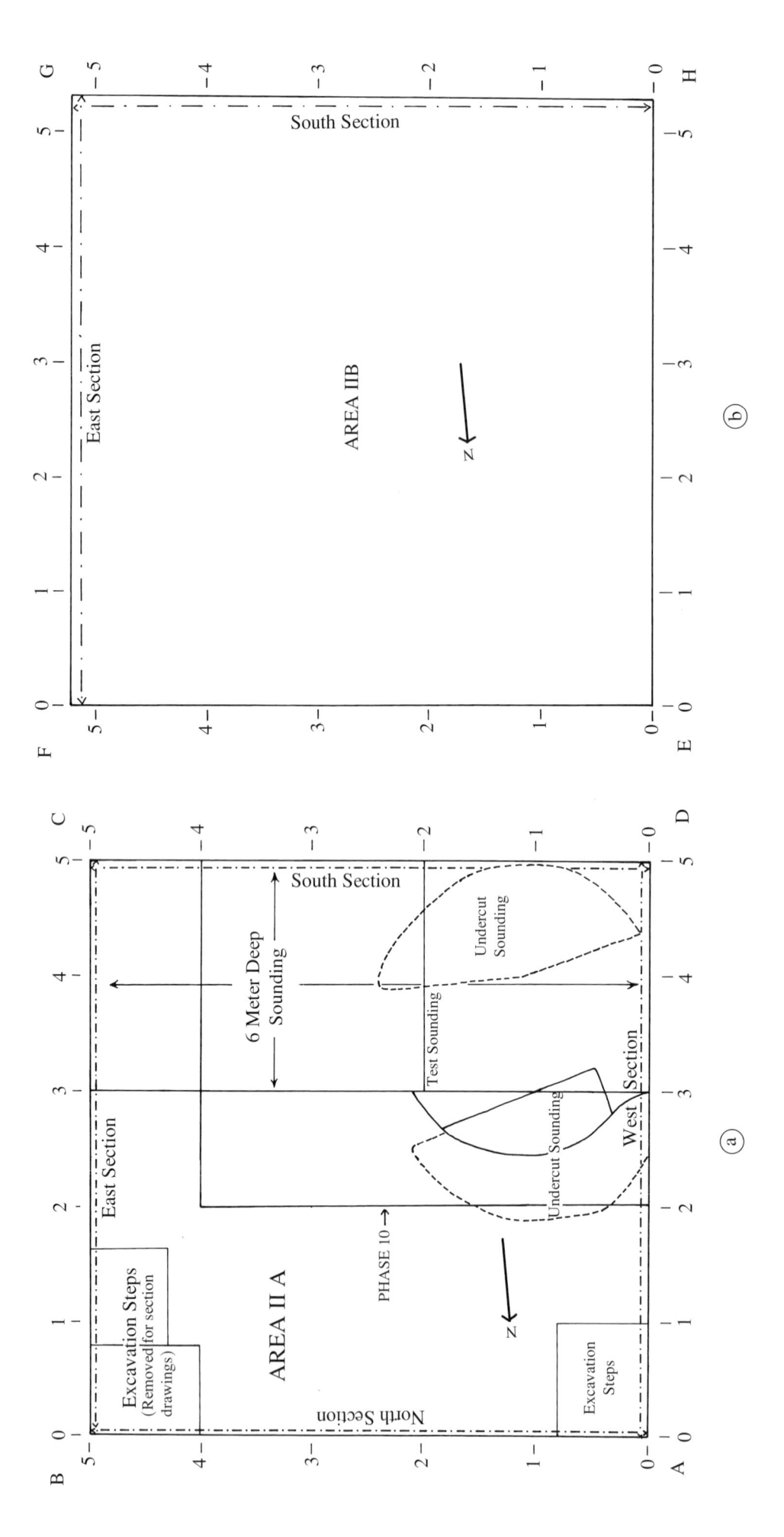

(*a*) Keys to Plans and Sections of Trench IIA and (*b*) Keys to Plans and Sections of Trench IIB. Scale 1:50

Plate 147

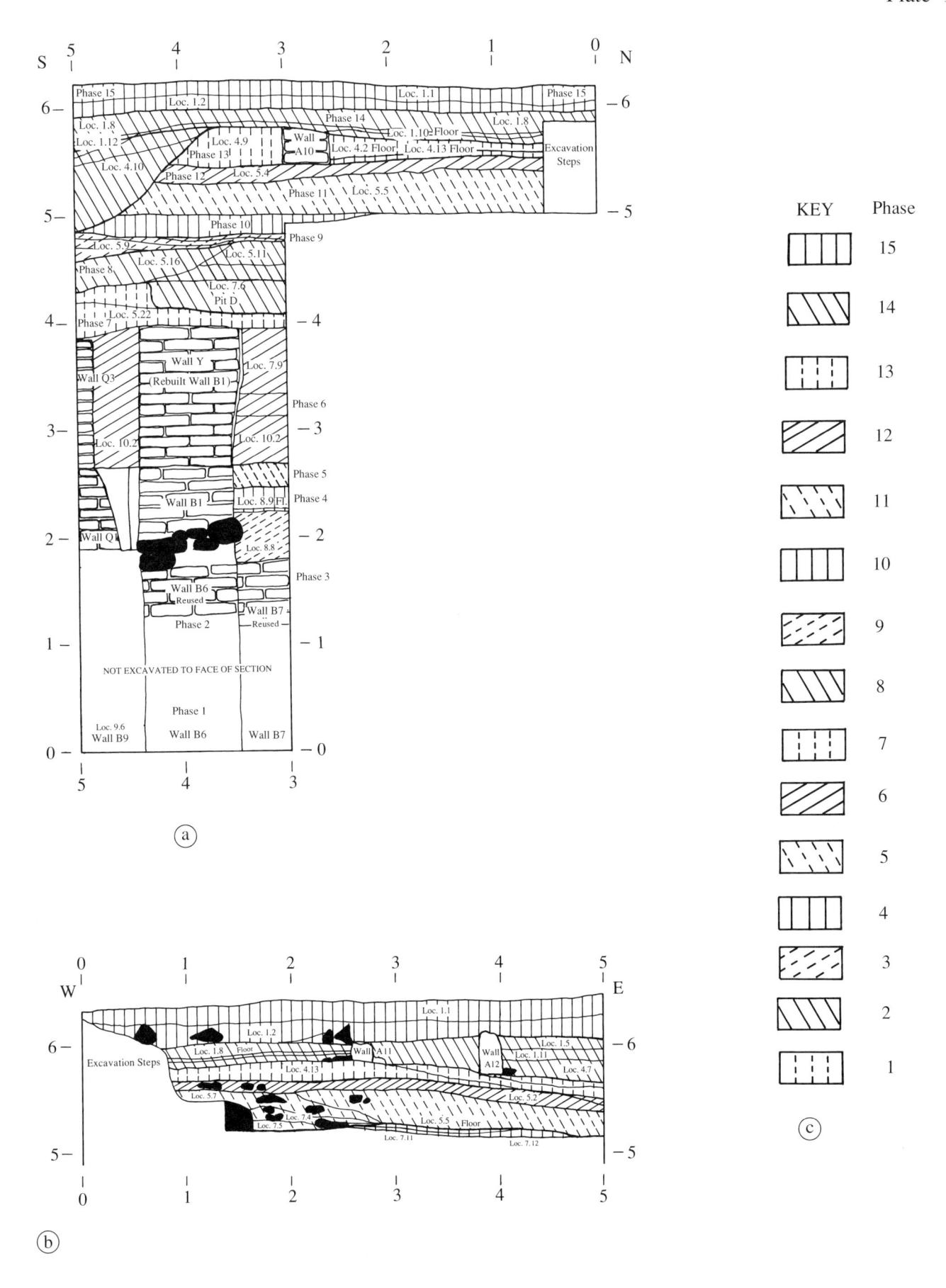

(a) Area IIA, West Section, (b) Area IIA, North Section, and (c) Key to Hatching of Phases on Section Drawings of Trenches IIA and IIB. Scale 1:50

Plate 148

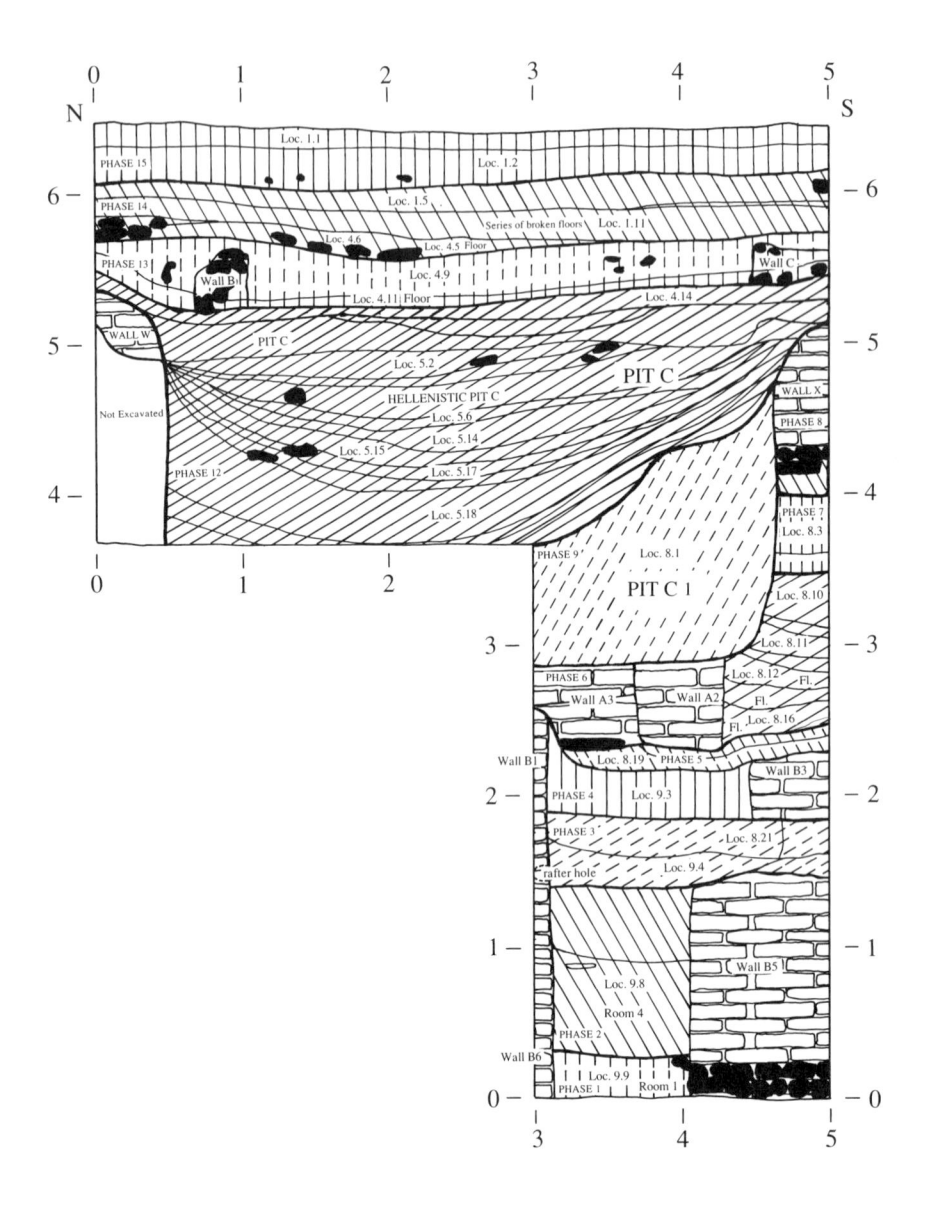

Trench IIA, East Section. Scale 1:50

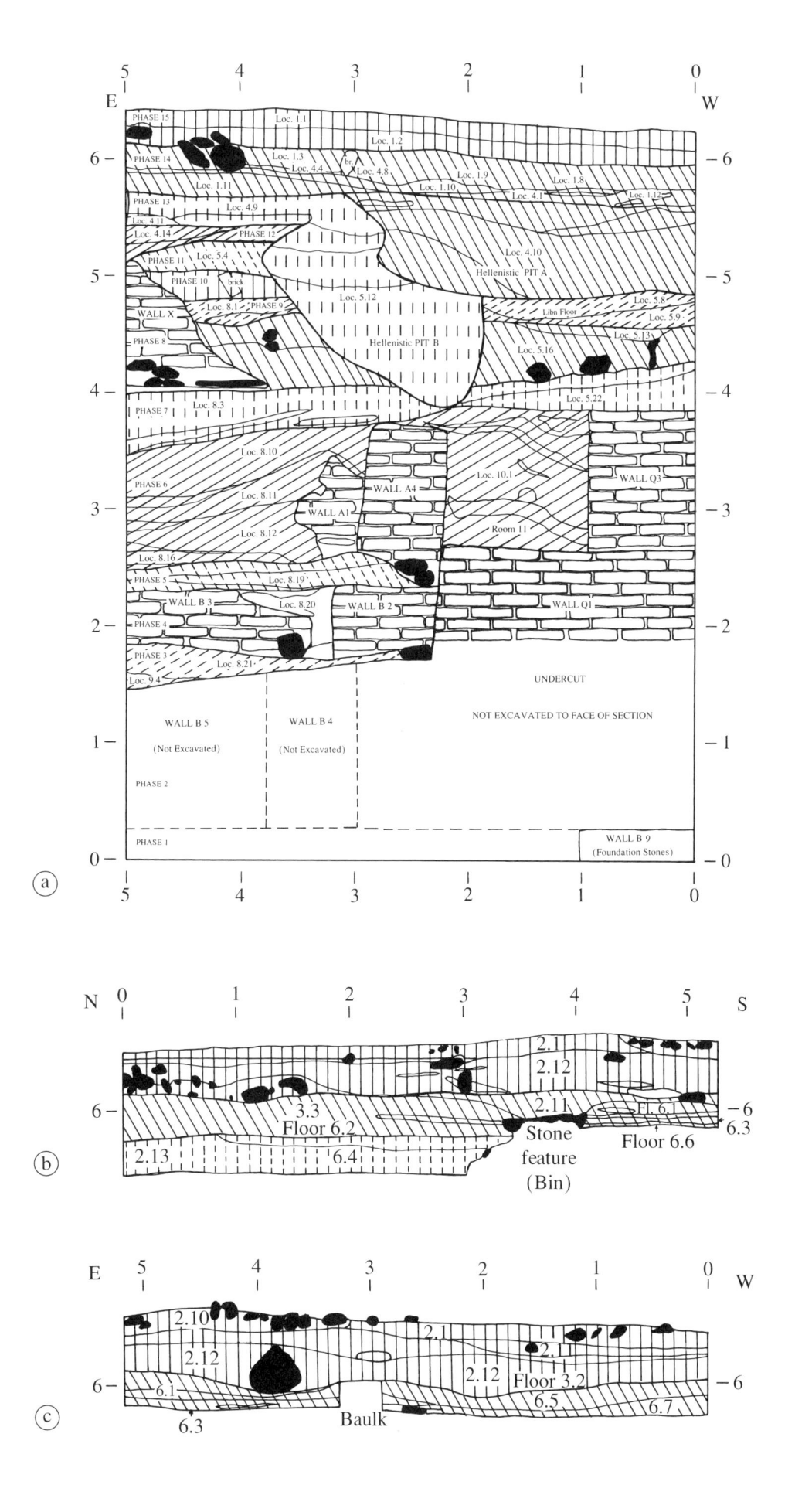

(*a*) Trench IIA, South Section, (*b*) Trench IIB, East Section, and (*c*) Trench IIB, South Section. Scale 1:50

Plate 150

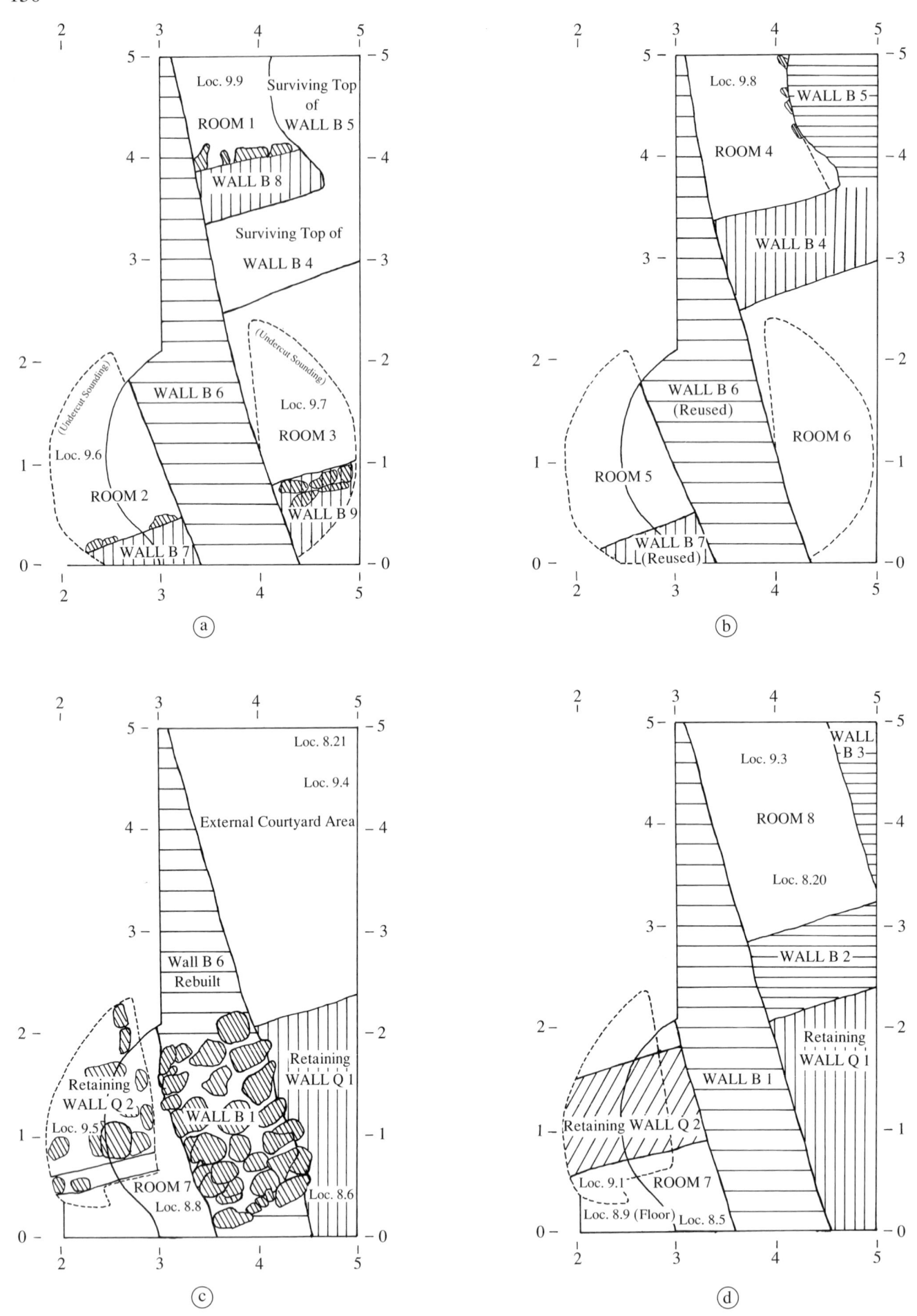

(a) Plan of Trench IIA, Phase 1, (b) Plan of Trench IIA, Phase 2, (c) Plan of Trench IIA, Phase 3, and (d) Plan of Trench IIA, Phase 4. Scale 1:50

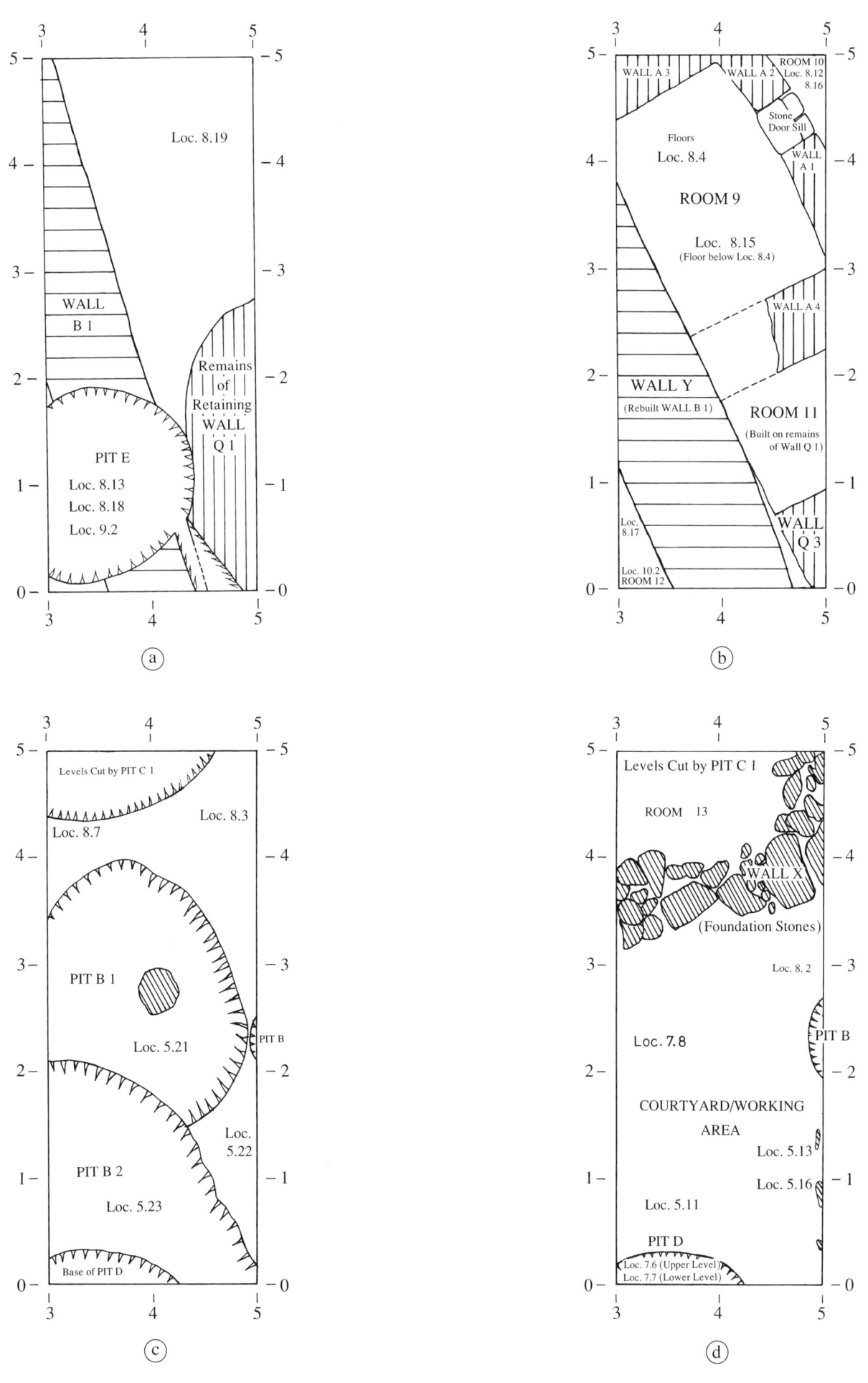

(*a*) Plan of Trench IIA, Phase 5, (*b*) Plan of Trench IIA, Phase 6, (*c*) Plan of Trench IIA, Phase 7, and (*d*) Plan of Trench IIA, Phase 8. Scale 1:50

Plate 152

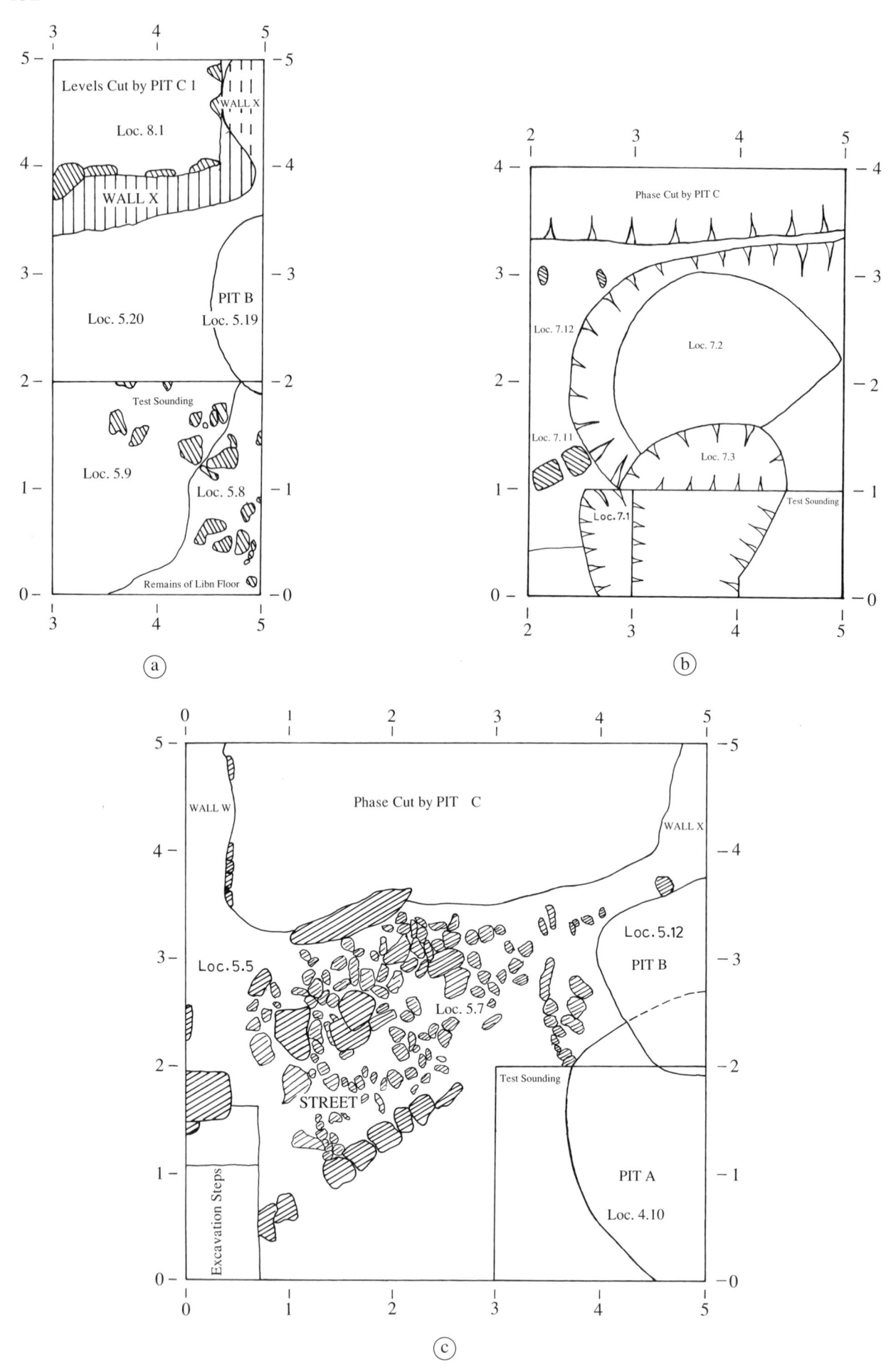

(*a*) Plan of Trench IIA, Phase 9, (*b*) Plan of Trench IIA, Phase 10, and (*c*) Plan of Trench IIA, Phase 11. Scale 1:50

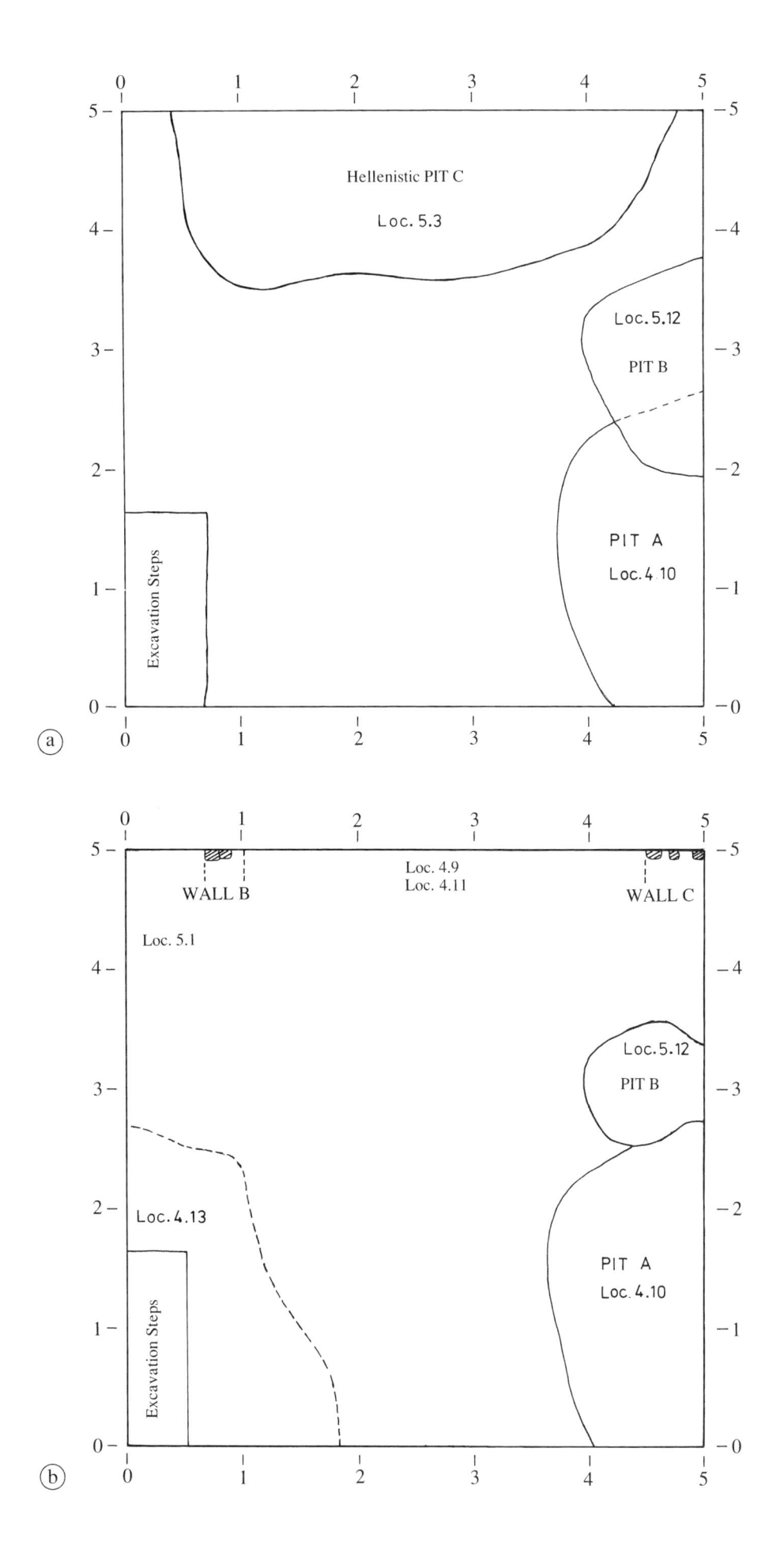

Plate 153

(*a*) Plan of Trench IIA, Phase 12, and (*b*) Plan of Trench IIA, Phase 13. Scale 1:50

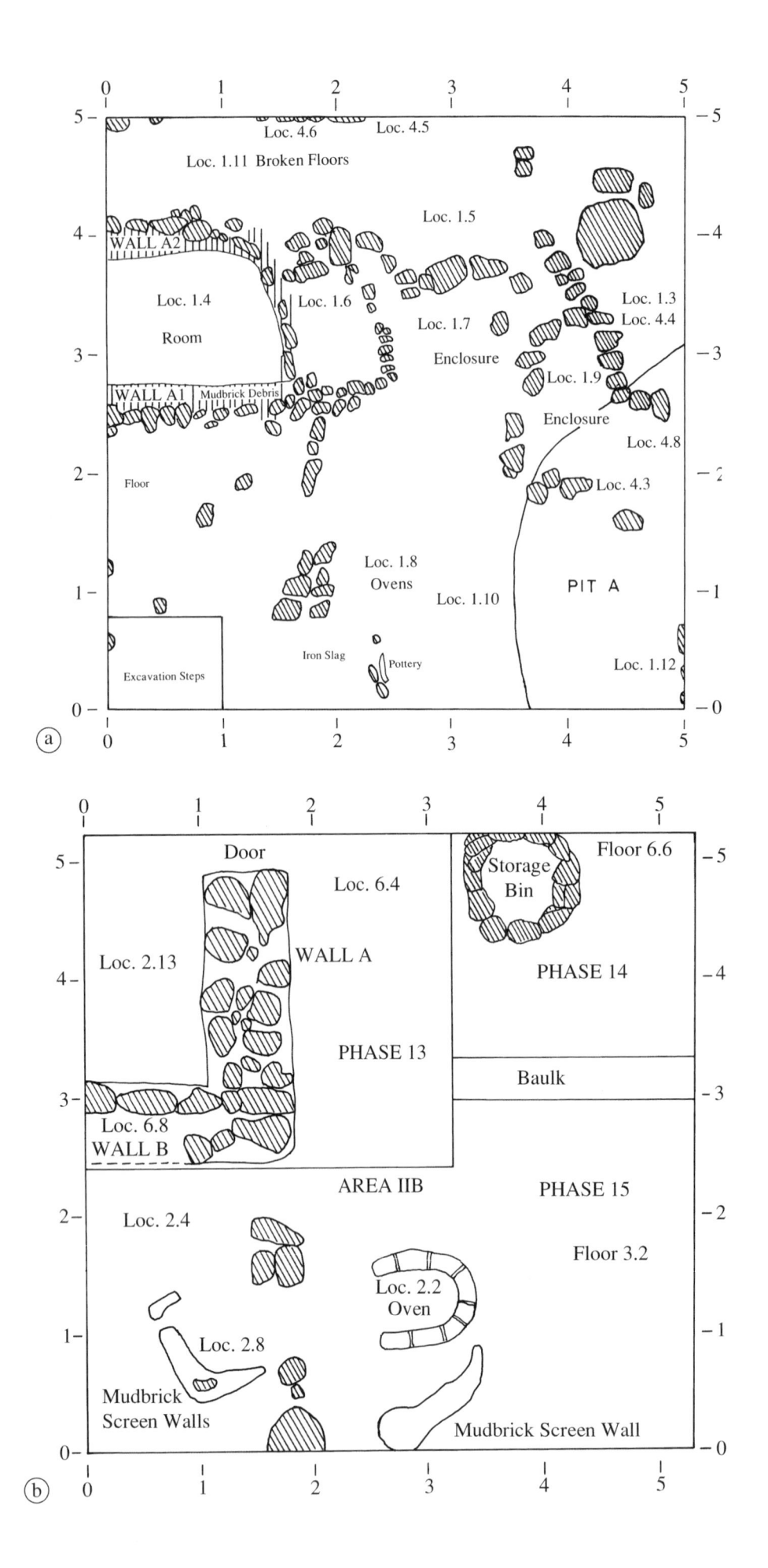

Plate 154

(*a*) Plan of Trench IIA, Phase 14, and (*b*) Plan of Trench IIB, Phases 13, 14, and 15. Scale 1:50

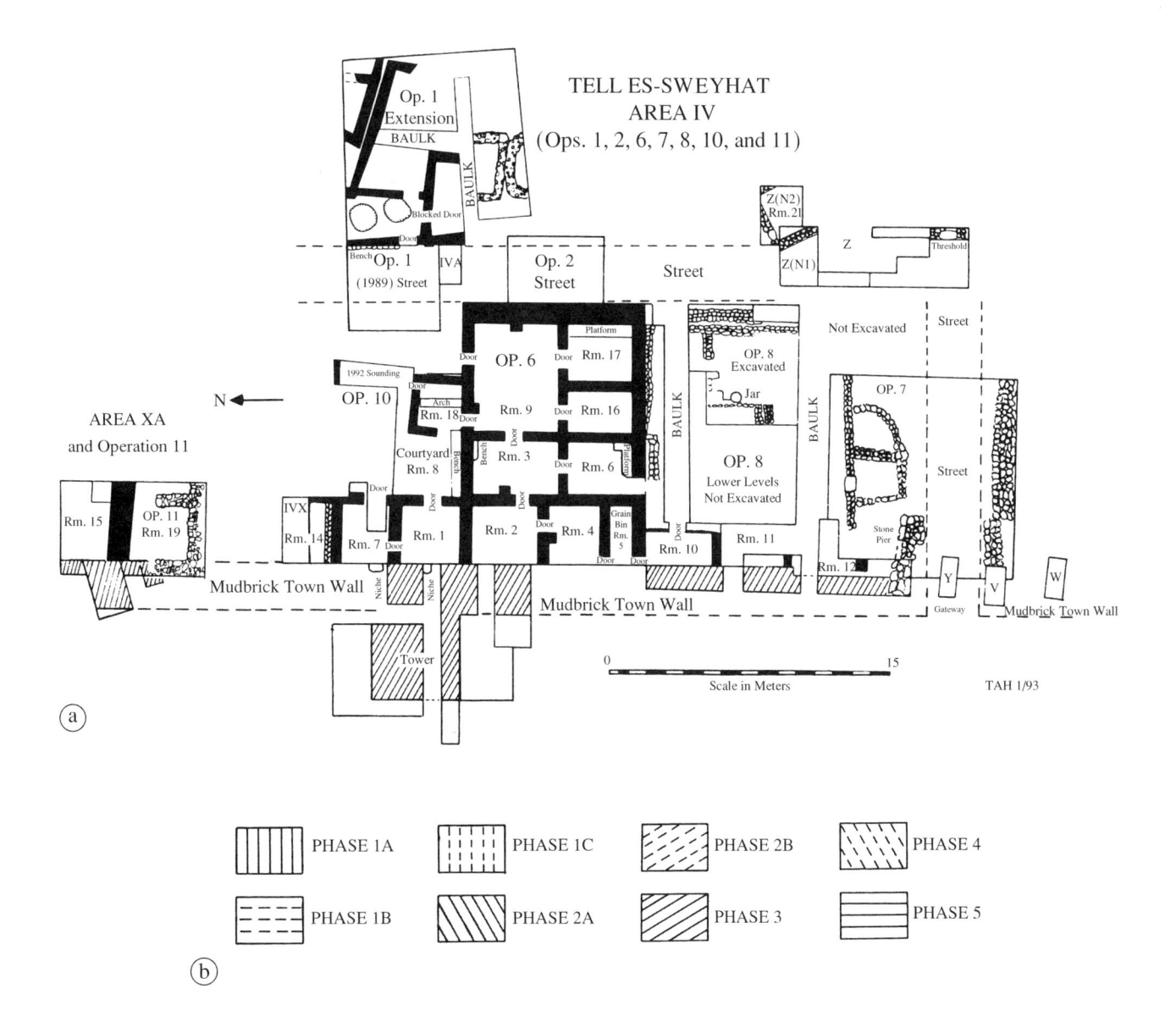

(*a*) Schematic Plan Showing Locations of Trenches, Operations, and Rooms in Area IV and Trench XA, and (*b*) Key to Hatching of Phases on Section Drawings of Area IV and Trench XA

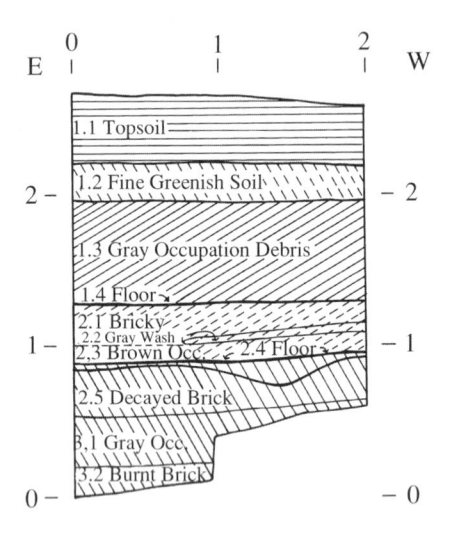

Plate 156

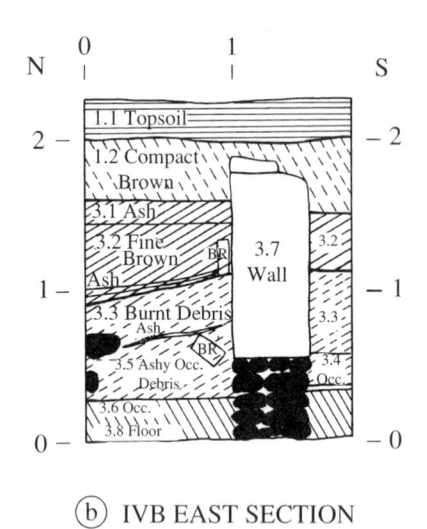

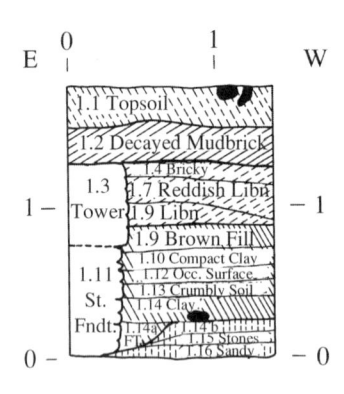

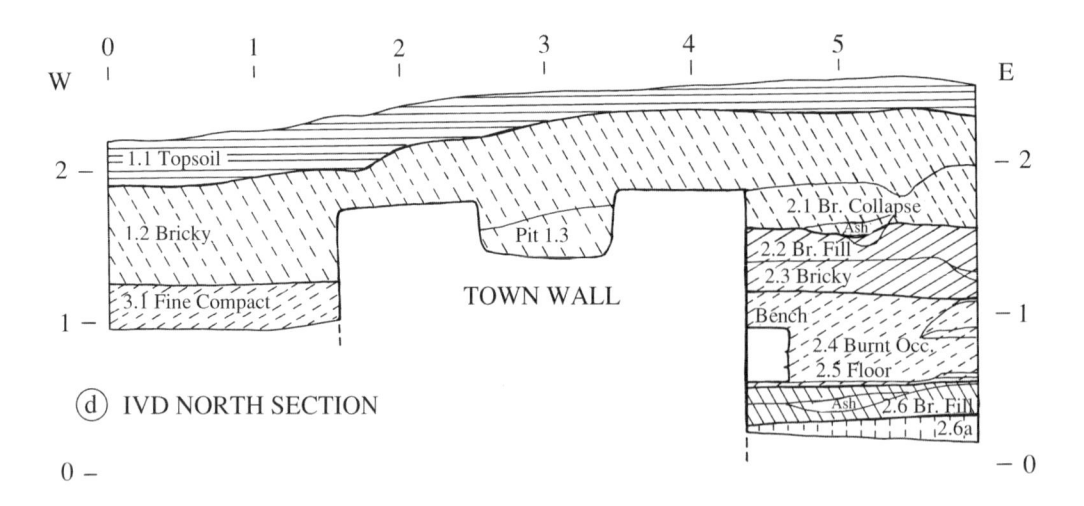

(*a*) Trench IVA, South Section, (*b*) Trench IVB, East Section of Sounding into Western Portions of Trench IVF (Room 1) and Trench IVK (Room 2), (*c*) Trench IVC, South Section Abutting Southwest Corner of Town Wall Tower, and (*d*) Trench IVD, North Section Showing Position of Town Wall and Western Portion of Trench IVK (Room 2). Scale 1:50

Plate 157

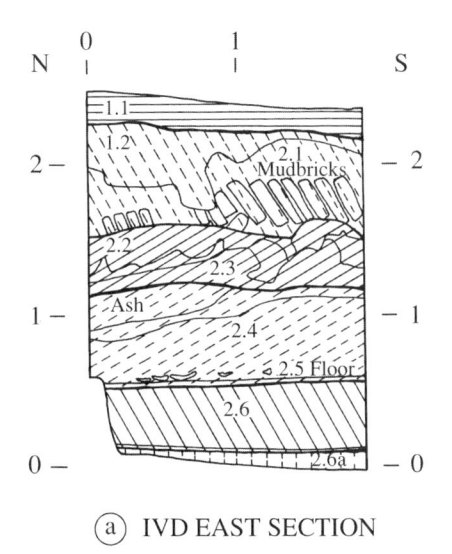

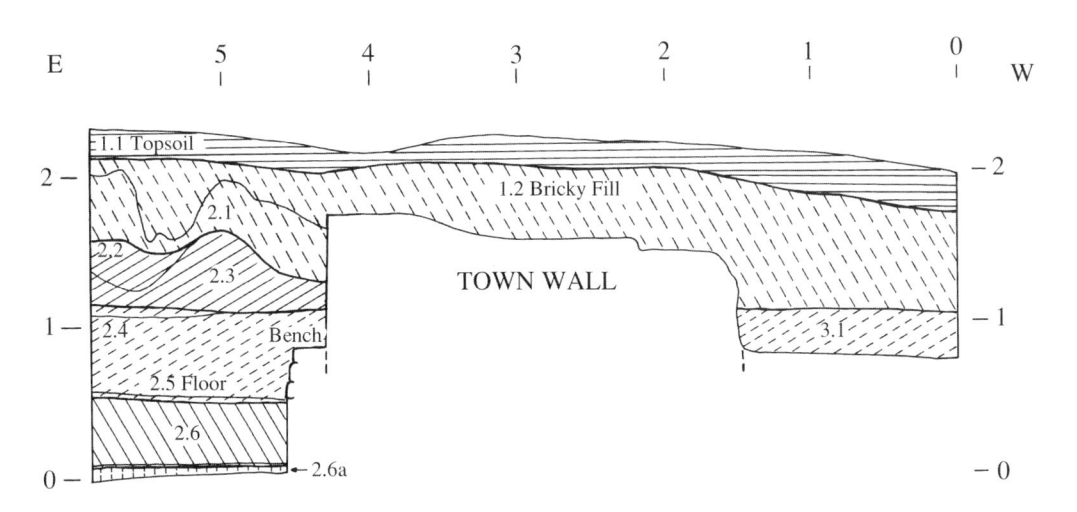

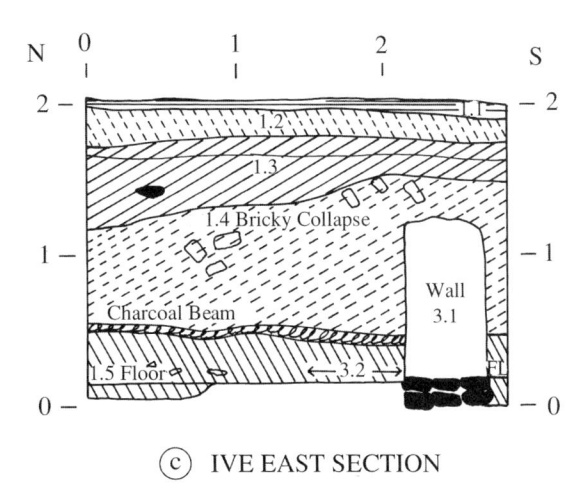

(*a*) Trench IVD, East Section Showing Central Portion of Trench IVK (Room 2), (*b*) Trench IVD, South Section Showing Position of Town Wall and Western Portion of Trench IVK (Room 2), and (*c*) Trench IVE, East Section of Sounding into Portions of Trench IVL (Room 3) and Trench IVQ (Room 6). Scale 1:50

Plate 158

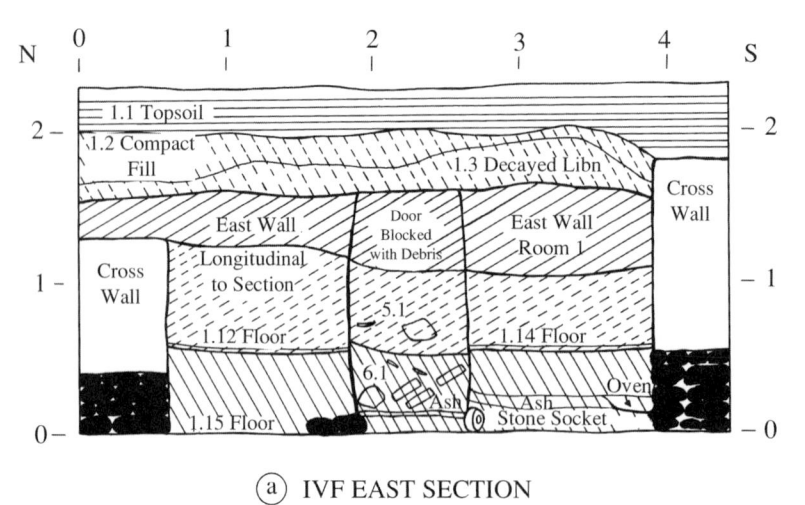

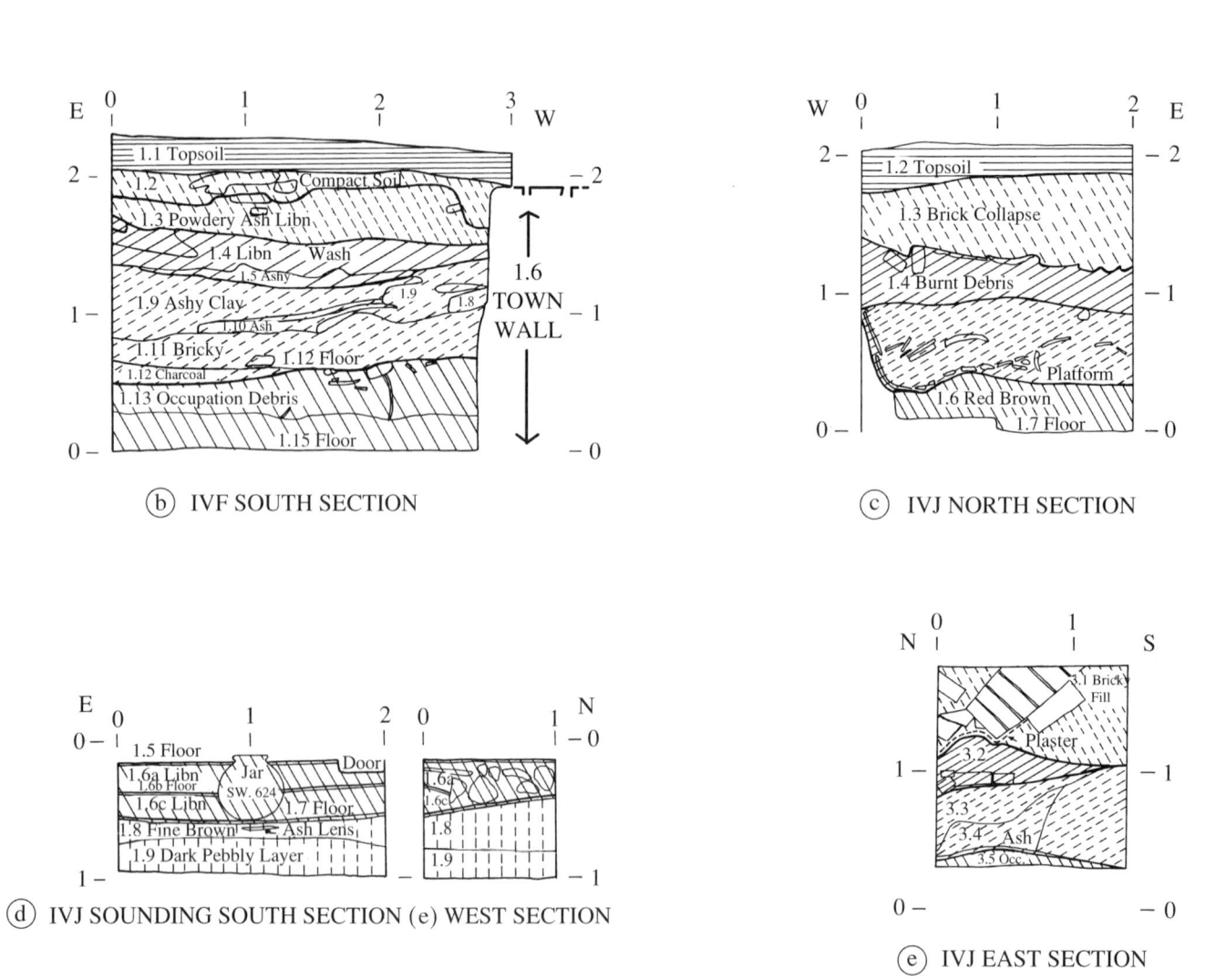

(a) IVF EAST SECTION

(b) IVF SOUTH SECTION

(c) IVJ NORTH SECTION

(d) IVJ SOUNDING SOUTH SECTION (e) WEST SECTION

(e) IVJ EAST SECTION

(*a*) Trench IVF, East Section Along Walls and Door Between IVF (Room 1) and IVN (Room 8), (*b*) Trench IVF, South Section of First Sounding in the North Portion of Room 1, (*c*) Trench IVJ, North Section Showing Position of Pottery on Platform in Northwestern Portion of Room 4, (*d*) Trench IVJ, South Section of Sounding on Southern Side of Room 4, (*e*) Trench IVJ, West Section of Sounding on Southern Side of Room 4, and (*f*) Trench IVJ, East Section Through Central Upper Portion of the Storage Bin (Room 5). Scale 1:50

Plate 159

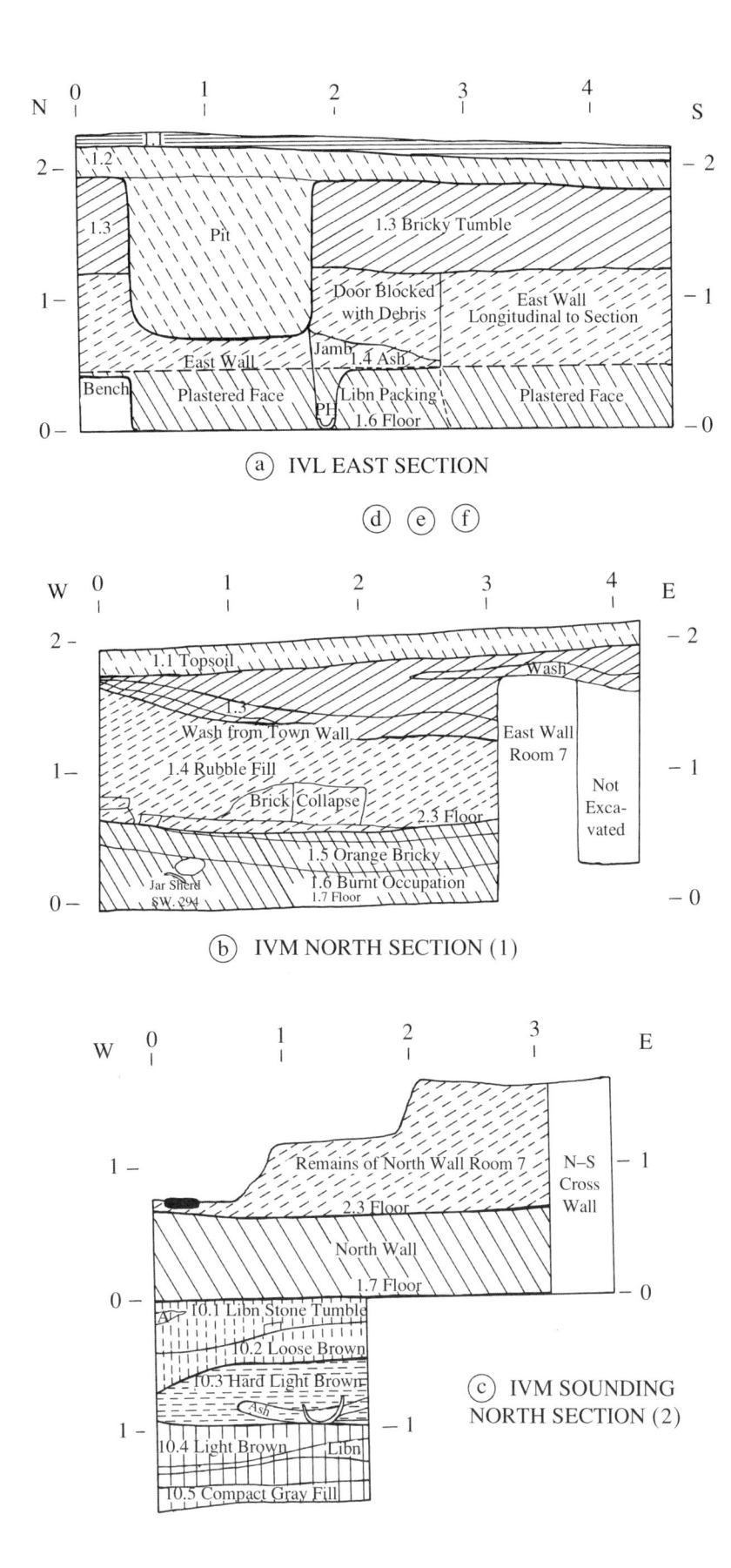

(a) IVL EAST SECTION

(b) IVM NORTH SECTION (1)

(c) IVM SOUNDING NORTH SECTION (2)

(a) Trench IVL, East Section Along Wall and Door Between Trench IVL (Room 3) and Trench IVP (Courtyard Room 9), (b) Trench IVM, North Section 1 Across Full Length of the Northern Portion of Room 7, and (c) Trench IVM, North Section 2 Showing Remains of North Wall (Room 7) and Sounding Below the Wall of Room 7. Scale 1:50

Plate 160

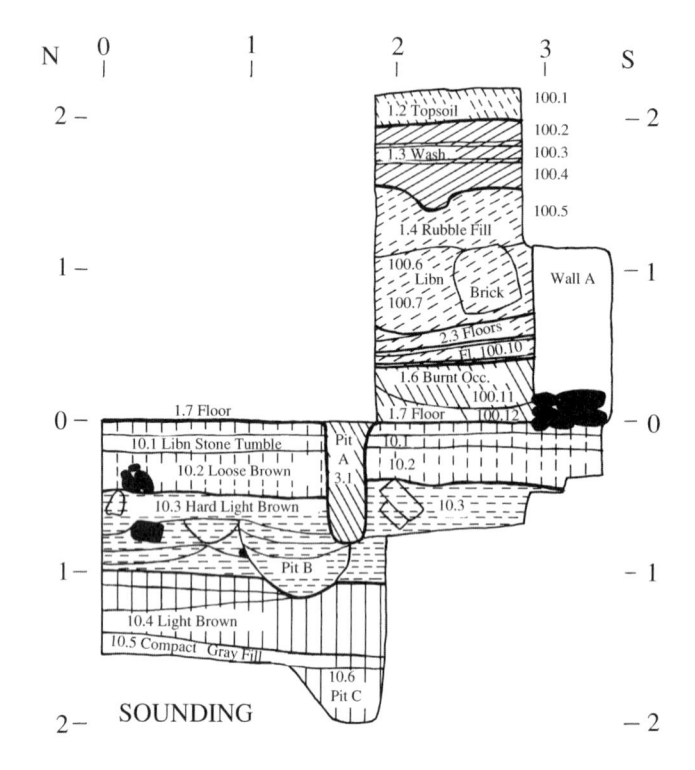

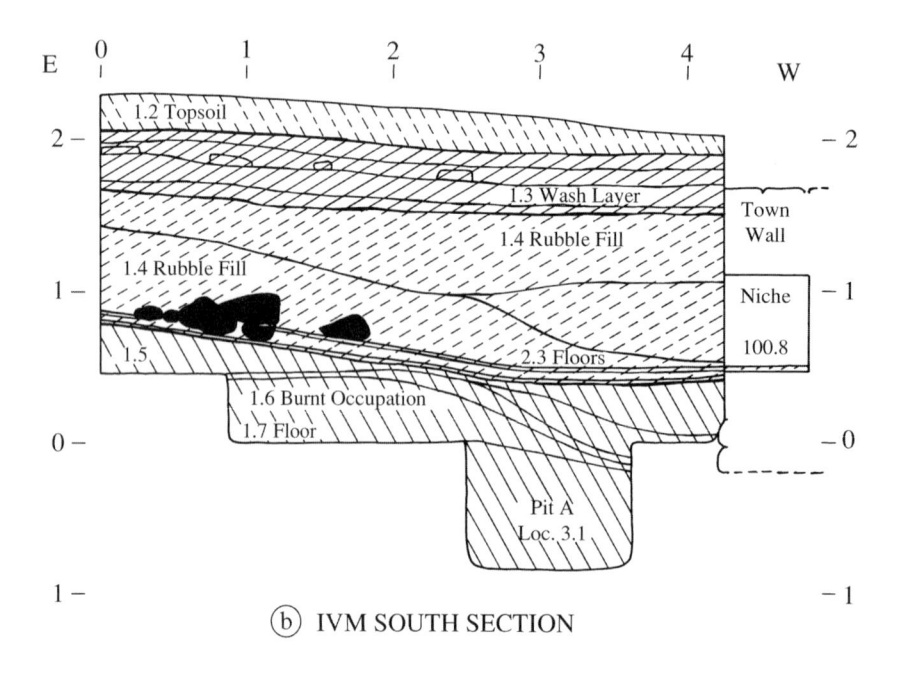

(a) Trench IVM, East Section of Southwest Portion of Room 7 and Sounding Below the Wall of Room 7, and
(b) Trench IVM, South Section Across the Central East–West Portion of Room 7. Scale 1:50

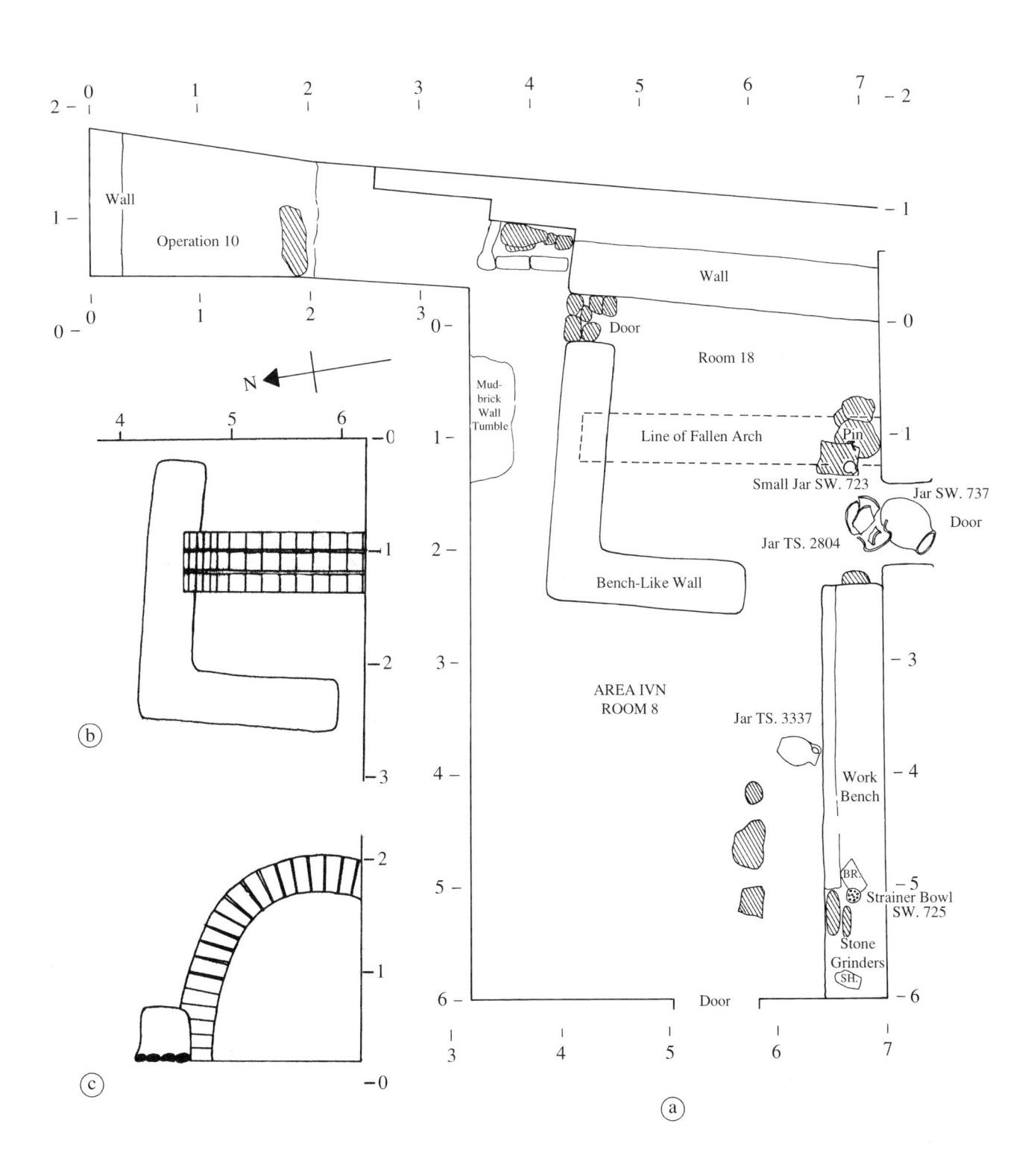

(*a*) Plan of Rooms 8 and 18 in Trench IVN and the Operation 10 Sounding at the Northeast Corner of Trench IVN, (*b*) Plan of Top View of Arch in Trench IVN, and (*c*) Elevation Plan of West Side of Arch in Trench IVN. Scale 1:50

Plate 162

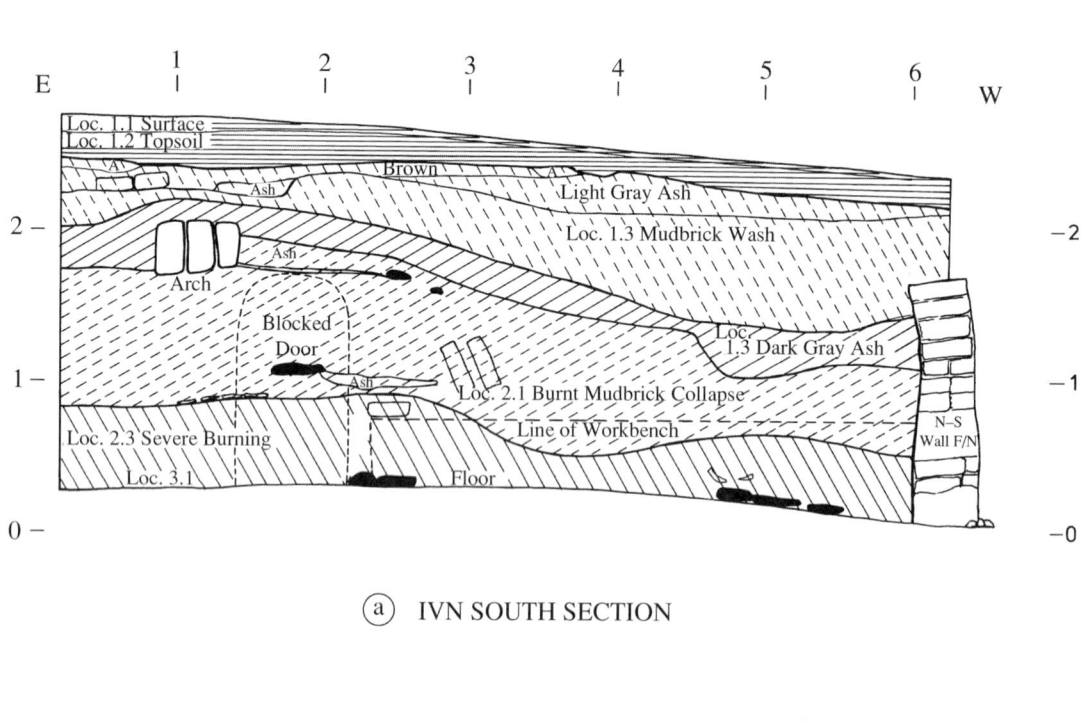

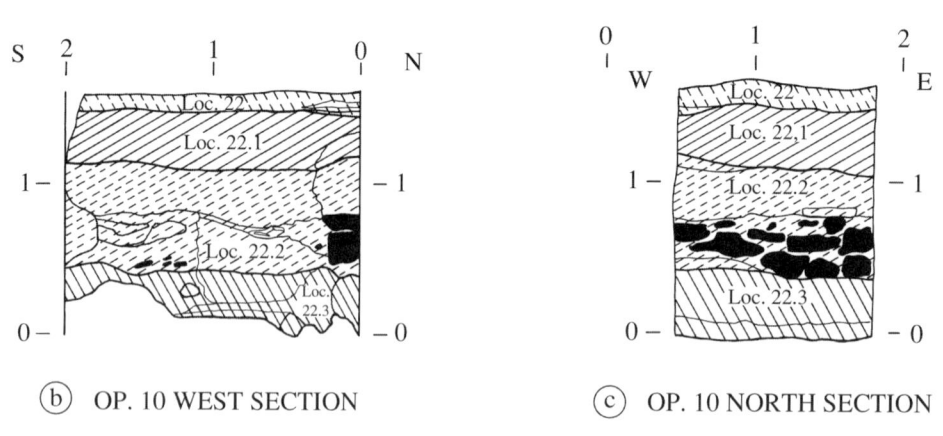

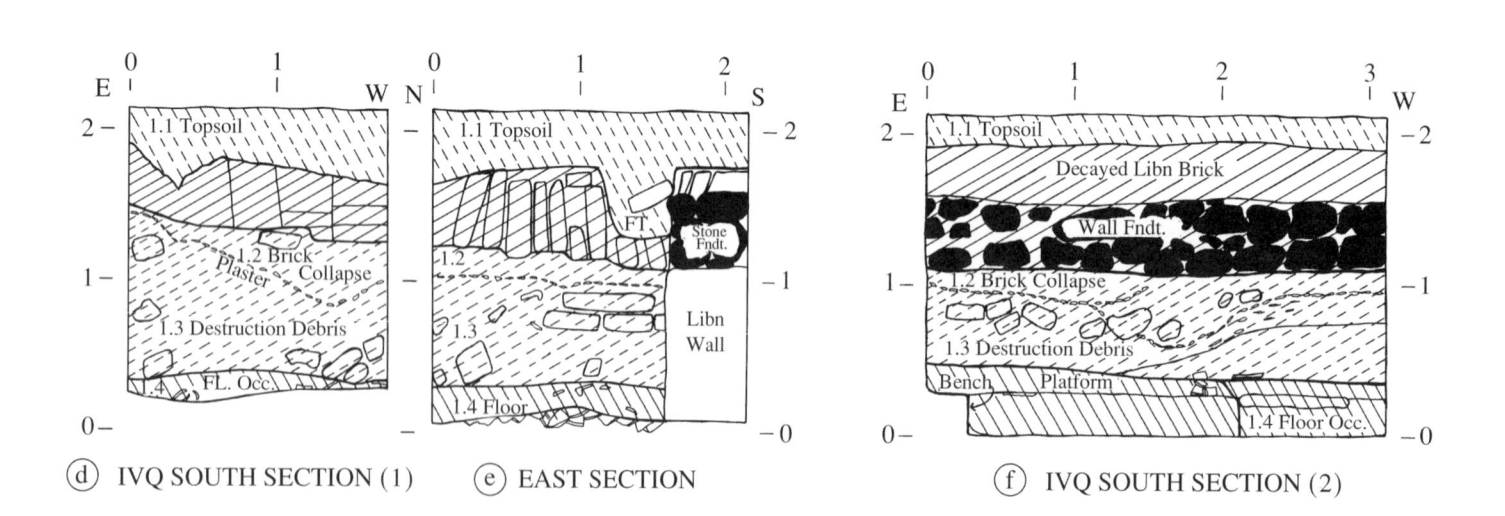

(a) IVN SOUTH SECTION

(b) OP. 10 WEST SECTION

(c) OP. 10 NORTH SECTION

(d) IVQ SOUTH SECTION (1)

(e) EAST SECTION

(f) IVQ SOUTH SECTION (2)

(*a*) Trench IVN, South Section of Rooms 8 and 18, (*b*) Operation 10, West Section, (*c*) Operation 10, North Section, (*d*) Trench IVQ, South Section 1 of Southeast Quadrant of Room 6, (*e*) Trench IVQ, East Section of Southeast Quadrant of Room 6, and (*f*) Trench IVQ, South Section 2 Along South Wall of Room 6. Scale 1:50

Plate 163

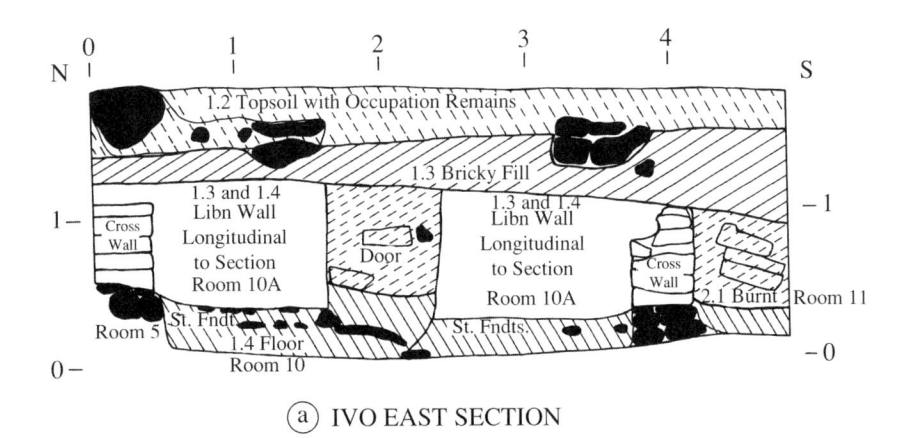

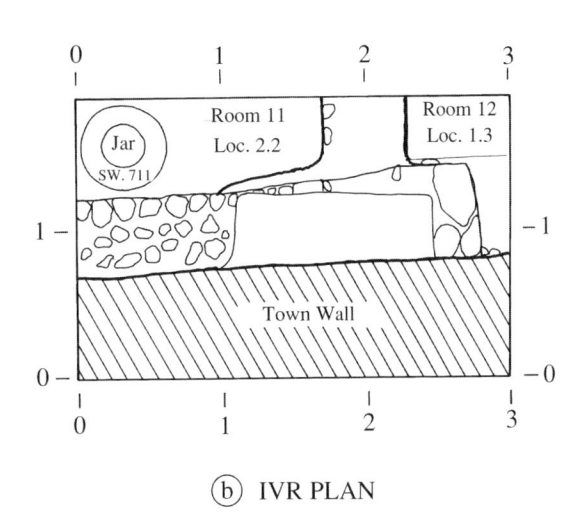

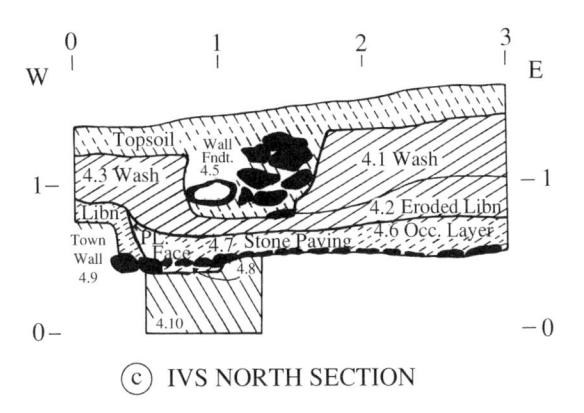

(*a*) Trenches IVO and R, East Section along Walls and Door of Rooms 10 and 11, (*b*) Trench IVR, Plan of Portions of Rooms 11 and 12 and the Town Wall, and (*c*) Trench IVS, North Section through the Middle of Room 12. Scale 1:50

Plate 164

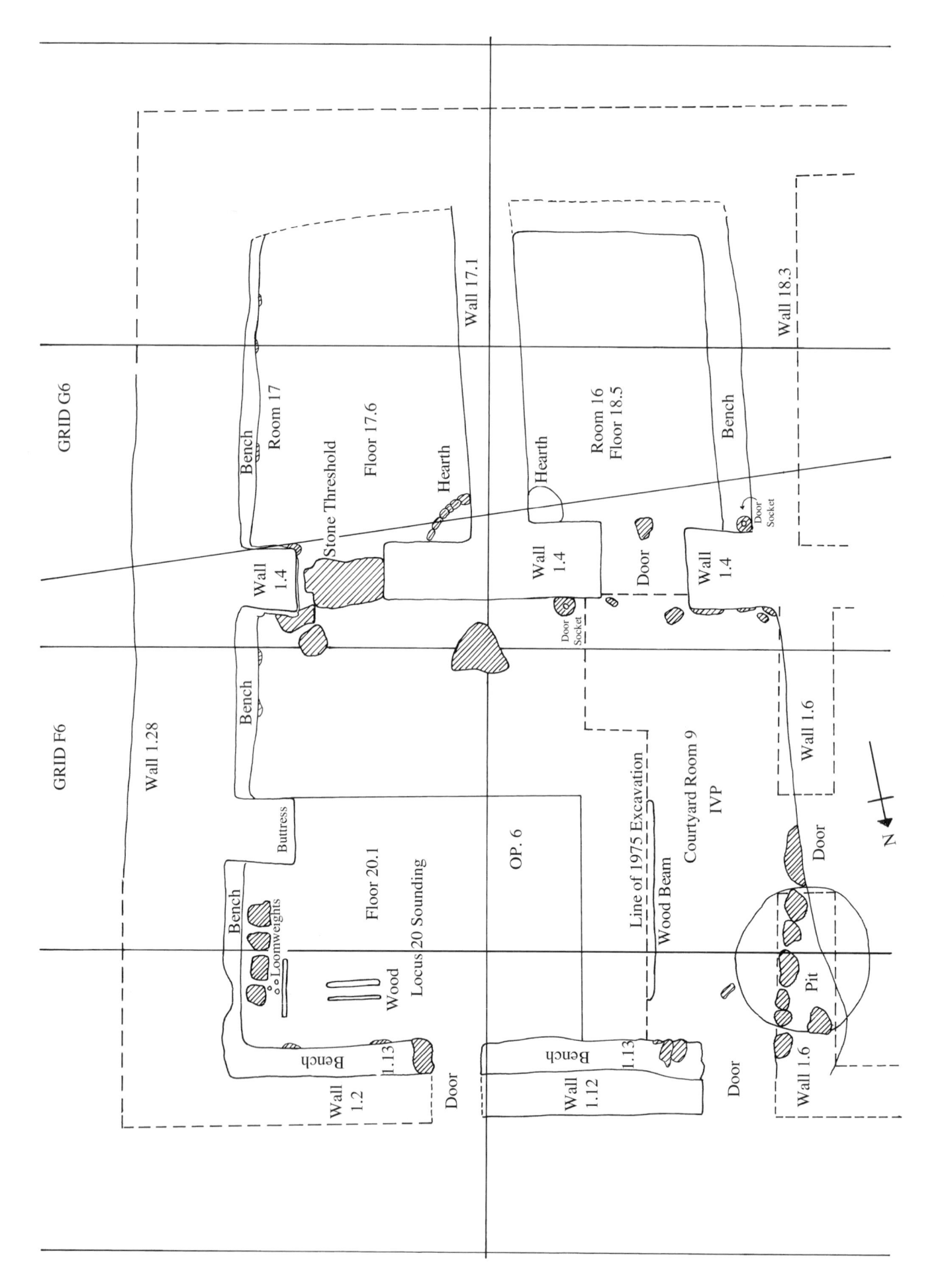

Phase 2A Plan of Courtyard Trench IVP, Room 9, and Operation 6, Rooms 16 and 17. Scale 1:50

Plate 165

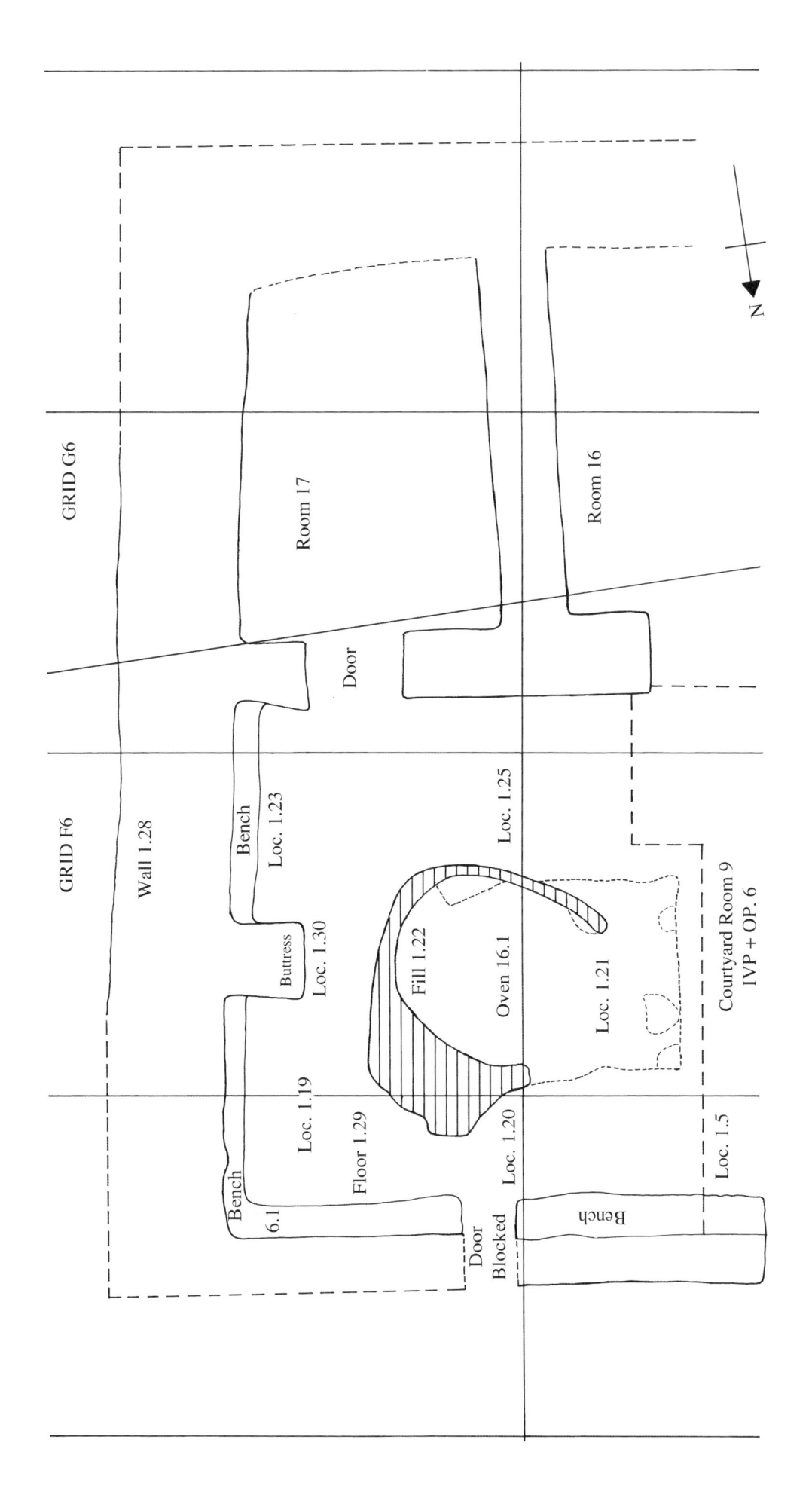

Phase 2B Plan of Trench IVP, Courtyard Room 9, and Operation 6, Oven 16.1 and Room 17. Scale 1:50

Plate 166

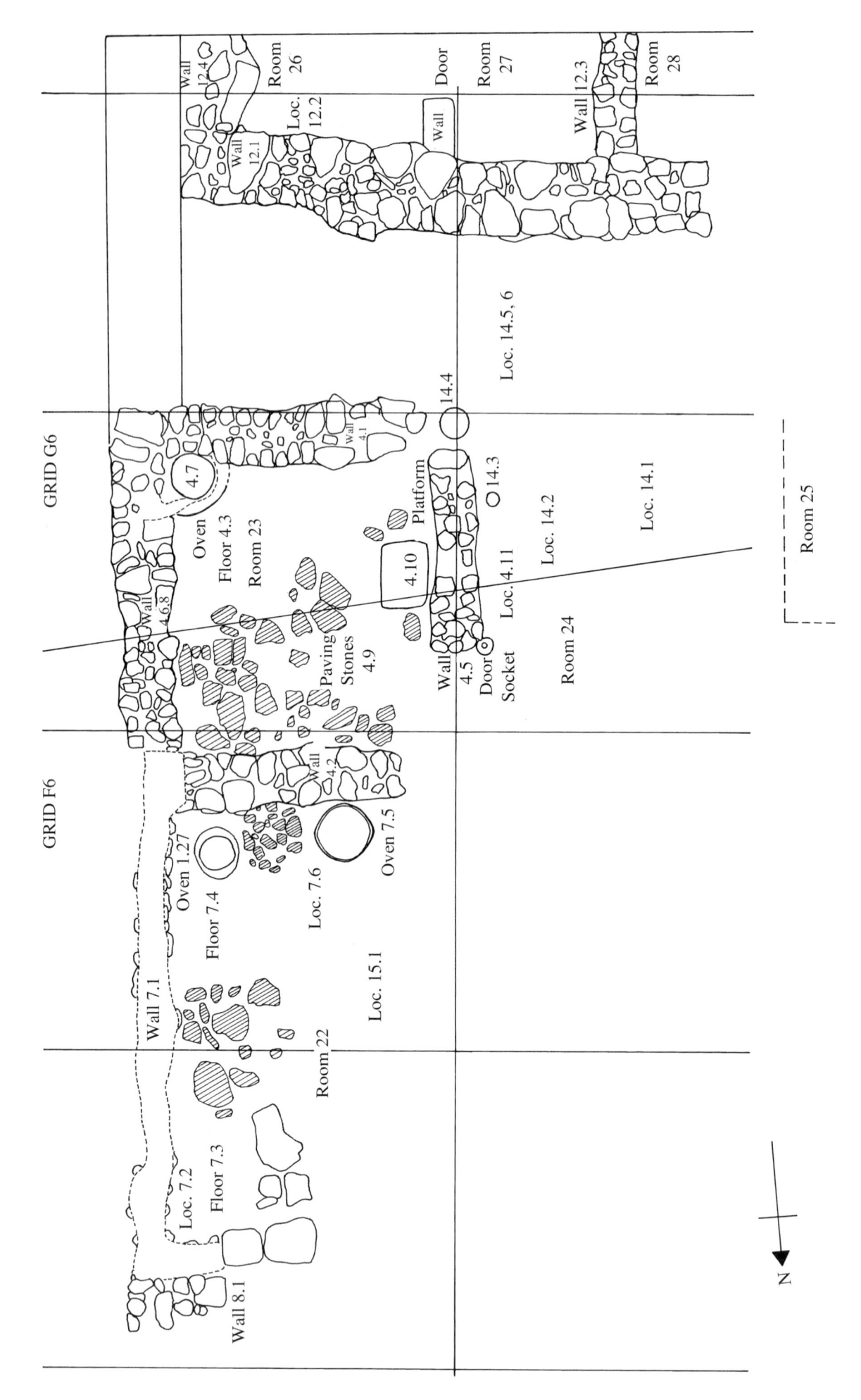

Phase 3 Plan of Operation 6, Rooms 22–28. Scale 1:50

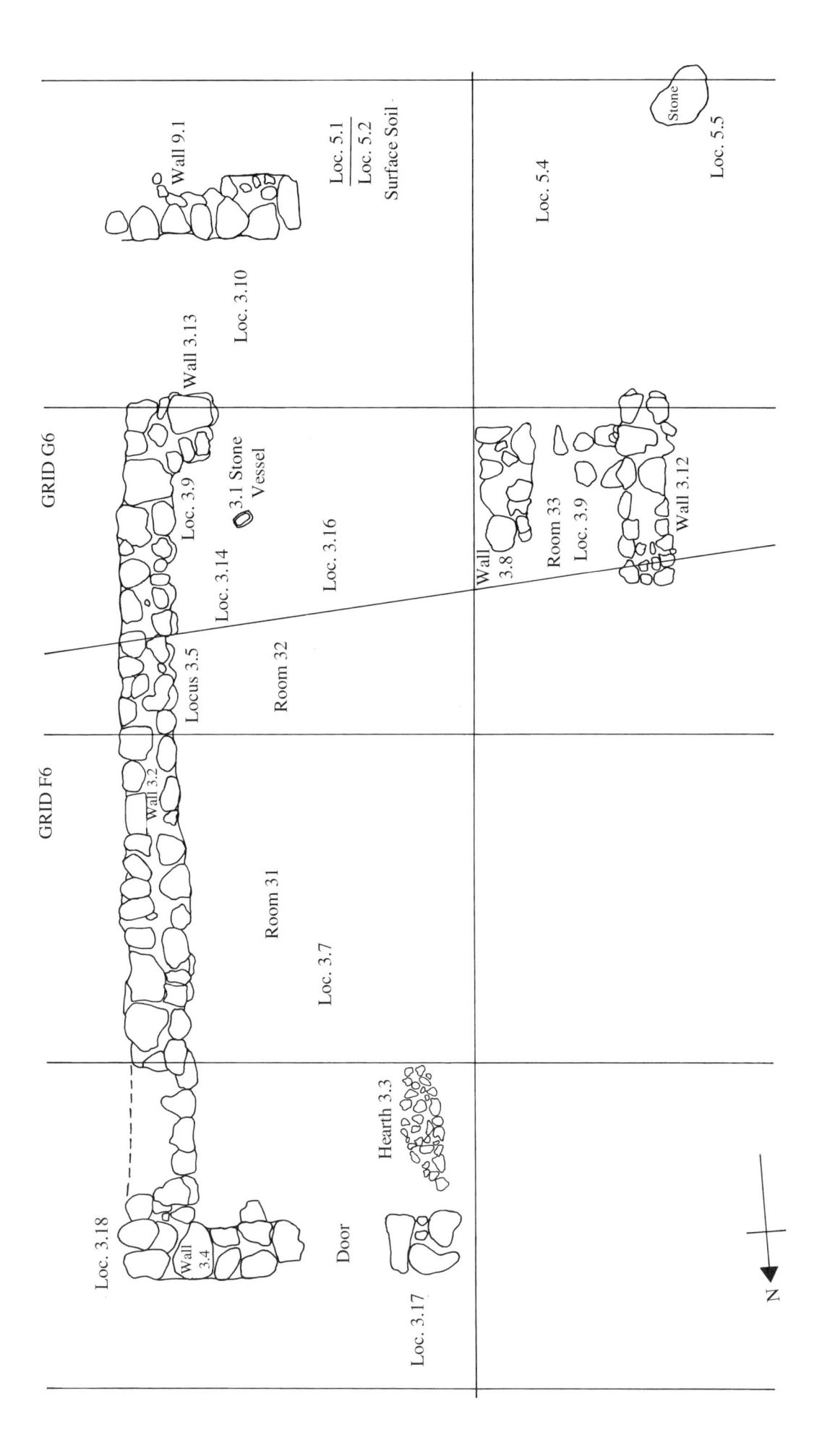

Phase 4 Plan of Operation 6, Rooms 31–33. Scale 1:50

Plate 168

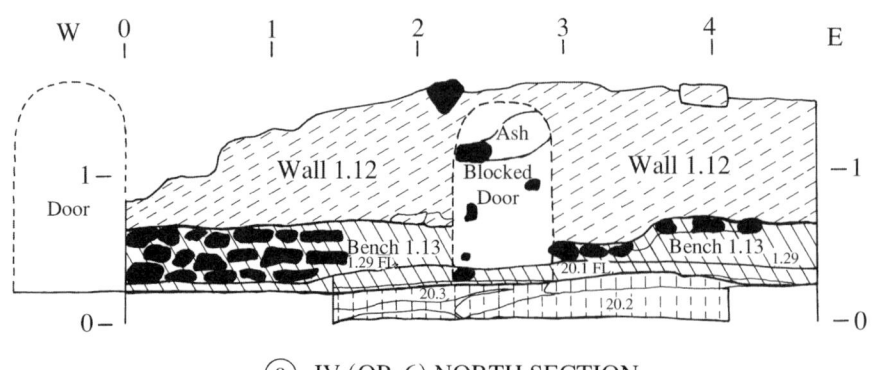

(a) IV (OP. 6) NORTH SECTION

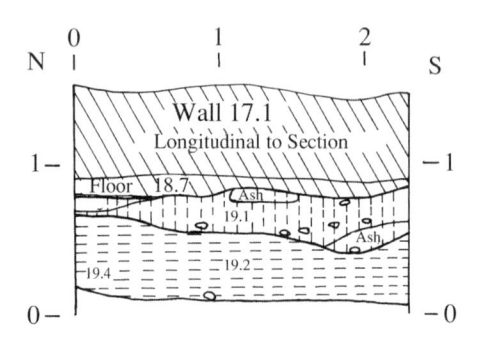

(b) IV (OP. 6) ROOM 16 EAST SECTION

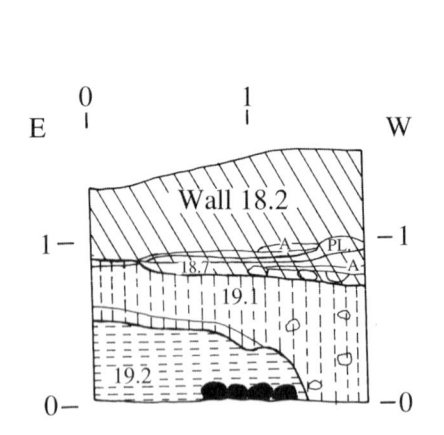

(c) IV (OP. 6) ROOM 16 SOUTH SECTION

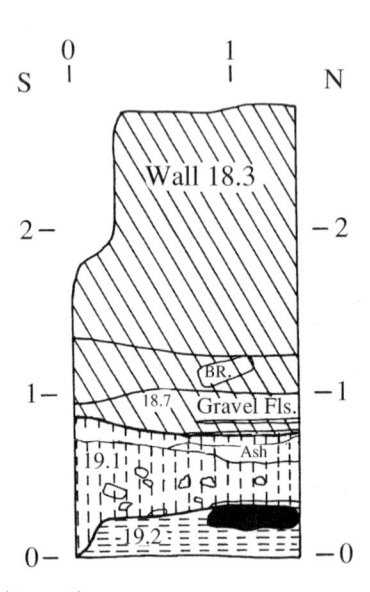

(d) IV (OP. 6) ROOM 16 WEST SECTION

(*a*) Trench IVP, Courtyard Room 9, North Section Showing Phases IC, 2A, and 2B, (*b*) Operation 6, Room 16, East Section, (*c*) Operation 6, Room 16, South Section, and (*d*) Operation 6, Room 16, West Section. Scale 1:50

Plate 169

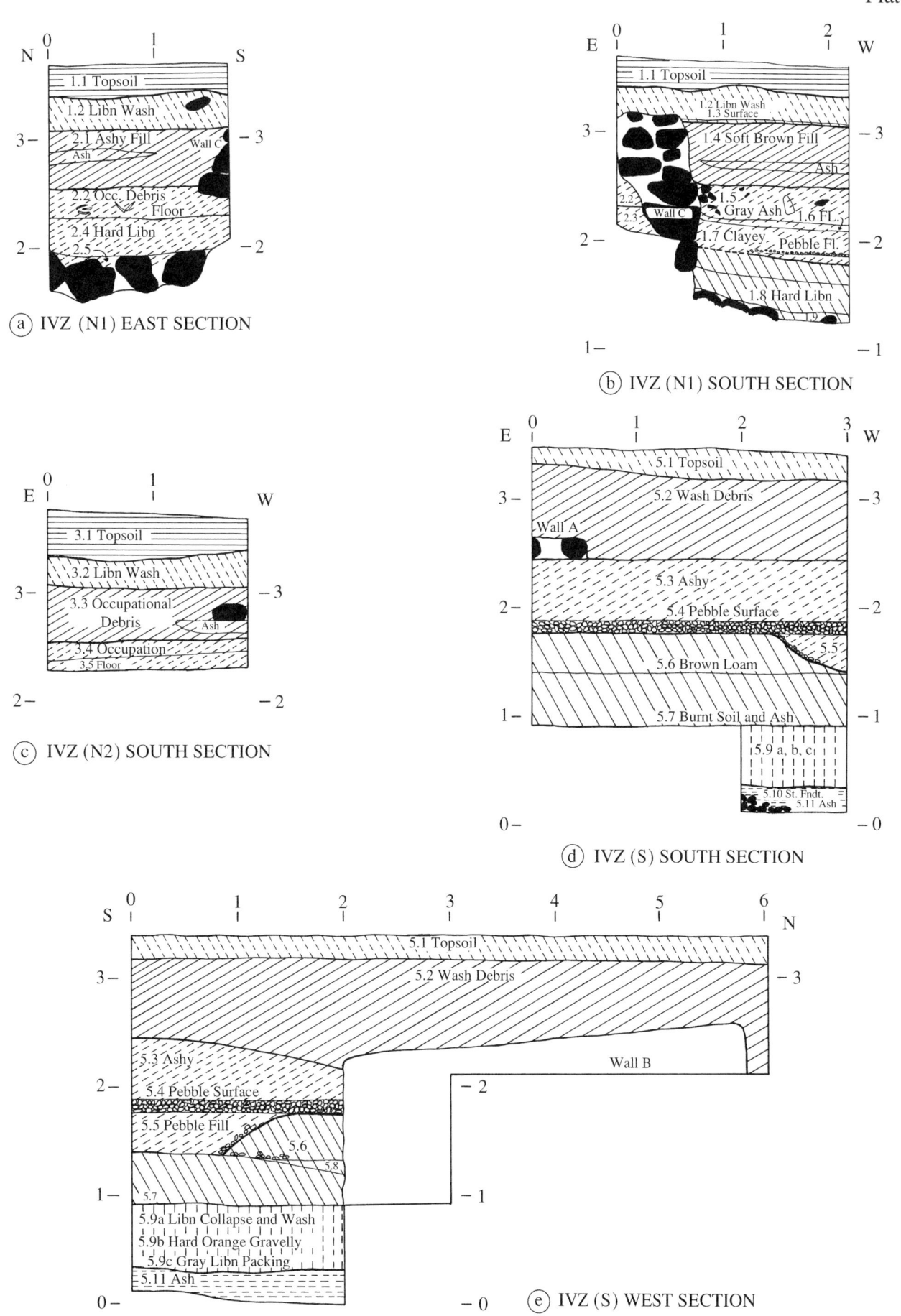

(a) Trench IVZ(N1), East Section, (b) Trench IVZ(N1), South Section, (c) Trench IVZ(N2), South Section, (d) Trench IVZ(S), South Section, and (e) Trench IVZ(S), West Section. Scale 1:50

Plate 170

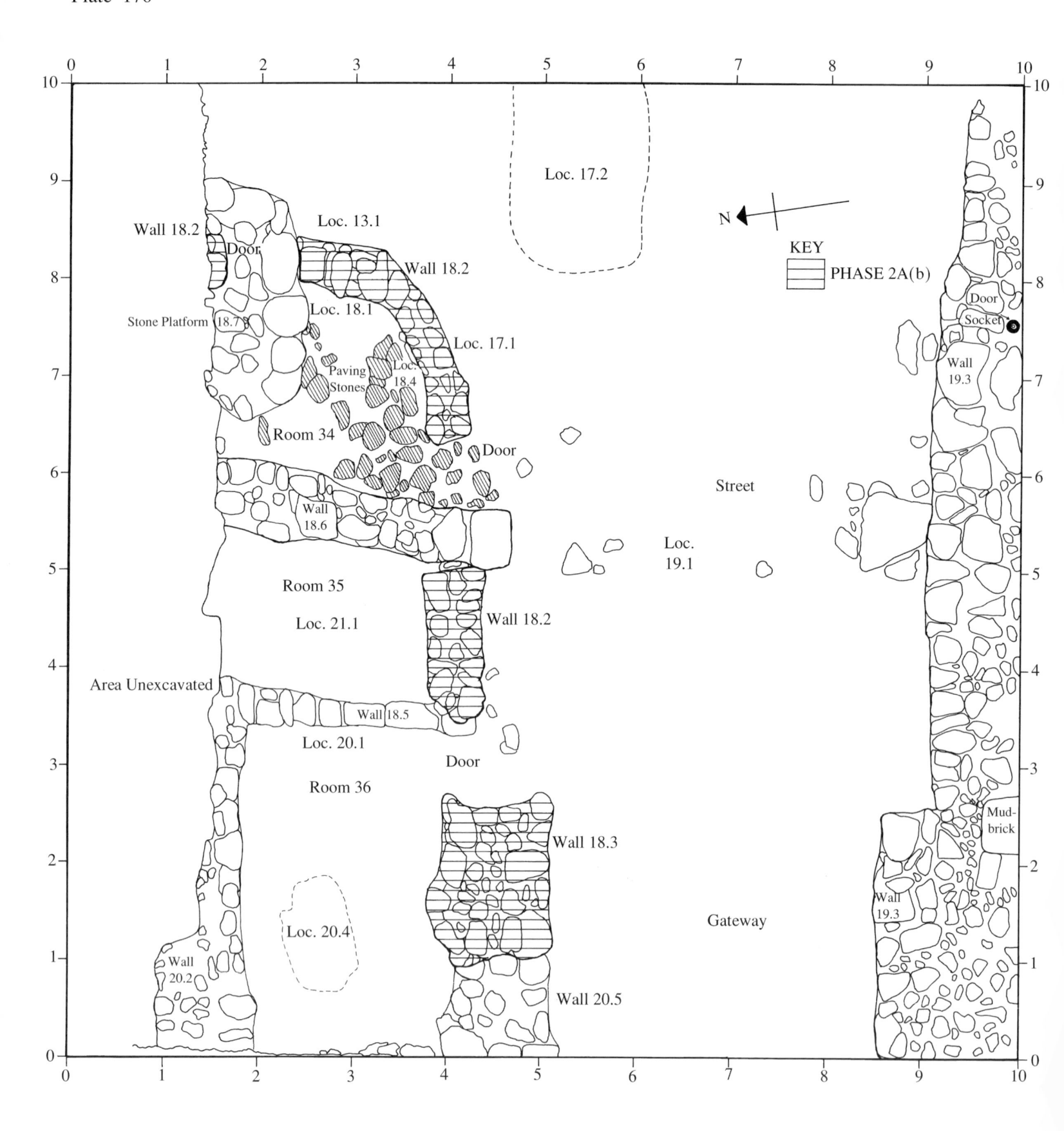

Plan of Operation 7, Rooms 34–36, Gateway, and Street through West Side of Town Wall During Phases 2A(a) and 2A(b). Scale 1:50

Plate 171

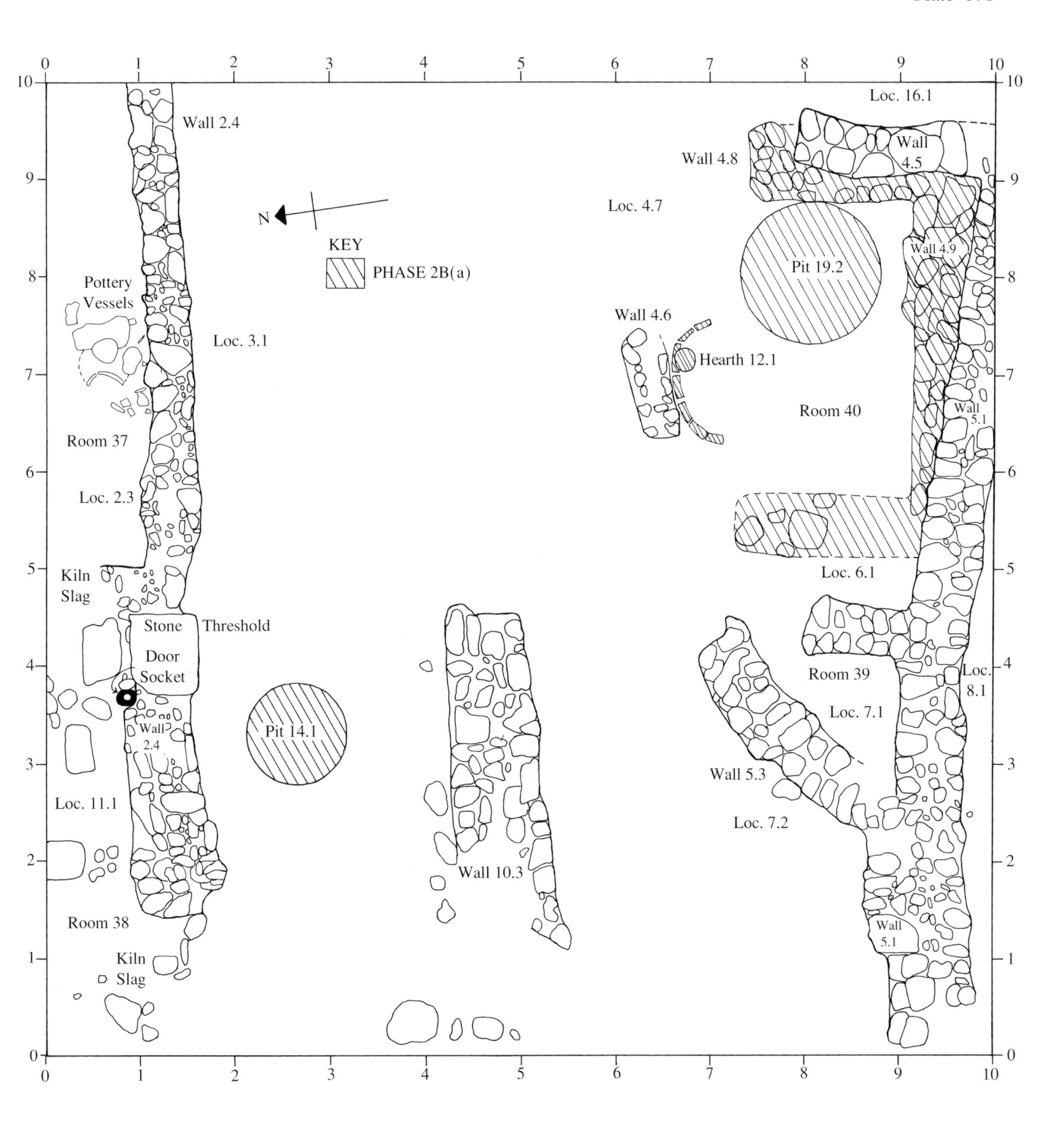

Phase 2B(a) Plan of Operation 7, Pits and Room 40, and Phase 2B(b) Plan of Operation 7, Rooms 37–39. Scale 1:50

Plate 172

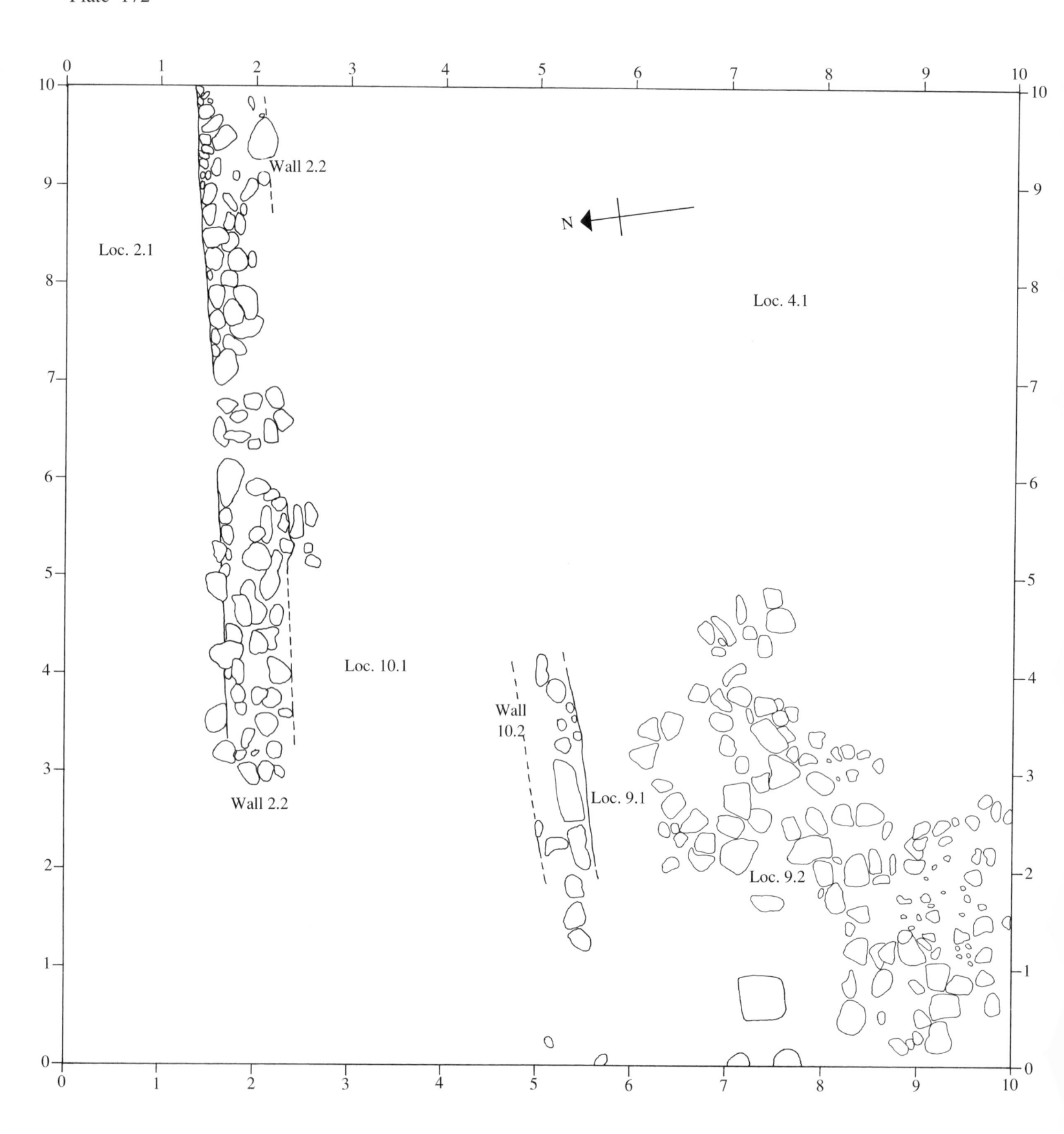

Plan of Operation 7, Phase 3 Walls and Phase 4 Stone Collapse, Loci 9.1 and 9.2. Scale 1:50

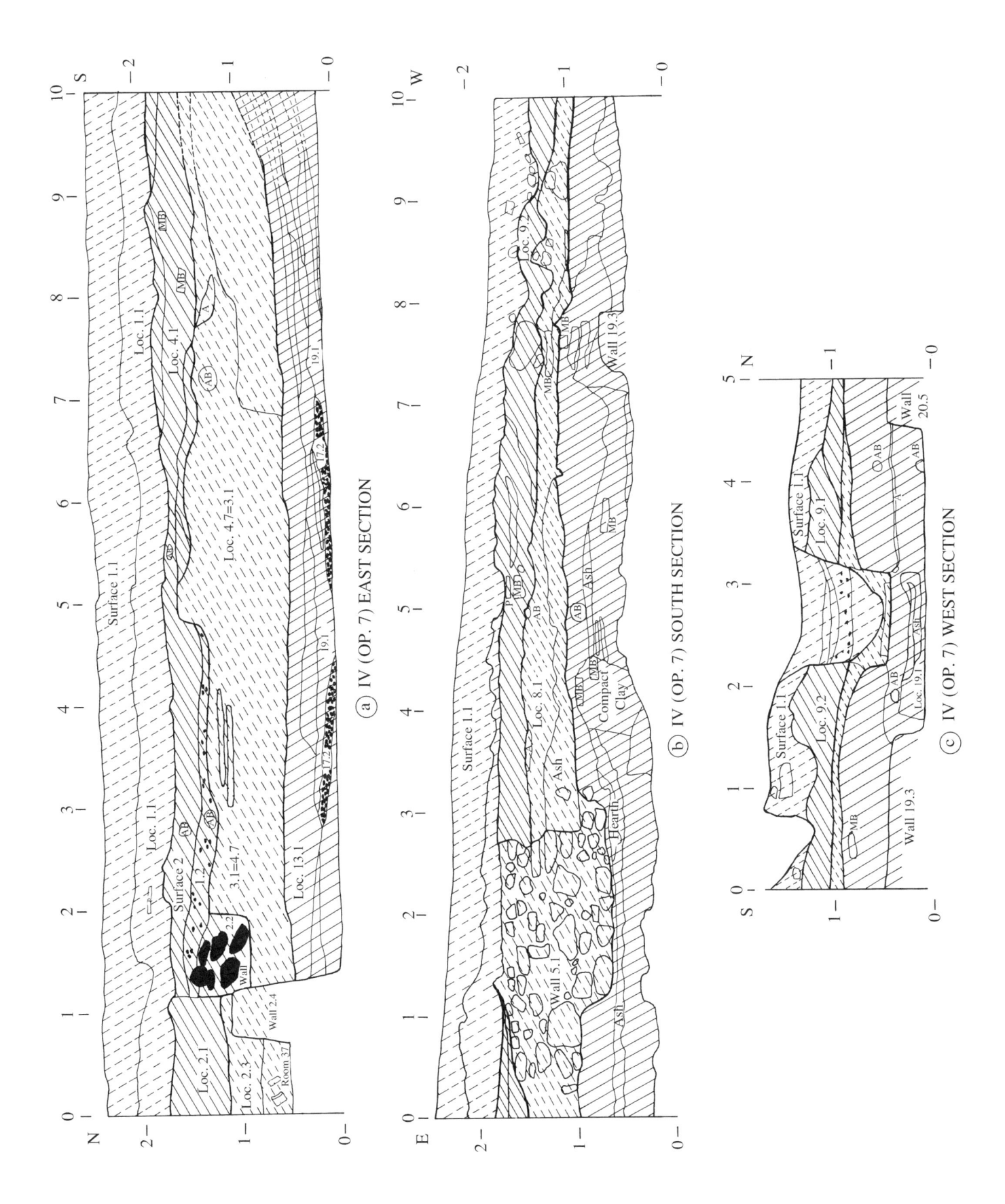

(*a*) Operation 7, East Section, (*b*) Operation 7, South Section, and (*c*) Operation 7, West Section. Scale 1:50

Plate 174

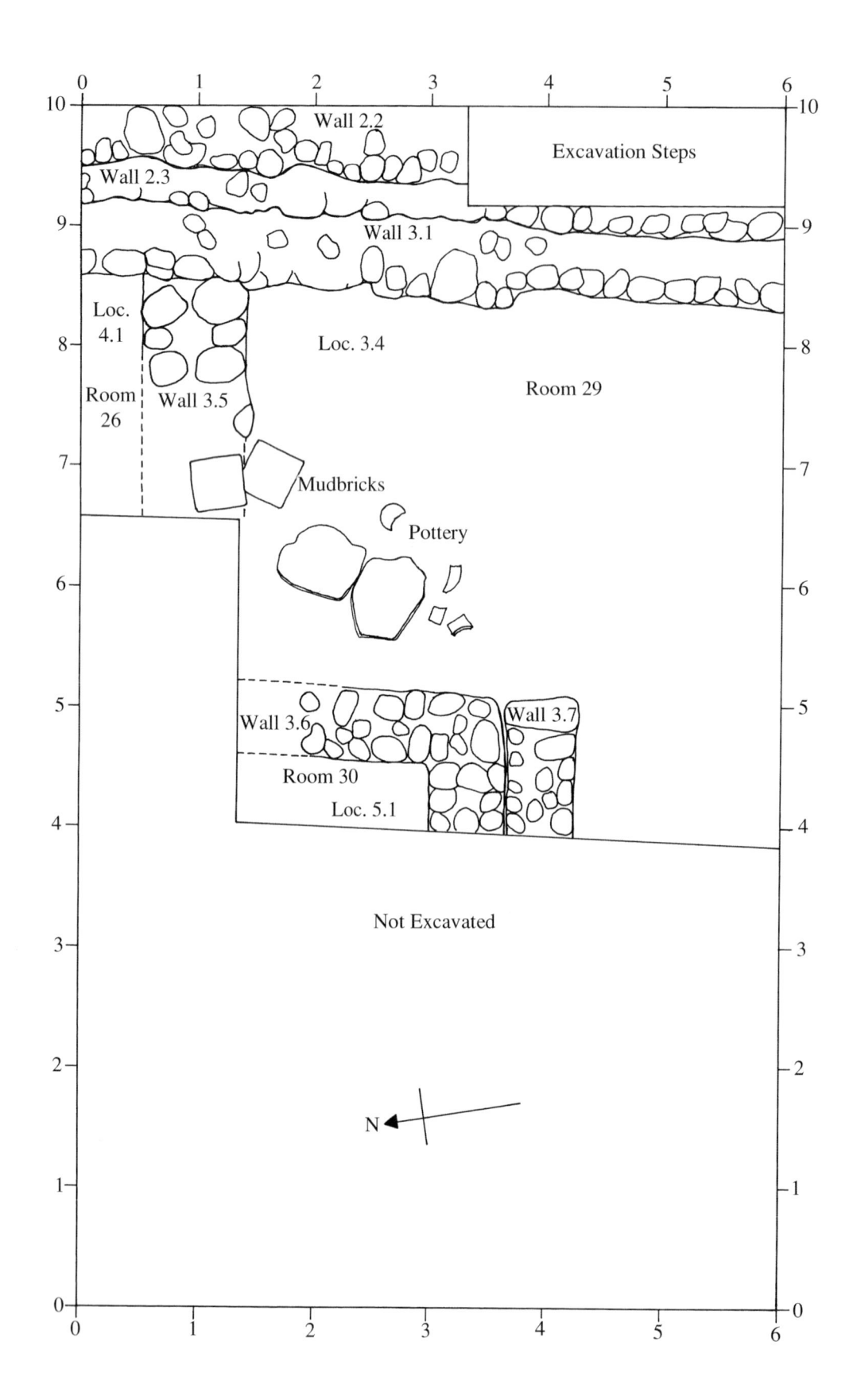

Phases 3 and 4 Plan of Operation 8, Portions of Rooms 26, 29, and 30. Scale 1:50

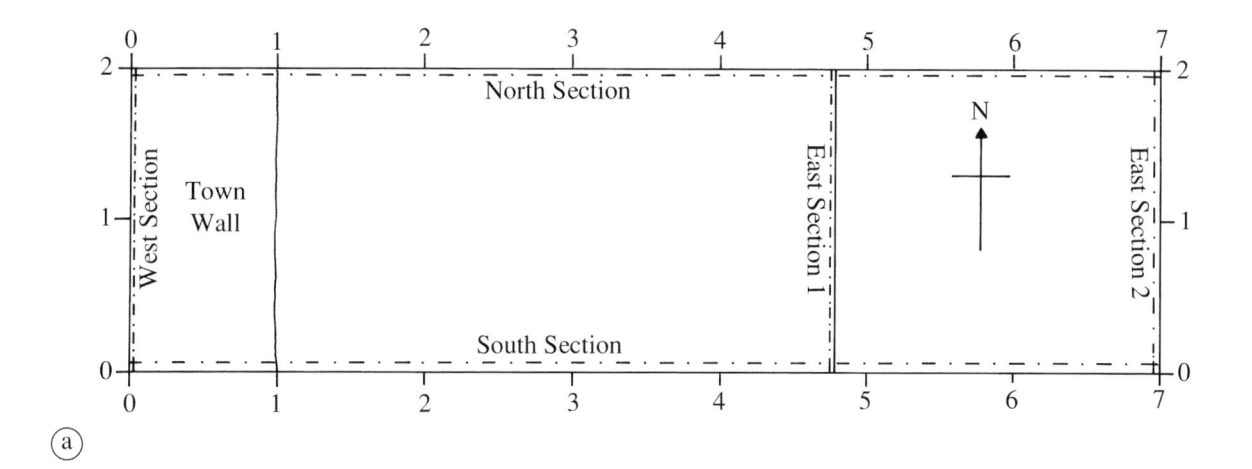

(*a*) Key to Plans and Positions of Sections in Trench IXA and (*b*) Key to Hatching of Phases on Sections. Scale 1:50

Plate 176

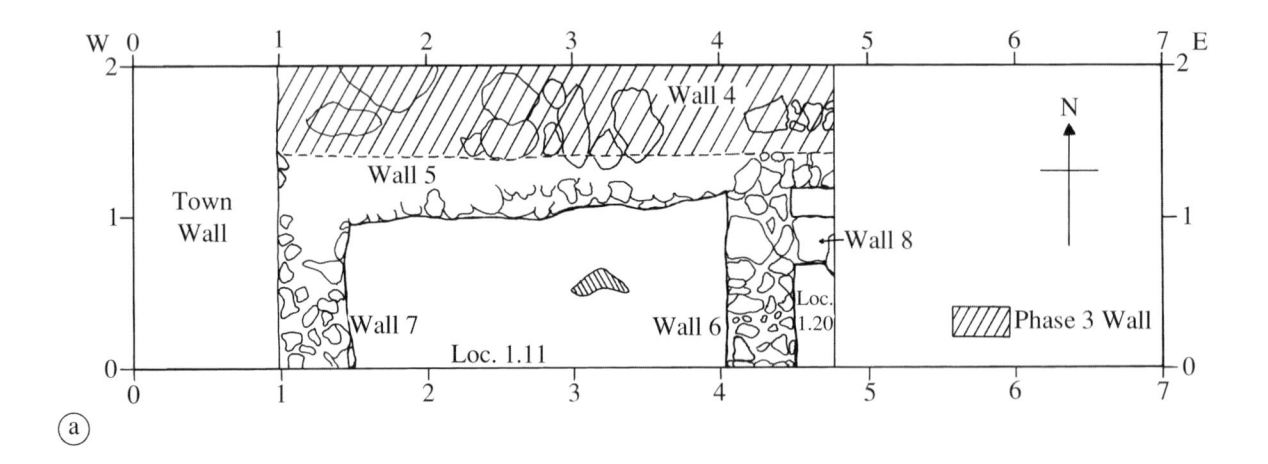

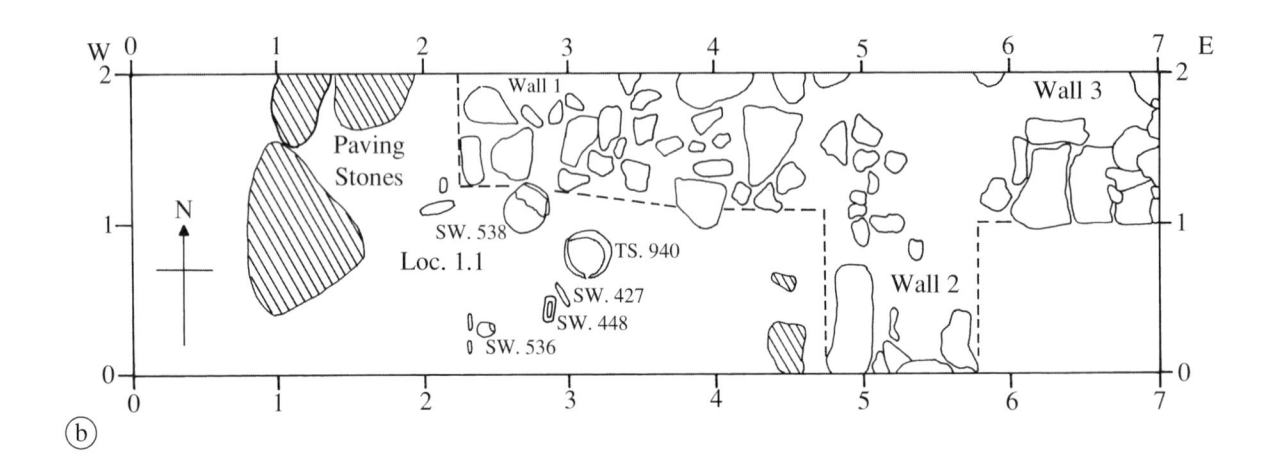

(*a*) Phases 2A and 3 Plan of Trench IXA and (*b*) Phase 4 Plan of Trench IXA. Scale 1:50

Plate 177

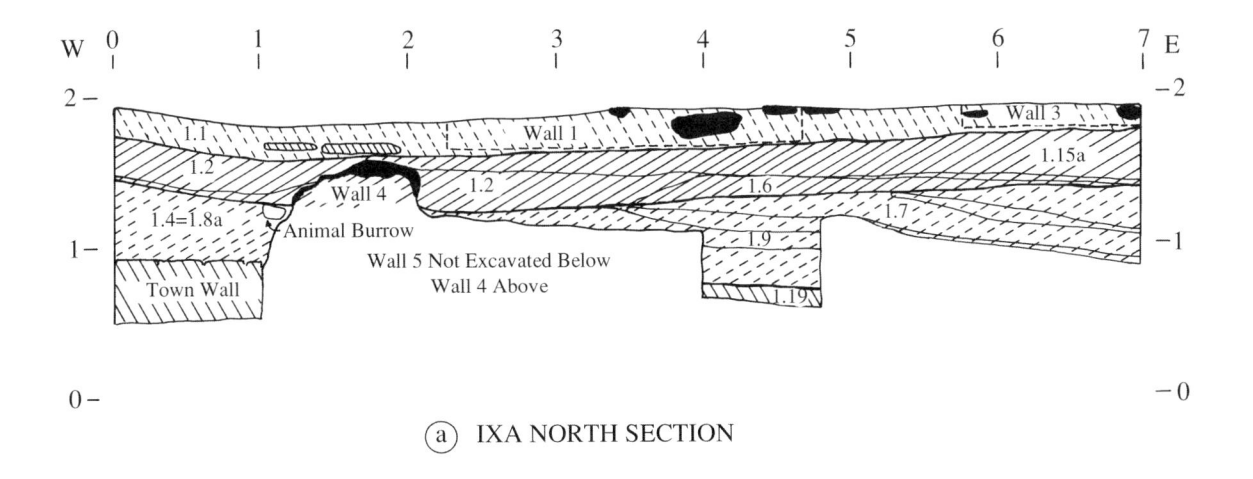

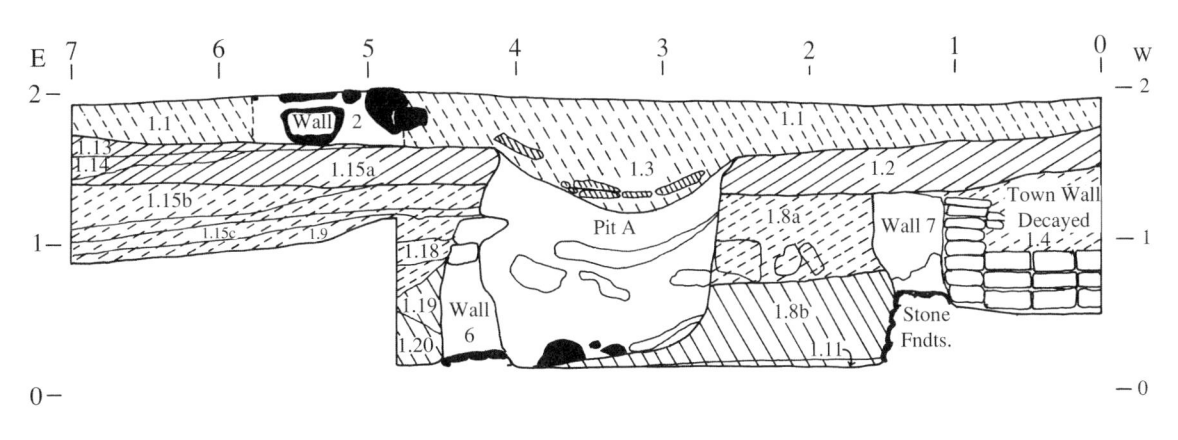

(a) IXA NORTH SECTION

(b) IXA SOUTH SECTION

(*a*) Trench IXA, North Section, and (*b*) Trench IXA, South Section

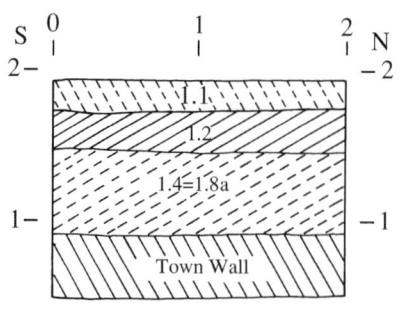

Plate 178

(*a*) Trench IXA, West Section, (*b*) Trench IXA, East Section 1, and (*c*) Trench IXA, East Section 2. Scale 1:50

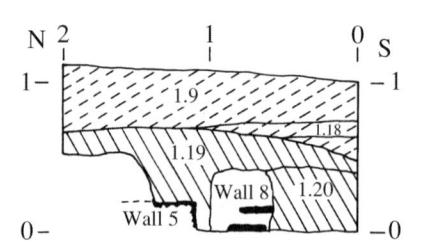

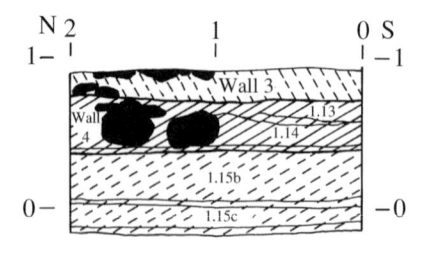

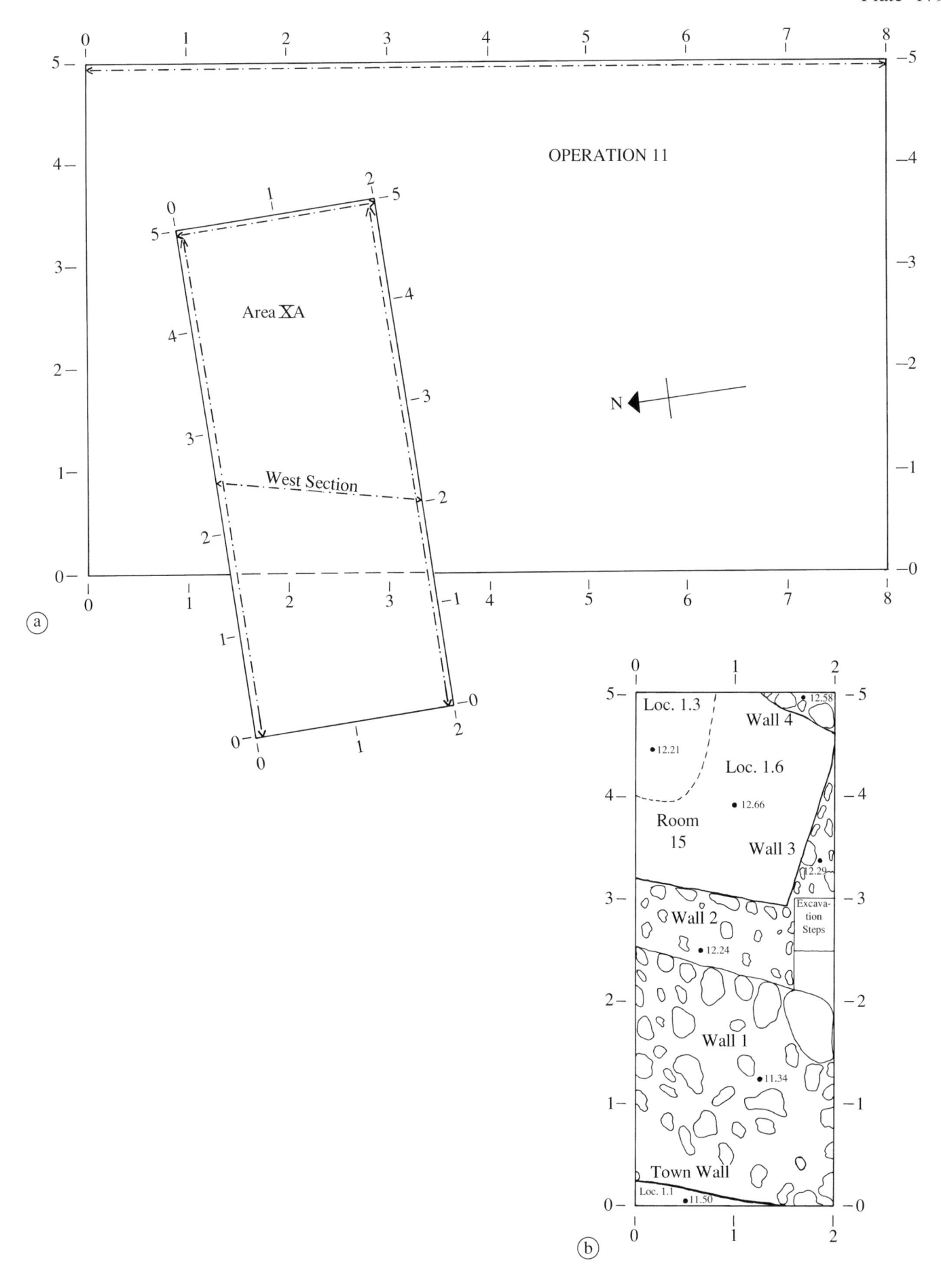

(*a*) Key to Plans and Sections of Trench XA and Operation 11 and (*b*) Plan of Trench XA, Phase 2A Town Wall and Southwestern Portion of Room 15. Scale 1:50

Plate 180

(a) Trench XA, West Section Against Inner Face of Town Wall, (b) Trench XA, North Section, (c) Trench XA, East Section, and (d) Trench XA, South Section. Scale 1:50

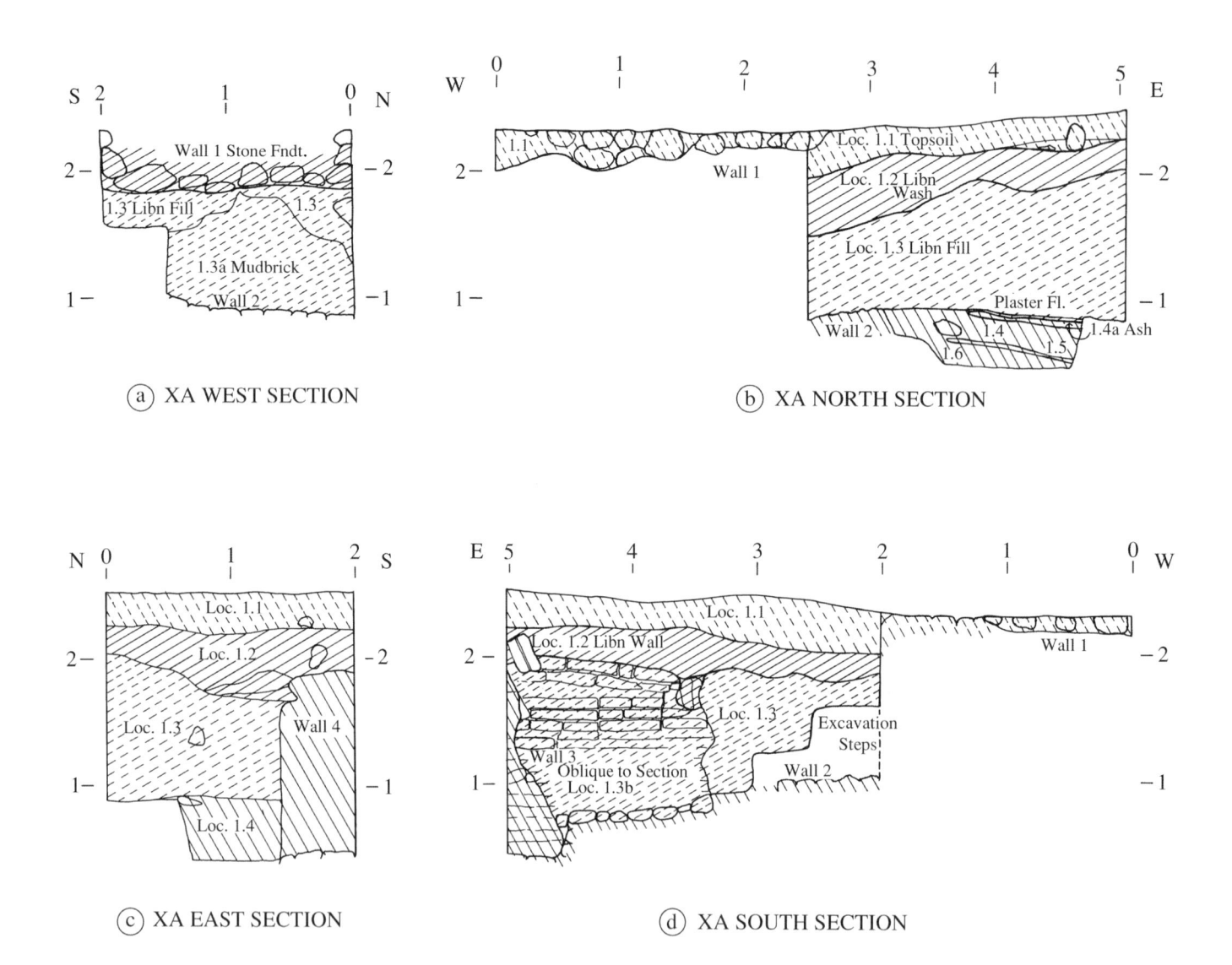

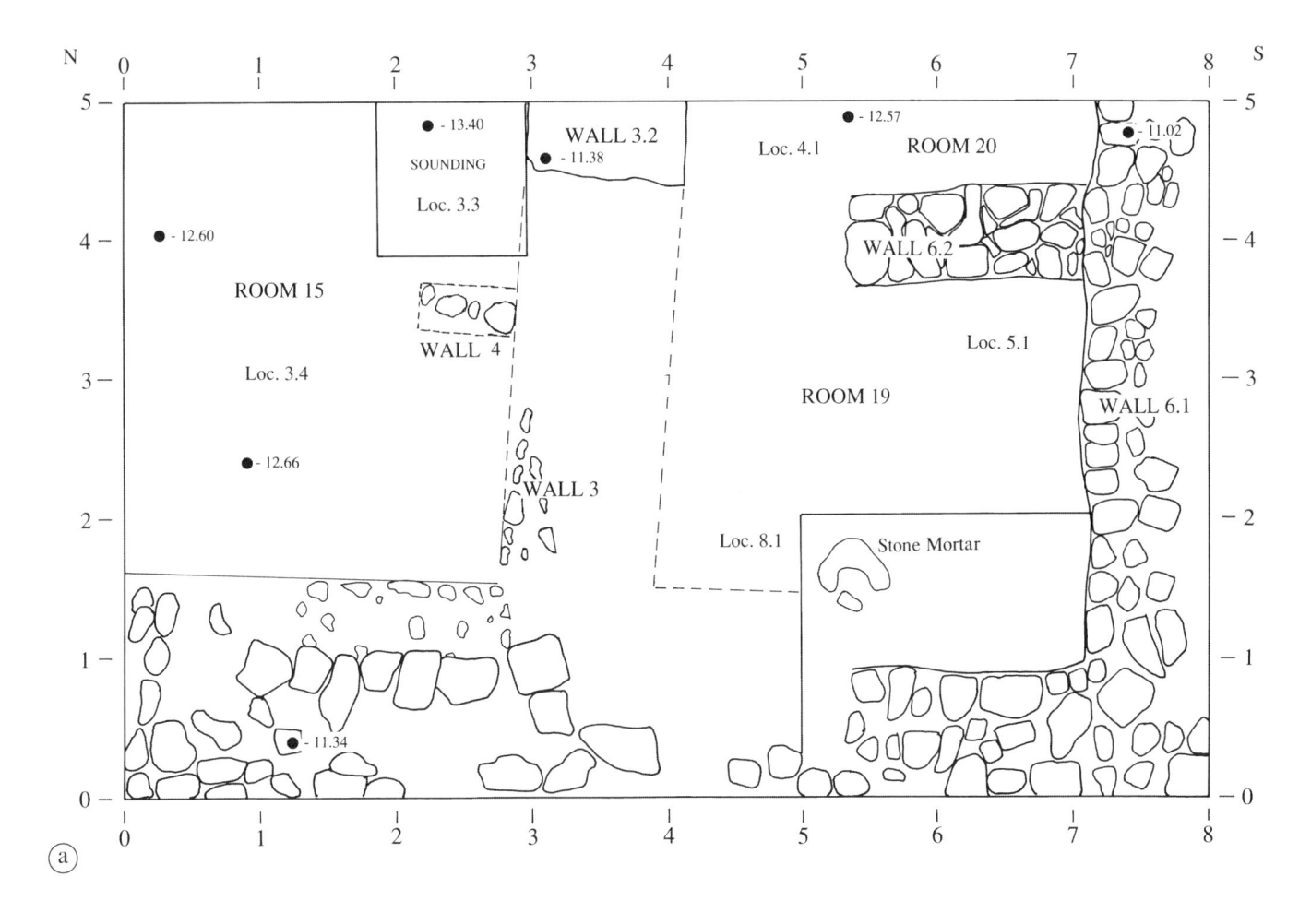

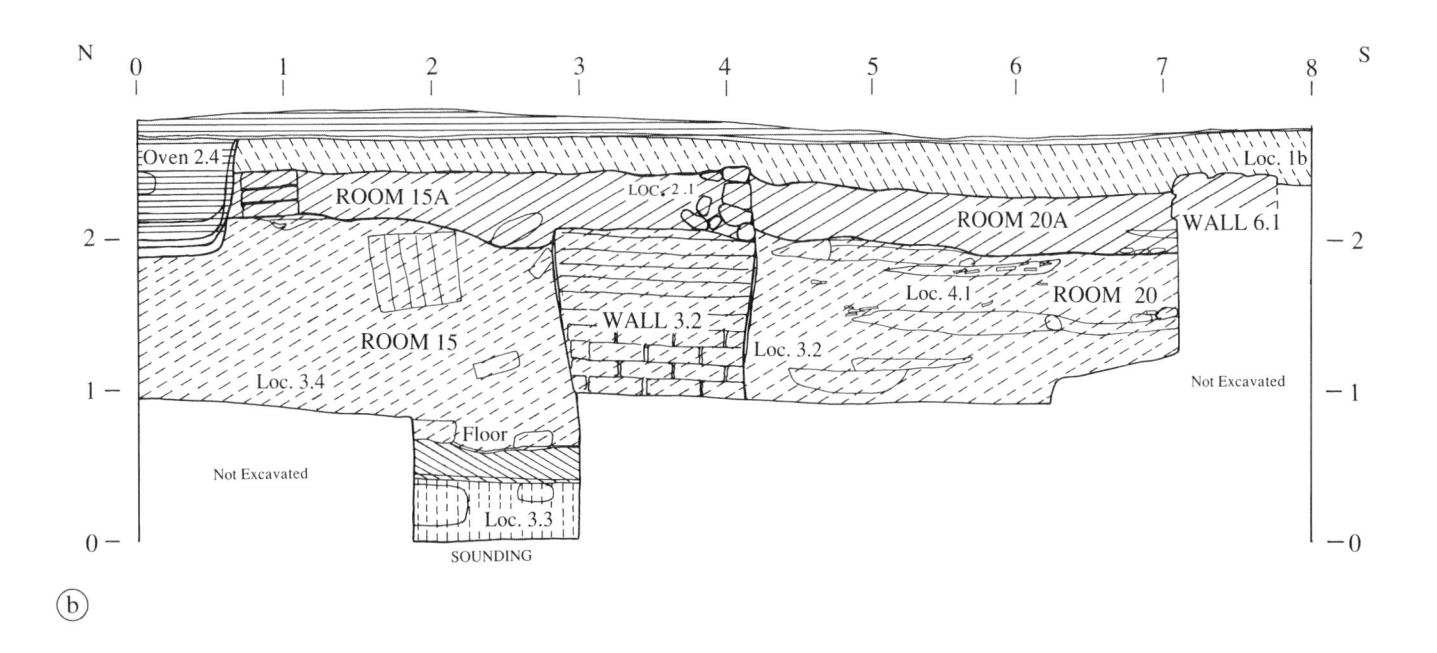

(*a*) Composite Plan of Trench XA and Operation 11 Showing Phases 1C and 2A Sounding, Phase 2B Rooms 15, 19, and 20, and Portions of Phase 3 Walls Belonging to Rooms 15A and 20A; and (*b*) Operation 11, East Section. Scale 1:50

Plate 182

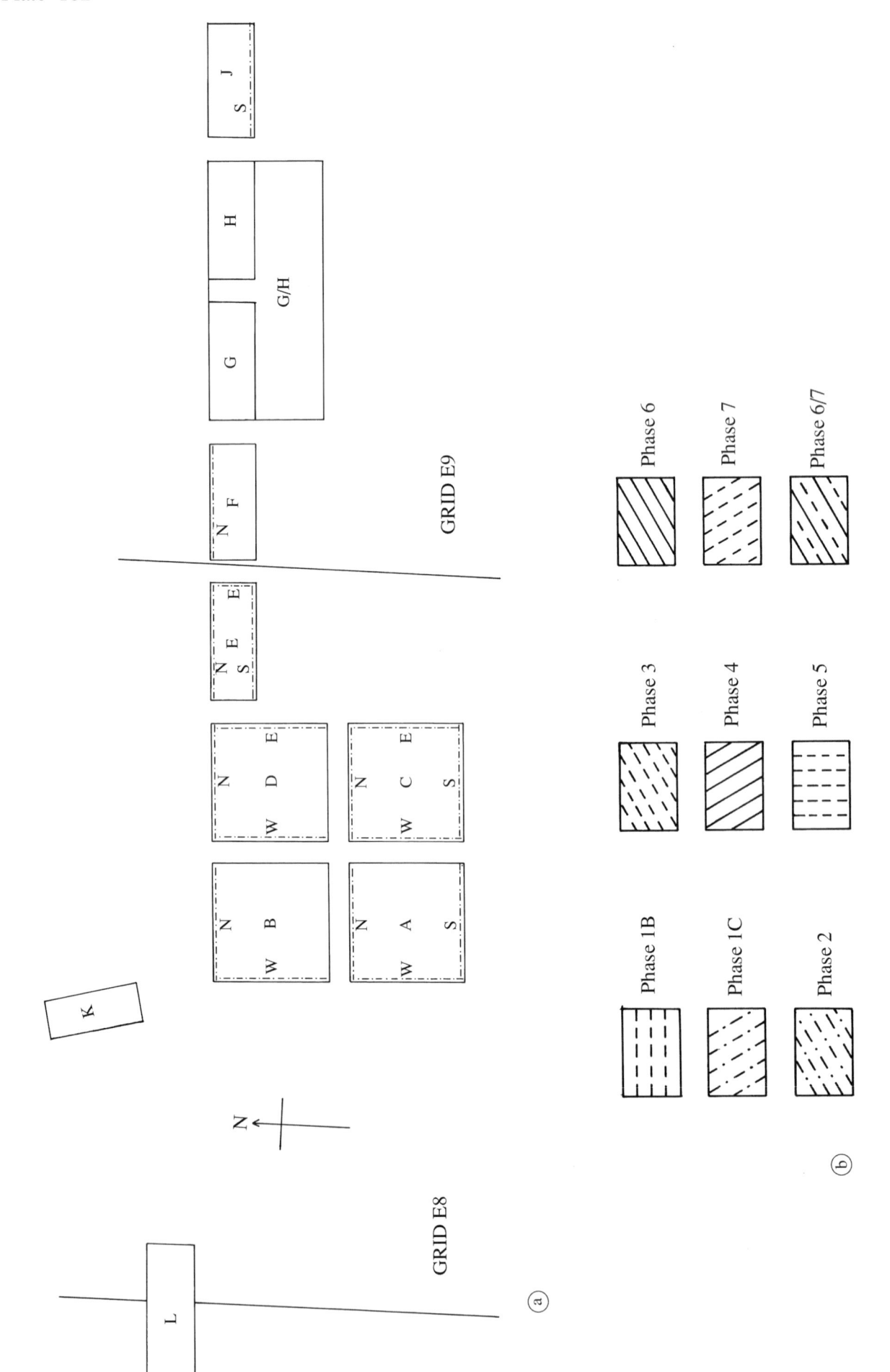

(a) Key to Plans and Sections of Area III (for Key to Trenches IIIG, H, and G/H, see pl. 191) and (b) Key to Hatching of Phases on Sections. Scale 1:50

Plate 183

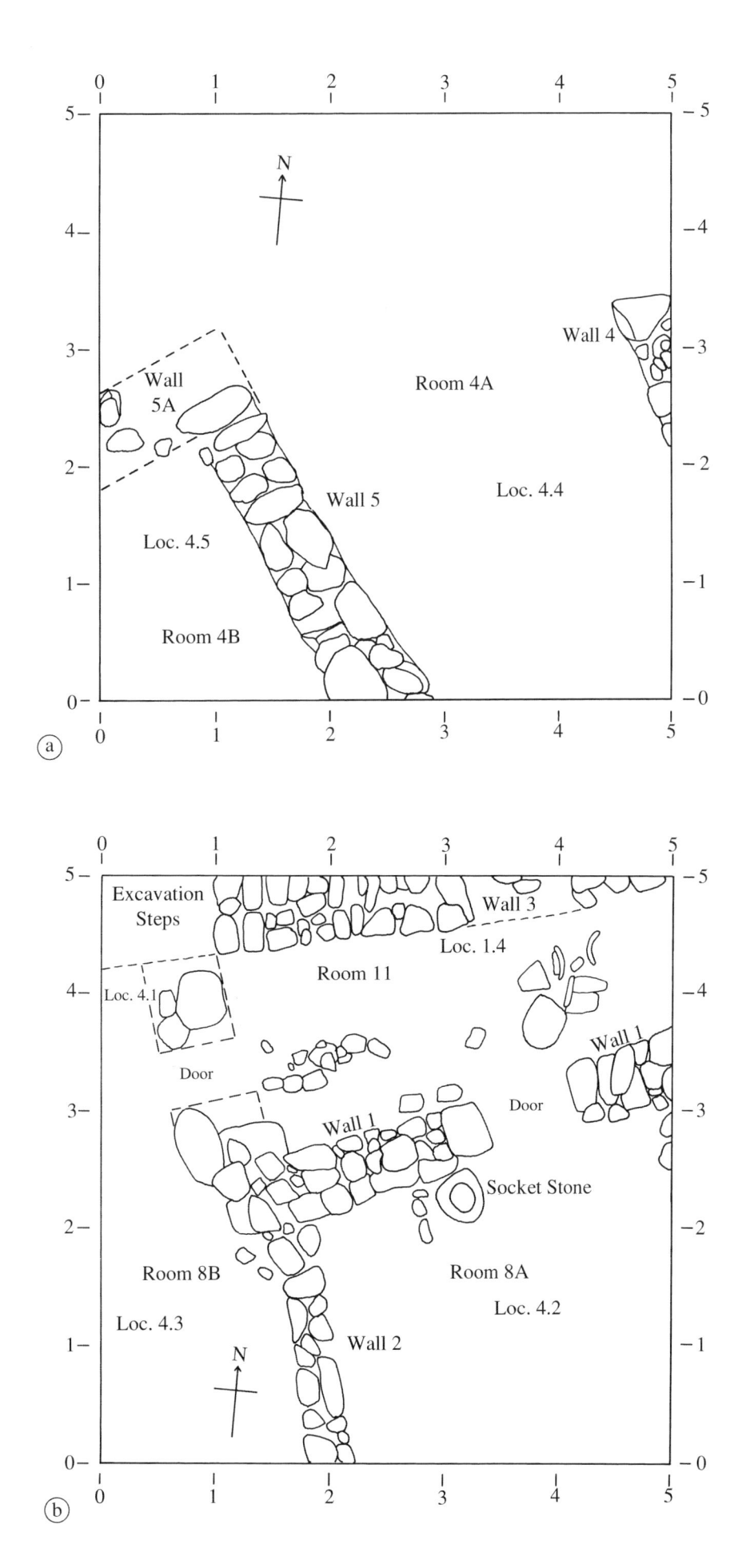

(*a*) Phase 3 Plan of Trench IIIA, Rooms 4A and 4B, Showing Walls 4, 5, and 5A, and (*b*) Phase 4 Plan of Trench IIIA, Rooms 8A, 8B, and 11, Showing Walls 1, 2, and 3. Scale 1:50

Plate 184

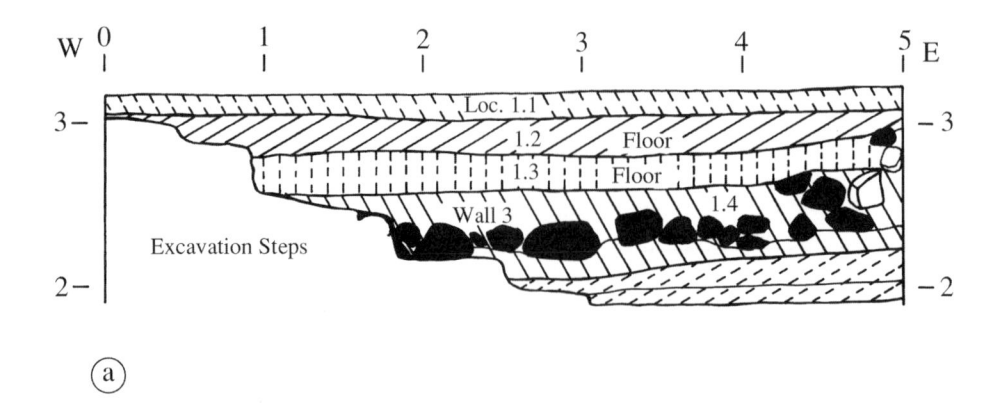

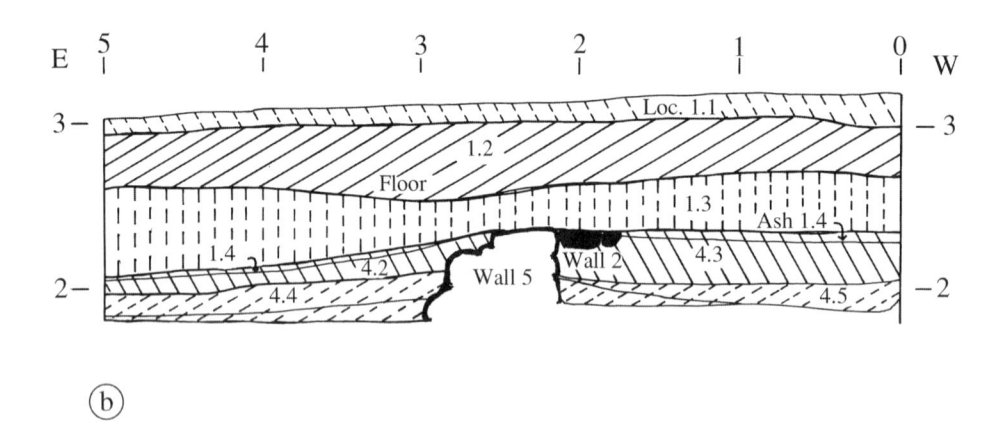

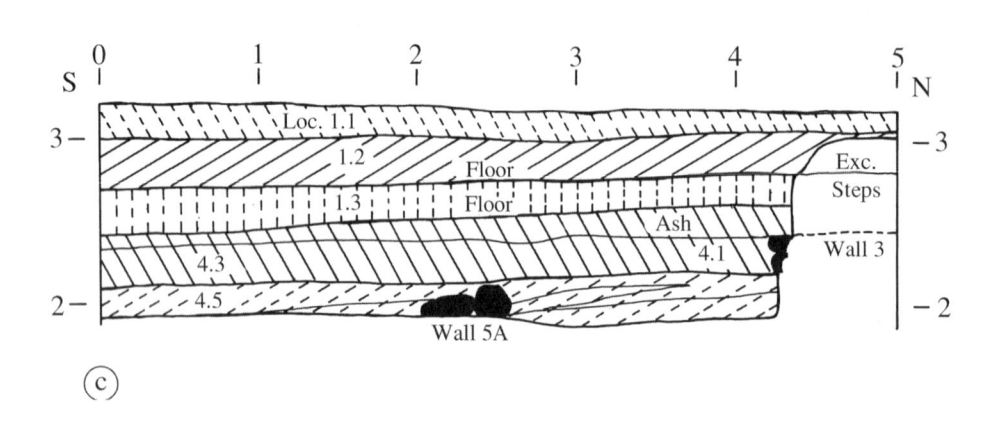

(*a*) Trench IIIA, North Section, (*b*) Trench IIIA, South Section, and (*c*) Trench IIIA, West Section. Scale 1:50

Plate 185

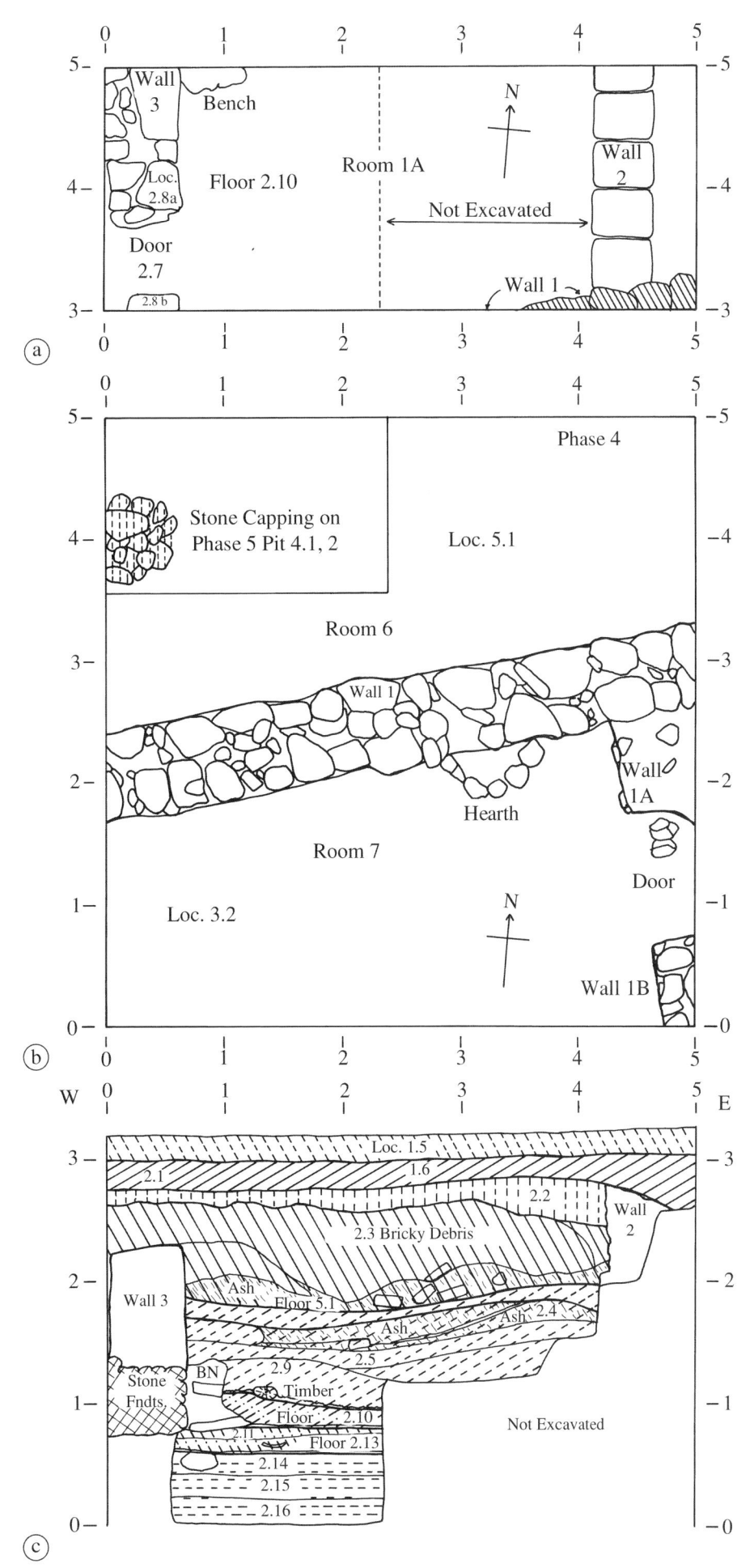

(*a*) Phases 2 and 3 Plan of Trench IIIB, Room 1A, Showing Walls 2 and 3 with Phase 4 Wall 1 in situ; (*b*) Phase 4 Plan of Trench IIIB, Rooms 6 and 7, Showing Walls 1, 1A, and 1B and Phase 5 Stone Capping on Pit 4.1 and 4.2; and (*c*) Trench IIIB, North Section. Scale 1:50

Plate 186

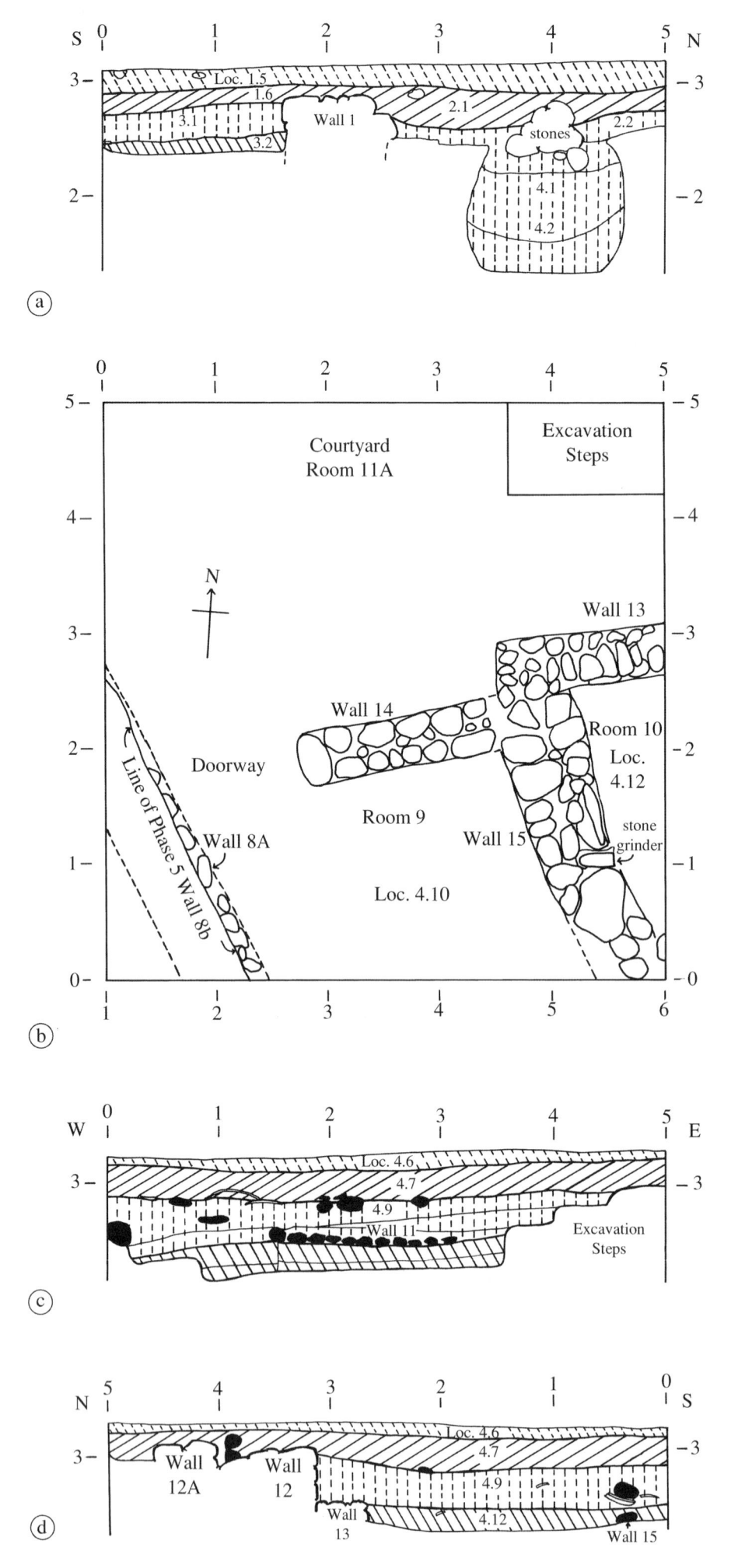

(*a*) Trench IIIB, West Section; (*b*) Phase 4 Plan of Trench IIIC, Rooms 9, 10, and 11A, Showing Walls 8A, 13, 14, and 15; (*c*) Trench IIIC, North Section; and (*d*) Trench IIIC, East Section. Scale 1:50

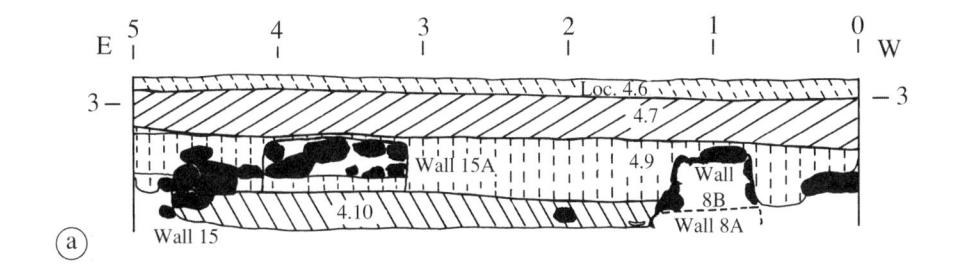

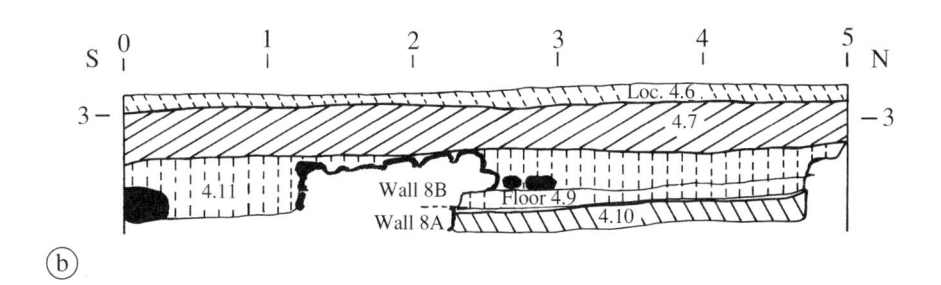

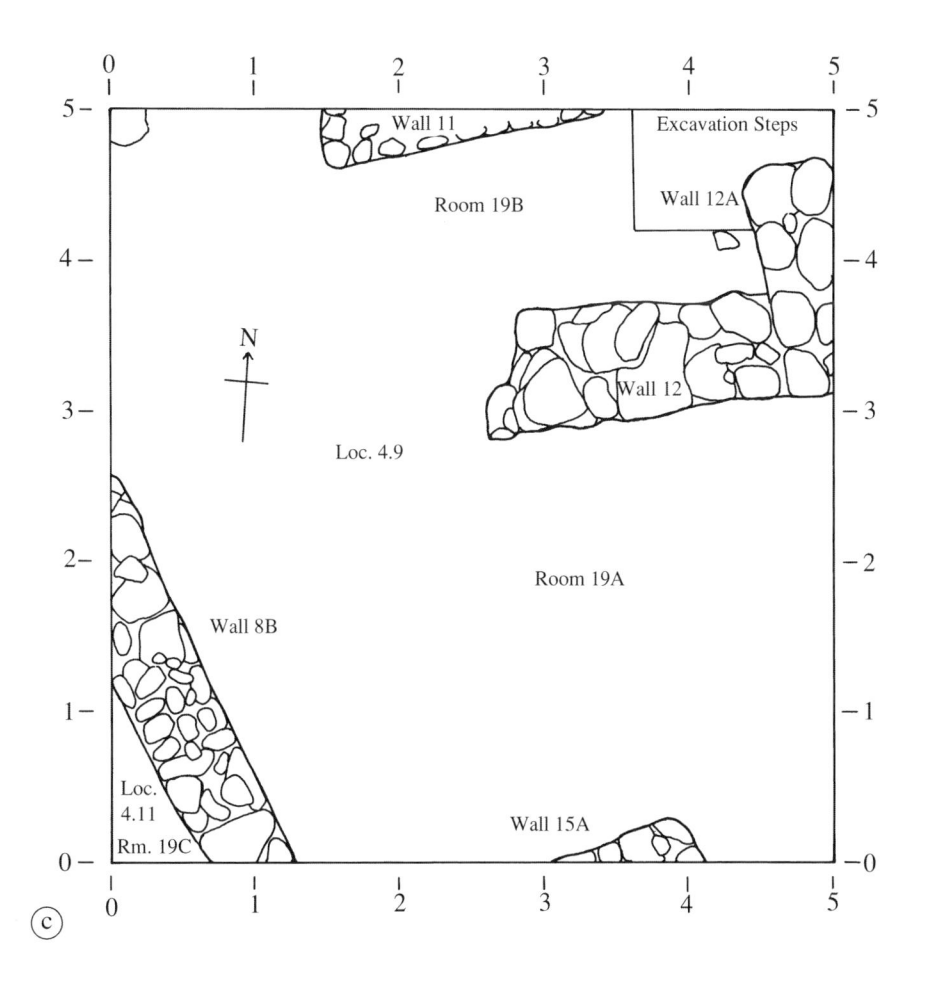

(*a*) Trench IIIC, South Section, (*b*) Trench IIIC, West Section, and (*c*) Phase 5 Plan of Trench IIIC, Rooms 19A–C, Showing Walls 8B, 11, 12, 12A, and 15A. Scale 1:50

Plate 188

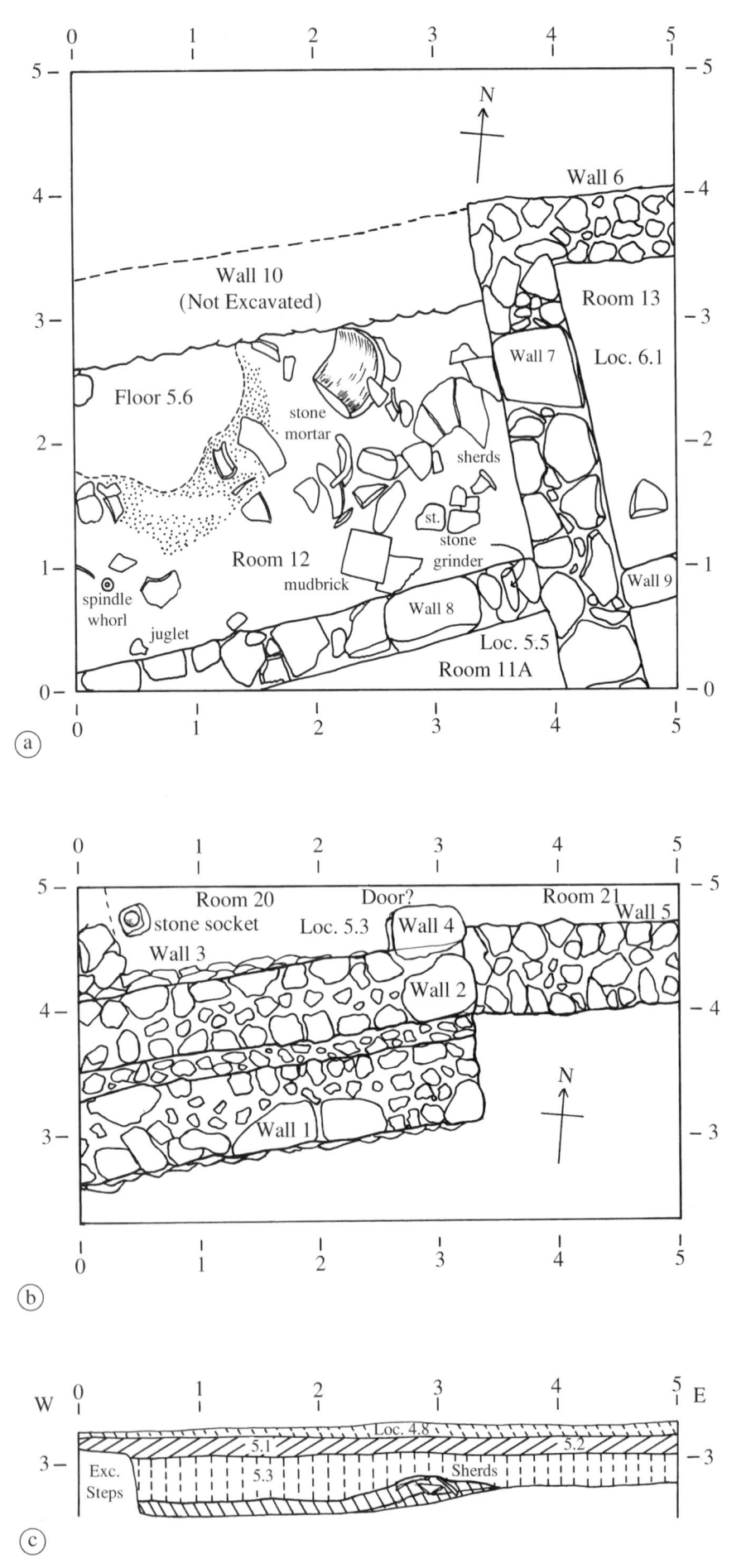

(a) Phase 4 Plan of Trench IIID, Rooms 11A, 12, and 13, Showing Walls 6, 7, 8, 9 and Position of Unexcavated Wall 10; (b) Phase 5 Plan of Trench IIID, Rooms 20 and 21, Showing Walls 1–5; and (c) Trench IIID, North Section. Scale 1:50

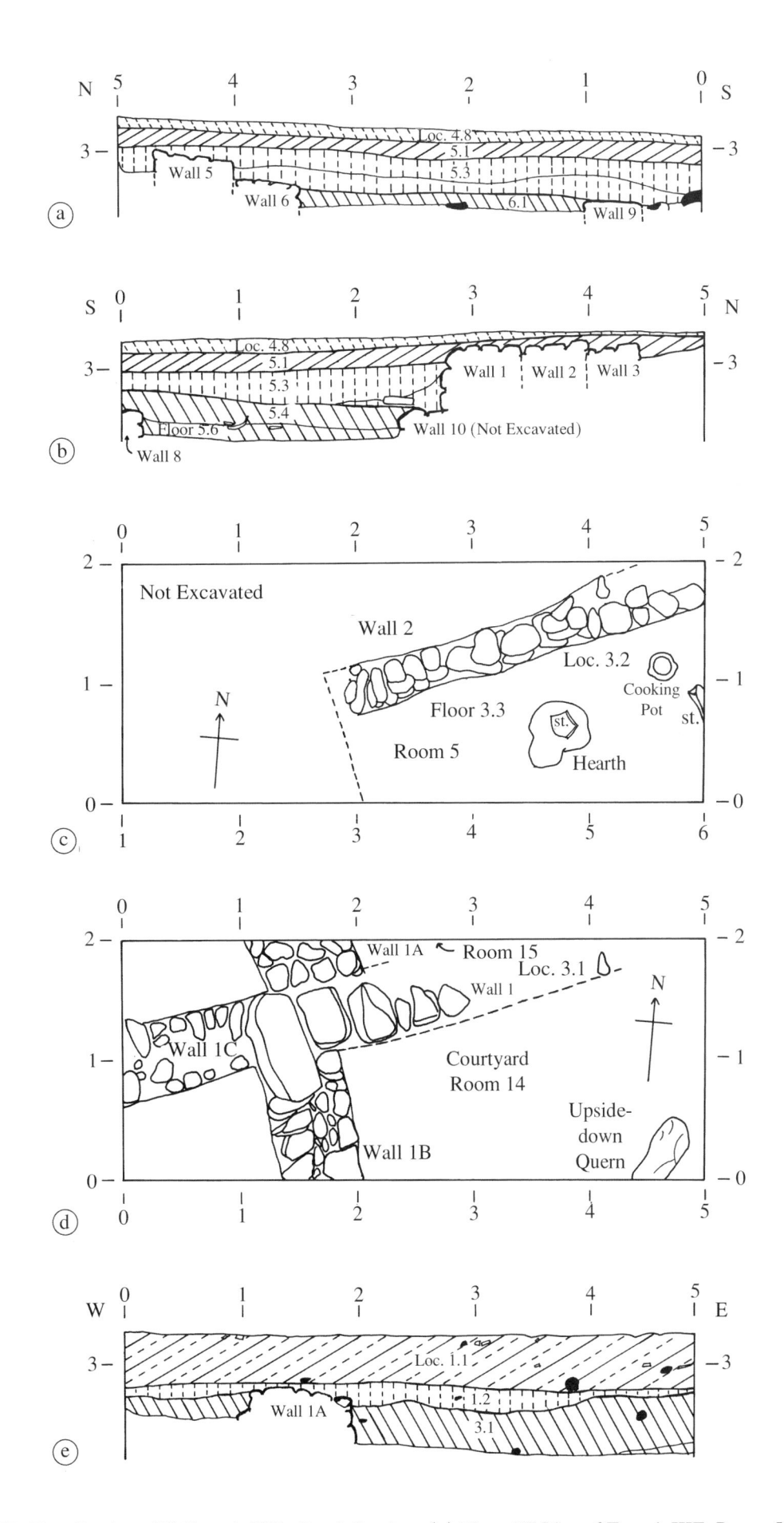

(*a*) Trench IIID, East Section; (*b*) Trench IIID, South Section; (*c*) Phase III Plan of Trench IIIE, Room 5, Showing Wall 2 and Unexcavated Portion of Trench; (*d*) Phase 4 Plan of Trench IIIE, Courtyard Room 14 and Room 15, Showing Walls 1, 1A, 1B, and 1C; and (*e*) Trench IIIE, North Section. Scale 1:50

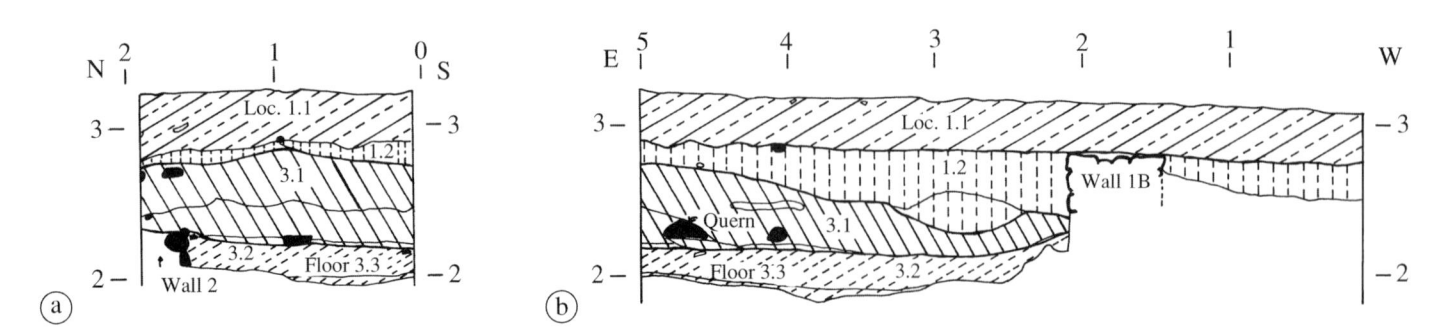

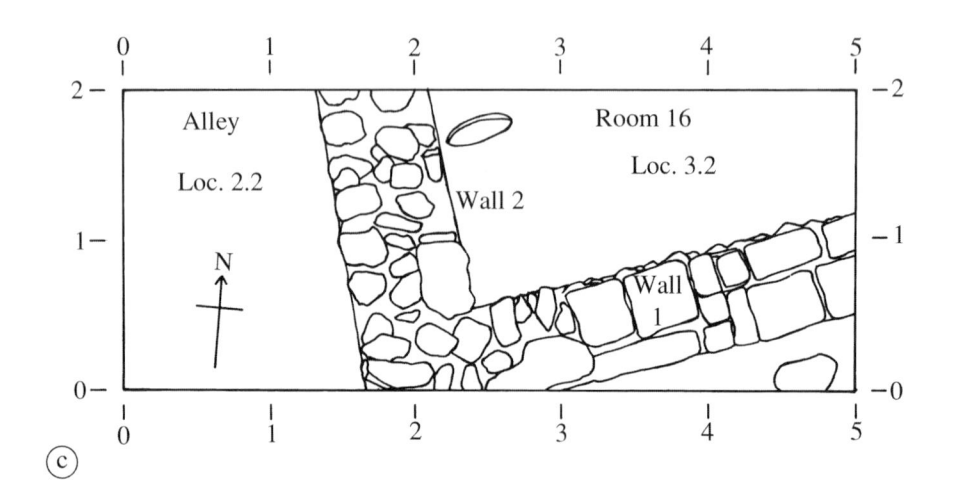

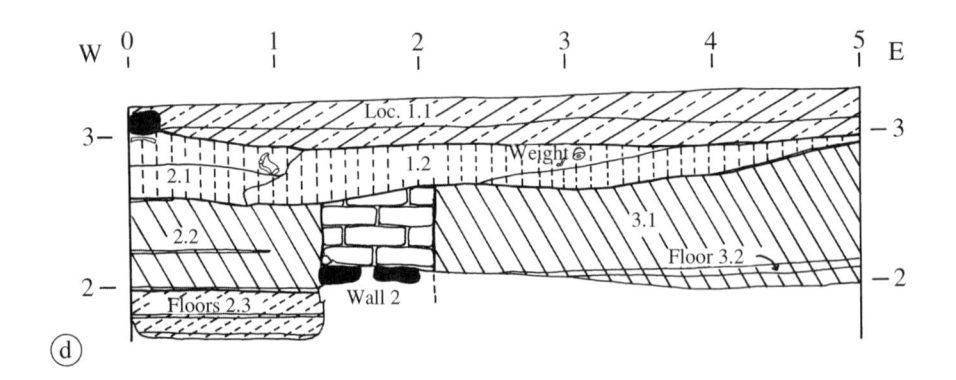

Plate 190

(*a*) Trench IIIE, East Section; (*b*) Trench IIIE, South Section; (*c*) Phase 4 Plan of Trench IIIF, Alley and Room 16, Showing Walls 1 and 2; and (*d*) Trench IIIF, North Section. Scale 1:50

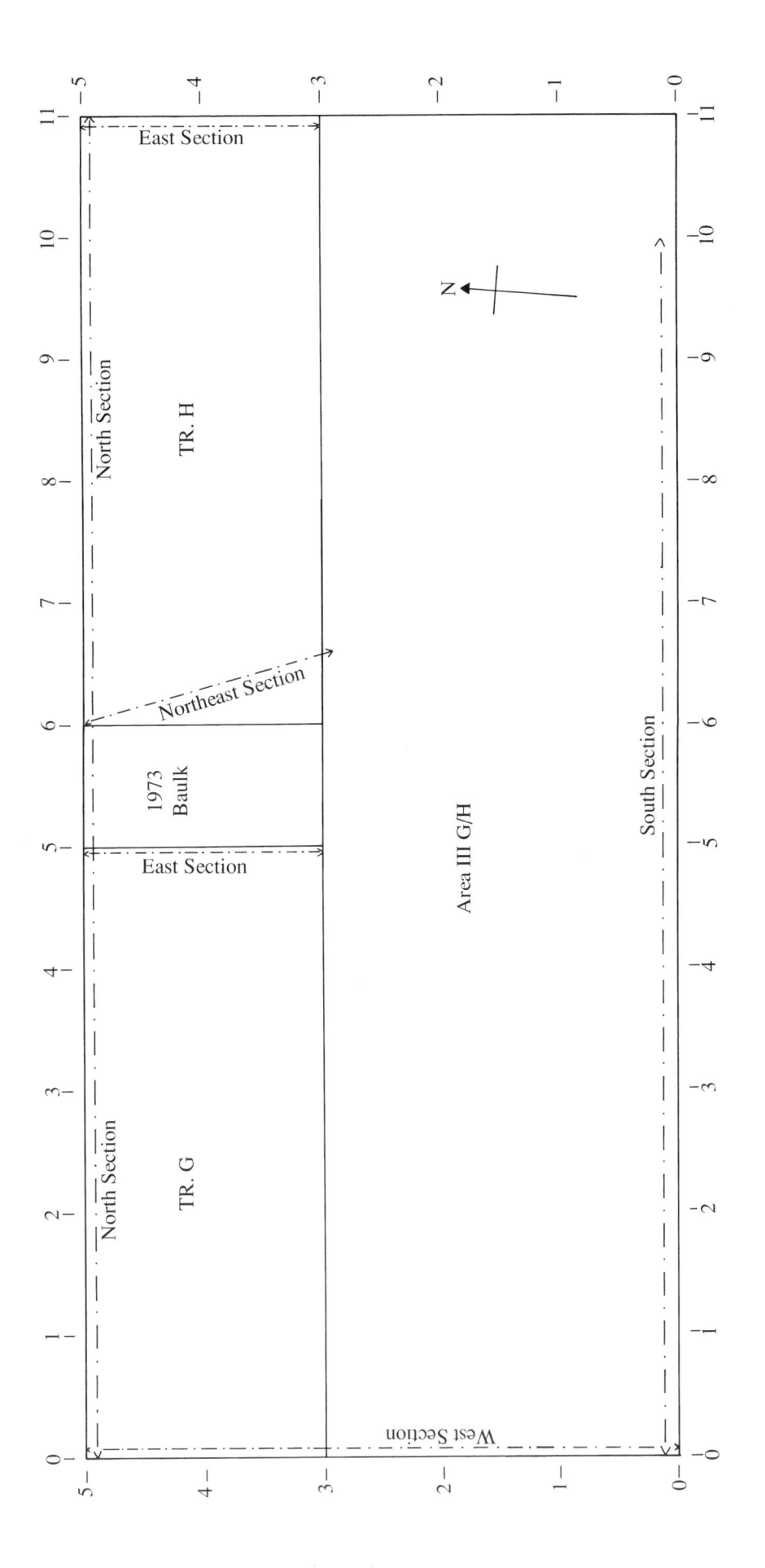

Key to Plan of Trenches IIIG, H, and Expanded Trench III G/H Showing Positions of Sections. Scale 1:50

Plate 192

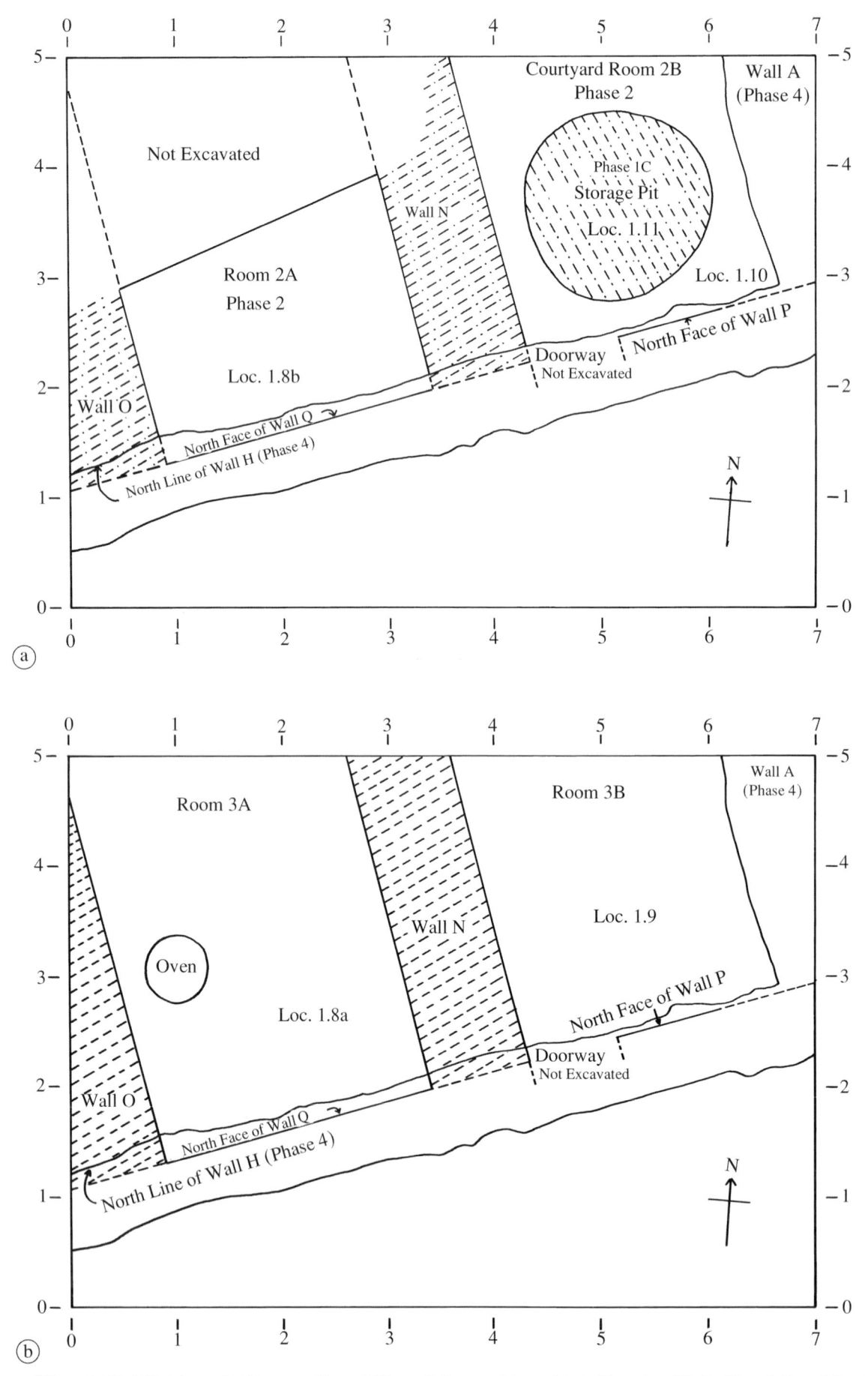

(*a*) Plan of Trench IIIG/H, Phase 1C Storage Pit and Phase 2 Rooms 2A and 2B, Showing Walls N and O and Positions of Walls P and Q; and (*b*) Plan of Trench IIIG/H, Phase 3 Rooms 3A and 3B, Showing Reused Walls N and O and Positions of Reused Walls P and Q. Scale 1:50

Plate 193

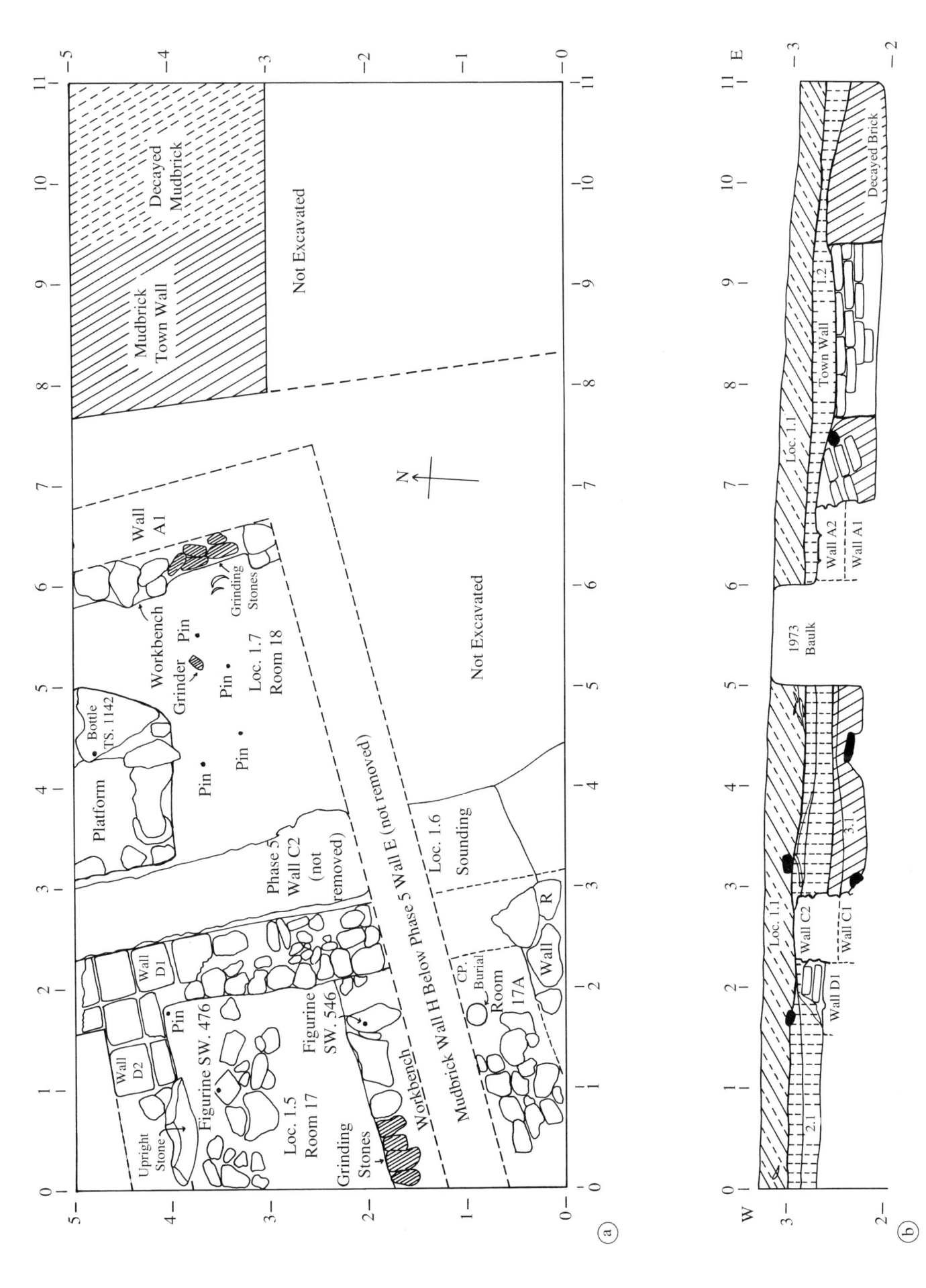

(a) Phase 4 Plan of Trench IIIG/H, Rooms 17, 17A, and 18, Showing Walls D1, D2, and R and Positions of Unexcavated Walls A1 and H and Remains of Mudbrick Town Wall on the Northeastern Side of the Main Mound; and (b) Trench IIIG/H, North Section. Scale 1:50

Plate 194

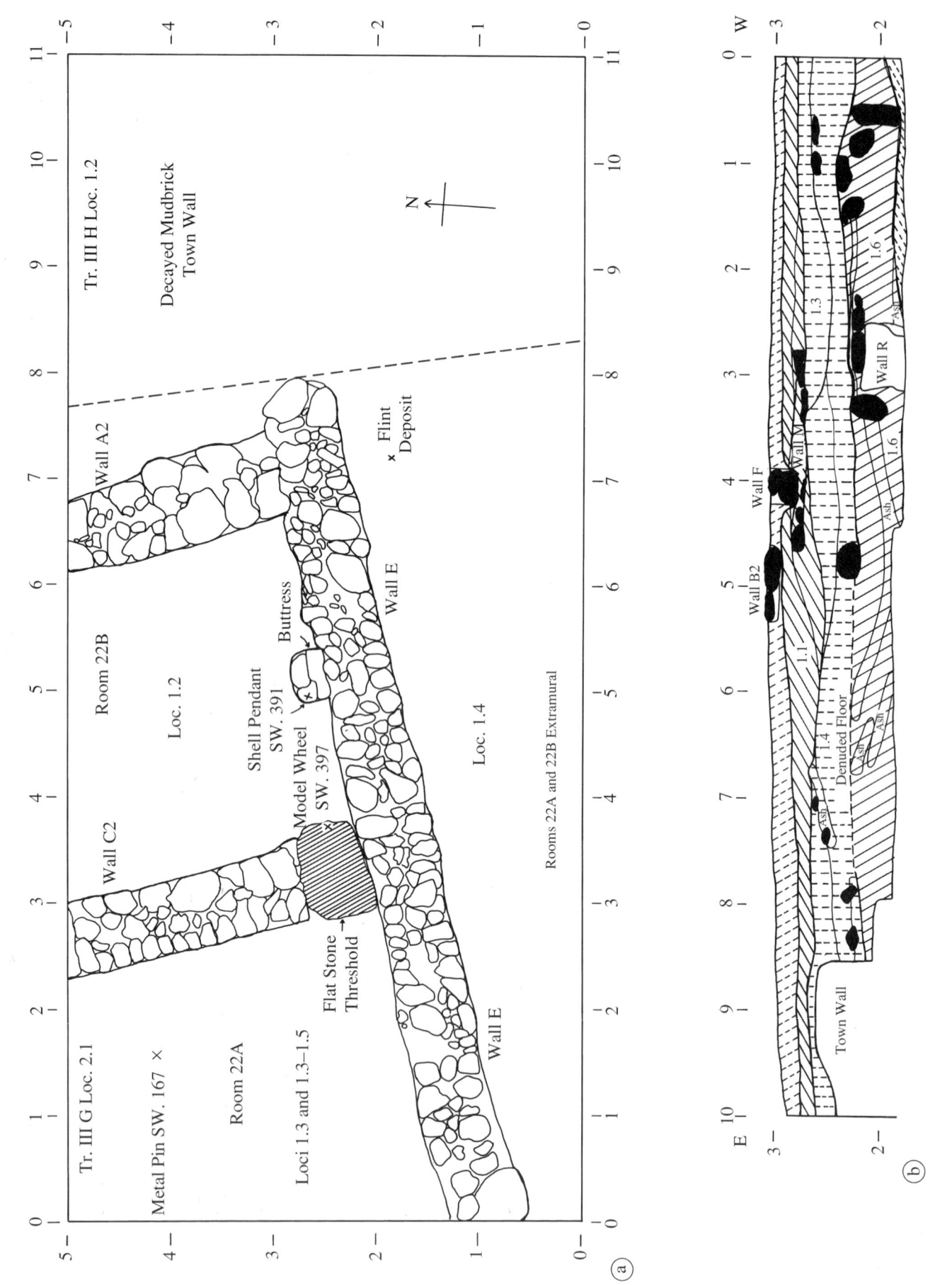

(a) Phase 5 Plan of Trench IIIG/H, Rooms 22A and 22B, Showing Walls A2, C2, and E, and (b) Trench IIIG/H, South Section. Scale 1:50

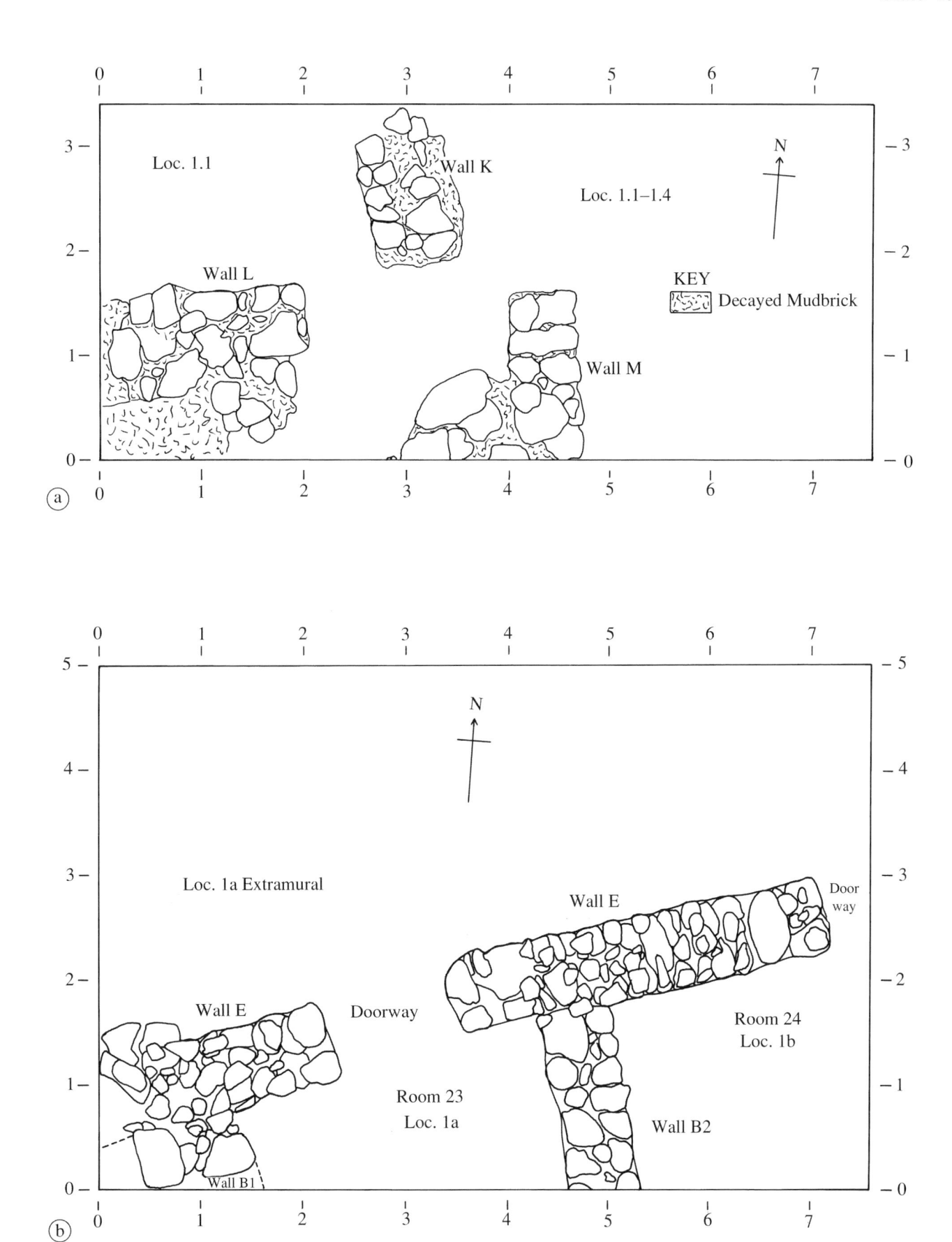

(*a*) Phase 6 Plan of Trench IIIG/H Showing Fragmentary Walls K, L, and M; and (*b*) Phase 7A Plan of Trench IIIG/H, Rooms 23 and 24, Showing Walls B1 and B2 and Reused Wall E. Scale 1:50

Plate 196

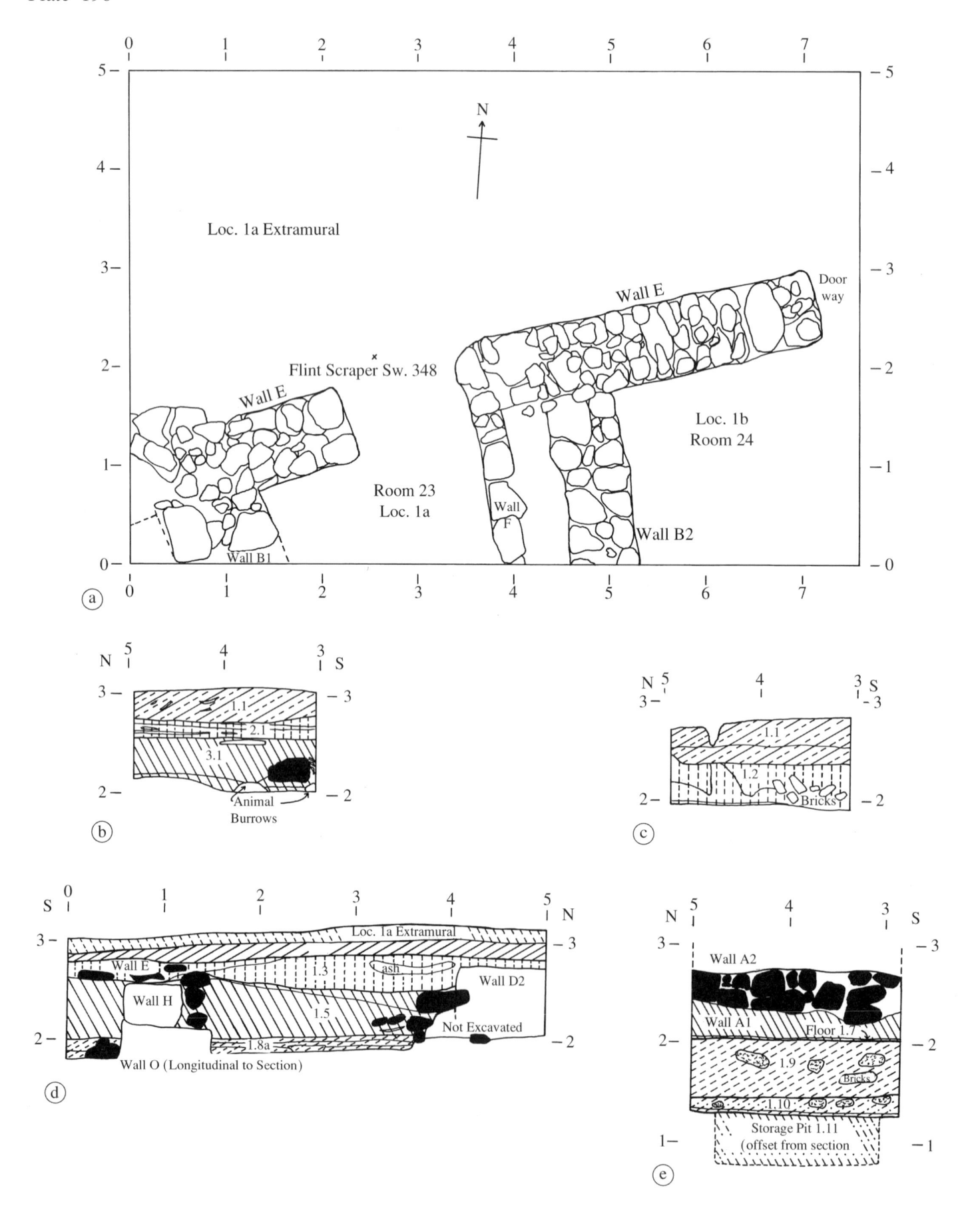

(*a*) Phase 7B Plan of Trench IIIG/H, Reused Rooms 23 and 24, Showing Reused Walls B1, B2, E, and Additional Wall F; (*b*) Trench IIIG, East Section; (*c*) Trench IIIH, East Section; (*d*) Trench IIIG/H, West Section; and (*e*) Trench IIIG/H, Northeast Section. Scale 1:50

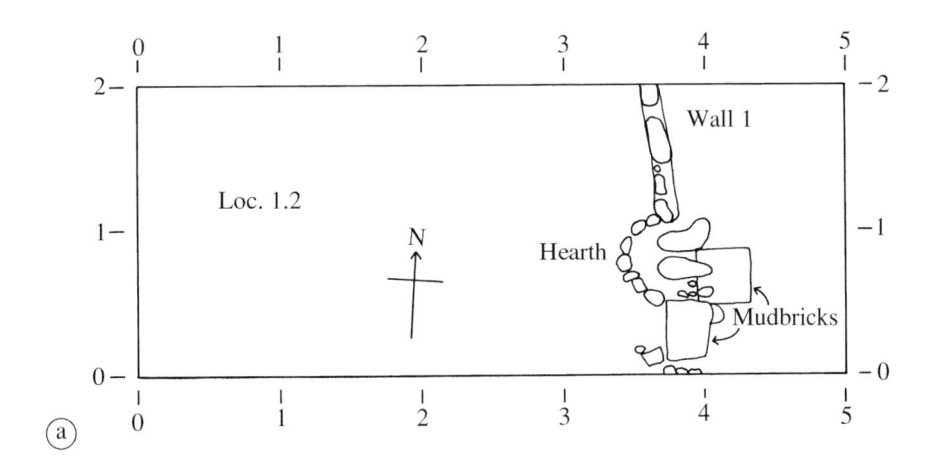

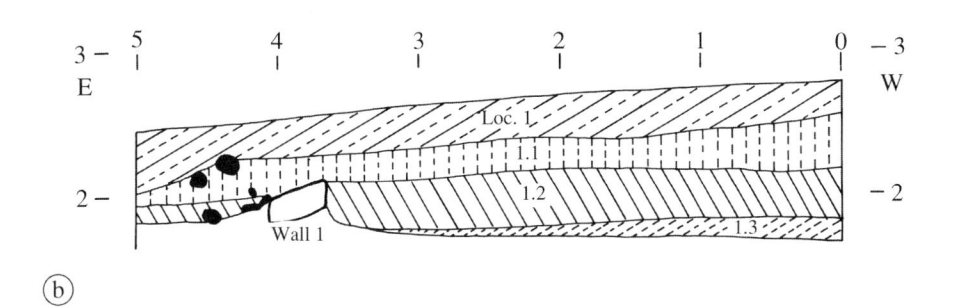

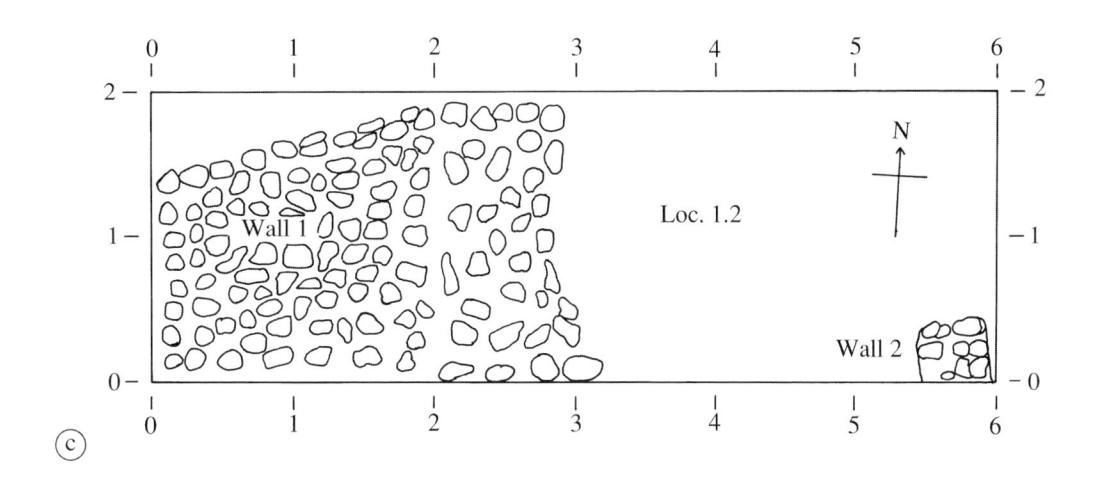

(*a*) Plan of Trench IIIJ Phase 4 Showing Wall 1 and Hearth; (*b*) Trench IIIJ, South Section; and (*c*) Phase 5 Plan of Trench IIIL Showing Walls 1 and 2. Scale 1:50

Plate 198

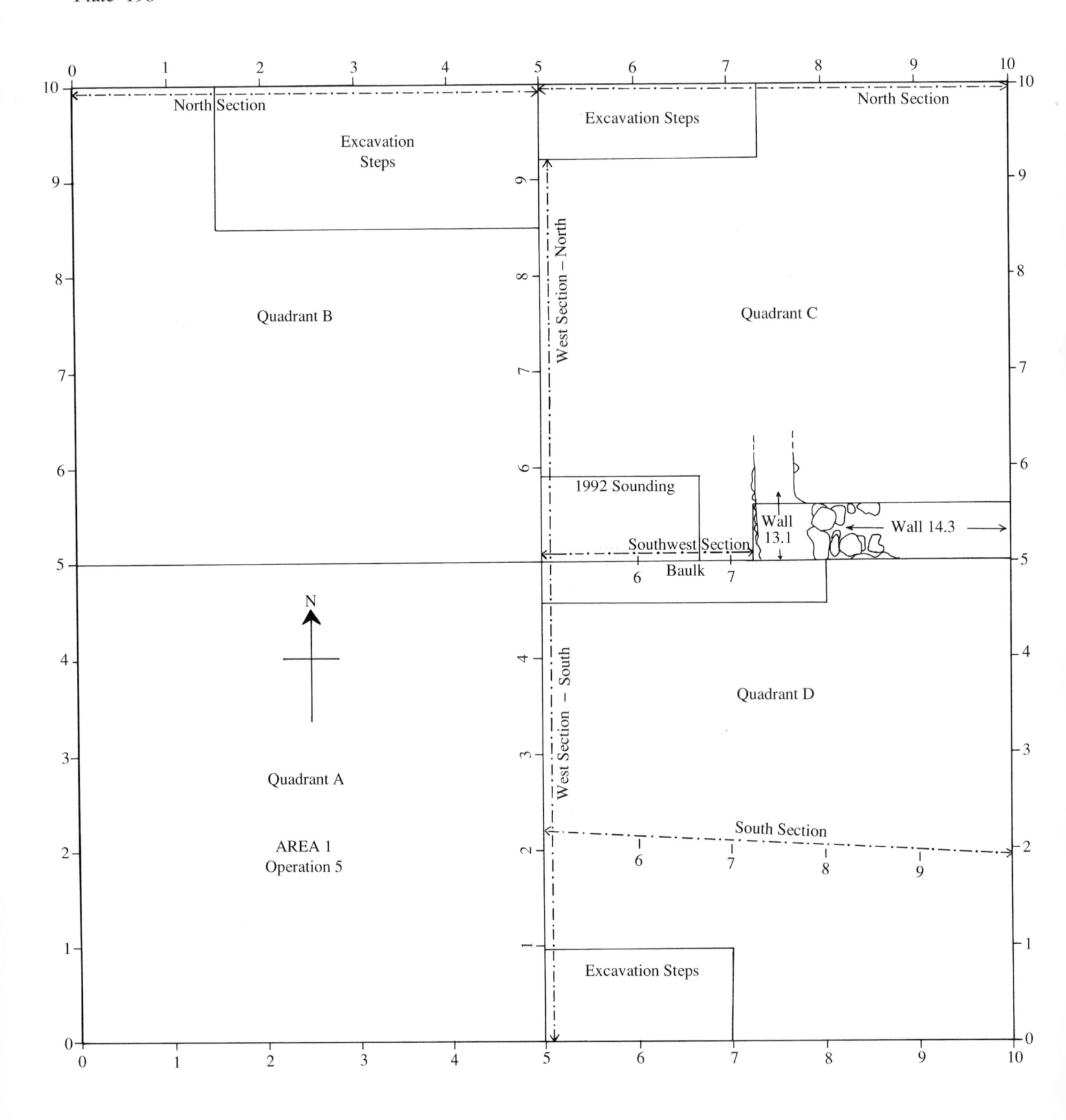

Key to Plans and Sections of Operation 5. Scale 1:50

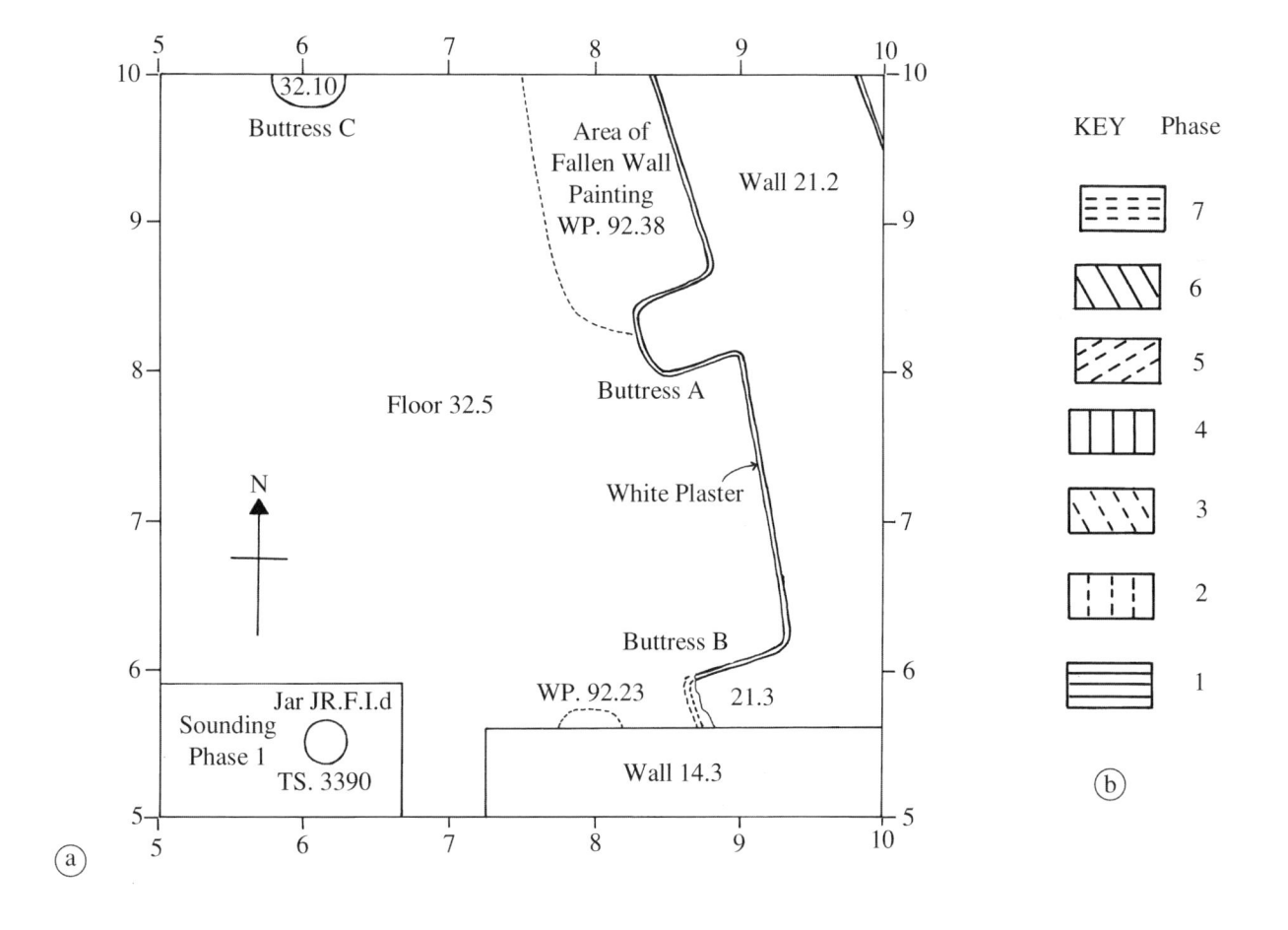

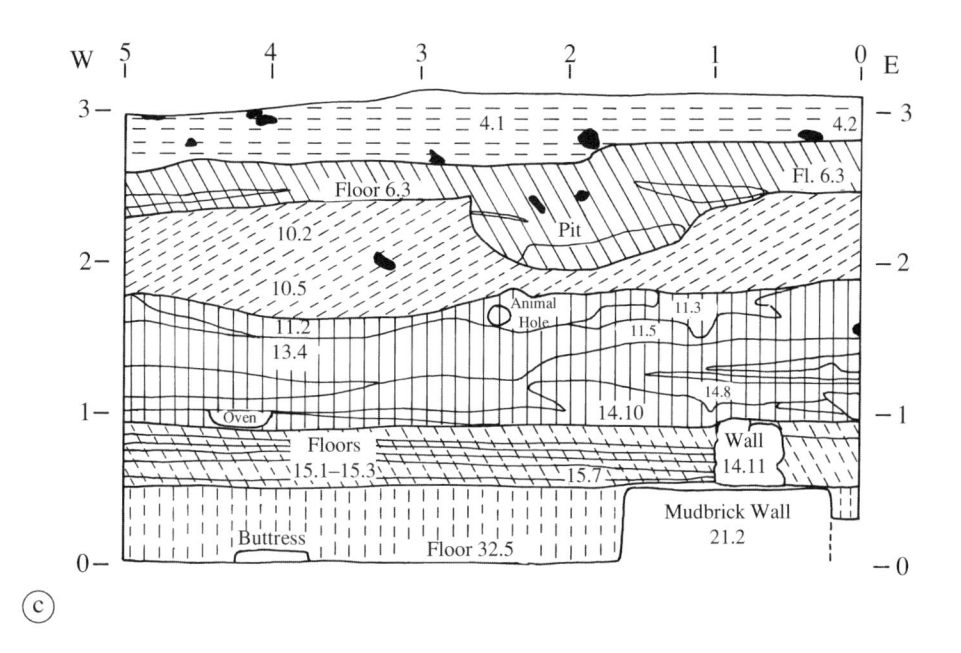

Plate 199

(*a*) Plan of Operation 5, Phase 2 Mudbrick Wall 21.2 with Fallen Wall Painting Fragments and Phase 1 Sounding in Southwest Corner of Quadrant C; (*b*) Key to Hatching of Phases on Sections; and (*c*) Operation 5, North Section of Quadrant C. Scale 1:50

Plate 200

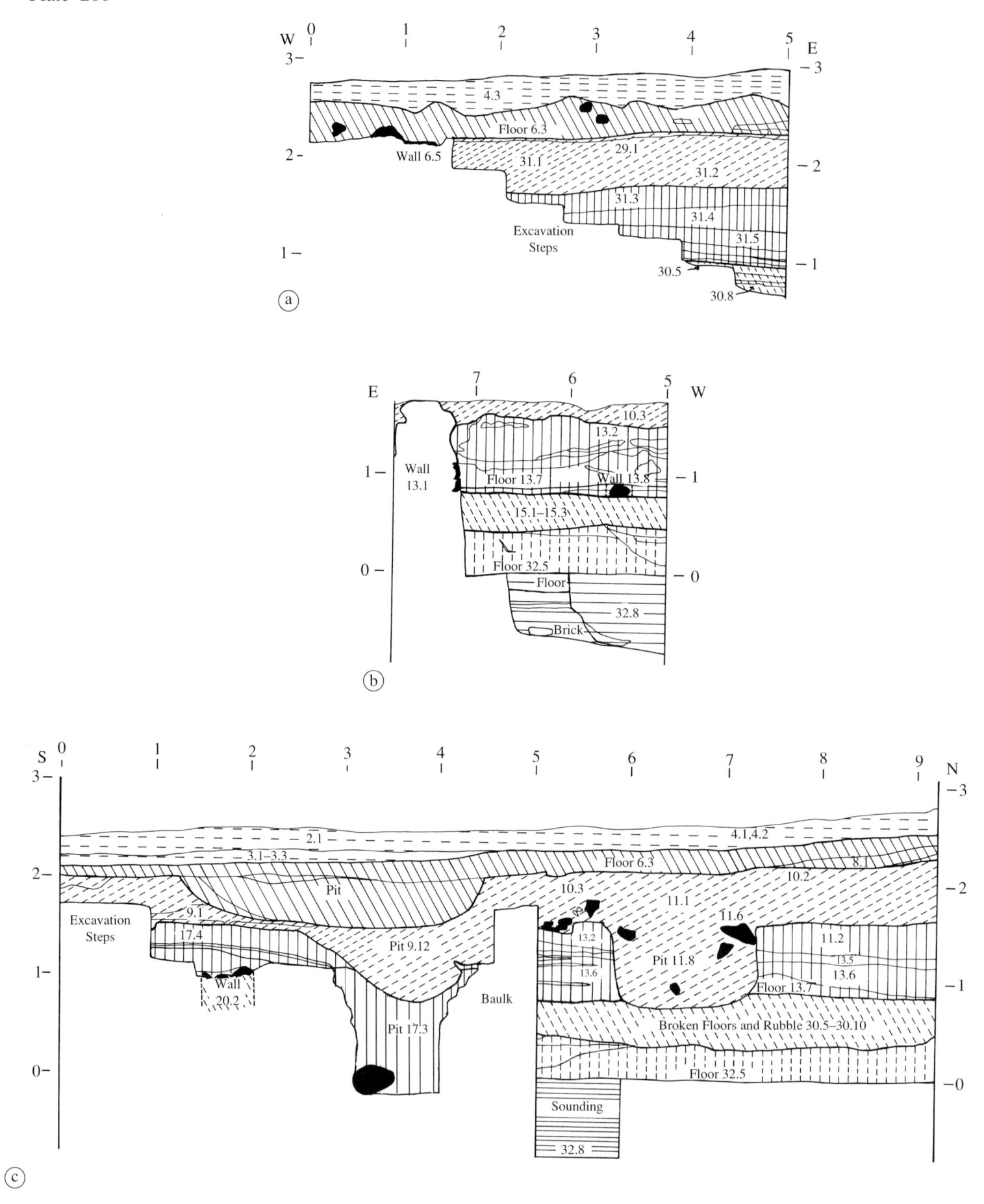

(*a*) Operation 5, North Section of Quadrant B, (*b*) Operation 5, Southwest Section of Quadrant C; and (*c*) Operation 5, West Section of Quadrants D and C. Scale 1:50

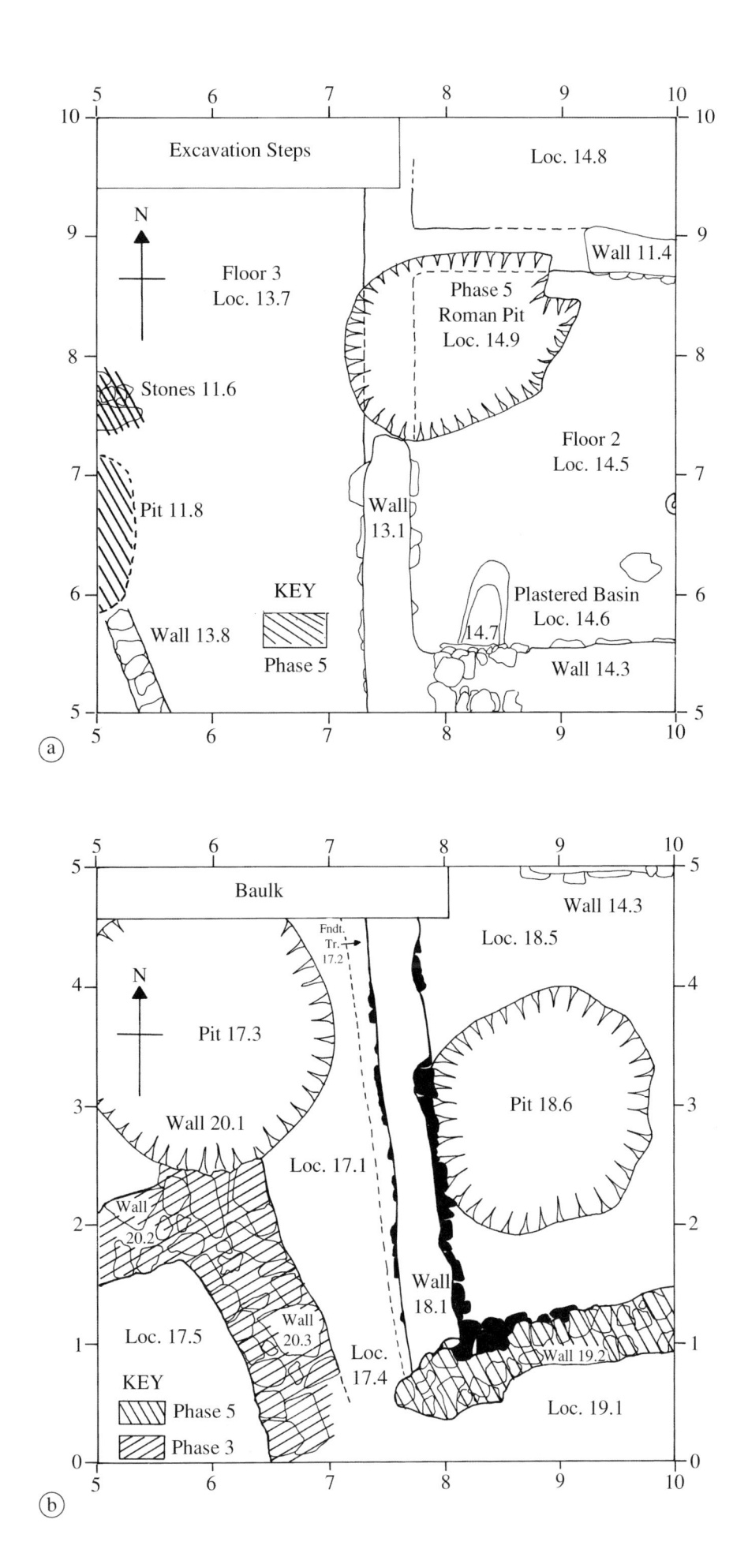

(*a*) Plan of Operation 5, Quadrant C, Showing Remnants of Phases 4 and 5; and (*b*) Plan of Operation 5, Quadrant D, Showing Phase 4 Pits 17.3 and 18.6 and Phases 3, 4 (Walls 14.3, 18.1) and 5 Walls. Scale 1:50

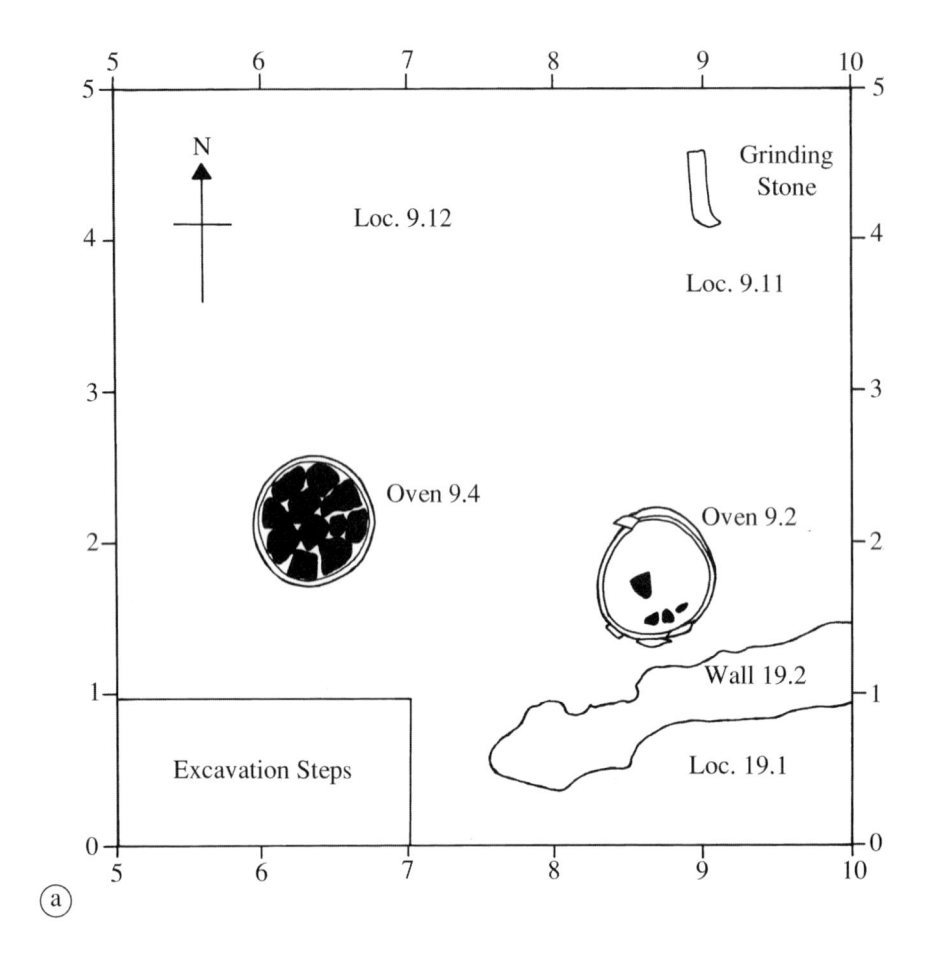

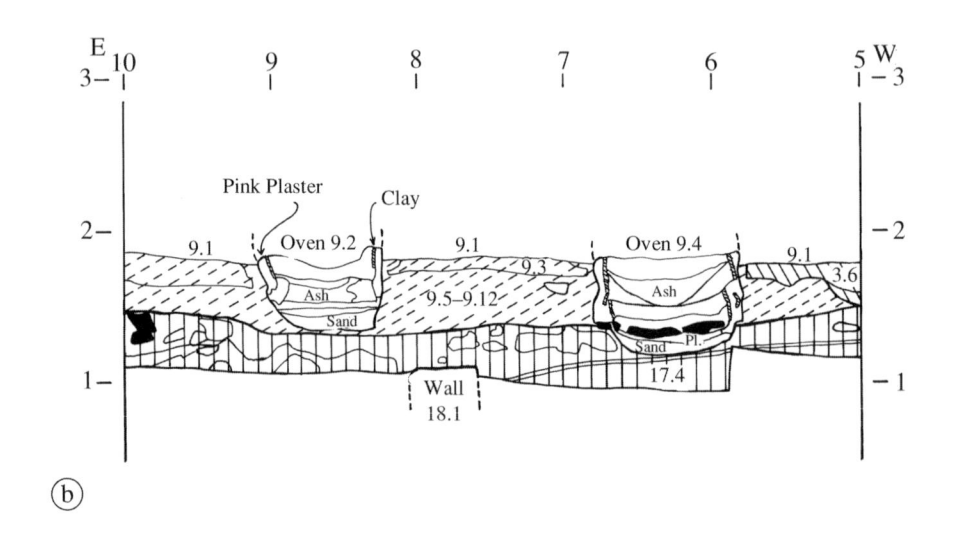

Plate 202

(*a*) Plan of Operation 5, Quadrant D, Showing Phase 5 Roman Ovens 9.2 and 9.4 and Wall 19.2; and (*b*) Operation 5, Quadrant D South Section through Roman Ovens 9.2 and 9.4. Scale 1:50

Plate 203

Plan of Operation 5, Quadrants A–D, Showing Phases 6 and 7. Scale 1:50

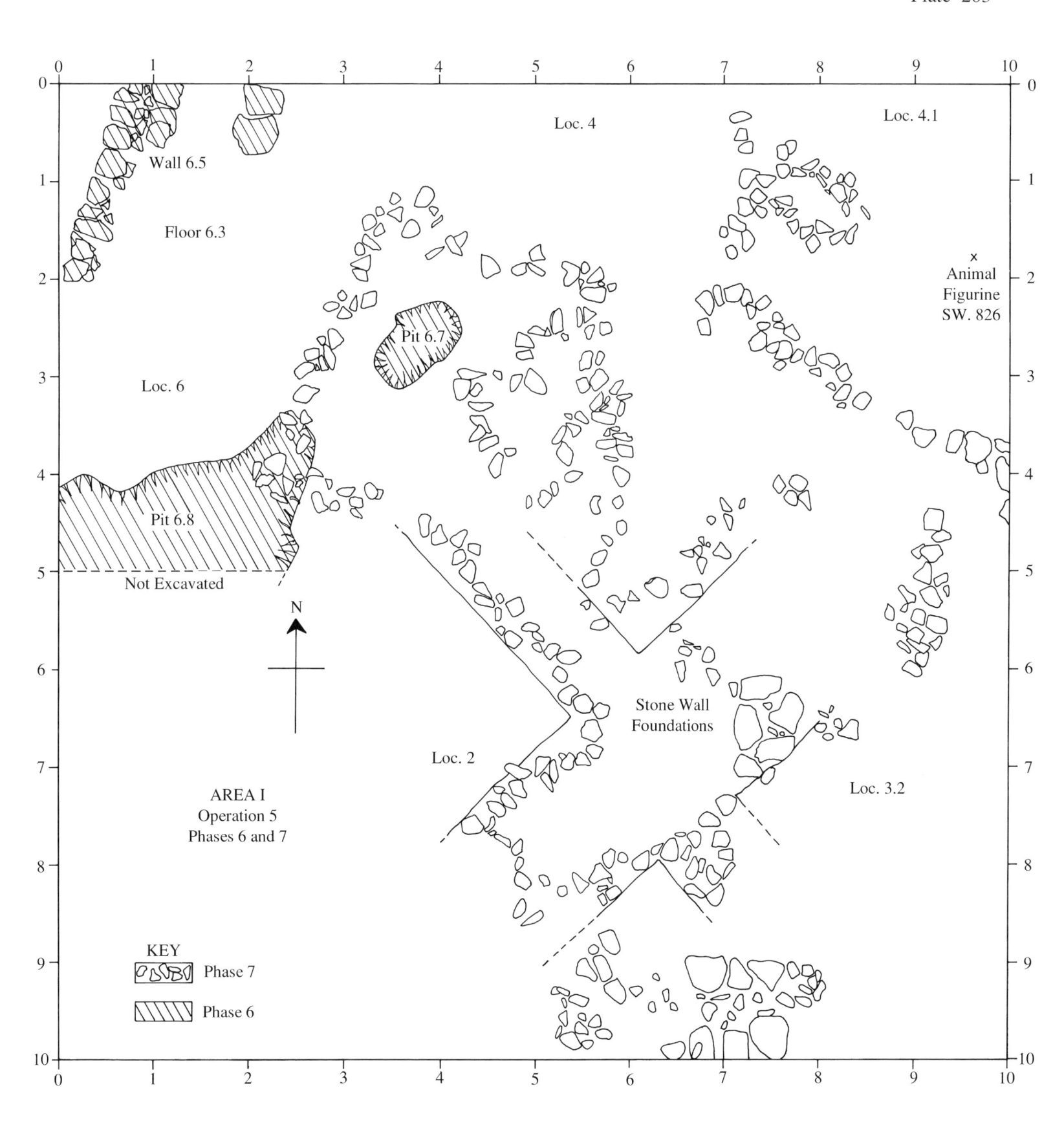

Plate 204

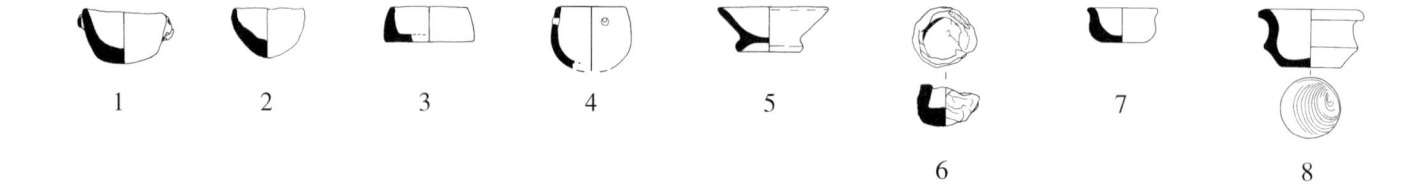

Bronze Age Miniature Bowl (MBR) Types A–D. Scale 1:5

1. MBR. A.I.a (SW. 483; IVO, 1.3, Fill). Phase 3 (see also pl. 89a). Complete, handmade. Four cord handles applied in pairs on opposite sides below rim. Fairly fine pink ware.
—. MBR. A.I.b (SC. 2638; IVP, 1.5, Room 9). Not illustrated. Phase 2B. About 1/10 rim and upper wall segment with a nearly complete rectangular ledge handle attached to outside top of rim and upper wall (0.5 m wide × 2.5 cm long). Fine buff ware with a few small lime grits, evenly fired. Self slip in and out.
2. MBR. A.II.a (SW. 262; IIIF, 1.2). Phase 5. One half extant, handmade. Coarse drab ware with many lime and mica grits, unevenly fired grayish in and over rim out, pinkish-brown on lower outer surface.
3. MBR. B.I.a (SW. 557; IVL/P, 1.3, Pit). Phase 3. One fourth extant, handmade. Fairly coarse brownish-pink ware, evenly fired.
4. MBR. B.I.b (TS. 1241; IIID, 5.3, Rooms 20/21). Phase 5. About 1/10 rim segment and most of wall profile with cord hole bored below rim before firing, handmade. Fairly fine buff ware, evenly fired. Self slip in and out.
5. MBR. B.II.a (SW. 498; IVM, 1.5, Room 7). Phase 2A. Mended to near completion, partially blackened out. Fairly coarse brown ware.
6. MBR. C.I.a (SW. 227; IIA, 9.3, Room 8). Phase 4. Complete, crudely handmade. Light brownish-buff ware with lime and mica grits, evenly fired.
7. MBR. D.I.a (TS. 3300; Op. 7, Surface 1.1). Phase 4. About 1/2 rim segment and complete wall profile. Handmade. Fairly coarse reddish-brown ware with fine gold- and silver-colored mica and lime grits, evenly fired. Self slip in and out.
8. MBR. D.II.a (SW. 810; Op. 7, 2.3, Room 37). Phase 2B(b). Complete, string-cut base. Ware description not available.

Plate 205

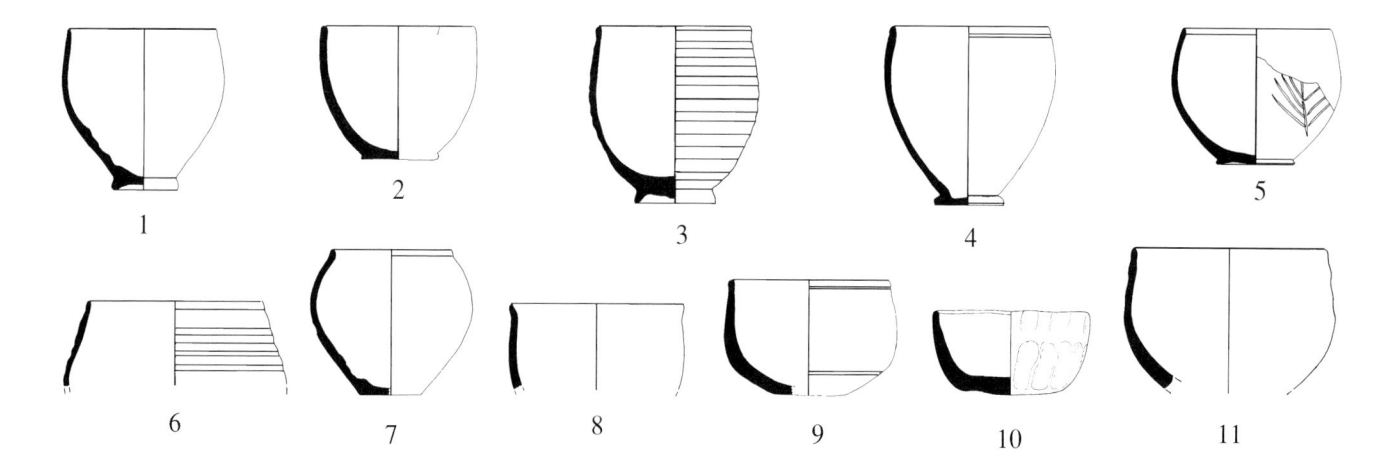

Bronze Age Small Bowl/Cup (SBR) Type A. Scale 1:5

1. SBR. A.I.a (SW. 246; IVD, 2.4, Room 2). Phase 2B. Nearly complete. Hard, grayish-green ware with lime grits, evenly fired. Creamy-green slip in and out.
2. SBR. A.I.b (PM. A.5; SW. 382; IVK, 2.4, Room 2). Phase 2B (see also pl. 89c). Mended to completion. Incised linear potter's mark on rim and string-cut base. Fine creamy-buff ware, fairly evenly fired.
3. SBR. A.I.c (SW. 568; IVJ, Bin, 3.5, Room 5). Phase 2A (see also pl. 35a, and pocket plan 3). Nearly complete. Fairly coarse buff ware. Cream slip in and out.
4. SBR. A.I.d (SW. 245; IIIB, 2.10, Room 1A). Phase 2. Complete profile, about 1/2 segment, string-cut base. Hard, fine buff ware with lime and mica grits, evenly fired.
5. SBR. A.I.e (IP [G.4] D.II; PM. D.19; SW. 732; IVQ, 1.6, Room 6). Phase 2A. Complete profile, about 2/3 body segment with tree or wheat stalk potter's mark incised on the outside wall before firing. Hard, fine buff ware with fine lime and mica grits, evenly fired. Self slip out.
6. SBR. A.I.f (TS. 1021; IXA, 1.3, stone floor). Phase 4. About 1/24 rim and upper wall segment. Fairly coarse pinkish-buff ware. Cream slip in and out.
7. SBR. A.I.g (SW. 301 = TS. 1742; IVD, 2.4 and IVK, 2.3, Room 2). Phases 2B and 3. Complete mended profile, about 1/4 rim segment. Slightly mended coarse buff ware with many lime and mica grits, evenly fired. Self slip out.
8. SBR. A.I.h (TS. 2024; IVC, 1.2). Phase 3. Small rim and upper wall segment. Fairly close buff ware, evenly fired. Creamy-buff slip in and out.
9. SBR. A.II.a (SW. 251; 1E, 1.10). Phase 3. Nearly complete profile except for central portion of the flat base. Fairly coarse pinkish-buff ware with lime and mica grits, unevenly fired creamy-green out.
10. SBR. A.II.b (SW. 64; IIIA, 4.5, Room 4B). Phase 3. Nearly complete. Handmade with potter's finger depressions fired into the outside wall of the vessel. Slightly coarse pinkish-buff ware with black mineral temper, evenly fired.
11. SBR. A.II.c (TS. 1601; IVJ, 1.5, Room 4). Phase 2B. About 1/4 rim segment and most of wall profile. Fairly fine pink ware, evenly fired. Cream slip in and out.

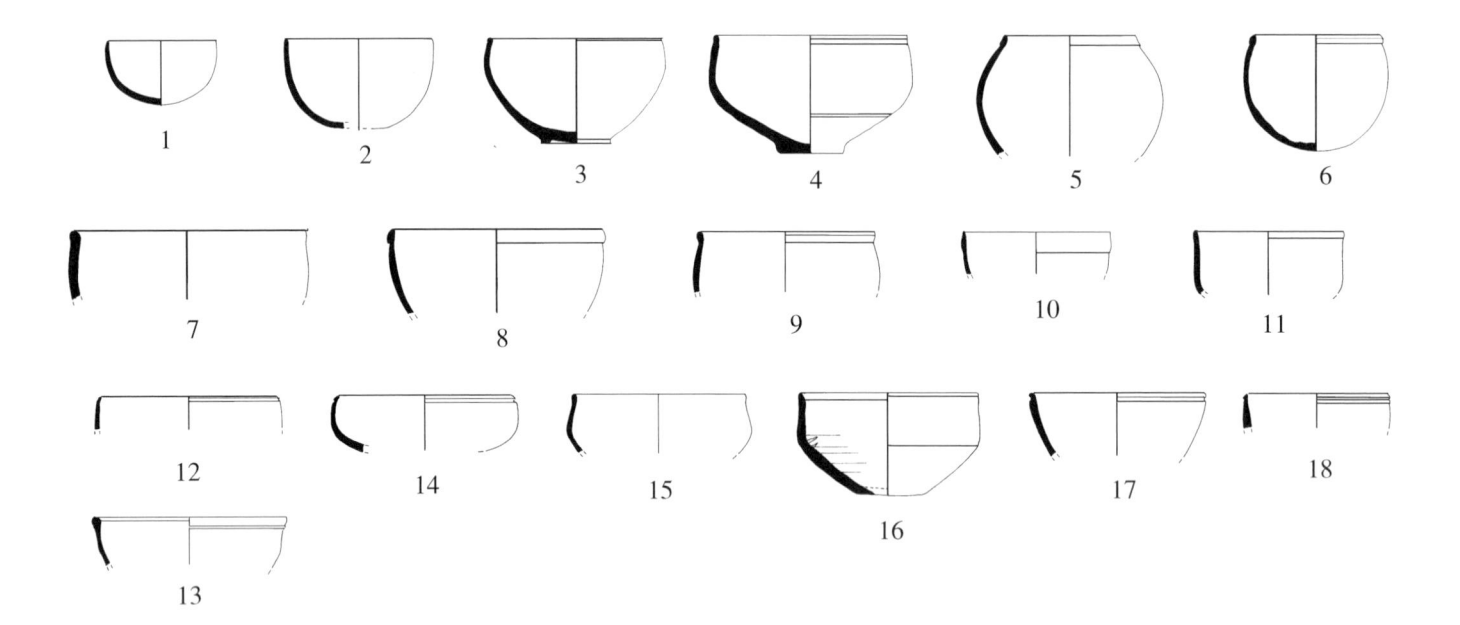

Bronze Age Small Bowl/Cup (SBR) Type B. Scale 1:5

1. SBR. B.I.a (TS. 2631; IVM, 10.4, Below Room 7). Phase 1A. Complete profile, about 1/3 segment. Fine pinkish-buff ware, evenly fired. Remains of cream slip out.
2. SBR. B.I.b (TS. 2131; VE, 1.3). Phase 4. Nearly complete profile. Slightly coarse buff ware, evenly fired. Self slip in and out.
3. SBR. B.I.c (SW. 327; IIIE, 3.3, Room 5). Phase 4. Complete profile, about 1/4 segment. Hard, fine cream ware, evenly fired.
4. SBR. B.I.d (SW. 59; IIIA, 1.4, Room 11). Phase 4. Complete profile. Buff-orange ware with black- and gold-colored mica grits.
5. SBR. B.I.e (TS. 2601 = TS. 2929; IVP, 1.5, 1.6 + IVJ, 1.5, Rooms 9 and 4; most vessel sherds come from Area IVP). Phase 2A. About 1/3 rim segment and most of wall profile with non-joining fragments. Fairly fine pinkish-buff ware, evenly fired. Creamy-buff slip in and out.
6. SBR. B.I.f (TS. 2555; IVM, 1.4, Room 7). Phase 2B. Complete profile, about 1/3 rim segment. Fairly fine ware, unevenly fired with gray core and pink at surfaces. Self slip in and out.
7. SBR. B.I.g (TS. 2019; IIIF, 2.1). Phase 5. Small rim and upper wall segment. Fairly coarse ware, unevenly fired with light gray core and buff at surfaces. Thick creamy-buff slip in and out.
8. SBR. B.I.h (TS. 2702; IVZ(S), 5.3). Phase 2B. About 1/8 rim and wall segment. Fine grayware, evenly fired. Self slip in and out.
9. SBR. B.I.i (TS. 2483; IC, 1.39). Phase 5. About 1/6 rim and upper wall segment. Fairly fine brownish-buff ware, evenly fired. Creamy-buff slip in and out.
10. SBR. B.I.j (TS. 2974; IVM, 10.1, Below Room 7). Phase 1C. Small rim and upper wall segment. Slightly coarse pinkish ware, evenly fired. Cream slip in and out.
11. SBR. B.I.k (TS. 475; IIIC, 4.10, Room 9). Phase 4. About 1/10 rim and upper wall segment. Fairly coarse buff ware.
12. SBR. B.I.l (TS. 1213; IIIG/H, 1.8a, Room 3A). Phase 3. Small rim and upper wall segment. Fine brown ware with self slip in and out. Traces of grayish-black substance inside, possibly bitumen.
13. SBR. B.I.m (TS. 815; IC, 1.40). Phase 4. About 1/32 rim and upper wall segment. Fairly coarse pink ware, unevenly fired with buff core. Cream slip out.
14. SBR. B.I.n (TS. 1085; XA, 1.4, Room 15). Phase 2A. About 1/6 rim segment and most of wall profile. Fairly fine pink ware. Cream slip on upper body out and thin buff slip in.
15. SBR. B.I.o (TS. 1981; IVG, 1.4, Room 3). Phase 2B. Small rim and wall segment. Fairly fine pink ware, evenly fired. Buff slip out.
16. SBR. B.I.p (PM. F; SW. 265; IVC, 1.5 = IVM, Room 7). Phase 2B. Nearly complete profile, about 1/2 rim segment. Slightly coarse grayish-buff ware with small lime and mica grits, evenly fired. Remains of a potter's mark incised on the inside wall before firing.
17. SBR. B.I.q (TS. 1361; IIID, 5.3, Rooms 20/21). Phase 5. Small rim and upper wall segment. Fairly fine pinkish-buff ware, evenly fired. Creamy-buff slip in and out.
18. SBR. B.I.r (TS. 2509; IC, 1.7). Phase 8. Small rim and upper wall segment. Fairly coarse grayware, evenly fired. Self slip in and out.

Plate 207

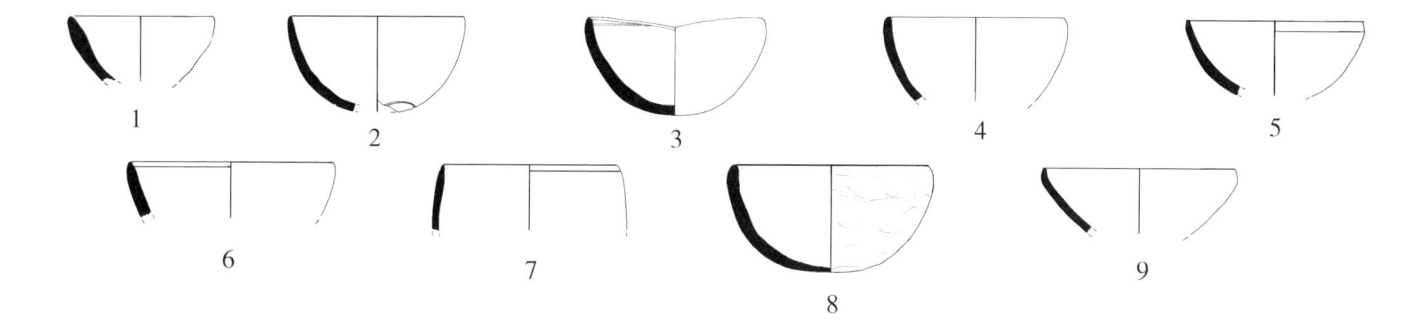

Bronze Age Small Bowl/Cup (SBR) Type C. Scale 1:5

1. SBR. C.I.a (TS. 169; IIA, 8.4, Room 9). Phase 6. Small rim segment and most of wall profile. Fine pinkish-brown ware with lime and mica grits, evenly fired. Creamy-buff slip out.
2. SBR. C.II.a (PM. B.1; TS. 1042; IC, 1.40 + 1.48). Phase 3. Nearly complete profile; round base with remains of a potter's mark incised on the outside of the base before firing. Fairly fine ware, unevenly fired buff in, pink out.
3. SBR. C.II.b (SW. 300; IIA, 9.9, Room 1). Phase 1. About 1/4 rim segment and complete wall profile. Slightly coarse pinkish-buff ware with mica and lime grits, evenly fired.
4. SBR. C.II.c (TS. 1039; IC, 1.48). Phase 3. About 1/5 rim and 2/3 wall segment. Fairly coarse pink ware, evenly fired.
5. SBR. C.II.d (TS. 312 = TS. 319; IIA, 8.17, Room 12). Phase 6. Two small non-joining rim segments and most of wall profile. Slightly coarse pinkish-buff ware with lime and mica grits, evenly fired. Self slip in and out.
6. SBR. C.II.e (TS. 116; IIA, 5.16, Courtyard). Phase 8. Small rim and upper wall segment. Fairly fine buff ware with lime and mica grits, evenly fired. Self slip in and out.
7. SBR. C.III.a (TS. 2447; IVG, 1.4, Room 3). Phase 2B. About 1/8 rim and upper wall segment. Slightly coarse buff ware, evenly fired. Self slip out.
8. SBR. C.III.b (SW. 299; IIA, 9.9, Room 1). Phase 1. About 1/2 rim segment and complete wall profile. Hard, slightly coarse greenish-buff ware with small, various colored, lime grits, fairly evenly fired. Self slip in and out.
9. SBR. C.IV.a (TS. 1984; IIA, 8.4, Room 9). Phase 6. Small rim and 2/3 wall segment. Slightly coarse pinkish-buff ware, evenly fired. Creamy-buff slip in and out.

Plate 208

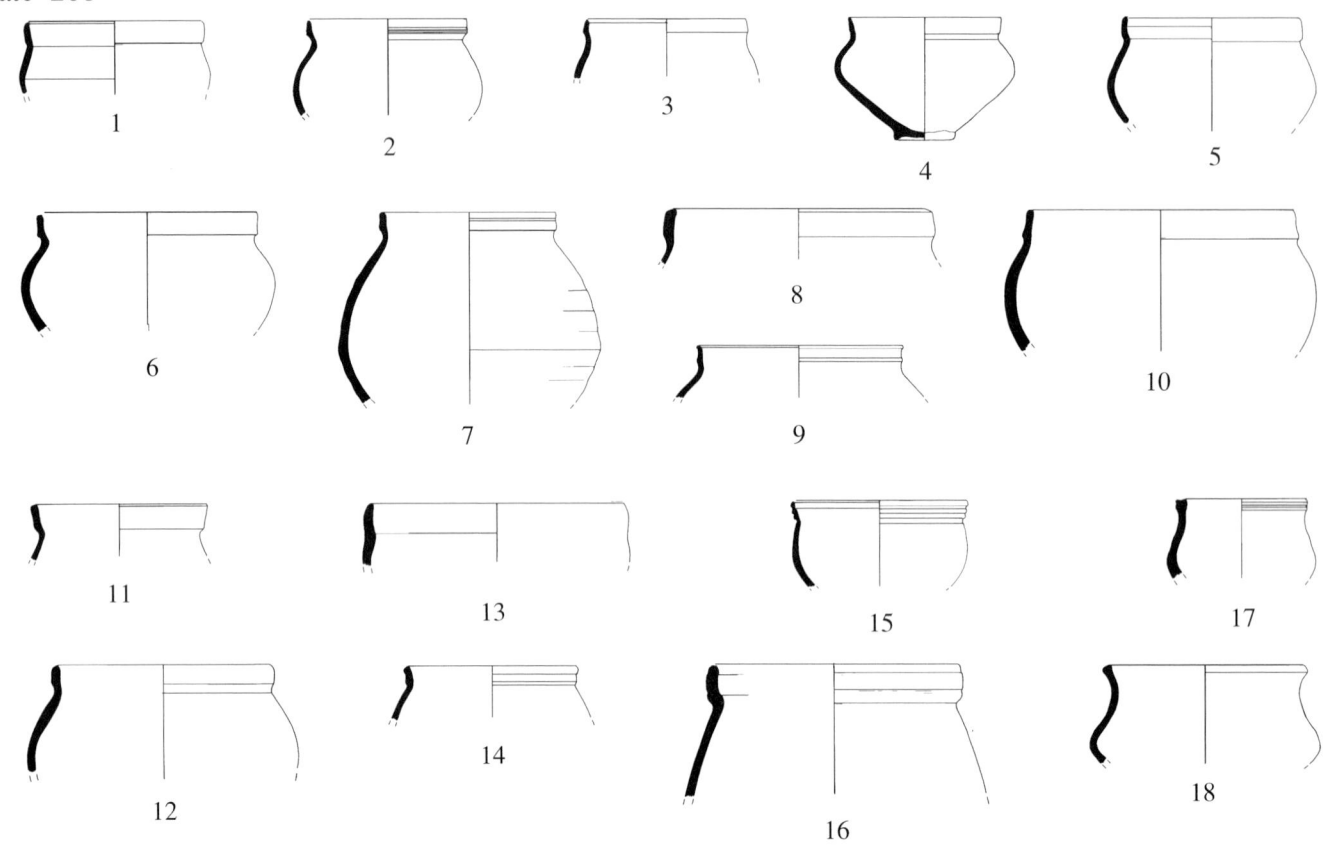

Bronze Age Small Bowl (SBR) Type D. Scale 1:5

1. SBR. D.I.a (TS. 1681; IVN, 2.3, Room 18). Phase 2A. About 1/3 rim and upper wall segment. Fine grayish-buff ware, evenly fired. Creamy-buff slip in and out.
2. SBR. D.I.b (TS. 1096; IIIG/H, 1.8b, Room 2A). Phase 2. About 1/2 rim and upper wall segment. Fine pinkish-orange ware, evenly fired. Self slip in and out.
3. SBR. D.I.c (TS. 1017; IXA, 1.8a). Phase 2B. About 1/2 rim and shoulder segment. Fairly coarse cream ware, evenly fired.
4. SBR. D.I.d (SW. 485; IIIG/H, 1.3 + 1.7, Room 22A + Room 18). Phases 5 and 4. Complete profile, about 1/6 rim segment with complete base and lower body. Fairly fine cream ware, evenly fired.
5. SBR. D.I.e (TS. 1682; IVN, 2.3, Room 18). Phase 2A. About 1/3 rim and 2/3 wall segment. Fine pinkish ware, evenly fired. Cream slip in and out.
6. SBR. D.I.f (TS. 2607; IVP, 1.5, Room 9). Phase 2B. About 1/6 rim and 2/3 wall segment. Slightly coarse pinkish-buff ware, evenly fired. Cream slip out.
7. SBR. D.I.g (TS. 2598; IVO, 1.3 + 1.4, Rooms 10, 10A). Phase 2B. About 1/2 rim and 2/3 wall segment. Fairly coarse grayish-green ware, evenly fired. Creamy-green slip out.
8. SBR. D.I.h (TS. 1245; IIID, 5.3, Rooms 20/21). Phase 5. Small rim and shoulder segment. Fine pink ware, unevenly fired with light brown core at rim fold. Creamy-buff slip out.
9. SBR. D.I.i (TS. 2821; IVP, 1.5, Room 9). Phase 2B. About 1/6 rim and shoulder segment. Fairly fine pinkish-buff ware, evenly fired. Cream slip in and out.
10. SBR. D.II.a (TS. 1268; IIIA, 4.1, Room 8B). Phase 4. About 1/4 rim and 2/3 wall segment with three joining rim pieces. Slightly coarse pinkish-buff ware, evenly fired. Creamy-buff slip in and out.
11. SBR. D.II.b (TS. 1922; IIID, 5.3, Rooms 20/21). Phase 5. Small rim and shoulder segment. Slightly coarse pinkish-buff ware, evenly fired. Thick creamy-yellow slip in and out.
12. SBR. D.II.c (TS. 1614; IVO, 1.3, Room 10A). Phase 2B. Small rim and 2/3 wall segment. Fairly fine buff ware, evenly fired. Cream slip in and out.
13. SBR. D.II.d (TS. 1809; IIIA, 1.1). Phase 7. Small rim and upper wall segment. Slightly coarse pinkish-buff ware, evenly fired. Creamy-buff slip out and to base of rim in.
14. SBR. D.II.e (TS. 1357; IIID, 5.3, Rooms 20/21). Phase 5. Small rim and shoulder segment. Slightly coarse grayish-buff ware, unevenly fired pinkish-buff in and grayish-buff out.
15. SBR. D.II.f (TS. 2822; IVN, 2.1, Room 8). Phase 2B. Small rim and 2/3 wall segment. Slightly coarse light pink ware, evenly fired. Creamy-pink slip out.
16. SBR. D.II.g (TS. 539; VIIA, 4.3). Phase 3. Large rim and upper wall segment. Fairly coarse pinkish-buff ware, evenly fired. Light greenish slip out and over rim in.
17. SBR. D.II.h (TS. 2625; IVY, 1.2). Phase 4. About 1/3 rim and 2/3 wall segment. Fairly fine pinkish-buff ware, evenly fired. Creamy-buff slip out and just over rim in.
18. SBR. D.III.a (TS. 779 = TS. 995; IIIG/H, 1.3, 1.5, Room 22A). Phases 4, 5. Two small joining rim fragments and 2/3 wall segment. Slightly coarse light grayware, evenly fired. Vertically burnished out and irregularly in.

Plate 209

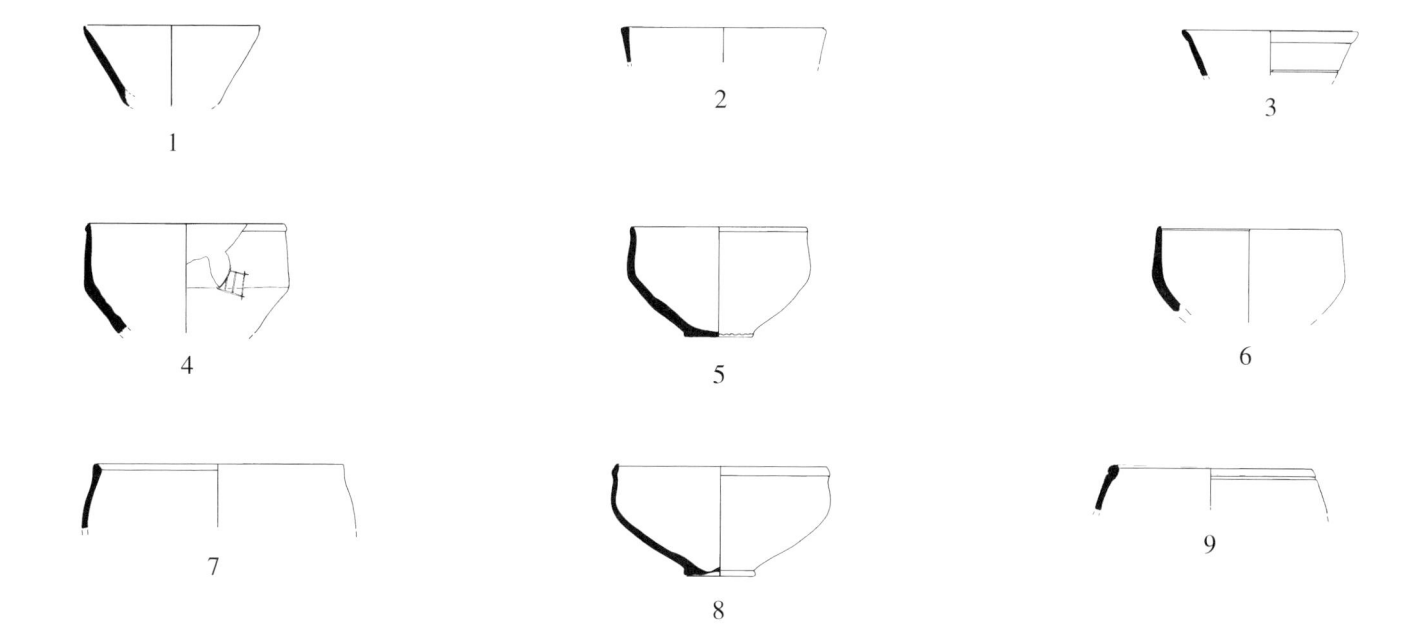

Bronze Age Small Bowl (SBR) Types E, F, and G. Scale 1:5

1. SBR. E.I.a (TS. 3539; Op. 7, 19.1, Street). Phase 2A(a). Small rim segment and most of wall profile. Fine pinkish-brown ware with gold- and silver-colored mica and small white lime grits, evenly fired. Creamy-buff slip out.
2. SBR. E.I.b (TS. 2471; IVF, 1.5, Room 1A). Phase 3. Small rim and upper wall segment. Fine flesh pink ware, evenly fired. Creamy-pink slip out and just over rim in.
3. SBR. E.I.c (TS. 1572; IIA, 9.2, Pit E). Phase 5. Small rim and upper wall segment. Fairly fine creamy-buff ware with fine lime and mica grits, evenly fired. Self slip in and out.
4. SBR. F.I.a (PM. D.15; TS. 571; IIIG/H, 1.4, Rooms 22A/B Extramural). Phase 5. Small rim segment and about 2/3 body segment with part of a potter's mark incised on the outside wall before firing. Coarse pink ware, evenly fired.
5. SBR. F.I.b (PM. C.20; SW. 149; IIID, 5.3, Rooms 20/21). Phase 5. Complete profile, about 1/3 rim segment with portion of circular-shaped potter's mark (not illustrated) incised on the base before firing. Orange-brown ware with much black- and gold-colored mineral temper, evenly fired. Light buff slip irregularly applied in and out from rim to carination.
6. SBR. F.I.c (TS. 1712; IVL, 2.1, Room 3A). Phase 3. Small rim and 2/3 wall segment. Fine pink ware, evenly fired. Cream slip in and out.
7. SBR. F.I.d (TS. 1707; IVN, 3.1, Room 18). Phase 2A. Small rim and upper wall segment. Hard, fine pink ware with a few lime grits, evenly fired. Self slip in and out.
8. SBR. F.I.e (TS. 3281; Op. 6, 3.1, Room 32). Phase 4. Mended to complete profile. Ware description not available.
9. SBR. G (TS. 3499; Op. 7, 17.2, Street). Phase 2A(a). About 1/6 rim and upper wall. Fairly fine pinkish-buff ware with lime grits, evenly fired. Cream slip in and out.

## Plate 210. Bronze Age Bowl (BR) Type A

1. BR. A.I.a (TS. 2633; IVM, 3.1, Room 7, Pit A). Phase 2A. About 1/8 rim segment and most of wall profile. Fairly fine grayish-green ware, evenly fired. Creamy-green slip in and out.
2. BR. A.I.b (TS. 2632; IVM, 10.6, Below Room 7). Phase 1A. About 1/4 rim segment and most of wall profile. Fine pinkish-buff ware, evenly fired. Thin self slip or wash in and out.
3. BR. A.I.c (TS. 2924; IVP, 1.4, Room 9A). Phase 3. About 1/4 rim and upper wall segment. Fairly fine pink ware, evenly fired. Self slip in and out.
4. BR. A.I.d (TS. 2942; IVZ(S), 5.3). Phase 2B. Small rim and upper wall segment. Slightly coarse pinkish-buff ware, evenly fired. Self slip in and out.
5. BR. A.I.e (TS. 2941; IVZ(S), 5.4, 5.5). Phase 2B. About 1/6 rim and upper wall segment. Slightly coarse pinkish-buff ware, evenly fired. Cream slip out and over rim in.
6. BR. A.I.f (TS. 2944; IVS, 4.1, Room 12A). Phase 3. Small rim and upper wall segment. Fine creamy-buff ware, evenly fired. Self slip in and out.
7. BR. A.II.a (TS. 1387; IIIB, 2.9, Room 1B). Phase 3. Small rim and uper wall segment. Slightly coarse pinkish-brown ware, evenly fired. Self slip in and out.
8. BR. A.II.b (TS. 437; IIIC, 4.10, Room 9). Phase 4. About 1/2 rim segment and most of wall profile. Fairly coarse pinkish-buff ware, evenly fired. Cream slip in and out.
9. BR. A.II.c (TS. 1196; IIIC, 4.7). Phase 6. Small rim and upper wall segment. Fine pinkish ware with lime and mica grits, evenly fired. Creamy-buff slip out.
10. BR. A.II.d (TS. 502; IIIC, 4.7). Phase 6. Small rim and upper wall segment. Fairly coarse pink ware, evenly fired. Cream slip in and out.
11. BR. A.II.e (TS. 1714; IVK, 1.3, Room 2A). Phase 3. Small rim and upper wall segment. Medium fine pink ware, evenly fired. Cream slip in and out.
12. BR. A.II.f (TS. 2069; IG, 1.15). Phase 6. Small rim and upper wall segment. Hard, fine dark pink ware, evenly fired. Buff slip in and out.
13. BR. A.II.g (TS. 3310; Op. 7, 4.7, Room 40). Phase 2B(b). About 1/8 rim segment and most of wall profile. Slightly coarse pinkish-buff ware with many gold- and silver-colored mica grits, lime grits, and vegetable temper, evenly fired. Creamy-buff slip in and out.
14. BR. A.III.a (TS. 832; IIIG/H, 1.4, Rooms 22A/B Extramural). Phase 5. Small rim segment and most of wall profile. Fairly coarse buff ware, evenly fired. Cream slip in and out.
15. BR. A.III.b (TS. 2955; IVK, 2.4, Room 2). Phase 2B. About 1/10 rim and upper wall segment. Fairly fine buff ware, evenly fired. Self slip in and out.
16. BR. A.IV.a (TS. 746; IIIG/H, 1.7, Room 18). Phase 4. Small rim and upper wall segment. Fairly coarse brown ware, evenly fired. Buff slip in. Partially blackened in and out.
17. BR. A.IV.b (TS. 2558; IVP, 1.2 + 1.3, Room 9B). Phase 4. Complete profile with about 3/5 rim segment and complete disk-type base. Fairly coarse grayware, evenly fired. Very worn self slip in and out.
18. BR. A.IV.c (PM. A.9; SW. 148; IIIC, 4.10, Room 9). Phase 4. Complete profile, about 2/3 segment with a potter's mark incised on the upper outside wall before firing. Light brown ware with black mineral temper, evenly fired. Buff slip in and greenish-buff slip out. Iron-colored stains on rim.
19. BR. A.IV.d (TS. 928; VIIIA, 1.1). Phase 3. Small rim and upper wall segment. Fairly coarse dark brown ware, evenly fired. Buff slip in.
20. BR. A.IV.e (TS. 1965; IVH, 1.3, Room 3). Phase 2B. Small rim and upper wall segment. Fairly fine pinkish-buff ware, evenly fired. Creamy-buff slip in and out.
21. BR. A.IV.f (TS. 1349; IIID, 5.4, Room 12). Phase 4. Small rim and 2/3 wall segment. Slightly coarse pink ware, evenly fired. Creamy-buff slip in and out.
22. BR. A.IV.g (TS. 1930; IVA, 2.3, Street). Phase 2B. Small rim and upper wall segment. Slightly coarse pinkish-buff ware, evenly fired. Self slip in and out.

Plate 210

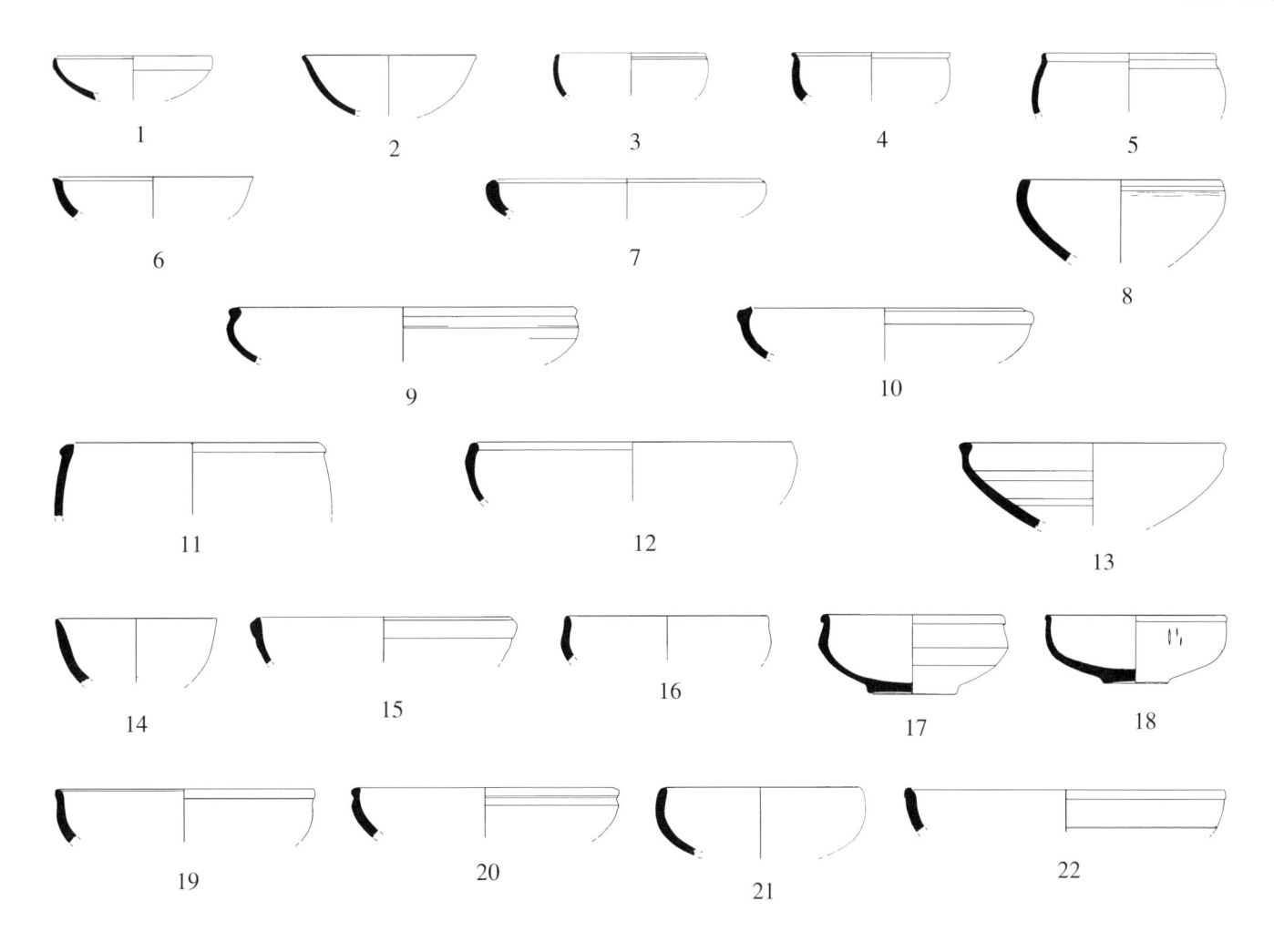

Bronze Age Bowl (BR) Type A. Scale 1:5

Plate 211

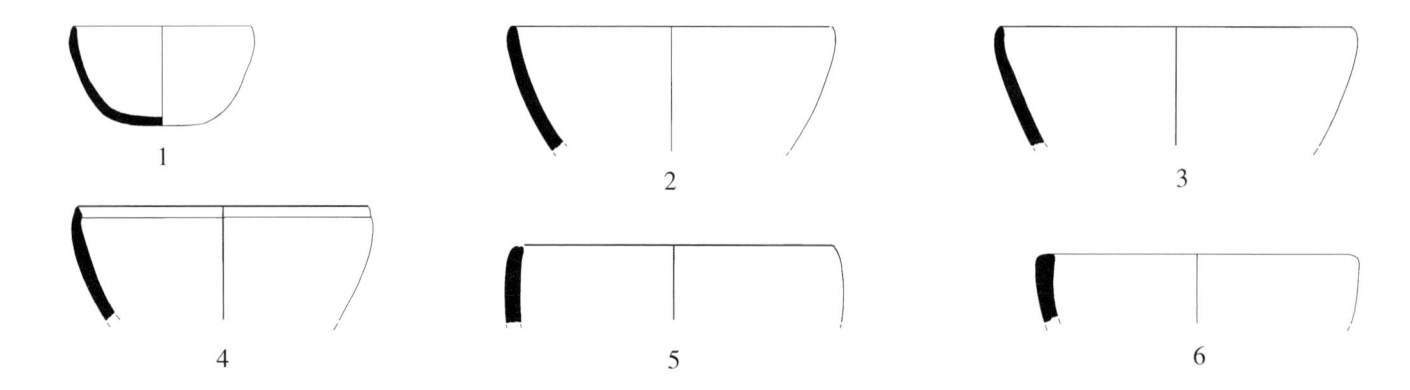

Bronze Age Bowl (BR) Type B. Scale 1:5

1. BR. B.I.a (SW. 474; IC, 1.48). Phase 3. Complete profile, about 1/2 rim segment. Fairly coarse brown-buff ware, evenly fired.
2. BR. B.II.a (TS. 1568; IIA, 9.8, Room 4). Phase 2. Small rim and 2/3 wall segment. Fairly fine ware with lime and mica grits, unevenly fired with gray core and pinkish-buff at surfaces. Creamy-buff slip in and out.
3. BR. B.II.b (TS. 428; VA, "1.1"). Phase 3. Large rim and 2/3 wall segment. Very hard, fine greenish-buff ware, evenly fired. Self slip in and out.
4. BR. B.II.c (TS. 1153; VC, 3.2). Phase 3. Large rim and 2/3 wall segment. Fairly coarse pink ware, evenly fired. Buff slip in and light cream slip out.
5. BR. B.II.d (TS. 1534; IIA, 10.2, Room 12). Phase 6. Small rim and upper wall segment. Hard, fine ware with lime and mica grits, unevenly fired with gray core and pinkish-buff at surfaces. Creamy-buff slip in and out.
6. BR. B.II.e (TS. 2457; IE, 1.41 = IC, 1.40). Phase 4. Small rim and upper wall segment. Fairly fine pink ware, evenly fired. Cream slip out.

Plate 212

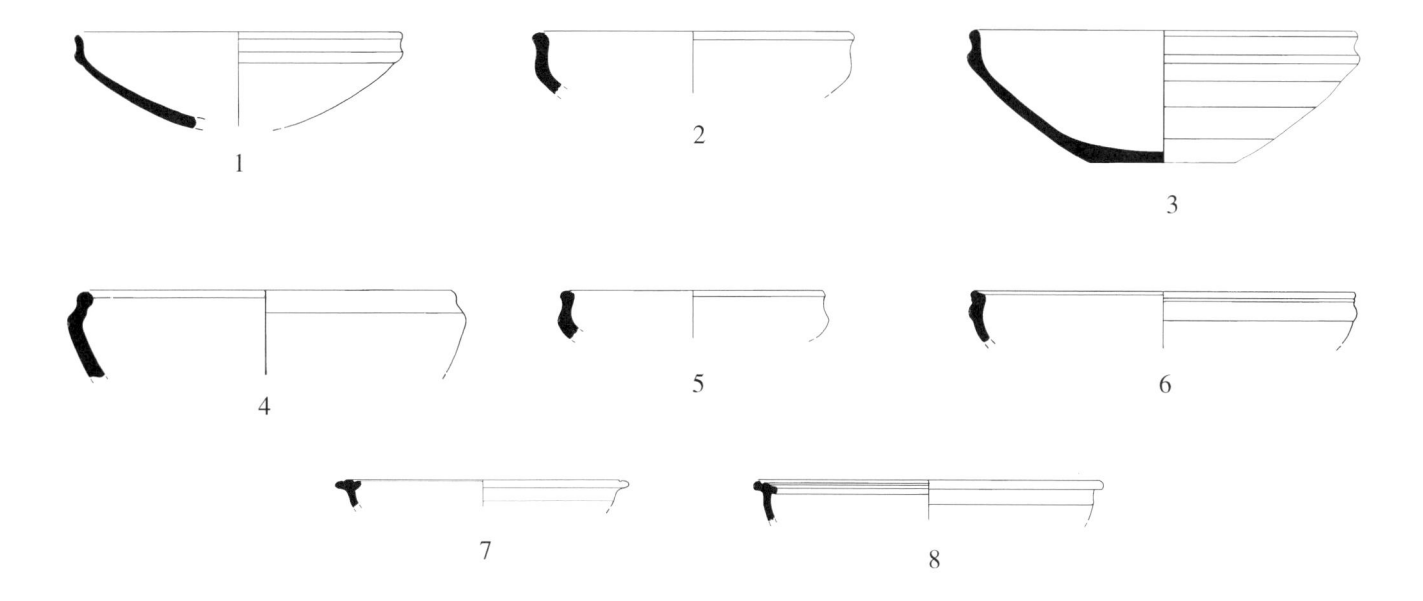

Bronze Age Bowl (BR) Type C. Scale 1:5

1. BR. C.I.a (TS. 1592; IVJ, 1.5, Room 4). Phase 2B. Large rim segment and most of wall profile. Hard, fine buff ware, evenly fired. Light cream slip in.
2. BR. C.I.b (TS. 1791; IIIA, 4.2, Room 8A). Phase 4. Small rim and upper wall segment. Slightly coarse purple-pink ware, evenly fired. Creamy-buff slip in and out.
3. BR. C.I.c (TS. 1797; IIIA, 1.4, Room 11). Phase 4. Small rim and upper wall segment. Slightly coarse buff-brown ware, evenly fired. Creamy-buff slip in and out.
4. BR. C.I.d (SW. 735; IVZ(N1), 2.2, Room 21). Phase 2B. Complete profile, about 1/3 rim segment. Fairly coarse pinkish-buff ware with lime and mica grits, evenly fired. Green slip in and out.
5. BR. C.I.e (TS. 1594; IVJ, 1.2). Phase 5. Small rim and upper wall segment. Fairly coarse buff ware, evenly fired. Self slip in and out.
6. BR. C.I.f (TS. 1608; IVJ, 1.5, Room 4). Phase 2B. Small rim and upper wall segment. Fine buff ware, evenly fired. Creamy-buff slip in and out.
7. BR. C.I.g (TS. 857; VC, 1.1). Phase 4 (Derived EBA). About 1/32 rim and upper wall segment. Fairly coarse buff ware, evenly fired. Cream slip out
8. BR. C.I.h (TS. 958; VC, 1.1). Phase 4 (Derived EBA). About 1/20 rim and upper wall segment. Fairly coarse buff ware evenly fired. Cream slip out.

## Plate 213. Bronze Age Bowl (BR) Type D

1. BR. D.I.a (TS. 1706; IVN, 1.4, Rooms 8A/18A). Phase 3. Small rim and upper wall segment. Hard, medium-fine charcoal grayware, evenly fired. Self slip in and out.
2. BR. D.I.b (TS. 2637; IVJ, 1.5, Room 4). Phase 2B. About 1/10 rim and 2/3 wall segment. Fairly fine buff ware, evenly fired. Creamy-buff slip in and out.
3. BR. D.I.c (TS. 2608; IVP, 1.5, Room 9). Phase 2B. About 1/8 rim and 2/3 wall segment. Fine buff ware, evenly fired. Cream slip in and out.
4. BR. D.II.a (TS. 983; XA, 1.3, Room 15). Phase 2B. Small rim and 2/3 wall segment. Fairly coarse green ware, evenly fired.
5. BR. D.II.b (TS. 1046; IIIG/H, 1.10, Room 2B). Phase 2. Large rim and 2/3 wall segment. Fairly coarse pink ware, evenly fired. Cream slip in and out. Partially blackened in and out.
6. BR. D.II.c (TS. 2744; IVW, 2.1). Phase 2A. Small rim and 2/3 wall segment. Slightly coarse ware, unevenly fired with brown core and pink at surfaces. Self slip in and out.
7. BR. D.II.d (TS. 1199; IIIH, 1.1). Phase 6/7 Extramural. Small rim and upper wall segment. Fairly fine pinkish-buff ware, evenly fired. Creamy-buff slip out.
8. BR. D.III.a (TS. 1973; IVH, 1.3, Room 3). Phase 2B. Small rim and upper wall segment. Fairly fine fine pink ware, evenly fired. Self slip in and out.
9. BR. D.III.b (TS. 1967; IVH, 1.3, Room 3). Phase 2B. Small rim and upper wall segment. Fairly fine buff ware, evenly fired. Self slip or wash in and out.
10. BR. D.IV.a (TS. 2639; IVM, 1.6 + 3.1, Room 7 + Pit A). Phase 2A. Two small non-joining rim and upper wall segments. Fairly fine buff ware, evenly fired. Creamy-buff slip in and out.
11. BR. D.V.a (TS. 888; IIIG/H, 1.4, Rooms 22A/B Extramural). Phase 5. Small rim and upper wall segment. Fairly fine black ware, evenly fired. Greenish slip in and out.
12. BR. D.VI.a (TS. 3568; Op. 7, 20.1, Room 36). Phase 2A(a). Small rim (4 cm) and upper wall segment. Hard, fine buff ware with gold and silver-colored mica and small lime grits, fired pinkish-red in, pinkish-buff out. Irregular spaced horizontal line burnish (band burnished) on outside of rim and on extant wall.
13. BR. D.VI.b (TS. 2605; IVY, 1.5). Phase 2B. About 1/2 rim and upper wall segment. Fairly coarse grayish-green ware, evenly fired. Self slip in and out.
14. BR. D.VI.c (TS. 1055; IIIG/H, 1.9, Room 3B). Phase 3. Small rim and upper wall segment. Fairly fine grayware, evenly fired. Horizontal burnish lines in and out.
15. BR. D.VII.a (TS. 1607; IVJ, 1.5, Room 4). Phase 2B. Small rim and 1/2 wall segment. Fairly fine buff ware, evenly fired. Self slip in and out.

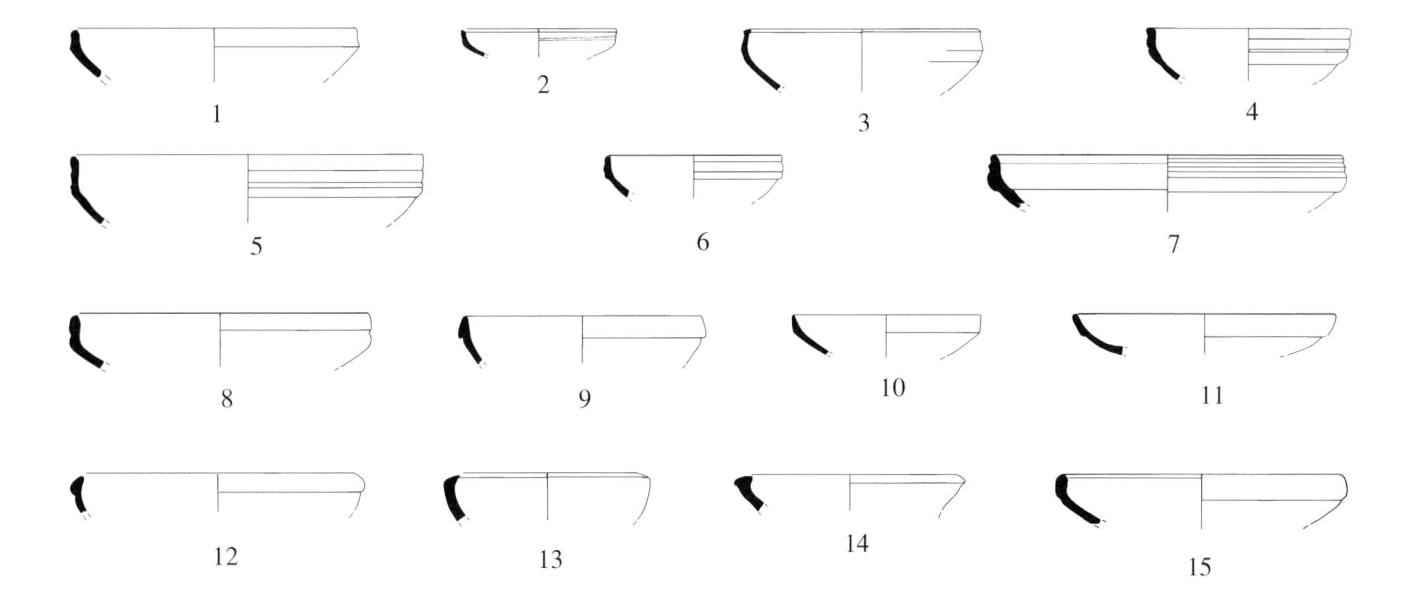

Plate 213

Bronze Age Bowl (BR) Type D. Scale 1:5

Plate 214. Bronze Age Bowl (BR) Type E

1. BR. E.I.a (TS. 2587; IVP, 1.3, Room 9B). Phase 4. About 1/6 rim and 2/3 wall segment. Hard, fine pink ware, evenly fired. Self slip in and out.
2. BR. E.I.b (TS. 2589; IVP, 1.5, Room 9). Phase 2B. About 1/6 rim and 2/3 wall segment. Hard, fine metallic-like grayish-green ware, evenly fired. Creamy-green slip out.
3. BR. E.I.c. (TS. 2592; IVP, 1.5, Room 9). Phase 2B. Small rim and 2/3 wall segment. Slightly coarse buff ware, evenly fired. Creamy-buff slip in and out.
4. BR. E.II.a (TS. 1674 = TS. 1690; IVL, 2.1 + 1.5, Rooms 3A and 3). Phases 3 and 2A. Complete profile, about 1/3 rim segment from 2.1 and non-joining rim and body fragments from 1.5. Medium coarse pink ware with mica grits, evenly fired. Cream slip in and out.
5. BR. E.II.b (TS. 1375; IIIC, 4.7). Phase 6. Small rim and upper wall segment. Slightly coarse pinkish-buff ware, evenly fired. Creamy-buff slip in and out.
6. BR. E.II.c (TS. 1304; IIIF, 1.1). Phase 6/7. Small rim and 1/2 wall segment. Slightly coarse pinkish-buff ware, evenly fired. Creamy-buff slip in and out.
7. BR. E.III.a (SW. 496; IVJ, 1.6, Room 4). Phase 2A (see also pl. 89d). About 1/2 rim segment and complete wall profile. Coarse pink ware, evenly fired. Light creamy-buff slip in and round rim out.
8. BR. E.III.b (TS. 1959; IVF, 1.5, Room 1A). Phase 3. Large rim and 1/2 wall segment. Slightly coarse grayish-brown ware, evenly fired. Creamy-buff slip out.
9. BR. E.III.c (TS. 1197; IIID, 5.3, Rooms 20/21). Phase 5. Large rim and 1/2 wall segment. Fairly fine buff ware, evenly fired. Creamy-buff slip out and over rim in.
10. BR. E.III.d (TS. 1238; IIIC, 4.7 + IIID, 5.3, Rooms 20/21). Phases 6 and 5. Large rim and 2/3 wall segment (four joining rim fragments). Slightly coarse and gritty pinkish-buff ware, evenly fired. Buff slip in and out.
11. BR. E.III.e (TS. 1301; IIIF, 2.1, Debris). Phase 5. Large rim and 1/2 wall segment. Fairly coarse buff ware, evenly fired. Creamy-buff slip in and out.
12. BR. E.III.f (TS. 1146; IIIG/H, 1.8a, Room 3A). Phase 3. Large rim and 1/2 wall segment. Fairly coarse pink ware, evenly fired. Creamy-buff slip out.
13. BR. E.III.g (TS. 2201; VIIA, 1.7). Phase 1. Small rim and upper wall segment. Fine pink ware, evenly fired. Creamy-buff slip in and out.
14. BR. E.III.h (TS. 1600; IVJ, 1.5, Room 4). Phase 2B. Small rim segment and most of wall profile which is slightly ribbed and with diagonally tool-scored lines on lower wall. Medium coarse pink ware, unevenly fired. Cream slip in and out.
15. BR. E.III.i (TS. 1722; IVL/P, 1.3, Pit). Phase 3. Large rim and upper wall segment. Medium coarse pink ware, unevenly fired. Cream slip out.
16. BR. E.III.j (TS. 2578; IVG, unstratified). About 1/8 rim and upper wall segment. Slightly coarse buff ware, evenly fired. Creamy-buff slip in and out.
17. BR. E.IV.a (TS. 1588; IVO, 1.2, Room 10B). Phase 4. About 1/6 rim and 2/3 wall segment. Medium coarse pink ware, evenly fired. Cream slip in and out.
18. BR. E.IV.b (TS. 1599; IVJ, 1.5, Room 4). Phase 2B. Large rim and 2/3 wall segment. Medium fine buff ware, unevenly fired. Cream slip in and out.
19. BR. E.IV.c (TS. 1640; IVM, 1.4, Room 7). Phase 2B. About 1/4 rim segment and most of wall profile. Pink ware, evenly fired. Cream slip in and out.

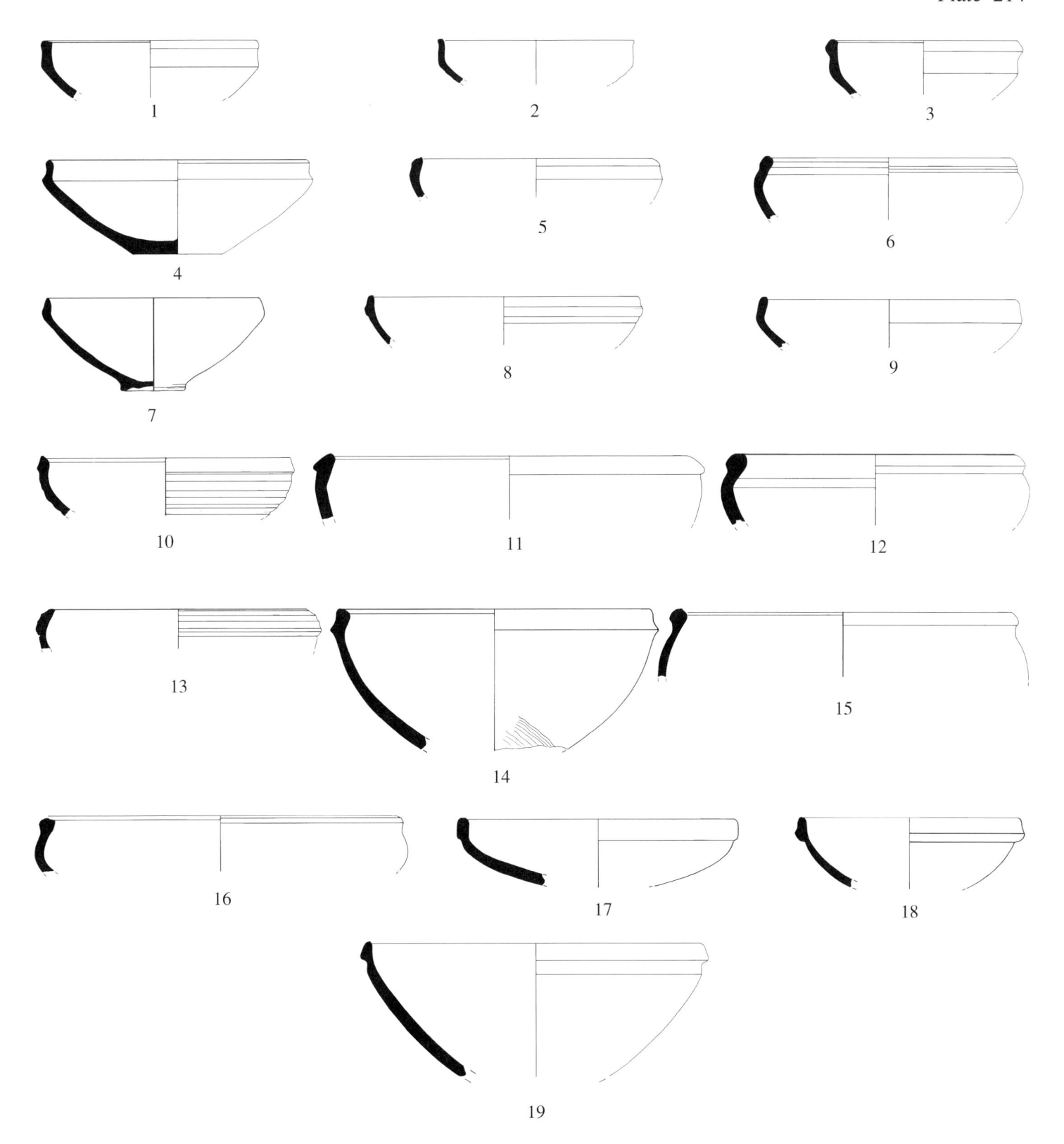

Plate 214

Bronze Age Bowl (BR) Type E. Scale 1:5

## Plate 215. Bronze Age Bowl (BR) Type F

1. BR. F.I.a (TS. 2532; XA, 1.3, Room 15). Phase 2B. About 1/10 rim and upper wall segment. Slightly coarse pinkish-buff ware, evenly fired. Creamy-green slip in and out.
2. BR. F.I.b (TS. 906; IC, 1.40). Phase 4. Small rim and upper wall segment. Fairly fine pink ware, evenly fired.
3. BR. F.I.c (TS. 2487; IIIH, 1.2, Town Wall Debris). Phase 5. About 1/10 rim and 2/3 wall segment. Very hard, fine pink ware, evenly fired. Creamy-buff slip in and out.
4. BR. F.I.d (TS. 2526; IVG, 1.3, Room 3A). Phase 3. About 1/12 rim and upper wall segment. Hard, fine pink ware, evenly fired. Creamy-buff slip in and out.
5. BR. F.I.e (TS. 2570; IVK, 1.2, Room 2B). Phase 4. Small rim and upper wall segment. Fine buff ware, evenly fired. Self slip in and out.
6. BR. F.II.a. (TS. 1963; IVD, 1.3). Phase 4. Small rim and upper wall segment. Slightly coarse pinkish-buff ware, evenly fired. Self slip in and out.
7. BR. F.II.b (TS. 1292; IIIG/H, 1.3, Room 22A). Phase 5. Large rim and 2/3 wall segment. Hard, fairly fine pinkish-buff ware, evenly fired. Creamy-buff slip in and out.
8. BR. F.II.c (TS. 2418; IC, 1.42, Destruction level). Phase 4. About 1/20 rim and upper wall segment. Fairly coarse pink ware, evenly fired. Creamy-yellow slip in and out.
9. BR. F.II.d (TS. 2662; IVD, 3.1, Room 2). Phase 2B. Small rim and upper wall segment. Slightly coarse ware, unevenly fired with greenish core and buff at surfaces. Creamy-green slip in and out.
10. BR. F.III.a (TS. 2766; IVO, 1.4, Room 10). Phase 2B. Small rim and upper wall segment. Fairly coarse pink ware, evenly fired. Self slip in and out.
11. BR. F.III.b (TS. 2046; IE, 1.18). Phase 1. Small rim and 2/3 wall segment. Hard, fine grayware, unevenly fired buff at surfaces. Heavily burned on outside wall.
12. BR. F.III.c (TS. 2529; VE, 1.4, Pit [bottom]). Phase 3. About 1/1 rim and 1/2 wall segment. Slightly coarse pinkish-buff ware, evenly fired. Creamy-buff slip out.
13. BR. F.III.d (TS. 2241; IXA, 1.8a). Phase 2B. Large rim and upper wall segment. Slightly coarse buff-brown ware, evenly fired. Creamy-green slip in and out.
14. BR. F.III.e (TS. 2191; IIID, 5.4, Room 12). Phase 4. Small rim and upper wall segment. Slightly coarse pink ware, evenly fired. Creamy-buff slip in and out.
15. BR. F.III.f. (TS. 2990; IVO, 1.4, Room 10). Phase 2B. Small rim and upper wall segment. Fairly fine buff ware, evenly fired. Creamy-green slip in and out.
16. BR. F.III.g. (TS. 1630; IVF, 4.1, Room 1). Phase 2A. Large rim and 1/2 wall segment. Fairly coarse pink ware, evenly fired. Cream slip in and out.
17. BR. F.III.h (TS. 1633; IVF, 1.11–13, Room 1). Phase 2B. Small rim and upper wall segment. Medium coarse pink ware, evenly fired. Light cream slip in and out.
18. BR. F.III.i (TS. 2648; IVJ, 1.3, Room 4B). Phase 4. About 1/10 rim and upper wall segment. Hard, fine light pink ware, evenly fired. Creamy-buff slip out.
19. BR. F.IV.a (TS. 2985; IVM, 1.4, Room 7). Phase 2B. Small rim and upper wall segment. Fairly fine pink ware, evenly fired. Light pink slip in and out.
20. BR. F.IV.b (TS. 1009; IIIG/H, 1.6, Room 17A). Phase 4. Small rim and upper wall segment. Fairly fine buff ware, evenly fired. Cream slip in and out.
21. BR. F.IV.c (TS. 1928; IVF, 1.11, Room 1). Phase 2B. Small rim and upper wall segment. Fairly fine pinkish-buff ware, evenly fired. Creamy-buff slip in and out.
22. BR. F.IV.d (TS. 2731; IVN, 2.3, Room 18). Phase 2A. About 1/5 rim and 2/3 wall segment. Fairly fine pinkish-buff ware, evenly fired. Cream slip in and out.
23. BR. F.IV.e (TS. 1754; IVN, 2.2, Room 8). Phase 2A. Large rim and upper wall segment. Slightly coarse pink ware with lime and mica grits, evenly fired. Cream slip in and out.
24. BR. F.V.a (TS. 2572; IVG, 1.5, Room 3). Phase 2A. Small rim and upper wall segment. Slightly coarse brownish-buff ware, fairly evenly fired. Self slip in and out.

Plate 215

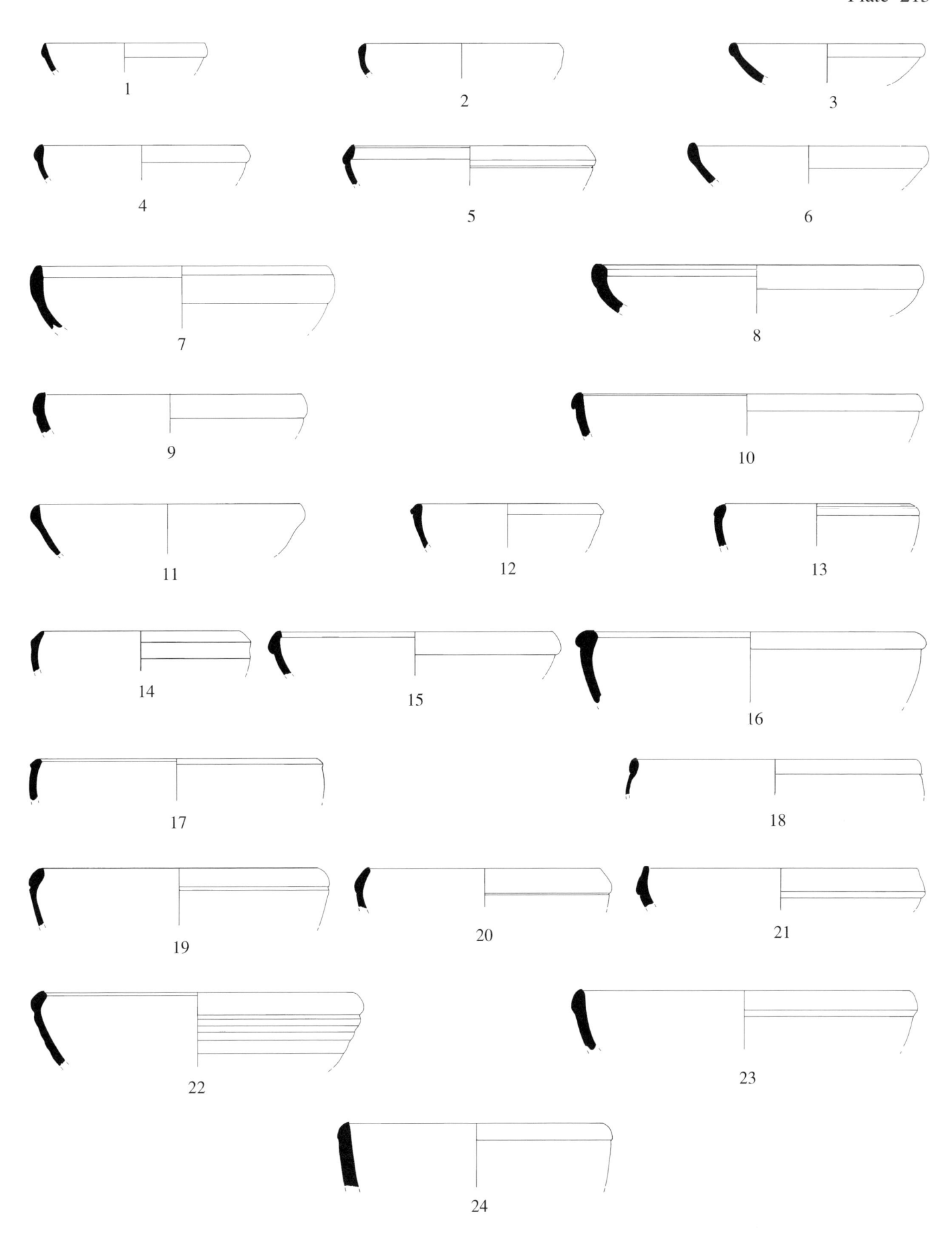

Bronze Age Bowl (BR) Type F. Scale 1:5

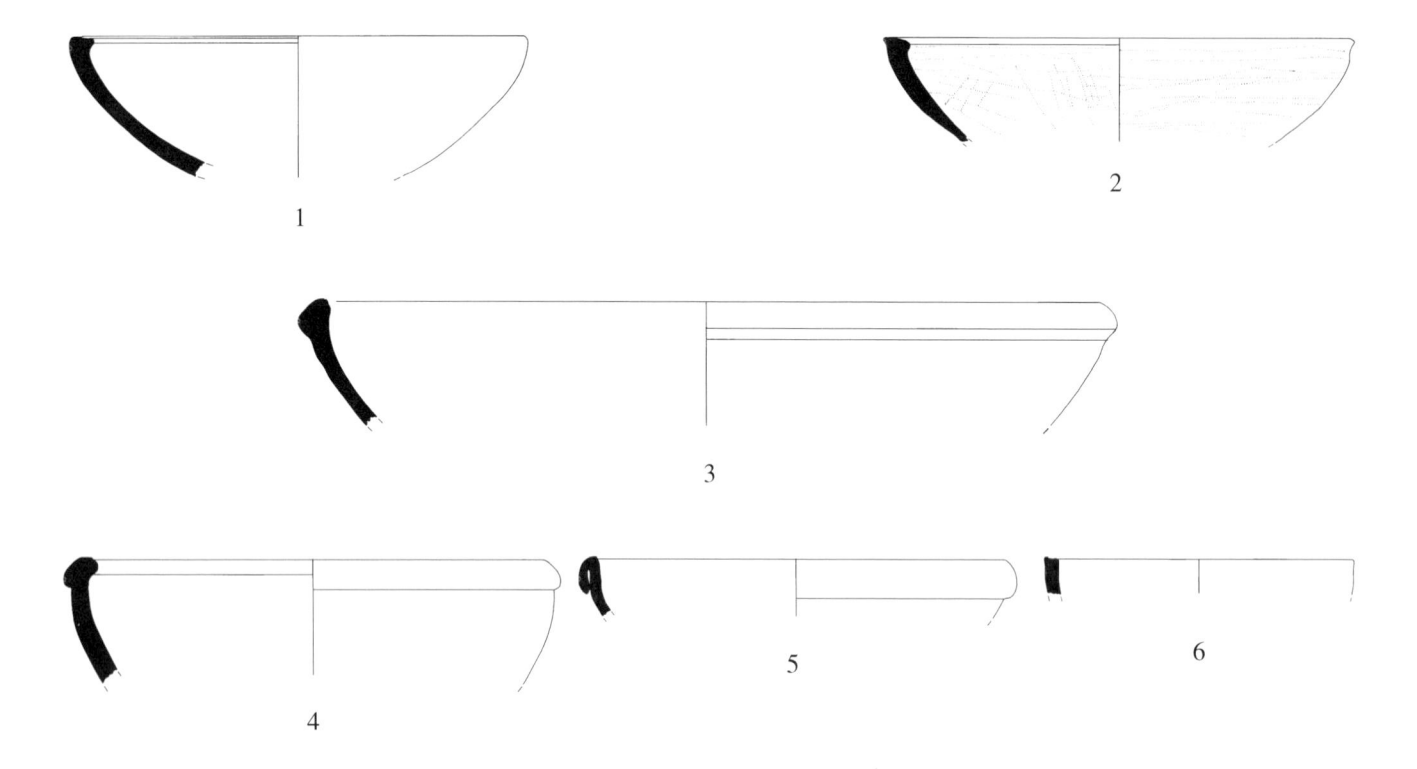

Plate 216

Bronze Age Bowl (BR) Type G. Scale 1:5

1. BR. G.I.a (TS. 602; IIIF, 3.1, Room 16). Phase 4. Large rim segment and most of wall profile. Fairly coarse pink ware, evenly fired.
2. BR. G.I.b (TS. 56; IIA, 5.11, Courtyard). Phase 8. About 1/8 rim and 2/3 wall segment. Slightly coarse pinkish-brown ware with lime and mica grits, evenly fired. Creamy-buff slip in and out. Irregular horizontal burnishing lines out and on rim and chordal burnishing on inside wall.
3. BR. G.I.c (TS. 769; IC, 1.34). Phase 5. About 1/12 rim and upper wall segment. Fairly coarse pink ware, evenly fired. Cream slip out.
4. BR. G.I.d (TS. 766; IIIG/H, 1.1, Courtyard). Phase 6. Large rim and 1/2 wall segment. Coarse pink ware, evenly fired. Cream slip out.
5. BR. G.I.e (TS. 1244; IIID, 5.4, Room 12). Phase 4. Small rim and upper wall segment. Slightly coarse pinkish-buff ware, evenly fired. Creamy-buff slip in and out.
6. BR. G.I.f (TS. 2671; IVL, 1.3, Room 3A). Phase 3. Small rim and upper wall segment. Fairly fine pink ware, evenly fired. Creamy-pink slip in and out.

Plate 217

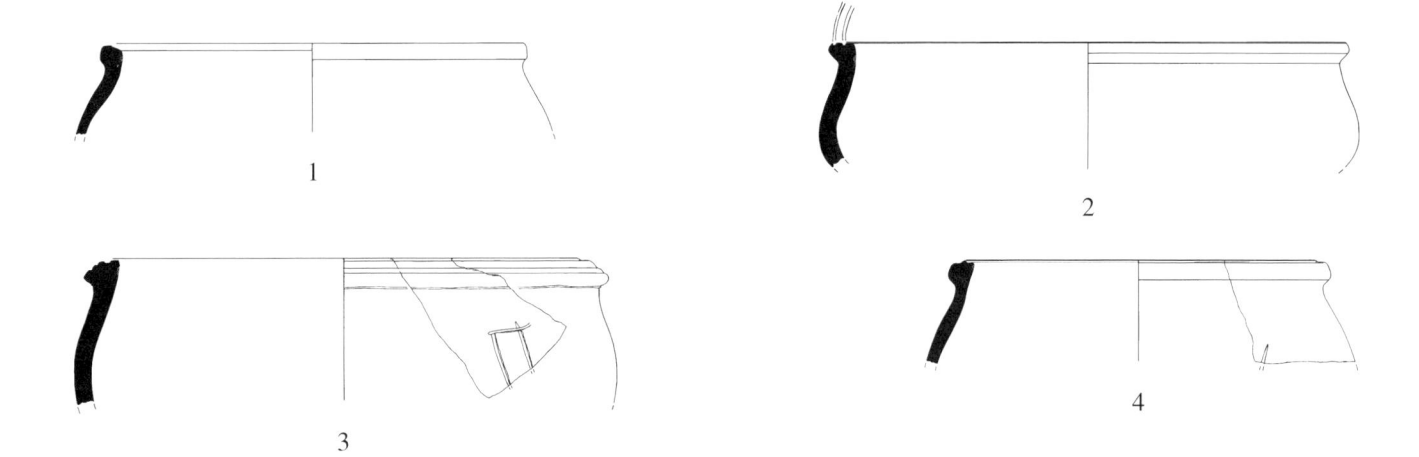

Bronze Age Bowl (BR) Type H. Scale 1:5

1. BR. H.I.a (TS. 1232; IIIG/H, 1.10, Room 2B). Phase 2. Large rim and upper wall segment. Slightly coarse pinkish-buff ware, evenly fired. Creamy-buff slip out and over rim in.
2. BR. H.I.b. (TS. 579; IC, 1.21). Phase 7. About 1/12 rim and 1/2 wall segment. Coarse pink ware, evenly fired.
3. BR. H.II.a (PM. D.3; TS. 550; IE, 1.5). Phase 4. Small rim and upper wall segment with portion of a potter's mark incised on the outside wall before firing. Coarse brownish-buff ware, evenly fired. Cream slip out.
4. BR. H.III.a (PM. A.11; TS. 2685; IVZ(N1), 1.5). Phase 2B. Small rim and upper wall segment with remains of a potter's mark incised on the outside wall before firing. Slightly coarse light pink ware, evenly fired. Very worn cream slip in and out.

Plate 218. Bronze Age Bowl (BR) Types J and K

1. BR. J.I.a (TS. 2581; IVP, 1.4, Room 9A). Phase 3. About 1/10 rim segment and most of wall profile. Fairly coarse pinkish-red ware, evenly fired. Creamy-buff slip in and out.
2. BR. J.I.b (TS. 505; IIIB, 2.2). Phase 5. Small rim and upper wall segment. Fairly coarse soft pinkish-light brown ware, unevenly fired gray at inside surface.
3. BR. J.I.c (SW. 182 = TS. 493; IIIE, 3.2 + IIIE, 3.3, Room 5). Phase 4. Large rim segment mended from five fragments and most of wall profile. Brown ware with black-, gold-, and white-colored mineral temper, evenly fired. Buff slip in and out.
4. BR. J.I.d (TS. 481= TS. 514; IIIC, 4.9, Room 19A and IIIA, 4.1). Phase 5. Two joining rim and upper wall segments. Coarse pinkish-buff ware, evenly fired. Cream slip in and out.
5. BR. J.II.a (TS. 2585; IVZ(N1), 1.4). Phase 3. About 1/4 rim and 1/2 wall segment. Slightly coarse pink ware, evenly fired. Creamy-green slip out.
6. BR. J.II.b (TS. 865; IIIG/H, 1.9, Room 3B). Phase 3. Small rim and upper wall segment. Fairly coarse pink ware, evenly fired. Cream slip out.
7. BR. K.I.a (TS. 1097; VF, 1.9). Phase 4. About 1/5 rim and 2/3 wall segment. Fairly fine pinkish-brown ware, unevenly fired with a darker core.
8. BR. K.I.b (TS. 3514; Op. 7, 18.1, Room 34). Phase 2A(a). About 1/8 rim and 2/3 wall segment. Fairly fine pinkish-buff ware with very small gold- and silver-colored mica and lime grits, evenly fired. Creamy-buff self slip in and out. Outside wall irregularly tool-shaved with broad horizontal bands at the leather-hard stage of manufacture.

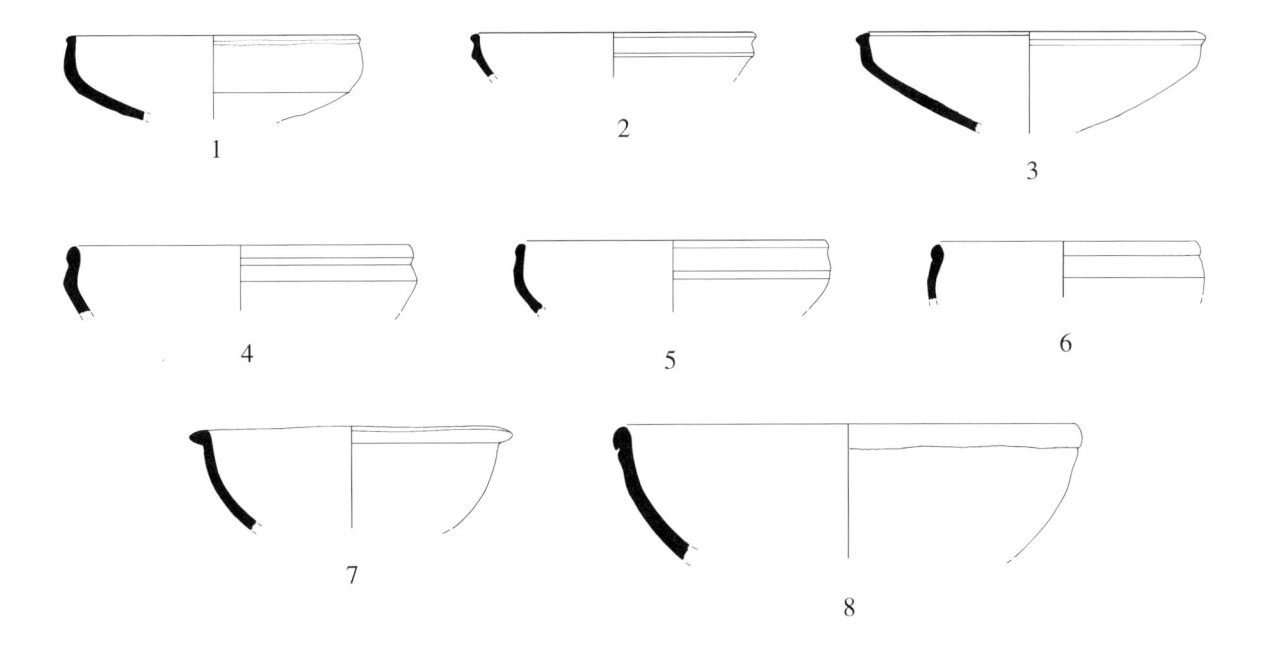

Plate 218

Bronze Age Bowl (BR) Types J and K. Scale 1:5

## Plate 219. Bronze Age Bowl (BR) Type L

1. BR. L.I.a (TS. 2915; IVN, 4.4, Room 18). Phase 2A. About 1/8 rim and upper wall segment. Slightly coarse pink ware, evenly fired. Creamy-buff slip out and over rim in.
2. BR. L.I.b (TS. 1606; IVJ, 1.5, Room 4). Phase 2B. Small rim and upper wall segment. Fairly fine buff ware, evenly fired. Self slip in and out.
3. BR. L.I.c (TS. 1184; IVF, 1.11, Room 1). Phase 2B. Small rim and 1/2 wall segment. Fine, fine pinkish-buff ware with lime and mica grits, evenly fired. Creamy-buff slip in and on top of rim.
4. BR. L.I.d (TS. 456 = TS. 1203; IIID, 5.2 = IIIE, 3.1, Room 15). Phases 6 and 5. Three fairly large rim and wall segments. Slightly coarse pinkish-buff ware with lime and mica grits, evenly fired. Remains of a gypsum coating inside, on top of rim, and in spots out.
5. BR. L.I.e (TS. 1926; IVB, 3.3, Room 1). Phase 2B. Small rim and upper wall segment. Slightly coarse pinkish-buff ware, evenly fired. Creamy-buff slip in and out.
6. BR. L.I.f (TS. 2468; VIIA, 2.5). Phase 1. Small rim and upper wall segment. Hard, fine, flesh-pink colored ware, evenly fired. Cream slip out.
7. BR. L.I.g (TS. 2458; IC, 1.28, Floor-like surface). Phase 6. About 1/6 rim and upper wall segment. Fairly coarse grayish-buff ware, evenly fired. Self slip in and out.
8. BR. L.I.h (PM. C.21; TS. 1610; IVJ, 1.5, Room 4). Phase 2B (see also pl. 100c). Small rim and upper wall segment with alphabetic-type potter's marks on the inside wall and a floral-like pattern incised on the outside wall after application of slip. Hard buff ware, evenly fired. Cream slip in and out.
9. BR. L.I.i (TS. 1923; IVD, 2.1). Phase 4. Small rim and 1/2 wall segment. Fairly fine pinkish-buff ware, evenly fired. Buff slip in and out.
10. BR. L.I.j (TS. 2899; IVP, 1.5, Room 9). Phase 2B. Small rim and upper wall segment. Fairly fine buff ware, evenly fired. Creamy-buff slip in and out.
11. BR. L.II.a (TS. 2056; IC, 1.21). Phase 7. Small rim and 2/3 wall segment. Fairly coarse grayish-buff ware, evenly fired. Self slip in and out.
12. BR. L.II.b (TS. 1123; VIIIB, 1.2). Phase 2. Small rim and upper wall segment. Fairly coarse pinkish-buff ware, evenly fired. Cream slip in and out.
13. BR. L.II.c (TS. 699; VIIIA, 1.2). Phase 2. Small rim and upper wall segment. Fairly coarse greenish-cream ware, evenly fired.
14. BR. L.II.d (TS. 2586; IVP, 1.3, Room 9B). Phase 4. Small rim and 2/3 wall segment. Slightly coarse pink ware, evenly fired. Creamy slip in and out.
15. BR. L.II.e (TS. 1936; IVB, 2.3, Below Room 1). Phase 1C. Small rim and upper wall segment. Slightly coarse pinkish-buff ware, evenly fired. Creamy-buff slip in and out.
16. BR. L.II.f (TS. 2467; VIIB, 1.1). Phase 5. Small rim and 1/2 wall segment. Slightly coarse ware with greenish-buff core, unevenly fired buff at surfaces. Creamy-buff slip in and out.
17. BR. L.II.g (TS. 2739; IVP, 1.2, Room 9B). Phase 4. About 1/6 rim and 2/3 wall segment. Slightly coarse pinkish-buff ware, evenly fired. Creamy-green slip in and out.
18. BR. L.II.h (Hd. C; TS. 2580; IVP, 1.3, Room 9B). Phase 4. About 1/3 rim and 2/3 wall segment with remains of one vertically positioned and pierced barrel-shaped handle or suspension lug. Hard, grayish-buff ware, fairly evenly fired. Creamy-green slip in and out.
19. BR. L.III.a (TS. 675; IIIJ, 1.2, 1.3). Phases 4 and 3. Two large rim and 2/3 wall segments. Fairly coarse pinkish-buff ware, evenly fired. Creamy-buff slip out.
20. BR. L.III.b (TS. 501; IIIB, 5.1, Room 6). Phase 4. Small rim and upper wall segment. Fairly coarse buff ware. Cream slip in and out.
21. BR. L.III.c (TS. 1925; IVF, 1.11, Room 1). Phase 2B. Small rim and upper wall segment. Slightly coarse pinkish-buff ware, evenly fired. Creamy-buff slip in and out.
22. BR. L.III.d (TS. 1071; IIIG/H, 1.4, Rooms 22A/B Extramural). Phase 5. Large rim and 1/2 wall segment. Fairly coarse pink ware, unevenly fired with brown core at fold of rim. Cream slip out and just over rim in.
23. BR. L.III.e (TS. 1386; IIIB, 2.9, Room 1B). Phase 3. Small rim and upper wall segment. Slightly coarse pinkish-brown ware, evenly fired. Very worn self slip in and out.
24. BR. L.III.f (TS. 706; VIIA, 4.1/4.2). Phase 4. Two small rim and upper wall segments. Fairly fine pink ware, unevenly fired with buff core. Cream slip out, partially blackened.
25. BR. L.III.g (TS. 2062; IF, 1.13). Phase 3. Large rim and 1/2 wall segment. Fairly coarse greenish-buff ware, evenly fired. Self slip in and out.
26. BR. L.III.h (TS. 1701; IVN, 2.2, Room 8). Phase 2A. Large rim and 1/2 wall segment. Slightly coarse buff ware with lime and mica grits, evenly fired. Cream slip in and out.

Plate 219

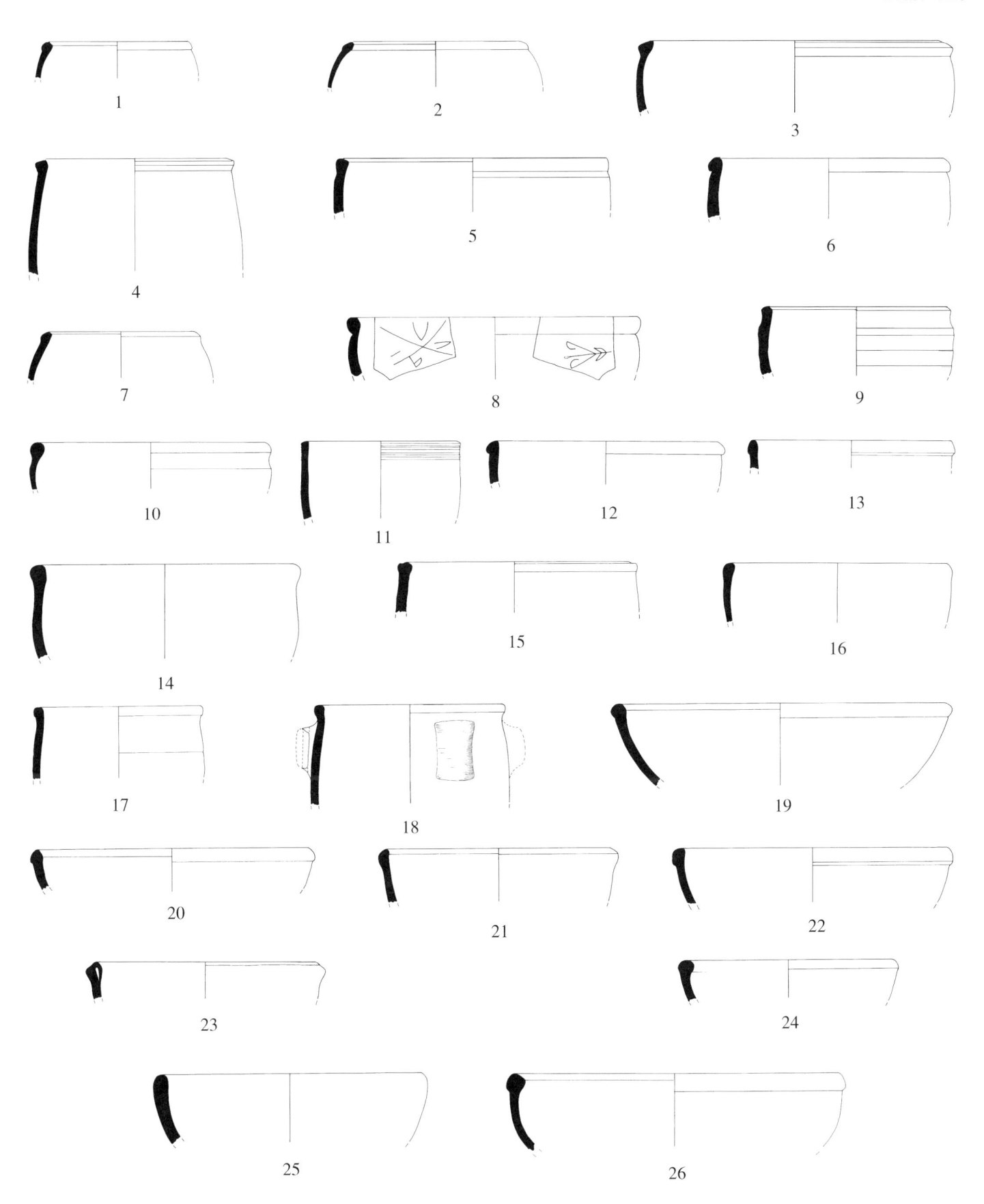

Bronze Age Bowl (BR) Type L. Scale 1:5

Plate 220

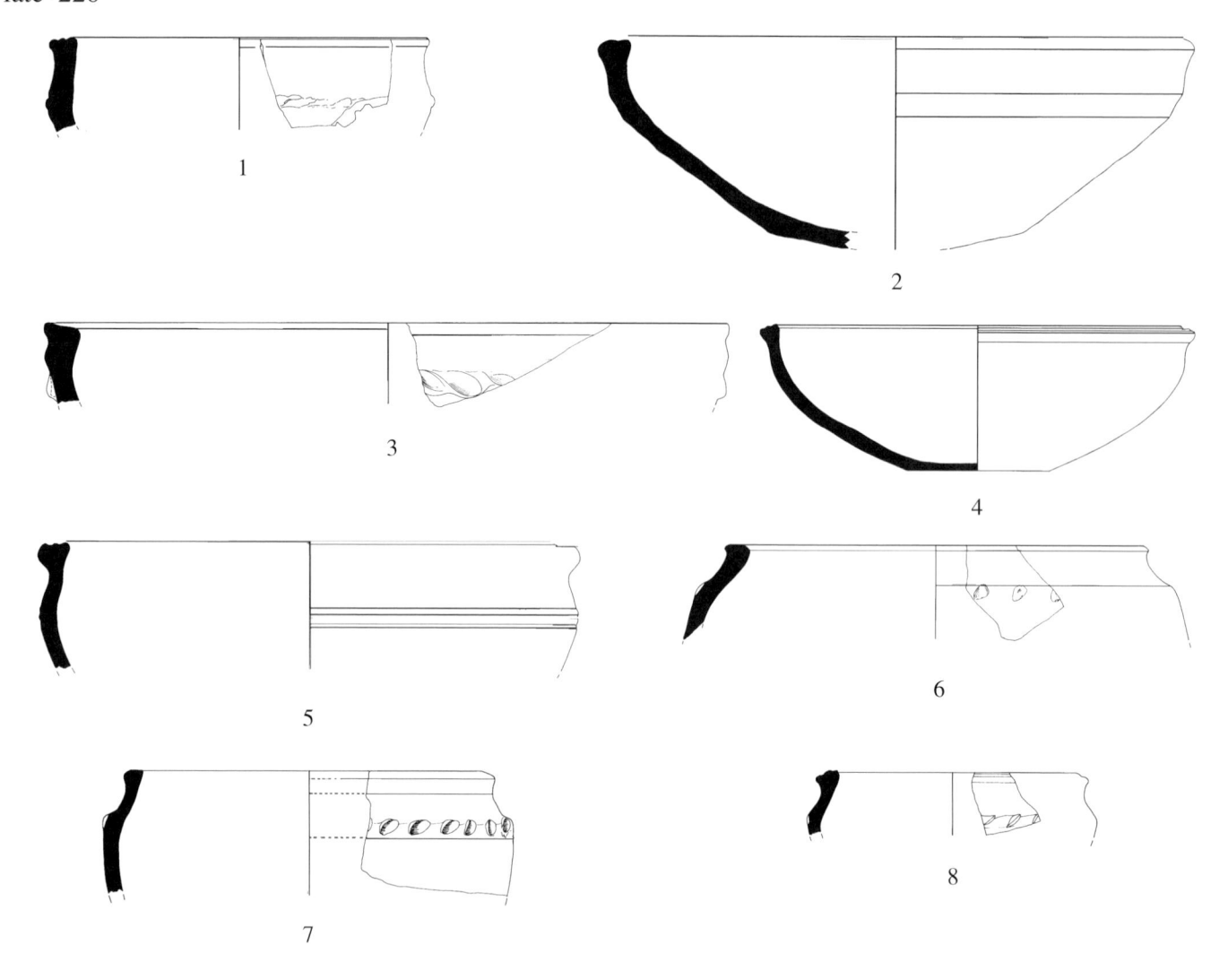

Bronze Age Bowl (BR) Types M and N. Scale 1:5

1. BR. M.I.a (TS. 3215; Op. 6, 20.1, Room 9). Phase 2A. About 1/12 rim and 1/2 wall segment with remains of a possible spout hole at the carination of the vessel wall. Slightly coarse pink ware with small gold- and white-colored mica grits, evenly fired. Creamy-pink self slip in and out.
2. BR. M.I.b (SW. 275; IIID, 5.3, Rooms 20/21). Phase 5. Large rim segment and nearly complete wall profile. Fairly fine pinkish-buff ware with fine lime and mica grits, unevenly fired buff at surfaces.
3. BR. M.II.a (TS. 2728; IVP, 1.4, Room 9A). Phase 3. Large rim and upper wall segment with applied finger-impressed rope-like band around the outside wall. Coarse pink ware, evenly fired. Creamy-buff slip in and out.
4. BR. M.III.a (TS. 1675; IVK, 1.3, Room 2A). Phase 3. About 1/4 segment of complete profile. Pink ware, unevenly fired. Cream slip in and out.
5. BR. N.I.a (TS. 3613; Op. 11, 3.1, Room 19A). Phase 3. About 1/8 rim and 1/2 wall segment. Slightly coarse pinkish-orange ware with many gold- and silver-colored mica and white lime grits, evenly fired. Creamy-buff slip in and out.
6. BR. N.II.a (TS. 2938; IVG, 1.4, Room 3). Phase 2B. Small rim and upper wall segment with tool-impressed decoration around shoulder. Slightly coarse pinkish-brown ware, evenly fired. Creamy-green slip in and out.
7. BR. N.II.b (TS. 542; IC, 1.5). Phase 9. About 1/8 rim and 1/2 wall segment with a finger-impressed band of decoration around the shoulder. Coarse brownish-buff ware, evenly fired. Cream slip out.
8. BR. N.II.c (TS. 846; IIIL, 1.1). Phase 6/7. Small rim and upper wall segment with a tool-impressed decorative band around the shoulder. Fairly coarse pink ware, evenly fired. Cream slip in and out.

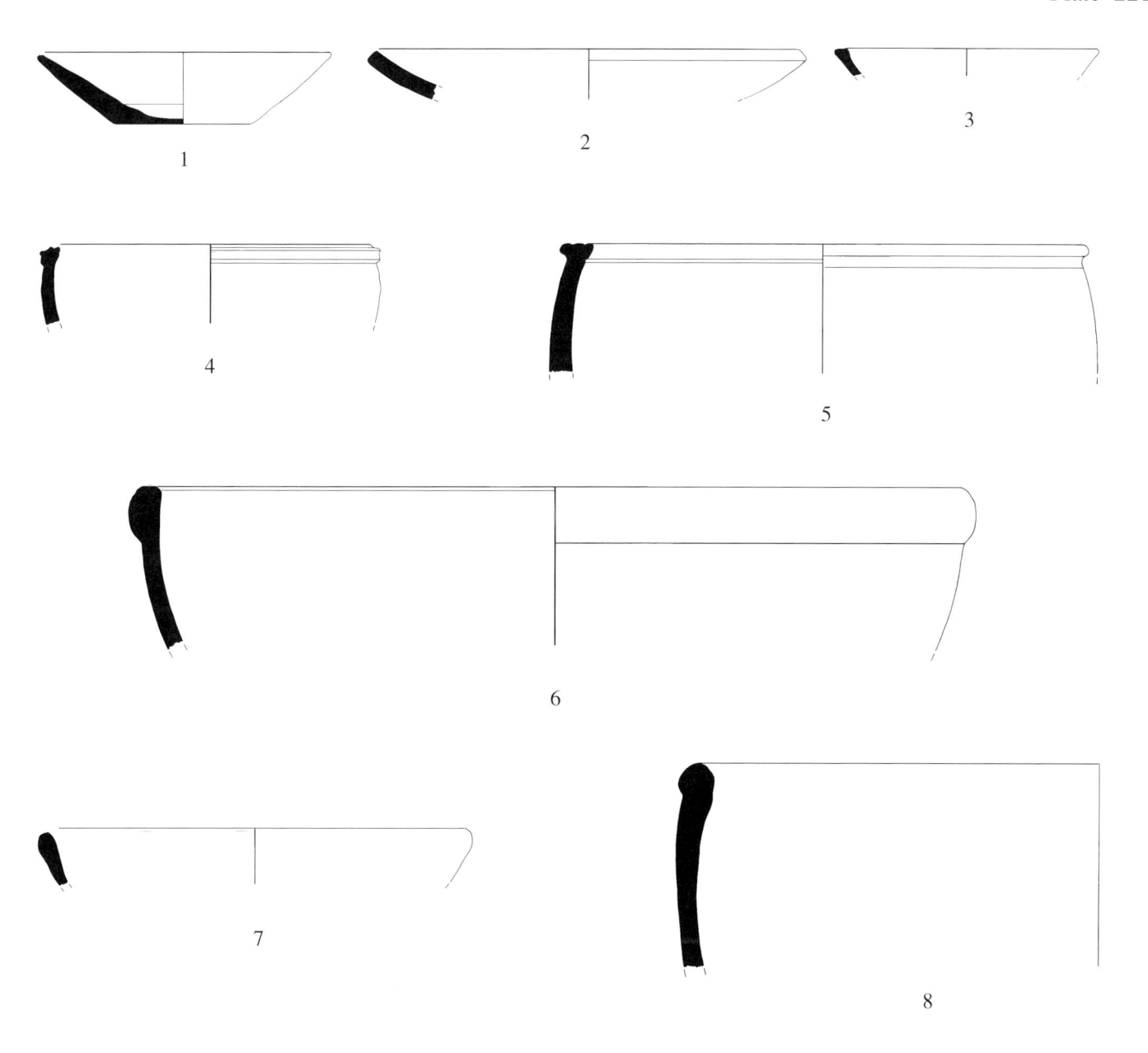

Bronze Age Bowl (BR) Types O, P, and Q. Scale 1:5

1. BR. O.I.a (TS. 1643; IVL, 1.2, Room 3B). Phase 4. Small rim segment and complete wall profile. Fairly coarse pink ware, unevenly fired. Self slip out.
2. BR. O.I.b (TS. 700; IIIG/H, 1.3, Room 22A). Phase 5. Small rim and upper wall segment. Fairly coarse creamy-buff ware, evenly fired. Light cream slip out.
3. BR. O.I.c (TS. 2952; IVJ, 1.8, Below Room 4). Phase 1C. Small rim and upper wall segment. Slightly coarse pinkish-buff ware, evenly fired. Creamy-green slip in and out.
4. BR. P.I.a (TS. 3455; Op. 6, 18.7, Room 16). Phase 2A. Small rim and 1/2 wall segment. Fine buff ware with white- and gold-colored mica grits, evenly fired. Creamy-buff slip in and out.
5. BR. P.I.b (TS. 595; IIID, 6.1, Room 13). Phase 4. Large rim and upper wall segment. Coarse pink ware, evenly fired. Cream slip in and out.
6. BR. Q.I.a (TS. 771; IC, 1.32C, Pit A + 1.43). Phases 4 and 7. About 1/24 rim and upper wall segments (two joining sherds). Fairly coarse pink ware, evenly fired. Cream slip in and out.
7. BR. Q.I.b (TS. 2464; IIIC, 4.9, Room 19A). Phase 5. About 1/8 rim and upper wall segment. Slightly coarse creamy-buff ware, evenly fired. Self slip in and out.
8. BR. Q.II.a (TS. 1026; IXA, 1.8a). Phase 2B. Large rim and upper wall segment. Fairly coarse creamy-buff ware, evenly fired.

Plate 222

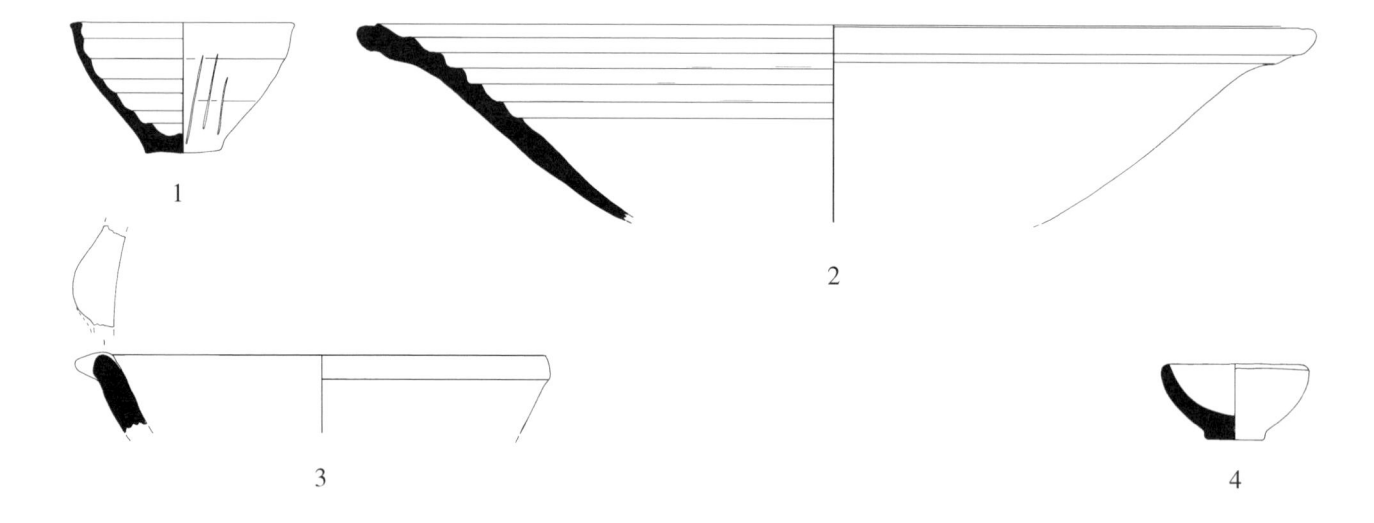

Bronze Age Bowl (BR) Types R, S, and T. Scale 1:5

1. BR. R.I.a (PM. A.17; SW. 501; IVO, 1.2, Room 10B). Phase 4 (see also pl. 89e). Mended to near completion with a potter's mark incised on outside wall before firing. String-cut base. Fairly fine pinkish-buff ware, evenly fired. Cream slip out.
2. BR. R.II.a (SW. 177; IB, 1.9). Phase 2. Large rim segment and most of wall profile. Coarse pinkish-buff ware with black mineral temper and large white grits, evenly fired. Yellow-green slip in and out.
3. BR. S.I.a (TS. 775; IC, 1.42, Destruction level). Phase 4. About 1/12 rim and upper wall segment with rounded ledge handle at top edge of rim. Fairly coarse pink ware, evenly fired. Buff slip in and out.
4. BR. T (TS. 2584; IVP, 1.2, Room 9B). Phase 4. About 1/10 rim segment and complete wall profile. Fairly coarse pinkish-buff ware, evenly fired. Buff slip out.

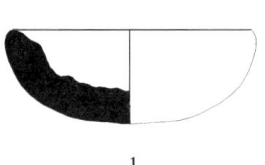

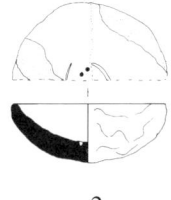

Plate 223

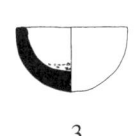

Bronze Age Crucible Bowl (CBR) Type A and Miniature Jar (MJR) Types (Not Classified). Scale 1:5

1. CBR. A.I.a (SW. 381; IVG, 1.4, Room 3). Phase 2A (see also pl. 90). About 1/6 segment with complete wall profile. Rough, handmade, friable, and heavily tempered ware. Thick residue remains inside from smelting of metal ore (for corrosive products, Cu, Sn, As, and Ni, see Holland 1976: 66).
2. CBR. A.II.a (PM. C.10; SW. 121; IIIA, 4.2, 4.3, Rooms 8A/8B). Phase 4. About 1/2 rim segment and complete wall profile. Handmade, with remains of punched holes and linear incisions on inside base. Coarse brown ware with fine black mineral temper.
3. CBR. A.II.b (SW. 551 = TS. 1891; IXA, 1.13 + 1.8a). Phases 2B, 3. About 1/2 segment mended with complete wall profile. Handmade, coarse, friable, gritty grayish-buff ware with chaff temper, unevenly fired with dark core.
4. MJR. 1 (SW. 86; IB, 1.7, Floor). Phase 3. Rim and neck missing, but body complete. Very gritty buff ware with black temper, evenly fired.
5. MJR. 2 (SW. 185; IIIG, 3.1, Room 18). Phase 4. Complete. Handmade, coarse ware with small grits and vegetable temper, unevenly fired pinkish-buff at surfaces.
6. MJR. 3 (SW. 433; IXA, 1.1). Phase 4. Nearly complete apart from a small piece of the rim. Fine buff ware, evenly fired. Partially blackened in and out.

Plate 224. Bronze Age Small Jar (SJR) Type A

1. SJR. A.I.a (TS. 2961; IVF, 4.1, Room 1). Phase 2A. Small rim and upper wall segment. Fine buff ware, evenly fired. Creamy-buff slip in and out.
2. SJR. A.I.b (TS. 672; IIIG/H, 1.7, Room 18). Phase 4. Small rim and upper wall segment. Fairly coarse pink ware, evenly fired. Cream slip out.
3. SJR. A.I.c (TS. 158; IIIB, 2.11). Phase 1C. About 1/3 rim segment and most of wall profile. Fairly coarse green ware with lime grit, evenly fired. Self slip out.
4. SJR. A.I.d (SW. 455; IVJ, 1.5, Room 4). Phase 2B. Complete. Fairly coarse greenish-buff ware, evenly fired. Handmade with base trimed on a potter's wheel.
5. SJR. A.II.a (SW. 263; IVE, 1.5, Room 3). Phase 2A. Complete. Light greenish-buff ware with fine grits, fairly evenly fired. Drainage hole manufactured in center of base.
6. SJR. A.II.b (TS. 2020; IIIB, 2.11). Phase 1C. Small rim and neck segment. Fairly fine pinkish-buff ware, evenly fired. Buff slip in and out.
7. SJR. A.II.c (TS. 1799; IIIB, 3.1). Phase 5. Small rim and upper wall segment. Fairly fine pinkish-buff ware, evenly fired. Creamy-buff slip in and out.
8. SJR. A.II.d (TS. 1308; IIIG, 1.1). Phase 6/7, Extramural. Small rim and upper wall segment with portion of round base; traces of bitumen inside and on rim outside. Slightly coarse pinkish-brown ware, evenly fired. Self slip in and out.
9. SJR. A.II.e (TS. 2102; IB, 1.12). Phase 1. Small rim and upper wall segment. Slightly coarse grayish-buff ware, fairly evenly fired.
10. SJR. A.II.f (TS. 1048; IIIG/H, 1.10, Room 2B). Phase 2. Large rim and 1/2 wall segment. Fairly coarse creamy-green ware, evenly fired. Self slip in and out.
11. SJR. A.II.g (TS. 1890; IXA, 1.13). Phase 3. Small rim and upper wall segment. Fairly fine light pinkish-buff ware, evenly fired. Creamy-buff slip in and out.
12. SJR. A.II.h (TS. 2437; IVM, 1.3, Room 7A). Phase 3. About 1/10 rim and upper wall segment. Fairly fine pink ware, evenly fired. Buff slip out.
13. SJR. A.II.i (TS. 1956; IVG, 1.5, Room 3). Phase 2A. Small rim and upper wall segment. Fine pinkish-buff ware, evenly fired. Creamy-buff slip in and out.
14. SJR. A.III.a (TS. 806 = TS. 889; IC, 1.48 + 1.47). Phase 3. About 1/4 rim and upper wall segment (two non-joining sherds). Slightly coarse pinkish-buff ware, evenly fired. Cream slip in and out.
15. SJR. A.III.b (TS. 881; VE, 1.1). Phase 9. Small rim and upper wall segment. Fairly coarse buff ware, evenly fired. Dark cream slip out.
16. SJR. A.III.c (TS. 2896; Lower Town Sounding: t.1, 12.89). Phase 1. Small rim and upper wall segment. Slightly coarse buff ware, evenly fired. Cream slip in and out.
17. SJR. A.III.d (TS. 2452; IC, 1.21). Phase 7. About 1/6 rim and upper wall segment. Slightly coarse pinkish-buff ware, evenly fired. Cream slip out.
18. SJR. A.III.e (TS. 3200; Op. 6, 3.1, Room 32). Phase 4. About 1/2 rim segment and most of wall profile. Fairly coarse pinkish-buff ware with black and white lime and gold-colored mica grits, evenly fired. Self slip out; very worn and pitted surface in.

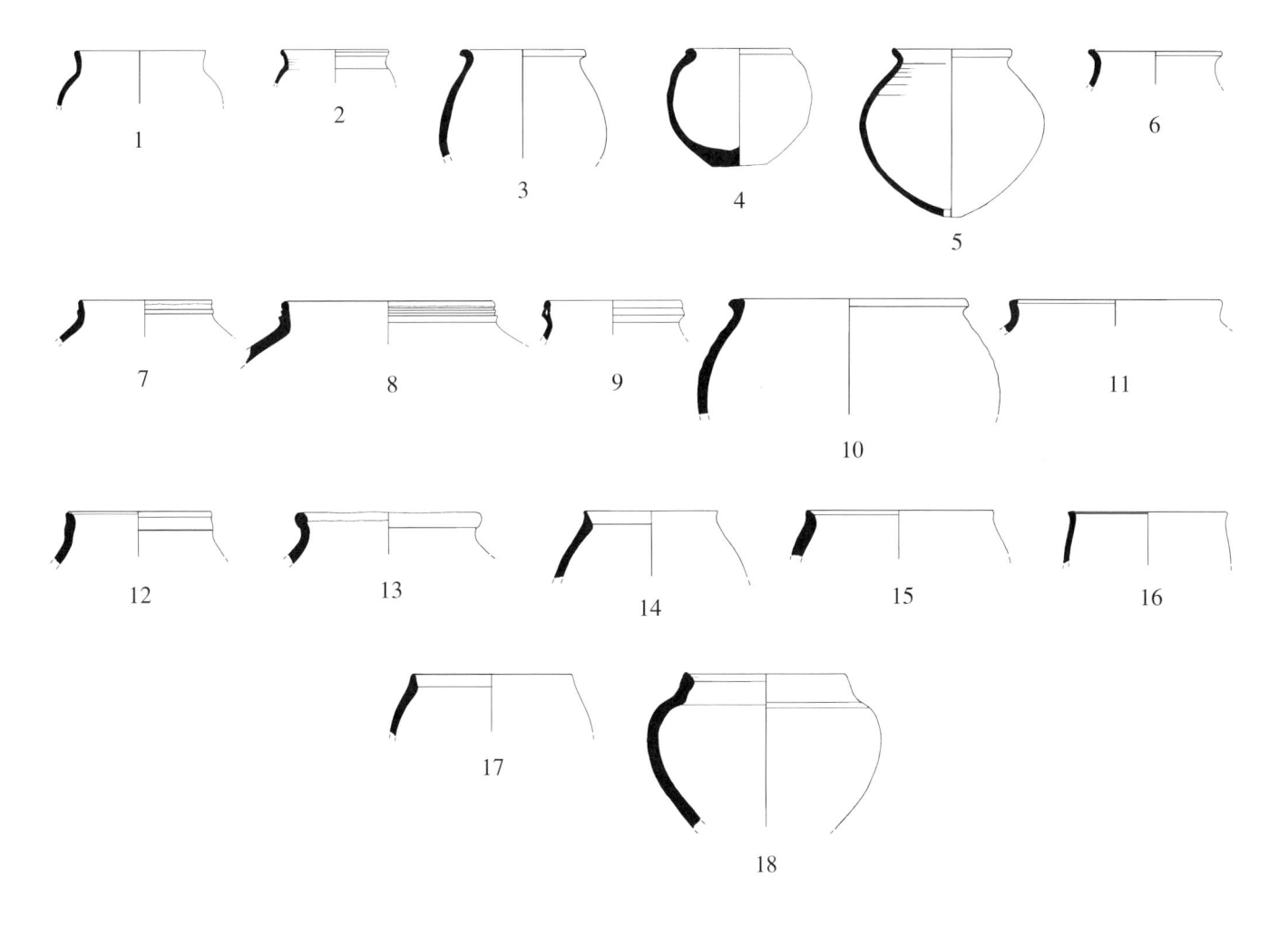

Plate 224

Bronze Age Small Jar (SJR) Type A. Scale 1:5

Plate 225. Bronze Age Small Jar (SJR) Type B

1. SJR. B.I.a (TS. 710; IIIG/H, 1.7, Room 18). Phase 4. Small rim and neck segment. Fairly coarse grayware, evenly fired. Burnished out.
2. SJR. B.I.b (TS. 1059; XA, 1.3, Room 15). Phase 2B. About 1/8 rim and neck segment. Fairly fine grayware. Burnished vertically on neck out and horizontally on rim and neck in.
3. SJR. B.I.c (Hd. G.2; SW. 129 = TS. 1378; IIIC, 4.6). Phase 7. Nearly complete with two horizontally pierced lug handles on opposite sides of upper wall. Fairly fine pinkish-buff ware, evenly fired. Creamy-buff slip in and out.
4. SJR. B.I.d (TS. 1978; IVF, 1.11, Room 1). Phase 2B. Small rim and neck segment. Fairly fine buff ware, evenly fired. Self slip or wash in and out.
5. SJR. B.II.a (TS. 3004; IVJ, 1.4, Room 4A). Phase 3. About 1/6 rim and neck segment. Fine creamy-buff ware, evenly fired. Self slip in and out.
6. SJR. B.II.b (TS. 1212; IIIG/H, 1.3–1.5, Room 22A). Phase 5. Small rim and neck segment. Fairly fine grayware, evenly fired. Vertically burnished on neck out.
7. SJR. B.II.c (SW. 264 = TS. 1760; IVE, 1.6 + IVK, 2.4, Room 2). Phases 2A and 2B. Nearly complete. Thin, slightly coarse dark grayish-brown ware with small lime and mica grits, evenly fired. Possibly burnished out, but surface too worn to identify with certainty.
8. SJR. B.II.d (TS. 1711; IVN, 1.3, Rooms 8B/18B). Phase 4. About 1/3 rim and 1/2 wall segment (two non-joining rim fragments). Fine buff ware, evenly fired. Cream slip in and out.
9. SJR. B.II.e (TS. 1098; IC, 1.56). Phase 2. About 1/6 rim and shoulder segment, handmade. Slightly gritty grayware, unevenly fired brown at surfaces. Self slip in and out, irregularly straw-wiped in and out during leather-hard stage of manufacture.
10. SJR. B.II.f (TS. 2018; IIIG/H, 1.3, Room 22A). Phase 5. Small rim and shoulder segment. Slightly coarse light pink ware, evenly fired. Buff slip out.
11. SJR. B.II.g (TS. 2316; IIIB, 2.11). Phase 1C. About 1/8 rim, neck, and upper shoulder segment with remains of a spout hole. Fairly fine pinkish-buff ware, evenly fired. Creamy-buff slip out.
12. SJR. B.II.h (TS. 955; XA, 1.3, Room 15). Phase 2B. Small rim and upper neck segment. Fairly fine pinkish-brown ware, evenly fired. Horizontally burnished in and irregularly on rim out.
13. SJR. B.II.i (TS. 2325; IIIG/H, 1.6, Room 17A). Phase 4. About 1/4 rim, neck, and upper shoulder segment. Fairly coarse pinkish ware, evenly fired. Buff slip in and out.
14. SJR. B.II.j (SW. 497; IVJ, 2.1, Room 4). Phase 2A. Nearly complete. Fairly coarse pink ware, evenly fired. Cream slip out and to mid-body inside.
15. SJR. B.II.k (TS. 2326; IC, 1.32C, Pit A). Phase 7. About 1/8 rim and neck segment. Fairly coarse grayish-buff ware, unevenly fired. Self slip burnished on top of rim and out.
16. SJR. B.III.a (TS. 751; IC, 1.41). Phase 4. About 1/12 rim and neck segment. Fairly fine pink ware, evenly fired.
17. SJR. B.III.b (TS. 811; IG, 1.12). Phase 1. Small rim and neck segment. Fine grayware, evenly fired. Narrow, horizontal black-painted bands out.
18. SJR. B.III.c (TS. 2479; IVA, 2.5). Phase 2A. Small rim and neck segment. Fine grayish-buff ware, evenly fired. Creamy-buff slip out and over rim in.
19. SJR. B.III.d (TS. 2548; IVD, 2.5, Room 2). Phase 2B. About 1/6 rim and neck segment. Fairly fine light brown ware, evenly fired. Buff slip in and out.
20. SJR. B.III.e (SW. 502; IVO, 1.2, Room 10B). Phase 4. Mended to about 1/2 completion. Fairly coarse pink ware, evenly fired. Cream slip in and out.
21. SJR. B.III.f (TS. 2828; IVY, 1.3). Phase 3. About 1/6 rim and neck segment. Slightly coarse buff ware, evenly fired. Self slip in and out.
22. SJR. B.IV.a (TS. 2829; IVX, 2.2, Room 14). Phase 2B. About 1/8 rim and shoulder segment. Slightly coarse creamy-buff ware, evenly fired. Self slip in and out.
23. SJR. B.IV.b (TS. 864; VF/G, 1.1). Phase 9. About 1/2 rim and 2/3 wall segment. Fairly fine creamy-buff ware, evenly fired.

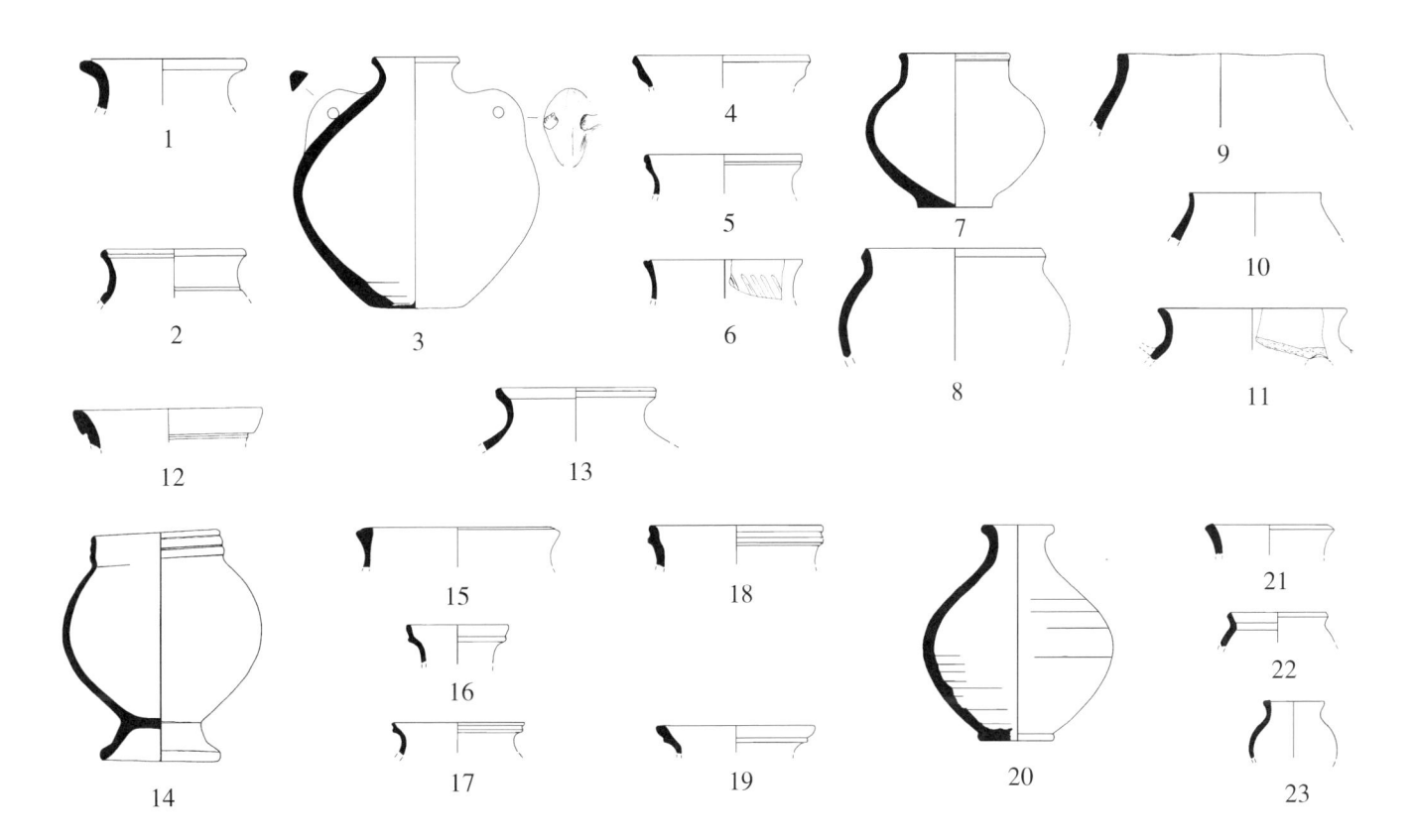

Plate 225

Bronze Age Small Jar (SJR) Type B. Scale 1:5

Plate 226. Bronze Age Small Jar (SJR) Type C

1. SJR. C.I.a (SW. 540; IVM, 1.7, Room 7). Phase 2A. Nearly complete, except for chips in rim. Fairly coarse brownish-buff ware, evenly fired. Cream slip in and out.
2. SJR. C.I.b (TS. 1013; IXA, 1.8a). Phase 2B. Small rim and neck segment. Fine buff ware, evenly fired. Creamy-buff slip in and out.
3. SJR. C.I.c (TS. 2964; IVM, 10.1, Below Room 7). Phase 1C. About 1/6 rim and neck segment. Fairly fine pinkish-brown ware, evenly fired. Cream slip in and out.
4. SJR. C.I.d (TS. 982, IG, 1.19). Phase 6. About 1/8 rim and neck segment. Fairly fine pink ware, evenly fired. Dark cream slip out.
5. SJR. C.I.e (SW. 461; IXA, 1.1). Phase 4. Mended almost to completion. String-cut base. Coarse buff ware, unevenly fired gray on inside. Burned patches on one side in and out.
6. SJR. C.I.f (TS. 2314; IVG, 1.5, Room 3). Phase 2A. About 1/8 rim and neck segment. Fairly fine pinkish-buff ware, evenly fired. Creamy-buff slip out and just over rim in.
7. SJR. C.I.g (TS. 2436; IC, 1.15). Phase 8. About 1/4 rim and neck segment. Coarse buff ware, evenly fired. Creamy-buff slip in and out.
8. SJR. C.I.h (TS. 2545; IC, 1.32B, Pit A). Phase 7. About 1/6 rim and neck segment. Hard, fine green ware, evenly fired. Self slip in and out.
9. SJR. C.II.a (TS. 2780; IVF, 4.1, Room 1). Phase 2A. About 1/8 rim and neck segment. Fairly fine flesh-pink ware, evenly fired. Pinkish-brown slip in and out. Irregularly-spaced horizontal line burnish outside.
10. SJR. C.II.b (TS. 1892; IXA, 1.8b). Phase 2A. Small rim and neck segment. Fairly fine pinkish-buff ware, evenly fired. Buff slip in and out.
11. SJR. C.II.c (TS. 1143; IVJ, 2.1, Room 4). Phase 2A. Small rim and neck segment. Fairly fine buff ware, evenly fired. Black slip in and out. Vertically burnished lines on extant portion of neck.
12. SJR. C.II.d (SW. 102; IIIA, 1.4, Room 11). Phase 4 (see also pl. 91b). Mended to near completion. Dark grayware with black mineral temper.
13. SJR. C.II.e (TS. 971; IIIG/H, 1.6, Room 17A). Phase 4. Small rim and neck segment. Fairly coarse pink ware, evenly fired. Buff slip in and out.
14. SJR. C.II.f (TS. 1388; IIIB, 2.4, Room 1B). Phase 3. Small rim and neck segment. Hard, fine creamy-buff ware, evenly fired. Self slip in and out.
15. SJR. C.II.g (TS. 1970; IVG, 1.3, Room 3A). Phase 3. Small rim and neck segment. Fairly fine buff ware, evenly fired. Creamy-buff slip in and out.
16. SJR. C.II.h (TS. 2694; IVZ(S), 5.3). Phase 2B. About 1/5 rim and neck segment. Slightly coarse purplish-buff ware, evenly fired. Self slip in and out.
17. SJR. C.II.i (SW. 10 = TS. 848; IIIG, 3.1, Room 18 + IIIG/H, 1.9, Room 3B). Phases 4 and 3 (see also pl. 91c). Many fragments mended to complete profile. The two shoulder segments extant are decorated with a cylinder seal impression. Fairly coarse grayware, evenly fired. Self slip burnished diagonally on rim out, horizontally below rim in.
18. SJR. C.II.j (TS. 2016; IVE, 1.2, Room 3B). Phase 4. Small segment. Fairly fine pinkish-buff ware, evenly fired. Buff slip in and out.
19. SJR. C.II.k (SW. 395 = TS. 1767; IVK, 2.4, 2.7, Room 2). Phases 2A and 2B (see also pl. 92a). Mended almost to completion. Thin fine greenish-cream ware, evenly fired. Self slip out.
20. SJR. C.II.l (SW. 247; IVE, 3.2, Room 3). Phase 2A. Complete. Hard, fine grayware with lime and mica grits, evenly fired. Bands of horizontal ring burnishing around outer rim and body. String-cut base.
21. SJR. C.II.m (SW. 723; IVN, 2.3, Room 18). Phase 2A (see also pl. 92b). Mended to completion. Hard, fine grayware, evenly fired. Self burnished slip outside.
22. SJR. C.II.n (TS. 143 = TS. 1343; IIID, 5.2). Phase 6. Two small rim and neck segments. Fairly fine buff ware, evenly fired. Creamy-buff slip in and out.
23. SJR. C.II.o (TS. 3341; Op. 11, 4.1, Room 20). Phase 2B. Complete rim and base mended to complete profile. Very hard-fired metallic-like ware with pinkish-red core, unevenly fired drab-brown at surfaces. Very many medium-sized white lime grits visible on outer surface and a few on the inner surface. Self slip in and out. Traces of burning on core after breakage in antiquity.
24. SJR. C.II.p (PM. A.14; TS. 520; IC, 1.1). Phase 10. About 1/10 rim, neck, and upper shoulder segment with potter's mark incised on neck before firing. Fairly coarse pink ware, unevenly fired. Self burnished on shoulder with irregular horizontal bands.
25. SJR. C.II.q (TS. 2541; IVE, 1.4, Room 3). Phase 2B. About 1/6 rim and neck segment. Hard, fine grayish-buff ware, evenly fired. Creamy-green slip in and out.
26. SJR. C.II.r (TS. 2543; IXA, 1.4). Phase 2B. About 1/12 rim and neck segment. Slightly coarse light brown ware, evenly fired.

Plate 226

Self slip out and over rim in.
27. SJR. C.II.s (TS. 2546; IF, 1.22). Phase 1. About 1/6 rim and neck segment. Fairly fine pinkish-buff ware, evenly fired. Creamy-buff slip just below rim in and out (only rim portion inserted into slip mixture). Self burnished below slip outside.
28. SJR. C.II.t (SW. 25 = TS. 2480; IIIA, 1.4, Room 11). Phase 4. Mended to near completion. Fairly fine buff ware, evenly fired. Creamy-buff slip in and out.
29. SJR. C.II.u (TS. 2878; Lower Town Sounding: t.1, 6.89). Phase 3. About 2/5 rim and neck segment. Fairly fine brownish-buff ware, evenly fired. Grayish olive-colored slip out. Horizontally burnished at leather-hard stage of manufacture.
30. SJR. C.II.v (TS. 1770; IVS, 4.3, Room 12A + IVW, 2.1). Phases 2A, 3. About 1/3 rim and neck segment and 2/3 wall profile. Buff porous ware with lime and mica grits, evenly fired. Self slip in and out.
31. SJR. C.III.a (TS. 939; VA, "1.1"). Phase 3. Small rim, neck, and upper shoulder segment. Fairly coarse greenish-cream ware,

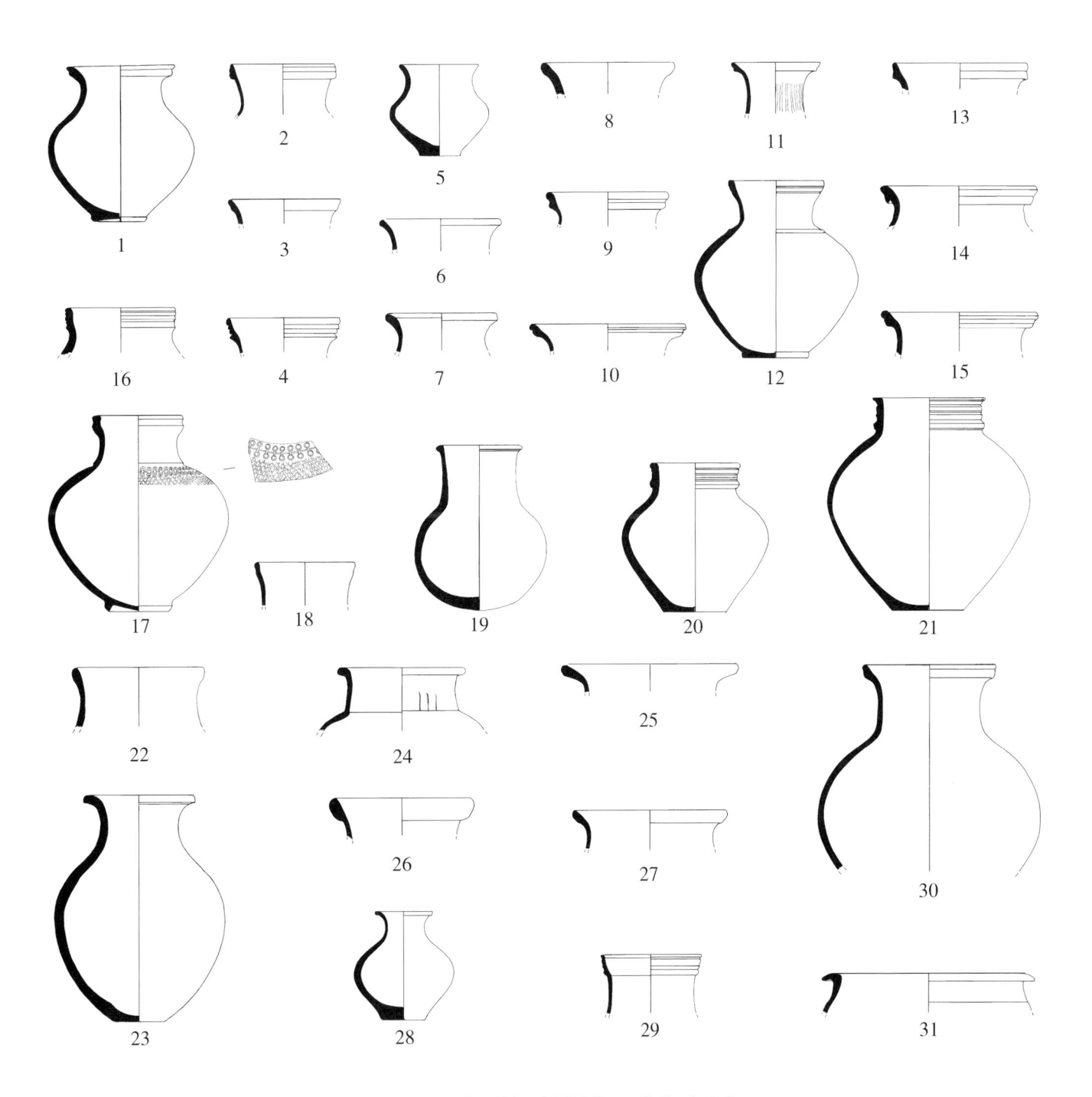

Bronze Age Small Jar (SJR) Type C. Scale 1:5

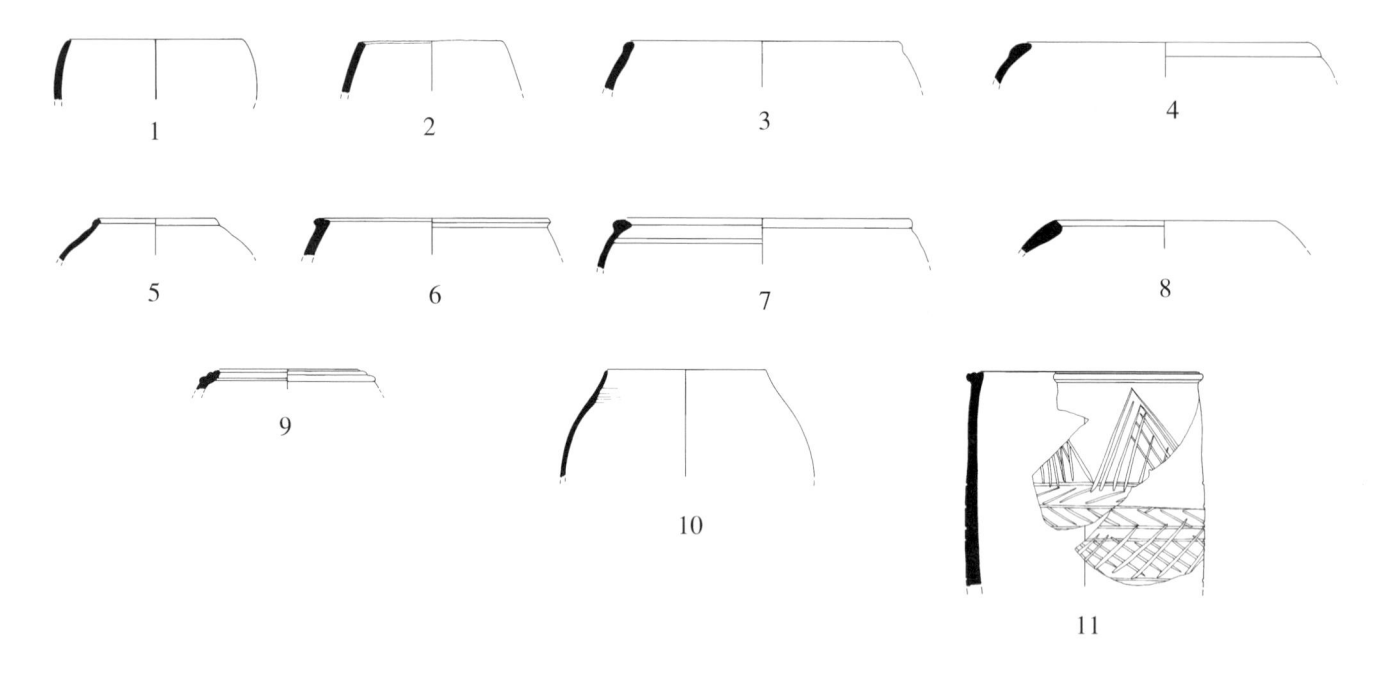

Bronze Age Small Jar (SJR) Types D, E, and F. Scale 1:5

1. SJR. D.I.a (TS. 1556; IIA, 9.9, Room 1). Phase 1. Small rim and upper wall segment. Fine light greenish-grayware with fine lime and mica grits, evenly fired.
2. SJR. D.I.b (TS. 1167; VE, 1.4, Pit [bottom]). Phase 3. Small rim and upper wall segment. Fairly coarse light cream ware, evenly fired. Self slip in and out.
3. SJR. D.I.c (TS. 2745; IVN, 2.3, Room 18). Phase 2A. About 1/10 rim and upper wall segment. Fairly fine pinkish-orange ware, evenly fired. Buff slip out.
4. SJR. D.I.d (TS. 2898; Lower Town Sounding: t.1, 9.89). Phase 2. Small rim and upper wall segment. Slightly coarse creamy-green ware, evenly fired. Self slip in and out.
5. SJR. D.II.a (TS. 2014; IVA, 2.2). Phase 2B. Small rim and upper wall segment. Fairly coarse ware, unevenly fired grayish-buff out, pinkish-buff in.
6. SJR. D.II.b (TS. 787; IIIG/H, 1.1, Courtyard). Phase 6. Small rim and upper wall segment. Coarse pink ware, evenly fired. Cream slip out.
7. SJR. D.II.c (TS. 2136; IIIH, 1.1). Phase 6/7, Extramural. Small rim and upper wall segment. Slightly coarse buff ware, evenly fired. Light white-buff slip in and out.
8. SJR. D.III.a (TS. 1800; IIIA, 4.4, Room 4A). Phase 3. Small rim and upper wall segment. Fairly coarse gritty buff-brown ware, evenly fired. Blackened inside.
9. SJR. D.III.b (TS. 2824; IVZ(N1), 1.1, 1.2). Phases 4 and 5. Small rim segment. Fine grayware, evenly fired. Self slip in and out.
10. SJR. E.I.a (TS. 2646; IVJ, 1.5, Room 4). Phase 2B. About 1/5 rim, neck, and upper wall segment. Fine pink ware, unevenly fired with gray core and pinkish-buff at surfaces. Thin self slip in and out.
11. SJR. F (IP [G.2] B.I.a; TS. 513 = TS. 531; IIIC, 4.7; IIIA, 1.3). Phases 6 and 5. Large rim and upper wall segment plus a large joining segment of the lower wall of a barrel-shaped jar with incised linear decoration out. Fairly coarse pink ware with mineral temper, evenly fired. Buff slip out.

Plate 228

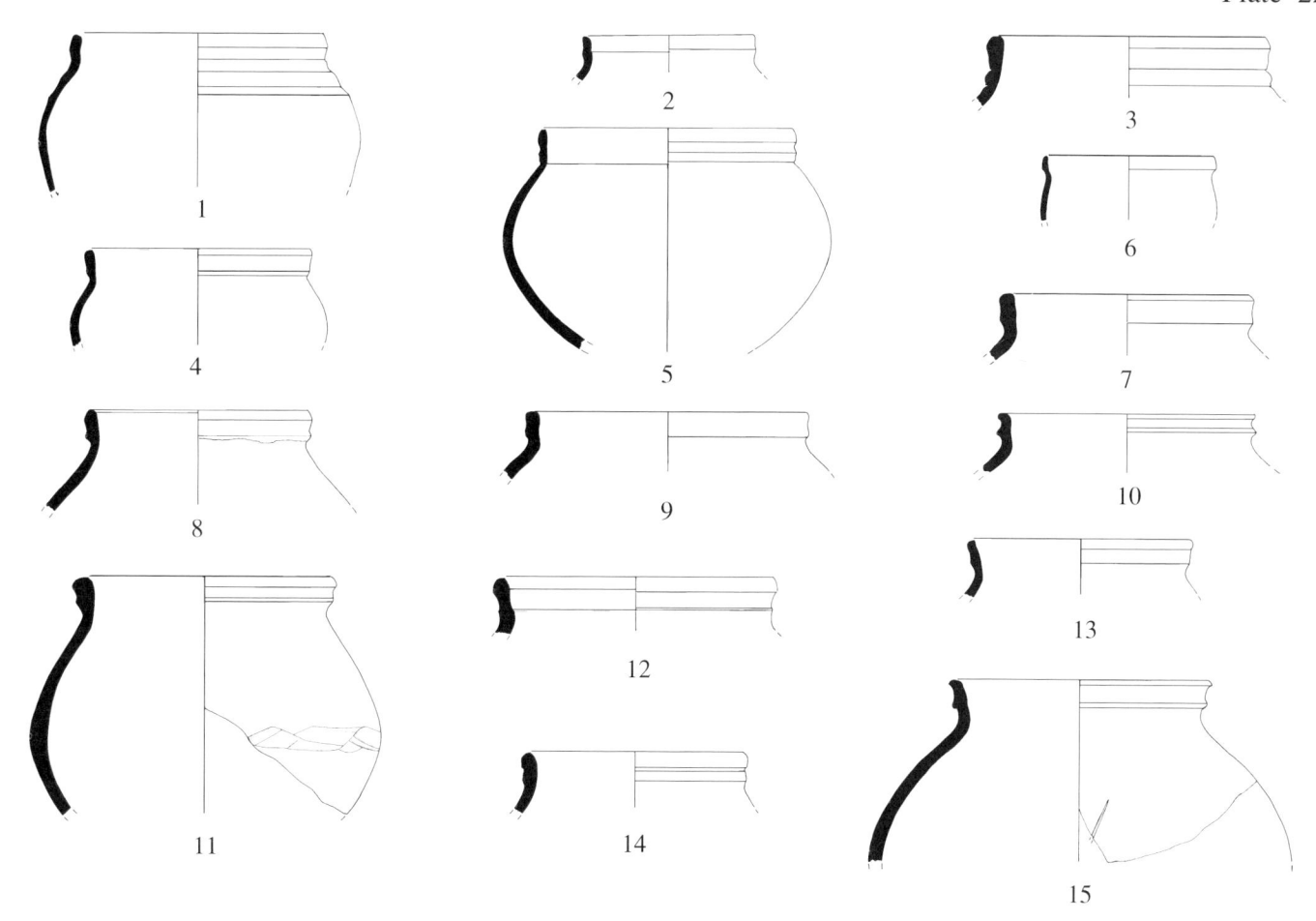

Bronze Age Jar (JR) Type A. Scale 1:5

1. JR. A.I.a (TS. 3363; Op. 10, 20, Room 18). Phase 2A. Large rim and neck segment and 2/3 wall profile. Ware description not available.
2. JR. A.II.a (TS. 3537; OP 7, 18.1 + 20.1, Rooms 34 and 36). Phase 2A(a). About 1/4 rim, neck, and segments of shoulder (two non-joining sherds). Fairly fine pinkish-orange ware with gold- and silver-colored mica and lime grits, evenly fired. Self slip in and out.
3. JR. A.II.b (TS. 1794; IIIB, 1.6). Phase 6. Small rim, neck, and upper shoulder segment. Slightly coarse pinkish-buff ware, evenly fired. Light creamy-yellow slip out.
4. JR. A.III.a (TS. 1905; IIIF, 1.2, Debris). Phase 5. Small rim segment and 1/2 wall profile. Slightly coarse buff ware, evenly fired. Creamy-buff slip in and out.
5. JR. A.III.b (TS. 596; IIIC, 4.7, 4.10, Room 9). Phases 6 and 4. Complete rim and nearly complete wall profile. Fairly coarse pink ware, evenly fired. Cream slip out and over rim in.
6. JR. A.III.c (TS. 3494; Op. 7, 17.1, Extramural). Phase 2A(b). About 1/6 rim and 1/2 wall segment. Fine buff ware with gold- and silver-colored mica and small lime grits, evenly fired. Self slip in and out.
7. JR. A.III.d (TS. 1904; IIID, 4.8). Phase 7. Small rim and upper shoulder segment. Fairly coarse buff ware, evenly fired. Self slip in and out.
8. JR. A.III.e (TS. 1867; IIID, 5.2). Phase 6. Small rim and shoulder segment. Slightly coarse pinkish-buff ware, evenly fired. Buff slip in and out. Charred on rim in.
9. JR. A.III.f (TS. 2188; IVA, 1.2). Phase 4. Small rim, neck, and upper shoulder segment. Fairly coarse pink ware, evenly fired. Thick creamy-buff slip out and just over rim in.
10. JR. A.IV.a (TS. 1757; IVL, 2.1, Room 3A). Phase 3. About 1/8 rim and upper shoulder segment. Medium pink ware with lime and mica grits, evenly fired. Self slip in and out.
11. JR. A.V.a (TS. 3271; Op. 6, 1.30, Room 9). Phase 2B. About 1/10 rim segment and most of wall profile. Fairly fine pink ware with large lime grit and pebbles and fine gold-colored mica inclusions, evenly fired. Irregularly shaved at girth. Creamy-buff slip out and just over rim in.
12. JR. A.V.b (TS. 1356; IIID, 5.3, Rooms 20/21). Phase 5. Small rim, neck, and upper shoulder segment. Slightly coarse buff ware, evenly fired. Creamy-green slip in and out.
13. JR. A.V.c (TS. 1903; IIIB, 1.6). Phase 6. Small rim, neck, and upper shoulder segment. Slightly coarse pinkish-buff ware, evenly fired. Self slip in and out.
14. JR. A.V.d (TS. 2655; IVF, 4.1, Room 1). Phase 2A. About 1/8 rim, neck, and upper shoulder segment. Fairly fine light pinkish-buff ware, evenly fired. Creamy-green slip out and over rim in.
15. JR. A.VI.a (PM. A.11; TS. 890; IIIG/H, 1.2, Room 22B). Phase 5. About 1/2 rim, neck, and 1/2 wall segment with remains of a potter's mark incised on outside wall before firing. Fairly coarse pink ware, even fired. Cream slip in and out.

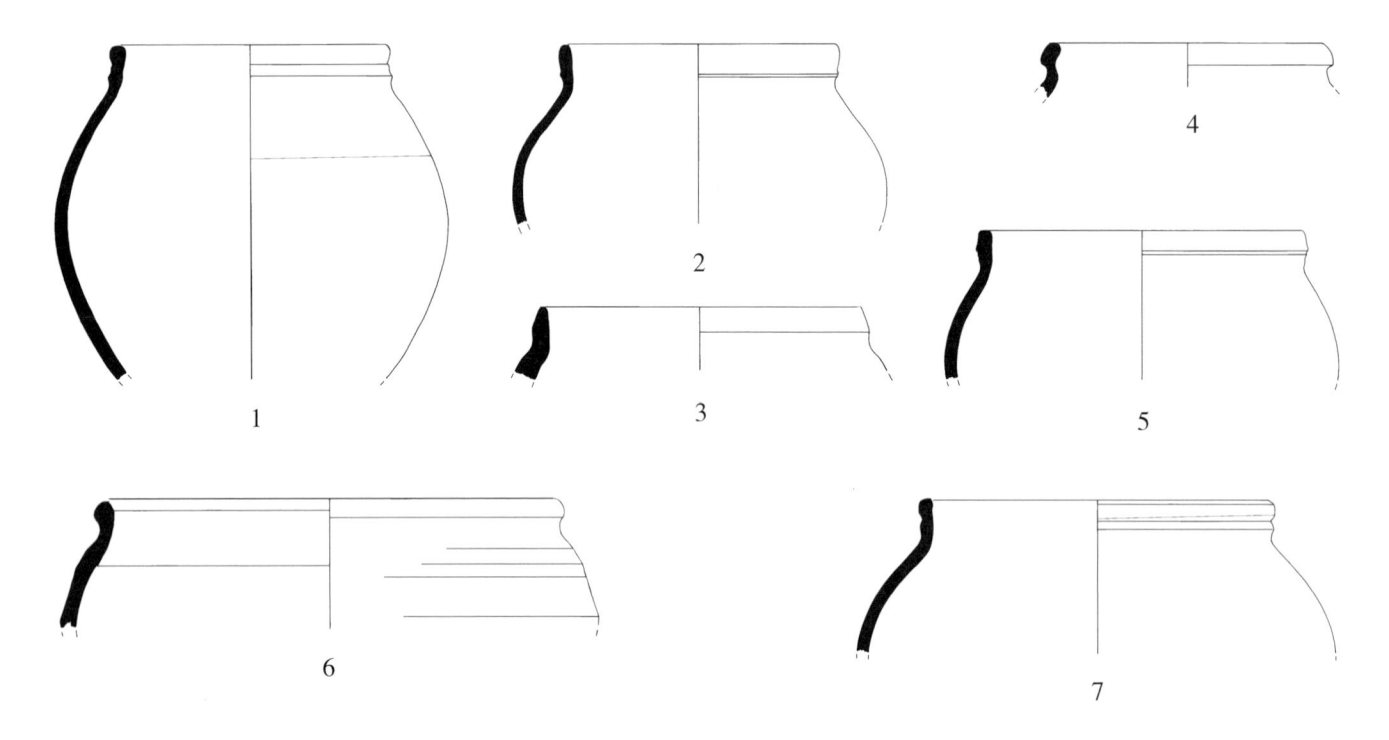

Bronze Age Jar (JR) Types B.I and B.II. Scale 1:5

1. JR. B.I.a (TS. 3615; Op. 5, 17.3, Pit). Phase 4. Large rim and neck segment and most of wall profile. Ware description not available.
2. JR. B.I.b (TS. 601; IIID, 4.8, 5.3, Rooms 20/21). Phases 7 and 5. About 1/2 rim, neck, and wall segment (four fragments). Fairly coarse buff ware. Cream slip out.
3. JR. B.II.a (TS. 1795; IIIA, 1.1). Phase 7. Small rim, neck, and upper wall segment. Fairly coarse buff ware, evenly fired. Creamy-buff slip in and out.
4. JR. B.II.b (TS. 3155; IIIA, 1.1). Phase 7. Small rim, neck, and upper wall segment. Slightly coarse and gritty grayish-buff ware, evenly fired. Creamy-green slip out.
5. JR. B.II.c (TS. 1344; IIIC, 4.6 + IIID, 5.4, Room 12). Phases 7 and 4. Fairly large rim and neck segment and 1/2 wall profile. Slightly coarse pinkish-brown ware, evenly fired. Self slip out.
6. JR. B.II.d (TS. 1275 + TS. 1380; IIIC, 4.6). Phase 7. About 1/2 rim, neck, and upper wall segment (four fragments). Fairly coarse pinkish-buff ware, evenly fired. Creamy-green slip out and over rim in.
7. JR. B.II.e (TS. 2042; IE, 1.8). Phase 3. Fairly large rim, neck, and upper wall segment. Hard, fine pink ware, evenly fired. Creamy-buff slip out.

Plate 230

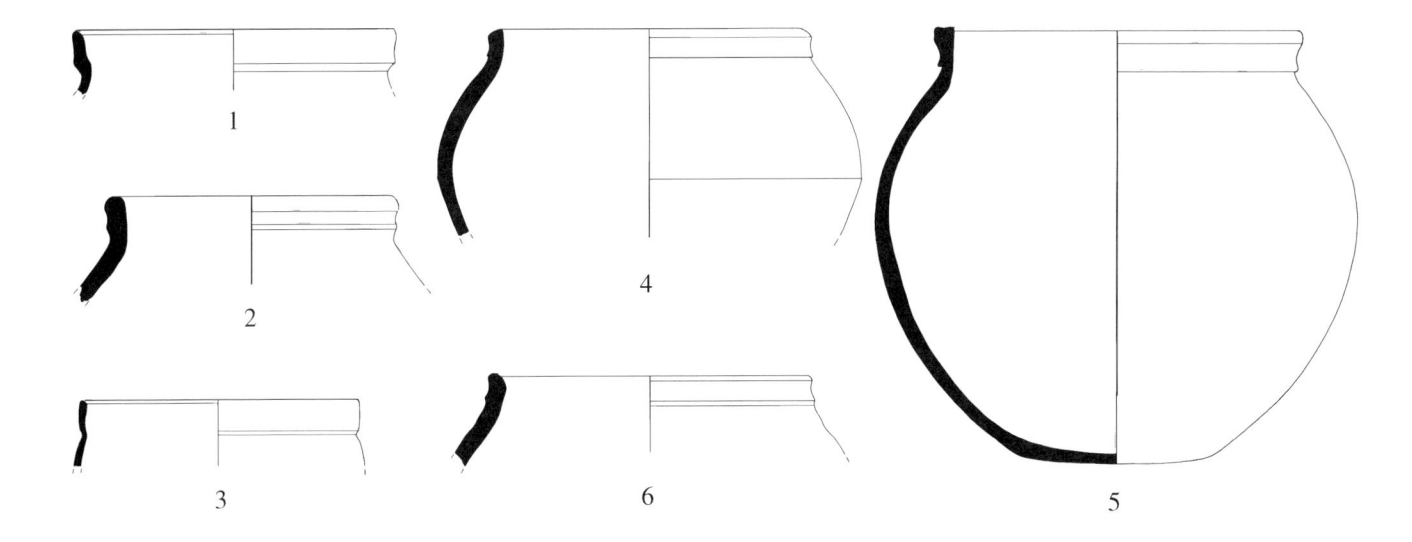

Bronze Age Jar (JR) Type B.III. Scale 1:5

1. JR. B.III.a (TS. 1879; IXA, 1.15a). Phase 3. Small rim, neck, and upper shoulder segment. Slightly coarse pink ware, evenly fired. Creamy-green slip out.
2. JR. B.III.b (TS. 1899; IIIA, 1.2). Phase 6. Small rim, neck, and upper shoulder segment. Slightly coarse pink ware, evenly fired. Self slip in and out.
3. JR. B.III.c (TS. 3451; Op. 6, 18.7, Room 16). Phase 2A. About 1/8 rim, neck, and upper wall segment. Fairly fine ware with gold- and silver-colored mica and a few small lime grits, unevenly fired buff in and pinkish-buff at surface out. Creamy-buff slip in and out.
4. JR. B.III.d (TS. 661 + TS. 821; IIIG/H, 1a, Room 23). Phase 7A. About 1/6 rim and neck segment and 2/3 wall profile. Fairly coarse buff ware, evenly fired. Cream slip out.
5. JR. B.III.e (TS. 1050; XA, 1.3, 1.4, Room 15). Phases 2B and 2A. Mended to near completion. Fairly coarse pink ware, evenly fired. Cream slip out.
6. JR. B.III.f (TS. 1900; IIIC, 4.6). Phase 7. Small rim, neck, and upper shoulder segment. Slightly coarse pink ware, evenly fired. Pinkish-buff slip out.

Plate 231

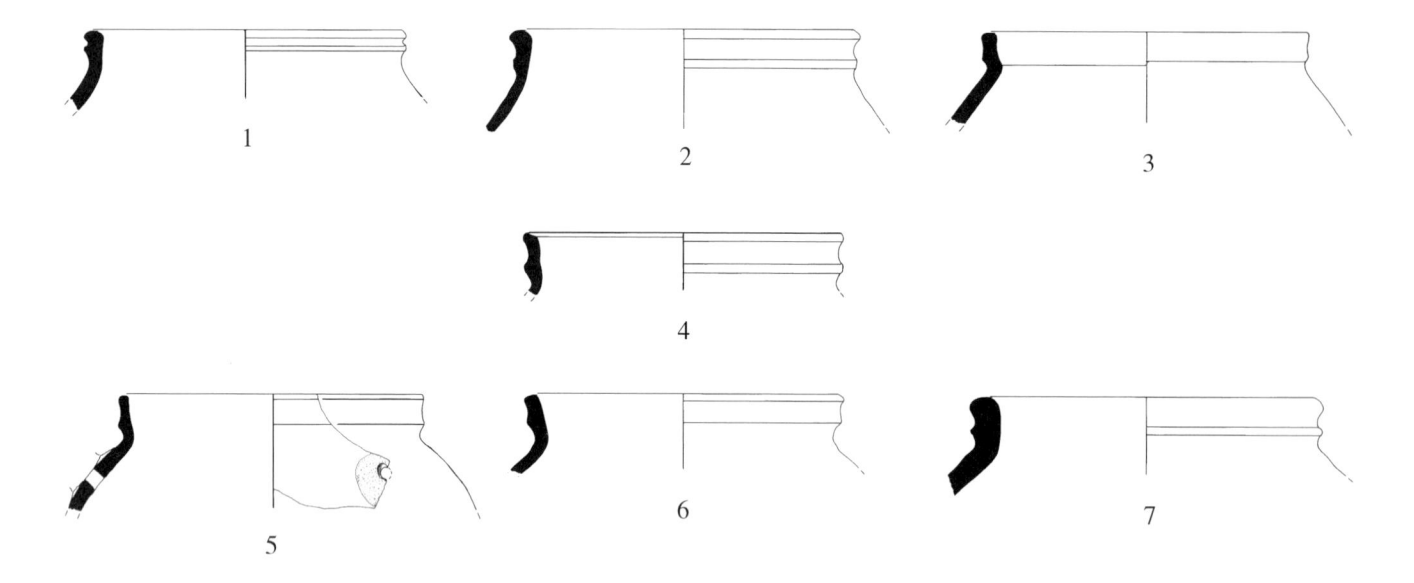

Bronze Age Jar (JR) Type B.IV. Scale 1:5

1. JR. B.IV.a (TS. 1796; IIIB, 1.6). Phase 6. Small rim, neck, and upper shoulder segment. Slightly coarse pinkish-buff ware, evenly fired. Creamy-buff slip out.
2. JR. B.IV.b (TS. 1373; IIIC, 4.7). Phase 6. Small segment. Fairly coarse grayish-buff ware evenly fired. Creamy-buff slip in and out.
3. JR. B.IV.c (TS. 408; VB, 1.2). Phase 3. Small rim, neck, and shoulder segment. Light brownish-buff ware, evenly fired. Cream slip out.
4. JR. B.IV.d (TS. 1790; IIIA, 4.1, Room 8B). Phase 4. Small rim, neck, and upper shoulder segment. Slightly coarse pinkish-gray-ware, evenly fired. Buff slip out and on top of rim.
5. JR. B.IV.e (TS. 600; IIIG, 3.1, Room 18). Phase 4. Fairly large rim, neck, and shoulder segment with remains of a spout on the shoulder. Fairly fine pink ware, evenly fired. Buff slip out and traces of bitumen in.
6. JR. B.IV.f (TS. 2683; IVZ(S), 5.7). Phase 2A. About 1/6 rim, neck, and upper shoulder segment. Fairly coarse pinkish-buff ware, evenly fired. Creamy-buff slip in and out.
7. JR. B.IV.g (TS. 1306; IIIB, 3.1). Phase 5. Small rim, neck, and supper shoulder segment. Hard, slightly coarse pinkish-buff ware, evenly fired. Creamy-buff slip out.

Plate 232

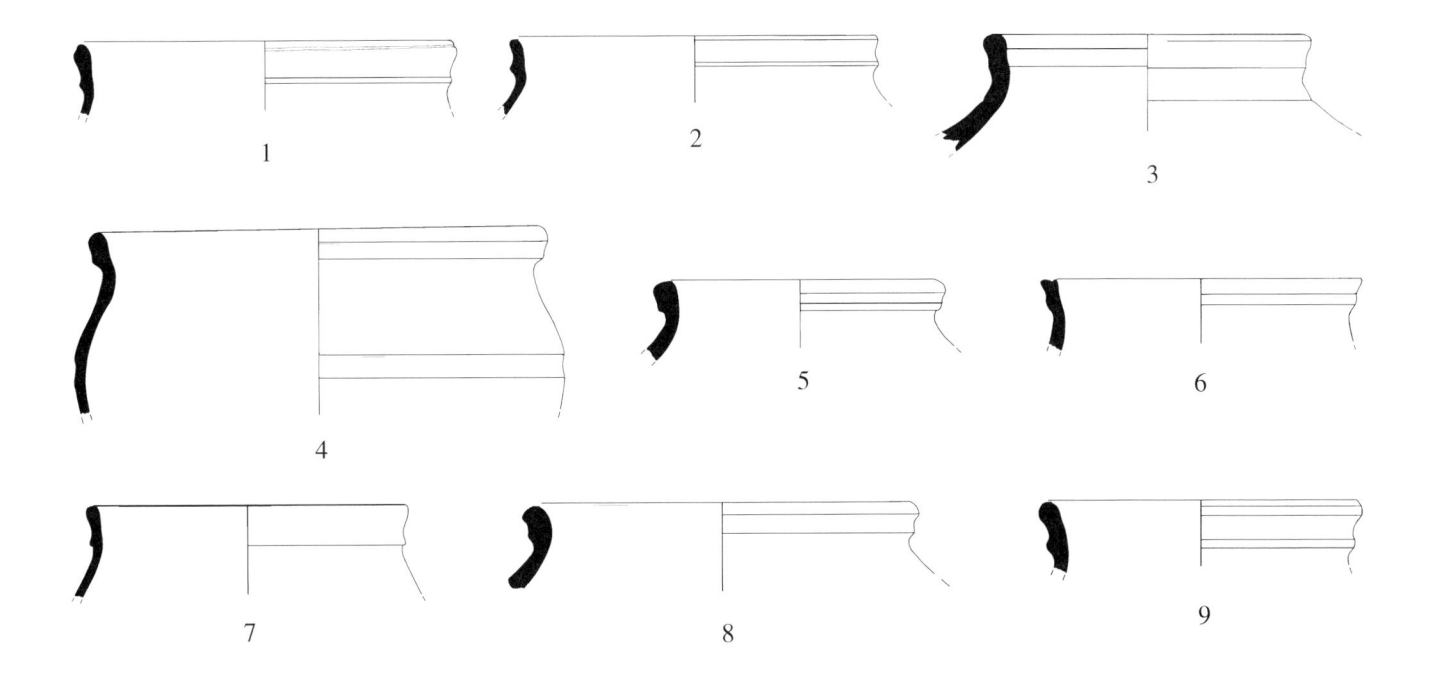

Bronze Age Jar (JR) Types B.V and B.VI. Scale 1:5

1. JR. B.V.a (TS. 1875; IIIA, 4.2/3, Rooms 8A/8B). Phase 4. Small rim, neck, and upper shoulder segment. Slightly coarse pink ware, evenly fired. Creamy-buff slip out and over rim in.
2. JR. B.V.b (TS. 2911; IVP, 1.4, Room 9A). Phase 3. Small rim, neck, and upper shoulder segment. Slightly coarse pink ware, evenly fired. Cream slip in and out.
3. JR. B.V.c (TS. 1339; IIID, 4.8). Phase 7. Small rim, neck, and shoulder segment. Slightly coarse pinkish-brown ware, fairly evenly fired. Buff slip out.
4. JR. B.V.d (TS. 431; IIIB, 3.2, Room 7). Phase 4. Fairly large rim, neck, and 1/2 wall segment. Fairly coarse grayish-brown ware, evenly fired. Cream slip in and out.
5. JR. B.V.e (TS. 1052; IIIL, 1.1). Phase 6/7. Small rim, neck, and upper shoulder segment. Fairly coarse brownish-buff ware, evenly fired. Green slip in and out.
6. JR. B.V.f (TS. 2689; IVY, 1.2). Phase 4. About 1/12 rim and neck segment. Slightly coarse pinkish-buff ware, fairly evenly fired. Grayish-buff slip out.
7. JR. B.VI.a (TS. 2909; IVP, 1.5, Room 9). Phase 2B. Small rim, neck, and upper shoulder segment. Slightly coarse pink ware, evenly fired. Cream slip in and out.
8. JR. B.VI.b (TS. 1646; IVL, 1.3, Room 3A). Phase 3. Small rim, neck, and upper shoulder segment. Medium coarse pink ware, evenly fired. Cream slip in and out. Tool-shaved marks below rim outside made during leather-hard stage of manufacture.
9. JR. B.VI.c (TS. 1874; IIIB, 1.6). Phase 6. Small rim and neck segment. Slightly coarse grayish-buff ware, evenly fired. Self slip in and out.

Plate 233. Bronze Age Jar (JR) Types C.I and C.II

1. JR. C.I.a (SW. 477; IVM, 1.5, Room 7). Phase 2A. Mended almost to completion. Fairly coarse creamy-buff ware, evenly fired.
2. JR. C.I.b (TS. 1067; XA, 1.4, Room 15). Phase 2A. Small rim, neck, and shoulder segment. Fairly fine buff ware, evenly fired. Cream slip in and out.
3. JR. C.I.c (TS. 1616; IVO, 1.2, Room 10B). Phase 4. Small rim, neck, and shoulder segment. Medium buff ware, evenly fired. Self slip in and out.
4. JR. C.I.d (TS. 1277; IIIC, 4.9, Room 19A). Phase 5. About 1/3 rim, neck, and shoulder segment. Fairly fine buff ware, evenly fired. Self slip in and out.
5. JR. C.I.e (SW. 394; IVK, 2.4, Room 2). Phase 2B. Complete (see also pls. 29b and 30a for in situ position). Fine creamy-buff ware with a little grit temper, evenly fired.
6. JR. C.I.f (TS. 1333; IIIL, 1.1). Phase 6/7. Small rim, neck, and upper shoulder segment. Slightly coarse buff ware, evenly fired. Tannish-buff slip out and over rim in.
7. JR. C.I.g (TS. 2623; IVP, 1.5, Room 9). Phase 2B. About 1/8 rim, neck, and shoulder segment. Slightly coarse buff ware, evenly fired. Self slip in and out.
8. JR. C.I.h (TS. 1620; IVO, 1.2, Room 10B). Phase 4. Nearly complete rim, neck, and about 1/2 wall profile. Fine pink ware, evenly fired. Cream slip in and out.
9. JR. C.I.i (TS. 2611; IVN, 1.3, Rooms 8B/18B). Phase 4. About 1/8 rim, neck, and shoulder segment, heavily burned with pitted surfaces. Fairly fine grayware, evenly fired. Self slip in and out.
10. JR. C.II.a (SW. 274; IIA, 8.5, Room 7). Phase 4 (intrusive late third millennium or misassigned on the pottery washing mats). Mended to complete profile. Pinkish-buff ware with fine lime grits, fairly evenly fired.
11. JR. C.II.b (TS. 2560; IVX, 10.7 = IVM, Room 7). Phase 2A. Complete profile mended from 1/5 rim and 1/2 base segments. Slightly coarse pink ware, evenly fired. Self slip in and out.
12. JR. C.II.c (TS. 1844; IIIC, 4.9, Room 19A). Phase 5. Small rim and neck segment. Slightly coarse pinkish-buff ware, evenly fired. Creamy-green slip in and out.
13. JR. C.II.d (TS. 1854; IIIF, 1.1). Phase 6/7. Small rim and neck segment. Slightly coarse greenish-buff ware, evenly fired. Light green slip in and out.
14. JR. C.II.e (TS. 1698; IVN, 2.1, Room 8). Phase 2B. About 1/2 rim, neck, and shoulder segment. Hard, fairly fine pink ware, evenly fired. Cream slip in and out.
15. JR. C.II.f (TS. 2218; IE, 1.5). Phase 4. Small rim, neck, and shoulder segment. Slightly coarse pinkish-brown ware, evenly fired. Creamy-buff slip out.

Plate 233

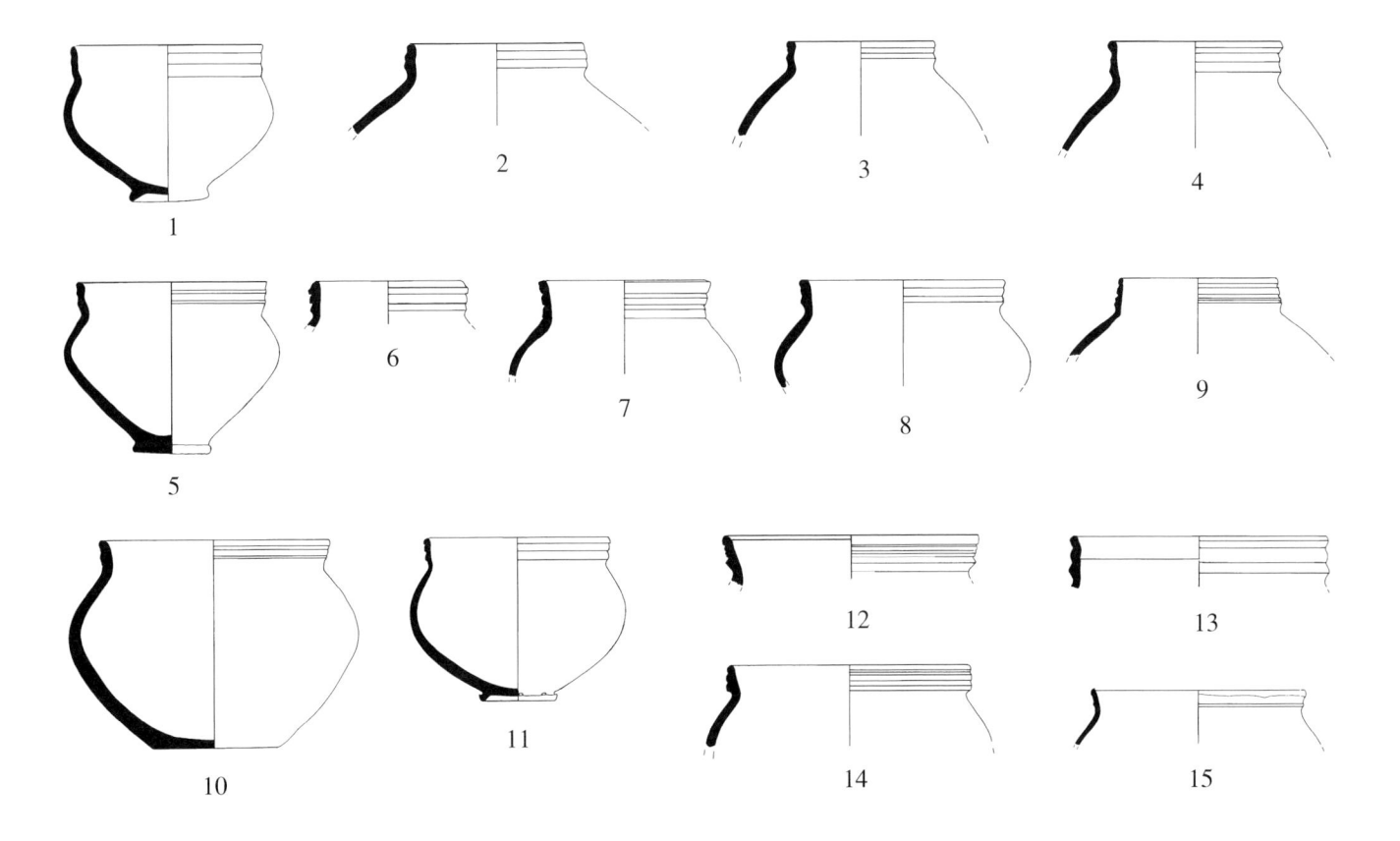

Bronze Age Jar (JR) Types C.I and C.II. Scale 1:5

Plate 234

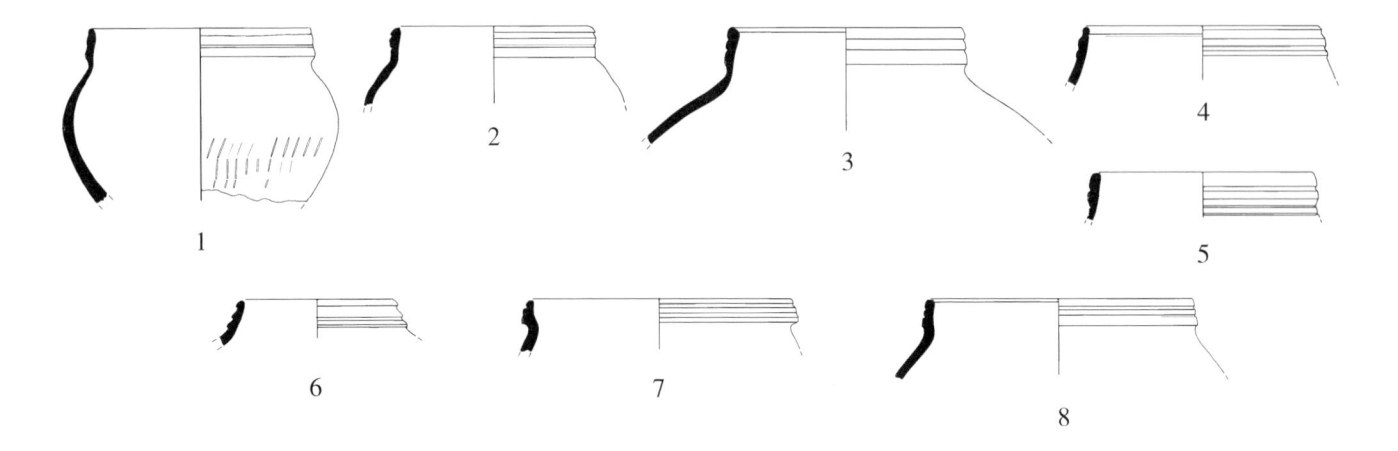

Bronze Age Jar (JR) Types C.III and C.IV. Scale 1:5

1. JR. C.III.a (TS. 118; IF, 1.16, 1.20). Phases 3 and 2. Large rim and neck segment and most of wall profile. Decorated with diagonally impressed stroke lines on lower outside wall. Fairly fine pinkish-buff ware with mica grits, evenly fired. Creamy-buff slip out.
2. JR. C.III.b (TS. 1839; IIIG/H, 1.3, Room 22A). Phase 5. Small rim, neck, and shoulder segment. Slightly coarse brownish-buff ware, evenly fired. Self slip in and out.
3. JR. C.III.c (TS. 1276; IIIC, 4.7). Phase 6. Large rim, neck, and shoulder segment. Fairly fine pinkish-buff ware, evenly fired. Creamy-buff slip out.
4. JR. C.III.d (TS. 1862; IIID, 5.2). Phase 6. Small rim and neck segment. Slightly coarse ware, unevenly fired with light gray core and pinkish-buff at surfaces. Creamy-buff slip out.
5. JR. C.III.e (TS. 2225; IE, 1.10). Phase 3. Small rim and neck segment. Slightly coarse dark buff ware, evenly fired. Creamy-buff slip out.
6. JR. C.IV.a (TS. 3590; Op. 8, 2.1, Room 29A). Phase 4. Small rim (3 cm), neck, and upper shoulder segment. Fairly fine ware with small gold- and silver-colored mica grits with gray core, unevenly fired pinkish-buff at surfaces. Creamy-buff slip in and out.
7. JR. C.IV.b (TS. 1882; IXA, 1.8b). Phase 2A. Small rim, neck, and upper shoulder segment. Fairly fine buff ware, unevenly fired pink on outside surface. Creamy-buff slip in and out.
8. JR. C.IV.c (TS. 2039; IF, 1.12). Phase 3. Small rim, neck, and shoulder segment. Slightly coarse dark brownish-buff ware, evenly fired. Grayish-buff slip out and over rim in.

Plate 235

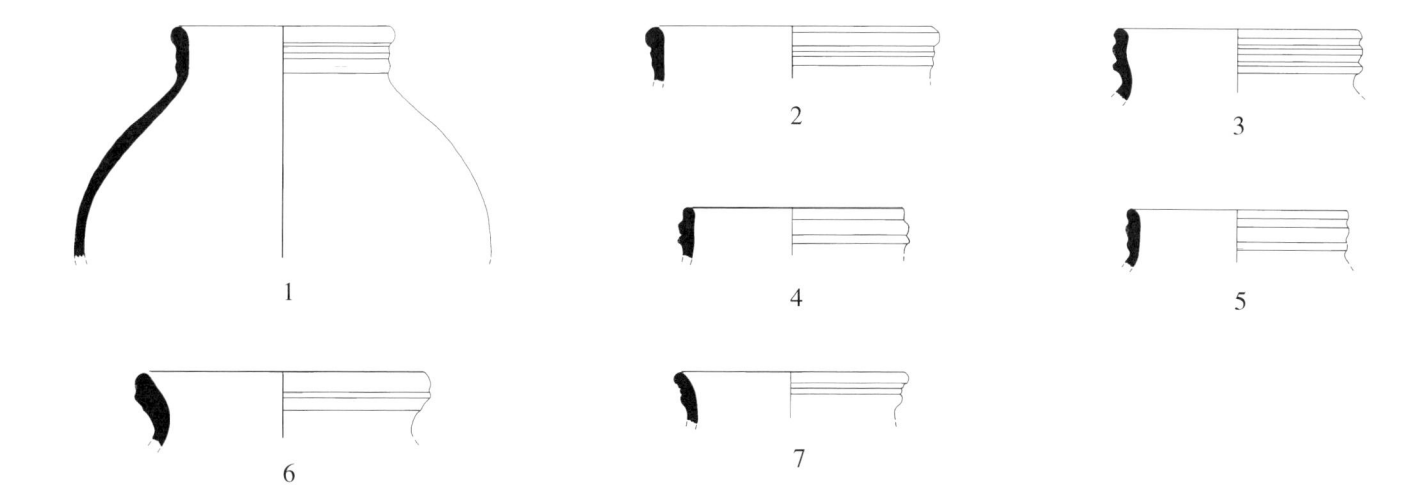

Bronze Age Jar (JR) Types C.V and C.VI. Scale 1:5

1. JR. C.V.a (SW. 325; IIIC, 4.10, Room 9). Phase 4. About 1/3 rim, neck, and 1/2 wall segment. Hard, fairly coarse pink ware with lime and mica grits, evenly fired. Light cream slip out.
2. JR. C.V.b (TS. 1390; IIIB, 2.3, Room 6). Phase 4. Small rim and neck segment. Slightly coarse light grayware, unevenly fired buff at surfaces. Creamy-buff slip in and out.
3. JR. C.V.c (TS. 1307; IIIE, 3.1, Room 15). Phase 5. Small rim, neck, and upper shoulder segment. Slightly coarse pinkish-buff ware, evenly fired.
4. JR. C.V.d (TS. 490; IIIC, 4.9, Room 19A). Phase 5. Small rim and neck segment. Fairly coarse pinkish-buff ware, evenly fired. Cream slip in and out.
5. JR. C.V.e (TS. 1819; IIIF, 2.2, Alley). Phase 4. Small rim, neck, and upper shoulder segment. Slightly coarse grayware, evenly fired. Grayish-buff slip in and out.
6. JR. C.VI.a (TS. 3598; Op. 8, 3.3, Room 29). Phase 3. Small rim (6 cm) and neck segment. Slightly coarse pinkish-buff ware with gold- and silver-colored mica and lime grits, evenly fired. Creamy-buff slip in and out.
7. JR. C.VI.b (TS. 1843; IIIC, 4.6). Phase 7. Small rim and neck segment. Slightly coarse buff ware, evenly fired. Self slip in and out.

Plate 236

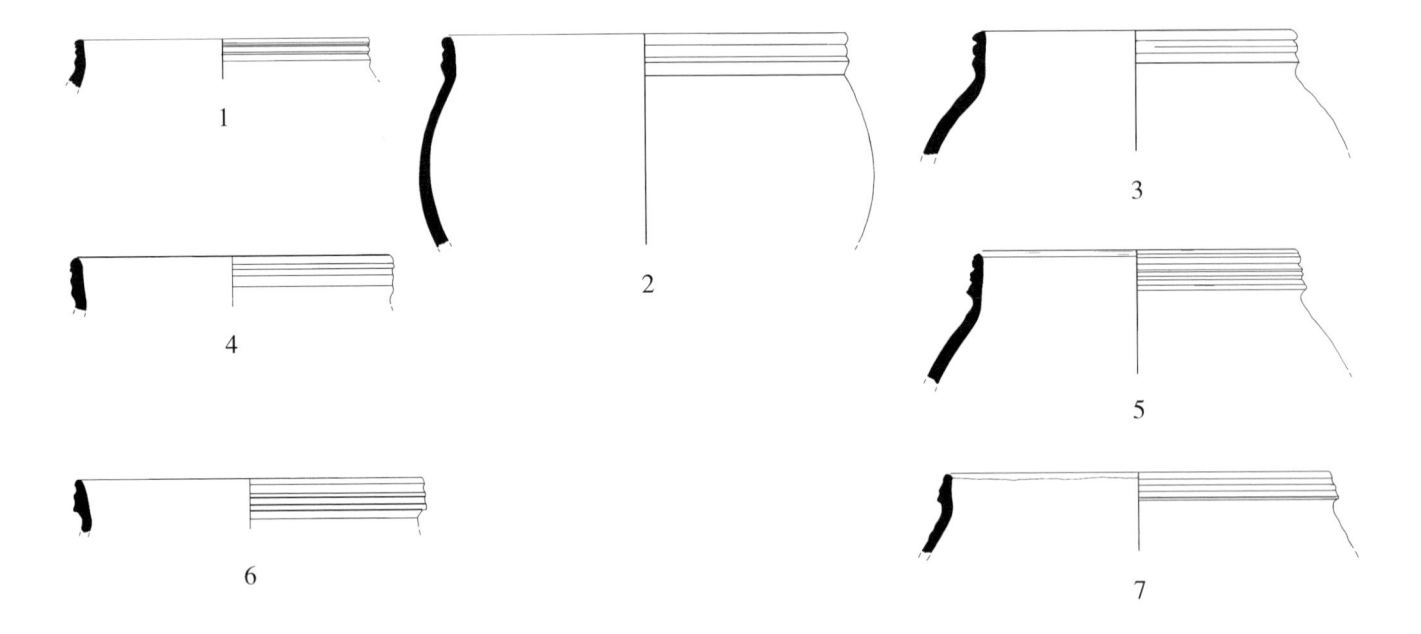

Bronze Age Jar (JR) Type D.I. Scale 1:5

1. JR. D.I.a (TS. 1852; IIIC, 4.6). Phase 7. Small rim, neck, and upper shoulder segment. Fairly fine pinkish-buff ware, evenly fired. Buff slip in and out.
2. JR. D.I.b (TS. 2052; IC, 1.32A, Pit A). Phase 7. Small rim, neck, and 2/3 wall segment. Fairly coarse grayish-buff ware, evenly fired. Creamy-green slip out and over rim in.
3. JR. D.I.c (TS. 1829; IIID, 5.2). Phase 6. Large rim, neck, and shoulder segment. Slightly coarse pinkish-buff ware, evenly fired. Creamy-buff slip out.
4. JR. D.I.d (TS. 1855; IIIF, 1.2, Debris). Phase 5. Small rim and neck segment. Slightly coarse pinkish-buff ware, evenly fired. Creamy-buff slip out.
5. JR. D.I.e (TS. 460; IIIC, 4.9, Room 19A). Phase 5. Large rim, neck, and shoulder segment. Fairly coarse buff ware, evenly fired. Cream slip out.
6. JR. D.I.f (TS. 2743 = TS. 2984; IVN, 2.2, Room 8 + IVF, 1.15, Room 1). Phase 2A. Small rim and neck segment. Slightly coarse creamy-green ware, evenly fired. Self slip in and out.
7. JR. D.I.g (TS. 754; IC, 1.41). Phase 4. About 1/28 rim, neck, and shoulder segment. Fairly coarse buff ware, evenly fired. Cream slip out.

Plate 237

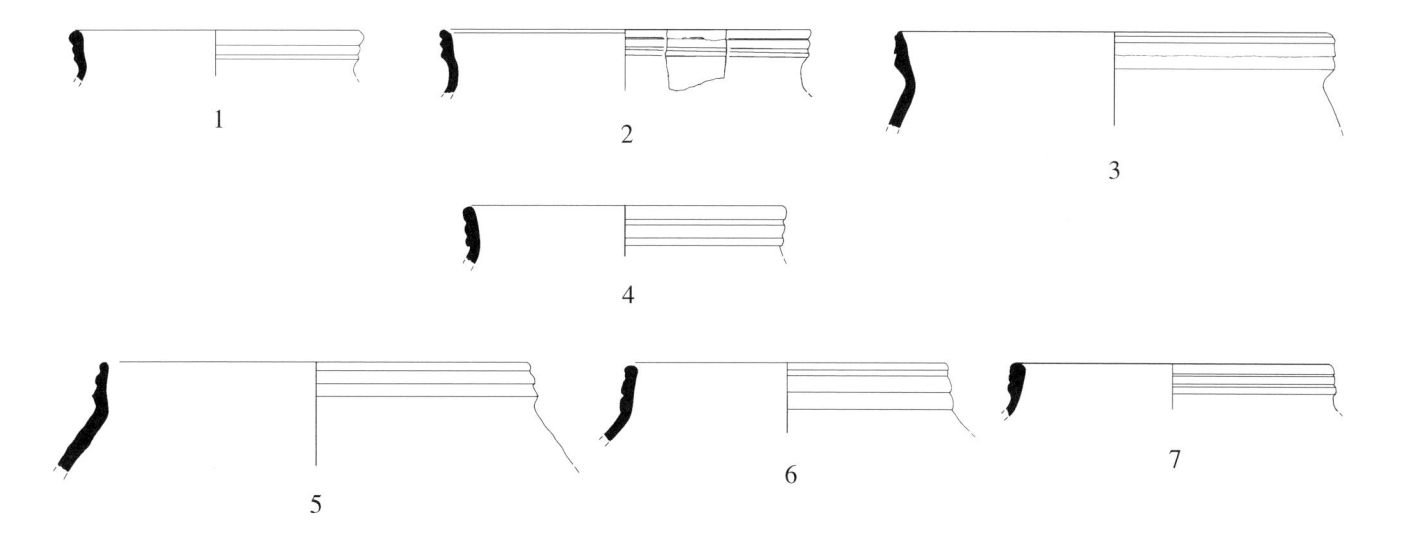

Bronze Age Jar (JR) Type D.II and D.III. Scale 1:5

1. JR. D.II.a (TS. 1850; IIIF, 1.1). Phase 6/7. Small rim and neck segment. Hard, fine grayware, unevenly fired buff at surfaces. Creamy-green slip out.
2. JR. D.II.b (TS. 507; IIIE, 1.1). Phase 6/7. Small rim and neck segment. Fairly coarse pinkish-buff ware, evenly fired. Cream slip in and out.
3. JR. D.II.c (TS. 1271; IIIA, 4.1, Room 8B + IIIC, 4.6). Phases 4 + 7. Two large joining rim, neck, and upper shoulder segments from IIIC and one non-joining rim fragment from IIIA. Slightly coarse buff ware, evenly fired. Creamy-buff slip out.
4. JR. D.II.d (TS. 2186; IVF, 1.11, Room 1). Phase 2B. Small rim and neck segment. Fairly close pinkish-buff ware, evenly fired. Creamy-buff slip in and out.
5. JR. D.III.a (TS. 994; IXA, 1.8b). Phase 2A. Large rim, neck, and shoulder segment. Fairly fine pinkish-buff ware, unevenly fired with light colored core. Creamish-buff slip out.
6. JR. D.III.b (TS. 1825; IIIG/H, 1a, Room 23). Phase 7A. Small rim, neck, and shoulder segment. Fairly fine buff ware, evenly fired. Creamy-buff slip out.
7. JR. D.III.c (TS. 1853; IIIF, 1.1). Phase 6/7. Small rim and neck segment. Fairly fine pink ware, evenly fired. Creamy-buff slip out.

Plate 238

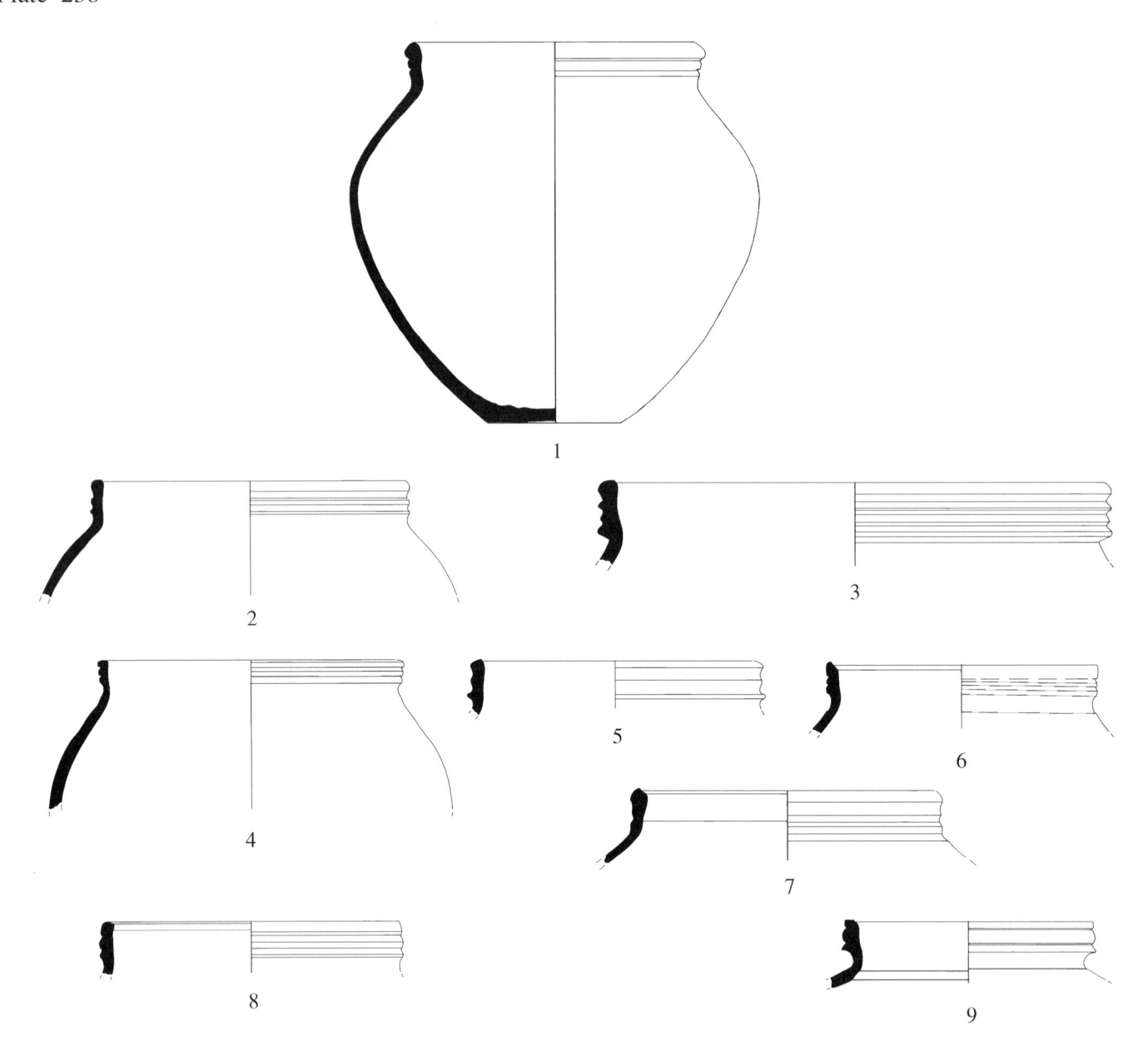

Bronze Age Jar (JR) Types D.IV and D.V. Scale 1:5

1. JR. D.IV.a (TS. 3389; Op. 11, 5.1, Room 19). Phase 2B. Nearly complete in situ. Ware description not available.
2. JR. D.V.a (TS. 1826; IIIG/H, 1.3, Room 22A). Phase 5. Large rim, neck, and shoulder segment. Fairly fine pinkish-buff ware, evenly fired. Light creamy-green slip out.
3. JR. D.V.b (TS. 607; IC, 1.21). Phase 7. About 1/12 rim and neck segment. Coarse pink ware, unevenly fired with buff core. Cream slip in and out.
4. JR. D.V.c (TS. 2619; IVZ(N2), 3.1). Phase 5. About 1/3 rim, neck, and 1/2 wall segment. Slightly coarse pinkish-orange ware, evenly fired. Self slip in and out.
5. JR. D.V.d (TS. 2183; IVF, 1.11, Room 1). Phase 2B. Small rim and neck segment. Slightly coarse pinkish-buff ware, evenly fired. Remains of creamy-buff slip out.
6. JR. D.V.e (TS. 2223; VE, 1.2). Phase 5. Small rim, neck, and shoulder segment. Hard, slightly coarse ware, unevenly fired with light gray core and buff at surfaces. Creamy-green slip out.
7. JR. D.V.f (TS. 1653; IVL/P, 1.3, Pit). Phase 3. About 1/4 rim, neck, and upper shoulder segment (two joining rim fragments). Pink ware, evenly fired. Cream slip in and out.
8. JR. D.V.g (TS. 1822; IIIA, 4.1, Room 8B). Phase 4. Small rim and neck segment. Hard grayware, fairly evenly fired. Grayish-buff slip in and out.
9. JR. D.V.h (TS. 914; IIIG/H, 1.4, Rooms 22A/B Extramural). Phase 5. Small rim, neck, and upper shoulder segment. Fairly coarse pink ware, evenly fired. Buff slip out and just over rim in.

Plate 239

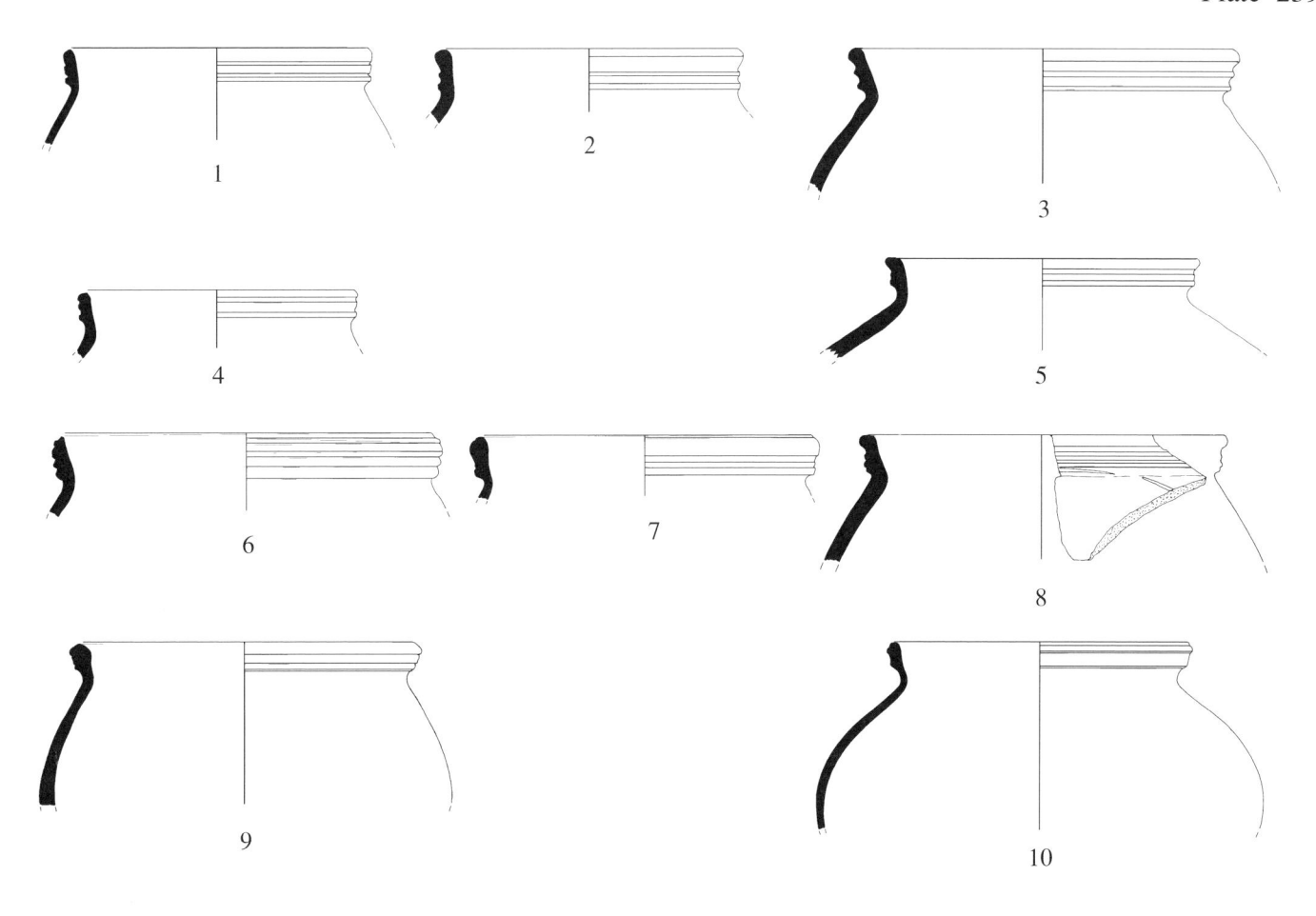

Bronze Age Jar (JR) Types D.VI and D.VII. Scale 1:5

1. JR. D.VI.a (TS. 1274; IIIC, 4.9, Room 19A). Phase 5. About 1/3 rim, neck, and shoulder segment (two non-joining rim fragments). Slightly coarse pinkish-buff ware, fairly evenly fired. Creamy-buff slip in and out.
2. JR. D.VI.b (TS. 1818; IIIG/H, 1.4, Rooms 22A/B Extramural). Phase 5. Small rim, neck, and upper shoulder segment. Slightly coarse pinkish-purple ware, evenly fired. Creamy-buff slip in and out.
3. JR. D.VI.c (TS. 2622; IVO, 1.3, Room 10A). Phase 3. About 1/8 rim, neck, and shoulder segment. Slightly coarse pinkish-orange ware, evenly fired. Creamy slip out and over rim to base of neck in.
4. JR. D.VI.d (TS. 1832; IIIA, 4.2/3, Rooms 8A/8B). Phase 4. About 1/2 rim, neck, and upper shoulder segment (five rim fragments). Fairly fine buff ware, evenly fired. Creamy-green slip in and out.
5. JR. D.VI.e (TS. 512; IB, 1.3). Phase 3, Wall A. About 1/2 rim, neck, and shoulder segment (three rim fragments). Fairly coarse light brownish-buff ware, evenly fired. Cream slip out.
6. JR. D.VII.a (TS. 3552; Op. 7, 19.1, Street). Phase 2A(a). About 1/10 rim, neck, and upper shoulder segment. Fairly fine dark pinkish-buff ware with gold- and silver-colored mica and lime grits, evenly fired. Self slip in and out.
7. JR. D.VII.b (TS. 1840; IIIF, 2.2, Alley). Phase 4. Small rim, neck, and upper shoulder segment. Slightly coarse pinkish-buff ware, evenly fired. Creamy-buff slip in and out.
8. JR. D.VII.c (PM. A.11; TS. 665; IIIG/H, 1a, Room 23). Phase 7A. About 1/5 rim, neck, and shoulder segment (two non-joining rim fragments) with a potter's mark at junction of neck and shoulder. Fairly coarse light brown ware, evenly fired. Creamy-green slip in and out.
9. JR. D.VII.d (TS. 3250; Op. 5, 17.1). Phase 4. Large segment of rim, neck, and shoulder, and 1/2 upper body. Ware description not available
10. JR. D.VII.e (TS. 3841; Op. 5, 11.2). Phase 4. Large segment of rim, shoulder, and 1/2 upper body. Ware description not available.

Plate 240

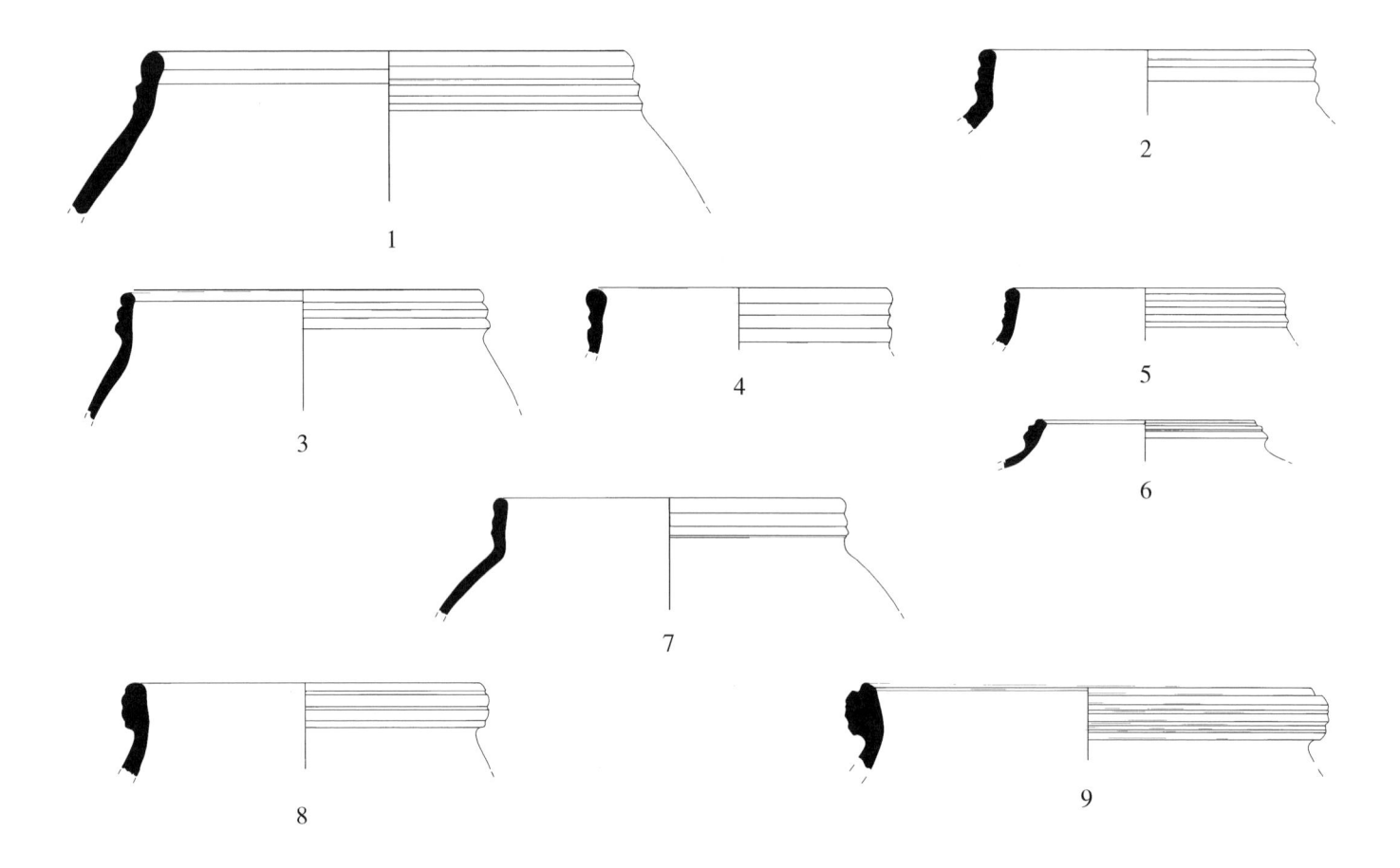

Bronze Age Jar (JR) Types D.VIII, D.IX, and D.X. Scale 1:5

1. JR. D.VIII.a (TS. 1775; IVZ(S), 5.2, 5.3). Phase 3. About 1/2 rim, neck, and shoulder segment (five joining rim fragments). Slightly coarse pinkish-buff ware with some lime and mica grits, evenly fired. Creamy-buff slip in and out.
2. JR. D.VIII.b (TS. 1834; IIIB, 2.2). Phase 5. Small rim, neck, and upper shoulder segment. Slightly coarse light green ware, evenly fired. Self slip in and out.
3. JR. D.VIII.c (TS. 1295; IIIG/H, 1.6, Room 17A). Phase 4. Large rim, neck, and shoulder segment. Fairly coarse pinkish-buff ware, evenly fired. Buff slip in and out.
4. JR. D.VIII.d (TS. 3156; IVZ(N1), 1.5). Phase 2B. Small rim and neck segment. Hard, fairly coarse and gritty grayish-buff ware, evenly fired. Creamy-green slip in and out.
5. JR. D.VIII.e (TS. 1845; IIIC, 4.9, Room 19A). Phase 5. Small rim and neck segment. Slightly coarse pinkish-buff ware, evenly fired. Creamy-buff slip in and out.
6. JR. D.VIII.f (TS. 3308; Op. 7, 4.7, Room 40). Phase 2B(b). About 1/5 rim, neck, and upper shoulder segment. Fine light pinkish-orange ware with gold- and silver-colored mica and lime grits, evenly fired. Cream slip out.
7. JR. D.IX.a (TS. 3469; Op. 6, 18.4, Room 16). Phase 2A. Large rim, neck, and shoulder segment. Ware description not available.
8. JR. D.X.a (TS. 469; IIIB, 2.3, Room 6). Phase 4. Small rim, neck, and upper shoulder segment. Coarse brownish-grayware, unevenly fired a darker shade inside.
9. JR. D.X.b (TS. 1743; IVN, 2.2, Room 8). Phase 2A. Small rim and neck segment. Medium coarse grayware with lime grits, unevenly fired. Pink slip in and out.

Plate 241

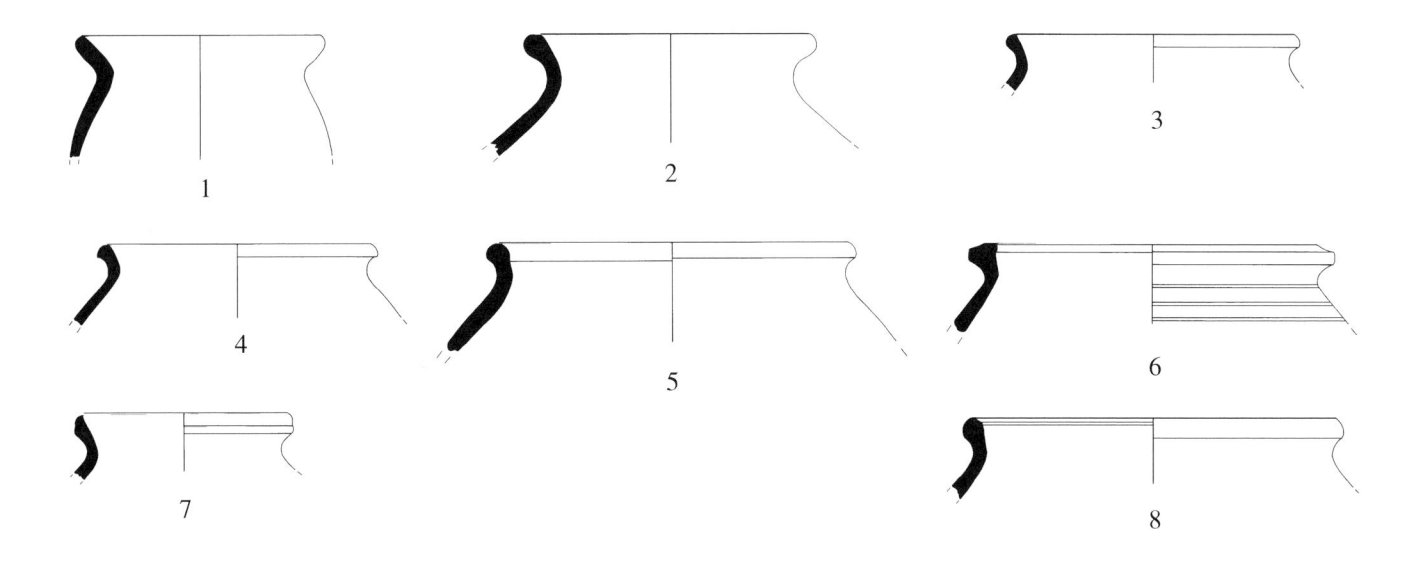

Bronze Age Jar (JR) Type E.I. Scale 1:5

1. JR. E.I.a (TS. 2125; IC, 1.35). Phase 5. Small rim, neck, and shoulder segment. Hard, fairly fine light greenish-buff ware, evenly fired. Self slip in and out.
2. JR. E.I.b (TS. 1374; IIIC, 4.10, Room 9). Phase 4. Large rim, neck, and shoulder segment. Slightly coarse pinkish-buff ware, evenly fired. Buff slip in and out.
3. JR. E.I.c (TS. 2211; IVE, 1.6, Room 2). Phase 2A. Small rim, neck, and upper shoulder segment. Fairly fine buff ware, evenly fired. Creamy-buff slip out.
4. JR. E.I.d (TS. 2262; IIIG/H, 1.3, Room 22A). Phase 5. Small rim, neck, and shoulder segment. Hard, slightly coarse grayish-green ware, evenly fired. Self burnished slip on rim and out.
5. JR. E.I.e (TS. 1656; IVK, 1.3, Room 2A). Phase 3. About 1/8 rim, neck, and shoulder segment. Medium coarse pink ware, evenly fired. Cream slip in and out.
6. JR. E.I.f (TS. 1665; IVL/P, 1.3, Pit). Phase 3. About 1/3 rim, neck, and shoulder segments (two joining fragments with three horizontal wheel-incised lines extant on shoulder. Fairly coarse grayish-buff ware, evenly fired. Cream slip in and out.
7. JR. E.I.g (TS. 2777; IVE, 1.6, Room 2). Phase 2A. About 1/8 rim, neck, and upper shoulder segment. Hard, fine pinkish-brown ware, evenly fired. Self slip, burnished in and out.
8. JR. E.I.h (TS. 2403; IVG, 1.2, Room 3B). Phase 4. About 1/10 rim, neck, and shoulder segment. Hard, fine creamy-green ware, evenly fired. Self slip in and out.

Plate 242. Bronze Age Jar (JR) Types E.II.a to E.II.h

1. JR. E.II.a (SW. 595; IVJ, 1.3, 1.4, Room 4A). Phase 3. Mended to completion. Fairly coarse buff ware, evenly fired. Cream slip out.
2. JR. E.II.b (TS. 2571; IVO, 1.4, Room 10). Phase 2B. Nearly complete profile with drainage hole manufactured in the center of the round base. Fairly fine greenish-buff ware, evenly fired. Self slip in and out.
3. JR. E.II.c (TS. 740; IC, 1.43, Ashy layer). Phase 4. About 1/8 rim, neck, and shoulder segment. Fairly fine pinkish-buff ware, evenly fired. Buff slip in and out.
4. JR. E.II.d (TS. 2845; IVN, 1.4, Rooms 8A/18A). Phase 3. About 1/8 rim, neck, and shoulder segment heavily burned. Slightly coarse grayish-brown ware, unevenly fired. Self slip in and out. Diagonally tool-scored lines on inner wall below the neck.
5. JR. E.II.e (TS. 719; IIIL, 1.2, Walls 1, 2). Phase 5. Small rim and neck segment. Fairly fine pinkish-buff ware, unevenly fired with buff core. Light cream slip out.
6. JR. E.II.f (TS. 2650; IVJ Bin, 3.5, Room 5). Phase 2A. About 1/6 rim, neck, and shoulder segment. Slightly coarse creamy-green ware, unevenly fired with buff patches. Creamy-green slip out.
7. JR. E.II.g (TS. 1731; IVM, 10.4, Below Room 7). Phase 1A. About 1/2 rim, neck, and shoulder segment with deep-ribbed upper wall. Fairly fine pinkish-red ware with lime grits, evenly fired. Buff slip out and just below rim in.
8. JR. E.II.h (TS. 1078; IC, 1.42, Destruction level). Phase 4. About 1/20 rim, neck, and shoulder segment. Fairly coarse pink ware, evenly fired. Cream slip out.

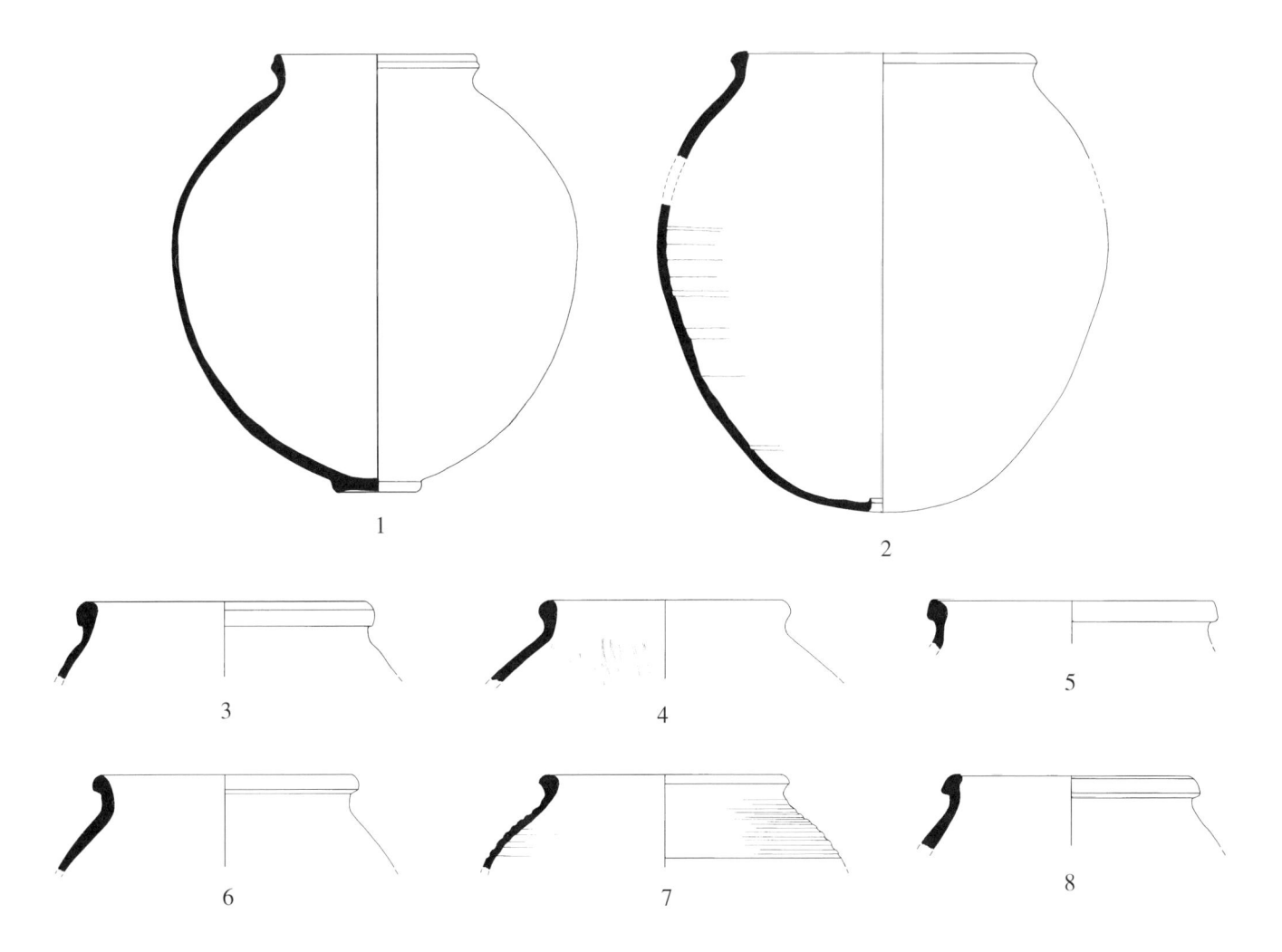

Plate 242

Bronze Age Jar (JR) Types E.II.a to E.II.h:. Scale 1:5

Plate 243. Bronze Age Jar (JR) Types E.II.i to E.II.z

1. JR. E.II.i (TS. 752; IE, 1.40 = IC, 1.40). Phase 4. About 1/8 rim, neck, and shoulder segment. Fairly coarse dark greenish-buff ware, evenly fired. Self slip in and out.
2. JR. E.II.j (TS. 2789; IVO, 1.3 + 1.4, Fill + Room 10). Phases 3, 2B. About 1/2 rim, neck, and shoulder segment. Fairly coarse pink ware, evenly fired. Self slip out.
3. JR. E.II.k (TS. 1696; IVJ, 1.6, Room 4). Phase 2A. Small rim, neck, and upper shoulder segment. Medium-fine buff ware, evenly fired. Cream slip in and out. Horizontal linear incisions scored into the clay below the inside lip of the rim and on top of the rim with a sharp fine combing tool at the leather-hard stage of manufacture.
4. JR. E.II.l (TS. 1587 = TS. 1671; IVJ, 1.3, 1.4 + IVK, 2.3, Rooms 4B and 2A). Phases 4, 3. Rim mended to completion with about 1/3 of neck and shoulder. Medium coarse grayish ware with mica grits, evenly fired. Cream slip in and out.
5. JR. E.II.m (TS. 2755; IVP, 1.3, Room 9B). Phase 4. About 1/3 rim, neck, and upper shoulder segment. Fairly coarse pinkish ware, evenly fired. Creamy-green slip in and out.
6. JR. E.II.n (TS. 3576; Op. 7, 20.1, Room 36). Phase 2A(a). Small rim, neck, and upper wall segment. Fairly coarse pinkish-buff ware with fine gold- and silver-colored mica and lime grits, evenly fired. Creamy-green slip out and over rim in.
7. JR. E.II.o (TS. 2682; IVZ(S), 5.7). Phase 2A. About 1/6 rim, neck, and shoulder segment. Fairly coarse salmon-pink colored ware, evenly fired. Creamy-yellow slip out.
8. JR. E.II.p (TS. 3885; Op. 5, 17.1). Phase 4. Small rim, neck, and upper shoulder segment. Ware description unavailable.
9. JR. E.II.q (TS. 2000; IIA, 9.7, Room 3). Phase 1. Small rim, neck, and upper shoulder segment. Close pink ware, fairly evenly fired. Pinkish-buff slip out and over rim in.
10. JR. E.II.r (SW. 524; IVJ, 2.1, Room 4). Phase 2A (see also pls. 32a and 92c). Mended to completion with a drainage hole manufactured in the center of the round base. Fairly coarse pink ware, evenly fired. Horizontally reserved bands of cream slip in and out.
11. JR. E.II.s (TS. 3616; Op. 5, 17.3, Pit). Phase 4. Large rim (diam. 32 cm) and neck segment with most of wall profile. Ware description unavailable.
12. JR. E.II.t (TS. 3852; Op. 5, 17.3, Pit). Phase 4. About 1/6 rim (diam. 26 cm) and upper body segment. Slightly coarse pink ware with very few small lime and white mica grits, evenly fired. Cream slip out.
13. JR. E.II.u (TS. 3316; Op. 8, 1.1, Room 29A). Phase 4. About 1/6 rim, neck, and upper shoulder segment. Slightly coarse pinkish-orange ware with very few small lime grits and a few small gold-colored mica grits, evenly fired. Creamy-buff slip out and on rim.
14. JR. E.II.v (TS. 2381; VC, 2.1). Phase 3. About 1/3 rim, neck, and shoulder segment. Slightly coarse pinkish-rose ware with lime grits, evenly fired. Creamy-green slip out.
15. JR. E.II.w (TS. 2291; IVD, 2.5, Room 2). Phase 2B. About 1/8 rim and neck segment. Slightly coarse buff ware, evenly fired. Self slip in and out.
16. JR. E.II.x (TS. 2762; IVO, 1.3, Room 10A + IVR, 1.2). Phases 3, 5. About 1/3 rim and neck segment from IVR with one non-joining and mis-shapened, overfired, fragment from IVO. Coarse ware, unevenly fired with gray core and buff at surface out. Creamy-green slip out.
17. JR. E.II.y (TS. 2676 = TS. 2735; IVY, 1.3 + IVS, 4.2, Room 12A). Phase 3. About 1/3 rim (manufactured with an oval shape from the top view), neck, and upper shoulder segment. Hard, fine pinkish-buff ware, evenly fired. Creamy-buff slip in and out.
18. JR. E.II.z (TS. 2675; IVP, 1.4, Room 9A). Phase 3. About 1/2 rim, neck, and shoulder segment. Hard, fine pink ware, evenly fired. Yellow-buff slip in and out.

Plate 243

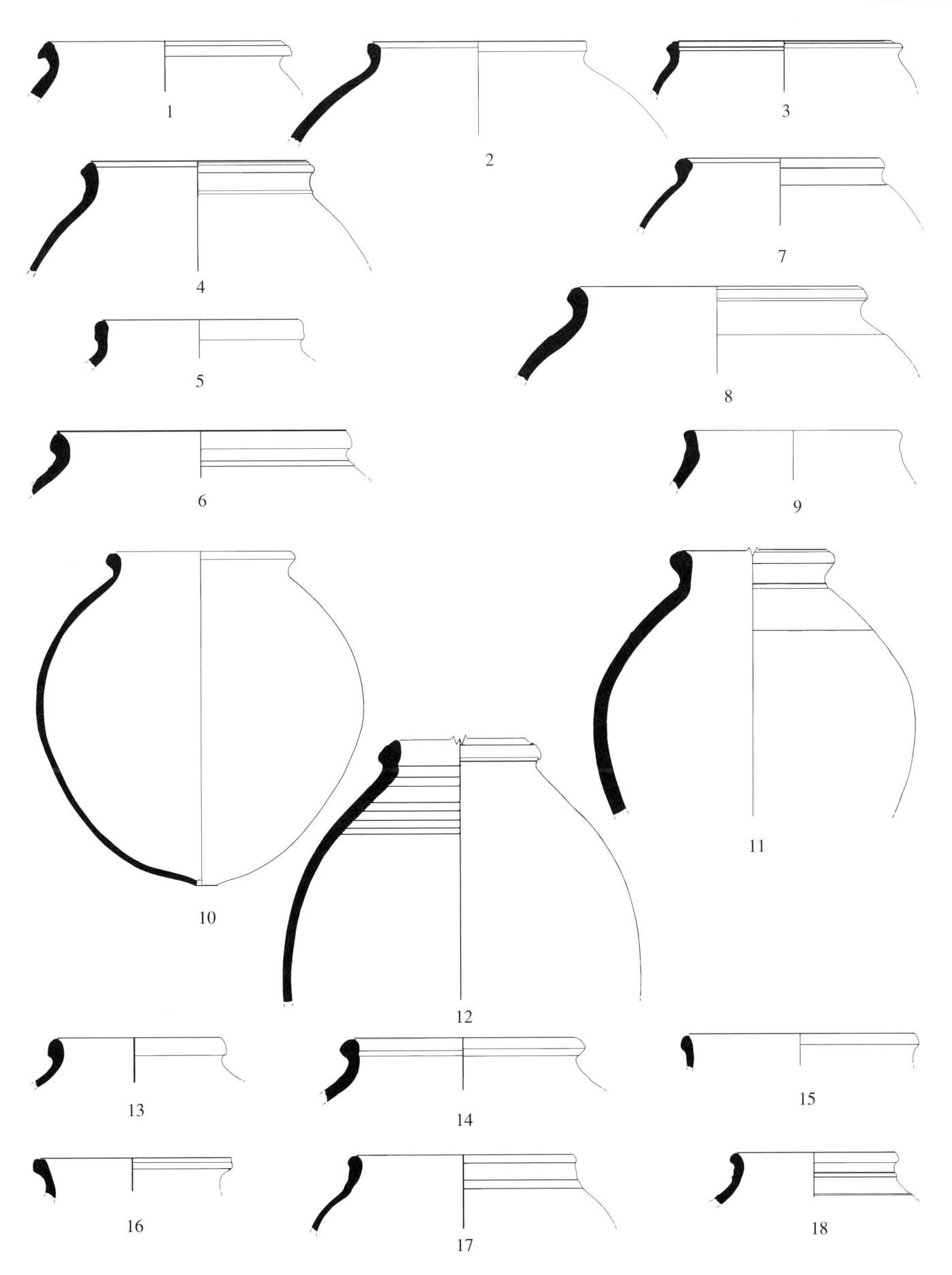

Bronze Age Jar (JR) Types E.II.i to E.II.z. Scale 1:5

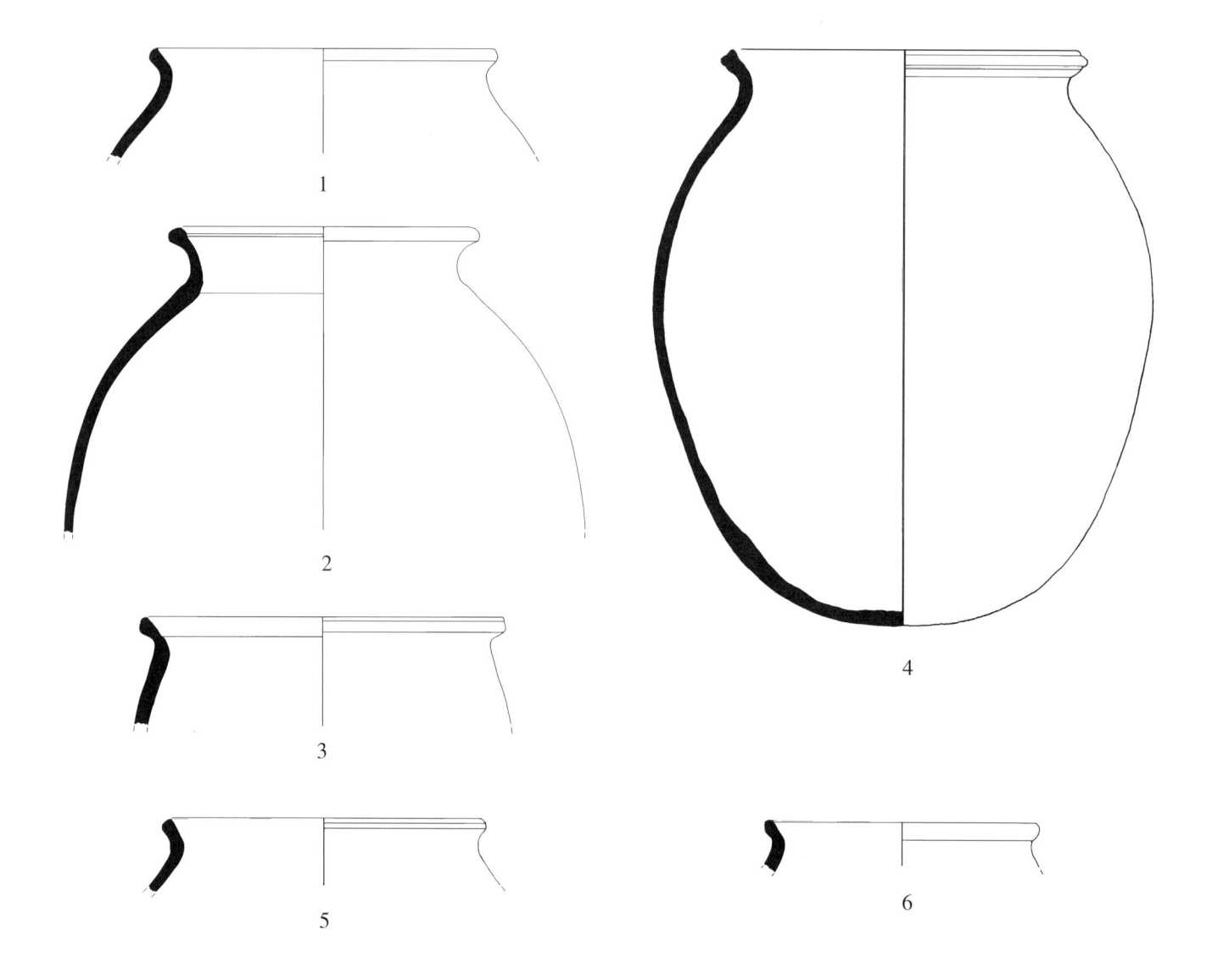

Plate 244

Bronze Age Jar (JR) Type F.I. Scale 1:5

1. JR. F.I.a (TS. 774; IC, 1.43, Ashy layer). Phase 4. About 1/40 rim and shoulder segment. Fairly coarse pinkish-buff ware, evenly fired.
2. JR. F.I.b (TS. 2774; IVM, 10.4, Below Room 7). Phase 1A. About 1/8 rim and neck segment and 1/2 wall profile. Fairly fine ware, unevenly fired with thin pinkish core and yellow-brown at surfaces. Thin cream slip out and on top of rim.
3. JR. F.I.c (TS. 801; IC, 1.48). Phase 3. About 1/16 rim and upper wall segment. Fairly coarse buff ware, evenly fired. Light cream slip out.
4. JR. F.I.d (TS. 3390; Op. 5, 32.5). Phase 2. Nearly complete in situ. Slightly coarse ware with black lime and gold- and silver-colored mica grits, unevenly fired with purplish-gray core and pinkish-brown at surfaces. Creamy-brown slip in and out.
5. JR. F.I.e (TS. 2654; IVF, 1.14, Room 1). Phase 2B. About 1/10 rim and upper wall segment. Light, fairly coarse buff ware, evenly fired. Creamy-green slip out and over rim in.
6. JR. F.I.f (TS. 1585; IIA, 9.2, Pit E). Phase 5. Small rim and upper wall segment. Fairly fine grayish-buff ware with lime and mica grits, evenly fired. Creamy-buff slip out.

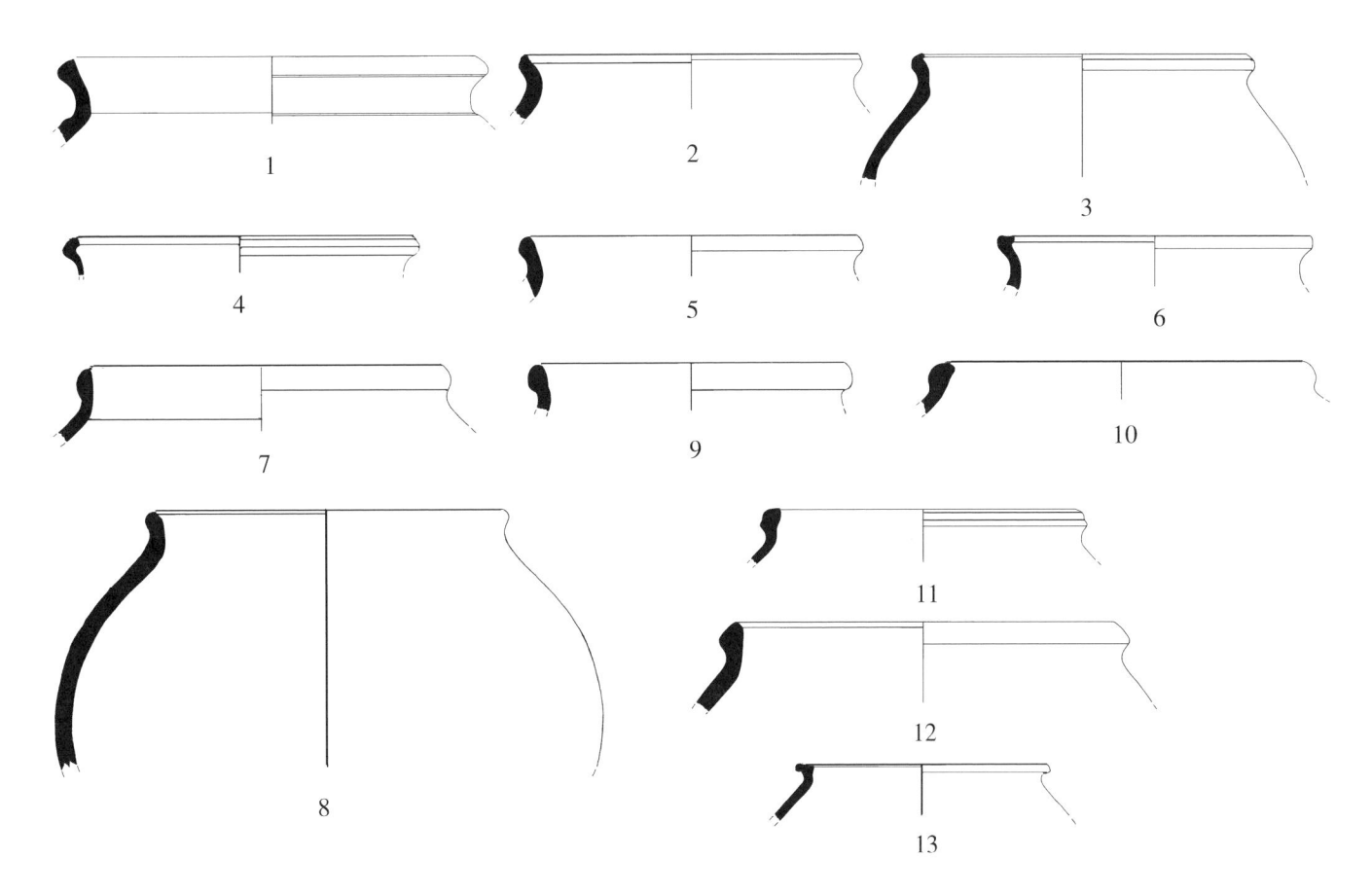

Bronze Age Jar (JR) Type F.II and F.III. Scale 1:5

1. JR. F.II.a (TS. 2734; IVZ(N1), 1.1). Phase 5. About 1/10 rim, neck, and shoulder segment. Hard, fine light pink ware, evenly fired. Creamy slip in and out.
2. JR. F.II.b (TS. 2538; IVF, 1.5, Room 1A). Phase 3. About 1/12 rim, neck, and shoulder segment. Hard, fine flesh-pink colored ware, evenly fired. Creamy-buff slip in and out.
3. JR. F.II.c (TS. 1093; IIIA + C, unstratified). Small rim, neck, and shoulder segments. Fairly coarse pink ware, evenly fired. Cream slip in and out.
4. JR. F.II.d (TS. 1933; IVD, 2.5, Room 2). Phase 2B. Small rim and neck segment. Slightly coarse grayish-buff ware, evenly fired. Self slip in and out.
5. JR. F.II.e (TS. 1555; IIA, 9.9, Room 1). Phase 1. Small rim and neck segment. Fairly fine ware with lime and mica grits, unevenly fired with buff core and pink at surfaces. Creamy-buff slip in and out.
6. JR. F.II.f (TS. 2236; IVG, 1.5, Room 3). Phase 2A. Small rim and neck segment. Fairly fine pink ware, evenly fired. Creamy-buff slip out and on top of rim.
7. JR. F.III.a (TS. 798; IC, 1.48). Phase 3. About 1/4 rim, neck, and shoulder segment (two joining fragments). Fairly fine buff ware, evenly fired. Light cream slip in and out.
8. JR. F.III.b (SW. 305; IIA, 9.8, Room 4). Phase 2. About 1/4 rim and neck segment and 1/2 wall profile. Hard pinkish-orange ware with lime grits, evenly fired. Creamy-buff slip in and out. Inside vertically wet-smoothed up to the neck.
9. JR. F.III.c (TS. 3438; Op. 11, 4.1, Room 20). Phase 2B. Small rim and neck segment. Fairly fine light pinkish-buff ware with gold-colored mica and a few small white lime grits, evenly fired. Self slip in and out.
10. JR. F.III.d (TS. 2998; IVJ, 1.8, Below Room 4). Phase 1C. Small rim and neck segment. Fairly fine creamy-grayish/green ware, evenly fired. Self slip in and out.
11. JR. F.III.e (TS. 2995; IVN, 1.4, Room 8A/18A). Phase 3. About 1/6 rim, neck, and upper shoulder segment. Fairly fine creamy-green ware, evenly fired. Self slip in and out.
12. JR. F.III.f (TS. 724; IIIJ, 1.2, West of Wall 1). Phase 4. Small rim, neck, and upper shoulder segment. Fairly fine pink ware, unevenly fired with lighter colored core. Buff slip out.
13. JR. F.III.g (TS. 3503 = TS. 4166; Op. 7, 18.1, Room 34 and Op. 7, 13.1, Extramural). Phase 2A(a). About 1/4 rim, neck, and shoulder segment (two joining fragments). Fairly fine dark greenish-buff ware with small gold- and silver-colored mica and lime grits, evenly fired. Self slip in and out.

Plate 246. Bronze Age Jar (JR) Types G.I, G.II, and G.III

1. JR. G.I.a (TS. 1159; VE, 1.4, Pit, bottom). Phase 3. Large rim, neck, and upper shoulder segment. Fairly fine pink ware, evenly fired.
2. JR. G.I.b (TS. 770; IC, 1.42). Phase 4. Large rim, neck, and upper shoulder segment. Fairly fine pink ware, evenly fired. Light cream slip out.
3. JR. G.I.c (TS. 1730; IVN, 2.2, Room 8). Phase 2A. Small rim, neck and upper shoulder segment. Medium-fine pinkish-buff ware, evenly fired. Cream slip in and out.
4. JR. G.II.a (TS. 4040; Op. 5, 32.1). Phase 2. Small rim, neck, and upper shoulder segment. Ware description unavailable.
5. JR. G.II.b (TS. 3187; Op. 5, 32.1). Phase 2. Large rim, neck, and upper shoulder segment. Ware description unavailable.
6. JR. G.II.c (TS. 91; IIA, 8.2, Courtyard). Phase 8. Large rim, neck, and shoulder segment. Hard, fine pink ware with lime and gold-colored mica grits, evenly fired. Yellow-buff slip out. Body of vessel smoothed by hand at the leather-hard stage of manufacture, vertically outside and diagonally inside.
7. JR. G.III.a (PM. C.8; TS. 14; IIA, 7.2, Pit). Phase 10. About 1/8 rim, neck, and upper shoulder segment with one extant potter's mark incised on the shoulder before firing. Fine, hard fired, pinkish-buff ware with lime and mica grits, evenly fired. Self slip out.

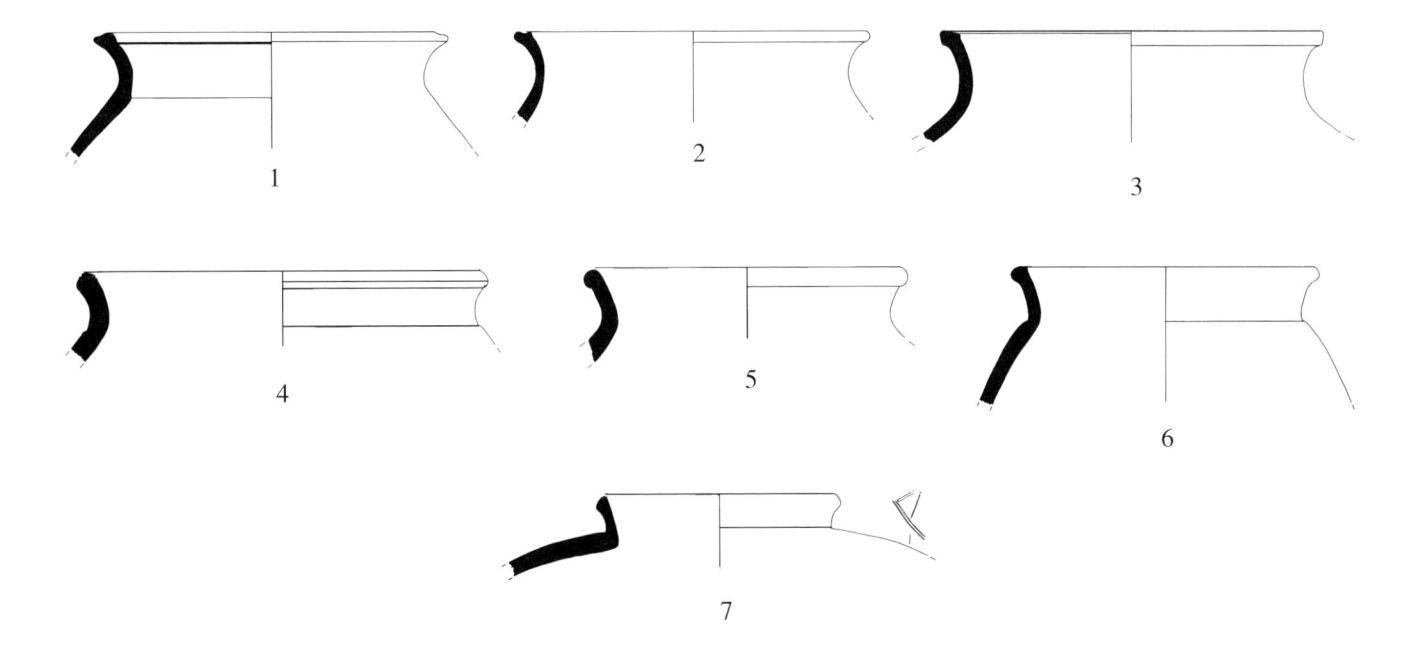

Plate 246

Bronze Age Jar (JR) Types G.I, G.II, and G.III. Scale 1:5

Plate 247. Bronze Age Jar (JR) Type H.I

1. JR. H.I.a (TS. 2906; IVK, 1.2, Room 2B). Phase 4. Small rim and upper shoulder segment. Fairly fine pink ware, evenly fired. Cream slip in and out.
2. JR. H.I.b (TS. 2242; IC, 1.40). Phase 4. Small rim and upper shoulder segment. Slightly coarse pinkish-red ware, evenly fired. Creamy-pink slip out.
3. JR. H.I.c (TS. 1939; IVF, 1.5, Room 1A). Phase 3. Small rim and upper shoulder segment. Slightly coarse buff ware, evenly fired. Creamy-buff slip out and over rim in.
4. JR. H.I.d (TS. 2900; IVN, 2.1, Room 8). Phase 2B. Small rim and upper shoulder segment. Fairly fine pinkish-buff ware, evenly fired. Cream slip in and out.
5. JR. H.I.e (SW. 728; IVM, 1.6 + IVX, 2.6, Room 7). Phase 2A. Mended to near completion. Slightly coarse pinkish-buff ware with many lime grits, evenly fired. Creamy-buff slip out.
6. JR. H.I.f (TS. 3515; Op. 7, 18.1, Room 34). Phase 2A(a). About 1/8 rim and upper shoulder segment. Slightly coarse buff ware with fine gold- and silver-colored mica and lime grits, evenly fired. Self slip in and out.
7. JR. H.I.g (PM. A.20; SW. 642; IVO, 1.4, Room 10). Phase 2B. About 1/8 rim and shoulder segment with one extant ledge handle on shoulder and another rim segment with the remains of a potter's mark incised outside before firing. Fairly coarse grayware, evenly fired. Green slip in and out.
8. JR. H.I.h (TS. 1961; IVH, 1.3, Room 3). Phase 2B. Small rim and shoulder segment. Slightly coarse buff ware, evenly fired. Self slip out.
9. JR. H.I.i (TS. 2815; IVM, 10.1, Below Room 7). Phase 1C. Small rim and shoulder segment. Hard, fine pink ware, evenly fired. Creamy-pink slip out and on top of rim.
10. JR. H.I.j (TS. 3959; Op. 5, 18.5). Phase 4. Small rim and upper shoulder segment. Ware description unavailable.
11. JR. H.I.k (TS. 3734; Op. 5, 14.5). Phase 4. Small rim and upper wall segment. Ware description unavailable.
12. JR. H.I.l (PM. E.2; TS. 3356; Op. 10, 22.1). Phase 3. Large rim and upper wall segment with a potter's mark incised outside before firing. Ware description unavailable.
13. JR. H.I.m (TS. 1593; IVJ, 1.6, Room 4). Phase 2A. Small rim and upper shoulder segment. Coarse grayish ware, evenly fired. Very worn slip, color indeterminate, in and out.
14. JR. H.I.n (IP [G.4] F.III.a; TS. 2556; IVX, 10.7 = IVM, Room 7). Phase 2A. About 1/5 segment of four joining rim and upper wall fragments with remains of animal drawings incised on the outside wall before firing (compare Jar JR. H.III.h, pl. 249:8). Slightly coarse pink ware, evenly fired. Creamy-buff slip out.

Plate 247

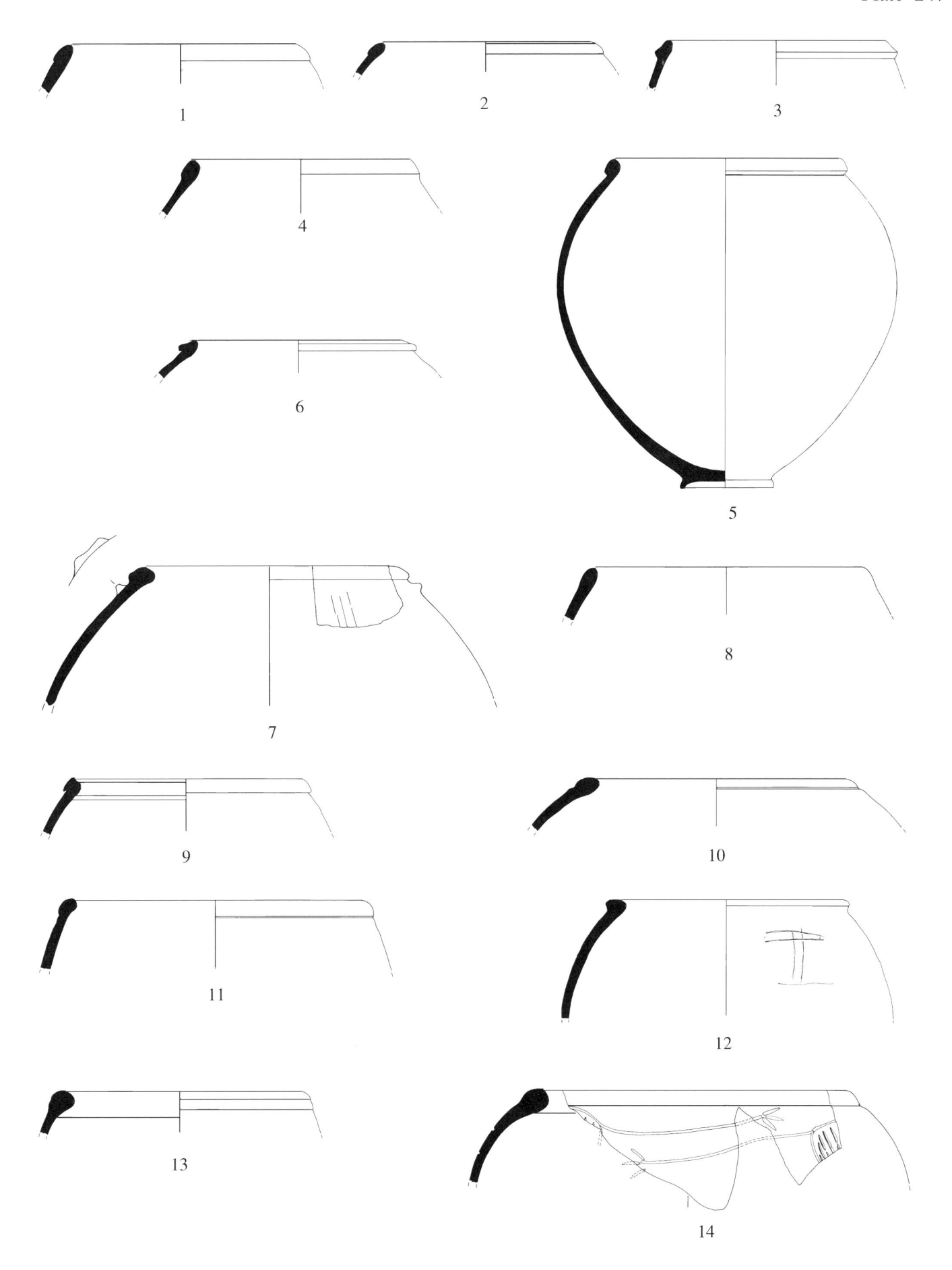

Bronze Age Jar (JR) Type H.I. Scale 1:5

Plate 248

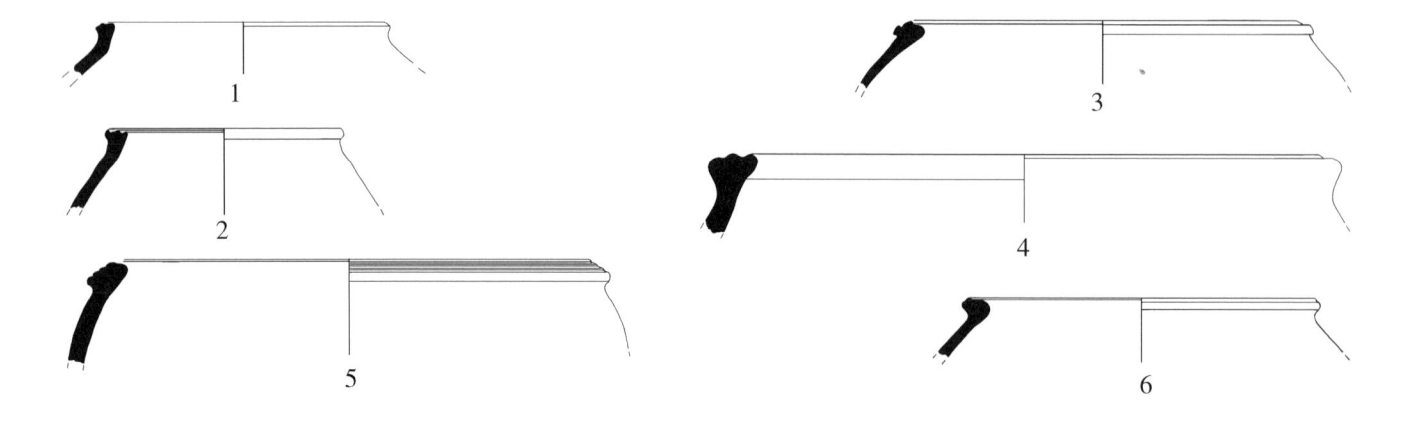

Bronze Age Jar (JR) Type H.II. Scale 1:5

1. JR. H.II.a (TS. 1764; IVL, 1.3, Room 3A). Phase 3. Small rim, neck, and upper shoulder segment. Slightly coarse buff ware, evenly fired. Cream slip in and out.
2. JR. H.II.b (TS. 759; IC, 1.39, Destruction level). Phase 5. About 1/12 rim, neck, and shoulder segment. Fairly coarse creamy-buff ware, evenly fired. Self slip out.
3. JR. H.II.c (TS. 3551; Op. 7, 19.1, Street). Phase 2A(a). About 1/12 rim and shoulder segment. Hard, fine light pink ware with very fine gold- and silver-colored mica and lime grits, evenly fired. Cream slip in and out.
4. JR. H.II.d (TS. 2763; IVP, 1.2, Room 9B). Phase 4. Small rim and neck segment. Fairly coarse grayish-buff ware, evenly fired. Creamy-green slip in and out.
5. JR. H.II.e (TS. 3347; Op. 5, 14.3, Wall). Phase 4. Large rim and upper shoulder segment. Ware description unavailable.
6. JR. H.II.f (TS. 1598; IVJ, 1.6, Room 4). Phase 2A. Small rim and upper shoulder segment. Medium-fine pink ware, evenly fired. Pinkish-buff slip in and out.

Plate 249

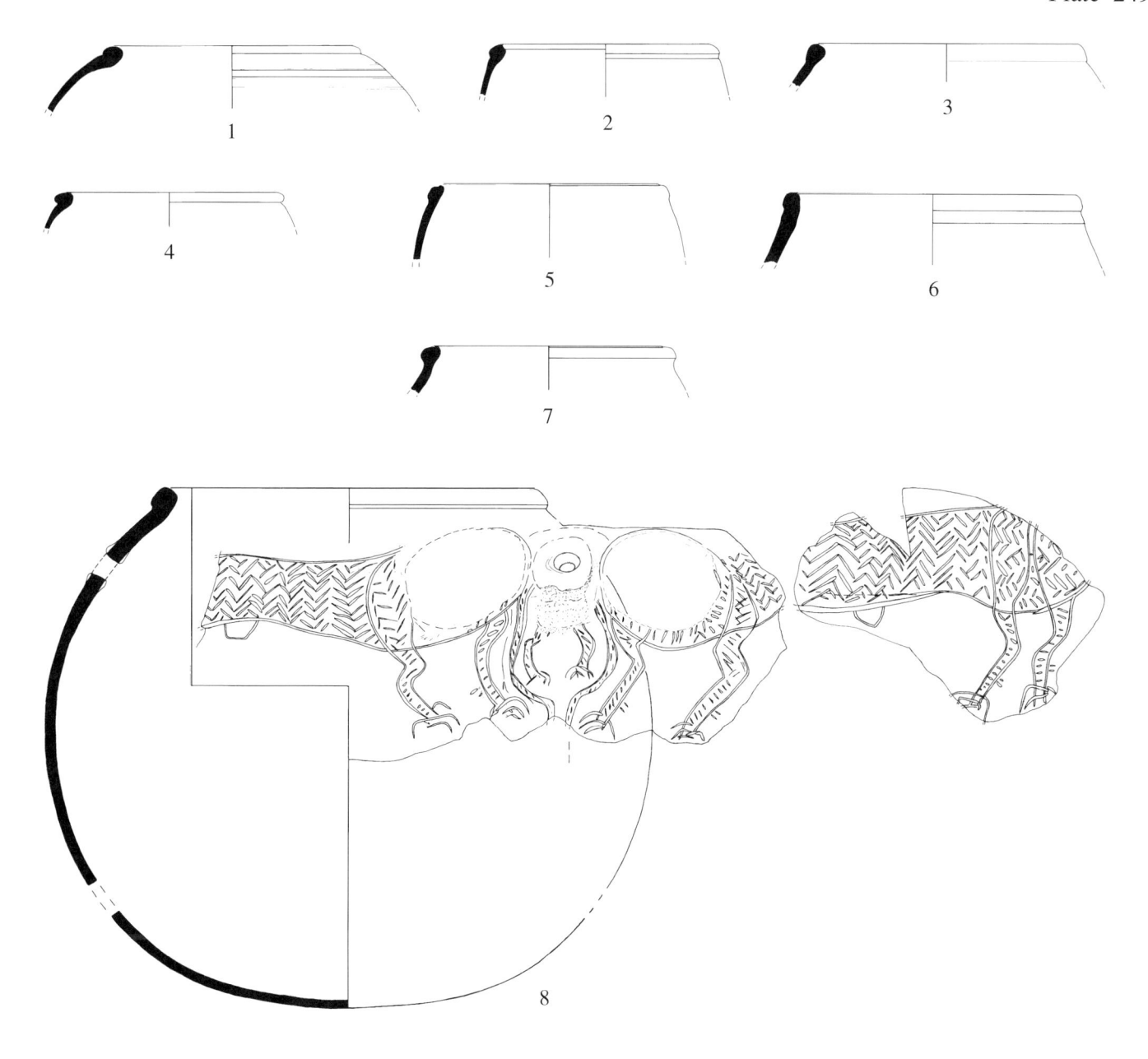

Bronze Age Jar (JR) Type H.III.a to H.III.h. Scale 1:5

1. JR. H.III.a (TS. 3262; Op. 5, 18.5). Phase 4. Large rim and shoulder segment. Ware description unavailable.
2. JR. H.III.b (TS. 2239; IC, 1.32A, Pit A). Phase 7. Small rim and shoulder segment. Fairly coarse gritty buff-brown ware, evenly fired. Creamy-buff slip in and out.
3. JR. H.III.c (TS. 2816; IVM, 10.1, Below Room 7). Phase 1C. About 1/10 rim and upper shoulder segment. Hard, fine buff ware, evenly fired. Creamy-buff slip in and out.
4. JR. H.III.d (TS. 992; IIIG/H, 1.4, Rooms 22A/B Extramural). Phase 5. Small rim and upper shoulder segment. Hard, fine ware, unevenly fired with black core and green at surfaces. Light green slip out.
5. JR. H.III.e (TS. 3509; Op. 7, 18.1, Room 34). Phase 2A(a). About 1/4 rim (two joining fragments) and upper wall segments. Fairly coarse pinkish-brown ware with many small gold- and silver-colored mica and lime grits, evenly fired. Creamy-buff slip in and out.
6. JR. H.III.f (TS. 734; IC, 1.43, Ashy layer). Phase 4. About 1/12 rim and shoulder segment. Fairly coarse pinkish-buff ware, evenly fired, Cream slip out and applied thinly in.
7. JR. H.III.g (TS. 2651; IVM, 1.4, Room 7). Phase 2B. About 1/8 rim and shoulder segment. Slightly coarse creamy-green ware, evenly fired. Self slip in and out.
8. JR. H.III.h (IP [G.4] F.III.a; TS. 3295; Op. 6, 1.32, 1.37, 1.38, Room 9). Phase 2A. Mended to near completion. Spouted vessel with incised remains of an eagle below spout and mythical "lion-like" figures on each side of the spout with appliqué heads broken off. The animal and bird bodies were incised before firing. Slightly coarse pinkish-orange ware with lime and mica grits, evenly fired. Self slip in and out. Heavily burned on inside surface.

Plate 250. Bronze Age Jar (JR) Type H.III.i to H.III.z

1. JR. H.III.i (TS. 2243; IC, 1.43, Ashy layer). Phase 4. Small rim and shoulder segment. Fairly coarse gritty pink ware, evenly fired. Self slip irregularly burnished in and out.
2. JR. H.III.j (TS. 1716; IVM, 1.4, Room 7). Phase 2B. About 1/8 rim, neck, and upper shoulder segment. Medium-fine pinkish-buff ware, evenly fired. Self slip in and out with irregular horizontal burnish strokes below neck out and traces on rim inside.
3. JR. H.III.k (TS. 2790; IVO, 1.3 + 1.4, Rooms 10, 10A). Phase 2B. About 1/2 rim and upper wall segment consisting of six fragments. Slightly coarse grayish-buff ware, fairly evenly fired. Creamy-green slip out.
4. JR. H.III.l (TS. 3642; Op. 5, 17.1). Phase 4. Small rim and upper shoulder segment. Ware description unavailable.
5. JR. H.III.m (TS. 3553; Op. 7, 19.1, Street). Phase 2A(a). About 1/8 rim and shoulder segment. Fairly fine pinkish-brown ware with gold- and silver-colored mica and lime grits, evenly fired. Creamy-pink slip out.
6. JR. H.III.n (TS. 314; IIA, 8.17, Room 12). Phase 6. Small rim and shoulder segment. Light brown ware, evenly fired. Creamy-buff slip out.
7. JR. H.III.o (TS. 2504; XA, 1.4, Room 15). Phase 2A. About 1/10 rim segment. Hard, flesh-pink colored ware, evenly fired. Self slip in and out.
8. JR. H.III.p (TS. 3624; Op. 5, 17.3, Pit). Phase 4. Small rim and upper shoulder segment with remains of a spout hole on the shoulder. Ware description unavailable.
9. JR. H.III.q (TS. 3716; Op. 5, 17.4). Phase 4. Large rim and shoulder segment. Ware description unavailable.
10. JR. H.III.r (TS. 124; IIA, 8.5, Room 7). Phase 4. Small rim and upper shoulder segment. Slightly coarse light brown ware with lime and mica grits, evenly fired. Dark buff slip in and out.
11. JR. H.III.s (TS. 3535; Op. 7, 18.4, Room 34). Phase 2A(a). Small rim and shoulder segment. Slightly coarse ware with small gold- and silver-colored mica and many lime grits, unevenly fired pinkish-brown out, pinkish-orange in. Creamy-brown slip out.
12. JR. H.III.t (TS. 2738; IVN, 2.3, Room 18). Phase 2A. About 1/10 rim and shoulder segment with remains of a spout hole on the shoulder. Slightly coarse buff ware evenly fired. Self slip in and out.
13. JR. H.III.u (TS. 2740; IVS, 4.10, Room 12). Phase 2A. About 1/8 rim and shoulder segment. Fairly fine pink ware, evenly fired. Cream slip out.
14. JR. H.III.v (TS. 3261; Op. 5, 18.5). Phase 4. About 1/6 rim and upper wall segment with remains of a small horizontal ledge handle below the rim. Ware description unavailable.
15. JR. H.III.w (TS. 3350 = TS. 3983; Op. 5, 13.7). Phase 4. Small rim and upper wall segments with remains of a knob-like handle or decoration on the upper part of the shoulder. Ware description unavailable.
16. JR. H.III.x (TS. 3243; Op. 5, 13.3). Phase 4. About 1/5 rim and upper wall segment with remains of a horizontal ledge handle on the shoulder. Ware description unavailable.
17. JR. H.III.y (TS. 3560; Op. 7, 19.1, Street). Phase 2A(a). Small rim and upper wall segment. Fairly fine pinkish-buff ware with gold-colored mica and lime grits, evenly fired. Creamy-buff slip in and out.
18. JR. H.III.z (TS. 3574; Op. 7, 20.1, Room 36). Phase 2A(a). About 1/8 rim and upper wall segment. Slightly coarse pinkish-orange ware with fine gold- and silver-colored mica and lime grits, evenly fired. Cream slip out.

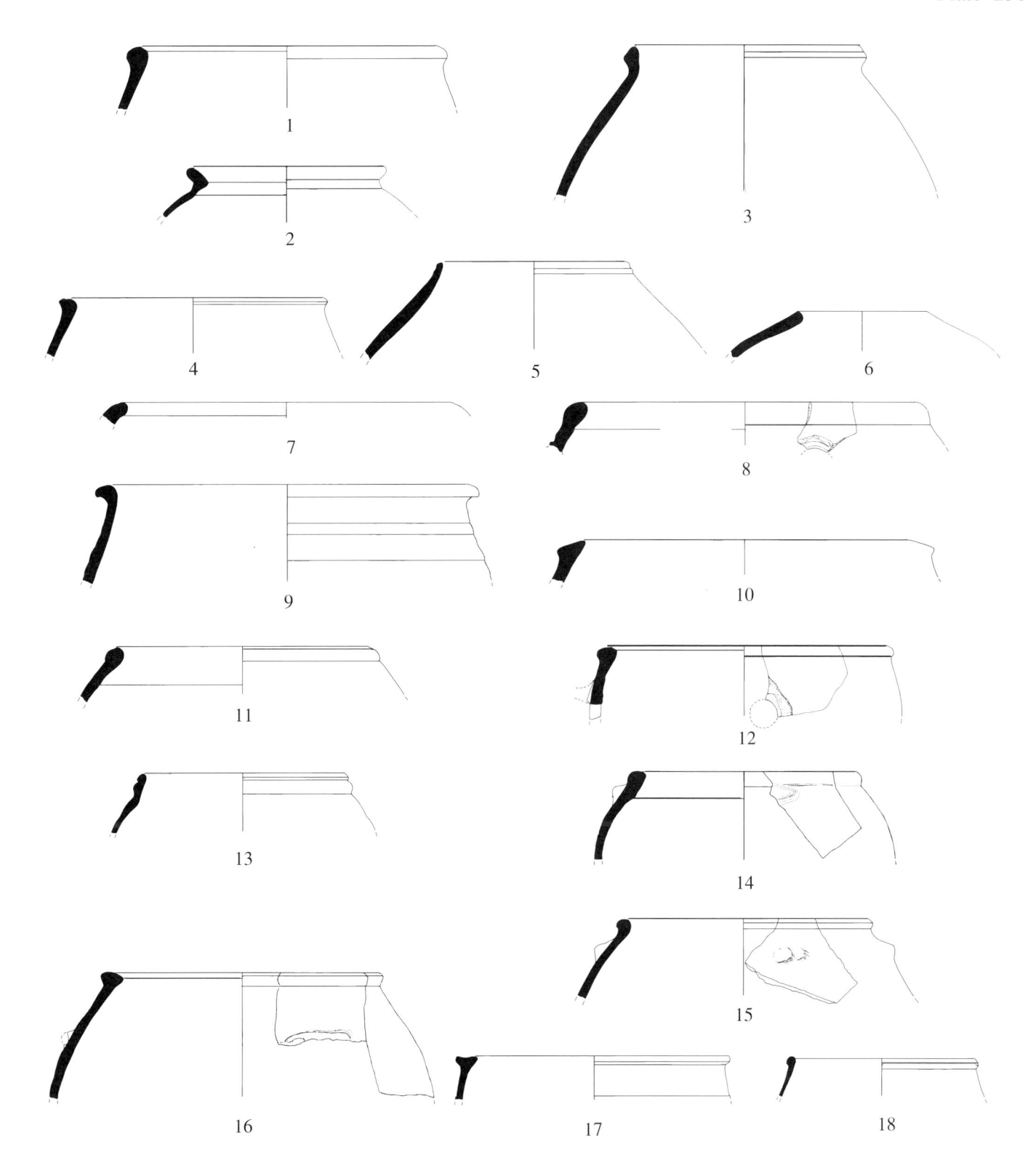

Plate 250

Bronze Age Jar (JR) Type H.III.i to H.III.z. Plate 1:5

Plate 251. Bronze Age Jar (JR) Type J.I

1. JR. J.I.a (TS. 2265; XA, 1.2, Room 15A). Phase 3. About 1/3 segment of two joining rim and shoulder fragments. Fairly fine pinkish-buff ware, evenly fired. Creamy-buff slip out and over rim in.
2. JR. J.I.b (TS. 2661; IVM, 1.4 + 100.13, Room 7). Phase 2A. About 1/4 segment of two joining rim and neck fragments. Slightly coarse buff ware, evenly fired. Self slip in and out.
3. JR. J.I.c (SW. 682; IVO, 1.4, Room 10). Phase 2A. Mended to near completion. Medium pink ware, evenly fired. Cream slip in and out with horizontal creamy-white slip lines in reserve on outside body.
4. JR. J.I.d (PM. B.8; SW. 295; IVD, 2.4, 2.5 + IVE, 1.6, Room 2). Phases 2B, 2A. Mended to near completion with a potter's mark incised on the shoulder before firing. Fairly fine pinkish-brown ware with lime and mica grits, evenly fired. Burnished smooth self slip out. Inside base and wall to shoulder diagonally wet-smoothed before firing.
5. JR. J.I.e (PM. D.27; SW. 292; IVD, 2.5, Room 2). Phase 2B (see also pl. 94). Mended to near completion, with potter's mark incised on the shoulder before firing. Fairly coarse grayish-buff ware with lime grits, evenly fired. Creamy-buff slip out, slightly ribbed on neck and upper shoulder due to turning of the vessel on a potter's wheel.
6. JR. J.I.f (TS. 1626; IVO, 1.4, Room 10). Phase 2A. About 2/3 rim, neck, and shoulder segment. Fairly hard, burnished, buff ware, unevenly fired. Traces of burning in and out.
7. JR. J.I.g (TS. 311; IIA, 8.18, Pit E). Phase 5. Small rim and neck segment. Buff ware, evenly fired.
8. JR. J.I.h (PM. D.10; SW. 733; IVE, 3.2 + IVG, 1.5 + IVL, 1.4, 1.5, Room 3). Phase 2A (see also pl. 95a). Mended to near completion with two potter's marks on opposite sides of the shoulder, one complete mark incised before firing and the incomplete mark painted red after firing. Fairly fine ware with lime and mica grits, unevenly fired with light gray core and light pinkish-brown at surfaces. Smooth self slip out and over rim to base of neck in.
9. JR. J.I.i (TS. 2295; IIIB, 2.3, Room 6). Phase 4. About 1/3 rim, neck, and shoulder segment. Fairly coarse yellow-buff ware, evenly fired. Self slip in and out.
10. JR. J.I.j (TS. 3958; Op. 5, 32.1). Phase 2. Small rim and neck segment. Ware description unavailable.
11. JR. J.I.k (TS. 2708; IVZ(N2), 3.1). Phase 5. Small rim and neck segment. Fine creamy-green ware, evenly fired. Self slip in and out.
12. JR. J.I.l (TS. 2764; IVP, 1.5, Room 9). Phase 2B. About 1/8 rim and neck segment. Slightly coarse pinkish-brown ware, evenly fired. Self slip in and out.

Plate 251

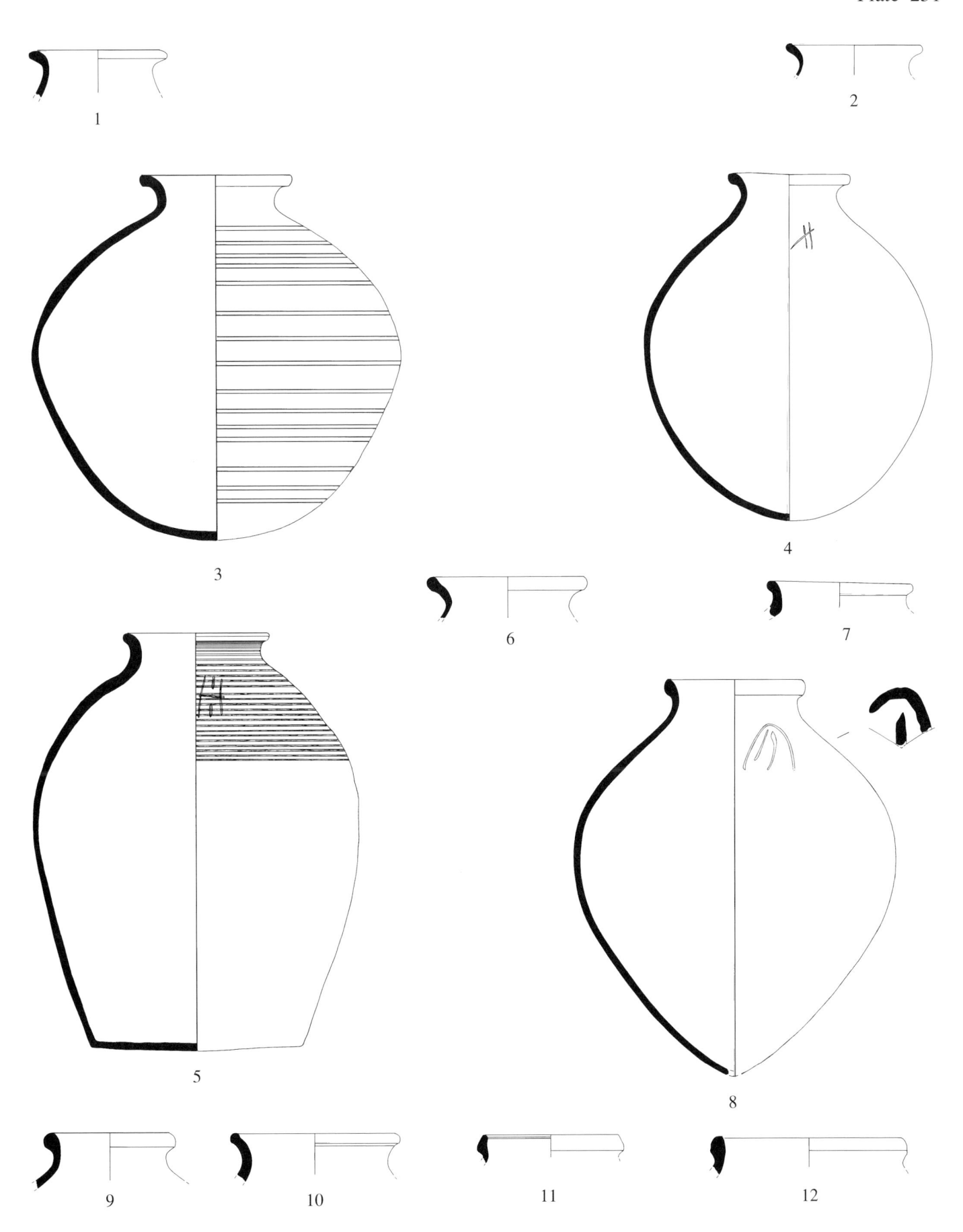

Bronze Age Jar (JR) Type J.I. Scale 1:5

Plate 252. Bronze Age Jar (JR) Type J.II

1. JR. J.II.a (TS. 2659; IVK, 1.3, Room 2A). Phase 3. About 1/10 rim, neck, and upper shoulder segment. Fine pinkish-brown ware, fairly evenly fired. Creamy-buff slip in and out.
2. JR. J.II.b (TS. 92; IIA, 8.2, Courtyard). Phase 8. Large rim, neck, and shoulder segment. Fairly fine pinkish-brown ware with lime and mica grits, evenly fired. Creamy-buff slip out and over rim in.
3. JR. J.II.c (TS. 3513; Op. 7, 18.1, Room 34). Phase 2A(a). About 1/2 rim, neck, and shoulder segment. Hard, fine light brown ware with gold- and silver-colored mica and lime grits, unevenly fired pinkish-orange at surfaces. Self slip. Irregular horizontal burnish on the shoulder and vertical burnish on the neck out; horizontal burnish on the outside edge of the rim and to the base of the neck inside.
4. JR. J.II.d (TS. 2405; IVC, 1.6, Pit in NE Tower). Phase 2B. About 1/12 rim and neck segment. Fairly fine ware, unevenly fired gray in and buff-brown out. Irregular horizontal burnish out.
5. JR. J.II.e (TS. 2629; IVK, 2.4, Room 2). Phase 2B. About 1/3 rim and neck segment. Hard, fairly fine pinkish-brown ware, evenly fired. Self slip in and out. Burnished horizontally below rim out.
6. JR. J.II.f (TS. 2404; IIIG/H, 1.4, Rooms 22A/B Extramural). Phase 5. About 1/10 rim and neck segment. Hard, fine pink ware, evenly fired.
7. JR. J.II.g (TS. 2289; IC, 1.32C, Pit A). Phase 7. About 1/4 rim, neck, and upper shoulder segment. Hard, fine ware, unevenly fired with grayish core and buff-green at surfaces. Creamy-green slip in and out.
8. JR. J.II.h (TS. 2407; IVD, 2.5, Room 2). Phase 2B. About 1/12 rim and neck segment. Slightly coarse pinkish-buff ware, evenly fired. Creamy-buff slip out.
9. JR. J.II.i (TS. 3371; Op. 11, 4.1, Room 20). Phase 2B. Small rim, neck, and upper shoulder segment. Ware description unavailable.
10. JR. J.II.j (PM. D.10; SW. 285; IIID, 5.3, Rooms 20/21). Phase 5. About 1/3 rim, neck, and large body segment with remains of decoration or a potter's mark incised on the shoulder before firing. Hard, fine drab ware with fine mica grits, unevenly fired grayish-brown out and over rim in. Possible self slip, but much worn.
11. JR. J.II.k (TS. 2396; IC, 1.42, Destruction level). Phase 4. About 1/10 rim and neck segment. Slightly coarse buff-brown ware, evenly fired. Creamy-green slip out and over rim in.
12. JR. J.II.l (PM. A.15; SW. 664; IVO, 1.4, Room 10). Phase 2A. Mended to near completion with a potter's mark incised on the shoulder before firing. Medium coarse pink ware, evenly fired. Horizontal cream slip lines in reserve on outside body and neck.
13. JR. J.II.m (TS. 3825; Op. 5, 32.1). Phase 2. Large rim, neck, and upper wall segment. Ware description unavailable.
14. JR. J.II.n (TS. 3354; Op. 10, 22.1, Room 8A). Phase 3. Small rim, neck, and upper shoulder segment. Ware description unavailable.

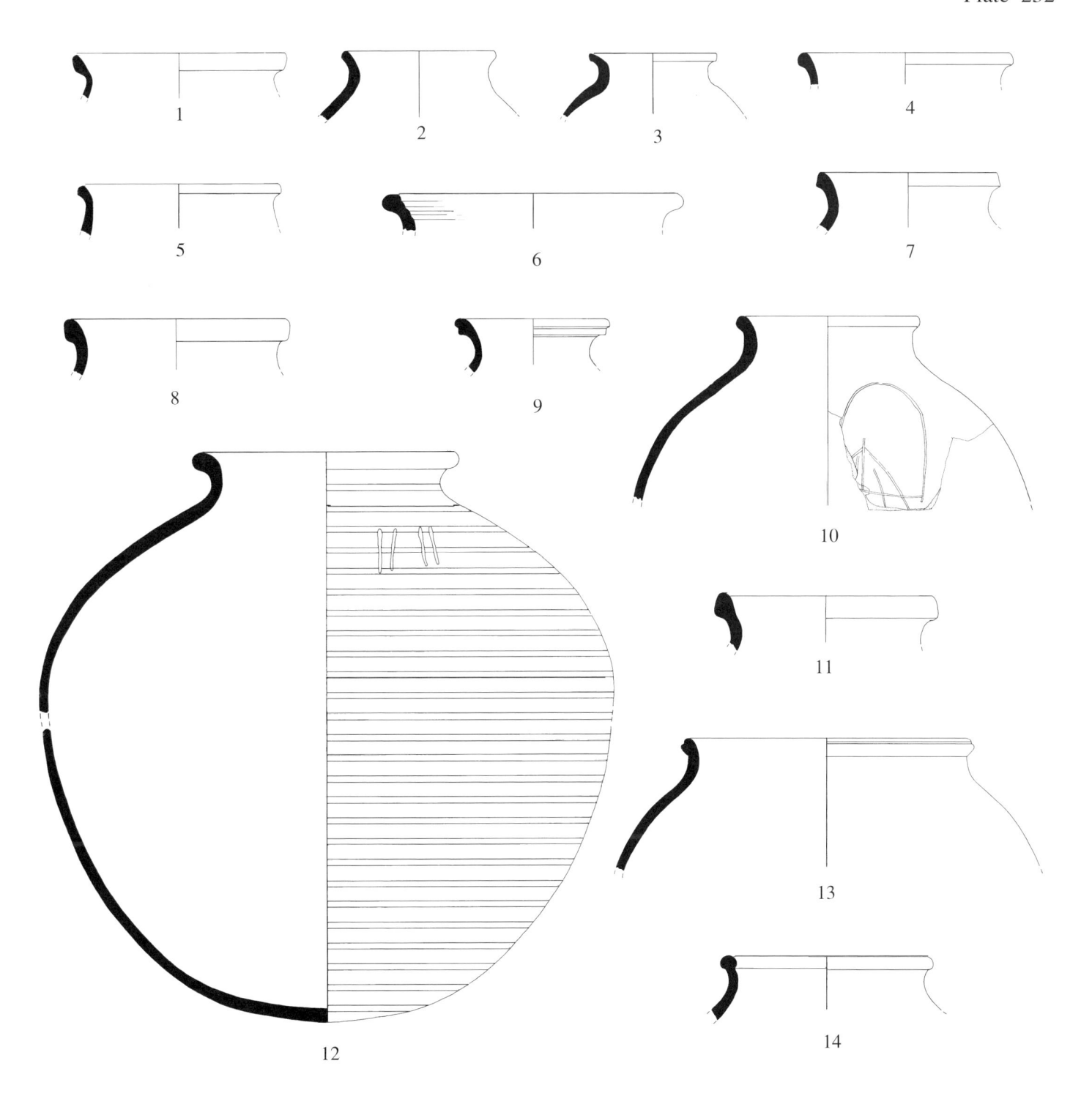

Plate 252

Bronze Age Jar (JR) Type J.II. Scale 1:5

Plate 253. Bronze Age Jar (JR) Type J.III.a to J.III.s

1. JR. J.III.a (SW. 552; IVJ, 2.1, Room 4). Phase 2A. Mended to completion. Fairly coarse buff ware, evenly fired. Cream slip in and out.
2. JR. J.III.b (TS. 1069; XA, 1.4, Room 15). Phase 2A. Small rim and neck segment. Fairly coarse buff ware, evenly fired. Creamy-buff slip out.
3. JR. J.III.c (TS. 1075; XA, 1.4, Room 15). Phase 2A. Two large joining rim, neck, and shoulder segments. Fairly coarse buff ware, evenly fired. Cream slip in and out.
4. JR. J.III.d (TS. 3023; IVQ, 2.4, Room 6). Phase 2A. Nearly complete rim, neck, and shoulder segment. Slightly coarse creamy-green ware, evenly fired. Self slip in and out.
5. JR. J.III.e (TS. 1787; IVP, 1.2, 1.3, Room 9B + IVL/P, 1.3, Pit). Phases 4 and 3. About 3/4 complete with three joining rim segments. Coarse pink ware with lime and mica grits, evenly fired. Creamy-buff slip out and just over rim in.
6. JR. J.III.f (TS. 3754; Op. 5, 18.2). Phase 4. Small rim, neck, and upper shoulder segment. Ware description unavailable.
7. JR. J.III.g (PM. C.11; TS. 794; IC, 1.48). Phase 3. About 1/4 rim, neck, and shoulder segment. Incomplete potter's mark incised on the shoulder before firing. Fairly fine buff ware, evenly fired. Light cream slip out.
8. JR. J.III.h (TS. 3019; IVM, 3.1, Room 7, Pit A). Phase 2A. About 1/8 rim, neck, and shoulder segment. Slightly coarse pinkish-buff ware, evenly fired. Cream slip in and out.
9. JR. J.III.i (TS. 3218; Op. 6, 18.5, Room 16). Phase 2A. About 1/6 rim, neck, and shoulder segment. Fine, fine pinkish-buff ware with a few very fine white-colored mica grits, evenly fired. Thick creamy-buff slip in and out.
10. JR. J.III.j (TS. 572; IVO, 1.2, Topsoil, 1.3, Fill). Phases 4 and 3. Complete rim and upper half of body and complete base. Fairly coarse pink ware, evenly fired. Cream slip in and out.
11. JR. J.III.k (TS. 2271; IVA, 2.3, Street). Phase 2B. About 1/4 rim, neck, and upper shoulder segment. Fairly coarse greenish-buff ware, evenly fired. Self slip in and out.
12. JR. J.III.l (TS. 1958; IVE, 1.4, Room 3). Phase 2B. Small rim and neck segment. Fairly fine light greenish-buff ware, evenly fired. Self slip in and out.
13. JR. J.III.m (PM. A.10; SW. 672; IVJ, 2.1, Room 4). Phase 2A. Mended to about 2/3 completion (round base not illustrated), with a potter's mark incised on the shoulder before firing. Slightly coarse pinkish-buff ware, evenly fired. Cream slip out.
14. JR. J.III.n (TS. 1066; XA, 1.2, 1.4, Rooms 15A and 15). Phases 3 and 2A. Two joining rim, neck, and shoulder segments. Fairly coarse buff ware, evenly fired. Cream slip in and out.
15. JR. J.III.o (TS. 1045; IC, 1.39, 1.40). Phases 5, 4. About 1/3 segment of rim, neck, and shoulder plus other non-joining body sherds. Fairly coarse pink ware, evenly fired. Cream slip out and just over rim; buff slip inside below rim.
16. JR. J.III.p (TS. 2324; IC, 1.36, 1.39). Phase 5. About 1/6 segment of two joining rim and neck fragments. Fine yellow-buff ware, evenly fired. Self slip in and out.
17. JR. J.III.q (TS. 1596 = TS. 1621; IVJ, 1.6, Room 4). Phase 2A. Small segment. Fairly fine buff ware evenly fired. Self slip out.
18. JR. J.III.r (PM. D.28; SW. 291; IVG, 1.4, Room 3). Phase 2B. Nearly complete except for a few body sherds. Potter's mark incised on the shoulder before firing. Hard, fine pinkish-buff ware with lime grits, evenly fired. Self slip in and out. Wet-smoothed from lower shoulder to base in and out.
19. JR. J.III.s (TS. 3368; Op. 11, 4.1, Room 20). Phase 2B. Small rim, neck, and upper shoulder segment. Ware description unavailable.

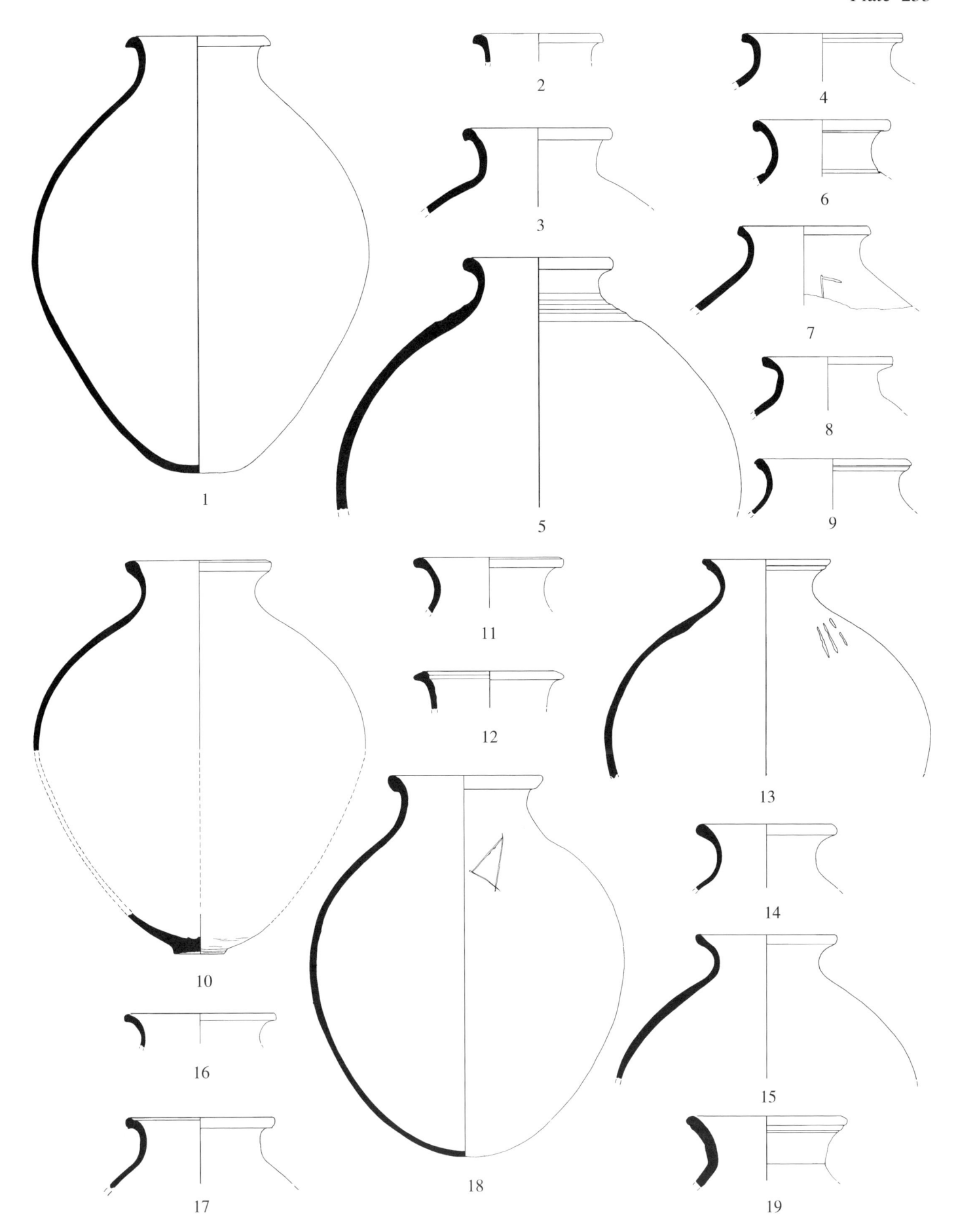

Plate 253. Bronze Age Jar (JR) Type J.III.a to J.III.s. Scale 1:5

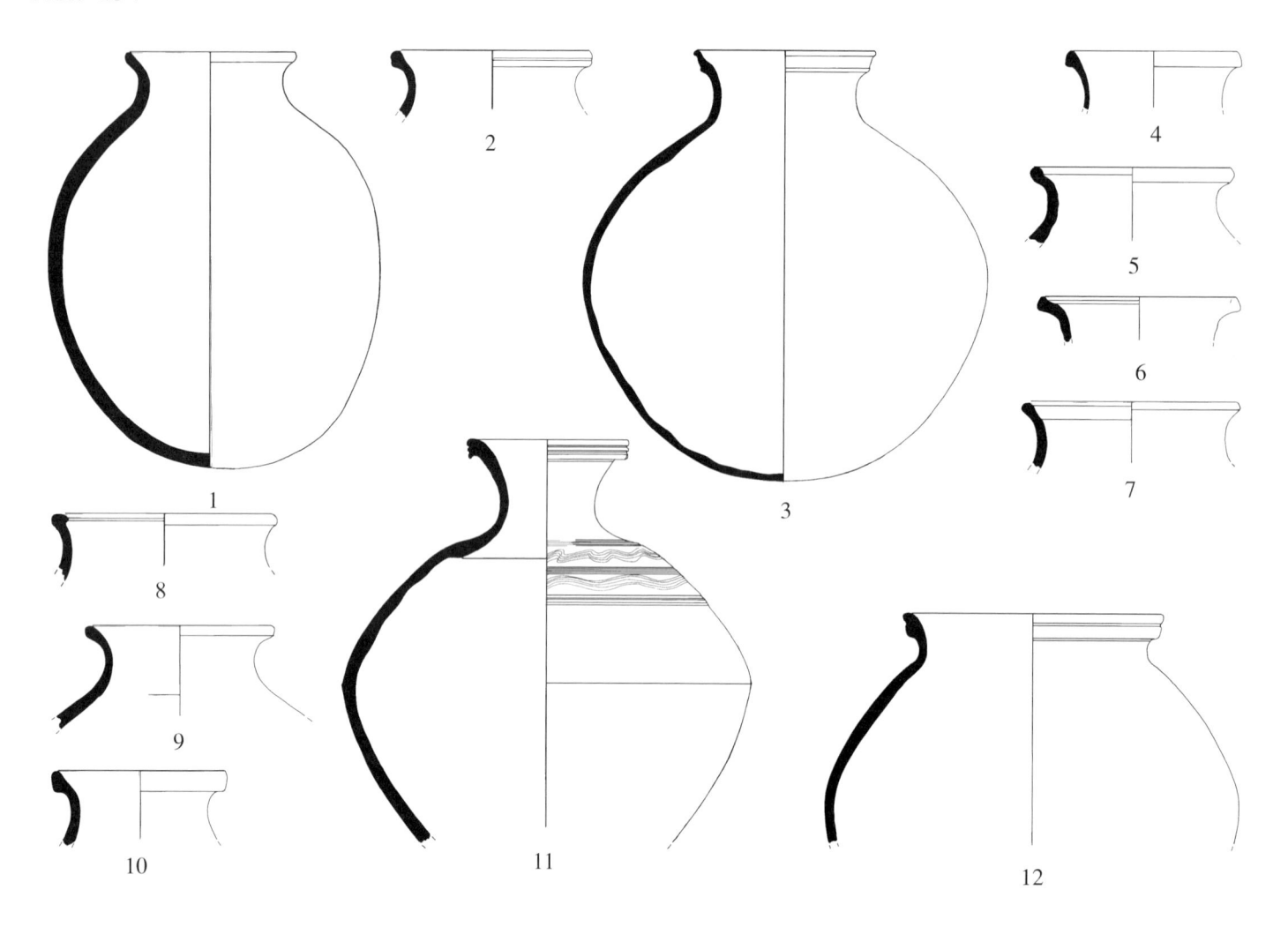

Plate 254

Bronze Age Jar (JR) Type J.III.t to J.III.ae. Scale 1:5

1. JR. J.III.t (SW. 567; IVJ Bin, 3.5, Room 5). Phase 2A (see also pls. 35a, 95c, and pocket plan 3). Jar found nearly complete (1/3 rim missing) in situ on grain bin floor with a small bowl/cup (SW. 568, see pl. 205:3) positioned in the rim. Fairly fine pink ware, evenly fired. Cream slip in and out.
2. JR. J.III.u (TS. 2954; IVJ, 1.6, Room 4). Phase 2A. About 1/4 rim, neck, and upper shoulder segment. Fairly fine pinkish-buff ware, evenly fired. Creamy-buff slip in and out.
3. JR. J.III.v (SW. 309; IVG, 1.5, Room 3). Phase 2A (see also pl. 95d). Mended to near completion. Very hard pink ware with fine lime and mica grits, unevenly fired creamy-buff in and out.
4. JR. J.III.w (TS. 2292; XA, 1.3, Room 15). Phase 2B. About 1/6 rim and neck segment. Fine pink ware, evenly fired. Buff slip out and just over rim in.
5. JR. J.III.x (TS. 2993; IVK, 2.4, Room 2). Phase 2B. Small rim, neck, and upper shoulder segment. Slightly coarse pink ware, evenly fired. Cream slip in and out.
6. JR. J.III.y (TS. 2335; IVA, 2.4, Street). Phase 2B. About 1/10 rim and neck segment. Slightly coarse creamy-yellow ware, evenly fired. Self slip out.
7. JR. J.III.z (TS. 2005; IVB, 3.8, Room 1). Phase 2A. Small rim and neck segment. Fine pink ware, evenly fired. Pinkish-buff slip out.
8. JR. J.III.aa (TS. 2987; IVM, 10.1, Below Room 7). Phase 1C. Small rim and neck segment. Slightly coarse creamy-green ware, evenly fired. Self slip in and out.
9. JR. J.III.ab (TS. 2283; IC, 1.40). Phase 4. About 1/5 rim, neck, and shoulder segment. Fine pink ware, evenly fired. Cream slip out and over rim in.
10. JR. J.III.ac (TS. 2883; t.1, 7.89). Phase 3. Small rim and neck segment. Slightly coarse buff ware, evenly fired. Creamy-green slip in and out.
11. JR. J.III.ad (TS. 3330 = TS. 3336; Op. 10, 22, Room 8B). Phase 4. Mended to near completion with horizontal and wavy band decoration comb-incised on the shoulder before firing. Ware description unavailable.
12. JR. J.III.ae (TS. 4024; Op. 10, 23, Room 8). Phase 2A. Large rim, neck, and upper half of body segment. Ware description unavailable.

Plate 255

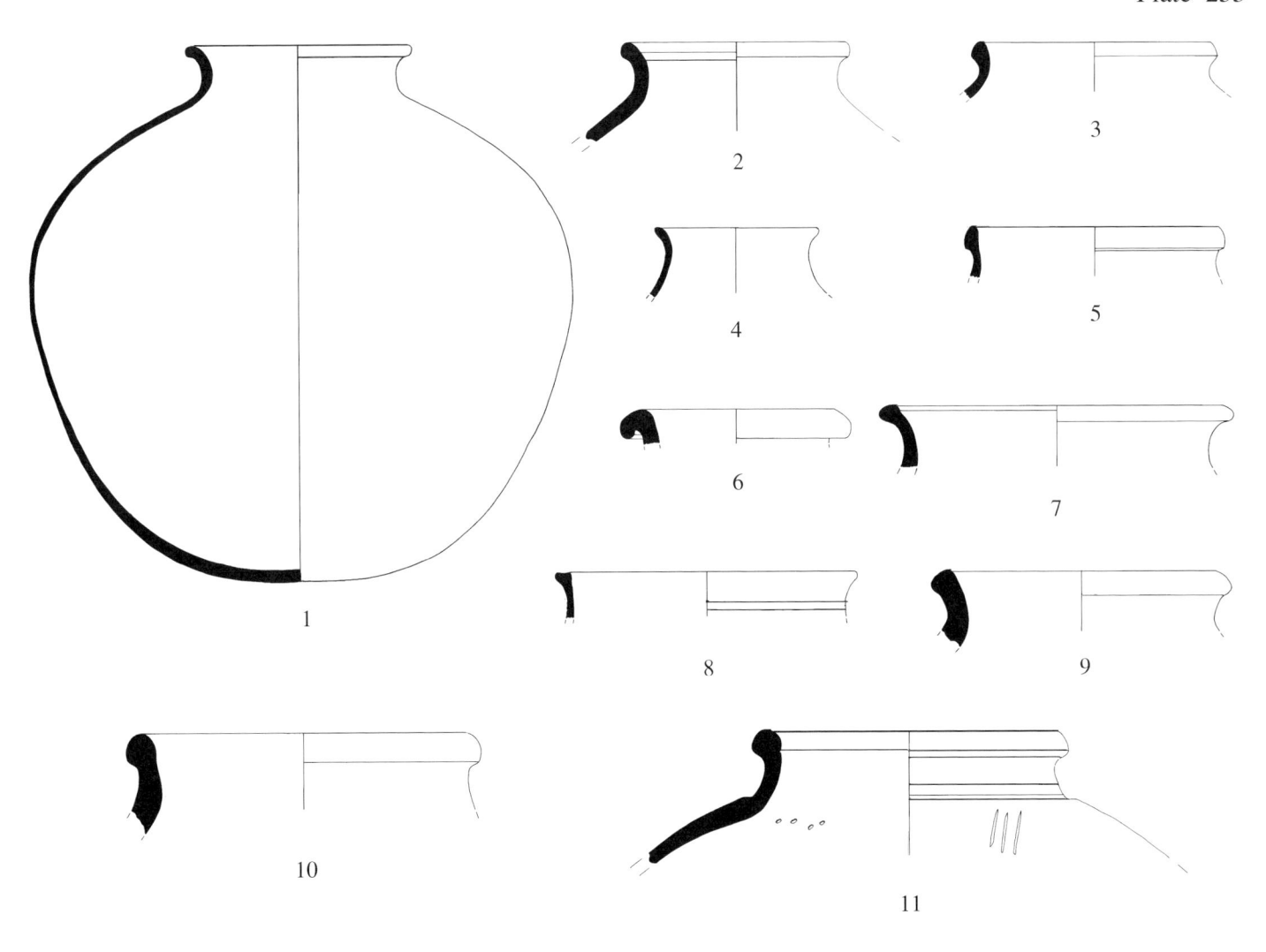

Bronze Age Jar (JR) Type J.IV. Scale 1:5

1. JR. J.IV.a (SW. 649; IVJ, 1.5, 2.1, Room 4). Phases 2A and 2B (see also pl. 96a). Mended to completion. Fairly fine buff ware, evenly fired.
2. JR. J.IV.b (TS. 1662; IVK, 1.3, Room 2A). Phase 3. Small rim, neck, and shoulder segment. Medium buff ware, evenly fired. Cream slip in and out.
3. JR. J.IV.c (TS. 2756; IVP, 1.2, Room 9B). Phase 4. About 1/8 rim, neck, and upper shoulder segment. Slightly coarse pinkish ware, evenly fired. Creamy-green slip in and out.
4. JR. J.IV.d (TS. 3219; Op. 6, 19.4, Below Room 16). Phase 1B. About 1/6 rim and neck segment. Fine buff ware with no visible grits; vegetable temper burned out during firing. Self slip in and out.
5. JR. J.IV.e (TS. 731; IIIG/H, 1.5, Room 17). Phase 4. Small rim and neck segment. Fairly coarse pink ware, evenly fired. Cream slip out and just over rim in.
6. JR. J.IV.f (TS. 2138; IC, 1.38). Phase 5. Small rim and upper neck segment. Coarse pinkish-buff ware, evenly fired. Light creamy-green slip in and out.
7. JR. J.IV.g (TS. 1111; VC, 3.1). Phase 3. About 1/10 rim and neck segment. Fairly coarse orange-pink ware, evenly fired.
8. JR. J.IV.h (TS. 492; IIIB, 2.3, Room 6). Phase 4. Small rim and neck segment. Fairly fine brownish-buff ware, evenly fired. Cream slip in and out.
9. JR. J.IV.i (TS. 2213; IC, 1.42, Destruction level). Phase 4. Small rim, neck, and upper shoulder segment. Hard, fine reddish-brown ware, evenly fired. Creamy-buff slip out.
10. JR. J.IV.j (TS. 2382; IVF, 1.9, Room 1). Phase 2B. About 1/8 rim and neck segment. Hard, fairly fine pink ware, evenly fired. Buff slip out.
11. JR. J.IV.k (PM. A.16; SW. 667; IVO, 1.4, Room 10). Phase 2A. Large rim, neck, and shoulder segment with a potter's mark incised on the shoulder before firing; also four small circles incised inside. Medium-coarse pink ware, evenly fired. Cream slip in and out.

Plate 256

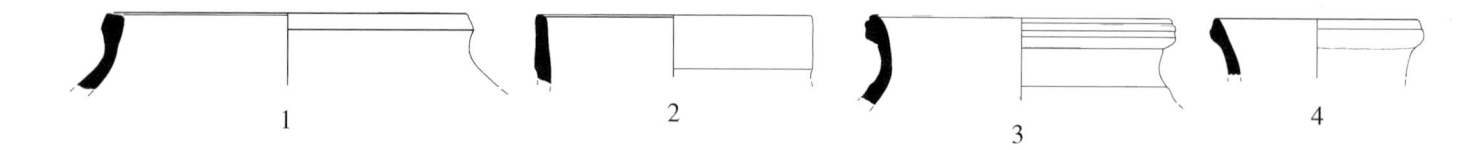

Bronze Age Jar (JR) Types J.V and J.VI. Scale 1:5

1. JR. J.V.a (TS. 3500; Op. 7, 17.2, Street). Phase 2A(a). About 1/6 rim and neck segment. Fairly fine buff ware with gold- and silver-colored mica and lime grits, fired buff-brown at surfaces. Creamy-buff slip in and out.
2. JR. J.V.b (TS. 2692; IVZ(S), 5.9b, c). Phase 1C. About 1/10 rim and neck segment. Slightly coarse pink ware, evenly fired. Creamy-buff slip out.
3. JR. J.VI.a (TS. 979; XA, 1.3, Room 15). Phase 2B. Small rim, neck, and upper shoulder segment. Fairly coarse brown ware, evenly fired. Reddish-orange slip in and out. Shoulder burnished outside.
4. JR. J.VI.b (TS. 2704; IVZ(N1), 1.8). Phase 2A. Small rim and neck segment. Coarse creamy-green ware, evenly fired. Self slip in and out.

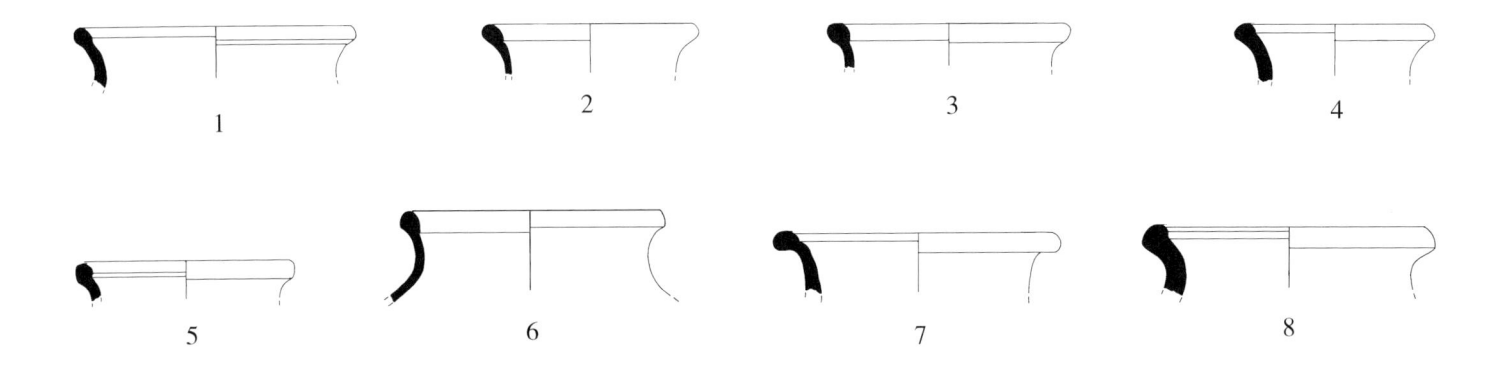

Bronze Age Jar (JR) Type K.I. Scale 1:5

1. JR. K.I.a (TS. 2338; XA, 1.4, Room 15). Phase 2A. About 1/10 rim and neck segment. Fairly fine pinkish ware, evenly fired. Creamy-buff slip out.
2. JR. K.I.b (TS. 2337; IC, 1.44). Phase 4. About 1/10 rim and neck segment. Fairly coarse yellowish-buff ware, evenly fired. Self slip in and out.
3. JR. K.I.c (TS. 2334; IVD, 2.1). Phase 4. About 1/10 rim and neck segment. Slightly coarse pink ware, evenly fired. Buff slip in and out.
4. JR. K.I.d (TS. 2340; XA, 1.2, Room 15A). Phase 3. About 1/12 rim and neck segment. Fairly fine greenish-buff ware, evenly fired. Self slip in and out.
5. JR. K.I.e (TS. 2332; IXA, 1.16). Phase 2B. About 1/14 rim and neck segment. Fairly fine yellow-buff ware, evenly fired. Self slip in and out.
6. JR. K.I.f (TS. 901; VIA, 1.2). Phase 4. Small rim, neck, and upper shoulder segment. Fairly fine pink ware, evenly fired. Cream slip out.
7. JR. K.I.g (TS. 1034; XA, 1.2, Room 15A). Phase 3. Small rim and neck segment. Fairly fine pinkish-buff ware, evenly fired. Cream slip out.
8. JR. K.I.h (TS. 2229; IIIG/H, 1.1–1.4, Courtyard). Phases 5 and 6. Small rim and joining neck segments. Hard, fine pinkish-buff ware, fairly evenly fired. Creamy-buff slip out.

Plate 258

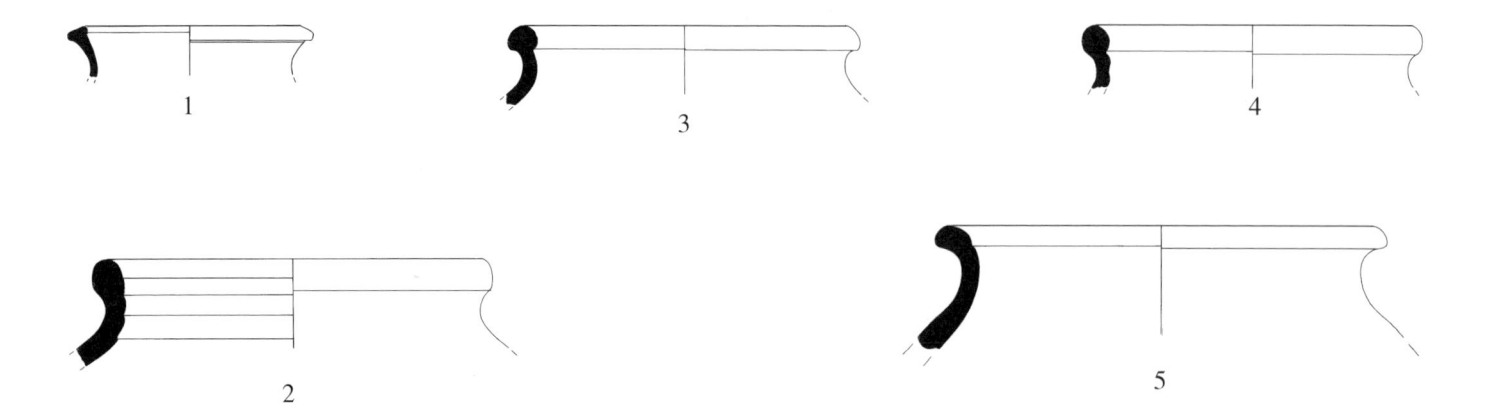

Bronze Age Jar (JR) Type K.II. Scale 1:5

1. JR. K.II.a (TS. 3726; Op. 5, 18.6, Pit). Phase 4. Small rim and neck segment. Ware description unavailable.
2. JR. K.II.b (TS. 2757; IVP, 1.5, Room 9). Phase 2B. About 1/10 rim, neck, and upper shoulder segment. Fairly fine pink ware, evenly fired. Cream slip out.
3. JR. K.II.c (TS. 2347; IVC, 1.5 = IVM, Room 7). Phase 2B. About 1/10 rim, neck, and upper shoulder segment. Slightly coarse buff ware, evenly fired. Light creamy-green slip in and out.
4. JR. K.II.d (TS. 2398; IVD, 2.5, Room 2). Phase 2B. About 1/6 rim and neck segment. Slightly coarse buff ware, evenly fired. Thick creamy-green slip out and just over rim in.
5. JR. K.II.e (TS. 1688; IVN, 2.1, Room 8). Phase 2B. About 1/4 rim, neck, and upper shoulder segment. Medium-coarse buff ware with lime and mica grits, unevenly fired. Cream slip in and out.

Plate 259

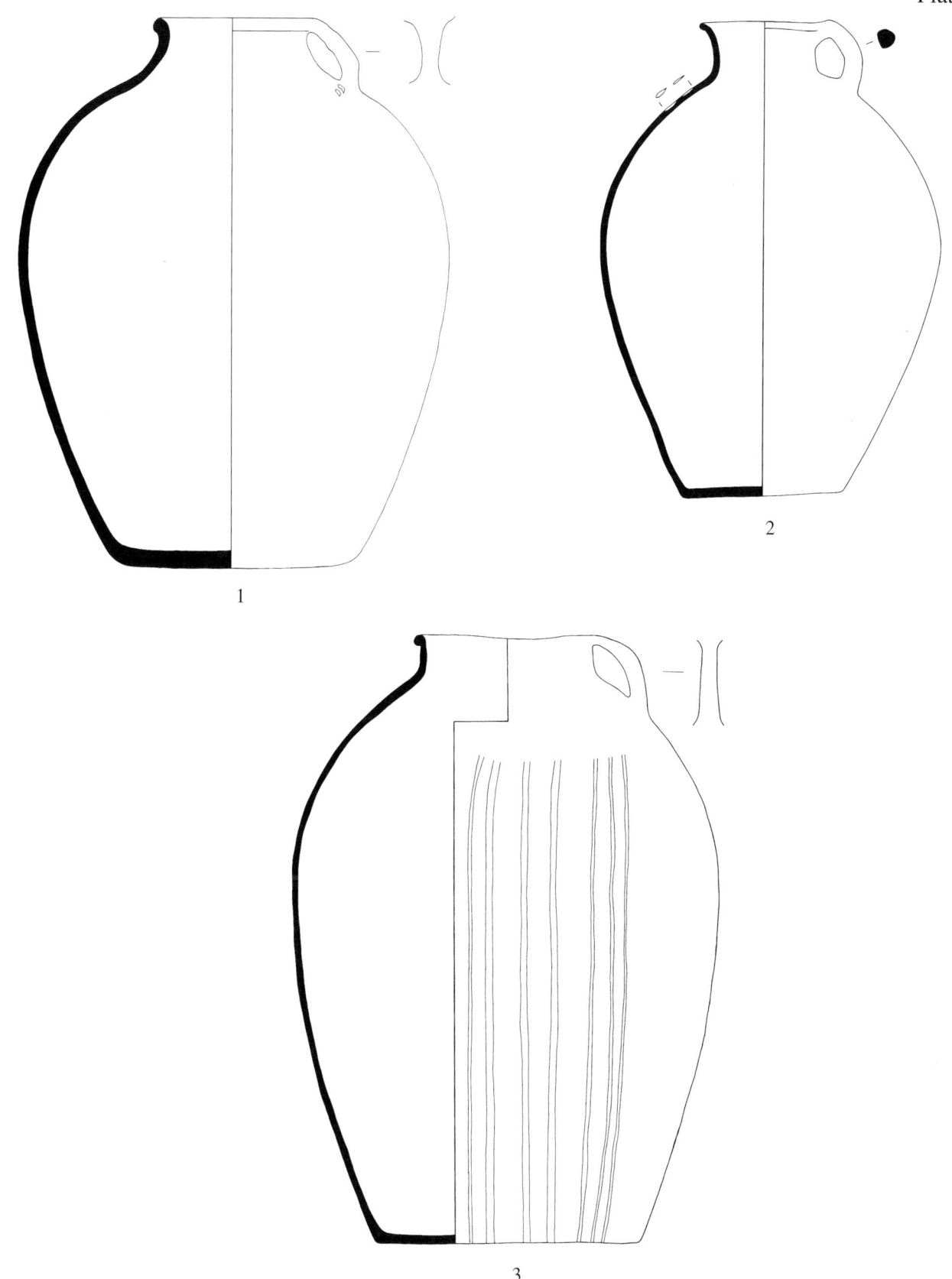

Bronze Age Jar (JR) Type L. Scale 1:5

1. JR. L.I.a (PM. A.1; SW. 676; IVJ, 1.5, Room 4). Phase 2B (see also pl. 96b). Nearly complete with one vertical loop handle and a potter's mark incised on the shoulder beside the handle before firing. Fine buff ware, evenly fired. Cream slip out.
2. JR. L.II.a (PM. A.2; SW. 651; IVJ, 1.5, 2.1, Room 4). Phases 2A and 2B (see also pl. 96c). Mended to completion with one vertical loop handle and an incised potter's mark on the shoulder before firing. Fairly coarse buff ware, evenly fired. Pink slip in and out.
3. JR. L.II.b (SW. 637; IVJ, 1.5, Room 4). Phase 2B. Mended to completion with one vertical loop handle. Fairly coarse cream ware, evenly fired. Light cream slip out with vertically painted darker cream slip line decoration.

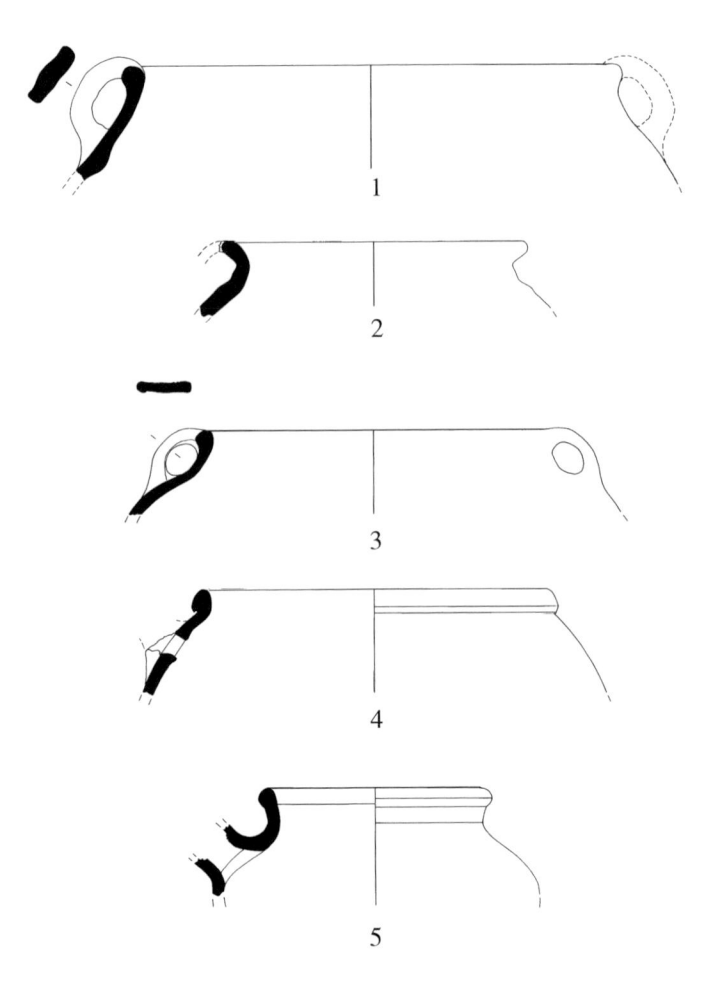

Bronze Age Jar (JR) Types M and N. Scale 1:5

1. JR. M.I.a (TS. 2626; IVM, 10.1, Below Room 7). Phase 1C. Small rim and shoulder segment with one wide vertical loop handle extant. Hard, fine greenish-buff ware, evenly fired. Creamy-yellow slip in and out.
2. JR. M.I.b (TS. 315; IIA, 8.7). Phase 7. Small rim, neck, and shoulder segment. Light brown ware, evenly fired. Inside rim slightly burnished.
3. JR. M.II.a (TS. 737; IE, 1.40 = IC, 1.40). Phase 4. Small rim, neck, and shoulder segment with complete vertical loop handle. Fairly coarse pinkish-buff ware, evenly fired. Buff slip in and out.
4. JR. N.I.a (TS. 3501; Op. 7, 17.2, Street). Phase 2A(a). Small rim and upper wall with remains of a spout on the shoulder. Fairly coarse light orange ware with many gold- and silver-colored mica and lime grits, evenly fired. Cream slip out.
5. JR. N.II.a (TS. 1652; IVL/P, 1.3, Pit). Phase 3. About 1/3 rim, neck, and shoulder segment with spout on shoulder. Fairly fine creamy-buff ware, evenly fired. Self slip in and out.

Plate 261

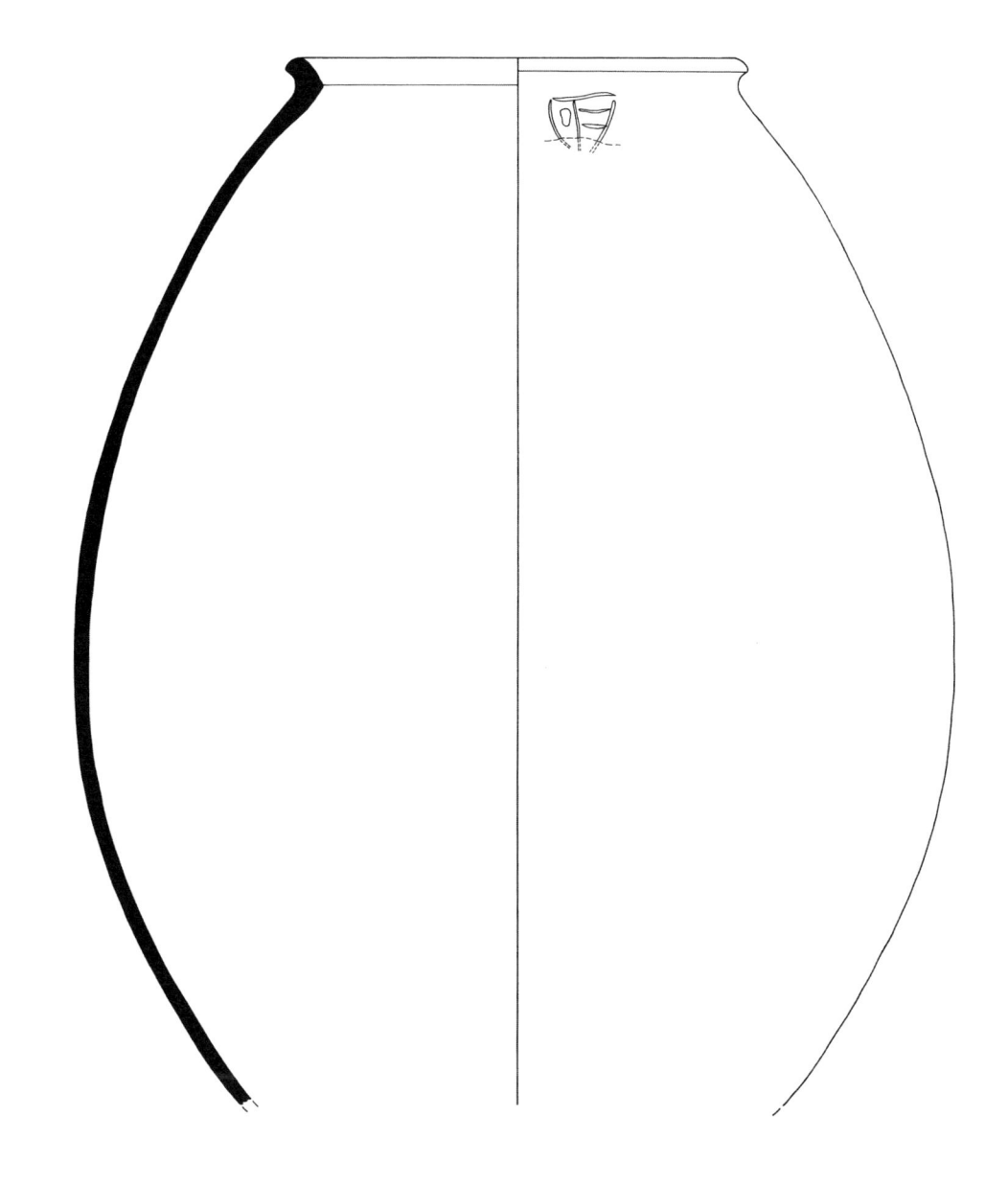

**Bronze Age Jar (JR) Type O.I.a. Scale 1:5**

JR. O.I.a (PM. D.6; SW. 695; IVM, 1.7, 2.6 + IVX, 3.1, 100.13, Room 7). Phase 2A (see also pl. 101b). Mended to near completion with most of a potter's mark incised on the shoulder just below the rim (joining body sherd missing during reconstruction of the vessel). Hard, charcoal-grayware, evenly fired. Burnished out.

Plate 262. Bronze Age Jar (JR) Types O.I.b to O.I.i

1. JR. O.I.b (SW. 668; IVJ, 1.3, 1.4, 1.5, Rooms 4A and 4B). Phase 3. Mended to completion. Fairly coarse pink ware, evenly fired. Cream slip out.
2. JR. O.I.c (TS. 791; IC, 1.54). Phase 3. About 1/20 rim and neck segment. Coarse buff ware, fairly evenly fired. Cream slip in and out.
3. JR. O.I.d (PM. D.30; TS. 1777; IVN, 4.1, Room 18B). Phase 4. About 1/5 rim and shoulder segment with a potter's mark incised on the shoulder before firing. Fine light brown ware, unevenly fired pinkish-brown in. Cream slip out.
4. JR. O.I.e (TS. 2656; IVX, 2.3 = IVM, Room 7). Phase 2B. About 1/10 rim and shoulder segment with remains of a ledge-like handle applied to the rim. Slightly coarse grayish-green ware, evenly fired. Creamy-green slip in and out.
5. JR. O.I.f (TS. 3443; Op. 11, 4.1, Room 20). Phase 2B. About 1/6 of two non-joining rim segments and about 1/4 of shoulder. Coarse purple-buff ware with lime grits, fairly evenly fired. Creamy-buff slip in and out.
6. JR. O.I.g (TS. 3362; Op. 10, 20, Room 18). Phase 2A. Large rim and shoulder segment. Ware description unavailable.
7. JR. O.I.h (TS. 4031; Op. 10, 20, Room 18). Phase 2A. Large rim and upper shoulder segment. Ware description unavailable.
8. JR. O.I.i (TS. 2793; IVJ, 1.5, Room 4). Phase 2B. Complete rim and shoulder segment. Handmade with coils of clay. Hard, fine ware, unevenly fired with gray core and pinkish-brown at surfaces. Grayish-buff slip out.

Plate 262

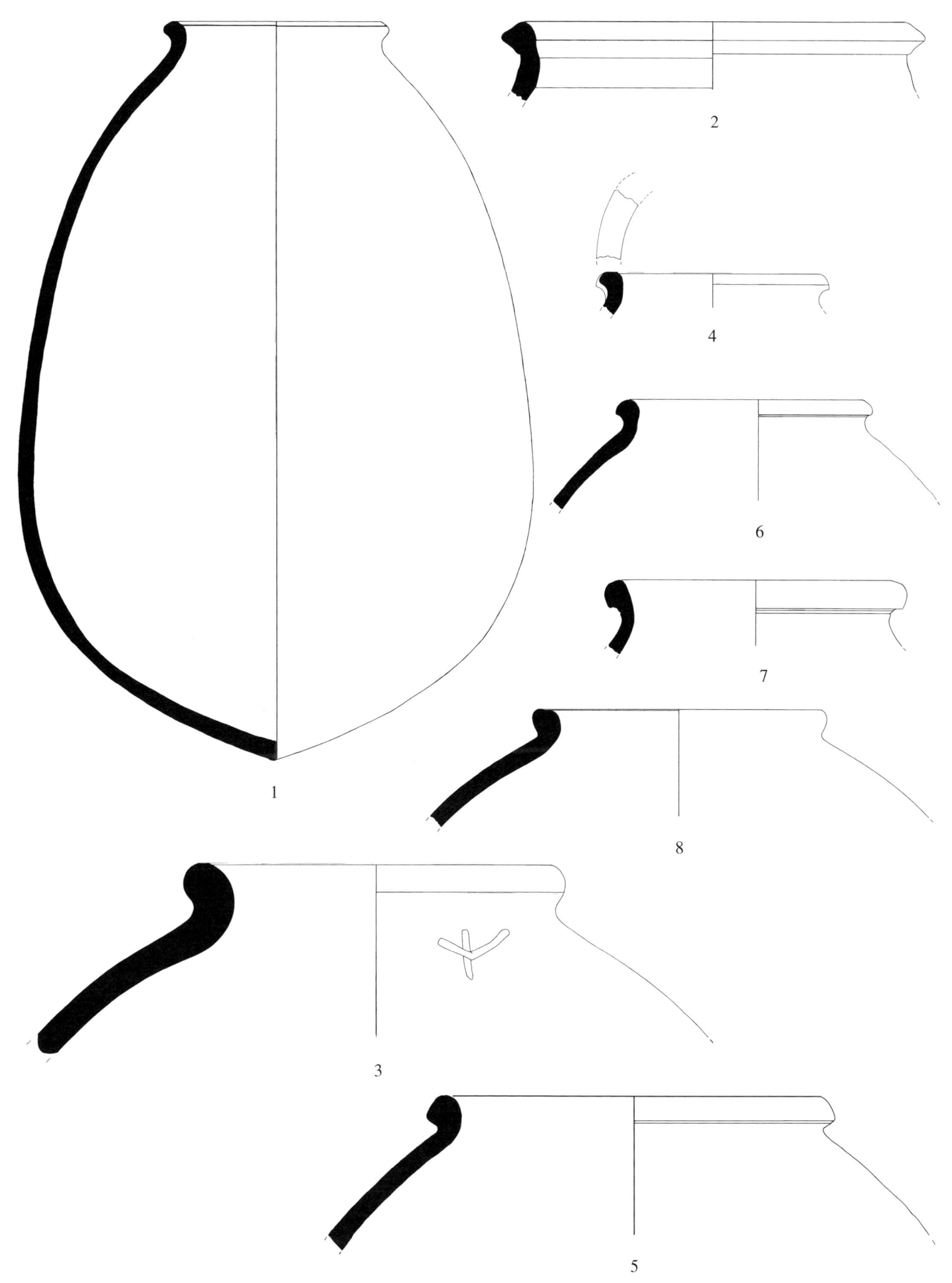

Bronze Age Jar (JR) Types O.I.b to O.I.i. Scale 1:5

Plate 263. Bronze Age Jar (JR) Types O.II.a to O.II.f

1. JR. O.II.a (PM. A.22; SW. 624; IVJ, 1.5, 1.7, Room 4). Phases 2B and 2A (see also pl. 96d). Found complete in situ, with a potter's mark incised on the shoulder before firing. Fairly coarse pink ware, evenly fired. Cream slip out.
2. JR. O.II.b (PM. E.2; SW. 711; IVR, 2.2, Room 11A). Phase 3. Mended to near completion with decoration or a potter's mark incised on the body after the vessel was fired. Medium-coarse pink ware with lime and mica grits, evenly fired. Cream slip in and out.
3. JR. O.II.c (PM. A.8; TS. 3384; Op. 11, 5.1, Room 19). Phase 2B. About 1/10 rim and shoulder segment with a potter's mark incised on the shoulder before firing. Slightly coarse pinkish-buff ware with gray and white lime grits and gold-colored mica grits, unevenly fired to a bright pink color inside. Creamy-buff slip out and on top of rim.
4. JR. O.II.d (TS. 1773; IVM, 1.4, Room 7). Phase 2B. About 2/3 rim segment and most of wall profile. Medium pink ware, evenly fired. Cream slip out and just below rim in.
5. JR. O.II.e (PM. A.6; TS. 2814; IVJ, 2.1, Room 4). Phase 2A. Complete rim and large shoulder segment with remains of a potter's mark incised on the upper shoulder before firing. Slightly coarse pinkish-orange ware, evenly fired. Creamy-green slip out.
6. JR. O.II.f (TS. 1209; XA, 1.3, Room 15). Phase 2B. Large rim and upper shoulder segment. Slighly coarse buff ware, evenly fired. Creamy-buff slip in and out.

Plate 263

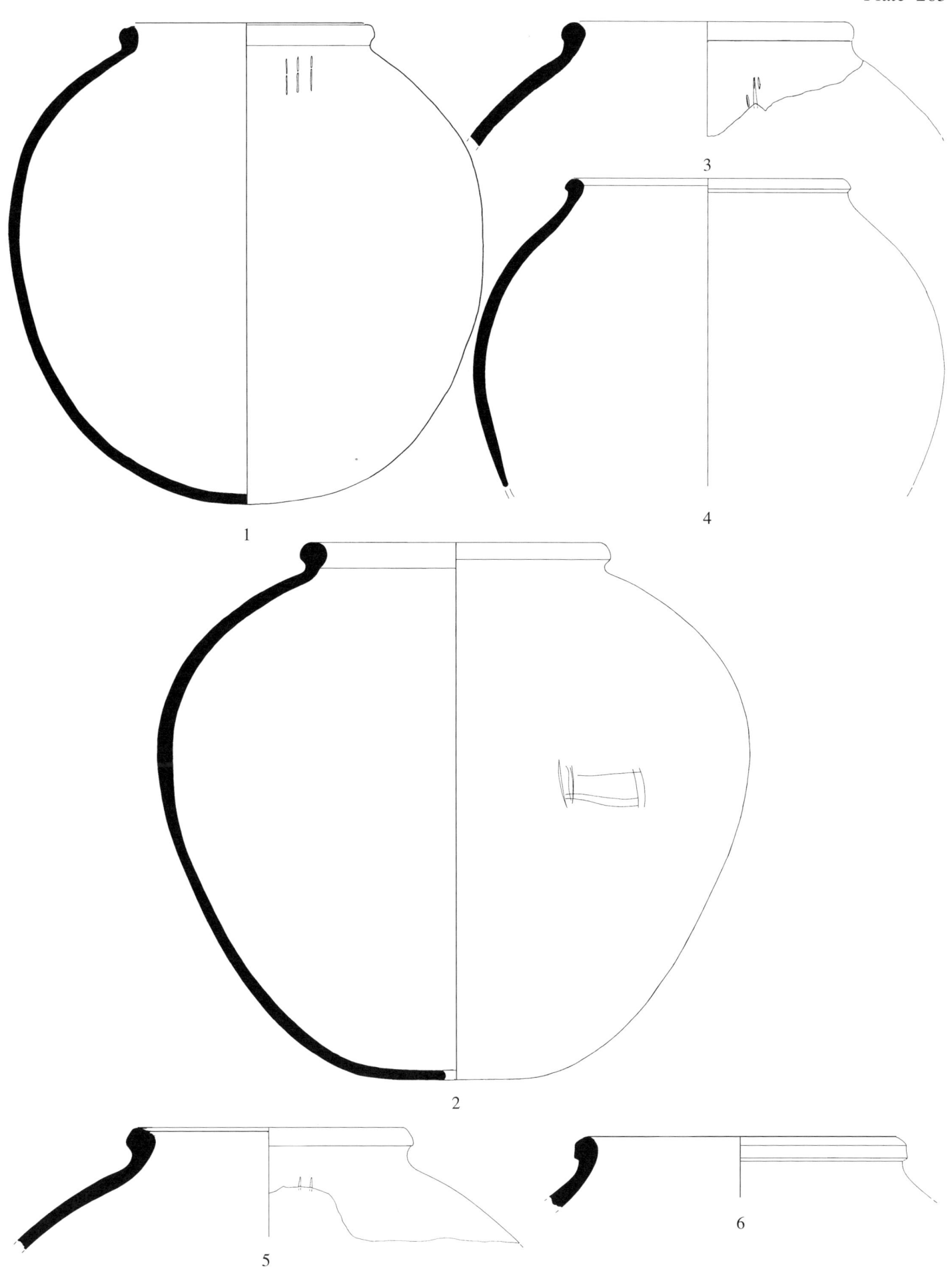

Bronze Age Jar (JR) Types O.II.a to O.II.f. Scale 1:5

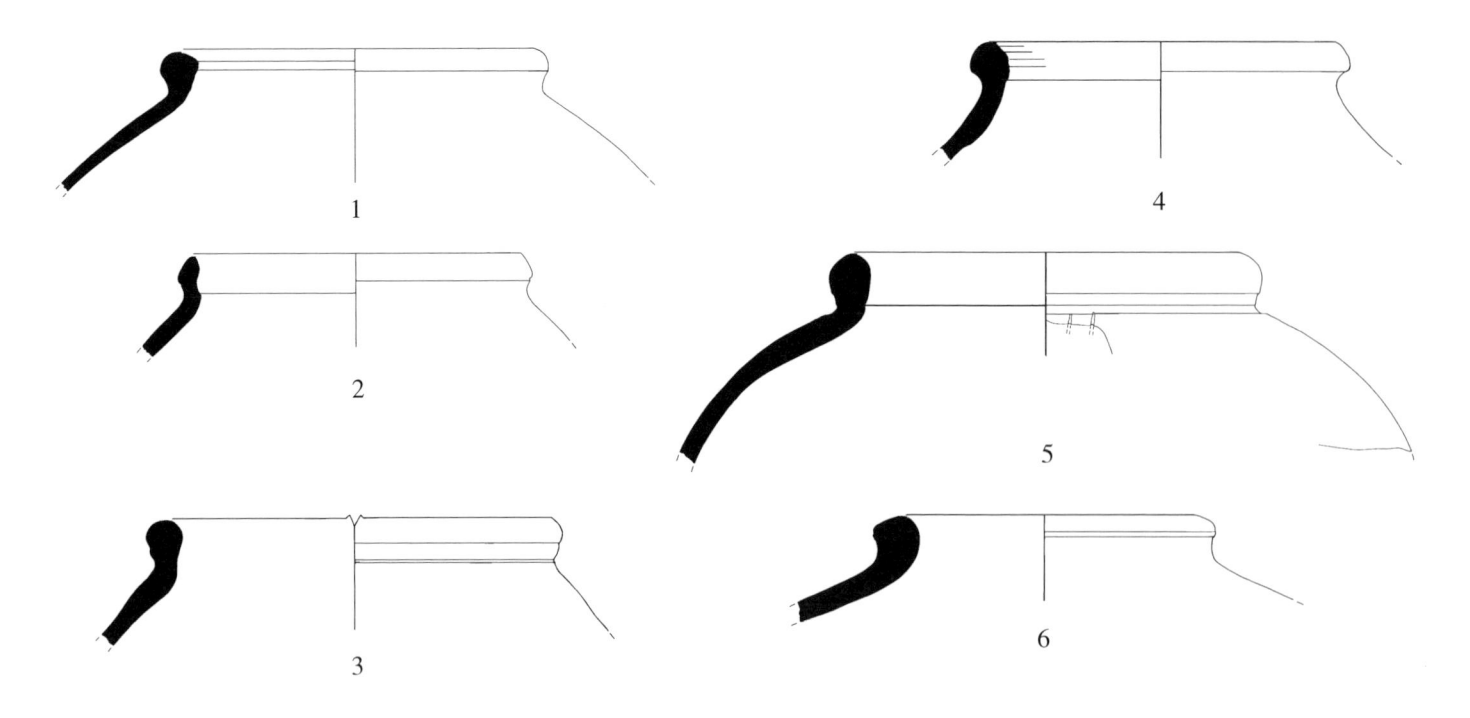

Plate 264

Bronze Age Jar (JR) Types O.II.g to O.II.l. Scale 1:5

1. JR. O.II.g (TS. 2813; IVJ, 1.5, 2.1, Room 4). Phase 2A. Complete rim and upper shoulder. Slightly coarse pinkish-buff ware, unevenly fired with gray core. Grayish-cream slip out.
2. JR. O.II.h (TS. 2732; IVZ(N1), 2.1). Phase 3. About 1/8 rim and upper shoulder segment. Slightly coarse pinkish-buff ware, evenly fired. Creamy-buff slip out and just over rim in.
3. JR. O.II.i (TS. 4030; Op. 10, 20, Room 18). Phase 2A. Large rim and upper shoulder segment. Rim diameter 28 cm. Ware description unavailable.
4. JR. O.II.j (TS. 443; IIIA, 1.4, Room 11). Phase 4. Large rim and shoulder segment. Coarse pink ware, unevenly fired with light brown core. Tannish-buff slip out.
5. JR. O.II.k (PM. A.6; TS. 2801; IVO, 1.3 + 1.4, Room 10A). Phase 2B. About 1/2 rim and upper shoulder segment with remains of a potter's mark incised on the shoulder before firing. Hard, fine ware, unevenly fired with partial gray core and pinkish-buff at surfaces. Creamy-green slip out.
6. JR. O.II.l (TS. 3211; Op. 6, 20.3, Room 9 Sounding). Phase 1C. About 1/10 rim and shoulder segment. Slightly coarse buff-brown ware with small and large-sized white lime grits, evenly fired. Self slip out.

Plate 265

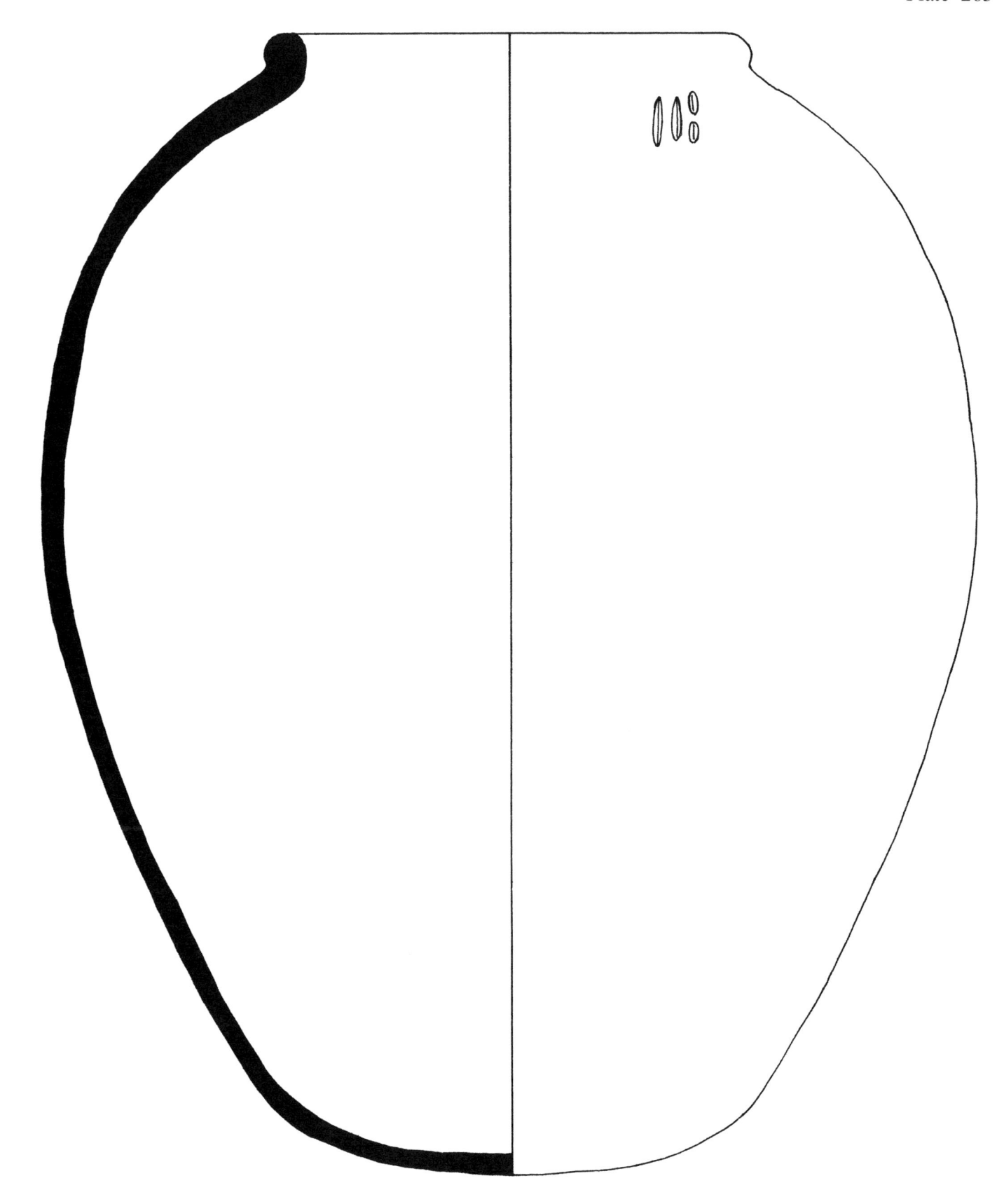

**Bronze Age Jar (JR) Type O.II.m. Scale 1:5**

JR. O.II.m (PM. A.10; SW. 368; IVD, 2.4, Room 2). Phase 2B. Mended to near completion with potter's mark incised on shoulder before firing. Coarse pink ware with lime and mica grits, evenly fired. Creamy-buff slip out and just over rim in.

Plate 266. Bronze Age Jar (JR) Type O.III

1. JR. O.III.a (PM. B.9; TS. 2807; IVN, 4.4, Room 18). Phase 2A. About 1/2 rim and shoulder segment with remains of a potter's mark incised on shoulder before firing. Slightly coarse pinkish-buff ware, evenly fired. Cream slip in and out.
2. JR. O.III.b (TS. 1663; IVK, 1.2, Room 2B). Phase 4. About 1/8 rim and shoulder segment. Very coarse pink ware with lime and mica grits, fairly evenly fired. Buff slip in and out.
3. JR. O.III.c (TS. 1685; IVN, 1.4, Rooms 8A/18A). Phase 3. Small rim and upper shoulder segment. Very coarse pinkish ware with lime grits, evenly fired. Cream slip in and out.
4. JR. O.III.d (TS. 3208; Op. 5, 30.5). Phase 3. Small rim segment. Ware description unavailable.
5. JR. O.III.e (PM. D.9; SW. 739; IVF, 4.1, Room 1). Phase 2A. Broken, but complete in situ (not fully mended) with a potter's mark incised on the shoulder before firing. Coarse brown ware with lime and mica grits, unevenly fired pink at surfaces. Thick creamy-green slip out and just over rim in.
6. JR. O.III.f (TS. 3632; Op. 5, 17.3, Pit). Phase 4. Small rim and neck segment. Ware description unavailable.
7. JR. O.III.g (TS. 3303; Op. 7, 2.2). Phase 3. Small rim (6 cm) and upper wall segment with zigzag linear decoration on the outside wall. Slightly coarse ware with fine gold- and silver-colored mica and lime grits. Unevenly fired with light gray core and pinkish-orange at surfaces. Creamy-pink slip out.
8. JR. O.III.h (TS. 2677; IVV, 1.1). Phase 4. About 1/8 rim and shoulder segment. Fairly coarse pink ware, evenly fired. Pinkish-buff slip in and out.

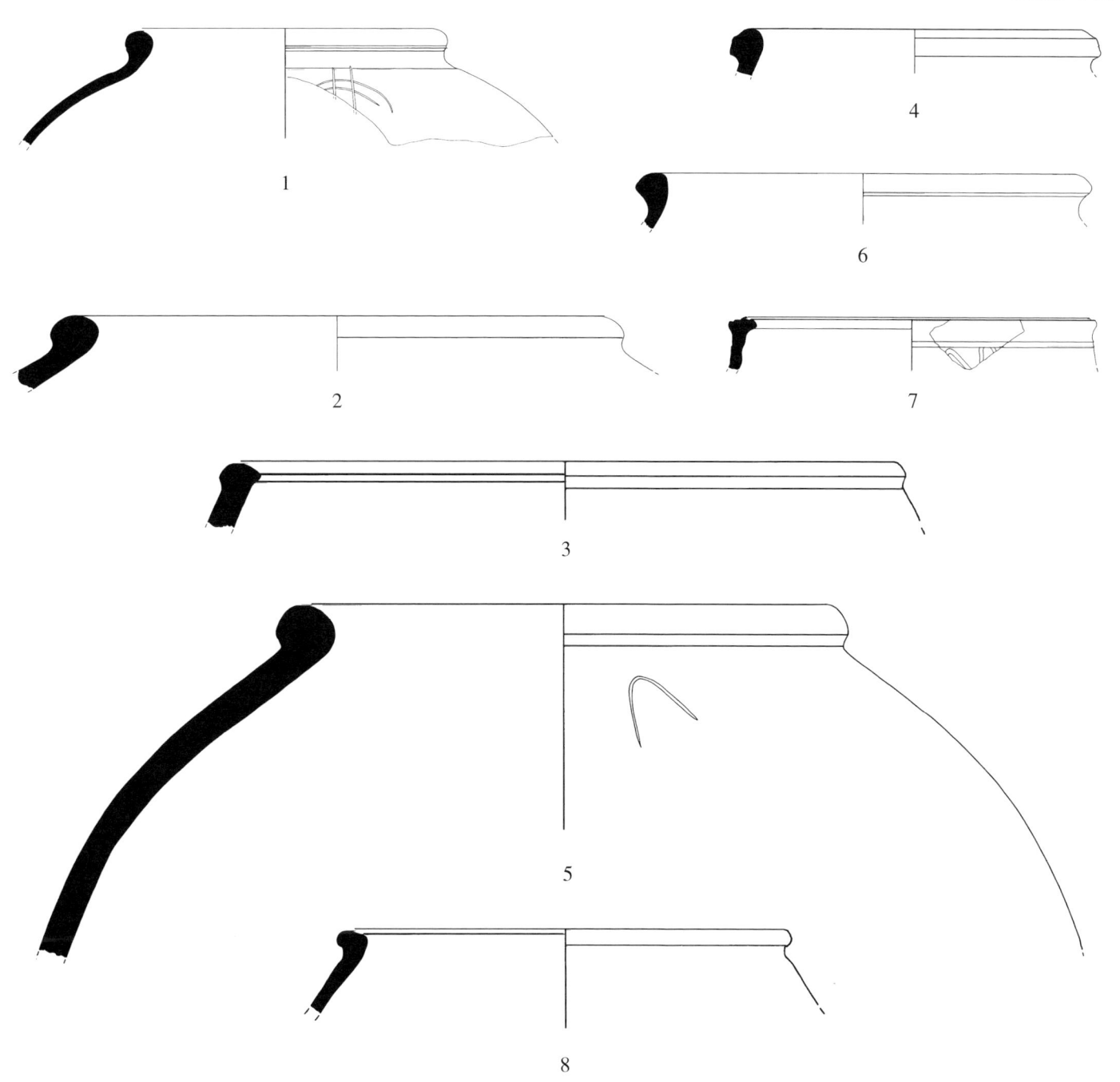

Plate 266

Bronze Age Jar (JR) Type O.III. Scale 1:5

Plate 267. Bronze Age Jar (JR) Type P.I

1. JR. P.I.a (TS. 2375; IVE, 1.4, Room 3). Phase 2B. About 1/8 rim, neck, and upper shoulder segment. Fairly coarse pinkish-buff ware, evenly fired. Creamy-buff slip out.
2. JR. P.I.b (PM. A.14; TS. 1642; IVG, 1.5, Room 3). Phase 2A. About 1/5 rim, neck, and shoulder segment with remains of a potter's mark incised on the shoulder before firing. Fairly fine brown ware with lime and mica grits, unevenly fired with some gray core. Cream slip in and out.
3. JR. P.I.c (TS. 2384; IVC, 1.2). Phase 3. About 1/6 rim, neck, and upper shoulder segment. Hard, fairly fine buff ware, evenly fired. Self slip out.
4. JR. P.I.d (SW. 326; IVG, 1.5, Room 3). Phase 2A. Mended to completion with drainage hole manufactured off center in the base. Very coarse, somewhat friable, pinkish ware with lime and mica grits, evenly fired. Cream slip out.
5. JR. P.I.e (PM. D.22; TS. 3387; Op. 11, 5.1, Room 19). Phase 2B. About 1/6 rim, neck, and shoulder segment with portion of a potter's mark incised on the outside wall before firing. Ware description unavailable.

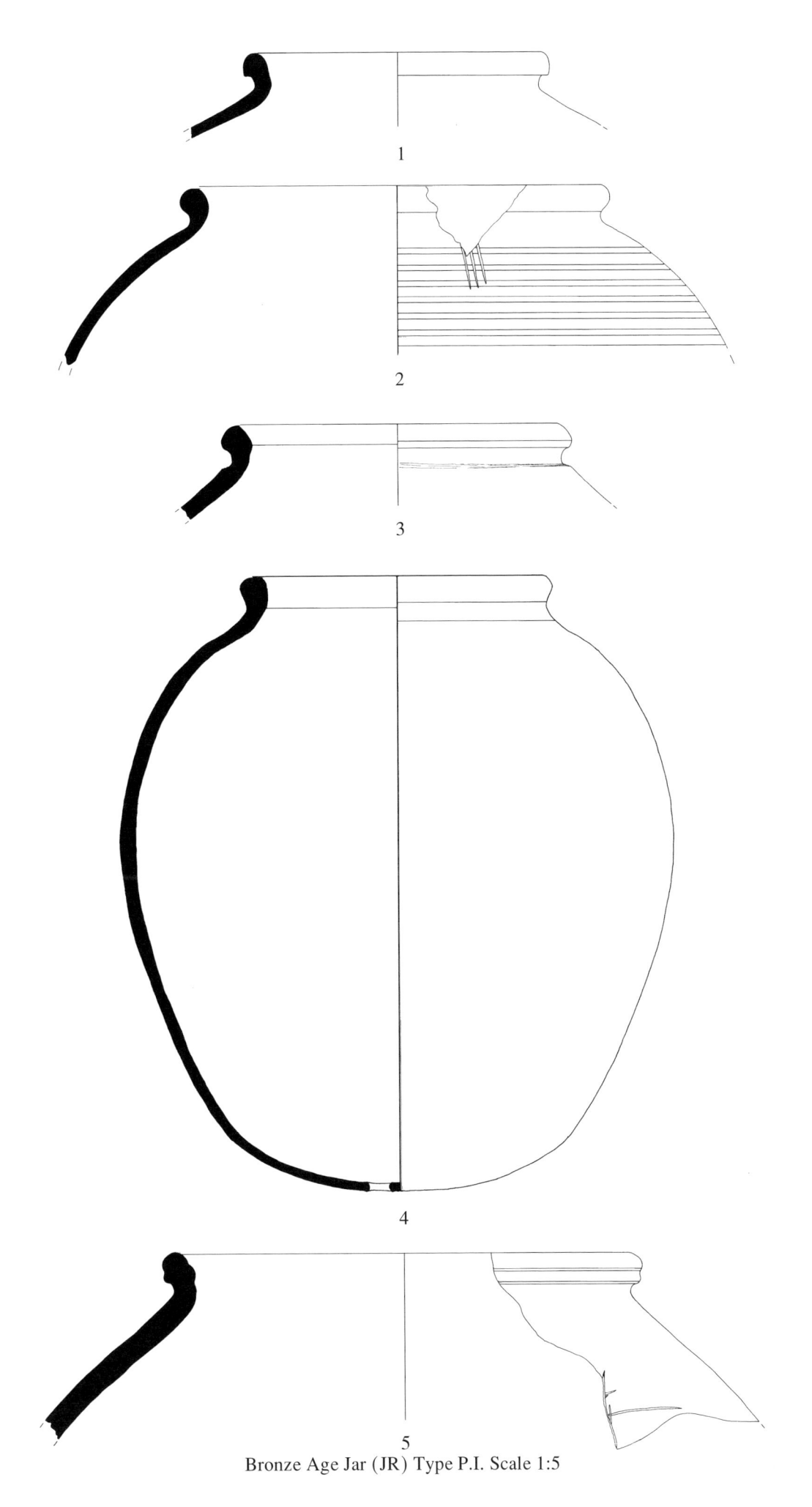

Plate 267

Bronze Age Jar (JR) Type P.I. Scale 1:5

Plate 268. Bronze Age Jar (JR) Types P.II.a to P.II.i

1. JR. P.II.a (TS. 2562; IVK, 2.4, Room 2). Phase 2B. About 1/3 rim, neck, and shoulder segment. Fairly coarse ware, unevenly fired with some gray core and pink at surfaces. Creamy-buff slip out.
2. JR. P.II.b (TS. 2804; IVN, 2.3, Room 18). Phase 2A. Complete rim, neck, and upper shoulder. Slightly coarse grayish-buff ware, unevenly fired pink in patches. Self slip in and out.
3. JR. P.II.c (PM. B.7; TS. 1627 = TS. 1735; IVN, 2.3, Room 18). Phase 2A. Rim and upper shoulder mended to completion with remains of a potter's mark incised on the shoulder before firing. Coarse pink ware with lime and mica grits, unevenly fired with some dark brown core. Cream slip out.
4. JR. P.II.d (TS. 2992; IVF, 1.14, Room 1). Phase 2B. About 1/8 rim and neck segment. Fairly fine pinkish and buff ware, unevenly fired. Cream slip in and out.
5. JR. P.II.e (TS. 1666 = TS. 2360; IVE, 1.6, Room 2). Phase 2A. About 1/3 rim, neck, and upper shoulder segment. Slightly coarse and gritty pinkish-brown ware, fairly evenly fired. Cream slip out.
6. JR. P.II.f (TS. 2361; IVB, 3.2, Room 1A). Phase 3. About 1/5 rim, neck, and upper shoulder segment. Fairly coarse buff ware, fairly evenly fired. Self slip out.
7. JR. P.II.g (TS. 2358; IC, 1.35). Phase 5. About 1/10 rim and neck segment. Fairly coarse and gritty dark pink ware, evenly fired. Creamy-buff slip in and out.
8. JR. P.II.h (TS. 3357; Op. 10, 22.1, Room 8A). Phase 3. Large rim, neck, and upper shoulder segment. Ware description unavailable.
9. JR. P.II.i (SW. 650; IVJ, 1.5, 2.1, Room 4). Phases 2B and 2A (compare Jar JR. P.II.j, pl. 269:1). Mended to completion. Fairly coarse creamy-buff ware, evenly fired. Horizontal reserved cream slip lines on outside wall.

Plate 268

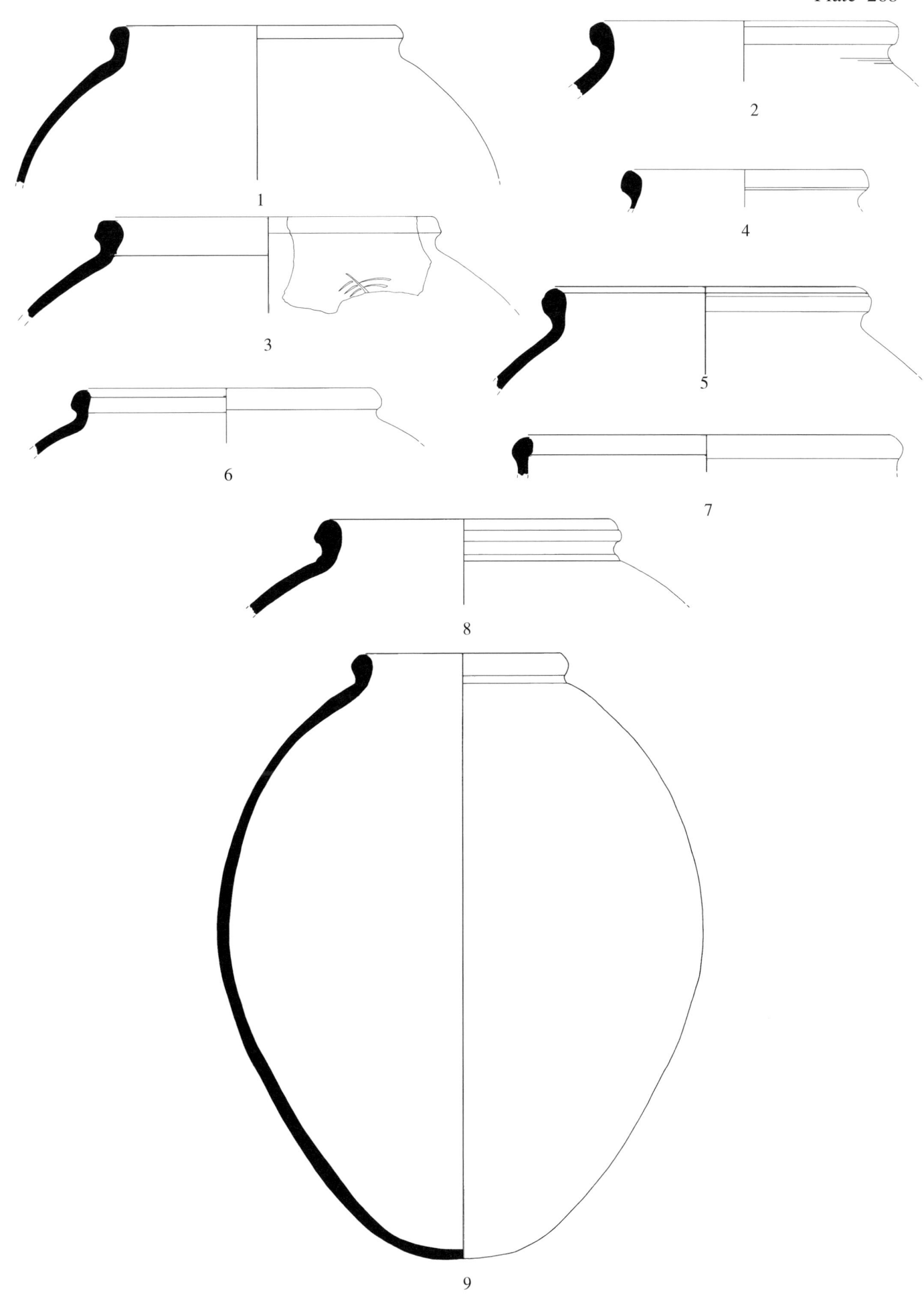

Bronze Age Jar (JR) Types P.II.a to P.II.i. Scale 1:5

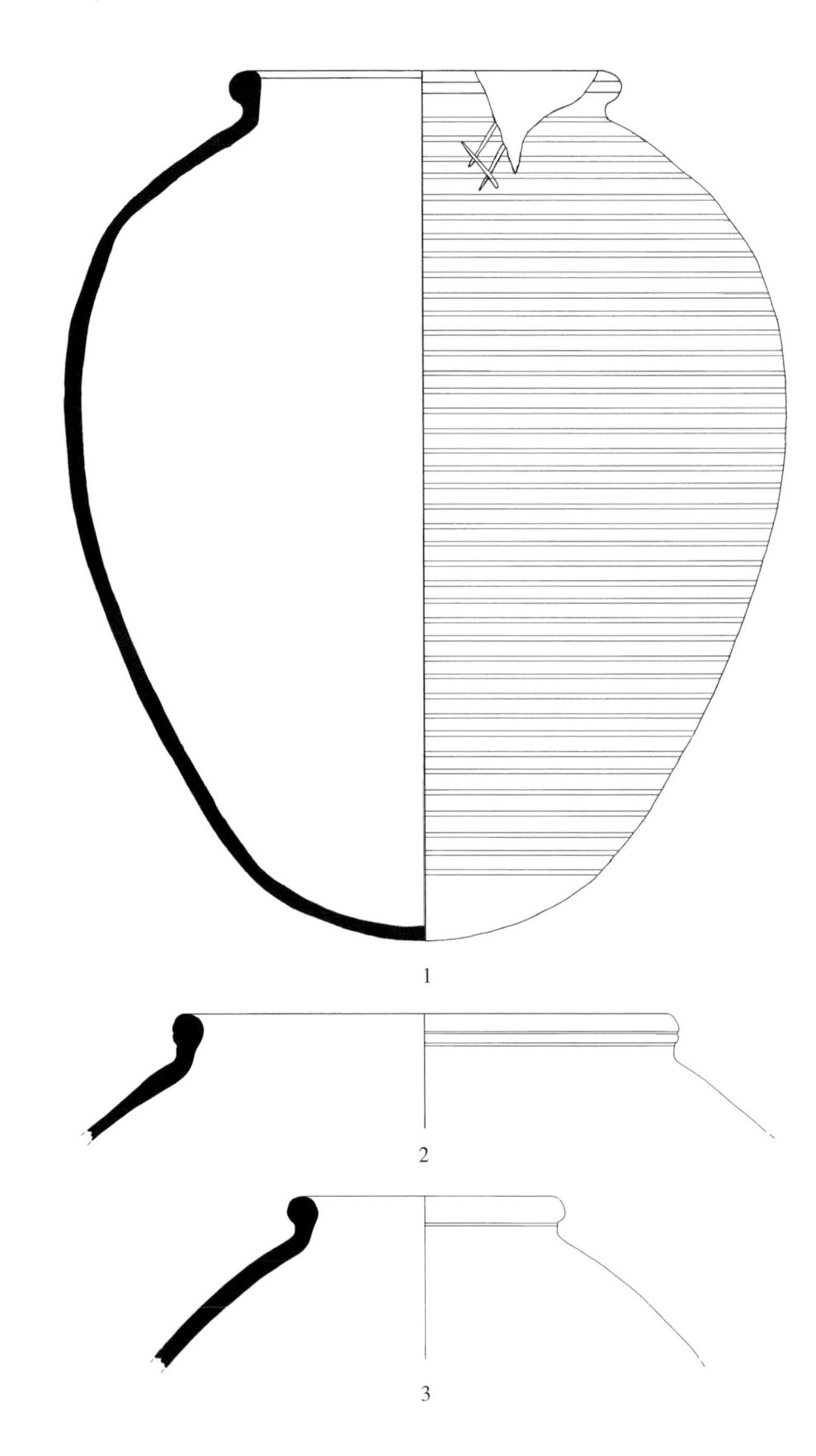

Plate 269

1

2

3

Bronze Age Jar (JR) Types P.II.j to P.II.l. Scale 1:5

1. JR. P.II.j (PM. D.22; SW. 311; IVE, 1.6, Room 2). Phase 2A. Mended to near completion except for small rim and shoulder segment. Remains of a potter's mark incised on the shoulder before firing. Fairly coarse brownish-grayware, unevenly fired pink in patches. Reserved cream slip lines out.
2. JR. P.II.k (TS. 4018; Op. 10, 20, Room 18). Phase 2A. Large rim, neck, and upper shoulder segment. Ware description unavailable.
3. JR. P.II.l (TS. 4029; Op. 10, 20, Room 18). Phase 2A. Large rim, neck, and shoulder segment. Ware description unavailable.

Plate 270

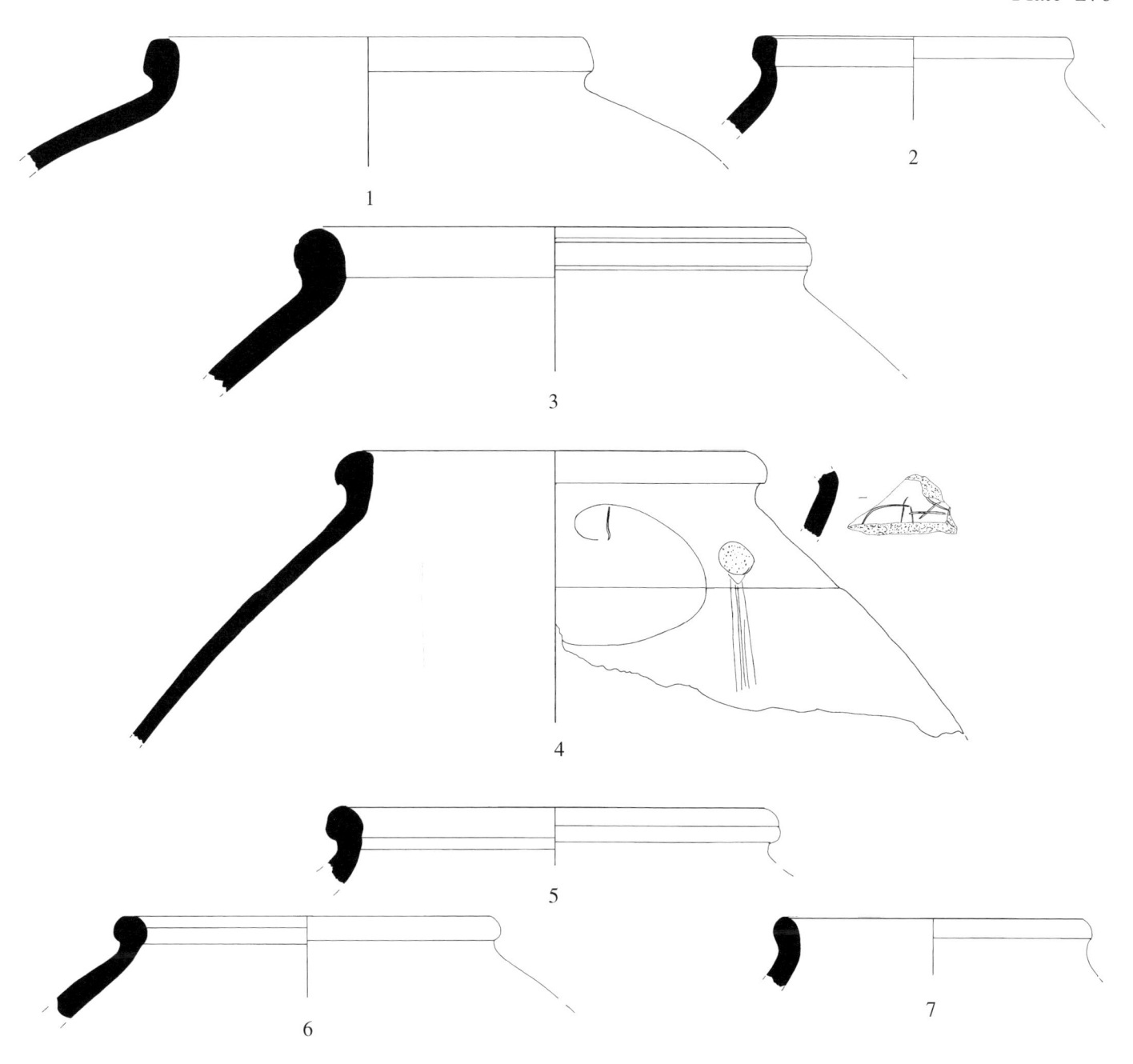

Bronze Age Jar (JR) Types P.II.m to P.II.s. Scale 1:5

1. JR. P.II.m (TS. 603; IVA, 2.4, Street). Phase 2B. Large rim, neck, and upper shoulder segment. Coarse brown ware, evenly fired. Cream slip in and out.
2. JR. P.II.n (TS. 2393; IC, 1.41). Phase 4. About 1/10 rim, neck, and shoulder segment. Hard, fine pinkish-brown ware, unevenly fired with some gray core. Buff slip out and over rim in.
3. JR. P.II.o (TS. 3879; Op. 5, 13.3). Phase 4. Large rim, neck, and upper shoulder segment. Ware description unavailable.
4. JR. P.II.p (PM. C.14, PM. D.4, and PM. D.17; TS. 3365; Op. 11, 5.1, Room 19). Phase 2B. About 1/4 rim, neck, and shoulder segment and one non-joining sherd. Decorative designs incised on the shoulder of the vessel and potter's marks incised on the non-joining sherd before firing. Slightly coarse pinkish-purple ware with black and white lime grits and silver-colored mica grits, fairly evenly fired. Creamy self slip in and out.
5. JR. P.II.q (TS. 1693; IVN, 1.4, Rooms 8A/18A). Phase 3. Small rim and neck segment. Very coarse pink ware with lime grits, unevenly fired. Cream slip in and out.
6. JR. P.II.r (TS. 1697; IVN, 2.1, Room 8). Phase 2B. Small rim, neck, and shoulder segment. Coarse pink ware, evenly fired. Cream slip in and out.
7. JR. P.II.s (TS. 2996; IVX, 10.7 = IVM, Room 7). Phase 2A. Small rim and neck segment. Fairly coarse pinkish-orange ware, evenly fired. Buff slip out and just over rim in.

Plate 271

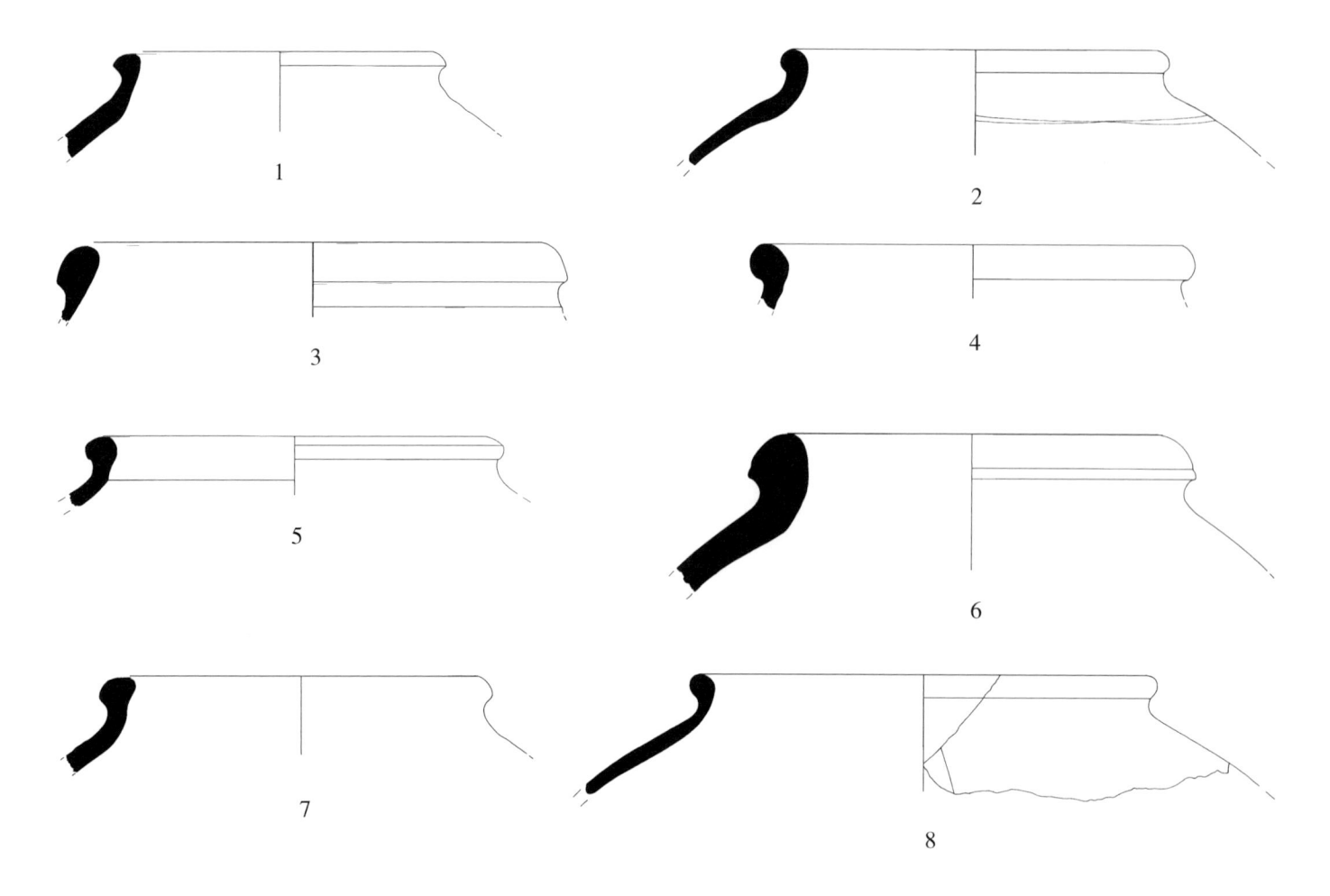

Bronze Age Jar (JR) Type P.III. Scale 1:5

1. JR. P.III.a (TS. 2752; IVP, 1.3, Room 9B). Phase 4. Small rim, neck, and upper shoulder segment. Slightly coarse pink ware, evenly fired. Creamy-green slip in and out.
2. JR. P.III.b (TS. 1636; IVF, 1.11–13, Room 1). Phase 2B. About 1/6 rim, neck, and shoulder segment. Medium coarse ware, unevenly fired with grayish core and brown at surfaces. Cream slip in and out.
3. JR. P.III.c (TS. 3277; Op. 6, 3.1, Room 32). Phase 4. Large rim and neck segment. Ware description unavailable.
4. JR. P.III.d (TS. 2758; IVP, 1.5, Room 9). Phase 2B. Small rim and neck segment. Fairly fine pink ware, evenly fired. Cream slip out and just over rim in.
5. JR. P.III.e (TS. 1704; IVK, 1.3, Room 2A). Phase 3. Small rim, neck, and shoulder segment. Medium coarse grayware with lime and mica grits, evenly fired. Self slip in and out.
6. JR. P.III.f (TS. 1718; IVX, 2.3 = IVM, Room 7). Phase 2B. Four large rim, neck, and shoulder segments. Very coarse pink ware, unevenly fired. Cream slip in and out.
7. JR. P.III.g (TS. 3323; Op. 8, 1.1, Room 29A). Phase 4. About 1/12 rim, neck, and upper shoulder segment. Slightly coarse pinkish-buff ware with white lime grits and a few small pebbles, evenly fired. Creamy-green slip out and just over rim in.
8. JR. P.III.h (PM. A.11; TS.1634; IVF, 1.13, Room 1). Phase 2A. Large rim, neck, and shoulder segment with remains of a potter's mark incised on the shoulder before firing. Coarse pinkish-brown ware, unevenly fired. Cream slip in and out.

Plate 272

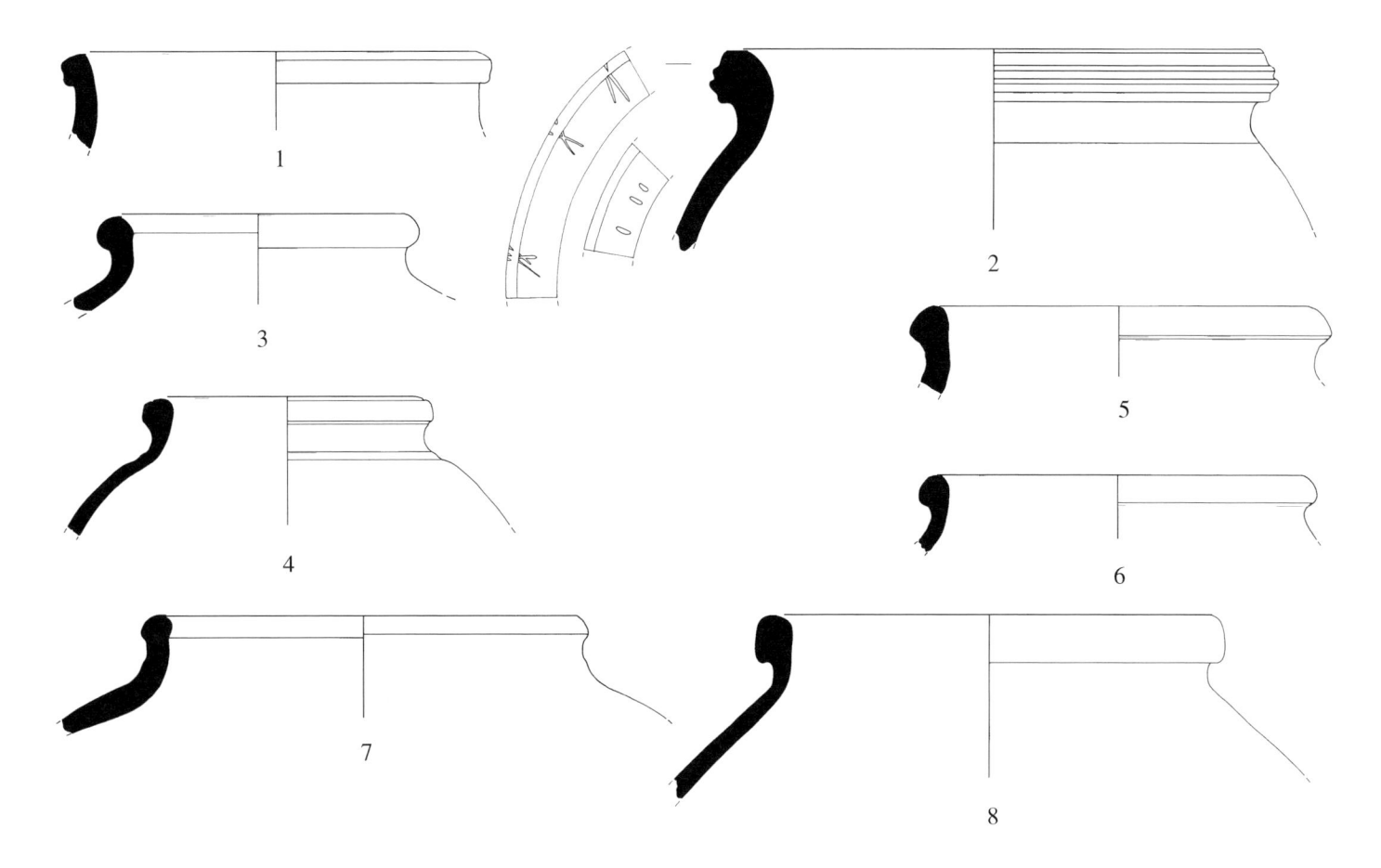

Bronze Age Jar (JR) Type Q. Scale 1:5

1. JR. Q.I.a (TS. 1579; IIA, 9.2, Pit E). Phase 5. Small rim and neck segment. Slightly coarse greenish-buff ware with lime and mica grits, evenly fired. Self slip in and out.
2. JR. Q.I.b (PM. A.1 and PM. C.14; SW. 684; IVO, 1.3 + 1.4, Room 10A). Phase 2B. Two large rim, neck, and shoulder segments with potter's marks incised on top of extant rim fragments before firing. Medium coarse buff ware, evenly fired. Light cream slip in and out.
3. JR. Q.II.a (TS. 1595; IVJ, 1.5, Room 4). Phase 2B. Small rim, neck, and upper shoulder segment. Coarse buff ware, evenly fired. Pink slip in and out.
4. JR. Q.II.b (TS. 4007; Op. 8, 3.3, Room 29). Phase 3. Large rim, neck, and shoulder segment. Ware description unavailable.
5. JR. Q.II.c (TS. 3367; Op. 11, 4.1, Room 20). Phase 2B. Small rim and neck segment. Ware description unavailable.
6. JR. Q.II.d (TS. 3444; Op. 11, 4.1, Room 20). Phase 2B. Small rim and neck segment. Fairly coarse ware with many gold- and silver-colored mica and white lime grits, unevenly fired with gray core and buff-brown at surfaces. Self slip in and out.
7. JR. Q.II.e (TS. 1589; IVJ, 1.5, Room 4). Phase 2B. Large rim, neck, and upper shoulder segment. Coarse grayish ware, unevenly fired. Cream slip in and out.
8. JR. Q.II.f (TS. 2798; IVO, 1.3, Fill). Phase 3. About 1/3 rim, neck, and shoulder segment. Slightly coarse buff ware, evenly fired. Creamy-green slip out.

Plate 273

1

2

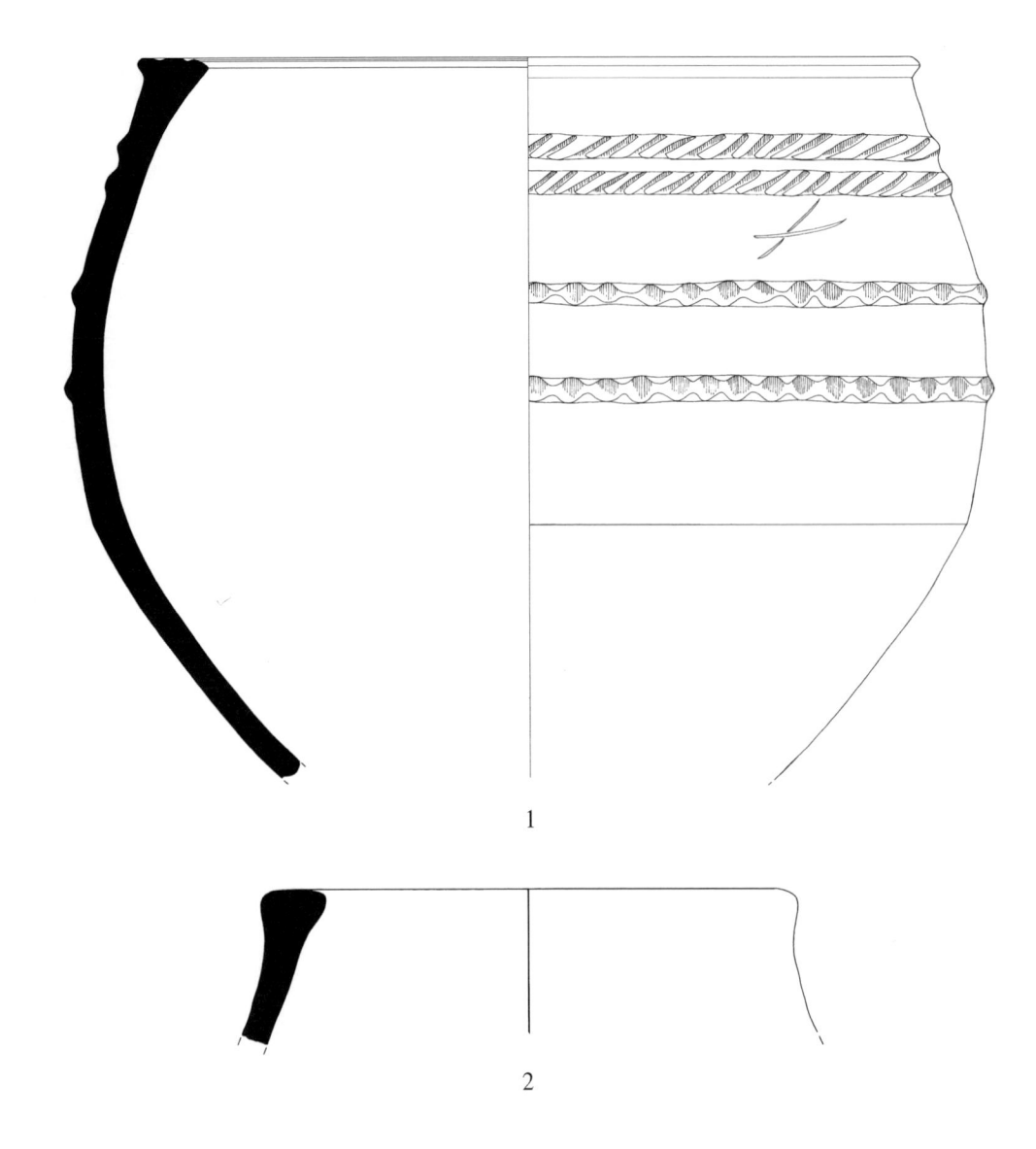

Bronze Age Jar (JR) Type R. Scale 1:5

1. JR. R.I.a (PM. C.14; SW. 730; IVZ(N1), 2.2, Room 21). Phase 2B. About 1/3 rim and nearly complete body profile. Applied rope-like bands decorated with finger- and tool-impressed decoration on upper wall of vessel; X-shaped potter's mark incised on wall before firing. Slightly coarse, heavy, light brown ware with lime and mica grits, evenly fired. Thick (2–3 mm) self slip in and creamy-buff slip out.
2. JR. R.II.a (TS. 1101; VD, 2.4, Pit, north end). Phase 9. About 1/10 rim and upper shoulder segment. Very coarse pinkish-brown ware with straw temper, fairly evenly fired. Cream slip in and out.

Plate 274

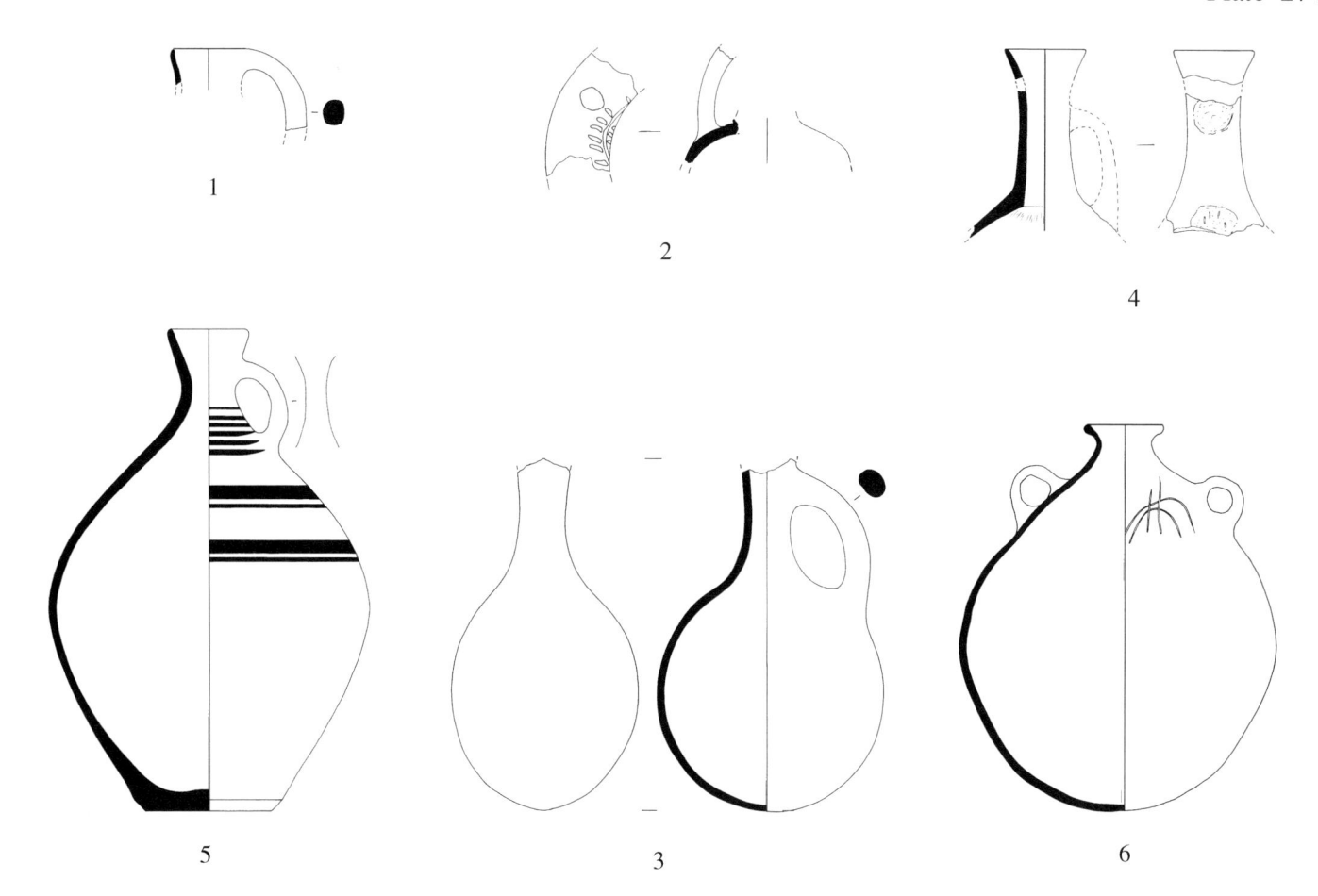

Bronze Age Flask (FL) Types A and B. Scale 1:5

1. FL. A.I.a (TS. 1720; IVM, 1.4, Room 7). Phase 2B. Rim and vertical loop handle segment. Pinkish-grayware, unevenly fired. Self slip out. Compare Til Barsip Hypogeum, (Thureau-Dangin and Dunand 1936, fig. 32, pl. 26:1).
2. FL. A.I.b (TS. 1236; IIIG/H, 1.8a, Room 3A). Phase 3. Segment of handle and shoulder with tool-impressed decoration at the base of the neck and on the upper part of the shoulder incised before firing. Fine buff ware, evenly fired. Creamy-buff slip out.
3. FL. A.II.a (SW. 722; IVS, 4.10, Room 12). Phase 2A (see also pl. 97a). Complete except for missing rim. Vessel contained charred grain. Medium buff ware with lime and mica grits, evenly fired. Self slip out.
4. FL. A.II.a (TS. 2563; IVF, 1.11–13, 3.1, Room 1). Phase 2A. Neck and upper shoulder extant with remains of a loop handle attached to the neck and shoulder of the vessel. Fairly fine pinkish-buff ware, evenly fired. Wet-smoothed and vertically burnished on neck and shoulder prior to firing.
5. FL. A.II.b (SW. 706; IVX, 2.6 = IVM, Room 7). Phase 2A (see also pl. 97b). Mended to near completion. Medium buff ware with lime grits, evenly fired. Cream slip in and out. Horizontally painted red bands on neck and shoulder.
6. FL. B.I.a (PM. B.9; SW. 537; IVJ, 1.5, Room 4). Phase 2B. Mended to near completion with a potter's mark or decoration incised on shoulder before firing. Two wide loop handles on opposite sides of the shoulder. Fairly coarse brown ware, evenly fired. Cream slip in and out.

Plate 275

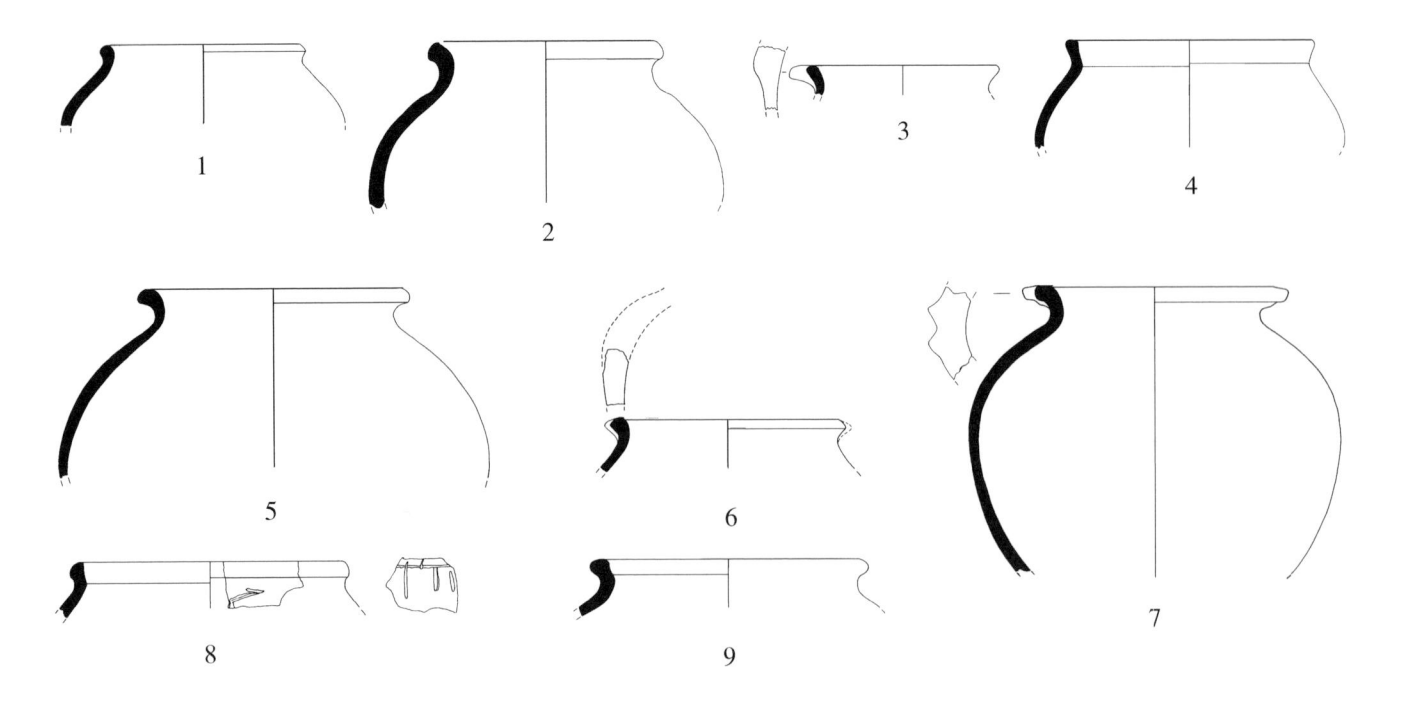

### Bronze Age Cooking Pot (CP) Type A.I. Scale 1:5

1. CP. A.I.a (TS. 2160; XA, 1.3, Room 15). Phase 2B. About 1/6 rim, neck, and shoulder segment. Fairly coarse gritty blackish-brown ware, evenly fired. Heavily charred in and out.
2. CP. A.I.b (TS. 326; IVD, 3.1, West side of Town Wall). Phase 2B. About 1/4 rim, neck, and upper wall segment. Coarse gritty brown ware, evenly fired. Charred on rim and outside wall.
3. CP. A.I.c (TS. 776; IC, 1.43, Ashy layer). Phase 4. About 1/12 rim and neck segment with remains of a ledge handle on the rim. Very coarse pink ware with lime and mica grits, evenly fired. Burnished in and out.
4. CP. A.I.d (TS. 1239; IIIF, 3.1, Room 16). Phase 4. Large rim, neck, and upper wall segment. Slightly coarse gritty brown ware, unevenly fired gray in. Burnished irregularly outside. Thick black-colored substance inside may be bitumen residue.
5. CP. A.I.e (TS. 712; IVF, 4.1, Room 1). Phase 2A. Large rim, neck, and upper wall segment. Coarse dark brown ware, evenly fired. Burnished out and just over rim in.
6. CP. A.I.f (TS. 1955; IVC, 1.5 = IVM, Room 7). Phase 2B. Small rim, neck, and upper shoulder segment with remains of triangular-shaped ledge handle on the rim. Fairly fine brown ware with small lime grits, evenly fired. Burnished out and just over rim in.
7. CP. A.I.g (SW. 671; IVO, 1.3 + 1.4, Room 10A). Phase 2B. Mended to 3/4 completion with two indented ledge handles on rim at opposite sides of the vessel. Pinkish-buff ware, evenly fired. Cream slip out.
8. CP. A.I.h (PM. A.15; TS. 859; IC, 1.52). Phase 3. Small rim, neck, and body segments with remains of a potter's mark incised on the shoulder and the non-joining body sherd before firing. Coarse brown ware, evenly fired. Charred out. Burnished in and out.
9. CP. A.I.i (TS. 2838; IVN, 2.1, Room 8). Phase 2B. About 1/5 rim, neck, and upper shoulder segment. Fairly coarse gritty pinkish-brown ware, evenly fired. Self slip in and out with irregular horizontal burnishing.

Plate 276

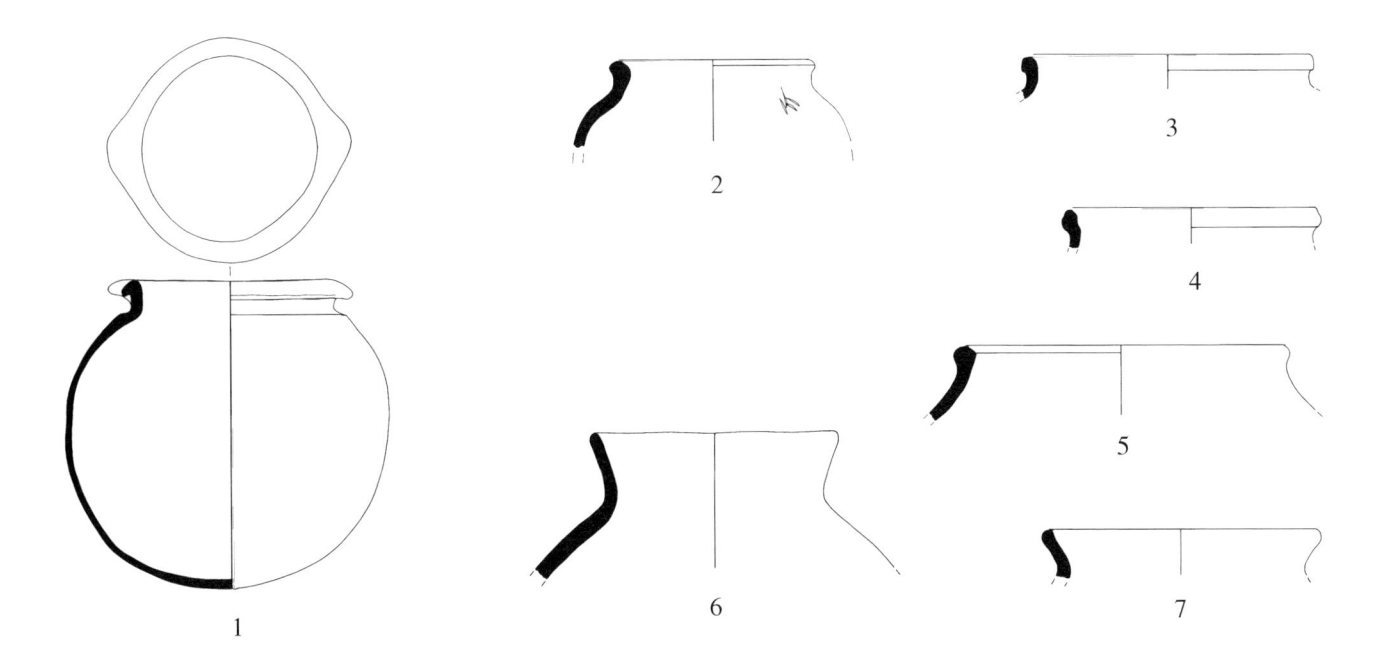

Bronze Age Cooking Pot (CP) Types A.II and A.III. Scale 1:5

1. CP. A.II.a (SW. 539; IVJ, 1.5, 2.1, Room 4). Phase 2A (see also pl. 98c and d). Mended to near completion with two triangular-shaped ledge handles attached to opposite sides of the rim. Fairly coarse pink ware, unevenly fired with black core. Burnished in and out.
2. CP. A.II.b (PM. E.2; TS. 1647; IVL/P, 1.3, Pit). Phase 3. About 1/6 rim, neck, and shoulder segment with a potter's mark incised on the shoulder before firing. Dark grayware with mica grits, evenly fired. Self slip in and out.
3. CP. A.II.c (TS. 2869; IVN, 1.4, 2.1, Rooms 8A/18A and 8). Phases 3 and 2B. About 1/5 rim, neck, and upper shoulder segment. Fairly coarse gritty pink ware, evenly fired. Self slip in and out.
4. CP. A.II.d (TS. 1941; IVF, 1.5, Room 1A). Phase 3. Small rim and neck segment. Fairly coarse gritty pinkish-brown ware, evenly fired.
5. CP. A.II.e (TS. 2841; IVZ(N2), 3.5, Room 21). Phase 2B. About 1/8 rim, neck, and upper shoulder segment. Fairly coarse gritty grayish-buff ware, evenly fired. Self slip in and out.
6. CP. A.III.a (TS. 1169; IIA, 9.8, Room 4). Phase 2. About 1/4 segment of rim, neck, and shoulder. Fairly coarse ware with straw temper and lime and mica grits, unevenly fired with light brown core and pinkish-brown at surfaces. Wet-smoothed and burnished below rim in and out.
7. CP. A.III.b (TS. 1548; IIA, 8.1, Pit C1). Phase 9. Small rim and neck segment. Slightly coarse drab ware, evenly fired.

Plate 277

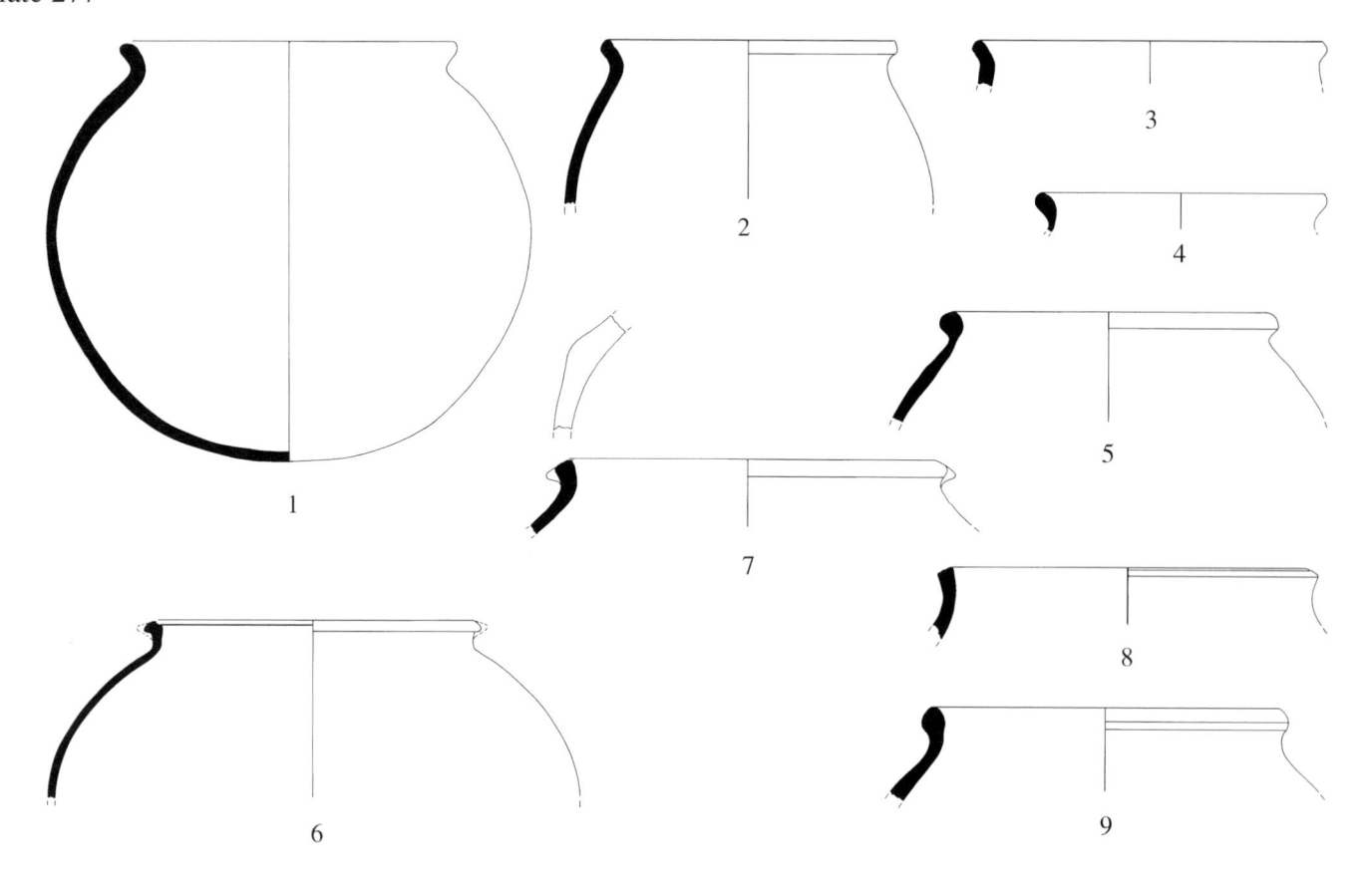

Bronze Age Cooking Pot (CP) Type B.I. Scale 1:5

1. CP. B.I.a (SW. 308 = TS. 1949; IVG, 1.4 + 1.5, Room 3). Phases 2B and 2A. About 1/2 rim and body sherds mended to complete profile. Hard, slightly coarse brown ware with lime and mica grits, fairly evenly fired. Girth of body outside wet-smoothed at leather-hard stage of manufacture. Wheelmade rim and shoulder, lower body handmade.
2. CP. B.I.b (TS. 820; IC, 1.56). Phase 2. About 1/2 rim and upper body. Very coarse ware with large grits, unevenly fired with gray core and brown at surfaces.
3. CP. B.I.c (TS. 1971; IVC, 1.4 = IVM, Room 7). Phase 2B. Small rim and upper shoulder segment. Slightly coarse gritty light brown ware, evenly fired.
4. CP. B.I.d (SC. 1824; IVF, 1.5, Room 1A). Phase 3. About 1/16 rim and neck segment. Slightly coarse brownish-buff ware with lime and small silver-colored mica grits, evenly fired. Self slip horizontally burnished out and around neck in.
5. CP. B.I.e (TS. 2249; IXA, 1.6). Phase 3. Large rim and shoulder segment. Fairly coarse gritty pinkish-brown ware, evenly fired. Surface very worn, but traces of burnishing on the rim.
6. CP. B.I.f (SW. 298 = TS. 555; IF, 1.16 + 1.19). Phases 3 and 2. Two large rim and upper wall segments with traces of triangular-shaped ledge handle attached to the rim. Fairly coarse brown ware with lime and mica grits, evenly fired. Wet-smoothed out and to below neck in during leather-hard stage of manufacture. Rim and body horizontally burnished.
7. CP. B.I.g (TS. 967; IIIG/H, 1.4, Rooms 22A/B Extramural). Phase 5. Large rim and shoulder segment with one triangular-shaped ledge handle attached to the rim. Coarse pink ware, unevenly fired with brown core. Buff slip out.
8. CP. B.I.h (TS. 1102 = TS. 2152; VD, 2.1). Phase 4. Two small joining rim and neck segments. Fairly coarse gritty reddish-brown ware, unevenly fired orange-buff in patches out.
9. CP. B.I.i (TS. 2836; IVP, 1.4, Room 9A). Phase 3. About 1/10 rim and upper shoulder segment. Coarse gritty pinkish-brown ware, evenly fired. Self slip in and out.

Plate 278

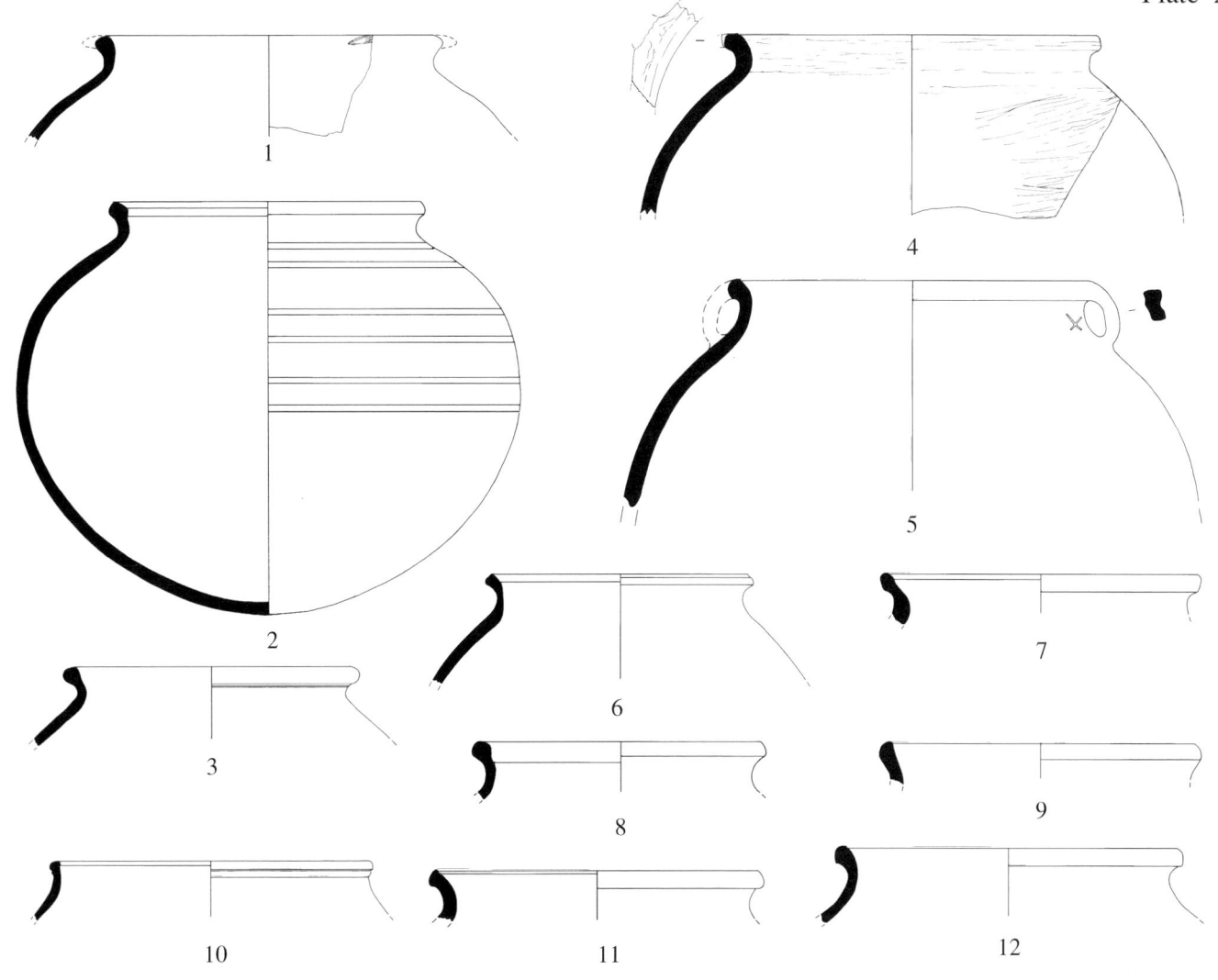

Bronze Age Cooking Pot (CP) Type B.II. Scale 1:5

1. CP. B.II.a (TS. 822; IC, 1.39). Occupation layer + 1.40). Phases 5 and 4. About 1/4 rim, neck, and shoulder segments; two joining fragments with remains of a triangular-shaped ledge handle on the rim. Coarse pink ware with lime and mica grits. Self burnished in and out.
2. CP. B.II.b (SW. 681 = TS. 649 and TS. 729; IVF, 1.3 + 4.1, Room 1). Phase 2A. Mended to completion. Coarse gritty light brown ware, evenly fired. Irregularly burnished with horizontal bands out and over rim in to the carination at the neck. Cream slip in and out.
3. CP. B.II.c (TS. 2840; IVN, 2.3, Room 18). Phase 2A. About 1/6 rim, neck, and shoulder segment. Fairly coarse gritty grayish-brown ware, unevenly fired. Self slip and irregular horizontal burnish out and just over rim in.
4. CP. B.II.d (SW. 284; IIIB, 2.9, Room 1B). Phase 3. About 1/2 rim, neck, and upper body segment with remains of triangular-shaped ledge handle on rim. Coarse, but hard fired, brown ware with many lime and mica grits, unevenly fired slightly gray inside. Wet-smoothed and irregularly burnished outside and around inside rim at leather-hard stage of manufacture.
5. CP. B.II.e (PM. C.14; TS. 648 = TS. 1625; IVF, 1.11–13, 4.1, Room 1). Phases 2A and 2B. Large rim, neck, and upper body segment with one handle extant and a potter's mark incised on the neck, near the one extant handle, before firing. Very coarse brown ware with mica grits, evenly fired. Irregular horizontal burnishing out and to depth of surviving profile in.
6. CP. B.II.f (TS. 2627; IVX, 10.7 = IVM, Room 7). Phase 2A. Large rim, neck, and shoulder segment. Coarse gritty, friable, brown ware, evenly fired. Self slip out irregularly burnished in crisscross fashion on body below neck out.
7. CP. B.II.g (TS. 1997; IIA, 9.8, Room 4). Phase 2. Segment. Coarse, gritty brown ware, fairly evenly fired. Blackened out and over rim in.
8. CP. B.II.h (TS. 1058; IC, 1.32A, 1.32B, Pit A). Phase 7. Two non-joining rim and neck segments. Coarse pink ware, unevenly fired with brown core. Burnished in and out.
9. CP. B.II.i (TS. 248; IIA, 5.2, Pit C, Derived EB). Phase 12. Small rim and neck segment. Slightly coarse pinkish-brown ware with line and mica grits, evenly fired.
10. CP. B.II.j (TS. 2628; IVM, 10.4, Below Room 7). Phase 1A. About 1/8 rim, neck, and upper shoulder segment. Hard, slightly gritty and coarse pinkish-brown ware, evenly fired. Plain self slip in and out.
11. CP. B.II.k (TS. 175; IIA, 8.6). Phase 3. Small rim and neck segment. Very coarse grayish-brown ware with large micaceous and lime grit temper, unevenly fired. Blackened in and out.
12. CP. B.II.l (TS. 2253; IIIG/H, 1.9, Room 3B). Phase 3. Large rim, neck, and shoulder segment. Slightly coarse and gritty pinkish-brown ware, evenly fired. Self burnished out and on rim.

Plate 279

1

2

3

4

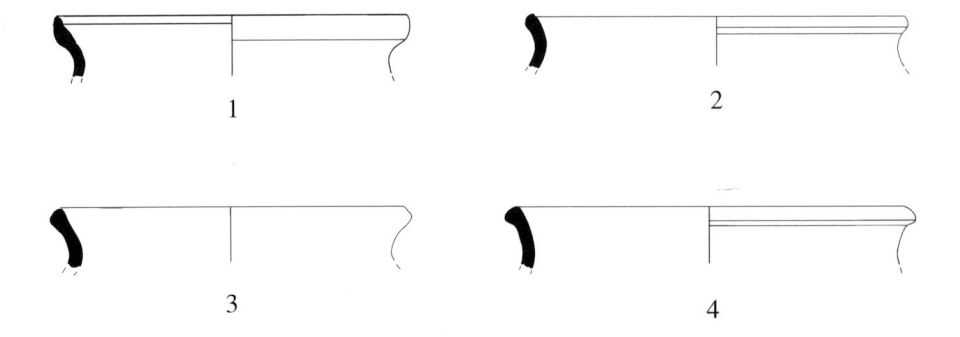

Bronze Age Cooking Pot (CP) Type B.III. Scale 1:5

1. CP. B.III.a (TS. 165; IIA, 8.2, Courtyard). Phase 8. Small rim and neck segment. Coarse brown ware with lime and mica grits and organic temper, evenly fired. Self slip in and out.
2. CP. B.III.b (TS. 2854; IVN, 2.3, Room 18). Phase 2A. About 1/12 rim and neck segment. Slightly coarse light pink ware, evenly fired. Thick creamy-pink slip out.
3. CP. B.III.c (TS. 325; IIA, 8.2, Courtyard). Phase 8. Small rim and neck segment. Coarse grayish-brown ware, evenly fired.
4. CP. B.III.d (TS. 1557; IIA, 9.9, Room 1). Phase 1. Small rim and neck segment. Slightly coarse dark brown ware with lime and mica grits, fairly evenly fired.

Plate 280

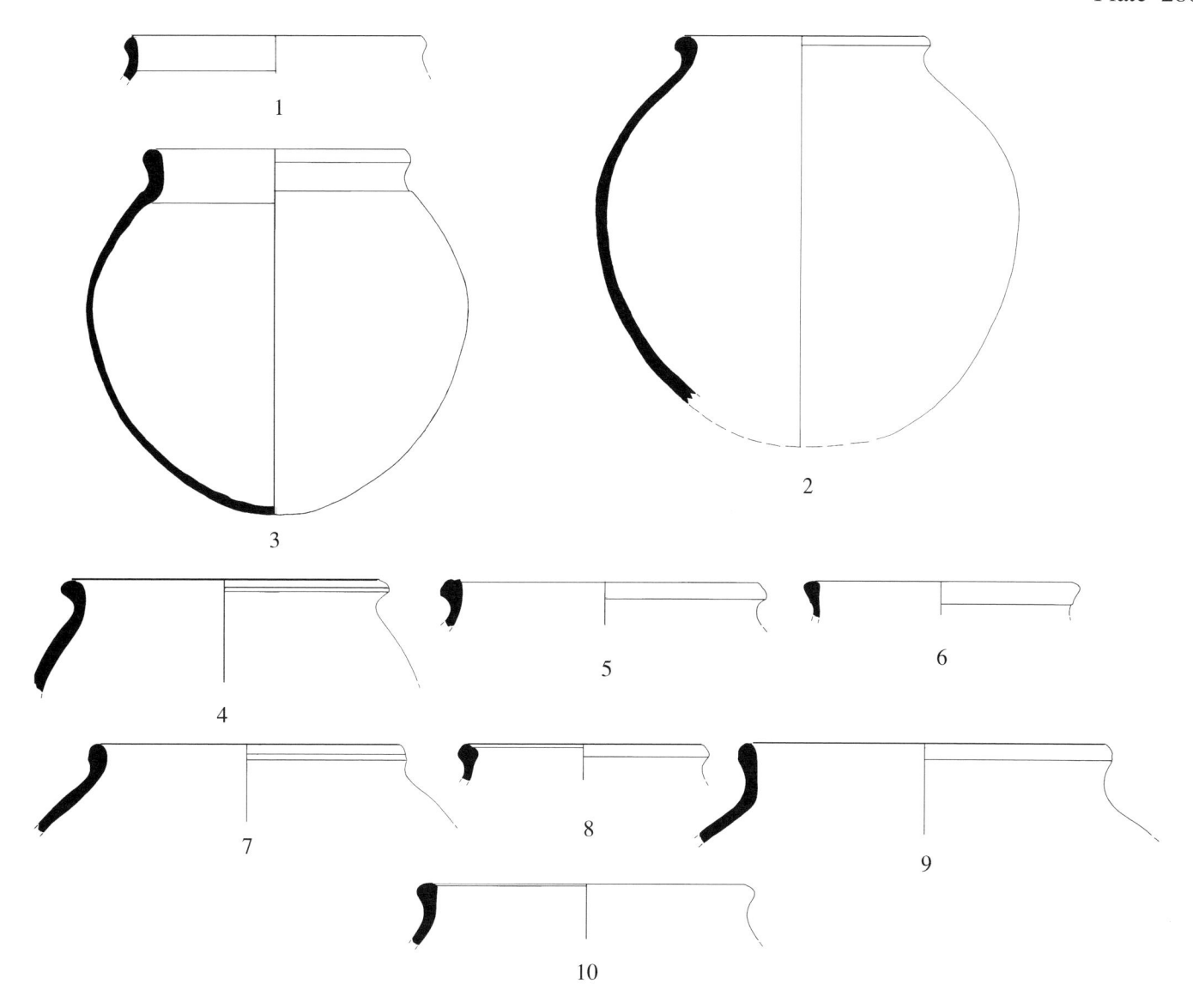

Bronze Age Cooking Pot (CP) Types B.IV and B.V. Scale 1:5

1. CP. B.IV.a (TS. 2857; IVO, 1.2, Room 10B). Phase 4. About 1/10 rim, neck, and upper shoulder segment. Fairly coarse gritty pinkish-brown ware, evenly fired. Self slip in and out. Burnished horizontally out.
2. CP. B.IV.b (SW. 132; IXB, Modern pit excavated for the expedition's drinking water barrel just east of the western inner town wall, Grid Square H 5). Phase 2B. Mended to 2/3 completion. The pot contained a baby's skeleton. Very coarse grayish-brown ware with large lime and mica grits, unevenly fired with dark gray and brown core. Wet-smoothed inside during leather-hard stage of manufacture.
3. CP. B.IV.c (SW. 761; Op. 11, 4.1, Room 20). Phase 2B (see also pl. 98e). Complete in situ apart from small delta-shaped body segment missing in base which was covered inside during antiquity by a broken jar sherd to enable further storage of some type of dry goods; flat-shaped irregular limestone lid covered most of rim in situ, but pot filled only with earth and some stones. Coarse brown ware with much white mica grits, evenly fired.
4. CP. B.IV.d (TS. 2852; IVL, 1.2, 1.3, Rooms 3A, 3B). Phases 3 and 4. About 1/4 segment of three joining rim, neck, and shoulder fragments. Fairly coarse gritty ware, unevenly fired grayish in and pink out. Self slip in and out.
5. CP. B.IV.e (TS. 899; XA, 1.1). Phase 4. Small rim and neck segment. Coarse ware with pink core, unevenly fired brown out and dark brown in.
6. CP. B.IV.f (TS. 2158; IA1, 2.5). Phase 1. Small rim and neck segment. Slightly coarse gritty light brown ware, evenly fired.
7. CP. B.IV.g (TS. 1710; IVN, 1.4, Rooms 8A/18A). Phase 3. Large rim, neck, and shoulder segment. Medium coarse grayware with lime grits, unevenly fired. Cream slip in and out.
8. CP. B.IV.h (TS. 2865; IVZ(N1), 1.3). Phase 4. Small rim and neck segment. Slightly coarse grayish-buff ware, evenly fired. Self slip in and out.
9. CP. B.V.a (TS. 1156 = TS. 1163; VE, 1.4, Pit, bottom). Phase 3. About 1/5 segment of two joining rim, neck, and upper shoulder fragments. Fairly coarse pink ware, unevenly fired with brown core.
10. CP. B.V.b (TS. 2848; IVJ, 1.5, Room 4). Phase 2B. About 1/5 segment of two joining rim, neck, and upper shoulder fragments. Slightly coarse pinkish-brown ware, evenly fired. Self slip in and out.

Plate 281

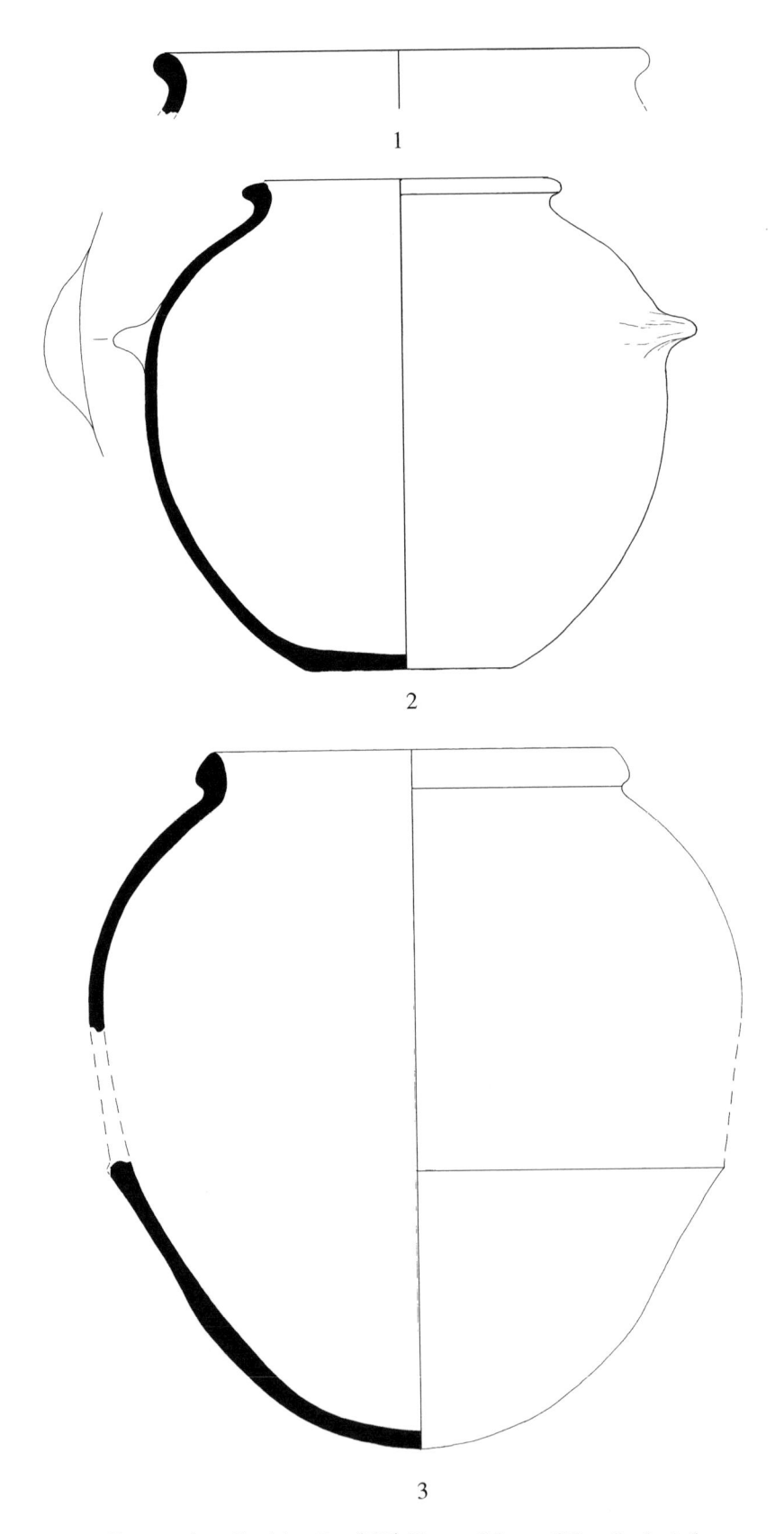

Bronze Age Cooking Pot (CP) Types C.I.a to C.I.c. Scale 1:5

1. CP. C.I.a (TS. 2851; IVM, 1.2, Room 7B). Phase 4. Small rim and upper shoulder segment. Coarse gritty ware with light gray core, unevenly fired pink at surfaces. Self slip in and out.
2. CP. C.I.b (SW. 484; IVK, 2.4, Room 2). Phase 2B. Mended to near completion with two broad ledge handles on opposite sides of the shoulder of the pot. Very coarse pink ware with lime and mica grits, evenly fired. Burnished outside.
3. CP. C.I.c (SW. 680; IVQ, 1.4, Room 6). Phase 2A. Mended to near completion. Very coarse gritty charcoal grayware, unevenly fired. Pinkish-cream slip in and out. Burnished out.

Plate 282

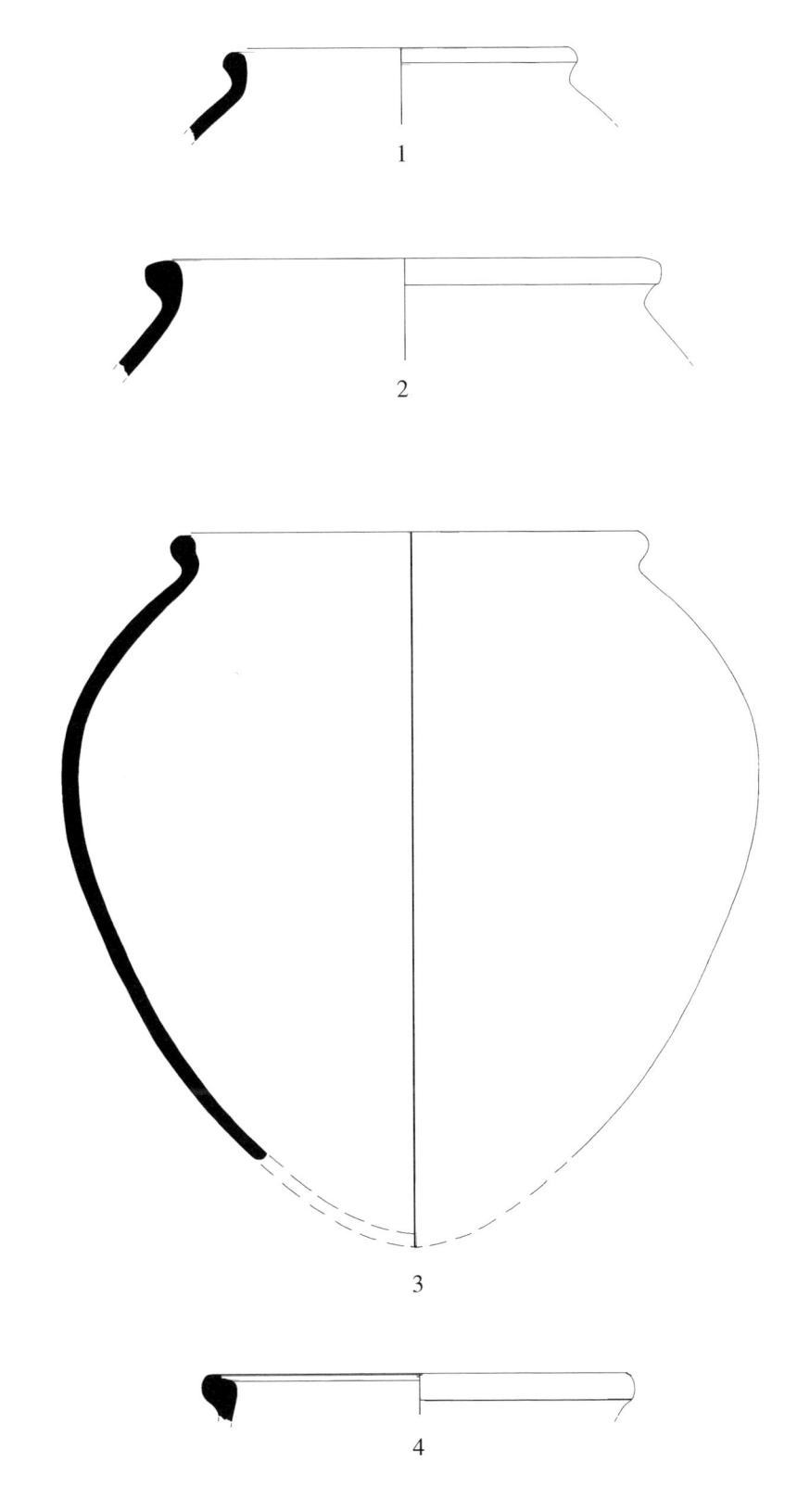

Bronze Age Cooking Pot (CP) Types C.I.d to C.I.g. Scale 1:5

1. CP. C.I.d (TS. 2817; IVZ(N2), 3.5, Room 21). Phase 2B. Large segment of two joining rim and upper shoulder fragments. Fairly coarse gritty pinkish-brown ware, evenly fired. Self slip in and out.
2. CP. C.I.e (TS. 2834; IVP, 1.3, Room 9B). Phase 4. About 1/6 segment of two joining rim and shoulder fragments. Fairly coarse gritty pinkish-brown ware, evenly fired. Remains of self slip out.
3. CP. C.I.f (SW. 678; IVQ, 1.4, Room 6). Phase 2A. Mended to near completion. Coarse gritty pinkish ware, evenly fired. Irregular horizontal burnishing in and out.
4. CP. C.I.g (TS. 2856; IVZ(N2), 3.3). Phase 3. Small rim segment. Coarse gritty pinkish-brown ware, evenly fired. Self slip in and out.

Plate 283

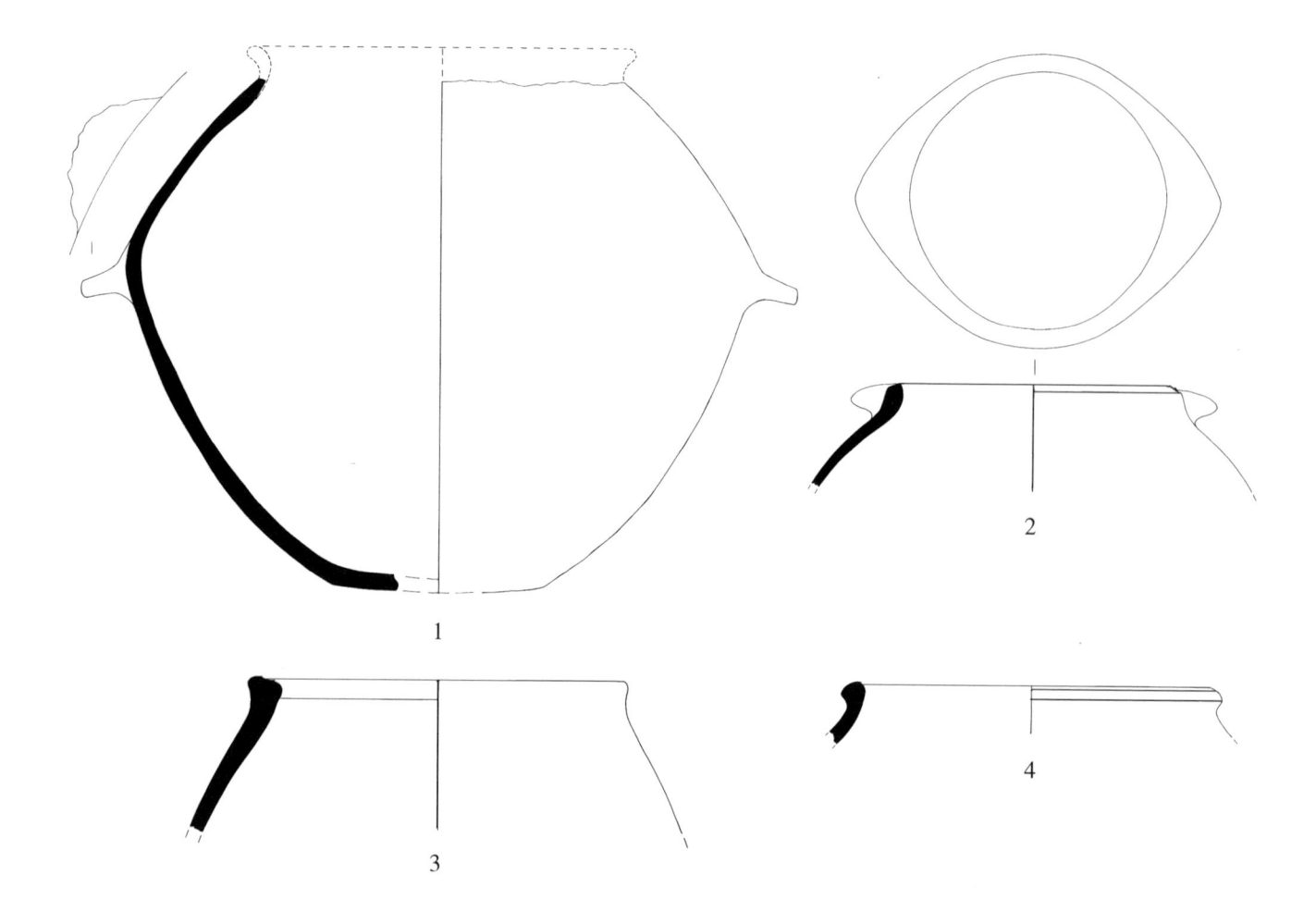

Bronze Age Cooking Pot (CP) Type C.II. Scale 1:5

1. CP. C.II.a (SW. 740; IVM, 1.7, Room 7). Phase 2A. Body mended to near completion, but rim is missing, which may be a "holemouth" type (but cf. rim type of cooking pot SW. 484, pl. 281:2). One plain ledge handle extant on lower part of the shoulder. Crumbly gritty grayware, fairly evenly fired.
2. CP. C.II.b (TS. 1590; IVJ, 1.5, 1.6, Room 4). Phases 2B and 2A. About 1/2 rim and shoulder segment with triangular-shaped ledge handles attached to opposite sides of rim. Medium coarse brown ware with lime and mica grits, evenly fired. Wet-smoothed with irregular horizontal burnish in and out.
3. CP. C.II.c (TS. 976; VE, 1.2 + VF, 1.9). Phases 5, 4. About 1/4 segment of two non-joining rim and shoulder fragments. Coarse pink ware, evenly fired. Buff slip out. Charred on rim.
4. CP. C.II.d (TS. 2870; IVJ Bin, 3.4, Room 5). Phase 2B. Ablut 1/10 rim and upper shoulder segment. Slightly coarse gritty brown ware, evenly fired. Self slip in and out. Burnished horizontally out and on top of rim.

Plate 284

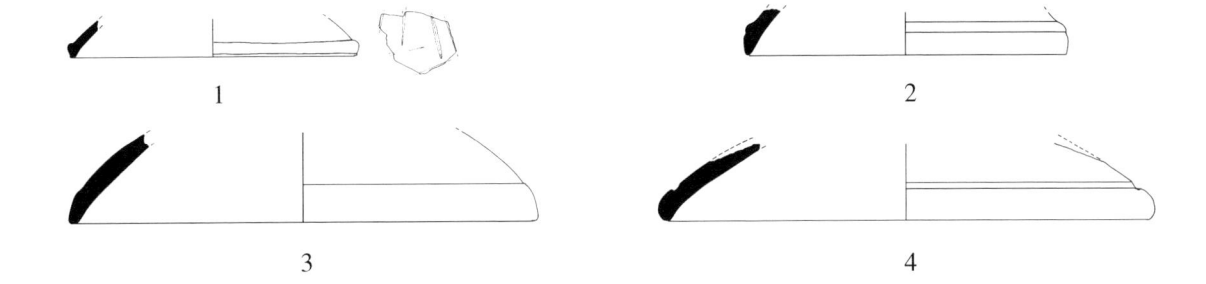

### Bronze Age Cooking Pot Lid (CP.Ld.) Type A. Scale 1:5

1. CP.Ld. A.I.a (TS. 2831; IVM, 1.5, Room 7). Phase 2A. Small rim and wall segment with two body sherds decorated on the outside wall with a linear pattern incised before firing. Coarse gritty brown ware, evenly fired. Self slip in and out.
2. CP.Ld. A.II.a (TS. 882; IC, 1.40). Phase 4. About 1/40 rim and wall segment. Coarse pinkish-brown ware, unevenly fired with dark core. Light brown slip out.
3. CP.Ld. A.II.b (TS. 2566; IVX, 2.3 = IVM, Room 7). Phase 2B. Small rim and wall segment. Coarse gritty brown ware, evenly fired. Charred out.
4. CP.Ld. A.II.c (TS. 488; IIIG/H, 1.3, Room 22A). Phase 5. About 1/5 rim and wall segment of two non-joining rim fragments. Coarse pinkish-brown ware with many mica grits, unevenly fired gray on inside half of core.

Plate 285

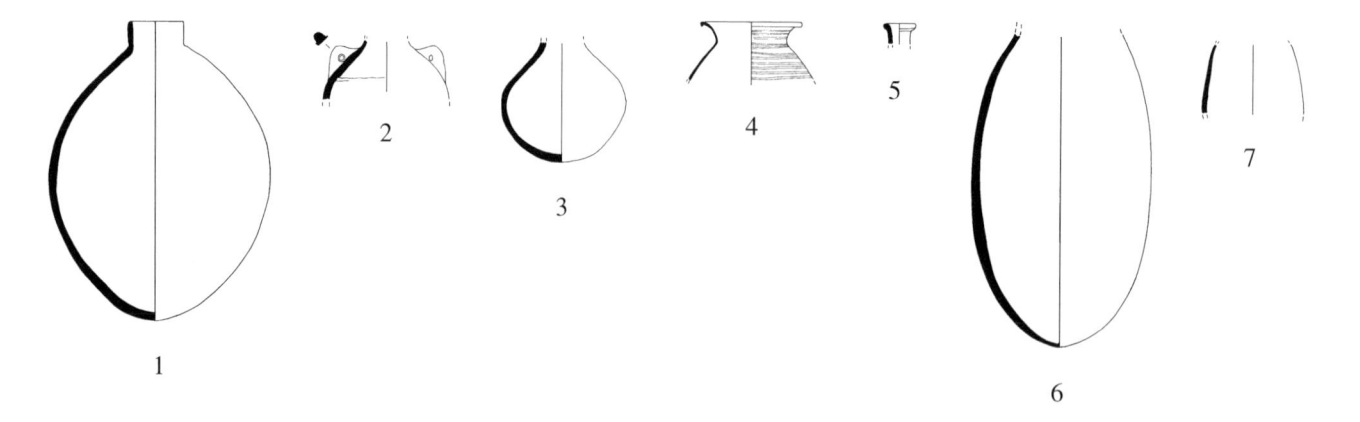

Bronze Age Bottle (Bt.) Types A and B. Scale 1:5

1. Bt. A.I.a (SW. 626; IVQ, 1.6, Room 6). Phase 2A. Mended to near completion. Fine ware, unevenly fired from light gray to light brown, buff, and pink. Burnished out.
2. Bt. A.I.b.1 (TS. 3527; Op. 7, 18.1, Room 34). Phase 2A(a). Shoulder segment with one extant pierced vertical lug handle. Fairly fine pinkish-buff ware with fine gold- and silver-colored mica and a few white lime grits, evenly fired. Creamy-buff slip out.
3. Bt. A.I.b.2 (TS. 3439; Op. 11, 4.1, Room 20). Phase 2B. Complete except for rim. Fairly fine buff ware with some white mica grits and a few white lime grits, evenly fired. Creamy-buff self slip in and out.
4. Bt. A.I.b.3 (TS. 1211; VE, 1.4, Pit, bottom). Phase 3. Small rim and shoulder segment. Fine grayware with lime and mica grits, evenly fired. Horizontally ring-burnished out and just over rim in.
5. Bt. A.I.b.4 (TS. 1142; IIIG/H, 1.7, Room 18). Phase 4. Small rim and neck segment. Fine light grayware, evenly fired. Cream slip in and out. Charred in and out.
6. Bt. B.I.1 (SW. 659 = SC. 3320; IVJ, 1.5, Room 4). Phase 2B. "Syrian Bottle"-type. Body mended to completion, but rim missing. Fairly fine light brown ware, evenly fired. Spaced horizontal line burnishing out.
7. Bt. B.I.2 (TS. 1215; VIIA, 3.6). Phase 1. "Syrian Bottle"-type. Body fragment. Fairly fine light grayware, evenly fired. Self burnished with irregular horizontal bands out.

Plate 286

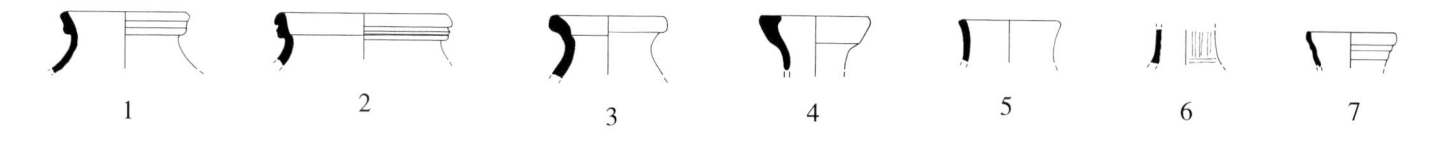

Bronze Age Jug (Jg.) Types A–C. Scale 1:5

1. Jg. A.I.a (TS. 2307; XA, 1.3, Room 15). Phase 2B. About 1/6 rim and neck segment. Slightly coarse green ware, evenly fired. Self slip out and just over rim in.
2. Jg. A.I.b (TS. 2221; IVC, 1.7). Phase 2B. Small rim and neck segment. Slightly coarse pinkish-buff ware, evenly fired. Self slip out.
3. Jg. B.I.a (TS. 2343; XA, 1.3, Room 15). Phase 2B. About 1/8 rim and neck segment. Fine pink ware, evenly fired. Creamy-yellow slip out and just over rim in.
4. Jg. C. 1 (TS. 1604; IVP, 1.4, Room 9A). Phase 3. Small rim and neck segment. Very hard pinkish ware with lime and mica grits, evenly fired. Self slip in and out.
5. Jg. C. 2 (TS. 3495; Op. 7, 17.1, Extramural). Phase 2A(b). About 1/5 rim and neck segment. Slightly coarse ware with many black and white lime grits, unevenly fired with pink core and light brown at surfaces. Self slip in and out.
6. Jg. C. 3 (TS. 1266; XA, 1.3, Room 15). Phase 2B. Neck segment. Fine grayware, unevenly fired black at surfaces. Irregular vertical burnish on neck and remains of horizontal burnish on upper fragment of shoulder.
7. Jg. C. 4 (SC. 3301; VIA, 3.1a). Phase 5. Small rim and neck segment.

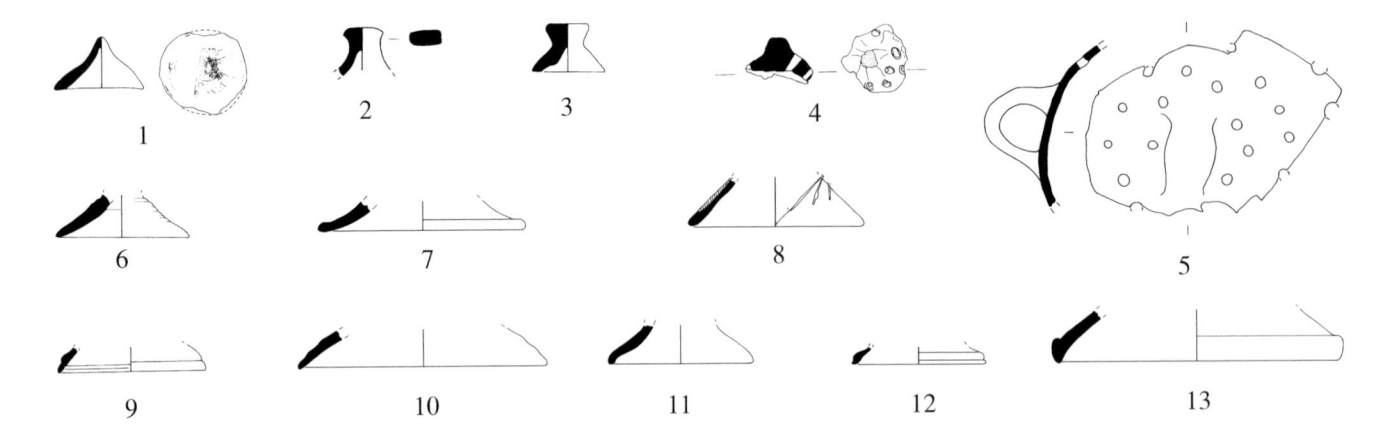

Bronze Age Lid (Ld.) Types A–C. Scale 1:5

1. Ld. A.I.a (TS. 1951; IVG, 1.3, Room 3A). Phase 3. Complete except for chips broken at edge of rim. Fairly fine pinkish-buff ware, evenly fired. Creamy-buff slip in and out.
2. Ld. A.II.a (TS. 3360; Op. 10, 22.2, Room 8). Phase 2B. Fragment with knob-like handle. Ware description unavailable.
3. Ld. A.III.a (TS. 3091; IVM, 3.1, Room 7, Pit A). Phase 2A. Complete with knob-like handle. Fairly coarse creamy-green ware, evenly fired. Self slip in and out.
4. Ld. B.I.a (SW. 216; VB, 1.1). Phase 4. Fragment with pierced strainer-like holes and a knob-like handle. Greenish ware with small black and white lime grits, evenly fired.
5. Ld. B.II.a (TS. 987; IC, 1.41). Phase 4. Fragment of a perforated lid with a complete loop handle. Fairly coarse buff ware, evenly fired. Cream slip in and out.
6. Ld. C.I.a (TS. 2670; IVX, 1.2, Room 14A). Phase 3. About 1/8 rim and wall segment. Slightly coarse pink ware, evenly fired. Creamy-pink slip out.
7. Ld. C.I.b (TS. 1762; IVL, 1.3, Room 3A). Phase 3. Small rim and wall segment. Medium fine pink ware with lime grits, evenly fired. Cream slip in and out.
8. Ld. C.II.a (PM. E.2; TS. 1746; IVL, 1.3, Room 3A). Phase 3. Small rim and wall segment with remains of a potter's mark incised on the outside wall before firing. Fairly fine pink ware, evenly fired.
9. Ld. C.II.b (SC. 1939; IVF/N, 5.1, Doorway between Rooms 1 and 8). Phase 2B. Small rim and wall segment. Ware description not available.
10. Ld. C.III.a (TS. 1747; IVN, 2.2, Room 8). Phase 2A. Small rim and wall segment. Fine dark pinkish ware with small lime grits, evenly fired. Cream slip in and out.
11. Ld. C.III.b (TS. 2672; IVF, 4.1, Room 1). Phase 2A. Small rim and wall segment. Fairly fine pink ware, evenly fired. Self slip in and out.
12. Ld. C.III.c (TS. 2830; IVC, 1.14b). Phase 1C. About 1/8 rim and wall segment. Fairly fine buff ware, evenly fired. Self slip in and out.
13. Ld. C.III.d (TS. 1564; IIA, 9.3, Room 8). Phase 4. Small rim and wall segment. Fairly fine pinkish-buff ware with lime and gold-colored mica grits, evenly fired. Self slip in and out.

Plate 288

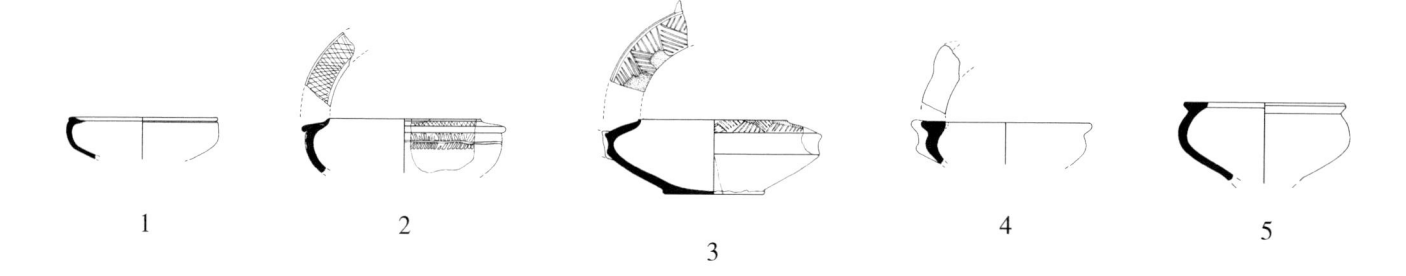

Bronze Age Lamp (Lp.) Types A and B. Scale 1:5

1. Lp. A.I.a (SW. 194; IE, 1.8). Phase 3. Small rim and wall segment. Fairly fine buff ware with some black grits, evenly fired. Ring burnished outside on the rim and body.
2. Lp. A.II.a.1 (IP [G.4] A.III.a; SW. 190; IIIG, 3.1, Room 18). Phase 4. Small rim and wall segment decorated with seal-rolled linear and herringbone patterns on top of rim and on upper wall of body. Fine ware with small black-, gold-, and white-colored grits, unevenly fired with brown core and gray at surfaces.
3. Lp. A.II.a.2 (IP [G.4] A.IV.a; SW. 145; IIIC, 4.9, Room 19A). Phase 5. About 1/5 rim segment and complete wall profile with remains of a lug-type handle on the extant portion of the vessel. Linear decoration on top of the rim probably hand-incised. Dark grayware with black and white grits, evenly fired. Burnished outside.
4. Lp. B.I.1 (SW. 343; IIIF, 2.1). Phase 5. Small rim and wall segment with remains of a vertically positioned double-winged handle from the top of the rim to below the carination of the wall. Fine grayware, evenly fired.
5. Lp. B.I.2 (TS. 1740; IVZ(S), 5.3, 5.4). Phase 2B. Large rim and wall segment. Medium fine grayware with lime and mica grits, evenly fired. Self slip in and out. Horizontally burnished on upper wall and vertically burnished on lower wall.

Plate 289

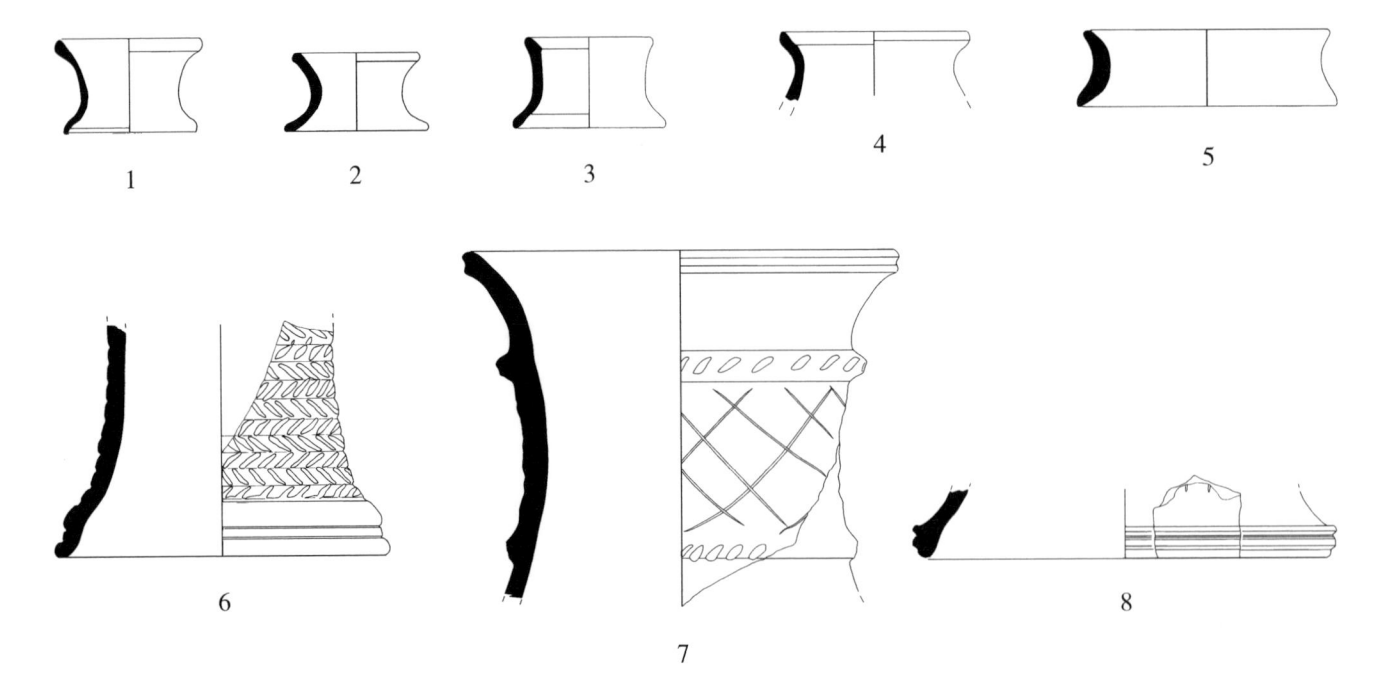

Bronze Age Pot Stand (PS) Types A and B. Scale 1:5

1. PS. A.I.a (SW. 560; IVQ, 1.4, 1.6, Room 6). Phase 2A (see also pl. 97d). Found nearly complete in situ. Fairly coarse pinkish-buff ware, evenly fired. Cream slip in and out.
2. PS. A.II.a (SW. 670 = TS. 2473; IVQ, 1.6, Room 6). Phase 2A. Mended almost to completion. Fairly fine buff ware, evenly fired. Cream slip out and blackish-brown slip in.
3. PS. A.II.b (SW. 727; IVP, 1.6, Room 9). Phase 2A. Complete profile segment. Slightly coarse grayish-buff ware with lime grits, evenly fired. Creamy-buff slip in and out.
4. PS. A.II.c (TS. 1745; IVN, 3.1, Room 18). Phase 2A. Small rim segment of either the top or bottom of the stand. Medium fine pink ware, evenly fired. Cream slip in and out.
5. PS. B.I.a (TS. 733; IIIJ, 1.2, West of Wall 1). Phase 4. Nearly complete. Fairly fine creamish-buff ware, evenly fired.
6. PS. B.I.b.1 (TS. 2557 = Op. 1, TS. 3396; IVP, 1.2, Room 9B). Phase 4. About 1/2 segment incised with registers of herringbone-style incisions before firing. Slightly coarse pink ware, evenly fired. Buff slip out.
7. PS. B.I.b.2 (TS. 3251; Op. 5, 17.1). Phase 4. About 1/2 rim segment and most of wall profile with incised checkerboard design bounded at top and bottom with applied and impressed rope-like bands. Ware description unavailable.
8. PS. B.I.b.3 (PM. F; TS. 3349 = TS. 3982; Op. 5, 13.5). Phase 4. Small rim and wall segment with remains of a potter's mark or decoration incised on outside wall before firing. Ware description unavailable.

Plate 290

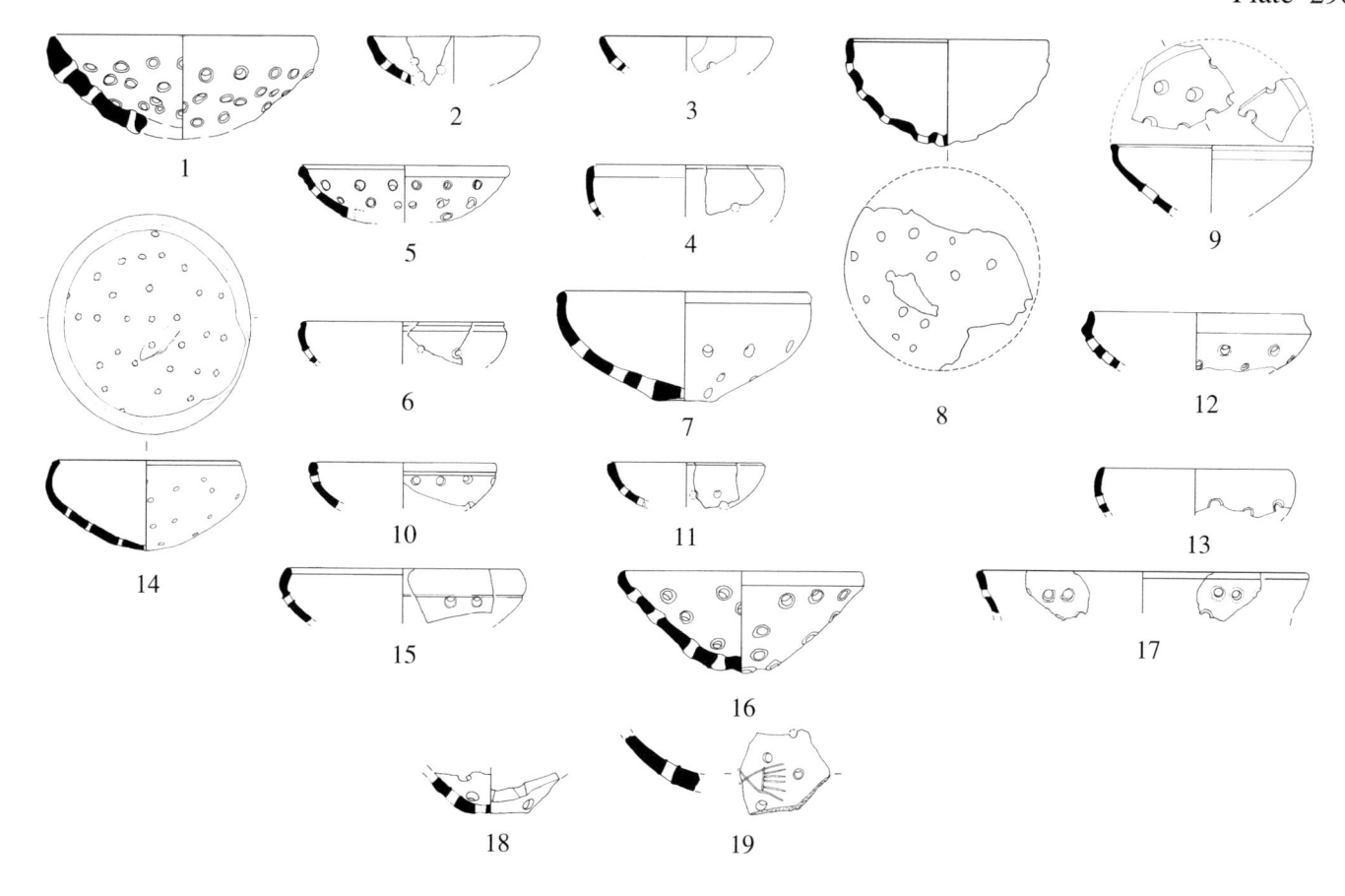

Bronze Age Strainer Bowl (SR) Types A–C and Strainer Bowl Base (SB) Type A. Scale 1:5

1. SR. A.I.a (TS. 1687; IVN, 2.1, Room 8). Phase 2B. Two large joining rim and wall segments; nearly complete profile. Pink ware, evenly fired.
2. SR. A.I.b (TS. 2104; IC, 1.25). Phase 6. Small rim and wall segment. Slightly coarse pinkish-buff ware, evenly fired.
3. SR. A.II.a (TS. 2432; IVC, 1.13). Phase 2A. About 1/5 rim and wall segment. Fairly fine pinkish-buff ware, evenly fired. Buff slip in and out.
4. SR. A.II.b (TS. 2935; IVP, 1.5, Room 9). Phase 2B. Small rim and wall segment. Slightly coarse pink ware, evenly fired. Self slip in and out.
5. SR. A.II.c (SW. 257; IVG, 1.3, Room 3A). Phase 3. About 1/6 rim and wall segment. Fairly coarse grayish-drab ware with lime and mica grits, evenly fired. Compare Hama J.4, Fugmann (1958), fig. 85 (3G466).
6. SR. A.II.d (TS. 2932; IVR, 2.5, Room 11). Phase 2A. Small rim and wall segment. Fairly fine buff ware, evenly fired. Creamy-buff slip in and out.
7. SR. B.I.a (SW. 21; IIIA, 1.3). Phase 5. Mended to complete profile. Very coarse buff ware with mineral temper, evenly fired.
8. SR. B.I.b (SW. 558; IVO, 1.3, Fill). Phase 3 (see also pl. 98a). Mended to complete profile. Fairly fine pinkish-buff ware, evenly fired. Cream slip in and out.
9. SR. B.I.c (TS. 2425; IIIA, 1.4, 4.2/3, Rooms 11 and 8A/8B). Phase 4. About 1/10 rim and wall segment (two non-joining rim fragments). Fairly fine pinkish-buff ware, evenly fired. Creamy-buff slip in and out.
10. SR. B.I.d (TS. 2427; IIIA, 1.4, Room 11). Phase 4. About 1/6 rim and wall segment. Slightly coarse pink ware, evenly fired. Pinkish-white slip out and on top of rim.
11. SR. B.I.e (TS. 2936; IVZ(S), 5.3). Phase 2B. Small rim and wall segment. Slightly coarse pinkish-buff ware, evenly fired. Buff slip in and out.
12. SR. B.II.a (TS. 3858; Op. 5, 5.2). Phase 7. About 1/2 rim and wall segment. Ware description unavailable.
13. SR. B.II.b (TS. 2430; IIIA, 1.4, 4.1, Rooms 8B and 11). Phase 4. About 1/2 rim and wall segment (three joining rim fragments). Fairly coarse light buff ware, evenly fired. Whitish-buff slip out.
14. SR. B.II.c (PM. D.8; SW. 346; VIIIA, 2.1). Phase 2. Nearly complete except for small segment of rim with a potter's mark incised on the inside base before firing. Fairly fine pink ware, evenly fired. Light brownish-buff slip in and out.
15. SR. B.II.d (TS. 2934; IVJ, 1.5, Room 4). Phase 2B. About 1/8 rim and wall segment. Slightly coarse buff ware, evenly fired. Cream slip in and out.
16. SR. C.I.a (SW. 725; IVN, 5.1, Room 8). Phase 2A (see also pl. 98b). Found complete in situ on workbench. Heavily charred from destruction of the building by fire. Fairly fine light brown ware, evenly fired.
17. SR. C.I.b (TS. 1249; IVB, 3.6, Room 1). Phase 2A. Small rim and wall segment. Fine pinkish-buff ware, evenly fired. Creamy-buff slip in and out.
18. SB. A.I.a (TS. 1210; XA, 1.3, Room 15). Phase 2B. About 1/2 base and lower wall segment. Medium fine buff ware, fairly evenly fired. Creamy-buff slip in and out.
19. SB. A.I.b (PM. D.13; TS. 2832; IVZ(N1), 1.3). Phase 4. Small segment of round base with a potter's mark incised on inner wall before firing. Slightly coarse pinkish-buff ware, evenly fired. Self slip in and out.

Plate 291

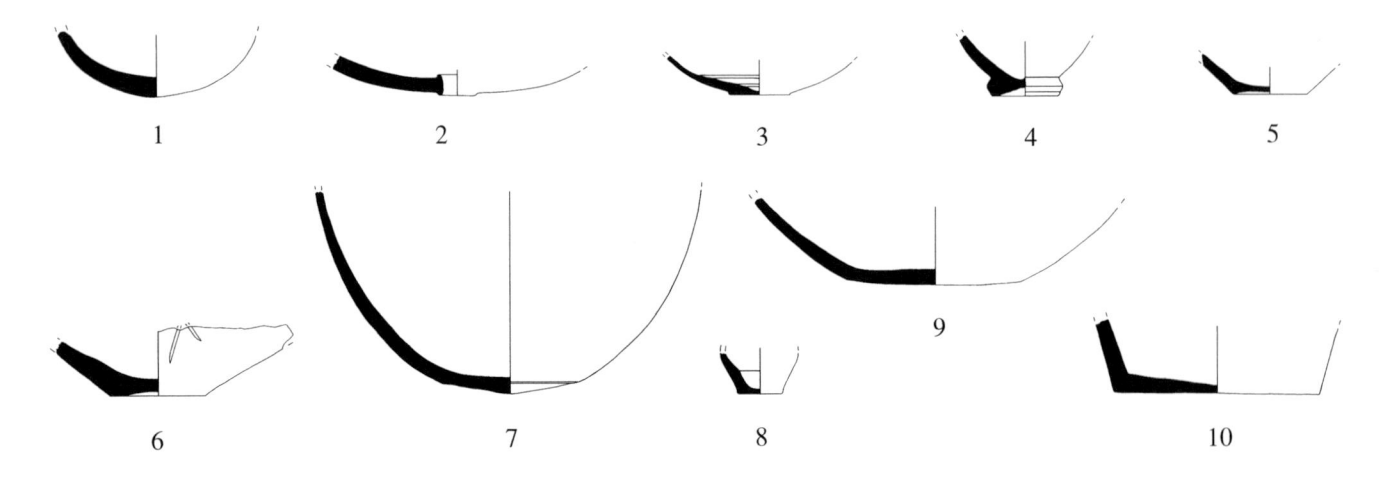

Bronze Age Base (BE) Types A.I to D.IV. Scale 1:5

1. BE. A.I (TS. 1650; IVL/P, 1.3, Pit). Phase 3. Large segment. Medium pink ware with lime and mica grits, evenly fired. Self slip out. Charred outside.
2. BE. A.II (TS. 3067; IVK, 1.3, Room 2A). Phase 3. Large segment with drainage hole manufacture in center of base before firing. Slightly coarse pink ware, evenly fired. Cream slip out.
3. BE. B.I (TS. 2768; IVN, 2.1, Room 8). Phase 2B. Complete base and lower wall. Fine light grayish-buff ware, evenly fired. Self slip in and out.
4. BE. B.II (TS. 3061; IVL, 2.1, Room 3A). Phase 3. About 1/2 segment. Fairly fine buff ware, evenly fired. Self slip in and out.
5. BE. C.I (TS. 3071; IVJ, 1.6, Room 4). Phase 2A. About 1/2 segment. Fine creamy-green ware, evenly fired. Self slip in and out.
6. BE. C.II (PM. C.14; TS. 1648; IVN, 1.2, Topsoil). Phase 5. About 1/2 segment with remains of a potter's mark incised on lower outside wall after firing. Fairly coarse buff ware, evenly fired. Self slip in and out.
7. BE. D.I (TS. 4036; Op. 5, 17.3, Pit). Phase 4. Nearly complete base with about 1/2 of body wall. Ware description unavailable.
8. BE. D.II (TS. 1261; XA, 1.3, Room 15). Phase 2B. Complete base and lower wall, string-cut off of the potter's wheel. Slightly coarse buff ware, evenly fired. Self slip out.
9. BE. D.III (TS. 1689; IVN, 1.3, Room 8B/18B). Phase 4. Complete base and lower wall. Pink ware, evenly fired. Cream slip in and out.
10. BE. D.IV (TS. 3991; Op. 5, 13.7). Phase 4. Lower wall segment of jar Type L with complete base profile. Ware description unavailable.

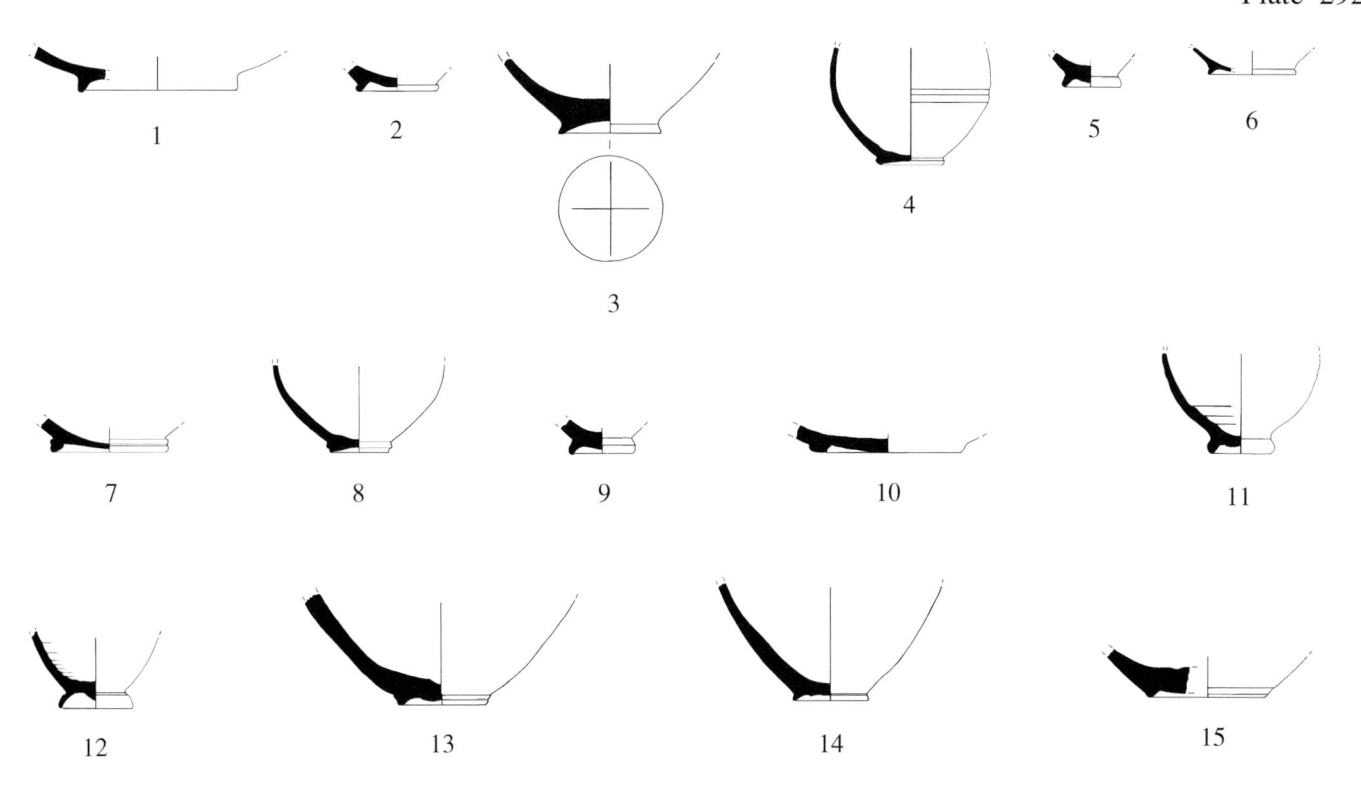

Bronze Age Base (BE) Types E.I.a to E.I.m. Scale 1:5

1. BE. E.I.a (TS. 3073; IVE, 1.4, Room 3). Phase 2B. About 1/6 segment. Fairly fine pinkish-buff ware, evenly fired. Cream slip out.
2. BE. E.I.b (TS. 3069; IVF, 1.2, Room 1B). Phase 4. About 1/2 segment. Fairly fine pinkish-brown ware, evenly fired. Self slip in and out.
3. BE. E.I.c (PM. C.14; TS. 1609; IVJ 1.5, 2.1, Room 4). Phase 2A (see also pl. 101a). Complete base with a large X-shaped potter's mark incised on underside before firing. Fairly fine buff ware with lime and mica grits, evenly fired. Buff slip in and out.
4. BE. E.I.d (TS. 3742; Op. 5, 17.1). Phase 4. Complete base with lower portion of wall attached. Fine drab buff-brown ware with a few gold- and white-colored mica grits, evenly fired.
5. BE. E.I.e (TS. 3221; Op. 6, 19.4, Room 16, Sounding). Phase 1B. Complete base with segment of lower wall of cup type vessel. Ware description unavailable.
6. BE. E.I.f (TS. 3072; IVM, 1.4, Room 7). Phase 2B. About 1/4 segment. Fine pinkish-grayware, evenly fired. Narrow orange-colored burnishing rings on outside wall of vessel.
7. BE. E.I.g (TS. 3578; Op. 7, 20.1, Room 36). Phase 2A(a). About 1/3 segment. Hard fine pinkish-brown ware with fine gold- and silver-colored mica and a few white lime grits, evenly fired. Creamy-buff slip out.
8. BE. E.I.h (TS. 3521; Op. 7, 18.1, Room 34). Phase 2A(a). Complete base and 1/3 segment of lower wall of vessel. Slightly coarse brownish-buff ware with gold- and silver-colored mica and many black and white lime grits, evenly fired. Self slip.
9. BE. E.I.i (TS. 3895; Op. 5, 15.1). Phase 3. Complete base with segment of lower wall of cup type vessel. Ware description unavailable.
10. BE. E.I.j.1 (TS. 3565; Op. 7, 19.2, Room 40, Pit). Phase 2B(a). Nearly 1/2 of base extant with small segment of wall of vessel. Slightly coarse dark rose-buff ware with gold- and silver-colored mica and lime grits, evenly fired. Self slip in and out.
11. BE. E.I.j.2 (TS. 3898; Op. 5, 9.14, 9.15). Phase 6. Nearly complete jar base with segment of lower wall. Ware description unavailable.
12. BE. E.I.k.1 (TS. 3900; Op. 5, 9.12). Phase 5. Complete base and lower half of wall of a cup type vessel. Ware description unavailable.
13. BE. E.I.k.2 (TS. 3224; Op. 6, 19.4, Room 16, Sounding). Phase 1B. Complete base and lower half of wall of a jar. Ware description unavailable.
14. BE. E.I.l (TS. 3851; Op. 5, 14.6). Phase 4. Complete base and lower half of wall of a jar. Ware description unavailable.
15. BE. E.I.m (TS. 3465; Op. 6, 18.5, Room 16). Phase 2A. Complete base and portion of lower wall of vessel. Hard, fine buff-brown ware with a few lime grits, evenly fired. Buff slip out and possibly in.

Plate 293

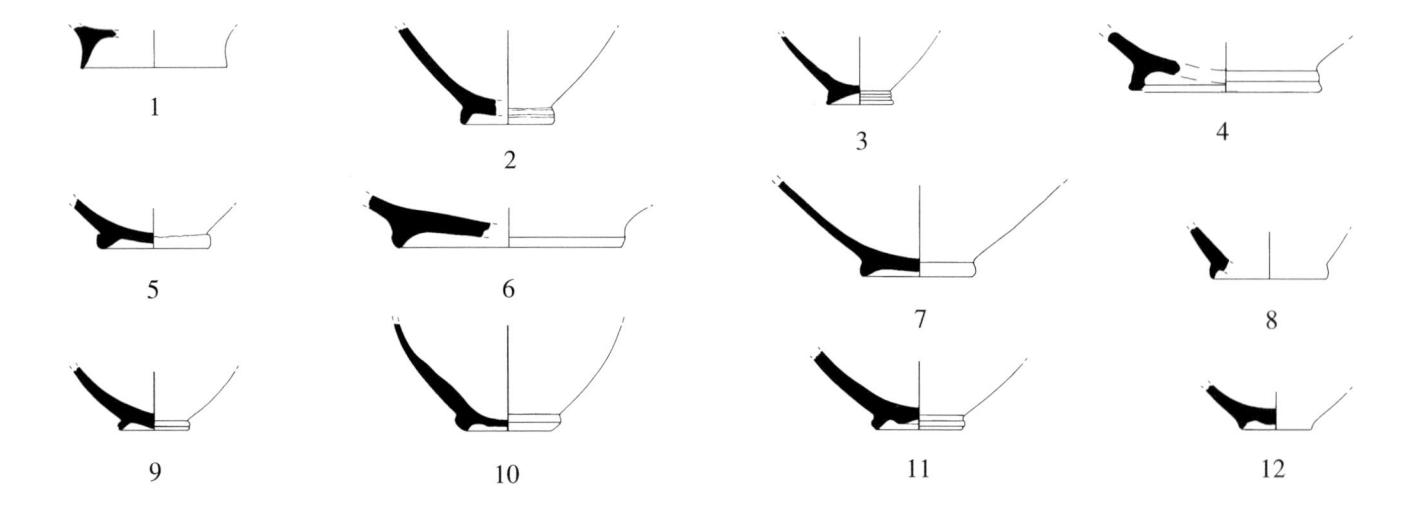

Bronze Age Base (BE) Types E.II.a to E.II.l. Scale 1:5

1. BE. E.II.a (TS. 3075; IIA, 9.2, Pit E). Phase 5. Small segment. Fairly fine ware, unevenly fired with brown core and reddish-brown at surfaces. Possible self slip in and out.
2. BE. E.II.b (TS. 3077; IVO, 1.4, Room 10). Phase 2A. About 1/3 segment. Slightly coarse pinkish-buff ware, evenly fired. Creamy-green slip out.
3. BE. E.II.c (TS. 3070; IVJ, 1.5, Room 4). Phase 2B About 1/2 segment. Fine light pink ware, evenly fired. Cream slip out.
4. BE. E.II.d (TS. 1673; IVL, 2.1, Room 3A). Phase 3. Small segment with incomplete profile. Medium fine pink ware with lime and mica grits, unevenly fired. Self slip in and out.
5. BE. E.II.e (TS. 3076; IVZ(S), 5.3). Phase 2B. About 1/2 segment. Slightly coarse creamy-green ware, evenly fired. Self slip in and out.
6. BE. E.II.f (TS. 3041; IVJ, 1.6, Room 4). Phase 2A. About 1/6 segment with nearly complete profile. Hard, fine pinkish-brown ware, unevenly fired pink at surfaces. Pink slip out.
7. BE. E.II.g (TS. 687; VIA, 3.1a). Phase 5. Complete base and lower wall. Fairly coarse pink ware, evenly fired. Buff slip out.
8. BE. E.II.h (TS. 3049; IVM, 10.1, Below Room 7). Phase 1C. Small segment with incomplete profile. Fine creamy-green ware, evenly fired. Self slip in and out.
9. BE. E.II.i (TS. 3074; IVN, 2.1, Room 8). Phase 2B. Complete base and lower wall. Fine light pink ware evenly fired. Remains of cream slip on wall above foot of base outside.
10. BE. E.II.j (TS. 2871; IVJ, 2.1, Room 4). Phase 2A. Complete base and about 1/2 of lower body. Slightly coarse, brittle, brown ware, evenly fired. Self slip in and out.
11. BE. E.II.k (TS. 3038; IVJ, 1.6, Room 4). Phase 2A. Complete base and lower portion of vessel. Fine pinkish-buff ware, evenly fired. Self slip in and out.
12. BE. E.II.l (TS. 3046; IVX, 10.8 = IVM, Room 7). Phase 2A. About 1/2 segment. Fairly fine pink ware, evenly fired. Self slip in and out.

Plate 294

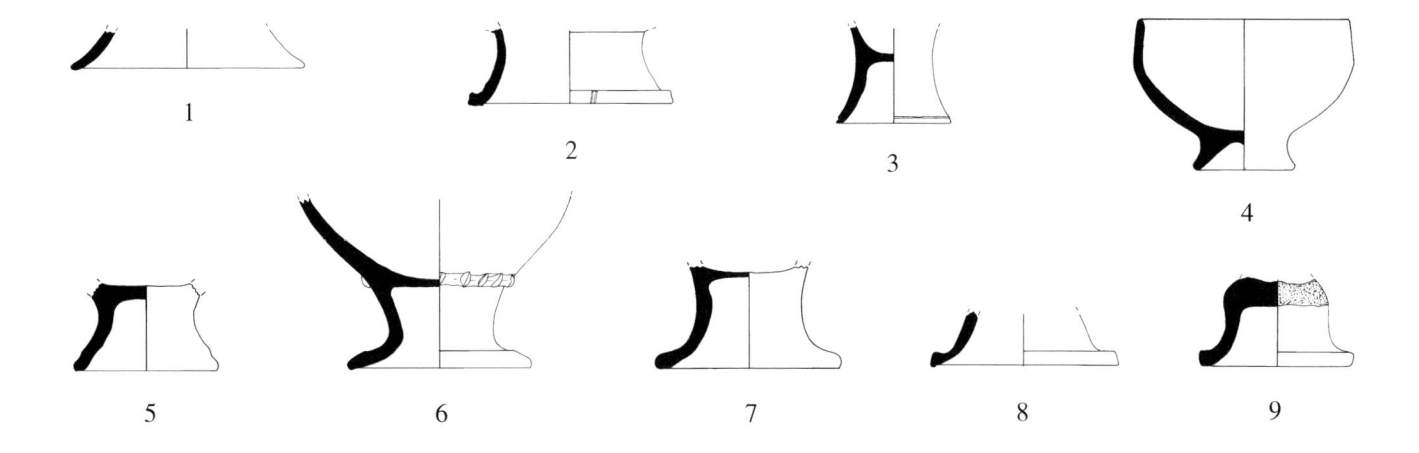

Bronze Age Base (BE) Types F.I.a to F.IV.b. Scale 1:5

1. BE. F.I.a (TS. 1559; IIA, 9.8, Room 4). Phase 2. Small segment. Close ware with fine lime and mica grits, unevenly fired with buff core and pink at surfaces. Creamy-buff slip in and out.
2. BE. F.I.b (PM. A.15; TS. 4070; Op. 10, 20, Room 18). Phase 2A. About 1/2 segment with a potter's mark consisting of two parallel lines incised on edge of the rim before firing. Fairly fine buff ware with small black and white lime grits, evenly fired. Creamy buff self slip in and out.
3. BE. F.II.a (TS. 2679; IVZ(N1), 1.5). Phase 2B. About 1/4 segment. Slightly coarse pinkish-brown ware, evenly fired. Pinkish-buff slip out.
4. BE. F.II.b.1 (SW. 679; IVW, 1.1). Phase 5. Found nearly complete in situ. Fairly fine pink ware, evenly fired. Cream slip in and out.
5. BE. F.II.b.2 (SW. 675; IVJ, 2.1, Room 4). Phase 2A. Complete pedestal-type base broken off from the lower wall of a vessel. Fairly coarse pink gritty ware, evenly fired. Cream slip out.
6. BE. F.III.a (SW. 279 = TS. 1798; IIIA, 1.4 + 4.1, Rooms 11 and 8B). Phase 4. About 1/4 segment of rim in two joining fragments and lower wall of vessel with impressed rope-like band decoration. Slightly coarse pinkish-buff ware with lime and gold- and silver-colored mica grits, evenly fired. Creamy-buff slip out.
7. BE. F.III.b (SW. 674; IVJ, 2.1, Room 4). Phase 2A. Base mended to completion. Coarse pinkish-buff ware, evenly fired. Dark self slip in and out.
8. BE. F.IV.a (TS. 2914; IVN, 2.2, Room 8). Phase 2A. About 1/6 segment. Slightly coarse pinkish-buff ware, evenly fired. Creamy-buff slip in and out.
9. BE. F.IV.b (SW. 249; IVD, 2.4, Room 2). Phase 2B. Complete base. Slightly coarse drab ware with lime and mica grits, unevenly fired grayish-buff at surfaces.

Plate 295

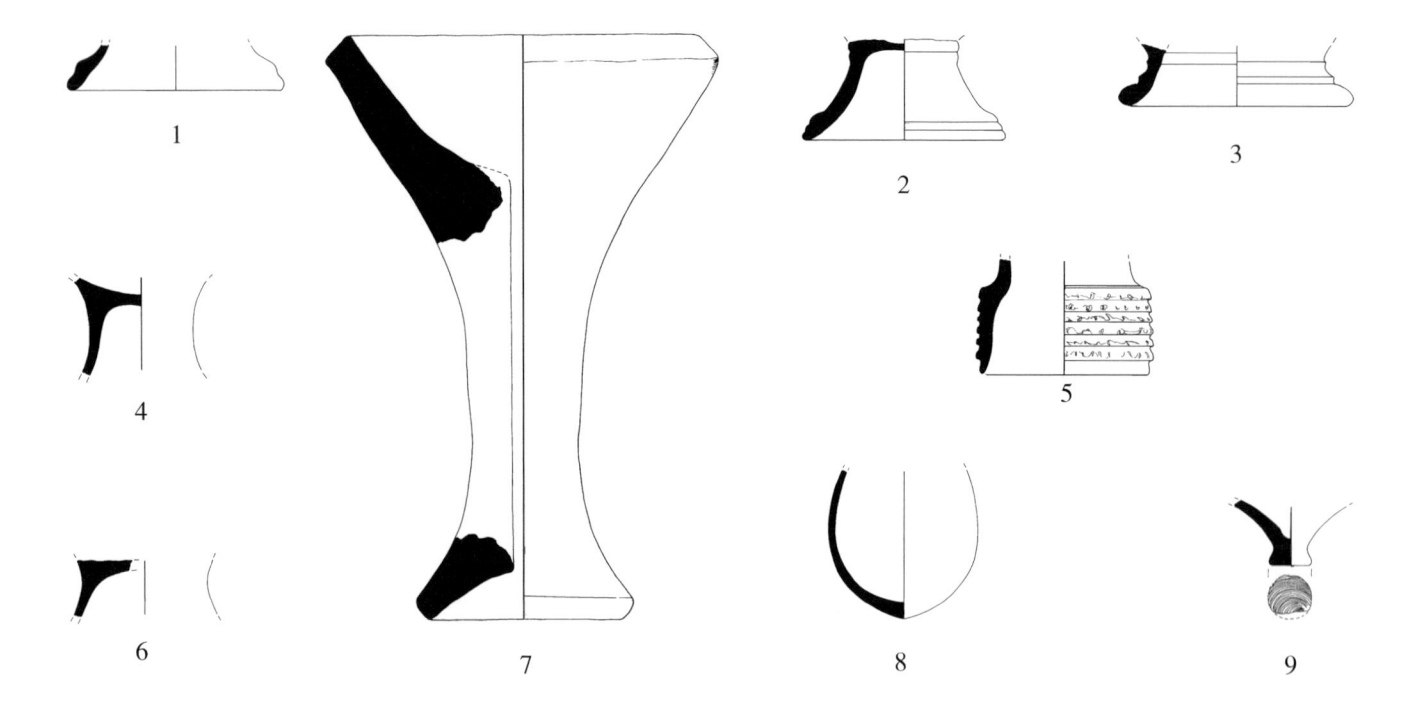

Bronze Age Base (BE) Types F.V.a to J. Scale 1:5

1. BE. F.V.a (TS. 2691; IVB, 1.3). Phase 5. About 1/8 segment. Slightly coarse light pinkish-buff ware, evenly fired. Creamy-green slip in and out.
2. BE. F.V.b (TS. 3311; Op. 1, Locus, Unstratified). About 2/3 segment of a pedestal base with complete profile. Ware description unavailable.
3. BE. F.VI.a (TS. 2664; IVJ, 1.5, Room 4). Phase 2B. About 1/8 segment. Slightly coarse pinkish ware, evenly fired. Self slip in and out.
4. BE. F.VII (TS. 738; IE, 1.40 = IC, 1.40). Phase 4. Incomplete segment. Fairly coarse pink ware, evenly fired. Cream slip in and out.
5. BE. F.VIII.a (TS. 3675; Op. 5, 5.1). Phase 7 (Derived EB–MB). Incomplete portion of the base. Ware description not available.
6. BE. F.VIII.b (TS. 544; IIIC, 4.9, Room 19A). Phase 5. Incomplete segment. Coarse pink ware with cream slip in and out.
7. BE. F.VIII.c (SW. 457b; IVK, 2.4, Room 2). Phase 2B. About 3/4 segment. Unbaked, heavily straw-tempered ware with lime plaster in and out. Drawing represents a possible reconstruction of this vessel.
8. BE. G (TS. 2785; IVQ, 1.4, Room 6). Phase 2A. Complete base and lower wall segment. Slightly coarse grayish-buff ware, evenly fired. Self slip in and out.
9. BE. H (TS. 3066; IVX, 10.7 = IVM, Room 7). Phase 2A. Nearly complete base with string-cut marks left on bottom when removed from the potter's wheel. Slightly coarse creamy-green ware, evenly fired. Self slip in and out.
—. BE. J (Miscellaneous): See Areas IIIF (Phase 5, SC. 3237), IIIG/H (Phase 3, SC. 3240; Phase 6, SC. 3234), IIIH (Phase 5, SC. 3239), IVB (Phase 5, TS. 3064), IVF (Phase 9, SC. 3236), IVG (Phase 6, SC. 3233), IVZ(N2) (Phase 3, TS 3035; Phase 4, TS. 3063).

Plate 296

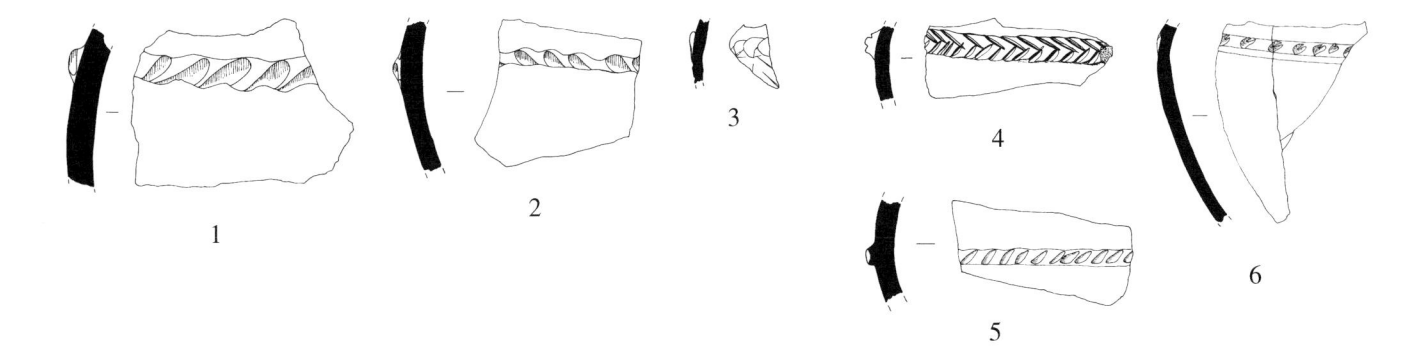

Bronze Age Applied-band Sherd (ABS) Types A–C. Scale 1:5

1. ABS. A.1 (TS. 1649; IVL, 2.1, Room 3A). Phase 3. Body segment. Coarse pink ware with lime grits, unevenly fired. Cream slip in and out.
2. ABS. A.2 (TS. 1670; IVL, 2.1, Room 3A). Phase 3. Body segment. Coarse pink ware with lime and mica grits, evenly fired. Buff slip in and out.
3. ABS. B.1 (SW. 631; IVN, 2.2, Room 8). Phase 2A. Small body segment. Fairly coarse cream ware, evenly fired.
4. ABS. B.2 (TS. 1070; IIIG/H, 1.10, Room 2B). Phase 2. Body segment. Fairly coarse pink ware. Cream slip out.
5. ABS. C.1 (TS. 1812; IIIA, 1.4, 4.2, Rooms 11 and 8A). Phase 4. Hard, fine buff ware, evenly fired. Creamy-buff slip in and out.
6. ABS. C.2 (TS. 1664; IVG, unstratified + IVL, 1.2, Room 3B). Phase 4. Two joining body segments. Coarse pink ware with lime and mica grits, evenly fired. Cream slip in and out.

Plate 297

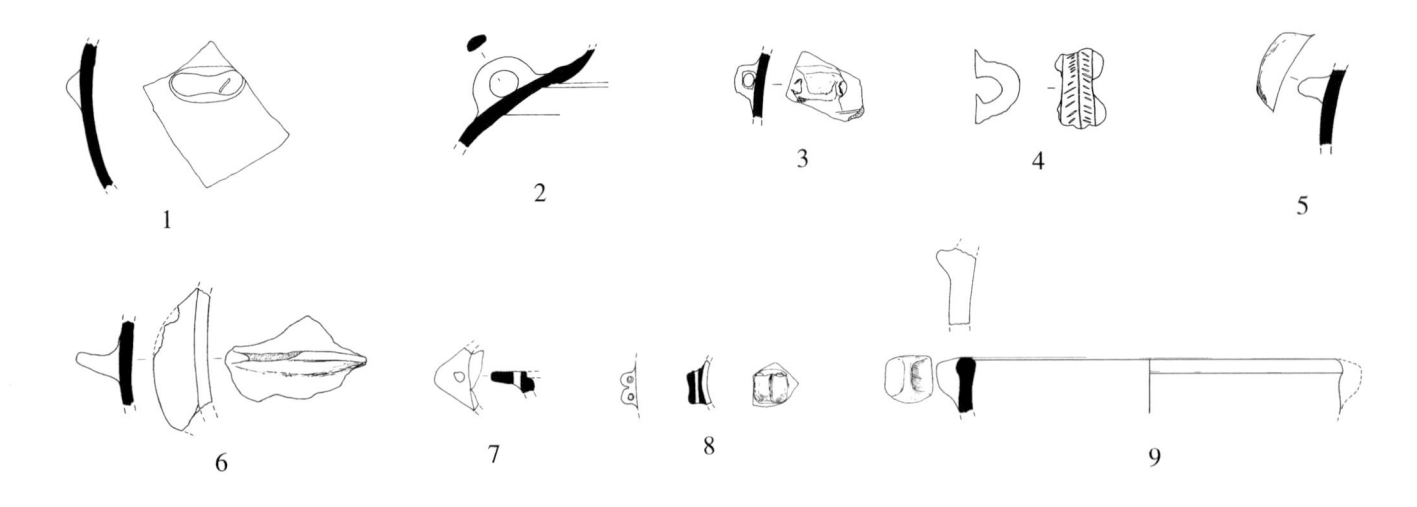

Bronze Age Handle (Hd.) Types A–G. Scale 1:5

1. Hd. A (TS. 1686; IVN, 1.3, Rooms 8B/18B). Phase 4. Fairly large body segment with one handle. Medium hard light grayware with lime and some mica grits, unevenly fired. Cream slip in and out.
2. Hd. B (TS. 1089; XA, 1.3, Room 15). Phase 2B. Large shoulder segment with complete loop handle. Fairly coarse pink ware. Creamy-buff slip out.
3. Hd. C (TS. 497; IIIE, 3.2, Room 5). Phase 4. Body sherd with complete lug handle, pierced horizontally. Fairly coarse creamy-buff ware with lime grits, unevenly fired with light brown core.
4. Hd. D.I (IP [G.3] A.II.a; SW. 641; IVO, 1.4, Room 10). Phase 2A. Complete loop handle with herringbone-style decoration on outside edge incised before firing of the vessel. Fairly coarse pink ware, evenly fired. Cream slip applied to handle and to extant portion of the outside wall
—. Hd. D.II (TS. 3511; Op. 7, 19.1, Street). Not illustrated. Phase 2A(a). (See fig. 145:22)
5. Hd. E.I a (TS. 557; IIIB, 3.2, Room 7). Phase 4. Small wall segment with complete ledge handle. Fairly fine pinkish-buff ware, evenly fired. Buff slip out.
6. Hd. E.I.b (TS. 3491; Op. 5, 18.2). Phase 4. Nearly complete ledge handle. Gritty, brown cooking pot-type ware, evenly fired.
7. Hd. E.II (TS. 2773; IVN, 2.1, Room 8). Phase 2B. Nearly complete, triangular-shaped, handle with suspension hole pierced in its center. Hard, fine grayware, evenly fired. Cream slip out.
8. Hd. F (TS. 2782; IVF, 3.1, Room 1). Phase 2A. Complete double barrel-type handle on small fragment of wall. Fairly fine light grayware, evenly fired. Self slip in and out. Metallic stoneware.
9. Hd. G.1 (TS. 2706; IVZ(N2), 3.3). Phase 3. Small segment of bowl rim and wall with vertical lug handle attached to rim and upper wall. Fairly fine pink ware, evenly fired. Self slip in and out.
—. Hd. G.2 (SW. 129 = TS. 1378; IIIC, 4.6). Not illustrated. Phase 7. (See pl. 225:3)

Plate 298

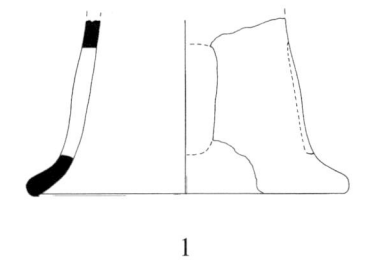

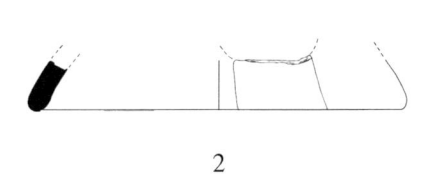

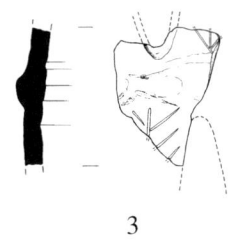

Bronze Age Windowed Pedestal Stand (WPS) Types A–C. Scale 1:5

1. WPS. A.I.a (TS. 704; VIIA, 4.1/4.2). Phase 4. About 1/4 segment of three joining rim fragments with remains of two windows in the wall. Fairly coarse brown ware. Cream slip in and out.
2. WPS. A.I.b (TS. 3081; IVX, 2.6 = IVM, Room 7). Phase 2A. Small segment with only a portion of the bottom window ledge. Slightly coarse ware, evenly fired. Buff slip in and out.
3. WPS. B (IP [G.4] D.IV; PM. D.19; TS. 1183; IVA, 2.4, Street). Phase 2B. Wall fragment with remains of two windows. Decorated on the outside wall with tree or wheat stalk potter's marks incised before firing. Fairly fine creamy-buff ware with fine lime and mica grits, evenly fired. Self slip in and out.
—. WPS. C (Type Uncertain): See Areas IC (Phase 8, TS. 636), IIIA (Phase 7, SC. 1949), IIIC (Phase 7, SC. 1946), IIIG (Phase 5, SC. 1947), IIIG/H (Phase 6, SC. 1953), IIIL (Phase 6/7, SC. 1951), IVF (Phase 2B, SC. 3253), IVX = IVM (Phase 2A, TS. 3081), and Operations 4 (Phase 1, TS. 3184), and 7 (Phase 3, TS. 4143).

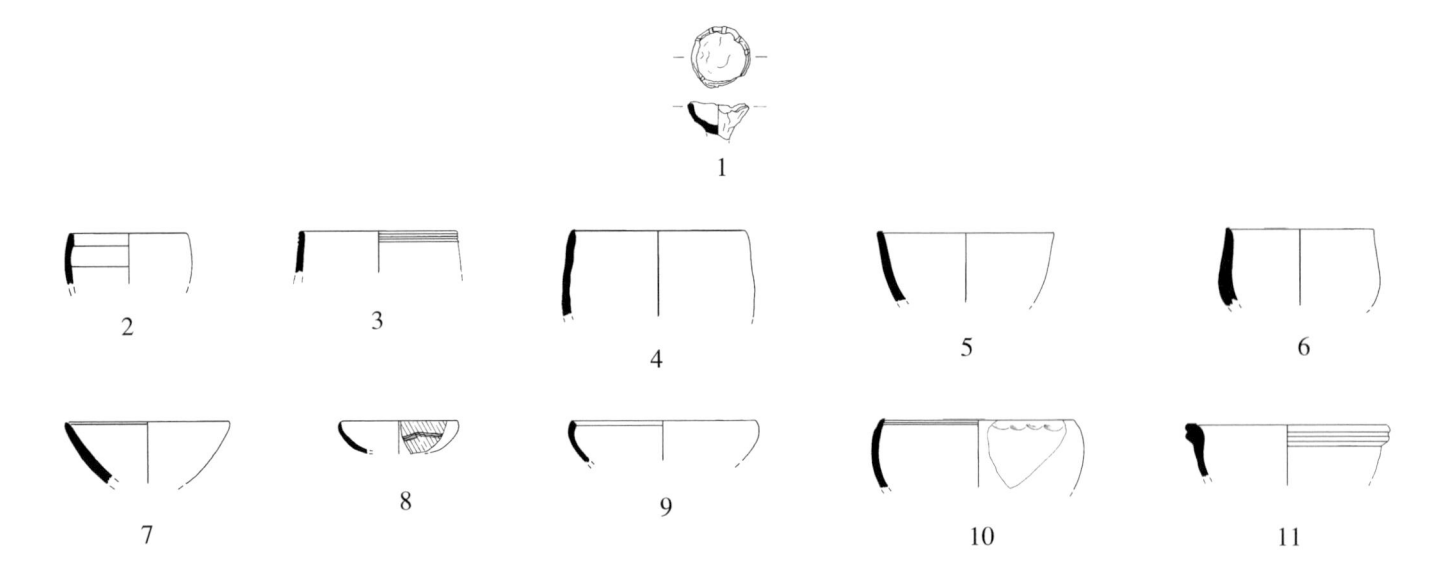

Hellenistic Miniature Bowl (H.MBR) and Small Bowl (H.SBR) Types A–C. Scale 1:5

1. H.MBR. (SW. 143; IIA, 1.1). Phase 15. Upper portion of miniature pottery container or goblet, handmade. The rim is decorated with transverse impressions, possibly made by a reed or stick. Buff ware with black lime temper, evenly fired. Light greenish-buff slip in and out.
2. H.SBR. A.I.a (TS. 1484; IIA, 4.1). Phase 14. Small rim and wall segment. Fairly fine greenish-buff ware evenly fired. Self slip in and out.
3. H.SBR. A.I.b (TS. 1417; IIB, 2.1). Phase 15. Small rim and wall segment. Fairly fine buff ware evenly fired. Self slip out and over rim in.
4. H.SBR. A.II.a (TS. 1985; IIA, 4.9). Phase 13. Fairly large rim and wall segment. Fairly fine pinkish-brown ware evenly fired. Grayish-buff slip in and out.
5. H.SBR. A.II.b (TS. 2112; VD, 1.1). Phase 5. Fairly large rim and wall segment. Slightly coarse buff ware evenly fired. Creamy-buff slip in and out.
6. H.SBR. A.II.c (TS. 1533; IIA, 7.5). Phase 11. Fairly large rim and wall segment. Hard, fine, light buff-brown ware with fine lime and mica grits, evenly fired. Buff slip out and just over rim in.
7. H.SBR. A.III.a (TS. 213; IIA, 5.5). Phase 11. Small rim and wall segment. Fairly fine pinkish-buff ware with lime and mica grits, evenly fired. Self slip in and out.
8. H.SBR. B.I.a (TS. 404; VF, 1.1). Phase 9. About 1/10 rim segment with band of comb-incised lines around body, made before firing. Fairly fine light brown ware with few visible grits, evenly fired.
9. H.SBR. B.I.b (TS. 335; IIA, 1.4). Phase 14. Small rim and wall segment. Grayish-buff ware with fine grits, evenly fired.
10. H.SBR. C.I.a (TS. 3008; IIA, 7.7, Pit D, lower). Phase 8. About 1/10 rim and wall segment with scallop-like decorative molding around the lip of the rim. Fairly fine creamy-green ware, evenly fired. Self slip in and out.
11. H.SBR. C.I.b (TS. 1444; IIB, 2.12). Phase 15. Small rim and upper wall segment. Fairly fine buff ware with fine mica grits, evenly fired. Creamy-buff slip out.

Plate 300

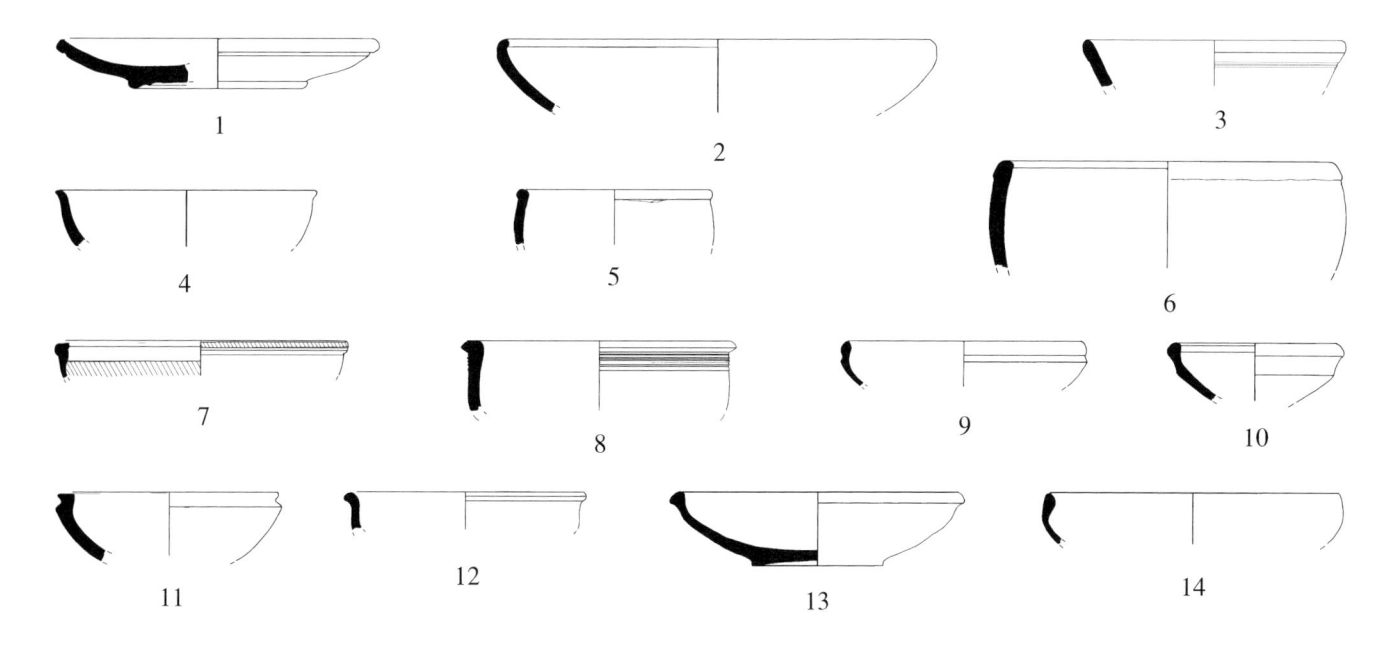

Hellenistic Bowl (H.BR) Type A. Scale 1:5

1. H.BR. A.I.a (TS. 974; VE, 1.2). Phase 5. About 1/10 rim segment with most of body profile. Fairly fine pinkish-buff ware. Cream slip in and out, partially burnished out.
2. H.BR. A.I.b (TS. 2122; IC, 1.1). Phase 10. Small rim and wall segment. Slightly coarse buff ware, evenly fired. Buff slip in and out.
3. H.BR.A.II.a (TS. 1475; IIA, 4.1). Phase 14. Small rim and upper wall segment. Fairly fine pinkish-buff ware with lime and mica grits, evenly fired. Self slip in and out.
4. H.BR. A.III.a (TS. 101; IIA, 5.6, Pit C). Phase 12. Small rim and wall segment. Fine pinkish-brown ware with silver-colored mica and lime grits, evenly fired. Very worn self slip in and out.
5. H.BR. A.III.b (TS. 240; IIA, 5.1). Phase 13. Small rim and upper wall segment. Slightly coarse buff ware with lime and mica grits, evenly fired. Creamy-buff slip out.
6. H.BR. A.III.c (TS. 211; IIA, 5.5). Phase 11. Small rim and wall segment. Slightly coarse pinkish-buff ware with lime and mica grits, evenly fired. Creamy-buff slip in and out.
7. H.BR. A.III.d (TS. 1993; IIB, 3.1). Phase 15. Small rim and upper wall segment. Fairly fine pink ware, evenly fired. Pink slip on outer wall with bands of red paint in, on top of rim, and on outside of rim.
8. H.BR. A.III.e (TS. 1450; IIA, 1.2). Phase 15. Small rim and wall segment. Fairly fine pinkish-buff ware, evenly fired.
9. H.BR. A.IV.a (TS. 1932; IVC, 1.2). Phase 3. Small rim and wall segment. Slightly coarse pinkish-buff ware, evenly fired. Self slip in and out.
10. H.BR. A.IV.b (TS. 259; IIA, 1.10). Phase 14. Small rim and wall segment. Fairly fine pinkish-buff ware with lime and mica grits, evenly fired. Self slip in and out.
11. H.BR. A.IV.c (TS. 100; IIA, 5.6, Pit C). Phase 12. Small rim and wall segment. Fairly fine buff ware with lime and mica grits, evenly fired. Self slip in and out.
12. H.BR. A.V.a (TS. 351; IIA, 1.1). Phase 15. Small rim and upper wall segment. Pinkish-buff ware, evenly fired.
13. H.BR. A.V.b (SW. 124; IIA, 4.9). Phase 13. Complete profile. Buff ware with black- and gold-colored mica grits, evenly fired. Pitted surfaces from burned out organic temper. Light buff slip in and out.
14. H.BR. A.V.c (TS. 1990; IIA, 7.2, Pit [unnumbered]). Phase 10. Small rim and wall segment. Slightly coarse brown ware, evenly fired. Buff slip in and out.

Plate 301. Hellenistic Bowl (H.BR) Type B

1. H.BR. B.I.a (TS. 18; IIA, 7.2, Pit [unnumbered]). Phase 10. Small rim and wall segment. Slightly coarse yellow-buff ware with lime grits, evenly fired. Self slip in and out.
2. H.BR. B.I.b (TS. 1113; VC, 2.1). Phase 3. Small rim and wall segment. Fairly coarse pink ware, evenly fired.
3. H.BR. B.I.c (TS. 249; IIA, 5.1). Phase 13. About 1/8 rim and upper wall segment. Slightly coarse pinkish-buff ware with lime and mica grits, evenly fired. Buff slip out.
4. H.BR. B.I.d (TS. 53 = TS. 370, IIA, 5.12 + 1.1). Phases 13 and 15. About 1/8 of two joining rim segments with mending hole in upper wall. Slightly coarse brownish-buff ware, evenly fired. Creamy-buff slip in and out.
5. H.BR. B.I.e (TS. 235; IIA, 5.2, Pit C). Phase 12. About 1/10 rim and upper wall segment. Slightly coarse buff ware with lime and mica grits, evenly fired. Self slip in and out.
6. H.BR. B.I.f (TS. 1465; IIB, 2.4). Phase 15. Small rim and upper wall segment. Fairly fine pinkish-buff ware, evenly fired.
7. H.BR. B.I.g (TS. 113; IIA, 5.6, Pit C). Phase 12. Small rim and upper wall segment. Coarse pinkish-brown ware with lime, mica, and organic temper, evenly fired. Creamy-buff slip out.
8. H.BR. B.II.a (TS. 948; VE, 1.1). Phase 9. About 1/24 rim and wall segment with diagonally impressed linear decoration on wall. Fairly coarse pink ware, evenly fired.
9. H.BR. B.II.b (TS. 1008; VG, 1.4). Phase 6. About 1/28 rim and upper wall segment. Fairly coarse brown ware, evenly fired. Cream slip out.
10. H.BR. B.II.c (TS. 959; VA, 1.1). Phase 4. Small rim and upper wall segment. Fairly coarse pink ware. Cream slip in and out.
11. H.BR. B.II.d (TS. 793; VF, 1.3). Phase 6. About 1/16 rim and wall segment. Fairly fine pink ware. Irregular burnished self slip out.
12. H.BR. B.III.a (TS. 111; IIA, 5.6, Pit C). Phase 12. About 1/5 rim and wall segment. Fairly fine dark brown ware with gold-colored mica and lime grits, evenly fired. Thin self slip or wash in and out.
13. H.BR. B.III.b (TS. 1964; IVC, 1.1). Phase 4. Small rim and wall segment. Fairly coarse pinkish-buff ware, evenly fired. Self slip in and out.
14. H.BR. B.III.c (TS. 131; IIA, 5.2, Pit C). Phase 12. About 1/6 rim and upper wall segment. Fairly fine pinkish-brown ware with lime and mica grits, evenly fired. Very worn self slip in and out.
15. H.BR. B.III.d (TS. 1531; IIB, 2.10). Phase 15. Small rim and upper wall segment. Fairly fine pinkish-buff ware, evenly fired. Buff slip in and out.
16. H.BR. B.III.e (TS. 390; IIB, 2.1). Phase 15. Small rim and upper wall segment. Pinkish-buff ware, evenly fired. Cream slip in and out.
17. H.BR. B.III.f (SC. 2832; VF/G, 1.1). Phase 9. About 1/12 rim segment. Fairly fine light buff ware with a few lime grits, evenly fired. Self slip in and out.
18. H.BR. B.III.g (TS. 883; VF/G, 1.1). Phase 9. About 1/20 rim and upper wall segment. Fairly coarse buff ware, evenly fired. Cream slip in and out.
19. H.BR. B.III.h (TS. 135; IIA, 4.2, Pit C). Phase 14. About 1/6 rim and wall segment. Hard, fairly fine pinkish-brown ware with lime and mica grits, evenly fired. Self slip in and out.
20. H.BR. B.III.i (TS. 1992; IIA, 5.6, Pit C). Phase 12. Large rim and wall segment. Fairly fine pink ware, evenly fired. Self slip in and out.
21. H.BR. B.III.j (TS. 208; IIB, 6.5). Phase 14. Small rim and upper wall segment. Fairly fine pinkish-buff ware with lime and mica grits, evenly fired. Buff slip in and out.
22. H.BR. B.III.k (TS. 855; VE, 1.1). Phase 9. About 1/24 rim and upper wall segment. Fairly fine pink ware, unevenly fired with buff core.
23. H.BR. B.III.l (TS. 964; VE, 1.1). Phase 9. About 1/8 rim and wall segment. Fairly coarse pink ware, evenly fired.
24. H.BR. B.III.m (TS. 222; IIB, 6.7). Phase 14. Small rim and upper wall segment. Hard, fine pinkish-brown ware with lime and mica grits, evenly fired. Tan slip out.
25. H.BR. B.III.n (TS. 145; IIA, 4.14, Pit C). Phase 12. About 1/4 rim and wall segment. Hard, fine pinkish-brown ware with lime and mica grits, evenly fired. Buff slip in and out.
26. H.BR. B.IV.a (TS. 66; IIA, 5.7, Street). Phase 11. Small rim and upper wall segment. Fine creamy-buff ware with very fine lime and mica grits, evenly fired. Self slip in and out.
27. H.BR. B.IV.b (TS. 727; VIIA, 1.3). Phase 3. Small rim and upper wall segment. Fairly fine buff ware. Creamy-buff slip out.
28. H.BR. B.IV.c (TS. 55; IIA, 5.21, Pit B1). Phase 7. About 1/5 rim and upper wall segment. Fairly fine pinkish-buff ware with lime and mica grits, evenly fired. Creamy-buff slip in and out.
29. H.BR. B.IV.d (TS. 3029; IIA, 4.1). Phase 14. Small rim and upper wall segment. Slightly coarse pinkish-buff ware, evenly fired. Creamy-green slip in and out.
30. H.BR. B.V.a (TS. 2147; VC, 1.1). Phase 4. Small rim and upper wall segment. Fairly fine buff ware, evenly fired. Self slip out.
31. H.BR. B.V.b (TS. 1438; IIB, 2.12). Phase 15. Small rim and upper wall segment. Fairly fine pinkish-buff ware, evenly fired. Creamy-buff slip out and on top of rim.
32. H.BR. B.V.c (TS. 2093; VD, 1.1). Phase 5. Small rim and upper wall segment. Slightly coarse pink ware, evenly fired. Creamy-buff

Plate 301

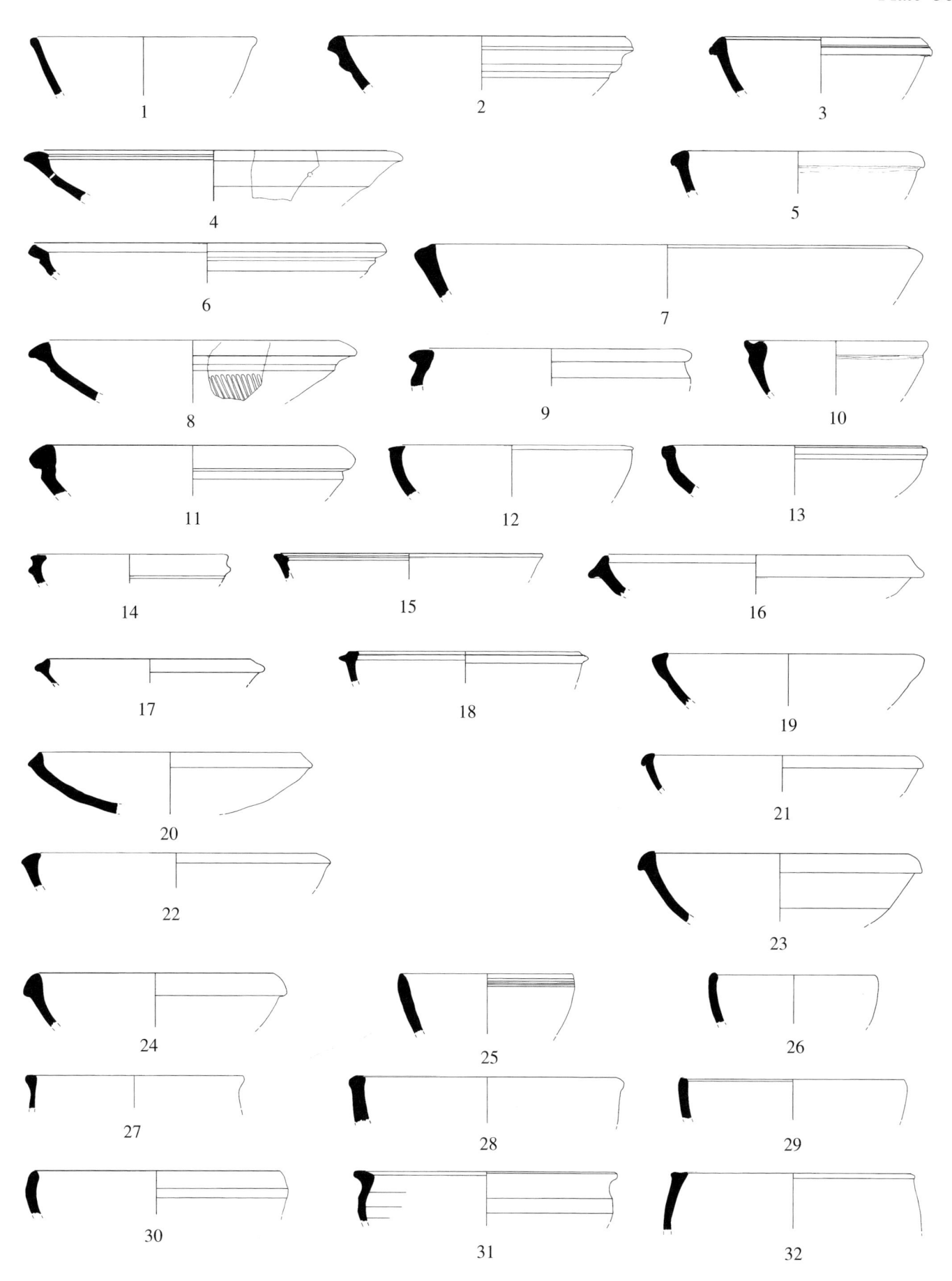

Hellenistic Bowl (H.BR) Type B. Scale 1:5

## Plate 302. Hellenistic Bowl (H.BR) Type C

1. H.BR. C.I.a (TS. 1035; VA/B Baulk). Phases 2–4. About 1/8 rim and 1/2 base fragment. Fairly coarse creamy-buff ware, evenly fired. Handmade.
2. H.BR. C.I.b (TS. 1439; IIB, 2.12). Phase 15. Small rim and upper wall segment. Fairly coarse ware with gray core fired pinkish-buff at surfaces. Self slip in and out.
3. H.BR. C.II.a (TS. 1422; IIA, 1.2). Phase 15. Small rim and upper wall segment. Slightly coarse buff ware fired creamy-buff at surfaces.
4. H.BR. C.II.b (TS. 986; VE, 1.2). Phase 5. About 1/12 rim and wall segment. Fairly coarse pink ware, evenly fired. Cream slip in and out.
5. H.BR. C.II.c (TS. 45; IIA, 5.18, Pit C). Phase 12. Small rim and upper wall segment. Coarse pinkish-grayware with lime, mica, and chaff temper, evenly fired. Self sip in and out.
6. H.BR. C.II.d (TS. 41; IIA, 5.18, Pit C). Phase 12. About 1/8 rim and wall segment. Coarse buff ware with lime, mica, and chaff temper, evenly fired. Creamy-buff slip in and out.
7. H.BR. C.II.e (TS. 1525; IIB, 2.10). Phase 15. Large rim and wall segment. Slightly coarse pinkish-buff ware with many lime and mica grits, evenly fired. Self slip in and on top of rim.
8. H.BR. C.II.f (TS. 1544; IIA, 8.1, Pit C1). Phase 9. Small rim and upper wall segment. Slightly coarse pinkish-buff ware, evenly fired. Buff slip out and on top of rim.
9. H.BR. C.II.g (TS. 99; IIA, 5.6, Pit C). Phase 12. Small rim and upper wall segment with remains of a ledge handle on the rim and a mending hole bored into the wall after the vessel was fired. Fairly coarse pinkish-brown ware, evenly fired. Self slip in and out.

Plate 302

Hellenistic Bowl (H.BR) Type C. Scale 1:5

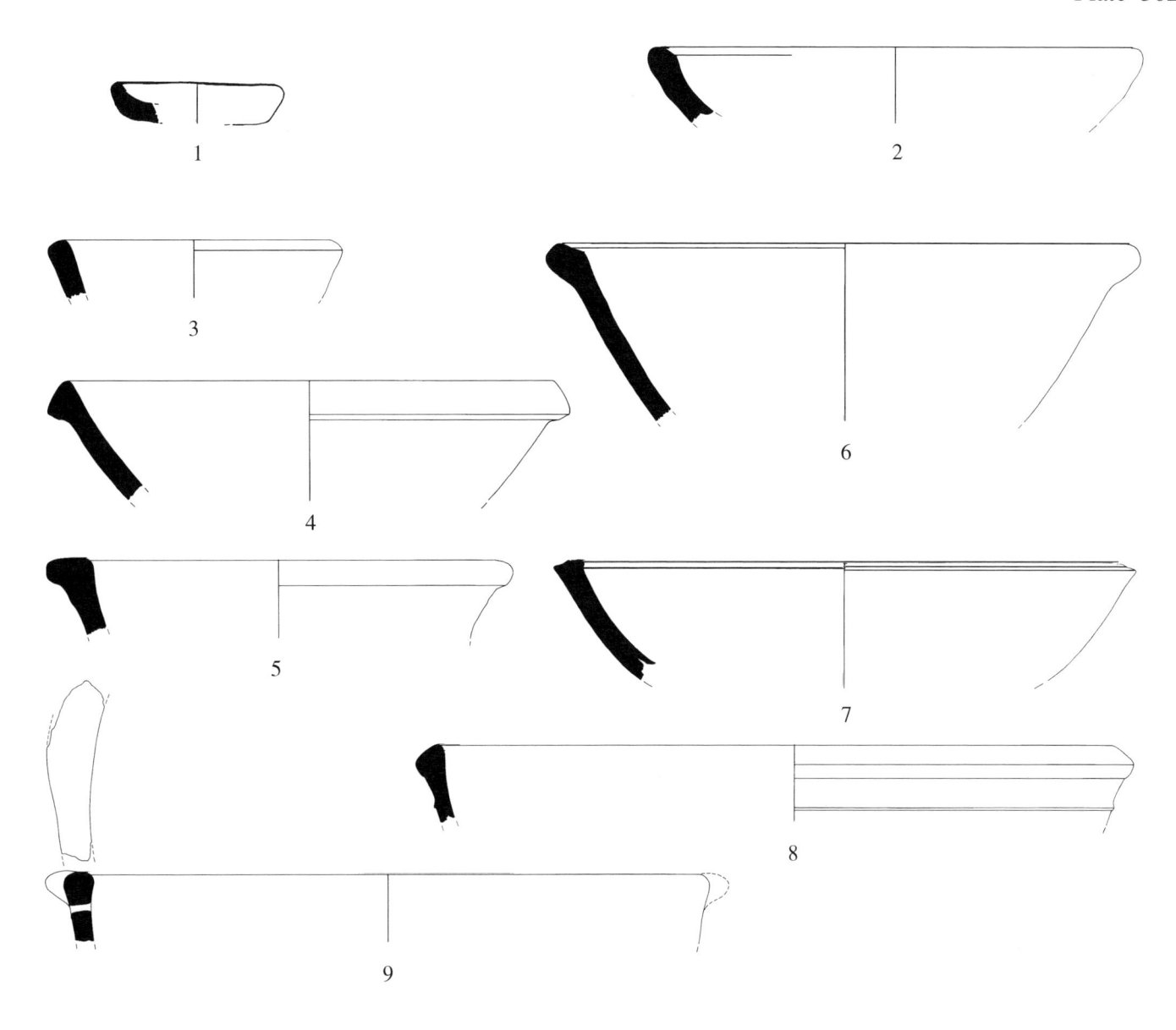

Plate 303. Hellenistic Red Slip Bowl (H.RSB) Types A.I.a to E.III.a and Red Slip Jar (H.RSJ) Types A.I.a to C.I.a.

1. H.RSB. A.I.a (TS. 1426; IIB, 2.12). Phase 15. Small rim and upper wall segment. Close, light buff ware with fine mica grits, evenly fired. Reddish-purple slip below rim in and out.
2. H.RSB. A.I.b (TS. 44; IIA, 5.23, Pit B2). Phase 7. About 1/8 rim and wall segment. Fine light brown ware with lime and mica grits, evenly fired. Red slip in and over rim out.
3. H.RSB. A.I.c (TS. 1944; IVC, 1.3). Phase 2A. Small rim and wall segment. Fairly fine pink ware, evenly fired. Reddish-brown slip in and out.
4. H.RSB. A.I.d.1 (TS. 1442; IIB, 2.12). Phase 15. Small rim and wall segment. Very fine light pink ware with no grit temper, evenly fired. Lustrous black-fired slip in and out. One millimeter wide band left in reserve 1 cm below rim on inside wall.
5. H.RSB. A.I.d.2 (TS. 988; VE, 1.2). Phase 5. About 1/6 rim and wall segment with red-painted, "festoon"-type, decoration on inside wall. Fairly fine brown ware, evenly fired.
6. H.RSB. A.II.a (SW. 126; IIA, 4.1). Phase 14. About 1/5 rim segment and nearly complete profile with two extant "leaf" stamp impressions on inside base. Fairly fine brown ware with mineral temper, evenly fired.
7. H.RSB. A.II.b (TS. 685; VIIA, 4.4). Phase 2. Small rim and upper wall segment. Fairly fine pinkish-buff ware, evenly fired. Red slip worn mostly off.
8. H.RSB. A.II.c (TS. 2145; VA, 1.1). Phase 4. Small rim and upper wall segment. Fine light grayware, evenly fired. Black slip in and out.
9. H.RSB. B.I.a (TS. 1419; IIB, 2.13, Room). Phase 13. Small rim and wall segment. Fine light buff ware with lime and mica grits, evenly fired. Burnished red slip in and out.
10. H.RSB. B.I.b (TS. 336; IIB, 2.1). Phase 15. Small rim and upper wall segment. Pinkish-buff ware, evenly fired. Red slip in and over rim out with irregular drip lines. Traces of burning on rim.
11. H.RSB. B.II.a (TS. 380; IIA, 1.1). Phase 15. Large rim and wall segment. Pinkish-buff ware, evenly fired. Red slip in and out and black paint over rim in and out.
12. H.RSB. B.II.b (TS. 256; IIB, 6.7). Phase 14. About 1/2 rim and wall segment. Light brown ware with lime and mica grits, evenly fired. Irregular red slip in and out.
13. H.RSB. B.II.c (TS. 310; IA1, 2.3). Phase 2. Small rim and wall segment. Light brown ware, evenly fired. Red slip in and out.
14. H.RSB. B.II.d (TS. 394; IIB, 2.3). Phase 15. Small rim and wall segment. Grayish-buff ware, evenly fired. Red slip irregularly applied in and out, but very worn with traces of burning.
15. H.RSB. C.I.a (TS. 401; VF, 1.1). Phase 9. Small rim and wall segment. Fine pinkish-orange ware with small gold-colored mica and lime grits, evenly fired. Red slip in and to below carination out.
16. H.RSB. C.II.a (TS. 1569; IIA, 5.1). Phase 13. Large rim and wall segment. Close, light brown ware with lime and mica grits, evenly fired. Reddish-brown slip irregularly applied in and out.
17. H.RSB. C.II.b (TS. 1400; IIB, 2.1). Phase 15. Large rim and wall segment. Close, light brown ware, evenly fired. Black slip in and red slip out to carination; dark red-painted band at line of carination with black slip below band.
18. H.RSB. D.I.a (TS. 956; VC, 1.1). Phase 4. About 1/12 rim and upper wall segment. Fine buff ware, evenly fired. Reddish-brown slip in and out.
19. H.RSB. D.I.b (TS. 1469; IIA, 1.2). Phase 15. Small rim and wall segment. Fairly fine buff ware, evenly fired. Very worn red slip in and just over lip of rim out.
20. H.RSB. D.II.a (TS. 398; IIB, 2.1). Phase 15. Small rim and wall segment. Fine buff ware, evenly fired. Imitation "black-glazed" ware. Red slip out and on lower portion of inside wall; upper inside black.
21. H.RSB. D.II.b (TS. 333; IIB, 2.16). Phase 15. Small rim and wall segment. Fine pinkish-brown ware, evenly fired. Reddish-brown slip in and irregularly applied out.
22. H.RSB. D.II.c (SW. 252; IIA, 5.23, Pit B2). Phase 7. Complete base and profile with about 1/2 rim extant. Hard, light brown ware with lime and mica grits, evenly fired. Dark reddish-brown slip in and irregularly applied out to carination line on upper wall.
23. H.RSB. D.II.d (TS. 357; IIB, 2.3). Phase 15. Small rim and wall segment. Fine buff ware, evenly fired. Red slip in and just over rim out.
24. H.RSB. D.II.e (SW. 116; IIA, 5.1). Phase 13. Complete base and profile with about 1/4 rim extant. Fine buff ware, evenly fired. Plum-brown slip in and irregularly applied out.
25. H.RSB. E.I.a (TS. 1428; IIB, 2.12). Phase 15. Small rim and wall segment. Very fine light pink ware, evenly fired. Red slip in and over rim out.
26. H.RSB. E.I.b (TS. 200; IIB, 6.6, Floor). Phase 14. Small rim and wall segment. Fine pinkish-brown ware with lime and mica grits, evenly fired. Red slip in and out, fired black in patches out.
27. H.RSB. E.II.a (TS. 426; VA, 1.1). Phase 4. Small rim and upper wall segment. Fairly fine buff ware, evenly fired. Red slip in, on top of rim, and out.
28. H.RSB. E.II.b (TS. 1418; IIA, 1.4). Phase 14. Small rim and upper wall segment. Fairly fine pinkish-buff ware, evenly fired. Red slip in and out.
29. H.RSB. E.II.c (TS. 327; IIA, 1.8). Phase 14. Large rim and wall segment. Pinkish-buff ware, evenly fired. Red slip in and on top of rim.
30. H.RSB. E.III.a (TS. 402; VB, 1.1). Phase 4. Small rim and upper wall segment with one loop handle. Hard, fine pink ware, evenly fired. Red slip in and creamy-buff slip on handle.
31. H.RSJ. A.I.a (TS. 1084; VA, 1.1). Phase 4. Small rim and shoulder segment. Fine pink ware, evenly fired. Burnished dark reddish-brown slip on upper wall in and all over out.
32. H.RSJ. B.I.a (TS. 354; IIB, 2.3). Phase 15. Shoulder fragment with complete horizontal loop handle. Fine light brown ware, evenly fired. Red slip in and out.
33. H.RSJ. B.I.b (SC. 3340; IIA, 7.1, Pit [unnumbered]). Phase 10. About 2/3 of the body (four non-joining sherds) with remains of a small vertical strap handle attached to the upper part of the carination of the vessel. Fine creamy-buff ware with very small white lime grits, evenly fired. Red slip in and out.
34. H.RSJ. C.I.a (SC. 3346; IIB, 2.3). Phase 15. About 1/10 rim segment. Fairly fine buff-brown ware with fine lime and gold-colored mica grits, evenly fired. Darkened reddish-brown slip on extant portion of the rim.

Plate 303

Red

Black

Very worn

Slip Color Key

Hellenistic Red Slip Bowl (H.RSB) Types A.I.a to E.III.a and Red Slip Jar (H.RSJ) Types A.I.a to C.I.a. Scale 1:5

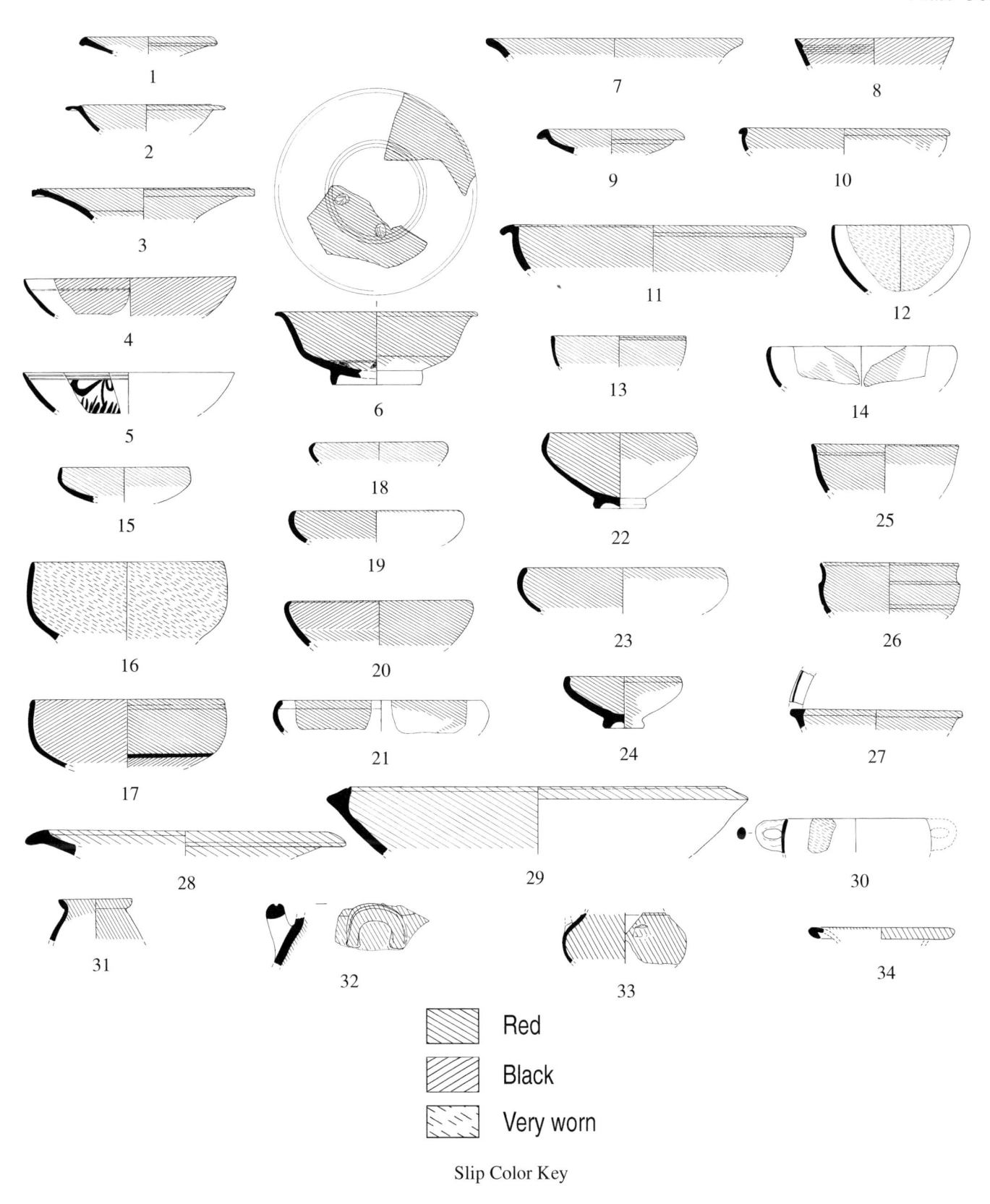

Plate 304

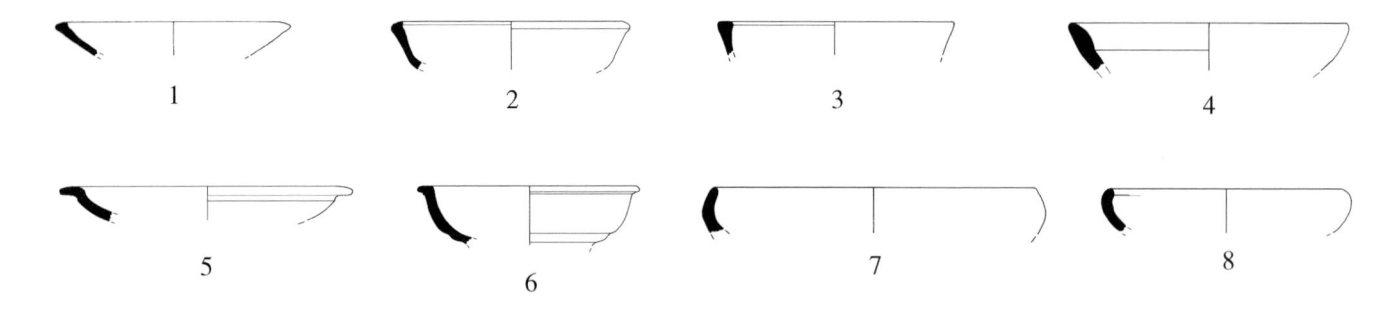

Hellenistic Burnished Gray Bowl (H.BGB) Types A and B. Scale 1:5

1. H.BGB. A.I.a (TS. 21; IIA, 7.2, Pit [unnumbered]). Phase 10. Small rim and upper wall segment. Fairly fine light grayware with lime and mica grits, evenly fired. Very worn self slip in and out with traces of burnishing.
2. H.BGB. A.I.b (TS. 239; IIA, 5.2, Pit C). Phase 12. Small rim and wall segment. Fine light grayware with lime and mica grits, evenly fired. Self slip in and out, burnished on top of rim and inside.
3. H.BGB. A.I.c (TS. 206; IVC, 1.6, Pit, NE Tower). Phase 2B. Small rim and upper wall segment. Hard, fine light grayware with lime grits, evenly fired. Grayish-brown slip in and out, very highly burnished.
4. H.BGB. A.I.d (TS. 1190; IIIF, 1.1). Phase 6/7. Small rim and upper wall segment. Fairly fine grayware with lime and mica grits, evenly fired. Burnished self slip in and out.
5. H.BGB. B.I.a (TS. 895; VC, 1.1). Phase 4. Small rim and upper wall segment. Fine grayware, evenly fired. Burnished self slip in and out.
6. H.BGB. B.I.b (TS. 229; IIB, 6.7). Phase 14. Small rim and wall segment. Fairly fine buff ware with lime grits, evenly fired. Self slip in and out with traces of burnishing below carination out.
7. H.BGB. B.I.c (TS. 827; VC, 1.1). Phase 4. Small rim and upper wall segment. Fine grayware, evenly fired. Horizontally burnished self slip in and out.
8. H.BGB. B.I.d (TS. 6; IIA, 7.2, Pit [unnumbered]). Phase 10. Small rim and upper wall segment. Grayware, evenly fired. Irregular horizontal burnish in and out.

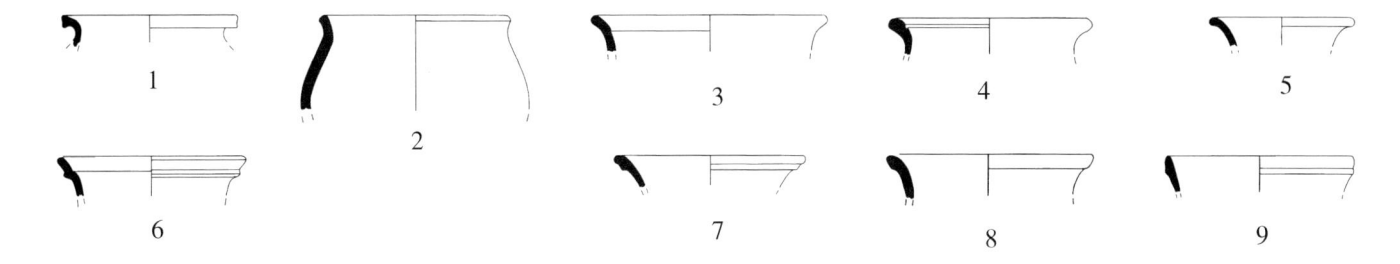

Hellenistic Small Jar (H.SJR) Types A and B. Scale 1:5

1. H.SJR. A.I.a (TS. 308; IIB, 2.3). Phase 15. Small rim and shoulder segment. Fine grayware, evenly fired.
2. H.SJR. A.I.b (TS. 1528; IIA, 1.2). Phase 15. Small rim and upper body segment. Fairly fine pinkish-buff ware, evenly fired. Self slip out and over rim in.
3. H.SJR. A.II.a (TS. 224 = TS. 388; IIB, 3.1 + 6.5). Phases 15 and 14. Two small joining rim and neck segments. Fairly fine pinkish-buff ware with lime and mica grits, evenly fired. Creamy-buff slip out.
4. H.SJR. A.II.b (SC. 2378; IIB, 2.3). Phase 15. About 1/12 rim and neck segment. Slightly coarse pinkish-buff ware with fine lime grits, evenly fired. Creamy slip in and out.
5. H.SJR. A.II.c (TS. 1539; IIA, 7.2, Pit [unnumbered]). Phase 10. Small rim and neck segment. Fairly fine buff ware, evenly fired.
6. H.SJR. A.II.d (TS. 1461; IIA, 1.2). Phase 15. Small rim and neck segment. Fine buff ware with lime and mica grits, evenly fired. Creamy-buff slip in and out.
7. H.SJR. A.II.e (TS. 340; IIB, 2.11). Phase 15. Small rim and neck segment. Buff ware, evenly fired. Self slip in and out.
8. H.SJR. A.II.f (SC. 2326; VE, 1.1). Phase 9. About 1/10 rim and neck segment. Coarse pinkish-buff ware with many lime and a few gold-colored mica grits, evenly fired. Thick self slip in and out.
9. H.SJR. B.I.a (TS. 247; IIA, 5.2, Pit C). Phase 12. About 1/4 rim and upper neck segment. Fairly fine buff ware with lime grits, evenly fired. Self slip in and out.

Plate 306

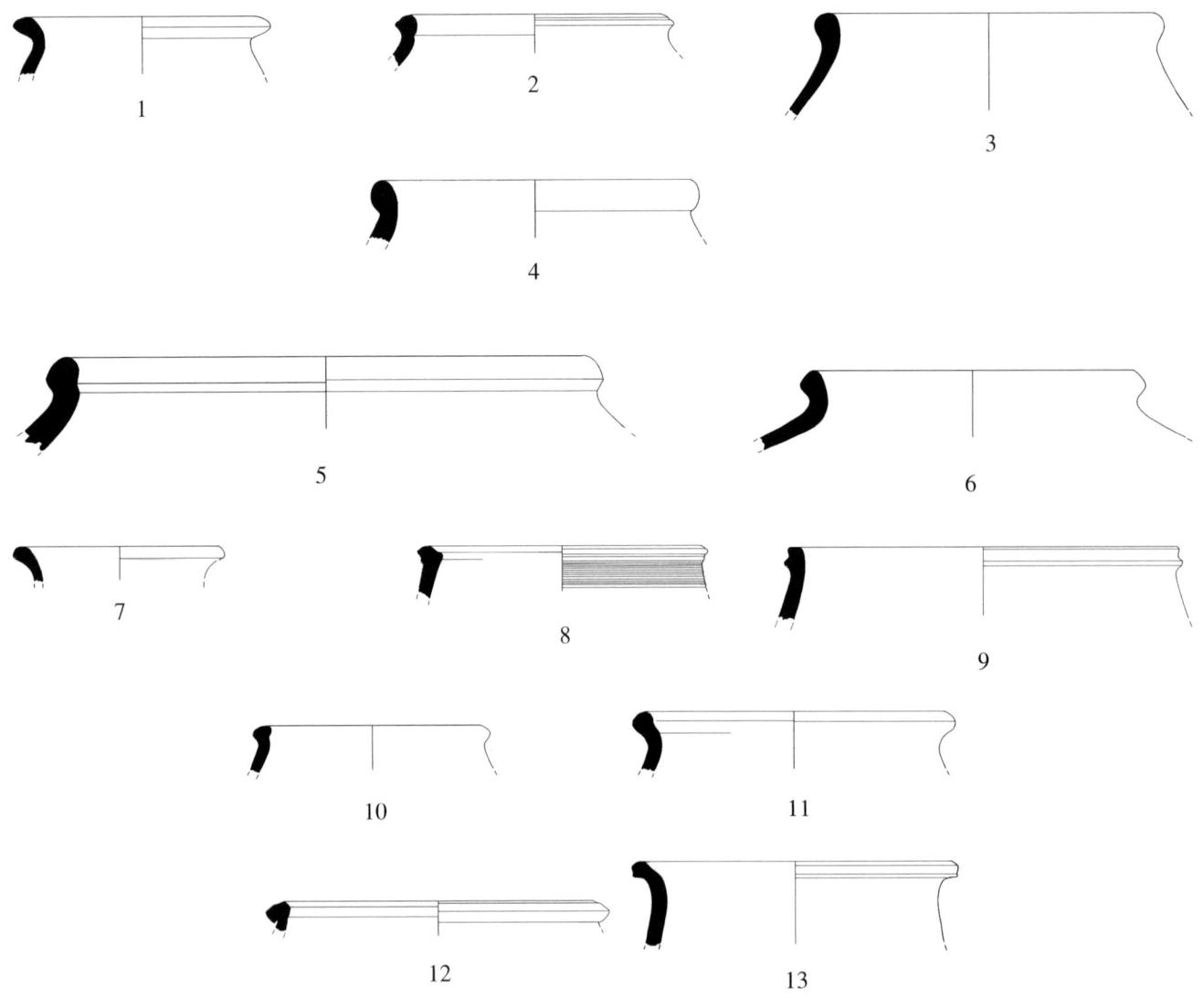

Hellenistic Jar (H.JR) Type A. Scale 1:5

1. H.JR. A.I.a (TS. 209; IIB, 6.5). Phase 14. Small rim and upper neck segment. Hard, fairly fine pinkish-brown ware with lime and mica grits, evenly fired. Wet-smoothed with self wash applied in and out.
2. H.JR. A.I.b (TS. 1540; IIA, 7.5). Phase 11. Small rim and shoulder segment. Hard, fine greenish-buff ware, evenly fired. Smooth greenish-cream slip in and out.
3. H.JR. A.I.c (TS. 2095; VC, 1.1). Phase 4. Large rim and shoulder segment. Fairly fine brown ware, evenly fired. Very worn light creamy-green slip out and possibly in.
4. H.JR. A.I.d (TS. 238; IIA, 5.1). Phase 13. Small rim and shoulder segment. Hard, slightly coarse pinkish-grayware with lime and mica grits, evenly fired. Light greenish-cream slip out.
5. H.JR. A.I.e (TS. 1452; IIB, 2.4). Phase 15. Large rim and shoulder segment. Slightly coarse light brown ware, evenly fired. Greenish-buff slip out.
6. H.JR. A.I.f (TS. 233; IIA, 5.5). Phase 11. Small rim, neck, and shoulder segment. Fairly fine pinkish-buff ware with lime and mica grits, evenly fired. Self slip out.
7. H.JR. A.II.a (SC. 2338; IIB, 2.1). Phase 15. Small rim and upper neck segment. Fairly coarse grayish-buff ware with fine lime grits, evenly fired.
8. H.JR. A.II.b (TS. 274; IIA, 4.9). Phase 13. Large rim and shoulder segment. Slightly coarse pinkish-buff ware, evenly fired. Buff slip in and out.
9. H.JR. A.II.c (TS. 1474; IIA, 4.1). Phase 14. Large rim and shoulder segment. Slightly coarse pink ware with lime and mica grits, evenly fired. Pinkish-buff slip out.
10. H.JR. A.II.d (TS. 1547; IIB, 6.4). Phase 13. Small rim and shoulder segment. Fairly fine pinkish-buff ware, evenly fired.
11. H.JR. A.II.e (TS. 142; IIA, 4.13). Phase 13. About 1/4 rim and neck segment with probable oval-shaped mouth. Hard, light pinkish-buff ware with lime and mica grits, evenly fired. Pinkish-buff slip in and out.
12. H.JR. A.II.f (TS. 330; IIB, 2.16). Phase 15. Small rim segment. Buff ware, evenly fired.
13. H.JR. A.II.g (TS. 2234; VB, 1.1). Phase 4. Small rim and upper neck segment. Slightly coarse creamy-green ware, evenly fired. Self slip out and over rim in.

Plate 307

Hellenistic Jar (H.JR) Type B. Scale 1:5

1. H.JR. B.I.a (TS. 148; IIA, 4.15). Phase 13. Small rim, neck, and shoulder segment. Slightly coarse pinkish-buff ware with lime and mica grits, evenly fired. Buff slip out.
2. H.JR. B.I.b (TS. 952; XIB, 2.1). Phase 1. Small rim and shoulder segment. Fairly fine pink ware. Cream slip in and out.

Plate 308

Hellenistic Jar (H.JR) Type C. Scale 1:5

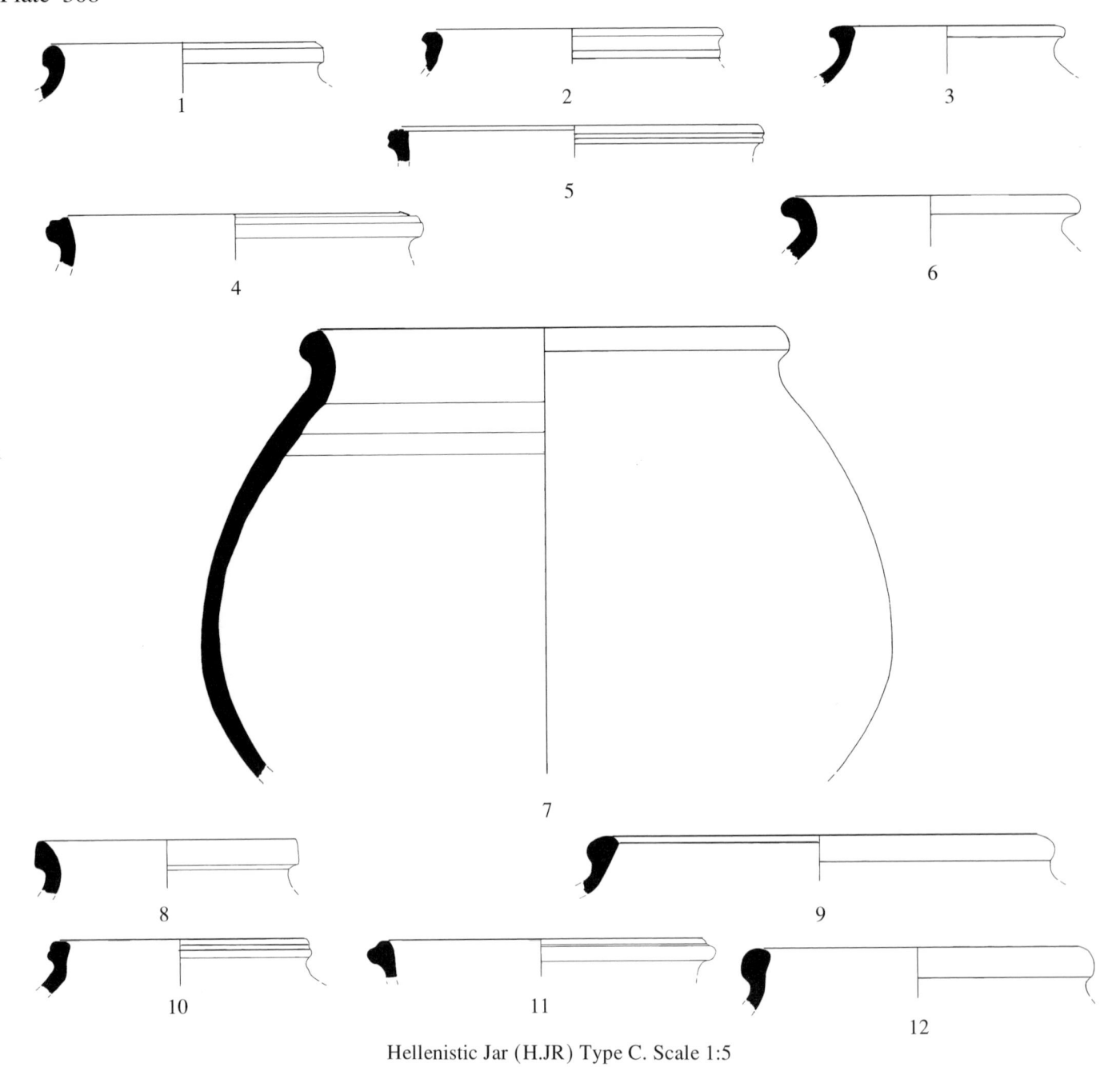

1. H.JR. C.I.a (SC. 1634; IIB, 3.1). Phase 15. About 1/8 rim and neck segment. Slightly coarse pinkish-orange ware with lime and gold- and silver-colored mica grits, evenly fired. Remains of self slip out.
2. H.JR. C.I.b (TS. 1412; IIB, 2.1). Phase 15. Small rim and neck segment. Fairly fine buff ware with fine lime and mica grits, evenly fired.
3. H.JR. C.I.c (TS. 110; IIB, 6.6, Floor). Phase 14. Small rim, neck, and shoulder segment. Hard, slightly coarse grayish-buff ware with lime and mica grits, evenly fired. Dark buff slip out and on top of rim.
4. H.JR. C.I.d (TS. 1430; IIB, 2.15). Phase 15. Small rim and neck segment. Slightly coarse buff ware, evenly fired. Creamy-buff slip in and out.
5. H.JR. C.I.e (TS. 963; VE, 1.1). Phase 9. Small rim and neck segment. Fairly coarse pink ware. Buff slip out and thinly applied in.
6. H.JR. C.I.f (TS. 268; IIA, 1.10). Phase 14. Small rim, neck, and shoulder segment. Hard, fine pinkish-buff ware with lime and mica grits, evenly fired. Self slip in and out.
7. H.JR. C.I.g (TS. 1025; XA, 1.1, Above Room 15A). Phase 4. Large rim and wall segment. Fairly coarse grayish-green ware. Thick creamy-green self slip in and out.
8. H.JR. C.I.h (TS. 1407; IIB, 2.1). Phase 15. Small rim and neck segment. Hard, fine light brown ware, evenly fired. Creamy-buff slip out.
9. H.JR. C.I.i (TS. 1449; IIA, 1.2). Phase 15. Small rim and neck segment. Slightly coarse dark pinkish-buff ware, evenly fired. Creamy-buff slip in and out.
10. H.JR. C.I.j (TS. 802; VIIIA, 1.1). Phase 3. Small rim, neck, and shoulder segment. Fairly coarse pink ware unevenly fired with brown core. Cream slip out.
11. H.JR. C.I.k (TS. 1332; IIIJ, 1). Phase 6/7. Small rim and neck segment. Slightly coarse buff ware, evenly fired. Creamy-green slip in and out.
12. H.JR. C.I.l (SC. 2462; IIB, 2.11). Phase 15. Small rim and neck segment. Fairly coarse grayish-buff ware with very small black and white lime grits, evenly fired. Traces of self slip in and out.

Plate 309

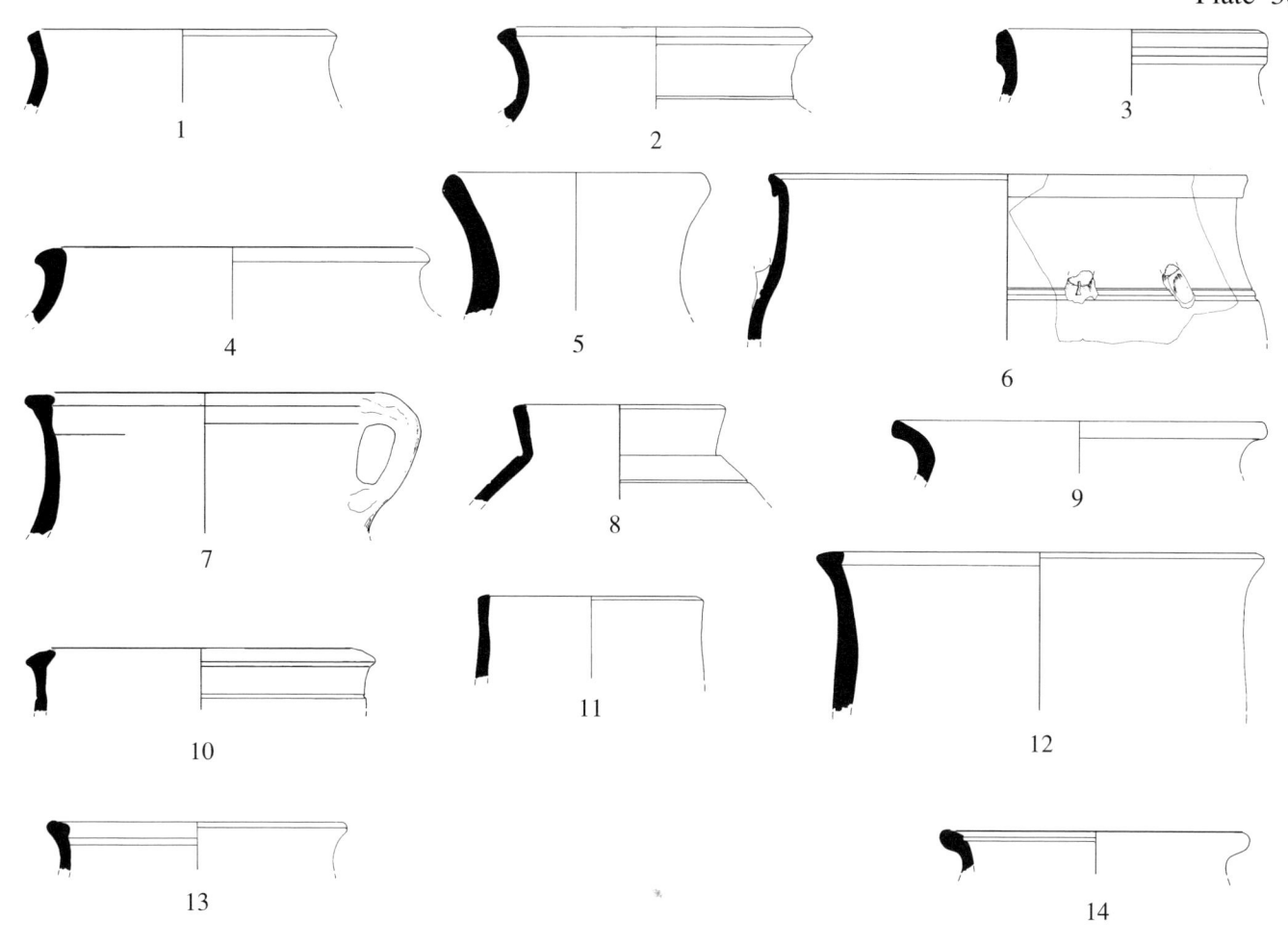

### Hellenistic Jar (H.JR) Type D. Scale 1:5

1. H.JR. D.I.a (TS. 1526 = TS. 1994; IIB, 2.10). Phase 15. Two small joining rim and shoulder segments. Slightly coarse pinkish-brown ware, fairly evenly fired. Grayish-buff slip out and over rim in.
2. H.JR. D.I.b (TS. 359; IIA, 4.3). Phase 14. Small rim, neck and shoulder segment. Fine pinkish-buff ware, evenly fired.
3. H.JR. D.I.c (TS. 196; IIB, 6.6, Floor). Phase 14. Small rim and neck segment. Hard, fine buff ware with lime and mica grits, evenly fired. Buff slip in and out.
4. H.JR. D.I.d (TS. 361; IIB, 2.3). Phase 15. Small rim and neck segment. Fine grayish-buff ware, evenly fired.
5. H.JR. D.I.e (TS. 184; IIA, 4.11). Phase 13. About 1/3 rim and neck segment. Coarse buff ware with lime, mica, and organic temper, unevenly fired pinkish at surfaces.
6. H.JR. D.I.f (TS. 98 =TS. 362; IIB, 6.6, Floor + 2.3). Phases 15 and 14. Small rim and joining wall segments with remains of horizontal loop handle on the shoulder. Fine pinkish-buff ware with mica grits, evenly fired. Creamy-buff slip out.
7. H.JR. D.I.g (TS. 180; IIA, 4.11). Phase 13. About 1/6 rim and neck segment with complete strap handle attached. Hard, fine pinkish-buff ware with lime and mica grits, evenly fired. Creamy-buff slip in and out.
8. H.JR. D.II.a (TS. 251; IIA, 5.2, Pit C). Phase 12. Small rim, neck, and shoulder segment. Hard, fairly fine buff ware with lime and mica grits, evenly fired. Buff slip out.
9. H.JR. D.II.b (TS. 1998; IIA, 4.11). Phase 13. Small rim and neck segment. Fairly fine pink ware, evenly fired. Ceamy-buff slip in and out.
10. H.JR. D.II.c (TS. 181; IIA, 4.11). Phase 13. About 1/8 rim and neck segment. Fairly fine light brown ware with lime and mica grits, evenly fired. Buff slip in and out.
11. H.JR. D.III.a (TS. 1028; IXA, 1.1). Phase 4. Small rim and neck segment. Fairly coarse greenish-cream ware, evenly fired.
12. H.JR. D.III.b (TS. 1424; IIA, 1.2). Phase 15. Large rim and neck segment. Fairly fine buff ware, evenly fired.
13. H.JR. D.III.c (TS. 234; IIB, 6.7). Phase 14. About 1/10 rim and neck segment. Fairly fine pinkish-buff ware, evenly fired. Creamy-buff slip out.
14. H.JR. D.IV.a (SC. 2398; IIB, 2.11). Phase 15. Small rim and upper neck segment. Slightly coarse pinkish-buff ware with black and white lime and a few small mica grits, evenly fired. Creamy-green slip in and out.

Plate 310

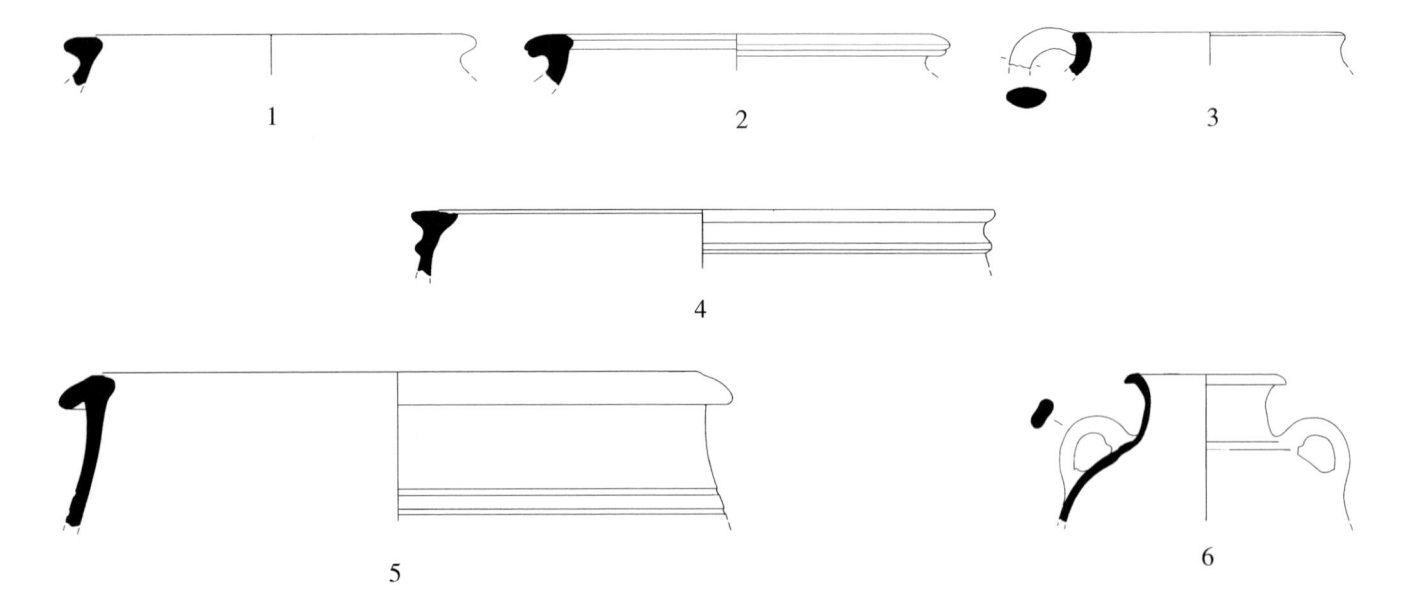

Hellenistic Jar (H.JR) Type E. Scale 1:5

1. H.JR. E.I.a (TS. 342; IIA, 1.1). Phase 15. Small rim and neck segment. Slightly coarse buff-brown ware, evenly fired.
2. H.JR. E.I.b (TS. 1454; IIB, 2.4). Phase 15. Small rim and neck segment. Fairly fine pinkish-buff ware, evenly fired. Creamy-buff slip in and out.
3. H.JR. E.I.c (TS. 934; VE, 1.1). Phase 9. Small rim and neck segment with portion of vertically-positioned loop handle attached to rim. Fairly coarse buff ware, evenly fired. Creamy slip out.
4. H.JR. E.II.a (TS. 836; VG, 1.2). Phase 8. About 1/30 rim and neck segment. Fairly coarse pink ware, evenly fired. Creamy-buff slip out.
5. H.JR. E.III.a (TS. 1005; XIA, 1.4). Phase 1. Large rim and neck segment. Fairly coarse pink ware, evenly fired. Cream slip in and out.
6. H.JR. E.IV.a (SW. 282 = TS. 34; IIA, 5.20). Phase 9. About 1/3 rim, neck, and remains of two vertical loop handles on opposite sides of shoulder. Coarse ware with lime and mica grits, fired grayish in and pink out. Pinkish-gray self slip in and out.

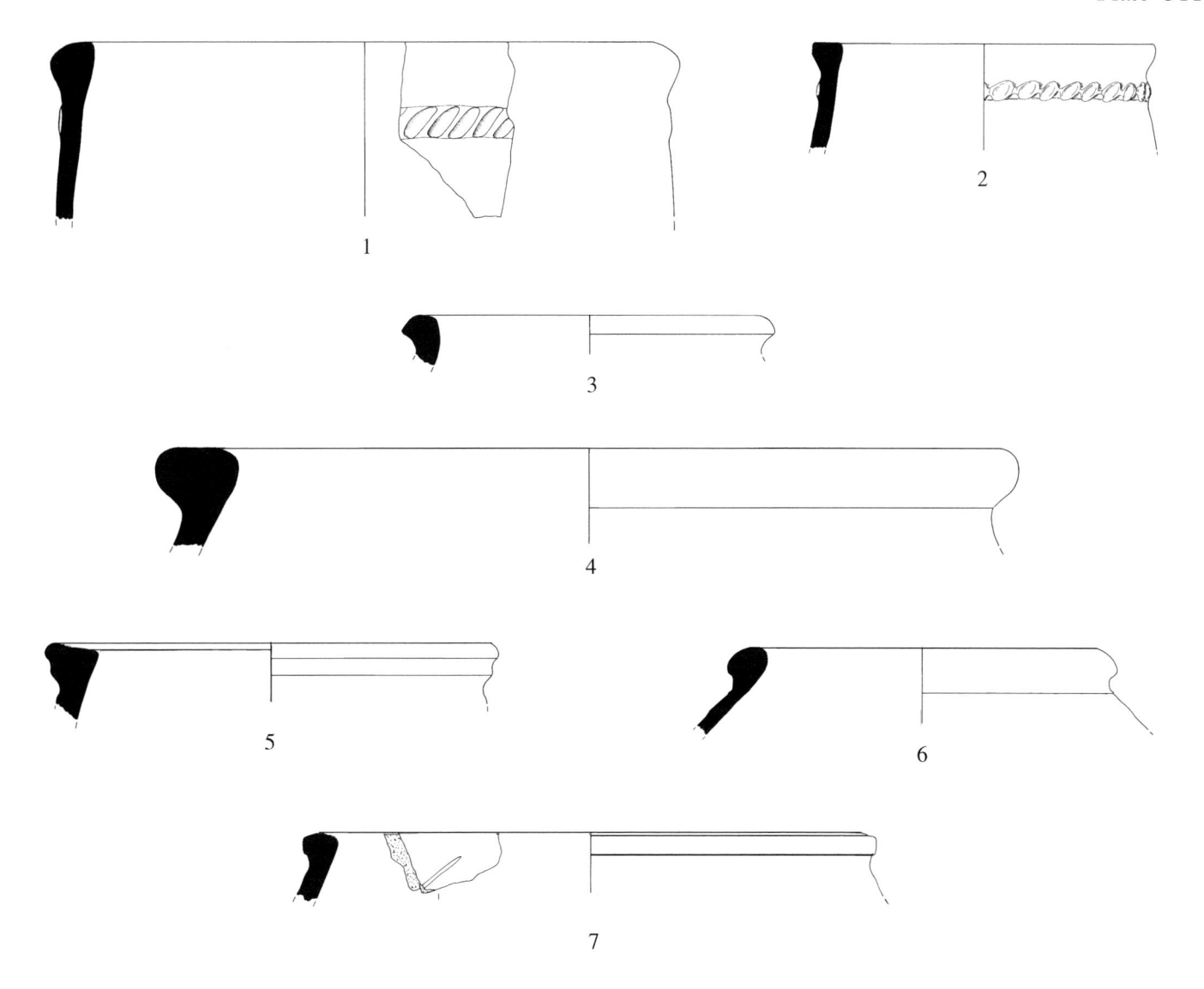

Hellenistic Jar (H.JR) Type F. Scale 1:5

1. H.JR. F.I.a (TS. 975; VE, 1.2). Phase 5. Small rim and upper wall segment with decorated applied band at top of neck. Fairly coarse pink ware. Buff slip out.
2. H.JR. F.I.b (TS. 40; IIA, 5.18, Pit C). Phase 12. About 1/8 rim and neck segment. Slightly coarse pinkish-brown ware with lime and mica grits, evenly fired. Creamy-buff slip in and out.
3. H.JR. F.II.a (SC. 1619; IIB, 6.7). Phase 14. About 1/10 rim and upper neck segment. Slightly coarse buff ware with a few visible lime grits and some burnt out chaff temper. Remains of creamy-green slip in and out.
4. H.JR. F.II.b (TS. 796; VF/G, 1.2). Phase 8. Small rim and neck segment. Fairly coarse ware fired pink in and to black out in section. Cream slip in and out, partially flaking off.
5. H.JR. F.II.c (TS. 907; VE, 1.1). Phase 9. Small rim and neck segment. Fairly coarse pink ware. Traces of cream slip out.
6. H.JR. F.II.d (TS. 46; IIA, 5.19, Pit B). Phase 9. Small rim, neck, and shoulder segment. Fairly fine pinkish-buff ware with lime and mica grits, evenly fired. Self slip out.
7. H.JR. F.II.e (SC. 1688; IIB, 2.12). Phase 15. About 1/16 rim and upper shoulder segment. Fairly coarse pinkish-rose ware with black and white lime grits, evenly fired. Remains of creamy-green slip in and out. Remains of a diagonal incision on upper inside wall, incised before firing, may represent a potter's mark.

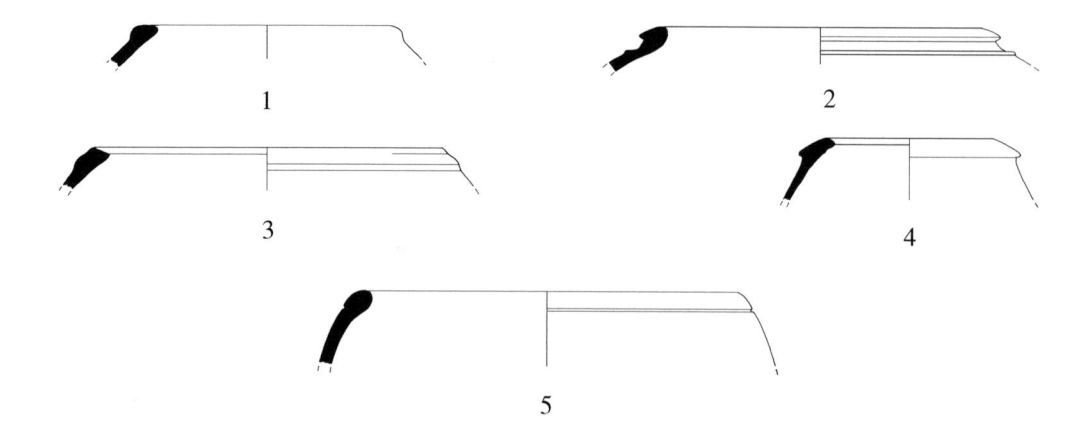

Hellenistic Jar (H.JR) Type G. Scale 1:5

1. H. JR. G.I.a (TS. 79; IIA, 8.3, Debris). Phase 7. Small rim and shoulder segment. Fairly fine light pink ware with lime and mica grits, evenly fired. Very worn self slip in and out.
2. H.JR. G.I.b (TS. 1115; VC, 2.1). Phase 3. Small rim and shoulder segment. Fairly coarse pinkish-brown ware. Cream slip in and out.
3. H.JR. G.II.a (TS. 409; VB, 1.1). Phase 4. About 1/12 rim and upper wall segment. Fairly coarse pink ware with lime and mica grits, unevenly fired with a brownish-colored core. Light tannish-brown slip in and out.
4. H.JR. G.II.b (TS. 199; IIB, 6.6, Floor). Phase 14. About 1/4 rim and shoulder segment. Fairly fine pinkish-brown ware with lime and mica grits, evenly fired. Creamy-buff slip out.
5. H.JR. G.III.a (SC. 1261; IIB, 2.4). Phase 15 (Possibly a derived Early Bronze Age holemouth jar). About 1/12 rim and upper shoulder segment. Fairly fine pinkish-buff ware with lime, gold- and silver-colored mica grits, evenly fired. Creamy-green slip out.

Plate 313

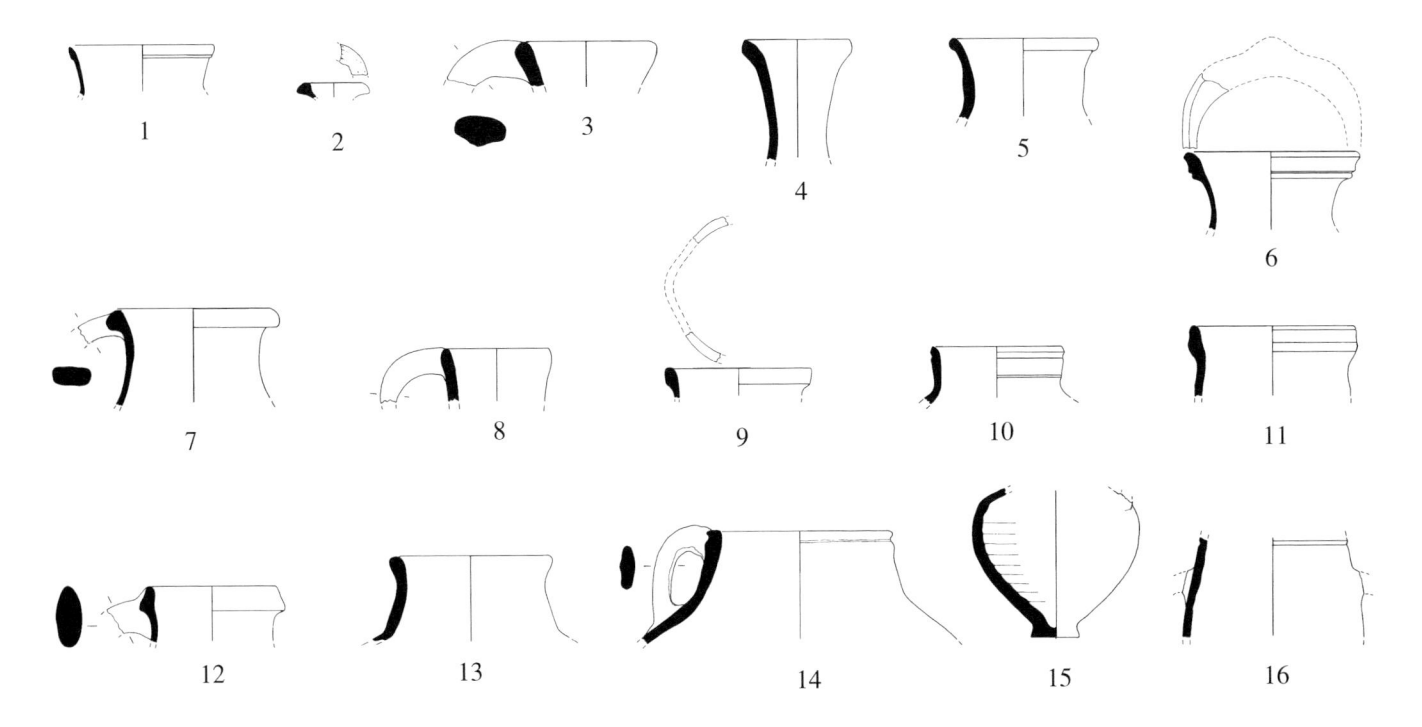

Hellenistic Jug (H.Jg) Types A–C. Scale 1:5

1. H.Jg. A.I.a (TS. 389; IIA, 1.1). Phase 15. Small rim and neck segment. Pinkish-buff ware, evenly fired. Self slip out.
2. H.Jg. A.I.b (SW. 50; IIB, 2.15). Phase 15. Small rim segment. Fairly fine buff ware with mineral temper, evenly fired. Burnished on upper surface of rim with three parallel lines of darker color.
3. H.Jg. B.I.a (TS. 937; VE, 1.1). Phase 9. Small rim and neck segment with remains of loop handle. Fairly coarse pink ware. Cream slip in and out and on handle.
4. H.Jg. B.I.b (TS. 416; VB, 1.2). Phase 3. Small rim and neck segment. Coarse light brownish-buff ware. Cream slip out.
5. H.Jg. B.I.c (TS. 216; IIA, 5.5). Phase 11. About 1/4 rim and neck segment. Fairly fine pinkish-buff ware with lime and mica grits, evenly fired.
6. H.Jg. B.I.d (TS. 231; IIB, 6.7). Phase 14. Small rim and neck segment with "pinched" lip for pouring. Hard, stone-like grayware with lime grits, evenly fired. Greenish-gray slip in and out.
7. H.Jg. B.I.e (TS. 946; VA, 1.1). Phase 4. Small rim and neck segment with remains of one loop handle. Fairly coarse brown ware, evenly fired. Cream slip in and out.
8. H.Jg. B.II.a (TS. 272; IIA, 4.9). Phase 13. About 1/4 rim and neck segment with 1/2 loop handle attached to rim. Slightly coarse buff ware with lime and mica grits, evenly fired. Self slip out.
9. H.Jg. B.II.b (TS. 2712; IVZ(N1), 1.1). Phase 5. Two small rim and upper neck segments with trefoil-shaped mouth. Slightly coarse pinkish-buff ware, evenly fired. Self slip in and out.
10. H.Jg. B.II.c (TS. 154; IIA, 4.14, Pit C). Phase 12. Small rim, neck, and shoulder segment. Fairly fine grayish-buff ware with lime and mica grits, evenly fired. Self slip out.
11. H.Jg. B.II.d (TS. 152; IIA, 4.14, Pit C). Phase 12. About 1/4 rim and neck segment. Fairly fine buff ware with lime grits, evenly fired. Self slip in and out.
12. H.Jg. B.II.e (TS. 2940; IVO, 1.2, Room 10B). Phase 4. About 1/3 rim and neck segment with remains of one loop handle. Slightly coarse pinkish-buff ware, evenly fired. Buff slip in and out.
13. H.Jg. B.III.a (TS. 343 = TS. 1437; IIB, 2.2, Oven). Phase 15. About 1/3 rim and neck of two non-joining segments. Light buff ware, evenly fired.
14. H.Jg. B.III.b (TS. 214; IIB, 6.5). Phase 14. About 1/6 rim, neck, and shoulder segment with complete strap handle. Fairly fine pinkish-buff ware with lime and mica grits, evenly fired. Buff slip out.
15. H.Jg. C.I.a (TS. 119, 120, 121; IIA, 7.1, Pit [unnumbered]). Phase 10. Complete base and most of body with stub of one loop handle on shoulder. Fairly fine pinkish-brown ware with gold-colored mica and lime grits, evenly fired. Light pinkish-cream slip out.
16. H.Jg. C.II.a (TS. 2028; IIB, 2.1, 2.3, 2.4). Phase 15. Three joining sherds, one with remains of a loop handle. Fairly fine grayware, evenly fired. Vertically burnished self slip out.

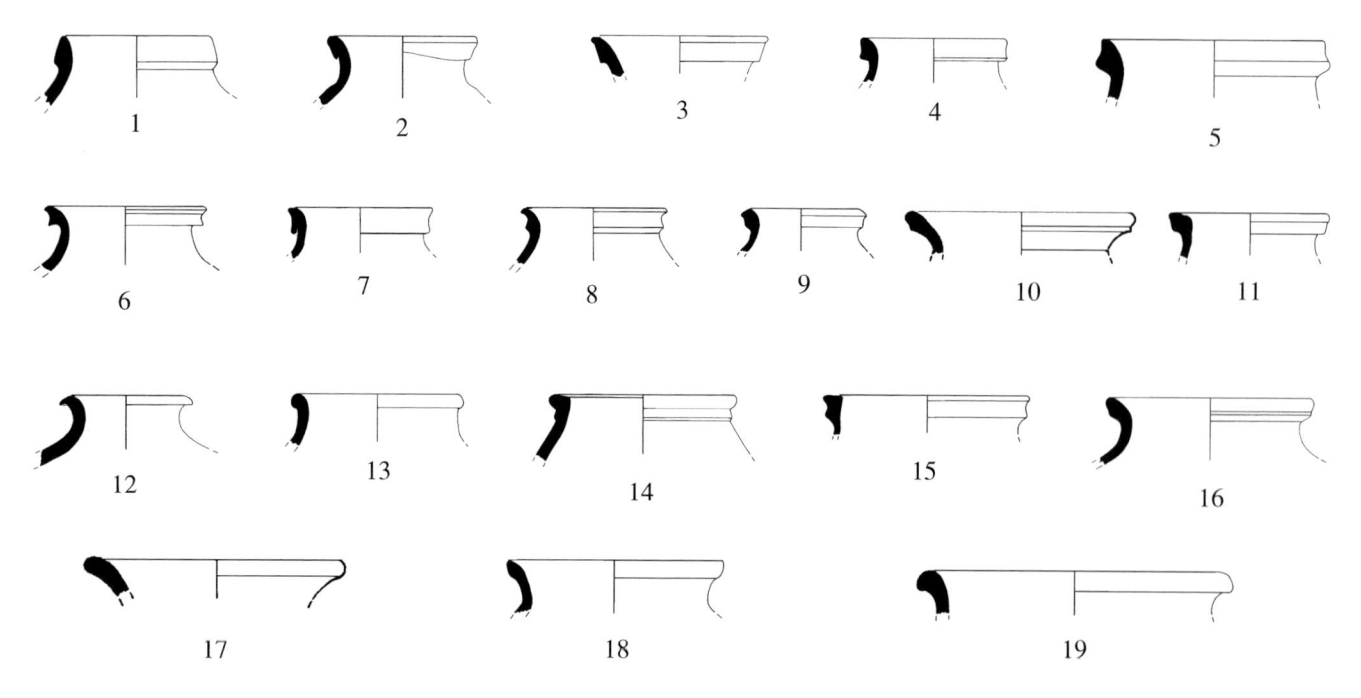

Hellenistic Storage Jar (H.St.J) Type A. Scale 1:5

1. H.St.J. A.I.a (TS. 1440; IIB, 2.12). Phase 15. Small rim and neck segment. Fine buff ware, evenly fired. Creamy-buff slip in and out.
2. H.St.J. A.I.b (TS. 355; IIB, 2.3). Phase 15. Small rim and neck segment. Pinkish-buff ware, evenly fired. Creamy-buff slip in and out.
3. H.St.J. A.I.c (TS. 329; IIB, 2.16). Phase 15. Small rim and neck segment. Buff ware, evenly fired.
4. H.St.J. A.I.d (TS. 1457; IIB, 2.4). Phase 15. Small rim and neck segment. Hard, fine pinkish-buff ware, evenly fired. Dark buff slip out and just over rim in.
5. H.St.J. A.I.e (TS. 1032; VA/B, Baulk). Phases 2–4. Small rim and neck segment. Fairly coarse cream ware.
6. H.St.J. A.I.f (TS. 1529; IIA, 1.2). Phase 15. Small rim and neck segment. Fairly fine pinkish-buff ware, evenly fired. Creamy-buff slip in and out.
7. H.St.J. A.I.g (TS. 366; IIB, 2.3). Phase 15. Small rim and neck segment. Creamy-buff ware, evenly fired.
8. H.St.J. A.I.h (TS. 1431; IIB, 2.12). Phase 15. Small rim and neck segment. Slightly coarse pinkish-buff ware, evenly fired. Self slip in and out.
9. H.St.J. A.I.i (TS. 210; IIA, 5.5, 5.11, Courtyard, 5.19, Pit B). Phases 11, 8 and 9. Four joining rim segments (two segments from 5.19); nearly complete rim and neck. Slightly coarse grayish-buff ware with lime and mica grits, evenly fired. Self slip out.
10. H.St.J. A.I.j (SC. 2665; VB, 1.1). Phase 4. About 1/16 rim and neck segment. Slightly coarse pinkish-buff ware with fine lime and mica grits, evenly fired. Self slip in and out.
11. H.St.J. A.I.k (TS. 900; VG, 1.4). Phase 6. Fairly coarse pinkish-buff ware, evenly fired. Cream slip in and out.
12. H.St.J. A.I.l (TS. 54; IIA, 5.21, Pit B1). Phase 7. About 1/4 rim, neck, and shoulder segment. Slightly coarse buff ware with lime and mica grits, evenly fired. Self slip in and out.
13. H.St.J. A.I.m (TS. 1435; IIB, 2.12). Phase 15. Small rim and neck segment. Slightly coarse grayish-buff ware, evenly fired. Self slip out.
14. H.St.J. A.I.n (TS. 2087; VF, 1.1). Phase 9. Small rim and neck segment. Slightly coarse buff ware, evenly fired. Light creamy-green slip out.
15. H.St.J. A.II.a (TS. 853; VG, 1.2). Phase 8. About 1/10 rim and neck segment. Fairly coarse pink ware, evenly fired. Cream slip in and out.
16. H.St.J. A.II.b (TS. 1427; IIB, 2.12). Phase 15. Small rim, neck, and shoulder segment. Fine pinkish-buff ware, evenly fired. Creamy-buff slip out.
17. H.St.J. A.II.c (SC. 2736; VB, 1.1). Phase 4. About 1/6 rim and upper neck segment. Slightly coarse pinkish-orange ware with a few lime and gold-colored mica grits, evenly fired. Remains of creamy-buff slip out.
18. H.St.J. A.II.d (TS. 278; IIB, 2.11). Phase 15. Two small joining rim and neck segments. Slightly coarse buff ware with lime grits, evenly fired. Creamy-buff slip out.
19. H.St.J. A.II.e (TS. 151; IIA, 4.13). Phase 13. About 1/6 rim and upper neck segment. Fairly fine buff ware with lime and mica grits, evenly fired. Creamy-buff slip in and out.

Plate 315

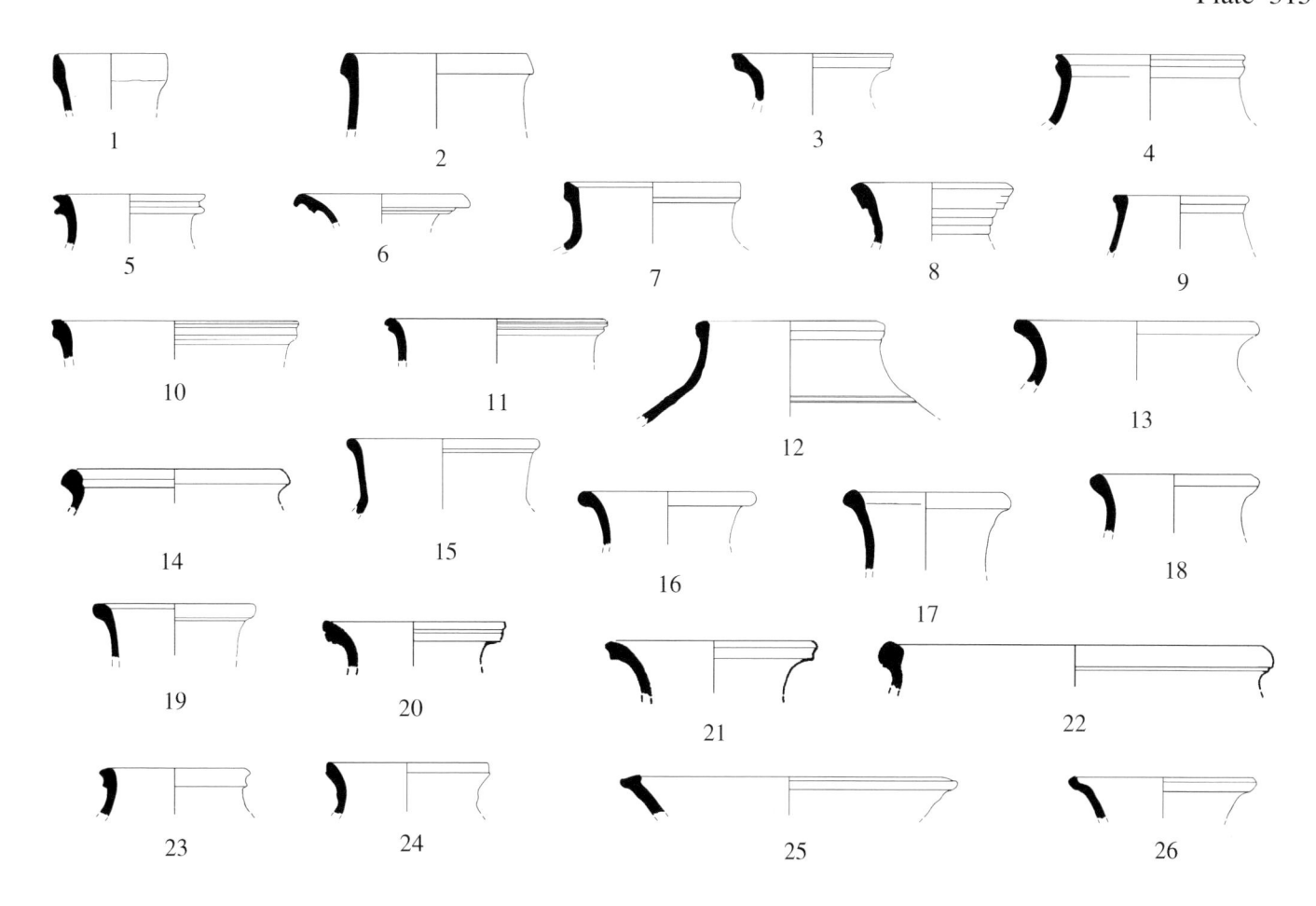

## Hellenistic Storage Jar (H.St.J) Type B. Scale 1:5

1. H.St.J. B.I.a (TS. 198; IIB, 6.6, Floor). Phase 14. Small rim and neck segment. Fine pink ware with lime and mica grits, evenly fired. Self slip in and out.
2. H.St.J. B.I.b (TS. 422; VA, 1.1). Phase 4. Small rim and neck segment. Fairly fine pink ware, evenly fired.
3. H.St.J. B.I.c (TS. 338; IIB, 2.11). Phase 15. Small rim and neck segment. Fairly fine buff ware, evenly fired.
4. H.St.J. B.I.d (TS. 1429 = SC. 2686; IIB, 2.12 + 2.13, Room). Phases 15 and 13. Two non-joining rim and neck segments. Fairly fine pinkish-buff ware, evenly fired. Buff slip in and out.
5. H.St.J. B.I.e (TS. 413; VF, 1.1). Phase 9. Small rim and neck segment. Fairly coarse pink ware with lime and mica grits, evenly fired. Light brownish-buff slip out.
6. H.St.J. B.I.f (TS. 879; VG, 1.4). Phase 6. Small rim and neck segment. Fairly coarse pinkish-brown ware, evenly fired. Cream slip in and out.
7. H.St.J. B.I.g (TS. 337; IIA, 1.8). Phase 14. Small rim, neck, and shoulder segment. Buff ware, evenly fired.
8. H.St.J. B.I.h (TS. 866; VG, 1.4). Phase 6. Small rim and neck segment. Fairly coarse pink ware, evenly fired. Cream slip in and out.
9. H.St.J. B.I.i (TS. 396; IIB, 2.1). Phase 15. Small rim and neck segment. Fine buff-brown ware, evenly fired. Creamy-buff slip in and out.
10. H.St.J. B.II.a (TS. 1477; IIA, 4.1). Phase 14. Small rim and upper neck segment. Fairly fine pinkish-buff ware, evenly fired.
11. H.St.J. B.II.b (TS. 254; IIA, 5.2, Pit C). Phase 12. About 1/6 rim and neck segment. Fairly fine buff ware with lime and mica grits, evenly fired. Self slip in and out.
12. H.St.J. B.II.c (SW. 26; IIB, 2.2, Oven). Phase 15. Large rim, neck, and shoulder segment. Orange ware, evenly fired. Cream slip out.
13. H.St.J. B.II.d (TS. 1434; IIB, 2.12). Phase 15. Small rim and neck segment. Fairly fine pinkish-buff ware, evenly fired. Creamy-buff slip in and out.
14. H.St.J. B.II.e (SC. 1164; VB, 1.1). Phase 4. About 1/8 rim and upper neck segment. Fairly fine pinkish-buff ware with small gold-colored mica grits, evenly fired. Remains of creamy-buff slip in and out.
15. H.St.J. B.II.f (TS. 331; IIA, 1.8). Phase 14. Small rim, neck, and shoulder segment. Pinkish-buff ware, evenly fired.
16. H.St.J. B.II.g (TS. 1402; IIB, 2.1). Phase 15. Small rim and neck segment. Fairly fine pinkish-buff ware, evenly fired. Creamy-buff slip in and out.
17. H.St.J. B.II.h (TS. 157; IVC, 1.1). Phase 4. Small rim and neck segment. Slightly coarse pinkish-brown ware with lime and mica grits, evenly fired. Pinkish-buff slip in and out.
18. H.St.J. B.II.i (TS. 197; IIB, 6.6, Floor). Phase 14. Small rim and neck segment. Fairly fine pinkish-buff ware with lime and mica grits, evenly fired. Self slip out.
19. H.St.J. B.II.j (TS. 1403; IIB, 2.1). Phase 15. Small rim and neck segment. Close buff ware fired pink at surfaces.
20. H.St.J. B.II.k (SC. 1427; VE, 1.1). Phase 5. About 1/8 rim and neck segment. Slightly coarse pinkish-buff ware with small lime grits, evenly fired. Creamy-buff slip in and out.
21. H.St.J. B.II.l (SC. 1425; VB, 1.2). Phase 3. About 1/6 rim and upper neck segment. Slightly coarse pinkish-buff ware with small gold-colored mica grits, evenly fired. Thick creamy-buff slip in and out.
22. H.St.J. B.II.m (SC. 2182; VB, 1.1). Phase 4. About 1/10 rim and upper neck segment. Fairly fine pinkish-buff ware with small black and white lime grits, evenly fired. Self slip in and out.
23. H.St.J. B.II.n (TS. 10; IIA, 7.3, Pit [unnumbered]). Phase 10. About 1/5 rim segment. Fairly fine pink ware with mica grits, evenly fired. Self slip in and out.
24. H.St.J. B.II.o (TS. 1038; VA/B, Baulk). Phases 2–4. Small rim and neck segment. Fairly coarse pink ware, evenly fired. Greenish-buff slip in and out.
25. H.St.J. B.II.p (TS. 1943; IVC, 1.2). Phase 3. Small rim and neck segment. Slightly coarse buff ware, evenly fired. Self slip in and out.
26. H.St.J. B.II.q (TS. 957; VC, 1.1). Phase 4. Small rim and neck segment. Fairly fine pink ware, evenly fired. Cream slip in and out.

Plate 316

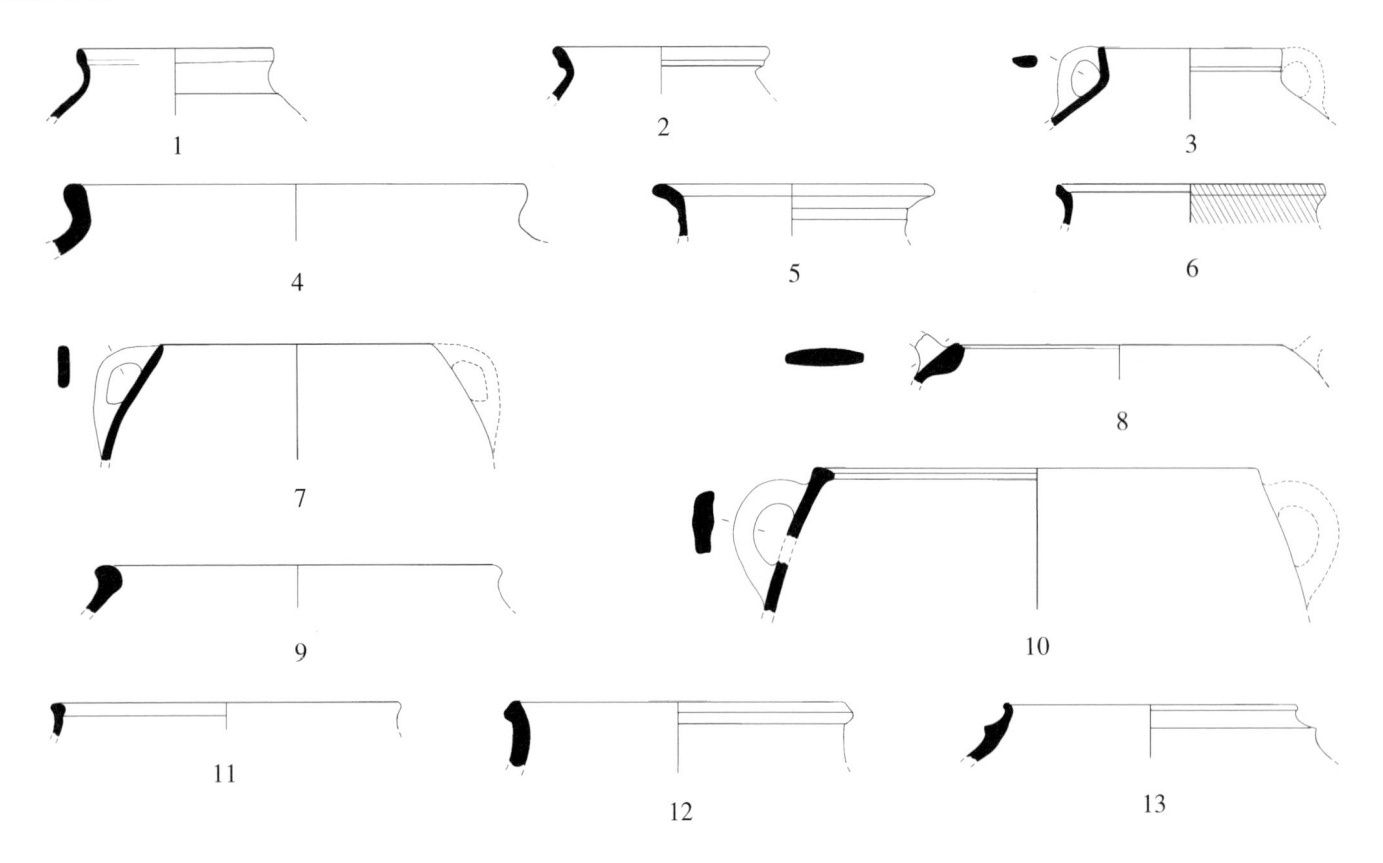

Hellenistic Cooking Pot (H.CP) Types A–E. Scale 1:5

1. H.CP. A.I.a (TS. 261; IIA, 1.10). Phase 14. Small rim, neck, and shoulder segment. Slightly coarse pinkish-brown ware with lime and mica grits, unevenly fired buff on inner surface.
2. H.CP. A.I.b (TS. 356; IIB, 2.3). Phase 15. Small rim and shoulder segment. Slightly coarse grayware fired reddish-brown out.
3. H.CP. B.I.a (TS. 228; IIB, 6.7). Phase 14. About 4/5 rim and shoulder segment with one complete loop handle. Coarse orange-brown ware with lime grits, evenly fired.
4. H.CP. B.II.a (TS. 48; IIA, 5.6, Pit C). Phase 12. Small rim, neck, and shoulder segment. Slightly coarse light brown ware with many lime and mica grits, evenly fired. Self slip out.
5. H.CP. C.I.a (TS. 904; VF, 1.5). Phase 5. About 1/10 rim and neck segment. Fairly coarse brown ware, evenly fired. Burnished on rim in.
6. H.CP. C.I.b (TS. 960 = TS. 1133; VC, 1.1 + VD, 2.4 + VB, 1.1). Phases 4, 9 (Pit), and 4 (Wall A). Three joining rim and neck segments. Coarse reddish-brown ware. Red slip out.
7. H.CP. D.I.a (TS. 281; IIA, 4.9). Phase 13. Small rim and wall segment with complete strap handle. Coarse pinkish-brown ware with lime and mica grits, evenly fired. Self slip out.
8. H.CP. D.I.b (TS. 189; IIA, 4.11). Phase 13. Small rim segment with remains of one wide strap handle. Coarse grayware with lime and mica grits, evenly fired. Charred or fired black at surfaces in and out.
9. H.CP. D.I.c (TS. 49; IIA, 5.8). Phase 9. Small rim and neck segment. Slightly coarse light brown ware with many lime and mica grits, evenly fired. Irregular horizontal burnish out.
10. H.CP. D.I.d (TS. 139; IIA, 5.2, Pit C). Phase 12. Small rim and shoulder segment with complete loop handle. Slightly coarse brown ware with lime and mica grits, evenly fired. Traces of burning in and out.
11. H.CP. E.I.a (TS. 395; IIB, 2.1). Phase 15. Small rim and upper wall segment. Fairly coarse grayish-brown ware, evenly fired.
12. H.CP. E.I.b (TS. 358 = TS. 386; IIB, 2.5 and 3.1). Phase 15. Small rim and upper wall segment. Fairly coarse grayish-brown ware, evenly fired. Traces of burning on upper rim in.
13. H.CP. E.I.c (TS. 961; VA, 1.1). Phase 4. Small rim and upper shoulder segment. Coarse reddish-brown ware, fairly evenly fired.

Plate 317

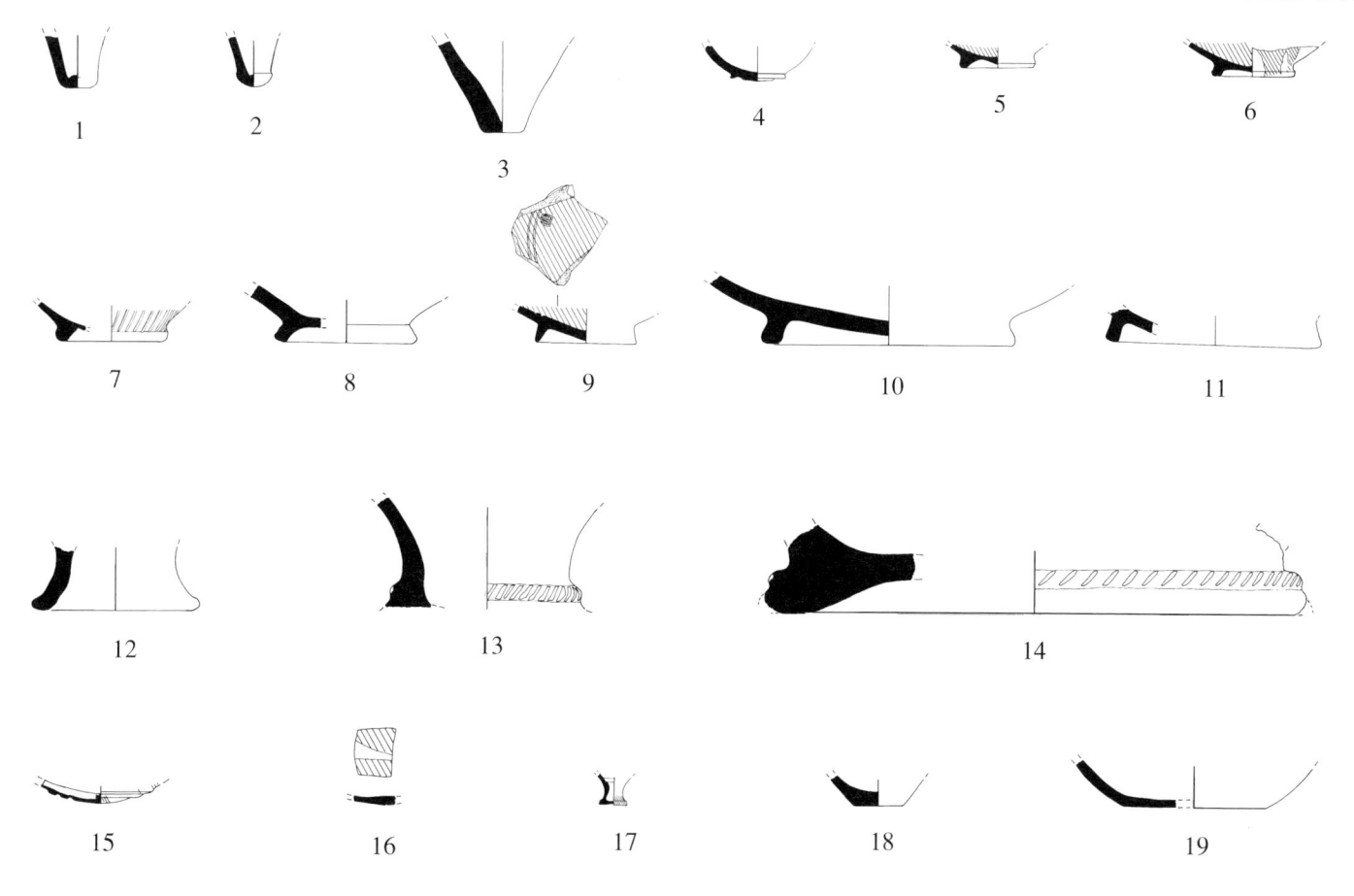

Hellenistic Base (BE) Types A–E. Scale 1:5

1. H.BE. A.I.a (TS. 1455; IIB, 2.4). Phase 15. Complete base and lower wall segment. Fairly fine buff ware, evenly fired.
2. H.BE. A.I.b (TS. 1803; IIIA, 1.1). Phase 7. Complete base and lower wall segment. Fairly fine pinkish-buff ware, evenly fired. Creamy-buff slip out.
3. H.BE. A.II.a (TS. 1405; IIB, 2.1). Phase 15. Complete base and lower wall segment. Hard, fine pinkish-buff ware, evenly fired. Buff slip out.
4. H.BE. B.I.a (TS. 377; IIA, 1.1). Phase 15. Complete base and lower wall segment. Fine buff ware, evenly fired. Thick self slip in and out.
5. H.BE. B.I.b (TS. 3090; IIB, 2.12). Phase 15. About 1/2 segment of base and lower wall. Slightly coarse light pink ware, evenly fired. Red slip in.
6. H.BE. B.I.c (SC. 3203; IIB, 2.2). Phase 15. Complete base and lower edges of vessel wall. Fine grayish-buff ware with a few small lime grits, evenly fired. Red slip on all of inner wall preserved and drip lines outside to bottom of base. Outside wall not covered by red slip is horizontally burnished.
7. H.BE. B.II.a (TS. 1223; IIB, 2.1). Phase 15. Small segment with portion of base wall inside ring missing. Vertically impressed linear decoration around base of vessel. Fairly fine pink ware, evenly fired. Creamy-buff slip out.
8. H.BE. B.II.b (TS. 1117; VC, 2.1). Phase 3. Small segment with portion of base wall inside ring missing. Fairly coarse pinkish-orange ware, evenly fired.
9. H.BE. B.II.c (TS. 3047; VG, 1.2). Phase 8. About 1/2 segment with stamped pattern on inside surface. Fine pinkish-orange ware, evenly fired. Remains of reddish-brown slip in.
10. H.BE. B.III.a (TS. 3043; VC, 1.1). Phase 4. About 1/3 segment. Fairly fine orange-buff ware, evenly fired. Heavily lime encrusted in and out.
11. H.BE. B.III.b (TS. 405; VB, 1.2). Phase 3. Small segment with portion of base wall, inside ring missing. Fairly coarse light brown ware, evenly fired. Cream slip in and out except on the outside bottom of the base.
12. H.BE. C.I.a (SC. 3078; IIB, 3.1). Phase 15. About 1/10 of pedestal rim and wall segment. Coarse pinkish-red ware with lime and mica grits, evenly fired. Creamy-buff slip in and out.
13. H.BE. C.II.a (SC. 3080; IIB, 2.3). Phase 15. About 1/4 segment of central portion of pedestal base with incised band of decoration at juncture with stand and missing vessel (note that drawing should possibly be turned upside down). Slightly coarse pinkish-red ware with a few large lime pebble inclusions and gold- and silver-colored mica grits, evenly fired. Cream slip out.
14. H.BE. C.II.b (TS. 943; VE, 1.1). Phase 9. Small segment. Fairly coarse pink ware, fairly evenly fired.
15. H.BE. D.I.a (SC. 3093; IIB, 2.4). Phase 15. About 1/2 segment of round, ribbed, base. Fairly fine pinkish-brown ware with very fine gold- and silver-colored mica grits, fired pinkish-orange at surfaces in and out. Remains of red slip on the outside of the base.
16. H.BE. D.I.b (SC. 3348; IIB, 6.5). Phase 14. About 1/2 segment of plain round base. Fairly fine pinkish-buff ware with a few lime and mica grits, evenly fired. Radiating bands of red slip applied on both the inner and outer surfaces.
17. H.BE. E.I.a (TS. 1393; IIB, 6.7). Phase 14. Complete base and lower wall segment. Fine reddish-brown ware, unevenly fired with gray core. Purple-brown slip out.
18. H.BE. E.I.b (SC. 3135; IIB, 2.3). Phase 15. Complete small flat base with fragment of lower wall of vessel. Fairly coarse grayish-buff ware with lime grits, evenly fired. Self slip in and out.
19. H.BE. E.I.c (SC. 3147; IIB, 6.6). Phase 14. About 1/6 segment of flat base and lower wall of vessel. Slightly coarse creamy-buff ware with a few lime grits, evenly fired. Buff slip out and light creamy-green slip in.

Plate 318. Hellenistic Miscellaneous Pottery Types (Unclassified): Bottles (H.Bt.), Pot Stands (H.PS), Handles (H.Hd.), Lids (H.Ld.), Lamps (H.Lp.), and Applied-band Sherd (H.ABS) Types A–E

1. H.Bt.1 (TS. 108; IIA, 5.6). Phase 12. Spout only from a probable baby feeding bottle. Brownish-buff ware, fairly evenly fired.
2. H.Bt.2 (SC. 3341; IIA, 5.1). Phase 13. Wall fragment. Hard, fine purple-red ware with a few very small lime grits, fired black on inside and outside surfaces. Outside highly burnished horizontally all over.
3. H.PS.1 (SW. 55; IIB, 2.4). Phase 15. Large segment of complete profile. Slightly coarse orange-buff ware with black mineral temper, evenly fired. Discolored white surface.
4. H.PS.2 (TS. 42 = TS. 212, 252, and 363; IIA, 5.19 (Pit B) + 5.5 + 5.1 and IIB, 2.3). Phases 9, 11, 13, and 15. Four joining rim segments making nearly complete diameter of one end of the stand. Hard, fairly fine pinkish-buff ware with lime and mica grits, evenly fired. Self slip in and out.
5. H.PS.3 (TS. 1462; IIA, 1.2). Phase 15. Small rim and portion of wall. Slightly coarse pinkish-buff ware, evenly fired. Creamy-buff slip out and on top of rim.
6. H.PS.4 (TS. 51; IIA, 5.9). Phase 9. About 1/8 segment with remains of a circular-shaped hole bored through the wall before firing. Fairly fine buff ware with micaceous grit temper, evenly fired.
7. H.Hd.1 (TS. 103; IIB, 6.6, Floor). Phase 14. Complete lug handle. Fairly fine light greenish-grayware with a few lime grits, evenly fired. Pinkish-buff slip out.
8. H.Hd.2 = H.CP. D.I.b (TS. 851; VG, 1.2). Phase 8. About 2/3 portion of broad strap handle. Fairly coarse pink ware, evenly fired.
9. H.Ld.1 (TS. 1543; IIA, 7.2). Phase 10. Small rim and wall segment. Fine buff ware, evenly fired.
10. H.Ld.2 (TS. 1542; IIA, 7.2). Phase 10. Small rim and wall segment. Fine pinkish-buff ware, evenly fired.
11. H.Ld.3 (TS. 393; IIB, 2.1). Phase 15. Small rim and wall segment. Pinkish-brown ware, evenly fired.
12. H.Ld.4 (TS. 1989; IIA, 4.15). Phase 13. Small rim and wall segment. Fairly fine pink ware, evenly fired. Pinkish-buff slip out.
13. H.Ld.5 (SW. 183; IIA, 7.1, Pit [unnumbered]). Phase 10. Incomplete knob-type lid. Fairly fine dark grayware with lime grits, evenly fired.
14. H.Ld.6 (SW. 174; IIA, 7.2, Pit [unnumbered]). Phase 10. Incomplete knob-type lid. Fine dark grayware with mineral temper, evenly fired. Burnished self slip.
15. H.Lp.1 (SW. 122; IIA, 4.9). Phase 13. Complete profile segment. Fairly fine brown ware with lime and mica grits, evenly fired. Plum-brown slip out.
16. H.Lp.2 (SW. 715; IVZ(N1), 1.1). Phase 5. Incomplete rim and wall segment with pierced lug-type handle. Fairly fine light grayware, evenly fired. Burnished self slip out.
17. H.ABS. A (TS. 237; IIA, 5.2, Pit C). Phase 12. Small wall segment. Slightly coarse light pink ware with lime and mica grits, evenly fired.
18. H.ABS. B (TS. 114; IIA, 5.6). Phase 12. Fairly large wall segment. Coarse pinkish-brown ware with lime and mica grits, evenly fired. Buff slip out.
19. H.ABS. C (TS. 1253; IIA, 4.9). Phase 13. Wall segment with diagonal impressions on three extant applied rope-like bands. Slightly coarse buff ware, evenly fired. Creamy-green slip out.
20. H.ABS. D (TS. 97; IIB, 6.6, Floor). Phase 14. Jar wall fragment with applied, thumb-impressed band of decoration, similar to jar type H.JR. F.I.b (pl. 311:2). Slightly coarse pinkish-brown ware with lime and mica grits and organic chaff temper, evenly fired. Self slip out.
21. H.ABS. E (TS. 1226; IIB, 2.1). Phase 15. Jar wall fragment with a slightly raised band of incised herringbone decoration. Slightly coarse pink ware fired buff at surfaces in and out. Creamy-buff slip in and out.

Plate 318

Hellenistic Miscellaneous Pottery Types (Unclassified): Bottles (H.Bt.), Pot Stands (H.PS), Handles (H.Hd.), Lids (H.Ld.), Lamps (H.Lp.), and Applied Band Sherd (H.ABS) Types A–E. Scale 1:5

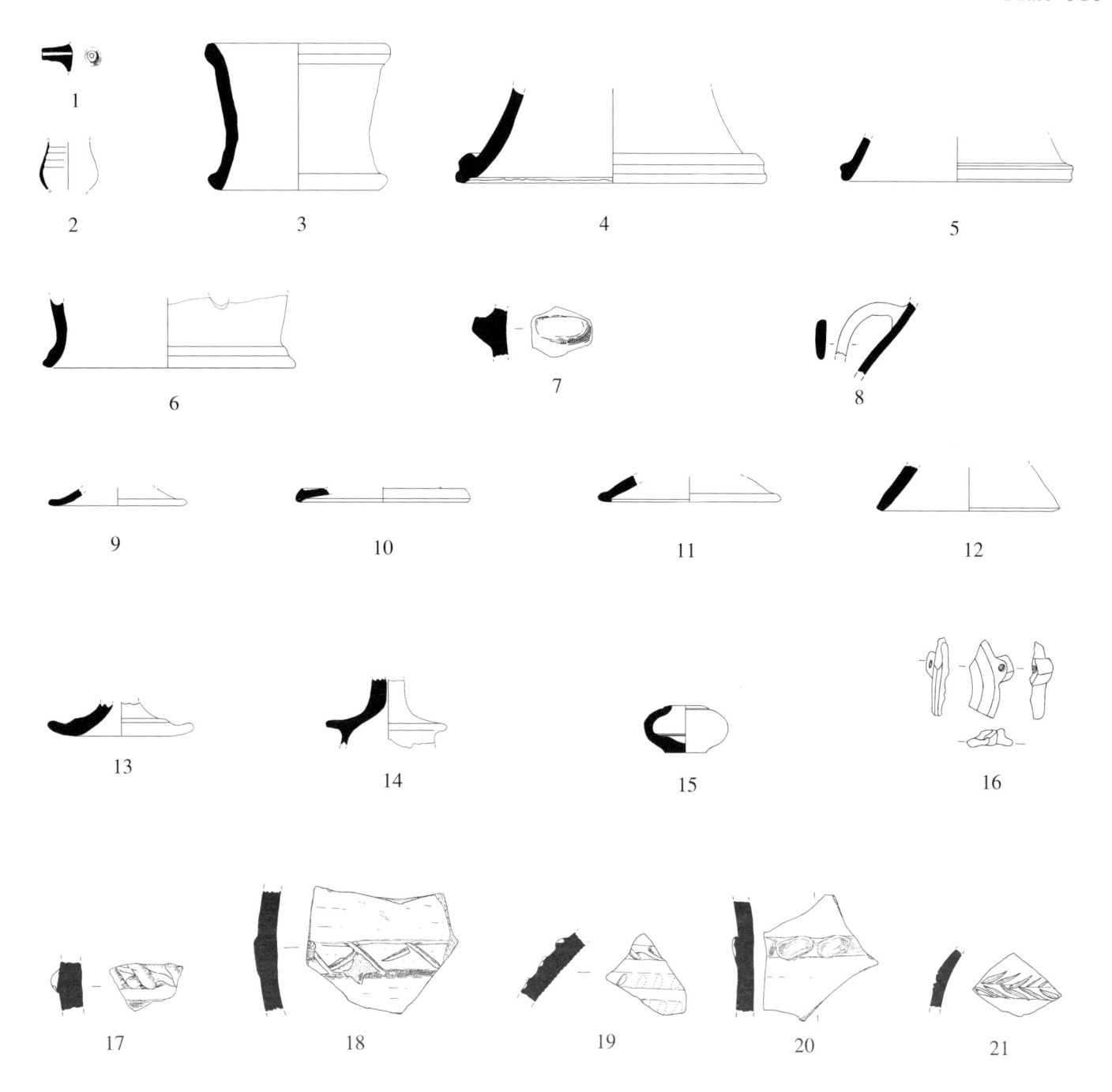

Plate 319. Roman Miniature Bowl (R.MBR) Types 1–5 (Unclassified) and Roman Small Bowl (R.SBR) Types A and B

1. R.MBR.1 (TS. 438; IA2, 4.3). Phase 2. Small rim and wall segment. Fairly coarse pink ware with lime and mica grits, evenly fired.
2. R.MBR.2 (TS. 1509; IA1, 1.3). Phase 3. Small rim and upper wall segment. Fairly fine buff ware, evenly fired. Self slip in and out.
3. R.MBR.3 (TS. 3984); Op. 5, 14.1). Phase 5. Small rim and upper wall segment. Ware description is unavailable.
4. R.MBR.4 (TS. 3803; Op. 5, 8.1). Phase 6. Complete bell-shaped base and lower portion of chalice-like vessel wall. Ware description is unavailable.
5. R.MBR.5 (SC. 3469; IA2, 3.1). Phase 4. Small rim and wall segment with a probable round base. Fairly coarse light grayware with lime and vegetable temper, evenly fired. Creamy-gray slip in and out.
6. R.SBR. A.I.a (TS. 2445; IA2, 3.3). Phase 3. About 1/10 rim and wall segment. Slightly coarse pink ware, evenly fired. Thick creamy-buff slip in and out.
7. R.SBR. A.II.a (TS. 652; IA2, 3.3). Phase 3. About 1/28 rim and upper wall segment. Fine pink ware, evenly fired. Red slip in and out.
8. R.SBR. A.III.a (TS. 2146; IB, 1.6, Floor). Phase 3. Small rim and wall segment. Fairly fine pink ware fired light brown on outside surface. Self slip in and out.
9. R.SBR. A.III.b (SC. 3444; IA2, 4.1). Phase 4. Small rim and upper wall segment. Fine light grayware with small lime grits, evenly fired. Dark creamy-buff slip in and out.
10. R.SBR. B.I.a (SC. 2927; IA1, 2.3). Phase 2. Small rim and upper wall segment. Slightly coarse buff ware with lime grits, evenly fired. Dark creamy-bull slip in and out.
11. R.SBR. B.I.b (SC. 3475; IB, 1.2). Phase 4. Small rim and upper wall segment. Slightly coarse buff ware with lime grits, evenly fired. Self slip in and out.

Plate 319. Roman Miniature Bowl (R.MBR) Types 1–5 and Roman Small Bowl (R.SBR) Types A and B. Scale 1:5

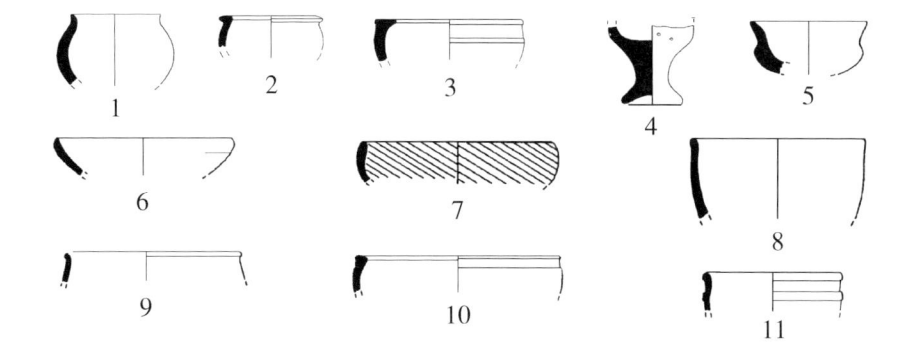

Plate 320. Roman Bowl (R.BR) Type A

1. R.BR. A.I.a (TS. 1516; IA2, 3.1). Phase 4. Small rim and upper wall segment. Fairly fine pinkish-buff ware, evenly fired. Creamy-buff slip in and out.
2. R.BR. A.I.b (TS. 577; IB, 3.1). Phase 4. Small rim and upper wall segment. Fairly fine pink ware, unevenly fired with dark core. Cream slip in and out.
3. R.BR. A.I.c (TS. 614; ID, 1.1). Phase 2. Small rim and upper wall segment. Fine pinkish-buff ware, evenly fired.
4. R.BR. A.I.d (TS. 637; IG, 1.1). Phase 6. Small rim and upper wall segment with applied piecrust-like edge below rim outside. Fairly coarse pink ware, evenly fired. Buff slip in and out.
5. R.BR. A.I.e (TS. 3681; Op. 5, 5.3). Phase 7. Small rim and upper wall segment. Ware description is unavailable.
6. R.BR. A.I.f (TS. 3652; Op. 5, 4.2). Phase 7. Small rim and upper wall segment. Ware description is unavailable.
7. R.BR. A.I.g (TS. 1490; IA2, 4.3). Phase 2. Small rim and upper wall segment. Slightly coarse pink ware with lime and mica grits, evenly fired. Creamy-buff slip in.
8. R.BR. A.I.h (TS. 2078; IG, 1.1). Phase 6. Small rim and upper wall segment. Slightly coarse pinkish-buff ware, evenly fired. Buff slip in and out.
9. R.BR. A.I.i (PM. C.15; SC. 2934; IB, 3.4). Phase 3. Small rim and upper wall segment with a pot mark on top of the rim, incised before firing. Slightly coarse rose-pink ware with lime grit temper, evenly fired. Creamy-buff slip in and out.
10. R.BR. A.II.a (TS. 638; IB, 1.1). Phase 4. Small rim and wall segment. Fairly coarse buff ware, evenly fired.
11. R.BR. A.II.b (TS. 969; IG, 1.19). Phase 6. Small rim and upper wall segment. Fairly coarse pink ware, evenly fired. Creamy-buff slip in and out.
12. R.BR. A.II.c (TS. 623; IA1, 2.1). Phase 4. Small rim and wall segment. Fairly fine pink ware, evenly fired. Thin reddish slip out.
13. R.BR. A.II.d (TS. 3698; Op. 5, 6.5, Wall + 6.6). Phase 6. Two joining rim and upper wall segments. Ware description is unavailable.
14. R.BR. A.II.e (TS. 3799; Op. 5, 8.1). Phase 6. Small rim and upper wall segment. Ware description is unavailable.
15. R.BR. A.II.f (TS. 3805; Op. 5, 9.3). Phase 5. Portion of rim and upper wall segment. Ware description is unavailable.
16. R.BR. A.II.g (TS. 3902; Op. 5, 9.1). Phase 5. Portion of rim and upper wall segment. Ware description is unavailable.
17. R.BR. A.II.h (TS. 1494; IA1, 1.3). Phase 3. Small rim and upper wall segment. Fairly fine pinkish-buff ware with lime and mica grits, evenly fired.
18. R.BR. A.III.a (SC. 2828; IB, 3.4). Phase 3. Small rim and upper wall segment. Slightly coarse pinkish-orange ware with many small mica inclusions, evenly fired. Self slip in and out, very worn.

Plate 320

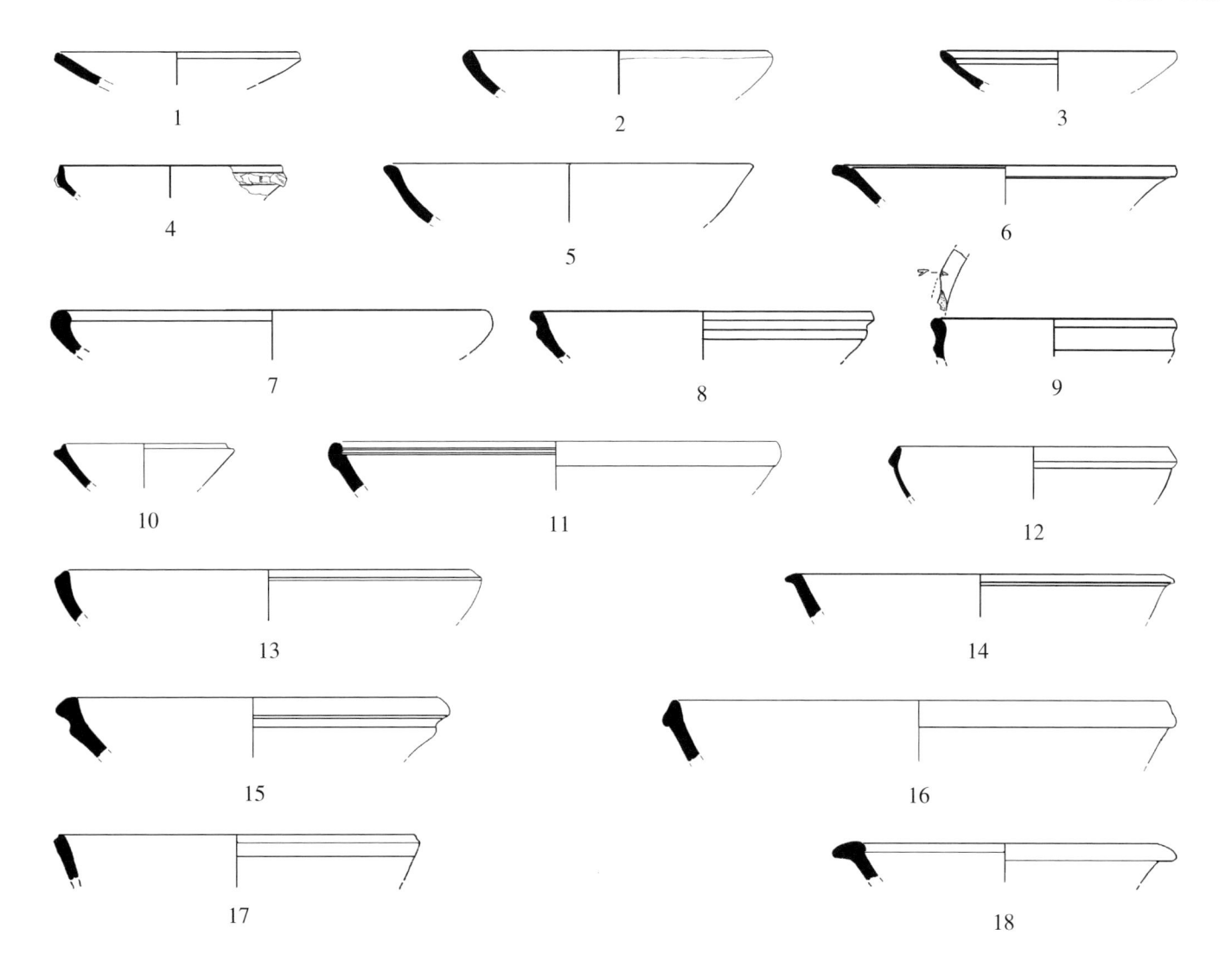

Roman Bowl (R.BR) Type A. Scale 1:5

Plate 321

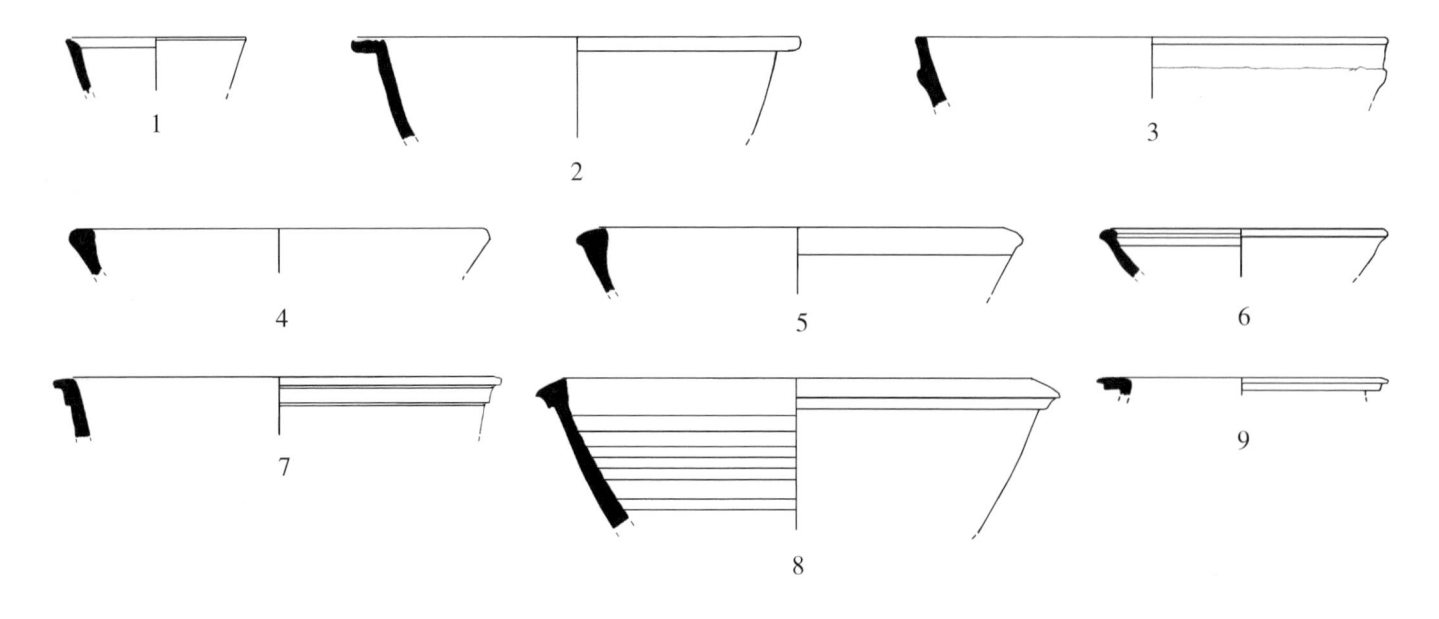

Roman Bowl (R.BR) Type B. Scale 1:5

1. R.BR. B.I.a (TS. 1515; IA2, 4.3). Phase 2. Small rim and wall segment. Fine buff ware, evenly fired. Self slip in and out.
2. R.BR. B.I.b (TS. 286; IA2, 4.1). Phase 4. About 1/8 rim and wall segment. Slightly coarse pinkish-buff ware with lime and mica grits, evenly fired. Yellow-buff slip in.
3. R.BR. B.I.c (TS. 629; IG, 1.1). Phase 6. About 1/20 rim and upper wall segment. Fairly fine pink ware, evenly fired.
4. R.BR. B.I.d (TS. 301; IA1, 2.3). Phase 2. Small rim and upper wall segment. Light brown ware, evenly fired.
5. R.BR. B.I.e (TS. 290; IA1, 2.3). Phase 2. About 1/8 rim and upper wall segment. Slightly coarse pinkish-buff ware with lime and mica grits, evenly fired. Self slip in and out.
6. R.BR. B.I.f (TS. 3940; Op. 5, 9.12). Phase 5. Small rim and upper wall segment. Ware description is unavailable.
7. R.BR. B.I.g (TS. 3874; Op. 5, 4.4). Phase 7. Small rim and upper wall segment. Ware description is unavailable.
8. R.BR. B.I.h (TS. 3235; Op. 5, 4.4). Phase 7. Large rim and most of wall segment. Ware description is unavailable.
9. R.BR. B.I.i (SC. 3516; IB, 1.3, Wall A). Phase 3. Small rim segment. Fairly fine light pink ware with small lime grits, evenly fired. Self slip in and out, very worn.

Plate 322

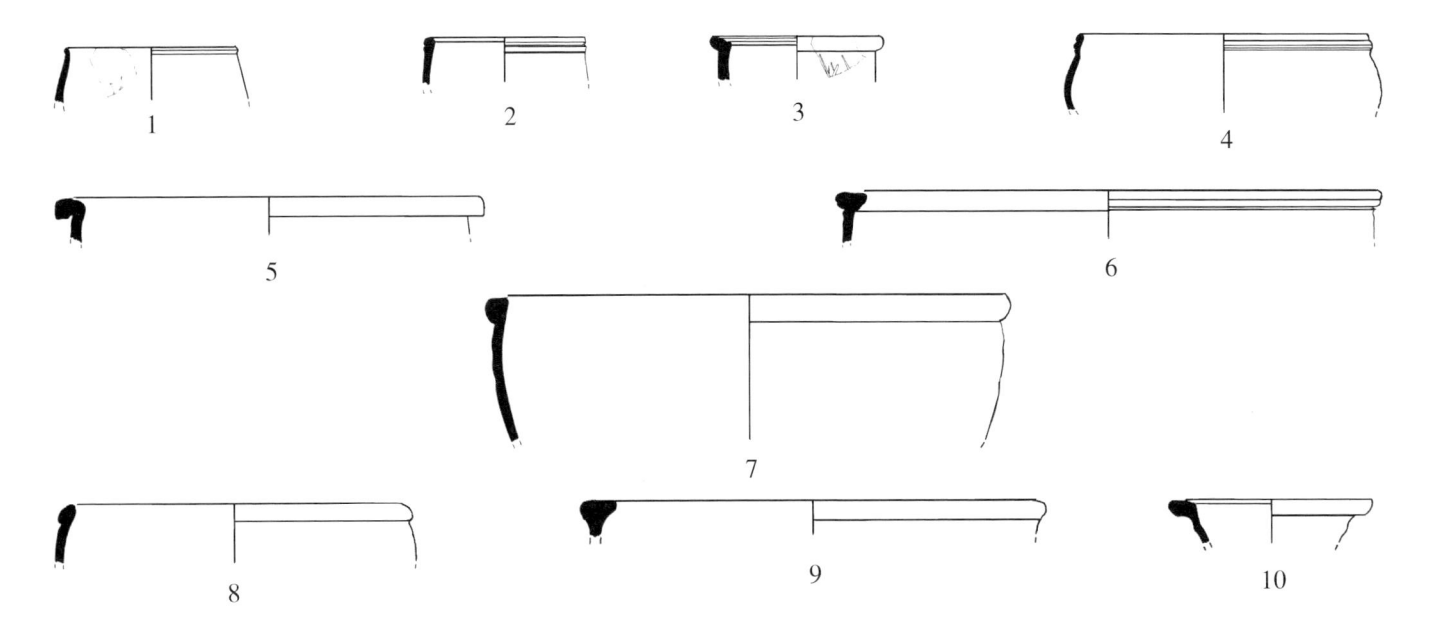

Roman Bowl (R.BR) Type C. Scale 1:5

1. R.BR. C.I.a (PM. A.6; TS. 1519; IA2, 5.1). Phase 1. Small rim and upper wall segment with portion of a potter's mark on inside wall incised before firing. Fairly fine pinkish-buff ware, evenly fired.
2. R.BR. C.I.b (TS. 1521; IA2, 3.1). Phase 4. Small rim and upper wall segment. Fairly fine buff ware, evenly fired. Self slip in and out.
3. R.BR. C.II.a (IP [G.4] A.VI.a ; TS. 1327; IIIG/H, 1a, Room 23). Phase 7A. Small rim and upper wall segment with incised linear decoration below rim outside. Slightly coarse buff ware, evenly fired. Self slip in and out.
4. R.BR. C.II.b (TS. 621; IA2, 4.4, Floor). Phase 2. Large rim and wall segment. Fairly fine pink ware, evenly fired. Cream slip in and out.
5. R.BR. C.II.c (TS. 295; IB, 3.4). Phase 3. Small rim and upper wall segment. Fairly fine pinkish-buff ware with lime and mica grits, evenly fired. Horizontally burnished self slip in and out.
6. R.BR. C.II.d (TS. 3890; Op. 5, 12.1). Phase 5. Large rim and most of wall segment. Ware description is unavailable.
7. R.BR. C.II.e (TS. 3800; Op. 5, 8.1). Phase 6. Small rim and upper wall segment. Ware description is unavailable.
8. R.BR. C.II.f (TS. 3348; Op. 5, 29.2). Phase 5. Small rim and upper wall segment. Ware description is unavailable.
9. R.BR. C.III.a (SC. 2925; IA2, 4.4, Floor). Phase 2. Small rim and upper wall segment. Fairly coarse pinkish-buff ware with many small lime and mica grits, evenly fired. Self slip in and out.
10. R.BR. C.III.b (SC. 3518; IB, 2.5). Phase 3. Small rim and upper wall segment. Slightly coarse buff ware with lime grits, evenly fired. Creamy-buff slip in and out.

Plate 323

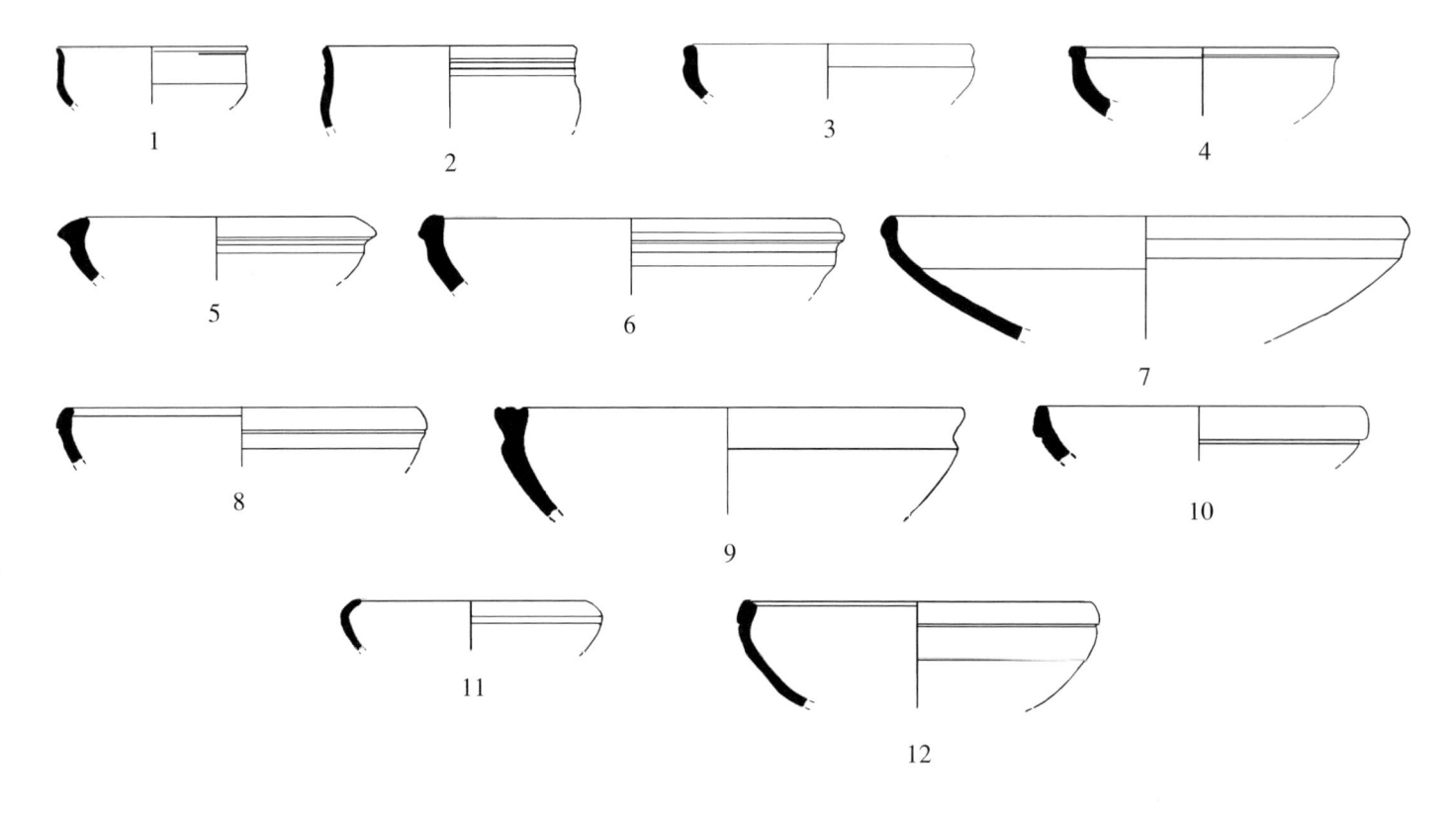

Roman Bowl (R.BR) Type D. Scale 1:5

1. R.BR. D.I.a (TS. 3193; Op. 5, 10.5). Phase 5. Small rim and carinated wall segment. Ware description is unavailable.
2. R.BR. D.I.b (TS. 3836; Op. 5, 29.1). Phase 5. Small rim and globular wall segment. Ware description is unavailable.
3. R.BR. D.II.a (TS. 1320; IIIF, 1.1). Phase 6/7. Small rim and upper wall segment. Fairly coarse and gritty pinkish-buff ware, evenly fired. Self slip in and out.
4. R.BR. D.II.b (TS. 3927; Op. 5, 10.3). Phase 5. Small rim and slightly carinated wall segment. Ware description is unavailable.
5. R.BR. D.II.c (TS. 3806; Op. 5, 9.3). Phase 5. Small rim and carinated upper wall segment. Ware description is unavailable.
6. R.BR. D.II.d (TS. 3190; Op. 5, 10.5). Phase 5. Small rim and carinated upper wall segment. Ware description is unavailable.
7. R.BR. D.II.e (TS. 3737; Op. 5, 10.5). Phase 5. Large rim and most of wall segment. Ware description is unavailable.
8. R.BR. D.II.f (TS. 2500; IE, 1.1a). Phase 5. Small rim and upper wall segment. Slightly coarse flesh-pink ware, evenly fired. Creamy-buff slip out.
9. R.BR. D.II.g (TS. 551; IA2, 4.3). Phase 2. Large rim and upper wall segment. Coarse pinkish-buff ware, evenly fired. Cream slip in and out. Three parallel grooves are on top of the rim.
10. R.BR. D.II.h (TS. 1496; IA1, 2.4a). Phase 2. Small rim and upper wall segment. Fairly fine buff ware with very fine lime and mica grits, evenly fired. Creamy-buff slip in and out.
11. R.BR. D.III.a (TS. 3702; Op. 5, 8.2). Phase 6. Small rim and upper wall segment. Ware description is unavailable.
12. R.BR. D.III.b (TS. 3808; Op. 5, 9.6). Phase 5. Small rim and most of globular wall segment. Ware description is unavailable.

Plate 324

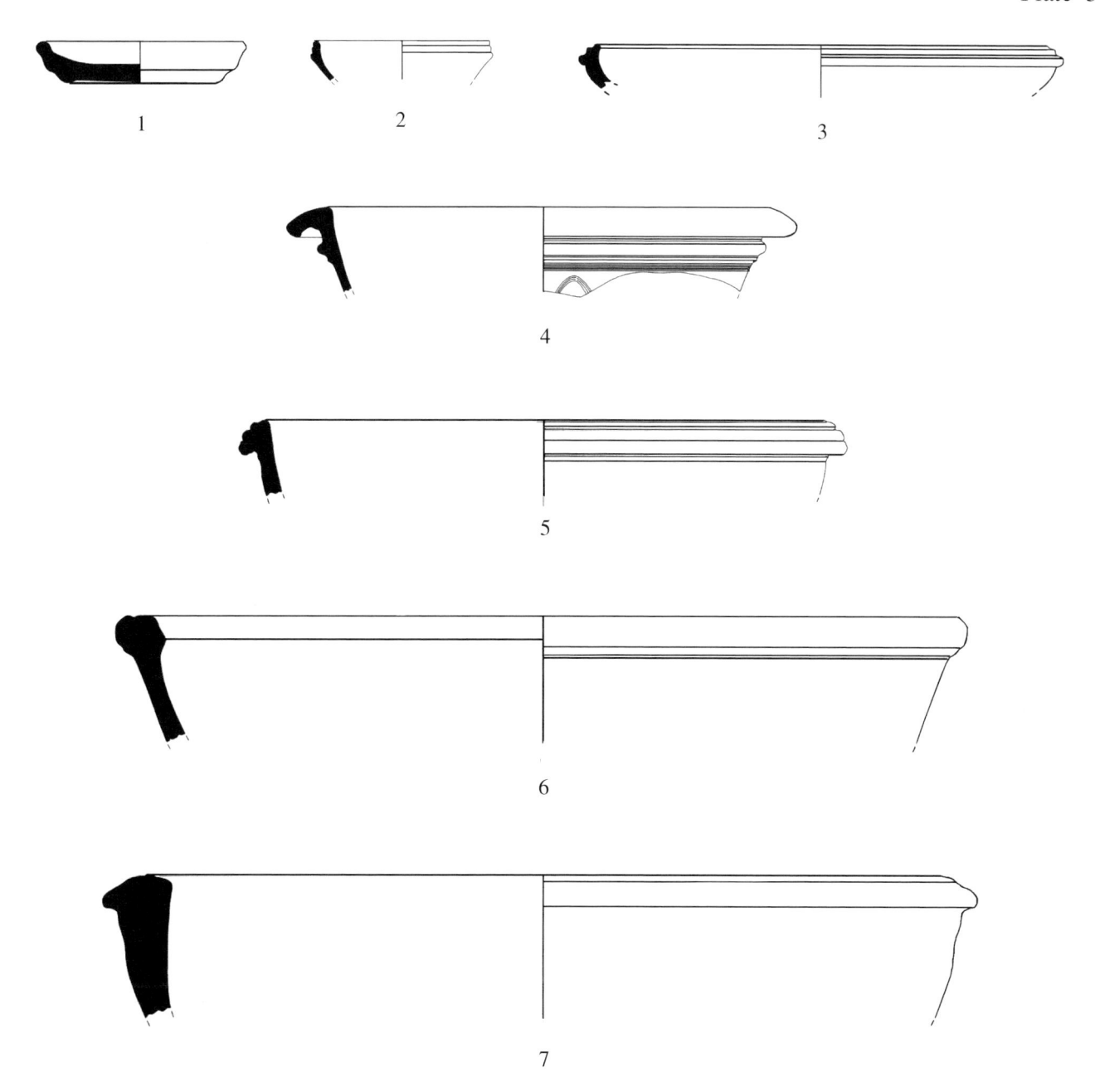

Roman Bowl (R.BR) Type E. Scale 1:5

1. R.BR. E.I.a (TS. 3933; Op. 5, 10.2). Phase 5. Nearly complete shallow bowl possibly made in imitation of a metal prototype. Ware description unavailable.
2. R.BR. E.I.b (TS. 4000; Op. 5, 12.1). Phase 5. Small rim and upper wall segment. Ware description unavailable.
3. R.BR. E.I.c (TS. 1500; IA2, 3.2). Phase 4. Small rim and upper wall segment. Fairly fine pinkish-buff ware with fine lime and mica grits, evenly fired. Creamy-buff slip in and out.
4. R.BR. E.II.a (IP [G.1] C.VI.a; TS. 3877; Op. 5, 10.5). Phase 5. Large rim and upper wall segment with comb-incised horizontal and wavy linear decoration on outside wall. Ware description unavailable.
5. R.BR. E.II.b (TS. 3869; Op. 5, 9.9). Phase 5. Small rim and upper wall segment. Ware description unavailable.
6. R.BR. E.II.c (TS. 3854; Op. 5, 4.4). Phase 7. Large rim and upper wall segment. Ware description unavailable.
7. R.BR. E.II.d (TS. 3792; Op. 5, 3.1). Phase 7. Large rim and upper wall segment. Ware description unavailable.

Plate 325

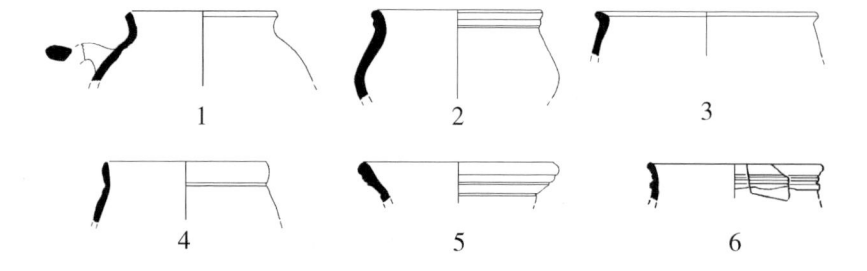

Roman Small Jar (R.SJR) Types A–C. Scale 1:5

1. R.SJR. A.I.a (TS. 587; IC, 1.1). Phase 10. Small rim and shoulder segment with portion of loop handle. Fairly coarse pink ware, evenly fired. Cream slip in and out.
2. R.SJR. A.I.b (TS. 3713; Op. 5, 9.6). Phase 5. Small rim and globular body segment. Ware description unavailable.
3. R.SJR. B.I.a (TS. 3891; Op. 5, 14.1). Phase 5. Small rim and upper wall segment. Ware description unavailable.
4. R.SJR. B.I.b (TS. 3950; Op. 5, 1.1). Phase 7. Small rim and upper wall segment. Ware description unavailable.
5. R.SJR. C.I.a (SC. 3312; XIA, 1.2). Phase 3. Small rim and neck segment. Hard, slightly coarse pinkish-buff ware with small black- and gold-colored mica grits, evenly fired.
6. R.SJR. C.I.b (SC. 3517; IB, 2.5). Phase 3. Small rim and neck segment. Fairly fine light grayware with small lime inclusions, evenly fired. Self slip in and out.

Plate 326

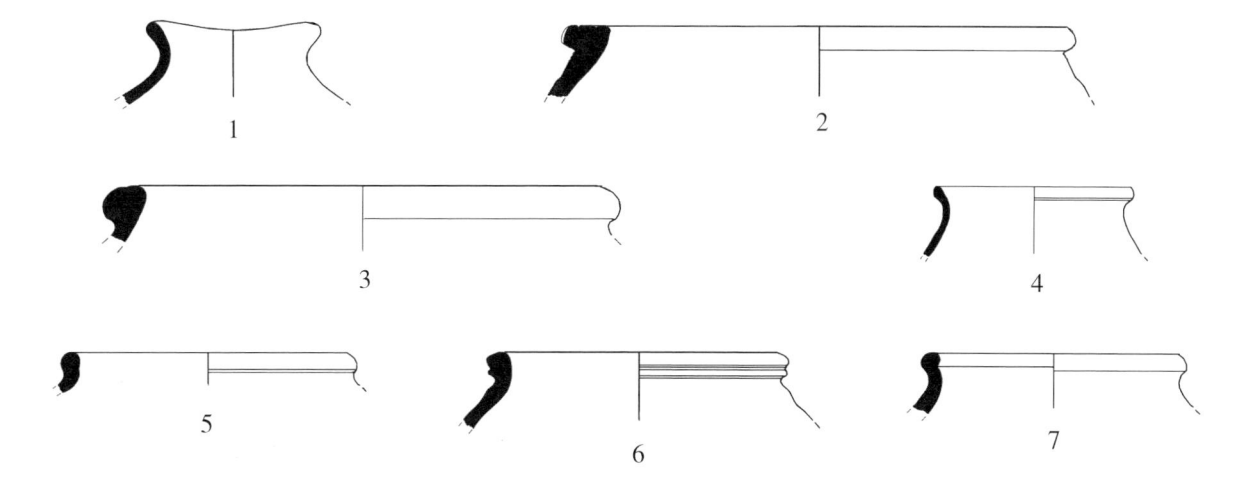

Roman Jar (R.JR) Type A. Scale 1:5

1. R.JR. A.I.a (TS. 1497; IA1, 1.3). Phase 3. Nearly 1/2 rim and neck fragment. Fairly fine pinkish-buff ware with lime and mica grits, evenly fired. Creamy-buff slip in and out.
2. R.JR. A.I.b (TS. 293; IA2, 4.3). Phase 2. Large rim and shoulder segment. Coarse pinkish-buff ware with lime and mica grits, evenly fired. Self slip in and out.
3. R.JR. A.I.c (TS. 1492; IA2, 4.3). Phase 2. Small rim and neck segment. Slightly coarse grayish-buff ware, fairly evenly fired.
4. R.JR. A.I.d (TS. 3860; Op. 5, 6.5, Wall). Phase 6. Small rim and upper wall segment. Ware description unavailable.
5. R.JR. A.I.e (TS. 3645; Op. 5, 10.5). Phase 5. Small rim and neck segment. Ware description unavailable.
6. R.JR. A.I.f (TS. 3818; Op. 5, 9.3). Phase 5. Small rim and shoulder segment. Ware description unavailable.
7. R.JR. A.I.g (TS. 3949; Op. 5, 1 + 4.1). Phase 7. Small rim and upper shoulder segment. Ware description unavailable.

Plate 327

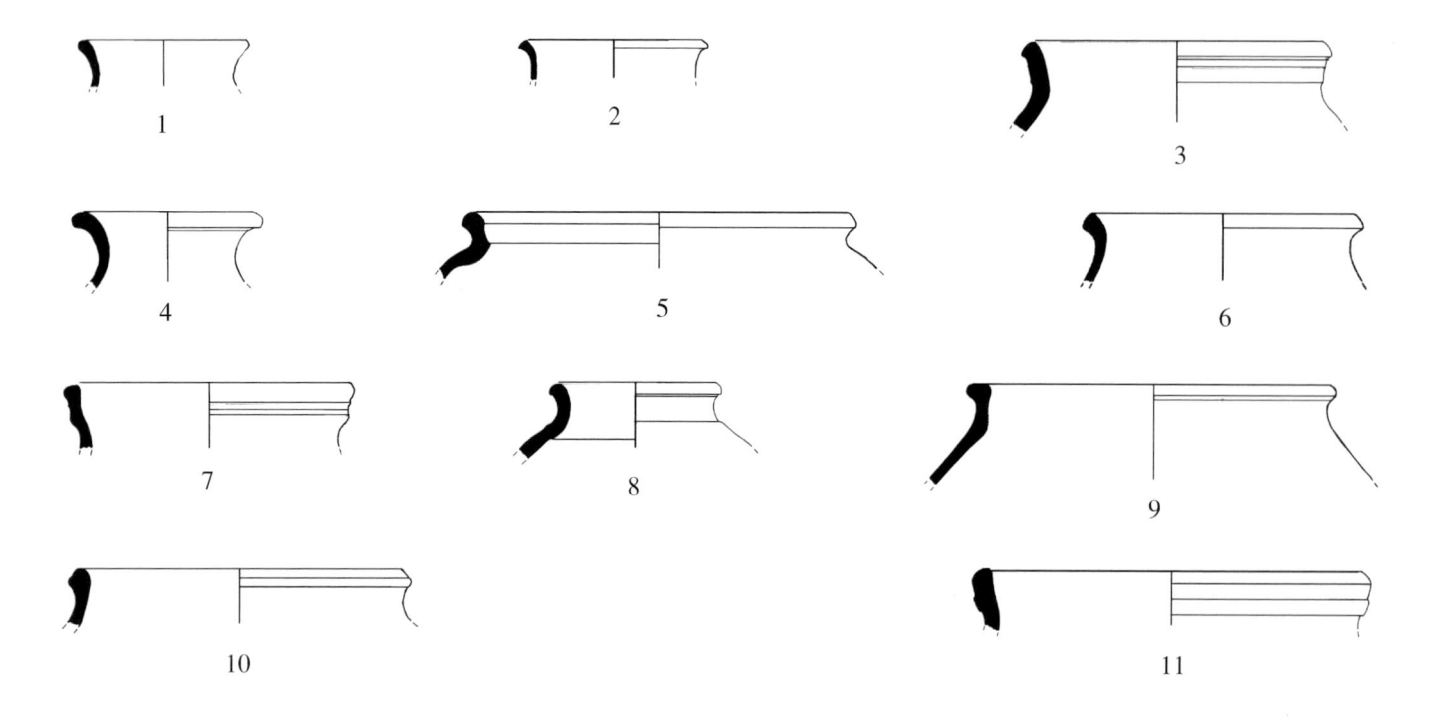

### Roman Jar (R.JR) Type B. Scale 1:5

1. R.JR. B.I.a (TS. 3923; Op. 5, 10.3). Phase 5. Small rim and neck segment. Ware description unavailable.
2. R.JR. B.I.b (TS. 3919; Op. 5, 11.1). Phase 5. Small rim and neck segment. Ware description unavailable.
3. R.JR. B.I.c (TS. 3859; Op. 5, 6.5, Wall). Phase 6. Large rim and upper shoulder segment. Ware description unavailable.
4. R.JR. B.I.d (TS. 3827; Op. 5, 29.1). Phase 5. Large rim, neck, and upper shoulder segment. Ware description unavailable.
5. R.JR. B.I.e (TS. 2108; IC, 1.1). Phase 10. Small rim, neck, and shoulder segment. Hard, fairly fine buff ware, evenly fired. Light creamy-green slip in and out.
6. R.JR. B.I.f (TS. 616; IG, 1.3). Phase 4. About 1/12 rim and upper shoulder segment. Fairly fine brown-buff ware, evenly fired. Greenish-buff slip in and out.
7. R.JR. B.II.a (TS. 659; IC, 1.7). Phase 8. Small rim and neck segment. Fairly coarse pink ware, evenly fired. Buff slip out and over rim in.
8. R.JR. B.II.b (TS. 3714; Op. 5, 9.1). Phase 5. Small rim and upper shoulder segment. Ware description unavailable.
9. R.JR. B.II.c (TS. 3870; Op. 5, 9.10. Phase 5. About 1/4 rim, neck, and shoulder segment. Ware description unavailable.
10. R.JR. B.II.d (TS. 434; IA1, 1.1). Phase 4. About 1/16 rim and shoulder segment. Fairly coarse pinkish-buff ware, evenly fired. Cream slip in and out.
11. R.JR. B.II.e (TS. 2081; IC, 1.5). Phase 9. Small rim and neck segment. Slightly coarse grayish-buff ware, evenly fired. Self slip out.

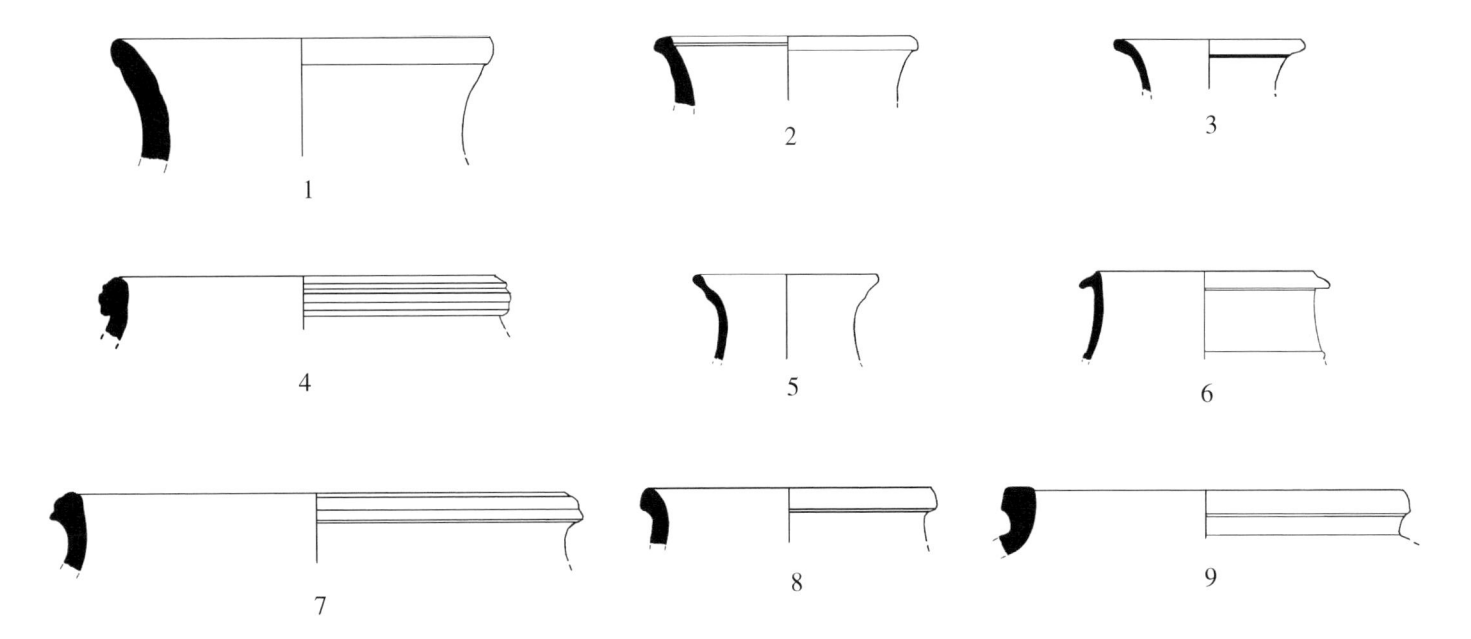

Roman Jar (R.JR) Type C. Scale 1:5

1. R.JR. C.I.a (TS. 573; IG, 1.3). Phase 4. Late Roman. Large rim and neck segment. Coarse pink ware, evenly fired. Buff slip in and out.
2. R.JR. C.I.b (TS. 3964; Op. 5, 5.3). Phase 7. Small rim and neck segment. Ware description unavailable.
3. R.JR. C.I.c (SC. 1458; IF, 1.1). Phase 6. About 1/3 rim and neck segment. Fairly coarse creamy-buff ware with lime inclusions, evenly fired.
4. R.JR. C.I.d (TS. 4060; IA1, 2.5). Phase 1. About 1/10 rim and upper neck segment. Hard, compact pinkish-grayware with many small gold-colored mica and a few lime grits, evenly fired. Very worn self slip on top of rim and outside.
5. R.JR. C.II.a (TS. 3930; Op. 5, 11.1). Phase 5. Small rim and neck segment. Ware description unavailable.
6. R.JR. C.II.b (TS. 3663; Op. 5, 8.1). Phase 6. Small rim and neck segment. Ware description unavailable.
7. R.JR. C.II.c (TS. 3700; Op. 5, 6.1). Phase 6. Small rim and neck segment. Ware description unavailable.
8. R.JR. C.II.d (TS. 3659; Op. 5, 1.2). Phase 7. Small rim and upper neck segment. Ware description unavailable.
9. R.JR. C.II.e (TS. 3651; Op. 5, 2 + 3.3). Phase 7. Small rim, neck, and upper shoulder segment. Ware description unavailable.

Plate 329

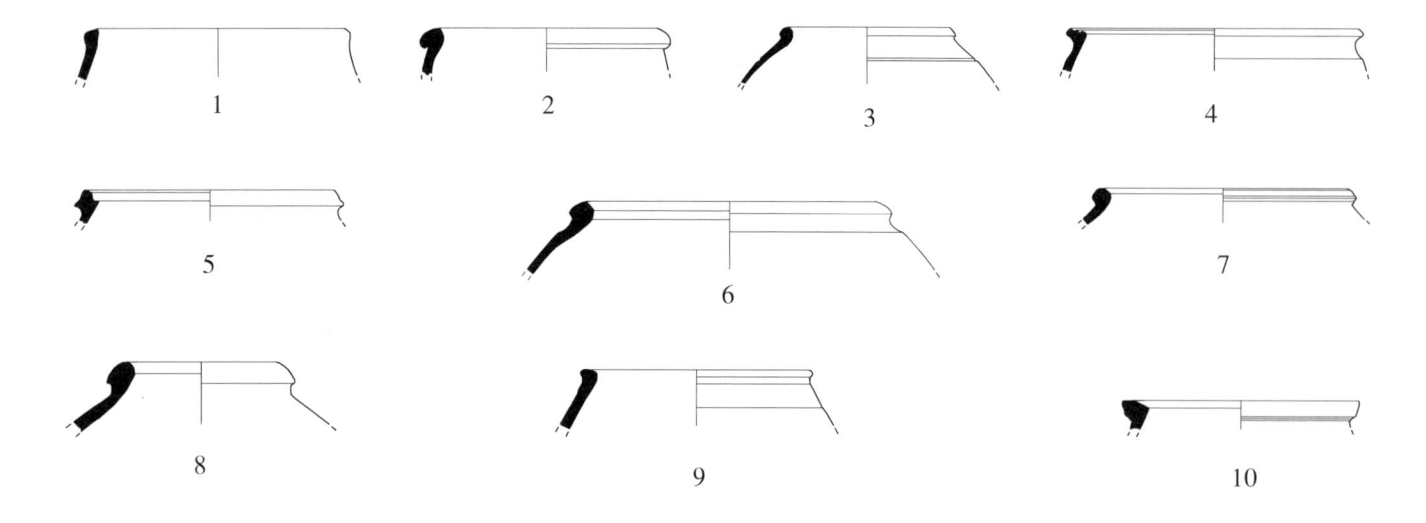

Roman Holemouth Jar (R.HMJ) Type A. Scale 1:5

1. R.HMJ. A.I.a (TS. 3160; IC, 1.6). Phase 9. Small rim and shoulder segment. Fairly fine pinkish-buff ware with a few white lime grits, evenly fired. Creamy-buff slip out.
2. R.HMJ. A.I.b (TS. 1513; IA2, 3.1). Phase 4. Small rim and shoulder segment. Fairly fine buff ware, evenly fired. Self slip in and out.
3. R.HMJ. A.II.a (TS. 2079; IB, 1.6, Floor). Phase 3. Small rim and shoulder segment. Hard, fine pinkish-buff ware, evenly fired. Buff slip out and over rim in.
4. R.HMJ. A.II.b (TS. 3162; IG, 1.1). Phase 6. Small rim and shoulder segment. Fairly fine buff ware, evenly fired. Creamy-green slip in and out.
5. R.HMJ. A.II.c (TS. 3164; IB, 1.6, Floor). Phase 3. Small rim and shoulder segment. Fairly fine greenish-buff ware, evenly fired. Creamy-green slip in and out.
6. R.HMJ. A.II.d (TS. 2414; IG, 1.3). Phase 4. About 1/6 rim and upper shoulder segment. Slight coarse buff ware, evenly fired. Self slip in and out.
7. R.HMJ. A.II.e (TS. 2076; IB, 3.1). Phase 4. Small rim and shoulder segment. Slightly coarse buff ware, evenly fired. Self slip in and out.
8. R.HMJ. A.II.f (TS. 564; IC, 1.1). Phase 10. Small rim and shoulder segment. Fairly coarse pink ware, evenly fired. Buff slip in and out.
9. R.HMJ. A.II.g (TS. 3704; Op. 5, 9.5). Phase 5. Small rim and upper shoulder segment. Ware description unavailable.
10. R.HMJ. A.II.h (TS. 3909; Op. 5, 9.12). Phase 5. Small rim segment. Ware description unavailable.

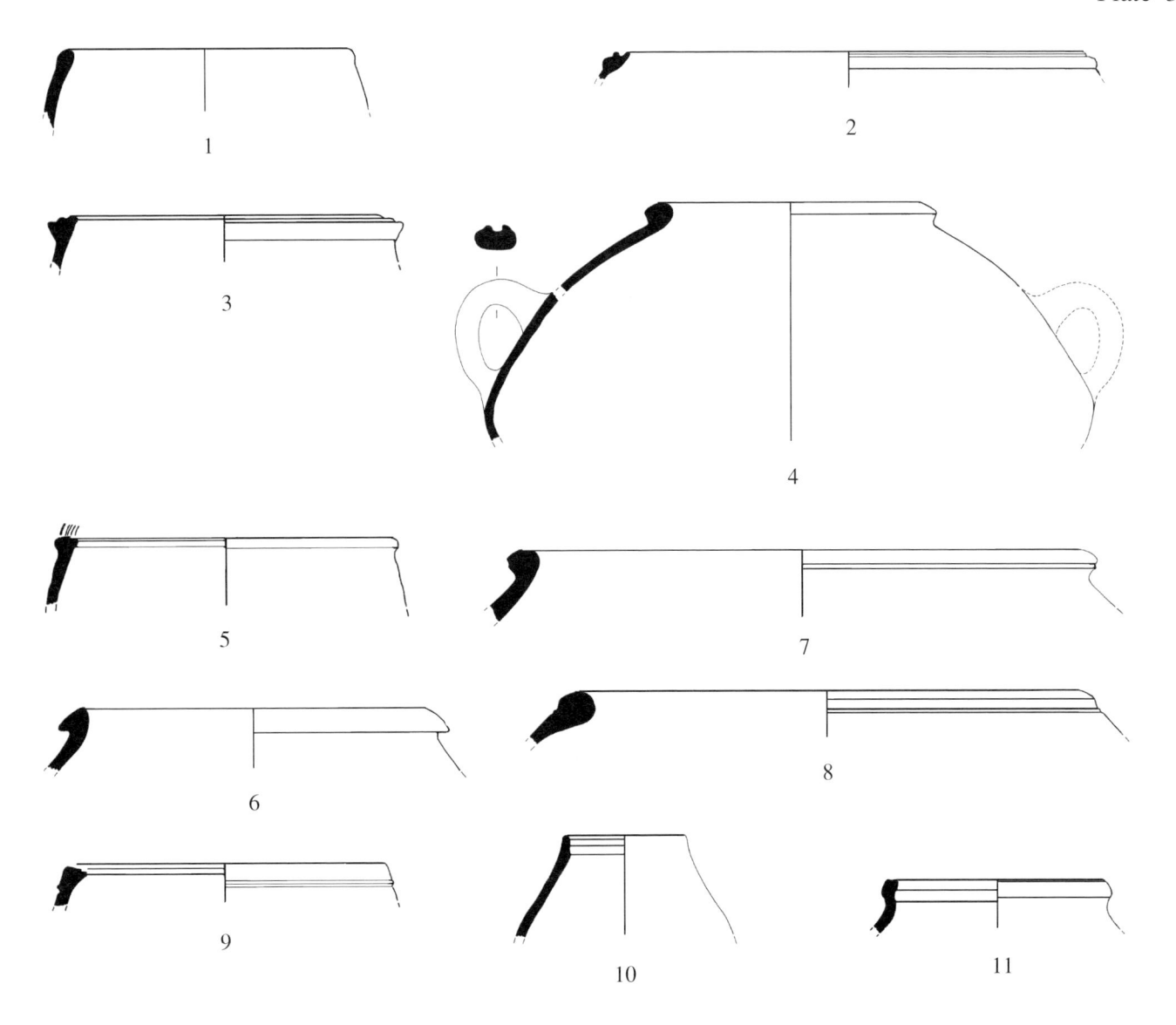

Plate 330. Roman Holemouth Jar (R.HMJ) Types B and C. Scale 1:5

1. R.HMJ. B.I.a (TS. 3163; IJ, 1.1). Phase 2. Small rim and upper wall segment. Hard, fine buff ware, evenly fired. Creamy-green slip in and out.
2. R.HMJ. B.I.b (TS. 1504; IA1, 1.2). Phase 3. Small rim segment. Close pinkish-buff ware, evenly fired. Self slip in and out.
3. R.HMJ. B.I.c (TS. 2065; IE, 1.1a). Phase 5. Small rim and upper shoulder segment. Hard, close pinkish-buff ware, evenly fired. Greenish-buff slip in and out.
4. R.HMJ. B.II.a (TS. 2061; IB, 1.6, Floor). Phase 3. Large rim and wall segment with one complete loop handle. Slightly coarse pinkish-buff ware, evenly fired. Horizontally burnished self slip out and over rim in.
5. R.HMJ. B.II.b (TS. 942; IJ, 1.1). Phase 2. About 1/20 segment of rim and upper wall. Fairly coarse pinkish-buff ware, evenly fired. Cream slip in and out.
6. R.HMJ. B.II.c (TS. 589; IB, 1.2). Phase 4. Small rim and shoulder segment. Coarse pink ware, evenly fired. Cream slip in and out.
7. R.HMJ. B.II.d (TS. 432; IA1, 2.5). Phase 1. Small rim and shoulder segment. Coarse pink ware, evenly fired. Cream slip out.
8. R.HMJ. B.II.e (TS. 289; IA1, 2.3). Phase 2. Small rim and shoulder segment. Hard, fairly fine light brown ware with lime and mica grits, evenly fired. Creamy-buff slip out.
9. R.HMJ. B.II.f (SC. 3044; IA2, 3.1). Phase 4. Small rim and upper wall segment. Fairly fine light pink ware with small lime and mica grits, evenly fired. Creamy-buff slip in and out.
10. R.HMJ. C.I.a (TS. 617; IB, 1.7, Floor). Phase 3. About 1/28 rim and shoulder segment. Fairly coarse pink ware, evenly fired. Cream slip out.
11. R.HMJ. C.I.b (TS. 2086; IA2, 4.3). Phase 2. Small rim, neck, and upper shoulder segment. Fairly coarse grayware, fired buff at surfaces.

Plate 331

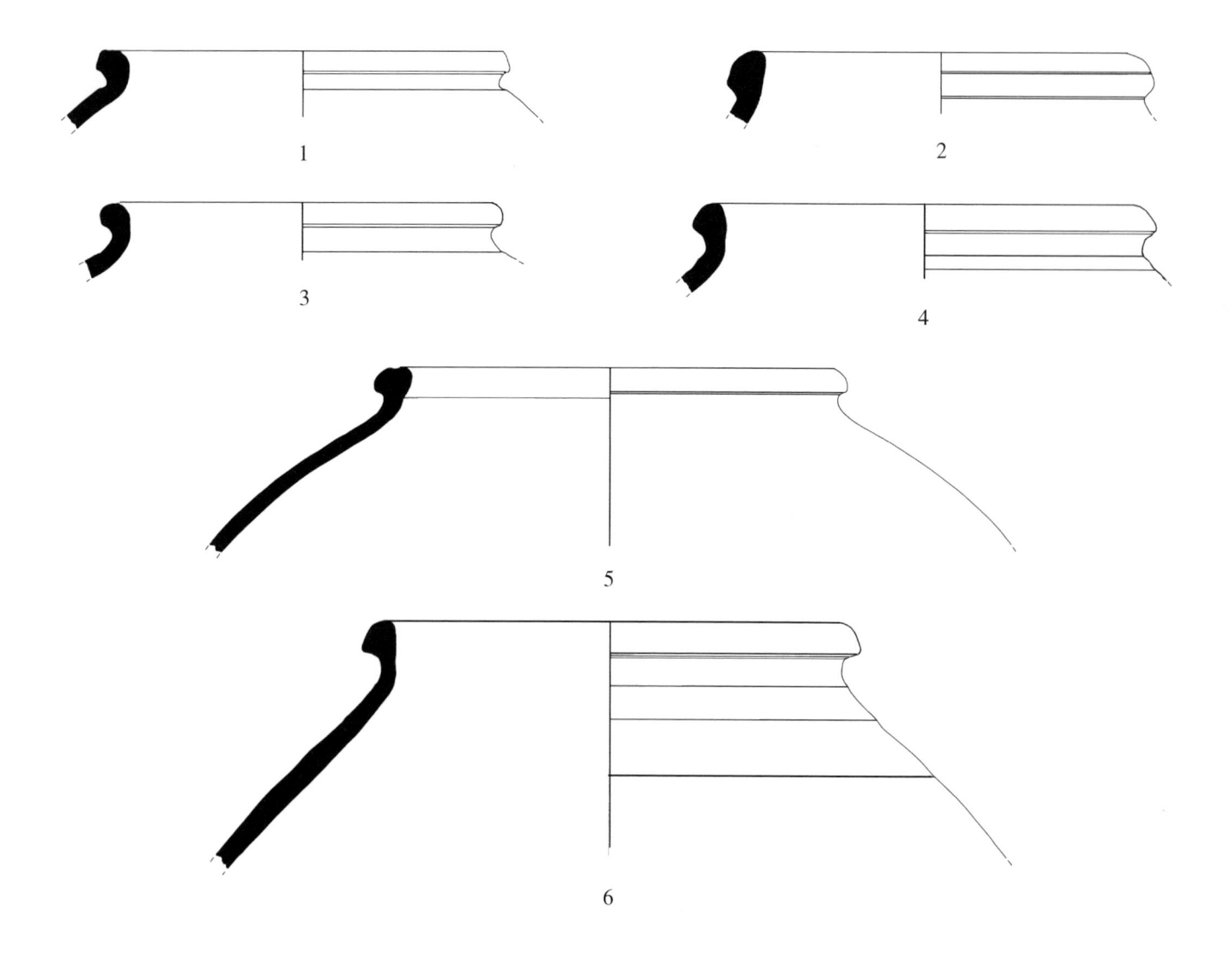

Roman Storage Jar (R.St.J) Types A–C. Scale 1:5

1. R.St.J. A.I.a (TS. 3815; Op. 5, 9.3). Phase 5. Small rim and upper shoulder segment. Ware description unavailable.
2. R.St.J. A.II.a (TS. 3646; Op. 5, 10.5). Phase 5. Small rim and upper shoulder segment. Ware description unavailable.
3. R.St.J. B.I.a (TS. 3647; Op. 5, 10.5). Phase 5. Small rim, neck, and upper shoulder segment. Ware description unavailable.
4. R.St.J. B.II.a (TS. 3648; Op. 5, 10.5). Phase 5. Small rim, neck, and upper shoulder segment. Ware description unavailable.
5. R.St.J. B.II.b (TS. 3880; Op. 5, 10.5). Phase 5. Large rim, neck, and most of shoulder segment. Ware description unavailable.
6. R.St.J. C.I.a (TS. 3746; Op. 5, 10.5). Phase 5. Large rim, neck, and most of shoulder segment. Ware description unavailable.

Plate 332

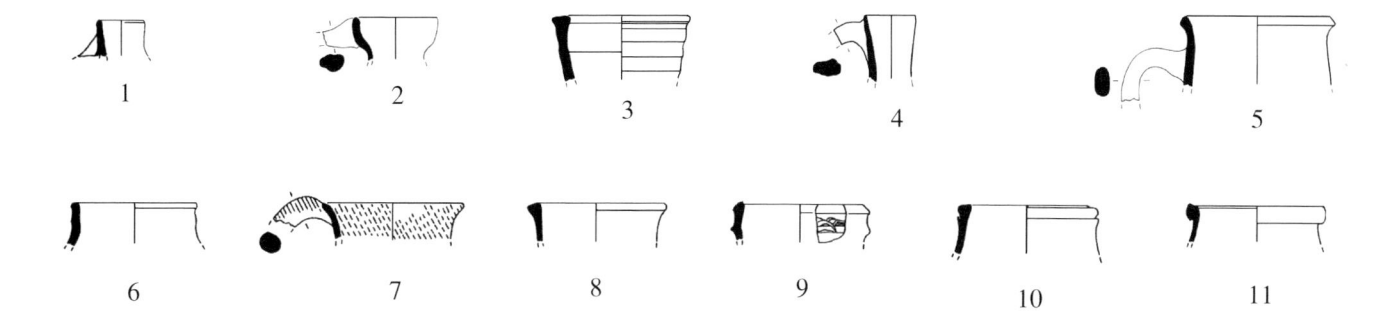

Roman Jug (R.Jg.) Type A. Scale 1:5

1. R.Jg. A.I.a (TS. 645; IG, 1.1). Phase 6. About 1/4 rim and neck segment with remains of upper portion of a loop handle. Fairly coarse buff ware, evenly fired. Cream slip in and out.
2. R.Jg. A.I.b (TS. 3157; IE, 1.1). Phase 6. Small rim and neck segment with remains of handle attached to side of rim. Fairly coarse buff ware, unevenly fired creamy-green at surfaces. Self slip in and out.
3. R.Jg. A.II.a (TS. 3669; Op. 5, 6.4). Phase 6. Small rim and neck segment. Ware description unavailable.
4. R.Jg. A.II.b (TS. 951; XIA, 1.3). Phase 2. Small rim and neck segment with remains of handle attached below lip of rim. Fairly coarse pink ware, evenly fired. Burnished cream slip out.
5. R.Jg. A.II.c (SW. 40; IA1, 1.3). Phase 3. About 1/2 rim and neck segment with 1/2 loop handle attached to neck. Buff ware, evenly fired.
6. R.Jg. A.III.a (SC. 2949; 1A2, 3.1). Phase 4. Small rim and neck segment. Slightly coarse pinkish-buff ware with lime grits, evenly fired. Creamy-buff slip in and out.
7. R.Jg. A.III.b (TS. 540; 1A2, 3.1). Phase 4. Small rim and upper neck segment with remains of a high loop handle. Fine buff-gray-ware, unevenly fired with a black core. Burnished brown paint or slip in and out.
8. R.Jg. A.III.c (SC. 2599; IB, 2.3). Phase 4. Small rim and neck segment. Slightly coarse pinkish-buff ware with many lime grits, evenly fired. Creamy-buff slip in and out.
9. R.Jg. A.III.d (SC. 2981; IB, 3.1). Phase 4. Small rim and upper neck segment with a decorated band around the center of the extant neck. Fairly fine pinkish-buff ware with a few small lime grits, evenly fired. Creamy-buff slip in and out.
10. R.Jg. A.III.e (SC. 3019; IA2, 4.3). Phase 2. Small rim and neck segment. Fairly fine light pinkish-buff ware with small lime grits, evenly fired. Creamy-buff slip in and out.
11. R.Jg. A.III.f (SC. 3519; IC, 1.1). Phase 10. Small rim and upper neck segment. Fairly fine light pink ware with small lime and mica grits, evenly fired. Creamy-buff slip in and out.

## Plate 333. Roman Jug (R.Jg.) Type B

1. R.Jg. B.I.a (TS. 2344, IB, 1.6, Floor). Phase 3. About 1/8 rim and neck segment. Slightly coarse buff ware, evenly fired. Creamy-yellow slip out and over rim in.
2. R.Jg. B.I.b (TS. 1520; IA2, 3.1). Phase 4. Small rim and neck segment. Fairly fine buff ware, evenly fired. Creamy buff slip in and out.
3. R.Jg. B.II.a (TS. 618; IB, 1.7, Floor). Phase 3. Small rim and neck segment. Fairly fine pink ware, evenly fired. Buff slip in and out.
4. R.Jg. B.II.b (TS. 804; VIIIA, 1.1). Phase 3. Small rim and neck segment. Fairly coarse pink ware, evenly fired. Cream slip in and out.
5. R.Jg. B.II.c (SW. 103; IB, 1.6, Floor). Phase 3. About 1/2 rim and neck segment with one incomplete loop handle attached to neck. Slightly coarse orange-brown ware with gold-colored mica grits and black mineral temper, fairly evenly fired.
6. R.Jg. B.II.d (TS. 296; IA1, 2.3). Phase 2. Small rim and neck segment with portion of loop handle attached just below lip of rim. Slightly coarse buff ware with lime and mica grits, evenly fired. Self slip out.
7. R.Jg. B.II.e (TS. 1064; XIA, 1.3). Phase 2. Small rim and neck segment with stub of one loop handle attached just below lip of rim. Fairly coarse pink ware, evenly fired. Cream slip out.
8. R.Jg. B.II.f (TS. 554; IC, 1.1). Phase 10. Small rim and neck segment with portion of loop handle attached to neck below rim. Coarse pinkish-buff ware, evenly fired. Cream slip in and out.
9. R.Jg. B.II.g (TS. 1501; IA1, 1.3). Phase 3. Small rim and neck segment with remains of handle attached to neck just below rim. Fairly fine buff ware, evenly fired.
10. R.Jg. B.II.h (TS. 1498; IA1, 1.3). Phase 3. Small rim and neck segment with about 1/2 of a loop handle attached to neck just below the rim. Fairly fine pinkish-buff ware, evenly fired.
11. R.Jg. B.II.i.(TS. 1506; IA1, 1.2). Phase 3. About 1/4 rim and neck segment with scar of handle attachment just below lip of rim. Fairly fine pinkish-buff ware, evenly fired.
12. R.Jg. B.II.j (TS. 518; IA1, 1.1). Phase 4. Small rim and neck segment. Fairly coarse greenish-buff ware, unevenly fired with darker core.
13. R.Jg. B.II.k (TS. 933; IH, 1.2). Phase 2. Small rim and neck segment with portion of loop handle attached to neck just below lip of rim. Fairly coarse buff ware, evenly fired. Cream slip out.
14. R.Jg. B.II.l (TS. 439; IA2, 3.4, Stone-lined pit). Phase 3. Small rim and neck segment with stub of handle attached to upper neck. Fairly coarse light brownish-buff ware, evenly fired. Cream slip in and out.
15. R.Jg. B.II.m (TS. 1512; IA1, 1.2). Phase 3. Small rim and neck segment. Fairly fine buff ware, evenly fired. Yellow-buff slip in and out.
16. R.Jg. B.II.n (TS. 300; IA2, 4.1). Phase 4. Small rim and neck segment. Soft, creamy-buff ware, evenly fired.
17. R.Jg. B.II.o (TS. 651; IB, 1.6, Floor). Phase 3. Small rim, neck, and shoulder segment. Fairly coarse pink ware, evenly fired. Cream slip out.
18. R.Jg. B.II.p (TS. 3158; IG, 1.1). Phase 6. Small rim and neck segment. Slightly coarse pink ware, evenly fired. Cream slip out.
19. R.Jg. B.II.q (TS. 1054; IG, 1.22). Phase 6. Small rim and neck segment with loop handle attached to rim and neck. Fairly coarse pink ware, evenly fired. Creamy-buff slip in and out.
20. R.Jg. B.II.r (TS. 3980; Op. 5, 12.1). Phase 5. About 1/5 rim and neck segment with portion of a loop handle attached. Ware description unavailable.

Plate 333

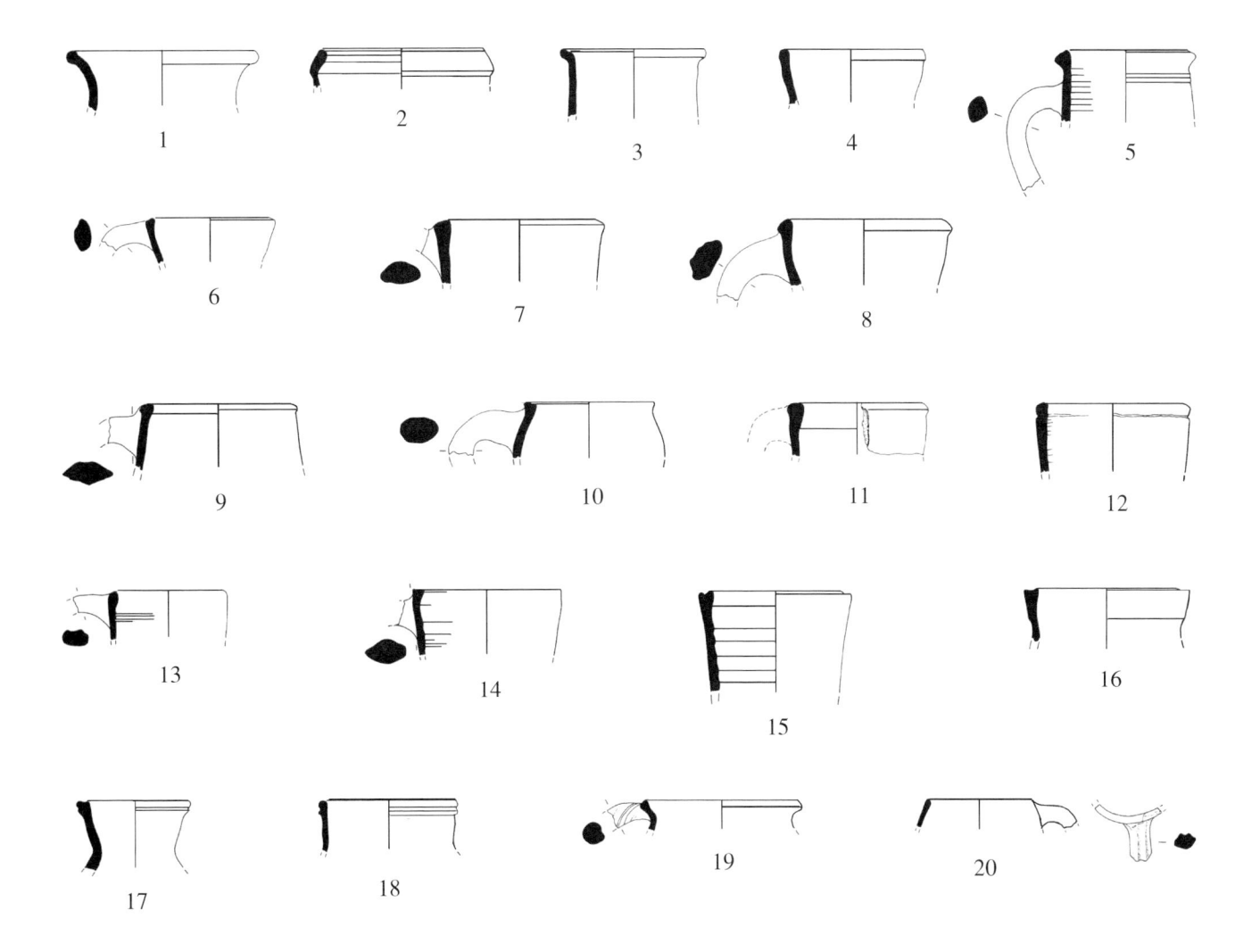

Roman Jug (R.Jg.) Type B. Scale 1:5

Plate 334

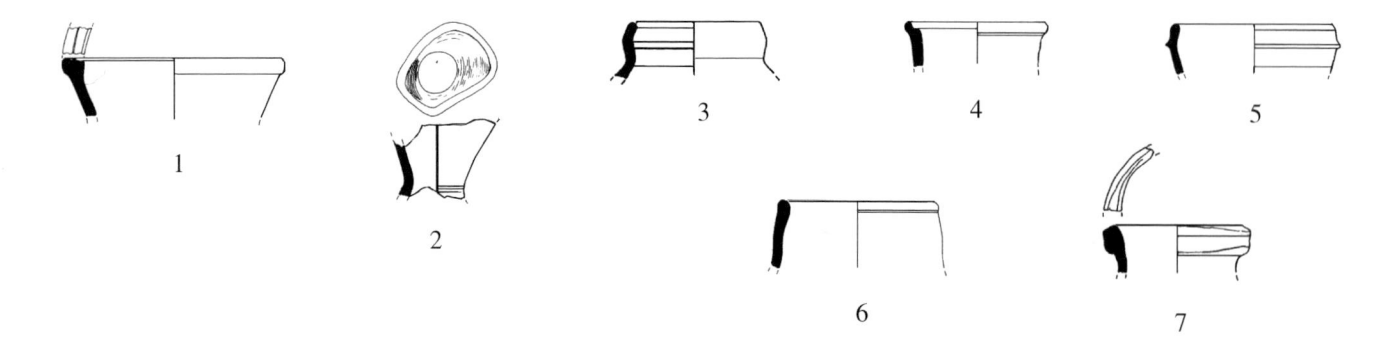

Roman Jug (R.Jg.) Type C. Scale 1:5

1. R.Jg. C.I.a (TS. 583; IC, 1.1). Phase 10. Small rim and neck segment. Fairly coarse pinkish-buff ware, evenly fired. Cream slip out.
2. R.Jg. C.I.b (TS. 440; IA1, 2.1). Phase 4. Nearly complete neck and shoulder segment. Fairly fine light brownish-buff ware, evenly fired. Cream slip out.
3. R.Jg. C.I.c (TS. 291; IA2, 4.1). Phase 4. About 1/4 rim, neck, and shoulder segment. Fairly fine light brown ware with lime and mica grits, evenly fired. Self slip in and out.
4. R.Jg. C.I.d (TS. 3658; Op. 5, 1.1). Phase 7. Small rim and neck segment. Ware description unavailable.
5. R.Jg. C.I.e (TS. 3661; Op. 5, 4.3). Phase 7. Small rim and neck segment. Ware description unavailable.
6. R.Jg. C.I.f (TS. 3781; Op. 5, 3.3). Phase 7. Small rim and neck segment. Ware description unavailable.
7. R.Jg. C.I.g (SC. 3394; IC, 1.1). Phase 10. Small rim and neck segment, with a pinched-type rim for pouring. Slightly coarse light pink ware with lime grits, evenly fired. Creamy-buff slip in and out.

Plate 335

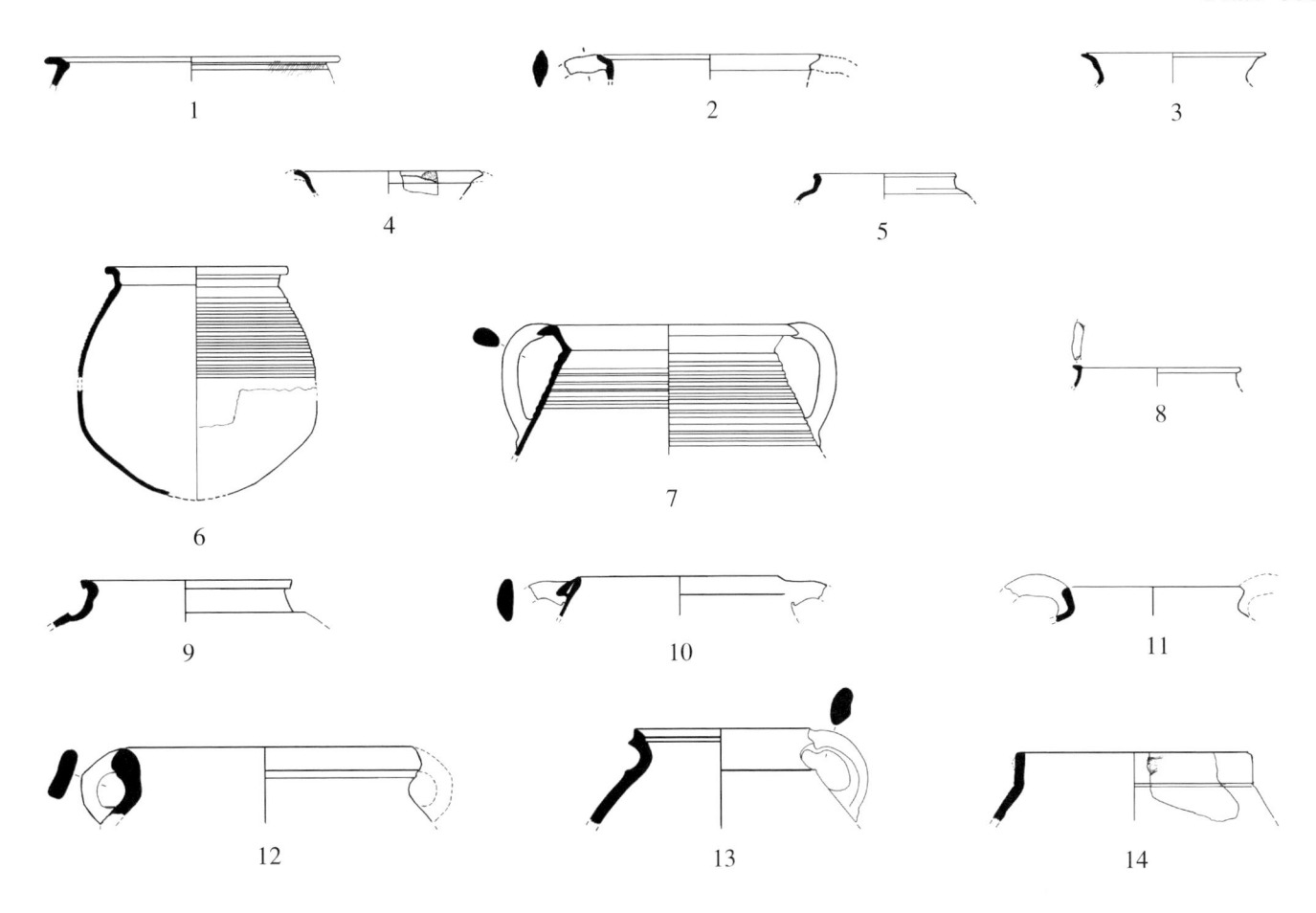

Roman Cooking Pot (R.CP) Types A and B. Scale 1:5

1. R.CP. A.I.a (SW. 1973+). Unstratified. Small rim segment. Fine reddish-orange ware, evenly fired. Self slip in and out.
2. R.CP. A.I.b (SC. 3050; IB, 1.6, Floor). Phase 3. Small rim and neck segment with the remains of a loop handle attached to the rim. Dark red brittle ware with many small lime and mica grits, evenly fired.
3. R.CP. A.II.a (TS. 447; IA2, 4.3). Phase 2. Small rim, neck, and shoulder segment. Fairly fine reddish-orange ware, evenly fired. Red slip in and out. Brown paint on edge of rim.
4. R.CP. A.II.b (SC. 3051; IA2, 4.3). Phase 2. Small rim and neck segment with remains of a loop handle attached to the rim. Hard dark red ware with lime and mica grits, unevenly fired with some gray core and grayish-black on outer surface and just over the inside of the rim.
5. R.CP. A.III.a (TS. 626; ID, 1.3). Phase 2. About 1/16 rim, neck, and upper wall segment. Fairly coarse reddish ware, evenly fired.
6. R.CP. A.IV.a (SW. 156; IB, 1.6, Floor). Phase 3. Many sherds mended to nearly complete profile. Dark reddish-brown ware with gold-colored mica and lime grits, evenly fired. Fired black with red patches outside.
7. R.CP. A.IV.b (TS. 3240; Op. 5, 10.1). Phase 6. Large rim and shoulder segment with one handle extant. For ware, compare R.CP. A.IV.a.
8. R.CP. A.IV.c (SC. 3069; IA2, 3.1). Phase 4. Small indented rim and neck segment. Slightly coarse brownish-buff ware with small lime and mica grits with evidence for destroyed vegetable temper. Irregular horizontal line-burnished self slip on top of rim and outside wall.
9. R.CP. A.V.a (TS. 449; IA2, 3.1). Phase 4. Small rim, neck, and shoulder segment. Fairly coarse red ware, unevenly fired black outside. Dark brownish-black line of paint on edge of rim.
10. R.CP. A.VI.a (TS. 3165; IC, 1.1). Phase 10. Small rim segment with portion of handle. Slightly coarse and gritty grayish "brittle" ware, fairly evenly fired. Self gray slip in and out.
11. R.CP. B.I.a (TS. 292; IC +). Unstratified. Small rim and shoulder segment with portion of one handle.
12. R.CP. B.II.a (TS. 3777; Op. 5, 11.1). Phase 5. Small rim, neck, and shoulder segment with one complete handle. Ware description unavailable.
13. R.CP. B.II.b (TS. 3234; Op. 5, 4.4). Phase 7. Large segment of upper body with one handle extant. For ware, compare R.CP. A.IV.a.
14. R.CP. B.III.a (TS. 625; IC, 1.1). Phase 10. Small rim, neck, and shoulder segment with part of upper part of handle attachment on neck just below the rim. Coarse blackish-brown ware, evenly fired.

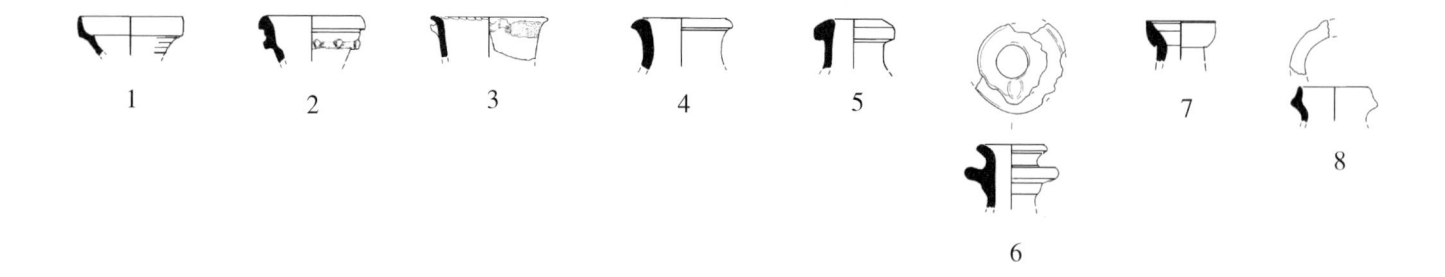

Roman Bottle (R.Bt.) Types A–C. Scale 1:5

1. R.Bt. A.I.a (TS. 655; IC, 1.28, Floor-like surface). Phase 6. Small rim and neck segment. Fairly fine buff ware, evenly fired. Green slip in and out.
2. R.Bt. A.I.b (TS. 3932; Op. 5, 10.2). Phase 5. About 1/2 rim and neck segment. Ware description unavailable.
3. R.Bt. B.I.a (TS. 2107; IB, 2.3). Phase 4. About 1/2 rim and neck segment with scar of handle attachment on upper neck below rim. Applied piecrust-type of band around neck. Fairly fine pinkish-buff ware, evenly fired. Buff slip in and out.
4. R.Bt. B.I.b (TS. 3194; Op. 5, 10.5). Phase 5. Small rim and neck segment. Ware description unavailable.
5. R.Bt. B.I.c (TS. 3159; IA1, 1.2, 2.5). Phases 3 and 1. About 1/2 segment of two joining rim and neck fragments. Fairly fine buff ware, evenly fired. Creamy-green slip in and out.
6. R.Bt. B.I.d (TS. 3786; Op. 5, 4.1). Phase 7. Nearly complete rim and neck segment with wide flange below the rim on the upper neck. Ware description unavailable.
7. R.Bt. C.I.a (TS. 1522; IA2, 3.1). Phase 4. Small rim and neck segment. Very hard, fine salmon-pink ware, evenly fired. Red slip in and out.
8. R.Bt. C.I.b (TS. 3166; XIA, 1.2). Phase 3. About 1/4 rim and neck segment with portion of pinched-type pouring lip at rim. Slightly coarse and gritty pinkish-red ware, evenly fired. Self slip in and out.

Plate 337

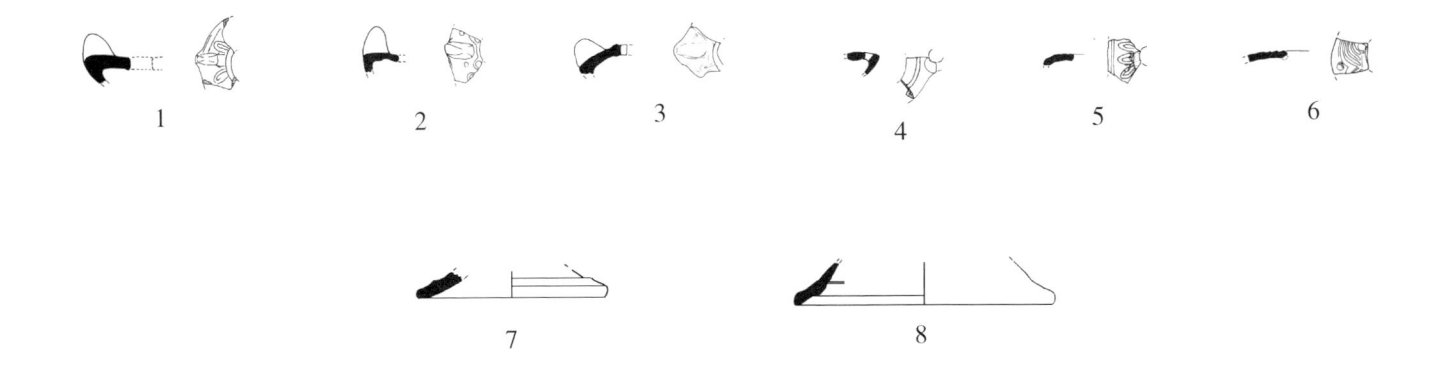

Roman Lamp (R.Lp.) Types (Unclassified) and Roman Lid (R.Ld.) Types (Unclassified). Scale 1:5

1. R.Lp. 1 (SW. 53; IA2, 4.3, 3.1). Phases 2 and 4. Handle segment, and part of upper surface decorated with leaf-like design on upper portion. Fine buff ware, evenly fired.
2. R.Lp. 2 (SW. 115; IA2, 3.1). Phase 4. Handle segment. Buff ware, evenly fired. Light greenish-buff slip out.
3. R.Lp. 3 (TS. 3677; Op. 5, 6.1). Phase 6. Small handle segment. Ware description unavailable.
4. R.Lp. 4 (SW. 155; IB, 1.7). Phase 3. Small shoulder segment. Fairly fine buff ware, evenly fired.
5. R.Lp. 5 (SW. 193; IC, 1.10). Phase 8. Upper surface segment with leaf-like design. Buff ware with small grits, evenly fired.
6. R.Lp. 6 (TS. 3876; Op. 5, 6.8, Pit). Phase 6. Small upper surface segment with linear decoration. Ware description unavailable.
7. R.Ld. 1 (TS. 1508; IA1, 1.3). Phase 3. About 1/2 segment. Fairly fine pinkish-buff ware with fine lime and mica grits, evenly fired. Creamy-buff slip in and out.
8. R.Ld. 2 (SW. 81; IB, 1.6, Floor). Phase 3. Small segment of rim and wall. Glazed ware. Light green glaze over all of clay, with white-irridescent weathering of glaze — craquelure.

Plate 338

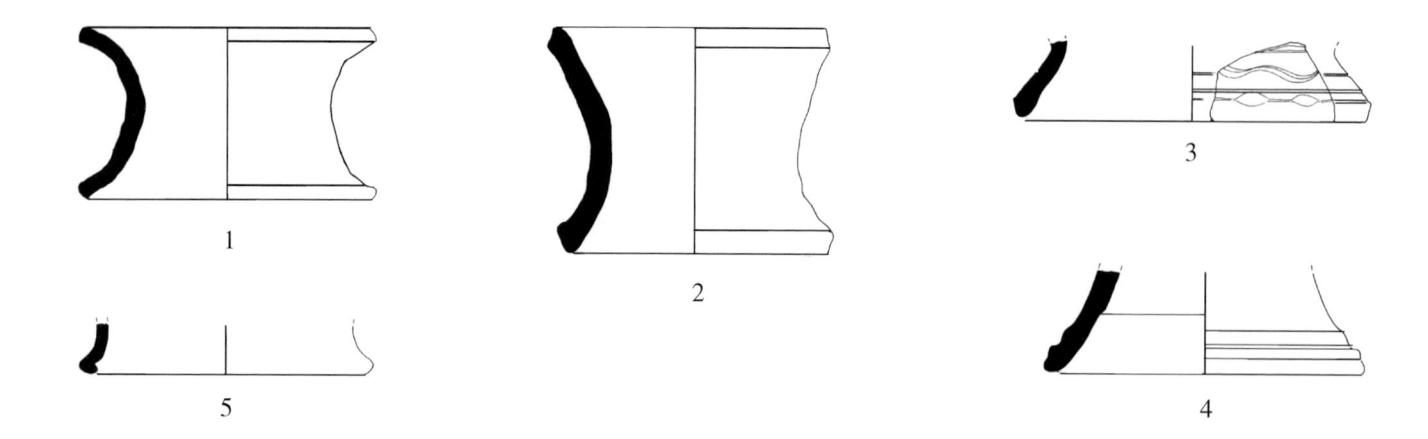

Roman Pot Stands (R.PS) Types (Unclassified). Scale 1:5

1. R.PS.1 (SW. 62; IB, 1.5, Floor). Phase 3. One end complete and about 1/3 of other end extant. Coarse buff ware with black- and gold- colored mineral temper, fairly evenly fired.
2. R.PS.2 (SW. 63; IB, 1.5, Floor). Phase 3. One end complete and about 1/3 of other end extant. Coarse buff ware with black-colored mineral temper and lime grits, fairly evenly fired.
3. R.PS.3 (TS. 3855; Op. 5, 5.1). Phase 7. About 1/8 segment of one end and portion of wall with incised wavy line decoration. Ware description unavailable.
4. R.PS.4 (TS. 3708; Op. 5, 9.6). Phase 5. Small rim and about 1/2 wall segment of one end. Ware description unavailable.
5. R.PS.5 (TS. 3707; Op. 5, 8.2). Phase 6. Small rim and portion of wall of one end. Ware description unavailable.

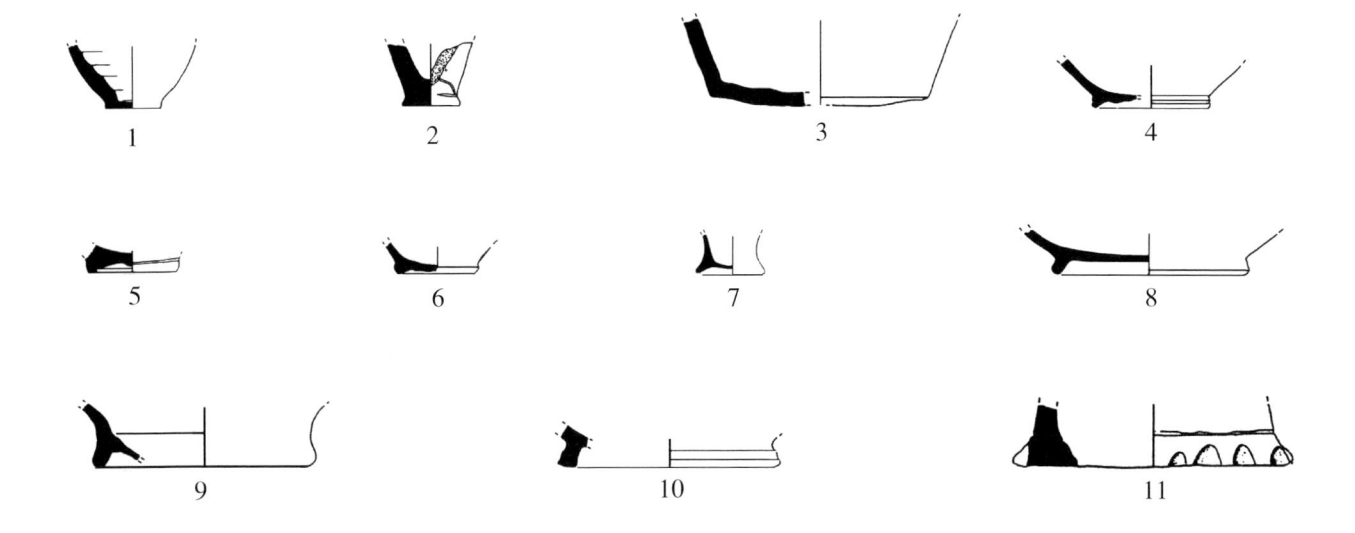

Roman Base (R.BE) Types A–C. Scale 1:5

1. R.BE. A.I.a (TS. 3899; Op. 5, 10.2). Phase 5. Complete disk base and lower portion of wall of vessel. Ware description unavailable.
2. R.BE. A.I.b (SC. 3229; IA2, 3.1). Phase 4. Nearly complete disk-type base with a portion of the diagonally splayed wall of the original vessel. Fairly fine pinkish-rose ware with gold-colored mica grits and some vegetable temper, evenly fired. Creamy-buff slip in and out.
3. R.BE. A.II.a (TS. 3655; Op. 5, 4.3). Phase 7. Nearly complete semi-flat base and lower portion of wall. Ware description unavailable.
4. R.BE. B.I.a (TS. 3689; Op. 5, 9.6). Phase 5. Nearly complete ring base with lower portion of wall of vessel. Ware description unavailable.
5. R.BE. B.I.b (TS. 538; IE, 1.1). Phase 6. About 1/2 of base profile extant. Fairly coarse pink ware with an unevenly fired buff core. Cream slip on outer surfaces.
6. R.BE. B.I.c (SC. 3189; IG, 1.19). Phase 6. About 1/3 of base profile extant. Ring base with an internal circular flat disk. Slightly coarse reddish-orange ware with a few lime inclusions, evenly fired.
7. R.BE. B.I.d (SC. 3158; IJ, 1.1). Phase 2. About 1/5 of base profile extant with remains of the lower wall of the original vessel. Fairly fine dark pinkish-buff ware with small lime grits, evenly fired. Self slip in and out.
8. R.BE. B.II.a (TS. 3913; Op. 5, 11.1). Phase 5. Complete ring base with lower portion of wall of vessel. Ware description unavailable.
9. R.BE. B.II.b.1 (TS. 3857; Op. 5, 5.1). Phase 7. Segment of ring base and lower wall of vessel. Ware description unavailable.
10. R.BE. B.II.b.2 (TS. 3701; Op. 5, 9.8). Phase 5. Segment of ring base and lower wall of vessel. Ware description unavailable.
11. R.BE. C.I.a (TS. 2094; IA1, 1.3). Phase 3. About 1/3 segment of base and lower wall of vessel. Fairly fine pinkish-buff ware, evenly fired. Creamy-buff slip in and out.

Plate 340. Incised Pottery (IP) Typology Groups G.1 to G.4

1. IP (G.1) A.I.a; JR. Q.II.b (TS. 985; VG, 1.4). Phase 6. Rim, neck, and shoulder segment. Fairly coarse pink ware, evenly fired. Cream slip out.
2. IP (G.1) A.II.a; R.JR.Sh. (TS. 1218; IA2, 3.1). Phase 4. Jar shoulder sherd. Fairly fine grayish-green ware, evenly fired. Traces of black paint or bitumen out.
3. IP (G.1) A.II.b; R.JR.Sh. (TS. 2057; IB, 1.6, Floor). Phase 3. Jar shoulder fragment with stub of upper portion of a loop handle. Slightly coarse buff ware, unevenly fired pink at surfaces. Pinkish-buff slip out.
4. IP (G.1) B.II.a; JR.Sh. (TS. 2170; VE, 1.4, Pit [bottom]). Phase 3. Jar shoulder sherd. Hard, fine buff ware, evenly fired. Greenish-buff slip out.
5. IP (G.1) C.II.b; R.JR.Sh. (TS. 2038; IE, 1.6). Phase 4. Jar shoulder sherd. Fairly coarse greenish-buff ware, evenly fired. Self slip in and out.
6. IP (G.1) C.IV.a; R.JR.Sh. (TS. 1221; IA2, 3.1). Phase 4. Jar shoulder sherd. Fine pink ware, evenly fired. Creamy-buff slip out.
7. IP (G.1) C.V.a; R.JR.Sh. (TS. 2037; IE, 1.1a). Phase 5. Jar shoulder sherd. Fairly coarse grayish-buff ware, evenly fired. Creamy-buff slip out.
8. IP (G.1) C.V.a; JR.Sh. (TS. 2167; VG, 1.4). Phase 6. Jar shoulder sherd. Fairly fine buff ware, evenly fired. Self slip out. Heavily charred.
9. IP (G.1) C.V.a; JR.Sh. (TS. 2168; VB, 1.2). Phase 3. Jar shoulder sherd. Hard, fine pink ware, evenly fired. Creamy-buff slip out.
10. IP (G.1) C.VI.a; H.JR. E.I.b (TS. 916 = TS. 1044; VG, 1.4 and VF/G, 1.5) Phases 6 and 8. About 1/4 rim, neck, and shoulder segment with large loop handle attached to upper shoulder. Comb-incised decoration applied before handle was attached. Fairly coarse pinkish-buff ware, unevenly fired brown-buff at surfaces.
11. IP (G.1) C.VI.b; H.JR. E.I.a (TS. 2124; VD, 1.1). Phase 5. Small rim, neck, and upper wall segment of a bowl or jar. Coarse buff ware, evenly fired. Light creamy-green slip out and on top of rim.
12. IP (G.1) C.VI.b; JR.Sh. (TS. 2165; VF, 1.1). Phase 9. Jar shoulder sherd with comb-incised decoration and an applied horizontal band around the outside wall. Hard, fairly fine buff ware, evenly fired. Light creamy-green slip out.
13. IP (G.1) C.VI.b; JR.Sh. (TS. 2161; VG, 1.3). Phase 7. Jar shoulder sherd. Hard, fine pink ware, fairly evenly fired. Thick cream slip out.
14. IP (G.1) D.I.a; R.JR.Sh. (TS. 1220; IA2, 3.1). Phase 4. Jar neck and shoulder sherd. Slightly coarse buff ware, evenly fired. Self slip in and out.
15. IP (G.1) D.I.b; R.JR.Sh. (TS. 1219; IA1, 2.4a). Phase 2. Jar shoulder sherd. Slightly coarse creamy-buff ware, evenly fired. Self slip out.
16. IP (G.1) D.I.c ; R.JR.Sh. (TS. 2033; IE, 1.6). Phase 4. Jar shoulder sherd. Slightly coarse grayish-buff ware, evenly fired. Self slip out.
17. IP (G.1) D.II.a; JR.Sh. (TS. 2166; VA, "1.1"). Phase 3. Jar shoulder sherd. Slightly coarse buff ware, evenly fired. Creamy-green slip out.
18. IP (G.1) D.III.b; R.JR.Sh. (TS. 2036; IA1, 2.5). Phase 1. Jar neck and shoulder sherd. Fairly coarse pink ware, evenly fired. Creamy-buff slip out.
19. IP (G.1) H.III.a; JR.Sh. (TS. 2070; VF/G, 1.1). Phase 9. Jar neck and shoulder sherd. Slightly coarse pink ware, evenly fired. Buff slip out. Very flaky surface.
20. H.IP (G.1) I.I.a; H.JR.Sh. (TS. 1224; IIB, 2.1). Phase 15. Jar shoulder sherd. Fairly fine pinkish-buff ware, evenly fired. Self slip out.
21. IP (G.1) J.I.a; JR.Sh. (TS. 2142; VA, "1.1"). Phase 3. Jar shoulder sherd. Fairly coarse light pinkish-buff ware, evenly fired. Creamy-buff slip in and out.
22. IP (G.1) J.II.a; R.JR.Sh. (TS. 2035; IF, 1.1). Phase 6. Jar shoulder sherd. Slightly coarse pink ware, evenly fired. Creamy-buff slip out.
23. IP (G.1) K.I.a; R.BR. B.I.b. (TS. 532; IA2, 3.1). Phase 4. Bowl. About 1/8 rim and upper wall segment. Fairly coarse pink ware, evenly fired. Creamy-buff slip in and out.
24. IP (G.1) K.I.b; R.BR. B.I.b (TS. 2119; IA1, 1.3). Phase 3. Bowl. Small rim and upper wall segment. Slightly coarse pinkish-buff ware, evenly fired. Buff slip in and out.
25. IP (G.2) A.III.a; R.JR.Sh. (TS. 474; IA2, 3.1). Phase 4. Jar shoulder sherd. Coarse pink ware, evenly fired. Self slip out.
26. IP (G.2) A.V.a; JR.Sh. (TS. 2135; VC, 1.1). Phase 4. Jar shoulder sherd. Fairly fine pink ware, evenly fired. Creamy-yellow slip out.
27. IP (G.2) A.VI.a; R.JR.Sh. (TS. 613; IB, 2.6, Floor). Phase 3. Jar shoulder sherd. Fairly coarse pink ware, evenly fired. Self slip out.
28. IP (G.2) B.II.a; JR.Sh. (TS. 880; VG, 1.3). Phase 7. Jar shoulder sherd. Slightly coarse pink ware, evenly fired. Creamy-pink slip out.
29. IP (G.3) B.II.a; JR.Sh. (TS. 425; VA, "1.1"). Phase 3. Jar shoulder sherd. Fairly coarse light grayish-buff ware, evenly fired. Light gray slip out.
30. IP (G.3) B.III.a; JR.Sh. (TS. 592; IA1, 2.5). Phase 1. Jar shoulder sherd. Fairly fine grayware, evenly fired. Self slip out with traces of burnishing.
31. H.IP (G.4) A.I.a; H.Lp.1 (TS. 353; IIB, 2.3). Phase 15. Lamp. About 1/8 rim and most of wall profile. Light grayware, evenly fired.
32. IP (G.4) A.II.a; Lp. B.I.2. (TS. 415; Surface). Lamp. Small rim and upper wall segment with small ledge handle attached to rim. Slightly coarse buff ware, fairly evenly fired. Creamy-green slip in and out.
33. IP (G.4) B.I.a; R.JR.Sh. (TS. 2034; IG, 1.19). Phase 6. Jar shoulder sherd. Hard, fine pinkish-buff ware, evenly fired.
34. IP (G.4) C.I.b; JR.Sh. (TS. 1139; IJ, 1.1). Phase 2. Jar body sherd. Fairly coarse buff ware, evenly fired. Cream slip out.
—. IP (G.4) D.III (PM. D.19); JR.Sh. (TS. 2169; VF, 1.3). Phase 6. (See fig. 260:9)
35. IP (G.4) E.I; JR.Sh. (TS. 2178; Surface). Jar shoulder sherd incised with a human figure. Hard, fine pinkish-buff ware, fairly evenly fired. Self slip out.

Plate 340

Incised Pottery (IP) Typology Groups G.1 to G.4. Scale 1:5, Except Sherd 35, Scale 1:3